YBM 실전토익
RC1000
2

YBM
실전토익
RC 1000 2

발행인 허문호
발행처 YBM

문항 개발 백주선, Marilyn Hook
편집 노경미
디자인 김혜경, DOTS
마케팅 정연철, 박천산, 고영노, 김동진, 박찬경, 김윤하

초판발행 2018년 2월 6일
14쇄발행 2024년 2월 1일

신고일자 1964년 3월 28일
신고번호 제 300-1964-3호
주소 서울시 종로구 종로 104
전화 (02) 2000-0515 [구입문의] / (02) 2000-0429 [내용문의]
팩스 (02) 2285-1523
홈페이지 www.ybmbooks.com

ISBN 978-89-17-22914-1

토익 주관사가 만든 고난도 적중실전

YBM 실전토익 RC 1000 2를 발행하며

지난 30여 년간 우리나라에서 토익 시험을 주관하면서 토익 시장을 이끌고, 꾸준히 베스트셀러를 출간해 온 YBM에서 〈YBM 실전토익 RC 1000 2〉를 출간하게 되었습니다.

YBM 토익은 이렇게 다릅니다!

YBM의 명성에 자부심을 가지고 개발했습니다!

YBM은 지난 1982년부터 우리나라의 토익 시험을 주관해온 토익 주관사로서, 지난 30여 년간 400여 권의 토익 베스트셀러를 출판해왔습니다. 그 오랜 시간 토익 문제를 분석하고 교재를 출판하면서 쌓아온 전문성과 실력으로 이번에 〈YBM 실전토익 RC 1000 2〉를 선보이게 되었습니다.

출제 예측 시스템을 기반으로 고득점 적중문제 위주로 개발했습니다!

정확한 예측 시스템을 토대로 신토익 최신 경향을 철저히 분석하여 〈YBM 실전토익 RC 1000 2〉를 개발하였습니다. 실제 시험과 가장 유사한 문제 유형을 반영하되, 고난이도 문제를 다수 포함시켜 단기간에 고득점을 달성할 수 있도록 구성했습니다.

ETS 교재를 출간한 노하우를 가지고 개발했습니다!

출제기관 ETS의 토익 교재를 독점 출간하는 YBM은 그동안 쌓아온 노하우를 바탕으로 〈YBM 실전토익 RC 1000 2〉를 개발하였습니다. 본 책에 실린 1000개의 문항은 출제자의 의도를 정확히 반영하였기 때문에 타사의 어떤 토익 교재와도 비교할 수 없는 퀄리티를 자랑합니다.

YBM의 모든 노하우가 집대성된 〈YBM 실전토익 RC 1000 2〉는 최단 시간에 최고의 점수를 수험자 여러분께 약속 드립니다.

YBM 토익연구소

토익의 구성과 수험 정보

TOEIC은
어떤 시험인가요?

Test of English for International Communication(국제적 의사소통을 위한 영어 시험)의 약자로서, 영어가 모국어가 아닌 사람들이 일상생활 또는 비즈니스 현장에서 꼭 필요한 실용적 영어 구사 능력을 갖추었는가를 평가하는 시험이다.

시험 구성

구성	Part	내용		문항수	시간	배점
듣기 (L/C)	1	사진 묘사		6	45분	495점
	2	질의 & 응답		25		
	3	짧은 대화		39		
	4	짧은 담화		30		
읽기 (R/C)	5	단문 빈칸 채우기(문법/어휘)		30	75분	495점
	6	장문 빈칸 채우기		16		
	7	독해	단일 지문	29		
			이중 지문	10		
			삼중 지문	15		
Total	7 Parts			200문항	120분	990점

TOEIC 접수는
어떻게 하나요?

TOEIC 접수는 한국 토익 위원회 사이트(www.toeic.co.kr)에서 온라인 상으로만 접수가 가능하다. 사이트에서 매월 자세한 접수 일정과 시험 일정 등의 구체적 정보 확인이 가능하니, 미리 일정을 확인하여 접수하도록 한다.

시험장에 반드시 가져가야 할 준비물은요?

신분증 규정 신분증만 가능
         (주민등록증, 운전면허증, 기간 만료 전의 여권, 공무원증 등)

필기구 연필, 지우개 (볼펜이나 사인펜은 사용 금지)

시험은 어떻게 진행되나요?

09:20	입실 (09:50 이후는 입실 불가)
09:30 – 09:45	답안지 작성에 관한 오리엔테이션
09:45 – 09:50	휴식
09:50 – 10:05	신분증 확인
10:05 – 10:10	문제지 배부 및 파본 확인
10:10 – 10:55	듣기 평가 (Listening Test)
10:55 – 12:10	독해 평가 (Reading Test)

TOEIC 성적 확인은 어떻게 하죠?

시험일로부터 19일 후, 오후 3시부터 인터넷과 ARS(060-800-0515)로 성적을 확인할 수 있다. TOEIC 성적표는 우편이나 온라인으로 발급 받을 수 있다(시험 접수시, 양자 택일). 우편으로 발급 받을 경우는 성적 발표 후 대략 일주일이 소요되며, 온라인 발급을 선택하면 유효기간 내에 홈페이지에서 본인이 직접 1회에 한해 무료 출력할 수 있다. TOEIC 성적은 시험일로부터 2년간 유효하다.

TOEIC은 몇 점 만점인가요?

TOEIC 점수는 듣기 영역(LC) 점수, 읽기 영역(RC) 점수, 그리고 이 두 영역을 합계한 전체 점수 세 부분으로 구성된다. 각 부분의 점수는 5점 단위이며, 5점에서 495점에 걸쳐 주어지고, 전체 점수는 10점에서 990점까지이며, 만점은 990점이다. TOEIC 성적은 각 문제 유형의 난이도에 따른 점수 환산표에 의해 결정된다.

신토익 경향 분석

PART1 사진 묘사 Photographs

총 6문제

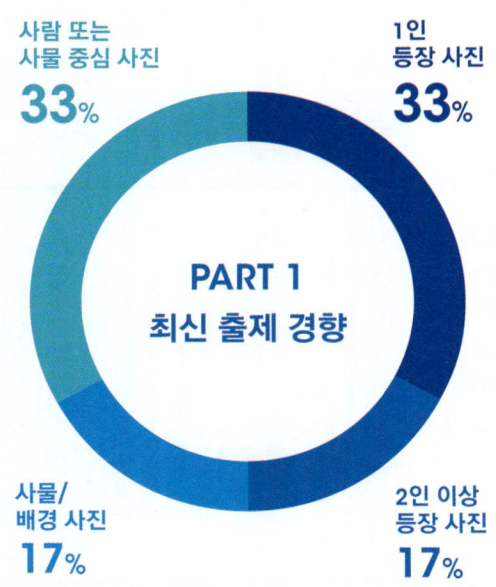

PART 1 최신 출제 경향

- 사람 또는 사물 중심 사진 **33**%
- 1인 등장 사진 **33**%
- 사물/배경 사진 **17**%
- 2인 이상 등장 사진 **17**%

1인 등장 사진
주어는 He/She, A man/woman, One of the men/women 등이며 주로 앞부분에 나온다.

2인 이상 등장 사진
주어는 They, Some men/women/people 등이며 주로 중간 부분에 나온다.

사물/배경 사진
주어는 A car, some chairs 등이며 주로 뒷부분에 나온다.

사람 또는 사물 중심 사진
주어가 일부는 사람, 일부는 사물이며 주로 뒷부분에 나온다.

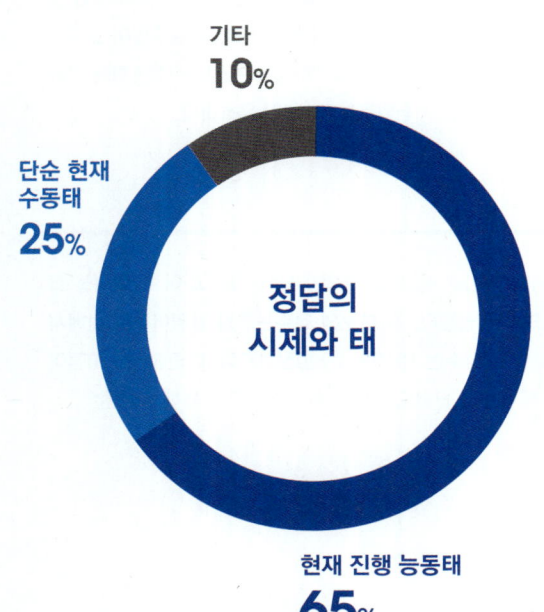

정답의 시제와 태

- 기타 **10**%
- 단순 현재 수동태 **25**%
- 현재 진행 능동태 **65**%

현재 진행 능동태
〈is/are + 현재분사〉 형태이며 주로 사람이 주어이다.

단순 현재 수동태
〈is/are + 과거분사〉 형태이며 주로 사물이 주어이다.

기타
〈is/are + being + 과거분사〉 형태의 현재 진행 수동태, 〈has/have + been + 과거 분사〉 형태의 현재 완료 수동태, '타동사 + 목적어' 형태의 단순 현재 능동태, There is/are와 같은 단순 현재도 나온다.

PART 2 질의 & 응답 Question-Response

평서문

질문이 아니라 객관적인 사실이나 화자의 의견 등을 나타내는 문장이다.

명령문

동사원형이나 Please 등으로 시작한다.

의문사 의문문

각 의문사마다 1~2개씩 나온다. 의문사가 단독으로 나오기도 하지만 What time ~?, How long ~?, Which room ~? 등에서처럼 다른 명사나 형용사와 같이 나오기도 한다.

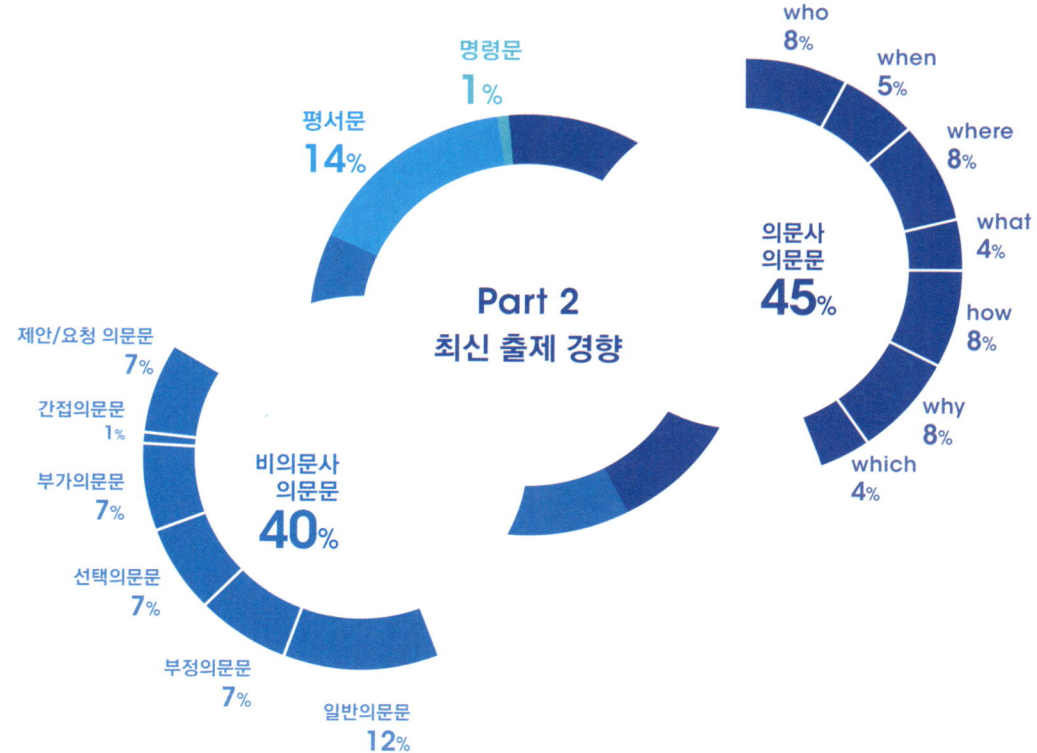

명령문 **1**%

평서문 **14**%

who **8**%

when **5**%

where **8**%

what **4**%

의문사 의문문 **45**%

how **8**%

why **8**%

which **4**%

제안/요청 의문문 **7**%

간접의문문 **1**%

부가의문문 **7**%

비의문사 의문문 **40**%

선택의문문 **7**%

부정의문문 **7**%

일반의문문 **12**%

Part 2 최신 출제 경향

비의문사 의문문

일반(Yes/No) 의문문 적게 나올 때는 한두 개, 많이 나올 때는 서너 개씩 나오는 편이다.

부정의문문 Don't you ~?, Isn't he ~? 등으로 시작하는 문장이며 일반 긍정 의문문보다는 약간 더 적게 나온다.

선택의문문 A or B 형태로 나오며 A와 B의 형태가 단어, 구, 절일 수 있다. 구나 절일 경우 문장이 길어져서 어려워진다.

부가의문문 ~ don't you?, ~ isn't he? 등으로 끝나는 문장이며, 일반 부정 의문문과 비슷하다고 볼 수 있다.

간접의문문 의문사가 문장 처음 부분이 아니라 문장 중간에 들어 있다.

제안/요청 의문문 정보를 얻기보다는 상대방의 도움이나 동의 등을 얻기 위한 목적이 일반적이다.

PART 3 짧은 대화 Short Conversations

총 13대화문 39문제 (지문당 3문제)

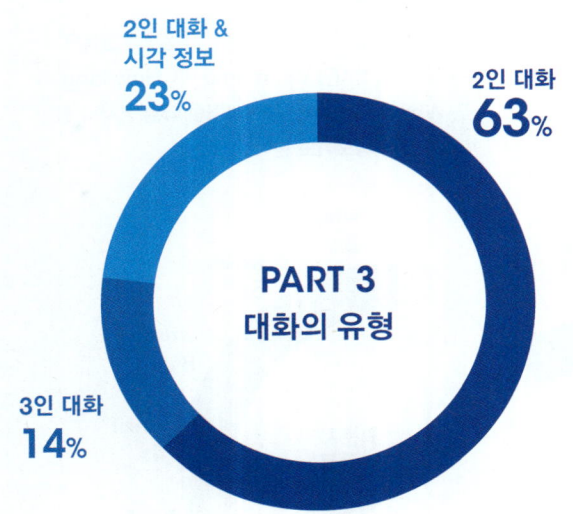

PART 3 대화의 유형

- 2인 대화 **63**%
- 2인 대화 & 시각 정보 **23**%
- 3인 대화 **14**%

- 3인 대화의 경우 남자 화자 두 명과 여자 화자 한 명 또는 남자 화자 한 명과 여자 화자 두 명이 나온다. 따라서 문제에서는 2인 대화에서와 달리 the man이나 the woman이 아니라 the men이나 the women 또는 특정한 이름이 언급될 수 있다.

- 대화 & 시각 정보는 항상 파트의 뒷부분에 나온다.

- 시각 정보의 유형으로 chart, map, floor plan, schedule, table, weather forecast, directory, list, invoice, receipt, sign, packing slip 등 다양한 자료가 골고루 나온다.

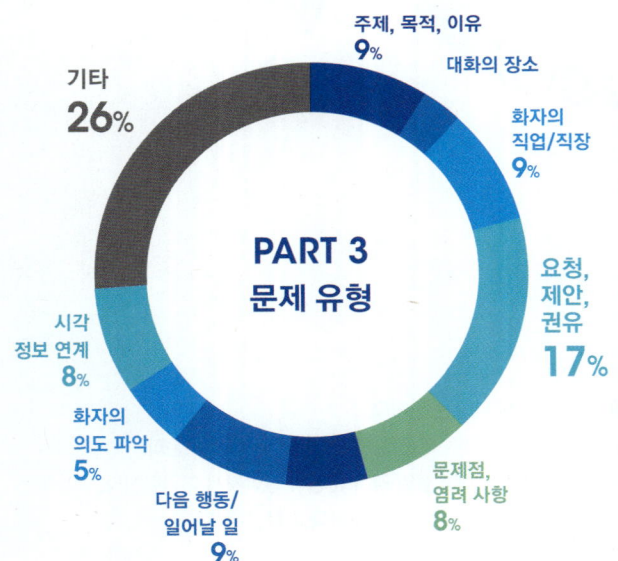

PART 3 문제 유형

- 주제, 목적, 이유 **9**%
- 대화의 장소
- 화자의 직업/직장 **9**%
- 요청, 제안, 권유 **17**%
- 문제점, 염려 사항 **8**%
- 다음 행동/일어날 일 **9**%
- 화자의 의도 파악 **5**%
- 시각 정보 연계 **8**%
- 기타 **26**%

- 주제, 목적, 이유, 대화의 장소, 화자의 직업/직장 등과 관련된 문제는 주로 대화의 첫 번째 문제로 나오며 다음 행동/일어날 일 등과 관련된 문제는 주로 대화의 세 번째 문제로 나온다.

- 화자의 의도 파악 문제는 주로 2인 대화에 나오지만, 가끔 3인 대화에 나오기도 한다. 시각 정보 연계 대화에는 나오지 않고 있다.

- Part 3 안에서 화자의 의도 파악 문제는 2개 나오고 시각 정보 연계 문제는 3개 나온다.

PART 4 짧은 담화 Short Talks

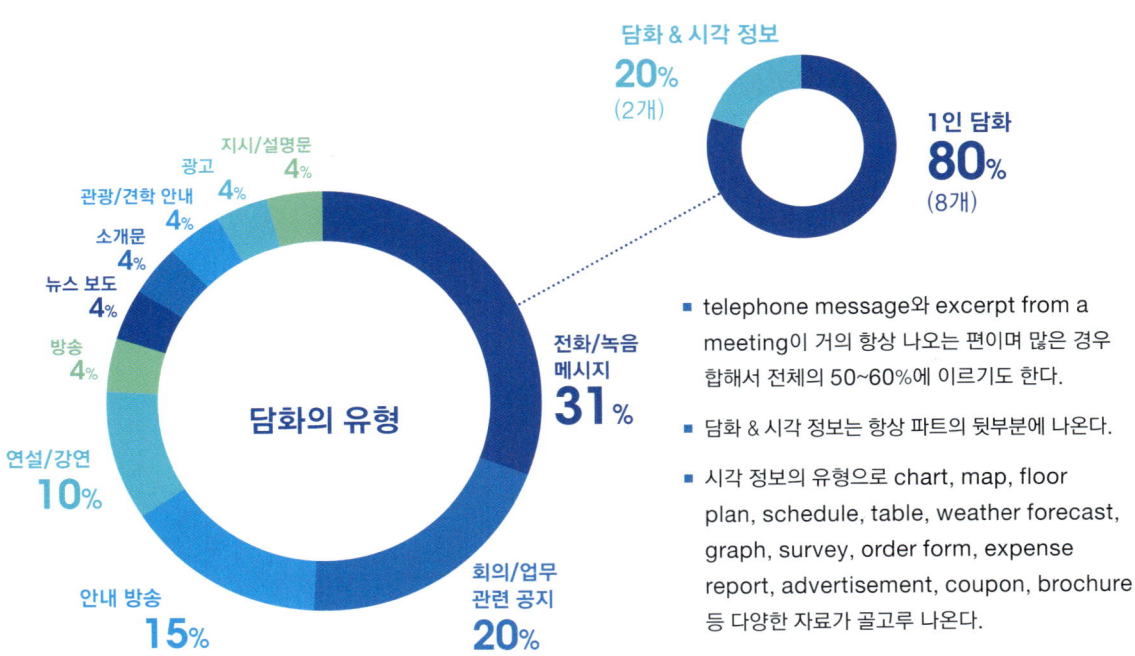

담화의 유형

- 담화 & 시각 정보 **20%** (2개)
- 1인 담화 **80%** (8개)
- 지시/설명문 **4%**
- 광고 **4%**
- 관광/견학 안내 **4%**
- 소개문 **4%**
- 뉴스 보도 **4%**
- 방송 **4%**
- 연설/강연 **10%**
- 안내 방송 **15%**
- 회의/업무 관련 공지 **20%**
- 전화/녹음 메시지 **31%**

- telephone message와 excerpt from a meeting이 거의 항상 나오는 편이며 많은 경우 합해서 전체의 50~60%에 이르기도 한다.

- 담화 & 시각 정보는 항상 파트의 뒷부분에 나온다.

- 시각 정보의 유형으로 chart, map, floor plan, schedule, table, weather forecast, graph, survey, order form, expense report, advertisement, coupon, brochure 등 다양한 자료가 골고루 나온다.

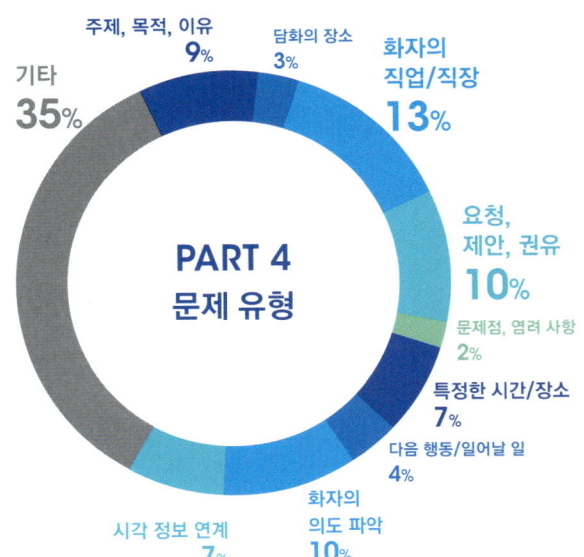

PART 4 문제 유형

- 주제, 목적, 이유 **9%**
- 담화의 장소 **3%**
- 화자의 직업/직장 **13%**
- 기타 **35%**
- 요청, 제안, 권유 **10%**
- 문제점, 염려 사항 **2%**
- 특정한 시간/장소 **7%**
- 다음 행동/일어날 일 **4%**
- 화자의 의도 파악 **10%**
- 시각 정보 연계 **7%**

- 문제 유형은 기본적으로 Part 3과 거의 비슷하다.

- 주제, 목적, 이유, 담화의 장소, 화자의 직업/직장 등과 관련된 문제는 주로 담화의 첫 번째 문제로 나오며 다음 행동/일어날 일 등과 관련된 문제는 주로 담화의 세 번째 문제로 나온다.

- Part 4 안에서 화자의 의도 파악 문제는 3개 나오고 시각 정보 연계 문제는 2개 나온다.

신토익 경향 분석

PART 5 단문 빈칸 채우기 Incomplete Sentences

총 30문제

문법 문제

시제와 대명사와 관련된 문법 문제가 2개씩, 한정사와 분사와 관련된 문법 문제가 1개씩 나온다. 시제 문제의 경우 능동태/수동태나 수의 일치와 연계되기도 한다. 그 밖에 한정사, 능동태/수동태, 부정사, 동명사 등과 관련된 문법 문제가 나온다.

어휘 문제

동사, 명사, 형용사, 부사와 관련된 어휘 문제가 각각 2~3개씩 골고루 나온다. 전치사 어휘 문제는 3개씩 꾸준히 나오지만, 접속사나 어구와 관련된 어휘 문제는 나오지 않을 때도 있고 3개가 나올 때도 있다.

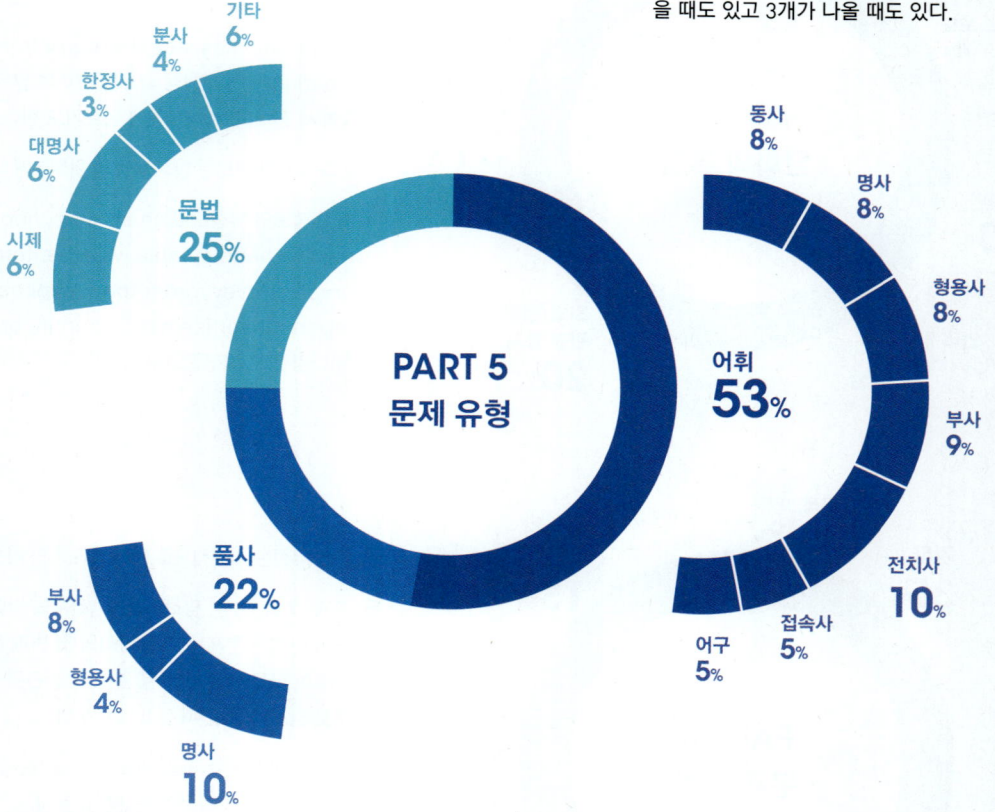

기타 6%
분사 4%
한정사 3%
대명사 6%
시제 6%
문법 25%

동사 8%
명사 8%
형용사 8%
부사 9%
전치사 10%
접속사 5%
어구 5%
어휘 53%

PART 5 문제 유형

품사 22%
부사 8%
형용사 4%
명사 10%

품사 문제

명사와 부사와 관련된 품사 문제가 2~3개씩 나오며, 형용사와 관련된 품사 문제가 상대적으로 적은 편이다.

PART 6 장문 빈칸 채우기 Text Completion

한 지문에 4문제가 나오며 평균적으로 어휘 문제가 2개, 품사나 문법 문제가 1개, 문맥에 맞는 문장 고르기 문제가 1개 들어간다. 문맥에 맞는 문장 고르기 문제를 제외하면 문제 유형은 기본적으로 파트 5와 거의 비슷하다.

어휘 문제

동사, 명사, 부사, 어구와 관련된 어휘 문제는 매번 1~2개씩 나온다. 부사 어휘 문제의 경우 therefore(그러므로)나 however(하지만)처럼 문맥의 흐름을 자연스럽게 연결해 주는 부사가 자주 나온다.

문맥에 맞는 문장 고르기

문맥에 맞는 문장 고르기 문제는 지문당 한 문제씩 나오는데, 나오는 위치의 확률은 4문제 중 두 번째 문제, 세 번째 문제, 네 번째 문제, 첫 번째 문제 순으로 높다.

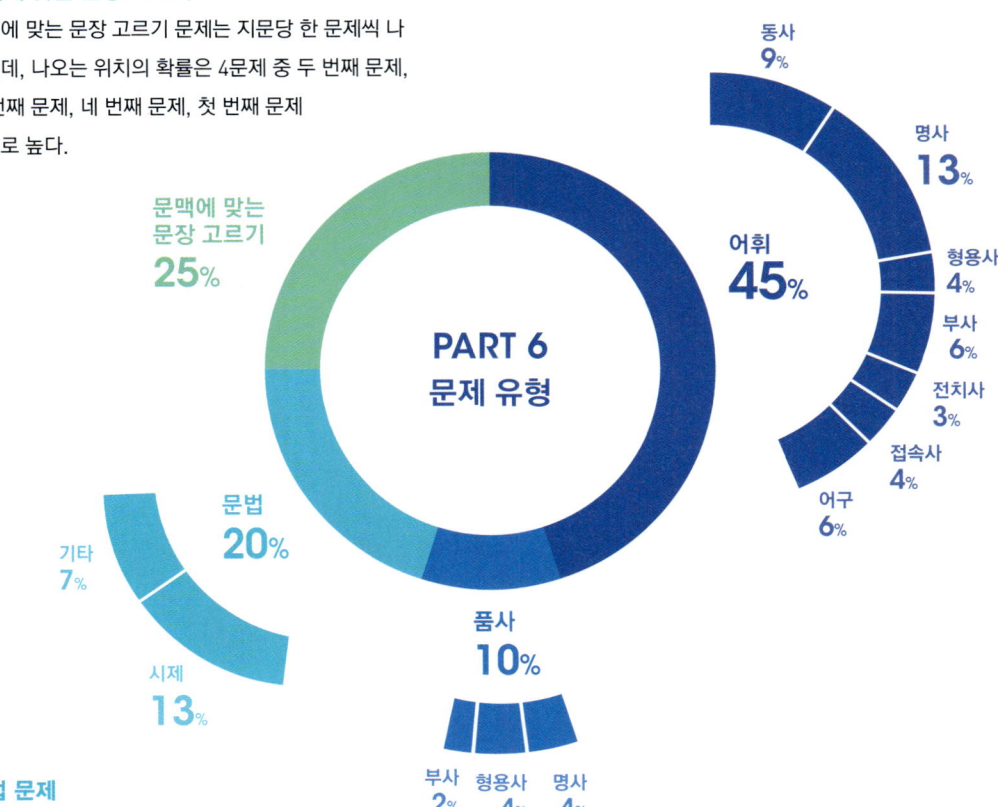

PART 6
문제 유형

문맥에 맞는
문장 고르기
25%

어휘
45%

동사
9%

명사
13%

형용사
4%

부사
6%

전치사
3%

접속사
4%

어구
6%

문법
20%

기타
7%

시제
13%

품사
10%

부사
2%

형용사
4%

명사
4%

문법 문제

문맥의 흐름과 밀접하게 관련이 있는 시제 문제가 2개 정도 나오며, 능동태/수동태나 수의 일치와 연계되기도 한다. 그 밖에 대명사, 능동태/수동태, 부정사, 접속사/전치사 등과 관련된 문법 문제가 나온다.

품사 문제

명사나 형용사 문제가 부사 문제보다 좀 더 자주 나온다.

PART 7 독해 Reading Comprehension

총 15지문 54문제 (지문당 2~5문제)

지문 유형	지문당 문제 수	지문 개수	비중 %
단일 지문	2문항	4개	약 15%
	3문항	3개	약 16%
	4문항	3개	약 22%
이중 지문	5문항	2개	약 19%
삼중 지문	5문항	3개	약 28%

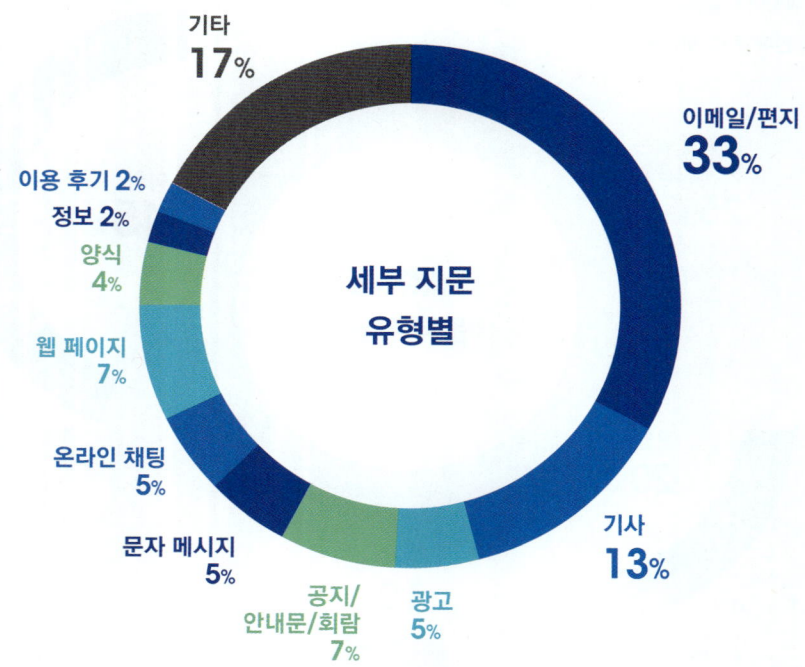

세부 지문 유형별

- 이메일/편지 33%
- 기사 13%
- 광고 5%
- 공지/안내문/회람 7%
- 문자 메시지 5%
- 온라인 채팅 5%
- 웹 페이지 7%
- 양식 4%
- 정보 2%
- 이용 후기 2%
- 기타 17%

- 이메일/편지, 기사 유형 지문은 거의 항상 나오는 편이며 많은 경우 합해서 전체의 50~60%에 이르기도 한다.

- 기타 지문 유형으로 agenda, brochure, comment card, coupon, flyer, instructions, invitation, invoice, list, menu, page from a catalog, policy statement, report, schedule, survey, voucher 등 다양한 자료가 골고루 나온다.

(이중 지문과 삼중 지문 속의 지문들을 모두 낱개로 계산함 − 총 23지문)

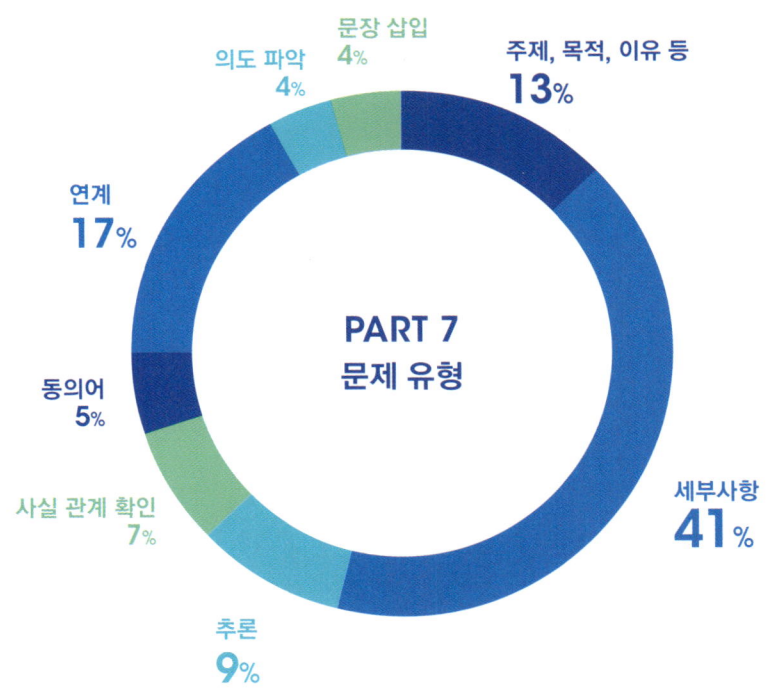

PART 7 문제 유형

- 주제, 목적, 이유 등 **13**%
- 세부사항 **41**%
- 추론 **9**%
- 사실 관계 확인 **7**%
- 동의어 **5**%
- 연계 **17**%
- 의도 파악 **4**%
- 문장 삽입 **4**%

- 동의어 문제는 주로 이중 지문이나 삼중 지문에 나온다.
- 연계 문제는 일반적으로 이중 지문에서 한 문제, 삼중 지문에서 두 문제가 나온다.
- 의도 파악 문제는 문자 메시지(text-message chain)나 온라인 채팅(online chat discussion) 지문에서 출제되며 두 문제가 나온다.
- 문장 삽입 문제는 주로 기사, 이메일, 편지, 회람 지문에서 출제되며 두 문제가 나온다.

점수 환산표

LISTENING Raw Score (맞은 개수)	LISTENING Scaled Score (환산 점수)	READING Raw Score (맞은 개수)	READING Scaled Score (환산 점수)
96–100	480–495	96–100	460–495
91–95	435–490	91–95	410–475
86–90	395–450	86–90	380–430
81–85	355–415	81–85	355–400
76–80	325–375	76–80	325–375
71–75	295–340	71–75	295–345
66–70	265–315	66–70	265–315
61–65	240–285	61–65	235–285
56–60	215–260	56–60	205–255
51–55	190–235	51–55	175–225
46–50	160–210	46–50	150–195
41–45	135–180	41–45	120–170
36–40	110–155	36–40	100–140
31–35	85–130	31–35	75–120
26–30	70–105	26–30	55–100
21–25	50–90	21–25	40–80
16–20	35–70	16–20	30–65
11–15	20–55	11–15	20–50
6–10	15–40	6–10	15–35
1–5	5–20	1–5	5–20
0	5	0	5

* 이 환산표는 본 교재에 수록된 Test용으로 개발된 것이다. 이 표를 사용하여 자신의 실제 점수를 환산 점수로 전환하도록 한다. 즉, 예를 들어 Reading Test의 실제 정답 수가 61~65개이면 환산 점수는 235점에서 285점 사이가 된다. 여기서 실제 정답 수가 61개이면 환산 점수가 235점이고, 65개이면 환산 점수가 285점임을 의미하는 것은 아니다. 본 책의 Test를 위해 작성된 이 점수 환산표가 자신의 영어 실력이 어느 정도인지 대략적으로 파악하는 데 도움이 되긴 하지만, 이 표가 실제 TOEIC 성적 산출에 그대로 사용된 적은 없다는 사실을 밝혀 둔다.

CONTENTS

TEST 1

READING TEST

In the Reading test, you will read a variety of texts and answer several different types of reading comprehension questions. The entire Reading test will last 75 minutes. There are three parts, and directions are given for each part. You are encouraged to answer as many questions as possible within the time allowed.

You must mark your answers on the separate answer sheet. Do not write your answers in your test book.

PART 5

Directions: A word or phrase is missing in each of the sentences below. Four answer choices are given below each sentence. Select the best answer to complete the sentence. Then mark the letter (A), (B), (C), or (D) on your answer sheet.

101. Diners at the Appleton Buffet have commented favorably on ------- wide variety of seafood dishes.

(A) we
(B) us
(C) our
(D) ours

102. Rev Furniture has high-quality handmade goods and reasonable delivery -------.

(A) routines
(B) trucks
(C) duties
(D) fees

103. The Fort Myers Garden Club ------- a monthly newsletter to its members to keep them informed.

(A) circulates
(B) was circulated
(C) to circulate
(D) has been circulated

104. Decorated with fascinating -------, the hotel's lobby is a great place to pass the time while waiting for someone.

(A) photographer
(B) photographed
(C) photographs
(D) photographic

105. At the end of the lease period, ------- keys to the apartment must be returned to the building owner.

(A) each
(B) all
(C) another
(D) others

106. The chemical can be hazardous if it gets in contact with bare skin, so be sure to handle it -------.

(A) carefully
(B) fairly
(C) currently
(D) barely

107. Tourism in Palm Valley has declined steadily ------- the past few years due to the rising cost of flights.

(A) over
(B) of
(C) beneath
(D) then

108. Most of the patient files are stored ------- secure cabinets on the fourth floor, which has a high level of security.

(A) as
(B) to
(C) in
(D) down

109. Because of a lack of space at the warehouse, some goods will be sent ------- to the store from the manufacturer.
(A) directs
(B) director
(C) directly
(D) direction

110. ------- the expansion to the Phoenix Building be approved, construction will begin at the beginning of March.
(A) Should
(B) Since
(C) Did
(D) While

111. Although the CEO spoke to reporters at the press conference, he failed to provide ------- answers to their questions.
(A) satisfies
(B) satisfactory
(C) satisfaction
(D) satisfactorily

112. Fans of the *Galaxy Battle* adventure series are ------- awaiting the release of the new film by director Rick Keller.
(A) fairly
(B) precisely
(C) repeatedly
(D) eagerly

113. The hotel works with several distributors in the region to ensure a ------- supply of cleaning products.
(A) constant
(B) portable
(C) reluctant
(D) previous

114. The office manager held a last-minute meeting ------- the sudden resignation of the company's president.
(A) concerning
(B) whereas
(C) until
(D) within

115. The first topic in the safety training covered ------- it is necessary to contact emergency medical personnel.
(A) when
(B) who
(C) what
(D) which

116. Ms. Lang uses Sky Couriers to send packages because she knows the service will be -------.
(A) prompts
(B) promptly
(C) promptness
(D) prompt

117. The parking policy that ------- by city officials last month resulted in a great deal of confusion among residents.
(A) had been implementing
(B) was implemented
(C) will have been implemented
(D) had implemented

118. The ticket allows you to visit all sections of the museum's permanent gallery ------- not its special exhibits.
(A) or
(B) but
(C) so
(D) as

119. Not until her book was published did the author speak ------- about her inspiration for writing it.
(A) publicity
(B) publicly
(C) public
(D) publicized

120. ------- its positive effect on the environment, the recycling program will generate extra income for the city.
(A) Besides
(B) Among
(C) Instead
(D) Toward

GO ON TO THE NEXT PAGE

121. The factory increased productivity by nearly thirty percent through equipment ------- made possible by a federal grant.

(A) modernize
(B) modernization
(C) modernized
(D) modernizes

122. Applicants must be at least eighteen years old ------- participate in the amateur photography contest.

(A) even though
(B) in order to
(C) on behalf of
(D) so that

123. All patrons of the Vanceville Public Library must agree to ------- by the library's rules and regulations.

(A) conform
(B) accompany
(C) establish
(D) abide

124. The news program is ------- to countries around the world in real time through a continuous satellite feed.

(A) featured
(B) equipped
(C) determined
(D) transmitted

125. Trash bins are ------- placed throughout the amusement park to reduce the amount of litter left on the ground.

(A) strategic
(B) strategized
(C) strategically
(D) strategy

126. The supervisor decided to introduce a relaxed dress code on Fridays in an attempt to improve staff -------.

(A) reimbursement
(B) appointment
(C) morale
(D) resource

127. A protective substance was applied to the new surface of the parking lot to keep it from ------- over time.

(A) revealing
(B) commuting
(C) overtaking
(D) deteriorating

128. The sales director believes that an eight percent increase in sales next quarter is a readily ------- goal.

(A) achieve
(B) achievable
(C) achievement
(D) achieving

129. Because Ms. Ferris did not have her ID card with her, the security guard ------- to allow her to enter the building.

(A) refuse
(B) refusal
(C) refusing
(D) refused

130. Although the logos had a ------- similar design, they were created by two completely unrelated companies.

(A) steadily
(B) remarkably
(C) consecutively
(D) unanimously

PART 6

Directions: Read the texts that follow. A word, phrase, or sentence is missing in parts of each text. Four answer choices for each question are given below the text. Select the best answer to complete the text. Then mark the letter (A), (B), (C), or (D) on your answer sheet.

Questions 131-134 refer to the following article.

March 12 — Starting from next month, street parking in the city center will be free. City council members chose ------- the use of parking meters downtown by a unanimous vote. Rising wages are
131.
needed for city workers to check parking meters and issue tickets, so the practice is no longer -------.
132.
Officials hope the change will also ------- development of the downtown area by encouraging more
133.
visitors, many of whom are shoppers from out of town. The change will go into effect on April 1,

though the meters won't be removed immediately. -------.
134.

131. (A) being discontinued
(B) discontinuing
(C) to discontinue
(D) discontinues

132. (A) economize
(B) economically
(C) economy
(D) economical

133. (A) adopt
(B) foster
(C) multiply
(D) publicize

134. (A) Signs will be posted to notify motorists.
(B) Traffic updates can be requested by text.
(C) The parking fee is considered reasonable.
(D) Please pay your parking fines promptly.

Questions 135-138 refer to the following e-mail.

To: Crucero Staff <stafflist@crucero.net>
From: Gabrielle Jensen <jensong@crucero.net>
Date: November 16
Subject: Overtime hours

The members of the finance team have ------- examined the budgets for our branch and, through
                                        135.
their meticulous work, determined that there is a significant shortfall. ------- this discovery, we must
                                                                           136.
reduce operating expenses by minimizing overtime hours. Please try to get all of your work -------
                                                                                            137.
within the usual business hours. In cases where overtime work cannot be avoided, it should be

approved in advance by a department head. -------. Thank you for your cooperation.
                                           138.

Sincerely,

Gabrielle Jensen

---

135. (A) thoroughly
    (B) urgently
    (C) adversely
    (D) solely

136. (A) Because
    (B) Due to
    (C) Consequently
    (D) Rather than

137. (A) completes
    (B) completed
    (C) completion
    (D) completing

138. (A) Please send in your detailed budgets as
       soon as possible.
    (B) Most employees prefer working on
       Saturdays over working on Sundays.
    (C) This applies to both sales and
       administration employees.
    (D) The additional payment has been
       deposited in your account.

Questions 139-142 refer to the following announcement.

Dawsonville in Motion, a nonprofit organization dedicated to promoting healthy lifestyles, ------- a **139.** Well-Being Festival for Saturday, August 18. The group wants to raise ------- of the methods for **140.** preventing heart disease and other conditions. The goal of many of the festival activities will be to show participants that they don't have to adhere strictly to a diet. -------. For example, a piece of fruit **141.** can replace a candy bar as an afternoon snack. -------, diners can swap French fries for a salad. **142.** Want more helpful tips? Come to the festival! It will be held at the Dawsonville Community Center, and admission is free to everyone.

139. (A) having organized
(B) would have organized
(C) has organized
(D) being organized

140. (A) awareness
(B) funds
(C) interest
(D) standards

141. (A) They can make small changes to improve their health.
(B) Organizers hope that the turnout is better than last year.
(C) The diet can be downloaded from the group's Web site.
(D) Rates of medical problems are on the rise in Dawsonville.

142. (A) As a result
(B) Similarly
(C) Regardless
(D) Unfortunately

GO ON TO THE NEXT PAGE

Questions 143-146 refer to the following notice.

CHARACK TOWERS: NOTICE

------- of Charack Towers should be aware that the power will be turned off to most of the complex
143.
on Thursday, September 18 at 9 A.M. to install new wiring. -------. The power should be restored by
144.
noon, but if the work takes longer than expected, it might affect ------- goods in your refrigerator. We
145.
will notify you if the work exceeds the estimated schedule so that you may check that your food is
still edible. Please note that this planned outage will affect all parts of Charack Towers ------- the
146.
South Tower, which was upgraded last quarter. Thank you for your patience and understanding.

---

143. (A) Occupy
(B) Occupations
(C) Occupying
(D) Occupants

144. (A) We must do so to comply with safety
regulations.
(B) If you would like to sign up, visit the
property office.
(C) The loss of power was caused by a severe
storm.
(D) Please wear protective gear while you are
working.

145. (A) durable
(B) renewable
(C) perishable
(D) exposed

146. (A) inside of
(B) owing to
(C) aside from
(D) such as

PART 7

Directions: In this part you will read a selection of texts, such as magazine and newspaper articles, e-mails, and instant messages. Each text or set of texts is followed by several questions. Select the best answer for each question and mark the letter (A), (B), (C), or (D) on your answer sheet.

Questions 147-148 refer to the following form.

Steam Masters Customer Rental Agreement
170 Malloy Street • (325) 555-0197

Customer: Iswara Gupte   Phone Number: (325) 555-0166
First-time Customer: No   Delivery ☐   Customer Pick-up ☒

Item	Description	Price
Dowler-405 carpet steam cleaner rental	Two-day rental	$95.00
Equipment rental deposit		$50.00
Concentrated carpet shampoo (12 oz.)	Purchase	$15.95
	Total	$160.95

Rental period valid until 5 P.M. on March 6. The deposit will be paid back once the device is returned.

---

147. What is true about Mr. Gupte?

(A) He rented two types of equipment.
(B) He can keep the device for one week.
(C) He recently changed his phone number.
(D) He has used Steam Masters before.

148. What will happen when Mr. Gupte returns the device?

(A) He will have to pay the remainder of his bill.
(B) He will be credited for unused shampoo.
(C) He will receive fifty dollars back.
(D) He will be charged a pick-up fee.

GO ON TO THE NEXT PAGE

Ramona Jackson
Ramona's Restaurant
552 Spring Haven Road
Santa Barbara, CA 93106

Dear Ms. Jackson,

Santa Barbara city officials have received several complaints regarding the outdoor patio you have set up in front of your restaurant, near the sidewalk. Because of your business hours, many of your patrons are having loud conversations outdoors late at night. Please ask your patrons to keep their conversations to a minimum volume after 9 P.M. You should also post a written announcement reminding them to be courteous of the residents in the area. I've enclosed one as an example. If you have any inquiries, please direct them to our non-emergency line at 555-0181.

Thank you for your cooperation.

Rita Salazar

Rita Salazar
Santa Barbara Police Department

---

149. What problem does Ms. Salazar mention?

(A) A neighborhood is for residential use only.
(B) Some tables are blocking a walkway.
(C) A restaurant's business license has expired.
(D) Customers are making too much noise.

150. What has Ms. Salazar included with the letter?

(A) A copy of an agenda
(B) An inquiry form
(C) A sample notice
(D) An invoice

Questions 151-152 refer to the following text-message chain.

Guo Xie, 2:05 P.M.
I'm on my way back from the meeting with the representatives from Largo Enterprises, but they're going to be accompanying me so that they can have a brief tour of our building.

Saskia Heyns, 2:06 P.M.
Is there anything you need me to do?

Guo Xie, 2:06 P.M.
Yes. Could you please check that the lobby looks presentable? It's their first time visiting our site, and I don't want them to form a poor opinion of our company right from the start.

Saskia Heyns, 2:07 P.M.
No problem. Several boxes of samples from our supplier arrived today. They're too big to fit in the storage closet. Maybe I can put them in someone's office.

Guo Xie, 2:08 P.M.
Good idea. I'm sure Ms. Hudson wouldn't mind.

Saskia Heyns, 2:09 P.M.
Okay. I'll make sure that's taken care of before you get here. How much time do I have?

Guo Xie, 2:10 P.M.
About half an hour. Thanks a lot!

151. What is Mr. Xie concerned about?

(A) Making an unfavorable first impression
(B) Meeting up with the representatives late
(C) Failing to find an employee to conduct a tour
(D) Having limited access to the building's lobby

152. At 2:08 P.M., what does Mr. Xie most likely mean when he says, "I'm sure Ms. Hudson wouldn't mind"?

(A) Ms. Hudson should help clean an area.
(B) Ms. Hudson can order more samples.
(C) Ms. Hudson has storage space in her office.
(D) Ms. Hudson should talk to the supplier.

GO ON TO THE NEXT PAGE

Please accept this coupon with the compliments of the new proprietor of **Starlight Bakery**.

This coupon can be used toward one of the following:

Buy one dozen cupcakes, and get two free cookies
Get 10% off fresh bread
Buy one cake and get another at half price

Expires July 31

Valid at our two locations: 349 Broad Street and 1709 Dellwood Avenue

153. What has recently changed at Starlight Bakery?

(A) Complimentary samples are distributed.
(B) The selection has been expanded.
(C) A second location has been opened.
(D) The business is under new ownership.

154. What is indicated on the coupon?

(A) Customers can buy two cakes for the price of one.
(B) The coupon is valid for a single offer.
(C) Free cookies are available with each purchase.
(D) The bakery's bread can be ordered in advance.

Questions 155-157 refer to the following advertisement.

TR2

You don't need to be a professional athlete to work out in comfort and style. At TR2, we offer the best apparel for basketball, soccer, baseball, and more. Whether you need lightweight running shorts for your next marathon or a warm-up suit for your exercise routine, we've got you covered. New owner Stephen Carbajal has participated in athletic competitions all over the world, and he is ready to bring his expertise and love of sports to you. In addition to our everyday low prices, we are offering a special coupon for 15% to anyone who registers for our mailing list to receive the TR2 monthly newsletter. Visit us daily from 9 A.M. to 9 P.M. at 1673 Davis Street.

155. What is being advertised?

(A) An athletic competition
(B) An exercise facility
(C) A sports stadium
(D) A clothing store

156. What is indicated about Mr. Carbajal?

(A) He was the winner of a sports competition.
(B) He recently purchased the business.
(C) He operates branches in several locations.
(D) He has moved to the area from another country.

157. How can customers take advantage of the special offer?

(A) By making a certain number of purchases
(B) By visiting the business on a particular day
(C) By signing up for a publication
(D) By recommending the business to a friend

GO ON TO THE NEXT PAGE

Fairmont Department Store

Thank you for taking the time to complete our annual questionnaire. To show our appreciation, we offer you this discount voucher.

15% off all cookware, bedding, and appliances in the store

Can be used at any Fairmont Department Store location. Does not include delivery or installation fees. Applicable to all brands, including TJ Home, coming October 1. Present your Fairmont Rewards Membership Card at the time of purchase to receive an additional 5% off.

Thank you for being a Fairmont Department Store customer!

158. What is indicated about the voucher?

(A) It is valid until October 1.
(B) It was issued to a survey participant.
(C) It can only be used at a certain branch.
(D) It cannot be combined with other offers.

159. What is NOT something that could be purchased with the voucher?

(A) A kitchen table
(B) A set of sheets
(C) A washing machine
(D) A frying pan

160. What is suggested about Fairmont Department Store?

(A) It has a customer loyalty program.
(B) It provides discounts to new customers.
(C) It offers free delivery for all products.
(D) It is the only store carrying the TJ Home brand.

NOTICE TO WOODFORD APARTMENT TENANTS:

On Wednesday, August 17, the Woodford Apartments maintenance crew will be testing the fire alarms and sprinkler system throughout the building. The testing is part of a quarterly check performed to fulfill the terms of the building owner's insurance policy and to ensure the safety of all tenants. The work will begin around 10 A.M. and is expected to take approximately two hours. During the testing procedures, the alarm system may sound continuously for up to a few minutes at a time. In addition, the hallways' emergency lights may flash on and off. You may ignore both of these signals, and there is no need to evacuate the building or take any further action. In the very unlikely event that an emergency presents itself during the testing, we will use the building's loudspeaker to instruct tenants to vacate the building. The procedures for evacuation can be obtained from the building manager. All questions about the testing should be directed to Scott Porter, as his team will be carrying out the work. Thank you for your cooperation.

161. What is the purpose of the work on August 17?

(A) To meet new government safety regulations
(B) To install fire prevention equipment for tenant use
(C) To comply with insurance requirements
(D) To replace a security system throughout the building

162. According to the notice, when should tenants take action during the August 17 work?

(A) If they hear an alarm sound
(B) If they see the hallway lights flashing
(C) If they hear an announcement
(D) If they receive a phone call

163. Who most likely is Mr. Porter?

(A) A maintenance manager
(B) A building owner
(C) A government official
(D) A building manager

GO ON TO THE NEXT PAGE

To: Department of Sanitation Employees
From: Larry Bozeman, Department Head
Date: September 3
Re: Update

Earlier this week, I visited the Brookville landfill to carry out an evaluation and determine the time left before space in the landfill runs out. — [1] —. The last estimate was made a decade ago, and at that time it was projected that the landfill would be able to meet Brookville's needs for another fifty years. Therefore, at this point, we would expect to have forty years left before having to make alternative plans for the management of solid waste. Unfortunately, as the number of residents in our community has nearly doubled in size in just a few short years, the landfill is getting used much more than originally anticipated. At the current rate, the remaining space at the site would only last for eighteen to twenty more years. — [2] —.

In order to curb overuse of the landfill and delay the date when the site will run out of space, I have already obtained approval to begin a food waste recycling program, which will be called the Brookville Compost Collection Program, or the BCC Program for short. — [3] —. This will involve collecting food scraps in special containers, to be picked up on the normal recycling collection days and used to create fertilizer. We will run a trial program in Warren Park, Oak Grove, and Rocklane beginning from next month. Once we work out the logistics, the program will be expanded to all neighborhoods in Brookville.

We will heavily promote recycling throughout Brookville, especially targeting businesses, whose commercial waste makes up approximately thirty percent of what is collected. — [4] —. This action alone could save tens of thousands of tons of waste. Homeowners and businesses would be encouraged to compost their yard waste on site instead.

164. What has Mr. Bozeman recently done?

    (A) Trained new sanitation department staff
    (B) Assessed a garbage disposal site
    (C) Gathered feedback from Brookville residents
    (D) Carried out employee evaluations

165. According to Mr. Bozeman, what has contributed to the problem?

    (A) Complex regulations
    (B) Rising recycling costs
    (C) Lack of public interest
    (D) Rapid population growth

166. What is indicated about the BCC Program?

    (A) It will be tested in a few neighborhoods initially.
    (B) It is aimed at teaching people how to prepare recyclables.
    (C) It may fail to be approved due to budget cuts.
    (D) It will be partially funded by the sale of fertilizer.

167. In which of the positions marked [1], [2], [3], and [4] does the following sentence best belong?

"Another possibility is not to allow grass clippings in the landfill."

    (A) [1]
    (B) [2]
    (C) [3]
    (D) [4]

GO ON TO THE NEXT PAGE

Yorkie Furniture Customer Assistance   — □ X

Gloria Cox (Staff ID: 413)   [3:09 P.M.]
Hello. I am a customer service agent for Yorkie Furniture. Are you writing about an old order or a pending order?

Sherman Holcomb   [3:10 P.M.]
An old order. I have already received the product.

Gloria Cox (Staff ID: 413)   [3:11 P.M.]
All right. What seems to be the problem?

Sherman Holcomb   [3:12 P.M.]
I'm having trouble assembling the shelves I ordered from you. In the past, I've paid for your pre-assembled goods, but this time I thought I'd try it myself.

Gloria Cox (Staff ID: 413)   [3:13 P.M.]
Please tell me the product name and whether there are any parts missing.

Sherman Holcomb   [3:16 P.M.]
It's the Rustic Beach Set shelving unit model. I'm not sure if anything is missing because it didn't come with any assembly instructions.

Gloria Cox (Staff ID: 413)   [3:17 P.M.]
I'm sorry about that. We've had numerous complaints about that model. During the packing process, the workers didn't put in the instructions or the product brochure.

Sherman Holcomb   [3:18 P.M.]
Could you mail the instructions to me?

Gloria Cox (Staff ID: 413)   [3:19 P.M.]
Of course, but if you have a printer at home, you can download them from our Web site instead and print them yourself.

Sherman Holcomb   [3:21 P.M.]
Are they the same instructions that would be shipped in the mail?

Gloria Cox (Staff ID: 413)   [3:22 P.M.]
Yes, and it's a lot easier.

Sherman Holcomb   [3:24 P.M.]
Okay, I'll do that now.

Gloria Cox (Staff ID: 413)   [3:25 P.M.]
I won't terminate this conversation until I know that you were able to get the document you need.

Sherman Holcomb   [3:26 P.M.]
Thank you.

168. What does Mr. Holcomb indicate about Yorkie Furniture?

(A) He thinks its prices are reasonable.
(B) Its selection has recently expanded.
(C) He has used its services before.
(D) It has a reputation for high-quality goods.

169. What does Ms. Cox suggest about the Rustic Beach Set?

(A) It is one of the company's most popular products.
(B) It is no longer being manufactured by the company.
(C) It was sent without all the necessary paperwork.
(D) It can be returned directly to the warehouse.

170. At 3:22 P.M., what does Ms. Cox mean when she writes, "it's a lot easier"?

(A) She recommends getting some information online.
(B) She wants Mr. Holcomb to set up an account.
(C) She plans to send an item by express mail.
(D) She thinks a different shelving unit would be better.

171. Why will Ms. Cox keep the chat open?

(A) To allow time to check an inventory list
(B) To wait for an order number
(C) To provide Mr. Holcomb with a progress update
(D) To confirm that Mr. Holcomb has received some paperwork

GO ON TO THE NEXT PAGE

Glass Containers to Be Banned

March 23—The Wynnedale City Council voted to enact a proposal that would ban glass containers at public beaches and parks. —[1]—. The measure, brought forward by Andrew McDowell, seeks to reduce injuries from broken glass, and it contained recommendations to fine those who disobey the ban up to $500 for the first violation. This original fine was considered excessive by many council members and was reduced to $100 before the final vote was taken.

Although the proposal received widespread support, it is not without its opponents. —[2]—. Ellen Jacobs voted against the proposal because she believed that it could disproportionately affect those living on the streets. Others raised concerns that the local police force does not have the manpower to make sure that people are following the regulation. This is because most discarded glass containers come from individuals or very small groups. Large-scale events such as concerts and festivals do not usually contribute to the litter problem. —[3]—.

The council plans to launch a public awareness campaign on April 3 to inform residents about the new regulation, which will go into effect the following month. —[4]—. It will include posting notices on the city's Web site, running public service announcements on the radio, and putting up signs in public places to spread the news.

172. What is indicated about Mr. McDowell's proposal?

(A) It will mainly apply to businesses.
(B) It will go into effect sometime in April.
(C) It was altered before receiving approval.
(D) It was unanimously supported by the city council.

173. What problem did Ms. Jacobs anticipate regarding the proposal?

(A) It could be applied unfairly to the homeless.
(B) It will cost too much to publicize the change.
(C) It would not result in cleaner public streets.
(D) It will be difficult for the local police to enforce it.

174. What is NOT a method that will be used in the public awareness campaign?

(A) Radio announcements
(B) Newspaper advertisements
(C) Online messages
(D) Publicly posted signs

175. In which of the positions marked [1], [2], [3], and [4] does the following sentence best belong?

"These require a detailed cleanup plan before a permit is issued."

(A) [1]
(B) [2]
(C) [3]
(D) [4]

GO ON TO THE NEXT PAGE

Rest and refresh with help from the Luna pillow from Odessa Housewares!

With the accelerated pace of modern life, getting enough sleep is more important than ever. Many people fail to realize that better sleep can result from keeping the body in the right position. Our team has meticulously researched sleeping habits to create a one-of-a-kind pillow that eliminates the most common sleeping problems. The Luna pillow is a memory foam pillow that is thinner in the middle for back sleepers and has high sides for side sleepers. This unique shape ensures that your head and neck are fully supported, and this also serves to ease discomfort and aching in your shoulders.

Each Luna pillow comes with an anti-bacterial cover that perfectly fits the pillow. The cover is made from a cotton and cashmere blend to maximize sweat absorption. Owing to the cover's patented Air-Flo technology, it keeps your head cool on hot nights and warm on cold nights, ensuring maximum comfort for hours. Visit www.odessahousewares.com for more information.

---

www.ratehomefurnishings.com ▼

Bedding >> Odessa Housewares >> Luna Pillow

Review posted by Jeff Payton

I made a purchase from Odessa Housewares before, so I opted into their monthly e-mail newsletter system. The most recent newsletter included advertisements for the Luna pillow, so I thought I'd give it a try. It took a few nights to get used to the firmness of the memory foam, but after the adjustment period, I started falling asleep more quickly and sleeping more soundly. The gentle touch of the cashmere and cotton case against my skin feels elegant and luxurious. I would highly recommend this pillow to anyone who has difficulty sleeping. I'm such a big fan of this pillow that I plan to purchase it as a gift for several of my family members.

176. According to the advertisement, what can help to improve sleep?

(A) Sleeping on a set schedule
(B) Positioning the body correctly
(C) Relaxing before bedtime
(D) Maintaining the right temperature

177. What benefit of the Luna pillow is mentioned in the advertisement?

(A) Building neck muscles
(B) Relieving joint pain
(C) Improving posture
(D) Reducing noise disturbances

178. What is NOT indicated about the Luna pillow's cover?

(A) It regulates body heat.
(B) It absorbs moisture.
(C) It can be machine washable.
(D) It is resistant to bacteria.

179. Which feature mentioned in the advertisement does Mr. Payton neglect to address?

(A) The pillow's shape
(B) The shipping process
(C) The pillow's material
(D) The cover's fabric

180. How did Mr. Payton originally find out about the Luna pillow?

(A) He was given the item as a gift from a family member.
(B) He saw an advertisement in a newspaper.
(C) He watched a demonstration in a store.
(D) He was e-mailed some promotional materials.

GO ON TO THE NEXT PAGE

Majestic Travel: Customer Invoice #8394

Customer: Kasis Rizal
Destination: Palm Island

Booking Date: May 3
First-Time Visitor: Yes

Accommodation: Hibiscus Corporation Room Type: Deluxe Number of Adults: 2, Number of Children: 0 Check in: July 19 / Check out: July 23	$700.00
Dining: Villa Complex All-Day Meal Pass, 2 Adults: July 20-22 Breakfast Meal Pass, 2 Adults: July 23	$185.00
Activity 1: Meridian Limited Private Boat Tour of Meridian Cove: July 21 Deposit of $100 received on May 3	$390.00
Activity 2: Orchid Enterprises Workshop: How to Prepare Regional Cuisine, 2 Adults: July 22	$60.00
Subtotal	$1,335.00
Remaining due	**$1,235.00**

Note: Plane tickets to be booked separately by the customer.

E-mail

To:	Kasis Rizal <krizal@stiles-inc.net>
From:	Raja Tahyadi <tahyadiraja@majestictravel.com>
Date:	May 8
Subject:	RE: Inquiry

Dear Ms. Rizal,

In response to your inquiry, I double-checked your invoice (#8394), and I can confirm that everything on the invoice is correct. I believe the source of confusion is that the price for the boat tour listed on our Web site is just a base fee, but a booking charge and additional valued added tax (VAT) were also applied, resulting in the total you see on the invoice. This was explained at the bottom of the booking page. Additionally, you are getting a discount on your meal passes because we are partners with that business, so the overall price of the vacation is quite reasonable. Nevertheless, if you would like to cancel the boat tour, you may do so, but the request must be made in writing by May 31, and you would lose half of your deposit. If you cancel after this date, you will be charged the full amount.

Attached you will find the instructions once again for paying the remaining balance by bank transfer. As I mentioned when you booked the trip, we no longer accept cash, checks, or credit cards.

I hope I have answered your questions to your satisfaction, but please do not hesitate to contact me if you have further inquiries.

Warmest regards,

Raja Tahyadi
Majestic Travel

181. What is indicated about Ms. Rizal?

(A) She will be on vacation for five nights.
(B) She has visited Palm Island in the past.
(C) She will share a room with two other people.
(D) She plans to participate in a cooking lesson.

182. What problem did Ms. Rizal most likely write to Mr. Tahyadi about?

(A) A payment receipt was not sent.
(B) A boat tour has been fully booked.
(C) A check-in date is incorrect.
(D) A fee was higher than expected.

183. How much would Ms. Rizal lose if she cancels the boat tour by May 31?

(A) $390.00
(B) $290.00
(C) $100.00
(D) $50.00

184. Which business is partnered with Majestic Travel?

(A) Hibiscus Corporation
(B) Villa Complex
(C) Meridian Limited
(D) Orchid Enterprises

185. What is suggested about Majestic Travel?

(A) It has a branch on Palm Island.
(B) It only accepts one form of payment.
(C) It mainly books vacation packages.
(D) It can provide discounts on airfares.

GO ON TO THE NEXT PAGE

History in Motion **Photography Contest**

History in Motion magazine is proud to announce its annual photography contest. This year's theme is "Transportation Then and Now." Entries must contain an image of a train, car, bus, etc. Images may be in color or black and white, and they will be judged by a panel of professional photographers along with our editorial team.

To enter the contest, visit www.historyinmotionmag.com/photo. There you can fill out an application form and upload your photo. You must also submit a statement affirming that the photo is your original work and that you hold all distribution rights to it. Participants may submit more than one entry, up to five total. Submissions must be received by June 30.

History in Motion Magazine Headquarters
Dodson Building, Suite 3001
489 Colony Street
Charlotte, South Carolina 28202

July 6

Samuel Goetz
1396 Valley View Drive
Boston, MA 02114

Dear Mr. Goetz,

Congratulations! You are a finalist in the *History in Motion* Photography Contest. Your photo entitled *Time over Time* was disqualified because it did not fit the contest's theme. However, *Face the Forest* really impressed the judging panel, so it has been selected as one of eight finalists.

You are invited to visit our headquarters on July 28 to take a tour, meet the other finalists, and participate in a photo shoot. We will cover your expenses for the flight to and from your home city as well as two nights of accommodations. Travel arrangements will be made by my assistant, and all contact regarding travel should go through her (contact details enclosed).

I hope you will be able to visit us!

Thomas Porter

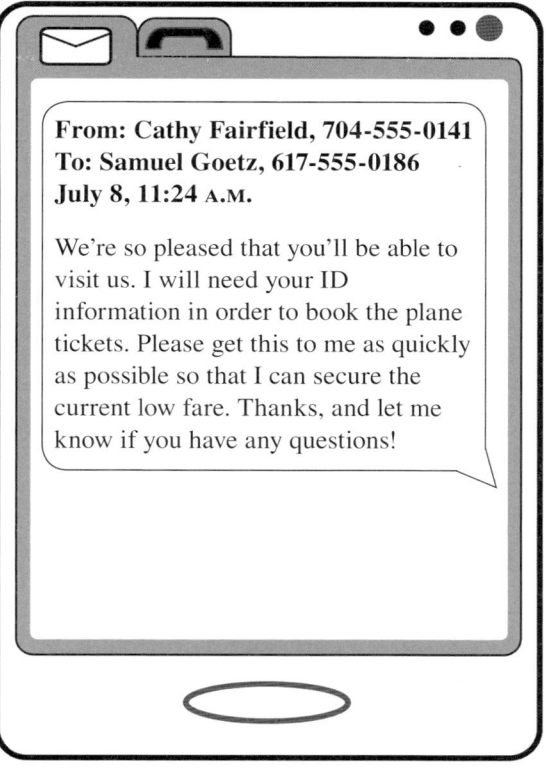

From: Cathy Fairfield, 704-555-0141
To: Samuel Goetz, 617-555-0186
July 8, 11:24 A.M.

We're so pleased that you'll be able to visit us. I will need your ID information in order to book the plane tickets. Please get this to me as quickly as possible so that I can secure the current low fare. Thanks, and let me know if you have any questions!

186. According to the information, what are contest entrants required to do?

(A) Declare that the submission is their own work
(B) Send a photograph of a particular size
(C) Include a description of their work with the entry
(D) Select an age category when signing up

187. What is suggested about *Time over Time*?

(A) It did not arrive before the deadline.
(B) It was well liked by the contest's judges.
(C) It was printed in black and white.
(D) It did not contain a form of transportation.

188. What does Mr. Porter say that his company will do?

(A) Take a trip to Mr. Goetz's hometown
(B) Inform the winners by e-mail
(C) Pay for a trip to South Carolina
(D) Give Mr. Goetz a job offer

189. Who most likely is Ms. Fairfield?

(A) A judge in the photo contest
(B) Mr. Goetz's business partner
(C) The editor of *History in Motion*
(D) Mr. Porter's assistant

190. In the text message, the word "secure" in paragraph 1, line 5, is closest in meaning to

(A) defend
(B) convince
(C) attach
(D) guarantee

GO ON TO THE NEXT PAGE

Viola Dalton
528 Coleman Road
Charlotte, NC 28210

July 6

Dear Ms. Dalton,

It was a pleasure to meet you at your interview on June 13. The entire hiring committee was impressed with your career history as well as your natural people skills. We are pleased that you have accepted the position of R&D Department Manager. Now that we have both signed the contract, it is official. Enclosed you will find a copy of the contract for your records.

For the orientation on July 17, you will be assigned to Group C. I look forward to seeing you there!

Sincerely,

Arina Saitou
Arina Saitou

HR Manager, Caldwell Corporation

To:	Undisclosed Recipients
From:	Arina Saitou
Date:	July 13
Subject:	Orientation at the Caldwell Corporation

Dear New Employees,

As we have just moved into our headquarters building, most of you have not seen it yet. The building has a spacious patio area for taking breaks or eating lunch outside, and the Lansing River runs right past it, so the views are amazing. I'm sure you will love it as much as the rest of the staff does.

To expedite the check-in process at the orientation on July 17, employees of each department should report to different rooms. Please see the table below:

Department(s)	Room
Graphic Design	Room 308
Research & Development, Accounting	Room 233
Marketing, Sales	Conference Room A
Administration, Human Resources	Conference Room B

I have attached a copy of the orientation schedule. Please do not hesitate to contact me with any questions you may have.

Sincerely,

Arina Saitou
HR Manager, Caldwell Corporation

Caldwell Corporation Ⓒⓦ
Staff Orientation, July 17

8:30 A.M.	Check-in (report to assigned rooms)
9:00 A.M.	Welcome speech, CEO Yan Huo
9:30 A.M.	Tax Paperwork and Vacation Policies, Ruth Bova
11:45 A.M.	Dress Code, Hamid Yemane
12:15 P.M.	Lunch: During the lunch break, groups should visit the security office to be assigned ID badges according to the following schedule: Group A 12:15 P.M., Group B 12:30 P.M., Group C 12:45 P.M., Group D 1:00 P.M.
1:15 P.M.	Online Activities from Work Computers, Jocelyn Lewis
2:30 P.M.	Split Session: Managers will hear a talk from Director Diego Barros, non-management full-time employees will have a question-and-answer session with Prabha Haldar, and part-time employees will watch a training video
4:45 P.M.	Building tour, Arina Saitou

191. Why did Ms. Saitou write the letter?

(A) To request further information
(B) To confirm a job appointment
(C) To make changes to a contract
(D) To set up an interview

192. Where should Ms. Dalton go first on July 17?

(A) Room 308
(B) Room 233
(C) Conference Room A
(D) Conference Room B

193. In the e-mail, the word "rest" in paragraph 1, line 4, is closest in meaning to

(A) relaxation
(B) majority
(C) halt
(D) remainder

194. What is implied about Ms. Dalton?

(A) She will get her questions answered by Ms. Haldar.
(B) She should go to the security office at 12:15 P.M.
(C) She will watch a video during the orientation.
(D) She will attend a session with Mr. Barros.

195. What is NOT indicated as a topic covered in the orientation?

(A) Internet usage
(B) Taking time off
(C) What to wear to work
(D) Corporate structure

GO ON TO THE NEXT PAGE

```
┌──────────────────────────── *E-Mail* ────────────────────────────┐
│  To:      │ Independent Filmmakers Club <memberslist@independentfilmc.com>│
│  From:    │ Roger Stratton <rstratton@palletpost.net>                     │
│  Date:    │ April 7                                                       │
│  Subject: │ Fresno Film Festival                                          │
└───────────────────────────────────────────────────────────────────┘
```

Dear Members,

As discussed at our last meeting, there is an exciting opportunity next month at the Fresno Film Festival. Attending this event will not only allow us to learn from the creative work of others, but it will also further our cause of supporting independent filmmakers.

Based on the interests expressed at the meeting, I think *The Message* on May 2 would be the best option for our group. We will meet at the Vargas Theater about half an hour before the show. I know many of you plan to drive, so please see the attached document, which includes parking information. Please e-mail me back to let me know if you'll be there so that I can purchase tickets for us all together.

Cheers!

Roger

Fresno Film Festival: May 2 Screenings

Again and Again, 7:00 P.M. @ the Atkinson Theater, Duration: 112 minutes
Participating in the Fresno Film Festival for the first time, director Claudia Emerson brings viewers the long-anticipated sequel to her movie *Again*, a love story from the 1800s.

Whispers of the Secrets, 7:00 P.M. @ the Vargas Theater, Duration: 87 minutes
Presenting his debut film, director Daniel Adams offers a unique sci-fi film about supernatural forces in a small Canadian town.

Everything I Am, 9:35 P.M. @ the Atkinson Theater, Duration: 93 minutes
Director Yuhan Zou continues to amaze audiences with his memorable characters and fast-moving plots in this crime drama.

The Message, 9:05 P.M. @ the Vargas Theater, Duration: 102 minutes
With her first-ever documentary, director Sara Compton branches out from her usual comedy films as she explores marketing in the modern age.

Parking for the Atkinson Theater is available on Webber Street and Cambridge Road. Parking for the Vargas Theater is available on McCray Street and Faulkner Avenue.

NOTICE OF CONSTRUCTION: April 18

The city of Fresno is announcing a planned closure of McCray Street from April 29 – May 31. The entire road will be closed to driving and parking for the duration of the construction. Workers will add five feet on both sides of the road so that a turning lane may be added. This will improve safety and relieve traffic congestion. Questions regarding the project should be directed to the Fresno Department of Transportation at 555-0133, extension 27.

196. In the e-mail, the word "further" in paragraph 1, line 3, is closest in meaning to

(A) publicize
(B) extend
(C) recommend
(D) advance

197. Who has made the fewest films?

(A) Claudia Emerson
(B) Daniel Adams
(C) Yuhan Zou
(D) Sara Compton

198. What is indicated about the Fresno Film Festival?

(A) It features films from a variety of genres.
(B) It does not charge audience members for admission.
(C) It will be held at three different locations.
(D) It was founded by the Independent Filmmakers Club.

199. Where will the Independent Filmmakers Club members most likely park on May 2?

(A) Webber Street
(B) Cambridge Road
(C) McCray Street
(D) Faulkner Avenue

200. According to the notice, what is the purpose of the construction work?

(A) To install some safety equipment
(B) To repair damaged areas
(C) To make a road wider
(D) To conform to new regulations

Stop! This is the end of the test. If you finish before time is called, you may go back to Parts 5, 6, and 7 and check your work.

RC

TEST 2

READING TEST

In the Reading test, you will read a variety of texts and answer several different types of reading comprehension questions. The entire Reading test will last 75 minutes. There are three parts, and directions are given for each part. You are encouraged to answer as many questions as possible within the time allowed.

You must mark your answers on the separate answer sheet. Do not write your answers in your test book.

PART 5

Directions: A word or phrase is missing in each of the sentences below. Four answer choices are given below each sentence. Select the best answer to complete the sentence. Then mark the letter (A), (B), (C), or (D) on your answer sheet.

101. The head office holds workshops that can prepare ------- to lead a team.

(A) you
(B) your
(C) yourself
(D) yourselves

102. Ms. Kingston decided to reserve transportation to the meeting venue ------- the clients.

(A) but
(B) off
(C) for
(D) down

103. ------- attempted to answer questions about local and national history.

(A) Contests
(B) Contestant
(C) Contesting
(D) Contestants

104. The "Business Plus" lecture will outline things you should do ------- after launching a new product.

(A) immediately
(B) nearly
(C) previously
(D) popularly

105. In its ------- scene, the contemporary musical *Picnic at the River* depicts a joyful family celebration.

(A) final
(B) finally
(C) finality
(D) finalize

106. Customers must write their initials on the dotted lines to indicate their ------- to the terms of the contract.

(A) consent
(B) receipt
(C) ability
(D) deal

107. The much-anticipated next episode of *Cat and Mouse* will be ------- tonight at nine on ZLTV.

(A) transformed
(B) entertained
(C) overcome
(D) broadcast

108. Noted chef Pierre Massasoit has ------- been awarded top prizes in famous cooking competitions.

(A) regular
(B) regularly
(C) regularity
(D) regularize

109. The employees were able to choose among a list of industrial machinery ------- the headquarters.

(A) from
(B) after
(C) into
(D) up

110. Because of the poor condition of its furniture, the small conference room is not considered ------- for formal meetings.

(A) appropriate
(B) timely
(C) competent
(D) responsible

111. We were surprised to learn that one of the boxes showed ------- damage after being shipped from the warehouse.

(A) noticeable
(B) noticeably
(C) notices
(D) noticing

112. Marlexia Shipping Co. will not ------- freight between trucks and trains any longer.

(A) transferred
(B) transfer
(C) transferring
(D) transfers

113. Onderik Garage carried out a ------- while the vehicle's owner was out of town.

(A) modification
(B) modify
(C) modified
(D) modifies

114. The chief technician had ------- to operate the laboratory's most sensitive instruments at his discretion.

(A) design
(B) request
(C) permission
(D) benefit

115. The vendor warned that the data conversion project would ------- fall behind schedule due to software issues.

(A) probably
(B) probable
(C) probabilities
(D) probability

116. Dalamet Publishing asks interviewees to send in salary requirements ------- their availability.

(A) also
(B) as well
(C) along with
(D) furthermore

117. The council requests that citizens limit themselves to remarks that are ------- to the topic under discussion.

(A) steady
(B) accustomed
(C) obvious
(D) relevant

118. With such a large ------- of tourists visiting the country every month, Narpan Tours Ltd. decided to open a new branch.

(A) role
(B) ground
(C) extent
(D) volume

119. Client support teams should always strive ------- customer satisfaction by offering excellent service.

(A) increased
(B) to increase
(C) increases
(D) is increasing

120. The building's roof was weakened during yesterday's storm and ------- must be repaired as soon as possible.

(A) occasionally
(B) consequently
(C) seldom
(D) easily

GO ON TO THE NEXT PAGE

121. The Airline Rewards Card is predicted to attract many new customers and lead to ------- profits for the bank.
(A) elevated
(B) practiced
(C) supervised
(D) illustrated

122. Agricultural drones can survey vast areas of farmland ------- a limited time frame.
(A) within
(B) toward
(C) about
(D) onto

123. The league's decision that some plays are not ------- during a game restricts coaches' opportunities to challenge referees.
(A) reviewable
(B) review
(C) reviews
(D) reviewing

124. During the factory tour, visitors must not ------- with any of the operations inside the production plant.
(A) attain
(B) interfere
(C) comply
(D) prevent

125. The red buses now in operation, ------- carry passengers to and from the city, are free for airline employees.
(A) which
(B) whose
(C) they
(D) their

126. According to the coordinator, several rooms remain ------- at our new branch office.
(A) experienced
(B) momentary
(C) yielding
(D) vacant

127. All throughout last month, Abla-Marc Ltd.'s operating profits ------- analysts' expectations.
(A) will be surpassing
(B) are being surpassed
(C) would have been surpassed
(D) have been surpassing

128. The first day of the Pinesville community festival is ------- the antiques flea market is held each year.
(A) any
(B) to
(C) since
(D) when

129. After detailed -------, scientists have determined the social systems of several species of wildlife.
(A) observation
(B) observed
(C) observe
(D) observant

130. Make sure to keep the loading area clear ------- forklift drivers can maneuver without difficulty.
(A) whether
(B) in view of
(C) due to
(D) so that

PART 6

Directions: Read the texts that follow. A word, phrase, or sentence is missing in parts of each text. Four answer choices for each question are given below the text. Select the best answer to complete the text. Then mark the letter (A), (B), (C), or (D) on your answer sheet.

Questions 131-134 refer to the following article.

Economics Department Newsletter

A new version of Professor Monique Harren's *Economics Principles* is set to be published in hardback this month. The original textbook is one of the most popular teaching materials for introductory economics classes. Professor Harren says she is excited for people to see the ------ 131. edition. When asked ------ it will contain, she explained, "It is similar to the first book in structure, but 132. the theories have been updated. I also tried to use real situations ------ imaginary ones to illustrate 133. each point. ------." The book will be available at the university library and bookstore from August 1. 134.

131. (A) digital
(B) revised
(C) older
(D) estimated

132. (A) how
(B) what
(C) where
(D) there

133. (A) owing to
(B) rather
(C) provided that
(D) instead of

134. (A) For example, the first chapter will be shortened.
(B) The department has promised to consider my proposal.
(C) I think instructors are going to find them very useful.
(D) I am proud of the work those students have done.

GO ON TO THE NEXT PAGE

From: Blake Wolney
To: All staff
Subject: Food drive
Date: April 22

I would like to announce that our company is partnering with Eiden Food Bank to hold a food donation drive in the first week of May. If you choose ------- with the drive, you will receive a durable
135.
nylon bag to take home and pack with food items. Once the bag has been -------, it should be
136.
brought to my office. Please note that donations will be kept unrefrigerated in our storage room until the end of the week. -------, bags should only include canned or dry foods. To sign up, please call me
137.
at extension 32. -------.
138.

Sincerely,

Blake Wolney
Human Resources

135. (A) being helped
    (B) having helped
    (C) to help
    (D) helps

136. (A) sewn
    (B) dried
    (C) filled
    (D) opened

137. (A) In response
    (B) Namely
    (C) Despite that
    (D) Therefore

138. (A) Try asking friends and family members for donations.
    (B) We thank volunteers in advance for their participation.
    (C) Bags have now been made in several more colors.
    (D) Eiden Food Bank is located at 905 Pecos Street.

Questions 139-142 refer to the following letter.

October 2

Vincent Hubbard
406 Paige Drive
Rulston, FL 32029

Dear Mr. Hubbard,

Last Thursday evening, two Water Department employees dismantled part of the sidewalk in your neighborhood, near the intersection of Jerden Road and Paige Drive. ------. Unfortunately, the time
139.
and way in which the work was performed alarmed area residents, who believed that the technicians were ------ an illegal act.
140.

This incident reflects a ------ oversight on our part, and we are taking steps to prevent its
141.
recurrence. Specifically, we have instituted new regulations that call for work crews to wear high-visibility uniforms at all times. Again, we are sorry for the ------.
142.

Thank you for your understanding in this matter.

Sincerely,

Aimee Ross
Director, Rulston Water Department

139. (A) Residents may be asked to move
vehicles away from the curb.
(B) A new treatment plant was expected to
improve the situation.
(C) They were attempting to find the source
of a nearby leak.
(D) Restructuring efforts are leading to larger
work crew sizes.

140. (A) exceeding
(B) committing
(C) violating
(D) merging

141. (A) majorly
(B) majored
(C) majors
(D) major

142. (A) confusion
(B) shortage
(C) postponement
(D) corruption

GO ON TO THE NEXT PAGE

Questions 143-146 refer to the following customer review.

I was shocked to find that several of the boxes I received from Carlisle Meal Boxes contained old, spoiled ingredients. This made it clear that the company wasn't concerned enough about the ------- of their food. -------. Carlisle refunded the cost of those boxes, but the problem kept occurring. I think **143.** **144.** shipping ingredients to customers so we can make meals at home is a fantastic idea, and I liked all of Carlisle's recipes. Still, I'll ------- my own food from now on. I cannot recommend ------- their **145.** **146.** service.

— Thomas Wilkinson

143. (A) freshness
(B) portions
(C) names
(D) diversity

144. (A) A lot of the dishes were too spicy for me.
(B) They had to mail me another copy of the form.
(C) The sign-up promotion was not offered in my city.
(D) Luckily, I had other meal options on those days.

145. (A) manufacture
(B) deliver
(C) buy
(D) discard

146. (A) user
(B) usage
(C) using
(D) use

PART 7

Directions: In this part you will read a selection of texts, such as magazine and newspaper articles, e-mails, and instant messages. Each text or set of texts is followed by several questions. Select the best answer for each question and mark the letter (A), (B), (C), or (D) on your answer sheet.

Questions 147-148 refer to the following advertisement.

Big Valley Point

Over 80 miles of marked hiking trails set among rolling hills
* Volunteer-led tours of landmark mansions built over 200 years ago
* Scenic ponds and picnic areas for relaxation
* Fully-restored Valley Museum showcasing our region's past

Big Valley Point is open year round. Entry is free, but a fee is charged for use of the adjacent parking area. Tours for groups of 20 or more must be reserved at least two weeks in advance — visit www.bigvalleypoint.org for details.

---

147. What is NOT listed as an attraction available at Big Valley Point?

(A) Walking paths
(B) Historic houses
(C) A history museum
(D) Various restaurants

148. According to the advertisement, what is there an extra charge for?

(A) Obtaining Internet access
(B) Parking in a neighboring area
(C) Using a facility on weekends
(D) Taking an indoor tour

GO ON TO THE NEXT PAGE

Hempel Alos

The Alos is a perfect example of Hempel Motors' award-winning design. The refined exterior complements a practical interior that includes a spacious trunk and leather seats for five people. Its powerful, fuel-efficient engine and sophisticated brakes ensure a safe, enjoyable driving experience. A large touchscreen display controls the radio and temperature systems, and includes many drivers' favorite feature—a video feed from the rearview camera.

This comfortable, dependable car is available now at Clegan City Auto. Come test-drive one today and speak to a salesperson about our customizable financing options.

149. What is the purpose of the information?

(A) To outline buyers' preferences
(B) To advertise a product on offer
(C) To supply customizing instructions
(D) To announce a committee's decision

150. What would the most popular feature most likely be used for?

(A) Cooling down the vehicle
(B) Allowing a passenger to sleep comfortably
(C) Moving the vehicle backwards safely
(D) Saving money on fuel

Questions 151-153 refer to the following memo.

To: Blandec Resources staff
From: Susan Moore, CEO
Re: Opportunity
Date: May 9

Dear all,

I'd like to let you know about an upcoming professional development opportunity. Andy Chambliss, a top consultant in our field, will lead a seminar on trends in information management on June 2 at the Demiralp Center. I met Mr. Chambliss at a conference recently, and was very impressed. He started out as an information officer for Ellis-Iversatt Ltd. before joining Recall Force Ltd. as a senior data management consultant. In this role, he has helped many companies, including the Hong Kong-based Mahlmar Industries, develop data storage solutions. He is an original member of the Information Science Association (ISA), and has twice won that organization's "Creative Data Solutions" award. He is also a member of the examination development team for the Information Management Competency Exam (IMCE), a new certification test scheduled for first administration soon at Inland Business University in Los Angeles.

I've directed Human Resources to assist any employees who want to participate in his seminar. Those interested should contact Jarrod Spalt.

151. Why most likely did Ms. Moore write the memo?

(A) To introduce an industry expert to staff
(B) To seek volunteers to lead workshops
(C) To discuss requirements for a job opening
(D) To announce the winner of an award

152. What will happen soon at Inland Business University?

(A) A conference will begin.
(B) An exam will be held.
(C) A certification will expire.
(D) A development team will be formed.

153. Which company is Mr. Chambliss currently employed by?

(A) Blandec Resources
(B) Ellis-Iversatt Ltd.
(C) Recall Force Ltd.
(D) Mahlmar Industries

GO ON TO THE NEXT PAGE

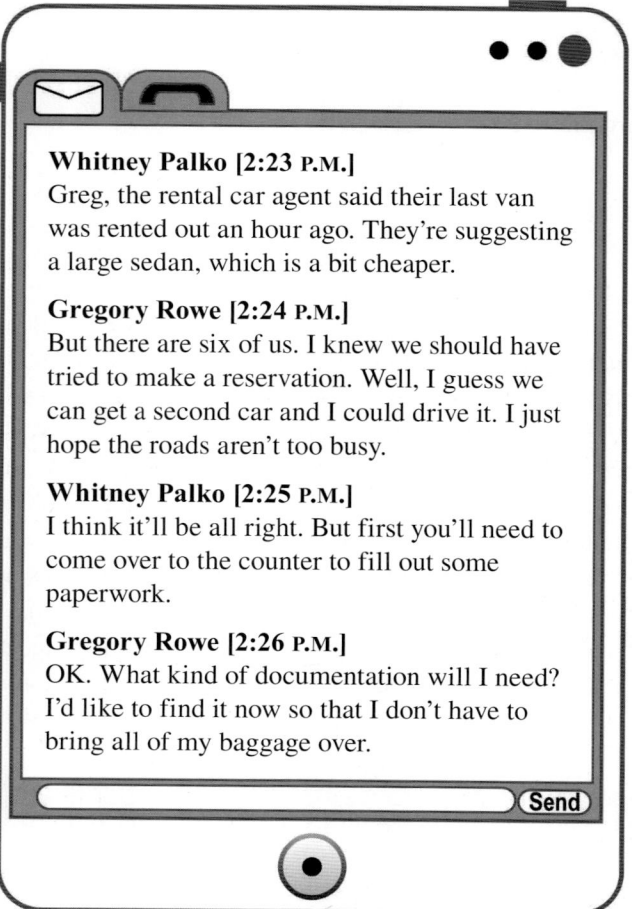

Whitney Palko [2:23 P.M.]
Greg, the rental car agent said their last van was rented out an hour ago. They're suggesting a large sedan, which is a bit cheaper.

Gregory Rowe [2:24 P.M.]
But there are six of us. I knew we should have tried to make a reservation. Well, I guess we can get a second car and I could drive it. I just hope the roads aren't too busy.

Whitney Palko [2:25 P.M.]
I think it'll be all right. But first you'll need to come over to the counter to fill out some paperwork.

Gregory Rowe [2:26 P.M.]
OK. What kind of documentation will I need? I'd like to find it now so that I don't have to bring all of my baggage over.

Send

154. At 2:24 P.M., what does Mr. Rowe most likely mean when he writes, "But there are six of us"?

(A) A price should be divided evenly.
(B) A car does not have sufficient capacity.
(C) There are larger groups waiting in line.
(D) Another person can take on a responsibility.

155. What will Ms. Palko's next message most likely contain?

(A) Descriptions of some luggage
(B) Directions to a counter
(C) A list of materials
(D) A reservation code

Byrne Museum of Art
242 Country Street
Sydney, NSW 2000
www.byrne-moa.au

3 January

Ms. Regina Traub
12 Lantern Avenue
Sydney, NSW 2000

Dear Ms. Traub,

Thank you for renewing your membership to the Byrne Museum of Art. — [1] —. All members are entitled to the special discounts listed in the enclosed brochure. In addition, you will get free admission to any weekly screening at the museum's first-ever film series, *Cinema Appreciated*, which runs from March to June. — [2] —. To view a schedule and reserve your complimentary tickets, visit www.byrne-moa.au/ca.

Membership also gives you special access to art experts. — [3] —. Several times a year, the museum invites local and international art critics and historians to give talks to our staff and members on themes of their choice. This year's first event, set for 9 January, will showcase the works of Mindy Naismith. — [4] —. Space is filling up quickly, so register soon.

If there is any way we can assist you in making full use of your member benefits, please let us know.

Regards,

Gretchen Firth
Public Outreach Director

---

156. What is indicated about Ms. Traub?

(A) She chose the least expensive type of membership.
(B) She is not a first-time member of the museum.
(C) She prefers not to be contacted by phone.
(D) She will receive a free gift in the mail.

157. According to the letter, what is new at the museum?

(A) A weekly film series
(B) A collection of sculptures
(C) An informative mobile app
(D) A line of branded stationery

158. In which of the positions marked [1], [2], [3], and [4] does the following sentence best belong?

"Her colorful paintings have won praise for their warm depiction of human relationships."

(A) [1]
(B) [2]
(C) [3]
(D) [4]

GO ON TO THE NEXT PAGE

E-Mail message	
To:	Arnaud Beaumont <abeaumont@limogesapparel.uk>
From:	Allison Neff <allisonneff@limogesapparel.uk>
Subject:	Anniversary
Date:	18 July

Dear Mr. Beaumont,

It's hard to believe that, in only a few weeks, we'll be celebrating Limoges Apparel's 30th anniversary. I want to let you know how preparations are coming along. To build excitement for this milestone, we've already released some retro-style advertisements on social media. Finally, we're almost finished putting together our selection of limited-edition Limoges Apparel merchandise that will be made available for purchase exclusively at the anniversary party.

I'm going to write you again next week, but please don't hesitate to contact me before then if you have any questions about these plans.

Sincerely,

Allison Neff
Marketing Director, Limoges Apparel

159. Why most likely was the e-mail written?

(A) To provide an update
(B) To prepare a survey
(C) To issue an invitation
(D) To postpone an event

160. Where will some special merchandise be sold?

(A) At a celebration
(B) On a social media site
(C) On a television show
(D) At a store's founding location

Questions 161-164 refer to the following article.

Pate Takes New Approach to OntMusic

TORONTO (June 8) — Pop star Leila Pate has posted a message on her personal Web site declaring a split from OntMusic, the leading online music seller.

Ms. Pate recently became a co-owner of Saroto, an up-and-coming rival music store. — [1] —. Her message explained that she and Saroto's other co-owners, who are also musicians, intend to "give power back to artists" by ensuring that they earn a larger share of the total profits from digital sales of their music. Similarly, she believes Saroto's users benefit from the greater technical sophistication of its platform. "We are improving the experience of buying music online," she claimed. — [2] —.

However, Ms. Pate also made it clear that she will not completely sever ties with OntMusic. "In appreciation of our long and mutually beneficial relationship, my previously-released songs and videos will continue to be sold on OntMusic," Ms. Pate wrote. — [3] —. "Nonetheless, my future albums will only be made available there three months after their original release dates." Music lovers who want to buy them before that time will have to use Saroto.

OntMusic has not yet made a public statement about the change. — [4] —. Purchases made through its store, one of the first entrants into the online music market, account for more than half of all digital music sales in Canada. Still, some warn that Saroto may be its most serious challenger to date.

161. According to the article, what is one reason for Ms. Pate's decisions?

(A) She wants to promote lesser-known musicians.
(B) She is concerned about falling album sales.
(C) She plans to retire from the music industry.
(D) She supports a technologically superior option.

162. What will OntMusic no longer do?

(A) Feature Ms. Pate on its main page
(B) Offer Ms. Pate's entire past catalog
(C) Sell Ms. Pate's new music immediately
(D) Allow Ms. Pate's works to be streamed for free

163. The phrase "account for" in paragraph 4, line 5, is closest in meaning to

(A) justify
(B) calculate
(C) represent
(D) perceive

164. In which of the positions marked [1], [2], [3], and [4] does the following sentence best belong?

"In the past, the company dismissed concerns about similar situations by citing its market domination."

(A) [1]
(B) [2]
(C) [3]
(D) [4]

GO ON TO THE NEXT PAGE

Rick Stayton [9:41 A.M.]
Ms. Ito, the flooring materials that were supposed to be delivered to us today won't arrive until Monday. That's going to push your renovations back several days.

Beth Ito [9:43 A.M.]
That's not good. Remember, the longer the restaurant is closed, the more likely it is that my employees will decide to quit and find other jobs.

Rick Stayton [9:44 A.M.]
Yes, I know. We're going to try to minimize the delay by working in other areas until the shipment comes. For example, we can get some of the outside work done.

Beth Ito [9:46 A.M.]
Oh, actually, I wanted to talk to you about the exterior. I think it would be better to hang the sign up higher on the north wall, so that it can be seen from farther away. Do you think it would make that wall look unbalanced, though?

Rick Stayton [9:47 A.M.]
Well, we're going to work on the roof today. I'll let you know when we're getting close to installing the sign.

Beth Ito [9:49 A.M.]
All right. Is there anything else you can do to speed up the process?

Rick Stayton [9:52 A.M.]
Well, I can phone Cook-Demi Ltd. early next week to start coordinating the installation of the kitchen appliances you had ordered from them.

Beth Ito [9:53 A.M.]
Terrific. I appreciate that.

165. According to Mr. Stayton, why is some work being delayed?

(A) The budget has been decreased.
(B) A supervisor is absent.
(C) A delivery has not arrived yet.
(D) The wrong type of materials was shipped.

166. Who most likely is Ms. Ito?

(A) A commercial architect
(B) A journalist for a newspaper
(C) An owner of a restaurant
(D) A local safety inspector

167. At 9:47 A.M., what does Mr. Stayton most likely mean when he writes, "we're going to work on the roof today"?

(A) Ms. Ito will not be able to enter the building.
(B) He is not sure about another crew's plans.
(C) A proposal can be discussed later.
(D) The renovations are almost finished.

168. What does Mr. Stayton offer to do for Ms. Ito?

(A) Lower the price of a service
(B) Refer customers to a business
(C) Contact an equipment supplier
(D) Lead an upcoming facility tour

Rec-Dek Plus

Are you looking for ways to increase the efficiency of your retail establishment? With Rec-Dek Plus, you can monitor how much merchandise you have on hand, see what products are selling well, and determine when your stock of certain items needs to be replenished.

Features:
- A fully detailed user's manual, plus a support team that is ready to assist you 24 hours a day, 7 days a week via online chat
- A handy "Add Image" feature that lets you select an image for a product and then show it alongside the item description for easy reference
- A "Large Quantity Pricing" feature that simplifies the process of calculating bulk discounts—for both wholesale purchases and sales to customers
- A streamlined "Client Care" feature that enables you to view a customer's name, e-mail address, mailing address, and phone number by pressing just one key

For more information about this program, go to www.rec-dekplus.com.

---

169. How would Rec-Dek Plus most likely be used?

(A) To edit promotional videos
(B) To manage inventory
(C) To improve data security
(D) To assist in a hiring process

170. What is indicated about customer support for Rec-Dek Plus?

(A) It is available at all times.
(B) It may be administered on site.
(C) It is complimentary for the first year.
(D) It receives excellent reviews from users.

171. What is NOT mentioned as a feature of Rec-Dek Plus?

(A) The ability to display images
(B) Comprehensive guidelines for users
(C) Access to customer contact information
(D) The automatic calculation of total sales

Questions 172-175 refer to the following post on a Web site.

Braydon Regional Park Authority (BRPA) update posting

Date: March 7

The five-year ecosystem improvement project for the western half of Braydon Regional Park is now in its second year, and the BRPA is pleased to announce that it is proceeding as planned. Under the leadership of Director Elaine Roteff, 500 trees of various species native to the area have been planted over a 20-acre stretch of the land, and efforts to combat the overpopulation of insects that harm such trees have succeeded. BRPA engineers are also stabilizing the slopes of hillsides that line Braydon Creek, thus improving the quality of the hills' soil and allowing the creek water to flow without blockages.

In fact, the project has been so successful that it has caught the attention of the International Forest Society, an organization dedicated to protecting the world's forests. Director Roteff has been invited to lead several sessions at its upcoming conference in Rio de Janeiro to pass on the insights that have been gained from the project, which is a tremendous honor.

Lastly, the BRPA is most excited to report that it has just lifted a restriction on accessing this part of the park. Thanks to the help of the BRPA's professional staff, it is now possible to take a two-hour guided walk around the twenty-acre area to view the project's progress. This free group tour will be offered at 10 A.M. every Saturday, except during the summer, when 1 P.M. and 3 P.M. tours will be added. The western area of the park may only be visited as part of this official tour. It remains off limits to the public at all other times to avoid interfering with work crews.

172. What is one purpose of the post?

(A) To apologize for a delay in park upgrades
(B) To give details about an amendment to a rule
(C) To explain a procedure for making donations
(D) To recruit volunteers for upcoming projects

173. What is NOT part of the ecosystem improvement project?

(A) Growing additional trees
(B) Increasing the stability of hillsides
(C) Reducing the population of certain insects
(D) Preventing farm animals from damaging plants

174. What has Ms. Roteff been asked to do?

(A) Give an interview on a radio broadcast
(B) Speak about a project at a conference
(C) Join the board of an international organization
(D) Accept an honorary degree from a local university

175. What is indicated about Braydon Regional Park?

(A) Part of it is normally closed to the public.
(B) It currently has two hiking trails.
(C) It will soon offer several picnic areas.
(D) Part of it borders a large lake.

GO ON TO THE NEXT PAGE

http://www.e-couponsltd.com

Welcome to E-Coupons Ltd. Our specialty is digital coupons for all types of businesses. Whatever kind of promotion your organization is holding, we can help you create the coupons you need. This can be done simply with our EC Services-Pro software package, which is yours for a one-time fee of $350. Use it to look through our collection of ready-made designs for coupons, and then personalize the coupon you chose by adding specific information.

☞ Tip: Want your coupons to be available only to a limited group of people? Add a verification bar code at no extra charge. This makes duplication impossible and guarantees that each coupon can only be used once.

EC Services-Pro also assists you to distribute coupons. In addition to classic options such as e-mail and text message, we recently developed a way to display coupons to visitors who connect to your business's Wi-Fi. Whichever delivery method you choose, the process will be simple for both you and your customers.

Click here to order EC Services-Pro and begin making attractive coupons today.

E-Coupons Ltd.

Customer Satisfaction Survey

Business name: __Broussard Books__   Customer name: __Stephanie Broussard__

1. How long have you been using EC Services-Pro? ✓ 0-1 year __ 1-2 years __ 2+ years

2. Have you ever used a different brand of coupon software? __Yes__
2a. What was it? __Tairov Digital__

2b. Please compare its features to those of EC Services-Pro.
Tairov Digital seemed to offer more tools, such as its range of ways to encourage customers to share coupons through social media. However, I no longer use it because it was often confusing and complicated. Switching to EC Services-Pro has saved me a lot of time.

3. Do you have any comments about EC Services-Pro?
This has already been brought up in your discussion forums, but you really should fix the software's "Options" menu so that it displays properly on all operating systems. Otherwise, I'm pleased with your new coupon distribution method, and hope you'll keep adding features like that.

176. According to the Web page, what does EC Services-Pro offer?

(A) Shipment tracking
(B) Design templates
(C) Industry news alerts
(D) Analyses of customer data

177. What is stated about coupons with a free additional feature?

(A) They cannot be copied.
(B) They are very popular.
(C) They are sold in a paper format.
(D) They require considerable extra production time.

178. What is suggested about Broussard Books?

(A) It will distribute new coupons to its investors.
(B) It provides wireless Internet access to visitors.
(C) It recently created a page on a social media Web site.
(D) It specializes in books on technology.

179. Why did Ms. Broussard stop using Tairov Digital?

(A) It is no longer available.
(B) It is not user-friendly.
(C) It does not have many features.
(D) It does not come with customer support.

180. What does Ms. Broussard ask E-Coupons Ltd. to do?

(A) Establish discussion forums
(B) Remove her from a mailing list
(C) Fix a flaw in its software
(D) Clarify the terms of a contract

GO ON TO THE NEXT PAGE

Mechling Fitness
Group Classes

http://www.mechlingfitness.com.au

In addition to top-notch personal training and facilities for self-directed exercise, Mechling Fitness is proud to offer free group classes to center members. The following classes are currently available five days per week:

Velocity

Want the scenery of an outdoor bike ride *and* the convenience of a cycling studio? With stationary bikes in front of a large screen that plays 30-minute videos of natural settings, Velocity allows you to have it all. Trainers ensure a vigorous workout by supplying instructions on when to speed up and when to coast.

Pure Exertion

In this short but lively class, participants do exercises at eight different stations, each focusing on a different area of the body, over a 30-minute period. To guarantee that everyone can visit each station, classes are capped at eight people.

Movement

Movement gently guides participants through simple yoga poses to improve flexibility. Including a short meditation period at the end, this 45-minute class is sure to leave you feeling relaxed yet energized.

Spark & Dazzle

This studio aerobics class is a fun way to get fit. Instructors lead participants through a high-energy dance routine set to the latest upbeat chart hits. Increase the difficulty of the hour-long class by using available hand weights.

Participants may reserve a place in selected classes ahead of time. Visit our front desk to do so, as well as to see a schedule of the classes above and those that meet less frequently. The front desk also provides loans of required materials, such as mats, for participants who do not bring their own.

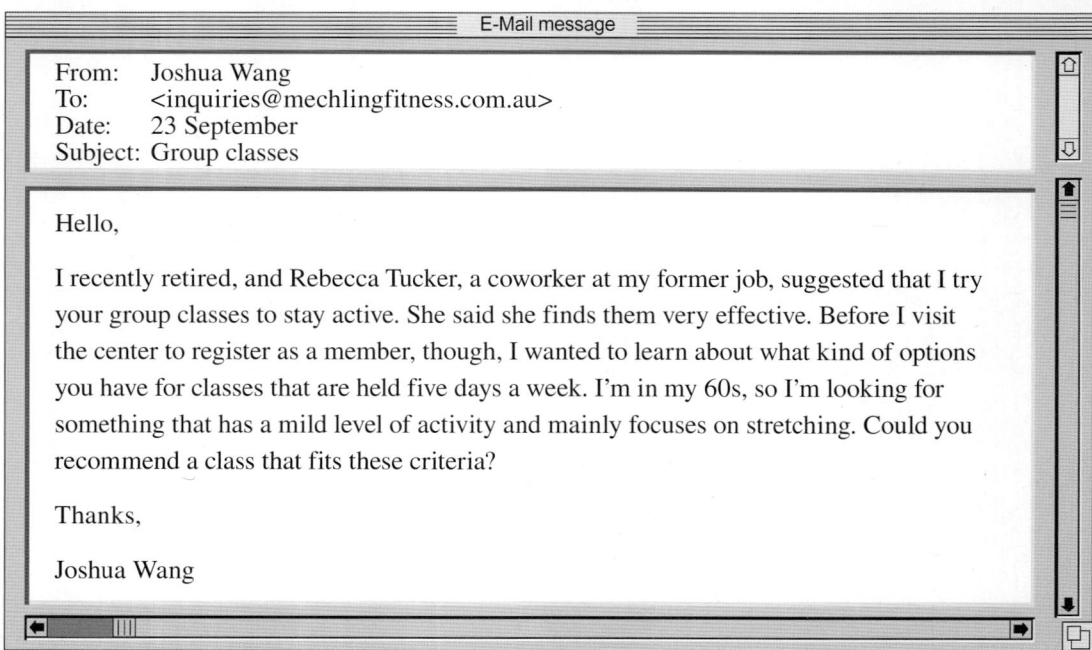

E-Mail message

From: Joshua Wang
To: <inquiries@mechlingfitness.com.au>
Date: 23 September
Subject: Group classes

Hello,

I recently retired, and Rebecca Tucker, a coworker at my former job, suggested that I try your group classes to stay active. She said she finds them very effective. Before I visit the center to register as a member, though, I wanted to learn about what kind of options you have for classes that are held five days a week. I'm in my 60s, so I'm looking for something that has a mild level of activity and mainly focuses on stretching. Could you recommend a class that fits these criteria?

Thanks,

Joshua Wang

181. What is NOT indicated about Mechling Fitness?

(A) It offers individualized fitness coaching.
(B) It allows non-members to buy one-day passes.
(C) It permits advance registration for some classes.
(D) It conducts more classes than are named in the flyer.

182. What is mentioned about Pure Exertion?

(A) It is accompanied by a video.
(B) It includes a warm-up period.
(C) It divides participants by skill level.
(D) It has a limited number of participants.

183. In the flyer, the word "routine" in paragraph 5, line 2, is closest in meaning to

(A) program
(B) habit
(C) trail
(D) load

184. What has Ms. Tucker most likely done recently?

(A) Started a new job
(B) Registered for an e-mail account
(C) Taken classes at Mechling Fitness
(D) Joined a social activities club

185. Which class will most likely be recommended to Mr. Wang?

(A) Velocity
(B) Pure Exertion
(C) Movement
(D) Spark & Dazzle

GO ON TO THE NEXT PAGE

Questions 186-190 refer to the following Web page, invoice, and e-mail.

---

http://www.grangerfurnishings.com

| **Home** | **CATEGORIES** | **ABOUT US** | **REVIEWS** |

Granger Furnishings

Thank you for considering Granger Furnishings. For more than 25 years, we have been providing the entire region with high-quality yet affordable furniture that adds distinction to any office. Click on "CATEGORIES" above to begin browsing our attractive workspace solutions by type, or check the space below for our monthly specials.

Sales for the month of March:
- 10% off all storage cabinets — use code STOCAB at checkout
- 5% off all Waycross-brand chairs — use code WAYCRO at checkout

---

Granger Furnishings

Customer name: Jeff Quinn
Phone number: (800) 555-0118
Delivery address: Girac Supply
17 Ivan Drive
Monroeville, PA 15147

Order number: B661879
Order date: March 28
Scheduled delivery: April 5, 1–5 P.M.

Product	Product description	Quantity	Price
DK21984	Traditional Wooden Desk	3	$2,985
SR88953B	Waycross Wood Bookcase (brown)	6	$1,986
FS25371	Collapsible Plastic Desk	10	$3,990
TC10004B	Steeltek Storage Cabinet (brown)	2	$1,402
		Total	$10,363

Delivery information: Unless we receive other instructions from you, our driver will park in front of the building at the address stated. The delivery team will then unload the furniture and carry it to the sites of your choosing. Please assist them by removing obstructions between the entrance and each site beforehand. Before leaving, they will remove the pieces' packaging and inspect them for damage sustained in transit.

```
╔═══════════════════════ E-Mail message ═══════════════════════╗
║  From:       │ Jeff Quinn <jquinn@girac-supply.com>            ║
║  To:         │ Diane Klavansky <dklavansky@girac-supply.com>   ║
║  Date:       │ April 5                                          ║
║  Subject:    │ Helping out                                      ║
║  Attachment: │ 📎 Invoice                                       ║
╚═══════════════════════════════════════════════════════════════╝
```

Hi Diane,

I won't be able to come to work today for personal reasons, so I need you to take over my duties. One of these, of course, is acting as a manager's assistant to Ms. Naquin, but since you've done that before, I won't go into detail about it.

The only unusual task will be accepting the furniture delivery this afternoon, but the attached invoice contains almost all the necessary information. Oh, and I should tell you that the delivery truck will park in our back lot.

Also, in case other people are out of the office and can't claim their furniture, remember that the wooden desks and bookcases go to the managers, the plastic desks go to staff, and the storage cabinets should be placed by the far wall of the office.

Finally, if Lance Gray comes by, give him the envelope on my desk.

Call my mobile phone if anything urgent comes up.

– Jeff

186. What is suggested about the Web page?

(A) It includes a link to a calendar.
(B) It is updated at least once a month.
(C) Its "CATEGORIES" menu lists 25 types of products.
(D) Its visitors can print special coupons.

187. Which product did Girac Supply most likely receive a discount on?

(A) DK21984
(B) SR88953B
(C) FS25371
(D) TC10004B

188. In the invoice, what is Mr. Quinn directed to do?

(A) Confirm his e-mail address
(B) Clear paths for the movers
(C) Indicate a packaging option
(D) Inspect items upon delivery

189. What is probably true about Mr. Quinn?

(A) He gave special instructions to Granger Furnishings.
(B) He is expecting a phone call from Mr. Gray.
(C) He added some items to his initial order.
(D) He will arrive at work by 1 P.M.

190. Who most likely will be issued a Traditional Wooden Desk?

(A) Mr. Quinn
(B) Ms. Klavansky
(C) Ms. Naquin
(D) Mr. Gray

GO ON TO THE NEXT PAGE ▶

ஃ South Africa National Ballet Competition ஃ

The South Africa National Ballet Competition (SANBC) is one of South African ballet's premier competitions for adults. Every other year, amateur dancers from all over the country gather to perform in front of discerning judges and enthusiastic live crowds. Please refer to the following schedule for information on participating in the SANBC.

10 December	Application deadline - Submissions should include a recent performance video
12 January	First regional competition - Dancers from eastern regions perform in Johannesburg
13 January	Second regional competition - Dancers from western regions perform in Cape Town - Judges' panel begins deliberations
18 January	Notification of finalists - The top five competitors in each division (individual and group) are invited to the national competition
17 February	National competition - Finalists perform in Durban - Judges announce top prize winners

	E-Mail	
To:	Sidra Kirmani	
From:	Shannon Kadick	
Date:	22 January	
Subject:	SANBC plans	

Hi Sidra,

I just wanted to share an idea I had for the national SANBC competition next month. Remember how I felt like our performance on the twelfth seemed to be lacking something? I think I've figured out what it is. Instead of having the foam blocks on stage to represent other people, we should use actual people. We could dress them in grey, and maybe even have them walk around a little bit. That would be much more visually memorable. We can use a few people from other local troupes that didn't make it past the regional round.

I know that this is a big change, but I really think we need to do something special to beat Donald Naidoo and the rest of Mastley Dance Company. Think about it tonight, and we can talk it over at practice tomorrow.

Shannon

Shannon Kadick
Ballet Earth, Co-Director & Performer

Ballet Earth Wins Top Award at SANBC

(18 February)—Ballet Earth was chosen as the group division winner of the most recent South Africa National Ballet Competition.

Sidra Kirmani, Ballet Earth's co-director and choreographer, expressed surprise at the group's victory, citing stiff competition from runner-up Mastley Dance Company and others. "I can't believe this is happening. Considering the pool this year, this is an incredible accolade. We'll try to live up to it."

The 13-person troupe was recognized for *Haunting the Pavement*, an eerie work set to a beautiful orchestral score. Dressed in flowing white clothing, the dancers moved gracefully among grey figures meant to symbolize busy pedestrians on a city street.

The SANBC, an event created to support nonprofessional ballet groups, will issue Ballet Earth a prize of R12,000, while Mastley Dance Company and second runner-up Ballet Gosnell will receive R9,000 and R6,000, respectively. The remaining troupes will take home R1,000 for their efforts.

191. What is stated about the SANBC?

(A) It is streamed live on the Internet.
(B) It is supported by a government agency.
(C) It takes place every two years.
(D) It is divided into age categories.

192. What is implied about Ballet Earth's performance in the regional competition?

(A) It was delivered in Johannesburg.
(B) It did not impress judges.
(C) It was one of five performances that day.
(D) It was recorded by a videographer.

193. What did Ms. Kadick want to change about a performance?

(A) The lighting
(B) The dancers' apparel
(C) The tempo of the music
(D) The stage decorations

194. In the article, the word "stiff" in paragraph 2, line 3, is closest in meaning to

(A) inflexible
(B) intense
(C) essential
(D) unsociable

195. How much prize money will Mr. Naidoo's troupe receive?

(A) R1,000
(B) R6,000
(C) R9,000
(D) R12,000

GO ON TO THE NEXT PAGE

Questions 196-200 refer to the following text message and e-mails.

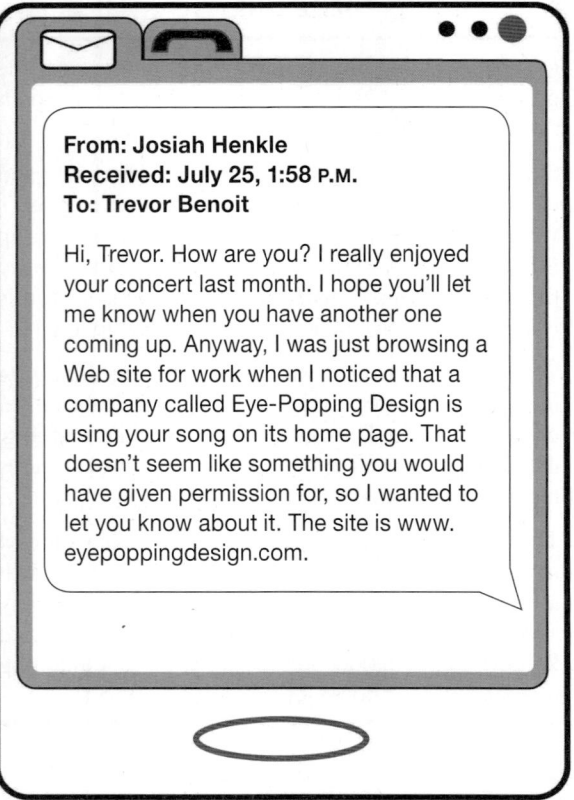

From: Josiah Henkle
Received: July 25, 1:58 P.M.
To: Trevor Benoit

Hi, Trevor. How are you? I really enjoyed your concert last month. I hope you'll let me know when you have another one coming up. Anyway, I was just browsing a Web site for work when I noticed that a company called Eye-Popping Design is using your song on its home page. That doesn't seem like something you would have given permission for, so I wanted to let you know about it. The site is www. eyepoppingdesign.com.

	E-Mail message
From:	Trevor Benoit <tbenoit@trevorbenoit.com>
To:	Audra Paxton <apaxton@eyepoppingdesign.com>
Subject:	Music issue
Date:	July 25

Dear Ms. Paxton,

I was disturbed to discover today that the promotional video on your graphic design company's home page contains a one-minute excerpt of my song, "From the Hills". I wrote, recorded, and released this song through my Web site last year, but I have not agreed to its use by a private company of any kind. Please replace my song with some other music or take down the entire video as soon as possible.

Sincerely,

Trevor Benoit

From:	Mark Fischlin <mark.fischlin@fischlinservices.com>
To:	Audra Paxton <apaxton@eyepoppingdesign.com>
Subject:	Mistake
Date:	July 26
Attachment:	Android; Time; Carriero

Dear Ms. Paxton,

We have investigated the matter you brought to our attention yesterday and determined that, unfortunately, Mr. Benoit is correct. Contrary to what she told you, the employee who handled your account, Ms. Stefanski, did not have permission to use his music. In fact, two of the other songs she chose were found to have the same issue. I apologize on behalf of Fischlin Services and want to assure you that Ms. Stefanski will face serious consequences for her actions.

Also, to show our commitment to providing excellent service, we have already looked through our files and found appealing, legally-available replacements for the songs in question. They are as follows:

Original	Replacement
"Bouncing Variations"	"To an Android"
"Patton's Song"	"Time Scattered Around"
"From the Hills"	"Carriero"

We have attached the new songs to this e-mail. Please let us know if they are to your satisfaction, and we will revise our work accordingly.

Yours truly,

Mark Fischlin
CEO, Fischlin Services

196. What is the purpose of the text message?

(A) To ask for permission to distribute some content
(B) To remind Mr. Benoit of an approaching deadline
(C) To suggest collaborating on a project
(D) To alert Mr. Benoit to a potential problem

197. What is suggested about Mr. Henkle?

(A) He watched a video about Ms. Paxton's firm.
(B) He hired Ms. Paxton to design his Web site.
(C) He is a personal friend of Ms. Paxton.
(D) He is Ms. Paxton's legal representative.

198. According to the first e-mail, what did Mr. Benoit do with a song?

(A) Released it on compact disc
(B) Played it at a concert
(C) Posted it on the Internet
(D) Agreed to its use in an advertisement

199. Which song is proposed as a replacement for Mr. Benoit's?

(A) "Bouncing Variations"
(B) "To an Android"
(C) "Time Scattered Around"
(D) "Carriero"

200. What is indicated about Eye-Popping Design?

(A) It will discipline an employee.
(B) It was misinformed by Ms. Stefanski.
(C) It has requested the closure of an account.
(D) It will give a public apology to Mr. Benoit.

Stop! This is the end of the test. If you finish before time is called, you may go back to Parts 5, 6, and 7 and check your work.

TEST 3

READING TEST

In the Reading test, you will read a variety of texts and answer several different types of reading comprehension questions. The entire Reading test will last 75 minutes. There are three parts, and directions are given for each part. You are encouraged to answer as many questions as possible within the time allowed.

You must mark your answers on the separate answer sheet. Do not write your answers in your test book.

PART 5

Directions: A word or phrase is missing in each of the sentences below. Four answer choices are given below each sentence. Select the best answer to complete the sentence. Then mark the letter (A), (B), (C), or (D) on your answer sheet.

101. Mr. Dola chose to take a ------- flight from Austin to Chicago in order to save time.

(A) direct
(B) precise
(C) durable
(D) formal

102. Guests at the international conference can request an interpreter if ------- do not understand spoken English.

(A) them
(B) they
(C) theirs
(D) their

103. ------- Ms. Lester nor her partner could find the updated contact details for the client.

(A) Both
(B) Not
(C) Neither
(D) Only

104. Prime Realty printed its logo on some ------- products for distribution to current and prospective customers.

(A) promotes
(B) promote
(C) promotionally
(D) promotional

105. The team leaders ------- by the head of the department based on seniority and experience.

(A) select
(B) are selecting
(C) are selected
(D) selected

106. If the severe storm hits the area as expected, the store's owner will ------- delay the grand opening ceremony.

(A) rather
(B) probably
(C) seldom
(D) ever

107. Unfortunately, just ten percent of the charity's fundraising goal has been collected -------.

(A) in brief
(B) so far
(C) even so
(D) at last

108. Mr. Woburn called the hotel's front desk to confirm that he planned to stay ------- than his original booking.

(A) longer
(B) long
(C) length
(D) lengthen

109. The fastest way to the Holt Shopping Center is to take Bus 409 from the stop ------- the pharmacy.

(A) since
(B) through
(C) opposite
(D) against

110. Southeast Utilities customers can ------- make their monthly payments by phone using our automated system.

(A) else
(B) now
(C) there
(D) well

111. There was some discussion ------- the shareholders as to whether the CEO was competently operating the business.

(A) inside
(B) at
(C) onto
(D) among

112. If the Caraway Electronics plant in Atlanta is not running ------- by December, it is at risk of closure.

(A) profiting
(B) profits
(C) profitable
(D) profitably

113. Ms. Choi's accountant explained that investing in a single company is ------- more dangerous than having a diverse portfolio of assets.

(A) such
(B) too
(C) far
(D) very

114. Thanks to strong revenues during its first year, Freshtime Bakery was able to pay off the ------- it incurred to cover opening costs.

(A) debt
(B) stock
(C) receipt
(D) term

115. Although the monthly salaries at Metz Tech are below average, the staff is ------- in other ways.

(A) compensated
(B) impressed
(C) emphasized
(D) congratulated

116. Whenever he is away from the office, Director Clement's ------- takes over any necessary duties that arise.

(A) assistant
(B) assistance
(C) assisted
(D) assisting

117. Most of the interns had their name badges pinned to their uniforms, but Ms. Naquin forgot to wear -------.

(A) her
(B) hers
(C) herself
(D) she

118. If the packages are not tied properly and securely, they will fall ------- when moved by the shipping team.

(A) apart
(B) quite
(C) across
(D) less

119. Housing prices in the city are still ------- more expensive than those in the suburb, but the commuting time is more reasonable.

(A) substantially
(B) unanimously
(C) respectfully
(D) accurately

120. The ------- submitted to the publisher was considered a possible best-seller due to its intriguing plot and charming characters.

(A) parcel
(B) contract
(C) bulletin
(D) manuscript

GO ON TO THE NEXT PAGE

121. The first step in building a positive work environment is sincerely ------- the contributions of each employee.

(A) acknowledges
(B) acknowledgement
(C) acknowledging
(D) acknowledged

122. During the interview, the job candidate described how he overcame a number of challenges ------- his career.

(A) aboard
(B) throughout
(C) between
(D) than

123. As the banners were needed -------, the customer opted to pay extra for the express printing service.

(A) steadily
(B) urgently
(C) typically
(D) entirely

124. Before entering the production area, it is our responsibility to caution ------- that industrial machinery may be in use.

(A) you
(B) yours
(C) your
(D) yourself

125. Hickory Restaurant had no choice but to discard all food that was in the refrigerator during the four-hour power -------.

(A) yield
(B) rating
(C) distribution
(D) outage

126. To maintain authenticity, the homeowner hired a contractor ------- in historic homes to renovate the property.

(A) specialized
(B) specialize
(C) specializing
(D) specialty

127. The dental clinic has added features to its Web site so that customers can make or change ------- online.

(A) appointed
(B) appointments
(C) appointing
(D) appointment

128. When the vehicle's engine started making an unusual sound, Mr. Patel immediately took it to a local ------- for inspection.

(A) mechanic
(B) mechanize
(C) mechanism
(D) mechanistic

129. Employees attending the Annual Engineering Trade Expo are welcome to travel to the event site ------- they choose.

(A) however
(B) afterward
(C) where
(D) once

130. Mr. Asano was not offered the financial consultant position ------- his extensive experience in the field and broad professional network.

(A) in spite of
(B) not to mention
(C) as much as
(D) on behalf of

PART 6

Directions: Read the texts that follow. A word, phrase, or sentence is missing in parts of each text. Four answer choices for each question are given below the text. Select the best answer to complete the text. Then mark the letter (A), (B), (C), or (D) on your answer sheet.

Questions 131-134 refer to the following notice.

NOTICE TO EMPLOYEES

------. This is required for the upcoming painting work on August 1. ------ the work crew only has the
131.   132.
weekend to complete the task, we want to do as much advance preparation as possible. Anything

left on the wall after 5 P.M. on Friday will be ------ abandoned. In that case, the cleaning staff will
133.
have to dispose of these items. To avoid this unnecessary ------, please be responsible for your own
134.
belongings. Please direct all questions to your immediate supervisor.

---

131. (A) Staff members can vote on their favorite colors.
(B) All signs and posters should be removed from the hallways.
(C) Funds have been allocated for some renovation work at the office.
(D) Work requests should be sent directly to the maintenance team.

132. (A) In addition
(B) As a result
(C) Given that
(D) Even though

133. (A) considered
(B) anticipated
(C) disputed
(D) finalized

134. (A) risk
(B) burden
(C) treatment
(D) precaution

www.bellinghamshelter.org/about_us
Bellingham Animal Shelter

We have been in ------- for about two years, providing veterinarian care, adoption services, and
135.
emergency housing for abandoned and unwanted pets. In addition to monetary donations, we need

pet food, blankets, cleaning products, and pet toys. ------- donations are tax deductible, as we are a
136.
registered charity.

Even if you do not have items or money to donate, you can make a difference at the shelter. We

need help with cleaning cages, exercising the pets, and providing obedience training. -------. To find
137.
out more about volunteering at the shelter, ------- us at 555-0176.
138.

135. (A) operation
(B) attraction
(C) publication
(D) investigation

136. (A) One
(B) Both
(C) All
(D) Each

137. (A) Let's work together to achieve our
fundraising goal.
(B) You can use your free time to assist with
these tasks.
(C) We can accept new and gently used items
at this time.
(D) Our staff is happy to find a pet that is right
for you.

138. (A) contacted
(B) contact
(C) to contact
(D) contacting

To: Karen Jankowski <kjankowski@metromail.net>
From: Selma Arcuri <selma@boonerentals.com>
Date: January 4
Subject: Unit 208

Dear Ms. Jankowski,

Thank you for giving written notice about your plans ------- your lease agreement on January 31.
139.

I have attached information about the process. ------- we visit your apartment for a final inspection,
140.

you should have all of your personal belongings removed from the property. Be sure to leave -------
141.

time to thoroughly clean the apartment. It should be in the same condition in which you received it,

with all surfaces dusted, carpets vacuumed, and countertops scrubbed. -------.
142.

Should you have any questions, please feel free to e-mail me at any time.

Sincerely,

Selma Arcuri
Property Manager, Boone Rentals

139. (A) terminate
(B) terminating
(C) terminated
(D) to terminate

140. (A) Now that
(B) As long as
(C) Before
(D) Even if

141. (A) imperative
(B) complete
(C) dependable
(D) adequate

142. (A) You can enjoy a tidy living environment.
(B) Therefore, the final rent payment will be in January.
(C) Our staff will attempt to fix it for you, if possible.
(D) We charge a housekeeping fee if this is not done.

Wilson Sporting Goods
1901 Echo Lane
White Plains, NY 10601

To Whom It May Concern:

I recently visited your store to purchase a wetsuit and some other surfing gear. I was assisted by Ken in the Water Sports department, and I was impressed with his patience and ------- behavior. He **143.** took the time to ask me about my preferences and intended usage. Taking these ------- into **144.** consideration, he recommended a few products. I can't tell you how much I ------- this personal **145.** attention. At most stores of your size, it is impossible to find someone to answer questions. -------. I **146.** will definitely recommend Wilson Sporting Goods to my friends and family.

Warmest regards,

Holly Mackenzie

143. (A) respects
(B) respectful
(C) respectfully
(D) respect

144. (A) amounts
(B) complaints
(C) assets
(D) needs

145. (A) celebrated
(B) satisfied
(C) appreciated
(D) promoted

146. (A) The item I purchased seems to be of high quality.
(B) Let's hope some of them will be resolved through this letter.
(C) I'm glad this is not the case at your establishment.
(D) The selection of seasonal goods was better than expected.

PART 7

Directions: In this part you will read a selection of texts, such as magazine and newspaper articles, e-mails, and instant messages. Each text or set of texts is followed by several questions. Select the best answer for each question and mark the letter (A), (B), (C), or (D) on your answer sheet.

Questions 147-148 refer to the following form.

Marigola Industries
Information Technology Department

Name: <u>Ravi Sehgal</u>   Employee ID: <u>1394</u>

Department: <u>Marketing</u>   Extension: <u>24</u>

Item #: <u>30429</u>

Description: <u>Portable projector</u>

Comments: <u>For use in Conference Room B</u>

Check-out Date: <u>January 18</u>

FOR OFFICE USE ONLY

Note: <u>To be returned by user within 24 hours. IT team will not retrieve the item.</u>

Approved by: <u>Kristin Neri</u>   Date: <u>January 18</u>

---

147. Why did Mr. Sehgal submit the form?

(A) To reserve a meeting space
(B) To place a supply order
(C) To borrow a device
(D) To ask for a repair service

148. What does Mr. Sehgal most likely plan to do?

(A) Inspect a conference room
(B) Drop off an item in person
(C) Revise a departmental budget
(D) Receive an express delivery

GO ON TO THE NEXT PAGE

Questions 149-150 refer to the following advertisement.

Ancworth Incorporated – Security at its finest
www.ancworthincorporated.com

At Ancworth Incorporated, we know that you want to protect your premises as well as your and your employees' peace of mind. We provide a wide range of security services, from popular brands of cameras and alarms to on-site personnel. We also maintain a constant connection with the local police department to maximize our effectiveness. Whether you need round-the-clock care or a simple system installation, accept nothing less than Ancworth Incorporated. Get a free quote by entering some basic details and preferences into our interactive online form. We look forward to serving you!

---

149. What is true about Ancworth Incorporated?

(A) It manufactures its own brand of alarms.
(B) Its employees used to be police officers.
(C) It works closely with local authorities.
(D) It is currently hiring security personnel.

150. According to the advertisement, what can readers do on a Web site?

(A) Request a price estimate
(B) Look at equipment photos
(C) Read customer testimonials
(D) Run a system test

Questions 151-152 refer to the following notice.

NOTICE: Book clubs now accepting new members at Comden Public Library.

It's recruitment time for the book clubs at Comden Public Library. From exciting novels to stimulating nonfiction works on a variety of topics, we've got something for everyone. We have one book club meeting every evening that we're open, and readers of all ages are welcome in any of the six groups. What's more, a library card is not required if you plan to bring your own copy of the book. However, you must fill out a registration form at the front desk and pay a charge of ten dollars, which covers your group membership for life. The group leader will then be in touch to let you know about upcoming meetings.

Join today and introduce yourself to a community of readers and a world of ideas!

151. What is suggested about the Comden Public Library?

(A) It hosts online forums for readers.
(B) It is closed one day a week.
(C) It sells some of its used books.
(D) It is currently seeking group leaders.

152. What is a requirement of book club membership?

(A) Being over a certain age
(B) Holding a valid library card
(C) Paying a one-time fee
(D) Undergoing an interview

GO ON TO THE NEXT PAGE

Questions 153-154 refer to the following text-message chain.

Arnoldo Siano [11:23 A.M.]
Lisandra, I looked into buying our tickets for the Devano Opera Company's visit to Ridgeway next month. I can't believe how fast they're selling.

Lisandra Condou [11:26 A.M.]
That doesn't surprise me. Locals have never had the opportunity to see the group before.

Arnoldo Siano [11:27 A.M.]
That's true. Anyway, I know you didn't want to spend more than $40 for your ticket, but the tickets in that price range are sold out for Friday, Saturday, and Sunday nights.

Lisandra Condou [11:28 A.M.]
Are there any other options?

Arnoldo Siano [11:31 A.M.]
We could go to one of the matinees on Saturday or Sunday. Or we can get the $60 tickets for Friday night.

Lisandra Condou [11:33 A.M.]
Well, I'm working all weekend.

Arnoldo Siano [11:36 A.M.]
All right. I'll book us tickets for Friday. We can just eat dinner at home instead of going out. That'll help us keep costs down.

---

153. What is implied about the Devano Opera Company?

(A) It plans to tour the country for one month.
(B) It will hold three shows in total.
(C) It has recently increased its ticket prices.
(D) It will perform in Ridgeway for the first time.

154. At 11:33 A.M., what does Ms. Condou most likely mean when she writes, "I'm working all weekend"?

(A) She is surprised that Mr. Siano will not work overtime.
(B) She is willing to purchase a more expensive ticket.
(C) She thinks Mr. Siano should invite someone else.
(D) She has traded shifts with one of her coworkers.

Questions 155-157 refer to the following schedule.

Spelter Martial Arts Center
Instructor Schedule: Monday, May 3

	Studio A	Studio B	Studio C
7 A.M.	Hapkido [Beginner] *Eric Charron*	Hapkido [Intermediate] *Alicia Kent*	Judo [Advanced] *Jeffrey Miranda*
8 A.M.	Kung Fu [Intermediate] *Jeffrey Miranda*	Taekwondo [Intermediate] *Eric Charron*	Taekwondo [Beginner] *Veronica Lawson*
9 A.M.	Hapkido [Intermediate] *Veronica Lawson*	Judo [Advanced] *Ian Scalia*	Hapkido [Beginner] *Alicia Kent*
1 P.M.	Taekwondo [Intermediate] *Eric Charron*	Kung Fu [Beginner] *Alicia Kent*	Judo [Intermediate] *Ian Scalia*
6 P.M.	Taekwondo [Beginner] *Veronica Lawson*	Krav Maga [Beginner] *Ian Scalia*	Taekwondo [Advanced] *Raymond Alvarez*
7 P.M.	Kung Fu [Intermediate] *Jeffrey Miranda*	Judo [Beginner] *Raymond Alvarez*	Kung Fu [Advanced] *Alicia Kent*
8 P.M.	Judo [Beginner] *Raymond Alvarez*	[none]	Taekwondo [Advanced] *Veronica Lawson*

Notes: Since we've just added Krav Maga to our class list, we're not sure how many people will be in attendance. Eric Charron may take on another evening class in this discipline if it proves to be popular. Before each session, make sure the mats, head guards, and gloves (if used) are in a good state of repair.

155. What is suggested about the center?

(A) Advanced classes are held exclusively in Studio C.
(B) Monday is its least busy day of the week.
(C) Hapkido is available at three different levels.
(D) Mr. Alvarez only teaches there in the evening.

156. Who is currently teaching the newest class?

(A) Mr. Charron
(B) Ms. Lawson
(C) Mr. Miranda
(D) Mr. Scalia

157. What are the instructors asked to do?

(A) Report scheduling errors to a manager
(B) Lock each studio's door at night
(C) Track some student numbers
(D) Examine some gear for damage

GO ON TO THE NEXT PAGE

Questions 158-160 refer to the following e-mail.

E-Mail message

To:	Jasmine Quinn
From:	Daniel Hsu
Date:	November 9
Subject:	Investment in online dictionary project

Dear Ms. Quinn,

Next week is the first meeting with investors regarding the online dictionary project proposed by our company. Thank you for agreeing to give a talk on the technology behind the project and the way that we have anticipated the needs of users interacting with the system. — [1] —. A laptop computer, projector, and projection screen will be available at the meeting, so you should prepare slides with text and graphics to accompany the talk. — [2] —. E-mailing the slides to yourself is an option, as you will have access to a Wi-Fi connection. However, to ensure that the talk can go forward even in the event of Internet complications, bringing the file on a USB flash drive is highly recommended.

Also, please limit the talk to 45 minutes, including ample time for questions. — [3] —. We will have four speakers on that day, all of whom have vital information to share with our valued guests. — [4] —. The meeting will be held off-site at Worlington Plaza, so more extensive preparations than usual are required. I will need a scan of your driver's license for the venue's security staff. Please e-mail it to me no later than Friday.

If you have any questions about this event, feel free to contact me at this address anytime.

Warmest regards,

Daniel Hsu

---

158. Why did Mr. Hsu write the e-mail?

(A) To describe the progress of a project
(B) To alert an investor to an opportunity
(C) To give instructions to a presenter
(D) To seek assistance with a task

159. What should Ms. Quinn send to Mr. Hsu by the end of the week?

(A) Driving directions to a meeting venue
(B) A list of graphics needed for some slides
(C) Confirmation of attendance at an event
(D) An image of an identification card

160. In which of the positions marked [1], [2], [3], and [4] does the following sentence best belong?

"Otherwise, we may easily fall behind schedule."

(A) [1]
(B) [2]
(C) [3]
(D) [4]

Questions 161-164 refer to the following online chat discussion.

Manuel Rocha [9:16 A.M.]
Hi, everyone. The HR director asked me to check how the planning is going for the staff retreat at Sunset Lodge.

Ranee Shah [9:18 A.M.]
We have a final head count. About half of the employees plan to go there the night before for the opening reception. The rest will travel in the morning and arrive by 10 A.M., in time for the compulsory workshops.

Lynette Crumpton [9:19 A.M.]
Is someone from the sales division presenting the first workshop?

Ranee Shah [9:20 A.M.]
No, that's in the afternoon. Public relations staff will hold the first one.

Lynette Crumpton [9:21 A.M.]
OK, then do we need someone from the IT department to set up equipment in the morning for them?

Ranee Shah [9:22 A.M.]
Ms. Galvan said that she can set things up herself. She only needs the microphone.

Manuel Rocha [9:25 A.M.]
Sounds good so far. And what about the caterer? Have you found one that can make meals for a group of our size?

Lynette Crumpton [9:26 A.M.]
Isn't that included?

Manuel Rocha [9:27 A.M.]
Only breakfast and lunch. We need to have the dinner catered.

Ranee Shah [9:28 A.M.]
How about Volkland Catering? They've helped us at other events, and I know they can work out of town. I have their business card around here somewhere. I'll e-mail you their contact details once I find it.

---

161. What is suggested about the opening reception?

(A) Its date has been moved.
(B) It is not mandatory.
(C) It will begin at 10 A.M.
(D) Its seating is limited.

162. In which department does Ms. Galvan most likely work?

(A) Human Resources
(B) Overseas Sales
(C) Public Relations
(D) Information Technology

163. At 9:26 A.M., what does Ms. Crumpton most likely mean when she writes, "Isn't that included"?

(A) She thought that food was part of a package.
(B) She is uncertain about the contents of a directory.
(C) She already sent the requested documents.
(D) She wants all employees to participate in an event.

164. What will Ms. Shah probably do next?

(A) Look for a business card
(B) E-mail a schedule
(C) Contact a caterer
(D) Consult a regional map

GO ON TO THE NEXT PAGE

http://www.teskdalefarms.com/ingredientsbox

Teskdale Farms Ingredients Box
~ Fresh food delivered right to your door ~

Teskdale Farms has partnered with nationally renowned chef Ramone Jacobs to create recipes made from fresh ingredients from our site and our local suppliers. Each Ingredients Box contains the ingredients for three home-cooked meals for two people—including the necessary spices and recipe cards with step-by-step instructions. The package is delivered every Monday or Thursday (your choice), and there is no extra fee for delivery.

Try our service with our three-month introductory period, during which time you face no fees in terminating the contract. In addition to the standard items, your first Ingredients Box will also include a wooden box for you to store your recipe cards, a large ceramic platter, and a coupon for 50% off frying pans at Evans Department Store.

Customers are billed monthly ($90 for the introductory rate, and $120 for the standard rate). Click here to join today and find out what *Myers Food Monthly* magazine called "the future of home cooking".

165. How often does each customer receive an Ingredients Box?

(A) Twice a week
(B) Once a week
(C) Twice a month
(D) Once a month

166. What is NOT mentioned as included in a customer's first Ingredients Box?

(A) A serving dish
(B) Some recipe cards
(C) A wooden container
(D) A cooking pan

167. What is implied about the Ingredients Box service?

(A) The cost of it rises in the fourth month.
(B) A charge is imposed on out-of-town customers.
(C) The company provides step-by-step videos.
(D) Customers are asked about their food allergies.

GO ON TO THE NEXT PAGE

Community News

(July 11)—The city of Bemmington is still feeling the effects of the heavy rainstorm that hit the area last week, dropping two-to-three inches of rain per hour for several days and causing the banks of the Tyson River to overflow. The flooding has resulted in the cancellation or postponement of several events, the most recent of which is the annual Regional Golf Tournament. —[1]—.

The tournament was originally scheduled to take place on Saturday, July 16, at Mendoza Park. Maintenance workers have pumped water from the most affected areas back into the adjacent sections of the river to speed up the drying process. —[2]—. However, the ground is still too damp. The tournament could not be moved to Pineview Park, which sits on much higher ground, because a baseball tournament was already scheduled for that day. Instead, the event has been moved to Saturday, August 6. —[3]—.

Participants in the tournament, including last year's champion James Lehman, will be contacted by the tournament's event planner. —[4]—. Local business owners hope that the change won't affect attendance at the event, as it is a big draw for tourists. "Whenever we have a lot of visitors in town, it's good for Bemmington," said Kang Shao, who contributed funding to the tournament. "I hope we see a similar turnout to last year's."

168. What is the article mainly about?

(A) A change to a sporting competition
(B) A new recreational facility
(C) A tournament registration process
(D) An issue with an upcoming fund-raiser

169. What is indicated about Mendoza Park?

(A) It has a baseball field.
(B) It is the city's largest park.
(C) It is located near a river.
(D) It will be closed until August.

170. Who most likely is Mr. Shao?

(A) A city official
(B) A maintenance worker
(C) A professional athlete
(D) An event sponsor

171. In which of the positions marked [1], [2], [3], and [4] does the following sentence best belong?

"They will have the option of participating or asking for a refund."

(A) [1]
(B) [2]
(C) [3]
(D) [4]

GO ON TO THE NEXT PAGE

Test 3

```
                              E-Mail message
```

To: Florian Krueger <f.krueger@kruegersconfections.com>
From: Hannah Choi <choihannah@almontebank.com>
Date: February 10
Subject: From Almonte Bank

Dear Mr. Krueger,

I'm sorry I missed your telephone call yesterday. In response to your question in the message that you left, I can confirm that your loan application is moving along nicely. We are awaiting confirmation of your credit score, and I have also determined that the debt-to-income ratio for this loan is reasonable.

There are a few documents that I still require. I know that you have six years' worth of business tax records, but we only require three for our purposes. These should be single certified copies of your yearly tax summary from the National Treasury Department. In addition, I need a detailed account of how the funds will be used. Your application only stated "building expansion," but we need a more thorough explanation, including an itemized list of services and materials. I've attached the form you need. You can visit www.almontebank.com/forms/b451.html to see a sample form that is filled out so you know what to do.

All completed documents should be mailed to my office, the address for which appears at the top of the attached form. You may submit the documents anytime, but the sooner you do, the sooner we can issue the funds. If you have any questions, please do not hesitate to contact me.

Best regards,

Hannah Choi
Loan Agent, Almonte Bank

172. Why did Mr. Krueger call Ms. Choi on February 9?

(A) To check the status of an application
(B) To introduce a small business
(C) To request a business loan
(D) To inquire about a tax document

173. What is suggested about Mr. Krueger's business?

(A) Its offices have undergone renovations.
(B) It has been in operation for six years.
(C) It supplies services to Almonte Bank.
(D) It recently moved to a different location.

174. Why should Mr. Krueger visit the Web site mentioned?

(A) To view an example
(B) To create an account
(C) To upload a form
(D) To see opening times

175. What is indicated about the relevant paperwork?

(A) It can be scanned and sent by e-mail.
(B) It must be signed in front of Ms. Choi.
(C) There must be multiple copies of each page.
(D) There is no deadline for its submission.

GO ON TO THE NEXT PAGE

Medolant

Medolant, a trusted name for commercial cleaning products, is pleased to announce an upgrade to our cleaning solutions. We've taken harmful substances out of our formulas and replaced them with non-toxic alternatives. Our cleaners remain affordable, however, and we still offer 15% off to registered charities, public schools, and aid organizations.

We welcome orders online at www.medolant.com or by phone at 555-0178. Customers may settle up-front or request to be billed once their goods have arrived. Those whose delivery address is within the state of California will receive two-day delivery. All other orders will be delivered approximately five days after the order is received. The shipping fee for bulk orders will be waived.

PRODUCTS:
Carpet Cleaners: Carpet Shampoo (#093), Odor-Absorbing Powder (#097)
Bathroom·Cleaners: All-Purpose Surface Cleaner (#113), Soap Scum Remover (#114), Mirror and Window Cleaner (#118), Toilet Bowl Cleaner (#119), Sink and Drain Gel (#120)
Kitchen Cleaners: All-Purpose Counter Cleaner (#124), Stainless Steel Polish (#125), No-Scrub Oven Cleaner (#129)
— NEW!!! — Stain Removers: Carpet Spot Treatment (#136), Upholstery Stain Remover (#137)

---

www.medolant.com/myorders/1021

Customer: Salguero Hotel
Phone Number: 555-0191
Shipping Address: 501 Saint Clair Street, Fresno, California, 93705
Billing Type: Credit Card XXXX-XXXX-XXXX-8859

Order Date: March 18

Product Code	Quantity	Price Per Unit	Total
093	3	$14.99	$44.97
113	2	$3.99	$7.98
114	4	$9.99	$39.96
120	1	$12.99	$12.99
125	2	$29.99	$59.98
136	4	$8.99	$35.96

[Click for Delivery Fees and Timing Estimates]

If you are not completely satisfied with your purchase, you may return it within 30 days for a full refund.

176. What has Medolant recently done?

(A) Adopted recyclable packaging
(B) Added new kitchen cleaners
(C) Started offering different bottle sizes
(D) Modified its products' ingredients

177. What is suggested about Medolant?

(A) It gives discounts to nonprofit organizations.
(B) It has the best-selling cleaning products on the market.
(C) It makes a separate line of residential cleaners.
(D) It also advertises via television commercials.

178. What is NOT indicated in the advertisement?

(A) Customers can pay after receipt of an order.
(B) There are two ways to place orders.
(C) Orders come with instructional booklets.
(D) Delivery is free for large orders.

179. Which type of item did Salguero Hotel purchase the most of?

(A) Carpet Cleaners
(B) Bathroom Cleaners
(C) Kitchen Cleaners
(D) Stain Removers

180. When most likely will Salguero Hotel receive its goods?

(A) On March 18
(B) On March 19
(C) On March 20
(D) On March 23

GO ON TO THE NEXT PAGE

Great Work Deserves Recognition!

It's time once again for the Ormolas Consulting employee awards. Nominate one of your fellow coworkers by filling out a form on the company Web site. Nominations will be accepted until November 20. CEO Dean Lockhart will present the awards at the annual employee banquet, but it is the awards committee that will review your comments and choose the winners.

Awards are available in four categories:

Award	Description	Eligibility Criteria
Shining Star Award	Awarded to a new employee who has built a positive reputation in a short time period	Hired within the past 12 months
Innovation Award	Awarded to an employee whose creative thinking has benefitted the company	None
Foundation Award	Awarded to an employee with a long track record of excellence	Minimum of five years of employment at Ormolas
Vision Award	Awarded to an employee whose guidance and direction helped to make his/her team stronger	Department manager or team leader only

---

www.ormolasconsulting.net/forms/378 ▶

Award Nomination Form

Person to Be Nominated: Amanda Wallace   **Department:** Marketing

Award Type: ☐ Shining Star ☐ Innovation ☒ Foundation ☐ Vision

Does the nominee meet the eligibility criteria? ☒ Yes ☐ No

Reason for Nomination: I've worked with Ms. Wallace for the past three years, and I have been extremely satisfied with her work. She always makes a good impression when representing the company. Just last month, she visited Buenos Aires to celebrate the first day of business for one of our new client's stores. She was favorably received and invited to return again. Also, her work reports are always accurate, as she reviews them meticulously to ensure they are error-free. I believe that Ms. Wallace is an excellent role model for all of us.

Submitted by: Ryan Demarco

181. Where would the information most likely be seen?

(A) In a company newsletter
(B) In a promotional brochure
(C) In a conference program
(D) In an industry magazine

182. What is suggested about Mr. Lockhart?

(A) He wrote an article for a Web site.
(B) He established a new award this year.
(C) He was not present at a previous banquet.
(D) He will not be involved in an award decision.

183. What is implied about Ms. Wallace?

(A) She has a reputation for producing creative ideas.
(B) She has worked at the company for at least five years.
(C) She is a team leader in the marketing department.
(D) She is interested in joining a committee.

184. What did Ms. Wallace do in Buenos Aires last month?

(A) Finalized a contract
(B) Attended a grand opening
(C) Accepted an award
(D) Selected a building site

185. What is mentioned as a characteristic of Ms. Wallace?

(A) Knowledge of various languages
(B) Commitment to teamwork
(C) Strong analytical skills
(D) Attention to detail

GO ON TO THE NEXT PAGE

NORFIELD (Feb. 15) — City officials have confirmed that the contamination levels at Augusta Pond, on the eastern side of town, are nearly ten times the level that is considered ideal. A test was carried out on February 2 by the Department of Rural Affairs (DRA). Officials determined that the increased use of pesticides and fertilizers on the surrounding farmland has likely contributed to the problem, and that a risk is being posed to the wildlife living in and around the pond as well as people using it for recreational purposes.

The city council plans to debate funding a cleanup project at the lake as well as passing new regulations to restrict the use of chemicals on farmland. The cleanup could cost as much as $3 million. While most council members are in favor of the project, citing health and environmental benefits, some council members oppose the proposal. Jesse Sierra fears that the financial burden will put the town at risk for bankruptcy. Marjorie Rowe is concerned that the work would cause other important projects to be postponed. The council hopes to make a decision soon.

E-Mail	
To:	Anya Teague <a.teague@stel-mail.com>
From:	Randall Moore <moorer@lurmonincorporated.com>
Date:	February 16
Subject:	Augusta Pond

Dear Ms. Teague,

Several members of the community have contacted me regarding the article about Augusta Pond in yesterday's edition of the *Norfield Times*. I was not contacted for a statement, but I share Ms. Rowe's opinion about the proposed work. It would be a good idea for us as city council members to hold an open forum for community members to share their opinions. I think everyone on the council appreciates that this is a complex topic, so the decision should not be taken lightly.

Sincerely,

Randall Moore

PUBLIC NOTICE

The Norfield City Council will hold a special meeting at the Norfield Community Center at 7 P.M. on Tuesday, March 1, to discuss the cleanup of Augusta Pond. Following the test conducted by Cheryl McVey and her team last month, a decision needs to be made about the proposal. Residents of Norfield and other interested parties are invited to attend the meeting and share their feedback. To avoid standing in the back, early arrival is recommended.

186. What is the purpose of the article?

(A) To highlight a local water pollution problem
(B) To encourage people to reduce their waste
(C) To introduce new farming regulations
(D) To recruit members for an environmental group

187. What is Mr. Moore concerned about?

(A) Financial difficulty
(B) Voter dissatisfaction
(C) Project delays
(D) Loss of habitat

188. In the e-mail, the word "appreciates" in paragraph 1, line 5, is closest in meaning to

(A) escalates
(B) thanks
(C) enjoys
(D) understands

189. What is suggested about Ms. McVey?

(A) She is a farmer near the town of Norfield.
(B) She is employed by the Department of Rural Affairs.
(C) She has been chosen to organize a volunteer event.
(D) She recently became a city council member.

190. What is implied about the March 1 meeting?

(A) The seating area is expected to be fully occupied.
(B) Ms. Teague will explain the results of a test.
(C) It is intended for Norfield residents only.
(D) The press will interview council members.

GO ON TO THE NEXT PAGE

Andrew Saldana
814 Cedar Lane
Columbus, OH 43035

Dear Mr. Saldana,

On behalf of the Crenton Art Museum, I would like to bring to your attention a number of upcoming events intended to raise money for the refurbishment of our presentation hall. Special events are usually limited to museum members only; however, we are inviting you to participate in them at no charge so you can cover them for your publication.

Every Friday evening throughout the month of September, we will be offering after-hours tours. For ticketholders, our regular hours of operations won't apply! Dasras Patel will give a presentation at the beginning of each tour, and then participants will be guided through the various sections of the museum by Barbara Fleming. Tickets are $100 and limited to 25 tickets per event to keep the group size small. Following each tour, refreshments will be served.

Please let me know if you are able to be in attendance by calling my office at 555-0177.

Sincerely,

Carrie Brighton
Carrie Brighton

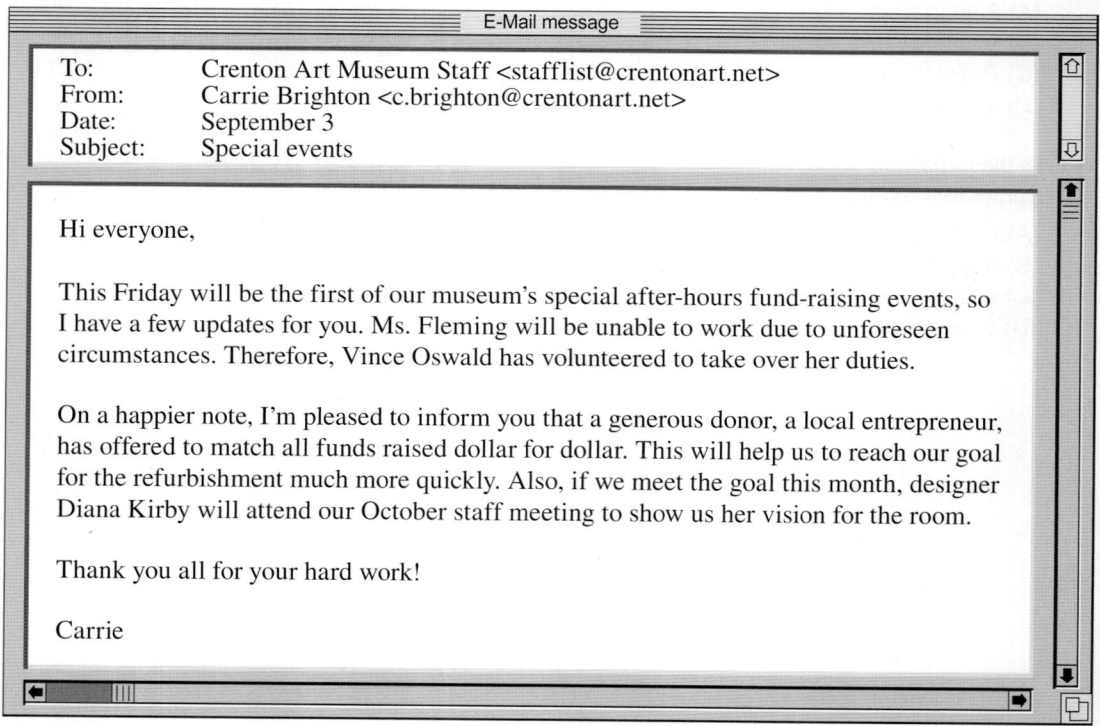

E-Mail message

To: Crenton Art Museum Staff <stafflist@crentonart.net>
From: Carrie Brighton <c.brighton@crentonart.net>
Date: September 3
Subject: Special events

Hi everyone,

This Friday will be the first of our museum's special after-hours fund-raising events, so I have a few updates for you. Ms. Fleming will be unable to work due to unforeseen circumstances. Therefore, Vince Oswald has volunteered to take over her duties.

On a happier note, I'm pleased to inform you that a generous donor, a local entrepreneur, has offered to match all funds raised dollar for dollar. This will help us to reach our goal for the refurbishment much more quickly. Also, if we meet the goal this month, designer Diana Kirby will attend our October staff meeting to show us her vision for the room.

Thank you all for your hard work!

Carrie

http://www.crentonart.net	◄ BACK HOME ►

HOME	EXHIBITS	SUPPORT US	**MUSEUM NEWS**	CONTACT

October 1

Fund-raiser Goal Reached!
With a combination of September's fund-raisers and a generous contribution from an anonymous donor, we have reached our goal of $20,000 for the updating of our presentation hall. Staff members will get a sneak peek at sketches of the redesign at the October 10 staff meeting. Further announcements, along with photos of the progress, will be posted to the public here on our Web site.

191. Who most likely is Mr. Saldana?

(A) A professional artist
(B) A museum supporter
(C) A print journalist
(D) A tourism official

192. In the letter, the word "apply" in paragraph 2, line 2, is closest in meaning to

(A) spread
(B) be in effect
(C) be eager
(D) devote

193. What will Mr. Oswald be responsible for at the special events?

(A) Conducting a survey
(B) Collecting donations
(C) Leading a tour
(D) Giving a presentation

194. What is suggested about Ms. Kirby?

(A) She will go to a meeting on October 10.
(B) She will post sketches on her Web site.
(C) She helped to plan the September fundraisers.
(D) She has designed other parts of the museum.

195. How much money did the anonymous donor most likely contribute?

(A) $100
(B) $2,500
(C) $10,000
(D) $20,000

GO ON TO THE NEXT PAGE

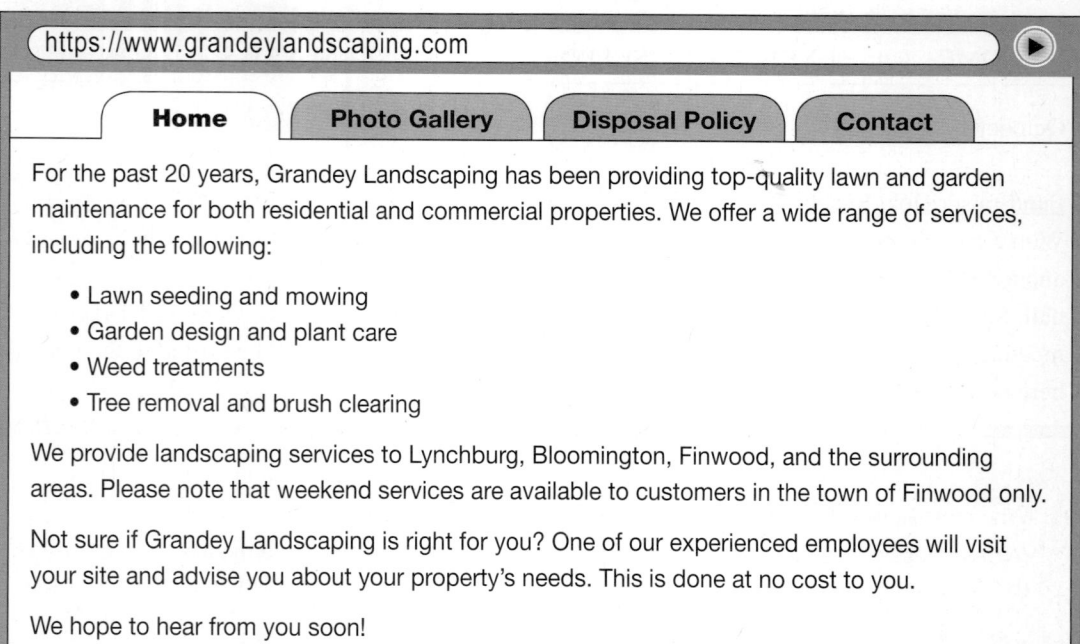

https://www.grandeylandscaping.com

Home | **Photo Gallery** | **Disposal Policy** | **Contact**

For the past 20 years, Grandey Landscaping has been providing top-quality lawn and garden maintenance for both residential and commercial properties. We offer a wide range of services, including the following:

- Lawn seeding and mowing
- Garden design and plant care
- Weed treatments
- Tree removal and brush clearing

We provide landscaping services to Lynchburg, Bloomington, Finwood, and the surrounding areas. Please note that weekend services are available to customers in the town of Finwood only.

Not sure if Grandey Landscaping is right for you? One of our experienced employees will visit your site and advise you about your property's needs. This is done at no cost to you.

We hope to hear from you soon!

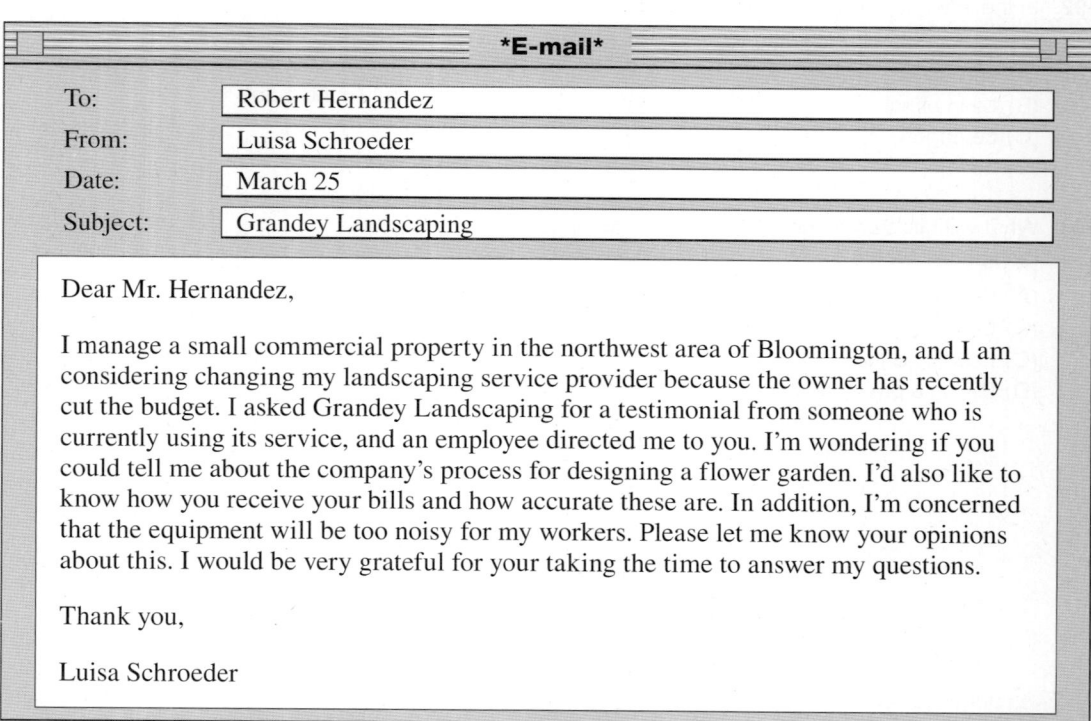

E-mail

To:	Robert Hernandez
From:	Luisa Schroeder
Date:	March 25
Subject:	Grandey Landscaping

Dear Mr. Hernandez,

I manage a small commercial property in the northwest area of Bloomington, and I am considering changing my landscaping service provider because the owner has recently cut the budget. I asked Grandey Landscaping for a testimonial from someone who is currently using its service, and an employee directed me to you. I'm wondering if you could tell me about the company's process for designing a flower garden. I'd also like to know how you receive your bills and how accurate these are. In addition, I'm concerned that the equipment will be too noisy for my workers. Please let me know your opinions about this. I would be very grateful for your taking the time to answer my questions.

Thank you,

Luisa Schroeder

```
┌─────────────────────────────────────────────────────────────┐
│                    ═══ E-Mail message ═══                    │
├──────────┬──────────────────────────────────────────────────┤
│ To:      │ Luisa Schroeder                                   │
├──────────┼──────────────────────────────────────────────────┤
│ From:    │ Robert Hernandez                                  │
├──────────┼──────────────────────────────────────────────────┤
│ Date:    │ March 26                                          │
├──────────┼──────────────────────────────────────────────────┤
│ Subject: │ RE: Grandey Landscaping                           │
└──────────┴──────────────────────────────────────────────────┘
```

Dear Ms. Schroeder,

I would not hesitate to recommend Grandey Landscaping. The company designed a flowerbed for my backyard and made recommendations based on the amount of shade the area receives. There was an extra charge for this service, but I think it was well worth it. I also had a dead tree between my house and my neighbor's fence, and the company's employees were able to remove it without any damage to the surrounding structures.

I currently have my lawn mowed and garden weeded twice a month, usually on Saturdays. The equipment is not very noisy, and the workers always clean up the lawn clippings and other debris before leaving. If you use this service, you will not be disappointed.

Best of luck,

Robert Hernandez

196. What is indicated about Grandey Landscaping?

(A) It has recently opened new branches in other towns.
(B) It offers a free consultation to new customers.
(C) It primarily provides maintenance for corporations.
(D) It has been in business for over three decades.

197. How did Ms. Schroeder obtain Mr. Hernandez's contact information?

(A) Through a commercial association
(B) Through a neighbor of Mr. Hernandez
(C) Through a hobby club for gardeners
(D) Through Grandey Landscaping

198. In the first e-mail, the word "cut" in paragraph 1, line 3, is closest in meaning to

(A) discontinued
(B) pierced
(C) decreased
(D) shortened

199. What topic mentioned by Ms. Schroeder is NOT addressed by Mr. Hernandez?

(A) Tree removal
(B) Billing methods
(C) Garden design
(D) Noise levels

200. What does the second e-mail imply about Mr. Hernandez?

(A) He is currently living in Finwood.
(B) His property was photographed for a Web site.
(C) He will visit Ms. Schroeder.
(D) His lawn was seeded by Grandey Landscaping.

Stop! This is the end of the test. If you finish before time is called, you may go back to Parts 5, 6, and 7 and check your work.

RC

TEST 4

READING TEST

In the Reading test, you will read a variety of texts and answer several different types of reading comprehension questions. The entire Reading test will last 75 minutes. There are three parts, and directions are given for each part. You are encouraged to answer as many questions as possible within the time allowed.

You must mark your answers on the separate answer sheet. Do not write your answers in your test book.

PART 5

Directions: A word or phrase is missing in each of the sentences below. Four answer choices are given below each sentence. Select the best answer to complete the sentence. Then mark the letter (A), (B), (C), or (D) on your answer sheet.

---

101. Before sending us your résumé, be sure to check that it meets our requirements -------.

(A) preciseness
(B) precise
(C) precision
(D) precisely

102. Most of the product photographs were taken by either the manufacturer ------- a freelance photographer.

(A) nor
(B) as
(C) and
(D) or

103. ------- about payments and account balances should be directed to our billing department.

(A) To inquire
(B) Inquired
(C) Inquiries
(D) Inquire

104. Girmus Airlines suspended several flights yesterday ------- issues with its aircraft.

(A) due to
(B) except for
(C) whereas
(D) although

105. Darablatt Ltd. ------- its earnings figures at its board meeting next Tuesday.

(A) being released
(B) was releasing
(C) will release
(D) released

106. Thanks to the new street signs, drivers' dependence on city landmarks for navigation will ------- be reduced.

(A) recently
(B) more
(C) soon
(D) early

107. The film *Greenmeadow Memories* has received warm praise ------- audiences and critics alike.

(A) from
(B) away
(C) during
(D) into

108. Steel bars placed inside the concrete should provide sufficient -------.

(A) reinforce
(B) reinforcement
(C) reinforced
(D) reinforceable

109. Set to open on Friday, the new Hagoya Shopping Mall ------- a variety of architectural styles and details.

(A) incorporations
(B) incorporating
(C) incorporation
(D) incorporates

110. After inspecting the artwork, please share your assessment of ------- authenticity and value.

(A) what
(B) whose
(C) there
(D) its

111. In one of the prize-winning posters currently on exhibition, a bicycle is shown leaning ------- a large oak tree.

(A) until
(B) between
(C) contrary
(D) against

112. Voter polls suggest that the two mayoral candidates are ------- likely to win the seat.

(A) normally
(B) equally
(C) formerly
(D) gradually

113. The ------- Fiona Lim has acquired enables her to deliver a persuasive talk to any audience.

(A) progress
(B) experience
(C) graduation
(D) instance

114. Folk singer Karen Watson is ------- considering appearing on the upcoming season of a popular music program.

(A) strengthen
(B) strongly
(C) strength
(D) strong

115. At Sebetich Mutual, employees may be given permission to telecommute if they have ------- at a superior level consistently.

(A) encountered
(B) assured
(C) understood
(D) performed

116. Despite his youth, Mark Brown has written one of the most ------- novels of recent times.

(A) engagement
(B) engaging
(C) engagingly
(D) engages

117. Bezotte, Inc.'s latest survey sought respondents' opinions on a ------- of economic and political topics.

(A) material
(B) range
(C) type
(D) distance

118. The Design Team made minor changes to the final version of the product, but overall it is not ------- different from the prototype.

(A) fundamentally
(B) approximately
(C) easily
(D) separately

119. The Product Support Department is on hand to assist customers ------- questions arise concerning warranty conditions.

(A) whenever
(B) rather than
(C) such as
(D) so that

120. Versoi Financial has denied claims that the investments are ------- risky.

(A) intentional
(B) intentionally
(C) intention
(D) intend

GO ON TO THE NEXT PAGE

121. This document details the factors that Mr. Zhao took into account for his ------- of the new employees.

(A) evaluate
(B) evaluation
(C) evaluated
(D) evaluates

122. The limited-edition Jeerab tea gift set will probably sell out fast, as the store has almost ------- supply remaining in inventory.

(A) no
(B) not
(C) nothing
(D) none

123. Although the restaurant's cuisine has become quite bold and adventurous, patrons agree that it is ------- delicious.

(A) much
(B) still
(C) far
(D) how

124. The Sales Team ------- in the all-employee meeting last month, but most of its members were away on business trips.

(A) have been participating
(B) would have participated
(C) can participate
(D) will be participating

125. We are working past regular hours to ensure the ------- resolution of the matter.

(A) steep
(B) prompt
(C) identical
(D) vague

126. During one impressive period in her directing career, Ms. Lu earned ------- Mauller Awards for *Hand to Hand* and *The Renwicks*.

(A) successive
(B) thorough
(C) mandatory
(D) compatible

127. By encouraging innovative promotional ideas, the company hopes to gain a ------- market share than it had previously.

(A) highly
(B) high
(C) higher
(D) highest

128. The city expects that the language classes will help newly-arrived international residents ------- their neighbors.

(A) apply for
(B) reach out
(C) interact with
(D) belong to

129. The Park Ecology Committee's weekly meeting is intended to provide a ------- in which attendees can discuss environmental issues.

(A) forum
(B) mission
(C) safeguard
(D) prediction

130. Festival organizers have ------- the crafts vendors that set-up assistance will be offered before the event.

(A) announced
(B) notified
(C) declared
(D) expressed

PART 6

Directions: Read the texts that follow. A word, phrase, or sentence is missing in parts of each text. Four answer choices for each question are given below the text. Select the best answer to complete the text. Then mark the letter (A), (B), (C), or (D) on your answer sheet.

Questions 131-134 refer to the following e-mail.

To: <jordan.bartlett@sweettree.com>
From: <linhbui@critespackaging.com>
Date: May 4
Subject: Packaging solutions

Dear Mr. Bartlett,

Thank you again for calling this morning to discuss our packaging solutions. Learning about Sweet Tree Catering's needs was very interesting. As promised, I ------- on the information to our design
131.
team. They responded that creating suitable packaging would not be -------. In fact, they could
132.
probably have samples ready for you in as little as one week. -------. If you are interested, the next
133.
step is to set up an in-person meeting ------- which you would describe your requirements in greater
134.
detail directly to the Design Team. Please call me or reply to this e-mail to confirm that that is what
you would like to do.

Sincerely,

Linh Bui
Crites Packaging

---

131. (A) passed
(B) pass
(C) will pass
(D) would have passed

132. (A) responsible
(B) challenging
(C) proportional
(D) inaccurate

133. (A) Do you know where they are being displayed?
(B) Are you certain that schedule is correct?
(C) Have you noticed any problems with them?
(D) Would you like to move ahead with this process?

134. (A) at
(B) on
(C) toward
(D) between

GO ON TO THE NEXT PAGE

Questions 135-138 refer to the following article.

CHICAGO (March 19)—Popular singer Kurt Glaize revealed this morning that the second single from his current album will be a remake of Stan Weber's classic "Sighs of Glass." ------. **135.**

Mr. Weber rose to fame upon releasing the ------ version of the song thirty years ago. It has been **136.** remade several times since then, in musical genres as diverse as jazz and rock. None of these

------ suit Mr. Glaize, however. The young singer describes his single as "actually pretty similar" to **137.**

Mr. Weber's, ------ his love for traditional ballads. "It's already such a beautiful song," he explained. **138.** "All I did was update it a little bit for modern audiences."

135. (A) Tickets may still be available for some of the April performances.
(B) The announcement was made during an interview on WLV Radio.
(C) The two musicians are expected to begin separate solo careers.
(D) Each song deals with a different aspect of young adulthood.

136. (A) newest
(B) adverse
(C) clarified
(D) original

137. (A) styles
(B) coupons
(C) instruments
(D) designs

138. (A) has reflected
(B) reflecting
(C) reflects
(D) will reflect

NOTICE TO CUSTOMERS

As you all know, the property surrounding Bracht Storage is fully fenced, and all areas ------

139.

continuously by a video surveillance system. Our meticulous cleaning practices also deter harmful

pests. However, our commitment to ------ no longer stops there. As an extra precaution, Bracht now

140.

requires storage unit contents to be insured. ------. The policy provides partial compensation for

141.

items damaged by fire, floods and other unexpected occurrences. For more comprehensive

coverage, customers may opt ------ a policy from a specialized insurance carrier. A consultant can

142.

help determine which option is suitable for you.

---

139. (A) to be filmed
(B) are filming
(C) were filmed
(D) are filmed

140. (A) courtesy
(B) security
(C) accessibility
(D) customization

141. (A) Nevertheless, many prefer the indoor facilities.
(B) Separate units must be rented for additional items.
(C) Customers may obtain a basic plan directly from us.
(D) A licensed repair worker is on call at all times.

142. (A) purchases
(B) that purchased
(C) to purchase
(D) purchaser

GO ON TO THE NEXT PAGE

Questions 143-146 refer to the following memo.

To: All library staff
From: Cameron Meach, Director
Subject: Budget and meeting
Date: December 5
Attachment: Proposals

This year, several of the events on which we usually spend the library's "Programs" budget have not taken place as expected. ------, our author readings scheduled for February were cancelled
143.
because of the heavy snowfall. This has left us with a sizable amount of money that must be spent on programs by the end of the year. In the attachment, I have listed a few ideas for how to do this. Please ------ them before Friday's meeting. We will discuss which one would best support the aim of
144.
------ the library's usefulness to the community. ------. With your valuable input, I feel certain we will
145. **146.**
be able to take full advantage of this situation.

143. (A) Otherwise
(B) As long as
(C) Owing to
(D) For instance

144. (A) transmit
(B) locate
(C) reserve
(D) examine

145. (A) enhanced
(B) enhancing
(C) enhancer
(D) enhance

146. (A) I also encourage you to make your own suggestions at that time.
(B) Thank you for the hard work you have put into planning this initiative.
(C) More recent patron surveys have tended to ask about other areas.
(D) Remember, we must take the reduced budget into account.

PART 7

Directions: In this part you will read a selection of texts, such as magazine and newspaper articles, e-mails, and instant messages. Each text or set of texts is followed by several questions. Select the best answer for each question and mark the letter (A), (B), (C), or (D) on your answer sheet.

Questions 147-148 refer to the following e-mail.

E-Mail message	
From:	<l.canfield@binniskphoto.com>
To:	<j.pham@signeteffect.com>
Subject:	Staff portraits
Date:	February 19

Dear Mr. Pham,

Thank you for choosing Binnisk Photography to create official portraits of Signet Effect Associates staff. We look forward to helping to shape the public image of your new business. As I mentioned when you booked the appointment, selecting a backdrop in advance ensures that the portraits look natural. Our photo retouching service is useful for making small changes to a subject's face or hair, but not for replacing an entire background. Please look over our background collection <u>here</u>, and inform us of your decision by the evening before the appointment.

Sincerely,

Leah Canfield
Client Services
Binnisk Photography

147. Why is Ms. Canfield writing to Mr. Pham?

(A) To find out a preference
(B) To recommend a business to him
(C) To confirm an appointment
(D) To apologize for a misunderstanding

148. What does Ms. Canfield mention is available?

(A) A nighttime studio session
(B) A professional makeup service
(C) Special lighting equipment
(D) Digital photograph editing

GO ON TO THE NEXT PAGE

Questions 149-150 refer to the following text message.

From: Alex Suu
Sent: May 31, 10:04 A.M.
To: Loreen Burton

Loreen, I need a small favor. I just met Ms. Tekle here at the Delpray Apartments, and she seems interested in leasing the vacant studio. I'm about to show her around the building. But I just realized that I don't have any of the sample rental contracts with me. Would you mind bringing one over? We'll be here a while.

149. What does Mr. Suu indicate will soon take place?

(A) A building tour
(B) A groundbreaking ceremony
(C) A safety inspection
(D) A training session

150. What is Ms. Burton asked to do?

(A) Review a contract
(B) Clean out a room
(C) Deliver a document
(D) Work overtime

Dermakk DXR Digital Camera

Congratulations on your purchase of a Dermakk DXR Digital Camera. We guarantee that its state-of-the-art technology will allow you to begin taking high-quality images in no time. To facilitate this, the attached manual describes how to use your digital camera and install the provided editing software. Please be sure that you have reviewed the manual's contents thoroughly before you use the camera. A searchable version of the manual is also available in several electronic file formats. Simply visit www.dermakk.com/support/manuals and type "DXR Digital Camera" into the box at the top of the page.

Test 4

151. For whom is the information most likely intended?

(A) A consumer attempting to make a purchasing decision
(B) An engineer developing digital editing software
(C) A salesperson who must explain a product's features
(D) A customer who owns a product

152. What is indicated about the DXR Digital Camera?

(A) It was previously sold by a different manufacturer.
(B) Its manual may be found on the Internet.
(C) Repair service is free within a certain amount of time.
(D) Its users can save photos in all standard formats.

GO ON TO THE NEXT PAGE

Questions 153-155 refer to the following Web page.

Dinajpur Food Processing Company's Web site

News update for: 2 February   **Posted by:** Tyler Sharma, Operations Manager

It's been two weeks since my last post, so I just want to inform everyone on what's going on with the construction of our new factory. We had a few setbacks during the installation of flooring materials in the main manufacturing area, but that work is now complete. Plumbing and electrical work are progressing as planned, and the inside partition walls will be put in soon. If the remaining work proceeds on schedule, the factory should be operational by late April.

I have been working closely with the Human Resources Team to recruit technical support staff for the plant. Last week, on behalf of the company, I attended the employment recruitment fair at Navi-Tech University in Mumbai to interview promising young candidates interested in careers in the industry. In addition, I have contacted a former colleague of mine, Giorgio Dutt, to handle the task of creating custom safety signs for the plant floor. The printing firm he owns specializes in high-visibility signs for work areas.

I will keep everyone posted as more news comes up.

153. Why most likely was the Web page written?

(A) To provide updates on a building project
(B) To outline a new manufacturing process
(C) To evaluate a corporate restructuring effort
(D) To propose more frequent all-staff meetings

154. According to the Web page, what did Mr. Sharma do in Mumbai?

(A) Demonstrated a new product
(B) Presented an employee award
(C) Toured a branch office
(D) Participated in a job fair

155. Who most likely is Mr. Dutt?

(A) A reporter for a business publication
(B) An intern at a head office
(C) A supervisor at a food processing plant
(D) An owner of a printing company

Aldac-D Ltd.
Customer Feedback Form

At Aldac-D Ltd., we value customers' opinions on our cleaning and repair services. Please share yours below.

Customer name: _Dan Martell_   **Item/Items serviced:** _Black leather dress shoes_

	Agree	Not sure	Disagree
Staff were friendly and helpful.		✓	
The cost of the service was reasonable.		✓	
The service was completed properly.	✓		
The service was completed swiftly.	✓		

Comments:

The service was very quick. My shoes were ready for pick-up just two days after I dropped them off at the service center. And I'm pleased with the results. The only problem is that the repair charges exceeded the original price quote I was given. I understand why this happened—the technician said that the shoes were in worse shape than he had expected—but I found it frustrating.

Thank you for your comments. We will use them to further develop our training methods for new and current staff and technicians.

156. What is indicated about Mr. Martell?

(A) He received the form by e-mail.
(B) He inquired about express shipping options.
(C) He communicated with staff via online chat.
(D) He visited a service center in person.

157. What problem does Mr. Martell describe?

(A) A confusing explanation
(B) A poor-quality repair
(C) A long wait time
(D) An incorrect cost estimate

158. According to the form, what will Aldac-D Ltd. do?

(A) Reward technicians who earn positive feedback
(B) Call Mr. Martell to discuss the form's contents
(C) Improve its employee education system
(D) Send Mr. Martell a free accessory

GO ON TO THE NEXT PAGE

Questions 159-160 refer to the following text-message chain.

Simone Powell, 10:34 A.M.
Gustavo—sorry to bother you on your day off, but we just heard from Wible. They've decided to target a different market, so they would like the TV campaign to present their products as cool and youthful, not classic and traditional. Can we do that? They'd like a reply by the end of the day.

Gustavo Limas, 10:35 A.M.
Of course, we're willing to accommodate them, but it won't be easy. If we're going to get the commercials done in time to air during the Teagarden Games, the team's going to need some help. I wonder if we could ask the director to lend us someone from another team.

Simone Powell, 10:36 A.M.
I don't see why not. It benefits the whole agency to keep Wible happy, so I think we'll be able to work something out.

Gustavo Limas, 10:37 A.M.
Plus, if they're finished in time, these ads will of course reach a much bigger audience. We want to create something impressive. I'll call him.

159. What does Wible hope to do?

(A) Appeal to a younger market
(B) Hire a celebrity spokesperson
(C) Respond to a rival campaign
(D) Conduct market research

160. At 10:36 A.M., what does Ms. Powell most likely mean when she writes, "I don't see why not"?

(A) She thinks an advertisement will be successful.
(B) She wants to request additional staffing.
(C) She prefers to borrow filming equipment.
(D) She expects a deadline to be extended.

Local Business News

March 23

The famously small Caravanne Café will soon increase its floor space by taking over a nearby building. — [1] —. Owner Ibraham Akkad says he is excited about his popular restaurant's expansion because it is too small at present to handle the large crowds wanting to eat there, especially on weekends.

Mr. Akkad has already begun updating the eatery's current dining area, located at 72 Clover Street. — [2] —. At the same time, he is busy remodeling the vacant structure next door, which was previously occupied by Kainer's Clothing Store. The opportunity to rent the larger neighboring storefront arose when, after 23 years at the same location, owner Roselyn Kainer decided to move her business to Marax Shopping Plaza. — [3] —. "I grabbed the chance to rent the space," Mr. Akkad said.

Mr. Akkad has not set a timeline for the completion of the expansion, but said that it will be celebrated with a large event. — [4] —. Its opening hours, menu, and other information can be found at www.caravannecafe.com.

161. What does the article mainly discuss?

(A) A local business event
(B) Changes to a restaurant's menu
(C) The expansion of a business
(D) The popularity of a weekend event

162. What is suggested about Kainer's Clothing Store?

(A) It is managed by Mr. Akkad.
(B) It used to be located on Clover Street.
(C) It used to occupy a smaller space than Caravanne Café.
(D) It opened a second branch in Marax Shopping Plaza.

163. In which of the positions marked [1], [2], [3], and [4] does the following sentence best belong?

"He would like patrons to know that the business will operate as usual until then."

(A) [1]
(B) [2]
(C) [3]
(D) [4]

GO ON TO THE NEXT PAGE

Barnotte Eye Clinic

www.barnotte-ec.com

Sherman Allsop
1735 Royal Road
Parma, MI 48089

Dear Mr. Allsop,

You may have heard that, after 40 years of service, Dr. Patrick Marsden will soon close his practice in order to travel and spend time with his family. I and the other physicians of Barnotte Eye Clinic are proud to announce that he chose us to continue to care for his patients in the Parma area. With your consent, I would be honored to begin serving your eye care needs. Let me tell you a little about myself.

I was raised nearby in Lansing, where much of my family still lives, and graduated from medical school at Goodrich University. I am board-certified and a regular contributor to the Michigan Academy of Ophthalmology's quarterly *Current Vision Research*. Upon joining Barnotte Eye Clinic, I committed myself to serving this community long-term. Should you decide to become my patient, I will review your medical records before we meet and take time to address your concerns during your appointments. Still, as a recipient of our clinic's "On-Time Doctor Award", I can assure you that you will not be kept waiting when you visit me.

To further facilitate us getting to know each other, I invite you to come to a reception for Dr. Marsden's former patients at our office on Thursday, July 15 at 5 P.M. It is sure to be an enjoyable affair, so I hope you can stop by. Otherwise, our desk staff will contact you soon to discuss setting up an appointment.

I look forward to meeting you.

Regards,

Dr. Hillary Vosburg

164. According to the letter, what will Dr. Marsden do?

(A) Retire from the workforce
(B) Start a new medical center
(C) Move to a different city
(D) Teach younger physicians

165. What did Dr. Vosburg receive an award for?

(A) Her research
(B) Her medical skills
(C) Her volunteer work
(D) Her punctuality

166. What is suggested about Dr. Vosburg?

(A) She is the founder of Barnotte Eye Clinic.
(B) Some of her family members are doctors.
(C) She has published articles in a professional journal.
(D) She used to teach at Goodrich University.

167. What is Mr. Allsop encouraged to do?

(A) Join a mailing list
(B) Attend a welcoming party
(C) Call to make an appointment
(D) Keep copies of his medical records

GO ON TO THE NEXT PAGE

Portala Stadium to Host USSL All-Star Game

US Soccer League (USSL) commissioner Joseph Mason, FC Santa Fe owner Octavia Yelnick, and Santa Fe mayor Idalia Ortiz held a joint press conference yesterday to announce that the city's Portala Stadium has been chosen as the site of the league's next all-star match.

The all-star game is a competition between the best players of the USSL's western and eastern divisions as determined by a poll of players and coaches. — [1] —. Last year, the Western Division Team, featuring current FC Santa Fe star Eric Gikunoo, narrowly beat the Eastern Division Team in a thrilling match in Nashville.

Mr. Mason explained that the league's decision reflects the skyrocketing local popularity of the sport since FC Santa Fe was formed two years ago. — [2] —. "We know that the city will provide a welcoming and exciting atmosphere for this event," he said.

During her turn to speak, Mayor Ortiz cited the quality of the stadium's facilities as another factor that influenced the USSL. An extensive renovation project to the stadium, which is also the home of the Santa Fe Streaks football team, was undertaken to accommodate FC Santa Fe, and was a major initiative of Ms. Ortiz's first term in office. — [3] —. The project drew concern from local officials and residents because of the high costs involved, but has been considered a success since its completion.

In addition to the game itself, the city will host several related special events throughout the week of the contest. These will be announced at a later date, but are likely to include concerts and player appearances. — [4] —.

168. What is suggested about Mr. Gikunoo?

(A) He will take part in a team selection process.
(B) He is the newest member of FC Santa Fe.
(C) He spoke at a press conference.
(D) He used to play for a Nashville-based team.

169. The word "drew" in paragraph 4, line 9, is closest in meaning to

(A) concluded
(B) attracted
(C) calculated
(D) portrayed

170. What is mentioned about Portala Stadium?

(A) It is also used as a concert venue.
(B) It is shared by two sports teams.
(C) It is currently undergoing renovations.
(D) Its construction was proposed by Ms. Ortiz.

171. In which of the positions marked [1], [2], [3], and [4] does the following sentence best belong?

"It is held in June each year."

(A) [1]
(B) [2]
(C) [3]
(D) [4]

Questions 172-175 refer to the following online chat discussion.

Ryan Etchison, 11:41 A.M.
Everyone, I'm going online now to buy tickets for the department's trip to the movies on Friday. How does *The Gates of Belief* sound? It's gotten excellent reviews from critics.

Hannah Kiehl, 11:42 A.M.
It's been in theaters for so long that I think most of us have seen it already. I'd prefer *The Adventures of Sam Driver*. My friend saw it last weekend and highly recommended it.

Mark Gaskins, 11:43 A.M.
The Adventures of Sam Driver does sound good, but I've heard that its second half is practically a horror movie.

Joy Lafferty, 11:44 A.M.
How about a more lighthearted option? *Goldfish Canteen* opens tomorrow.

Hamdan Al Neyadi, 11:44 A.M.
I'd be happy to see *Goldfish Canteen* or *Blizzard Connection*.

Ryan Etchison, 11:46 A.M.
It looks like there's a 4:30 showing of *Goldfish Canteen*. Does that sound all right?

Hannah Kiehl, 11:47 A.M.
Wait, will there be dinner afterwards? I was hoping to leave by 7 o'clock sharp.

Ryan Etchison, 11:48 A.M.
It looks like the movie's only 90 minutes, and we're eating at that Chinese restaurant next to the theater. I think you'll be fine.

172. Why is Mr. Etchison asking for film recommendations?

(A) For an office outing
(B) For a fundraising opportunity
(C) For an analytical article
(D) For a decorating theme

173. What does Mr. Gaskins suggest about *The Adventures of Sam Driver*?

(A) It is not being shown at local theaters.
(B) It has not been praised by critics.
(C) It is the sequel to another film.
(D) It includes frightening scenes.

174. Which film has not yet been released?

(A) *The Gates of Belief*
(B) *The Adventures of Sam Driver*
(C) *Goldfish Canteen*
(D) *Blizzard Connection*

175. At 11:47 A.M., what does Ms. Kiehl most likely mean when she writes, "will there be dinner afterwards"?

(A) She is feeling hungry.
(B) She is concerned about a schedule.
(C) She would like to volunteer to serve food.
(D) She thinks a budget for an event is too high.

GO ON TO THE NEXT PAGE

http://www.ste-a.org/tcc

Town Center Contest Information

The Small Town Enrichment Association organizes this annual contest to support America's small towns. If you know a community that is working hard to create a welcoming town center, we want to hear about it!

Entries can be submitted <u>here</u>. They must be titled and include a brief explanation of the town's past and present, and two to three photographs that show its overall character.

Note: Employees of the Small Town Enrichment Association, Rood Web Services, or Sakos Hardware may not enter the contest.

As usual, submissions are accepted until March 31. Towns chosen as finalists in April by a popular vote at www.ste-a.org/tcc/vote then host our judges for daylong visits in May. This year, judges will award the following prizes:

Prize name	Contents
Grand Prize	A check for $20,000
Gold Prize	A yearlong subscription to Rood Web Services
Silver Prize	A $500 gift card for Sakos Hardware
Bronze Prize	An elegant recognition plaque

E-Mail message

From:	<r.ayers@ste-a.org>
To:	<t.maddux@lio-mail.com>
Subject:	Town Center Contest Results
Date:	June 15
Attachment:	📎 Form

Dear Mr. Maddux,

Congratulations! You have won Gold Prize in the Small Town Enrichment Association's Town Center Contest. Judges were impressed with Bahr Hills' unique, locally-owned shops and restaurants. We hope that the winnings help to fulfill your goal of bringing more visitors to the area. I will contact you soon with detailed instructions about how to claim your prize.

Also, please know that the contents of your entry will be preserved on a "Winner's Page" on our Web site. We also encourage you to e-mail us a paragraph early next year about how participating in the Town Center Contest has benefitted Bahr Hills. It will be added to your entry to bring further positive publicity to your town, and attract applicants to future contests.

Sincerely,

Rose Ayers
Small Town Enrichment Association

176. What is NOT a required part of a contest submission?

(A) A heading
(B) A map of a town
(C) Some pictures of an area
(D) Some historical information

177. According to the Web page, who are not allowed to enter the contest?

(A) People who moved to a location recently
(B) People who have won the Grand Prize in the past
(C) People employed by certain organizations
(D) People in a town with over 20,000 residents

178. According to the Web page, what happens in May?

(A) Entries are collected.
(B) Rules are determined.
(C) Judges visit towns.
(D) The public votes online.

179. What did Mr. Maddux win?

(A) A decorative tablet
(B) A service subscription
(C) A store voucher
(D) A gift certificate

180. What is Mr. Maddux invited to do next year?

(A) Supply a written update
(B) Apply to the contest again
(C) Appear at an award ceremony
(D) Participate in a study

Test 4

GO ON TO THE NEXT PAGE

http://www.valmirebooks.com

Valmire Books
News and Updates

Friday, September 23

We are kicking off the fall season with something new to enhance your in-store shopping experience. Starting next Monday, we will produce a weekly flyer highlighting books that are strongly endorsed by our store's staff. Every book featured in the flyers will be 10% off, but you must visit the store to enjoy these discounts. The offer will not be valid for online purchases. We also encourage you to browse through our shop's vast inventory—including hundreds of titles that are not sold on our Web site.

For our first flyer, our employees chose some of their favorite how-to books from the store's business section. Among the selections for the week is the classic reference volume *Inspirations for Logo Design*, as well as Gretchen Silva's latest chart-topper. All of the selected titles are guaranteed to help aspiring entrepreneurs, so come in and check them out.

Valmire Books – Flyer for week of September 26

• *How to Lead a Team* by Denise Knapp

This easy-to-follow guide makes team management seem easy with the help of clear explanations and colorful flowcharts. Take the personality test provided in the appendix for extra insight.

• *Make Your Business Eco-Friendly* by Gretchen Silva

Filled with case studies of actual business owners' experiences in "going green", this book offers a six-part model for creating an environmentally-friendly company.

• *Inspirations for Logo Design* by Keith Gerlack

This authoritative volume showcases logos from 27 countries and serves as an invaluable reference tool for graphic designers looking to pick up new ideas.

• *Retail Display Tips* by Bart Dunstan

This highly informative book includes step-by-step instructions, accompanied by detailed sketches, for creating a memorable window display. Updated edition includes a new chapter covering Web site design for online shops.

181. What is suggested about Valmire Books?

(A) It has expanded hours during the summer.
(B) It plans to open a new store location.
(C) Its online and offline store inventories differ.
(D) Its staff members attend a nearby business university.

182. In the Web page, what is NOT indicated about the flyers?

(A) They are posted in the store window.
(B) They feature discounted books.
(C) They list books recommended by staff.
(D) They are a new project of the store.

183. Which book has been republished in a revised version?

(A) *How to Lead a Team*
(B) *Make Your Business Eco-Friendly*
(C) *Inspirations for Logo Design*
(D) *Retail Display Tips*

184. What is implied about *Make Your Business Eco-Friendly*?

(A) It was printed on recycled paper.
(B) It has exactly six chapters.
(C) It is a recent bestseller
(D) It contains helpful graphics.

185. In the flyer, the phrase "pick up" in paragraph 3, line 2, is closest in meaning to

(A) recover
(B) accelerate
(C) gain
(D) remove

Test 4

GO ON TO THE NEXT PAGE

ALBRIGHT FONNER BANK

About Us

Since our first location was opened on Peak Street in Auckland just over two years ago, Albright Fonner Bank has established additional branches in Whangarei, Tauranga, and Hamilton. Throughout this process, we have maintained an excellent record of service. In an online poll of New Zealanders by Glaspell Alliance, Albright Fonner was voted the bank with the best customer support.

Credit Card Solutions

If you are looking for a credit card with great benefits from an institution you can trust, check out our offerings below.

AF Blue Card Get 2% cash back on all grocery store purchases, and 1% cash back everywhere else.	**AF Glint Card** With every dollar you spend, earn 1.5 points that can be used on flights, hotels, cruises, etc.
AF White Card Enjoy a 0% annual interest rate for your first two years as a cardholder.	**AF Premium Card** For a small annual fee, earn 2 points per dollar and spend them on anything.

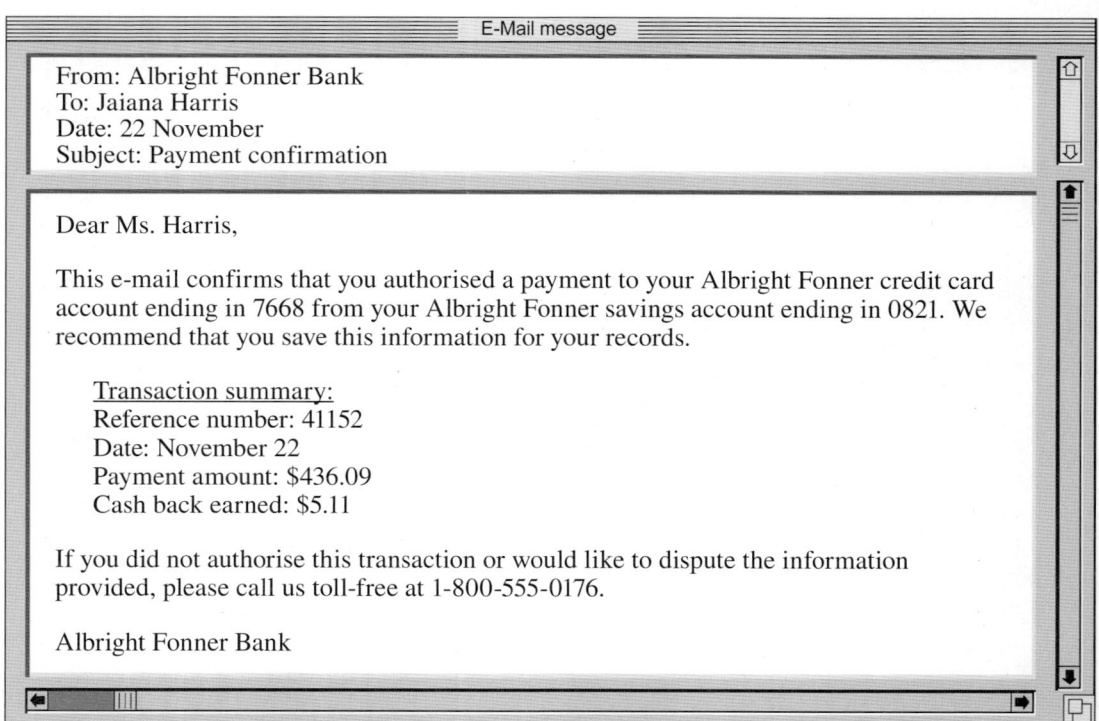

E-Mail message

From: Albright Fonner Bank
To: Jaiana Harris
Date: 22 November
Subject: Payment confirmation

Dear Ms. Harris,

This e-mail confirms that you authorised a payment to your Albright Fonner credit card account ending in 7668 from your Albright Fonner savings account ending in 0821. We recommend that you save this information for your records.

Transaction summary:
Reference number: 41152
Date: November 22
Payment amount: $436.09
Cash back earned: $5.11

If you did not authorise this transaction or would like to dispute the information provided, please call us toll-free at 1-800-555-0176.

Albright Fonner Bank

ALBRIGHT FONNER BANK
Anniversary Celebration during January

Albright Fonner Bank turns three years old this month. In honour of this milestone, we are offering special promotions that benefit both new and returning customers. Throughout January, customers at any of our branches who open a checking account with a deposit of at least $1,000 in it will earn a bonus deposit of $200.

Furthermore, all savings account holders have been entered into a lottery for a brand-new Arcuri N-680 sedan. The winner will be announced at a customer appreciation party held in front of our Auckland branch on Saturday, 25 January. Starting at 1 P.M. and continuing until the prize ceremony at 5 P.M., games and refreshments will be available to all Albright Fonner customers and their families. We hope you will join us to celebrate three years of successful growth, and to build relationships for our community's future.

Test 4

186. What is stated about Albright Fonner Bank?

(A) It was highly ranked in a nationwide survey.
(B) It has expanded through acquisitions of local banks.
(C) It mainly serves small business owners.
(D) It will launch an online investing tool.

187. According to the brochure, what can an AF Glint Card cardholder do?

(A) Sign up for automatic balance payments
(B) Pay a 1.5% interest rate
(C) Earn extra points for food purchases
(D) Save money on travel

188. Which credit card does Ms. Harris most likely have?

(A) The AF Blue Card
(B) The AF Glint Card
(C) The AF White Card
(D) The AF Premium Card

189. What is implied about Ms. Harris?

(A) She lives in Auckland.
(B) She will have to call a hotline.
(C) She has been entered into a drawing.
(D) She recently opened a new bank account.

190. What will be part of the anniversary celebration?

(A) Checking account holders will receive a gift.
(B) Employees at some branches will be given bonus pay.
(C) A gathering will be held for the bank's customers.
(D) A donation will be made to a community organization.

GO ON TO THE NEXT PAGE

Questions 191-195 refer to the following e-mail, text message, and article.

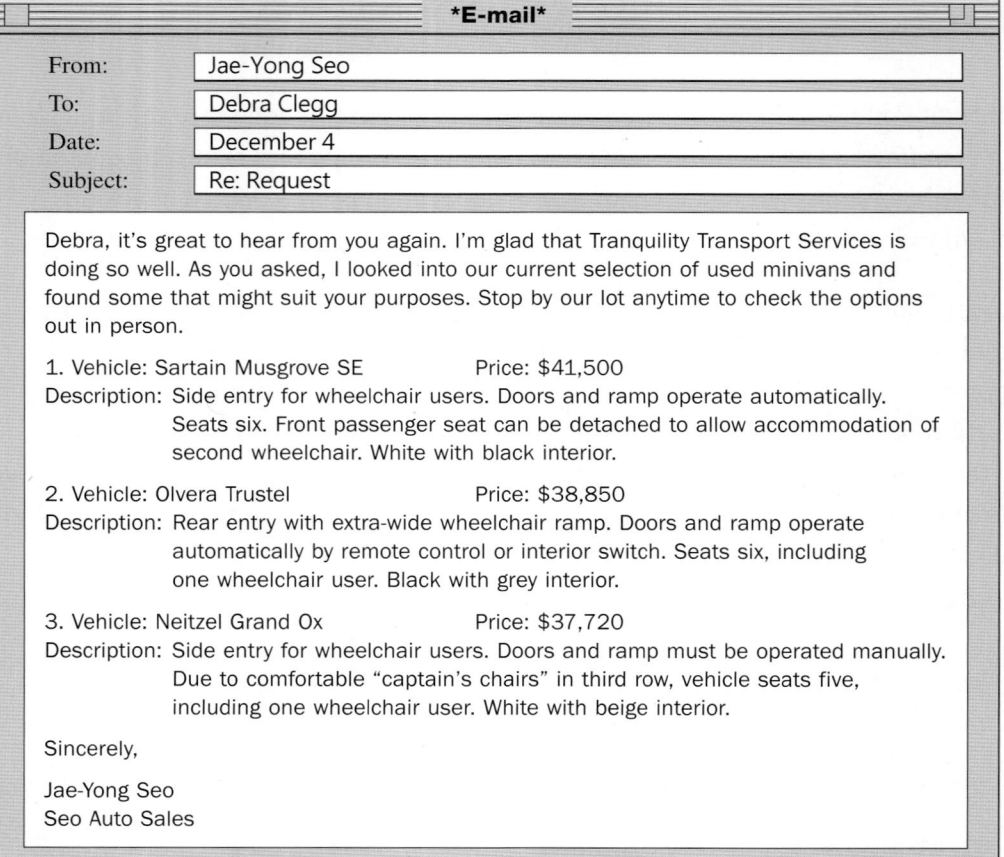

E-mail

From:	Jae-Yong Seo
To:	Debra Clegg
Date:	December 4
Subject:	Re: Request

Debra, it's great to hear from you again. I'm glad that Tranquility Transport Services is doing so well. As you asked, I looked into our current selection of used minivans and found some that might suit your purposes. Stop by our lot anytime to check the options out in person.

1. Vehicle: Sartain Musgrove SE   Price: $41,500
Description: Side entry for wheelchair users. Doors and ramp operate automatically.
           Seats six. Front passenger seat can be detached to allow accommodation of
           second wheelchair. White with black interior.

2. Vehicle: Olvera Trustel   Price: $38,850
Description: Rear entry with extra-wide wheelchair ramp. Doors and ramp operate
           automatically by remote control or interior switch. Seats six, including
           one wheelchair user. Black with grey interior.

3. Vehicle: Neitzel Grand Ox   Price: $37,720
Description: Side entry for wheelchair users. Doors and ramp must be operated manually.
           Due to comfortable "captain's chairs" in third row, vehicle seats five,
           including one wheelchair user. White with beige interior.

Sincerely,

Jae-Yong Seo
Seo Auto Sales

From: Matt Paulk
To: Debra Clegg
Received: December 7, 11:10 A.M.

I'd like to say again that I'm sorry that I can't go with you to Seo Auto Sales today to look at the vehicles. I really want to help you out, though, so here's a little advice on what to ask about the vans. Along with obvious things like cost, it's good to know how many people can fit in each one, with or without wheelchairs. I'd also find out what kind of repairs and servicing the vans have had in the past, and their total mileage. Then, tomorrow, we can talk over what you find out. Good luck!

Taking a Ride with Tranquility Transport Services

By Stephanie Oxner

· ·

LULEY (December 29)—Residents of Luley are about to see more white minivans with cheerful blue logo stickers. Tranquility Transport Services is a local company that provides transportation for non-emergency medical situations to people with or without disabilities. Now, after just six months in business, it has increased the size of its fleet from one vehicle to three.

I spoke with Tranquility Transport staff about this impressive growth. As driver Matt Paulk showed me an Olvera Trustel that the company had recently purchased, he explained that the foundation of the business was reliability. "People have learned that they can trust us to be on time and properly equipped," he said.

Debra Clegg, the company's owner, said she was excited about its future, noting, "We're now able to transport passengers to locations outside of Luley, such as Averin Hospital." She encourages those interested to call 555-0147 to learn about Tranquility Transport Services' offerings.

191. What is the purpose of the e-mail?

(A) To respond to an inquiry
(B) To confirm an order
(C) To advertise an upcoming sale
(D) To explain a service delay

192. What information is Ms. Clegg advised to ask for that is NOT provided in the e-mail?

(A) The vehicles' price
(B) The vehicles' mileage per gallon
(C) The vehicles' maintenance history
(D) The vehicles' seating capacity

193. What is most likely true about a Tranquility Transport Services vehicle?

(A) Its front passenger seat has been removed.
(B) It has a video entertainment system.
(C) It has been repainted.
(D) Its doors must be opened by hand.

194. In the article, the word "foundation" in paragraph 2, line 5, is closest in meaning to

(A) segment
(B) institute
(C) creation
(D) basis

195. How is Tranquility Transport Services changing?

(A) Its pricing strategy is being adjusted.
(B) Its service territory is increasing.
(C) It now caters to passengers with special needs.
(D) It is forming a partnership with a medical clinic.

GO ON TO THE NEXT PAGE

From:	Jeanne Dubois
To:	Rachel Freund
Date:	May 4
Subject:	CLS Results
Attachment:	📎 CLS Summary

Dear Rachel,

I've finished this semester's Campus Life Survey. A detailed report of my findings is attached to this e-mail, but I can summarize the main points for you as follows:

- The service or facility that received the lowest approval rating was parking. Students say there are not enough spaces, especially near Scheyd Auditorium.

- Most students rate Morton Cafeteria as their favorite dining hall, but express concerns about overcrowding there. They would like our other dining halls to offer special food items like its burrito bowls.

- Especially among students majoring in science, there continues to be demand for themed dormitories for those who share particular interests.

Please take a look at the attachment and let me know when we can meet to discuss the information. Obviously, I can't take on major projects in the short time that I have left in this position, but I will make sure my successor is well-informed of all issues raised.

Thanks,

Jeanne Dubois
Residential Life Manager, Carroway University

Residential Life Manager

Carroway University — Pittsburgh, Pennsylvania

The Department of Student Residential Life at Carroway University is seeking a residential life manager (RLM). The RLM's main responsibility is overseeing all aspects of life in the university's student residence halls. Occasional night and weekend work will be required, as the RLM must respond to residence-hall related problems as soon as they arise. In addition, the position involves serving as a liaison to several student-run committees, as well as designing and administering feedback surveys to assess satisfaction with campus life. Candidates must possess a master's degree or higher in an education-related field, and have worked in a university setting for a minimum of five years. For more information about the position, visit www.carroway.edu/hr.

Carroway University
New Student Orientation Schedule – Day 2

Time	Activity	Location
7 A.M.–8:30 A.M.	Breakfast	Belva Dining Hall
9 A.M.–10:30 A.M.	Icebreaker activities led by resident assistants	Each residence hall
11 A.M.–12 P.M.	Speech: "The History of Carroway" (Wentao Li, Carroway University President)	Scheyd Auditorium
12 P.M.–1:00 P.M.	Lunch	Morton Cafeteria
1:15 P.M.–2:30 P.M.	Speech: "Basics of Campus Living" (Peter Travis, Residential Life Manager)	Scheyd Auditorium
2:45 P.M.–4 P.M.	Speech: "Classroom Do's and Don'ts" (Professor Christine Wren, Social Science Department)	Scheyd Auditorium
4 P.M.–5:15 P.M.	Panel discussion: "Making the Most of Social Opportunities" (Returning students)	Scheyd Auditorium
6 P.M.–7:30 P.M.	Dinner	Belva Dining Hall
8 P.M.–10 P.M.	Welcoming party	Sloman Square

196. According to the e-mail, what do Carroway University students want?

(A) Themed housing
(B) A reduction in parking fees
(C) A new restaurant on campus
(D) Tutoring for science majors

197. What is one duty of the position described in the advertisement?

(A) Translating documents into another language
(B) Working outside of normal business hours
(C) Designing training programs for staff
(D) Driving long distances occasionally

198. What is implied about the New Student Orientation lunch?

(A) Students will be led to the venue by resident assistants.
(B) It will be held in the university's most popular dining hall.
(C) It will be hosted by the university president.
(D) Students must choose their meal in advance.

199. What is suggested about Mr. Travis?

(A) He lives on the university campus.
(B) He is the head of a finance committee.
(C) He has a master's degree in social science.
(D) He has at least five years of work experience.

200. When would an orientation participant start learning about academic policies?

(A) At 11:00 A.M.
(B) At 1:15 P.M.
(C) At 2:45 P.M.
(D) At 4:00 P.M.

Stop! This is the end of the test. If you finish before time is called, you may go back to Parts 5, 6, and 7 and check your work.

TEST 5

READING TEST

In the Reading test, you will read a variety of texts and answer several different types of reading comprehension questions. The entire Reading test will last 75 minutes. There are three parts, and directions are given for each part. You are encouraged to answer as many questions as possible within the time allowed.

You must mark your answers on the separate answer sheet. Do not write your answers in your test book.

PART 5

Directions: A word or phrase is missing in each of the sentences below. Four answer choices are given below each sentence. Select the best answer to complete the sentence. Then mark the letter (A), (B), (C), or (D) on your answer sheet.

101. The new beverage from the Elmhurst Corporation can be described ------- a nutritional energy drink.

(A) for
(B) by
(C) as
(D) to

102. The upfront investment in the manufacturing sector will ------- result in the creation of hundreds of jobs.

(A) commonly
(B) constantly
(C) ultimately
(D) formerly

103. The office manager hoped to ------- the changes to the dress code policy at the meeting.

(A) clarified
(B) clarifies
(C) clarifying
(D) clarify

104. The noise from the construction equipment outside of Mr. Polanco's office made it difficult to -------.

(A) lower
(B) concentrate
(C) obtain
(D) obstruct

105. Due to the very competitive nature of the field, the managers are seeking new and unique ------- to reaching customers.

(A) approachable
(B) approaches
(C) approach
(D) approached

106. After receiving ------- complaints about the device overheating, Wayvon Electronics recalled its new smartphone.

(A) numerated
(B) number
(C) numerate
(D) numerous

107. The originality of Ms. Lanham's entry could not be denied, ------- she did not make it to the final round of the art competition.

(A) for
(B) so
(C) yet
(D) and

108. Staff members at this company are expected to give as much notice as possible whenever ------- need time off work for a vacation.

(A) ourselves
(B) we
(C) our
(D) ours

109. After reviewing the two submitted bids, council members selected the more ------- option because of the company's reputation for reliability.
(A) costing
(B) costlier
(C) cost
(D) costly

110. The physician explained that a feeling of dizziness ------- accompanies increased thirst when a patient has not drunk enough water.
(A) next
(B) either
(C) much
(D) often

111. The emphasis placed ------- teamwork helps Espinoza International's employees feel supported.
(A) on
(B) to
(C) of
(D) among

112. For safety reasons, all employees and customers must ------- the building when the fire alarm sounds.
(A) decline
(B) dispose
(C) vacate
(D) suspend

113. Those who are familiar with the jazz trio's first album may find its latest release to be ------- similar.
(A) recognized
(B) recognizably
(C) recognizable
(D) recognizes

114. Analysts predict that Bolman Automotive will have a ------- for its hybrid vehicles for at least the next few years.
(A) demands
(B) demanded
(C) demanding
(D) demand

115. Ms. Jang was offered a promotion after handling the emergency procedures during the power outage -------.
(A) admiring
(B) admirably
(C) admiration
(D) admirable

116. The annual community softball tournament welcomes teams of all ages and ------- abilities.
(A) athletic
(B) athlete
(C) athletically
(D) athletes

117. Owing to the package's ------- contents, the courier was instructed not to stack anything heavy on top of it.
(A) fragile
(B) sudden
(C) vivid
(D) shallow

118. Once the sales personnel were informed that the product launch exceeded projections, they realized they had been ------- worried.
(A) obviously
(B) lastingly
(C) needlessly
(D) strategically

119. All massage therapists working at the Sunset Spa are required to have valid state ------- as well as three years of experience.
(A) certify
(B) certified
(C) certifiable
(D) certification

120. Surprisingly, Mr. Saraf can ------- arrive faster by train because traveling by air requires a long security procedure.
(A) whether
(B) both
(C) still
(D) despite

GO ON TO THE NEXT PAGE

121. The jet ski is unlikely to flip over when in operation, but users must nonetheless take the necessary -------.
   (A) resources
   (B) precautions
   (C) announcements
   (D) descriptions

122. Most tenants agree that the landlord made the right decision ------- the addition of motion-sensor lights near the side entrances.
   (A) since
   (B) regarding
   (C) into
   (D) underneath

123. The creators of the product claim that if you spray it evenly on carpeting or curtains, any odor ------- within a few minutes.
   (A) to eliminate
   (B) to be eliminated
   (C) will eliminate
   (D) will be eliminated

124. PG Internet was able to expand its network exponentially thanks to a number of important ------- in technology.
   (A) promotions
   (B) advancements
   (C) elevations
   (D) enlargements

125. Local art enthusiasts were delighted at the news that the museum procured a rare painting ------- to be worth over two million euros.
   (A) estimating
   (B) has estimated
   (C) was estimated
   (D) estimated

126. Officials are taking extraordinary measures to prevent some people from putting more ------- currency into circulation.
   (A) biased
   (B) negligent
   (C) reckless
   (D) counterfeit

127. Consumers were encouraged to return all battery packs to the manufacturer during its recall, however ------- they may be.
   (A) operational
   (B) operation
   (C) operationally
   (D) operates

128. The general consensus is that too much television near bedtime is bad for one's health, but Dr. Iversen set out to prove -------.
   (A) instead
   (B) opposite
   (C) otherwise
   (D) else

129. Because she enjoys learning about other cultures, Ms. Fernandez prefers to take vacations overseas ------- stay closer to home.
   (A) in order that
   (B) as if
   (C) whereas
   (D) rather than

130. Thanks to their beautiful illustrations and charming storylines, Alice Boyd's children's books have been ------- popular.
   (A) willingly
   (B) enduringly
   (C) hastily
   (D) scarcely

PART 6

Directions: Read the texts that follow. A word, phrase, or sentence is missing in parts of each text. Four answer choices for each question are given below the text. Select the best answer to complete the text. Then mark the letter (A), (B), (C), or (D) on your answer sheet.

Questions 131-134 refer to the following notice.

TO ALL CHESTER'S STEAKHOUSE CUSTOMERS

Chester's Steakhouse ------- to bringing you the best dining experience, so it's welcome news that
_____131._____
our patio is finally open for the summer. While dining in the fresh air, please keep in mind that

sections of this neighborhood are zoned as residential. Therefore, you should be ------- by
_____132._____
monitoring your voice volume in the late evening, especially when walking past the apartments

opposite our main entrance. Thank you in advance for your cooperation; it will help us to maintain a

positive ------- with those living nearby. Should you prefer to move indoors at any time, we can easily
_____133._____
accommodate you. -------.
_____134._____

---

131. (A) is committed
    (B) being committed
    (C) to commit
    (D) committing

132. (A) courteousness
    (B) courteously
    (C) courteous
    (D) courtesy

133. (A) impact
    (B) relationship
    (C) proof
    (D) service

134. (A) Just inform your server that you wish to do
       so.
    (B) We appreciate your bringing this problem
       to our attention.
    (C) As a result, the opening of the patio will be
       delayed.
    (D) It may take longer to prepare the dish than
       usual.

GO ON TO THE NEXT PAGE

To: Armando Michaud <armando@michauddrycleaning.com>
From: Ashville Bank <loans@ashvillebank.com>
Date: January 18
Subject: Small Business Loan

Dear Mr. Michaud,

Thank you for your interest in a small business loan from Ashville Bank. Please fill out the attached ------- , which afford us information about your business model as well as your personal credit history.
135.
It is essential that you ------ accurate information on the form. Failure to do so could result in the
136.
delay or ------ the rejection of your application. While we do our best to accommodate all requests,
137.
we may not be able to issue you the full amount. ------.
138.

Sincerely,

The Ashville Bank Loans Team

---

135. (A) form
(B) formed
(C) forming
(D) forms

136. (A) provide
(B) to provide
(C) provided
(D) are provided

137. (A) more
(B) rather
(C) yet
(D) even

138. (A) For this reason, our bank has received high customer service ratings.
(B) Nevertheless, we took your personal circumstances into consideration.
(C) In that case, there may still be other options available to you.
(D) Alternatively, you can check your balance to confirm that it was received.

Norcross Sleep Center

1200 Hanifan Lane • 461-555-0138

It is estimated that up to twenty percent of people suffer from a sleep problem. Many sleep issues may not be ------- to the affected person, so we recommend testing yourself even if you do not have
139.
severe symptoms. To have your condition assessed, visit our center in person, where our technicians can ------- a wide variety of sleep disorders. On the other hand, you may ------- test your
140. **141.**
sleep at home by renting a monitor. We will analyze the data after one week. A prescription is required for some of our devices, such as our continuous positive airway pressure (CPAP) machines. -------.
142.

139. (A) susceptible
(B) apparent
(C) tentative
(D) adequate

140. (A) interpret
(B) conduct
(C) diagnose
(D) inherit

141. (A) comfortably
(B) partially
(C) evidently
(D) abundantly

142. (A) Each week, you will receive an updated report.
(B) Most reported success after a few weeks.
(C) Please take care of this as soon as possible.
(D) Others are available to general consumers.

GO ON TO THE NEXT PAGE

Questions 143-146 refer to the following article.

October 6—Nicole Walt has accepted the role of National Transportation Advisor, replacing Leon Hixon, who is stepping down to start his own consulting business. Ms. Walt is ------- respected for **143.** her impressive security expertise. She ------- transportation in the southeast region of the country for **144.** several years, and supporters believe she will easily adapt to her larger-scale role. Analysts predict that she will soon push parliament to sell a section of the rail line to a corporation. A sale such as this would generate immediate profit for the national transportation system. -------. However, Walt will **145.** face strong opponents of the ------- of the system, as many believe publicly used services should **146.** stay in public hands.

143. (A) high
(B) higher
(C) highly
(D) height

144. (A) will have been managed
(B) was managed
(C) is managing
(D) has been managing

145. (A) It is also expected to result in more reliable journey times.
(B) Fortunately, this is considered to be an unlikely scenario.
(C) For instance, she plans to focus on modernizing ticket processing.
(D) Each one would benefit the thousands of daily passengers.

146. (A) privatization
(B) renewal
(C) evaluation
(D) operation

Directions: In this part you will read a selection of texts, such as magazine and newspaper articles, e-mails, and instant messages. Each text or set of texts is followed by several questions. Select the best answer for each question and mark the letter (A), (B), (C), or (D) on your answer sheet.

Questions 147-148 refer to the following invitation.

Regent Museum cordially invites you to the pre-opening of

Lightness and Darkness
An exhibit of paintings by Leslie Diaz

Friday, January 20, 7 P.M.

The Regent Museum is pleased to have these amazing paintings on display. Ms. Diaz's latest exhibition is inspired by her travels through Southeast Asia, where she observed the remarkable seaside and mountain landscapes that are central to her paintings. Your membership entitles you to attend this event and see the artwork ahead of the press and the general public.

147. What is indicated about Ms. Diaz?

(A) She is making her debut at the Regent Museum.
(B) Her paintings will be sold by auction.
(C) She used to live in Southeast Asia.
(D) Her artwork depicts scenes from nature.

148. Who most likely is the recipient of the invitation?

(A) A museum supporter
(B) An art critic
(C) An art student
(D) A member of the press

https://www.piedlantclothing.com/account ▶

Your account has been updated.

Name: | Diana Peters |

E-mail Address: | dpeters@kemberyco.com |

You have successfully unsubscribed from the Piedlant Clothing free monthly newsletter. You will still receive e-mails from Piedlant Clothing about the status of the orders you place and any policy changes that affect our Terms of Use for online customers. If you would like to undo this action, please click here. Please take a moment to let us know why you no longer wish to receive the newsletter.

Comments: I have been a regular customer of Piedlant Clothing for years, but the recent increase in prices has changed the way I plan to interact with the brand. While I'll still consider Piedlant Clothing for apparel for special occasions, it's more practical for me to purchase my casual clothing elsewhere.

149. Why did Ms. Peters visit the Web page?

(A) To leave a review of an order
(B) To complain about a service
(C) To remove herself from a mailing list
(D) To contribute ideas to a newsletter

150. What does Ms. Peters mention about Piedlant Clothing?

(A) It does not sell casual clothing anymore.
(B) Its marketing strategy is old-fashioned.
(C) It sends e-mails to customers too frequently.
(D) Its merchandise has become less affordable.

Questions 151-152 refer to the following text-message chain.

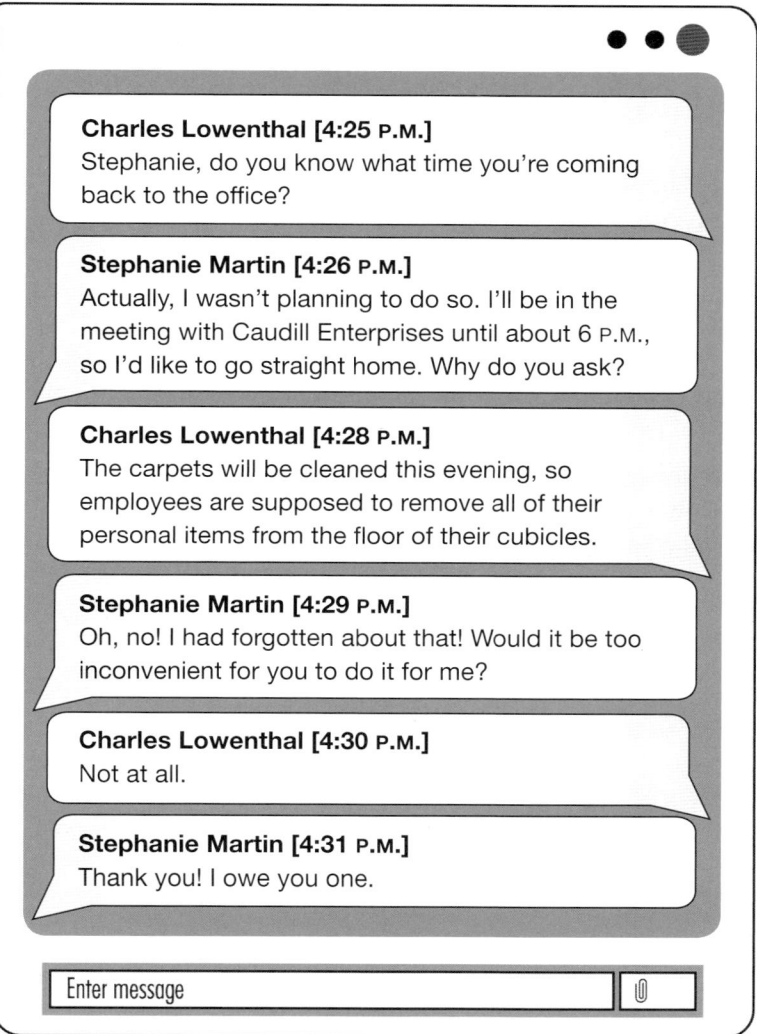

Charles Lowenthal [4:25 P.M.]
Stephanie, do you know what time you're coming back to the office?

Stephanie Martin [4:26 P.M.]
Actually, I wasn't planning to do so. I'll be in the meeting with Caudill Enterprises until about 6 P.M., so I'd like to go straight home. Why do you ask?

Charles Lowenthal [4:28 P.M.]
The carpets will be cleaned this evening, so employees are supposed to remove all of their personal items from the floor of their cubicles.

Stephanie Martin [4:29 P.M.]
Oh, no! I had forgotten about that! Would it be too inconvenient for you to do it for me?

Charles Lowenthal [4:30 P.M.]
Not at all.

Stephanie Martin [4:31 P.M.]
Thank you! I owe you one.

Enter message

Test 5

151. What does Mr. Lowenthal ask Ms. Martin?

(A) When she will return
(B) Which office is hers
(C) How a meeting went
(D) What tasks must be done

152. At 4:30 P.M., what does Mr. Lowenthal most likely mean when he writes, "Not at all"?

(A) He will clear Ms. Martin's work space.
(B) He has run out of some supplies.
(C) He was unable to speak with some clients.
(D) He will amend a cleaning schedule.

GO ON TO THE NEXT PAGE

To: All Roane Incorporated Employees
From: Rahul Shevade, Human Resources Director
Date: October 6
Re: 25 years in business

Dear Staff Members,

At the end of next month, Roane Incorporated will be celebrating its twenty-fifth anniversary. We want to hold a party to commemorate this achievement. I am currently looking for six people to join our planning board so that we can make the preparations for the event. Please note that this opportunity is open to staff members in every department. If you are interested, please e-mail me no later than Wednesday, October 15, with notes about when you would be able to take part in group meetings. After the deadline, I will review everyone's availability and select a time and day that works for all of us. Thank you for your consideration.

153. What is the purpose of the memo?
(A) To invite employees to a celebration
(B) To announce a job opening
(C) To seek committee members
(D) To congratulate the staff on an achievement

154. What does Mr. Shevade indicate will be determined after October 15?
(A) The timing of a meeting
(B) The size of a budget
(C) The goals of a group
(D) The location of a banquet

McDorwell Supplies

www.mcdorwellsupplies.com ▽ 1-800-555-0100

Business Name: Atchley's   **Point of Contact:** Michael Atchley
Phone Number: 901-555-0127   **Date of Order:** July 9
Billing Address: 875 Myrtle Avenue, Memphis, TN 38018
Shipping Address: 1299 Baldwin Street, Memphis, TN 38018
Shipping Type: Overnight Express   **Return Cutoff Date:** July 16
McDorwell Supplies Loyalty Program Number: 5498-7319

Item Description	Quantity	Price Per Unit	Total
18-inch wire hangers (pack of 500)	5	$21.99	$109.95
Cardboard shoulder guards (pack of 500)	3	$28.49	$85.47
Liquid stain remover (5L)	4	$29.99	$119.96
All-in-one detergent (20L)	3	$189.99	$569.97
Thank you for your purchase. To help us better serve you, please take a moment to complete a brief customer service questionnaire at www.mcdorwellsupplies.com/survey. Your feedback is important to us.	Subtotal		$885.35
	Taxes and Delivery		$83.75
	Total Due		$969.10

155. What kind of business most likely is Atchley's?

(A) A delivery company
(B) A clothing shop
(C) A dry-cleaning service
(D) A hair salon

156. When will Mr. Atchley's delivery most likely arrive?

(A) On July 9
(B) On July 10
(C) On July 11
(D) On July 16

157. What is implied in the invoice?

(A) Atchley's is collecting loyalty points.
(B) Mr. Atchley has completed a survey.
(C) A shipping fee has been decreased.
(D) The order will be sent to two addresses.

GO ON TO THE NEXT PAGE

Test 5

NOTICE TO REIMELT GYM MEMBERS

Reimelt Gym members who use our on-site parking lot should make alternative arrangements from September 1 to 7, as the lot will be off limits in order to accommodate work crews who will be repaving sections of the lot and sealing minor cracks. During this time, the main entrance will remain locked, and all members will need to use the employee entrance at the west end of the building. Updates regarding progress on the parking lot will be posted on our Web site. The schedule of fitness classes that we offer throughout the week will not be affected.

A private parking lot is located near the gym on Radcliffe Avenue. Unfortunately, we are unable to reimburse you for any costs incurred. We apologize for any inconvenience this work may cause, and we appreciate your patience. Also, this is one of many projects we intend to carry out over the next six months. We are always willing to hear from our members about further building upgrades that would make your workout experience more enjoyable. To put forward your ideas, please talk to Site Manager Dwayne Bailey directly or e-mail him at dbailey@reimeltgym.com.

158. What is the notice mainly about?

(A) The expansion of a parking lot
(B) A revision to a parking policy
(C) Repairs to a parking area
(D) An increase in parking charges

159. What is suggested about Reimelt Gym employees?

(A) They will be ready to answer questions about the change.
(B) They will share an entrance with members for one week.
(C) They will lead fewer classes than usual in September.
(D) They will be assigned parking spaces in the gym's lot.

160. According to the notice, why should gym members contact Mr. Bailey?

(A) To upgrade their membership status
(B) To suggest a facility improvement
(C) To learn how to receive reimbursement
(D) To inquire about the progress of a project

Questions 161-163 refer to the following e-mail.

E-Mail message

To:	Theresa Burgess <burgess.t@monticello1.eu>
From:	Beranston <info@beranstoncamping.eu>
Date:	February 1
Subject:	Products you'll love!

Dear Ms. Burgess,

We understand that there is a vast array of options to choose from when selecting camping gear, so we have compiled some product suggestions based on your recent orders. Aldrin is our newest addition to Beranston Camping, and this brand has already become a best-seller. If you purchase any Aldrin products this month, their shipping fee will be waived. Click the link to be taken to our Web site and buy your items in just minutes!

- Aldrin Battery-Operated Lantern [€45]: This lantern is safe to use inside or outside your tent, and one charge can provide up to 350 hours of light on the lowest setting.
- Aldrin Sleeping Bag [€150]: The perfect blend of comfort and practicality, this bag is suitable for temperatures down to −10°C and can be compressed into a size of just 15 × 30 centimeters for easy transport.
- Aldrin Stove [€50]: This stove is lightweight and small, but it fits pots of all sizes to make outdoor cooking easy.

Please note that we now accept returned items for up to 45 days from the purchase date, as feedback from our customers indicated that 30 days was not enough, especially for items given as gifts that may not be opened right away.

Happy shopping!

The Beranston Team

---

161. Why did Ms. Burgess receive the e-mail?

(A) She commented on a social media page.
(B) She asked for some product updates.
(C) She contacted the customer service department.
(D) She previously made purchases on a Web site.

162. What is NOT indicated about the Aldrin brand's items?

(A) They have become popular with customers.
(B) They are offered at a discounted price.
(C) They are eligible for free delivery in February.
(D) They include a heating device.

163. What has Beranston changed about its return policy?

(A) The amount of store credit that can be earned
(B) The documentation required for returning gifts
(C) The cost of mailing back items
(D) The period for making returns

GO ON TO THE NEXT PAGE

Test 5

Join the Fun at the Fall Festival!
Prairie Park, Saturday, October 20, 9 A.M.–7 P.M.

The Fall Festival is an annual celebration full of fun for all ages. This year, it will take place at Prairie Park on Saturday, October 20. Everyone in town is welcome to attend, and we encourage you to also participate in the festival's many activities. — [1] —.

One way to take part is to show your creativity by making and decorating your own scarecrow. Businesses, schools, and charities can enter this event. The registration fee is $20, and this includes the wooden frame (5' × 8') and a mini bale of straw for stuffing. — [2] —. We ask for one entry per group so that as many people as possible can participate. You may register and pick up your materials at City Hall anytime during regular business hours. Charities will only be charged $10.

Calling all bakers! The festival will include a pie-baking contest. — [3] —. Bring your pie(s) to the booth near the soccer fields at the northern end of the park at 10 A.M. on the day of the festival. Containers will not be returned, so please use a disposal pie tin for your pie. — [4] —. Judging will take place at 2 P.M., with the top three winners receiving a basket of $100 worth of baking accessories. Free pie and ice cream will be served after the winners have been announced. Advanced registration for the baking event is not necessary; however, if you would like to be one of the lucky people critiquing the entries, please call Cassie Shaw at 555-0199. We are looking for a panel of about five people.

A complete list of festival activities can be found on the city's Web site at www.westover.gov.

164. Where would this announcement most likely appear?

    (A) On an entry form
    (B) In a local newsletter
    (C) On a travel Web site
    (D) In a hobby magazine

165. What benefit for nonprofit organizations is mentioned?

    (A) Assistance from volunteers
    (B) Advertising space in a pamphlet
    (C) An opportunity to win a prize
    (D) A reduced registration fee

166. Why should people contact Ms. Shaw?

    (A) To apply to be a competition judge
    (B) To enter a baking contest
    (C) To arrange to pick up materials
    (D) To request the full festival schedule

167. In which of the positions marked [1], [2], [3], and [4] does the following sentence best belong?

    "There are a limited number of spots available."

    (A) [1]
    (B) [2]
    (C) [3]
    (D) [4]

GO ON TO THE NEXT PAGE

Questions 168-171 refer to the following online chat discussion.

Virginia Lietz [1:18 P.M.]
OK, I rang Mr. McFarlin right after our morning staff meeting to see whether he wanted to go forward with contract negotiations.

Jude Doyle [1:19 P.M.]
How did it go?

Virginia Lietz [1:19 P.M.]
Well, he decided to hire Rooker Computing instead since it has the lowest prices in the industry.

Megan Howell [1:20 P.M.]
We spent days on that sales pitch!

Virginia Lietz [1:21 P.M.]
I know. Everyone worked so hard. It's a big letdown.

Jude Doyle [1:21 P.M.]
To be honest, I'm not surprised that Mr. McFarlin preferred a well-established business like Rooker over a start-up. They have nearly five times the number of employees we do. But they also have more clients. I don't think they're able to provide the focused, personal service that we offer.

Megan Howell [1:22 P.M.]
You have a point. Most customers eventually figure out that it's worth the slightly higher cost to have a dependable tech support team like ours.

Virginia Lietz [1:23 P.M.]
Mr. McFarlin informed me that they signed a one-year contract. Therefore, we'll have another opportunity to secure a contract next year during the renewal period.

Megan Howell [1:26 P.M.]
I guess we need to put this defeat behind us and focus on preparing the presentation for Stalford Industries.

Jude Doyle [1:27 P.M.]
Exactly. And instead of making a completely new one, we can just adapt the one we have to address Stalford's specific needs.

168. What did Ms. Lietz do in the morning?

(A) Made a phone call
(B) Visited Mr. McFarlin's business
(C) Checked her e-mail inbox
(D) Wrote a memo

169. At 1:20 P.M., what does Ms. Howell most likely mean when she writes, "We spent days on that sales pitch"?

(A) She is surprised that a meeting ended quickly.
(B) She is frustrated that an appointment was postponed.
(C) She is disappointed with an employment decision.
(D) She is confident that negotiations will go well.

170. What is NOT indicated about Rooker Computing?

(A) It has more staff than the writers' company.
(B) It is known for providing good customer service.
(C) Its prices are lower than those of its competitors.
(D) It has been in operation longer than the writers' company.

171. What does Mr. Doyle suggest doing?

(A) Renewing a service contract
(B) Addressing a technical problem
(C) Adjusting a presentation
(D) Hiring Stalford Industries

GO ON TO THE NEXT PAGE

Carlsbrook Children's Hospital
1077 Gwent Road
Arlington, VA 20330

June 15

Dr. Katherine James
896 Cardiff Street
Arlington, VA 22210

Dear Dr. James,

Please accept this letter of appreciation for all the work your charity has done to contribute to the success of our new annex for children with special conditions. We could not have done it without your support. It was also wonderful to finally meet you in person at the opening ceremony last week. — [1] —.

As promised, I am sending you the research on creating a nurturing environment for children with progressive conditions. The first enclosure is a study from Wichita University led by Dr. Steven Chapman that describes the effects of color and music on recuperation periods. Although this trial was done with adults, we believe the effects would be similar for younger groups as well. That means the choice of paint in patients' rooms should be taken into consideration. — [2] —. The second enclosure is a joint study between our hospital and the local technical college. Run by Dr. Adele Diop, this research shows a strong link between providing specialized facilities and medical outcomes. — [3] —.

These studies should be useful to you when you help Arlington Hospital write their grant application for upgrading their facilities for children next month. Let me also congratulate you on this, your first consultancy work. — [4] —. I am sure that a number of my counterparts at other hospitals around the country would benefit from your help on similar projects, so please let me know if you are interested in doing more of this grant application assistance work.

Yours sincerely,

Dr. Ursula Augustin

Head of Pediatrics, Carlsbrook Children's Hospital
Enclosures

172. Where does Dr. James work?

(A) At a children's hospital
(B) At a laboratory
(C) At a technical college
(D) At a charity

173. What did Dr. Augustin agree to do?

(A) Donate money to an organization
(B) Contact some local universities
(C) Carry out a medical treatment trial
(D) Forward the results of some studies

174. What is indicated about Dr. James?

(A) She is an experienced consultant.
(B) She will be changing employers next month.
(C) She will be involved in obtaining some financing.
(D) She is responsible for conducting some medical research.

175. In which of the positions marked [1], [2], [3], and [4] does the following sentence best belong?

"It is amazing that this had not happened yet, considering that you and I have been working on many of the same projects."

(A) [1]
(B) [2]
(C) [3]
(D) [4]

GO ON TO THE NEXT PAGE

Questions 176-180 refer to the following e-mail and letter.

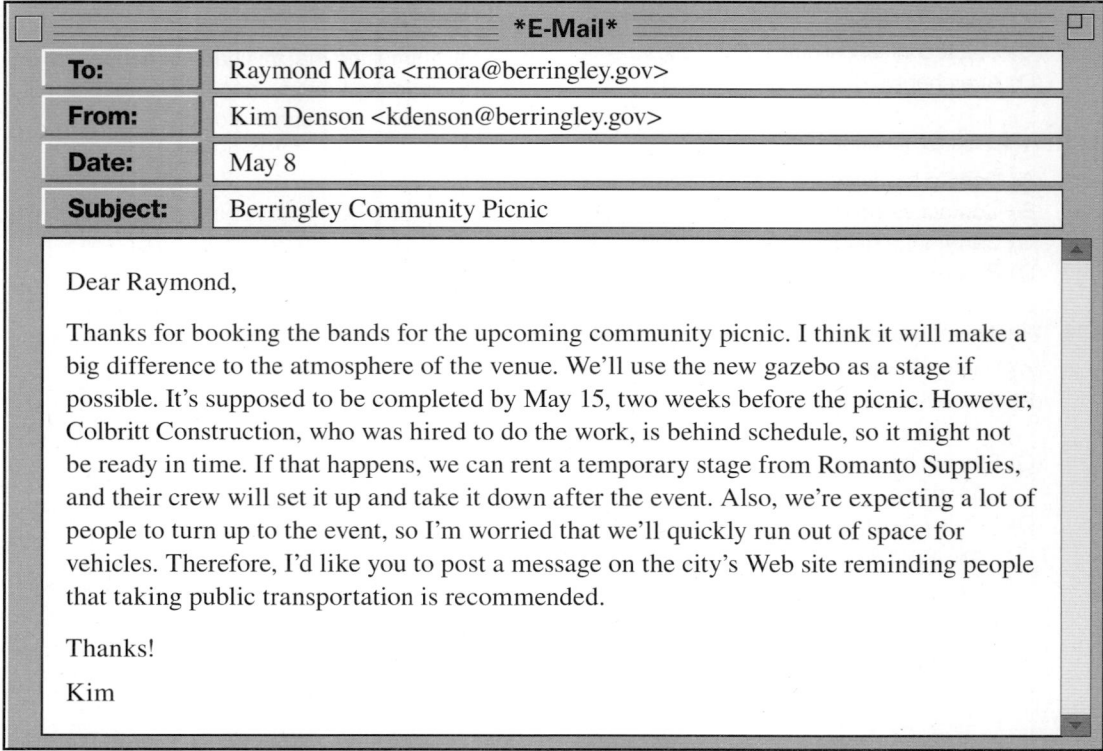

E-Mail

To:	Raymond Mora <rmora@berringley.gov>
From:	Kim Denson <kdenson@berringley.gov>
Date:	May 8
Subject:	Berringley Community Picnic

Dear Raymond,

Thanks for booking the bands for the upcoming community picnic. I think it will make a big difference to the atmosphere of the venue. We'll use the new gazebo as a stage if possible. It's supposed to be completed by May 15, two weeks before the picnic. However, Colbritt Construction, who was hired to do the work, is behind schedule, so it might not be ready in time. If that happens, we can rent a temporary stage from Romanto Supplies, and their crew will set it up and take it down after the event. Also, we're expecting a lot of people to turn up to the event, so I'm worried that we'll quickly run out of space for vehicles. Therefore, I'd like you to post a message on the city's Web site reminding people that taking public transportation is recommended.

Thanks!

Kim

Vera Fleming
214 Blackwell Street
Berringley, VT

Dear Ms. Fleming,

On behalf of the Berringley Event Planning Committee, I would like to cordially invite you to the 14th Annual Berringley Community Picnic on May 30. You may bring your own food or make a purchase from one of the booths sponsored by a local restaurant. I would be happy to reserve a seat for you and up to three guests in the VIP section designated for city council members. You would have a perfect view of the temporary stage, which will be set up at the northern end of Turner Park. If you would like to attend, please send back the enclosed postcard by May 27.

We hope to see you there!

Kim Denson

176. What has Mr. Mora done?

(A) Arranged some live entertainment
(B) Reserved an outdoor venue
(C) Recommended some musical groups
(D) Created an advertisement

177. What is Ms. Denson concerned about?

(A) Insufficient funds
(B) Low attendance
(C) A lack of parking spaces
(D) A poor review

178. Who most likely is Ms. Fleming?

(A) A restaurant owner
(B) An event planner
(C) A city politician
(D) A famous musician

179. What is implied about Colbritt Construction?

(A) It proposed safety features for a gazebo.
(B) Its office is located near Turner Park.
(C) It regularly does work for the city.
(D) It failed to finish a project on time.

180. Why should Ms. Fleming send back the postcard?

(A) To request some special seats
(B) To give feedback about a concert
(C) To show interest in renting a booth
(D) To cast a vote on a community issue

GO ON TO THE NEXT PAGE

Custom-made curtains now available at Anfield Furnishings!

Anfield Furnishings is pleased to introduce Bryker, our new line of custom-made curtains. We understand that each home is different, and our standard lines of curtains and drapes may not suit your home exactly. That's why we are offering this new service. In addition to being customized to the exact specifications of your window, Bryker curtains also come with a thick insulated layer to keep heat in, meaning you'll pay less for energy to heat your home in the winter. These stylish and high-quality curtains are available in several colors and over 250 patterns.

Book an appointment with us and we will have an employee visit your home or office to take precise measurements. The session will last for approximately half an hour, and we can begin producing your curtains within just a few days — no express service needed! Customers must put down a $25 deposit when booking the appointment, but these funds can be used toward your purchase.

To find out more, call 1-800-555-0176, or visit www.anfieldfurn.com. Please note that for most Anfield Furnishing products, we accept returns within two months of the purchase date, but this does not apply to the Bryker line.

Anfield Furnishings
Confirmation of Appointment for Taking Measurements

Customer: Pamela Alessi

Phone number: 555-0133

Address: 6795 Townes Lane, Austin, TX 78730

E-mail address: allessip@balconeco.com

Appointment Date/Time: October 8, 1:30 P.M.   **Property type:** Residential

Notes: To expedite the data-collection process, please leave a minimum of two feet of space between the windows and any sofas, tables, etc. so that the technician has easy access to them.

181. What is mentioned about Bryker curtains?

(A) They are the company's top-selling item.
(B) They are produced domestically.
(C) They can reduce energy bills.
(D) They are available in 250 colors.

182. What is implied about Anfield Furnishings?

(A) It does not allow returns of customized products.
(B) Its Web site has discussion forums for customers.
(C) It has made an agreement with a new supplier.
(D) Its showroom is restocked every two months.

183. What is suggested about Ms. Alessi?

(A) Her appointment was booked by phone.
(B) She has made an initial payment.
(C) A consultation will take place at her business.
(D) She will choose an express option.

184. When most likely will Ms. Alessi's appointment end on October 8?

(A) At 1:30 P.M.
(B) At 2:00 P.M.
(C) At 2:30 P.M.
(D) At 3:00 P.M.

185. What should Ms. Alessi do prior to the appointment?

(A) Remove furniture from a room
(B) Provide an access code
(C) Select a pattern and fabric
(D) Clear areas near the windows

GO ON TO THE NEXT PAGE

NOTICE

Attention, Colba Footwear shoppers:

The Namara Building branch of Colba Footwear will hold its final day of business on Sunday, April 30. Although we enjoy providing casual and formal footwear for our Edendale customers, we could not avoid this closure because the owner of our building plans to sell the structure for the sake of the upcoming stadium project. Merchandise will be discounted in the week leading up to the closure (Namara Building branch only). Thank you for your many years of patronage at this branch, and we look forward to continuing to serve you at the Tennyson Mall branch, where business will carry on as usual.

—Gaurav Kaul
Owner, Colba Footwear

---

https://www.mylocalshopreviews.com/bellcity

Bell City >> Retail >> Shoes >> Colba Footwear

Colba Footwear has an impressive range of goods, and I believe it is the best place in the city to buy shoes. Its attentive salespeople genuinely listen to your needs and make recommendations tailored to your specific situation. The business is now down to just one branch, since its original store closed a few weeks ago, but the second branch provides the same level of service, despite being open for a much shorter amount of time.

Posted May 18 by R.P.

Bell City Stadium Project Moves Forward . . . .

BELL CITY, May 30—The construction of a stadium in the Edendale neighborhood is moving forward, as all permits have been approved and the land acquisition deals have been finalized. Willins Development, the company overseeing the project, has purchased a number of buildings in the area, all of which will be demolished in order to make room for the 50,000-seat stadium designed by architect Anja Lindelauf.

The stadium, which will be named once city officials sell its naming rights to generate further income for the project, will be owned by the city and will be used not just for sports, but also concerts, festivals, and more, making it a welcome addition to the community. It will feature a retractable roof so that it can be used year-round regardless of the weather conditions. "I'm pleased not only with the functionality of this building but also its appearance," said Ms. Lindelauf. "It will blend in with the buildings and environment around it so as not to take away from the already stunning skyline of Bell City."

186. What is true about the Namara Building?

(A) It will be torn down.
(B) It is next to Tennyson Mall.
(C) It has been sold by Mr. Kaul.
(D) It is closed on Sundays.

187. What is indicated about Colba Footwear?

(A) It is the oldest shoe store in Bell City.
(B) Some of its sales are made online.
(C) Its staff needs more training.
(D) Its first store was in Edendale.

188. In the online review, the word "impressive" in paragraph 1, line 1, is closest in meaning to

(A) imminent
(B) talented
(C) meaningful
(D) extensive

189. What is mentioned about the stadium?

(A) It will replace a conference complex.
(B) It is intended to be used for various events.
(C) It will be named by the city's voters.
(D) Its construction was delayed by weather conditions.

190. What is Ms. Lindelauf pleased about?

(A) Designing a sturdy rooftop
(B) Using environmentally friendly materials
(C) Complementing nearby structures
(D) Achieving a budgetary goal

GO ON TO THE NEXT PAGE

Take a journey back in time with a visit to Aberporth Castle!

Aberporth Castle is a majestic stone structure built in the late thirteenth century as a military outpost. Guided tours of the castle itself and its meticulously manicured gardens are offered daily, with two guides assigned to groups exceeding 20 people to facilitate answering questions.

Other activities available daily include the following:
- Sampling examples of medieval cuisine at a traditional lunch hosted by Fritz Pinard
- Watching a pottery-making demonstration by Sophie Johnston
- Attending a lecture from the site's master gardener, Marilyn Clayton
- Horseback-riding through the surrounding woodlands with Aja Devi*
- Participating in a sword-fighting lesson given by Joseph Manzo*

Please note that starred activities (*) require pre-registration.

Find out more at www.aberporthcastle.com.

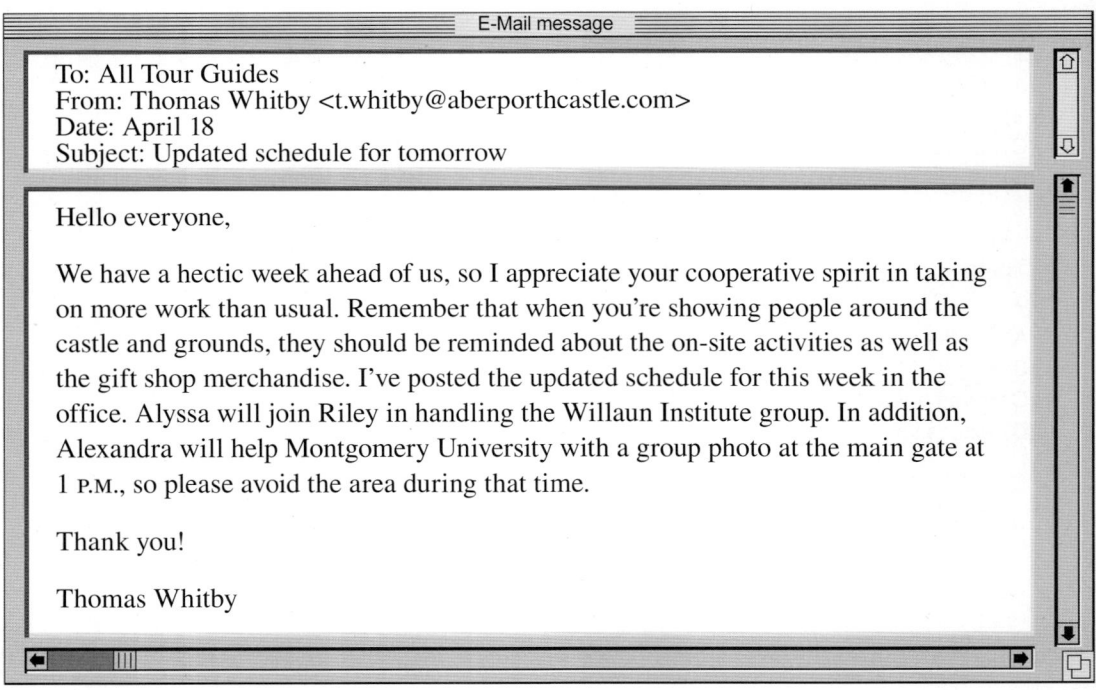

E-Mail message

To: All Tour Guides
From: Thomas Whitby <t.whitby@aberporthcastle.com>
Date: April 18
Subject: Updated schedule for tomorrow

Hello everyone,

We have a hectic week ahead of us, so I appreciate your cooperative spirit in taking on more work than usual. Remember that when you're showing people around the castle and grounds, they should be reminded about the on-site activities as well as the gift shop merchandise. I've posted the updated schedule for this week in the office. Alyssa will join Riley in handling the Willaun Institute group. In addition, Alexandra will help Montgomery University with a group photo at the main gate at 1 P.M., so please avoid the area during that time.

Thank you!

Thomas Whitby

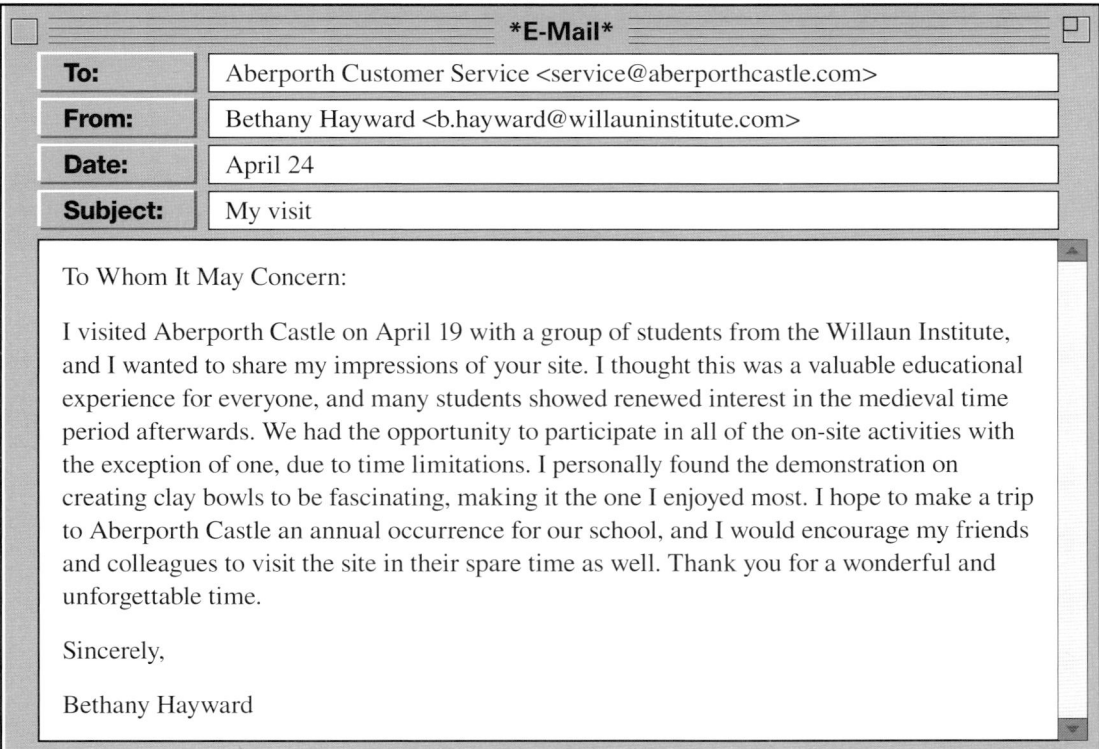

```
*E-Mail*
```

To:	Aberporth Customer Service <service@aberporthcastle.com>
From:	Bethany Hayward <b.hayward@willauninstitute.com>
Date:	April 24
Subject:	My visit

To Whom It May Concern:

I visited Aberporth Castle on April 19 with a group of students from the Willaun Institute, and I wanted to share my impressions of your site. I thought this was a valuable educational experience for everyone, and many students showed renewed interest in the medieval time period afterwards. We had the opportunity to participate in all of the on-site activities with the exception of one, due to time limitations. I personally found the demonstration on creating clay bowls to be fascinating, making it the one I enjoyed most. I hope to make a trip to Aberporth Castle an annual occurrence for our school, and I would encourage my friends and colleagues to visit the site in their spare time as well. Thank you for a wonderful and unforgettable time.

Sincerely,

Bethany Hayward

191. According to the advertisement, what must visitors do to take a sword-fighting lesson?

(A) Put on safety gear
(B) Pay an extra fee
(C) Register in advance
(D) Sign a consent form

192. What is implied about Aberporth Castle?

(A) Its main gate is being remodeled.
(B) It has a retail establishment.
(C) It is always busy in April.
(D) Its tour guides wear costumes.

193. What does Mr. Whitby imply about the group from the Willaun Institute?

(A) Some of its members are under 13 years of age.
(B) Its members will pose for a photograph.
(C) It will arrive too late for a special meal.
(D) There will be more than 20 people in it.

194. In the second e-mail, the word "share" in paragraph 1, line 2, is closest in meaning to

(A) express
(B) sponsor
(C) distribute
(D) divide

195. Who led the activity that Ms. Hayward enjoyed most?

(A) Mr. Pinard
(B) Ms. Johnston
(C) Ms. Clayton
(D) Ms. Devi

GO ON TO THE NEXT PAGE

Questions 196-200 refer to the following instructions, e-mail, and forum post.

Pensler House Runway Competition

Congratulations! Your design has been accepted for our amateur fashion show. This means that our preliminary judging panel was intrigued by the drawings you submitted and would like to see the finished outfit come down the runway. You now have a chance to become one of the ten winners that will be selected on the event day.

The finished entries must arrive at our headquarters (Galtway Building) by 5 P.M. on March 1 so that they can be photographed in the week prior to the runway show. To ensure that the clothing doesn't get lost, it must be brought by you; do not send it through the mail.

You should also e-mail a short description of yourself and your entry to mjensen@penslerhouse.com. If you plan to supply your own model, please complete the attached Contact Information Card for that person and send it back to us. Otherwise, we will supply a model for you.

E-Mail message	
To:	Yolanda Sanchez <yosanchez@ma103.com>
From:	Malcolm Jensen <mjensen@penslerhouse.com>
Date:	March 3
Subject:	Pensler House Runway Competition

Dear Ms. Sanchez,

Regarding the upcoming runway show on March 7, we have received your Contact Information Card, but we are still waiting for the short description of your work and design history. It should be between 80 and 100 words. Please e-mail it to me as soon as possible.

All designers should visit the Pensler House headquarters the day before the event at 5 P.M. in order to try the clothes on the models and make the necessary adjustments. One of our in-house designers, Genevieve Massey, will make recommendations about getting the most flattering fit. On the event day, everyone should report to the Wylona Center at 3 P.M. to leave plenty of time to prepare the models' hair and makeup.

If you have any further questions, please feel free to e-mail me anytime.

Malcolm Jensen

156

www.penslerhouse.com/events/runwaycompetition/forum

Posted: March 8   Post written by: Gemma Byrum

I had a great time at the Pensler House Runway Competition at the Wylona Center yesterday. There were so many unique designs on the runway that it was remarkable that the work was done by amateurs. If you didn't get the chance to catch the show, stop by the lobby of the Almeta Building to see the best outfit made by each of the winners. The host of the runway show announced that they would be on display there for the rest of the month. Don't pass up this opportunity to see some amazing fashions!

196. What do the instructions indicate that designers are required to do?

(A) Select their favorite outfit
(B) Make a list of fabrics
(C) Deliver items in person
(D) Prove their eligibility

197. What is suggested about Ms. Sanchez?

(A) She e-mailed some questions to Mr. Jensen.
(B) Her description was over 100 words.
(C) Her drawings were seen by Ms. Massey.
(D) She recruited a model for the runway show.

198. According to Mr. Jensen, what will happen on March 6?

(A) A clothing fitting session
(B) A tour of a design studio
(C) A hair and makeup lesson
(D) A practice runway walk

199. What is implied about the Almeta Building?

(A) It is the headquarters of Pensler House.
(B) It will display ten outfits in March.
(C) It is Ms. Byrum's workplace.
(D) It was the site of the runway show.

200. In the forum post, the phrase "pass up" in paragraph 1, line 6, is closest in meaning to

(A) transfer
(B) miss
(C) cease
(D) overtake

Stop! This is the end of the test. If you finish before time is called, you may go back to Parts 5, 6, and 7 and check your work.

TEST 6

READING TEST

In the Reading test, you will read a variety of texts and answer several different types of reading comprehension questions. The entire Reading test will last 75 minutes. There are three parts, and directions are given for each part. You are encouraged to answer as many questions as possible within the time allowed.

You must mark your answers on the separate answer sheet. Do not write your answers in your test book.

PART 5

Directions: A word or phrase is missing in each of the sentences below. Four answer choices are given below each sentence. Select the best answer to complete the sentence. Then mark the letter (A), (B), (C), or (D) on your answer sheet.

101. Won-Joon will handle receptionist duties ------- a more urgent matter requires his attention.

(A) along
(B) unless
(C) after
(D) beyond

102. Bexcan Ltd.'s consulting programs are tailored to meet the needs of ------- clients.

(A) individualization
(B) individual
(C) individuality
(D) individually

103. Upon completion, nonfiction manuscripts are carefully ------- for publication by an expert team of editors.

(A) preparing
(B) preparation
(C) prepared
(D) prepare

104. North-Metro Transit Authority ticket machines sell regular ------- special bus passes.

(A) and
(B) off
(C) both
(D) across

105. The ------- to join the poetry workshop will be handled in the order that they arrive.

(A) applies
(B) apply
(C) application
(D) applications

106. Users of this software appreciate having their travel expenses ------- recorded in the database.

(A) systematic
(B) systematize
(C) systematizes
(D) systematically

107. Participants are issued a swift refund in the event that a course is cancelled without advance -------.

(A) contribution
(B) interruption
(C) notification
(D) distribution

108. The merger with Walo Fashions is expected ------- our operating profit by ten million dollars this year.

(A) boosts
(B) boosting
(C) to boost
(D) will boost

109. Each potential client is given a ------- of the gym's personal training programs.

(A) descriptive
(B) describable
(C) description
(D) described

110. ------- more fully understand the market, Panaski Products has undertaken a consumer survey.

(A) Based on
(B) In case
(C) In order to
(D) Except for

111. ------- mistakes can result in serious consequences, legal documents are quite difficult to translate.

(A) Rather
(B) Just
(C) Because
(D) Any

112. Mr. Bang's nomination is a well-deserved ------- of his strong commitment to the Nyer Foundation's mission.

(A) inspiration
(B) acknowledgment
(C) allowance
(D) depiction

113. Lori Retton knows Mr. Vargas personally and so will remove ------- from the hiring committee.

(A) she
(B) her
(C) hers
(D) herself

114. The data show that Frosta Lite is ------- the top soft drink among teenagers.

(A) now
(B) more
(C) early
(D) long

115. The can's label should direct users to spray the paint ------- to prevent small paint bubbles from forming.

(A) lightens
(B) lighten
(C) lightly
(D) lightest

116. A former television star, Mr. Noah explained that he chose to act in the play because of ------- multicultural themes.

(A) it
(B) which
(C) something
(D) its

117. On Saturday, the first group of visitors toured around the city's ------- opened historical park.

(A) densely
(B) newly
(C) generally
(D) solely

118. Critchley Distributing price quotes expire one month ------- the date they are issued.

(A) when
(B) from
(C) onto
(D) despite

119. To make the best impression in the job interview, candidates should bring ------- of their artistic skills in the form of a portfolio.

(A) reduction
(B) cover
(C) reply
(D) evidence

120. The interns were asked to ------- the list of reports into sections by research topic.

(A) discuss
(B) demand
(C) delete
(D) divide

GO ON TO THE NEXT PAGE

121. Thanks to the city's generous spending on infrastructure, all types of public transportation are readily ------- in central Melwood City.

(A) availability
(B) availabilities
(C) availably
(D) available

122. At yesterday's meeting, the board of directors decided to ------- our contract with Egbele Consulting.

(A) insist
(B) exceed
(C) terminate
(D) agree

123. All of the hotel's deluxe suites are ------- with separate kitchens and work areas.

(A) subscribed
(B) equipped
(C) accelerated
(D) conducted

124. The courier delivered the urgent package directly to Ms. Uhm, so the standard sign-in protocol -------.

(A) disregards
(B) disregarding
(C) was disregarded
(D) is disregarding

125. The need to renovate some of the older store locations has been ------- among our management's concerns.

(A) attentive
(B) maximum
(C) executive
(D) foremost

126. The increase in Goshu Jam's brand recognition is likely due to the television ------- it has received.

(A) expose
(B) exposes
(C) exposed
(D) exposure

127. Through the demonstration, Diravi hopes to stimulate a multimillion-dollar ------- in the company's mobile platform.

(A) objective
(B) investment
(C) affiliation
(D) statement

128. ------- you indicate your region, the Web site will personalize the contents of your news feed.

(A) Whether
(B) Later
(C) Mostly
(D) Once

129. The museum is attempting to collect portable CD players and other ------- products before they disappear entirely.

(A) reversible
(B) anonymous
(C) tentative
(D) obsolete

130. Economists have noted that the region's unusually plentiful orange harvest this season will ------- lower prices for the fruit at supermarkets.

(A) inquire into
(B) complain about
(C) correspond to
(D) participate in

PART 6

Directions: Read the texts that follow. A word, phrase, or sentence is missing in parts of each text. Four answer choices for each question are given below the text. Select the best answer to complete the text. Then mark the letter (A), (B), (C), or (D) on your answer sheet.

Questions 131-134 refer to the following e-mail.

To: Carol Knapton <c-knapton@arf-mail.com>
From: Ned Becker <ned-becker@varpowbank.com>
Date: July 21
Subject: Your card

Dear Ms. Knapton,

Varpow Bank is sorry to hear that your Varpow Platinum credit card can no longer be recognized by card reading devices. I ------- it as per your request. A ------- card will be sent out by express mail in
      131.   **132.**
the next 24 hours. You can expect to receive it within three business days. Also, please rest assured that the benefits and protections you have been enjoying up to this point will ------- to your new
            133.
Varpow Platinum card. -------.
      134.

If you have any questions about this process, please respond to this e-mail.

Sincerely,

Ned Becker
Customer Service

---

131. (A) be canceling
(B) was being canceled
(C) have canceled
(D) would have been canceled

132. (A) replaces
(B) replaceability
(C) replace
(D) replacement

133. (A) share
(B) extend
(C) acquire
(D) qualify

134. (A) It has a much lower monthly interest rate.
(B) For security reasons, we recommend destroying it.
(C) Reward points must now be spent by the end of the year.
(D) All that will change is your credit card number.

GO ON TO THE NEXT PAGE

Questions 135-138 refer to the following instructions.

Recording a voicemail greeting on your Brihm 310 Answering Machine is simple. After preparing your message, press and hold the red "Record" button on the machine. ------ the recording tone
135.

sounds, begin speaking. ------. For your convenience, the display flashes when ------ ten seconds
136.   137.

are remaining. Release the button to end the recording. The new greeting ------ automatically. If you
138.

are unsatisfied with it, simply press and hold the "Record" button again. A tone will sound to indicate

that the greeting has been deleted. The process may then be started over.

---

135. (A) Even
　　　(B) Besides
　　　(C) In spite of
　　　(D) As soon as

136. (A) Greetings may be up to one minute
　　　　long.
　　　(B) Next, press "Clock" to set the display
　　　　time.
　　　(C) Voice prompts are given in English or
　　　　Spanish.
　　　(D) This will cause damage to your
　　　　microphone.

137. (A) only
　　　(B) most
　　　(C) still
　　　(D) enough

138. (A) is playing
　　　(B) played
　　　(C) will play
　　　(D) was playing

Questions 139-142 refer to the following note.

Bosic Dental Center

To improve our dental care services, we are now ------- feedback from patients about their visits.
139.

------- you recently had a routine dental cleaning at our clinic, it would be helpful if you would
140.

complete the attached questionnaire about your experience. -------. When you are finished, simply
141.

place the questionnaire in the self-addressed stamped envelope provided and drop it in a mailbox.

Although participation is strictly voluntary, we urge you to take the time to contribute, and to give full,

honest answers. After all, your efforts ------- with better service. Thank you.
142.

---

139. (A) modifying
     (B) gathering
     (C) treating
     (D) assisting

140. (A) While
     (B) Until
     (C) As
     (D) Therefore

141. (A) We will perform comprehensive exams during your visit.
     (B) This step is required when applying for open positions.
     (C) It will take about ten minutes of your time to complete.
     (D) Please schedule appointments two weeks in advance.

142. (A) to be rewarded
     (B) will be rewarded
     (C) have been rewarded
     (D) having rewarded

Test 6

GO ON TO THE NEXT PAGE

Questions 143-146 refer to the following e-mail.

From: Asif Bhuiyan
To: All Human Resources staff
Date: March 4
Subject: Workshop

Hi team,

On April 17, Repko Employers will hold a workshop on an innovative method of employee recognition. From the advertisement I was sent, it seems like something the company _____. I'd like
                                                                                                                    143.
to send two members of our team there to learn about this _____ in depth. The attendees will then be
                                                                                           144.
responsible for producing a report on it for the rest of us.

We will need to choose our representatives quickly. _____. Reply to this e-mail by 11 A.M. on
                                                                          145.
Thursday if you would like to attend. Preference will be given to senior employees and those who
are not involved in urgent projects. _____, I encourage anyone interested to volunteer.
                                                          146.

Asif

143. (A) that utilized
     (B) utilization
     (C) utilizable
     (D) could utilize

144. (A) technique
     (B) recipient
     (C) behavior
     (D) profession

145. (A) The company will pay for transportation for the whole team.
     (B) In my experience, Repko events are enormously popular.
     (C) Likewise, it can be difficult to find well-trained instructors.
     (D) Final reports should then be uploaded to a shared folder.

146. (A) Accordingly
     (B) However
     (C) Instead
     (D) Specifically

Directions: In this part you will read a selection of texts, such as magazine and newspaper articles, e-mails, and instant messages. Each text or set of texts is followed by several questions. Select the best answer for each question and mark the letter (A), (B), (C), or (D) on your answer sheet.

Questions 147-148 refer to the following invoice.

Kuznetzov Services

Bill to: Nigel Wilcox
Lindler Financial
42 Clary Road
London W11 2DY

Invoice: 85061
Issued: 4 July
Payment due: 4 August

Date	Service provided	Quantity	Rate	Amount
30 June	Translation of financial document from Russian to English by Darya Kuznetzov	1347 words	£0.08 / word	£1077.60
30 June	15% surcharge for same-day completion of above			£161.64
			TOTAL	£1239.24

Test 6

147. What did Ms. Kuznetzov do on June 30?

(A) Provided investment advice
(B) Converted the language of a text
(C) Made travel arrangements for Mr. Wilcox
(D) Printed some presentation documents

148. Why was a surcharge added to the invoice?

(A) For international shipping
(B) For an undersized order
(C) For an overdue payment
(D) For expedited service

GO ON TO THE NEXT PAGE

Questions 149-150 refer to the following Web page.

http://eplincitymusicfestival.com

Eplin City Music Festival 𝄞

The Eplin City Music Festival supplies complimentary tickets to individuals and businesses with Platinum Sponsorship status or higher. In addition, audience groups of ten or larger are eligible for a 15% reduction in ticket price, which is applied at the time of payment. Finally, under our "Festival Pass" system, visitors who plan to attend at least three events can receive a 25% discount on their tickets. Simply visit this page to register for a pass before beginning the booking process. Limit one offer per customer or group — offers may not be combined.

149. What is the purpose of the Web page?

(A) To attract festival sponsors
(B) To compare venue amenities
(C) To describe ticket promotions
(D) To explain a booking system

150. What is suggested about sponsorships?

(A) They are separated into levels.
(B) They may be purchased online.
(C) They are only offered to corporations.
(D) They require a certain minimum contribution.

Locker Usage

· ·

In the wake of some recent misunderstandings, Adamston Fitness would like to refresh members' memory of our locker usage policies:

Lockers are available on a first-come, first-served basis. Members should not expect to be able to use the same locker regularly, or to leave items in a locker past the duration of a single visit. Property that is left in lockers this way may be disposed of at any time. All lockers are outfitted with high-security padlocks, and keys will be provided by the attendant. The use of an outside lock to secure the locker is prohibited. Any outside locks that are discovered will be cut and removed. Adamston Fitness also reserves the right to inspect the contents of lockers to ensure that they are not being misused.

We thank you for your compliance.

– Adamston Fitness

151. Why was the notice posted?

(A) To give a reminder
(B) To ask for suggestions
(C) To recommend a brand
(D) To publicize a service

152. What is suggested about some of the members of Adamston Fitness?

(A) They are expected to bring additional security devices.
(B) They pay an extra fee for access to lockers.
(C) They have complained about the size of the lockers.
(D) They have attempted to use lockers for long-term storage.

GO ON TO THE NEXT PAGE

Questions 153-154 refer to the following text-message chain.

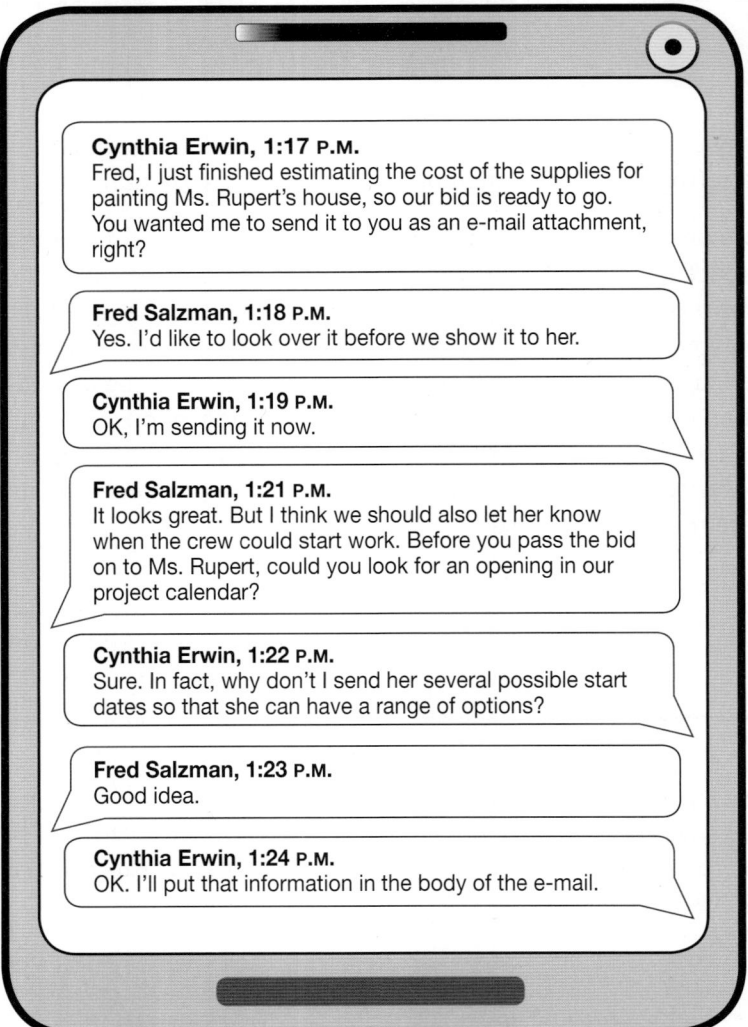

Cynthia Erwin, 1:17 P.M.
Fred, I just finished estimating the cost of the supplies for painting Ms. Rupert's house, so our bid is ready to go. You wanted me to send it to you as an e-mail attachment, right?

Fred Salzman, 1:18 P.M.
Yes. I'd like to look over it before we show it to her.

Cynthia Erwin, 1:19 P.M.
OK, I'm sending it now.

Fred Salzman, 1:21 P.M.
It looks great. But I think we should also let her know when the crew could start work. Before you pass the bid on to Ms. Rupert, could you look for an opening in our project calendar?

Cynthia Erwin, 1:22 P.M.
Sure. In fact, why don't I send her several possible start dates so that she can have a range of options?

Fred Salzman, 1:23 P.M.
Good idea.

Cynthia Erwin, 1:24 P.M.
OK. I'll put that information in the body of the e-mail.

153. What did Ms. Erwin do before sending the first message?

(A) Responded to a homeowner
(B) Calculated a potential cost
(C) Met with some painters
(D) Picked up some supplies

154. At 1:23 P.M., what does Mr. Salzman most likely mean when he writes, "Good idea"?

(A) He wants to give a customer some choices.
(B) He likes the vendor that Ms. Erwin suggested.
(C) He will postpone the start of a project.
(D) He will check a calendar for Ms. Erwin.

Starting immediately, there will be a limit on the amount of unused paid vacation time that may be rolled over from one year to the next. — [1] —. Employees may now carry over only one-half of their previously accrued leave time. This change does not apply to unpaid types of time off, such as medical leave and some less common varieties.

We hope that by announcing this policy early in the year, vacation plans may be modified without much trouble. If an adjustment is necessary, please make it far in advance. — [2] —.

For further information on the policy, refer to the new version of the company handbook. — [3] —. If you did not receive a copy, you may contact me at extension 302. We ask that you read the policy before submitting inquiries about it. — [4] —.

Thank you,

Joanna Do

155. What is indicated about medical leave?

(A) It is not available to all types of employees.
(B) It does not require a doctor's note.
(C) Employees do not take it frequently.
(D) Employees are not compensated for it.

156. According to the memo, what might employees need to do?

(A) Submit some documents to Ms. Do
(B) Rearrange their vacation schedules
(C) Receive advance approval for some expenses
(D) Attend a yearly training session on company policies

157. In which of the positions marked [1], [2], [3], and [4] does the following sentence best belong?

"It should have been placed in your inbox this morning."

(A) [1]
(B) [2]
(C) [3]
(D) [4]

GO ON TO THE NEXT PAGE

Test 6

Questions 158-160 refer to the following notice.

Notice

All Ketron Green Condos residents are invited to gather in room 102 of the main building on March 26 at 7 P.M. for a special discussion on an upcoming construction project.

The complex's board of directors recently voted to remove the artificial waterfall near the west entrance for the purpose of reducing unnecessary water usage. After considering several options, the board decided that a sculpture of an important figure would be an attractive use of the vacant space. This also has the advantage of affordable long-term maintenance costs.

The purpose of the in-person discussion, therefore, is to come up with a shortlist of sculpture subjects that all complex residents will later be able to choose from. We urge attendees to research potential candidates in advance and prepare brief arguments in their favor.

Thank you.

158. What is the purpose of the notice?

(A) To warn residents of an inconvenience
(B) To notify residents of an upcoming meeting
(C) To welcome a new member of the board of directors
(D) To advocate for a conservation campaign

159. What is mentioned about the housing complex?

(A) A statue will be installed on its grounds.
(B) One of its entrances will be closed temporarily.
(C) It has hired extra maintenance staff.
(D) Its water pipes have been damaged.

160. What are some residents encouraged to do before March 26?

(A) Develop a proposal
(B) Sign a consent form
(C) Visit a complex representative
(D) Remove items from a common area

Nationwide Rise in Guest Nights

DUBLIN (June 23)—Statistics Ireland (SI) announced yesterday that accommodation providers throughout the country saw a small surge in customers throughout May. According to an SI spokesperson, the increase was mainly due to visitors from overseas. These tourists spent 4.7 million nights in paid accommodations, a rise of 1.8% over the same month last year. This offset a 2.3% decrease in the number of domestic tourists' guest nights, which were down to 2.6 million.

SI also revealed the types of accommodations that were most popular. At 30%, hotels claimed the largest share of guest nights. However, this actually represented a slight drop from the same month last year. The proportion of guest nights spent at cheaper options such as guesthouses (23%) and youth hostels (11%), as well as outdoor alternatives such as campgrounds (16%), grew slightly.

A full report of SI's findings, including details about tourists' activities and expenditures, will be discussed on tonight's episode of *Ireland Issues*, broadcast by IBN.

161. What is indicated about the rise in guest nights?

(A) It offset a decline in restaurant spending.
(B) It was driven by international travelers.
(C) It occurred during the month of June.
(D) It resulted in additional revenues of €4.7 million.

162. What type of lodging did NOT enjoy a rise in its share of guest nights?

(A) Hotels
(B) Guesthouses
(C) Youth hostels
(D) Campgrounds

163. According to the article, how can readers obtain further information on this subject?

(A) By visiting a Web site
(B) By ordering a printed report
(C) By watching a television show
(D) By attending a lecture

GO ON TO THE NEXT PAGE

Questions 164-167 refer to the following online chat discussion.

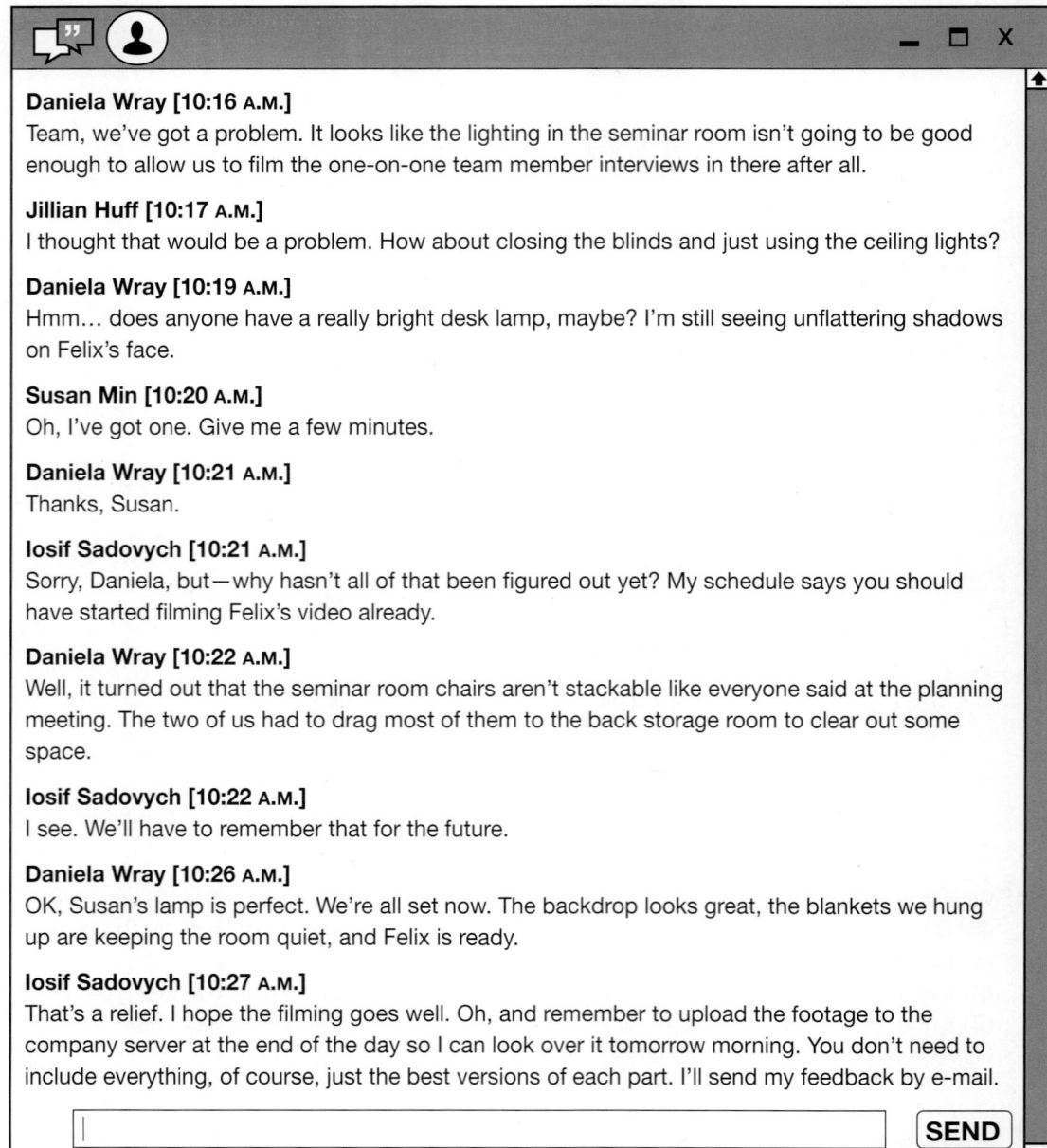

Daniela Wray [10:16 A.M.]
Team, we've got a problem. It looks like the lighting in the seminar room isn't going to be good enough to allow us to film the one-on-one team member interviews in there after all.

Jillian Huff [10:17 A.M.]
I thought that would be a problem. How about closing the blinds and just using the ceiling lights?

Daniela Wray [10:19 A.M.]
Hmm… does anyone have a really bright desk lamp, maybe? I'm still seeing unflattering shadows on Felix's face.

Susan Min [10:20 A.M.]
Oh, I've got one. Give me a few minutes.

Daniela Wray [10:21 A.M.]
Thanks, Susan.

Iosif Sadovych [10:21 A.M.]
Sorry, Daniela, but—why hasn't all of that been figured out yet? My schedule says you should have started filming Felix's video already.

Daniela Wray [10:22 A.M.]
Well, it turned out that the seminar room chairs aren't stackable like everyone said at the planning meeting. The two of us had to drag most of them to the back storage room to clear out some space.

Iosif Sadovych [10:22 A.M.]
I see. We'll have to remember that for the future.

Daniela Wray [10:26 A.M.]
OK, Susan's lamp is perfect. We're all set now. The backdrop looks great, the blankets we hung up are keeping the room quiet, and Felix is ready.

Iosif Sadovych [10:27 A.M.]
That's a relief. I hope the filming goes well. Oh, and remember to upload the footage to the company server at the end of the day so I can look over it tomorrow morning. You don't need to include everything, of course, just the best versions of each part. I'll send my feedback by e-mail.

SEND

164. At 10:20 A.M., what does Ms. Min most likely mean when she writes, "I've got one"?

(A) She has an idea that has not been considered yet.
(B) She knows how to fix an item.
(C) She can lend Ms. Wray an item.
(D) She is having the same problem as Ms. Wray.

165. Who most likely is Felix?

(A) The moderator of a videoconference
(B) A member of Ms. Wray's team
(C) A visiting technology consultant
(D) The president of Ms. Wray's company

166. What caused a delay in some preparations?

(A) An assistant went to the wrong place.
(B) Some equipment was in a storeroom.
(C) A room was being used for a seminar.
(D) Some furniture had to be moved.

167. What does Mr. Sadovych indicate that he would like to do?

(A) Send out a companywide e-mail
(B) Upload a file to a social media page
(C) Read some feedback
(D) View some videos

GO ON TO THE NEXT PAGE

```
═══════════════════════ E-Mail message ═══════════════════════
```

To:	Travis Jarrett
From:	Merna Adams
Date:	October 10
Subject:	Exciting announcement

Dear Mr. Jarrett,

As a valued customer of Kingston Walcott Services, we wanted Robinson & Jarrett Associates to be among the first to learn about our exciting news. We are expanding our range of service packages. Starting immediately, we will offer outdoor maintenance services on top of our janitorial packages. You have seen how conscientiously we take care of the inside of your building—now let us take responsibility for the outside too. Our enlarged, fully-certified workforce has been provided with training that goes far beyond local licensing requirements. This allows us to give our customers the best cutting-edge service in the industry.

Should you choose to make use of our new services, Kingston Walcott will even offer you a reduced rate available exclusively to current customers. The combined cost of your outdoor and indoor services will be just J$17,000 per month. Considering that they would total nearly J$22,000 if obtained individually, this will result in J$5,000 in savings each month. Also, we can get to work as early as November 5, the beginning of your next billing period.

We are eager to begin serving more of your needs. Please call me at 555-0194 when you are ready to move forward.

Sincerely,

Merna Adams
Sales Representative, Kingston Walcott Services

168. Which is one of the services promoted?

(A) Cafeteria operation
(B) Groundskeeping
(C) Building security
(D) Personal transport

169. What is emphasized about Kingston Walcott Services?

(A) It has expanded over a large region.
(B) Its headquarters are relocating.
(C) It gives real-time updates.
(D) Its employees are well-trained.

170. According to the e-mail, what is Mr. Jarrett eligible to do?

(A) Obtain a discount for existing customers
(B) Request an exclusive account manager
(C) Enjoy a free month of services
(D) Join a tour of a facility

171. What will happen on November 5?

(A) A company will be officially launched.
(B) A financial cycle will start anew.
(C) A demonstration will be given.
(D) A trial period will begin.

GO ON TO THE NEXT PAGE

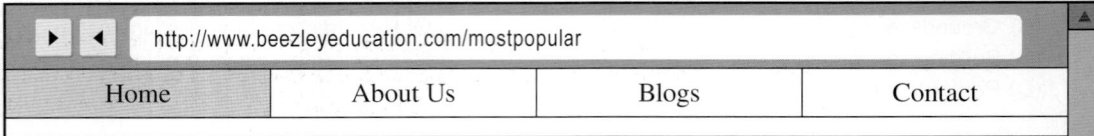

| Home | About Us | Blogs | Contact |

Beezley Education

Beezley Education conducts on-site seminars for professional organizations. Our offerings, which cover a range of interpersonal and technical skills, are taught by expert lecturers. —[1]—.

The four seminars listed below are our most popular; a complete list of our subjects is available <u>here</u>. —[2]—. For more information about a particular offering, send an e-mail to the relevant field coordinator. When you are ready to set up a seminar, you may fill out <u>this form</u>.

<u>Business Skills</u> (Coordinator: Julien Zito, j.zito@beezleyeducation.com)

Teamwork Basics
This seminar invests teams with the skills needed to work together efficiently. It covers the ways that different personality types interact, and teaches awareness of communication styles. Participants act out scenarios related to brainstorming and dispute resolution.

Effective Management
Meant for managers or supervisors of groups of any size, this seminar gives coaching on how to establish authority while maintaining cordial relationships with subordinates. —[3]—. Special focus is put on delivering an effective performance evaluation.

<u>Computer Skills</u> (Coordinator: Grace Adenaike, g.adenaike@beezleyeducation.com)
Please be advised that if your organization's computers are not equipped with the appropriate programs, participants will receive printed instructions for later individual practice.

Delisle Desktop Publishing Software
Users at all but the most advanced level will find this seminar useful. It familiarizes participants with the numerous tools Delisle offers, as well as with shortcuts that can significantly increase productivity.

Femia Presentation Software
This seminar explains how to use Femia to give presentations that are polished and persuasive. —[4]—. It includes a section on the newer functions of the software that is guaranteed to bring longtime users up to speed.

172. According to the Web page, what can readers ask Mr. Zito to do?

(A) Organize an on-site seminar
(B) List the company's full range of offerings
(C) Provide details about a certain seminar
(D) Resolve a technical issue with the Web page

173. What is mentioned as part of the Teamwork Basics seminar?

(A) Taking a personality quiz
(B) Writing a peer evaluation
(C) Setting group goals
(D) Engaging in role plays

174. What is implied about computer skills seminars?

(A) None of them are appropriate for beginner software users.
(B) They may be shortened according to client preference.
(C) Beezley Education does not supply software for them.
(D) Their contents are also available through personal tutoring.

175. In which of the positions marked [1], [2], [3], and [4] does the following sentence best belong?

"Each one has years of experience in the subject in question."

(A) [1]
(B) [2]
(C) [3]
(D) [4]

GO ON TO THE NEXT PAGE

http://cierrasonthelake.com/catering   ▼

Cierra's on the Lake
Catering Packages

Our catering packages let you experience the mouth-watering cuisine of Cierra's on the Lake in any location within the Garrell area. They have been carefully developed to form balanced meals with complimentary tastes. As with our in-restaurant meals, the ingredients are obtained from Garrell-based suppliers to guarantee that they are as fresh as possible.

Cierra's on the Lake's logistics and service expertise enables customers to enjoy our edible delights in a leisurely fashion. Whether you opt for a buffet or a sit-down meal, our staff will complete the setup and cleanup processes quickly, and remain on hand in between to take care of any issues that may arise. Please note, however, that the only non-food items we provide are plates, glasses, cutlery, and napkins.

In addition to our year-round packages listed at the bottom of the page, we are pleased to offer customers two options specially devised for the summer season:

Summer Fresh	**Summer Deluxe**
Comes with cold chicken, fruit salad, green salad, and corn on the cob. Perfect for cooling down in the middle of a hot day.	Comes with grilled hamburgers, fruit salad, green salad, macaroni salad, and corn on the cob. Requires access to electricity.

These packages also come with hand-squeezed lemonade, as well as our usual drink options.

Cierra's on the Lake
Catering Order Form

Customer: _Maja Kaminski_   Phone: _(651) 555-0190_

Package: _Summer Deluxe_   Number of guests: _24_
Serving method: Buffet ___✓___   Sit-down _____

Event date: _July 29_   Event duration*: _1 P.M. – 3 P.M._
Event location: _1002 Langer Road, Garrell, MN 55076_

Special instructions: Please park just inside the front gate.

Order received by: _Ian O'Brien_

Assigned to: _Caleb Ames_

* _Event durations do not include setup and cleanup times._

176. What is suggested about Cierra's on the Lake?

(A) It is a family-owned business.
(B) It does not cater formal functions.
(C) It recently entered the catering industry.
(D) It does not furnish guest seating.

177. What does Cierra's on the Lake do to guarantee the quality of its food?

(A) It cooks with organic ingredients.
(B) It buys from local vendors.
(C) It undergoes frequent inspections.
(D) It employs a special refrigeration system.

178. In the Web page, the word "fashion" in paragraph 2, line 2, is closest in meaning to

(A) trend
(B) mold
(C) manner
(D) category

179. What will caterers most likely do at Ms. Kaminski's event?

(A) Set out plates of chicken
(B) Stay for only two hours
(C) Use a power source
(D) Park indoors

180. According to the order form, what is probably true about Ms. Kaminski's guests?

(A) They have been invited to a wedding.
(B) They have special dietary requirements.
(C) They will leave their tables to serve themselves.
(D) They will come into contact with Mr. O'Brien.

GO ON TO THE NEXT PAGE

To:	Clint Weimer
From:	Madeline Stein
Date:	April 10
Subject:	Informational booklet launch

Dear Mr. Weimer,

The Office of International Students has spent the past year reworking the *Information for International Students* to create a comprehensive booklet called *"Guide to Royland University for International Students"*, or "GRUIS". GRUIS contains extensive information about dormitories and apartments, common financial and language issues, the municipal bus system, and more. Our office even spoke with local employees of mobile network operators to secure up-to-date details on their contract requirements and offerings. We are confident that GRUIS will allow international students to adjust more easily and fully to life here.

To celebrate and publicize the booklet's release, we are holding a launch party on April 23 at 7 P.M. Please join us in the foyer of Parziale Hall to pick up your copy of GRUIS and watch a short presentation by our director, or by me if the director is unavailable. As the president of one of Royland's most popular student organizations, your support for this project would be invaluable. We hope to see you there.

Sincerely,

Madeline Stein
Office of International Students

E-Mail message

To:	Madeline Stein
From:	Clint Weimer
Date:	April 26
Subject:	Re: Informational booklet launch

Dear Ms. Stein,

Now that I have had a chance to look over the copy of GRUIS that I received at the launch party, I would like to express my thoughts on the booklet's content. I think it does an excellent job of introducing life at Royland. As you said during your presentation, it will help minimize the challenges that our international students would be typically expected to face. I will definitely recommend it with enthusiasm to my acquaintances. Please let me know if there is anything else I can do for the Office of International Students in the future.

Sincerely,

Clint Weimer

181. What is indicated about GRUIS?

    (A) It was written by a student association.
    (B) It is a revision of an earlier publication.
    (C) It will also be distributed in digital form.
    (D) It is being published in multiple languages.

182. What is NOT listed as covered in GRUIS?

    (A) Housing
    (B) Mobile phone service
    (C) Public transportation
    (D) Employment

183. Who is Mr. Weimer?

    (A) A university club leader
    (B) A university official
    (C) An international student
    (D) A professor of tourism studies

184. What is implied about the launch party?

    (A) There were not enough copies of GRUIS for all attendees.
    (B) A presentation had some technical difficulties.
    (C) It was moved to a larger building.
    (D) An administrator was not present.

185. What does Mr. Weimer say he will do?

    (A) Introduce Ms. Stein to some acquaintances
    (B) Assist Ms. Stein with some research
    (C) Advise other people to read GRUIS
    (D) Suggest topics for a future edition of GRUIS

GO ON TO THE NEXT PAGE

Questions 186-190 refer to the following article, report, and e-mail.

New Library Survey to Take Place

PRANTON (September 23) — Chomsley residents' days of travelling as much as ten miles to the nearest public library may soon come to an end. Yesterday, the Daiglen County Library Commission announced that the town has been chosen as the site of a possible new branch.

As a first step, the commission will poll Chomsley's citizens on the features that they would most like to be included in a new library. It will then incorporate the study's findings into a project proposal to be submitted to the County Board of Supervisors for approval.

"Construction and maintenance of a seventh branch would probably require raising the county sales tax," said Corinne Speck, president of the nine-member commission. "That's why putting together an appealing proposal is a very important task for us."

Report Summary

Vosting Associates

On behalf of the Daiglen County Library Commission, Vosting Associates surveyed residents of the city of Chomsley on potential features of a new county library. Data was collected from 653 people via telephone interview during the one-month period from September 28 to October 27. The following chart summarizes the survey's major findings:

Proposed feature	% of respondents expressing interest
Computers, printers, and scanners	92%
Private meeting rooms	85%
Audiovisual materials and media stations	74%
A café	70%
A children's play area	66%
An automated check-in/check-out system	51%

From:	Corinne Speck
To:	Library Commission members
Date:	November 7
Subject:	Survey findings
Attachment:	📎 Report

Hi everyone,

Vosting Associates just sent over their survey report. As you'll see in the chart in the summary, there were six proposed features favored by more than half of the respondents. Despite this, I think we should take the automated borrowing system out of consideration, as its rating is still quite low. Also, as we know from its inclusion in the last new county library in Rudliss, it may not actually be used very often. The other top results are mostly what we expected, though the demand for access to DVDs and CDs is much greater than we had predicted.

Anyway, please read through the report and be prepared to discuss it at our closed meeting next Wednesday.

Regards,

Corinne

186. According to the article, what did Ms. Speck say may be necessary?

(A) An increase in a tax obligation
(B) A pay raise for library staff
(C) The sale of county property
(D) The formation of a task force

187. How did Vosting Associates employees conduct the survey?

(A) They mailed questionnaires.
(B) They called participants.
(C) They went to Chomsley residences.
(D) They interviewed people in county libraries.

188. What is implied about the library branch in Rudliss?

(A) It has the smallest number of regular patrons.
(B) It is ten miles from Chomsley city limits.
(C) It was the sixth county library that was built.
(D) It has shut down its automated borrowing terminals.

189. Which figure in the chart does Ms. Speck indicate is unexpected?

(A) 92%
(B) 85%
(C) 74%
(D) 70%

190. In her e-mail, what does Ms. Speck suggest the commission do?

(A) Dismiss a relatively unpopular option
(B) Delay a discussion until after a public event
(C) Ask Vosting Associates for more information
(D) Prepare simplified visual aids for a handout

GO ON TO THE NEXT PAGE

E-Mail message

From: Jasmine Nesbit
To: Drake Sanders
Date: December 8
Subject: Changes

Dear Mr. Sanders,

I just wanted to tell you again how excited I am to become the new executive producer of *Comedy Nightly News*. Now that I've spoken with the full cast, I feel I can guarantee that my plans to modernize the show to appeal to a younger audience will succeed. With the help of my experiences at other shows, the creative staff and I will begin updating the look, sound, and content of the show, without exceeding its current budget. As we discussed, the changes will be made all at once to increase their impact; I have set January 4 as the target date for the premiere of this new version of *Comedy Nightly News*.

Thank you again for this opportunity.

Sincerely,

Jasmine Nesbit

What's on Tonight
February 3

8 P.M.	(Ch. 5) *A Fresh Look* "Daan Goettsch" An introduction to the abstract painter's life and work.
9 P.M.	(Ch. 40) *On Melvin Street* A girl faces her final year of high school. Winner of several film festival awards.
9:30 P.M.	(Ch. 2) *The Franklin Family* "Monkey Business" Rob and Harley get into trouble during a trip to the zoo.
10 P.M.	(Ch. 8) *Space Net* "Empty Plains" The crew of the S.S. *Wanderer* lands on a planet that has no inhabitants.
11 P.M.	(Ch. 24) *Comedy Nightly News* The news parody show debuts big transformations. Guest: Lynn Sam.

Professional Reviewers   **Audience Reviewers**

The New *Comedy Nightly News*
By Chad Frosch, February 3

As a longtime viewer of *Comedy Nightly News*, I have mixed feelings about the changes to the show. The opening theme music is much more energetic, and a monitor featuring a digital map of the globe has replaced the out-of-date city skyline backdrop. But the problem is that these positive changes seem to be accompanied by really silly jokes. I felt like I was watching that show I caught a moment of earlier tonight, where the characters were behaving ridiculously with some animals. Don't the people running *Comedy Nightly News* know that many of us enjoy this award-winning show because of the sophisticated humor that most other comedy shows lack? It would be a pity if it lost that quality.

191. What does Ms. Nesbit write that she intends to do?

(A) Attract a new group of viewers to the show
(B) Recruit talented creative staff from other shows
(C) Make changes gradually to avoid disruption
(D) Seek ways to reduce production expenses

192. What is implied about the changes to the show?

(A) They received mostly positive responses.
(B) They took place later than planned.
(C) They resulted in longer episodes.
(D) They are being imitated by other shows.

193. In the review, the word "mixed" in paragraph 1, line 1 is closest in meaning to

(A) united
(B) repetitive
(C) conflicting
(D) false

194. Which broadcast does Mr. Frosch compare *Comedy Nightly News* to?

(A) *A Fresh Look*
(B) *On Melvin Street*
(C) *The Franklin Family*
(D) *Space Net*

195. What does Mr. Frosch mention about *Comedy Nightly News*?

(A) Its cast seems more energetic.
(B) Its humor has become less sophisticated.
(C) Its new set backdrop is unappealing.
(D) Its host has been replaced.

GO ON TO THE NEXT PAGE

Goffney Connections

Inspections to Take Place

Part of Goffney's exciting new agreement to manufacture appliances for Hadrick Home calls for regular machinery inspections. Both plants that will be involved in manufacturing for Hadrick will be visited by outside inspectors who will test factory machinery. Any equipment that receives a "U" grade, for "unsatisfactory", will need to be replaced or repaired.

The first of these visits will take place while these facilities are still finishing the most recent order from another appliance brand. The Darlington plant will undergo an inspection in June and the Fansville plant will be visited in July, though the exact dates have not been confirmed yet. On these days, production may be slowed or suspended. We hope that all affected employees will be patient during this process and take extra care to please this important client.

From: Sandra Culley, Manager
To: Production Department
Date: June 16
Re: Inspection results

As you may have heard, the recent inspection of our plant determined that the cutting machine and foam injector on one of our lines need to have components replaced. The necessary parts have been ordered and will arrive before noon tomorrow. Josh Fetty, the line manager involved, will notify his employees and follow our standard maintenance procedures.

This will put us slightly behind schedule on shipping the Kalluri order, but I have already spoken with Scott Fonseca to resolve this problem. His line is going to work some overtime to compensate. Questions or concerns about this situation may be addressed to me.

Finally, headquarters sends congratulations on passing the inspection with so few issues. Let's continue to be a credit to the Goffney name.

```
┌─────────────────────────────────────────────────────────────────────┐
│                            *E-Mail*                                   │
│  ┌──────────┐  ┌───────────────────────────────────────────────────┐ │
│  │ From:    │  │ Joshua Fetty                                      │ │
│  └──────────┘  └───────────────────────────────────────────────────┘ │
│  ┌──────────┐  ┌───────────────────────────────────────────────────┐ │
│  │ To:      │  │ Thomas Chun                                       │ │
│  └──────────┘  └───────────────────────────────────────────────────┘ │
│  ┌──────────┐  ┌───────────────────────────────────────────────────┐ │
│  │ Date:    │  │ June 16                                           │ │
│  └──────────┘  └───────────────────────────────────────────────────┘ │
│  ┌──────────┐  ┌───────────────────────────────────────────────────┐ │
│  │ Subject: │  │ A favor                                           │ │
│  └──────────┘  └───────────────────────────────────────────────────┘ │
│                                                                       │
│  Hi Tom,                                                              │
│                                                                       │
│  Sorry to bother you in the evening, but I know you're usually the    │
│  first person at the factory in the mornings. Could you make a sign   │
│  and post it near the entrance before everyone else arrives? I need   │
│  to let my operators know that the line will be shut down from 12     │
│  P.M. to 3 P.M. tomorrow. The sign should say clearly that Line 1     │
│  employees should wait in the employee break room after their lunch   │
│  hour and then report to their stations at 3.                         │
│                                                                       │
│  Thanks,                                                              │
│                                                                       │
│  Josh                                                                 │
└─────────────────────────────────────────────────────────────────────┘
```

196. According to the notice, what has Goffney recently done?

(A) Purchased a new set of equipment
(B) Directed its technicians to carry out inspections
(C) Opened its second manufacturing plant
(D) Made a deal with a new client

197. What is NOT implied about a cutting machine?

(A) It is used to manufacture appliances.
(B) It is in the Darlington factory.
(C) It was expensive.
(D) It was issued a "U" grade.

198. What is suggested about Ms. Culley?

(A) She is supervised by Mr. Fonseca.
(B) She was asked to relay a message.
(C) She is concerned about an overtime plan.
(D) She has postponed a shipment.

199. Why most likely will Mr. Chun send Line 1 employees to a break area?

(A) To allow time for repairs
(B) To view an updated schedule
(C) To hear about safety regulations
(D) To await a delivery of raw materials

200. In the e-mail, the expression "report to" in line 5 is closest in meaning to

(A) collect
(B) inform
(C) object to
(D) appear at

Stop! This is the end of the test. If you finish before time is called, you may go back to Parts 5, 6, and 7 and check your work.

TEST 7

READING TEST

In the Reading test, you will read a variety of texts and answer several different types of reading comprehension questions. The entire Reading test will last 75 minutes. There are three parts, and directions are given for each part. You are encouraged to answer as many questions as possible within the time allowed.

You must mark your answers on the separate answer sheet. Do not write your answers in your test book.

PART 5

Directions: A word or phrase is missing in each of the sentences below. Four answer choices are given below each sentence. Select the best answer to complete the sentence. Then mark the letter (A), (B), (C), or (D) on your answer sheet.

101. Mr. Pritchard called the bank to ask about the savings account ------- had opened last month.

(A) he
(B) him
(C) his
(D) himself

102. Most people in the office choose to ------- the bus to work because there is limited parking near the building.

(A) travel
(B) cross
(C) ride
(D) run

103. For safety reasons, the kitchen ------- on display in the showroom are not kept plugged in.

(A) utensils
(B) appliances
(C) tiles
(D) counters

104. Surprisingly, the cost of repairing the vehicle after the accident was ------- than purchasing a new one.

(A) greatly
(B) great
(C) greater
(D) greatness

105. The small business loan from Renata Bank is what helped ------- café make some much-needed refurbishments.

(A) our
(B) ours
(C) we
(D) us

106. The negotiator position requires a ------- understanding of the internal conflicts in the organization.

(A) sole
(B) deep
(C) private
(D) severe

107. As the two products were ------- identical, the manager ordered the one with the lower price.

(A) nearer
(B) nearly
(C) nearest
(D) nearness

108. Customers using the laundry facility for the ------- time may need assistance in operating the machines.

(A) first
(B) each
(C) single
(D) once

109. Langley Software ------- its user agreement later this year to make the terms easier for customers to understand.
(A) modified
(B) modifying
(C) will modify
(D) having modified

110. The spokesperson seemed to respond to reporters' inquiries ------- though he were unfamiliar with the company's history.
(A) if
(B) so
(C) as
(D) when

111. Everyone who completes the customer ------- within the time frame will be entered into a prize drawing.
(A) demand
(B) questionnaire
(C) loyalty
(D) service

112. Small bags can be placed in the overhead compartments or ------- the seat in front of you.
(A) under
(B) between
(C) toward
(D) among

113. Guests who do not want to leave ------- items in their rooms can use the hotel's safe while they're away.
(A) fluent
(B) attentive
(C) prompt
(D) valuable

114. The report had to be rewritten because a piece of ------- information about the budget had been omitted.
(A) critics
(B) critically
(C) criticize
(D) critical

115. Cottage Farms specializes in ------- produce organically, without harmful fertilizers or pesticides.
(A) cultivates
(B) cultivating
(C) cultivation
(D) cultivate

116. The weekday lunch special at Paradise Café is served ------- a choice of side salad or the soup of the day.
(A) by
(B) with
(C) to
(D) until

117. When responding to the invitation, please indicate your meal ------- if you will be in attendance.
(A) preference
(B) preferred
(C) preferable
(D) preferably

118. ------- safer than other cutting machines on the market, it's no wonder that the Y-881 is a top-selling product.
(A) Demonstration
(B) Demonstrate
(C) Demonstrably
(D) Demonstrable

119. ------- Rochester Boulevard has been expanded, traffic jams are rarely seen in the area.
(A) Whenever
(B) Only if
(C) Once
(D) Now that

120. To prevent cross-contamination of the food, raw meat and fresh vegetables should be kept ------- at all times.
(A) separate
(B) further
(C) nearby
(D) opposite

GO ON TO THE NEXT PAGE

121. ------- wishes to upgrade a standard class ticket to first class may do so at the station or on board.

(A) Anything
(B) Every
(C) Whoever
(D) Those

122. ------- made from plated copper are becoming more popular in the fashion world these days.

(A) Accessorized
(B) Accessorizes
(C) Accessorize
(D) Accessories

123. Dr. Madison was unable to complete the experiment ------- some of the necessary equipment was malfunctioning.

(A) through
(B) since
(C) neither
(D) although

124. The airline's ticketing agent should ------- your luggage on the scale at the time of check-in.

(A) weighing
(B) have weighed
(C) be weighed
(D) have been weighed

125. Some of the items sold by Henrietta Gifts are more fragile than others, so they should be packaged -------.

(A) absolutely
(B) flexibly
(C) accordingly
(D) mutually

126. The team led by Ms. Gibbons ------- a memorable slogan to use in the Westbury Beverages commercial.

(A) came up with
(B) took off
(C) ran out of
(D) relied on

127. During the lecture, biologist Joanne Marquez outlined ------- that this songbird has made to adjust to living near highly populated areas.

(A) adaptations
(B) adapting
(C) adapt
(D) adapted

128. Ms. Richards performs the majority of her writing in the ------- garage that she uses as a home office.

(A) convert
(B) converting
(C) converts
(D) converted

129. Most of the city council members nodded their heads ------- as Mr. Vidalia spoke about the need to reduce taxes.

(A) agreeable
(B) agreement
(C) agree
(D) agreeably

130. Because the new employee information is so complicated, Mr. Conley ------- it down into four training sessions.

(A) withdrew
(B) ensured
(C) broke
(D) shared

PART 6

Directions: Read the texts that follow. A word, phrase, or sentence is missing in parts of each text. Four answer choices for each question are given below the text. Select the best answer to complete the text. Then mark the letter (A), (B), (C), or (D) on your answer sheet.

Questions 131-134 refer to the following article.

Ector Foods, one of the country's largest food processing companies, has announced ------- plans to **131.** meet 100% of its energy needs from renewable sources within five years. The move ------- the first of **132.** the company's three-step environmental initiative. Experts working in the field are not surprised that Ector Foods is the first of its kind to take such measures. -------. **133.**

"We have a responsibility to produce our goods responsibly," said CEO Morgan Parker in a press conference yesterday. "------- should not be taken lightly." Ector Foods will make use of on-site solar **134.** power as well as purchase electricity from wind farms in the area.

131. (A) altered
(B) similar
(C) ambitious
(D) motivated

132. (A) marks
(B) marking
(C) to mark
(D) will have marked

133. (A) The company has always led the industry in innovation.
(B) Investors want to branch out into other markets.
(C) A great deal of knowledge is needed for the change.
(D) The grand opening ceremony is set for later this month.

134. (A) What
(B) He
(C) These
(D) It

GO ON TO THE NEXT PAGE

Questions 135-138 refer to the following e-mail.

To: Asher Larson <a.larson@larsonflowers.com>
From: Emily Eilers <emily@lilacvalleydeals.com>
Date: October 10
Subject: Promote your business!

Dear Mr. Larson,

The number of tourists to the area has ------- increased over the past few years. *Lilac Valley Deals*
                                          135.
can help your business stand out! Our magazine has a ------- of 20,000, and we reach hotels, tourist
                                                      136.
information centers, and public transportation facilities. You can advertise a special offer for your

business on a quarter, half, or full page. -------. Please note that ------- you do not have an ad
                                            137.   **138.**
prepared, you can still advertise with us, as our in-house graphics team can create something for

you. Please e-mail me back if you are interested.

Sincerely,

Emily Eilers

---

135. (A) steady
(B) steadied
(C) steadily
(D) steadiness

136. (A) deposit
(B) circulation
(C) wage
(D) turnout

137. (A) I enjoyed learning about your business.
(B) The largest size is the best value.
(C) This is the majority of seasonal tourists.
(D) Simply present this coupon for a discount.

138. (A) owing to
(B) whether
(C) before
(D) even if

196

Nicole Hudson

Cupcake Express

312 Capital Avenue

New Castle, IN 47362

Dear Ms. Hudson,

I'd like to invite you to the New Castle Baking Festival. ------. However, if we reach the level of
139.

participation that we are expecting, we can make it an annual tradition. This is an excellent way to

promote your business because visitors will try your ------. To find out more about the event, please
140.

watch our ------ video online at www.newcastlebaking.org. Just a few minutes of your time will teach
141.

you everything you need to know. We also plan to post a list of businesses that ------ the festival.
142.

We hope to add you to that list!

Sincerely,

Maya Fischer

139. (A) Last year's festival was an enormous
    success.
(B) Please respond with your intention to
    enter.
(C) This is our first time organizing such an
    event.
(D) Each booth features a different kind of
    food.

140. (A) competitions
(B) recipes
(C) routines
(D) methods

141. (A) brief
(B) live
(C) minor
(D) similar

142. (A) will be attended
(B) attends
(C) will be attending
(D) is attending

Test 7

New Members Welcome at Glendale Support

Glendale Support is currently seeking new members. ------. However, attendance at all meetings is
143.

not required. Our organization ------ community members to work together toward improving public
144.

sites in Glendale. This ------ approach can maximize our impact on schools, libraries, parks, and
145.

more. To become a part of our group, please attend our next meeting, which will be held on June 18

at 7 P.M. at the Filbert Center, room 104. You can also e-mail our Membership Director, Kyle

Thompson, at k.thompson@glendalesupport.org. To read more about projects ------ our group has
146.

carried out in the past, please visit our Web site at www.glendalesupport.org.

---

143. (A) Each project receives public as well as private funding.
(B) Your membership fee can be waived in some cases.
(C) We get together on the first and third Monday of every month.
(D) This service has been growing in popularity.

144. (A) is urged
(B) to urge
(C) urges
(D) urge

145. (A) cooperative
(B) reversible
(C) occasional
(D) imaginary

146. (A) what
(B) who
(C) that
(D) where

PART 7

Directions: In this part you will read a selection of texts, such as magazine and newspaper articles, e-mails, and instant messages. Each text or set of texts is followed by several questions. Select the best answer for each question and mark the letter (A), (B), (C), or (D) on your answer sheet.

Questions 147-148 refer to the following receipt.

– **Customer Receipt** –
Crawton Hall
1265 Rosetti Lane ▽ 555-0188

Date: August 12
Purchase Location: Box Office, In-Person, Agent #081
Customer Name: Tessa Fortney
Payment Type: Credit card XXXX-XXXX-XXXX-0734

Description

Buenos Aires Theatre Orchestra, Aug. 31	Seat C51	£28.00
Buenos Aires Theatre Orchestra, Aug. 31	Seat C52	£28.00
Handling Charge		£1.50
Theatre Restoration and Construction*		£5.00
	TOTAL	£62.50

Thank you for your optional contribution! Your support will help us to carry out essential renovations and build an extension to our existing structure.

147. For what kind of event did Ms. Fortney purchase tickets?

(A) An academic lecture
(B) A musical performance
(C) A film screening
(D) A comedy show

148. What is indicated about Ms. Fortney on the receipt?

(A) She was charged £1.50 in city taxes.
(B) She made a donation to a building project.
(C) She placed her order one month in advance.
(D) She bought the tickets over the phone.

GO ON TO THE NEXT PAGE

Luciano Garcia [10:23 A.M.]
Hello, this is Luciano from Southfield Incorporated. We are scheduled to make a delivery to your home today between 12:30 P.M. and 1:30 P.M.

Melanie Walters [10:26 A.M.]
I'll be home to accept the delivery. It's the queen-sized mattress, right?

Luciano Garcia [10:27 A.M.]
That's correct. It is from order #95871.

Melanie Walters [10:28 A.M.]
There might be one problem, though. My apartment is on the fourth floor, and there's no elevator in this building.

Luciano Garcia [10:29 A.M.]
Oh, there are two of us.

Melanie Walters [10:30 A.M.]
That should be fine, then. See you later today. Thanks!

149. What most likely is Southfield Incorporated?

(A) A car rental company
(B) An electronics repair service
(C) A real estate agency
(D) A furniture store

150. At 10:29 A.M., what does Mr. Garcia most likely mean when he writes, "there are two of us"?

(A) There is competition to provide a service.
(B) An item can be moved without difficulty.
(C) An administrative error has been made.
(D) Some goods will arrive separately.

Brian Silva
403 Liberty Street
Fort Worth, TX 76111

Dear Mr. Silva,

We have received your application to renew your driver's license by mail. Unfortunately, we are unable to process your request because it does not meet our renewal criteria. Drivers are only allowed two consecutive renewals by mail, after which they must visit a Motor Vehicles Authority office in person to have a new photograph taken. Please be sure to complete this task before your license expires. Otherwise, you could be subject to a penalty charge. A list of sites that issue state driver's licenses is printed on the back of this letter.

Sincerely,

Robert Nelson

Robert Nelson
Renewals Department

---

151. Why was Mr. Silva's request refused?

(A) He has already renewed his license by mail twice.
(B) He sent a photograph that was the wrong size.
(C) He did not include the necessary payment.
(D) He no longer lives at the same address.

152. What might happen if Mr. Silva allows his current license to expire?

(A) A driving exam may become required.
(B) An application may be rejected.
(C) A fine may be imposed.
(D) A deadline may be extended.

GO ON TO THE NEXT PAGE

Thank you for joining the Home-Meals team! Our deliveries of daily hot meals to the elderly prevent isolation and allow them to maintain their independence. On the days that you are assigned a shift, you should report to our commercial kitchen in Reston at 8 A.M. You may assist with meal preparation there or be asked to transport goods from our storage facility at the head office in Calverton. Once the meals are prepared, you will be assigned a delivery route of between 10 and 15 stops. These routes cover the neighborhoods of Reston, Calverton, Fairfax, and Landover. Should you have any questions, please speak to the manager on duty, or contact Audrey Vogel at the head office at 555-0176.

153. For whom is the information most likely intended?

(A) New workers
(B) Potential volunteers
(C) Charity donors
(D) Elderly people

154. Where does Ms. Vogel most likely work?

(A) In Reston
(B) In Calverton
(C) In Fairfax
(D) In Landover

Questions 155-157 refer to the following advertisement.

Bike Tour Guides Needed!

Spend your summer in the great outdoors by becoming a bike tour guide at Wiedl Parks Plus. As a guide, you will conduct tours in and around Utica National Park and work with a wide range of group sizes and abilities. Housing in our modern dormitory is provided for the entire summer season; depending on the tour and location, you may also be housed at hotels or lodges near the park at no cost to you. Bike tour guides are paid $95 dollars per day on tour days, and all meals are provided. We are happy to answer any questions you may have about compensation at the initial interview. All guides must be physically fit and knowledgeable about bicycle maintenance and repair. To apply, send an e-mail to Human Resources Director Philip Norris at pnorris@wiedl-pp.com. Please note that those who accept the position must purchase a travel insurance policy before the first day of employment.

155. What is indicated about the accommodations offered to bike tour guides?

(A) They are situated within a national park.
(B) The buildings sites may vary by tour.
(C) They are only available for free on tour days.
(D) The rooms must be shared with other guides.

156. What should candidates with payment questions do?

(A) Include them in an e-mail to Mr. Norris
(B) Download a sample contract
(C) Watch a recruitment video
(D) Ask them during an interview

157. According to the advertisement, what must new employees do before starting work?

(A) Pass a physical fitness test
(B) Review the company's safety policy
(C) Show proof of relevant experience
(D) Buy some travel insurance

GO ON TO THE NEXT PAGE

BCP – Your Parcel, Your Way

You can rely on BCP to make sure your parcel gets there on time and in good condition. We have the lowest rate of lost or damaged items in the industry, and we've recently changed to a flat fee based on box size so that the price is clear from the beginning. At our service points, envelopes, boxes, and tape are freely available so that you can get your package ready without any hassle. After your items are sent, you can track the shipment in real time on our Web site. Remember, certain things cannot be transported through the mail due to safety issues or restrictions set by international law. To find out what is and is not allowed, visit www.bcp-mail.com/before_sending.

We are always searching for ways to improve our services. Customers who have sent a package through BCP anytime in the past month may complete a short questionnaire in May to receive a voucher for 15% off their next transaction. To do so, call 1-800-555-0144.

158. What is NOT mentioned as available to BCP customers?

(A) Compensation for lost packages
(B) An online tracking system
(C) Complimentary packing supplies
(D) A simplified pricing structure

159. According to the advertisement, what can be found on the Web page mentioned?

(A) A map of service points
(B) A pick-up scheduling form
(C) A list of prohibited items
(D) An estimate of transportation times

160. How can customers get a discount coupon?

(A) By referring a friend
(B) By using a service frequently
(C) By joining for a mailing list
(D) By filling out a survey

```
===================== E-Mail message =====================

To:          Carrie Keaton <ckeaton@drilbyskiresort.com>

From:        Evan Barnett <ebarnett@drilbyskiresort.com>

Date:        September 4

Subject:     Magazine advertisement

Attachment:  📎 maxfuntravelsubmissions.doc
```

Dear Carrie,

Thanks for agreeing to design the advertisement for our resort that will appear in the October issue of *Max Fun Travel* magazine. — [1] —. We want the advertisement to inform both new and existing customers of changes that will affect this season— namely, that our dining hall has reopened after renovations throughout the summer, and that a complimentary session with a ski instructor will now be included with every lift ticket.

I have contacted the submissions department of *Max Fun Travel* to request the latest guidelines and have attached a copy for your reference. — [2] —. Please feel free to use any of the images in our company database. The file sent to *Max Fun Travel* must be completely ready for publication and in the correct format when it is submitted. — [3] —. We only have enough room in the budget for a half-page advertisement. It can be in full color, but the magazine only offers horizontal half-page ads, so the design must be wider than it is tall. — [4] —. If you run into any obstacles, don't hesitate to e-mail me.

Thank you,

Evan

161. What is Drilby Ski Resort about to offer for the first time?

(A) Free skiing lessons
(B) On-site dining
(C) Summer tours
(D) Overnight lodging

162. What does Mr. Barnett mention about the advertisement?

(A) It should feature several images.
(B) It must be submitted by the end of the month.
(C) It should have a limited number of colors.
(D) It must have a specific shape.

163. In which of the following positions marked [1], [2], [3], and [4] does the following

sentence best belong?

"The magazine charges a significant fee to make changes after that point."

(A) [1]
(B) [2]
(C) [3]
(D) [4]

GO ON TO THE NEXT PAGE

Jimenez-Wright Enterprises to Expand Its Horizons

July 29 — In a press briefing held yesterday, activewear manufacturer Jimenez-Wright Enterprises confirmed that it will add a new line of clothing in order to branch into the children's clothing market, an idea pushed by recently appointed CEO Jesse Stegman. Jimenez-Wright Enterprises is the parent company of the popular retailers Chaskell and Krismore, whose clothing is produced domestically for men and women, respectively. Based on feedback from loyal customers who attended Jimenez-Wright's first-ever beach volleyball competition at Daytona Beach last year, the company began developing clothing suitable for children.

"There has been an increase in obesity rates among children over the past few years, as they have few opportunities for exercise while being in school all day" said pediatrician Jordan Downey, a consultant for the company. "Fortunately, parents are starting to wake up to this problem and take action, adopting a healthy lifestyle for the whole family."

Jimenez-Wright Enterprises hopes to capitalize on this trend by introducing Marilou, a line of activewear for children ages 5 to 13. The apparel will be manufactured in Jimenez-Wright Enterprises' existing factories, with up to 40% of the fabrics made from reprocessed plastic bottles. While many of the items in the adult stores must be hand-washed to maintain the performance of the fabric, all items in the Marilou line will be machine-washable and resistant to staining. Initially, the line will be rolled out in stores with the company's women's clothing to test consumers' interest, but the long-term plan is to have retail stores that sell Marilou exclusively.

164. What is true about Jimenez-Wright Enterprises?
(A) It recently acquired a rival manufacturer.
(B) It is developing some exercise equipment.
(C) It hosted a sports competition last year.
(D) It will create a sports organization for children.

165. Who most likely is Ms. Downey?
(A) A financial consultant
(B) A medical professional
(C) The principal of a school
(D) The CEO of a company

166. What is NOT suggested about Marilou products?
(A) They will be too delicate for machine washing.
(B) They will be produced domestically.
(C) They will be partially made from recycled materials.
(D) They will be made of stain resistant fabrics.

167. Where will the Marilou line first be sold?
(A) On a special Web site
(B) In a seasonal catalog
(C) In Chaskell stores
(D) In Krismore stores

PUBLIC NOTICE OF ROADWORK

On Monday, October 7, work will begin on nearly 2,000 feet of water pipes under Cecil Boulevard. — [1] —. Aging concrete pipes that date back several decades will be swapped for those made of galvanized steel. The $750,000 project was approved by the city council earlier this year, and it will be funded in part by a federal grant for infrastructure development.

During the project, the water supply to certain neighborhoods must be turned off. In those cases, a temporary water supply will be provided via a series of rubber hoses, and individual households will be affected for approximately 48 hours at most. — [2] —.

Sections of Cecil Boulevard will be torn up, resulting in partial road closures with single-lane use. Crews will work from 6:30 P.M. to 6:30 A.M. to minimize interruptions to the flow of traffic. Still, motorists in the area should expect delays, as alternative routes will be busier than usual, and they should watch for notices and signage in the area indicating detours. — [3] —. They are also reminded that fines for speeding are doubled in a construction zone. The work is expected to take six weeks, though adverse weather could delay some tasks. Updates of closures, progress, and alternative route recommendations can be found on the Department of Transportation's Web site. — [4] —.

Test 7

168. What is being announced in the notice?

(A) The addition of railings to a roadway
(B) The widening of Cecil Boulevard
(C) The replacement of outdated pipes
(D) The installation of water purification filters

169. What is indicated about the work crews?

(A) They will complete the work within one month.
(B) They will post pictures of the progress online.
(C) They will not work during peak periods.
(D) They will fully shut down a busy street.

170. According to the notice, what should drivers do within the construction zone?

(A) Look out for informational signs
(B) Keep their windows closed
(C) Report speeding violations
(D) Avoid parking near detours

171. In which of the following positions marked [1], [2], [3], and [4] does the following sentence best belong?

"The occupants of those residences have already been notified by the city."

(A) [1]
(B) [2]
(C) [3]
(D) [4]

GO ON TO THE NEXT PAGE

Questions 172-175 refer to the following online chat discussion.

Sidney Lee [11:25 A.M.]
The grand opening of our company's newly constructed manufacturing plant will take place this Friday, August 10. Mr. Finch wants three people from our team to be in attendance, so we need to figure out which of the four of us will stay behind.

Charlotte Mackenzie [11:27 A.M.]
Mr. Finch's memo said there will be five special guests, so we can all go as well as invite someone from another team, perhaps the head of marketing.

Nakula Goyal [11:28 A.M.]
You're right that there will be five people in total, but the memo said that Mr. Finch plans to be there himself and that CEO Gaia Tieben is going along as well in order to give a brief speech.

Charlotte Mackenzie [11:29 A.M.]
Oh, I must have missed that.

Min Cheng [11:31 A.M.]
I'm interested in seeing the new state-of-the-art equipment that will be used at the plant, but I'll volunteer to be the one who doesn't go. I can't go, really—I've got an employee evaluation report due soon.

Sidney Lee [11:32 A.M.]
All right. That works out perfectly. Mr. Finch and Ms. Tieben will travel to the site on their own because they're leaving for a business trip directly from the site. Charlotte, Nakula, what would you prefer to do about transportation?

Nakula Goyal [11:33 A.M.]
Let's meet at the office and then carpool there.

Charlotte Mackenzie [11:34 A.M.]
Good idea. I think it's about a two-hour drive, so it could be boring on our own.

Min Cheng [11:35 A.M.]
Have a great time! Let me know how it was.

172. What will happen on August 10?

(A) A factory will be inspected.
(B) A new product will be launched.
(C) A facility will officially open.
(D) An executive will present an award.

173. At 11:29 A.M., what does Ms. Mackenzie most likely mean when she writes, "I must have missed that"?

(A) She did not read a memo carefully.
(B) She misplaced a document from Mr. Finch.
(C) She does not remember attending an event.
(D) She realizes that a due date has passed.

174. Why is Ms. Cheng unable to go to an event?

(A) She received a poor score on an evaluation.
(B) She has to finish writing a report.
(C) She is preparing for a business trip.
(D) She does not know how to use some tools.

175. What does Mr. Goyal suggest doing?

(A) Taking public transportation
(B) Traveling to a site together
(C) Arriving two hours early
(D) Borrowing a company vehicle

GO ON TO THE NEXT PAGE

To:	Freya Kent <f.kent@abbotmail.com>
From:	Harrison Stein <harrison_stein@colimabank.com>
Date:	February 10
Subject:	Colima Bank

Dear Ms. Kent,

On behalf of Colima Bank, I would like to thank you for considering using our services for your personal banking needs. It was a pleasure speaking to you at the Aurora branch this afternoon, and, as promised, I am sending the details of the individual savings accounts we offer. Please be aware of the following, should you choose to move forward with opening an account:

- We limit the number of personal accounts to one per person, but you are welcome to change account types at any time.
- I have verified your basic personal information and mailing address from your driver's license. I may need a copy of your passport information page for additional verification, depending on the account type you choose.
- Interest payments will be deposited automatically in your account on the last day of every month.

	Minimum Opening Deposit	Interest Rate	Maximum Annual Withdrawals
Colima Basic	$50	.01%	5
Colima Gold	$250	.025%	8
Colima Priority	$1,000	.03%	10
Colima Platinum	$2,500	.05%	Unlimited

You can reach me on my direct line, which is 555-0175, extension 33. I look forward to hearing from you.

Harrison Stein
Accounts Officer, Colima Bank

To:	Harrison Stein <harrion_stein@colimabank.com>
From:	Freya Kent <f.kent@abbotmail.com>
Date:	February 11
Subject:	Re: Colima Bank

Dear Mr. Stein,

I have reviewed the options, and I think the best account for me would be the Colima Priority account. If I am pleased with the quality of service I receive, I may also switch over my corporate account to your bank. Interest rates are also important, but—to me—good service is what really counts.

Sincerely,

Freya Kent

176. Why did Mr. Stein send the first e-mail?

(A) To fulfill a promise
(B) To correct an error
(C) To explain a change
(D) To confirm an appointment

177. What does Mr. Stein mention in his e-mail?

(A) Further identification checks may be necessary.
(B) Paperwork must be completed at the Aurora branch.
(C) An offer will only be available for a limited time.
(D) Colima Basic is the most popular account type.

178. What is implied about Ms. Kent?

(A) She plans to upgrade her account later.
(B) She currently operates her own business.
(C) She posted a review on Colima Bank's Web site.
(D) She has been disappointed by Colima Bank's services.

179. What is true about the account that Ms. Kent selected?

(A) It does not permit deposits over a certain amount.
(B) It has the highest interest rate among the options.
(C) It requires an initial balance of $2,500.
(D) It allows money to be taken out ten times a year.

180. In the second e-mail, the word "counts" in paragraph 1, line 4, is closest in meaning to

(A) calculates
(B) regards
(C) matters
(D) relies

GO ON TO THE NEXT PAGE

| | HOME | SEARCH | **NEWS** | SUBSCRIBE | CONTACT |

www.megaphotosearch.com

Mega Photo Search (MPS) is pleased to open our photo library to individuals and small businesses for the first time ever. This collection was previously only offered to large corporations, but we have adapted our Web site for more general use. With an extensive network of freelance photographers, MPS is well on its way to becoming the largest collection of high-quality images online. Also, with our technical team available to answer questions around the clock via online chat, we are confident that we can serve our customers well.

Although we do not offer single purchases of photographs, our subscriptions are reasonably priced to fit your budget. For any photograph that you download through your subscription, you can retain permanent—though not exclusive—ownership of the license. Prices are listed below, and you can terminate your service agreement at any time without penalty. Your first bill will include a sign-up fee of $25, and from that point you will be billed once a month.

Subscription Type	Monthly Downloads	Users	Monthly Fee	Bonus
Standard	50	1	$75	—
Standard Plus	300	1	$150	100 bonus photos after one year
Partner	700	2	$280	Advance notice of new photos
Team	700	3–5	$310	Free access to Rainbox*

*Rainbox is MPS's online software program that allows you to adjust the color and size of photos and combine multiple images into one.

www.megaphotosearch.com

| HOME | SEARCH | NEWS | **SUBSCRIBE** | CONTACT |

Mega Photo Search – New Subscriber

Name: Dane Mullins   **Company (if applicable):** Bellin Publishing
E-mail Address: dmullins@bellin-publ.com   **Daytime Phone Number:** 469-555-0172
Billing Address: 975 Marion Avenue, Cambridge, MA 02142

Billing details: $25 sign-up fee + $310 monthly fee
Billed to credit card ending in 5539. Recurring charges will be made to this card monthly.

Thank you for choosing Mega Photo Search. As a welcome gift, we are offering a free e-book that gives you tips on how to search our collection efficiently. Click <u>here</u> to download it.

181. What is the main purpose of the information in the Web page?

(A) To encourage customers to make an upgrade
(B) To give an update on a corporate merger
(C) To announce the expansion of a service
(D) To seek submissions from freelance photographers

182. What is indicated about MPS?

(A) It has a larger collection than any of its competitors.
(B) It offers customer support twenty-four hours a day.
(C) It provides workshops for small business owners.
(D) It has recently opened a branch in Cambridge.

183. What is mentioned about subscriptions in the Web page?

(A) They enable users to download illustrations.
(B) They are only sold to individuals.
(C) They are billed on the first day of every month.
(D) They can be canceled without incurring a fee.

184. What is implied about Mr. Mullins?

(A) He will receive 100 free photos after a year.
(B) He will make his regular payments by bank transfer.
(C) He will be notified about additions to the collection.
(D) He will have access to image editing software.

185. According to the online form, what is available in a downloadable file?

(A) Advice for conducting searches
(B) A book on photography
(C) Information on copyright law
(D) A receipt for a subscription

GO ON TO THE NEXT PAGE

Test 7

Laredo Community Festival Returns

LAREDO (May 5)—The Laredo Community Festival (LCF), which has been growing in popularity, is scheduled to return this summer, from June 27 to June 28 at Roland Park. In addition to the usual booths from local restaurants and retail businesses, this year there will be a section for charities to raise money and promote their work.

Event planner Anita Gutierrez confirmed that feedback from Laredo residents prompted the change. "This is an opportunity for us to support the less fortunate members of our community," said Ms. Gutierrez, who will take photos during the opening ceremony and speak at the start of the *Laredo Live* episode being filmed at the festival.

Registration for all booths runs until June 1, and a number of groups have already signed up. One is Coffee-B, a charity devoted to supporting low-income people in coffee-growing regions. Along with its signature coffee drinks, Coffee-B has created a special drink—an espresso topped with honeycomb—that will be sold exclusively at its LCF booth.

Laredo Community Festival Special Events
Saturday, June 27

The Laredo Community Festival (LCF) celebrates our people and our passions. In addition to browsing the 200+ booths, don't miss these special events on the main stage:

10:00 A.M.	**Opening Ceremony** Featuring the mayor and city council members
1:00 P.M.	**Laredo Spoken Word Contest** Contestants of all ages share poems, short stories, and speeches
2:30 P.M.	**Filming of *Laredo Live*** Hour-long television program hosted by Tracy Ratcliff, with special guests from the area
7:00 P.M.	**Battle of the Bands** Local musicians show their talents in this free outdoor concert

Get Buzzing with Coffee-B!

Coffee-B is a charity that teaches people in coffee-growing regions how to raise bees as a source of income. Bees, which pollinate coffee flowers, are the perfect complement to coffee. The honey and wax they produce create a steady source of income for beekeepers in a way that doesn't require land ownership.

Check out our booth at the Laredo Community Festival at Roland Park. We'll be raising money by selling the Honey Dream, a coffee-flavored milkshake with a twist of honey; the Sweet Shot, a freshly-brewed espresso with real honeycomb on top; the Buzzy Bomb, a double espresso with cinnamon and beeswax stirring stick; and the Caffeine Cooler, an iced coffee that can be infused with a variety of flavored syrups.

---

186. According to the article, what will be different about this year's LCF?

(A) It will be held earlier in the summer.
(B) A new type of organization will be involved.
(C) A wider selection of foods will be sold.
(D) It will include a fund-raising contest.

187. In the article, the word "prompted" in paragraph 2, line 2, is closest in meaning to

(A) hurried
(B) convinced
(C) asked
(D) caused

188. When will Ms. Gutierrez give a talk on June 27?

(A) At 10:00 A.M.
(B) At 1:00 P.M.
(C) At 2:30 P.M.
(D) At 7:00 P.M.

189. Which drink will only be available at LCF?

(A) Honey Dream
(B) Sweet Shot
(C) Buzzy Bomb
(D) Caffeine Cooler

190. What is mentioned in the flyer about beekeepers?

(A) They produce wax for coffee growers.
(B) They can rent equipment from Coffee-B.
(C) They usually work in coffee-growing areas.
(D) They do not need to own property.

GO ON TO THE NEXT PAGE

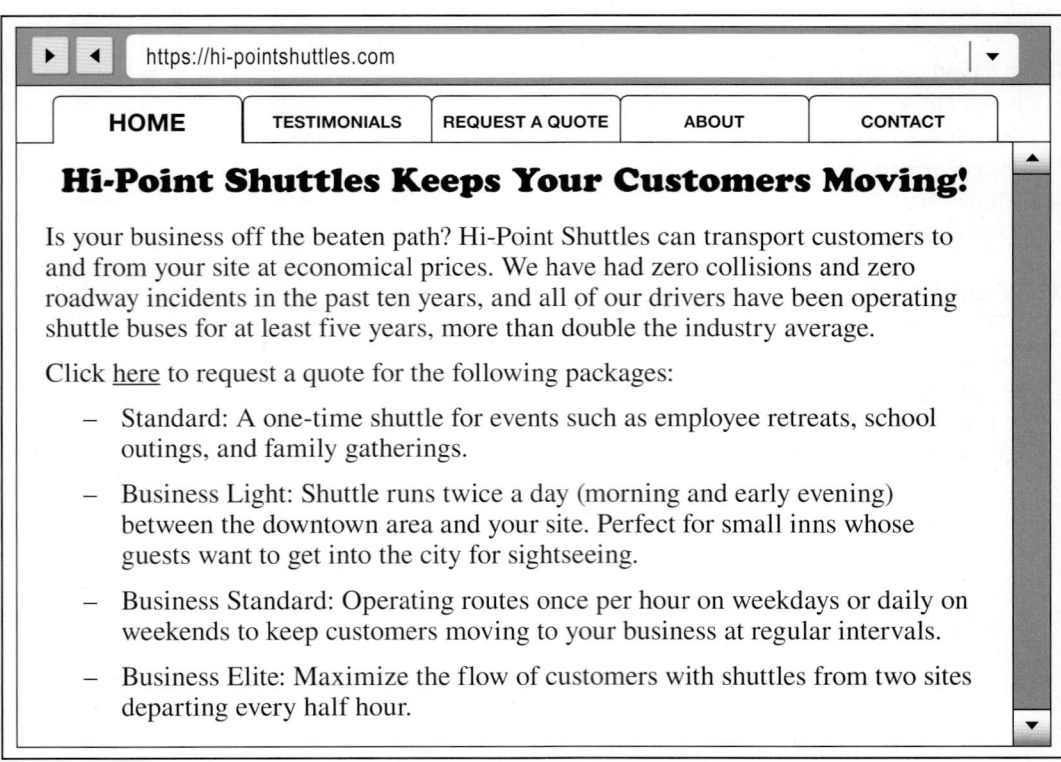

www.vivabotanicalgardens.com/customer_feedback ▶

Viva Botanical Gardens Customer Feedback

← Previous Posts   **Posted Today**

As an avid gardener, I was looking forward to seeing the wide variety of flowers and plants at Viva Botanical Gardens. The admission fee is quite reasonable, as you can spend an entire day exploring the exhibits. However, it is a challenge to reach the gardens from the city center. There are no public buses or trains, and the taxi fares are very expensive. I spoke to the manager, who was very friendly, and suggested that he hire a transportation service that was used by another tourist site I had gone to earlier in my trip. I hope he takes this advice into consideration.

– Christina Saunders, July 18

I'm not sure that I would recommend this attraction to others. The admission fee is very expensive, and it's hard to get there unless you have your own car. Very inconvenient! Next time, I'll skip this site and visit the Amherst Nature Reserve instead.

–Venkata Thakur, July 18

▶ ◀   https://hi-pointshuttles.com   ▼

| HOME | TESTIMONIALS | REQUEST A QUOTE | ABOUT | CONTACT |

Hi-Point Shuttles Keeps Your Customers Moving!

Is your business off the beaten path? Hi-Point Shuttles can transport customers to and from your site at economical prices. We have had zero collisions and zero roadway incidents in the past ten years, and all of our drivers have been operating shuttle buses for at least five years, more than double the industry average.

Click here to request a quote for the following packages:

- Standard: A one-time shuttle for events such as employee retreats, school outings, and family gatherings.

- Business Light: Shuttle runs twice a day (morning and early evening) between the downtown area and your site. Perfect for small inns whose guests want to get into the city for sightseeing.

- Business Standard: Operating routes once per hour on weekdays or daily on weekends to keep customers moving to your business at regular intervals.

- Business Elite: Maximize the flow of customers with shuttles from two sites departing every half hour.

Hi-Point Shuttles
Customer Review Form

Name: _Dave Bates_   Details: _Viva Botanical Gardens Manager_

Overall rating: _5_ / 5

Comments: _One of my customers recommended Hi-Point Shuttles after using it to visit_ _a textile factory, and I'm so glad I gave the company a chance. My customers love the_ _hourly shuttle option, and this has brought a lot of business to my site. The estimates of_ _the journey time have a high degree of accuracy, and the shuttles are comfortable._

May we post your review on our Web site? Yes _x_   No ____

---

191. In the first Web page, what issue with Viva Botanical Gardens do both posters mention?

(A) The small number of exhibits
(B) The high price of admission tickets
(C) The difficulty of getting to the site
(D) The inconvenient hours of operation

192. What is NOT indicated about Hi-Point Shuttles?

(A) It charges affordable rates.
(B) Its staff members are experienced.
(C) Its vehicles are cleaned frequently.
(D) It has an excellent safety record.

193. What did Ms. Saunders most likely visit before Viva Botanical Gardens?

(A) A flower shop
(B) A textile factory
(C) A nature reserve
(D) A city museum

194. Which service package did Mr. Bates most likely purchase?

(A) Standard
(B) Business Light
(C) Business Standard
(D) Business Elite

195. In the customer review, the word "degree" in paragraph 1, line 4, is closest in meaning to

(A) level
(B) step
(C) diploma
(D) temperature

Test 7

GO ON TO THE NEXT PAGE

Q-Rewards — Shop your way to savings!

Quincy Supermarket is pleased to introduce its new loyalty program—Q-Rewards. Join this program to earn one point for every dollar you spend at Quincy Supermarket and one point for every two dollars you spend at any of the businesses in our partner network. Enroll in the program at www.quincysupermarket.com/qrewards, and you'll instantly be issued a temporary card by e-mail, with a physical card following later in the mail. New members can get a bonus of 300 points just for signing up, and we'll also send you a voucher for $5 if you register to receive our monthly newsletter and other occasional store offers by e-mail. Once you are enrolled in the program, you will automatically be sent a $10 voucher every time your account reaches 1,000 points.

To earn points, simply present your Q-Rewards card at the time of checkout. You can also download the Q-Rewards smartphone application, which allows you to claim your points by scanning a store receipt within 48 hours of its issuance. Sign up today and watch the points pile up!

Carol Faulk
1607 Wescam Avenue
Grofflan, OH 45231

Dear Ms. Faulk,

Thank you for signing up for our Q-Rewards program. Please find enclosed your Q-Rewards card, as well as the $5 voucher that you are entitled to. This voucher can be used at any Quincy Supermarket store as well as online at www.quincysupermarket.com. Please treat it as you would treat cash of equivalent value, as we will not be able to issue you a new voucher if you misplace this one.

Don't forget to check out the newest brands in our product lineup:
- Plincus cleaning products: countertop cleaner, glass cleaner, and wood polish
- Vispant gourmet cheeses: the finest cheeses imported from France
- Lankdon juices: cranberry, apple, and grape varieties in 355ml bottles
- Charking daily vitamin supplements: separate formulas for adults and children

We hope to see you soon at Quincy Supermarket!

Sincerely,

Todd Hampton
Customer Service, The Q-Rewards Team

```
+----------------------------------------------------------+
|                                                          |
|  $5      Quincy Supermarket      $5                      |
|                                                          |
|  This voucher is valid for FIVE DOLLARS off              |
|            at Quincy Supermarket.                        |
|                                                          |
|  Please note that the purchase must exceed five          |
|  dollars, and no change will be given. Not valid         |
|  for home appliances or beverages. See reverse           |
|  side for further terms and conditions.                  |
|                                                          |
+----------------------------------------------------------+
```

196. What is true about the Q-Rewards program?

(A) Members are eligible for monthly coupons.
(B) Members receive two points for each dollar they spend.
(C) Points can be collected up to two days after a purchase.
(D) Points may be claimed by filling out a form.

197. What did Ms. Faulk most likely do?

(A) Inquired about Q-Rewards enrollment
(B) Accumulated 1,000 rewards points
(C) Damaged her Q-Rewards card
(D) Signed up for an e-mail newsletter

198. What is suggested about Quincy Supermarket?

(A) It is the largest grocery store in Grofflan.
(B) It recently started selling its goods online.
(C) It has partnered with a local restaurant.
(D) It consists of multiple branch locations.

199. What does Mr. Hampton warn Ms. Faulk about?

(A) The voucher will not be valid after the expiration date.
(B) Lost vouchers will not be replaced by the store.
(C) Vouchers cannot be exchanged for cash.
(D) Purchases made with vouchers do not earn rewards points.

200. Which brand's products cannot be purchased with the voucher?

(A) Plincus's
(B) Vispant's
(C) Lankdon's
(D) Charking's

Stop! This is the end of the test. If you finish before time is called, you may go back to Parts 5, 6, and 7 and check your work.

TEST 8

READING TEST

In the Reading test, you will read a variety of texts and answer several different types of reading comprehension questions. The entire Reading test will last 75 minutes. There are three parts, and directions are given for each part. You are encouraged to answer as many questions as possible within the time allowed.

You must mark your answers on the separate answer sheet. Do not write your answers in your test book.

PART 5

Directions: A word or phrase is missing in each of the sentences below. Four answer choices are given below each sentence. Select the best answer to complete the sentence. Then mark the letter (A), (B), (C), or (D) on your answer sheet.

101. Several local food makers offer ------- own products to employees at reduced prices.

(A) themselves
(B) they
(C) them
(D) their

102. Fawley Academy's ------- on absences caused by medical issues are explained in the student handbook.

(A) solutions
(B) classrooms
(C) instructors
(D) guidelines

103. Check that the lid of the container is ------- sealed to prevent its contents from leaking.

(A) firm
(B) firmly
(C) firming
(D) firmness

104. It is ------- that the accuracy of measuring instruments be tested yearly.

(A) active
(B) initial
(C) vital
(D) fluent

105. The new law will not affect homeowners whose property has been ------- at less than $80,000 in value.

(A) assess
(B) assessed
(C) assessor
(D) assessment

106. Taxi service should ------- be used when there is cheaper alternative transportation available during your business travel.

(A) overly
(B) too
(C) never
(D) ever

107. This technique is meant to be ------- in treating muscle-related soreness.

(A) employment
(B) employed
(C) employs
(D) employing

108. ------- this summer's unusual weather, it is no surprise that ice cream sales fell.

(A) Into
(B) Until
(C) Given
(D) Amid

109. To minimize any negative impact on tourism, the ------- of the famous statue will require careful timing.
(A) relocate
(B) relocates
(C) relocation
(D) relocated

110. Ms. Migliacio asked that corrections to online articles be made ------- upon noticing errors.
(A) accidentally
(B) chiefly
(C) promptly
(D) highly

111. All of our products undergo ------- inspections at our manufacturing facility to ensure they meet high quality standards.
(A) strict
(B) bent
(C) aware
(D) vacant

112. Dr. Itaru Matsuda's studies have proven the ------- effects of the new medication on patients.
(A) advantageously
(B) advantageous
(C) advantage
(D) advantages

113. You are provided a license to use Crombee until the end of next month under the ------- of this agreement.
(A) conditions
(B) penalties
(C) approaches
(D) phrases

114. A company that is ------- for its corporate values will have greater success in attracting qualified job candidates.
(A) respecting
(B) respects
(C) respect
(D) respected

115. Although relatively few surveyed residents commute to work by bike, recreational bicycle use is -------.
(A) impatient
(B) widespread
(C) talented
(D) empty

116. Managers must submit revised deadline schedules ------- their projects face delays.
(A) behind
(B) when
(C) over
(D) whereas

117. The traffic sign was ------- visible from the road until the branches of a nearby tree obscured it.
(A) clearest
(B) clearer
(C) clearly
(D) cleared

118. Deenad Import-Export Ltd. operates a modern warehouse with floor space ------- 27,000 square meters.
(A) finishing
(B) obtaining
(C) developing
(D) covering

119. Clothing sales revenues are ------- even though the store's home goods remain popular.
(A) declining
(B) declines
(C) declined
(D) decline

120. The executive committee is proud to announce that ------- will soon resume negotiations with Pruneda Holdings.
(A) we
(B) us
(C) our
(D) ourselves

GO ON TO THE NEXT PAGE

121. Human Resources reports that staff in a majority of departments are ------- absent during weeks that include national holidays.

(A) persisted
(B) persisting
(C) persistent
(D) persistently

122. Tours of select apartments ------- now that construction on the complex has been completed.

(A) are allowing
(B) to allow
(C) have allowed
(D) will be allowed

123. ------- you find our mobile app satisfactory, please tap on the button below to leave a five-star review.

(A) If
(B) Either
(C) Regardless
(D) So that

124. The Karvex-K's advanced features are ------- with what professional photographers expect from a digital camera.

(A) incapable
(B) excited
(C) thankful
(D) consistent

125. Shoppers are encouraged to look around our store's entire showroom floor ------- they decide not to purchase anything.

(A) even if
(B) in case
(C) now that
(D) such as

126. The IT team ------- that all database systems be upgraded monthly.

(A) expires
(B) believes
(C) recalls
(D) advises

127. Quality control officials found defects in a Phung's Apparel item just ------- over the course of a weeklong visit.

(A) yet
(B) for
(C) about
(D) once

128. ------- to package a new food product depends heavily on the item's brand image and target customer.

(A) Which
(B) How
(C) Nothing
(D) Whatever

129. Patient records ------- with "Confidential" in red ink are subject to stronger protection measures.

(A) stamping
(B) stamped
(C) that stamp
(D) are stamped

130. The Snell Herald's career advice column enables readers to seize opportunities they may ------- at work.

(A) come across
(B) take apart
(C) go through
(D) back up

Directions: Read the texts that follow. A word, phrase, or sentence is missing in parts of each text. Four answer choices for each question are given below the text. Select the best answer to complete the text. Then mark the letter (A), (B), (C), or (D) on your answer sheet.

Questions 131-134 refer to the following e-mail.

From: Harold Bjorneby <h.bjorneby@oue-mail.com>
To: Reba Shelton <r.shelton@tpead.com>
Subject: Response
Date: March 18

Dear Ms. Shelton,

Thank you for your application to rent my two-bedroom property located at 349 Forest Way. I agree that you are a good match for the ------. As you authorized, I will proceed immediately with your
131.
credit check. ------, I cannot promise that your wish to move in before the end of the month can be
132.
accommodated. Please understand that my main priority is to confirm that you will be a satisfactory tenant. I ------ to take as much time as necessary to do that. ------. In the meantime, please feel free
133.   **134.**
to e-mail me with any questions you may have.

Sincerely,

Harold Bjorneby

131. (A) unit
(B) post
(C) major
(D) vehicle

132. (A) Still
(B) Therefore
(C) Furthermore
(D) Luckily

133. (A) had
(B) have
(C) will have had
(D) have had

134. (A) The attached report explains the reasons
for this refusal.
(B) Your e-mail did not clarify where to pay
these fees.
(C) I will contact you again once the process is
complete.
(D) We require the contract to be signed in
person.

GO ON TO THE NEXT PAGE

From: Human Resources
To: All Staff
Subject: Re: Survey

Last year, some of you refused to fill out Oakhan Corporation's yearly employee satisfaction survey due to worries that expressing _____ would have a negative effect on your careers. Without candid
135.
feedback, however, we cannot make necessary improvements to our current systems. _____, we
136.
have decided to conduct the survey anonymously this year. Your individual answers _____ only by
137.
Ramagos Surveys. It is a company that specializes in compiling sets of completed forms to create a
comprehensive report, which is the only document that Oakhan management will receive. _____.
138.

Please visit www.ramagossurveys.com/2937 between February 19 and 25 to participate.

135. (A) displeases
(B) displeasing
(C) displeased
(D) displeasure

136. (A) Namely
(B) Accordingly
(C) Additionally
(D) Formerly

137. (A) seen
(B) see
(C) will be seen
(D) have been seen

138. (A) Last year, its findings were mostly positive.
(B) We hope that this puts your concerns to rest.
(C) It may take time to give thoughtful answers.
(D) Finally, organize the data collected into graphs.

226

To: <r.abrantes@nov-mail.com>
From: <membership@underwoodhome.com>
Subject: Membership confirmation
Date: July 25

Dear Ms. Abrantes,

Welcome to the Underwood Home Forums. You will now be able to discuss home improvement issues and projects with people all around the world. To begin commenting, simply find a forum that interests you. This should not be difficult considering the wide variety of ------- available.
139.

For an optimal using experience, -------, there is one step you may want to take first. -------. Our
140. **141.**
longtime posters have created numerous shorthand terms that are incomprehensible to outsiders. That is why we recommend ------- the customized dictionary accessible via the "UnderSpeak" icon
142.
on our home page before getting started.

Good luck!

Sincerely,

The Underwood Home Forums Team

---

139. (A) estimates
(B) replacements
(C) venues
(D) topics

140. (A) for instance
(B) likewise
(C) though
(D) in fact

141. (A) The terms of use agreement forbids the replication of our content.
(B) While using the site, you may encounter unfamiliar expressions.
(C) Although debate is encouraged, we ask that you remain polite.
(D) We do not verify claims made in member profiles or posts.

142. (A) reviewing
(B) a review
(C) reviewers
(D) that review

GO ON TO THE NEXT PAGE

Coffee Machines in the Office   *Resnell Company Newsletter*

The coffee fans among us are now enjoying a new benefit of being a Resnell employee. Earlier this month, the coffee pot in each pantry of the building was replaced with a state-of-the-art machine. ------. The new machines, Hulford Brewing Systems, produce single cups in a variety of flavors.
143.
Their appearance ------ with nearly universal delight. Several employees say the café mocha is the
144.
best coffee they have tasted. ------, trips to the pantry have become more frequent for members of
145.
many departments. Regardless, company administration says there are currently no plans to limit ------ of the machines. They urge all employees to try a cup.
146.

143. (A) Pantries will be off-limits while they are installed.
     (B) The reusable cups must be washed regularly.
     (C) Interested employees should speak to their managers.
     (D) The move is meant as a reward for a great first quarter.

144. (A) was greeted
     (B) will be greeting
     (C) have greeted
     (D) is greeting

145. (A) Nevertheless
     (B) Consequently
     (C) Conversely
     (D) Previously

146. (A) transportation
     (B) development
     (C) ranking
     (D) usage

PART 7

Directions: In this part you will read a selection of texts, such as magazine and newspaper articles, e-mails, and instant messages. Each text or set of texts is followed by several questions. Select the best answer for each question and mark the letter (A), (B), (C), or (D) on your answer sheet.

Questions 147-148 refer to the following note.

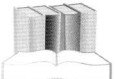

A Word from the Publisher

This week, Drager's takes a break from current affairs to honor some of the groundbreaking scientists of the past decades. More than 50 pages of articles explain these great figures' achievements in a variety of fields, and consider their effects on the world today. We were also fortunate enough to speak directly with several of them about their experiences; a complete list is available on page four. So, without further comment, we invite you to begin enjoying this unique issue of *Drager's Weekly*.

147. Where would the note most likely appear?

(A) In a science journal
(B) In a laboratory newsletter
(C) In a book of collected writings
(D) In a news magazine

148. What can be found on the page mentioned?

(A) A photograph of a ceremony
(B) A republished article
(C) The names of some interviewees
(D) The results of a reader poll

GO ON TO THE NEXT PAGE

THE K270 SPEAKER BY PRAUSS

What backyard barbecue or pool party would be complete without music? Despite being just ten inches in length, the portable K270 produces crystal-clear sound wherever it is placed. A tough aluminum shell allows it to withstand sunlight and other hazards of summer events, while any of the shell's available brilliant shades add a touch of fun. What's more, the K270 is compatible with a variety of devices and has wireless connectivity with a range of up to 30 feet. Want to try it out? Visit any Prauss Electronics store nationwide today.

149. For whom is the advertisement most likely intended?

(A) People who enjoy spending time outdoors

(B) People who are seeking discount electronics

(C) People who listen to music while driving

(D) People who play music professionally

150. What is stated about the K270 Speaker?

(A) It is large.

(B) It is sold online.

(C) It is brightly colored.

(D) It comes with a carrying case.

Questions 151-152 refer to the following text-message chain.

Valeria Kwon [10:24 A.M.]
Don, where are you?

Don Trousdale [10:25 A.M.]
I'm at one of the houses on the east end of the development. I had to fix a loose door handle for a tenant. Why?

Valeria Kwon [10:25 A.M.]
The potential homebuyer, Ms. Ponti, just arrived here at the office.

Don Trousdale [10:26 A.M.]
Well, it's going to take me at least a half hour to get back there.

Valeria Kwon [10:27 A.M.]
OK. It seems like Ms. Ponti is on a tight schedule, so maybe I could start showing her around the model home myself. I have the keys.

Don Trousdale [10:28 A.M.]
Go right ahead. I'll catch up.

151. Who most likely is Mr. Trousdale?

(A) A property manager
(B) An administrative assistant
(C) A potential buyer
(D) An interior designer

152. At 10:28 A.M., what does Mr. Trousdale most likely mean when he writes, "Go right ahead"?

(A) He is happy to lend out a vehicle.
(B) A street may be inaccessible.
(C) Ms. Kwon should lead a house tour.
(D) He will return some keys to Ms. Kwon later.

GO ON TO THE NEXT PAGE

Working at the Counter

In order to provide excellent service to customers, counter clerks at all Maire Laundry locations should adhere to the following basic procedures.

- Greet customers in a friendly manner.
- Receive the customer's items, clarifying which are to be laundered and which are to be dry cleaned, and whether special services such as stain removal are required.
- Enter all information gathered into the electronic ticketing system.
- Show the resulting price to the customer and obtain full payment.
- Print the ticket. Detach the part marked "Customer to retain this portion of ticket" and give it to the customer. Explain that they will need to show it when retrieving their items, and point out the "Ready by" date.
- End the interaction pleasantly.
- Attach tickets to the customer's items and place them into the appropriate bins. (See the next section for sorting instructions.)

153. What is indicated about Maire Laundry?

(A) It serves commercial enterprises.
(B) It is a chain business.
(C) It has self-service machines.
(D) It sends out electronic notifications.

154. What are clerks instructed to do before accepting payment?

(A) Print a claim ticket
(B) Sort clothing into bins
(C) Estimate a completion date
(D) Ask about special requests

Busbyton Mall has grown! Check out our new additions!

Busbyton Mall now boasts more than 55 shops and ample parking! Shoppers are sure to find just what they are looking for here. You can also browse at a leisurely pace to discover new products. For a time-out from shopping, stop by one of our 17 on-site restaurants, or take in the sensational music performances held frequently on our first-floor stage.

But that's not all. Busbyton Mall is:

Historic: Built nearly 100 years ago, our beautiful main building has been photographed for numerous design publications, and later structures have been carefully conceived to complement it.

Kid-friendly: Our indoor playground offers free, safe fun for younger visitors. Also available are The Wenman Store, which sells items related to Wenman's classic cartoons, and our video game arcade, located on the second floor.

Already a fan? Become a Busbyton VIP! For a small annual fee, you will gain access to exclusive discounts and be invited to unwind in our VIP lounge. Visit an Information Desk for details.

Busbyton Mall: Shopping made fun for all!

155. What is indicated about Busbyton Mall?

(A) It recently expanded.
(B) It produces a monthly publication.
(C) It has more than two floors.
(D) It has changed ownership.

156. What is NOT mentioned as a feature of Busbyton Mall?

(A) Easy access to public transportation
(B) A play facility for children
(C) Charming architecture
(D) A concert venue

157. What are visitors who hold special memberships allowed to do?

(A) Enter prize drawings
(B) Use a relaxation room
(C) Accumulate rewards points
(D) Park in the closest area

Test 8

Questions 158-160 refer to the following e-mail.

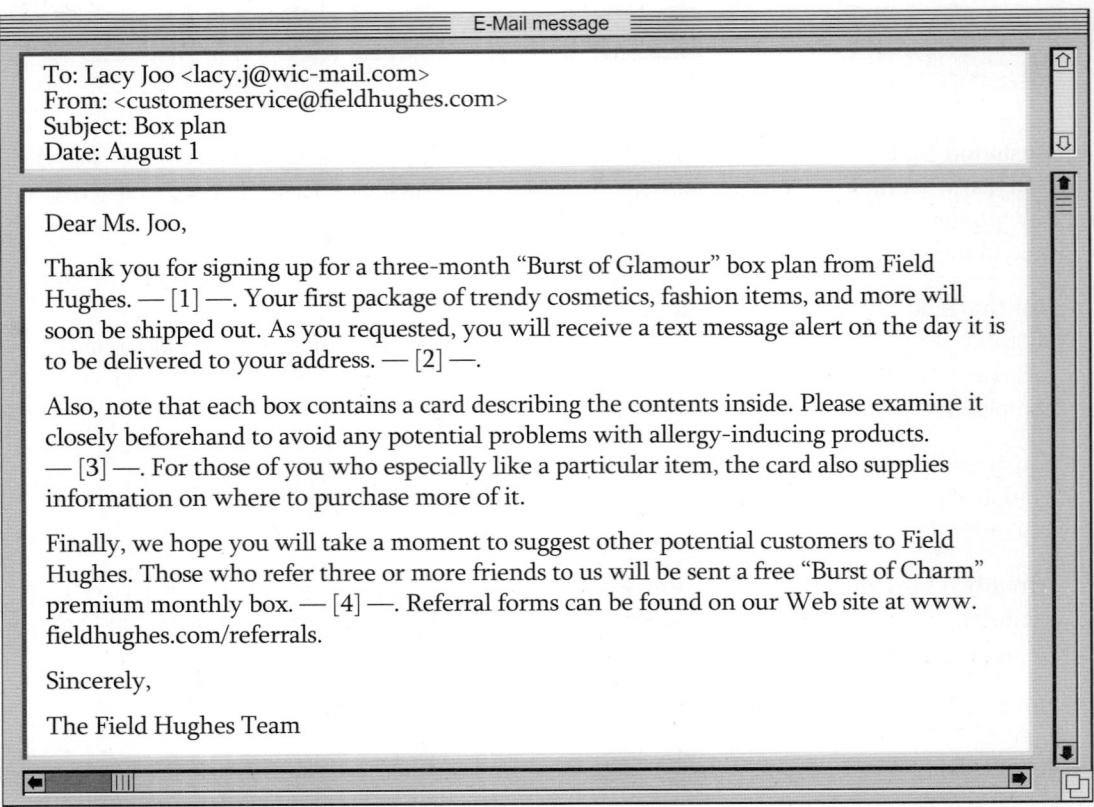

To: Lacy Joo <lacy.j@wic-mail.com>
From: <customerservice@fieldhughes.com>
Subject: Box plan
Date: August 1

Dear Ms. Joo,

Thank you for signing up for a three-month "Burst of Glamour" box plan from Field Hughes. — [1] —. Your first package of trendy cosmetics, fashion items, and more will soon be shipped out. As you requested, you will receive a text message alert on the day it is to be delivered to your address. — [2] —.

Also, note that each box contains a card describing the contents inside. Please examine it closely beforehand to avoid any potential problems with allergy-inducing products. — [3] —. For those of you who especially like a particular item, the card also supplies information on where to purchase more of it.

Finally, we hope you will take a moment to suggest other potential customers to Field Hughes. Those who refer three or more friends to us will be sent a free "Burst of Charm" premium monthly box. — [4] —. Referral forms can be found on our Web site at www.fieldhughes.com/referrals.

Sincerely,

The Field Hughes Team

---

158. What is one purpose of the e-mail?

(A) To respond to an inquiry
(B) To confirm a subscription
(C) To alert Ms. Joo to a shipping delay
(D) To recommend a new product

159. What is Ms. Joo instructed to read carefully?

(A) A Web page
(B) A product label
(C) A text message
(D) A package insert

160. In which of the positions marked [1], [2], [3], and [4] does the following sentence best belong?

"The ingredients of all cosmetics and edible goods are listed in full."

(A) [1]
(B) [2]
(C) [3]
(D) [4]

Questions 161-163 refer to the following e-mail.

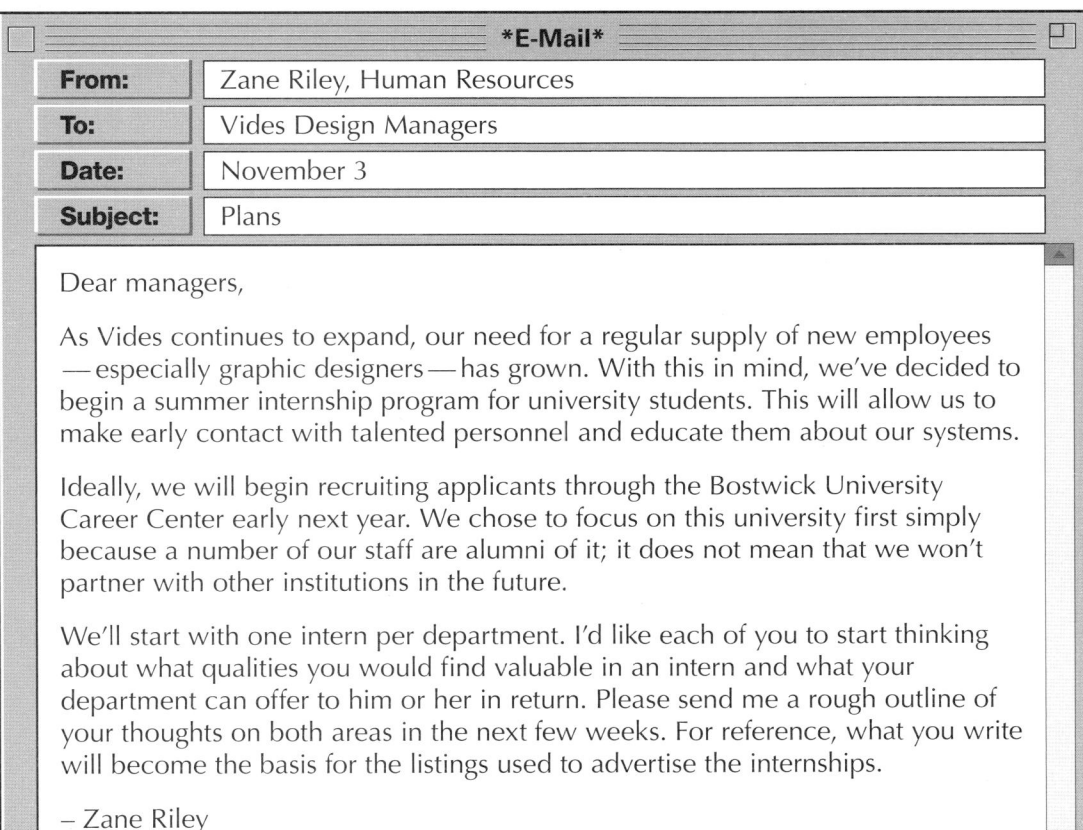

E-Mail

From: Zane Riley, Human Resources

To: Vides Design Managers

Date: November 3

Subject: Plans

Dear managers,

As Vides continues to expand, our need for a regular supply of new employees —especially graphic designers—has grown. With this in mind, we've decided to begin a summer internship program for university students. This will allow us to make early contact with talented personnel and educate them about our systems.

Ideally, we will begin recruiting applicants through the Bostwick University Career Center early next year. We chose to focus on this university first simply because a number of our staff are alumni of it; it does not mean that we won't partner with other institutions in the future.

We'll start with one intern per department. I'd like each of you to start thinking about what qualities you would find valuable in an intern and what your department can offer to him or her in return. Please send me a rough outline of your thoughts on both areas in the next few weeks. For reference, what you write will become the basis for the listings used to advertise the internships.

– Zane Riley

161. Why was the e-mail written?

(A) To recruit speakers for a seminar series
(B) To announce an internship program
(C) To describe the purpose of a new branch office
(D) To correct misunderstandings about a hiring process

162. What is indicated about Bostwick University?

(A) It has an excellent Graphic Design Department.
(B) It leads professional development courses in the summer.
(C) Vides Design is collaborating with it on a public art project.
(D) Several Vides Design employees graduated from it.

163. What are readers of the e-mail asked to consider?

(A) The mutual benefits of a possible relationship
(B) The qualities of successful leaders
(C) The basis for a customer complaint
(D) The best channel through which to advertise a position

GO ON TO THE NEXT PAGE

Welcome to the One-Day Workshop with Sophia Hong!

Now that you have checked in, please take a seat and prepare to begin learning. From 10 A.M. to 12:30 P.M., Ms. Hong will share the story of her path to becoming a successful author, in a conversational format in which questions are encouraged. From 1:30 P.M. until the workshop ends at 4:30 P.M., she will supply personalized advice to all five of our workshop's participants, based on the story proposal that each of you submitted prior to attending. In addition to the one-hour lunch period, ten-minute breaks will take place at 11:15 A.M. and 3 P.M. In order not to disturb our patrons, we ask that you take breaks in the lobby near the circulation desk. This area has benches and lounge chairs for your comfort and convenience.

Participants who provide post-workshop feedback in the box below will be given their choice of the gifts listed.

----------------------------------- Detach here -----------------------------------

Comments:

Gift: _____ spiral notebook   _____ canvas bookbag

---

164. What is the workshop most likely about?

(A) How to give effective presentations
(B) Starting a carpentry business
(C) How to succeed as a writer
(D) Various ways to make handicrafts

165. What were participants required to do before the workshop?

(A) Gather in the lobby of a building
(B) Submit questions for Ms. Hong
(C) Purchase a set of note-taking tools
(D) Prepare ideas for a potential project

166. What information is NOT included on the form?

(A) The schedule for rest times
(B) The number of participants
(C) The location of the workshop
(D) The topic of the morning discussion

167. What is indicated about participants who give feedback?

(A) They can receive a cloth sack.
(B) They probably disliked the workshop.
(C) They must send in a form by post.
(D) They may register for a future event.

Questions 168-171 refer to the following online chat discussion.

Andre Jones, 9:02 A.M.
Hey, everyone. I just got word that Mr. Boliek will be attending our meeting this morning, so please be prepared.

Bharat Laghari, 9:02 A.M.
OK, thanks for the heads-up. I'll let Chisato know when she arrives with the snacks.

Carole Hauser, 9:03 A.M.
I'll check that the conference room is set up. And should I revise the agenda to allow time for Mr. Boliek to speak?

Andre Jones, 9:04 A.M.
No, that's all right, Carole. Actually, he wants us to act as if he wasn't there. But it's been a long time since someone at the vice-president level has sat in on our weekly meeting, so I'd like to ensure that, at a minimum, we don't make a bad impression.

Yvette Curley, 9:05 A.M.
In that case, could we possibly move my presentation on the buying habits of our target consumers to next week? I've been really busy with the product launch….

Andre Jones, 9:05 A.M.
I think that would make the meeting too short. Did you make an electronic slideshow, at least?

Yvette Curley, 9:06 A.M.
Yes, but it could be better.

Andre Jones, 9:07 A.M.
Hmm… please e-mail the file to me and then come to my office to talk it over. Carole, I'll let you know what we decide.

---

168. What is indicated about Mr. Boliek?

(A) He is a high-ranking executive.
(B) He called Mr. Jones directly.
(C) He has an announcement to make.
(D) He has returned from a long business trip.

169. What is Ms. Hauser most likely responsible for doing?

(A) Obtaining refreshments
(B) Making a timetable
(C) Preparing electronic equipment
(D) Reserving a conference room

170. What field do the writers most likely work in?

(A) Law
(B) Medicine
(C) Accounting
(D) Marketing

171. At 9:06 A.M., what does Ms. Curley most likely mean when she writes, "it could be better"?

(A) Mr. Jones may be disappointed by a research finding.
(B) She is dissatisfied with the current state of some work.
(C) She wants to use visual aids to explain some data.
(D) Mr. Jones should consider cancelling a meeting.

GO ON TO THE NEXT PAGE

Test 8

Attuso Food Truck Festival to Expand
by Abigail Davies

ATTUSO (August 31) — Citing the remarkable success of the inaugural Attuso Food Truck Festival in May, the city of Attuso has revealed plans to add a second day to next year's event, while the venue remains the same.

The first Attuso Food Truck Festival was organized to attract visitors to Montar Park, which the city had finished constructing in January. —[1]—. More than 20 trucks served a variety of foods to an estimated crowd of 1,000 people, while musicians and arts-and-crafts tents provided entertainment.

The change was announced in a press release posted yesterday on the festival's Web site, www.attuso-ftf.com. City officials wrote that the extra day will have a large impact on the second celebration of the festival by giving more visitors a chance to attend. —[2]—.

Drake Ryu, owner of Kimchi Curry, one of the most popular trucks to participate in this year's festival, voiced excitement about the news. "We'll definitely be at next year's festival," he said. —[3]—. "The first one introduced our food to a lot of new people, and it sounds like it's only going to get better."

The city also hopes to widen the range of entertainment options offered. Businesses and organizations will be sought to sponsor additional activities tents, and there will be more opportunities for musical performances by groups and individuals. —[4]—. The press release promises that application forms are coming soon and encourages those interested to check the Web site regularly.

172. What is implied about the festival?

(A) Ms. Davies has taken part in it.
(B) Mr. Ryu is one of its organizers.
(C) It has been held twice before.
(D) It takes place in a public park.

173. What is suggested about a Web site?

(A) It does not yet contain necessary documents.
(B) It is not maintained by the city of Attuso.
(C) It was designed for out-of-town visitors.
(D) It will give live updates during the next festival.

174. The word "introduced" in paragraph 4, line 4, is closest in meaning to

(A) instituted
(B) assigned
(C) presented
(D) generated

175. In which of the positions marked [1], [2], [3], and [4] does the following sentence best belong?

"They also predict that it will make the event more attractive to trucks from outside of the Attuso area."

(A) [1]
(B) [2]
(C) [3]
(D) [4]

GO ON TO THE NEXT PAGE

	E-Mail message
From:	<promotions@aledonshoes.com>
To:	Grant Hudec
Date:	January 29
Subject:	Aledon Shoes Huckley

Dear Mr. Hudec,

We are pleased to announce that, after two years of rapid growth online, Aledon Shoes is launching its first offline location. Aledon Shoes Huckley, located on fashionable Tarpey Street, will open its doors this Saturday. As a loyal customer in the Huckley region, we wanted you to be among the first to know about this exciting development. Come by on opening weekend to collect a free Shoe Cleaner Set with any purchase!

But even if you can't visit us so soon, we encourage you to stop in later between 10 A.M. and 7 P.M., Tuesdays through Sundays. An authority on footwear design will always be on hand to give you an in-person consultation. And, as a proud member of the Huckley City Chamber of Commerce, we'll offer a standing 10% discount to holders of Huckley City Commerce Preferred Customer Cards.

We hope to see you soon.

Sincerely,

Alisa Shipp
CEO, Aledon Shoes

Order Receipt

Aledon Shoes Huckley
907 Tarpey Street

Customer name: Grant Hudec
Customer #: 000325

Date: February 3
Salesclerk: Jillian Stafford

Thank you for shopping at Aledon Shoes Huckley. We will construct the items below using the specifications listed and the sizing measurements we have taken. You may pick up your order on or after Tuesday, February 12.

Model #	Information	Quantity	Price Per Unit	Total
5439	Premium Leather Dress Shoes; black with black stitching	1	$121.00	$121.00
8167	Canvas Sneakers; navy with white soles	1	$108.00	$108.00
3402	Shoe Cleaner Set	1	0.00	$0.00

	Discount	-$0.00
	Total Amount Due	$229.00
	Amount Received	-$229.00
	Balance Due	**$0.00**

Payment type: __x__ Credit Card _____ Cash _____ Other

176. What is mainly being advertised in the e-mail?

(A) A seasonal sale
(B) A line of merchandise
(C) A customer loyalty card
(D) A grand opening

177. According to the e-mail, what is available to Aledon Shoes Huckley customers?

(A) Advice from a specialist
(B) Footwear repair
(C) A 3D foot-scanning device
(D) A variety of matching accessories

178. What is NOT mentioned about Aledon Shoes Huckley?

(A) It is closed one day per week.
(B) It sells custom-made shoes.
(C) It operates a home delivery service.
(D) It grew out of an Internet business.

179. What is indicated about the purchased items?

(A) Ms. Stafford gift-wrapped them.
(B) They are in an extra-narrow width.
(C) They are made of the same material.
(D) Mr. Hudec did not receive them on February 3.

180. What is implied about Mr. Hudec?

(A) He shopped during a sales promotion.
(B) He carries a local commerce card.
(C) He used to reside on Tarpey Street.
(D) He paid for his purchases with cash.

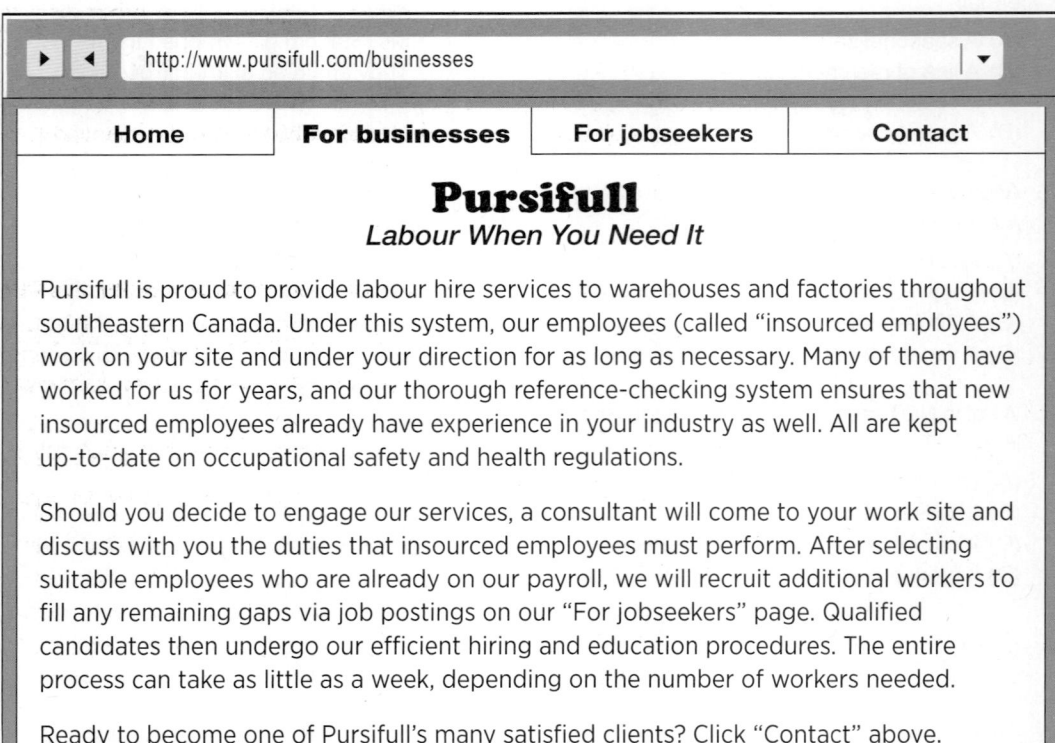

http://www.pursifull.com/businesses

| Home | **For businesses** | For jobseekers | Contact |

Pursifull
Labour When You Need It

Pursifull is proud to provide labour hire services to warehouses and factories throughout southeastern Canada. Under this system, our employees (called "insourced employees") work on your site and under your direction for as long as necessary. Many of them have worked for us for years, and our thorough reference-checking system ensures that new insourced employees already have experience in your industry as well. All are kept up-to-date on occupational safety and health regulations.

Should you decide to engage our services, a consultant will come to your work site and discuss with you the duties that insourced employees must perform. After selecting suitable employees who are already on our payroll, we will recruit additional workers to fill any remaining gaps via job postings on our "For jobseekers" page. Qualified candidates then undergo our efficient hiring and education procedures. The entire process can take as little as a week, depending on the number of workers needed.

Ready to become one of Pursifull's many satisfied clients? Click "Contact" above.

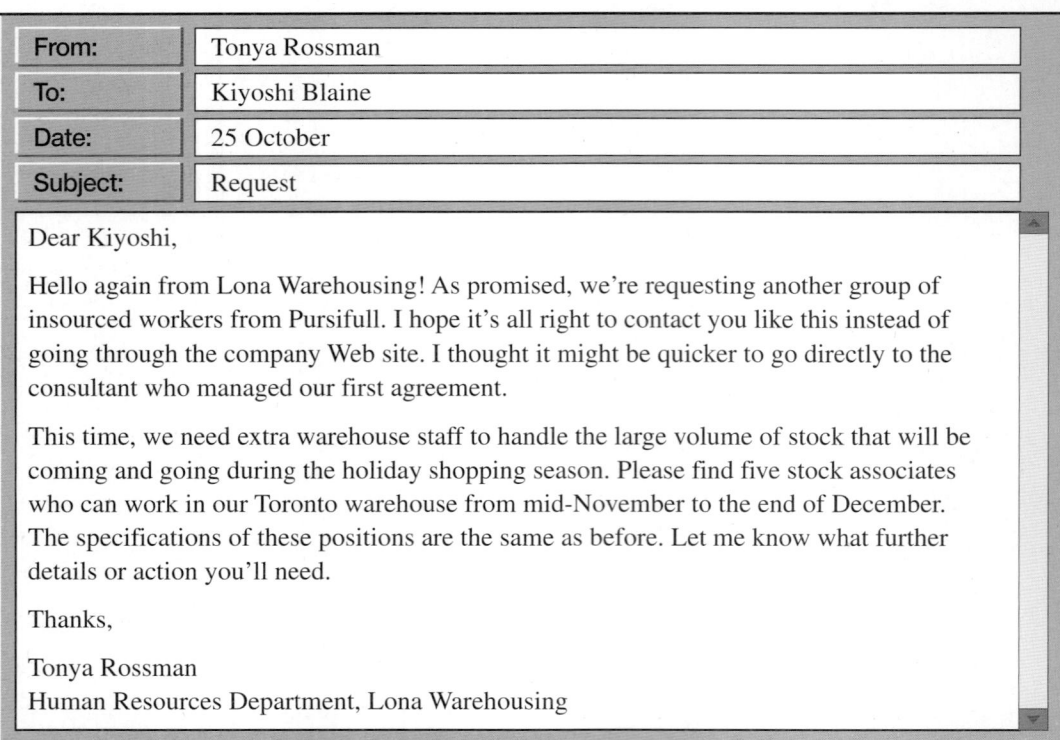

From:	Tonya Rossman
To:	Kiyoshi Blaine
Date:	25 October
Subject:	Request

Dear Kiyoshi,

Hello again from Lona Warehousing! As promised, we're requesting another group of insourced workers from Pursifull. I hope it's all right to contact you like this instead of going through the company Web site. I thought it might be quicker to go directly to the consultant who managed our first agreement.

This time, we need extra warehouse staff to handle the large volume of stock that will be coming and going during the holiday shopping season. Please find five stock associates who can work in our Toronto warehouse from mid-November to the end of December. The specifications of these positions are the same as before. Let me know what further details or action you'll need.

Thanks,

Tonya Rossman
Human Resources Department, Lona Warehousing

181. What is NOT indicated about insourced employees?

(A) They are given safety education.
(B) They have relevant work experience.
(C) They have provided job references.
(D) They are sent all over the country.

182. In the Web page, the word "direction" in paragraph 1, line 3, is closest in meaning to

(A) route
(B) evidence
(C) oversight
(D) recovery

183. According to the Web page, what can be found on Pursifull's Web site?

(A) Job advertisements
(B) Learning resources
(C) Résumés posted by jobseekers
(D) A list of current clients

184. What is implied about Mr. Blaine?

(A) He will train some stock associates.
(B) He was transferred to the Toronto branch of Pursifull.
(C) He will need over a week to fulfill a request.
(D) He has been inside a Lona Warehousing facility.

185. What reason does Ms. Rossman give for her request?

(A) Anticipation of an annual busy period
(B) Difficulty with staffing a new warehouse
(C) The malfunctioning of some machines
(D) The departure of some employees

GO ON TO THE NEXT PAGE

Test 8

http://www.auengineeringconference.co.au/seminars/2204 ▶

Australia Civil Engineering Conference
Seminar Schedule for Friday, 19 June

Click on underlined titles for further information.

9 A.M. – 10:20 A.M.	"Energy-Efficient Railways" Sang-Woo Jeong, South Korea Wing C, Room 102
10:40 A.M. – 12 P.M.	"Materials and Durability" Elsa Koenig, Germany Wing C, Room 105
1:30 P.M. – 2:50 P.M.	"Ethics in Civil Engineering" (Additional fee: AU$30) Jirou Shields, Australia Wing C, Room 103
3:10 P.M. – 4:30 P.M.	"Improving Water Supply Systems" Sylvia Watson, Canada Wing C, Room 102

E-Mail message

From:	Nigel Rollins
To:	Wendy Vincent
Date:	19 June
Subject:	Question

Hi Wendy,

I'm at the Australia Civil Engineering Conference, as you know, and I'm writing to get your opinion on a proposal. Right now, I'm sitting in a seminar about high-performance concrete and other new construction materials. I think we might want to incorporate some of them into the Storvick Bridge project. They could solve the problem we're having with the land on the Gouldley side of the river. When the seminar ends, I'd like to ask the speaker to act as a consultant for the bridge committee. What do you think?

Please get back to me soon, because I don't have much time left for that kind of networking. My train departs early this evening.

Thanks,

Nigel

Storvick Bridge Opens to the Public

SYDNEY (22 April)—Cricket fans now have more ways to get to the Wendell Cup final that will take place next month. Storvick Bridge, which opened to pedestrian and bicycle traffic with a small ceremony yesterday, connects West Cricket Ground with the Cressell neighborhood across the Gilmour River.

The bridge's beautifully-patterned railings enhance visitors' views of the river, while a 25-metre segment at its midpoint can rotate 90 degrees to give a clear way for tall ships to pass through. Local residents and enterprises also appreciate that it links two major cycling paths.

Storvick Bridge represents a great improvement to the region's infrastructure, and will benefit its economy long after the Wendell Cup is over.

---

186. On the Web page, what is suggested about "Improving Water Supply Systems"?

(A) It takes place in the same room as another seminar.
(B) There is an extra fee to register for it.
(C) The speaker is from Australia.
(D) It was originally scheduled for a different day.

187. Whose seminar was Mr. Rollins attending when he wrote the e-mail?

(A) Mr. Jeong's
(B) Ms. Koenig's
(C) Mr. Shields's
(D) Ms. Watson's

188. What does Mr. Rollins mention he intends to do in the evening?

(A) Conduct a seminar
(B) Leave a conference
(C) Speak to an event coordinator
(D) Go to a networking dinner

189. What is probably true about West Cricket Ground?

(A) It is located in Gouldley.
(B) It was built recently.
(C) It always hosts the Wendell Cup.
(D) It is near a conference complex.

190. What is indicated about Storvick Bridge?

(A) It has two lanes for automobiles.
(B) Its railings are decorated with model ships.
(C) It was named for a popular cricket player.
(D) Its center section is movable.

Questions 191-195 refer to the following e-mail, notification message, and article.

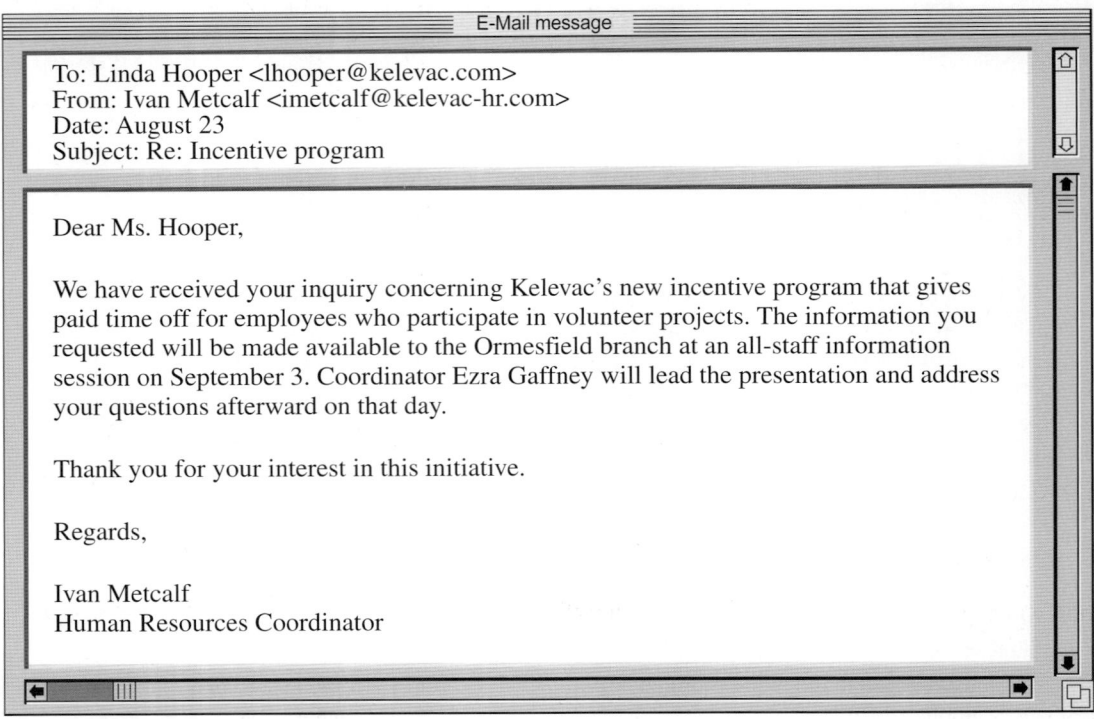

E-Mail message

To: Linda Hooper <lhooper@kelevac.com>
From: Ivan Metcalf <imetcalf@kelevac-hr.com>
Date: August 23
Subject: Re: Incentive program

Dear Ms. Hooper,

We have received your inquiry concerning Kelevac's new incentive program that gives paid time off for employees who participate in volunteer projects. The information you requested will be made available to the Ormesfield branch at an all-staff information session on September 3. Coordinator Ezra Gaffney will lead the presentation and address your questions afterward on that day.

Thank you for your interest in this initiative.

Regards,

Ivan Metcalf
Human Resources Coordinator

Your Time-Off Request Has Been Approved

Name: Linda Hooper   **Department:** Finance

Start Date: October 13   **Time:** 1 P.M.
End Date: October 13   **Time:** 5 P.M.
Total Hours: 4
Type of Time Off: Volunteer Time Off

Comments: I will use the time to help with an event that United Ormesfield is holding on that day. I have not previously used any Volunteer Time Off.

- - - - -   - - - - - -   - - - - - -   - - - - -

Reviewed by: Olivia Clark
Date: October 11
Approved: Yes ☑   No ☐
Comments: Please give notice at least five days in advance next time. Also, remember that you must print out the "Volunteer Service Confirmation Form", have it signed by a member of the organization you are assisting, and submit it to me. Remaining Volunteer Time Off for this year: 36 hours.

Kelevac Gives Back to the Community

ORMESFIELD (October 30) — Ormesfield is now reaping the benefits of a new policy recently adopted by Kelevac. The pharmaceuticals giant, which is based in Thielberg, decided in August to allow its staff one week of paid leave to engage in volunteer work. Many of the 200 employees working at its Ormesfield branch are taking advantage of the opportunity.

According to Chris Jimenez, an official at the branch, Kelevac employees have volunteered for Ormesfield Beach clean-up efforts and helped United Ormesfield put on an auction earlier this month to raise money for its community food bank.

Tristan Liu, a quality assurance assistant, has signed up for a program providing tutoring for struggling students at Ormesfield schools. "I just completed the orientation process, and I can't wait to get started," he said.

Mr. Jimenez predicts that the number of volunteers will continue to grow as employees hear about their coworkers' rewarding experiences.

191. What is the purpose of the e-mail?

(A) To report on the success of an initiative
(B) To thank Ms. Hooper for signing up for a program
(C) To urge Ms. Hooper to wait for some information
(D) To suggest volunteering to give a presentation

192. In the notification message, the word "holding" in paragraph 1, line 2, is closest in meaning to

(A) presiding over
(B) remaining true
(C) grasping
(D) enduring

193. What did Ms. Hooper most likely do during her time off?

(A) Cleaned up a local beach
(B) Organized shelves in a food bank
(C) Joined an orientation session
(D) Assisted with a fundraiser

194. What does the article indicate about Kelevac?

(A) Its headquarters are in Ormesfield.
(B) Its staff are eligible for a week of vacation leave.
(C) It acquired another company in August.
(D) It is in a healthcare-related industry.

195. What is probably true about Mr. Liu?

(A) He replied to an e-mail from Mr. Metcalf.
(B) He attended a meeting led by Mr. Gaffney.
(C) He is a member of Mr. Jimenez's department.
(D) He finished high school in Ormesfield.

GO ON TO THE NEXT PAGE

http://www.underbrinktours.com/tours-by-theme/city-tour-b

| Home | Attractions Overview | **Tours by Theme** | Tours by Length | FAQ |

City Tour B

As one of our two-day general city tours, City Tour B affords a comprehensive introduction to Underbrink in a relatively short time. It offers all the same activities as City Tour A, but requires participants to arrange their own accommodations. They are picked up and dropped off at Lowis Station, which is near many major hotels.

City Tour B starts with a walk through Underbrink's historical Bristaw neighborhood. An afternoon visit to Schimming Hill, the home of Beth Estepp, will delight fans of her novels, while giving plenty to see to non-fans as well. In the evening, participants will cruise down the Staylen River. The second day boasts a trip to the Denato Art Museum and a bus ride through nearby Staylen Valley. Each of these activities is led by a different specialist guide, leaving the tour director free to assist tour participants as necessary. Throughout the tour, various lunch and dinner options are provided.

The price of this tour varies depending on the season. Click here to see information on pricing and availability.

Underbrink Tours Customer Satisfaction Survey

Tour: City Tour A   **Name:** Asa Sloman

	Poor	Fair	Good	Excellent
Accommodations			X	
Activities				X
Guides				X
Meals		X		
Transportation			X	

Comments:

I had some trouble with the heaviness of the food. In particular, the lunch we had in Bristaw made me feel so unwell that I had to rest in the hotel instead of going to Schimming Hill. But all of the activities that I did participate in were very enjoyable. I think it's great that you have specialist guides. Each one really knew a lot about their subject. I certainly plan to recommend Underbrink Tours to friends.

```
┌─────────────────────── *E-mail* ───────────────────────┐
```

From:	Lance Ntchobo <l.ntchobo@underbrinktours.com>
To:	All tour guides
Date:	April 27
Subject:	Survey results

Hi everyone,

The customer survey forms we've been collecting have now given us a good sense of customers' opinions about our offerings. First, I'm happy to tell you all that you're consistently praised for your deep understanding of the attractions on our tours. Well done!

That said, there have been some comments about your explanations lacking excitement and humor. I'm hoping we can all meet in our offices on Monday, May 9, at 4 P.M. to talk about ways to resolve this issue. Please respond to this e-mail to confirm your attendance.

Sincerely,

Lance Ntchobo
Executive Director, Underbrink Tours

---

196. What is indicated about City Tour B?

(A) It begins with a tour of Lowis Station.
(B) It does not include lodging.
(C) It is longer than City Tour A.
(D) It is not administered in every season.

197. Which activity was Mr. Sloman unable to participate in?

(A) An outdoor walking tour
(B) An evening river cruise
(C) A visit to a famous house
(D) An art museum outing

198. What is suggested about Mr. Sloman?

(A) He has made plans to meet friends in Underbrink.
(B) His opinion of the guides is mostly shared by others.
(C) His survey form was submitted on April 26.
(D) He had a special meal option during his tour.

199. In the e-mail, the word "sense" in paragraph 1, line 1, is closest in meaning to

(A) capacity
(B) logic
(C) doubt
(D) idea

200. What does Mr. Ntchobo want to discuss at a meeting?

(A) How to make tours more entertaining
(B) Who can give a tour of a new attraction
(C) Whether to change the order of an itinerary
(D) Why the number of customers is decreasing

Stop! This is the end of the test. If you finish before time is called, you may go back to Parts 5, 6, and 7 and check your work.

TEST 9

READING TEST

In the Reading test, you will read a variety of texts and answer several different types of reading comprehension questions. The entire Reading test will last 75 minutes. There are three parts, and directions are given for each part. You are encouraged to answer as many questions as possible within the time allowed.

You must mark your answers on the separate answer sheet. Do not write your answers in your test book.

PART 5

Directions: A word or phrase is missing in each of the sentences below. Four answer choices are given below each sentence. Select the best answer to complete the sentence. Then mark the letter (A), (B), (C), or (D) on your answer sheet.

---

101. Invited guests must confirm their intention to attend the banquet ------- the end of the week.

(A) behind
(B) by
(C) on
(D) across

102. Applicants will be asked to provide proof of ------- accounting certification at the first interview.

(A) they
(B) them
(C) their
(D) themselves

103. ------- resembling sculptures from previous eras, Mr. Florence's artwork depicts everyday scenes.

(A) Closer
(B) Close
(C) Closely
(D) Closest

104. Mr. Parza will take part in a contract ------- in Singapore to finalize the details of the acquisition.

(A) negotiate
(B) negotiation
(C) negotiates
(D) negotiator

105. The audience gave an enthusiastic round of applause when the musicians stepped ------- the stage.

(A) onto
(B) until
(C) with
(D) as

106. Hikers should bring ------- they need with them, as there are no shops along the trail.

(A) wherever
(B) this
(C) everything
(D) then

107. Upon examination, Ms. Seo discovered that the figures her department ------- last week were incorrect.

(A) has calculated
(B) calculates
(C) will calculate
(D) calculated

108. Partnering with Apor Footwear could be a profitable ------- for Pasadena Department Store thanks to the retailer's excellent reputation.

(A) atmosphere
(B) content
(C) arrangement
(D) source

109. ------- the merger is authorized by the board members, an official valuation of the company must be made.

(A) Before
(B) Despite
(C) Nor
(D) How

110. Fairnay Manufacturing ------- standards set by the National Health and Safety Association regarding exposure to chemicals.

(A) insisted
(B) conducted
(C) adopted
(D) underwent

111. The increase in mobile phone usage brought ------- the need for stricter laws against texting while driving.

(A) among
(B) toward
(C) down
(D) about

112. Visitors to Bellucci Orchard can become active ------- in the harvest process by registering for a VIP tour.

(A) participants
(B) participate
(C) participatory
(D) participation

113. The resort offers a daily pass and a season ticket, ------- of which can be used to access the ski lift.

(A) either
(B) it
(C) those
(D) what

114. The company's CEO reacted ------- to the news that stockholders had called for a last-minute meeting.

(A) predictable
(B) predictably
(C) predicts
(D) prediction

115. An extensive construction project on Highway 17 has ------- the exit ramps to improve motorist safety.

(A) broad
(B) broaden
(C) broadly
(D) broadened

116. The community basketball tournament is ------- supported by city government funds, with local businesses making up the remainder.

(A) partially
(B) approximately
(C) overly
(D) briefly

117. Only employees with ------- sales of $30,000 for domestic and international goods will be eligible for promotions.

(A) combines
(B) combined
(C) to have combined
(D) to combine

118. The upcoming city council meeting is intended for residents ------- wish to voice concerns about the proposed commercial district expansion.

(A) several
(B) others
(C) but
(D) who

119. Although the costs of the top-selling hybrid vehicles differ -------, the gas mileage results are nearly the same.

(A) signify
(B) significant
(C) significantly
(D) signifying

120. Many passengers choose to travel solely with a carry-on bag ------- than pay the required fee for checked luggage.

(A) whenever
(B) rather
(C) better
(D) regardless

GO ON TO THE NEXT PAGE

Test 9

121. Driven by demand for ways to share information quickly, a number of new social media sites ------- in the past year alone.

(A) to emerge
(B) are emerged
(C) have emerged
(D) will emerge

122. An online education platform, Eleshade allows users to take technology courses from the ------- of their own home.

(A) appreciation
(B) decoration
(C) layout
(D) comfort

123. Management chose to ------- the office picnic due to a forecast of adverse weather.

(A) call off
(B) fill out
(C) back up
(D) hand in

124. The San Marino Ballet Company will perform at Welburn Theater, and troupe members will sign autographs -------.

(A) somewhat
(B) afterward
(C) alike
(D) otherwise

125. Attendees of the International Unity Summit come from ------- cultural backgrounds and speak a variety of languages.

(A) ongoing
(B) conscious
(C) adjustable
(D) diverse

126. The report demonstrated that rush hour traffic downtown and the average congestion on Nicall Bridge are roughly -------.

(A) compares
(B) comparable
(C) comparing
(D) comparison

127. Each club official must remain in office ------- to the expiration date of his or her term of office until a successor can be found.

(A) prospective
(B) subsequent
(C) likely
(D) eager

128. When she concludes her assignment overseas on June 30, Ms. Adrian ------- over one hundred production facilities.

(A) would inspect
(B) will be inspected
(C) is inspecting
(D) will have inspected

129. Items that do not meet customers' expectations may be returned for a refund or exchanged for merchandise of ------- value.

(A) competent
(B) receptive
(C) initial
(D) equivalent

130. University administration asked the committee to analyze the ------- of the change for faculty and students.

(A) implications
(B) alliances
(C) aptitudes
(D) supplements

PART 6

Directions: Read the texts that follow. A word, phrase, or sentence is missing in parts of each text. Four answer choices for each question are given below the text. Select the best answer to complete the text. Then mark the letter (A), (B), (C), or (D) on your answer sheet.

Questions 131-134 refer to the following notice.

NOTICE OF CONSTRUCTION

Routine maintenance work on the rail lines ------- for October 3 to 7 on Line 3 of the Metropolitan
                                            131.

Subway System. ------- who is traveling during the project should check the updated schedules
                132.

posted online and throughout the stations, as there will be some delays and interruptions. No trains

will be running between Sunnyvale Station and Campbell Station. There will be a replacement bus

service operating regularly. -------. If you need any assistance or have concerns about the work,
                             133.

please speak to a staff member. We will try to minimize the inconvenience ------- we can.
                                                                          134.

---

131. (A) is planned
     (B) was being planned
     (C) to plan
     (D) has been planning

132. (A) Other
     (B) One another
     (C) Those
     (D) Anyone

133. (A) We appreciate the patience you showed
        during the project.
     (B) Passengers may use it by presenting a
        valid train ticket.
     (C) The subway system transports commuters
        daily.
     (D) The route depends on your driver's license
        category.

134. (A) so that
     (B) as much as
     (C) aside from
     (D) whether

GO ON TO THE NEXT PAGE

To: All Newhall Inc. Employees
From: Marvin Montano, Branch Manager
Date: April 14
Re: Brian Whitaker

Brian Whitaker will be retiring from the position of director on the last day of this month. In spite of this, you will still see him around the office regularly, as he will work for the company part-time in an ------- role. This will involve providing financial advice as well as recommending ------- to existing **135.** **136.** contracts. By using ------- expertise even after retirement, the company can ensure profitability going **137.** forward. Although Mr. Whitaker will continue working for us, we want to acknowledge the contributions he has made in a formal celebration. -------. We hope to see you there. **138.**

135. (A) adequate
(B) estimated
(C) advisory
(D) equal

136. (A) revised
(B) revisable
(C) revisions
(D) revises

137. (A) his
(B) their
(C) our
(D) your

138. (A) We couldn't have reached our goals without the staff.
(B) A reception will be held at 4 P.M. on April 30.
(C) Several new clients have enrolled with us.
(D) He developed policies to improve efficiency.

Questions 139-142 refer to the following advertisement.

Get your tickets to see Silvana Russo!

The Ramke Gallery is pleased to host a talk by painter Silvana Russo on June 2 at 7 P.M. ------. Ms.
                                                                                              139.
Russo does not often make public appearances, but during the event she will talk about her ------
                                                                                              140.
from a hotel housekeeper to a world-renowned artist, a career path that has resulted in decades of

successful art installations. Following the talk, she will respond to questions from the audience.

Audience members who prefer handing in their questions in advance ------ them by e-mail to info@
                                                                     141.
ramkegallery.com no later than May 30. To get your ticket to see this ------ artist in person, call the
                                                                      142.
Ramke Gallery at 555-0144.

---

139. (A) This is a rare opportunity for art lovers.
      (B) Each one is signed by the artist herself.
      (C) These paintings are valued in the
          thousands.
      (D) Regular lectures help to inform the
          public.

140. (A) involvement
      (B) absence
      (C) journey
      (D) release

141. (A) will submit
      (B) be submitted
      (C) must submit
      (D) had submitted

142. (A) rejected
      (B) originated
      (C) undiscovered
      (D) talented

Test 9

GO ON TO THE NEXT PAGE

Questions 143-146 refer to the following e-mail.

To: Venita Yang <vyang@crestonco.com>
From: Sebastian Nadeau <snadeau@crestonco.com>
Date: February 20
Subject: Staff meeting

Dear Venita,

I noticed that you were not able to attend the weekly staff meeting. ------. The meeting was mainly
                                                                      143.
centered on plans to have a new logo designed, as ours is ------ similar to that of Terilyn
                                                         144.
Enterprises. We want to set ourselves ------ from our competitors with a new logo. Our in-house
                                      145.
graphics team will ------ with designers from BC Art in order to produce a number of samples.
                   146.
Employees will have the opportunity to share their opinions on the samples at a later time.

Sebastian

143. (A) Even so, attendance is mandatory for
         everyone.
     (B) It has been rescheduled for Friday at
         4 P.M.
     (C) Therefore, I wanted to give you an
         update.
     (D) Your presentation was extremely
         informative.

144. (A) strikingly
     (B) strike
     (C) struck
     (D) striking

145. (A) beyond
     (B) against
     (C) upon
     (D) apart

146. (A) identify
     (B) collaborate
     (C) uphold
     (D) coincide

PART 7

Directions: In this part you will read a selection of texts, such as magazine and newspaper articles, e-mails, and instant messages. Each text or set of texts is followed by several questions. Select the best answer for each question and mark the letter (A), (B), (C), or (D) on your answer sheet.

Questions 147-148 refer to the following advertisement.

Do you have a high-school diploma and consider yourself to be a great team player?

If this sounds like you, why not to work at Sandhill & Co.? We are the leading law firm in Wisconsin, representing a client base of over 50 large corporations. We consider our expert legal team to be the finest in the country.

As our business has experienced continued success for a sustained period, we are looking to expand our team further. As such, a position is available at the reception desk of our newly opened Milwaukee office. Your responsibilities will include greeting walk-in clients, answering the phone, corresponding with clients via e-mail and mail, and assisting our legal professionals.

To apply for this position, please send an up-to-date résumé and cover letter to our human resources manager, Andy Stewart, at astewart@sandhill.com by March 31. Shortlisted applicants will be contacted by telephone by April 10.

147. What position is being advertised?

(A) PR assistant
(B) Lawyer
(C) Receptionist
(D) HR manager

148. What are interested individuals encouraged to do?

(A) Send an e-mail
(B) Complete an online form
(C) Visit the business
(D) Make a phone call

GO ON TO THE NEXT PAGE

Questions 149-150 refer to the following memo.

MEMO

From: Sue Paulsen, Personnel Manager
To: Remley Bank Employees
Date: March 2
Re: Stanley Cooper's Retirement Party

To all employees,

As you know, Mr. Cooper's retirement party was due to take place this Friday evening at the Diamond Ballroom downtown. Unfortunately, I have had to cancel this reservation and make a new one elsewhere, as the guest list has grown too large. Therefore, the event will now be held in the banquet hall of the Marigold Hotel. Frank Grimey has spoken directly with the hotel manager, and he promises that the food served at the party will be of the finest quality. The music will be provided by local band *The Funky Flutes*. Frank will visit each of you at your desks on Wednesday to obtain your menu preferences. As many of you know, Mr. Cooper has been the head of the sales team for over thirty years, so let's make sure we make Friday an evening to remember!

Thanks,

Sue Paulsen

---

149. Why was the memo sent?
   (A) To inform staff of alterations to arrangements
   (B) To encourage employees to bring refreshments to an event
   (C) To announce that an event has been canceled
   (D) To request suggestions for event entertainment

150. What is Frank Grimey planning to do on Wednesday?
   (A) Contact a catering manager
   (B) Practice a musical performance
   (C) Attend a sales meeting
   (D) Speak to staff about dinner options

Conference Hall C, Twittledon Convention Center
Thursday, November 28, 8:00 P.M.

The Twittledon town council would like to invite all residents to attend an awards ceremony at the Twittledon Convention Center this coming Thursday. This event is to mark the achievements of our young volunteers, whose hard work has included clearing trash from our streets and providing a catering service to the elderly. Twittledon mayor Tony Gribbons will present the awards.

On Thursday, anyone who comes to the evening will receive:
- A complimentary soft drink
- A copy of the most recent town council newsletter
- A booklet containing discount vouchers for a number of local businesses

Tickets are expected to sell out fast. To reserve your place, please e-mail Jo Buckwheat at j.buckwheat@twittledontc.net.

---

151. What is the main purpose of the event?

(A) To mark the opening of a catering company
(B) To outline a new trash collection policy
(C) To discuss planning permission for local businesses
(D) To celebrate the achievements of volunteers

152. What is NOT indicated about the event?

(A) Elderly residents may enter free of charge.
(B) It will be attended by the town mayor.
(C) Tickets can be reserved by e-mail.
(D) Drinks will be provided.

GO ON TO THE NEXT PAGE

Questions 153-154 refer to the following text message chain.

PETER REDMOND   2:52 P.M.
Hi, Susan. I didn't see you at this morning's training workshop. All staff had to attend. Did you forget about it? Don't worry, you can make it up next month.

SUSAN BARKLEY   2:54 P.M.
Hi, Peter. I was on my way to the meeting this morning, but I got stuck in a traffic jam. There was an accident involving two trucks, so I couldn't make it in on time.

PETER REDMOND   3:02 P.M.
Oh, I heard about that on the news. That's a valid excuse. Shall I book you in for the training workshop in September?

SUSAN BARKLEY   3:06 P.M.
I've checked the dates of that one, and it seems I am attending a trade fair on the day of the workshops. How about I attend one in October?

PETER REDMOND   3:21 P.M.
Sure thing. I'll contact Robert in HR and get him to make the necessary arrangements.

SUSAN BARKLEY   3:33 P.M.
Thanks, Peter. Could you fax across the minutes from this morning's meeting?

PETER REDMOND   3:38 P.M.
You'll have to ask Caroline for those. I believe she was in charge of taking them this morning.

153. What is indicated about Ms. Barkley?

(A) She is currently attending a trade fair.
(B) She led a workshop in the morning.
(C) She was late for work.
(D) She was in a car accident.

154. At 3:21 P.M., what does Mr. Redmond mean when he writes, "Sure thing"?

(A) He believes that the HR manager is in his office.
(B) He is accepting Ms. Barkley's request for a document.
(C) He is certain that a trade fair will produce many sales.
(D) He is agreeing that Ms. Barkley can attend an October workshop.

GO ON TO THE NEXT PAGE

Test 9

The Stanberg Museum for Arts & Crafts this week announced it has taken out a contract to improve facilities for all patrons. —[1]—. Ms. Jessie Katzen, a representative of the museum, told reporters that this was made possible through a grant from local business tycoon Charlie Hamilton. —[2]—. The substantial sum of money donated will fund the building of a new museum wing, in which the museum plans to house its collection of arts and crafts from the Renaissance era. —[3]—.

Ms. Katzen also noted that the investment came at the perfect time for the Stanberg Museum. Speculation had been mounting that the museum was experiencing financial difficulties, with its twenty employees fearing it would not be viable for it to continue operating if the situation wasn't rectified. —[4]—. Now both local residents and tourists will be free to enjoy the stunning works on display for many years to come.

155. What is the main topic of the article?

(A) The life of a famous artist
(B) The expansion of a museum
(C) A town hall meeting
(D) The art of the Renaissance era

156. What is suggested about the Stanberg Museum?

(A) It currently employs over one hundred staff members.
(B) It is changing its name to the Charlie Hamilton Museum.
(C) Its exhibits have been moved to a different building.
(D) It was recently assumed to be near the point of bankruptcy.

157. In which of the positions marked [1], [2], [3], and [4] does the following sentence best belong?

"Some of these pieces have been held in storage for several months due to a lack of space."

(A) [1]
(B) [2]
(C) [3]
(D) [4]

Questions 158-160 refer to the following memo.

To: Robert Walsh, Trevor Partridge, Annie Taylor
From: Kerry Grahams, Training Officer
Date: August 3
Re: Mandatory Training

For all of us at Remical Ltd., it is vital that we constantly improve and update our facilities in order to remain at the cutting edge of field innovations. Yesterday, we received a delivery of a large volume of lab equipment. This includes new measuring beakers, test tubes, and microscopes. There is also a new high-powered heating device. Once this equipment is installed, you will be able to use it to conduct your experiments. However, before being able to use this expensive piece of machinery, all staff will need to undergo mandatory training as is stated in your employee handbook. Training will be conducted on Friday. In the meantime, please familiarize yourselves with the agenda for Friday that I have attached. As you can see, we are due to start at 9:00 A.M. Please ensure you arrive promptly at this time.

Our safety inspector Bill Kenright has also issued us some new safety apparel to use within the lab. These luminous yellow outfits are important, as they have been tested and found to be heatproof. You can choose from small, medium, or large sizes of safety gear. Please let me know your preference by e-mail, and I will bring the items on Friday.

Regards,

Kerry Grahams

158. Who is the memo most likely intended for?

(A) Scientists
(B) Delivery drivers
(C) Safety inspectors
(D) Training officers

159. What has Ms. Grahams included with the memo?

(A) An invoice
(B) A training schedule
(C) New equipment
(D) An employee handbook

160. What is NOT indicated about the safety apparel?

(A) It is available in a range of sizes.
(B) It is brightly colored.
(C) It is heat resistant.
(D) It will be paid for by employees.

GO ON TO THE NEXT PAGE

November 1 (Jonesville) — After much speculation surrounding the future of the plot of land that is the current site of the Jonesville Automotive factory, property developer Righthome Ltd. today purchased the land for a fee estimated to be at around $20 million. Upon purchasing the land, Righthome immediately submitted blueprints to the city's planning department in order to receive permission to build 100 luxury condos on the site. These properties will be targeted at the many young professionals moving to Jonesville to work in the thriving legal sector here.

Righthome Ltd. was founded by Miguel Lopez twenty years ago. After retiring, he trained as his successor his son, Pablo Lopez, who is now CEO of the company. At a press conference yesterday, Pablo Lopez gave further details on the development project. According to Mr. Lopez, a five-story condominium building named Melwood Grove will be constructed. In addition, a communal swimming pool and gym facilities will be built on the site for all residents to use. Mr. Lopez also confirmed that each apartment will be provided with complimentary high-speed Internet access. He finished the conference by outlining the timescale of the project, which he hopes will be completed within eighteen months. This latest development is just one of many in recent years that have yielded the dramatic rejuvenation of the Jonesville town center.

161. What is the article mainly about?

    (A) The construction of a car factory
    (B) The founding of a law firm
    (C) The opening of a gym
    (D) The building of some new structure

162. Who most likely is Pablo Lopez?

    (A) A lawyer
    (B) A town planner
    (C) A property developer
    (D) An Internet salesman

163. What is NOT indicated about Melwood Grove?

    (A) It contains leisure facilities.
    (B) It will require keycard access.
    (C) It will be targeted at young professionals.
    (D) It will have free Internet access.

GO ON TO THE NEXT PAGE

Test 9

Questions 164-167 refer to the following online chat discussion.

DALE WINSOR	4:12 P.M.
Good afternoon, Wayne. I've just been on a conference call with our directors. They are really upset about the lack of progress on building our warehouse.	
WAYNE HENNESY	4:14 P.M.
Did they say why exactly they are unhappy? I thought the timeframe for completion was fairly flexible.	
DALE WINSOR	4:21 P.M.
It was, but they have since set a deadline of June 1. Otherwise, we won't be able to store enough clothes, and it will take longer to deliver our clothes to customers.	
WAYNE HENNESY	4:29 P.M.
Wait a minute. I'll add Beth…	
(BETH TOADIE JOINED THE GROUP CHAT)	4:30 P.M.
WAYNE HENNESY	4:34 P.M.
Hi, Beth. I think we're going to have to source a new construction company for the warehouse project. The current one is struggling to meet the deadline.	
BETH TOADIE	4:40 P.M.
That's a pain in the neck. It took a long time to agree on the contract with the current firm. Were the directors firmly set on changing constructors?	
DALE WINSOR	4:46 P.M.
I'm afraid so. I tried to explain that the changes to the deadline were unreasonable, but they wouldn't change their minds.	
BETH TOADIE	4:50 P.M.
I see. Well, I'll have to tell them my opinion on the matter at the meeting next week.	
DALE WINSOR	4:57 P.M.
Good luck. If anyone can convince them, it's you!	

164. What is the main topic of the discussion?

(A) The arrangements for a meeting
(B) The appointing of a director
(C) The construction of a warehouse
(D) The manufacturing of some clothing

165. What is one issue the directors are concerned about?

(A) Terms of a contract may be changed.
(B) Delivery times may be increased.
(C) Building materials may become more expensive.
(D) Planning permission may not be granted.

166. What can be inferred about Ms. Toadie?

(A) She is involved in clothing design.
(B) She conducted a conference call earlier today.
(C) She is the manager of a construction firm.
(D) She is meeting with some directors next week.

167. At 4:40 P.M., what does Ms. Toadie mean when she writes, "That's a pain in the neck"?

(A) She would prefer to take a break.
(B) She believes a construction site is too far away.
(C) She thinks a change will be inconvenient.
(D) She is concerned about a budget limit.

GO ON TO THE NEXT PAGE

Test 9

◀ ▶

| **Our Packages** | **CEO Profile** | **Customer Testimonials** | **Destinations** |

We at Touchstar have 25 years of experience helping all of our clients to fulfill their dreams. We are well known throughout the local community for providing tour packages of supreme quality, and our customers often go on to recommend us to friends. —[1]—. Under the direction of our CEO, Bob Anderson, we are confident that our staff will be able to assist you in finding something to suit you, whether you are a group of young friends or a senior couple.

When making your choice, we recommend taking plenty of time to reflect on what you want from your summer. Individuals with very young families may find some of our more adventurous packages unsuitable. Likewise, those in search of an adrenaline-packed summer may have a disappointing experience with one of our family packages. We have dedicated experts available 24 hours a day to answer any queries that you may have before booking. —[2]—.

This summer, we are pleased to announce a range of different options. Our Caribbean Dreamliner package allows you to visit several islands over the course of a week, and engage in a number of leisure activities. This package is often popular with older travelers who enjoy whale-watching and bird-spotting. —[3]—. Conversely, our Tropical Rush package allows thrill seekers to take part in a number of extreme hobbies, including skydiving and bungee jumping. Our Mini Adventurer deal is best suited for young families, and it includes accommodation at a 5-star resort complete with a private swimming pool. Expert guides will be present on all packages to ensure the smooth running of activities. —[4]—.

168. What kind of company most likely is Touchstar?

(A) A tour company
(B) A family law firm
(C) An accountancy firm
(D) A newspaper office

169. What does the Web page suggest that customers do?

(A) Consider their goals carefully
(B) Read testimonials from customers
(C) Request an experienced employee
(D) Confirm a payment by phone

170. What is NOT indicated about Touchstar?

(A) It has been in business for over two decades.
(B) It offers some exciting activities.
(C) It has received favorable media reviews.
(D) It caters to clients from a range of age groups.

171. In which of the positions marked [1], [2], [3], and [4] does the following sentence best belong?

"They are standing by to take your call."

(A) [1]
(B) [2]
(C) [3]
(D) [4]

The Baltimore Herald
Induction Schedule

Location: Herald Offices Training Suite – Level B
Date: Monday, March 19

Why? It is vital that you quickly become familiar with the various departments of our newspaper company, and the work that they do, before commencing your role. This induction package has been designed as the most efficient way to provide you with this experience.

Agenda: The schedule for the day has been designed by executive director Dennis Furman and has been included below. If you have any questions about the agenda, please call Mr. Furman at extension 3299.

Time	Activity	Additional Details	Location
9:00 – 10:00	Meet and Greet	Staff members will be introduced to the executive director in person.	Breezdale Conference Room
10:00 – 12:00	Writing Style	An introduction to the formatting styles and techniques commonly employed by our newspaper.	Seminar Room C
1:00 – 3:00	Legislation	A discussion over our legal obligation on issues such as confidentiality. Tea and coffee served.	Yammin Media Suite
3:00 – 4:00	Systems and Control	Instruction in using a variety of software, including our word-processing, database, and spreadsheet packages.	The Levy Suite
4:00 – 5:00	Field Integrity	Brian Cranfield will give a talk on how to ensure that the reputation of the newspaper and the ethics of the field are maintained when interviewing subjects.	Seminar Room C

172. What is the main purpose of the March 19 event?

(A) To advertise vacant positions
(B) To gather information to be used in a story
(C) To provide training to new employees
(D) To collect statistics on newspaper circulation

173. Where will staff participate in activities related to computing?

(A) The Levy Suite
(B) Breezdale Conference Room
(C) Seminar Room C
(D) The Yammin Media Suite

174. When will some beverages be available?

(A) Between 9:00 and 10:00
(B) Between 10:00 and 12:00
(C) Between 1:00 and 3:00
(D) Between 3:00 and 4:00

175. What will event attendees most likely do at 9 A.M.?

(A) Listen to a lecture by Brian Cranfield
(B) Discuss legal obligations
(C) Meet Dennis Furman
(D) Practice writing an article

Test 9

GO ON TO THE NEXT PAGE

Huffleton Food Market a Huge Hit

· ·

Huffleton, IL (July 15)—Huffleton opened the doors of its long-awaited food market last week. The first-ever session of the market, which organizers now hope to run on the last weekend of every month, was deemed a huge success, attracting over 10,000 visitors to the town on a gloriously sunny day. Types of food sold by vendors included German sausage, French cheese, British fish and chips, and Turkish kebabs. The market was part of an initiative by the town mayor to attract higher volumes of tourists to the area. To promote the event, a local film star was recruited to distribute complimentary hamburgers to patrons.

In addition to the market, several food-related events were also held. The most popular of these was the cooking demonstration by Japanese chef Akemi Suki. Mr. Suki delighted crowds by displaying his expert slicing techniques before cooking pieces of fish in oil to produce mesmerizing, brightly colored flames. Another popular event was the cooking contest. Competition categories included making the best soup, chicken dish, sandwich, and cake, with prizes awarded to the winning chef in each category.

Mr. Akemi Suki
86 Horston Avenue
Huffleton, IL 60415

Dear Mr. Suki,

Firstly, I would like to state how much I enjoyed my time at the Huffleton Food Market, which I attended last weekend. My family and I enjoyed eating lots of amazing food—we still can't believe we were served hamburgers by the famous Dale Springfield!

The reason I am writing is that I am currently in the process of opening a Japanese restaurant in the downtown area of Huffleton and would very much like it if you would join our team.

I'll provide some further details about my company. We just opened last year, and we serve a range of Asian cuisine inspired by flavor profiles from all over the continent. We already have recruited chef Sally Bergstrom to produce our desserts. You may remember she won a related competition at the recent food market. If you were to come on board, I am confident that this venture would be extremely successful for all of us.

I feel that we have much to talk about. I would appreciate it if you could give me a call on 560-2219-8282 as soon as you are able.

All the best,

Adele Walsh

Adele Walsh
Far Eastern Restaurant

176. What is indicated about the Huffleton Food Market?

(A) It was attended by the mayor.
(B) It was open to town residents only.
(C) It had never been held before.
(D) It was postponed due to bad weather.

177. In the article, the word "run" in paragraph 1, line 2, is closest in meaning to

(A) sprint
(B) flow
(C) compete
(D) operate

178. What is indicated about Mr. Springfield?

(A) He is a film star.
(B) He is the town mayor.
(C) He is a renowned chef.
(D) He was born in Germany.

179. Why did Ms. Walsh get in contact with Mr. Suki?

(A) To make a complaint
(B) To offer him a job
(C) To ask his advice on a menu
(D) To invite him to dinner

180. Which competition did Ms. Bergstrom most likely win?

(A) Best ice cream
(B) Best soup
(C) Best chicken dish
(D) Best cake

GO ON TO THE NEXT PAGE

To:	inquiries@homecomfort.net
From:	cmcree@hnmail.com
Date:	September 2, 3:49 P.M.
Subject:	Recent Purchase
Attachment:	📎 invoice

Dear Sir or Madam,

Last week, I ordered a new kitchen unit from Home Comfort's furnishing department. I was ecstatic with the prompt installation of the unit. The fittings team visited my house for two days this week and completed the installation on schedule. Nevertheless, I noticed one piece (#9422) has a large scratch across its surface, which is obviously unacceptable. The item's style meets my expectations, and I would therefore like an identical replacement installed at your earliest convenience. Please find my receipt attached to this e-mail. My account number is AG5929.

Just to note, I am going on vacation in two weeks, so I would really like this issue resolved by then. Nobody would be at home to let in the installation team after this period, so I would prefer it to be taken care of prior to my travels. Thanks in advance for your assistance.

Sincerely,

Charlie McRee

RECEIPT

Home Comfort
18 Greenfield Park
Seattle, WA 98107
United States

Order Date: August 25
Order No: 92919
Installation Date(s): August 29–30

Client Billing and Delivery Address

Name:	Charlie McRee	Account No: AG5929
Address:	302 Black Forest Avenue	Telephone: 501-533-6669
City:	Portland	
County/State:	OR 97230	
Country:	United States	

Items Purchased

#3218	Marble Kitchen Counter	$800
#7032	(24 Pack) Granite Floor Tiles	$400
#9422	Metallic Kitchen Sink	$350
#1305	Quickburn Gas Stove	$900

Subtotal: $2,450
Installation Fee: $300
Total: $2,750

Thank you for choosing Home Comfort!

181. What is the purpose of the e-mail?

(A) To report a change of address
(B) To demand a refund
(C) To provide some directions
(D) To request a replacement item

182. What does Mr. McRee say pleased him?

(A) The quality of the items
(B) The speed of the installation
(C) The friendliness of the sales staff
(D) The ease of using a Web site

183. In the e-mail, the phrase "meets" in paragraph 1, line 5, is closest in meaning to

(A) gathers
(B) introduces
(C) agrees
(D) satisfies

184. What item purchased by Mr. McRee is specifically referred to in the e-mail?

(A) Marble Kitchen Counter
(B) Granite Floor Tiles
(C) Metallic Kitchen Sink
(D) Quickburn Gas Stove

185. How much extra did Mr. McRee pay to have some items installed?

(A) $300
(B) $350
(C) $900
(D) $2,750

GO ON TO THE NEXT PAGE

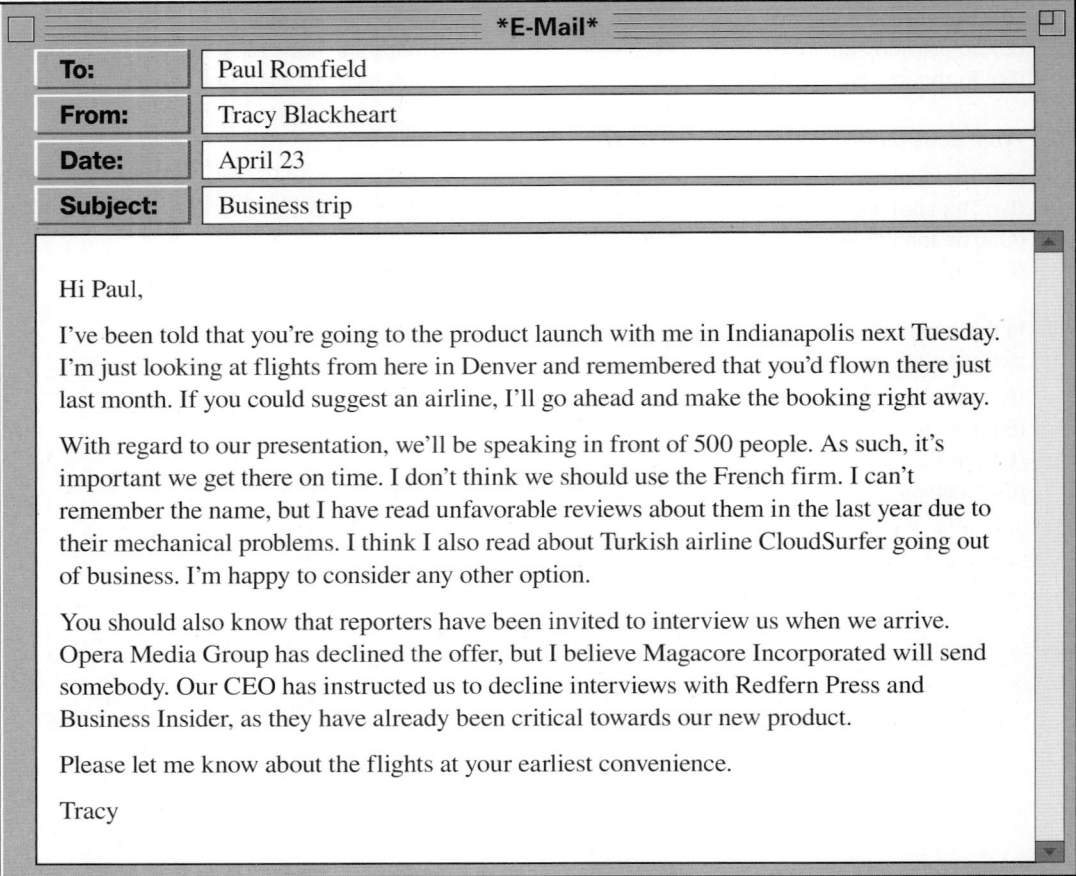

E-Mail

To:	Paul Romfield
From:	Tracy Blackheart
Date:	April 23
Subject:	Business trip

Hi Paul,

I've been told that you're going to the product launch with me in Indianapolis next Tuesday. I'm just looking at flights from here in Denver and remembered that you'd flown there just last month. If you could suggest an airline, I'll go ahead and make the booking right away.

With regard to our presentation, we'll be speaking in front of 500 people. As such, it's important we get there on time. I don't think we should use the French firm. I can't remember the name, but I have read unfavorable reviews about them in the last year due to their mechanical problems. I think I also read about Turkish airline CloudSurfer going out of business. I'm happy to consider any other option.

You should also know that reporters have been invited to interview us when we arrive. Opera Media Group has declined the offer, but I believe Magacore Incorporated will send somebody. Our CEO has instructed us to decline interviews with Redfern Press and Business Insider, as they have already been critical towards our new product.

Please let me know about the flights at your earliest convenience.

Tracy

---

http://www.skysearcher.com/results/e0302555

Rapidfly Deluxe: **Overall rating – 4.5/5.** Recently recognized for its outstanding customer service in the Aviation Honors ceremony, German firm Rapidfly has now established itself as a major player in the travel sector. Despite this, bookings have declined so far this year, perhaps in part due to the discontinuing of food service on flights.

GoldenWings: **Overall rating – 2/5.** The flight operator from the south of France has experienced a downturn in ticket sales in the last year. Many customers are unconvinced by Robert Pier's statement that the company has turned a corner, and flights continue to be undersubscribed.

SilverJet: **Overall rating – 3/5.** In a bid to boost dwindling sales figures, Swedish company SilverJet has recently announced a discounted range of flights. This offer extends to its Early Bird flight—the only flight to arrive into Indianapolis from Denver each day before lunchtime.

Directors fly in for Technospark product launch

By Beverly Shimmer

This morning, I met with Technospark directors Paul Romfield and Tracy Blackheart shortly after their flight from Denver touched down in Indianapolis at 10:30 A.M. Mr. Romfield claimed he was "extremely excited" to be unveiling the new model of notebook computer at this afternoon's product launch and predicted that it would quickly become a market leader.

For the full interview with Mr. Romfield, including exclusive pictures of the forthcoming product, please turn to page 5.

186. What is the purpose of the e-mail?

(A) To extend an invitation
(B) To discuss a schedule change
(C) To seek a colleague's advice
(D) To suggest revising a presentation

187. What is indicated about GoldenWings?

(A) It has gone bankrupt.
(B) Its planes have experienced mechanical issues.
(C) It has recently won an award.
(D) It is launching a new product next week.

188. What do all the companies on the Web page have in common?

(A) They have all experienced decreased ticket sales.
(B) They originate from the same country.
(C) A hot meal is served on each flight.
(D) They have all been awarded the same rating.

189. Which airline did Mr. Romfield most likely recommend to Ms. Blackheart?

(A) GoldenWings
(B) Rapidfly
(C) SilverJet
(D) CloudSurfer

190. What media outlet does Ms. Shimmer most likely work for?

(A) Redfern Press
(B) Opera Media Group
(C) Business Insider
(D) Magacore Incorporated

Test 9

GO ON TO THE NEXT PAGE

Questions 191-195 refer to the following notice, e-mail, and survey.

For the attention of:
ALL LUXURHOME EMPLOYEES

This is a reminder that all employees are to attend mandatory training on March 19. The management team wants to ensure that everybody is aware of our new sales policy when it comes to letting property. Unfortunately, we have been unable to book Cincinnati Convention Center this year. We also inquired about renting the boardroom at the Crystal Hotel, but this was fully booked for our preferred date. As such, we have provisionally booked a room at the Clark Technical Institute. However, this will be altered to the conference suite at Cincinnati University if we need to move the training to a weekend.

The training day will include advice on closing deals provided by business expert Paula Flores. Ryan Bertrand will be on hand to lend his expertise in the area of contract negotiation, and Terry Felz will give a lecture on the new city property regulations. Last but not least, Eileen Rashford will provide advice on delivering successful presentations.

We hope you enjoy the day, and that the information serves you well in your career with Luxurhome.

E-Mail message

To: Wayne Hendersey <w.hendersey@luxurhome.net>
From: Susan Zeperlin <s.zeperlin@luxurhome.net>
Subject: Training Day
Date: April 5
Attachment: Questionnaire

Dear Wayne,

Firstly, I'd like to thank you and the rest of the management team for organizing the recent company training day. The speakers were all very knowledgeable, and I thought the facilities on hand at Cincinnati University were first class. Please find attached my completed questionnaire.

In light of how much I enjoyed the day, I'd like to meet with you at some point next week. As a new employee, I am now extremely excited about my future career with Luxurhome and would like the opportunity to discuss career strategies with you. If you could find time in your busy schedule to accommodate me, I would greatly appreciate it.

Regards,

Susan Zeperlin
Junior Sales Associate

Luxurhome

	Strongly agree	Somewhat agree	Somewhat disagree	Strongly disagree
The training day has prepared me well for my future career	✗			
The training day was well organized	✗			
The venue was easily accessible				✗
The speakers were knowledgeable		✗		

Additional Feedback: Fantastic day. However, I should point out that I got lost finding the venue, as the directions on the Web site were incorrect. As such, I only arrived in time for the second lecture; I thought Paula Flores provided invaluable information. I was a little disappointed to find out that Terry Felz was sick and couldn't make it, but thought Amelia Song delivered a very competent lecture using Mr. Felz's notes.

Susan Zeperlin

---

191. What is the purpose of the notice?

(A) To seek speakers for a training workshop
(B) To provide an update on an event
(C) To describe a new company policy
(D) To announce a change of schedule

192. On what day of the week was the training day most likely held?

(A) Monday
(B) Wednesday
(C) Thursday
(D) Saturday

193. In the e-mail, the word "accommodate" in paragraph 2, line 4, is closest in meaning to

(A) house
(B) contain
(C) assist
(D) adapt

194. What is suggested about Ms. Zeperlin?

(A) She is a managing director.
(B) She was late to the training day.
(C) She would like to become a university lecturer.
(D) She felt the training day was poorly organized.

195. On which subject did Amelia Song most likely lecture?

(A) Contract negotiation
(B) Giving presentations
(C) Closing the deal
(D) Property regulations

GO ON TO THE NEXT PAGE

Technology Convention

In March, the city of Boise will welcome thousands of visitors to the annual technology convention that takes place in the city. Last year's event was a huge success, with over 3,000 visitors attending seminars, and lectures spread over the duration of the seven day convention. We are hoping to beat this attendance record this time around, with 1,500 advance tickets sold already. This year's event will be held in the Stephenson Hall as usual, and events will be spread over two weeks this time around.

Many attendees fall in love with our city and choose to spend an extended period of time here, taking in the riverside view and beautiful surrounding countryside. With this in mind, we are delighted to announce local firm Galaxy Cars as our official rental firm for the event. Special discounts will be available to those attending the conference, and vehicles will be delivered directly to your hotel for your convenience. The Galaxy Cars Web site can be found at www.galaxycars.com.

Prices for this year's convention are set as the following:

Gold Pass – Attendance at all talks, seminars and workshops: $85
Silver Pass – Attendance at evening events only: $40
Bronze Pass – Online access to Web broadcast: $15

To book your place, please call our dedicated hotline at 208-555-0143. We will be eagerly awaiting your call and hope to see you in person at the convention.

---

http://www.galaxycars.com

Special Offer: Boise Technology Convention

We at Galaxy Cars always seek to embrace technological advancements in the motor industry, and we strive to provide our customers with the best customer service as well as the latest gadgets in our rental cars. This is why we are delighted to support this year's technology convention.

To celebrate this important event, we have decided to offer a reward scheme for attendees of the convention. Reserving a vehicle in advance will entitle you to receive a special discount on your rental price. Please quote the code "SAVERDEAL" at the time of booking. The following offers are currently available:

Bookings made before September 25: 20% discount
Bookings made between September 25 and September 30: 15% discount
Bookings made between October 1 and October 7: 10% discount
Bookings made after October 8: 5% discount

Receipt Printed: September 29
Guest: Terrence Burnette
Address: 49 Beachy Lane, Chicago IL, 60605
Guest Pass Level: Silver
Vehicle booked (Y/N): Yes
Vehicle make and model: Advance Speedway T400 Deluxe
Reward program member: 2388 MAH
Grand Total: $169.95
Vehicle Return Date: October 7
Date of Booking: September 23
Bank card: XXXXXXXXXXXX5939
Card expiry: October 15

Passes may be picked up from the official reception desk prior to the event starting.

196. What is implied about this year's technology convention?

(A) It is being held at a new venue in Boise.
(B) Its tickets have already sold out completely.
(C) Complimentary airport transportation is included.
(D) It will be held for longer than last year's event.

197. What is suggested about Galaxy Cars?

(A) It will operate a display booth at the convention.
(B) It equips its vehicles with advanced devices.
(C) It is celebrating being in business for one year.
(D) It will offer a shuttle service at the convention.

198. What must guests do in order to receive discounted car rental?

(A) Sign in to an online account
(B) Display a guest pass
(C) Book a hotel room with a particular company
(D) Quote a reference code

199. What is true about Mr. Burnette?

(A) He is unable to attend this year's event.
(B) He recently accepted a job at Galaxy Cars.
(C) He will be allowed to attend only the evening events.
(D) He is a guest speaker at the technology convention.

200. How much of a discount will Mr. Burnette receive on car rental?

(A) 5%
(B) 10%
(C) 15%
(D) 20%

Stop! This is the end of the test. If you finish before time is called, you may go back to Parts 5, 6, and 7 and check your work.

TEST 10

READING TEST

In the Reading test, you will read a variety of texts and answer several different types of reading comprehension questions. The entire Reading test will last 75 minutes. There are three parts, and directions are given for each part. You are encouraged to answer as many questions as possible within the time allowed.

You must mark your answers on the separate answer sheet. Do not write your answers in your test book.

PART 5

Directions: A word or phrase is missing in each of the sentences below. Four answer choices are given below each sentence. Select the best answer to complete the sentence. Then mark the letter (A), (B), (C), or (D) on your answer sheet.

101. The passenger was asked to place ------- luggage in the overhead compartments after boarding the plane.

(A) her
(B) she
(C) hers
(D) herself

102. ------- the initial prototype and the final model of the keyboard featured customizable media keys.

(A) None
(B) Either
(C) Both
(D) That

103. Executives at the Cedal Corporation ------- negotiations for the acquisition of Nevix Industries two months ago.

(A) begins
(B) began
(C) beginning
(D) will begin

104. Our associates searched the file cabinet for nearly an hour and finally found the missing receipts ------- some travel documents.

(A) at
(B) onto
(C) during
(D) among

105. The fund for maintaining the community's public parks will run out ------- if the city council does not make it a top priority.

(A) entire
(B) entirety
(C) entireness
(D) entirely

106. ------- hotels charge a fee for cancellation within 24 hours of check-in, but the Renora Inn does not.

(A) Other
(B) Each
(C) Which
(D) Another

107. A legitimate ------- of residency in the city can be proven via a valid apartment rental lease.

(A) is claiming
(B) claimed
(C) claim
(D) claims

108. Please ------- the sources for all of the statistics included in your report.

(A) base
(B) direct
(C) fulfill
(D) cite

109. The candidate had already won a majority by a large margin, but election officials counted the rest of the votes -------.

(A) otherwise
(B) ever
(C) nonetheless
(D) rather

110. Even when the drone unexpectedly encountered a storm, its operator remained in ------- and kept the machine on course.

(A) control
(B) shape
(C) force
(D) order

111. Many construction firms delegate portions of their work to ------- who can complete the job more cost-effectively.

(A) contractually
(B) contractors
(C) contractual
(D) contracts

112. The branch manager called for an emergency meeting to tell staff ------- the change in government policy.

(A) for
(B) through
(C) behind
(D) about

113. Fortunately, the inventory taken by the aid organization found that the shelter had ------- levels of reserve supplies.

(A) willing
(B) acceptable
(C) skillful
(D) rapid

114. Owing to strong competition in the industry, the new smartphone designed by Vamiant Electronics must be marketed -------.

(A) consecutively
(B) recently
(C) strictly
(D) aggressively

115. The natural history museum's VIP members are ------- to enter the workshop and see the curators in action.

(A) permitted
(B) permitting
(C) permits
(D) permit

116. Roonelot Manufacturing installed solar panels on its rooftops ------- it could generate some of its own energy on site.

(A) such as
(B) regardless of
(C) no matter what
(D) so that

117. Due to the prestigious nature of the award, even Ms. Donnelly's most ------- colleagues traveled to watch her accept it.

(A) distances
(B) distance
(C) distant
(D) distantly

118. The owner of Hedley Tower may ------- the building if it does not pass the upcoming safety inspection.

(A) demolish
(B) demolishing
(C) demolished
(D) demolishes

119. Despite the IT director ------- warning the company president of issues with the e-mail system, he did not allocate funds to fix it.

(A) repetition
(B) repetitive
(C) repeatedly
(D) repeating

120. By signing a sponsorship agreement with a highly respected athlete, Ferdan Sports was able to ------- its status.

(A) divide
(B) recruit
(C) attach
(D) elevate

Test 10

GO ON TO THE NEXT PAGE

121. Most analysts agree that all three of the suggested tax measures offer ------- alternatives to the system that is currently in place.

(A) preferences
(B) preferring
(C) preferable
(D) prefer

122. The client complained that our technicians left ------- scratches on the glass in the process of transporting it.

(A) vital
(B) visible
(C) reduced
(D) accessible

123. ------- for the economic summit must have a professional certificate and be native speakers of the target language.

(A) Interpreting
(B) Interpretation
(C) Interprets
(D) Interpreters

124. When opportunities for promotion at the university are insufficient, the rate of faculty ------- rises significantly.

(A) dissatisfying
(B) dissatisfaction
(C) dissatisfies
(D) dissatisfy

125. Members of Parliament are expected to pass proposed ------- to conserve the natural habitat of a rare bird species in the southwest region.

(A) regulations
(B) transactions
(C) affiliations
(D) admissions

126. If the grant for the project is not renewed by the Kogara Science Foundation, the lab's research will have to stop -------.

(A) lately
(B) altogether
(C) almost
(D) much

127. Employees at the Soracune Corporation were encouraged ------- their cubicles to create a pleasant work environment.

(A) being personalized
(B) to personalize
(C) personalized
(D) personalizing

128. In order to ensure that the participants are treated fairly by the judging panel, their identities are ------- until a winner has been selected.

(A) defined
(B) concealed
(C) verified
(D) prohibited

129. More than half of older adults still have a landline phone in their home, ------- younger consumers depend solely on mobile technology.

(A) whereas
(B) instead of
(C) before
(D) so as to

130. Although Gassett Pharmaceuticals has experienced a great deal of success in the past few years, its revenues are predicted to ------- in the foreseeable future.

(A) criticize
(B) revolve
(C) shrink
(D) deduct

PART 6

Directions: Read the texts that follow. A word, phrase, or sentence is missing in parts of each text. Four answer choices for each question are given below the text. Select the best answer to complete the text. Then mark the letter (A), (B), (C), or (D) on your answer sheet.

Questions 131-134 refer to the following letter.

January 22

Dear Mr. Cardoso,

I am pleased to offer you the position of senior financial analyst at Stanton Advisors. The members of the hiring committee ------- for a qualified candidate, and you most certainly surpassed our
131.
expectations. The investment portfolios you showed us were well-balanced and expertly developed.
-------. We also received a glowing recommendation from ------- former employer. I have enclosed
132.   **133.**
the standard employment contract. ------- signing it, please look it over carefully and let me know if
134.
you have any questions.

Sincerely,

Harold Carney

---

131. (A) will have searched
(B) had been searching
(C) were searched
(D) are searching

132. (A) The earning potential of the position is very attractive to job seekers.
(B) Similarly, we follow a strict ethics code to avoid potential issues.
(C) Please submit a copy of your résumé for our review.
(D) Furthermore, you have a deep understanding of market conditions.

133. (A) their
(B) our
(C) its
(D) your

134. (A) Prior to
(B) Except for
(C) Because of
(D) Such as

GO ON TO THE NEXT PAGE

Test 10

Scott Graham
859 Walwyn Road
HALIFAX
HX1 5TW

Dear Mr. Graham,

Thank you for joining the Sinclair Airlines Frequent Flyer Program. Through excellent customer service and the support of our loyal customers, our business ------- to become one of the top fifteen
135.
airlines in the world.

Although most airlines offer a rewards program these days, ------- have the benefits we provide. We
136.
have a wide network of partners from hotels to car rental companies. These ------- have set their own
137.
earning levels. You can boost your points by supporting these businesses or rely solely on your
points from flights. -------. Please see the enclosed brochure for further details.
138.

Sincerely,

The Sinclair Airlines Team

135. (A) has grown
(B) grown
(C) to grow
(D) growing

136. (A) those
(B) neither
(C) which
(D) few

137. (A) subscribers
(B) affiliates
(C) passengers
(D) attendants

138. (A) In fact, most of our members choose to do so.
(B) Therefore, comfort and convenience are our top priorities.
(C) Either way, you'll be enjoying a free flight in no time.
(D) As a result, our safety record is the best in the industry.

Anaheim Sharpening Steel: How to Use

In one hand, hold the handle of the steel ------- in a vertical position. In the other hand, hold the knife
                                              139.

with the tip of the blade pointing upward. Place the blade against the steel with the widest part of the

blade in contact with the base. ------- light pressure as you move the blade up the steel along the
                                140.

cutting edge, maintaining an angle of twenty degrees. -------. Alternate sides for each stroke to
                                                      141.

ensure even sharpening. Test the blade's sharpness ------- approximately fifteen strokes on each
                                                   142.

side. Regular sharpening is recommended to enhance the performance of your knives.

---

139. (A) tightening
(B) tightly
(C) tighten
(D) tightness

140. (A) Relieve
(B) Force
(C) Withstand
(D) Apply

141. (A) Sharp knives contribute to faster food
preparation.
(B) This will maximize the effectiveness of the
tool.
(C) A user manual is included with each item.
(D) If it is not hot enough, the process will not
work.

142. (A) through
(B) into
(C) after
(D) since

GO ON TO THE NEXT PAGE

Questions 143-146 refer to the following e-mail.

To: Undisclosed Recipients
From: Goldstein Dental Clinic
Date: February 1
Subject: Big news!

Dear Goldstein Dental Clinic Patients,

Goldstein Dental Clinic is proud to announce that our new Web site has been launched. Now patients ------- their appointments online. -------. Simply click here and fill out the text boxes. It only
     143.   **144.**
takes a moment, and you'll enjoy the convenience of having your patient information ------- available.
                                               145.
The ------- of our booking process frees up our reception staff to provide better quality service at the
     146.
clinic. However, those of you who prefer to make appointments by phone will still be able to do so.

Sincerely,

The Goldstein Dental Clinic Staff

---

143. (A) can book
(B) have booked
(C) must book
(D) to book

144. (A) We are sorry if the Web site crash caused any confusion.
(B) A new dentist will be joining our distinguished team next month.
(C) No special computer skills are needed to set up your account.
(D) Confirmation of your appointment is attached to this e-mail.

145. (A) noticeably
(B) widely
(C) primarily
(D) readily

146. (A) continuation
(B) interval
(C) automation
(D) stability

Directions: In this part you will read a selection of texts, such as magazine and newspaper articles, e-mails, and instant messages. Each text or set of texts is followed by several questions. Select the best answer for each question and mark the letter (A), (B), (C), or (D) on your answer sheet.

Questions 147-148 refer to the following advertisement.

Hillock Shopping Mall – Retail Spaces for Rent

We have several retail spaces available on the first and second floor. Some of the second-floor spaces boast a magnificent view across Arnott River. All of the retail spaces at Hillock Shopping Mall feature brand-new fixtures and fittings, including display lighting, security systems, and counters. Our shopping center is situated in a prime location, right in between two subway stations and next to Centro Park Bus Terminal.

Contact Barry Galloway at bgalloway@starrealty.com to schedule an evening viewing.
Available viewing periods: Weekdays, 7 P.M. to 10 P.M., Weekends, 8 P.M. to 11 P.M.

147. What is mentioned as an advantage of Hillock Shopping Mall?

(A) It contains a wide variety of affordable stores.
(B) Its business hours are longer than those of other malls.
(C) Some of its retail spaces have multiple floors.
(D) It has convenient access to public transportation.

148. Why are people encouraged to send an e-mail?

(A) To inquire about the mall's opening hours
(B) To request to hold an event at the mall
(C) To find out information about store discounts
(D) To arrange to see vacant retail spaces

Test 10

Questions 149-150 refer to the following sign.

To preserve the delicate condition of all paintings and sculptures, and to avoid spoiling the enjoyment of other visitors, please behave respectfully and courteously while visiting the gallery.

✔ Place all food and drink wrappers or containers in a trash can.
✔ Do not use your flash when taking photos.
✔ Speak only at a low volume during exhibition tours.
✔ Do not touch or pick up any exhibits or lighting apparatus.

We truly appreciate your cooperation. Thank you.

149. What is the purpose of the sign?

(A) To give directions to an art gallery
(B) To provide guidelines for visitors
(C) To inform visitors about new exhibits
(D) To remind staff of job duties

150. What activity is prohibited?

(A) Eating food
(B) Talking during tours
(C) Taking photographs
(D) Handling exhibits

```
≡ E-Mail message ≡
```

From:	Lynne Kozlowski <lkozlowski@filmfest.com>
To:	Vernon Hogan <vhogan@widemail.net>
Subject:	Film festival
Date:	March 9

Hi, Vernon,

As I mentioned to you last week, we have begun preparing for the fourth annual Oregon Independent Film Festival, which will take place on Saturday, May 4 and Sunday, May 5. As was the case with previous festivals, critics and reviewers from various newspapers, magazines, and Web sites will be invited to attend.

Please take a look at our previous guest lists and e-mail me the names of all the film critics who attended past festivals. Then, I will contact them and confirm their attendance this year. The movie theater we are using this year will reserve seats by name on the opening night of the event, so the proprietor asked me to send a guest list as soon as possible. Later this week, I'll send you the finalized guest list so that you can start preparing formal invitations for the opening night. You should submit these to Arnie Loomis for distribution by March 31.

Thanks,

Lynne

151. Why did Ms. Kozlowski send the e-mail?

(A) To change the dates of a festival
(B) To encourage Mr. Hogan to attend a festival
(C) To explain why the theater is holding a festival
(D) To seek assistance with organizing a festival

152. What does the e-mail suggest Ms. Kozlowski has already done to prepare for the festival?

(A) Selected films to show on the opening night
(B) Sent invitations to special guests
(C) Communicated with a theater owner
(D) Compiled a list of attending film critics

GO ON TO THE NEXT PAGE

Test 10

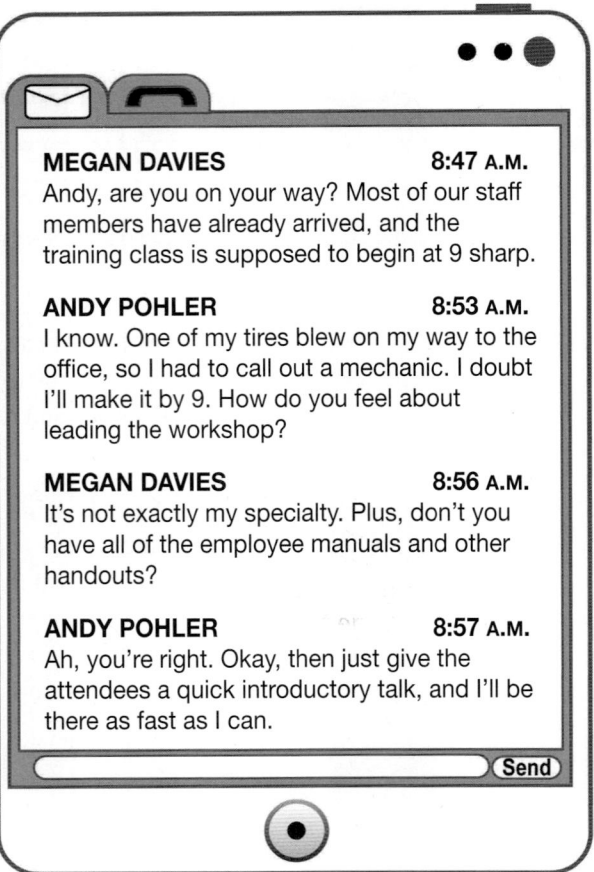

MEGAN DAVIES   8:47 A.M.

Andy, are you on your way? Most of our staff members have already arrived, and the training class is supposed to begin at 9 sharp.

ANDY POHLER   8:53 A.M.

I know. One of my tires blew on my way to the office, so I had to call out a mechanic. I doubt I'll make it by 9. How do you feel about leading the workshop?

MEGAN DAVIES   8:56 A.M.

It's not exactly my specialty. Plus, don't you have all of the employee manuals and other handouts?

ANDY POHLER   8:57 A.M.

Ah, you're right. Okay, then just give the attendees a quick introductory talk, and I'll be there as fast as I can.

Send

153. What can be inferred about Mr. Pohler?

(A) He wants to reschedule the workshop.
(B) He offered to give Ms. Davies a ride to work.
(C) He went to the wrong location.
(D) He had trouble with his vehicle.

154. At 8:56 A.M., what does Ms. Davies mean when she writes, "It's not exactly my specialty"?

(A) She feels that she requires more training.
(B) She is unable to offer Mr. Pohler any advice.
(C) She is reluctant to fill in for Mr. Pohler.
(D) She does not know how to create a manual.

Questions 155-157 refer to the following notice.

INFOTEC DEVELOPMENT INSTITUTE
EDUCATIONAL EXCELLENCE

The Infotec Development Institute has been in operation for over twenty years. With a range of courses and seminars, we provide exceptional opportunities for the development skills by those in the legal profession. Thousands of lawyers and attorneys have chosen us to help them take the next step in their careers. —[1]—.

Each of our ten courses runs once a month. Although some courses can be accessed online, others require participants to attend in person in order to take part in discussions and practical activities. All handouts and training packs will be included in the cost of the course. —[2]—.

Until the end of the month, if you purchase an Infotec membership, you will receive a complimentary pack of luxury stationery, as well as be given the e-mail address of an Infotec personal tutor in order to help you with your learning. Members are also eligible to receive generous savings on courses they participate in. —[3]—. However, members must now arrange their own transportation to and from the airport, as this service has now been discontinued.

We hope to see you soon and look forward to providing you with the skills to take your career to the next level. —[4]—. To book your place, please call 545-555-0125.

---

155. What is indicated about the educational courses?

(A) They can all be accessed remotely through a Web site.
(B) They are targeted at medical professionals.
(C) They are delivered several times a year.
(D) Course materials must be purchased additionally.

156. What is NOT mentioned as a benefit of Infotec membership?

(A) A staff member's contact details
(B) Discounted tuition fees
(C) A free gift
(D) A complimentary shuttle service

157. In which of the positions marked [1], [2], [3], and [4] does the following sentence best belong?

"These will be provided to you upon arrival at the institute."

(A) [1]
(B) [2]
(C) [3]
(D) [4]

Eat-Sleep-Play – Available Soon!

★ ★ ★ ★ ★

If you are looking for recommendations for restaurants, hotels, or fun activities around town, then *Eat-Sleep-Play* is for you! Starting with our first issue, *Eat-Sleep-Play*'s pages will feature in-depth articles and reviews that will be of interest to both local residents and the soaring number of tourists who come to Hartsville. Each month, we will try to bring you thought-provoking news, so you won't want to miss out on a single issue!

In addition to purchasing *Eat-Sleep-Play* from newsstands and supermarkets, you can subscribe to ensure that you never miss out. The first monthly issue comes out on October 1 and includes an interview with the owner of Zap Zone Laser Tag, the only business of its kind in Hartsville.

An 18-month subscription costs just $75, which gives you savings of $36 compared to the regular retail price. When subscribing by e-mail, provide the promo code ESP111 in the subject line to get a free coffee mug with your first issue. Contact us now at inquiries@ eatsleepplay.com. If you are interested in employment opportunities, visit www.eatsleepplay. com/vacancies.

---

158. What is the main purpose of the advertisement?

(A) To announce a company's expansion
(B) To promote a new publication
(C) To recommend businesses in Hartsville
(D) To seek new employees for a business

159. What is suggested about Hartsville?

(A) It is home to several laser tag facilities.
(B) Its restaurant scene is increasingly competitive.
(C) It has a convenient public transportation system.
(D) It has been experiencing a rise in tourism.

160. How can someone receive a complimentary gift?

(A) By visiting a Web site
(B) By subscribing by a specific date
(C) By entering a special code
(D) By signing up for a one-year subscription

Corolla's Bistro

3009 Glendale Park Road, San Francisco, CA 94118   Tel: 555-0133

September 4

Ms. Aida Yurawat
237 Hilson Avenue,
San Francisco, CA 94103

Dear Ms. Yurawat,

I was delighted to receive your letter regarding your recent visit to our restaurant and the excellent service provided to you by a member of our wait staff, Ms. Alice Lee. Ms. Lee has not been with us long, so it is very pleasing for me to hear that she is displaying such professionalism and attentiveness to our customers. I particularly enjoyed your description of the way she handled the mix-up with your party's food order.

As the owner of the business, I highly value the comments that I receive from my diners, as they help me to make good business decisions in the future when trying to improve my restaurant. Ms. Lee will be personally thanked when I hold a staff meeting this Thursday. And, to thank you for your letter, I have included a voucher in the envelope. When you visit my restaurant again, you can use it to receive fifty percent off your total bill.

Again, thanks for bringing my staff member's dedication and professional attitude to my attention.

Kindest regards,

Adrian Corolla
Adrian Corolla

---

161. What is the purpose of the letter?

(A) To express gratitude to a customer for providing feedback
(B) To address a customer's complaint about unsatisfactory service
(C) To approve a customer's request to hold a party at a business
(D) To answer a question from a customer about menu changes

162. What can be inferred about Ms. Lee?

(A) She prepared food for Ms. Yurawat.
(B) She will be awarded a bonus.
(C) She is the manager of a restaurant.
(D) She is a relatively new employee.

163. What has Mr. Corolla enclosed with the letter?

(A) A revised bill
(B) A partial refund
(C) A sample menu
(D) A discount voucher

Test 10

GO ON TO THE NEXT PAGE

Questions 164-167 refer to the following online chat discussion.

RACHEL BECKETT	**11:02 A.M.**
Hi, Brad. I've just arrived at the convention hall to deliver my presentation, but I don't have everything I need to start it.	
BRAD NAVAL	**11:07 A.M.**
What do you need? Do you have the presentation slides?	
RACHEL BECKETT	**11:14 A.M.**
Yes, I have those. But I don't have the handouts I was going to give to the audience. Could you print some and bring them over for 12:30 P.M.?	
BRAD NAVAL	**11:17 A.M.**
It's a bit last minute. Do they not have printing facilities there?	
RACHEL BECKETT	**11:21 A.M.**
I've already checked. I can't do it here because their printer is experiencing a fault. They are waiting for an engineer to service it.	
BRAD NAVAL	**11:28 A.M.**
Oh, that's too bad. I won't be able to make it in time. How about we e-mail the handout to people instead?	
RACHEL BECKETT	**11:31 A.M.**
Okay, that's probably the best solution. I'll go ahead and do that.	

164. Why did Ms. Beckett contact Mr. Naval?

(A) To tell him she is stuck in traffic
(B) To check the address of a venue
(C) To request that he deliver some documents
(D) To request a computer login code

165. At 11:17 A.M., what does Mr. Naval mean when he writes, "It's a bit last minute"?

(A) He is telling Ms. Beckett to hold on a moment.
(B) It is too late to do as Ms. Beckett asks.
(C) It will be a quick task to carry out.
(D) He is asking Ms. Beckett what time it is.

166. What problem does Ms. Beckett mention?

(A) She has forgotten her e-mail password.
(B) Some presentation materials contain errors.
(C) Some machinery is out of order.
(D) Audience members have not arrived yet.

167. What does Mr. Naval suggest?

(A) Postponing the event
(B) Going to a different lecture room
(C) Meeting at the office
(D) Sending a document electronically

GO ON TO THE NEXT PAGE

Mr. Bryan Hughes
14 Fairfield Avenue
Blackpool, UK
BL3 9FH

Dear Mr. Hughes,

I am a long-term customer of Econobuild and regularly buy my work supplies from your company. I often find the parts I purchase to be extremely reliable to use when I am repairing sink and toilet units. Unfortunately, in this instance, I have several complaints to make. — [1] —.

Firstly, the package I received from your company arrived a day later than scheduled. As somebody who works with strict time deadlines, this caused significant problems for my business, as I had to reschedule some appointments. — [2] —. I would, therefore, be grateful if you could refund the £9.99 charge for express delivery, as this service clearly wasn't fulfilled by your company. I was at least pleased to find that the parts were of their usual high quality. — [3] —.

Secondly, I spoke to one of your customer service employees on the phone, who put me through to your complaints department. I tried to explain my issue to the member of staff there. However, I found him to be extremely rude and unhelpful. In addition to this, he didn't really offer a solution to my problem, hence my writing you this letter.

Lastly, when I logged in to check my balance on your Web site's member's section, I noticed I had been charged for some items that I did not order on my last invoice. As such, I seem to have been overcharged by about £60. — [4] —.

As stated above, I was disappointed to encounter these problems, as I have always been pleased with the service provided by you in the past. If you would like to contact me to discuss anything I've mentioned, please call me at 558-555-0117.

Yours sincerely,

Paul Gravel
Gravel Industries

168. What is suggested about Mr. Gravel?

(A) He is currently unemployed.
(B) He works as a plumber.
(C) He is late in paying an invoice.
(D) He would like to apply for a job at Econobuild.

169. What issue does Mr. Gravel NOT make a complaint about?

(A) The conduct of a staff member
(B) The contents of an invoice
(C) The quality of some products
(D) The time taken to deliver some items

170. What is indicated about Econobuild?

(A) It offers an online service to members.
(B) It has branches in several countries.
(C) Its complaints department is unstaffed.
(D) It is advertising for more delivery drivers.

171. In which of the positions marked [1], [2], [3], and [4] does the following sentence best belong?

"I'd appreciate it if you would see to it that this is amended immediately."

(A) [1]
(B) [2]
(C) [3]
(D) [4]

GO ON TO THE NEXT PAGE

Seventh Annual Munro Mountain Firefly Festival – June 13

Park rangers are getting ready for Munro Mountain's most famous cultural event: the Firefly Festival! This year's event will be held on June 13, from 4 P.M. to 10 P.M., and we expect peak conditions for firefly viewing. Those interested in attending the event must be aware of the following:

Trail sections closed to the general public during the festival:
Stony Bridge Trail: The entire trail, starting from the Visitor Center
Conifer Trail: From Rowan Shelter onward to Douglas Peak
Manford Trail: The entire trail, starting from the Visitor Center
Eden Trail: From Sherwood Campground onward to Barnes Ridge

Parking Pass Lottery:
In order to prevent congestion on surrounding roads, visitors must obtain a parking pass through our lottery system or use public transportation. Applications for passes will be accepted from May 1 to June 1, subject to availability, through our Web site at www. munromountainpark.com/parking. There is no fee for entering the lottery this year. The results of the lottery will be announced via e-mail on June 2. Passes are non-refundable, non-transferable, and good only for the date of the event.

Parking Area and Visitor Center:
Those permitted to bring a vehicle to the festival may park in the main parking lot in front of the Visitor Center. The building itself will not be open that evening, but a temporary booth will be set up on the north side of the parking lot. A park employee will be on hand to answer your questions and provide pamphlets.

Admission:
Tickets are priced at $8.50 for adults and $3.50 for children. They may be obtained from the Visitor Center, the Parks and Recreation office at city hall, and the public library. In all cases, cash or credit cards are acceptable forms of payment. Please note that tickets are limited to four per person. Visit our Web site for more details.

172. For whom is the notice mainly intended?

(A) Park employees
(B) Event attendees
(C) Parking lot attendants
(D) Festival organizers

173. What is NOT suggested about parking passes?

(A) The lottery can be entered free of charge.
(B) The passes may only be used on June 13.
(C) The successful applicants will be notified by e-mail.
(D) The passes are only good for specific types of vehicles.

174. What is indicated about the Visitor Center?

(A) It has several different parking areas.
(B) It will be closed during the event.
(C) It can provide maps of the park.
(D) It is located next to a campground.

175. What is true about event tickets?

(A) They will be mailed to recipients.
(B) They can be reserved via a Web site.
(C) They must be paid for by credit card.
(D) They can be purchased at various locations.

GO ON TO THE NEXT PAGE

A Design for Life
By Sam Maxton

(October 10) Boston—Caroline Burgess has been employed locally as an interior designer for nearly two decades. Recently, she made the decision to found her own company in Boston, and already has a large client base in the local area. "Interior design has always been my passion," Burgess says. "I take a great amount of pleasure in developing something special with customers, and providing them with a living space that they are truly happy with." Burgess' work often attracts glowing reviews from her clients. Recently, she worked on a project with the governor of Massachusetts to help renovate his family home.

"I'm really pleased with how my own business is going. The work I did on the governor's mansion was great for attracting some publicity towards my company. I've had a lot more inquiries since then." Burgess is well known for the attention to detail she provides to each project. Every aspect is personalized, and the customer's wishes are always taken into consideration. The one downside of her role, she claims, is that she sometimes has to spend days away from home. "I miss my parents and siblings sometimes. But they are very understanding", she says.

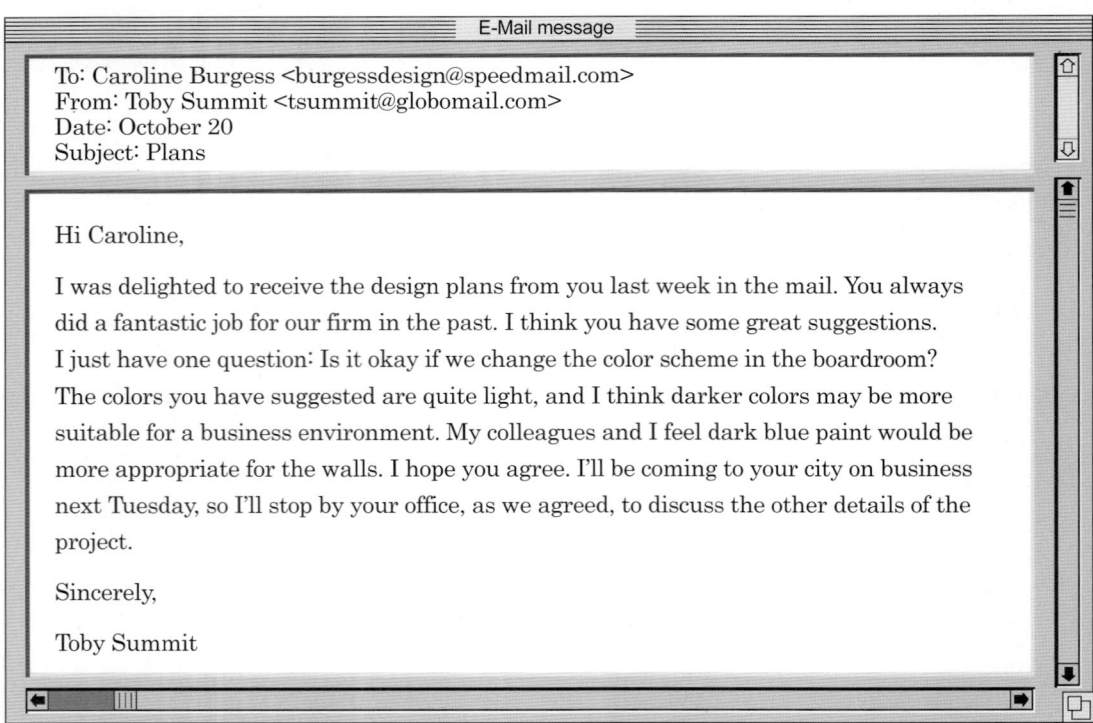

E-Mail message

To: Caroline Burgess <burgessdesign@speedmail.com>
From: Toby Summit <tsummit@globomail.com>
Date: October 20
Subject: Plans

Hi Caroline,

I was delighted to receive the design plans from you last week in the mail. You always did a fantastic job for our firm in the past. I think you have some great suggestions. I just have one question: Is it okay if we change the color scheme in the boardroom? The colors you have suggested are quite light, and I think darker colors may be more suitable for a business environment. My colleagues and I feel dark blue paint would be more appropriate for the walls. I hope you agree. I'll be coming to your city on business next Tuesday, so I'll stop by your office, as we agreed, to discuss the other details of the project.

Sincerely,

Toby Summit

176. What is the purpose of the article?

(A) To announce a job opportunity
(B) To describe an upcoming design project
(C) To profile an entrepreneur
(D) To promote the opening of a building

177. What does Ms. Burgess say is a disadvantage of her job?

(A) She has to spend time away from her family.
(B) She finds some clients difficult to work with.
(C) She has had to take a recent pay cut.
(D) She often has to work through the night.

178. What has Mr. Summit asked Ms. Burgess to design?

(A) A performance venue
(B) A seminar hall
(C) A personal residence
(D) An office space

179. What does Mr. Summit ask Ms. Burgess to change?

(A) The layout of some furniture
(B) The dimensions of some curtains
(C) The color scheme of a room
(D) The time of a board meeting

180. What is indicated about Mr. Summit?

(A) He has never worked with Ms. Burgess before.
(B) He will be traveling to Boston next week.
(C) He has sent some product samples to Ms. Burgess.
(D) He would like Ms. Burgess to visit his workplace.

GO ON TO THE NEXT PAGE

Modern Art Fans:
The Watson Exhibit is coming to Rockford!
Syril Watson to display his groundbreaking modern paintings

Venue: Stephenson Convention Center

Dates: Monday, September 16 to Wednesday, September 18

Time: 5:00 P.M.—8:00 P.M.

Cost: $25 adults / Free for children under thirteen

If you want to reserve tickets ahead of time, you can do so by calling our ticket office at 553-555-0195 and selecting option 3 when you hear the automated message. To pay, you can opt to use a credit card over the phone, or send a money order to our head office. Any unsold tickets will be available for purchase on the day of the exhibits. Unfortunately, we are only able to accept cash as payment when tickets are purchased at the door.

To find out more, contact our information line at 553-555-0132, or e-mail Johnny Coleman at jcoleman@rockfordarts.org.

E-Mail message	
To:	Johnny Coleman <jcoleman@rockfordarts.org>
From:	Rachel Lingford <rlingford@trimail.net>
Subject:	Syril Watson Show
Date:	September 3

Dear Mr. Coleman,

I was extremely excited to find out that Syril Watson will be bringing his artwork to Rockford. I have followed his career since his very first exhibition, and I cannot wait to share this opportunity with my family.

I would like to buy four tickets for the second evening of the exhibit. I'd like to receive my tickets well in advance, but I don't have access to a credit card right now. Can you please clarify the mailing address of your head office?

Thank you,

Rachel Lingford

181. What was NOT mentioned as a payment option?

(A) By credit card
(B) By money order
(C) By personal check
(D) In cash

182. What is indicated in the flyer?

(A) Tickets are likely to sell out.
(B) The exhibit will last for 3 days.
(C) The artist will answer questions.
(D) There are no parking facilities available.

183. In the e-mail, the word "followed" in paragraph 1, line 2, is closest in meaning to

(A) searched
(B) conformed
(C) watched
(D) advanced

184. On which day does Ms. Lingford plan to attend the exhibit?

(A) Monday
(B) Tuesday
(C) Wednesday
(D) Thursday

185. What is indicated about Ms. Lingford?

(A) She has previously viewed the exhibit in another city.
(B) She spoke to a sales representative on the phone.
(C) She plans to pay for her tickets by mail.
(D) She will display some artwork at the exhibition.

GO ON TO THE NEXT PAGE

Ms. Rosemary Reid
39 Holebas Lane
Albuquerque, NM 87114

Dear Ms. Reid,

As a regular customer of Gomes Car Rentals, we thought you would be interested in hearing about the latest upgrades that we have made to our service. Through working closely with Yasmin Gallas of car manufacturer Rapidrive, we have been able to obtain a new fleet of vehicles at a discounted price. Our CEO Greg Perkins is determined that these savings be passed on to our customers. To this end, we have devised a range of packages priced at different levels so that all drivers will be able to find a vehicle to suit their particular needs. Anybody can take advantage of one of our deals by calling our customer service representative Billy Carroll at 555-0178 or by stopping by one of our stores at Charleston, Albuquerque, or Princeville. Business clients are advised to speak to Helen Patterson, who manages the accounts of these customers, at 555-0179. Additionally, as a special promotion, all those booking by phone will receive some complimentary cinema tickets to a screening of their choice.

We look forward to serving you soon.

Best Wishes,

Robert Hargrove

Sales Director, Gomes Car Rentals

Gomes Car Rentals
In Association with Rapidrive

The Solo - For clients who need a vehicle for a single day
Price: $55
Vehicles available: Rapi Micro, Rapi T100

The Weekender - Ideal for customers looking to escape the city for a few days (2-3 days)
Price: $45 per day
Vehicles available: Rapi T100, Rapi Experience

The Road Tripper - For those requiring a vehicle for a longer trip (10-day minimum)
Price: $40 per day
Vehicles available: Rapi Experience, Rapi Roadster

The Explorer - Perfect for those looking for a longer-term rental (1-month minimum)
Price: $35 per day
Vehicles available: Rapi Roadster, Rapi Deluxe Plus

To:	Robert Hargrove <rhargrove@gomescars.com>
From:	Rosemary Reid <r.reid@speedymail.net>
Date:	August 3
Subject:	Recent car rental

Dear Mr. Hargrove,

I recently rented one of your new vehicles, and I thought you'd appreciate some feedback on my experience. I thought the Rapidrive vehicle that I rented handled really nicely, and the interior was clean and luxurious. I feel they are a real upgrade on your last models. Secondly, I found your staff to be very accommodating. I spoke to one of your advisors on the phone on July 5, who was able to book the Road Tripper package for me and charge it to my business account. However, I had to call back after some changes were made to my business trip, which meant it was shortened to last just three days. Your advisor was very accommodating and chose a more suitable package for me immediately. Although my experience was largely positive, I am yet to receive the complimentary cinema tickets that you advertised. Could you look into this for me?

Regards,

Rosemary Reid

186. Why was the letter sent?

(A) To request customer feedback
(B) To announce a business relocation
(C) To describe service improvements
(D) To promote a new model of car

187. What is indicated about Gomes Car Rentals?

(A) It has further discounts on its Web site.
(B) It has stores in multiple locations.
(C) It has been sold to Rapidrive.
(D) It has an on-site movie screen.

188. Whom did Ms. Reid most likely speak with on July 5?

(A) Helen Patterson
(B) Greg Perkins
(C) Billy Carroll
(D) Yasmin Gallas

189. Which package did Ms. Reid most likely pay for?

(A) The Road Tripper
(B) The Solo
(C) The Weekender
(D) The Explorer

190. What problem does Ms. Reid mention in her e-mail?

(A) A member of staff was rude to her.
(B) The interior of the car was unclean.
(C) Her vehicle was hard to drive.
(D) She has not received a free gift.

GO ON TO THE NEXT PAGE

Sharpline Stationery Company – Memo

To: All Employees
From: Amy Whitehouse, Human Resources

Dear Team Members,

As you are aware, our annual employee retreat has been arranged for next weekend. This offers an excellent opportunity for staff members from different departments to get to know each other personally while enjoying some fun activities in a beautiful setting. The retreat will last for two days. You may recall I sent around a document with some menu choices. If anybody requires the vegetarian option, please let me know by the end of business today. Team-building events are to be led by Sharpline managers. Robert Polson will be leading an obstacle-course fitness event, and Natalie Porter will host a map-reading exploration session. Emily Daggard and Colin Himaa have volunteered to host a quiz for us. This is subject to change, as Ms. Daggard has made us aware that she may have to attend to some urgent business. We are also still looking for another manager to lead the water polo session. Hopefully, this will be confirmed at our managerial meeting tomorrow.

We hope you enjoy the retreat!

SHARPLINE STATIONERY COMPANY EMPLOYEE RETREAT
Saturday, April 18
Wellington Resort

Event	Session Leaders	Start Time	Location
Orienteering	Natalie Porter	8:00 A.M.	Wellington Downs
Obstacle Course	Robert Polson	10:30 A.M.	Blackforest Woods
Water Polo Tournament	To be confirmed	2:00 P.M.	Resort Pool
General Knowledge Quiz	Colin Himaa & Michael Oxley	7:30 P.M.	Diamond Function Room

To:	Amy Whitehouse <amywhitehouse@sharpline.net>
From:	Bradley Welsh <bradleywelsh@sharpline.net>
Date:	April 21
Subject:	Company Retreat

Hi Amy,

I just want to thank you for all the work you put into organizing the company retreat. I really enjoyed the weekend, and I know lots of other staff members did too. I also really enjoyed hosting the water polo event. I must admit, I was a little reluctant when you first suggested it at the meeting, as I had never played the sport before, but I was surprised by how much I liked it. I also just want to apologize for having to rush away before the evening event. I had to take my daughter to the hospital because she was feeling unwell. Although I was disappointed not to be able to attend for the entire retreat, this family emergency had to take priority. I hope you understand.

Thanks again,

Bradley Welsh

191. What are Sharpline Stationery Company's employees encouraged to do?

(A) Make a payment
(B) Specify dietary requirements
(C) Invite family members
(D) Suggest retreat events

192. In the memo, the word "recall" in paragraph 1, line 4, is closest in meaning to

(A) bring
(B) find
(C) order
(D) remember

193. Who most likely took Ms. Daggard's place at the retreat?

(A) Robert Polson
(B) Bradley Welsh
(C) Michael Oxley
(D) Natalie Porter

194. Which event did Mr. Welsh most likely miss?

(A) Obstacle Course
(B) Water Polo Tournament
(C) General Knowledge Quiz
(D) Orienteering

195. What can be inferred about Mr. Welsh?

(A) He used to be a professional athlete.
(B) He is a manager at Sharpline.
(C) He is a qualified doctor.
(D) He has several children.

Test 10

Questions 196-200 refer to the following Web page, review, and response.

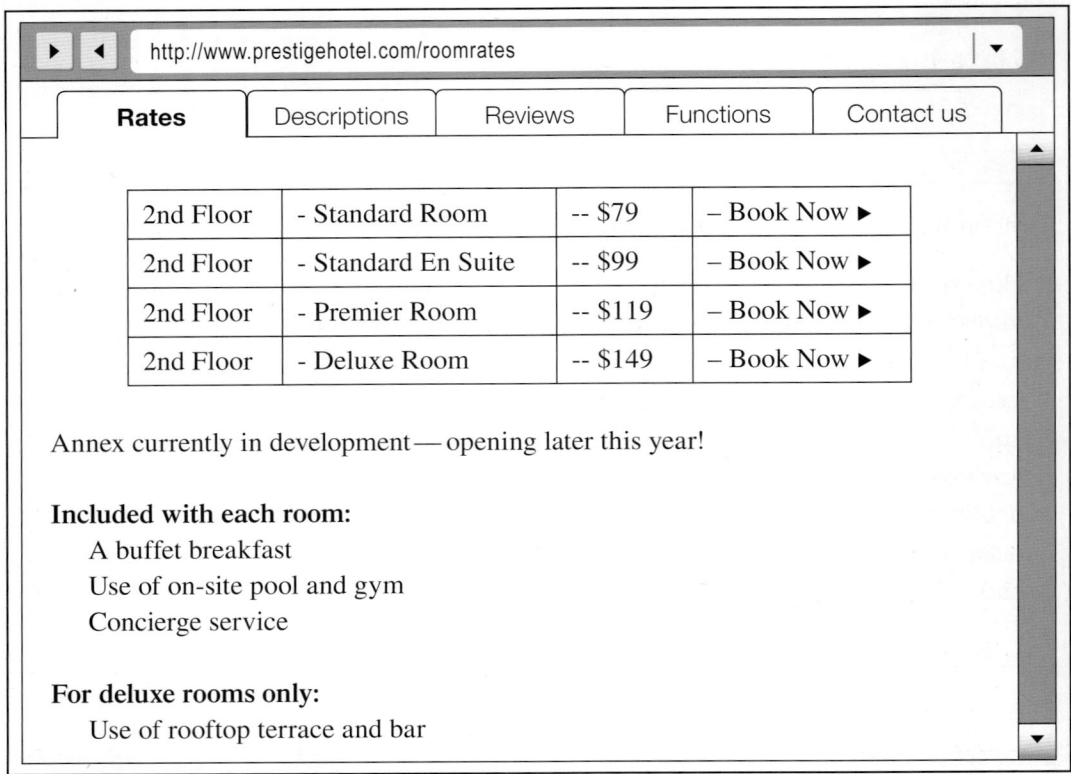

http://www.prestigehotel.com/roomrates

| Rates | Descriptions | Reviews | Functions | Contact us |

2nd Floor	- Standard Room	-- $79	– Book Now ▶
2nd Floor	- Standard En Suite	-- $99	– Book Now ▶
2nd Floor	- Premier Room	-- $119	– Book Now ▶
2nd Floor	- Deluxe Room	-- $149	– Book Now ▶

Annex currently in development—opening later this year!

Included with each room:
    A buffet breakfast
    Use of on-site pool and gym
    Concierge service

For deluxe rooms only:
    Use of rooftop terrace and bar

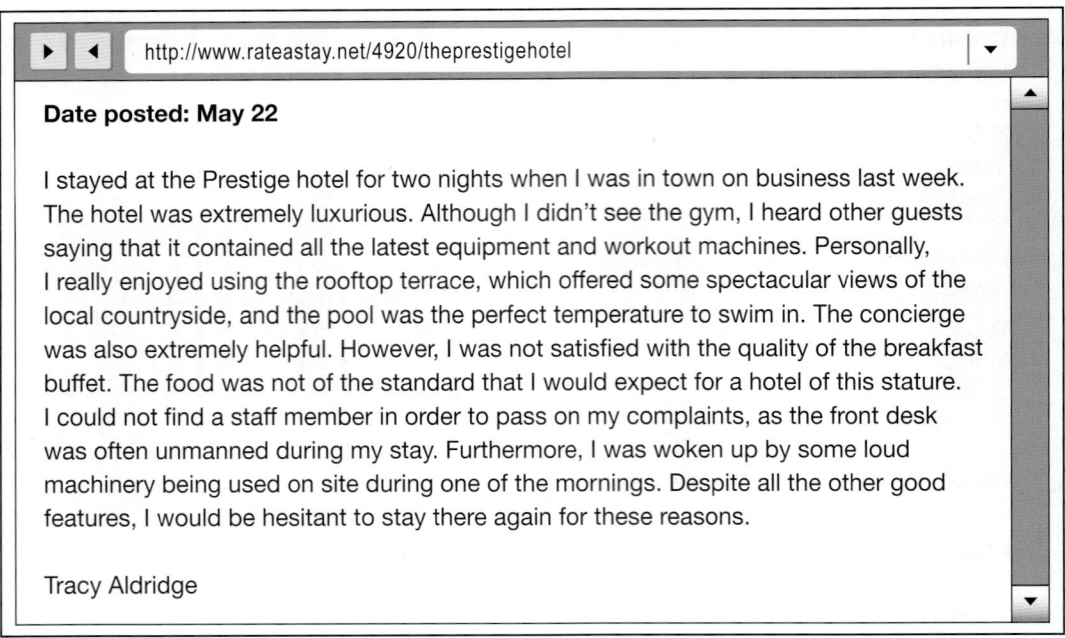

http://www.rateastay.net/4920/theprestigehotel

Date posted: May 22

I stayed at the Prestige hotel for two nights when I was in town on business last week. The hotel was extremely luxurious. Although I didn't see the gym, I heard other guests saying that it contained all the latest equipment and workout machines. Personally, I really enjoyed using the rooftop terrace, which offered some spectacular views of the local countryside, and the pool was the perfect temperature to swim in. The concierge was also extremely helpful. However, I was not satisfied with the quality of the breakfast buffet. The food was not of the standard that I would expect for a hotel of this stature. I could not find a staff member in order to pass on my complaints, as the front desk was often unmanned during my stay. Furthermore, I was woken up by some loud machinery being used on site during one of the mornings. Despite all the other good features, I would be hesitant to stay there again for these reasons.

Tracy Aldridge

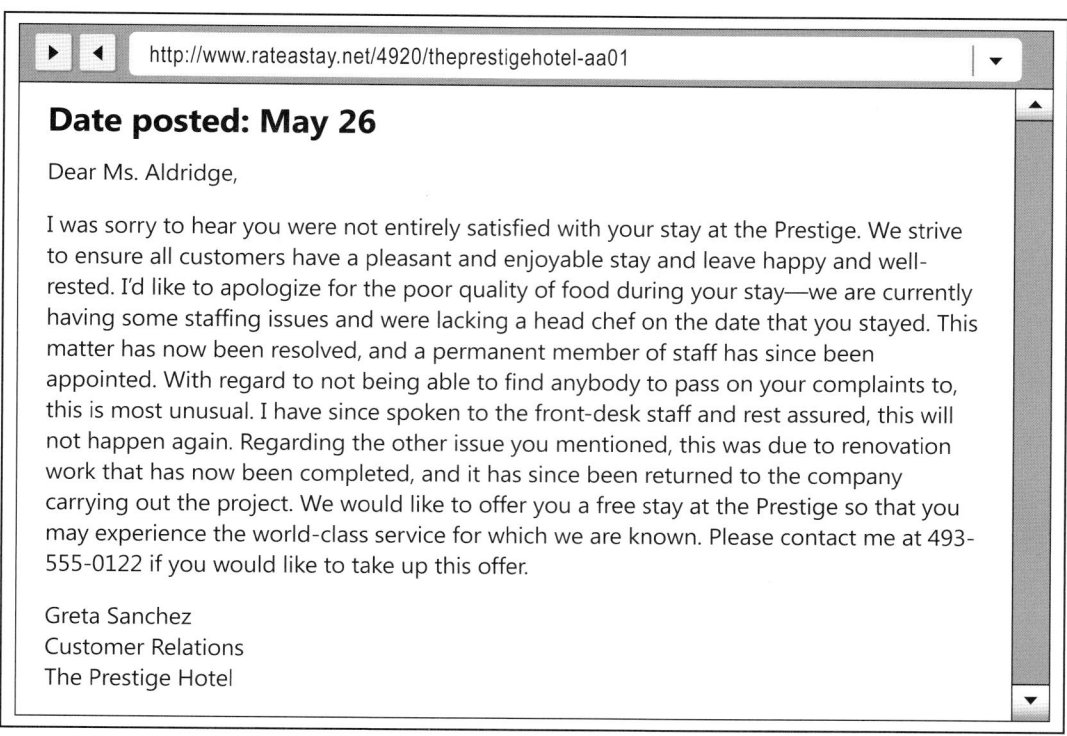

Date posted: May 26

Dear Ms. Aldridge,

I was sorry to hear you were not entirely satisfied with your stay at the Prestige. We strive to ensure all customers have a pleasant and enjoyable stay and leave happy and well-rested. I'd like to apologize for the poor quality of food during your stay—we are currently having some staffing issues and were lacking a head chef on the date that you stayed. This matter has now been resolved, and a permanent member of staff has since been appointed. With regard to not being able to find anybody to pass on your complaints to, this is most unusual. I have since spoken to the front-desk staff and rest assured, this will not happen again. Regarding the other issue you mentioned, this was due to renovation work that has now been completed, and it has since been returned to the company carrying out the project. We would like to offer you a free stay at the Prestige so that you may experience the world-class service for which we are known. Please contact me at 493-555-0122 if you would like to take up this offer.

Greta Sanchez
Customer Relations
The Prestige Hotel

196. What is indicated about the hotel rooms listed on the Web page?

(A) Some are offered at a discounted price.
(B) They are all located on the same level.
(C) Rooms on the first floor are more expensive.
(D) Some do not have access to concierge services.

197. Which of the following features did Ms. Aldridge NOT personally use?

(A) The concierge
(B) The swimming pool
(C) The gym
(D) The roof terrace

198. In the review, the word "offered" in paragraph 1, line 4, is closest in meaning to

(A) provided
(B) discounted
(C) volunteered
(D) passed

199. In what type of room did Ms. Aldridge most likely stay?

(A) Standard
(B) Standard En Suite
(C) Premier
(D) Deluxe

200. What does Ms. Sanchez indicate about the machinery on site?

(A) It has now been removed.
(B) It has been relocated to the gym.
(C) It will be insulated to make it quieter.
(D) A staff member has been employed to fix it.

Stop! This is the end of the test. If you finish before time is called, you may go back to Parts 5, 6, and 7 and check your work.

ANSWER SHEET

YBM 실전토익 RC 1000 (2)

수험번호

응시일자 : 20 년 월 일

성명
한글
한자
영자

Test 01 (Part 5~7)

101	102	103	104	105	106	107	108	109	110	111	112	113	114	115	116	117	118	119	120
121	122	123	124	125	126	127	128	129	130	131	132	133	134	135	136	137	138	139	140
141	142	143	144	145	146	147	148	149	150	151	152	153	154	155	156	157	158	159	160
161	162	163	164	165	166	167	168	169	170	171	172	173	174	175	176	177	178	179	180
181	182	183	184	185	186	187	188	189	190	191	192	193	194	195	196	197	198	199	200

Test 02 (Part 5~7)

101	102	103	104	105	106	107	108	109	110	111	112	113	114	115	116	117	118	119	120
121	122	123	124	125	126	127	128	129	130	131	132	133	134	135	136	137	138	139	140
141	142	143	144	145	146	147	148	149	150	151	152	153	154	155	156	157	158	159	160
161	162	163	164	165	166	167	168	169	170	171	172	173	174	175	176	177	178	179	180
181	182	183	184	185	186	187	188	189	190	191	192	193	194	195	196	197	198	199	200

ANSWER SHEET

YBM 실전토익 RC 1000 (2)

수험번호

응시일자 : 20 년 월 일

성명 한글 / 한자 / 영자

Test 03 (Part 5~7)

101–120, 121–140, 141–160, 161–180, 181–200

Test 04 (Part 5~7)

101–120, 121–140, 141–160, 161–180, 181–200

ANSWER SHEET

YBM 실전토익 RC 1000 (2)

수험번호

응시일자 : 20   년   월   일

성명 한글
한자
영자

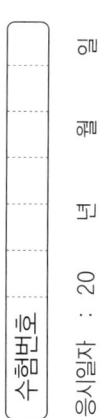

Test 05 (Part 5~7)

101 102 103 104 105 106 107 108 109 110 111 112 113 114 115 116 117 118 119 120

121 122 123 124 125 126 127 128 129 130 131 132 133 134 135 136 137 138 139 140

141 142 143 144 145 146 147 148 149 150 151 152 153 154 155 156 157 158 159 160

161 162 163 164 165 166 167 168 169 170 171 172 173 174 175 176 177 178 179 180

181 182 183 184 185 186 187 188 189 190 191 192 193 194 195 196 197 198 199 200

Test 06 (Part 5~7)

101 102 103 104 105 106 107 108 109 110 111 112 113 114 115 116 117 118 119 120

121 122 123 124 125 126 127 128 129 130 131 132 133 134 135 136 137 138 139 140

141 142 143 144 145 146 147 148 149 150 151 152 153 154 155 156 157 158 159 160

161 162 163 164 165 166 167 168 169 170 171 172 173 174 175 176 177 178 179 180

181 182 183 184 185 186 187 188 189 190 191 192 193 194 195 196 197 198 199 200

ANSWER SHEET

YBM 실전토익 RC 1000 (2)

수험번호

응시일자 : 20   년   월   일

성명
한글
한자
영자

Test 07 (Part 5~7)

Test 08 (Part 5~7)

ANSWER SHEET

YBM 실전토익 RC 1000 (2)

수험번호

응시일자 : 20 년 월 일

성명		
	한글	
	한자	
	영자	

Test 09 (Part 5~7)

101 ~ 120	121 ~ 140	141 ~ 160	161 ~ 180	181 ~ 200

Test 10 (Part 5~7)

101 ~ 120	121 ~ 140	141 ~ 160	161 ~ 180	181 ~ 200

ANSWER SHEET

YBM 실전토익 RC 1000 (2)

수험번호						

응시일자 : 20 년 월 일

성명	한 글	
	한 자	
	영 자	

Test (Part 5~7)

101	ⓐ ⓑ ⓒ ⓓ	121	ⓐ ⓑ ⓒ ⓓ	141	ⓐ ⓑ ⓒ ⓓ	161	ⓐ ⓑ ⓒ ⓓ	181	ⓐ ⓑ ⓒ ⓓ
102	ⓐ ⓑ ⓒ ⓓ	122	ⓐ ⓑ ⓒ ⓓ	142	ⓐ ⓑ ⓒ ⓓ	162	ⓐ ⓑ ⓒ ⓓ	182	ⓐ ⓑ ⓒ ⓓ
103	ⓐ ⓑ ⓒ ⓓ	123	ⓐ ⓑ ⓒ ⓓ	143	ⓐ ⓑ ⓒ ⓓ	163	ⓐ ⓑ ⓒ ⓓ	183	ⓐ ⓑ ⓒ ⓓ
104	ⓐ ⓑ ⓒ ⓓ	124	ⓐ ⓑ ⓒ ⓓ	144	ⓐ ⓑ ⓒ ⓓ	164	ⓐ ⓑ ⓒ ⓓ	184	ⓐ ⓑ ⓒ ⓓ
105	ⓐ ⓑ ⓒ ⓓ	125	ⓐ ⓑ ⓒ ⓓ	145	ⓐ ⓑ ⓒ ⓓ	165	ⓐ ⓑ ⓒ ⓓ	185	ⓐ ⓑ ⓒ ⓓ
106	ⓐ ⓑ ⓒ ⓓ	126	ⓐ ⓑ ⓒ ⓓ	146	ⓐ ⓑ ⓒ ⓓ	166	ⓐ ⓑ ⓒ ⓓ	186	ⓐ ⓑ ⓒ ⓓ
107	ⓐ ⓑ ⓒ ⓓ	127	ⓐ ⓑ ⓒ ⓓ	147	ⓐ ⓑ ⓒ ⓓ	167	ⓐ ⓑ ⓒ ⓓ	187	ⓐ ⓑ ⓒ ⓓ
108	ⓐ ⓑ ⓒ ⓓ	128	ⓐ ⓑ ⓒ ⓓ	148	ⓐ ⓑ ⓒ ⓓ	168	ⓐ ⓑ ⓒ ⓓ	188	ⓐ ⓑ ⓒ ⓓ
109	ⓐ ⓑ ⓒ ⓓ	129	ⓐ ⓑ ⓒ ⓓ	149	ⓐ ⓑ ⓒ ⓓ	169	ⓐ ⓑ ⓒ ⓓ	189	ⓐ ⓑ ⓒ ⓓ
110	ⓐ ⓑ ⓒ ⓓ	130	ⓐ ⓑ ⓒ ⓓ	150	ⓐ ⓑ ⓒ ⓓ	170	ⓐ ⓑ ⓒ ⓓ	190	ⓐ ⓑ ⓒ ⓓ
111	ⓐ ⓑ ⓒ ⓓ	131	ⓐ ⓑ ⓒ ⓓ	151	ⓐ ⓑ ⓒ ⓓ	171	ⓐ ⓑ ⓒ ⓓ	191	ⓐ ⓑ ⓒ ⓓ
112	ⓐ ⓑ ⓒ ⓓ	132	ⓐ ⓑ ⓒ ⓓ	152	ⓐ ⓑ ⓒ ⓓ	172	ⓐ ⓑ ⓒ ⓓ	192	ⓐ ⓑ ⓒ ⓓ
113	ⓐ ⓑ ⓒ ⓓ	133	ⓐ ⓑ ⓒ ⓓ	153	ⓐ ⓑ ⓒ ⓓ	173	ⓐ ⓑ ⓒ ⓓ	193	ⓐ ⓑ ⓒ ⓓ
114	ⓐ ⓑ ⓒ ⓓ	134	ⓐ ⓑ ⓒ ⓓ	154	ⓐ ⓑ ⓒ ⓓ	174	ⓐ ⓑ ⓒ ⓓ	194	ⓐ ⓑ ⓒ ⓓ
115	ⓐ ⓑ ⓒ ⓓ	135	ⓐ ⓑ ⓒ ⓓ	155	ⓐ ⓑ ⓒ ⓓ	175	ⓐ ⓑ ⓒ ⓓ	195	ⓐ ⓑ ⓒ ⓓ
116	ⓐ ⓑ ⓒ ⓓ	136	ⓐ ⓑ ⓒ ⓓ	156	ⓐ ⓑ ⓒ ⓓ	176	ⓐ ⓑ ⓒ ⓓ	196	ⓐ ⓑ ⓒ ⓓ
117	ⓐ ⓑ ⓒ ⓓ	137	ⓐ ⓑ ⓒ ⓓ	157	ⓐ ⓑ ⓒ ⓓ	177	ⓐ ⓑ ⓒ ⓓ	197	ⓐ ⓑ ⓒ ⓓ
118	ⓐ ⓑ ⓒ ⓓ	138	ⓐ ⓑ ⓒ ⓓ	158	ⓐ ⓑ ⓒ ⓓ	178	ⓐ ⓑ ⓒ ⓓ	198	ⓐ ⓑ ⓒ ⓓ
119	ⓐ ⓑ ⓒ ⓓ	139	ⓐ ⓑ ⓒ ⓓ	159	ⓐ ⓑ ⓒ ⓓ	179	ⓐ ⓑ ⓒ ⓓ	199	ⓐ ⓑ ⓒ ⓓ
120	ⓐ ⓑ ⓒ ⓓ	140	ⓐ ⓑ ⓒ ⓓ	160	ⓐ ⓑ ⓒ ⓓ	180	ⓐ ⓑ ⓒ ⓓ	200	ⓐ ⓑ ⓒ ⓓ

Test (Part 5~7)

101	ⓐ ⓑ ⓒ ⓓ	121	ⓐ ⓑ ⓒ ⓓ	141	ⓐ ⓑ ⓒ ⓓ	161	ⓐ ⓑ ⓒ ⓓ	181	ⓐ ⓑ ⓒ ⓓ
102	ⓐ ⓑ ⓒ ⓓ	122	ⓐ ⓑ ⓒ ⓓ	142	ⓐ ⓑ ⓒ ⓓ	162	ⓐ ⓑ ⓒ ⓓ	182	ⓐ ⓑ ⓒ ⓓ
103	ⓐ ⓑ ⓒ ⓓ	123	ⓐ ⓑ ⓒ ⓓ	143	ⓐ ⓑ ⓒ ⓓ	163	ⓐ ⓑ ⓒ ⓓ	183	ⓐ ⓑ ⓒ ⓓ
104	ⓐ ⓑ ⓒ ⓓ	124	ⓐ ⓑ ⓒ ⓓ	144	ⓐ ⓑ ⓒ ⓓ	164	ⓐ ⓑ ⓒ ⓓ	184	ⓐ ⓑ ⓒ ⓓ
105	ⓐ ⓑ ⓒ ⓓ	125	ⓐ ⓑ ⓒ ⓓ	145	ⓐ ⓑ ⓒ ⓓ	165	ⓐ ⓑ ⓒ ⓓ	185	ⓐ ⓑ ⓒ ⓓ
106	ⓐ ⓑ ⓒ ⓓ	126	ⓐ ⓑ ⓒ ⓓ	146	ⓐ ⓑ ⓒ ⓓ	166	ⓐ ⓑ ⓒ ⓓ	186	ⓐ ⓑ ⓒ ⓓ
107	ⓐ ⓑ ⓒ ⓓ	127	ⓐ ⓑ ⓒ ⓓ	147	ⓐ ⓑ ⓒ ⓓ	167	ⓐ ⓑ ⓒ ⓓ	187	ⓐ ⓑ ⓒ ⓓ
108	ⓐ ⓑ ⓒ ⓓ	128	ⓐ ⓑ ⓒ ⓓ	148	ⓐ ⓑ ⓒ ⓓ	168	ⓐ ⓑ ⓒ ⓓ	188	ⓐ ⓑ ⓒ ⓓ
109	ⓐ ⓑ ⓒ ⓓ	129	ⓐ ⓑ ⓒ ⓓ	149	ⓐ ⓑ ⓒ ⓓ	169	ⓐ ⓑ ⓒ ⓓ	189	ⓐ ⓑ ⓒ ⓓ
110	ⓐ ⓑ ⓒ ⓓ	130	ⓐ ⓑ ⓒ ⓓ	150	ⓐ ⓑ ⓒ ⓓ	170	ⓐ ⓑ ⓒ ⓓ	190	ⓐ ⓑ ⓒ ⓓ
111	ⓐ ⓑ ⓒ ⓓ	131	ⓐ ⓑ ⓒ ⓓ	151	ⓐ ⓑ ⓒ ⓓ	171	ⓐ ⓑ ⓒ ⓓ	191	ⓐ ⓑ ⓒ ⓓ
112	ⓐ ⓑ ⓒ ⓓ	132	ⓐ ⓑ ⓒ ⓓ	152	ⓐ ⓑ ⓒ ⓓ	172	ⓐ ⓑ ⓒ ⓓ	192	ⓐ ⓑ ⓒ ⓓ
113	ⓐ ⓑ ⓒ ⓓ	133	ⓐ ⓑ ⓒ ⓓ	153	ⓐ ⓑ ⓒ ⓓ	173	ⓐ ⓑ ⓒ ⓓ	193	ⓐ ⓑ ⓒ ⓓ
114	ⓐ ⓑ ⓒ ⓓ	134	ⓐ ⓑ ⓒ ⓓ	154	ⓐ ⓑ ⓒ ⓓ	174	ⓐ ⓑ ⓒ ⓓ	194	ⓐ ⓑ ⓒ ⓓ
115	ⓐ ⓑ ⓒ ⓓ	135	ⓐ ⓑ ⓒ ⓓ	155	ⓐ ⓑ ⓒ ⓓ	175	ⓐ ⓑ ⓒ ⓓ	195	ⓐ ⓑ ⓒ ⓓ
116	ⓐ ⓑ ⓒ ⓓ	136	ⓐ ⓑ ⓒ ⓓ	156	ⓐ ⓑ ⓒ ⓓ	176	ⓐ ⓑ ⓒ ⓓ	196	ⓐ ⓑ ⓒ ⓓ
117	ⓐ ⓑ ⓒ ⓓ	137	ⓐ ⓑ ⓒ ⓓ	157	ⓐ ⓑ ⓒ ⓓ	177	ⓐ ⓑ ⓒ ⓓ	197	ⓐ ⓑ ⓒ ⓓ
118	ⓐ ⓑ ⓒ ⓓ	138	ⓐ ⓑ ⓒ ⓓ	158	ⓐ ⓑ ⓒ ⓓ	178	ⓐ ⓑ ⓒ ⓓ	198	ⓐ ⓑ ⓒ ⓓ
119	ⓐ ⓑ ⓒ ⓓ	139	ⓐ ⓑ ⓒ ⓓ	159	ⓐ ⓑ ⓒ ⓓ	179	ⓐ ⓑ ⓒ ⓓ	199	ⓐ ⓑ ⓒ ⓓ
120	ⓐ ⓑ ⓒ ⓓ	140	ⓐ ⓑ ⓒ ⓓ	160	ⓐ ⓑ ⓒ ⓓ	180	ⓐ ⓑ ⓒ ⓓ	200	ⓐ ⓑ ⓒ ⓓ

YBM
실전토익
RC1000

2
정답·해설

YBM
실전토익
RC1000
2

YBM

TEST 1

101 (C)	**102** (D)	**103** (A)	**104** (C)	**105** (B)
106 (A)	**107** (A)	**108** (C)	**109** (C)	**110** (A)
111 (B)	**112** (D)	**113** (A)	**114** (A)	**115** (A)
116 (D)	**117** (B)	**118** (B)	**119** (B)	**120** (A)
121 (B)	**122** (B)	**123** (A)	**124** (D)	**125** (C)
126 (C)	**127** (D)	**128** (C)	**129** (D)	**130** (B)
131 (C)	**132** (D)	**133** (D)	**134** (A)	**135** (A)
136 (B)	**137** (B)	**138** (C)	**139** (C)	**140** (A)
141 (A)	**142** (B)	**143** (D)	**144** (A)	**145** (C)
146 (C)	**147** (D)	**148** (C)	**149** (B)	**150** (C)
151 (A)	**152** (C)	**153** (D)	**154** (B)	**155** (D)
156 (C)	**157** (D)	**158** (D)	**159** (B)	**160** (C)
161 (C)	**162** (C)	**163** (A)	**164** (D)	**165** (D)
166 (A)	**167** (D)	**168** (C)	**169** (D)	**170** (D)
171 (D)	**172** (B)	**173** (A)	**174** (B)	**175** (C)
176 (B)	**177** (D)	**178** (C)	**179** (A)	**180** (D)
181 (D)	**182** (D)	**183** (D)	**184** (B)	**185** (B)
186 (A)	**187** (D)	**188** (C)	**189** (D)	**190** (D)
191 (B)	**192** (D)	**193** (D)	**194** (D)	**195** (D)
196 (D)	**197** (B)	**198** (A)	**199** (D)	**200** (C)

PART 5

101 인칭대명사의 격 _ 소유격

해설 빈칸 뒤에 나오는 명사(variety)를 한정 수식하는 자리이므로, 정답은 소유격 인칭대명사 (C) our이다.

번역 애플턴 뷔페에서 식사하신 고객들은 저희의 다양한 해산물 요리를 호평해왔습니다.

어휘 diner 식사 손님 comment favorably on ~을 호평하다 [a / 소유격] wide variety of 다양한 seafood dish 해산물 요리

102 명사 어휘

해설 빈칸 앞 명사(delivery)와 함께 복합명사를 이루는 명사 자리로, 앞에 있는 형용사(reasonable)의 수식을 받는다. 문맥상 '저렴한 배송비'라는 의미가 자연스러우므로, 정답은 (D) fees(수수료, 요금)이다. '배송비(delivery fee)'라는 관용적인 표현으로 묶어서 기억하자. (A) routines (일과, 일상적인 일), (B) trucks(트럭), (C) duties(업무, 직무, 세금)는 의미상 적합하지 않다.

번역 레브 가구는 질 좋은 수제 상품을 갖추었으며 배송비가 저렴하다.

어휘 furniture 가구 high-quality 고급, 질 좋은 handmade goods 수제 상품 reasonable 합리적인, 저렴한 delivery fee 배송비

103 동사 어형 _ 태

해설 빈칸은 주어(The Fort Myers Garden Club) 뒤의 동사 자리로, 뒤에 나오는 명사구(a monthly newsletter)를 목적어로 취한다. 문맥상 '월간 소식지를 배포한다'라는 능동의 의미가 자연스러우므로, 정답은

(A) circulates이다. 수동의 의미를 나타내는 동사 (B) was circulated와 (D) has been circulated는 목적어를 취할 수 없고, to부정사 (C) to circulate는 동사 자리에 들어갈 수 없다.

번역 포트 마이어스 가든 클럽은 회원들에게 정보를 알리기 위해 월간 소식지를 배포한다.

어휘 monthly 한 달에 한 번의, 매월의 newsletter 소식지 keep + 사람 + informed ~에게 계속 알려주다 circulate 배포[유포]하다

104 명사 자리

해설 빈칸은 형용사(fascinating)의 수식을 받는 명사 자리이다. 명사 (A) photographer와 (C) photographs 중에 문맥상 '흥미로운 사진들로 장식된 로비'가 의미가 자연스러우므로, 정답은 (C) photographs이다. 명사 (A) photographer(사진작가)는 의미상 적합하지 않고, 형용사 (D) photographic(사진의)은 품사상 적합하지 않다.

번역 흥미로운 사진들로 장식되어 있어서 호텔 로비는 누군가를 기다리는 동안 시간을 보내기에 아주 좋은 장소이다.

어휘 decorate 장식하다 fascinating 흥미로운 pass the time 시간을 보내다 wait for ~을 기다리다 photograph 사진; 사진을 찍다, 촬영하다

105 수량형용사

해설 빈칸 뒤 복수명사(keys)를 한정 수식하는 자리이므로, 정답은 (B) all이다. (A) each와 (C) another는 단수명사를 한정 수식하고, 부정대명사 (D) others는 형용사 자리에 나올 수 없다. 참고로 (B) all은 복수명사 외에 셀 수 없는 명사도 한정 수식한다.

번역 임대 기간이 끝나면 아파트의 모든 열쇠는 건물주에게 반환되어야 한다.

어휘 at the end of ~말에, ~이 끝날 때 lease period 임대[대여] 기간 return 돌려주다, 반환하다 building owner 건물주

106 부사 어휘

해설 빈칸은 to부정사(to handle)의 목적어(it) 뒤에서 to부정사(to handle)를 수식하는 부사 자리이다. 문맥상 '조심해서 다루다'라는 의미가 자연스러우므로, 정답은 (A) carefully(조심해서, 주의 깊게)이다. (B) fairly(상당히, 꽤, 정당하게), (C) currently(현재), (D) barely(간신히, 가까스로, 거의 ~ 없이)는 의미상 적합하지 않다.

번역 그 화학물질은 맨살에 닿으면 위험할 수 있으므로 반드시 조심해서 다루어야 한다.

어휘 chemical 화학물질 hazardous 위험한 get in contact with ~와 접촉하다, ~에 닿다 bare skin 맨살 be sure to + 동사원형 반드시 ~하다 handle 다루다, 취급하다 carefully 조심해서, 주의 깊게

107 전치사 어휘

해설 빈칸은 명사구(the past few years) 앞에 위치하는 전치사 자리이다. 전치사 (A) over(~ 동안, ~ 위로), (B) of(~의, ~ 중에), (C) beneath (~ 아래에) 중에 문맥상 '지난 몇 년 동안 쇠퇴해왔다'라는 의미가 자연스

러우므로, 정답은 (A) over이다. 접속부사 (D) then(그때, 그리고는)은 목적어를 취할 수 없으므로 적합하지 않다.

번역 팜밸리의 관광산업은 항공비 상승으로 지난 몇 년 동안 꾸준히 쇠퇴해왔다.

어휘 tourism 관광산업 decline 쇠퇴하다 steadily 꾸준히 due to ~ 때문에 rising 상승하는, 오르는 cost of flights 항공비

108 전치사 어휘

해설 빈칸은 명사구(secure cabinets) 앞에 올 수 있는 전치사 자리이다. 문맥상 '안전한 캐비닛 안에 보관되어 있다'라는 의미가 자연스러우므로, 정답은 (C) in이다.

번역 환자 진료기록부는 대부분 4층의 안전한 캐비닛에 보관되어 있는데, 이는 그곳의 보안 수준이 높기 때문이다.

어휘 most of ~의 대부분[대다수] patient file (환자) 진료기록부 store 보관하다 secure 안전한 a high level of security 높은 보안 수준

109 부사 자리

해설 앞의 동사구(wil be sent)를 수식하는 부사 자리로, 정답은 (C) directly이다. 동사 (A) directs, 명사 (B) director와 (D) direction은 품사상 적합하지 않다.

번역 창고 공간이 부족해서 일부 상품은 제조업체에서 바로 매장으로 보낼 것이다.

어휘 a lack of ~의 부족 space 공간 warehouse 창고 goods 상품 manufacturer 제조업체, 제조사 direct 지시하다 director 감독 directly 바로, 직접 direction 지시, 방향

110 가정법 미래 _ 도치

해설 빈칸은 가정법 미래의 접속사(if)가 생략되어 주어(the expansion to the Phoenix)와 조동사(should)가 도치된 절의 조동사 자리이므로, 정답은 조동사 (A) Should이다. 가정법 미래의 접속사(If)를 포함한 절은 〈If the expansion to the Phoenix Building should be approved〉로 나타낼 수 있다.

번역 피닉스 빌딩의 확장이 혹시 승인된다면 3월 초에 건설공사가 시작될 것이다.

어휘 expansion 확장, 확대 approve 승인하다, 허가하다 construction 건설공사 since ~이므로, ~ 이래로 while ~하는 동안: ~인 반면

111 형용사 자리

해설 빈칸 뒤 명사(answers)를 수식하는 형용사 자리이므로, 정답은 (B) satisfactory이다. 동사 (A) satisfies, 명사 (C) satisfaction, 부사 (D) satisfactorily는 품사상 적합하지 않다.

번역 CEO가 기자회견에서 기자들에게 이야기했지만 그들의 질문에 흡족한 답변을 하지는 못했다.

어휘 although ~에도 불구하고 speak to ~에게 말하다 reporter 기자 press conference 기자회견 fail to + 동사원형 ~하지 못하다, ~하는 데 실패하다 provide 제공하다 satisfy 만족시키다 satisfactory 만족스러운, 흡족한 satisfaction 만족 satisfactorily 만족스럽게, 흡족하게

112 부사 어휘

해설 빈칸은 현재진행시제 동사를 이루는 are와 awaiting 사이에서, 동사(awaiting)를 수식하는 부사 자리이다. 문맥상 '손꼽아 기다리다'라는 의미가 자연스러우므로, 정답은 (D) eagerly(간절히, 손꼽아, 열심히)이다. (A) fairly(상당히, 꽤, 정당하게), (B) precisely(정확하게, 정밀하게), (C) repeatedly(거듭, 반복해서)는 의미상 적합하지 않다.

번역 〈갤럭시 배틀〉 모험 시리즈의 팬들은 릭 켈러 감독의 신작 영화가 개봉되기를 손꼽아 기다리고 있다.

어휘 galaxy 은하계 battle 전투 adventure 모험, 어드벤처 series 연작[연재물], 시리즈 await 기다리다(= wait for) release 개봉 director 감독 eagerly 간절히, 손꼽아

113 형용사 어휘

해설 빈칸 앞에 있는 to부정사(to ensure)의 목적어 역할을 하는 명사(supply)를 수식하는 형용사 자리이다. 문맥상 '꾸준한 공급을 확실히 하기 위해'라는 의미가 자연스러우므로, 정답은 (A) constant(꾸준한, 지속적인)이다. (B) portable(휴대할 수 있는), (C) reluctant(주저하는, 망설이는), (D) previous(이전의, 먼저의)는 의미상 적합하지 않다.

번역 그 호텔은 청소용품을 꾸준히 공급 받기 위해 지역의 몇몇 유통업체와 협업한다.

어휘 work with ~와 함께 일하다, 협력하다 several 몇몇의 distributor 유통업자, 배급업자 region 지역 ensure 반드시 ~하다, 보장하다 supply 공급 cleaning product 청소용품 constant 꾸준한, 지속적인

114 전치사

해설 빈칸 뒤 목적어(the sudden resignation of the company's president)와 함께 앞에 있는 명사(meeting)를 수식하는 전치사 자리이다. 전치사 (A) concerning(~에 관한), (C) until(~까지), (D) within(~ 이내에, ~ 안에) 중에 문맥상 '사장의 갑작스런 사임에 관한 회의'라는 의미가 자연스러우므로, 정답은 (A) concerning이다. 부사절 접속사 (B) whereas(반면에) 뒤에는 완전한 절이 나와야 한다.

번역 팀장은 사장의 갑작스러운 사임을 두고 막판에 회의를 열었다.

어휘 office manager 팀장, 부장 hold a meeting 회의를 열다 last-minute 막판의 sudden 갑작스런 resignation 사임, 사직 president 사장 concerning ~에 관해

115 명사절 접속사

해설 빈칸 뒤에 나오는 완전한 절(it is necessary to contact emergency medical personnel)을 이끌면서 앞에 있는 타동사(covered)의 목적어 역할을 하는 명사절 접속사 자리이므로, 정답은 (A) when이다. 명사절 접속사 (B) who, (C) what, (D) which 뒤에는 주어 또는 목적어가 없는 불완전한 절이 나온다.

번역 안전교육의 첫 주제로 언제 응급의료진에게 연락할 필요가 있는지를 다루었다.

safety training 안전교육 cover 다루다, 포함하다 necessary 필요한 contact 연락하다, 접촉하다 emergency medical personnel 응급의료진

116 형용사 자리 _ 주격 보어

해설 빈칸은 동사(will be)의 주어(the service)를 보충 설명하는 형용사 자리이므로, 정답은 형용사 (D) prompt이다. 동사 (A) prompts, 부사 (B) promptly, 명사 (C) promptness는 품사상 적합하지 않다.

번역 랭 씨는 서비스가 신속하다는 점을 알기 때문에 스카이 택배를 이용해 소포를 보낸다.

어휘 courier 택배 package 소포, 짐꾸러미 prompt 즉각적인, 신속한; 촉발하다, 유도하다 promptly 신속하게 promptness 신속함

117 동사 자리 _ 태 / 시제

해설 빈칸은 주격 관계대명사(that)이 이끄는 관계대명사절의 동사 자리로, 수, 태, 시제를 따져가며 정답을 선택해야 한다. 과거 시간을 나타내는 부사(last month)가 있고, 문맥상 '지난달에 시행된 주차정책'이라는 수동의 의미가 자연스러우므로, 정답은 수동의 과거시제 동사 (B) was implemented이다.

번역 지난달 시 공무원들이 실시한 주차정책의 결과로 주민들이 많은 혼란을 겪었다.

어휘 parking policy 주차정책 city official 시 공무원 result in 결과 ~이 되다 a great deal of 많은 confusion 혼란, 혼동 resident 주민 implement 시행[실시]하다

118 상관접속사

해설 빈칸에는 부정어(not)와 함께 상관접속사를 이루어 앞에 있는 to부정사(to visit)의 목적어(all sections of the museum's permanent gallery)와 목적어(its special exhibits)를 연결하는 등위접속사가 들어가야 한다. 따라서 정답은 (B) but이다. 상관접속사 B but not A(A가 아니라 B)는 상관접속사(not A but B)의 형태로도 나타낼 수 있다. 등위접속사 (A) or는 either와 짝을 이루어 쓰인다.

번역 입장권이 있으면 박물관 상설 전시실의 모든 구역을 구경할 수 있지만 특별 전시회는 볼 수 없다.

어휘 allow 허용[허락]하다 visit 방문하다, 구경하러 다니다 section 구역 permanent 상설의, 영구적인 special exhibit 특별 전시회

119 부사 자리

해설 빈칸 앞 동사원형(speak)을 수식하는 부사 자리이므로, 정답은 부사 (B) publicly이다. 명사 (A) publicity, 형용사 (C) public, 과거시제 동사/과거분사 (D) publicized는 품사상 적합하지 않다. 참고로 부정어(Not)가 부사절(until her book was published)의 맨 앞에 나오면, 주절은 〈조동사(did)+주어(the author)+동사(speak)〉의 형태로 도치된다.

번역 그 작가는 자신의 책이 출판되고 나서야 비로소 집필에 영감을 준 대상을 공개적으로 밝혔다.

어휘 not until + 도치구문 ~하고 나서야 비로소 ~하다 publish 출판[출간, 발표]하다 author 저자, 작가 inspiration 영감 publicity 선전, 홍보 publicly 공개적으로 public 공개적인, 공공의 publicize 선전[홍보]하다, 알리다

120 전치사 어휘

해설 빈칸은 명사구(its positive effect on the environment) 앞 전치사 자리이다. 문맥상 '환경에 긍정적 효과를 미치는 것 외에도 시에 부가 수입을 창출한다'라는 의미가 자연스러우므로, 정답은 (A) Besides(~외에, ~에 더하여)이다. 전치사 (B) Among(~ 사이에, ~ 중에)와 (D) Toward(~을 향해)는 의미상 적합하지 않고, 부사 (C) Instead(대신에)는 전치사(of)와 결합하여 전치사(~대신에)로 쓰인다.

번역 그 재활용 프로그램은 환경에 긍정적 효과를 미치는 것 외에도 시에 부가 수입을 창출할 것이다.

어휘 positive 긍정적인 effect on ~에 미치는 효과 environment 환경 recycling 재활용 generate 창출하다 extra income 부가 수입 besides ~ 외에, ~에 더하여

121 명사 자리 _ 전치사의 목적어

해설 빈칸 앞 명사(equipment)와 함께 복합명사를 이루는 명사 자리로, 빈칸을 포함한 복합명사는 앞에 있는 전치사(through)의 목적어 역할을 한다. 또한 뒤에 나오는 과거분사 구문(made possible by a federal grant)의 수식을 받는다. 따라서 정답은 명사 (B) modernization이다. 동사원형 (A) modernize, 과거시제 동사/과거분사 (C) modernized, 3인칭 단수 현재형 동사 (D) modernizes는 품사상 적합하지 않다.

번역 그 공장은 연방 지원금 덕에 장비를 현대화해서 생산성을 30% 가까이 올렸다.

어휘 factory 공장 increase 올리다, 증가시키다 productivity 생산성 nearly 거의, ~ 가까이 through ~을 통해 equipment 장비 modernization 현대화 possible 가능한 federal grant 연방 지원금 modernize 현대화하다

122 to부정사

해설 빈칸 뒤 동사원형(participate)과 함께 쓰일 수 있는 표현을 선택해야 한다. 따라서 정답은 (B) in order to이다. 부사절 접속사 (A) even though와 (D) so that 뒤에는 주어와 동사로 이루어진 완전한 절이 와야 하고, 전치사 (C) on behalf of 뒤에는 동사원형이 올 수 없다. '~하기 위해'라는 관용 표현으로 'in order to 동사원형/so as to 동사원형/to 동사원형'을 묶어서 기억하자.

번역 지원자들이 아마추어 사진대회에 참가하려면 나이가 적어도 18살은 돼야 한다.

어휘 applicant 지원자 at least 적어도, 최소한 participate in ~에 참가[참여]하다 photography contest 사진대회 even though (설령) ~일지라도 in order to + 동사원형 ~하기 위해 on behalf of ~을 대신[대표]해 so that + 주어 + 동사 ~하기 위해

123 동사 어휘

해설 빈칸 뒤 전치사(by)와 결합하여 '준수하다, 지키다'라는 의미를 나타내는 동사를 선택해야 한다. 따라서 정답은 (D) abide이다. 자동사 (A) conform(따르다, 순응하다)은 전치사(to)와 함께 쓰이고, (B) accompany는 be accompanied by(~을 동반하다)의 형태로 쓰이며, (C) establish(설립하다, 제정하다, 확립하다)는 주로 타동사로 쓰인다.

번역 밴스빌 공립도서관을 이용하는 모든 사람은 도서관 규정을 지키는 데 동의해야 한다.

어휘 **patron** 이용객, 손님, 후원자 **public library** 공립[공공] 도서관 **rules and regulations** 규정, 규약 **conform to** ~을 따르다 **abide by** ~을 지키다

124 동사 어휘

해설 빈칸 앞 동사(is)와 함께 수동의 의미를 나타내는 과거분사 자리로, 문맥에 어울리는 어휘를 선택해야 한다. 문맥상 '세계 여러 나라에 실시간 중계된다'라는 의미가 자연스러우므로, 정답은 (D) transmitted(전송하다, 중계하다, 방송하다)이다. (A) featured(~을 특징으로 하다, 특별히 포함하다), (B) equipped(장비를 갖추다), (C) determined(결정하다, 판단하다, 확정하다)는 의미상 적합하지 않다.

번역 그 뉴스 프로그램은 지속적인 위성 송출로 세계 여러 나라에 실시간 중계된다.

어휘 **in real time** 실시간으로 **continuous** 끊임없는, 지속적인 **satellite feed** 위성 송출[방송] **transmit** 중계하다, 전송하다

125 부사 자리

해설 빈칸은 수동의 의미를 나타내는 동사(are)과 과거분사(placed) 사이에서 뒤의 과거분사(placed)를 수식하는 부사 자리이므로, 정답은 (C) strategically이다. 형용사 (A) strategic, 과거시제 동사/과거분사 (B) strategized, 명사 (D) strategy는 품사상 적합하지 않다.

번역 땅바닥에 버려지는 쓰레기의 양을 줄이기 위해 놀이공원 전역에 쓰레기통이 전략적으로 배치되어 있다.

어휘 **trash bin** 쓰레기통 **place** 놓다, 배치하다 **throughout** ~ 전역에 **amusement park** 놀이공원 **reduce** 줄이다 **amount** 양 **litter** 쓰레기 **left on the ground** 땅바닥에 버려진 **strategic** 전략적인 **strategize** 전략을 짜다, 빈틈없이 계획하다 **strategically** 전략적으로 **strategy** 전략

126 명사 어휘

해설 빈칸은 명사(staff)와 함께 복합명사를 이루는 명사 자리이다. 문맥상 '직원들의 사기를 높이기 위해'라는 의미가 자연스러우므로, 정답은 (C) morale(사기, 의욕)이다. (A) reimbursement(상환, 배상), (B) appointment(예약, 약속), (D) resource(자원, 수완)는 의미상 적합하지 않다.

번역 관리자는 직원들의 사기를 높이기 위해 금요일마다 완화된 복장 규정을 도입하기로 했다.

어휘 **supervisor** 감독관, 관리자, 상사 **decide** 결정[결심]하다 **introduce** 도입하다 **relaxed** 완화된 **dress code** 복장 규정 **in an attempt to** + 동사원형 ~하기 위해, ~하려는 시도로 **improve** 높이다, 향상시키다 **staff morale** 직원 사기

127 동사 어휘

해설 빈칸 앞 전치사(from)의 목적어 역할을 하는 동명사 자리로, 문맥에 어울리는 어휘를 선택해야 한다. 문맥상 '손상되는 것을 막기 위해'라는 의미가 자연스러우므로, 정답은 (D) deteriorating(악화되다, 더 나빠지다)이다. (A) revealing(폭로하다, 밝혀내다, 드러내다), (B) commuting(통근하다), (C) overtaking(추월하다, 앞지르다, 능가하다)은 의미상 적합하지 않다.

번역 주차장의 새 표면이 시간이 지나면서 손상되는 것을 막기 위해 보호 물질이 도포되었다.

어휘 **protective** 보호하는 **substance** 물질 **be applied to** ~에 도포하다, 바르다 **surface** 표면 **parking lot** 주차장 **keep ~ from -ing** ~가 …하는 것을 막다[방지하다] **over time** 시간이 지나면서

128 형용사 자리 _ 명사 수식

해설 빈칸은 명사(goal)를 수식하는 형용사 자리이므로 정답은 (B) achievable(달성할 수 있는, 성취 가능한)이다. 동사 (A) achieve, 명사 (C) achievement, 동명사/현재분사 (D) achieving은 품사상 적합하지 않다.

번역 영업이사는 다음 분기 매출을 8% 높이는 것이 쉽게 달성할 수 있는 목표라고 생각한다.

어휘 **sales director** 영업이사 **increase** 증가 **sales** 매출, 판매 **quarter** 분기 **readily** 쉽게 **achieve** 달성하다 **achievable** 달성할 수 있는 **achievement** 업적, 성취

129 동사 자리 _ 시제

해설 빈칸은 단수 주어(the security guard) 뒤 동사 자리이다. 동사 (A) refuse와 (D) refused 중에 주절의 과거 시제(did not have)와 어울리는 시제를 찾아야 하므로 정답은 과거시제 동사 (D) refused이다. 현재 시제 복수동사 (A) refuse는 단수 주어(the security guard)와 수일치하지 않고, 시제상으로도 적합하지 않다. 명사 (B) refusal과 동명사/현재분사 (C) refusing은 품사상 적합하지 않다.

번역 페리스 씨가 신분증을 소지하지 않아서 경비원이 그녀를 건물에 들여보내지 않았다.

어휘 **ID card** 신분증 **security guard** 경비원, 보안요원 **allow** 허락[허용]하다 **enter** 들어가다 **refuse** 거부[거절]하다 **refusal** 거부, 거절

130 부사 어휘

해설 빈칸 뒤 형용사(similar)를 수식하는 부사 자리로, 문맥에 어울리는 어휘를 선택해야 한다. 문맥상 '눈에 띄게 비슷한 디자인'이라는 의미가 자연스러우므로, 정답은 (B) remarkably(눈에 띄게, 두드러지게)이다. (A) steadily(꾸준히, 착실히), (C) consecutively(연달아, 연속적으로), (D) unanimously(만장일치로, 이의 없이)는 의미상 적합하지 않다.

번역 그 로고들은 도안이 눈에 띄게 비슷해도 전혀 관련 없는 회사들이 만든 것이었다.

어휘 **although** 비록 ~일지라도 **logo** 로고, 상표 **similar** 비슷한 **create** 창조하다, 만들다 **completely unrelated** 전혀 관련 없는 **remarkably** 눈에 띄게, 확연히

PART 6

131-134 기사

> 3월 12일—다음 달부터 도심 거리 주차가 무료가 된다. 시의원들은 만장일치 투표로 시내에서 주차료 징수기 사용을 **131중단하기로** 했다. 시 공무원들이 주차료 징수기를 확인하고 주차권을 발행하기 위해서는 임금 인상이 필요해서 이런 관행이 더 이상 **132경제적이지** 않게 된 것이다. 공무원들은 이번 변화를 계기로 시 외곽에서 온 쇼핑객이 다수인 방문자들이 더 많아져 도심지역 개발을 **133촉진하기를** 바라고 있다. **134주차료 징수기가 당장 없어지지는 않겠지만 이번 변화는 4월 1일부터 시행된다.** 안내판을 부착해 운전자들에게 공지할 예정이다.

> **어휘** street parking 거리 주차 city center 도심 free 무료의, 공짜의 city council 시의회 choose to+동사원형 ~하기로 하다 parking meter 주차료 징수기 by a unanimous vote 만장일치 투표로 wage 임금 city worker 시 공무원 check 확인하다 issue 발행[발급]하다 practice 관행, 실천 no longer 더 이상 ~ 않다 official 공무원, 관리 development 개발 encourage 장려하다 shopper 쇼핑객 out of town 시외에서 go into effect 발효되다 remove 제거하다 immediately 당장, 즉시

131 to부정사

해설 빈칸은 앞에 있는 동사(chose)의 목적어 역할을 하는 자리로, 뒤에 나오는 명사(the use)를 목적어로 취한다. 동사(chose)는 to부정사를 목적어로 취하는 동사이므로, 정답은 능동의 to부정사 (C) to discontinue이다.

어휘 discontinue 중단하다

132 형용사 자리 _ 주격 보어

해설 빈칸은 앞에 있는 주어(the practice)를 보충 설명하는 형용사 자리이므로, 정답은 (D) economical(경제적인, 절약하는)이다. 명사 (C) economy(경제, 경기)는 주어(the practice)와 동격 관계를 이루지 않고, 동사 (A) economize(절약하다)와 부사 (B) economically(경제적으로)는 품사상 적합하지 않다.

어휘 economical 경제적인, 실속 있는, 절약하는

133 동사 어휘

해설 빈칸은 조동사(will) 뒤에 나오는 동사원형 자리로, 문맥에 어울리는 어휘를 선택해야 한다. 문맥상 '방문자들이 더 많아져 도심지역 개발을 촉진하다'라는 의미가 자연스러우므로, 정답은 (B) foster(촉진하다, 조성하다, 육성하다)이다. (A) adopt(채택하다, 입양하다), (C) multiply(증가시키다, 늘리다, 곱하다), (D) publicize(광고하다, 홍보하다, 알리다)는 의미상 적합하지 않다.

어휘 foster 촉진하다, 장려하다

134 문맥에 맞는 문장 고르기

번역 (A) 안내판을 부착해 운전자들에게 공지할 예정이다.
(B) 문자로 최신 교통 정보를 요청할 수 있다.
(C) 주차료는 저렴하다고 여겨진다.
(D) 주차 위반 과태료를 즉시 납부하시기 바랍니다.

해설 빈칸 앞 문장 '주차료 징수기가 당장 없어지지는 않겠지만 이번 변화는 4월 1일부터 시행된다(The change will go into effect on April 1, though the meters won't be removed immediately)'를 통해 무료 주차가 시행되는 시점과 주차료 징수기 철거에 따른 문제점을 알 수 있다. 따라서 빈칸에는 이에 대해 운전자들에게 알리는 방법을 언급하는 것이 문맥상 자연스러우므로, 정답은 (A)이다.

어휘 sign 안내표지판 post 게시하다 notify 알리다, 공지하다 motorist 운전자 parking fee 주차비 reasonable 합리적인, 저렴한 parking fine 주차위반 과태료 promptly 즉시

135-138 이메일

> 수신: 크루세로 전 직원 (stafflist@crucero.net)
> 발신: 가브리엘 젠슨 (jensong@crucero.net)
> 날짜: 11월 16일
> 제목: 초과근무 시간
>
> 재무팀 직원들이 우리 지점의 예산을 **135철저히** 살펴보았으며, 세심한 작업을 통해 상당히 부족한 부분이 있다고 판단했습니다. 이번 발견 **136때문에** 우리는 초과근무 시간을 최소화해서 운영비를 절감해야만 합니다. 모든 업무가 통상적인 근무시간 안에 **137완료되도록** 애써 주시기 바랍니다. **138초과근무가 불가피한 경우에는 부서장에게 미리 승인을 받아야 합니다.** 이는 영업부와 총무부 직원 모두에게 해당됩니다. 여러분의 협조에 감사합니다.
>
> 가브리엘 젠슨

> **어휘** overtime hours 초과근무 시간 finance 재무, 재정 examine 살펴보다, 조사하다 budget 예산 branch 지사, 지점 meticulous 꼼꼼한, 세심한 determine 판단하다, 결정하다 significant 상당한, 중요한 shortfall 부족(분) discovery 발견 reduce 줄이다, 절감하다 operating expense 운영비, 영업비 business hours 영업시간, 근무시간 overtime work 초과근무 avoid 피하다 approve 승인하다, 허가하다 in advance 미리, 사전에 department head 부서장 cooperation 협조, 협력

135 부사 어휘

해설 빈칸은 현재완료시제 동사를 이루는 have와 examined 사이에서 동사를 수식하는 부사 자리이다. 뒤에 나오는 앞뒤 순서를 나타내는 등위접속사(and) 뒤 전치사구(through their meticulous work)는 앞에서 있었던 일을 가리키고 있으므로, 빈칸에는 이와 유사한 의미의 부사를 선택해야 한다. 따라서 정답은 (A) thoroughly(철저히, 완전히)이다. (B) urgently(긴급히), (C) adversely(불리하게, 반대로), (D) solely(오직, 단독으로)는 의미상 적합하지 않다.

어휘 thoroughly 철저히

136 전치사

해설 빈칸은 명사구(this discovery) 앞 전치사 자리이다. 전치사 (B) Due to(~ 때문에, ~로 인해)와 (D) Rather than(~ 대신에) 중에 문맥상 '이번 발견 때문에 우리는 초과근무 시간을 최소화해서 운영비를 절감해야 한다'라는 의미가 자연스러우므로, 정답은 (B) Due to이다. 부사절 접속사 (A) Because 뒤에는 완전한 절이 나와야 하고, 부사 (C) Consequently(결과적으로, 따라서)는 목적어를 취할 수 없다.

어휘 due to ~ 때문에

137 형용사 자리 _ 목적격 보어

해설 빈칸 앞에 있는 to부정사(to get)의 목적어(all of your work)를 보충 설명하는 목적격 보어 자리이다. 목적격 보어로 쓰일 수 있는 과거분사 (B) completed와 현재분사 (D) completing 중에 문맥상 '모든 업무가 완료되도록 하다'라는 수동의 의미가 자연스러우므로, 정답은 과거분사 (B) completed이다. 동사 (A) completes는 품사상 적합하지 않고, 명사 (C) completion은 목적어(all of your work)와 동격 관계를 이루지 않는다.

138 문맥에 맞는 문장 고르기

번역 (A) 상세한 예산을 되도록 빨리 제출하시기 바랍니다.
(B) 대다수 직원이 일요일 근무보다 토요일 근무를 선호합니다.
(C) 이는 영업부와 총무부 직원 모두에게 해당됩니다.
(D) 추가 급여는 여러분의 계좌에 입금되었습니다.

해설 빈칸 앞 문장 '초과근무가 불가피한 경우에는 부서장에게 미리 승인을 받아야 합니다(In cases where overtime work cannot be avoided, it should be approved in advance by a department head)'를 통해 빈칸에는 초과근무의 경우 승인을 받아야 하는 대상을 구체적으로 언급하는 것이 문맥상 자연스러우므로 정답은 (C)이다.

어휘 apply to ~에게 적용되다, 해당하다

139-142 안내문

건강한 생활방식 장려에 헌신하는 비영리단체 도슨빌 인 모션이 8월 18일 토요일에 웰빙 축제를 139마련했습니다. 도슨빌은 심장병과 여타 질환 예방법에 관한 140인식을 높이길 원합니다. 축제의 많은 활동들의 목표는 참가자들에게 한 가지 식단을 엄격하게 고수할 필요가 없음을 보여주는 것입니다. 참가자들은 작은 변화로 건강을 증진할 수 있습니다. 141예를 들어, 오후 간식으로 먹는 초코바를 과일 한 조각으로 대체할 수 있습니다. 142마찬가지로, 감자 튀김을 샐러드로 바꿀 수 있습니다. 도움이 되는 조언을 더 원하십니까? 축제에 오세요! 축제는 도슨빌 지역주민회관에서 열릴 예정이며, 누구나 무료로 입장할 수 있습니다.

어휘 in motion 움직이는, 행동하는 nonprofit organization 비영리단체[기관] dedicated to ~에 헌신하는, 전념하는 promote 증진하다, 고취하다 raise awareness 인식[관심]을 높이다[제고하다] method 방법 prevent 예방하다, 방지하다 heart disease 심장병 condition 질환 participant 참가자 adhere to ~을 지키다[고수하다] strictly 엄격하게, 철저하게 for example 예를 들어 replace 대체하다 candy bar 초코바 snack 간식 swap A for B A를 B로 바꾸다[대체하다] admission 입장(료)

139 동사 어형

해설 빈칸은 주어(Dawsonville in Motion) 뒤에 나오는 동사 자리로, 앞에 있는 삽입구문(a nonprofit organization dedicated to promoting healthy lifestyles)은 주어와 동격 관계를 이룬다. 문맥상 주어 (Dawsonville in Motion)가 한 일을 나타내고 있으므로, 정답은 현재완료시제 동사 (C) has organized이다. 가정법 과거완료시제 동사 (B) would have organized(~했을 텐데)는 과거에 하지 못한 일을 나

타내므로, 의미상 적합하지 않고, 동명사/분사 (A) having organized와 (D) being organized는 동사 자리에 들어갈 수 없다.

어휘 organize 조직하다, 마련하다

140 명사 어휘

해설 빈칸 앞 to부정사(to raise)의 목적어 역할을 하는 명사 자리로, 뒤에 나오는 전치사구(of the methods for preventing heart disease and other conditions)와 잘 어울리는 어휘를 골라야 한다. 문맥상 '심장병과 여타 질환 예방법에 관한 인식을 높이다'라는 의미가 자연스러우므로, 정답은 (A) awareness(인식, 관심, 의식)이다. (B) funds(자금), (C) interest(관심, 흥미, 이해관계, 이익), (D) standards(기준, 수준, 규범)는 의미상 적합하지 않다.

141 문맥에 맞는 문장 고르기

번역 (A) 참가자들은 작은 변화로 건강을 증진할 수 있습니다.
(B) 주최측은 지난해보다 많은 사람이 참가하기를 기대합니다.
(C) 식단은 단체의 웹사이트에서 내려 받을 수 있습니다.
(D) 도슨빌에서 의료 문제의 비율이 상승하고 있습니다.

해설 빈칸 뒤에 나오는 문장 '예를 들어, 오후 간식으로 먹는 초코바를 과일 한 조각으로 대체할 수 있다(For example, a piece of fruit can replace a candy bar as an afternoon snack)'에서 변경사항의 구체적인 예(For example)를 제시하고 있다. 따라서 빈칸에는 포괄적인 내용(small changes)을 언급하는 것이 문맥상 자연스러우므로, 정답은 (A)이다.

어휘 turnout 참가자 수 rate 비율, 요금

142 부사 어휘 _ 문장 수식

해설 빈칸은 문장 전체를 수식하는 부사 자리로 문맥에 맞는 어휘를 선택해야 한다. (A) As a result(결과적으로), (B) Similarly(마찬가지로), (C) Regardless(개의치 않고), (D) Unfortunately(안타깝게도) 중에 앞에 나온 구체적인 예(For example, a piece of fruit can replace a candy bar as an afternoon snack)에 이어 시도해 볼 수 있는 또 다른 예(diners can swap French fries for a salad)를 들고 있으므로 정답은 (B) Similarly이다.

143-146 공지

차랙 타워스: 공지

144전기배선 신규 설치를 위해 9월 18일 목요일 오전 9시에 단지 대부분에 전력이 차단되오니 차랙 타워스 143입주민들께서는 양지하시기 바랍니다. 안전규정을 준수하려면 그렇게 해야 합니다, 정오까지는 전력이 복구되겠지만, 예상보다 작업이 길어지면 댁내 냉장고에 있는 145상하기 쉬운 식품들에 영향을 미칠 수도 있습니다. 작업이 예상 일정을 초과하면 귀대의 식품이 여전히 먹을 만한지 확인하시도록 공지해 드리겠습니다. 이번 계획된 정전은 지난 분기에 업그레이드된 사우스 타워를 146제외한 차랙 타워스 전 구역에 영향을 미치게 되니 유념하시기 바랍니다. 여러분의 인내와 이해에 감사드립니다.

143 명사 자리 _ 동사의 주어

해설 빈칸 뒤에 나오는 동사(should be aware)의 주어 역할을 하는 명사 자리로, 뒤에 나오는 전치사구(of Charack Towers)의 수식을 받는다. 문맥상 '차락 타워스 입주민들께서는 양지하시기 바랍니다'라는 의미가 자연스러우므로, 정답은 사람을 나타내는 명사 (D) Occupants(입주자, 사용자)이다. 명사 (B) Occupations(직업, 점령, 점유)는 의미상 적합하지 않고, 타동사의 동명사 (C) Occupying은 전치사(of) 없이 바로 목적어를 취한다.

어휘 occupy 점령[점유]하다, 차지하다 occupation 직업; 점령[점유]
occupant 입주민

144 문맥에 맞는 문장 고르기

번역 (A) 안전규정을 준수하려면 그렇게 해야 합니다.
(B) 가입을 원하시면 관리사무소를 찾아주십시오.
(C) 강한 폭풍으로 전력 공급이 중단되었습니다.
(D) 작업 중에는 보호장구를 착용하시기 바랍니다.

해설 빈칸 앞 문장 '전기배선 신규 설치를 위해 9월 18일 목요일 오전 9시에 단지 대부분에 전력이 차단되니 차락 타워스 입주민들께서는 양지하시기 바랍니다(Occupants of Charack Towers should be aware that the power will be turned off to most of the complex on Thursday, September 18 at 9 A.M. to install new wiring)'에서 전기배선의 신규 설치를 위한 전력차단을 언급하고 있다. 따라서 빈칸에는 그렇게 하는(do so) 이유를 밝히는 것이 문맥상 자연스러우므로, 정답은 (A)이다.

145 형용사 어휘

해설 빈칸 뒤 명사(goods)를 수식하는 형용사 자리로, 문맥에 맞는 어휘를 선택해야 한다. 문맥상 '냉장고에 있는 상하기 쉬운 식품들에 영향을 미칠 수 있다'라는 의미가 자연스러우므로, 정답은 (C) perishable(상하기 쉬운)이다. (A) durable(내구성이 있는, 오래 가는), (B) renewable(재생할 수 있는, 갱신 가능한), (D) exposed(노출된)는 의미상 적합하지 않다.

어휘 perishable 상하기 쉬운, 부패하기 쉬운

146 전치사 어휘

해설 빈칸은 명사(the South Tower) 앞에 오는 전치사 자리이다. 문맥상 '지난 분기에 업그레이드된 사우스 타워를 제외한 차락 타워스 전 구역'이라는 의미가 자연스러우므로, 정답은 (C) aside from(~을 제외하고)이다. (A) inside of(~의 안에), (B) owing to(~ 때문에, ~ 덕분에), (D) such as(~ 같은)는 의미상 적합하지 않다.

어휘 aside from ~을 제외하고

PART 7

147-148 양식

스팀 매스터스 고객 임대차 계약
멀로이 스트리트 170번지 · (325) 555-0197

고객: 이스와라 굽테   전화번호: (325) 555-0166
147신규 고객: 아니요   배송 ☐   방문 수령 ☒

품목	설명	가격
다울러-405 카펫 스팀 청소기 임대	2일 임대	95.00달러
148장비 임대 보증금		50.00달러
농축 카펫 샴푸 (12온스)	구입	15.95달러
	합계	160.95달러

유효 임대 기간은 3월 6일 오후 5시까지입니다. **148**보증금은 일단 기기가 반환되면 돌려받게 됩니다.

147 사실 관계 확인

번역 굽테 씨에 관해 사실인 것은?
(A) 두 가지 장비를 임차했다.
(B) 기기를 일주일 동안 보유할 수 있다.
(C) 최근에 전화번호를 바꿨다.
(D) 전에 스팀 매스터스를 이용한 적이 있다.

해설 양식에서 신규 고객(First-time Customer)인지 여부를 표시하는 자리에 '아니요(No)'라고 응답하고 있으므로, 정답은 (D)이다.

▶▶ Paraphrasing 지문의 **First-time Customer: No**
→ 정답의 **has used Steam Masters before**

148 세부 사항

번역 굽테 씨가 기기를 반환하면 어떻게 되겠는가?
(A) 남은 요금을 지불해야 할 것이다.
(B) 사용하지 않은 샴푸 값을 공제받을 것이다.
(C) 50달러를 돌려받게 될 것이다.
(D) 방문 수령비를 물게 될 것이다.

해설 마지막 단락에서 보증금은 일단 기기가 반환되면 돌려받게 될 것(The deposit will be paid back once the device is returned)이라고 했다. 따라서 굽테 씨가 기기를 반환할 경우 항목(Item)의 장비 임대 보증금(Equipment rental deposit)인 50달러를 돌려받는다는 것을 알 수 있으므로, 정답은 (C)이다.

▶▶ Paraphrasing 지문의 **be paid back**
→ 정답의 **receive fifty dollars back**

149-150 편지

러모나 잭슨
러모나 식당
스프링헤이븐 로드 552번지
93106 캘리포니아 주 샌타바버라

잭슨 씨께,

귀하가 식당 앞 인도 가까이에 설치한 실외 파티오와 관련해 샌타바버라 시 공무원들이 몇 차례 불편신고를 접수했습니다. **149**귀하의 영업시간 때문에 고객 다수가 밤 늦게 옥외에서 시끄럽게 대화하고 있습니다. 오후 9시 이후에는 대화하는 소리를 최대한 낮추도록 고객들에게 요청해 주시기 바랍니다. **150**또한 서면 공지를 붙여서 고객들이 지역 주민에게 예의를 갖추도록 일깨워야 합니다. 제가 공지 예문 하나를 동봉했습니다. 문의하실 내용이 있으면 저희의 비긴급 전화 회선인 555-0181로 연락해 주십시오.

협조해 주셔서 감사합니다.

리타 살라자 배상
샌타바버라 경찰국

어휘 city official 시 공무원 complaint 불편신고, 민원 regarding ~에 관해 outdoor 옥외의, 야외의 (*cf.* outdoors 옥외[야외]에서, 밖에서) patio (주변 바닥과 높이가 같고 포장된) 파티오 (*cf.* terrace 포장 혹은 비포장으로 주변 바닥보다 높이가 높은 테라스) set up 설치하다, 세우다 in front of ~ 앞에 sidewalk 보도, 인도 because of ~ 때문에, ~ 탓에 business hour 영업시간, 근무시간 patron 고객, 손님 loud 시끄러운, 소란스러운 conversation 대화 late at night 밤 늦게 keep ~ to a minimum volume ~ 소리를 최소한으로 유지하다 post a written announcement 서면 공지를 붙이다[게시하다] be courteous of ~에게 예의를 갖추다, ~를 정중히 대하다 inquiry 질문, 문의사항 direct A to B A를 B에게 연락하다[보내다] non-emergency line 비긴급[비응급] 전화

149 세부 사항

번역 살라자 씨가 언급하는 문제는 무엇인가?
(A) 동네가 주거 전용이다.
(B) 일부 테이블이 통로를 막고 있다.
(C) 식당의 영업허가가 만료되었다.
(D) 손님들이 소음을 너무 많이 낸다.

해설 귀하의 영업시간 때문에 고객 다수가 밤 늦게 옥외에서 시끄럽게 대화하고 있다(Because of your business hours, many of your patrons are having loud conversations outdoors late at night)고 했으므로 고객들이 밤 늦게까지 소음을 발생시킨다는 것을 알 수 있다. 따라서 정답은 (D)이다.

▶▶ Paraphrasing 지문의 **many of your patrons are having loud conversations** → 정답의 **Customers are making too much noise.**

150 세부 사항

번역 살라자 씨가 편지에 포함시킨 것은?
(A) 안건 사본
(B) 질의 양식
(C) 공지 견본
(D) 청구서

해설 서면 공지를 붙여서 고객들이 지역 주민에게 예의를 갖추도록 일깨워야 한다며 공지 예문 하나를 동봉했다(You should also post a written announcement reminding them to be courteous of the residents in the area. I've enclosed one as an example)고 했으므로, 서면 공지의 견본을 동봉했음을 알 수 있다. 따라서 정답은 (C)이다.

▶▶ Paraphrasing 지문의 **an example**
→ 정답의 **A sample notice**

151-152 문자 메시지

궈 시에, 오후 2:05
라고 엔터프라이지스 직원들과 회의를 하고 돌아오는 길인데, 그 사람들이 잠시 우리 건물을 구경하려고 나와 동행할 예정이에요.
새스키아 헤인스, 오후 2:06
내게 시킬 일이 있나요?
궈 시에, 오후 2:06
네. 로비 상태가 괜찮은지 확인 좀 해 줄래요? **151**우리 회사를 처음 방문하는 거라서 나는 그들이 처음부터 우리 회사를 좋지 않게 생각하지 않았으면 해요.
새스키아 헤인스, 오후 2:07
걱정 마세요. 납품업체에서 오늘 견본 몇 상자가 도착했어요. 크기가 너무 커서 수납 벽장에 들어가지 않아요. **152**아마 누군가의 사무실에 넣어둘 수 있을 거예요.
궈 시에, 오후 2:08
152좋은 생각이로군요. 허드슨 씨라면 분명히 언짢아하지 않을 거예요.
새스키아 헤인스, 오후 2:09
좋아요. 당신이 이곳에 오기 전에 꼭 처리되게 할게요. 내게 시간이 얼마나 있나요?
궈 시에, 오후 2:10
한 30분 정도요. 정말 고마워요!

어휘 be on one's way back from ~에서 돌아오는 길이다 representative 대리, 대표, 직원 accompany 동행하다, 따르다 have a brief tour of ~을 잠시 구경하다[둘러보다] check 확인하다, 점검하다 presentable 남 앞에 내놓을 만한, 보기 흉하지 않은 form a poor opinion of ~을 좋지 않게 생각하다 right from the start 처음부터, 초장부터 No problem. 걱정 마세요. supplier 공급업체, 납품업자 fit in ~을 맞추다, ~이 들어갈 공간을 만들다 storage closet 수납 벽장 mind 꺼리다, 언짢게 여기다 make sure that 꼭[반드시] ~하다

151 세부 사항

번역 시에 씨가 우려하는 것은?
(A) 좋지 않은 첫 인상을 남기는 것
(B) 해당 직원들과 늦게 만나는 것
(C) 안내해 줄 직원을 찾지 못하는 것
(D) 건물 로비 출입에 제한을 받는 것

해설 시에 씨의 오후 2시 6분 메시지에서 그들이 우리 회사를 처음 방문하는 거라서 처음부터 우리 회사를 좋지 않게 생각하지 않았으면 한다(It's their first time visiting our site, and I don't want them to form a poor opinion of our company right from the start)고 했으므로, 라고 엔터프라이지스의 직원들에게 좋지 않은 첫 인상을 줄까 봐 염려하고 있음을 알 수 있다. 따라서 정답은 (A)이다.

▶▶ **Paraphrasing** 지문의 **form a poor opinion of our company right from the start** → 정답의 **Making an unfavorable first impression**

152 의도 파악

번역 오후 2시 08분에 시에 씨가 "허드슨 씨라면 분명히 언짢아하지 않을 거예요" 라고 말할 때, 그 의도는 무엇인가?
(A) 허드슨 씨가 청소를 도와줘야 한다.
(B) 허드슨 씨가 견본을 더 주문할 수 있다.
(C) 허드슨 씨의 사무실에 보관 공간이 있다.
(D) 허드슨 씨가 납품업자에게 말해야 한다.

해설 헤인스 씨의 오후 2시 7분 메시지에서 아마 누군가의 사무실에 넣어둘 수 있을 것(Maybe I can put them in someone's office)이라고 했고, 이에 대해 시에 씨가 좋은 생각(Good idea)이라고 동의한 후 허드슨 씨라면 분명히 언짢아하지 않을 것(I'm sure Ms. Hudson wouldn't mind)이라는 구체적인 대안을 제시하고 있으므로, 정답은 (C)이다.

153-154 쿠폰

> [153]새로운 주인이 증정하는 이 쿠폰을 받아주시기 바랍니다.
> **스타라이트 제과점**
>
> [154]이 쿠폰은 다음 중 한 가지에 사용될 수 있습니다:
> 컵케이크 12개 구입 시 무료 쿠키 2개 증정
> 갓 구운 빵 10% 할인
> 케이크 1개 구입 시 반값에 하나 더 구입
>
> 7월 31일 만료
>
> 두 군데 유효 지점: 브로드 스트리트 349번지와 델우드 애비뉴 1709번지

어휘 accept 받아주다, 수락하다 with the compliments of ~가 증정하는 proprietor 주인, 소유주 bakery 제과점, 빵집 the following 다음에 적은[말하는] 것, 하기 dozen 12개의 fresh bread 갓 구운 빵 another 또 하나, 하나 더 at half price 반값에 expire 만료되다 valid 유효한, 효력이 있는 location 지점, 점포, 매장 complimentary 무료의, 증정의 distribute 나눠주다, 배포하다 selection 구비 품목 expand 확장하다, 늘이다 under new ownership 주인이 바뀐

153 세부 사항

번역 스타라이트 제과점에서 최근에 바뀐 점은?
(A) 증정품을 나눠준다.
(B) 제과 종류가 늘었다.
(C) 지점을 하나 더 열었다.
(D) 가게 주인이 새로 바뀌었다.

해설 쿠폰의 첫 번째 문장에서 새로운 주인이 증정하는 이 쿠폰을 받아주기 바란다(Please accept this coupon with the compliments of the new proprietor)고 했으므로 주인이 바뀌었다는 것을 알 수 있다. 따라서 정답은 (D)이다.

▶▶ **Paraphrasing** 지문의 **of the new proprietor** → 정답의 **under new ownership**

154 사실 관계 확인

번역 쿠폰에 명시되어 있는 것은?
(A) 고객들이 케이크 한 개 가격으로 두 개를 살 수 있다.
(B) 쿠폰을 한 번만 쓸 수 있다.
(C) 구입할 때마다 쿠키를 무료로 받을 수 있다.
(D) 제과점의 빵을 미리 주문할 수 있다.

해설 두 번째 단락에서 이 쿠폰은 다음 중 한 가지에 사용될 수 있다(This coupon can be used toward one of the following)고 했으므로, 정답은 (B)이다.

▶▶ **Paraphrasing** 지문의 **can be used toward one** → 정답의 **is valid for a single offer**

155-157 광고

> 편안하고 멋진 모습으로 운동하기 위해 전문 운동선수가 될 필요는 없습니다. [155]TR2에서는 농구, 축구, 야구 등에 가장 좋은 운동복을 갖추고 있습니다. 다음 번 마라톤 경주에 입을 가벼운 경기용 반바지이든, 평소 운동할 때 입을 땀복이든 저희가 해결해 드립니다. [156]새 점주 스티븐 카바잘은 전 세계의 운동 경기들에 참가해왔으며, 스포츠에 관한 자신의 전문성과 애정을 여러분에게 전해 드릴 준비가 되어 있습니다. [157]저희는 평소의 저렴한 가격 외에도 저희의 메일링 리스트에 등록해 TR2의 월간 소식지를 받아 보시는 모든 분께 15% 할인 특별 쿠폰을 제공하고 있습니다. 매일 오전 9시부터 오후 9시까지 데이비스 스트리트 1673번지에 있는 저희 매장을 찾아주세요.

어휘 professional athlete 프로[전문] 운동선수 work out 운동하다 in comfort and style 편안하고 멋있게 offer 제공[제안]하다, 팔려고 내놓다 apparel 의복, 옷 lightweight 가벼운 running shorts (경기용) 반바지 warm-up suit 땀복, 트레이닝복 exercise routine 규칙적인 운동 We've got you covered. 우리가 해결해[도와] 드립니다.(= We'll take care of the situation.) owner 주인, 소유주 participate in ~에 참가[참여]하다(= take part in) athletic competition 운동 경기[시합] be ready to+ 동사원형 ~할 준비가 되어 있다 expertise 전문성, 전문지식 in addition to ~ 외에, ~에 더하여 everyday 매일의, 일상의, 평소의 register for ~에 등록하다 mailing list 우편물/이메일 수신자 명단 monthly newsletter 월간 소식지 daily 매일

155 주제 / 목적

번역 무슨 광고인가?
(A) 운동 경기
(B) 운동 시설
(C) 운동 경기장
(D) 옷 가게

해설 두 번째 문장에서 TR2에서는 농구, 축구, 야구 등에 가장 좋은 운동복을 갖추고 있다(At TR2, we offer the best apparel for basketball, soccer, baseball, and more)고 했으므로, TR2가 옷 가게임을 알 수 있다. 따라서 정답은 (D)이다.

156 사실 관계 확인

번역 카바잘 씨에 관해 명시된 것은?
(A) 운동 경기의 우승자였다.
(B) 최근에 업체를 매입했다.
(C) 몇 군데에서 지점을 운영한다.
(D) 다른 나라에서 이 지역으로 이주했다.

해설 광고 중반부에서 새 점주 스티븐 카바잘은 전 세계의 운동 경기들에 참가해 왔으며, 스포츠에 관한 자신의 전문성과 애정을 여러분에게 전해 드릴 준비가 되어 있다(New owner Stephen Carbajal has participated in athletic competitions all over the world, and he is ready to bring his expertise and love of sports to you)고 했으므로, 카바잘 씨가 새로 업체를 인수했다는 것을 알 수 있다. 따라서 정답은 (B)이다.

▶▶ **Paraphrasing** 지문의 **New owner**
→ 정답의 **recently purchased the business**

157 세부 사항

번역 고객들이 특별 할인을 받는 방법은?
(A) 일정 수를 구매함으로써
(B) 특정한 날 업체를 방문함으로써
(C) 출판물을 신청함으로써
(D) 친구에게 이 업체를 추천함으로써

해설 후반부에서 평소의 저렴한 가격 외에도 메일링 리스트에 등록해 TR2의 월간 소식지를 받아 보는 모든 분께 15% 할인 특별 쿠폰을 제공하고 있다(In addition to our everyday low prices, we are offering a special coupon for 15% to anyone who registers for our mailing list to receive the TR2 monthly newsletter)고 했으므로, 정답은 (C)이다.

▶▶ **Paraphrasing** 지문의 **a special coupon**
→ 질문의 **the special offer**
지문의 **registers for our mailing list to receive the TR2 monthly newsletter**
→ 정답의 **signing up for a publication**

158-160 할인권

페어몬트 백화점

158시간을 내서 저희의 연례 설문지를 작성해 주셔서 감사합니다. 감사의 표시로 이 할인권을 제공해 드립니다.

159B, C, D백화점 내 조리기구, 침구, 가전제품 전 품목 15% 할인

페어몬트 백화점의 모든 지점에서 사용할 수 있습니다. 배송료나 설치비는 포함되어 있지 않습니다. TJ 홈을 비롯해 10월 1일에 판매되는 모든 브랜드에 적용됩니다. **160**5% 추가 할인을 받으려면 구매 시 페어몬트 리워드 회원 카드를 제시하십시오.

페어몬트 백화점의 고객이 되어 주셔서 감사합니다!

어휘 take the time to+동사원형 시간[짬]을 내서 ~하다 complete 완성하다; 기입[작성]하다 annual 연례의, 1년에 한 번의 questionnaire 설문(지) appreciation 감사 discount voucher 할인권, 할인 쿠폰 cookware 조리기구, 취사도구 bedding 침구 appliance 가전제품 location 지점; 장소 include 포함하다 delivery 배송 installation 설치 fee 수수료 applicable to ~에 적용되는[해당하는] brand 브랜드, 상표 come 나오다, 팔리다 present 제시하다, 보여주다 reward 보상 purchase 구매, 구입 receive an additional ~% off ~%를 추가로 할인받다 customer 고객, 손님

158 사실 관계 확인

번역 할인권에 관해 명시된 것은?
(A) 10월 1일까지 유효하다.
(B) 설문조사 참여자에게 발급되었다.
(C) 특정 지점에서만 사용할 수 있다.
(D) 다른 할인과 결합할 수 없다.

해설 첫 번째 단락에서 시간을 내어 연례 설문지를 작성해 준 데 대해 감사하다(Thank you for taking the time to complete our annual questionnaire)며 감사의 표시로 이 할인권을 제공한다(Thank you for taking the time to complete our annual questionnaire. To show our appreciation, we offer you this discount voucher)고 했으므로, 설문조사 참여자에게 할인권을 준다는 것을 알 수 있다. 따라서 정답은 (B)이다.

159 사실 관계 확인

번역 할인권으로 구입할 수 있는 물건이 아닌 것은?
(A) 식탁
(B) 침대 시트 세트
(C) 세탁기
(D) 프라이팬

해설 두 번째 단락에서 백화점 내 조리기구, 침구, 가전제품 전 품목 15% 할인(15% off all cookware, bedding, and appliances in the store)이라고 명시했으므로 (B) 침대 시트 세트, (C) 세탁기, (D) 프라이팬은 쿠폰 할인 품목임을 확인할 수 있다. 따라서 정답은 (A)이다.

▶▶ **Paraphrasing** 지문의 **bedding** → 보기의 **A set of sheets**
지문의 **appliances**
→ 보기의 **A washing machine**
지문의 **cookware** → 보기의 **A frying pan**

160 추론 / 암시

번역 페어몬트 백화점에 관해 암시된 것은?
(A) 고객 충성 프로그램이 있다.
(B) 신규 고객에게 할인을 제공한다.
(C) 모든 제품을 무료로 배송해 준다.
(D) TJ 홈 브랜드를 취급하는 유일한 매장이다.

해설 마지막 단락에서 구매 시 5% 추가 할인을 받기 위해 페어몬트 리워드 회원 카드를 제시하라(Present your Fairmont Rewards Membership Card at the time of purchase to receive an additional 5% off)고 했으므로, 백화점이 고객 유지를 위해 회원 카드 제도를 운용하고 있음을 유추할 수 있다. 따라서 정답은 (A)이다.

▶▶ **Paraphrasing** 지문의 **Fairmont Rewards Membership Card**
→ 정답의 **a customer loyalty program**

161-163 공지

우드퍼드 아파트 세입자 공지:

1618월 17일 수요일에 우드퍼드 아파트 보수정비반이 건물 전체의 화재 경보와 스프링클러 시스템을 검사할 예정입니다. 이 검사는 건물주의 보험 계약 조건을 이행하고 모든 세입자의 안전을 확보하기 위해 실시하는 분기별 점검의 일환입니다. 작업은 오전 10시쯤 시작되어 2시간 정도 걸릴 것으로 예상됩니다. 검사 절차를 진행하는 동안 경보 시스템이 한 번에 최대 몇 분까지 계속 울릴 수도 있습니다. 게다가 복도의 비상등까지 점멸할 수 있습니다. 이 신호들은 둘 다 무시하셔도 되며, 건물에서 대피하거나 추가 조치를 취할 필요가 없습니다. **162**가능성이 매우 낮지만 검사를 하는 동안 응급 상황이 발행할 경우에는 저희가 건물의 확성기를 사용하여 세입자들에게 건물을 비우도록 지시할 것입니다. 대피 절차는 건물 관리인에게서 얻으실 수 있습니다. **163**검사와 관련된 모든 문의는 스콧 포터 씨의 팀이 작업을 수행할 예정이므로 포터 씨에게 해 주시기 바랍니다. 협조해 주셔서 감사합니다.

어휘 notice 공지, 공고 tenant 세입자 maintenance crew 보수정비반 test 검사하다, 시험하다 fire alarm 화재 경보 sprinkler 스프링클러, 살수 장치 quarterly check 분기별 점검 perform 실시[시행]하다 fulfill the terms of ~의 조건을 이행하다[준수하다] building owner 건물 소유주 insurance policy 보험 계약 ensure 확보하다, 보장하다 safety 안전 be expected to+동사원형 ~할 것으로 예상[기대]되다 approximately 대략 testing procedure 검사 절차 alarm system 경보 시스템 continuously 지속[계속]해서, 끊이지 않고 up to 최대 ~까지 in addition 덧붙여, 게다가 hallway 복도 emergency light 비상등 flash on and off 켜졌다 꺼졌다 하다[점멸하다] ignore 무시하다 signal 신호 evacuate 대피하다 take further action 추가 조처를 취하다 unlikely 개연성이 낮은, ~할 것 같지 않은 present oneself 발생하다, 생기다 loudspeaker 확성기 instruct 지시하다 vacate 비우다 evacuation 대피 obtain 얻다, 획득하다, 입수하다 building manager 건물 관리인 direct 보내다, 송신하다 carry out 수행하다 cooperation 협조, 협동

---

161 세부 사항

번역 8월 17일에 하는 작업의 목적은?
(A) 새로운 정부안전규정 준수
(B) 세입자용 화재 예방장비 설치
(C) 보험 요건 준수
(D) 건물 전체 보안 시스템 교체

해설 지문의 초반부에서 8월 17일 수요일에 우드퍼드 아파트 보수정비반이 건물 전체의 화재 경보와 스프링클러 시스템을 검사할 예정(On Wednesday, August 17, the Woodford Apartments maintenance crew will be testing the fire alarms and sprinkler system throughout the building)이며, 이 검사는 건물 소유주의 보험 계약 조건을 이행하고 모든 세입자의 안전을 확보하기 위해 실시하는 분기별 점검의 일환(The testing is part of a quarterly check performed to fulfill the terms of the building owner's insurance policy and to ensure the safety of all tenants)이라고 했다. 따라서 이 검사는 보험 계약 조건 이행의 일환임을 알 수 있으므로, 정답은 (C)이다.

▶▶ **Paraphrasing** 지문의 **to fulfill the terms of the building owner's insurance policy**
→ 정답의 **To comply with insurance requirements**

---

162 세부 사항

번역 공지에 따르면, 8월 17일 작업 동안 세입자들이 조치를 취해야 하는 때는?
(A) 경보 소리가 들리면
(B) 복도의 불빛이 깜박거리는 것을 보면
(C) 안내방송을 들으면
(D) 전화를 받으면

해설 중반부에서 가능성이 매우 낮지만 검사를 하는 동안 응급 상황이 발행할 경우 건물의 확성기를 사용해 세입자들에게 건물을 비우도록 지시하겠다(In the very unlikely event that an emergency presents itself during the testing, we will use the building's loudspeaker to instruct tenants to vacate the building)고 했다. 따라서 응급 상황 발생 시 안내방송을 한다는 것을 알 수 있으므로, 정답은 (C)이다.

▶▶ **Paraphrasing** 지문의 **vacate the building**
→ 질문의 **take action**

---

163 추론 / 암시

번역 포터 씨는 누구이겠는가?
(A) 보수 정비 관리자
(B) 건물주
(C) 정부 공무원
(D) 건물 관리인

해설 후반부에서 검사 관련 모든 문의는 스콧 포터 씨의 팀이 작업을 수행할 예정이므로 포터 씨에게 하라(All questions about the testing should be directed to Scott Porter, as his team will be carrying out the work)고 했다. 따라서 포터 씨가 보수 정비반의 관리자임을 유추할 수 있으므로, 정답은 (A)이다.

164-167 회람

수신: 위생국 직원들
발신: 래리 보즈먼 국장
날짜: 9월 3일
제목: 새로운 소식

164이번 주 초, 나는 평가 작업을 하고 매립지 공간이 고갈되기 전 남은 시간을 판단하기 위해 브룩스빌 매립지를 방문했습니다. 가장 최근의 평가는 10년 전에 한 것으로, 그 당시에는 이 매립지가 브룩스빌의 필요를 50년은 더 채울 수 있을 것으로 예측됐습니다. 그러므로 현 시점에서 우리는 남은 40년이 지나야 일반 쓰레기 관리를 위해 대체 계획을 세워야 하는 상황이 올 것으로 예상할 법도 합니다. **165**하지만 유감스럽게도, 우리 지역사회의 주민 수가 불과 몇 년 새 규모가 거의 두 배가 되면서 매립지가 애초 예상보다 훨씬 더 많이 사용되고 있습니다. 지금 속도라면 남은 매립 공간이 18~20년 동안만 더 지속될 뿐입니다.

과도한 매립지 사용을 억제하고 매립 공간이 고갈되는 시점을 늦추기 위해 나는 음식물 쓰레기 재활용 프로그램을 시작하도록 이미 허가를 받았는데, 이 사업은 브룩스빌 퇴비 수거 프로그램, 줄여서 BCC 프로그램이라고 불리게 될 것입니다. 여기에는 평소 재활용품 수거일에 음식물 찌꺼기를 수거해서 비료를 만드는 데 사용하도록 특수 용기에 음식물 찌꺼기를 모으는 일이 포함됩니다. **166**우리는 다음 달부터 워런 파크, 오크 그로브, 로크레인에서 시험 프로그램을 운영할 것입니다. 일단 세부 계획을 마련하는 대로 브룩스빌 전 지역으로 프로그램을 확대하게 됩니다.

브룩스빌 전역에서, 특히 업소들을 대상으로 재활용을 매우 장려할 예정인데, 이들이 배출하는 상업 쓰레기가 수거물의 약 30%를 차지하기 때문입니다. 또 다른 가능성은 매립지에 깎아낸 풀의 반입을 허용하지 않는 것입니다. **167**이런 조치만으로 수만 톤의 쓰레기를 줄일 수 있습니다. 대신에 자택 소유자들과 업소들을 장려해 정원 쓰레기를 현장에서 퇴비로 만들도록 할 것입니다.

어휘 Department of Sanitation 위생국 department head 국장, 부장 update 최신 정보, 새로운 소식 landfill 매립지 carry out an evaluation 평가하다 determine 판단하다, 측정하다 space 공간 run out 고갈되다, 다 쓰다 estimate 추정, 추산, 평가 decade 10년 project 예측하다, 내다보다 meet 충족하다, 만족시키다 needs 필요 at this point 이 시점에, 현재 expect 기대[예상]하다 make alternative plans 대체[대안] 계획을 세우다 management 관리, 경영 solid waste 고형 폐기물, 일반 쓰레기 unfortunately 유감스럽게, 안타깝게, 불행히도 resident 주민, 거주민 community 지역사회, 공동체 nearly 거의 double in size 규모[크기]가 두 배가 되다 originally 원래, 애초에 anticipate 예상[기대]하다 at the current rate 현재 속도로 remaining 남은 site 현장, 장소 last 지속되다, 유지되다 curb 억제하다, 제한하다 overuse 과용 delay 지연하다, 늦추다 obtain approval 승인을 받다, 허가를 얻다 food waste 음식물 쓰레기 recycling 재활용 compost 퇴비 collection 수집, 수거 for short 줄여서 involve 포함하다, 수반하다 food scraps 음식물 찌꺼기 special container 특수 용기 pick up 수거하다, 가져가다 normal 평소의, 보통의 recycling collection day 재활용품 수거일 create fertilizer 비료를 만들다 run a trial program 시험 프로그램을 운영하다 work out the logistics 세부 (실행) 계획을 마련하다, 물류를 해결하다 expand 확대[확장]하다 neighborhood 동네 heavily promote 매우 장려하다 target 표적[대상]으로 삼다 commercial waste 상업 쓰레기 make up 구성하다, 차지하다 action 조치, 조처 save 줄이다, 절감하다 homeowner 자택 소유자 encourage 장려하다, 용기를 북돋우다 yard waste 정원 쓰레기 on site 현장에서

164 세부 사항

번역 보즈먼 씨가 최근에 한 일은?
(A) 위생국 신입 직원 교육
(B) 쓰레기 처리장 평가
(C) 브룩스빌 주민들의 의견 수집
(D) 직원 평가 수행

해설 첫 번째 단락에서 보즈먼 씨는 이번 주 초, 평가 작업을 하고 매립지 공간이 고갈되기 전 남은 시간을 판단하기 위해 브룩스빌 매립지를 방문했다(Earlier this week, I visited the Brookville landfill to carry out an evaluation and determine the time left before space in the landfill runs out)고 했으므로, 정답은 (B)이다.

▶▶ Paraphrasing 지문의 **Earlier this week** → 질문의 **recently**
지문의 **carry out an evaluation**
→ 정답의 **Assessed**
지문의 **landfill**
→ 정답의 **a garbage disposal site**

165 세부 사항

번역 보즈먼 씨에 따르면, 문제의 원인은 무엇인가?
(A) 복잡한 규제
(B) 재활용 비용 증가
(C) 대중의 관심 부족
(D) 빠른 인구 증가

해설 첫 번째 단락의 후반부에서 유감스럽게도, 우리 지역사회의 주민 수가 불과 몇 년 새 거의 두 배가 되면서 매립지가 애초 예상보다 훨씬 더 많이 사용되고 있다(Unfortunately, as the number of residents in our community has nearly doubled in size in just a few short years, the landfill is getting used much more than originally anticipated)고 했으므로, 급속한 주민 수의 증가로 인해 매립지 사용에 문제가 발생했음을 알 수 있다. 따라서 정답은 (D)이다.

▶▶ Paraphrasing 지문의 **the number of residents in our community has nearly doubled in size in just a few short years**
→ 정답의 **Rapid population growth**

166 사실 관계 확인

[번역] BCC 프로그램에 관해 명시된 것은?
(A) 처음에 몇몇 동네에서 시범 운영될 것이다.
(B) 사람들에게 재활용품 준비 방법을 가르치는 게 목적이다.
(C) 예산 삭감으로 승인을 못 받게 될 수도 있다.
(D) 비료 판매로 재원 일부를 마련할 것이다.

해설 두 번째 단락에서 다음 달부터 워런 파크, 오크 그로브, 로크레인에서 시험 프로그램을 운영할 예정(We will run a trial program in Warren Park, Oak Grove, and Rocklane beginning from next month)이라고 했으므로, 정답은 (A)이다.

▶▶ Paraphrasing 지문의 **run a trial program in Warren Park, Oak Grove, and Rocklane** → 정답의 **be tested in a few neighborhoods**

167 문장 삽입

번역 [1], [2], [3], [4]로 표시된 곳 중에서 다음 문장이 들어가기에 가장 적합한 곳은?

"또 다른 가능성은 매립지에 깎아낸 풀의 반입을 허용하지 않는 것입니다."

(A) [1]
(B) [2]
(C) [3]
(D) [4]

해설 삽입 문장 '또 다른 가능성은 매립지에 깎아낸 풀의 반입을 허용하지 않는 것입니다(Another possibility is not to allow grass clippings in the landfill)'를 통해 뒤에서 이 또 다른 가능성(Another possibility)에 대해 구체적으로 설명할 것임을 알 수 있다. [4] 뒤에 나오는 문장에서 이런 조치만으로 수만 톤의 쓰레기를 줄일 수 있고, 대신에 자택 소유자들과 업소들을 장려해 정원 쓰레기를 현장에서 퇴비로 만들도록 할 것(This action alone could save tens of thousands of tons of waste. Homeowners and businesses would be encouraged to compost their yard waste on site instead)이라고 명시하고 있다. 즉 매립지에 깎아낸 풀의 반입을 허용하지 않는 것(This action)의 효과와 대안을 제시하고 있으므로, 정답은 (D)이다.

168-171 온라인 채팅

요키 가구 고객 지원	
글로리아 콕스 (직원 ID: 413)	[오후 3:09]
안녕하세요. 저는 요키 가구의 고객 서비스 관리자입니다. 문자로 문의하시는 내용이 기존 주문에 관한 건가요, 대기 주문에 관한 건가요?	
셔먼 홀콤	[오후 3:10]
기존 주문이에요. 제품은 이미 받았어요.	
글로리아 콕스 (직원 ID: 413)	[오후 3:11]
그러셨군요. 무엇이 문제인가요?	
셔먼 홀콤	[오후 3:12]
제가 귀사에서 주문한 선반을 조립하는 데 애를 먹고 있어요. **168**예전에는 사전 조립 상품을 구입했는데, 이번에는 제가 직접 해 보고 싶은 생각이 들었어요.	
글로리아 콕스 (직원 ID: 413)	[오후 3:13]
제품명과 빠진 부품이 있는지 여부를 말씀해 주십시오.	
셔먼 홀콤	[오후 3:16]
169러스틱 비치 세트 선반 모델이에요. 조립설명서가 없어서 뭐가 빠졌는지 확실히 알 수가 없네요.	
글로리아 콕스 (직원 ID: 413)	[오후 3:17]
그렇다면 죄송합니다. 그 모델에 대해 저희가 많은 불만을 접수했습니다. **169**포장 과정에서 작업자들이 설명서나 제품 안내서를 넣지 않았거든요.	
셔먼 홀콤	[오후 3:18]
우편으로 설명서를 보내주실 수 있나요?	
글로리아 콕스 (직원 ID: 413)	[오후 3:19]
170물론입니다. 하지만 댁에 프린터가 있으면 저희 웹사이트에서 다운로드하셔서 직접 프린트하실 수도 있습니다.	
셔먼 홀콤	[오후 3:21]
우편으로 배송될 설명서와 같은 건가요?	
글로리아 콕스 (직원 ID: 413)	[오후 3:22]
네, 그리고 그게 훨씬 더 쉽습니다.	
셔먼 홀콤	[오후 3:24]
좋아요. 지금 해 볼게요.	
글로리아 콕스 (직원 ID: 413)	[오후 3:25]
171고객님께서 필요한 문서를 입수하셨다는 것을 제가 알 때까지 이 대화를 종료하지 않겠습니다.	
셔먼 홀콤	[오후 3:26]
고맙습니다.	

어휘 furniture 가구 customer assistance 고객 지원 customer service agent 고객 서비스 관리자 order 주문(품) pending order 대기 주문 product 제품 have trouble (in) 동명사 ~하는 데 애를 먹다 assemble 조립하다 shelf 선반 (pl. shelves) pay for ~의 값을 치르다 pre-assembled goods 사전 조립 상품 try 시험 삼아 해 보다, 시도하다 part 부품 missing 빠진, 실종된 shelving unit 선반 assembly instructions 조립설명서 numerous 수많은 complaint 불만, 불평 packing process 포장 과정 put in 넣다 product brochure 제품 안내서 mail 우편으로 보내다 ship 배송하다 terminate 종료하다, 끝내다 conversation 대화 document 문서

168 사실 관계 확인

번역 요키 가구에 관해 홀콤 씨가 명시하는 것은?
(A) 가격이 적당하다고 생각한다.
(B) 최근에 상품 구색이 늘었다.
(C) 이전에 서비스를 이용한 적이 있다.
(D) 질 좋은 상품으로 유명하다.

해설 오후 3시 12분 메시지에서 홀콤 씨가 예전에는 사전 조립 상품을 구입했는데, 이번에는 직접 해 보고 싶다는 생각이 들었다(In the past, I've paid for your pre-assembled goods, but this time I thought I'd try it myself)고 했다. 따라서, 홀콤 씨가 전에 요키 가구에서 상품을 구매했다는 것을 알 수 있으므로, 정답은 (C)이다.

▶▶ **Paraphrasing** 지문의 In the past, I've paid for your pre-assembled goods → 정답의 He has used its services before.

169 추론 / 암시

번역 러스틱 비치 세트에 대해 콕스 씨가 암시하는 것은?
(A) 회사에서 가장 인기 있는 제품 중 하나다.
(B) 회사가 더 이상 제작하지 않는 물건이다.
(C) 필요한 문서를 다 구비하지 못한 채 보내졌다.
(D) 창고로 직접 반환할 수 있다.

해설 홀콤 씨가 오후 3시 16분 메시지에서 러스틱 비치 세트 선반 모델을 언급했고, 이에 오후 3시 17분 응답 메시지에서 콕스 씨는 포장 과정에서 작업자들이 설명서나 제품 안내서를 넣지 않았다(During the packing process, the workers didn't put in the instructions or the product brochure)고 했다. 따라서, 필요한 문서를 동봉하지 않았음을 알 수 있으므로, 정답은 (C)이다.

▶▶ **Paraphrasing** 지문의 didn't put in the instructions or the product brochure → 정답의 without all the necessary paperwork

170 의도 파악

번역 오후 3시 22분에 콕스 씨가 "그게 훨씬 더 쉽습니다"라고 쓸 때, 그 의도는 무엇인가?
(A) 온라인으로 정보를 얻기를 권한다.
(B) 홀콤 씨가 계정을 만들기를 바란다.
(C) 속달 우편으로 물건을 보낼 계획이다.
(D) 다른 선반이 더 낫겠다고 생각한다.

해설 콕스 씨가 오후 3시 19분 메시지에서 집에 프린터가 있으면 웹사이트에서 다운로드해 직접 프린트해도 된다(but if you have a printer at home, you can download them from our Web site instead and print them yourself)고 해결책을 제시하고 있다. 후에 콕스 씨는 그게 훨씬 더 쉽다(it's a lot easier)며 다시 한 번 웹사이트 다운로드의 편리함을 강조하고 있으므로, 정답은 (A)이다.

171 세부 사항

번역 콕스 씨가 대화창을 열어 두려고 하는 이유는?
(A) 재고 목록을 확인할 시간을 주려고
(B) 주문번호를 기다리려고
(C) 홀콤 씨에게 최신 진행 정보를 제공하려고
(D) 홀콤 씨가 서류를 받았는지 확인하려고

해설 콕스 씨의 오후 3시 25분 메시지에서 고객님이 필요한 문서를 입수하셨다는 것을 제가 알 때까지 이 대화를 종료하지 않겠다(I won't terminate this conversation until I know that you were able to get the document you need)고 했으므로 홀콤 씨가 필요한 문서를 입수했는지 확인하고자 한다는 것을 알 수 있다. 따라서 정답은 (D)이다.

▶▶ **Paraphrasing** 지문의 won't terminate this conversation
→ 질문의 keep the chat open
지문의 get the document
→ 정답의 received some paperwork

172-175 기사

유리 용기 금지되다

3월 23일 – 윈데일 시의회는 공공 해변과 공원에서 유리 용기를 금지하는 발의안을 표결로 법제화했다. 앤드루 맥도웰이 제안한 이 조치는 깨진 유리로 인한 부상을 줄이려는 시도이며, 금지령을 어기는 사람들에게 최초 위반 시 최대 500달러까지 벌금을 물리게 하는 권고안을 포함하고 있었다. **172**이 최초 벌금액은 시의원 다수가 과도하다고 여겨서 최종 표결을 하기 전에 100달러로 줄였다.

발의안은 널리 지지를 받았지만 반대자가 없는 것은 아니다. **173**엘렌 제이컵스는 발의안이 노숙인들에게 과도하게 영향을 줄 수 있다고 생각해서 그것에 반대 투표를 했다. 사람들이 규정을 따르고 있는지 확인할 만한 인력이 지역 경찰에 없다고 우려를 제기하는 이들도 있었다. 그 이유는 버려진 유리 용기가 대부분 개인이나 규모가 아주 작은 집단에서 나오기 때문이다. **175**콘서트와 축제 같은 대규모 행사는 대개 쓰레기 문제를 일으키지 않는다. 이런 행사들은 허가를 받기 전에 세부적인 청소 계획이 필요하다.

시의회는 주민들에게 새로운 규정을 알리기 위해 4월 3일 대국민 캠페인을 벌일 계획이며, 새 규정은 다음 달에 발효될 예정이다. **174A, C, D**캠페인에는 시 웹사이트에 공지를 올리고, 라디오로 공익광고를 내보내고, 공공 장소에 표지판을 부착해서 소식을 널리 알리는 작업이 포함될 것이다.

어휘 glass container 유리 용기[그릇] ban 금지하다
city council 시의회 vote 투표하다, 표결하다 enact 제정하다
proposal 발의, 제안 public 공공의, 대중의 measure 조치, 대책
bring forward 제안[제시]하다 seek to + 동사원형 ~하려고
시도하다[추구하다] reduce 줄이다 injury 부상 contain 포함하다
recommendation 권고, 권장 fine 벌금을 물리다 disobey
위반하다 up to 최대, ~까지 violation 위반, 범칙 original
처음의; 원래의 consider 여기다, 간주하다; 고려하다 excessive
과도한, 지나친 council member 시의원 widespread 폭넓은
support 지지, 지원 opponent 반대자 vote against ~에
반대 투표하다 disproportionately 불균형하게, 지나치게 affect
영향을 주다 those living on the streets 노숙인 raise
concerns 우려를 제기하다 local 현지의, 지역의 police force
경찰(력) manpower 인력 make sure 반드시 ~하도록 하다,
확인하다 regulation 규정 discarded 버려진 individual 개인
large-scale 대규모의 contribute to ~의 원인이다 litter 쓰레기
launch a public awareness campaign 대국민 캠페인을
시작하다 inform 알리다 resident 주민 go into effect 발효되다
include 포함하다 post a notice 공지를 올리다 run a public
service announcement 공익광고를 하다 put up a sign
표지판을 설치하다 spread 퍼뜨리다, 널리 알리다

172 사실 관계 확인

번역 맥도웰 씨의 발의에 관해 명시된 것은?
(A) 주로 업체들에 적용될 것이다.
(B) 4월 중으로 발효될 것이다.
(C) 승인을 받기 전에 수정되었다.
(D) 시의회가 만장일치로 지지했다.

해설 첫 번째 단락의 마지막 문장에서 최초 벌금액은 시의원 다수가 과도하다고 여겨 최종 표결을 하기 전에 100달러로 줄였다(This original fine was considered excessive by many council members and was reduced to $100 before the final vote was taken)고 했으므로, 벌금액이 승인되기 전 수정되었음을 알 수 있다. 따라서 정답은 (C)이다.

▶▶ **Paraphrasing** 지문의 reduced to $100 before the final vote was taken → 정답의 altered before receiving approval

173 세부 사항

번역 발의와 관련해 제이컵스 씨가 예상한 문제는?
(A) 노숙인들에게 부당하게 적용될 수도 있다.
(B) 변화를 홍보하는 비용이 너무 많이 들 것이다.
(C) 그렇다고 공공 도로가 더 깨끗해지지는 않을 것이다.
(D) 지역 경찰이 그것을 집행하기 어려울 것이다.

해설 두 번째 단락에서 엘렌 제이컵스는 발의안이 노숙인들에게 과도하게 영향을 줄 수 있다고 생각해 그것에 반대 투표를 했다(Ellen Jacobs voted against the proposal because she believed that it could disproportionately affect those living on the streets)고 했다. 따라서 정답은 (A)이다.

▶▶ **Paraphrasing** 지문의 disproportionately affect those living on the streets → 정답의 be applied unfairly to the homeless

174 사실 관계 확인

번역 대국민 캠페인에 사용될 방법이 아닌 것은?
(A) 라디오 발표
(B) 신문 광고
(C) 온라인 메시지
(D) 공공 표지판

해설 마지막 단락에서 캠페인에는 시 웹사이트에 공지를 올리고, 라디오로 공익 광고를 내보내고, 공공 장소에 표지판을 부착해서 소식을 널리 알리는 작업이 포함될 것(It will include posting notices on the city's Web site, running public service announcements on the radio, and putting up signs in public places to spread the news)이라고 했으므로 (A) 라디오 발표, (C) 온라인 메시지, (D) 공공 표지판은 캠페인에 사용될 방법임을 확인할 수 있다. 따라서 정답은 (B)이다.

▶▶ **Paraphrasing** 지문의 running public service announcements on the radio → 보기의 Radio announcements
지문의 posting notices on the city's Web site → 보기의 Online messages
지문의 putting up signs in public places → 보기의 Publicly posted signs

175 문장 삽입

번역 [1], [2], [3], [4]로 표시된 곳 중에서 다음 문장이 들어가기에 가장 적합한 곳은?

"이런 행사들은 허가를 받기 전에 세부적인 청소 계획이 필요하다."

(A) [1]
(B) [2]
(C) [3]
(D) [4]

해설 삽입 문장 '이런 행사들은 허가를 받기 전에 세부적인 청소 계획이 필요하다(These require a detailed cleanup plan before a permit is issued)'를 통해 앞에서 이런 행사들(These)에 대해 구체적으로 언급할 것임을 알 수 있다. [3]의 앞 문장에서 콘서트와 축제 같은 대규모 행사는 대개 쓰레기 문제를 일으키지 않는다(Large-scale events such as concerts and festivals do not usually contribute to the litter problem)'고 했으므로, 정답은 (C)이다.

176-180 광고 + 후기

오데사 하우스웨어에서 루나 베개로 휴식과 활기를 찾으세요!

빨라진 현대 생활 탓에 충분한 수면이 그 어느 때보다 더 중요합니다. **176**많은 사람이 자세를 바르게 유지하면 잠을 더 잘 잘 수 있다는 사실을 깨닫지 못합니다. 저희 팀은 수면 습관을 꼼꼼하게 연구해 가장 흔한 수면 문제들을 없애 주는 독보적인 베개를 만들었습니다. **179**루나 베개는 바로 누워 자는 분들을 위해 가운데가 더 얇고, 옆으로 누워 자는 분들을 위해 가장자리는 높은 메모리폼 베개입니다. **177**이 독특한 모양은 귀하의 머리와 목이 온전히 받쳐지게 해주며, 불편함과 어깨 통증을 더는 데도 도움이 됩니다.

178D각각의 루나 베개에는 꼭 맞는 항균 베갯잇이 포함됩니다. **178B, 179**베갯잇은 땀 흡수를 극대화하는 면과 캐시미어 혼방 재질입니다. **178A**베갯잇의 특허받은 에어-플로 기술 덕에 더운 밤에는 머리를 시원하게, 추운 밤에는 따뜻하게 유지해 여러 시간 동안 최대의 편안함을 누리도록 보장합니다. 더 많은 정보를 원하시면 www.odessahousewares.com을 방문하세요.

어휘 rest 휴식 refresh 활기[생기]를 되찾다 pillow 베개 houseware 가정용품 accelerated 빨라진, 가속화된 pace 속도, 걸음 than ever 그 어느 때보다 fail to+동사원형 ～하지 못하다, 실패하다 realize 깨닫다, 인식하다 result from ～에서 비롯되다 keep the body in the right position 자세를 바르게 유지하다 meticulously 꼼꼼하게 research 연구하다 sleeping habit 수면 습관, 잠버릇 one-of-a-kind 독보적인, 단 하나뿐인 eliminate 제거하다, 없애다 common 흔한 thinner 더 얇은 in the middle 가운데에, 중간에 back sleeper 바로 누워 자는 사람 side sleeper 옆으로 누워 자는 사람 unique 독특한 shape 모양, 형태 ensure 보장하다 support 지지하다, 받치다 ease 덜다, 완화하다 discomfort 불편함 aching 통증 anti-bacterial 항균의 perfectly fit 완벽하게 맞다 cotton 면 cashmere 캐시미어 blend 혼방, 혼합 maximize 극대화하다 sweat absorption 땀 흡수 owing to ～ 덕분에 patented 특허를 받은 maximum 최대의 information 정보

---

www.ratehomefurnishings.com

침구 ≫ 오데사 하우스웨어 ≫ 루나 베개

제프 페이튼이 올린 사용 후기

저는 전에 오데사 하우스웨어에서 제품을 구매한 적이 있어서 매달 나오는 이메일 소식지를 받아보려고 시스템에 가입했어요. **180**가장 최근에 나온 소식지에 루나 베개 광고가 실려 있길래 한번 써보기로 했죠. 단단한 메모리폼에 익숙해지는 데 며칠 밤이 걸렸지만, 적응기가 지나자 더 빨리, 더 깊이 잠들기 시작했어요. **179**캐시미어와 면으로 된 베갯잇이 부드럽게 피부에 닿는 감촉이 안락하고 쾌적하게 느껴집니다. 수면장애로 고생하는 분들께 이 베개를 적극 추천합니다. 저는 이 베개가 너무 마음에 들어서 가족 중 몇 명에게 줄 선물로 그것을 구입할 계획이에요.

어휘 review 사용 후기, 평가 make a purchase 구입하다 opt into ～에 가입하다 monthly 월간의, 매월의 newsletter 소식지 recent 최근의 include 포함하다 advertisement 광고 give it a try 한번 해 보다 get used to ～에 익숙해지다 firmness 단단함 adjustment period 적응기 fall asleep 잠들다 soundly 곤하게, 깊이 gentle touch 부드러운 감촉 elegant 안락한, 우아한 luxurious 호화로운; 쾌적한 recommend 추천하다 have difficulty in -ing ～하는 데 어려움이 있다 a big fan of ～의 열혈 팬 plan to+동사원형 ～할 계획이다 purchase 구입[구매]하다 gift 선물

176 세부 사항

번역 광고에 따르면, 잠을 개선하는 데 도움이 될 수 있는 것은?
(A) 정해진 시간에 자기
(B) 몸의 자세를 바르게 하기
(C) 자기 전에 긴장 풀기
(D) 적정 온도 유지하기

해설 광고의 첫 번째 단락에서 많은 사람들이 자세를 바르게 유지하면 잠을 더 잘 잘 수 있다는 사실을 깨닫지 못한다(Many people fail to realize that better sleep can result from keeping the body in the right position)고 했다. 즉 바른 자세가 수면 개선에 도움이 된다는 의미 이므로, 정답은 (B)이다.

▶▶ Paraphrasing 지문의 **keeping the body in the right position**
→ 정답의 **Positioning the body correctly**

177 세부 사항

번역 광고에 언급된 루나 베개의 장점은?
(A) 목 근육 키우기
(B) 관절 통증 완화
(C) 자세 개선
(D) 소음 장해 줄이기

해설 광고의 첫 번째 단락에서 루나 베개의 독특한 모양은 머리와 목을 온전히 받쳐주며, 불편함과 어깨 통증을 더는 데도 도움이 된다(This unique shape ensures that your head and neck are fully supported, and this also serves to ease discomfort and aching in your shoulders)고 했으므로, 정답은 (B)이다.

▶▶ Paraphrasing 지문의 **to ease discomfort and aching in your shoulders**
→ 정답의 **Relieving joint pain**

178 사실 관계 확인

번역 루나 베개의 베갯잇에 관해 명시되지 않은 것은?
(A) 체온을 조절한다.
(B) 수분을 흡수한다.
(C) 세탁기로 빨 수 있다.
(D) 세균에 저항력이 있다.

해설 광고의 두 번째 단락에서 베갯잇의 특허받은 에어-플로 기술 덕에 더운 밤에는 머리를 시원하게, 추운 밤에는 따뜻하게 유지해 여러 시간 동안 최대의 편안함을 누리도록 보장한다(Owing to the cover's patented Air-Flo technology, it keeps your head cool on hot nights and warm on cold nights, ensuring maximum comfort for hours)고 했으므로 (A)를, 베갯잇은 땀 흡수를 최대화하는 면과 캐시미어 혼방 재질(The cover is made from a cotton and cashmere blend to maximize sweat absorption)이라고 했으므로 (B)를, 각각의 루나 베개에는 꼭 맞는 항균 베갯잇이 포함된다(Each Luna pillow comes with an anti-bacterial cover that perfectly fits the pillow)고 했으므로 (D)를 확인할 수 있다. 따라서 정답은 (C)이다.

▶▶ Paraphrasing 지문의 **keeps your head cool on hot nights and warm on cold nights**
→ 보기의 **regulates body heat**
지문의 **sweat absorption**
→ 보기의 **absorbs moisture**
지문의 **anti-bacterial**
→ 보기의 **resistant to bacteria**

179 연계

번역 광고에 언급되지만 페이튼 씨가 잊고서 다루지 않은 특징은?
(A) 베개의 모양
(B) 배송 과정
(C) 베개의 재료
(D) 베갯잇의 천

해설 광고의 첫 번째 단락에서 루나 베개는 바로 누워 자는 사람들을 위해 가운데가 더 얇고, 옆으로 누워 자는 사람들을 위해 가장자리는 높은 메모리폼 베개(The Luna pillow is a memory foam pillow that is thinner in the middle for back sleepers and has high sides for side sleepers)라며 (A) 베개의 모양을, 두 번째 단락에서는 베갯잇은 땀 흡수를 최대화하는 면과 캐시미어 혼방 재질(The cover is made from a cotton and cashmere blend to maximize sweat absorption)이라며 (D) 베갯잇의 소재를 언급하고 있다. 하지만 페이튼 씨는 이용 후기에서 캐시미어와 면으로 된 베갯잇이 부드럽게 피부에 닿는 감촉이 안락하고 쾌적하게 느껴진다(The gentle touch of the cashmere and cotton case against my skin feels elegant and luxurious)며 (D) 베갯잇의 천을 언급하고 있으므로, 광고에 언급되지만 페이튼 씨가 다루지 않은 특징은 정답 (A) 베개의 모양이다. (B) 배송 과정과 (C) 베개 재료는 광고에서 언급되지 않았다.

180 세부 사항

번역 페이튼 씨는 처음에 루나 베개에 관해 어떻게 알게 되었나?
(A) 가족에게서 선물로 받았다.
(B) 신문 광고를 보았다.
(C) 상점에서 시연하는 것을 보았다.
(D) 홍보 자료 몇 가지를 이메일로 받았다.

해설 이용 후기에서 페이튼 씨는 가장 최근에 나온 소식지에 루나 베개 광고가 실려 있어 한번 써보기로 했다(The most recent newsletter included advertisements for the Luna pillow, so I thought I'd give it a try)고 언급했으므로 이메일 소식지에서 정보를 얻었다는 것을 알 수 있다. 따라서 정답은 (D)이다.

▶▶ Paraphrasing 지문의 **newsletter**
→ 정답의 **some promotional materials**

181-185 송장 + 이메일

머제스틱 여행사: 고객용 송장 #8394		
고객: 카시스 리갈		예약일: 5월 3일
목적지: 팜 아일랜드		신규 방문객: 예

숙소: 히비스커스 주식회사		
	방 종류: 디럭스	700달러
	성인 수: 2, 어린이 수: 0	
	투숙: 7월 19일 / 퇴실: 7월 23일	
184식사: 빌라 콤플렉스		
	종일 식권, 성인 2명: 7월 20-22일	185달러
	아침 식권, 성인 2명: 7월 23일	
활동 1: 메리디안 리미티드		
	183메리디안 코브 개인 보트 여행: 7월 21일	390달러
	5월 3일에 보증금 100달러 수령	

활동 2: 오키드 엔터프라이즈		
181워크숍: 지역 요리 만드는 법, 성인 2명: 7월 22일		60달러
	소계	1,335.00달러
	남은 요금	1,235.00달러

주의: 비행기표는 고객이 별도 예약

어휘 travel 여행 customer invoice 고객용 송장[청구서]
booking date 예약일 destination 행선지, 목적지 first-time
visitor 신규 방문객 accommodation 주거 deluxe 고급의,
우아한 adult 어른, 성인 check in 투숙하다 meal pass 식권
activity 활동 meridian 자오선의 limited 한정된 private
개인적인 deposit 예치금, 보증금 enterprise 기업 workshop
워크숍 prepare 준비하다 regional cuisine 지역[향토] 요리
subtotal 소계 remaining 남은 due 요금 separately 별도로

수신: 카시스 리잘 〈krizal@stiles-inc.net〉
발신: 라자 타야디 〈tahyadiraja@majestictravel.com〉
날짜: 5월 8일
제목: 답장: 문의

리잘 씨께,

문의를 받고 제가 귀하의 송장(#8394)을 재확인했으며, 송장의 모든 내용이 정확하다는 사실을 확인해 드릴 수 있습니다. **182**제 생각에는 저희 웹사이트에 기재된 보트 여행 가격이 기본 요금이라서 혼동이 생겼지만, 예약 수수료와 부가가치세(VAT)를 더하면 송장에 보이는 합계가 나옵니다. 이는 예약 페이지 하단에서 설명이 되었습니다. **184**아울러, 귀하께서는 저희가 그 회사의 파트너라서 식권을 할인받고 계시므로, 전체 휴가 비용이 매우 적정한 수준입니다. **183**그럼에도, 보트 여행을 취소하고 싶다면 그렇게 하셔도 되지만, 취소 요청은 5월 31일까지 서면으로 하셔야 하며, 보증금의 절반을 잃게 되실 것입니다. 이 날짜가 지난 뒤에 취소하시면 보증금 전액을 비용으로 내셔야 합니다.

185은행 계좌 이체로 남은 금액을 납부하는 데 필요한 설명서를 다시 한 번 첨부합니다. 여행을 예약하셨을 때 제가 언급했듯이 저희는 현금이나 수표, 신용카드를 더 이상 받지 않습니다.

제가 귀하의 질문에 만족스럽게 답변해 드렸기를 바라지만, 문의하실 내용이 더 있으면 주저하지 마시고 제게 연락하시기 바랍니다.

라자 타야디
머제스틱 여행사

어휘 in response to ~에 응하여[답하여] inquiry 문의, 질문
double-check 재확인하다 invoice 송장, 청구서 confirm
확증[확인]하다 correct 정확한 source 원천, 근원 confusion
혼동, 혼란 price 가격, 값 list 기재하다 a base fee 기본 요금
a booking charge 예약 수수료 additional 추가적인 value
added tax(VAT) 부가가치세 apply 적용하다 result in 그
결과 ~이 되다 explain 설명하다 at the bottom of ~ 하단에
additionally 더욱이, 아울러 get a discount on ~을 할인
받다 overall price 전체 가격 reasonable 적정한, 비싸지 않은
nevertheless 그럼에도 cancel 취소하다 attached 첨부된
instructions 설명, 지시 remaining balance 남은 금액 bank
transfer 은행 계좌 이체 mention 언급하다 no longer 더 이상
~ 아니다 cash 현금 check 수표 to one's satisfaction ~가
만족하게 hesitate 망설이다, 주저하다 contact 연락하다

---

181 사실 관계 확인

번역 리잘 씨에 관해 명시된 것은?
(A) 휴가로 닷새 밤을 보낼 것이다.
(B) 과거에 팜 아일랜드를 방문한 적이 있다.
(C) 다른 두 사람과 한 방을 쓸 것이다.
(D) 요리 강습에 참가할 계획이다.

해설 고객용 송장의 활동 2(Activity 2)에서 지역 요리 만드는 법에 대한 워크숍(Workshop: How to Prepare Regional Cuisine)을 신청했음을 알 수 있다. 즉 리잘 씨가 요리 강습에 참여한다는 것을 나타내고 있으므로, 정답은 (D)이다.

▶▶ **Paraphrasing** 지문의 **Workshop: How to Prepare Regional Cuisine**
→ 정답의 **a cooking lesson**

---

182 추론 / 암시

번역 리잘 씨가 무슨 문제로 타야디 씨에게 이메일을 보냈겠는가?
(A) 납부 영수증이 송부되지 않았다.
(B) 보트 여행의 예약이 다 찼다.
(C) 투숙 날짜가 부정확하다.
(D) 요금이 예상보다 더 많았다.

해설 이메일의 첫 번째 단락에서 타야디 씨는 웹사이트에 기재된 보트 여행 가격이 기본 요금이라서 혼동이 생겼지만, 예약 수수료와 부가가치세(VAT)를 적용하면 송장에 보이는 합계가 나온다(I believe the source of confusion is that the price for the boat tour listed on our Web site is just a base fee, but a booking charge and additional valued added tax (VAT) were also applied, resulting in the total you see on the invoice)고 했다. 즉 리잘 씨가 예상보다 많이 부가된 요금에 대해 먼저 이메일로 문제를 제기했음을 유추할 수 있으므로, 정답은 (D)이다.

---

183 연계

번역 리잘 씨가 3월 31일까지 보트 여행을 취소하면 얼마를 잃게 되는가?
(A) 390달러
(B) 290달러
(C) 100달러
(D) 50달러

해설 이메일의 첫 번째 단락에서 보트 여행을 취소하고 싶다면 그렇게 해도 되지만, 취소 요청은 5월 31일까지 서면으로 해야 하며, 보증금의 절반을 잃게 될 것(if you would like to cancel the boat tour, you may do so, but the request must be made in writing by May 31, and you would lose half of your deposit)이라고 했다. 그리고 송장의 활동 1(Activity 1)에서 보트 여행의 보증금(Deposit)이 100달러임을 확인할 수 있으므로, 정답은 절반인 (D) 50달러이다.

---

184 연계

번역 어떤 업체가 머제스틱 여행사와 제휴하고 있나?
(A) 히비스커스 주식회사
(B) 빌라 콤플렉스
(C) 메리디안 리미티드
(D) 오키드 엔터프라이즈

해설 이메일의 첫 번째 단락에서 저희가 그 회사의 파트너라서 귀하께서는 식권을 할인받고 계시므로, 전체 휴가 비용이 매우 적정한 수준(Additionally, you are getting a discount on your meal passes because we are partners with that business, so the overall price of the vacation is quite reasonable)이라는 언급을 통해 식사 업체와 제휴를 맺고 있음을 알 수 있다. 아울러 송장의 식사(Dining) 항목에서 빌라 콤플렉스가 제휴사임을 확인할 수 있으므로, 정답은 (B)이다.

185 추론 / 암시

번역 머제스틱 여행사에 관해 암시된 것은?
(A) 팜 아일랜드에 지사가 있다.
(B) 요금 납부 방식이 한 가지뿐이다.
(C) 휴가 패키지를 주로 예약한다.
(D) 항공 요금을 할인해 줄 수 있다.

해설 머제스틱 여행사에서 보낸 이메일의 두 번째 단락에서 은행 계좌 이체로 남은 금액을 납부하는 데 필요한 설명서를 다시 한 번 첨부한다(Attached you will find the instructions once again for paying the remaining balance by bank transfer)면서, 여행 예약 당시 언급했듯이 현금이나 수표, 신용카드를 더 이상 받지 않는다(As I mentioned when you booked the trip, we no longer accept cash, checks, or credit cards)고 이야기했다. 즉 요금 납부는 은행 계좌 이체로만 가능하다는 것을 알 수 있으므로, 정답은 (B)이다.

▶▶ **Paraphrasing** 지문의 **paying ~ by bank transfer**
→ 정답의 **one form of payment**

186-190 안내문 + 편지 + 문자 메시지

〈움직이는 역사〉 사진 공모전

〈움직이는 역사〉 잡지는 연례 사진 공모전을 알리게 되어 뿌듯합니다. [187]올해의 주제는 "운송의 과거와 현재"입니다. 응모작에는 기차, 자동차, 버스 등의 사진이 들어가야 합니다. 사진은 컬러나 흑백이어야 하며, 저희 편집팀과 함께 전문 사진작가들로 구성된 심사위원단의 심사를 받게 됩니다.

공모전에 출품하려면 www.historyinmotionmag.com/photo를 방문하시기 바랍니다. 거기에서 신청서 양식을 작성하고 사진을 올리실 수 있습니다. [186]해당 사진이 자신의 독창적 저작물이며 사진 배포권이 자신에게 있음을 확인하는 진술서도 제출해야 합니다. 참가자들은 응모작을 한 편 이상, 최대 다섯 편까지 출품할 수 있습니다. 작품은 6월 30일까지 제출해야 합니다.

어휘 in motion 움직이는, 이동하는 photography contest 사진 공모전 magazine 잡지 announce 발표하다, 알리다 annual 연례의, 일년에 한 번 열리는 theme 주제, 테마 transportation 운송 then and now 과거와 현재 entry 출품작 contain 포함하다, 담다 in color 컬러로 in black and white 흑백으로 judge 심사하다, 판단하다 professional 전문적인 photographer 사진작가 editorial team 편집부 enter a contest 공모[시합]에 참가하다 fill out 작성하다 application form 신청 양식 submit 제출하다 statement 진술서 affirm 단언하다, 확증하다 original work 독창적 작품 distribution right 배포권 participant 참가자 submission 제출

[188]〈움직이는 역사〉 잡지 본사

도슨 빌딩 3001호
콜로니 스트리트 489번지
[188]28202 사우스캐롤라이나 주 샬럿

7월 6일

새뮤얼 고츠
밸리뷰 드라이브 1396번지
02114 매사추세츠 주 보스턴

고츠 씨께,

축하합니다! 〈움직이는 역사〉 사진 공모전의 결선 진출자가 되셨습니다. [187]"시간 위의 시간"이라는 제목이 붙은 귀하의 사진은 공모전 주제에 부합하지 않아 실격되었습니다. 하지만 "숲과 마주하다"가 심사위원단에게 정말 깊은 인상을 남겨서 여덟 점의 결선 진출작 중 하나로 뽑혔습니다.

[188]7월 28일에 저희의 본사를 방문해 회사를 둘러보시고, 다른 결선 진출자들과 만나고, 사진 촬영에 참여하시도록 귀하를 초청합니다. [188]이틀간의 숙박비뿐만 아니라 왕복 항공비도 저희가 부담하겠습니다. [189]제 비서가 여행을 주선할 예정이니 여행과 관련한 연락은 모두 그녀를 통하셔야 합니다(자세한 연락 정보 동봉).

귀하가 저희를 방문하실 수 있기를 바랍니다!

[189]토머스 포터 드림

어휘 congratulation 축하 finalist 결선 진출자 entitled 제목이 ~인 disqualify 실격 처리하다 fit 부합하다, 맞다 face 마주하다 impress 감동을 주다, 깊은 인상을 남기다 judging panel 심사위원단 select 선발하다, 고르다, 뽑다 be invited to+동사원형 ~하도록 초대받다 headquarters 본사, 사령부 take a tour 둘러보다, 여행하다 participate in ~에 참가[참여]하다 photo shoot 사진 촬영 cover one's expenses ~의 경비[비용]을 부담하다 flight to and from 왕복 항공편 A as well as B B는 물론 A도 accommodation 숙박 travel arrangement 여행 준비 assistant 조수, 비서 regarding ~에 관해 contact detail 자세한 연락처 enclosed 동봉된

[189]발신: 캐시 페어필드, 704-555-0141
수신: 새뮤얼 고츠, 617-555-0186
7월 8일, 오전 11:24

저희를 방문하실 수 있다니 매우 기쁩니다. [189]제가 항공권을 예매하려면 귀하의 신분증 정보가 필요할 것입니다. [190]현재의 저가 요금으로 확보할 수 있게 가능한 한 빨리 신분증 정보를 주십시오. 감사드리고, 문의 사항이 있으면 제게 알려주시기 바랍니다!

어휘 pleased 기쁜, 기분 좋은 be able to+동사원형 ~할 수 있다 ID information 신분증 정보 book 예약[예매]하다 as quickly as possible 가능한 한 빨리 secure 확보하다 current 현재의 fare 요금

186 세부 사항

번역 안내문에 따르면, 공모전 참가자들이 해야 하는 일은?
(A) 출품작이 자신의 작품이라고 선언한다.
(B) 특정한 크기의 사진을 보낸다.
(C) 응모작에 작품 설명을 포함시킨다.
(D) 등록할 때 연령대를 선택한다.

해설 안내문의 두 번째 단락에서 참가자들은 해당 사진이 본인의 독창적 저작물이며 사진 배포권이 본인에게 있음을 확인하는 진술서도 제출해야 한다(You must also submit a statement affirming that the photo is your original work and that you hold all distribution rights to it)고 했으므로 정답은 (A)이다.

▶▶ **Paraphrasing** 지문의 **affirming that the photo is your original work** → 정답의 **Declare that the submission is their own work**

187 연계

번역 "시간 위의 시간"에 관해 암시된 것은?
(A) 마감시한 전에 도착하지 않았다.
(B) 공모전 심사위원들의 호감을 샀다.
(C) 흑백으로 인화되었다.
(D) 교통수단을 포함하지 않았다.

해설 편지의 첫 번째 단락에서 "시간 위의 시간"이라는 제목이 붙은 사진은 공모전 주제에 부합하지 않아 실격되었다(Your photo entitled *Time over Time* was disqualified because it did not fit the contest's theme)고 했다. 그리고 안내문의 첫 번째 단락에서 올해의 주제는 "운송의 과거와 현재"이며, 응모작에는 기차, 자동차, 버스 등의 사진이 들어가야 한다(This year's theme is "Transportation Then and Now." Entries must contain an image of a train, car, bus, etc)고 교통수단을 포함할 것을 언급하고 있다. 따라서 정답은 (D)이다.

188 세부 사항

번역 포터 씨는 회사가 무엇을 할 것이라고 말하는가?
(A) 고츠 씨의 고향으로 찾아간다.
(B) 우승자들에게 이메일로 알린다.
(C) 사우스캐롤라이나로 오는 경비를 지불한다.
(D) 고츠 씨에게 일자리를 제안한다.

해설 편지의 두 번째 단락에서 회사로 초청한다면서 이틀 밤 숙박비는 물론 왕복 항공비까지 회사가 부담하겠다(We will cover your expenses for the flight to and from your home city as well as two nights of accommodations)고 했다. 편지 상단에서 회사는 사우스캐롤라이나 주의 샬럿(Charlotte, South Carolina)에 위치한다는 것을 알 수 있으므로, 정답은 (C)이다.

▶▶ **Paraphrasing** 지문의 **cover your expenses for the flight to and from your home city as well as two nights of accommodations** → 정답의 **Pay for a trip**

189 연계

번역 페어필드 씨는 누구이겠는가?
(A) 사진 공모전의 심사위원
(B) 고츠 씨의 동업자
(C) 〈움직이는 역사〉의 편집자
(D) 포터 씨의 비서

해설 페어필드 씨는 문자 메시지의 발신인(From: Cathy Fairfield)이며, 제가 항공권을 예매하려면 귀하의 신분증 정보가 필요할 것(I will need your ID information in order to book the plane tickets)이라는 문자 메시지를 통해 여행 관련 업무를 담당한다는 것을 유추할 수 있다. 포터 씨가 쓴 편지의 두 번째 단락에서 비서가 여행을 주선할 예정이니 여행과 관련한 연락은 모두 그녀를 통해 해 달라(Travel arrangements will be made by my assistant, and all contact regarding travel should go through her)는 언급을 통해 페어필드 씨는 포터 씨의 비서임을 확인할 수 있다. 따라서 정답은 (D)이다.

190 동의어 찾기

번역 문자 메시지에서 첫 번째 단락 5행의 "secure"와 의미가 가장 가까운 단어는?
(A) 방어하다
(B) 설득하다
(C) 첨부하다
(D) 보장하다

해설 해당 문장은 '현재의 저가 요금으로 확보할 수 있게 가능한 한 빨리 신분증 정보를 주십시오(Please get this to me as quickly as possible so that I can secure the current low fare)'와 같이 해석되므로, 여기서 secure는 '확보하다, 보장하다'라는 의미이다. 따라서 정답은 (D) guarantee(보장하다, 확실하게 하다)이다.

191-195 편지 + 이메일 + 일정표

비올라 돌턴
콜먼 로드 528번지
28210 노스캐롤라이나 주 샬럿
7월 6일

돌턴 씨 귀하,

6월 13일 면접에서 귀하를 만나 즐거웠습니다. 채용위원회 전원이 귀하의 자연스러운 사교술은 물론 이력에 깊은 인상을 받았습니다. **191, 192, 194**우리는 귀하가 연구개발부장 자리를 수락해 주셔서 기쁩니다. **191**양측이 계약서에 서명했으므로 이것은 공식적인 계약입니다. 귀하의 보관용 계약서 사본을 동봉합니다.

7월 17일 오리엔테이션에서 귀하는 C그룹에 배정될 것입니다. 그곳에서 만나 뵙기를 고대합니다!

아리나 사이토우 배상
콜드웰 주식회사 인력관리부장

어휘 It is a pleasure to+동사원형 ~해서 기쁩니다 interview 면접, 인터뷰 entire 전체의 hiring committee 채용위원회, 고용위원회 be impressed with ~에 깊은 인상을 받다 career history 이력 B as well as A A뿐만 아니라 B도, A는 물론 B도 natural 자연스러운, 타고난 people skills 사교술, 대인(관계) 기술

accept 수락하다, 받아들이다 position 지위, 자리 R&D Department Manager 연구개발부장 now that ~이기 때문에, ~이므로 sign a contract 계약서에 서명하다 official 공식적인, 정식의 Enclosed you will find ~을 동봉합니다 copy 사본 for one's record 보관용으로 orientation 오리엔테이션, 예비 교육 be assigned to ~에 배정[편성]되다 look forward to ~을 고대하다 HR Manager 인력관리부장, 인사부장 corporation 주식회사, 법인

수신: 비공개 수신자들
발신: 아리나 사이토우
날짜: 7월 13일
제목: 콜드웰 주식회사 오리엔테이션

신입사원 귀하,

우리가 본사 건물에 막 입주한 상태라 여러분 대다수는 아직 본사 건물을 본 적이 없습니다. 건물에는 잠시 쉬거나 옥외에서 점심식사를 할 수 있는 널찍한 파티오가 있으며, 옆에 랜싱 강이 흘러서 경치가 근사합니다. 나는 여러분이 **193**나머지 다른 직원들만큼 그것을 좋아할 것이라고 확신합니다.

1927월 17일 오리엔테이션에서 입장 절차에 속도를 더하기 위해 각 부서의 직원들은 서로 다른 방으로 출석해야 합니다. 아래 있는 표를 보시기 바랍니다.

부서	방
그래픽 디자인	308호
192연구개발, 회계	233호
마케팅, 영업	A 회의실
총무, 인력관리	B 회의실

오리엔테이션 일정 사본을 첨부했습니다. 질문이 있으면 망설이지 말고 저에게 연락하시기 바랍니다.

아리나 사이토우 배상
콜드웰 주식회사 인력관리부장

어휘 undisclosed recipients 비공개 수신자들 employee 사원, 직원 move into ~에 입주하다 headquarters building 본사 건물 spacious 널찍한 patio 파티오 take a break 잠시 쉬다 view 전망, 경치 amazing 놀라운, 멋진 the rest of the staff 나머지 직원들 expedite 신속히 처리하다, 촉진하다 check-in process 입장 절차 report to ~에 출두하다, 출석[도착]을 알리다 department 부서 accounting 회계, 경리 sales 영업, 판매 administration 총무; 행정 human resources 인적 자원 conference room 회의실 attach 첨부하다 schedule 시간표, 일정 hesitate 망설이다, 주저하다 contact 연락하다, 접촉하다

콜드웰 주식회사
직원 오리엔테이션, 7월 17일

오전 8:30 입장 수속 (배정된 방으로 출석)
오전 9:00 환영사, CEO 안 훠
오전 9:30 **195B**세금 서류작업과 휴가 정책, 루스 보바
오전 11:45 **195C**복장 규정, 해미드 예메인
오후 12:15 점심식사: 점심 시간 동안 그룹들은 다음 시간표에 따라 경비실에 가서 신분증 배지를 배정받아야 합니다: A그룹 오후 12:15, B그룹 오후 12:30, C그룹 오후 12:45, D그룹 오후 1:00

오후 1:15 **195A**업무용 컴퓨터로 하는 온라인 활동, 조슬린 루이스
오후 2:30 분할 모임: **194**관리자들은 디에고 배러스 이사의 강연을 듣고, 일반 정규 직원들은 프라바 할다르와 질의응답 시간을 가지며, 비정규 직원들은 교육용 동영상을 시청할 것이다.
오후 4:45 사옥 탐방, 아리나 사이토우

어휘 report to ~에 출두하다, 출석[도착]을 알리다 assigned 배정된, 할당된 welcome speech 환영사 tax 세금 paperwork 서류 작업 vacation 휴가 policy 정책 dress code 복장 규정 lunch break 점심 시간 security office 경비실 assign 배정하다, 할당하다 according to ~에 따라 work computer 업무용 컴퓨터 split session 분할 모임 non-management employee (관리자가 아닌) 일반 직원 full-time employee 정규 직원, 상근 직원 part-time employee 비정규 직원, 시간제 근무자 question-and-answer session 질의응답 시간 training video 교육용 동영상

---

191 주제 / 목적

번역 사이토우 씨가 편지를 쓴 이유는?
(A) 추가 정보를 요청하려고
(B) 임용을 확인해 주려고
(C) 계약서를 변경하려고
(D) 면접 약속을 잡으려고

해설 편지의 첫 번째 단락에서 우리는 귀하가 연구개발부장 자리를 수락해서 기쁘고, 양측이 계약서에 서명했으므로 이것은 공식적인 계약이다(We are pleased that you have accepted the position of R&D Department Manager. Now that we have both signed the contract, it is official)라고 했다. 따라서 돌턴 씨의 임용 확인을 위해 편지를 썼음을 알 수 있으므로, 정답은 (B)이다.

---

192 연계

번역 7월 17일에 돌턴 씨가 가장 먼저 가야 하는 곳은?
(A) 308호
(B) 233호
(C) A 회의실
(D) B 회의실

해설 편지의 첫 번째 단락에서 우리는 귀하가 연구개발부장 자리를 수락해서 기쁘다(We are pleased that you have accepted the position of R&D Department Manager)라고 했으므로 돌턴 씨는 연구개발부서에서 근무할 것임을 알 수 있다. 이메일의 7월 17일 오리엔테이션 장소를 공지하는 표(table)를 통해 연구개발부서(Research & Development)의 신입직원들은 233호(Room 233)로 가야 한다는 것을 확인할 수 있으므로, 정답은 (B)이다.

---

193 동의어 찾기

번역 이메일에서 첫 번째 단락 4행의 "rest"와 의미가 가장 가까운 단어는?
(A) 이완
(B) 대다수
(C) 중단
(D) 나머지

해설 해당 문장은 '나는 여러분이 나머지 다른 직원들만큼 그것을 좋아할 것이라고 확신합니다(I'm sure you will love it as much as the rest of the staff does)'라는 의미로 해석되므로, 여기서 rest는 '나머지, 다른 사람들'이라는 의미가 자연스럽다. 따라서 정답은 (D) remainder(나머지)이다.

194 연계

번역 돌턴 씨에 관해 암시된 것은?
(A) 질문에 대한 답변을 할다르 씨에게 듣게 될 것이다.
(B) 오후 12시 15분에 경비실에 가야 한다.
(C) 오리엔테이션 동안 동영상을 시청할 것이다.
(D) 배러스 씨와 함께하는 모임에 참석할 것이다.

해설 편지의 첫 번째 단락에서 귀하가 연구개발부장 자리를 수락해서 기쁘다(We are pleased that you have accepted the position of R&D Department Manager)고 했으므로 돌턴 씨는 연구개발부장으로 근무할 것임을 알 수 있다. 일정표의 오후 2시 30분 분할 모임(Split Session)에서 관리자들은 디에고 배러스 이사의 강연을 들을 것(Managers will hear a talk from Director Diego Barros)이라고 했으므로 연구개발부장인 돌턴 씨는 배러스 씨의 강연에 참석할 것임을 유추할 수 있다. 따라서 정답은 (D)이다.

▶▶ **Paraphrasing** 지문의 **hear a talk**
→ 정답의 **attend a session**

195 사실 관계 확인

번역 오리엔테이션에서 다루는 주제로 명시되지 않은 것은?
(A) 인터넷 사용
(B) 휴가 내기
(C) 근무 복장
(D) 기업 구조

해설 일정표의 오후 1시 15분 '업무용 컴퓨터로 하는 온라인 활동(Online Activities from Work Computers)'을 통해 (A)를, 오전 9시 30분 '세금 서류작업과 휴가 정책(Tax Paperwork and Vacation Policies)'을 통해 (B)를, 오전 11시 45분 '복장 규정(Dress Code)'을 통해 (C)를 오리엔테이션에서 다룬다는 것을 확인할 수 있으므로, 정답은 (D)이다.

▶▶ **Paraphrasing** 지문의 **Online Activities**
→ 보기의 **Internet usage**
지문의 **Vacation** → 보기의 **Taking time off**
지문의 **Dress Code** → 보기의 **What to wear**

196-200 이메일 + 안내문 + 공지

수신: 독립영화 제작자 클럽 〈memberslist@independentfilmc.com〉
발신: 로저 스트래턴 〈rstratton@palletpost.net〉
날짜: 4월 7일
제목: 프레즈노 영화제

친애하는 회원 여러분께,

지난 모임에서 논의한 대로 다음달 프레즈노 영화제에 흥미진진한 기회가 있습니다. 이 행사에 참석하면 우리가 다른 사람들의 창작물로부터 배울 수 있을 뿐

더러 독립영화 제작자들을 지원한다는 우리의 대의명분도 **196**촉진할 수 있을 것입니다.

199모임에서 표출된 관심사를 바탕으로, 저는 5월 2일에 상영되는 〈더 메시지〉가 우리 모임에 가장 좋은 선택이 되리라고 생각합니다. 우리는 영화가 상영되기 약 30분 전에 바거스 극장에서 모일 것입니다. 제가 알기로 회원 다수가 차를 몰고 올 계획이니, 주차 정보가 나와 있는 첨부된 문서를 살펴보시기 바랍니다. 제가 입장권을 한꺼번에 구입할 수 있도록 그곳에 참석하는지의 여부를 이메일로 제게 알려주시기 바랍니다.

고맙습니다!

로저

어휘 independent filmmaker 독립영화 제작자[감독] film festival 영화제 as discussed 논의된 대로 exciting opportunity 흥미진진한 기회 attend 참석[참가]하다 event 행사 not only A but also B A뿐만 아니라 B도 creative work 창작품 further 발전시키다, 촉진하다, 조성하다 cause 대의명분 support 지원하다 based on ~을 바탕으로, 근거로 option 선택 theater 극장 plan to+동사원형 ~할 계획이다 attached document 첨부 문서 include 포함하다, 담다 parking information 주차 정보 e-mail back 이메일로 답장하다 purchase 구입[구매]하다

프레즈노 영화제: 5월 2일 상영표

어게인 앤 어게인, 오후 7:00 장소: 앳킨슨 극장, 상영시간: 112분
198프레즈노 영화제에 처음으로 참여하는 클로디아 에머슨 감독이 1800년대를 배경으로 한 러브 스토리로, 관객들이 오랫동안 고대하던 영화 〈어게인〉의 후속편을 선보인다.

비밀의 속삭임, 오후 7:00 장소: 바거스 극장, 상영시간: 87분
197, 198데뷔작을 발표하는 대니얼 애덤스 감독이 캐나다의 작은 도시에서 벌어지는 초자연적인 현상을 독특한 공상과학 영화로 담아낸다.

나의 모든 것, 오후 9:35 장소: 앳킨슨 극장, 상영시간: 93분
198유한 주 감독은 이 범죄 드라마에서 인상적인 등장인물과 빠른 전개로 관객에게 계속 놀라움을 선사한다.

더 메시지, 오후 9:05 장소: 바거스 극장, 상영시간: 102분
198새러 콤튼 감독이 생애 첫 다큐멘터리로 평소의 코미디 영화에서 벗어나 현대의 마케팅을 탐구한다.

앳킨슨 극장 이용자는 웨버 스트리트와 케임브리지 로드에 주차할 수 있다. **199**바거스 극장 이용자는 맥크레이 스트리트와 포크너 애비뉴에 주차할 수 있다.

어휘 screening 상영 duration 지속; 상영시간 participate in ~에 참여[참가]하다 for the first time 처음으로 director 감독 viewer 시청자, 관람객 long-anticipated 오랫동안 고대하던 sequel 속편 whisper 속삭임 present 발표하다, 선보이다 debut film (영화) 데뷔작 offer 제공하다, 내놓다 unique 독특한 sci-fi film 공상과학 영화 supernatural forces 초자연적인 힘 continue 계속하다 amaze 놀라게 하다 audience 관객 memorable 인상적인, 기억에 남을 만한 character 등장인물 fast-moving plot 전개가 빠른 구성 crime drama 범죄 드라마 first-ever 생애[사상] 첫 branch out from ~에서 벗어나다, 가지를 치다 usual 평소의, 보통의 explore 탐구하다 modern age 현대 parking 주차 available 이용할 수 있는

공사 안내: 4월 18일

199프레즈노 시는 4월 29일부터 5월 31일까지 맥크레이 스트리트를 폐쇄할 계획임을 알려 드립니다. 공사 기간 중에 도로 전체에서 자동차 주행과 주차가 금지됩니다. **200**공사반원들이 도로 양쪽을 5피트 넓혀 회전 차선을 추가할 것입니다. 이렇게 하면 안전이 증진되고 교통체증도 줄게 됩니다. 공사에 관한 문의는 프레즈노 시 교통국 전화 555-0133, 내선 27번으로 해 주십시오.

어휘 announce 공표[공지]하다, 알리다 planned 계획된
closure 폐쇄 entire 전체의 road 도로 be closed to ~이
금지되다, ~을 할 수 없다 driving (자동차) 주행 duration 지속
construction 공사 add 추가하다, 더하다 both sides 양측, 양쪽
turning lane 회전 차선 improve 향상시키다, 개선[개량]하다
safety 안전 relieve 덜다, 경감하다, 줄이다 traffic congestion
교통 체증 regarding ~에 관한 project 프로젝트, 사업, 계획
direct 보내다, (~ 앞으로) 하다 Department of Transportation
교통국 extension 내선

196 동의어 찾기

번역 이메일에서 첫 번째 단락 3행의 "further"와 의미가 가장 가까운 단어는?
(A) 홍보하다
(B) 연장하다
(C) 추천하다
(D) **촉진하다**

해설 해당 문장은 '이 행사에 참석하면 우리가 다른 사람들의 창작물로부터 배울 수 있을뿐더러 독립영화 제작자들을 지원한다는 우리의 대의명분도 촉진할 수 있을 것입니다(Attending this event will not only allow us to learn from the creative work of others, but it will also further our cause of supporting independent filmmakers)'라는 의미로 해석되므로, 여기서 further는 '촉진하다, 추진하다'라는 의미이다. 따라서 정답은 (D) advance(촉진하다, 추진하다, 개선하다, 발전시키다)이다.

197 세부 사항

번역 영화를 가장 적게 만든 사람은?
(A) 클로디아 에머슨
(B) **대니얼 애덤스**
(C) 유한 주
(D) 새러 콤튼

해설 안내문에 있는 두 번째 영화 소개에서 데뷔작을 발표하는 대니얼 애덤스 감독이 캐나다의 작은 도시에서 벌어지는 초자연적인 현상을 독특한 공상과학 영화로 담아낸다(Presenting his debut film, director Daniel Adams offers a unique sci-fi film about supernatural forces in a small Canadian town)고 했으므로, '비밀의 속삭임(Whispers of the Secrets)'은 대니얼 애덤스의 첫 작품임을 알 수 있다. 따라서 정답은 (B)이다.

198 사실 관계 확인

번역 프레즈노 영화제에 관해 명시된 것은?
(A) **다양한 장르의 영화를 상영한다.**
(B) 관객 회원들에게는 입장료를 받지 않는다.
(C) 서로 다른 장소 세 곳에서 열릴 것이다.
(D) 독립영화 제작자 클럽이 설립했다.

해설 안내문의 영화 소개를 통해 '어게인 앤 어게인(Again and Again)'과 같은 러브스토리(love story), '비밀의 속삭임(Whispers of the Secrets)'과 같은 공상과학 영화, '나의 모든 것(Everything I Am)'과 같은 범죄 드라마, '더 메시지(The Message)'와 같은 코미디 영화 등 다양한 장르의 영화를 영화제에서 상영한다는 것을 알 수 있으므로, 정답은 (A)이다.

199 연계

번역 독립영화 제작자 클럽 회원들은 5월 2일에 어디에 주차하겠는가?
(A) 웨버 스트리트
(B) 케임브리지 로드
(C) 맥크레이 스트리트
(D) **포크너 애비뉴**

해설 이메일의 두 번째 단락에서 5월 2일에 상영되는 〈더 메시지〉가 우리 모임에 가장 좋은 선택이 되리라 생각한다(I think The Message on May 2 would be the best option for our group)며, 영화가 상영되기 약 30분 전에 바거스 극장에서 모이자(We will meet at the Vargas Theater about half an hour before the show)고 했으므로 클럽 회원들은 5월 2일 바거스 극장에서 영화를 볼 예정임을 알 수 있다. 안내문의 마지막 단락에서 바거스 극장 이용자는 맥크레이 스트리트와 포크너 애비뉴에 주차할 수 있다(Parking for the Vargas Theater is available on McCray Street and Faulkner Avenue)며 주차가 가능한 두 곳을 언급하고 있다. 하지만 공지에서 프레즈노 시는 4월 29일부터 5월 31일까지 맥크레이 스트리트를 폐쇄할 계획(The city of Fresno is announcing a planned closure of McCray Street from April 29–May 31)이라고 했으므로, 남은 장소인 포크너 애비뉴에 주차할 것임을 유추할 수 있다. 따라서 정답은 (D)이다.

200 세부 사항

번역 공지에 따르면, 건설 공사의 목적은 무엇인가?
(A) 안전장비 설치
(B) 피해지역 복구
(C) **도로 확장**
(D) 새로운 법규 준수

해설 공지에서 공사반원들이 도로 양쪽을 5피트 넓혀 회전 차선을 추가할 것(Workers will add five feet on both sides of the road so that a turning lane may be added)이라고 했으므로, 정답은 (C)이다.

▶▶ **Paraphrasing** 지문의 **add five feet on both sides of the road** → 정답의 **make a road wider**

TEST 2

101 (A)	102 (C)	103 (D)	104 (A)	105 (A)
106 (A)	107 (D)	108 (B)	109 (A)	110 (A)
111 (A)	112 (B)	113 (A)	114 (C)	115 (A)
116 (C)	117 (D)	118 (D)	119 (B)	120 (B)
121 (A)	122 (A)	123 (A)	124 (B)	125 (A)
126 (D)	127 (D)	128 (D)	129 (A)	130 (D)
131 (B)	132 (B)	133 (D)	134 (C)	135 (C)
136 (C)	137 (D)	138 (B)	139 (C)	140 (B)
141 (D)	142 (A)	143 (A)	144 (D)	145 (C)
146 (D)	147 (B)	148 (B)	149 (B)	150 (C)
151 (A)	152 (B)	153 (C)	154 (B)	155 (C)
156 (B)	157 (A)	158 (C)	159 (A)	160 (C)
161 (C)	162 (C)	163 (C)	164 (B)	165 (C)
166 (C)	167 (C)	168 (C)	169 (B)	170 (C)
171 (D)	172 (B)	173 (C)	174 (B)	175 (A)
176 (B)	177 (A)	178 (B)	179 (D)	180 (C)
181 (B)	182 (D)	183 (A)	184 (C)	185 (B)
186 (B)	187 (D)	188 (B)	189 (A)	190 (D)
191 (C)	192 (D)	193 (D)	194 (B)	195 (C)
196 (D)	197 (A)	198 (C)	199 (D)	200 (B)

PART 5

101 인칭대명사의 격 _ 목적격

해설 빈칸 앞에 있는 동사(can prepare)의 목적어 자리이므로, 정답은 목적격 인칭대명사 (A) you이다. 동사(can prepare)의 주어(workshops)와 빈칸이 서로 일치하지 않으므로, 재귀대명사인 (C) yourself와 (D) yourselves는 적합하지 않다.

번역 본사에서 여러분이 팀을 이끌 수 있도록 준비시키는 워크숍을 엽니다.

어휘 head office 본사 hold (회의·시합 등을) 열다 prepare 준비시키다

102 전치사 어휘

해설 명사 the clients 앞 전치사 자리이다. 문맥상 '고객들을 위해 교통편을 예약하다'라는 의미가 자연스러우므로, 정답은 (C) for이다.

번역 킹스턴 씨는 고객들을 위해 회의 장소로 가는 교통편을 예약하기로 결정했다.

어휘 decide to + 동사원형 ~하기로 결정[결심]하다 reserve 예약하다 transportation 교통 venue (행사 등이 개최되는) 장소 client 고객

103 명사 자리 _ 주어

해설 빈칸은 동사(attempted) 앞 주어 자리이다. 빈칸 앞에 한정사가 없으므로, 셀 수 있는 명사의 복수형인 (A) Contests(대회)와 (D) Contestants(참가자)가 적합하다. 문맥상 '참가자들이 대답하려고 애쓸 것이다'라는 의미가 자연스러우므로, 정답은 (D) Contestants이다.

번역 참가자들은 지역 및 국가의 역사에 관한 질문에 대답하려고 애썼다.

어휘 attempt to + 동사원형 ~하려고 시도하다[애쓰다] contestant (대회) 참가자

104 부사 어휘

해설 빈칸은 뒤에 나오는 전치사구(after launching a new product)를 강조하는 부사 자리이다. 문맥상 '신제품 출시 직후'라는 의미가 자연스러우므로, 정답은 (A) immediately이다. (B) nearly(거의), (C) previously (전에), (D) popularly(일반적으로, 널리)는 의미상 적합하지 않다.

번역 '비즈니스 플러스' 강의는 신제품 출시 직후 여러분이 해야 할 일을 개괄적으로 설명해 줄 것이다.

어휘 lecture 강의 outline 개요를 설명하다 immediately after ~ 직후에 launch (제품을) 출시하다 product 제품, 상품

105 형용사 자리 _ 명사 수식

해설 빈칸 뒤의 명사(scene)를 수식하는 형용사 자리이다. 따라서 정답은 형용사 (A) final이다. 부사 (B) finally, 명사 (C) finality, 동사 (D) finalize는 품사상 적합하지 않다.

번역 현대 뮤지컬 〈강가의 소풍〉은 마지막 장면에서 즐거운 가족 행사를 그리고 있다.

어휘 contemporary 당대의, 현대의 depict 묘사하다, 그리다 joyful 즐거운 celebration 기념 행사

106 명사 어휘

해설 빈칸은 앞에 있는 to부정사(to indicate)의 목적어 역할을 하는 명사 자리로, 뒤의 전치사구(to the terms of the contract)의 수식을 받는다. 문맥상 '계약 조건에 동의를 표하다'라는 의미가 자연스러우므로, 정답은 명사 (A) consent이다. (B) receipt(영수증, 수령), (C) ability(능력), (D) deal(거래)은 의미상 적합하지 않다.

번역 고객들은 계약 조건에 동의를 표한다는 의미로 점선 위에 자신의 이름 머리글자를 적어야 한다.

어휘 initials (성명의) 머리글자 dotted line 점선 indicate 보이다, 나타내다 consent to ~에 대한 동의 terms of a contract 계약 조건

107 동사 어휘

해설 빈칸 앞의 주어(The much-anticipated next episode of *Cat and Mouse*)와 의미가 가장 잘 통하는 수동의 의미를 나타내는 과거분사를 선택해야 한다. 문맥상 '다음 에피소드가 방영되다'라는 의미가 가장 자연스러우므로, 정답은 (D) broadcast이다. 참고로 broadcast(방송하다)는 동사원형, 과거형, 과거분사형 모두 broadcast이다. (A) transformed (변형하다), (B) entertained(즐겁게 하다), (C) overcome(극복하다)은 의미상 적합하지 않다.

번역 고대하시던 〈고양이와 쥐〉 다음 에피소드가 오늘 밤 9시 ZLTV에서 방영됩니다.

어휘 anticipate 기대하다, 고대하다 broadcast (라디오·TV로) 방송하다 (broadcast – broadcast – broadcast)

108 부사 자리 _ 동사 수식

해설 빈칸은 현재완료 시제를 나타내는 동사인 has been awarded 사이에서 동사를 수식하는 부사 자리이다. 따라서 정답은 부사 (B) regularly이다. 형용사 (A) regular, 명사 (C) regularity, 동사 (D) regularize는 품사상 적합하지 않다.

번역 유명한 요리사 피에르 매사소잇은 명망 있는 요리 경연대회들에서 여러 차례 1등상을 받았다.

어휘 noted 유명한, 저명한 be awarded 상을 받다, 수상하다
competition (경연) 대회 regularly 자주

109 전치사 어휘

해설 빈칸 뒤의 목적어(the headquarters)와 함께 앞의 명사(industrial machinery)를 수식하는 전치사 자리이다. 문맥상 '본사에서 나오는 산업 장비'라는 의미가 자연스러우므로, 정답은 (A) from이다.

번역 직원들은 본사에서 나오는 산업 장비 목록에서 선택할 수 있었다.

어휘 choose 선택하다 industrial machinery 산업 장비
headquarters 본사, 본부

110 형용사 어휘

해설 빈칸은 앞에 있는 주어(the small conference room)를 보충 설명하는 형용사 자리로, 주어와 의미가 가장 잘 통하는 형용사를 선택해야 한다. 문맥상 '작은 회의실이 정식 회의에는 적합하지 않다'라는 의미가 자연스러우므로, 정답은 (A) appropriate이다. (B) timely(시기 적절한), (C) competent(유능한), (D) responsible(책임이 있는)은 의미상 적합하지 않다.

번역 작은 회의실은 가구 상태가 변변찮아서 정식 회의에는 적합하지 않다고 사료된다.

어휘 condition 상태 conference room 회의실 formal 정식의, 공식적인 appropriate 적합한

111 형용사 자리 _ 명사 수식

해설 빈칸은 동사(showed)의 목적어 역할을 하는 명사(damage)를 수식하는 형용사 자리이므로, 정답은 형용사 (A) noticeable이다. 부사 (B) noticeably, 명사/동사 (C) notices, 동명사 (D) noticing은 품사상 적합하지 않다. 현재분사 (D) noticing은 명사를 수식하는 형용사 역할을 할 수 있으나, 여기서는 '인지되는 손상'이라는 수동의 의미가 되어야 하므로 과거분사인 noticed가 정답으로 가능하다.

번역 우리는 상자 중 하나가 창고에서 배송된 후 뚜렷한 손상이 있는 것을 알고 놀랐다.

어휘 ship 운송하다, 배송하다 warehouse 창고 noticeable 눈에 띄는, 뚜렷한

112 동사 어형 _ 조동사 + 동사원형

해설 빈칸 앞의 조동사(will) 뒤에는 동사원형이 이어져야 한다. 따라서 정답은 동사원형 (B) transfer이다.

번역 말렉시아 운송 사는 트럭과 열차 간에는 더 이상 화물 운송을 하지 않을 예정입니다.

어휘 freight 화물 transfer 운송하다

113 명사 자리 _ 동사의 목적어

해설 빈칸은 앞의 부정관사(a)와 함께 동사(carried out)의 목적어 역할을 하는 명사 자리이므로, 명사 (A) modification이 적합하다. 동사 (B) modify, (D) modifies, 과거시제 동사/과거분사 (C) modified는 품사상 적합하지 않다.

번역 온데릭 거라지에서는 차 주인이 다른 도시에 가 있는 동안 차를 튜닝했다.

어휘 carry out 수행하다 vehicle 차량, 탈 것 be out of town (업무 등으로) 사는 곳에서 벗어나다 modification 변경, (차량) 튜닝(소유자의 취향에 따라 차량의 외형에 변화를 줌)

114 명사 어휘

해설 빈칸 앞에 있는 동사(had)의 목적어 역할을 하는 명사 자리로, 뒤에 나오는 to부정사 구문(to operate the laboratory's most sensitive instruments at his discretion)의 수식을 받는다. 문맥상 '재량에 따라 조작할 수 있는 승인을 받다'라는 의미가 자연스러우므로, 정답은 (C) permission이다. (A) design(디자인), (B) request(요청), (D) benefit(혜택)은 의미상 적합하지 않다.

번역 수석 기사는 실험실에서 가장 민감한 도구들을 재량에 따라 조작할 수 있도록 승인을 받았다.

어휘 technician 기사 permission 허가, 승인 operate 조작하다, 가동하다 laboratory 실험실 sensitive (자극·변화에) 민감한 instrument 도구 at one's discretion ~의 재량에 따라

115 부사 자리 _ 동사 수식

해설 빈칸 앞의 조동사(would)와 뒤의 동사원형(fall) 사이에서 동사를 수식하는 부사 자리이다. 따라서 정답은 부사 (A) probably이다. 형용사 (B) probable, 명사 (D) probability는 품사상 적합하지 않다.

번역 판매사에서는 소프트웨어 문제로 데이터 변환 작업이 예정보다 늦어질 가능성이 있다고 경고했다.

어휘 vendor (제품·서비스의) 판매인, 판매 회사 conversion 전환 fall behind schedule 예정보다 늦어지다 issue 문제, 쟁점

116 전치사 자리 _ 전치사 / 부사 구분

해설 빈칸은 뒤에 나오는 명사(their availability)를 목적어로 취할 수 있는 전치사 자리이다. 따라서 정답은 전치사 (C) along with이다. "면접 가능한 시간과 함께 급여 조건을 제출하라"는 의미가 되어 문맥상으로도 자연스럽다. 부사 (A) also(또한), (B) as well(또한), (D) furthermore(더욱이)는 품사상 적합하지 않다. 참고로 (B) as well은 as well as(~과 마찬가지로, ~에 더하여)로 고치면 정답으로 가능하다.

번역 델러멧 출판은 면접 대상자들에게 면접 가능한 시간과 함께 급여 조건을 제출하라고 요구한다.

어휘 interviewee 면접 대상자, 면접 받는 사람(*cf.* interviewer 면접관) send in ~을 제출하다 salary requirements 급여 조건 availability 이용 가능한 시간[사람] along with ~와 함께, ~에 덧붙여

117 형용사 어휘

해설 빈칸은 주격 관계대명사(that) 앞에 있는 명사(remarks)를 보충 설명하는 형용사 자리로, 뒤의 전치사구(to the topic)의 수식을 받는다. 문맥상 '주제와 관련 있는 발언'이라는 의미가 자연스러우므로, 정답은 (D) relevant이다. (A) steady(꾸준한), (B) accustomed(익숙한), (C) obvious(명백한)는 의미상 적합하지 않다.

번역 위원회는 주민들에게 논의 중인 주제와 관련 있는 발언만 해달라고 요청한다.

어휘 council 위원회, 협의회 limit oneself to (소유하거나 행동하는 것을) ~로 제한하다 remark 발언, 언급 relevant to ~에 관련된 under discussion 논의 중인, 토의 중인

118 명사 어휘

해설 빈칸은 앞의 형용사 large의 수식을 받는 명사 자리로 뒤에 나오는 tourists와 어울리는 어휘를 골라야 한다. 문맥상 '관광객이 많아서 새 지점을 열기로 했다'라는 의미가 자연스러우므로, 정답은 명사 (D) volume (양)이다. 명사 (A) role(역할), (B) ground(기초, 근거), (C) extent(정도)는 의미상 적합하지 않다.

번역 매달 그 나라를 방문하는 관광객이 아주 많아서 나르판 여행사는 새 지점을 열기로 결정했다.

어휘 branch 지점 volume 부피, 양 a large volume of 다량의, 많은 양의

119 to부정사 _ 명사 역할

해설 빈칸은 뒤의 명사(customer satisfaction)를 목적어로 취하면서, 앞에 있는 동사(strive)의 목적어 역할을 하는 자리이다. 따라서 정답은 명사와 같은 역할을 할 수 있는 to부정사 (B) to increase이다. 과거동사/과거분사 (A) increased, 현재동사 (C) increases, 현재진행동사 (D) is increasing은 동사의 목적어 역할을 할 수 없다.

번역 고객 지원팀은 최상의 서비스를 제공해 고객 만족도를 높이려고 항상 노력해야 한다.

어휘 support 지원, 지지 strive to + 동사원형 ~하려고 분투하다, 애쓰다 customer satisfaction 고객 만족

120 부사 어휘

해설 빈칸 앞의 등위접속사(and)와 함께 앞뒤를 자연스럽게 이어주는 부사를 선택해야 한다. 문맥상 '따라서 가능한 신속하게 수리되어야 한다'라는 의미가 자연스러우므로, 정답은 (B) consequently이다. (A) occasionally(가끔), (C) seldom(거의 ~없이), (D) easily(손쉽게)는 의미상 적합하지 않다.

번역 건물 지붕이 어제의 폭풍우로 약해졌으므로 가능한 신속하게 수리되어야 한다.

어휘 weaken 약해지다 storm 폭풍우 consequently 그로 인해, 따라서

121 형용사 어휘 _ 과거분사

해설 빈칸 앞에 있는 전치사(to)의 목적어 역할을 하는 명사(profits)를 수식하는 형용사 자리이다. 문맥상 '수익률 향상을 가져오다'라는 의미가 자연스러우므로, 정답은 (A) elevated이다. (B) practiced(숙련된), (C) supervised(감독을 받는), (D) illustrated(삽화를 넣은)는 의미상 적합하지 않다.

번역 항공사 보상 카드가 신규 고객을 많이 끌어들여 은행의 수익이 높아지리라 전망된다.

어휘 predict 예측하다, 전망하다 attract 끌다, 유치하다 lead to ~로 이어지다 elevated 높은, 높아진 profit 수익

122 전치사 어휘

해설 빈칸 뒤의 목적어(a limited time frame)와 함께 앞의 동사(survey)를 수식하는 전치사 자리이다. 문맥상 '제한된 기간 내에 조사하다'라는 의미가 자연스러우므로 정답은 (A) within이다.

번역 농업용 드론은 제한된 기간 내에 광대한 농지 구역을 조사할 수 있다.

어휘 agricultural 농업의 drone 드론, 무인 비행기 survey 조사하다, 측량하다 farmland 농지 time frame 기간

123 형용사 자리 _ 주격 보어

해설 빈칸 앞에 있는 주어(some plays)를 보충 설명하는 형용사 자리이므로, 형용사 (A) reviewable과 현재분사 (D) reviewing(검토중인)이 적합하다. 문맥상 '재검토할 수 없는'이라는 의미가 자연스러우므로, 정답은 형용사 (A) reviewable이다.

번역 경기 중에 일부 플레이는 재검토할 수 없다는 연맹의 결정은 코치가 심판에게 이의를 제기할 수 있는 기회를 제한한다.

어휘 league 리그, 연맹 restrict 제한하다 challenge 이의를 제기하다, 도전하다 referee 심판 reviewable 재검토할 수 있는

124 동사 어휘

해설 빈칸은 조동사(must) 뒤의 동사원형 자리로, 뒤의 전치사(with)와 함께 명사(any of the operations)를 목적어로 취하는 자동사를 선택해야 한다. 문맥상 '작업을 방해하지 않아야 한다'라는 의미가 자연스러우므로, 정답은 자동사 (B) interfere이다. 전치사 with와 함께 주로 쓰이는 자동사 (C) comply(준수하다)는 의미상 적합하지 않고, 타동사 (A) attain(달성하다), (D) prevent(막다, 예방하다)는 전치사 없이 바로 목적어를 취한다.

번역 공장 견학 중에 방문객들은 생산 공장 안에서 어떤 작업도 방해해서는 안 된다.

어휘 interfere with ~을 방해하다 operation 작업 production plant 생산 공장

125 주격 관계대명사

해설 빈칸 뒤에 나오는 주어가 없는 불완전한 절(carry passengers to and from the city)을 이끌면서, 앞에 있는 사물명사(The red buses)를 수식하는 주격 관계대명사 자리이다. 따라서 정답은 (A) which이다. 소유격 관계대명사 (B) whose는 주어가 없는 불완전한 절을 이끌 수 없고, 인칭대명사 (C) they, (D) their는 접속사의 기능이 없다.

번역 승객들을 시내까지 싣고 오가는, 현재 운행 중인 빨간 버스는 항공사 직원들에게는 무료이다.

어휘 in operation 운영[가동] 중인 free 무료의 employee 직원

126 형용사 어휘

해설 빈칸은 앞에 있는 주어(several rooms)를 보충 설명하는 형용사 자리이다. 문맥상 '몇몇 방들은 여전히 비어 있다'라는 의미가 자연스러우므로, 정답은 (D) vacant이다. (A) experienced(숙련된), (B) momentary(순간의), (C) yielding(유연한, 수확이 많은)은 의미상 적합하지 않다.

번역 진행자에 따르면 새 지사의 몇몇 방들은 여전히 비어 있다.

어휘 according to ~에 따르면 coordinator 진행자, 코디네이터 branch office 지점, 지사 vacant 비어 있는

127 동사 어형 _ 시제 / 태

해설 빈칸은 주어(Abla-Marc Ltd.'s operating profits)와 목적어(analysts' expectations) 사이의 동사 자리이다. 앞에 있는 기간을 나타내는 전치사구(All throughout last month)의 수식을 받고, 문맥상 '지난달 내내 영업 이익이 분석가들의 예상을 뛰어넘고 있다'라는 능동의 의미를 나타내고 있다. 따라서 정답은 과거부터 현재까지 계속의 의미를 나타내는 능동의 현재완료진행 동사 (D) have been surpassing이다. 미래 동사 (A) will be surpassing, 수동의 현재진행 동사 (B) are being surpassed, 수동의 가정법 과거완료 동사 (C) would have been surpassed는 시제나 태가 적합하지 않다.

번역 지난달 내내 아블라-마크 사의 영업 이익이 경제 분석가들의 예상을 뛰어넘고 있다.

어휘 throughout ~ 동안 죽, 내내 operating profit 영업 이익 surpass (기대·예상 등을) 뛰어넘다[능가하다]

128 명사절 접속사

해설 빈칸은 뒤에 나오는 완전한 절(the antique flea market is held each year)과 함께 주격 보어를 이루는 명사절 접속사 자리이다. 따라서 정답은 명사절을 이끌 수 있는 의문부사 (D) when이다.

번역 파인즈빌 지역 축제 첫날은 매년 골동품 벼룩시장이 열리는 날이다.

어휘 community 지역사회, 공동체 community festival 지역 축제 antique 골동품 flea market 벼룩시장

129 명사 자리 _ 전치사의 목적어

해설 빈칸은 형용사(detailed)와 함께 전치사(After)의 목적어 역할을 하는 명사 자리이므로, 정답은 명사 (A) observation이다. 과거분사/과거시제 동사 (B) observed, 동사 (C) observe, 형용사 (D) observant는 품사상 적합하지 않다.

번역 자세한 관찰을 거쳐 과학자들은 몇몇 야생동물 종의 사회 체제를 밝혀냈다.

어휘 detailed 자세한, 상세한 determine 밝히다, 알아내다 social system 사회 제도[체제] species (동식물의) 종 wildlife 야생동물 observation 관찰

130 부사절 접속사와 전치사의 구분

해설 빈칸은 뒤에 나오는 완전한 절(forklift drivers can maneuver without difficulty)을 이끌면서 앞에 있는 명령문을 수식하는 부사절 접속사 자리이므로, 정답은 부사절 접속사 (D) so that이다. 접속사 (A) whether(~인지 아닌지)는 의미상 적합하지 않고, 전치사 (B) in view of(~을 고려하여), (C) due to(~ 때문에)는 절을 이끌 수 없다.

번역 지게차 운전자들이 어려움 없이 차를 조종할 수 있도록 반드시 적재 구역을 깨끗하게 치워두세요.

어휘 make sure to + 동사원형 반드시 ~하다, 확실히 ~하다 loading area 적재 구역, 짐 싣는 구역 so that + 절 ~하기 위해서 forklift 지게차 maneuver (차량·도구 등을) 다루다, 조종하다

Part 6

131-134 기사

경제학과 소식지

모니크 하렌 교수의 〈경제학 원리〉 신판이 이번 달 양장본으로 출간될 예정이다. 원본은 경제학 입문 강의 교수용 교재로 가장 인기 있는 서적 중 하나이다. 하렌 교수는 사람들이 **131**개정판을 볼 것이 기대된다고 밝혔다. **132**어떤 내용이 수록될지 묻는 질문에 "구성은 처음 책과 비슷하지만 이론이 새로워졌습니다. **134**각 요점을 분명히 하기 위해 가상 사례 **133**대신 실제 상황을 활용하려고 노력했습니다. 교수들이 이를 매우 유용하게 여기리라고 생각합니다."라고 답했다. 해당 서적은 8월 1일부터 대학교 도서관 및 서점에서 찾아볼 수 있다.

어휘 be set to + 동사원형 ~하도록 예정되어 있다 hardback 양장본(표지가 두꺼운 책) teaching material 교육 교재 theory 이론 imaginary 가상의 illustrate (실례, 도해 등을 이용해) 분명히 보여주다

131 형용사 어휘

해설 빈칸은 정관사(the)와 명사(edition) 사이에서 명사(edition)를 수식하는 형용사 자리로, 빈칸을 포함한 명사구는 앞에 있는 to부정사(to see)의 목적어 역할을 한다. 빈칸 뒤에 나오는 인용문장 '구성은 처음 책과 비슷하지만 이론이 새로워졌다(It is similar to the first book in structure, but the theories have been updated)'를 통해 개정판임을 알 수 있으므로, 정답은 (B) revised(수정된, 개정된)이다. (A) digital(디지털 방식을 쓰는), (C) older(더 낡은, 더 오래된), (D) estimated(추정된, 견적의)는 의미상 적합하지 않다.

132 명사절 접속사

해설 빈칸은 뒤에 나오는 동사(will contain)의 목적어가 없는 불완전한 절을 이끌면서, 앞에 있는 과거분사(asked)의 목적어 역할을 하는 명사절 접속사 자리이므로, 정답은 (B) what이다. 명사절 접속사 (A) how와 (C) where 뒤에는 완전한 절이 나와야 하고, 부사 (D) there는 절을 이끌 수 없다. 참고로 타동사 ask는 간접목적어와 직접목적어 모두를 목적어로 취하는 4형식 동사로 쓰일 수 있으므로, 수동의 의미를 나타내는 과거분사(asked) 뒤에 직접목적어가 나올 수 있다.

133 전치사 / 부사 / 부사절 접속사 구분

해설 빈칸 뒤의 목적어(imaginary ones)와 함께 앞에 있는 to부정사 구문(to use real situations)을 수식하는 전치사 자리이므로, 전치사 (A) owing to(~ 때문에)와 (D) instead of(~ 대신에)가 적합하다. 문맥상 '가상 사례 대신 실제 상황을 활용하다'라는 의미가 자연스러우므로, 정답은 (D) instead of이다. 부사 (B) rather(다소, 약간)와 부사절 접속사 (C) provided that(~라면)은 품사상 적합하지 않다.

134 문맥에 맞는 문장 고르기

번역 (A) 예를 들어 제1장은 짧아질 것입니다.
(B) 경제학과에서 내 제안을 고려하기로 약속했습니다.
(C) 교수들이 이를 매우 유용하게 여기리라고 생각합니다.
(D) 학생들이 한 일이 자랑스럽습니다.

해설 빈칸 앞 문장 '각 요점을 분명히 하기 위해 가상 사례 대신 실제 상황을 활용하려고 노력했다(I also tried to use real situations instead of imaginary ones to illustrate each point)'에서 실제 상황의 활용을 언급하고 있다. 따라서 빈칸에는 실제 상황(them)의 활용에 따른 기대효과 또는 의견 등을 제시하는 것이 문맥상 자연스러우므로, 정답은 (C)이다.

135-138 이메일

발신: 블레이크 볼네이
수신: 전 직원
제목: 음식 나눔 운동
날짜: 4월 22일

저희 회사에서 아이덴 푸드 뱅크와 협력해 5월 첫째 주에 음식 기부 운동을 벌인다는 것을 여러분께 알리고 싶습니다. 운동에 **135**도움을 주시고자 하는 분은 튼튼한 나일론 가방을 받게 됩니다. 가방을 집에 가져가 음식들을 채우십시오. 가방을 **136**채우면 제 사무실로 갖다 주십시오. 기부품은 이번 주말까지 저장실에 냉장되지 않은 상태로 보관된다는 점에 유의해 주십시오. **137**그렇기 때문에, 가방에는 통조림 식품이나 건조 식품만 담으셔야 합니다. **138**참가하시려면 내선번호 32번으로 제게 전화 주십시오. 참여해 주신 자원자들께 미리 감사드립니다.

블레이크 볼네이
인사부

어휘 announce 알리다 partner with ~와 협력하다 food (donation) drive 음식 나눔기 운동 choose to+동사원형 ~하기로 결정하다 durable 질긴, 내구성이 있는 pack 채우다, 꾸리다 once 일단 ~하면 unrefrigerated 냉장하지 않은 storage room 저장고, 창고 canned 통조림으로 된 sign up 참가하다, 신청하다 extension 내선 번호

135 to부정사

해설 빈칸은 앞에 있는 동사(choose)의 목적어 자리이므로, 목적어 역할을 할 수 있는 동명사 (A) being helped, (B) having helped와 to부정사 (C) to help, 명사의 복수형 (D) helps 모두가 정답 후보이다. choose는 to부정사를 목적어로 취하는 동사이므로, 정답은 (C) to help이다.

136 동사 어휘

해설 빈칸은 주어(the bag) 뒤 동사 자리로 수동태 문장이다. 앞에서 '튼튼한 나일론 가방을 받은 후, 가방을 집에 가져가 음식들을 채우다(will receive a durable nylon bag to take home and pack with food items)'라고 언급하고, 뒤에는 '사무실로 가져오다(it should be brought to my office)'라는 내용이 이어지고 있다. 따라서 앞뒤의 가방의 상태를 자연스럽게 이어줄 수 있는 동사가 빈칸에 들어가야 하므로, 정답은 (C) filled이다. (A) sewn(바느질한, 봉합한), (B) dried(건조된), (D) opened(열린)는 의미상 적합하지 않다.

137 부사 어휘

해설 빈칸에는 앞뒤의 문장을 자연스럽게 이어주는 접속부사가 필요하다. 앞에서 '기부품은 냉장되지 않은 상태로 보관된다(donations will be kept unrefrigerated)'라는 이유를 언급하고, 뒤에는 '가방에는 통조림 식품이나 건조 식품만 담아야 한다(bags should only include canned or dry foods)'라는 결과의 내용이 이어지고 있다. 따라서 정답은 (D) Therefore(그래서)이다. 부사 (A) In response(응답하여)와 (B) Namely(즉)는 의미상 적합하지 않다.

138 문맥에 맞는 문장 고르기

번역 (A) 친구와 가족들에게 기부를 요청해 보세요.
(B) 참여해 주신 자원자들께 미리 감사드립니다.
(C) 가방은 여러 가지 색깔로 제작되었습니다.
(D) 아이덴 푸드 뱅크는 페코스 거리 905번지에 있습니다.

해설 빈칸 앞의 문장 '참가하시려면, 제게 전화 주십시오(To sign up, please call me)'를 통해 참가를 권하고 있음을 알 수 있다. 따라서 빈칸에는 참여에 대한 감사를 표하는 내용이 이어지는 것이 자연스러우므로, 정답은 (B)이다.

어휘 donation 기증, 기부 volunteer 자원자 in advance 미리 participation 참가

139-142 편지

10월 2일

빈센트 허버드
페이지 드라이브 406번지
럴스턴, 플로리다 32029

허버드 씨께

139지난 목요일 저녁 수도국 직원 두 명이 여러분 동네 저든 로드와 페이지 드라이브 교차로 인근에서 인도 일부를 뜯어냈습니다. 그들은 근처에 발생한 누수 원인을 찾고 있었습니다. 유감스럽게도, 작업이 벌어진 시간과 방식이 지역 주민들을 놀라게 했습니다. 그분들은 기술자들이 불법 행위를 **140**저지르고 있다고 생각한 것입니다.

이 사건은 저희 측의 **141**중대한 불찰을 드러냅니다. 따라서 이런 일이 재발하지 않도록 막기 위한 조치를 취하고 있습니다. 특히 저희는 작업반원들이 항상 눈에 잘 띄는 제복을 입도록 하는 새로운 규정을 도입했습니다. 다시 한 번, **142**혼란을 일으킨 데 대하여 사과드립니다.

이 문제를 양해해 주셔서 감사합니다.

에이미 로스
국장, 럴스턴 수도국

어휘 dismantle 해체하다, 철거하다 sidewalk 인도
intersection 교차로 perform 수행하다 alarm 놀라게 하다
resident 거주민 technician 기술자, 기사 incident 일, 사건
reflect 나타내다 oversight 실수, 간과, 불찰 take steps 조치를
취하다 recurrence 되풀이, 재발 specifically 특별히 institute
(제도 등을) 도입하다 regulation 규제 call for 요청하다 work
crew 작업반원 high-visibility 높은 가시성의, 잘 보이는 uniform
제복

139 문맥에 맞는 문장 고르기

번역 (A) 주민들은 도로 경계석에 있는 차량을 치워달라는 요청을 받을 것입니다.
(B) 새로운 정수장이 상황을 개선하리라 예상되었습니다.
(C) 그들은 근처에 발생한 누수 원인을 찾고 있었습니다.
(D) 개편 노력이 작업조의 규모 확대로 이어지고 있습니다.

해설 빈칸 앞에서 '수도국 직원 두 명이 인도 일부를 뜯어냈다(two Water Department employees dismantled part of the sidewalk)'고 언급하고 있다. 따라서 빈칸에는 그 행동의 이유가 이어지는 것이 문맥상 자연스러우므로, 정답은 (C)이다.

어휘 vehicle 차량 treatment plant 정수장, 처리장 source 근원
leak 누수, 누출 restructuring 개편, 구조조정 work crew
작업조, 작업반

140 동사 어휘

해설 빈칸 뒤의 목적어(an illegal act)와 의미가 가장 잘 통하는 현재분사를 선택해야 한다. 문맥상 '불법 행위를 저지르고 있다'는 의미가 자연스러우므로, 정답은 (B) committing(저지르다)이다. (A) exceeding(초과하다), (C) violating(위반하다), (D) merging(합병하다)은 의미상 적합하지 않다.

어휘 commit (범죄·불법 행위를) 저지르다

141 형용사 자리 _ 명사 수식

해설 빈칸 앞의 부정관사(a)와 뒤의 명사(oversight) 사이에서 명사 (oversight)를 수식하는 형용사 자리이므로, 과거분사 (B) majored와 형용사 (D) major가 적합하다. 문맥상 '중대한 불찰'이라는 의미가 자연스러우므로, 정답은 (D) major이다.

어휘 major 큰, 중대한

142 명사 어휘

해설 빈칸 앞에 있는 형용사(sorry)에 대한 이유를 밝히는 명사를 선택해야 한다. 앞에서 '그분들은 기술자들이 불법 행위를 저지르고 있다고 생각했다(area residents, who believed that the technicians were committing an illegal act)'를 통해 판단의 착오를 일으킬 원인을 제공했음을 알 수 있다. 따라서 정답은 (A) confusion이다. (B) shortage(부족), (C) postponement(연기), (D) corruption(부정부패)은 의미상 적합하지 않다.

어휘 confusion 혼란

143-146 고객 후기

칼리슬 밀 박시스에서 받은 상자 몇 개에 오래되고 상한 재료가 들어 있어서 충격을 받았습니다. **144**이는 회사에서 음식의 **143**신선도에는 제대로 관심을 갖지 않았다는 걸 명백하게 보여준 겁니다. 다행히 그 며칠간 저한테 다른 식사 대안이 있었습니다. **144**칼리슬이 그 박스들에 해당하는 돈을 환불해 주었지만 이 문제는 계속 발생했습니다. 고객이 집에서 식사를 준비할 수 있도록 고객에게 재료를 배달해 준다는 발상은 아주 멋지고 칼리슬의 조리법 모두 좋아합니다. 하지만 이제부터는 음식을 제가 직접 **145**구입할 생각입니다. 그들의 서비스를 **146**이용하라고 추천하지는 못하겠습니다.

– 토마스 윌킨슨

어휘 contain 함유하다, ~이 들어 있다 spoiled (음식이) 상한
ingredient (음식의) 재료 be concerned about ~을 우려하다,
~에 관심을 기울이다 refund 환불해 주다 keep -ing 계속해서 ~하다
occur 발생하다 fantastic 환상적인, 굉장한 recipe 조리법 still
그럼에도 recommend 추천하다

143 명사 어휘

해설 빈칸은 뒤에 나오는 전치사구(of their food)의 수식을 받고, 앞의 전치사(about)와 함께 앞에 있는 형용사(concerned)를 수식한다. 앞의 '오래되고 상한 재료(old, spoiled ingredients)'를 통해 음식의 상태에 대해 언급하고 있음을 알 수 있으므로, 정답은 (A) freshness이다. (B) portions(부분), (C) names(이름), (D) diversity(다양성)는 의미상 적합하지 않다.

어휘 freshness 신선도

144 문맥에 맞는 문장 고르기

번역 (A) 많은 음식들이 제게는 너무 매웠습니다.
(B) 그들은 제게 양식을 한 장 더 보내야 했습니다.
(C) 가입 판촉 행사를 우리 시에서는 하지 않았습니다.
(D) 다행히 그 며칠간 저한테 다른 식사 대안이 있었습니다.

해설 빈칸 앞에서 음식의 신선도에 대해 이야기했고, 빈칸 뒤에는 환불 (refund)에 대해 언급하고 있다. 따라서 빈칸에는 취소에 따른 해결책을 제시하는 것이 문맥상 자연스러우므로, 정답은 (D)이다.

어휘 spicy 매운 sign-up 가입, 등록 luckily 다행히 meal 식사

145 동사 어휘

해설 빈칸 앞에서 고객이 집에서 식사를 준비할 수 있도록 고객에게 재료를 배달해 준다는 발상은 아주 멋지고 칼리슬의 조리법 모두 좋아한다(I think shipping ingredients to customers so we can make meals at home is a fantastic idea, and I liked all of Carlisle's recipes)라고 한 뒤 Still(그러나)이 나왔다. Still은 앞 문장과 반대되는 내용을 이어주므로 뒤에는 칼리슬의 서비스를 이용하지 않겠다는 내용이 이어져야 한다. 따라서 문맥상 '앞으로는 직접 음식을 구입하겠다'라는 내용이 자연스러우므로, 정답은 (C) buy이다. (A) manufacture(제조하다), (B) deliver(배달하다), (D) discard(버리다)는 의미상 적합하지 않다.

146 동명사를 목적어로 취하는 동사

해설 빈칸은 앞에 나온 동사 recommend의 목적어 자리이다. recommend는 뒤에 that절 또는 동명사를 목적어로 취하므로 정답은 (C) using이다.

Part 7

147-148 광고

빅 밸리 포인트

147A완만한 구릉들 사이로 이어지는 80마일 이상의 길이 표시된 등산로

* **147B**자원봉사자의 안내로 지은 지 200년이 넘는 랜드마크 대저택 투어
* 느긋하게 휴식할 수 있는 경치 좋은 연못들과 소풍 구역
* **147C**지역의 과거를 보여주는 완벽하게 복원된 밸리 박물관

빅 밸리 포인트는 1년 내내 개방됩니다. **148**입장은 무료이지만 인근 주차장 이용에는 요금이 부과됩니다. 20인 이상의 단체 투어는 적어도 2주 전에 예약해야 합니다. 자세한 내용은 www.bigvalleypoint.org를 방문하세요.

어휘 marked (위치 등이) 표시가 된 hiking trail 등산로 rolling 완만하게 경사진 mansion 대저택 scenic 경치가 아름다운 relaxation 휴식, 이완 restore 복원하다 showcase 보여주다, 전시하다 past 과거 year round 1년 내내 free 무료인 charge 부과하다 adjacent 인접한 reserve 예약하다 in advance 사전에

---

147 사실 관계 확인

번역 빅 밸리 포인트에서 볼 수 있는 명소로 나열되지 않은 것은?
(A) 산책로
(B) 유서 깊은 저택
(C) 역사 박물관
(D) 다양한 음식점

해설 첫 번째 단락에 나열된 명소들을 보면 음식점에 관한 언급은 없으므로 정답은 (D)이다. 완만한 구릉들 사이로 이어지는 80마일 이상의 길이 표시된 등산로(Over 80 miles of marked hiking trails set among rolling hills)에서 (A), 지은 지 200년이 넘는 랜드마크 대저택 투어(landmark mansions built over 200 years ago)에서 (B), 지역의 과거를 보여주는 완벽하게 복원된 밸리 박물관(Fully-restored Valley Museum showcasing our region's past)에서 (C)가 언급되었으므로, 정답은 (D)이다.

▶▶ Paraphrasing 지문의 hiking trails → 보기의 Walking paths
지문의 landmark mansions built over 200 years ago → 보기의 Historic houses
지문의 Valley Museum showcasing our region's past → 보기의 A history museum

148 세부 사항

번역 광고에 따르면 추가 요금이 있는 경우는?
(A) 인터넷 이용
(B) 주변 지역 주차
(C) 주말 시설 이용
(D) 실내 투어

해설 두 번째 단락에서 근처에 있는 주차장 이용에는 요금이 부과된다(a fee is charged for use of the adjacent parking area)를 통해 주변 지역 주차에 대해 추가 요금이 발생한다는 것을 알 수 있으므로, 정답은 (B)이다.

▶▶ Paraphrasing 지문의 use of the adjacent parking area
→ 정답의 Parking in a neighboring area

149-150 정보문

헴펠 알로스

알로스는 수상 경력이 있는 헴펠 모터스 디자인의 훌륭한 본보기입니다. 세련된 외형에, 널찍한 트렁크와 5인용 가죽 의자 같은 실용적인 내부가 결합되어 있습니다. 강력하면서 연료 효율성이 높은 엔진, 그리고 정교한 브레이크가 안전하고 즐거운 운전을 보장합니다. **150**대형 터치스크린 화면은 라디오와 온도 장치를 조절할 수 있음은 물론, 많은 운전자들이 원하는 기능, 즉 후방 카메라에서 전송되는 동영상까지 나옵니다.

149편안하면서 믿음직한 이 차는 클레건 시티 오토에서 지금 구매할 수 있습니다. 오늘 와서 시승해 보시고 저희의 고객 맞춤형 융자 옵션에 대해 영업사원과 상담하세요.

어휘 award-winning 상을 받은 refined 세련된, 다듬어진 exterior 외부 complement 상호 보완하다, 합쳐져 더 좋게 만들다 practical 실용적인 interior 실내 spacious 널찍한 fuel-efficient 연료 효율성이 높은 sophisticated (기계가) 정교한 ensure 보장하다 display 디스플레이, 화면 표시 feature 기능, 특성 rearview camera 후방 카메라 comfortable 편안한 dependable 신뢰할 만한 test-drive 시승하다 customizable 고객 맞춤형의 financing option 자금 조달[융자] 옵션

---

149 주제 / 목적

번역 정보문의 목적은 무엇인가?
(A) 구매자들의 선호도 개괄
(B) 제공하는 상품 광고
(C) 고객 맞춤형 설명서 제공
(D) 위원회 결정 통보

해설 두 번째 단락에서 편안하면서 믿음직한 이 차는 현재 클레건 시티 오토에서 구매할 수 있다. 오늘 와서 시승해 보고 고객 맞춤형 융자 옵션에 대해 영업사원과 상의하라(This comfortable, dependable car is available now at Clegan City Auto. Come test-drive one today and speak to a salesperson about our customizable financing options)고 했다. 따라서 자동차 광고를 위한 글임을 알 수 있으므로, 정답은 (B)이다.

150 추론 / 암시

번역 가장 인기 있는 기능은 어떤 용도로 사용되겠는가?
(A) 차량 식히기
(B) 승객이 편안하게 잠들게 하기
(C) 차를 안전하게 후진시키기
(D) 연료비 절약하기

해설 첫 번째 단락 마지막 문장에 대형 터치스크린 화면은 라디오와 온도 장치를 조절할 수 있음은 물론, 많은 운전자들이 원하는 기능, 즉 후방 카메라에서 전송되는 동영상까지 나온다(A large touchscreen display controls the radio and temperature systems, and includes many drivers' favorite feature—a video feed from the rearview camera)라고 했다. 따라서 후방 카메라에서 전송되는 동영상(a video feed from the rearview camera)을 통해 인기 있는 기능은 후진 시 사용한다는 것을 유추할 수 있으므로, 정답은 (C)이다.

▶▶ Paraphrasing 　지문의 many drivers' favorite feature
→ 질문의 the most popular feature

151-153 회람

수신: 블랜덱 리소시즈 직원
발신: 수잔 무어, CEO
제목: 기회
날짜: 5월 9일

여러분께,

다가오는 전문성 개발 기회에 대해 알려드리고자 합니다. **151**이 분야 최고의 컨설턴트인 앤디 챔블리스 씨가 6월 2일 데미랄프 센터에서 정보 관리 동향에 관한 세미나를 주관합니다. 최근 회의에서 챔블리스 씨를 만났는데, 아주 인상 깊었습니다. **151, 153**그는 엘리스-이버샛 주식회사에서 정보 책임자로 출발해 이후 리콜 포스 주식회사에 데이터 관리 선임 컨설턴트로 입사했습니다. 해당 직책을 맡아 홍콩에 기반을 둔 맬머 인더스트리즈를 비롯한 수많은 회사를 도와 데이터 저장 솔루션을 개발했습니다. 그는 정보과학협회(ISA) 원년 회원이며 ISA '창의적 데이터 솔루션' 상을 2회 수상한 바 있습니다. **152**또한 로스앤젤레스 인랜드 경영 대학교에서 곧 최초로 시행될 예정인 새 자격증 시험, 정보관리능력시험(IMCE)의 시험 개발팀의 일원이기도 합니다.

저는 그의 세미나에 참가를 원하는 직원을 지원하라고 인사팀에 지시했습니다. 관심 있는 분은 제로드 스폴트 씨에게 연락하십시오.

어휘 upcoming 다가오는　professional development 전문성 개발, 신장　competency 능력　certification 자격증
administration 집행

151 추론 / 암시

번역 무어 씨가 회람을 작성한 이유는 무엇이겠는가?
(A) 직원들에게 업계 전문가를 소개하려고
(B) 워크숍을 이끌 자원봉사자를 찾으려고
(C) 공석의 자격요건에 대해 이야기하려고
(D) 수상자를 발표하려고

해설 첫 번째 단락 두 번째 문장에서 이 분야 최고의 컨설턴트인 앤디 챔블리스 씨가 6월 2일 데미랄프 센터에서 정보 관리 동향에 관한 세미나를 주관한다(Andy Chambliss, a top consultant in our field, will lead a seminar on trends in information management on June 2 at the Demiralp Center)고 했고 이어서 엘리스-이버샛 주식회사에서 정보 책임자로 출발해 이후 리콜 포스 주식회사에 데이터 관리 선임 컨설턴트로 입사했다(He started out as an information officer for Ellis-Iversatt Ltd. before joining Recall Force Ltd. as a senior data management consultant)고 했다. 이 문장들을 통해 챔블리스 씨를 소개하기 위해 회람을 작성하고 있음을 유추할 수 있으므로, 정답은 (A)이다.

▶▶ Paraphrasing 　지문의 a top consultant in our field
→ 정답의 an industry expert

152 세부 사항

번역 인랜드 경영 대학교에 곧 어떤 일이 있을 것인가?
(A) 회의가 시작될 것이다.
(B) 시험이 시행될 것이다.
(C) 자격증이 만료될 것이다.
(D) 개발팀이 꾸려질 것이다.

해설 첫 번째 단락 마지막 문장에서 그는 또한 로스앤젤레스 인랜드 경영 대학교에서 곧 최초로 시행될 예정인 새 자격증 시험, 정보관리능력시험(IMCE)의 시험 개발팀의 일원이기도 하다(He is also a member of the examination development team for the Information Management Competency Exam (IMCE) ~ first administration soon at Inland Business University in Los Angeles)고 했다. 따라서 인랜드 경영 대학교에서 새 자격증 시험이 시행될 예정임을 알 수 있으므로, 정답은 (B)이다.

▶▶ Paraphrasing 　지문의 a new certification test scheduled for first administration
→ 정답의 An exam will be held

153 세부 사항

번역 챔블리스 씨는 현재 어떤 회사에 고용되어 있는가?
(A) 블랜덱 리소시즈
(B) 엘리스-이버샛 주식회사
(C) 리콜 포스 주식회사
(D) 맬머 인더스트리즈

해설 첫 번째 단락 중반부에서 엘리스-이버샛 주식회사에서 정보 책임자로 출발해 이후 리콜 포스 주식회사에서 데이터 관리 선임 컨설턴트로 입사했다(He started out as an information officer for Ellis-Iversatt Ltd. before joining Recall Force Ltd. as a senior data management consultant)고 했다. 따라서 챔블리스 씨는 현재 리콜 포스 주식회사에서 근무하고 있음을 알 수 있으므로, 정답은 (C)이다.

▶▶ Paraphrasing 　지문의 joining → 질문의 employed by

154-155 문자 메시지

휘트니 팔코 [오후 2:23]
154그렉, 렌터카 중개인 말로는 마지막 밴이 한 시간 전에 대여됐대요. 그들이 큰 세단을 권하는데, 좀 더 저렴하답니다.

그레고리 로우 [오후 2:24]
하지만 우리가 여섯 명이잖아요. 나는 우리가 예약을 했어야 한다고 생각했어요. **154**음, 두 번째 차를 빌리면 될 거 같네요. 내가 운전할 수도 있고요. 길이 너무 막히지나 않았으면 좋겠어요.

휘트니 팔코 [오후 2:25]
괜찮을 거예요. 그런데 서류를 작성하려면 우선 카운터까지 가셔야 되겠는데요.

그레고리 로우 [오후 2:26]

알겠어요. **155어떤 서류가 필요하죠?** 짐을 다 들고 갈 필요가 없도록 지금 찾아 놓으려고요.

> **어휘** rental car agent 렌터카 중개인 rent (차를) 빌려주다[빌리다]
> a bit 약간 come over to ~로 가다 fill out (서류를) 작성하다
> paperwork 서류, 서류 작업 documentation (증빙을 위한) 서류
> bring ~ over ~을 가지고 가다

154 의도 파악

번역 오후 2시 24분에 로우 씨가 "하지만 우리가 여섯 명이잖아요"라고 쓸 때, 그 의도는 무엇이겠는가?
(A) 비용을 균등하게 배분해야 한다.
(B) 차에 수용 공간이 부족하다.
(C) 더 많은 사람들이 줄을 서서 기다리고 있다.
(D) 다른 사람이 책임을 맡을 수 있다.

해설 팔코 씨의 오후 2시 23분 메시지에서 렌터카 중개인 말로는 마지막 밴이 한 시간 전에 대여되었고, 큰 세단을 권하는데, 좀 더 저렴하다(the rental car agent said their last van was rented out an hour ago. They're suggesting a large sedan, which is a bit cheaper)라고 한 말에 대해, 로우 씨가 두 번째 차를 빌리면 될 것 같다. 내가 운전할 수도 있다(I guess we can get a second car and I could drive it)라며 해결책을 제시하고 있다. 따라서 하지만 우리가 여섯 명이다(But there are six of us)는 인원에 비해 차가 작다는 문제점을 제기하고자 했다는 것을 유추할 수 있으므로, 정답은 (B)이다.

155 추론 / 암시

번역 팔코 씨의 다음 메시지에는 어떤 내용이 담기겠는가?
(A) 짐에 대한 설명
(B) 카운터까지 가는 길
(C) 자료 리스트
(D) 예약 번호

해설 로우 씨의 오후 2시 26분 메시지에서 어떤 서류가 필요한지(What kind of documentation will I need) 물어본 말에 대해 팔코 씨가 문의에 응답할 것이라고 유추할 수 있으므로, 정답은 (C)이다.

> ▶▶ **Paraphrasing** 지문의 **documentation**
> → 정답의 **A list of materials**

156-158 편지

번 미술관
컨트리 스트리트 242
시드니, NSW 2000
www.byrne-moa.au

1월 3일

레지나 트라우브 씨
랜턴 애비뉴 12
시드니, NSW 2000

트라우브 씨께,

156번 미술관 회원증을 갱신해 주셔서 감사합니다. 모든 회원에게는 동봉한 책자에 열거된 특별 할인을 받을 자격이 부여됩니다. **157아울러 3월부터 6월까지 상영하는 미술관 최초의 시리즈 영화 〈시네마 어프리시에이티드〉 매주 상영 시 무료 입장이 가능합니다.** 시간표 확인이나 무료 입장권 예약은 www.byrne-moa.au/ca를 방문해 주십시오.

회원에게는 미술 전문가들을 만날 특별 기회도 드립니다. 미술관에서는 일 년에 여러 차례 지역과 해외의 미술 비평가와 미술사가들을 초청하여 직원 및 회원이 선정한 주제에 관해 강연을 펼칩니다. **158올해 첫 행사로 1월 9일에 민디 네이스미스의 작품을 전시할 예정입니다.** 이 작가의 다채로운 색감을 지닌 그림은 인간관계를 따뜻하게 묘사했다는 호평을 받았습니다. 자리가 금방 차니 서둘러 등록하시기 바랍니다.

회원 특전을 최대로 활용하실 수 있도록 저희가 도와드릴 방법이 있다면 알려주십시오.

그레첸 퍼스
공공 봉사 담당

> **어휘** be entitled to ~할 자격이 있다 enclosed 동봉한
> screening 상영 complimentary 무료의 expert 전문가
> critic 비평가 historian 사학자 register 등록하다 make full
> use of ~을 충분히 활용하다

156 사실 관계 확인

번역 트라우브 씨에 대해 명시된 것은?
(A) 회원권 중 가장 저렴한 것을 선택했다.
(B) 미술관에 처음 등록한 회원이 아니다.
(C) 전화 연락을 원치 않는다.
(D) 우편으로 무료 선물을 받을 것이다.

해설 첫 번째 단락의 번 미술관 회원증을 갱신해 주셔서 감사하다(Thank you for renewing your membership to the Byrne Museum of Art)를 통해 트라우브 씨가 미술관의 기존 회원임을 알 수 있으므로, 정답은 (B)이다.

157 세부 사항

번역 편지에 따르면 미술관에 새로 도입된 것은 무엇인가?
(A) 주간 영화 시리즈
(B) 조각품 모음
(C) 정보를 제공하는 모바일 앱
(D) 유명 상표 문구류

해설 첫 번째 단락의 중반부에서 아울러 3월부터 6월까지 상영하는 미술관 최초의 시리즈 영화 〈시네마 어프리시에이티드〉 매주 상영 시 무료 입장이 가능하다(In addition, you will get free admission to any weekly screening at the museum's first-ever film series, *Cinema Appreciated*, which runs from March to June)고 했으므로 영화의 주간 상영이 새로 도입되었음을 알 수 있다. 따라서 정답은 (A)이다.

> ▶▶ **Paraphrasing** 지문의 **first-ever** → 질문의 **new**
> 지문의 **any weekly screening at the museum's first-ever film series**
> → 정답의 **A weekly film series**

158 문장 삽입

번역 [1], [2], [3], [4]로 표시된 곳 중에서 다음 문장이 들어가기에 가장 적합한 곳은?

"이 작가의 다채로운 색감을 지닌 그림은 인간관계를 따뜻하게 묘사했다는 호평을 받았습니다."

(A) [1]
(B) [2]
(C) [3]
(D) [4]

해설 삽입 문장 '이 작가의 다채로운 색감을 지닌 그림은 인간관계를 따뜻하게 묘사했다는 호평을 받았습니다(Her colorful paintings have won praise for their warm depiction of human relationships)'를 통해 앞에서 그림을 그린 작가(Her)를 언급할 것임을 알 수 있다. [4]의 앞 문장 '올해 첫 행사로 1월 9일에 민디 네이스미스의 작품을 전시할 예정입니다(This year's first event, set for 9 January, will showcase the works of Mindy Naismith)'에서 작가를 특정하고 있으므로, 정답은 (D)이다.

159-160 이메일

수신: 아노드 뷰몬트 〈abeaumont@limogesapparel.uk〉
발신: 앨리슨 네프 〈allisonneff@limogesapparel.uk〉
제목: 기념일
날짜: 7월 18일

뷰몬트 씨께,

믿기 어렵지만 몇 주만 있으면 저희 리모지스 어패럴이 창립 30주년을 맞습니다. **159**준비가 어떻게 되어가는지 알려드리고자 합니다. 멋진 기념일을 만들기 위해, 저희는 이미 소셜미디어에 광고를 냈습니다. **160**마침내 저희는 기념 파티에서 독점 판매될 리모지스 어패럴 한정판 상품 준비를 드디어 거의 끝냈습니다.

다음 주에 다시 메일을 드리겠지만 그 전이라도 이러한 계획에 대한 질문이 있으시면 언제든 연락 주십시오.

앨리슨 네프
리모지스 어패럴 마케팅 책임자

어휘 come along 되어가다 milestone 중요한 단계, 시점 retro-style 복고풍의 limited-edition 한정판 merchandise 상품 exclusively 독점적으로

159 추론 / 암시

번역 이메일을 쓴 이유는 무엇이겠는가?

(A) 새로운 진행 상황을 알리기 위해
(B) 설문조사를 준비하기 위해
(C) 초청장을 보내기 위해
(D) 행사를 연기하기 위해

해설 첫 번째 단락의 두 번째 문장에서 준비가 어떻게 되어가는지 알려드리고자 한다(I want to let you know how preparations are coming along)고 했다. 따라서 준비 진행 상황을 알리기 위해 이메일을 쓰고 있음을 유추할 수 있으므로, 정답은 (A)이다.

▶▶ **Paraphrasing** 지문의 to let you know how preparations are coming along
→ 정답의 To provide an update

160 세부 사항

번역 특별 상품은 어디서 판매될 것인가?

(A) 기념행사
(B) 소셜미디어 사이트
(C) TV 프로그램
(D) 매장 설립장소

해설 첫 번째 단락의 마지막 문장에서 마침내 기념 파티에서 독점 판매될 리모지스 어패럴 한정판 상품 준비를 드디어 거의 끝냈다(Finally, we're almost finished putting together our selection of limited-edition Limoges Apparel merchandise that will be made available for purchase exclusively at the anniversary party)고 했다. 따라서 기념 파티에서 한정판 상품이 판매된다고 언급하고 있으므로, 정답은 (A)이다.

▶▶ **Paraphrasing** 지문의 limited-edition Limoges Apparel merchandise that will be made available for purchase → 질문의 some special merchandise be sold 지문의 at the anniversary party
→ 정답의 At a celebration

161-164 기사

페이트, 온트뮤직에 새롭게 접근하다

토론토(6월 8일) – 팝스타 레일라 페이트가 온라인 음악 판매의 선두주자인 온트뮤직과 결별을 선언하는 메시지를 자신의 개인 웹사이트에 게시했다.

페이트 씨는 최근 미래가 유망한 경쟁 음악사 사로토의 공동 소유주가 되었다. 그녀는 메시지에서 자신은 역시 음악가들인 사로토의 다른 공동소유주들과 함께 아티스트들이 디지털 음반 판매 총수익 중에서 더 큰 몫을 차지할 수 있도록 보장함으로써 "아티스트들에게 힘을 되돌려주려" 한다고 설명했다. **161**마찬가지로 페이트는 사로토 이용자들 또한 그곳 플랫폼의 더 나은 기술적 정교함 때문에 이득을 보리라고 믿는다. "우리는 온라인 음악 구입 체험을 더욱 개선할 겁니다."라고 그녀는 주장했다.

그러나 페이트 씨는 자신이 온트뮤직과 완전히 단절되지는 않을 것이라는 점 역시 분명히 했다. **162**"오랫동안 상호 이익이 되어 왔던 관계에 감사하며 예전에 발표된 제 노래와 비디오는 계속 온트뮤직에서 판매될 것입니다." 페이트 씨는 이렇게 적었다. "하지만, 앞으로 새 앨범은 출시일 이후 3개월이 지나야만 그곳에서 구입이 가능합니다." 그 이전에 구입하고 싶은 음악 애호가들은 사로토를 이용해야 할 것이다.

온트뮤직은 이러한 변화를 아직 공식적으로 발표하지는 않았다. 과거에 회사는 시장 지배를 인용하며 비슷한 상황에 대한 우려를 일축한 바 있다. **164**온라인 음반 시장에 최초로 진입한 판매처들 중 하나인 온트뮤직을 통한 음악 구매가 캐나다 디지털 음악 판매의 절반 이상을 **163**차지한다. 하지만 일각에서는 현재까지 사로토가 가장 중대한 도전자일지도 모른다고 경고한다.

161 세부 사항

번역 기사에 따르면, 페이트 씨가 결정을 내린 이유에 해당하는 것은?
(A) 덜 알려진 음악가들을 알리고 싶다.
(B) 앨범 판매 감소를 우려한다.
(C) 음악 산업에서 손을 뗄 계획이다.
(D) 기술적으로 우수한 쪽을 지지한다.

해설 두 번째 단락 후반부에서 마찬가지로 페이트는 사로토 이용자들 또한 그곳 플랫폼의 더 나은 기술적 정교함 때문에 이득을 보리라고 믿는다(Similarly, she believes Saroto's users benefit from the greater technical sophistication of its platform)고 했다. 이를 통해 페이트 씨가 사토로의 기술적인 우수함 때문에 변경 결정을 내렸음을 알 수 있으므로, 정답은 (D)이다.

▶▶ Paraphrasing 지문의 **the greater technical sophistication** → 정답의 **a technologically superior option**

162 세부 사항

번역 온트뮤직은 무엇을 더 이상 하지 않을 것인가?
(A) 페이트 씨를 메인 페이지에 싣기
(B) 페이트 씨의 지난 카탈로그 전체를 제공하기
(C) 페이트 씨의 음악을 출시 즉시 판매하기
(D) 페이트 씨의 저작물이 무료로 스트리밍되도록 허용하기

해설 세 번째 단락에서 오랫동안 상호 이익이 되어 왔던 관계에 감사하며 예전에 발표된 제 노래와 비디오는 계속 온트뮤직에서 판매될 것이다. 하지만, 앞으로 새 앨범은 출시 이후 3개월이 지나야만 그곳에서 구입이 가능하다(In appreciation of our long and mutually beneficial relationship ~ my future albums will only be made available there three months after their original release dates)고 했다. 따라서 새 앨범은 출시 즉시 온트뮤직을 통해 판매되지 않는다는 것을 알 수 있으므로, 정답은 (C)이다.

▶▶ Paraphrasing 지문의 **my future albums will only be made available** → 정답의 **Sell Ms. Pate's new music**

163 동의어 찾기

번역 네 번째 단락 5행의 "account for"와 의미가 가장 가까운 단어는?
(A) 정당화시키다   (B) 계산하다
(C) 해당하다   (D) 인지하다

해설 해당 문장은 온라인 음반 시장에 최초로 진입한 판매처들 중 하나인 온트뮤직을 통한 음악 구매가 캐나다 디지털 음악 판매의 절반 이상을 차지한다(Purchases made through its store, one of the first entrants into the online music market, account for more than half of all digital music sales in Canada)라는 의미로 해석되는데, 여기서 account for는 문맥상 '차지하다, 해당하다'라는 의미가 자연스러우므로, 정답은 (C) represent(나타내다, 대표하다, 해당하다)이다.

164 문장 삽입

번역 [1], [2], [3], [4]로 표시된 곳 중에서 다음 문장이 들어가기에 가장 적합한 곳은?

"과거에 회사는 시장 지배를 인용하며 비슷한 상황에 대한 우려를 일축한 바 있다."

(A) [1]
(B) [2]
(C) [3]
(D) [4]

해설 삽입 문장의 '과거에 회사는 시장 지배를 인용하며 비슷한 상황에 대한 우려를 일축한 바 있다(In the past, the company dismissed concerns about similar situations by citing its market domination)'를 통해 시장 점유율을 뺏길 것에 대한 우려를 일축했음을 알 수 있다. 따라서 시장 점유율에 관한 이야기 앞에 인용문이 나오는 것이 적절하므로 시장 점유율에 관한 언급이 있는 문장을 찾는다. 네 번째 단락에 온라인 음반 시장에 최초로 진입한 판매처들 중 하나인 온트뮤직을 통한 음악 구매가 캐나다 디지털 음악 판매의 절반 이상을 차지한다(Purchases made through its store, one of the first entrants into the online music market, account for more than half of all digital music sales in Canada)에서 시장 점유율에 관해 언급하고 있으므로, 정답은 (D)이다.

165-168 문자 메시지

릭 스테이턴 [오전 9:41] 165이토 씨, 오늘 저희에게 배송되기로 한 바닥재가 월요일까지 도착하지 못할 겁니다. 그래서 이토 씨의 개조 작업이 며칠 미뤄질 예정입니다.
베스 이토 [오전 9:43] 유감이군요. 166식당 문을 오래 닫을수록 저희 직원들이 그만두고 다른 일자리를 찾아갈 것 같습니다.
릭 스테이턴 [오전 9:44] 네, 알고 있습니다. 배송이 될 때까지 저희가 다른 구역을 작업해서 지연을 최소화하려고 합니다. 예를 들어 옥외 작업 일부를 마칠 수 있습니다.
베스 이토 [오전 9:46] 아, 사실 외관에 대해 말씀드리고 싶었어요. 167북향 담에 표지판을 좀 더 높게 달아서 더 멀리서도 보일 수 있게 하면 좋을 것 같아요. 그렇게 하면 벽의 균형이 맞지 않게 보일까요?
릭 스테이턴 [오전 9:47] 음, 저희가 오늘 지붕 작업을 할 텐데요, 167표지판을 설치할 때가 다 되면 알려드리겠습니다.
베스 이토 [오전 9:49] 알겠습니다. 작업을 더 빨리 진행할 수 있는 부분이 있나요?

릭 스테이턴 [오전 9:52]

168글쎄요, 쿡-데미 주식회사에 다음 주 초에 전화해서 주문하신 주방용품 설치를 진행할 수 있는지 알아봐 드릴게요.

베스 이토 [오전 9:53]

좋아요. 감사합니다.

어휘 flooring material 바닥재 renovation 개조 shipment 배송 install 설치하다 kitchen appliance 주방용품

165 세부 사항

번역 스테이턴 씨에 따르면 작업이 지연되는 이유는 무엇인가?
(A) 예산이 삭감됐다.
(B) 감독관이 나오지 않았다.
(C) 아직 배송이 되지 않았다.
(D) 맞지 않은 자재가 배송됐다.

해설 스테이턴 씨의 오전 9시 41분 메시지에 오늘 배송되기로 한 바닥재가 월요일까지 도착하지 못할 것이다. 그래서 이토 씨의 개조 작업이 며칠 미뤄질 예정이다(Ms. Ito, the flooring materials that were supposed to be delivered to us today won't arrive until Monday. That's going to push your renovations back several days)라고 했으므로 배송 지연으로 작업이 미뤄졌음을 알 수 있다. 따라서 정답은 (C)이다.

▶▶ Paraphrasing 지문의 **push your renovations back several days** → 질문의 **some work being delayed**
지문의 **the flooring materials that were supposed to be delivered**
→ 정답의 **A delivery**
지문의 **won't arrive until Monday**
→ 정답의 **has not arrived yet**

166 추론 / 암시

번역 이토 씨는 누구이겠는가?
(A) 상업 건축가
(B) 신문기자
(C) 식당 소유주
(D) 지역 안전 검사관

해설 이토 씨의 오전 9시 43분 메시지에 식당 문을 오래 닫을수록 직원들이 그만두고 다른 일자리를 찾아갈 것 같다(Remember, the longer the restaurant is closed, the more likely it is that my employees will decide to quit and find other jobs)고 했다. 따라서 이토 씨가 식당 소유주임을 유추할 수 있으므로, 정답은 (C)이다.

167 의도 파악

번역 오전 9시 47분에 스테이턴 씨가 "저희가 오늘 지붕 작업을 할 텐데요"라고 쓸 때, 그 의도는 무엇인가?
(A) 이토 씨는 건물 출입을 할 수 없을 것이다.
(B) 다른 작업자의 계획에 대해 잘 모른다.
(C) 제안에 대해 추후 논의할 수 있다.
(D) 개조작업이 거의 완료됐다.

해설 이토 씨는 오전 9시 46분 메시지에서 북향 담에 표지판을 좀 더 높게 달아서 더 멀리서도 보일 수 있게 하면 좋을 것 같다. 그렇게 하면 벽의 균형이

맞지 않게 보일까(I think it would be better to hang the sign up higher on the north wall, so that it can be seen from farther away. Do you think it would make that wall look unbalanced, though)라고 하며 표지판 설치 작업에 대해 스테이턴 씨의 의견을 구하고 있다. 이에 대해 스테이턴 씨가 오늘 지붕 작업을 할 예정(we're going to work on the roof today)이라며 다른 작업을 제시한 후 표지판을 설치할 때가 다 되면 알려주겠다(I'll let you know when we're getting close to installing the sign)고 했으므로, 정답은 (C)이다.

168 세부 사항

번역 스테이턴 씨는 이토 씨를 위해 무엇을 하겠다고 제안하는가?
(A) 서비스 금액 삭감하기
(B) 고객들에게 업체 상황 알리기
(C) 장비 제공업체에 연락하기
(D) 다가오는 시설 견학 주관하기

해설 스테이턴 씨의 오전 9시 52분 메시지에서 쿡-데미 주식회사에 다음 주 초에 전화해서 주문한 주방용품 설치를 진행할 수 있는지 알아봐 준다(Well, I can phone Cook-Demi Ltd. early next week to start coordinating the installation of the kitchen appliances you had ordered from them)고 하며 설치 관련 진행 상황을 알아보기 위한 업체 연락을 제안하고 있으므로, 정답은 (C)이다.

▶▶ Paraphrasing 지문의 **phone Cook-Demi Ltd.**
→ 정답의 **Contact an equipment supplier**

169-171 광고

렉덱 플러스

소매점의 효율을 높일 방법을 찾고 계신가요? **169**렉덱 플러스와 함께라면 현재 얼마나 많은 상품을 보유하고 있는지 관찰하고, 어떤 제품이 잘 팔리는지 알아서, 특정 품목의 재고를 언제 다시 채워야 할지 판단할 수 있습니다.

특징:

- **170, 171B**빠짐없이 상세한 사용자 설명서와 함께 온라인 채팅을 통해 일주일 내내, 하루 24시간 고객을 도울 준비가 된 지원팀
- **171A**제품의 이미지를 선택하면 쉽게 참조할 수 있도록 품목 명세가 함께 나오는 유용한 "이미지 추가" 기능
- 도매 구입과 개별 고객 판매 모두에서, 대량 할인 계산 절차를 간소화시켜 주는 "대량 상품 가격 결정" 기능
- **171C**키 하나만 누르면 고객의 이름, 이메일 주소, 우편 주소, 전화번호를 볼 수 있게 해 주는 효율적인 "고객 관리" 기능

이 프로그램에 관해 자세한 내용을 원하시면 www.rec-dekplus.com을 방문하세요.

어휘 efficiency 효율(성) retail establishment 소매점 establishment 영업소, 점포 monitor 관찰하다, 감시하다 merchandise 상품 on hand 소유하여, 수중에 determine 알아내다, 결정하다 replenish 다시 채우다 handy 쓸모 있는 alongside ~과 더불어 item description 품목 명세 reference 참고 pricing 가격 결정 calculate 계산하다 bulk 대량, 대규모 wholesale 도매의, 대량의 streamlined (단순화시켜) 효율적인

169 추론 / 암시

번역 렉덱 플러스는 어떻게 이용되겠는가?
(A) 홍보용 비디오 편집에
(B) 재고를 관리하는 데
(C) 데이터 보안을 개선하는 데
(D) 고용 절차를 돕는 데

해설 첫 번째 단락의 두 번째 문장에서 렉덱 플러스와 함께라면 현재 얼마나 많은 상품을 보유하고 있는지 관찰하고, 어떤 제품이 잘 팔리는지 알아서, 특정 품목의 재고를 언제 다시 채워야 할지 판단할 수 있다(With Rec-Dek Plus, you can monitor how much merchandise you have on hand, see what products are selling well, and determine when your stock of certain items needs to be replenished)고 했다. 이를 통해 렉덱 플러스 프로그램이 재고관리를 위해 사용됨을 유추할 수 있으므로, 정답은 (B)이다.

170 사실 관계 확인

번역 렉덱 플러스의 고객 지원에 관해 명시된 것은?
(A) 언제나 이용할 수 있다.
(B) 현장에서 관리될 수 있다.
(C) 첫째에는 무료이다.
(D) 사용자로부터 아주 좋은 평가를 받는다.

해설 두 번째 단락의 빠짐없이 상세한 사용자 설명서와 함께 온라인 채팅을 통해 일주일 내내, 하루 24시간 고객을 도울 준비가 된 지원팀(A fully detailed user's manual, plus a support team that is ready to assist you 24 hours a day, 7 days a week via online chat)을 통해 항시 지원을 제공한다는 것을 알 수 있으므로, 정답은 (A)이다.

▶▶ **Paraphrasing** 지문의 **24 hours a day, 7 days a week** → 정답의 **at all times**

171 사실 관계 확인

번역 렉덱 플러스의 특징으로 언급되지 않은 것은?
(A) 이미지 표시 기능
(B) 사용자들을 위한 포괄적인 지침
(C) 고객 연락 정보 접근
(D) 총매출액 자동 계산

해설 두 번째 단락의 두 번째 특징인 제품의 이미지를 선택하면 쉽게 참조할 수 있도록 품목 명세가 함께 나오는 유용한 "이미지 추가" 기능(A handy "Add Image" feature that lets you select an image for a product and then show it alongside the item description for easy reference)을 통해 (A)를, 첫 번째 특징인 빠짐없이 상세한 사용자 설명서(A fully detailed user's manual)를 통해 (B)를, 네 번째 특징인 키 하나만 누르면 고객의 이름, 이메일 주소, 우편 주소, 전화번호를 볼 수 있게 해 주는 효율적인 "고객 관리" 기능(A streamlined "Client Care" feature that enables you to view a customer's name, e-mail address, mailing address, and phone number by pressing just one key)을 통해 (C)를 확인할 수 있다. 따라서 정답은 (D)이다.

▶▶ **Paraphrasing** 지문의 **Add Image** → 보기의 **display images**
지문의 **A fully detailed user's manual** → 보기의 **Comprehensive guidelines for users**
지문의 **to view a customer's name, e-mail address, mailing address, and phone number** → 보기의 **Access to customer contact information**

172-175 웹사이트 게시물

브레이던 지역공원 관리당국 (BRPA) 최근 게시물

날짜: 3월 7일

저희 BRPA는 브레이던 지역공원 서부 생태계 개선 5개년 프로젝트의 그 두 번째 해를 맞아 그것이 계획대로 진행 중임을 알려드리게 되어 기쁩니다. **173A, 173C**엘레인 로테프 담당관의 지휘 아래, 지역 고유의 다양한 수종 500그루를 20에이커 면적에 심었으며 이러한 나무에 해를 끼치는 벌레의 과잉 서식을 막기 위한 노력이 성공을 거뒀습니다. **173B**또한 BRPA 기술자들은 브레이던 개울을 따라 서 있는 산비탈을 안정화하여 토양의 질을 높이고 개울이 막힘 없이 흐르도록 하고 있습니다.

사실 프로젝트가 매우 큰 성공을 거둬, 세계 삼림 보호에 헌신하는 단체인 국제삼림협회의 주목을 받았습니다. **174**로테프 담당관이 다가오는 리우데자네이루 회의에서 여러 세션을 맡아 프로젝트에서 얻은 식견을 전수해 달라는 초청을 받았습니다. 매우 영광스러운 일입니다.

172끝으로 BRPA는 공원의 해당 구역 접근 금지를 해제했다는 소식을 전하게 되어 무엇보다 기쁩니다. BRPA 전문가들의 도움 덕분에 이제 20에이커에 해당하는 구역을 두 시간 동안 가이드와 함께 둘러보며 프로젝트 진행 상황을 볼 수 있습니다. 이 무료 단체 투어는 여름철을 제외하고 매주 토요일 오전 10시에 제공되며 여름에는 오후 1~3시 투어가 추가될 예정입니다. **175**공원 서부 지역은 공식 투어의 일환으로만 방문 가능합니다. 작업자들을 방해하지 않기 위해 다른 때는 일반인에게 출입금지구역으로 계속 유지됩니다.

어휘 ecosystem 생태계 proceed 진행하다 combat (악화를) 방지하다 overpopulation 과잉 인구 stabilize 안정시키다 slope 비탈 blockage 막는 것, 장애 catch the attention of ~의 주목을 받다 dedicated to ~에 헌신하는 pass on 전수하다 tremendous 엄청난, 대단한 lift a restriction on ~에 대한 제한을 풀다, 해제하다 off limits 출입 금지 구역 interfere with ~를 방해하다

172 주제 / 목적

번역 게시물의 목적 한 가지는 무엇인가?
(A) 공원 개선작업에 지연이 발생한 것을 사과하려고
(B) 규정 변경에 대한 세부 사항을 전달하려고
(C) 기부 절차에 대해 설명하려고
(D) 다가오는 프로젝트의 자원봉사자를 모집하려고

해설 마지막 단락에서 끝으로 BRPA는 공원의 해당 구역 접근 금지를 해제했다는 소식을 전하게 되어 무엇보다 기쁘다(Lastly, the BRPA is most excited to report that it has just lifted a restriction on accessing this part of the park)를 통해 접근 금지 해제와 관련한 세부 사항도 알리기 위한 게시물임을 알 수 있으므로, 정답은 (B)이다.

▶▶ **Paraphrasing**　지문의 it has just lifted a restriction on accessing this part of the park → 정답의 an amendment to a rule

173 사실 관계 확인

번역 생태계 개선 프로젝트의 일부가 아닌 것은?
(A) 추가로 나무 기르기
(B) 비탈의 안정성 높이기
(C) 특정 벌레 개체수 줄이기
(D) 해로운 식물로부터 농장 동물 보호하기

해설 첫 번째 단락의 엘레인 로테프 담당관의 지휘 아래, 지역 고유의 다양한 수종 500그루를 20에이커 면적에 심었으며 이러한 나무에 해를 끼치는 벌레의 과잉 서식을 막기 위한 노력이 성공을 거뒀다(Under the leadership of Director Elaine Roteff, 500 trees of various species native to the area have been planted over a 20-acre stretch of the land, and efforts to combat the overpopulation of insects that harm such trees have succeeded)를 통해 (A)와 (C)를, 또한 BRPA 기술자들은 브레이던 개울을 따라 서 있는 산비탈을 안정화하여 토양의 질을 높이고 개울이 막힘 없이 흐르도록 하고 있다(BRPA engineers are also stabilizing the slopes of hillsides that line Braydon Creek, thus improving the quality of the hills' soil and allowing the creek water to flow without blockages)를 통해 (B)를 확인할 수 있으므로, 정답은 (D)이다.

▶▶ **Paraphrasing**　지문의 500 trees of various species native to the area have been planted → 보기의 Growing additional trees 지문의 stabilizing the slopes of hillsides → 보기의 Increasing the stability of hillsides 지문의 efforts to combat the overpopulation of insects that harm such trees → 보기의 Reducing the population of certain insects

174 세부 사항

번역 로테프 씨는 무엇을 하도록 요청받는가?
(A) 라디오 방송 인터뷰하기
(B) 회의에서 프로젝트에 대해 발표하기
(C) 국제단체 이사회 가입하기
(D) 지역 대학교에서 명예학위 수여받기

해설 두 번째 단락에서 로테프 담당관이 다가오는 리우데자네이루 회의에서 여러 세션을 맡아 프로젝트에서 얻은 식견을 전수해 달라는 초청을 받았다. 매우 영광스러운 일이다(Director Roteff has been invited to lead several sessions at its upcoming conference in Rio de Janeiro to pass on the insights that have been gained from the project, which is a tremendous honor)라고 했으므로 로테프 담당관이 회의에서 프로젝트 관련 세션을 맡아 달라는 요청을 받았다는 것을 알 수 있다. 따라서 정답은 (B)이다.

▶▶ **Paraphrasing**　지문의 been invited → 질문의 been asked 지문의 pass on the insights that have been gained from the project → 정답의 Speak about a project

175 사실 관계 확인

번역 브레이던 지역공원에 대해 명시된 것은?
(A) 공원 일부는 보통 때 일반인 출입이 금지된다.
(B) 현재 두 개의 등반로가 있다.
(C) 여러 곳의 소풍 구역이 곧 제공된다.
(D) 공원 일부는 큰 호수와 경계를 이룬다.

해설 마지막 단락에서 공원 서부 지역은 공식 투어의 일환으로만 방문 가능하다. 작업자들을 방해하지 않기 위해 다른 때는 일반인 출입금지구역으로 계속 유지된다(The western area of the park may only be visited as part of this official tour. It remains off limits to the public at all other times to avoid interfering with work crews)고 했다. 공식투어를 제외한 외부인 출입금지를 언급하고 있으므로, 정답은 (A)이다.

▶▶ **Paraphrasing**　지문의 The western area of the park → 정답의 Part of it 지문의 remains off limits to the public at all other times → 정답의 is normally closed to the public

176-180 웹페이지 + 양식

---

http://www.e-couponsltd.com

E-쿠폰 주식회사에 오신 것을 환영합니다. 저희는 모든 업종을 위한 디지털 쿠폰 전문업체입니다. 귀하의 단체가 어떤 종류의 판촉행사를 진행하시든 필요한 쿠폰을 만들 수 있도록 도와 드립니다. 저희 EC 서비스-프로 소프트웨어 패키지를 통해 쉽게 만들 수 있으며 1회 비용은 350달러입니다. **176**이미 만들어진 저희의 쿠폰 디자인 모음을 살펴보시고 선택한 쿠폰에 특정 정보를 추가하여 개인의 필요에 맞추십시오.

☛ 조언: 한정된 단체만 귀하의 쿠폰을 사용하기를 바라십니까? **177**추가 비용 없이 확인 바코드를 추가하세요. 이렇게 하면 복제가 되지 않고 각 쿠폰이 한 번만 사용될 수 있도록 보장됩니다.

EC 서비스-프로는 쿠폰 배포도 도와 드립니다. **178**이메일이나 문자 메시지 같은 전통적 선택사항에, 최근에는 귀사의 와이파이에 접속하는 방문자들에게 쿠폰을 보여주는 방식까지 개발했습니다. 어떤 전달 방식을 선택하시든 귀사와 귀사의 고객 모두에게 간단한 절차입니다.

여기를 클릭해 오늘 EC 서비스-프로를 주문하고 멋진 쿠폰을 만들어 보세요.

어휘 specialty 전문 promotion 홍보, 판매 촉진 one-time 1회의 look through 훑어보다, 살펴보다 ready-made 이미 만들어진, 기성품의 personalize 개인화하다, 개인의 기호[필요]에 맞추다 verification 확인 at no extra charge 추가 비용 없이 duplication 복제 guarantee 보장하다 distribute 배포하다, 나눠주다 attractive 매력적인

176 세부 사항

번역 웹페이지에 따르면 EC 서비스-프로는 무엇을 제공하는가?
(A) 배송 추적
(B) 디자인 템플릿
(C) 업계 뉴스 특보
(D) 고객 데이터 분석

해설 웹페이지의 첫 번째 단락 마지막 문장에서 이미 만들어진 쿠폰 디자인 모음을 살펴보고 선택한 쿠폰에 특정 정보를 추가하여 개인의 필요에 맞추라(Use it to look through our collection of ready-made designs for coupons, and then personalize the coupon you chose by adding specific information)를 통해 EC 서비스-프로가 쿠폰 디자인 템플릿을 제공한다는 것을 알 수 있으므로, 정답은 (B)이다.

▶▶ **Paraphrasing**   지문의 **ready-made designs**
→ 정답의 **Design templates**

177 사실 관계 확인

번역 무료 추가 기능이 있는 쿠폰에 대해 명시된 것은?
(A) 복제가 불가능하다.
(B) 인기가 매우 높다.
(C) 종이 형태로 판매된다.
(D) 상당한 추가 생산 시간이 필요하다.

해설 웹페이지의 두 번째 단락에서 추가 비용 없이 확인 바코드를 추가하면 복제가 되지 않고 각 쿠폰이 한 번만 사용될 수 있도록 보장한다(Add a verification bar code at no extra charge. This makes duplication impossible and guarantees that each coupon can only be used once)고 했으므로 무료로 제공되는 확인 바코드 기능으로 쿠폰의 복제를 막을 수 있음을 언급하고 있다. 따라서 정답은 (A)이다.

▶▶ **Paraphrasing**   지문의 **Add a verification bar code at no extra charge**
→ 질문의 **a free additional feature**
지문의 **makes duplication impossible**
→ 정답의 **cannot be copied**

178 연계

번역 브루사드 북스에 대해 암시된 것은?
(A) 투자자들에게 새 쿠폰을 나눠줄 예정이다.
(B) 방문자들에게 무선 인터넷 접속을 제공한다.
(C) 최근 소셜미디어 웹사이트상에서 페이지를 개설했다.
(D) 기술 서적에 특화되어 있다.

해설 두 번째 지문인 브루사드 북스가 작성한 고객 의견 중 3번 항목에서 그것만 아니라면 새로운 쿠폰 배포 방식은 만족스럽다. 이런 기능을 계속 추가해 주기 바란다(Otherwise, I'm pleased with your new coupon distribution method, and hope you'll keep adding features like that)와 같이 새로운 쿠폰 배포 방식에 대한 만족도를 언급하고 있다. 새로운 쿠폰 배포 방식에 관한 정보는 첫 번째 지문인 웹페이지를 통해 확인할 수 있다. 웹페이지의 세 번째 단락에서 이메일이나 문자 메시지와 같은 전통적 선택사항에 더해, 최근에는 귀사의 와이파이에 접속하는 방문자들에게 쿠폰을 보여주는 방식까지 개발했다(In addition to classic options such as e-mail and text message, we recently developed a way to display coupons to visitors who connect to your business's Wi-Fi)를 통해 브루사드 북스가 방문자들에게 와이파이 이용 서비스를 제공한다는 것을 알 수 있으므로, 정답은 (B)이다.

▶▶ **Paraphrasing**   지문의 **connect to your business's Wi-Fi**
→ 정답의 **wireless Internet access**

179 세부 사항

번역 브루사드 씨가 타이로프 디지털을 이용하지 않게 된 이유는 무엇인가?
(A) 더 이상 이용할 수 없어서
(B) 사용하기 어려워서
(C) 기능이 많지 않아서
(D) 고객 지원이 없어서

해설 두 번째 지문의 고객 의견 중 2번 항목에서 타이로프 디지털을 사용해 본 적이 있다(Tairov Digital)고 했고, 종종 헷갈리고 복잡해서 더 이상 이용하지 않는다(However, I no longer use it because it was often confusing and complicated)에서 헷갈리고 복잡해서 타이로프 디지털을 이용하지 않게 되었다고 언급하고 있으므로, 정답은 (B)이다.

▶▶ **Paraphrasing**   지문의 **no longer use** → 질문의 **stop using**
지문의 **often confusing and complicated**
→ 정답의 **not user-friendly**

180 세부 사항

번역 브루사드 씨가 E-쿠폰 주식회사에 요청한 것은 무엇인가?
(A) 토론 포럼을 개최할 것
(B) 메일 수신 리스트에서 자신을 삭제할 것
(C) 소프트웨어 결함을 수정할 것
(D) 계약조건을 명확히 할 것

해설 두 번째 지문의 고객 의견 중 3번 항목, 이미 토론 포럼에서 제기된 문제인데 소프트웨어의 "옵션" 메뉴를 고쳐서 모든 운영체제에서 제대로 보이도록 해야 한다(This has already been brought up in your discussion forums, but you really should fix the software's "Options" menu so that it displays properly on all operating systems)에서 소프트웨어의 문제점을 고치도록 요청하고 있으므로, 정답은 (C)이다.

181-185 전단지 + 이메일

메클링 피트니스   http://www.mechlingfitness.com.au

단체 수업

181A최고 수준의 개인지도 훈련과 자기주도적 운동을 위한 시설 이외에도, 메클링 피트니스는 센터 회원들에게 무료 단체 수업을 제공하는 것을 자랑스럽게 생각합니다. 아래 수업은 현재 매주 5일간 운영됩니다.

속도

야외에서 자전거 탈 때의 경치, 거기에다 실내 자전거의 편리함을 원하세요? 자연 속의 장면이 30분간 비디오로 펼쳐지는 대형 스크린 앞에서 헬스 자전거를 타는 '속도'는 이 모든 것을 가질 수 있게 해줍니다. 트레이너들이 속도를 내야 할 때와 부드럽게 움직여야 할 때를 지시해 줌으로써 활기찬 운동이 될 수 있게 해줍니다.

순전한 노력

짧지만 활기찬 수업으로, 참가자들은 각기 신체의 다른 부분에 집중하는 8개 스테이션을 돌며 30분에 걸쳐 운동하게 됩니다. **182**누구나 빠짐없이 각 스테이션에 들 수 있도록 수업 인원은 8명으로 제한됩니다.

동작

185참가자들을 단순한 요가 동작으로 부드럽게 유도해 유연성을 기를 수 있게 해줍니다. 마지막에 짧은 명상 시간이 포함되는 이 45분 수업은 이완되면서도 힘이 나는 느낌을 틀림없이 갖게 해 줄 것입니다.

생기와 현란함

실내 에어로빅 수업은 재미있게 탄력을 찾을 수 있는 방법입니다. 강사들이 신나는 최신 히트곡에 맞춰 고강도 에너지 댄스 한 **183**코스를 마칠 수 있게 지도합니다. 한 시간 수업 중 아령을 사용해 난이도를 점점 높여주세요.

181C참가자들은 선택한 수업의 자리를 미리 예약할 수 있습니다. **181D**위의 수업들과 더 뜸하게 만나는 수업 시간표 확인뿐만 아니라 자리 예약을 위해 프런트 데스크로 오세요. 프런트 데스크에서는 자신의 것을 챙겨오지 못한 참가자들을 위해 매트 같은 필요 물품도 대여합니다.

어휘 top-notch 일류의, 최고 수준의 facilities 시설 self-directed 스스로 주도하는 velocity 속도 scenery 경치 outdoor 야외의 cycling studio 실내 자전거 시설 stationary bike 헬스 자전거 setting 환경, 배경 vigorous 격렬한, 활기찬 workout 운동 coast 부드럽게[저절로] 움직이다 exertion 분투, 있는 힘을 다함 lively 활기찬 cap 한도를 정하다 flexibility 유연성 meditation 명상 be sure to+동사원형 반드시 ~하다 energized 기운이 나는 fit (체력·몸매가) 건강한, 탄탄한 instructor 강사 routine 루틴(처음부터 끝까지 코스가 정해진 동작이나 행동) upbeat 신나는, 활기찬 chart hit (차트에 오른) 히트곡 hour-long 1시간 걸리는 hand weights 아령, 덤벨 ahead of time 사전에 loan 대여

발신: 조슈아 왕
수신: 〈inquiries@mechlingfitness.com.au〉
날짜: 9월 23일
제목: 단체 수업

안녕하세요,

저는 최근에 은퇴를 했는데, **184**제가 일하던 직장의 동료인 레베카 터커가 활력을 유지하기 위해 여기 단체 수업을 들어보라고 권했습니다. 수업이 매우 효과적이라고 하면서요. 그런데 센터에 들러 회원 등록을 하기 전에 주 5일 하는 수업들에 어떤 선택 사항이 있는지 알고 싶었습니다. **185**저는 60대입니다. 그러다 보니 가벼운 수준의 활동이 따르고 주로 스트레칭에 집중하는 수업을 찾고 있습니다. 이런 기준에 맞는 수업을 추천해 주실 수 있는지요?

감사합니다.

조슈아 왕

어휘 recently 최근에 retire 은퇴하다 former 이전의 register 등록하다 focus on ~에 집중하다, 주력하다 fit the criteria 기준에 맞다 criteria 기준

181 사실 관계 확인

번역 메클링 피트니스에 관해 명시되지 않은 것은?
(A) 개별적으로 피트니스 지도를 해 준다.
(B) 비회원은 1일 사용권을 구매할 수 있다.
(C) 일부 수업은 사전 등록을 허용한다.
(D) 전단지에 밝힌 것보다 더 많은 수업을 운영한다.

해설 전단지의 단체 수업(Group Classes)에서 최고 수준의 개인지도 훈련과 자기주도적 운동을 위한 시설 이외에도(In addition to top-notch personal training and facilities for self-directed exercise)를 통해 (A)를, 전단지 마지막 단락의 참가자들은 선택한 수업의 자리를 미리 예약할 수 있다(Participants may reserve a place in selected classes ahead of time)에서 (C)를, 전단지 마지막 단락에서 위의 수업들과 더 뜸하게 만나는 수업들(the classes above and those that meet less frequently)을 통해 (D)를 확인할 수 있다. 따라서 정답은 (B)이다.

▶ **Paraphrasing** 지문의 **personal training** → 보기의 **individualized fitness coaching**
지문의 **reserve a place in selected classes ahead of time** → 보기의 **advance registration for some classes**
지문의 **the classes above and those that meet less frequently** → 보기의 **more classes than are named in the flyer**

182 사실 관계 확인

번역 '순전한 노력'에 관하여 언급된 것은 무엇인가?
(A) 비디오가 동반된다.
(B) 준비운동 시간이 포함된다.
(C) 기술 수준에 따라 참가자를 구분한다.
(D) 참가자 수에 제한이 있다.

해설 세 번째 단락의 순전한 노력(Pure Exertion)에서 누구나 빠짐없이 각 스테이션에 들 수 있도록 수업 인원은 8명으로 제한된다(To guarantee that everyone can visit each station, classes are capped at eight people)를 통해 참가자 수에 제한을 둔다는 것을 알 수 있으므로, 정답은 (D)이다.

> ▶▶ **Paraphrasing** 지문의 **classes are capped at eight people** → 정답의 **It has a limited number of participants.**

183 동의어 찾기

번역 다섯 번째 단락 2행의 "routine"과 의미가 가장 가까운 단어는?
(A) 프로그램
(B) 습관
(C) 자취
(D) 짐

해설 해당 문장은 강사들이 신나는 최신 히트곡에 맞춰 고강도 에너지 댄스 한 코스를 마칠 수 있게 지도한다(Instructors lead participants through a high-energy dance routine set to the latest upbeat chart hits)라는 의미로 해석되는데, 여기서 routine은 문맥상 '코스, 프로그램'이라는 의미가 자연스러우므로, 정답은 (A) program이다.

184 추론 / 암시

번역 터커 씨는 최근에 무엇을 했겠는가?
(A) 새로운 일을 시작했다
(B) 이메일 계정을 등록했다
(C) 메클링 피트니스에서 수업을 받았다
(D) 사교 활동 모임에 가입했다

해설 이메일에서 전에 일하던 직장의 동료인 레베카 터커가 건강을 유지하기 위해 여기 단체 수업을 들어보라고 권했는데 수업이 매우 효과적(Rebecca Tucker, a coworker at my former job, suggested that I try your group classes to stay active. She said she finds them very effective)이라고 했다. 이를 통해 터커 씨가 직접 수업을 들은 후 권했다는 것을 유추할 수 있으므로, 정답은 (C)이다.

185 연계

번역 어떤 수업이 왕 씨에게 추천되겠는가?
(A) 속도
(B) 순전한 노력
(C) 동작
(D) 생기와 현란함

해설 이메일 후반부에서 왕 씨는 나는 60대로 가벼운 수준의 활동이 따르고 주로 스트레칭에 집중하는 수업을 찾고 있다(I'm in my 60s, so I'm looking for something that has a mild level of activity and mainly focuses on stretching)고 했다. 전단지에서 왕 씨의 조건에 부합하는 수업을 찾아야 한다. 동작(Movement) 수업이 참가자들을 단순한 요가 동작으로 부드럽게 유도해 유연성을 기를 수 있게 해 준다(Movement gently guides participants through simple yoga poses to improve flexibility)고 했으므로, 정답은 (C)이다.

186-190 웹페이지 + 청구서 + 이메일

http://www.grangerfurnishings.com

| 홈 | 카테고리 | 소개 | 후기 |

그레인저 가구

그레인저 가구를 고려해 주셔서 감사합니다. 저희는 25년이 넘는 세월 동안, 어떤 사무실도 돋보이게 할 고품질이면서 가격이 적당한 가구를 이 지역 전체에 공급해 왔습니다. **186**상단의 "카테고리"를 클릭하셔서 멋진 사무 공간 솔루션을 유형별로 검색하시거나, 하단에서 월별 특별 상품을 확인하십시오.

1873월 할인 판매
파일 캐비닛 일체 10% 할인 - 계산 시 STOCAB 코드 이용
웨이크로스 브랜드 의자 일체 5% 할인 - 계산 시 WAYCRO 코드 이용

어휘 **affordable** 가격이 적당한 **distinction** 차별, 구별, 탁월함 **browse** 검색하다 **storage cabinet** 파일 캐비닛

그레인저 가구

고객명: 제프 퀸	주문번호: B661879
전화번호: (800) 555-0118	**187**주문일자: 3월 28일
배송지 주소: 지락 서플라이	배송 예정일: 4월 5일 오후 1~5시
아이번 드라이브 17	
먼로빌, PA 15147	

제품	제품 설명	수량	가격
DK21984	전통 나무 책상	3	2,985달러
SR88953B	웨이크로스 나무 책장 (갈색)	6	1,986달러
FS25371	접이식 플라스틱 책상	10	3,990달러
187TC10004B	스틸텍 파일 캐비닛 (갈색)	2	1,402달러
		합계	10,363달러

배송 정보: **189**귀하로부터 다른 지시사항이 없는 한, 저희 운전기사가 명시된 주소에 있는 건물 앞에 차를 세울 것입니다. 그러고 나서 저희 배송팀이 가구를 내리고 선택하신 장소로 운반합니다. **188**출구와 장소 사이의 장애물을 미리 치워서 배송팀을 도와주시기 바랍니다. 출발하기 전에 배송팀이 가구 포장지를 치우고 가구 운반 중 손상이 생겼는지 점검할 것입니다.

어휘 **collapsible** (공간을 덜 차지하도록) 접을 수 있는 **unload** (짐을) 내리다 **obstruction** 장애물 **beforehand** 미리 **packaging** 포장 **sustain** (손상·피해 등을) 입다, 당하다 **in transit** 수송 중에

발신: 제프 퀸 (jquinn@girac-supply.com)
수신: 다이앤 클라반스키 (dklavansky@girac-supply.com)
날짜: 4월 5일
제목: 도움
첨부: 청구서

안녕하세요 다이앤 씨,

제가 오늘 개인적인 사유로 출근하지 못해 제 업무를 맡아주셔야 합니다. **190**물론 그중 하나는 관리자 나린 씨의 비서 업무를 하는 것이지만 다이앤 씨가 이전에 그 일을 하신 적이 있기에 자세히 쓰지 않겠습니다.

일상적이지 않은 업무 단 한 가지는 오늘 오후 가구 배송을 받는 일입니다만, 첨부한 청구서에 필요한 정보가 거의 다 들어 있습니다. **189**아, 배송 트럭이 우리 건물 뒤편에 주차될 예정임을 알려드려야겠군요.

190아울러 다른 사람들이 사무실을 비워 가구를 찾아갈 수 없을 경우, 나무 책상과 책장은 관리자들에게, 플라스틱 책상은 직원들에게 가야 하며 파일 캐비닛은 사무실 저쪽 벽 옆에 두어야 합니다.

끝으로 랜스 그레이 씨가 들르면 그에게 제 책상에 있는 봉투를 주십시오.

급한 일이 생기면 제 휴대전화로 연락 주세요.

― 제프

> **어휘** invoice 청구서 take over 인계받다 come by 잠깐 들르다

186 추론 / 암시

번역 웹페이지에 대해 암시된 것은?
(A) 일정표로 연결되는 링크가 있다.
(B) 최소 월 1회 업데이트된다.
(C) "카테고리" 메뉴에는 25가지 종류의 제품이 있다.
(D) 방문자들은 특별 쿠폰을 인쇄할 수 있다.

해설 웹페이지의 첫 번째 단락, 상단의 "카테고리"를 클릭해 멋진 사무 공간 솔루션을 유형별로 검색하거나, 하단에서 월별 특별 상품을 확인하라(Click on "CATEGORIES" above to begin browsing our attractive workspace solutions by type, or check the space below for our monthly specials)를 통해 월별 특별 상품으로 인해 적어도 월 1회는 웹페이지가 업데이트됨을 유추할 수 있으므로, 정답은 (B)이다.

▶▶ **Paraphrasing** 지문의 **monthly** → 정답의 **once a month**

187 연계

번역 지락 서플라이는 어떤 제품에 대해 할인을 받겠는가?
(A) DK21984
(B) SR88953B
(C) FS25371
(D) TC10004B

해설 지락 서플라이로 발행된 청구서의 '주문일자: 3월 28일(Order date: March 28)'과 '제품 설명(Product description)', 웹페이지의 두 번째 단락 '3월 할인 판매(Sales for the month of March)'의 '파일 캐비닛 일체 10% 할인―계산 시 STOCAB 코드 이용(10% off all storage cabinets―use code STOCAB at checkout)'을 통해 TC10004B 캐비닛 제품에 대해 할인을 받았음을 유추할 수 있으므로, 정답은 (D)이다.

▶▶ **Paraphrasing** 지문의 **Sales** → 질문의 **a discount**

188 세부 사항

번역 청구서에서 퀸 씨는 무엇을 하라고 지시받았는가?
(A) 이메일 주소 확인하기
(B) 가구 옮기는 사람들을 위해 길 치워두기
(C) 포장 선택사항 지시하기
(D) 배송 시 제품 점검하기

해설 청구서의 '배송 정보(Delivery information)' 중 출입구와 장소 사이의 장애물을 미리 치워서 배송팀을 도와주기 바란다(Please assist them by removing obstructions between the entrance and each site beforehand)에서 출입구와 설치 장소 사이의 물건들을 치우도록 고객인 퀸 씨에게 요청하고 있으므로, 정답은 (B)이다.

▶▶ **Paraphrasing** 지문의 **removing obstructions between the entrance and each site** → 정답의 **Clear paths**

189 연계

번역 퀸 씨에 대해 맞는 것은?
(A) 그레인저 가구에 특별 지시사항을 전달했다.
(B) 그레이 씨에게 전화가 올 것으로 예상한다.
(C) 최초 주문에 몇 가지 물품을 추가했다.
(D) 오후 1시까지 회사에 도착할 예정이다.

해설 퀸 씨가 쓴 이메일의 두 번째 단락, 배송 트럭이 우리 건물 뒤편에 주차될 예정임을 알려드린다(I should tell you that the delivery truck will park in our back lot)에서 가구 배송 트럭의 주차 장소를 언급하고 있다. 배송 트럭의 주차 장소에 대한 정보는 청구서의 배송 정보를 통해 확인할 수 있다. 청구서의 '배송 정보(Delivery information)' 중 다른 지시사항이 없는 한, 운전기사가 명시된 주소에 있는 건물 앞에 차를 세울 것이다(Unless we receive other instructions from you, our driver will park in front of the building at the address stated)를 통해 퀸 씨가 그레인저 가구에 주차 장소와 관련해 별도 지시를 했음을 유추할 수 있으므로, 정답은 (A)이다.

▶▶ **Paraphrasing** 지문의 **we receive other instructions from you** → 정답의 **He gave special instructions to Granger Furnishings**

190 추론 / 암시

번역 누가 전통 나무책상을 지급받겠는가?
(A) 퀸 씨
(B) 클라반스키 씨
(C) 나퀸 씨
(D) 그레이 씨

해설 이메일의 세 번째 단락, 아울러 다른 사람들이 사무실을 비워 가구를 찾아갈 수 없을 경우, 나무 책상과 책장은 관리자들에게, 플라스틱 책상은 직원들에게 가야 하며 파일 캐비닛은 사무실 저쪽 벽 옆에 두어야 한다(Also, in case other people are out of the office and can't claim their furniture ~ the storage cabinets should be placed by the far wall of the office)에서 나무 책상은 관리자를 위한 것임을 언급하고 있다. 이메일의 첫 번째 단락에서 물론 그중 하나는 관리자 나퀸 씨의 비서 업무를 하는 것이지만 이전에 다이앤 씨가 그 일을 한 적이 있기에 자세히 쓰지 않겠다(One of these, of course, is acting as a manager's assistant to Ms. Naquin, but since you've done that before, I won't go into detail about it)를 통해 나퀸 씨는 관리자임을 알 수 있다. 따라서 그녀에게 나무 책상이 지급될 것으로 유추할 수 있으므로, 정답은 (C)이다.

▶▶ **Paraphrasing** 지문의 **go to** → 질문의 **be issued**

남아프리카공화국 전국 발레대회

남아프리카공화국 전국 발레대회(SANBC)는 남아프리카공화국 제일의 성인 발레대회 중 하나입니다. [191]2년마다 전국의 아마추어 무용수들이 모여 식견 높은 심사위원과 열정적인 관중 앞에서 공연을 펼칩니다. SANBC 참가에 관한 정보는 다음 일정표를 참조하십시오.

12월 10일	지원 마감 – 제출물에 최근 공연 동영상을 포함해야 함
[192]1월 12일	지역 1차 대회 – 동부 지역 무용수들 요하네스버그에서 공연
1월 13일	지역 2차 대회 – 서부 지역 무용수들 케이프타운에서 공연 – 심사위원단 숙의 개시
1월 18일	결선 진출자 공지 – 각 부문별 (개인 및 단체) 상위 5위까지 전국 대회에 초청
2월 17일	전국 대회 – 결선 진출자들 더반에서 공연 – 심사위원단 우승자 발표

어휘 premier 최고의, 제1의 every other year 2년마다 discerning 식견 있는, 안목이 높은 enthusiastic 열정적인 refer to ~을 참조하다 deadline 마감 기한 submission 제출물 deliberation 숙고, 숙의 finalist 결선 진출자

수신: 시드라 커머니
발신: 섀넌 카딕
날짜: 1월 22일
제목: SANBC 계획

안녕하세요 시드라 씨,

다음 달에 있을 전국 SANBC 대회에 대해 제가 가진 아이디어를 공유하고 싶습니다. [192]12일 저희 공연에서 제가 뭔가 부족한 것 같다고 했던 것, 기억하세요? 그게 무엇인지 알 것 같습니다. [193]다른 사람들을 표현하기 위해 무대에 폼 블록을 쓰는 대신 진짜 사람을 쓰는 게 낫겠어요. 그들에게 회색 옷을 입히고 조금씩 걸어 다니게 할 수도 있을 겁니다. 그 편이 시각적으로 훨씬 더 기억에 남을 듯합니다. 지역 예선을 통과하지 못한 다른 지역 공연단에서 몇 명을 활용할 수 있을 겁니다.

[195]큰 변화일 테지만 도널드 나이두를 비롯해 마스틀리 댄스 컴퍼니의 나머지 무용수들을 이기려면 우리가 뭔가 특별한 것을 해야 한다고 생각합니다. 오늘밤에 생각해 보시고 내일 연습 때 이야기해요.

섀넌
섀넌 카딕
발레 어스 공동 감독 겸 공연자

어휘 lack 부족하다 figure out 알아내다 represent 대표하다 visually 시각적으로 troupe 공연단 make it past 통과하다

발레 어스, SANBC 우승

(2월 18일) – 최근 남아프리카공화국 전국 발레대회에서 발레 어스가 단체부문 우승자로 선정됐다.

발레 어스 공동 감독이자 안무가인 시드라 커머니는 차점자인 마스틀리 댄스 컴퍼니와 다른 무용수들의 [194]치열한 경쟁을 언급하며 팀의 우승에 놀라움을 표했다. "이런 일이 생기다니 믿을 수가 없습니다. 올해 무용단을 생각해 보면 믿기 힘든 상입니다. 저희는 이에 부응하고자 노력하겠습니다."

13인으로 구성된 공연단 발레 어스는 아름다운 오케스트라 음악에 맞춘 으스스한 작품 (유령이 출몰하는 보도)로 인정을 받았다. 늘어뜨린 흰 옷을 입은 무용수들은 도심 거리의 바쁜 행인을 상징하는 회색 사람들 틈을 우아하게 움직였다.

[195]SANBC는 프로가 아닌 발레 단체를 후원하기 위해 만들어진 행사로, 발레 어스에게 R12,000의 상금을 수여하며 마스틀리 댄스 컴퍼니와 두 번째 차점자 발레 고스펠은 각각 R9,000과 R6,000의 상금을 받는다. 나머지 공연단은 노력의 대가로 R1,000을 받게 된다.

어휘 choreographer 안무가 stiff competition 치열한 경쟁 runner-up 차점자 accolade 칭찬, 포상 live up to ~에 부응하다 haunting 뇌리에서 사라지지 않는 pavement 인도, 보도 eerie 괴상한, 으스스한 flowing 흐르는 듯한, 늘어뜨린 pedestrian 행인 nonprofessional 프로가 아닌, 아마추어의 respectively 각각

---

191 사실 관계 확인

번역 SANBC에 대해 명시된 것은?
(A) 인터넷에서 생중계로 방송된다.
(B) 정부 기관이 후원한다.
(C) 2년마다 개최된다.
(D) 연령별로 구분한다.

해설 정보문의 첫 번째 단락, 2년마다 전국의 아마추어 무용수들이 모여 식견 높은 심사위원과 열정적인 관중 앞에서 공연을 펼친다(Every other year, amateur dancers from all over the country gather to perform in front of discerning judges and enthusiastic live crowds)를 통해 SANBC가 2년마다 개최된다는 것을 알 수 있으므로, 정답은 (C)이다.

▶▶ **Paraphrasing** 지문의 **Every other year**
→ 정답의 **every two years**

---

192 연계

번역 지역 대회에서 발레 어스의 공연에 대해 암시된 것은?
(A) 요하네스버그에서 공연했다.
(B) 심사위원들에게 감동을 주지 못했다.
(C) 해당일에 이뤄진 공연 5개 중 하나였다.
(D) 비디오 예술가에 의해 녹화됐다.

해설 발레 어스의 카딕 씨가 쓴 이메일의 첫 번째 단락. 12일 저희 공연에서 제가 뭔가 부족한 것 같다고 했던 것, 기억하세요(Remember how I felt like our performance on the twelfth seemed to be lacking something)에서 발레 어스의 12일 공연을 언급하고 있다. 정보문의 일정표 중 1월 12일(12 January)의 지역 1차 대회 - 동부 지역 무용수들 요하네스버그에서 공연(First regional competition - Dancers from eastern regions perform in Johannesburg)을 통해 발레 어스가 요하네스버그에서 공연했음을 유추할 수 있으므로, 정답은 (A)이다.

193 세부 사항

번역 카딕 씨는 공연에서 무엇을 바꾸고 싶어 했는가?

(A) 조명
(B) 무용수의 의상
(C) 음악의 속도
(D) 무대 장식

해설 카딕 씨가 쓴 이메일의 첫 번째 단락, 다른 사람들을 표현하기 위해 무대에 폼블록을 쓰는 대신 진짜 사람을 쓰는 게 낫겠다(Instead of having the foam blocks on stage to represent other people, we should use actual people)를 통해 무대 장식의 변경을 원한다는 것을 알 수 있으므로, 정답은 (D)이다.

194 동의어 찾기

번역 기사에서 두 번째 단락 3행의 "stiff"와 의미가 가장 가까운 단어는?

(A) 융통성이 없는
(B) 치열한
(C) 필수적인
(D) 무뚝뚝한

해설 해당 문장은 발레 어스 공동 감독이자 안무가인 시드라 커마니는 차점자인 마스틀리 댄스 컴퍼니와 다른 무용수들의 치열한 경쟁을 언급하며 팀의 우승에 놀라움을 표했다(Sidra Kirmani, Ballet Earth's co-director and choreographer, expressed surprise at the group's victory, citing stiff competition from runner-up Mastley Dance Company and others)라는 의미로 해석되는데, 여기서 stiff는 '심한, 치열한'이라는 의미가 자연스러우므로, 정답은 (B) intense(치열한, 극심한, 강렬한)이다.

195 연계

번역 나이두 씨의 공연단이 받을 상금은 얼마인가?

(A) R1,000
(B) R6,000
(C) R9,000
(D) R12,000

해설 카딕 씨가 쓴 이메일의 두 번째 단락, 큰 변화일 테지만 도널드 나이두를 비롯해 마스틀리 댄스 컴퍼니의 나머지 무용수들을 이기려면 뭔가 특별한 것을 해야 한다고 생각한다(I know that this is a big change, but I really think we need to do something special to beat Donald Naidoo and the rest of Mastley Dance Company)를 통해 나이두 씨가 마스틀리 댄스 컴퍼니의 일원임을 알 수 있다. 상금에 대한 정보는 기사를 통해 확인할 수 있다. 기사의 마지막 단락, SANBC는 프로가 아닌 발레 단체를 후원하기 위해 만들어진 행사로, 발레 어스에게 R12,000의 상금을 수여하며 마스틀리 댄스 컴퍼니와 두 번째 차점자 발레 고스넬은 각각 R9,000과 R6,000의 상금을 받는다(The SANBC, an event created to support nonprofessional ballet groups, will issue Ballet Earth a prize of R12,000, while Mastley Dance Company and second runner-up Ballet Gosnell will receive R9,000 and R6,000, respectively)를 통해 나이두 씨가 속한 마스틀리 댄스 컴퍼니가 상금으로 R9000을 받는다는 것을 알 수 있으므로, 정답은 (C)이다.

196-200 문자 메시지 + 이메일 + 이메일

발신: 조시아 헨클
7월 25일 오후 1:58에 수신됨
수신: 트레버 베노아

안녕하세요, 트레버 씨. 잘 지내세요? 지난달 콘서트는 정말 즐거웠습니다. 다른 콘서트가 있을 때 알려 주셨으면 좋겠습니다. **196, 197**그런데 제가 일 때문에 웹사이트를 검색하다가 아이-팝핑 디자인이라는 업체에서 홈페이지에 베노아 씨의 노래를 사용하고 있는 것을 알았습니다. **196**허가하셨을 것 같지 않아서 알려 드리고 싶었어요. 사이트는 www.eyepoppingdesign.com입니다.

어휘 browse 검색하다 give permission 허가하다

발신: 트레버 베노아 〈tbenoit@trevorbenoit.com〉
수신: 오드라 팩스턴 〈apaxton@eyepoppingdesign.com〉
제목: 음악 문제
날짜: 7월 25일

팩스턴 씨께,

197, 199저는 오늘 귀하의 그래픽디자인 업체 홈페이지의 홍보 동영상에 제 노래 "언덕에서"의 1분짜리 발췌 부분이 들어 있는 것을 발견하고 마음이 편치 않습니다. **198**저는 작년에 이 노래를 작곡, 녹음하고 제 웹사이트를 통해 발표했지만, 어떠한 개인업체에도 이를 사용하는 데 동의한 적이 없습니다. 가능한 한 빨리 제 노래를 다른 음악으로 대체하거나 동영상 전체를 내려 주십시오.

트레버 베노아

어휘 promotional 홍보의 excerpt 발췌 (부분) replace A with B A를 B로 대체하다

발신: 마크 피쉴린 〈mark.fischlin@fischlinservices.com〉
200수신: 오드라 팩스턴 〈apaxton@eyepoppingdesign.com〉
제목: 실수
날짜: 7월 26일
첨부: 안드로이드; 시간; 카리에로

팩스턴 씨께,

어제 저희에게 제기하신 문제를 검토했으며 안타깝게도 베노아 씨의 말이 맞다고 결론내렸습니다. **200**귀하의 계정을 관리했던 직원 스테판스키 씨는 귀하에게 말씀드린 것과 달리 베노아 씨의 음악을 사용할 권한을 받지 않았습니다. 사실 선택한 다른 음악 중 두 곡도 같은 문제가 있는 것으로 밝혀졌습니다. 피쉴린 서비스를 대표해 사과의 말씀을 드리며, 스테판스키 씨가 자신의 행동에 대해 반드시 심각한 결과에 처하도록 하겠습니다.

아울러 좋은 서비스를 제공하겠다는 저희의 약속을 보여 드리기 위해, 저희는 이미 파일을 검토하여 문제의 음악을 대체할 매력적이면서도 법적으로 이용 가능한 음악을 찾아 두었습니다. 아래와 같습니다.

원곡	대체곡
"활기찬 변주곡"	"안드로이드로"
"패턴의 노래"	"흩뿌려진 시간"
199"언덕에서"	"카리에로"

본 이메일에 새 음악들을 첨부했습니다. 마음에 드는지 알려 주시면, 그에 맞춰 작업을 변경하겠습니다.

마크 피쉴린
피쉴린 서비스 CEO

196 주제 / 목적

번역 문자 메시지의 목적은 무엇인가?
(A) 일부 콘텐츠를 배포하는 데 허가를 요청하려고
(B) 베노아 씨에게 다가오는 마감기한을 상기시키려고
(C) 프로젝트 협업을 제안하려고
(D) 베노아 씨에게 잠재적인 문제점을 알리려고

해설 문자 메시지에서 일 때문에 웹사이트를 검색하다가 아이-팝핑 디자인이라는 업체에서 홈페이지에 베노아 씨의 노래를 사용하고 있는 것을 알았다. 허가했을 것 같지 않아서 알려 주고 싶었다(Anyway, I was just browsing a Web site for work when I noticed that a company called Eye-Popping Design is using your song on its home page ~ so I wanted to let you know about it)를 통해 베노아 씨에게 노래의 무단 사용을 알리기 위한 문자 메시지임을 알 수 있으므로, 정답은 (D)이다.

▶▶ **Paraphrasing** 지문의 **to let you know about** → 정답의 **To alert Mr. Benoit to**

197 연계

번역 헨클 씨에 대해 암시된 것은?
(A) 팩스턴 씨의 회사에 대한 동영상을 시청했다.
(B) 웹사이트 디자인을 위해 팩스턴 씨를 고용했다.
(C) 팩스턴 씨의 개인적인 친구이다.
(D) 팩스턴 씨의 법률 대리인이다.

해설 헨클 씨가 베노아 씨에게 쓴 문자 메시지에서 일 때문에 웹사이트를 검색하다가 아이-팝핑 디자인이라는 업체에서 홈페이지에 베노아 씨의 노래를 사용하고 있는 것을 알았다(I was just browsing a Web site for work when I noticed that a company called Eye-Popping Design is using your song on its home page)고 했으므로, 헨클 씨가 아이-팝핑 디자인의 홈페이지를 방문했음을 알 수 있다. 베노아 씨가 쓴 첫 번째 이메일에서 오늘 귀하의 그래픽디자인 업체 홈페이지의 홍보 동영상에 내 노래 "언덕에서"의 1분짜리 발췌 부분이 들어 있는 것을 발견하고 마음이 편치 않다(I was disturbed to discover today that the promotional video on your graphic design company's home page contains a one-minute excerpt of my song, "From the

Hills")를 통해 헨클 씨가 팩스턴 씨의 아이-팝핑 디자인 홍보 동영상을 시청했음을 유추할 수 있으므로, 정답은 (A)이다.

198 세부 사항

번역 첫 번째 이메일에 따르면, 베노아 씨는 음악으로 무엇을 했는가?
(A) CD로 발표했다
(B) 콘서트에서 연주했다
(C) 인터넷에 올렸다
(D) 광고에 사용하는 데 동의했다

해설 베노아 씨가 쓴 첫 번째 이메일에서 나는 작년에 이 노래를 작곡, 녹음하고 제 웹사이트를 통해 발표했다. 하지만 어떠한 개인업체에도 이를 사용하는 데 동의한 적이 없다(I wrote, recorded, and released this song through my Web site last year, but I have not agreed to its use by a private company of any kind)고 했다. 따라서 정답은 (C)이다.

▶▶ **Paraphrasing** 지문의 **released this song through my Web site** → 정답의 **Posted it on the Internet**

199 연계

번역 베노아 씨 음악의 대체 음악으로 어떤 노래가 제안되었는가?
(A) "활기찬 변주곡"
(B) "안드로이드로"
(C) "흩뿌려진 시간"
(D) "카리에로"

해설 베노아 씨가 쓴 첫 번째 이메일에서 나는 오늘 귀하의 그래픽디자인 업체 홈페이지의 홍보 동영상에 내 노래 "언덕에서"의 1분짜리 발췌 부분이 들어 있는 것을 발견하고 마음이 편치 않다(I was disturbed to discover today that the promotional video on your graphic design company's home page contains a one-minute excerpt of my song, "From the Hills")라고 하며 자신의 곡이 "언덕에서"임을 언급하고 있다. 두 번째 이메일의 표를 통해 "언덕에서"의 대체 음악으로 "카리에로"가 제안된 것을 확인할 수 있으므로, 정답은 (D)이다.

200 사실 관계 확인

번역 아이-팝핑 디자인에 대해 명시된 것은?
(A) 직원을 징계할 것이다.
(B) 스테판스키 씨에게 잘못된 정보를 받았다.
(C) 계정 폐쇄를 요청했다.
(D) 베노아 씨에게 공개 사과할 것이다.

해설 두 번째 이메일의 첫 번째 단락, 귀하의 계정을 관리했던 직원 스테판스키 씨는 귀하에게 말씀드린 것과 달리 베노아 씨의 음악을 사용할 권한을 받지 않았다(Contrary to what she told you, the employee who handled your account, Ms. Stefanski, did not have permission to use his music)를 통해 수신인(you)인 아이-팝핑 디자인의 팩스턴 씨가 거짓 정보를 제공받았음을 알 수 있으므로, 정답은 (B)이다.

▶▶ **Paraphrasing** 지문의 **Contrary to what she told you** → 정답의 **It was misinformed by Ms. Stefanski**

TEST 3

101 (A)	102 (B)	103 (C)	104 (D)	105 (C)
106 (B)	107 (B)	108 (A)	109 (C)	110 (B)
111 (D)	112 (D)	113 (C)	114 (A)	115 (A)
116 (A)	117 (B)	118 (A)	119 (A)	120 (D)
121 (C)	122 (B)	123 (B)	124 (A)	125 (D)
126 (C)	127 (B)	128 (A)	129 (A)	130 (A)
131 (B)	132 (C)	133 (A)	134 (B)	135 (A)
136 (C)	137 (B)	138 (D)	139 (D)	140 (C)
141 (D)	142 (D)	143 (B)	144 (D)	145 (C)
146 (C)	147 (B)	148 (B)	149 (C)	150 (D)
151 (B)	152 (C)	153 (D)	154 (B)	155 (C)
156 (D)	157 (B)	158 (C)	159 (D)	160 (C)
161 (B)	162 (C)	163 (A)	164 (A)	165 (B)
166 (D)	167 (A)	168 (D)	169 (C)	170 (D)
171 (D)	172 (A)	173 (B)	174 (A)	175 (D)
176 (D)	177 (A)	178 (C)	179 (B)	180 (C)
181 (A)	182 (D)	183 (B)	184 (B)	185 (C)
186 (A)	187 (C)	188 (D)	189 (B)	190 (A)
191 (C)	192 (B)	193 (C)	194 (A)	195 (C)
196 (B)	197 (D)	198 (C)	199 (B)	200 (A)

PART 5

101 형용사 어휘

해설 빈칸은 뒤의 명사(flight)를 수식하는 형용사 자리로, 문맥에 가장 알맞은 형용사 어휘를 찾아야 한다. 문맥상 '시간을 절약하려고 직항편을 타기로 했다'라는 의미가 자연스러우므로, 정답은 (A) direct이다. '직항편을 타다(take a direct flight)'라는 관용적인 표현으로 묶어서 기억하자. (B) precise(정확한, 정밀한), (C) durable(내구성 있는, 단단한), (D) formal(공식적인)은 의미상 적합하지 않다.

번역 돌라 씨는 시간을 절약하려고 오스틴에서 시카고행 직항편을 타기로 했다.

어휘 take a direct flight 직항편을 타다 in order to + 동사원형 ~하기 위해, ~하려고 save time 시간을 절약하다

102 인칭대명사의 격 _ 주격

해설 빈칸은 부사절 접속사(if)가 이끄는 부사절의 동사(do not understand) 앞 주어 자리이다. 주격 인칭대명사 (B) they와 소유대명사 (C) theirs 중에 앞에 있는 주절의 주어(Guests)를 대신 가리키고 있으므로, 정답은 (B) they이다.

번역 국제회의 손님들은 회화체 영어를 이해하지 못할 경우 통역사를 요청할 수 있다.

어휘 international conference 국제회의 request 요청하다 interpreter 통역사 spoken English 회화체[구어체] 영어

103 상관접속사

해설 빈칸 뒤에 나오는 접속사(nor)와 짝을 이루어 nor 앞의 명사(Ms. Lester)와 뒤의 명사(her partner)를 연결하는 단어를 선택해야 한다. 따라서 정답은 (C) Neither이다. (A) Both는 and와, (B) Not은 but과 짝을 이루어 쓰인다.

번역 레스터 씨도 그녀의 동업자도 그 고객의 최신 연락 정보를 찾지 못했다.

어휘 neither A nor B A도 B도 아니다 updated 최신의 contact details (자세한) 연락 정보 client 고객 both 둘 다

104 형용사 자리 _ 명사 수식

해설 빈칸 앞 한정사(some)와 명사(products) 사이에서 명사(products)를 수식하는 형용사 자리이므로, 정답은 (D) promotional이다. 동사 (A) promotes와 (B) promote, 부사 (C) promotionally는 품사상 적합하지 않다.

번역 프라임 부동산은 현재 및 유망 고객들에게 배포하려고 일부 판촉용품에 로고를 인쇄했다.

어휘 realty 부동산 print 인쇄하다 logo 로고, 상표 promotional product 판촉용품 distribution 배포 current 현재의 prospective customer 유망[잠재] 고객 promote 홍보[판촉]하다; 승진시키다

105 동사 어형 _ 태

해설 빈칸은 주어(The team leaders) 뒤 동사 자리로, 뒤에 나오는 전치사구(by the head of the department)의 수식을 받는다. 문맥상 '팀장들은 부서장에 의해 선발된다'라는 수동의 의미가 자연스러우므로, 정답은 (C) are selected이다. 능동 의미의 동사 (A) select, (B) are selecting, (D) selected는 주어와 동사의 능동관계를 나타내므로, 적합하지 않다.

번역 팀장들은 연공과 경력에 근거해 부서장에 의해 선발된다.

어휘 select 선발하다 the head of the department 부서장 based on ~에 근거[기초]해 seniority 연공(서열) experience 경험

106 부사 어휘

해설 빈칸은 조동사(will)와 동사원형(delay) 사이에서 동사 구문(delay the grand opening ceremony)을 수식하는 부사 자리이다. 문맥상 '강한 폭풍이 강타하면, 아마도 개업식을 미룰 것이다'라는 의미가 자연스러우므로, 정답은 (B) probably(아마, 십중팔구)이다. (A) rather(약간, 다소, 차라리), (C) seldom(좀처럼 ~ 않는), (D) ever(늘, 언제나)는 의미상 적합하지 않다.

번역 예상대로 강한 폭풍이 그 지역을 강타하면 매장 주인은 아마 개업식을 미룰 것이다.

어휘 severe storm 강한 폭풍 as expected 예상대로 delay 연기하다 grand opening ceremony 개업식 probably 아마, 십중팔구

107 부사 어휘

해설 빈칸 앞의 과거부터 현재까지의 의미를 나타내는 현재완료시제 동사(has been collected)를 수식하는 부사 자리이다. 문맥상 '현재까지 모금되었다'는 의미가 자연스러우므로, 정답은 (B) so far(지금까지, 현재까지)이다. (A) in brief(간단히), (C) even so(그렇지만, 그렇다고 해서), (D) at last(마침내, 드디어)는 의미상 적합하지 않다.

번역 안타깝게도, 현재까지 그 자선단체의 모금 목표 중 10%만 모금되었다.

어휘 unfortunately 안타깝게도, 유감스럽게도   charity 자선단체
fundraising 모금   collect 모으다, 수집하다   so far 현재[지금]까지

108 비교급

해설 빈칸은 앞에 있는 to부정사 to stay를 수식하는 부사 자리이다. 부사의 비교급 (A) longer와 원급 (B) long 중에 뒤에 비교급과 함께 쓰이는 접속사(than)가 있으므로, 정답은 (A) longer이다. 명사 (C) length와 동사 (D) lengthen은 품사상 적합하지 않다.

번역 워번 씨는 호텔 안내 데스크에 전화해 원래 예약한 것보다 더 오래 머물 계획이라고 확정했다.

어휘 front desk 안내 데스크   confirm 확정하다, 확인하다   plan to + 동사원형 ~할 계획이다   stay 머물다   original 원래의 booking 예약   length 길이   lengthen 늘이다, 길게 하다

109 전치사 어휘

해설 빈칸은 명사(the pharmacy) 앞에 올 수 있는 전치사 자리이다. 문맥상 '약국 맞은편 정거장'이라는 의미가 자연스러우므로, 정답은 (C) opposite (맞은편의)이다. (A) since(~ 이래로), (C) through(~을 통해), (D) against(~에 반대하여)는 의미상 적합하지 않다.

번역 홀트 쇼핑센터에 가는 가장 빠른 방법은 약국 맞은편 정거장에서 409번 버스를 타는 것이다.

어휘 fastest 가장 빠른   pharmacy 약국   opposite 맞은[반대]편의

110 부사 어휘

해설 빈칸 앞 조동사(can)와 동사원형(make) 사이에서 동사 구문(make their monthly payments)을 수식하는 부사 자리이다. 문맥상 '이제 전화로 월 공과금을 납부할 수 있다'라는 의미가 자연스러우므로, 정답은 (B) now(지금, 이제)이다. (A) else(또 다른, 그 밖의), (C) there(거기), (D) well(잘, 좋게)은 의미상 적합하지 않다.

번역 사우스이스트 유틸리티즈 고객들은 이제 우리 자동화 시스템을 이용해 전화로 월 공과금을 납부할 수 있다.

어휘 utilities (전기, 수도, 가스 등의) 공공 서비스   customer 고객, 손님 make a payment 지불[납부]하다   monthly 월별의, 한 달에 한 번 by phone 전화로   automated system 자동화 시스템

111 전치사 어휘

해설 빈칸은 명사(the shareholders) 앞에 올 수 있는 전치사 자리이다. 문맥상 '주주들 사이에 논의가 있었다'라는 의미가 자연스러우므로, 정답은 (D) among(~ 사이에, ~ 중에)이다. 참고로 전치사(among) 뒤에는 주로 복수명사가 나온다. (A) inside(~ 안의), (B) at(~에), (C) onto(~ 위로)는 의미상 적합하지 않다.

번역 CEO가 유능하게 회사를 운영하고 있는지를 놓고 주주들 사이에 얼마간 논의가 있었다.

어휘 discussion 논의, 토론   shareholder 주주   as to ~에 관해 whether ~인지 아닌지   competently 유능하게, 괜찮게   operate 운영하다   business 사업(체), 회사

112 부사 자리 _ 동사 수식

해설 빈칸 앞에 있는 동사(is not running)를 수식하는 부사 자리이므로, 정답은 (D) profitably이다. 동명사/현재분사 (A) profiting, 명사/동사 (B) profits, 형용사 (C) profitable은 품사상 적합하지 않다.

번역 애틀랜타에 있는 캐러웨이 일렉트로닉스 공장은 12월까지 수익을 내지 못하면 폐쇄될 위기에 처해 있다.

어휘 electronics 전자   profit 수익, 이윤   profitable 수익성 있는, 이익을 내는   profitably 수익성 있게, 이익이 되게   at risk of ~의 위험이 있는, ~의 위기에 처한   closure 폐쇄, 폐업

113 비교급 강조 부사

해설 빈칸 뒤 비교급(more dangerous)을 강조하는 부사 자리이므로 정답은 비교급 강조 부사인 (C) far이다. 참고로 비교급을 강조하는 부사로는 far 외에 much, even, still, a lot 등이 있다. (B) too, (D) very는 비교급을 수식할 수 없다.

번역 최 씨의 회계사는 한 회사에 투자하는 것이 자산을 다양하게 분산 투자하는 것보다 더 위험하다고 설명했다.

어휘 accountant 회계사   explain 설명하다   invest in ~에 투자하다 single 하나의, 단일한   far + 비교급 훨씬 더 ~한   dangerous 위험한   diverse 다양한   portfolio 분산 투자, 포트폴리오   asset 자산

114 명사 어휘

해설 빈칸은 to부정사(to pay off)의 목적어 역할을 하는 명사 자리로, 뒤에 나오는 생략된 관계대명사(which/that)가 이끄는 절(it incurred to cover opening costs)의 수식을 받는다. 문맥상 '개업 비용을 마련하기 위해 빚진 돈'이라는 의미가 자연스러우므로, 정답은 (A) debt(빚, 부채)이다. (B) stock(주식, 재고), (C) receipt(영수증, 수령), (D) term(기간, 용어)은 의미상 적합하지 않다.

번역 첫 해 동안 수익이 많았던 덕에 프레쉬타임 제과점은 개업 비용을 마련하기 위해 빚진 돈을 다 갚을 수 있었다.

어휘 thanks to ~덕분에   strong revenue 많은 수익   bakery 제과점, 빵집   be able to + 동사원형 ~할 수 있다   pay off 다 갚다, 청산하다 incur (비용을) 발생시키다, 초래하다   cover (돈을) 대다, 마련하다 debt 빚, 부채

115 동사 어휘

해설 빈칸 앞 동사(is)와 함께 수동태 동사를 나타내는 과거분사 자리로, 문맥에 어울리는 어휘를 찾아야 한다. 문맥상 '월급이 평균 이하이지만, 다른 식으로 보상을 받는다'라는 의미가 자연스러우므로 정답은 (A) compensated(보상하다, 벌충하다)이다. (B) impressed(인상을 남기다), (C) emphasized(강조하다), (D) congratulated(축하하다)는 의미상 적합하지 않다.

번역 메츠 테크는 월급이 평균 이하이지만 직원들이 다른 식으로 보상을 받는다.

어휘 monthly salary 월급   below average 평균 이하   staff 직원 compensate 보상하다, 벌충하다

116 명사 자리 _ 동사의 주어

해설 빈칸 뒤 동사(takes over)의 주어 자리이며, Director Clement's의 수식을 받는 명사 자리이다. 명사 (A) assistant(비서, 보조)와 (B) assistance(지원, 보조) 중에 문맥상 '비서가 넘겨받는다'라는 의미가 자연스러우므로, 정답은 (A) assistant이다. 과거시제 동사/과거분사 (C) assisted와 동명사/현재분사 (D) assisting은 품사상 적합하지 않다.

번역 클레멘트 이사가 사무실을 비울 때마다, 필요한 업무가 발생하면 비서가 넘겨받아 처리한다.

어휘 whenever ~할 때마다 be away from 자리를 비우다 director 이사 take over 인수하다, 인계 받다 necessary 필요한 duty 직무, 업무 arise 발생하다, 생기다 assistant 비서, 보조 assistance 지원, 보조 assist 돕다, 보조하다

117 인칭대명사의 격 _ 소유대명사

해설 빈칸은 앞에 위치한 to부정사(to wear)의 목적어 자리이다. 목적어 자리에 올 수 있는 목적격 인칭대명사 (A) her, 소유대명사 (B) hers, 재귀대명사 (C) herself 중에 문맥상 '그녀의 것(그녀의 이름표)을 착용하다'라는 의미가 자연스러우므로, 정답은 소유대명사 (B) hers(her name badge)이다. to wear는 사람을 나타내는 명사를 목적어로 취할 수 없으므로, 사람을 나타내는 인칭대명사 (A) her와 (C) herself는 적합하지 않다.

번역 대부분의 인턴은 유니폼에 핀으로 이름표를 달았지만, 네이퀸 씨는 깜빡 잊고 이름표를 착용하지 않았다.

어휘 most of 대부분의 name badge 이름표 pin 핀으로 고정하다 uniform 유니폼, 제복 forget to + 동사원형 ~하는 것을 잊다, 깜빡 잊고 ~하지 않다 wear 착용하다

118 부사 어휘

해설 빈칸 앞 동사원형(fall)과 짝을 이루어 '부서지다, 망가지다, 무너지다'라는 의미를 나타내는 부사를 선택해야 한다. 따라서 정답은 (A) apart이다. (C) across는 fall과 짝을 이루어 '우연히 만나다'라는 의미를 나타낸다. (B) quite와 (D) less는 의미상 어색하므로 적합하지 않다.

번역 소포들이 제대로 안전하게 묶여 있지 않으면 배송팀이 운반할 때 망가질 것이다.

어휘 package 짐, 소포 tie 묶다 properly 제대로, 적절하게 securely 안전하게 fall apart 부서지다, 허물어지다, 망가지다 move 운반하다 shipping team 배송팀

119 부사 어휘

해설 빈칸 앞의 부사(still)와 함께 형용사의 비교급(more expensive)을 수식하는 부사 자리이다. 문맥상 '여전히 상당히 더 비싼'이라는 의미가 자연스러우므로, 정답은 (A) substantially(상당히, 크게)이다. (B) unanimously(만장일치로), (C) respectfully(정중하게), (D) accurately(정확하게)는 의미상 적합하지 않다.

번역 시내 집값은 여전히 교외보다 상당히 더 비싸지만 통근 시간은 더 적절하다.

어휘 housing price 집값 substantially 크게, 상당히 suburb 교외 commuting time 통근 시간 reasonable 합당한, 적절한

120 명사 어휘

해설 빈칸 뒤에 나오는 동사(was considered)의 주어 자리로, 빈칸 뒤 과거분사 구문(submitted to the publisher)의 수식을 받는다. 문맥상 뒤에 나오는 명사(a possible best seller)와 동격 관계 나타내는 명사를 선택해야 하므로, 정답은 (D) manuscript(원고)이다. (A) parcel(꾸러미, 소포), (B) contract(계약, 계약서), (C) bulletin(게시, 공고)은 의미상 적합하지 않다.

번역 출판사에 제출된 원고는 흥미로운 줄거리와 매력적인 등장인물 덕에 베스트셀러가 될 가능성이 있다고 간주되었다.

어휘 submit 제출하다 publisher 출판사 consider 간주하다, 여기다, 고려하다 possible 가능성 있는 due to ~ 때문에 intriguing 흥미로운 plot 줄거리, 구성 charming 매력적인 character 등장인물 manuscript 원고

121 동명사

해설 빈칸은 앞에 있는 주어(The first step)와 동격 관계를 이루는 주격보어 자리이다. 빈칸 뒤 명사구(the contribution of each employee)를 목적어로 취하면서, 빈칸 앞 부사(sincerely)의 수식을 받으므로, 정답은 동명사 (C) acknowledging이다. 명사 (B) acknowledgement는 목적어를 취할 수 없고, 부사의 수식을 받지 않는다. 동사 (A) acknowledges와 과거분사/과거시제 동사 (D) acknowledged는 품사상 적합하지 않다.

번역 긍정적인 근무환경을 만드는 첫 단계는 직원 각자의 기여를 진심으로 인정하는 것이다.

어휘 step 단계 positive 긍정적인 work environment 근무환경 sincerely 진심으로 contribution 기여, 공헌 employee 사원, 직원 acknowledge 인정하다 acknowledgement 인정

122 전치사 어휘

해설 빈칸은 명사(his career) 앞에 올 수 있는 전치사 자리이다. 문맥상 '경력 내내 많은 도전을 극복했다'는 의미가 자연스러우므로, 정답은 (B) throughout(내내, 전역에)이다. (A) aboard(탑승하여, 승선하여), (C) between(~ 중간에, 사이에), (D) than(~보다)은 의미상 적합하지 않다.

번역 면접을 치르는 동안 그 구직자는 자신의 경력 내내 어떻게 많은 도전을 극복했는지 설명했다.

어휘 during ~ 동안 job candidate 구직자 describe 설명하다, 기술하다 overcome 극복하다 a number of 많은 challenge 도전, 어려움 career 경력, 이력

123 부사 어휘

해설 빈칸은 부사절 접속사(As)가 이끄는 부사절의 동사(were needed)를 수식하는 부사 자리이다. 문맥상 '긴급히 필요해서 빠른 인쇄 서비스를 받기로 했다'라는 의미가 자연스러우므로, 정답은 (B) urgently(긴급하게)이다. (A) steadily(꾸준히), (C) typically(일반적으로, 전형적으로), (D) entirely(완전히, 전적으로)는 의미상 적합하지 않다.

번역 그 고객은 현수막이 급히 필요해서 추가 요금을 내고 빠른 인쇄 서비스를 받기로 했다.

어휘 banner 현수막 need 필요하다 customer 고객, 손님 opt
to + 동사원형 ~하기로 (택)하다 pay extra 추가 요금을 내다
express 빠른, 급행 printing 인쇄 urgently 긴급하게

124 인칭대명사의 격 _ 목적격

해설 빈칸은 to부정사(to caution)의 목적어 자리이다. 목적어 자리에 올 수 있
는 인칭대명사 (A) you, 소유대명사 (B) yours, 재귀대명사 (D) yourself
중에 문맥상 '귀하에게 주의를 주는 것'이라는 의미가 자연스러우므로, 정
답은 (A) you이다. 재귀대명사 (D) yourself는 to부정사(to caution)의
생략된 주어(for us)와 일치하지 않으므로, 적합하지 않다.

번역 생산구역에 들어가기 전, 산업용 기계가 가동되고 있을지도 모른다고 주의를
주는 것이 우리의 책임이다.

어휘 production area 생산구역, 제조구역 responsibility 책임
caution 주의를 주다, 경고하다 industrial machinery 산업용 기계
in use 사용중인

125 명사 어휘

해설 빈칸 앞 명사(power)와 함께 복합명사를 이루는 명사 자리로, 빈칸
을 포함한 복합명사는 앞의 전치사(during)의 목적어 역할을 한다. 문
맥상 '정전이 일어난 4시간 동안'이라는 의미가 자연스러우므로, 정답은
(D) outage(공급정지)이다. '정전(power outage)'이라는 관용적인 표현
으로 묶어서 기억하자. (A) yield(산출량, 수익률), (B) rating(순위, 평가),
(C) distribution(분배, 분포, 유통)은 의미상 적합하지 않다.

번역 히코리 식당은 정전이 일어난 4시간 동안 냉장고 안에 있던 식품을 전부 버릴
수밖에 없었다.

어휘 have no choice but to + 동사원형 ~할 수밖에 없다 discard
버리다, 폐기하다 refrigerator 냉장고 power outage 정전

126 분사 자리

해설 빈칸 뒤 전치사구(in historic homes)와 함께 앞에 있는 명사(a
contractor)를 수식하는 분사 자리이다. 과거분사 (A) specialized와 현
재분사 (C) specializing 중에 문맥상 '고택 보수를 전문으로 하는 도급업
체'라는 능동의 의미가 자연스러우므로, 정답은 (C) specializing이다. 동
사 (B) specialize와 명사 (D) specialty는 품사상 적합하지 않다.

번역 원래 모습을 유지하기 위해 집주인은 건물을 보수하는 데 고택 전문업체를 고
용했다.

어휘 maintain 유지하다 authenticity 진품임, 원본임 homeowner
자택 소유자, 집주인 hire 고용하다 contractor 도급업자, 하청업자
specialize in ~ 전문이다 historic home 고택 renovate
보수[수리]하다, 개조하다 property 부동산, 건물, 재산 specialty
전문, 장기; 특산품

127 명사 자리 _ 동사의 목적어

해설 빈칸 앞 동사원형(make or change)의 목적어 역할을 하는 명사 자리
이다. 복수명사 (B) appointments와 단수명사 (D) appointment 중
에 빈칸 앞에 한정사가 없으므로 정답은 복수명사 (B) appointments이
다. 셀 수 있는 명사의 단수형인 (D) appointment 앞에는 한정사가 나
와야 하고, 과거시제 동사/과거분사 (A) appointed와 동명사/현재분사

(C) appointing은 품사상 적합하지 않다.

번역 그 치과는 고객이 온라인으로 진료약속을 잡거나 변경할 수 있도록 웹사이트
에 새로운 기능들을 추가했다.

어휘 dental clinic 치과 add A to B B에 A를 더하다[추가하다]
feature 기능, 특징 customer 고객, 손님 appointment (진료)
약속[예약], 임명 appoint 임명[지명]하다

128 명사 자리 _ 전치사의 목적어

해설 빈칸 앞 전치사(to)의 목적어 역할을 하고, 형용사(local)의 수식
을 받는 명사 자리이다. 명사 (A) mechanic(정비사, 수리공)과
(C) mechanism(기계장치, 구조) 중에 문맥상 '정비사에게 가져갔
다'라는 의미가 자연스러우므로, 정답은 (A) mechanic이다. 동사
(B) mechanize와 형용사 (D) mechanistic은 품사상 적합하지 않다.

번역 자동차 엔진이 이상한 소리를 내기 시작하자 페이텔 씨는 자동차를 즉시 지역
정비사에게 가져가 점검을 받았다.

어휘 vehicle 자동차, 탈것 unusual 이상한 immediately 즉시, 당장
local 지역의, 현지의 inspection 점검, 조사 mechanic 정비사,
수리공 mechanize 기계화하다 mechanism 기제, 장치, 체계
mechanistic 기계(론)적인

129 복합관계부사

해설 빈칸은 앞뒤의 문장을 한 문장으로 연결할 수 있는 접속사 자리이다. 접
속사 역할을 할 수 있는 (A) however(어떤 방법으로든, 어떻게라도, 아
무리 ~해도)와 (D) once(일단 ~하면) 중에 문맥상 '어떤 방식을 선택
하든지'라는 의미가 자연스러우므로, 정답은 (A) however이다. 부사
(B) afterward와 명사절/부사절 접속사 (C) where는 품사상 적합하지
않다.

번역 연례 엔지니어링 무역박람회에 참가하는 직원들은 어떤 방식을 선택하든 행사
현장으로 가면 된다.

어휘 attend 참가하다 site 장소, 현장

130 전치사

해설 빈칸은 명사구(his extensive experience) 앞에 올 수 있는 전치사 자리
이다. 문맥상 '광범위한 업계 경험과 폭넓은 인맥에도 불구하고'가 자연스
러우므로 정답은 (A) in spite of(~에도 불구하고)이다. 부사 (B) not to
mention(~은 말할 것도 없이)과 (C) as much as(~만큼 많이)는 품사
상 적합하지 않고, 전치사 (D) on behalf of(~을 대신하여, ~을 대표하
여)는 의미상 적합하지 않다.

번역 아사노 씨는 광범위한 업계 경험과 폭넓은 전문 인맥에도 불구하고 재무 컨설
턴트 자리를 제안 받지 못했다.

어휘 offer 제안[제공]하다 financial 재무의, 금융의 in spite of ~에도
불구하고 extensive 광범위한 experience 경험 broad 폭넓은
professional network 전문 인맥[네트워크]

PART 6

131-134 공지

어휘 require 필요하다 upcoming 다가오는, 곧 있을 crew 작업반 complete 완료하다, 마치다 task 작업, 일 advance preparation 사전준비 as much as possible 가능한 한 많이 left 남아 있는 abandoned 버려진, 폐기된 in that case 그럴 경우, 그렇게 되면 cleaning staff 청소 직원들 dispose of ~을 처분하다 item 품목, 항목, 물건 avoid 피하다, 방지하다 unnecessary 불필요한, 필요 없는 be responsible for ~을 책임지다 belongings 소지품, 소유물 direct A to B A를 B에게 보내다 immediate supervisor 직속 상사[상관]

131 문맥에 맞는 문장 고르기

번역 (A) 직원들은 가장 마음에 드는 색을 투표로 정할 수 있습니다.
(B) 모든 표지판과 포스터를 복도에서 철거해야 합니다.
(C) 사무실 보수작업을 위해 자금이 편성되었습니다.
(D) 작업 요청서는 정비팀으로 직접 보내야 합니다.

해설 빈칸 뒤에 나오는 문장 '이는 8월 1일에 있을 페인트칠 작업을 위해 필요한 일입니다(This is required for the upcoming painting work on August 1)'를 통해 페인트칠을 위한 사전작업(This)이 필요하다는 것을 알 수 있다. 따라서 빈칸에는 This에 대해 구체적으로 밝히는 것이 문맥상 자연스러우므로, 정답은 (B)이다.

어휘 vote on ~에 대해 투표하다 remove 제거[철거]하다, 없애다 allocate 편성하다, 배정하다 renovation 개보수, 수리 directly 직접, 바로 maintenance team 정비팀

132 부사절 접속사

해설 빈칸은 두 개의 완전한 절을 연결할 수 있는 부사절 접속사 자리이다. 부사절 접속사 (C) Given that(~을 고려하면, ~을 감안하면)과 (D) Even though(~에도 불구하고, 비록 ~일지라도) 중에 문맥상 '작업반이 작업을 끝낼 시간이 주말밖에 없다는 점을 감안하면'이라는 의미가 자연스러우므로, 정답은 (C) Given that이다. 참고로 given that은 considering that(~을 고려하면)과 바꾸어 쓸 수도 있다. 접속부사 (A) In addition (덧붙여, 게다가)과 (B) As a result(결과적으로)는 품사상 적합하지 않다.

133 동사 어휘

해설 빈칸 앞 동사(will be)와 함께 수동태 동사를 나타내는 과거분사 자리이다. 문맥상 '금요일 오후 5시 이후 벽에 남아 있는 물건은 무엇이든 버려진 것으로 간주된다'는 의미가 자연스러우므로, 정답은 (A) considered(간주

하다, ~로 여기다, 고려하다)이다. (B) anticipated(기대하다, 예상하다), (C) disputed(논쟁하다, 다투다), (D) finalized(결말짓다, 마무리하다)는 의미상 적합하지 않다.

어휘 consider 간주하다, 여기다

134 명사 어휘

해설 빈칸 앞에 있는 to부정사(To avoid)의 목적어 역할을 하는 명사 자리로, 앞의 지시형용사(this)와 형용사(unnecessary)의 수식을 받는다. 앞의 지시형용사(this)는 앞 문장(the cleaning staff will have to dispose of these items)을 대신 가리키고 있으므로, 빈칸에는 이를 포괄적으로 나타내는 명사를 선택해야 한다. 따라서 정답은 (B) burden(짐, 부담)이다. (A) risk(위험), (C) treatment(치료, 처치, 대우), (D) precaution (예방책, 예방 조치)은 의미상 적합하지 않다.

어휘 burden 짐, 부담

135-138 웹페이지

어휘 animal shelter 동물보호소 in operation 운영[영업/작동] 중인 provide 제공하다 veterinarian care 동물 치료[돌봄] adoption 입양 emergency housing 긴급 주거, 임시 거처 abandoned 버려진, 유기된 unwanted 원치 않는 pet 반려동물 in addition to ~ 외에, ~에 더하여 monetary donation 금품 기부 blanket 담요 cleaning product 청소용품 pet toy 반려동물 장난감 tax deductible 세금[세액]을 공제받을 수 있는 registered 등록된 charity 자선단체 item 물품, 품목 donate 기부[기증]하다 make a difference 도움을 주다, 영향을 미치다, 효과를 내다 cage 우리 exercise 운동하다[시키다] obedience training 복종 훈련 find out more about ~에 관해 더 알아보다 volunteer 자원봉사하다

135 명사 어휘

해설 빈칸 앞 전치사(in)의 목적어 역할을 하는 명사 자리로, 문맥에 자연스러운 명사를 찾아야 한다. 문맥상 '약 2년 동안 운영해 왔다'는 의미가 자연스러우므로 정답은 (A) operation(운영, 영업, 작동)이다. (B) attraction(매력, 명소), (C) publication(출판, 발행), (D) investigation(조사, 수사)은 의미상 적합하지 않다.

136 수량형용사

해설 빈칸 뒤 복수명사(donations)를 한정 수식하는 수량형용사 자리이다. 복수명사를 한정 수식할 수 있는 (B) Both(둘 다)와 (C) All(모든) 중에 앞 문장(In addition to monetary donations, we need pet food, blankets, cleaning products, and pet toys)에서 둘 이상의 다양한 기부방식을 언급하고 있으므로, 정답은 (C) All이다. (A) One과 (D) Each 는 셀 수 있는 명사의 단수형을 한정 수식한다.

137 문맥에 맞는 문장 고르기

번역 (A) 힘을 합쳐 우리의 모금 마련 목표액을 달성합시다.
(B) 시간 나실 때 이 일들을 도와 주실 수 있습니다.
(C) 이번에는 저희가 새 물품과 사용 흔적이 별로 없는 물품을 받을 수 있습니다.
(D) 저희 직원들이 귀하께 맞는 반려동물을 찾아드리게 되어 기쁩니다.

해설 빈칸 앞의 두 문장 '기증품이나 기부금이 없더라도 동물보호소에서 도움을 주실 수 있다. 우리 청소, 반려동물 운동시키기, 복종 훈련에 도움이 필요하다(Even if you do not have items or money to donate, you can make a difference at the shelter. We need help with cleaning cages, exercising the pets, and providing obedience training)'에서 금전적인 방법 외에 도움을 줄 수 있는 다양한 방법을 나열하고 있다. 따라서 빈칸에는 이러한 일(these tasks)의 실행과 관련된 내용이 이어지는 것이 문맥상 자연스러우므로, 정답은 (B)이다.

어휘 free time 자유시간 assist 돕다, 지원하다 gently used items 별로 사용하지 않은 물건

138 동사 어형 _ 명령문

해설 빈칸은 명령문의 생략된 주어(you) 뒤에 나오는 동사원형 자리이므로, 정답은 (B) contact이다. 과거동사 (A) contacted 앞에는 주어(you)를 생략할 수 없다.

어휘 contact 연락하다, 접촉하다

139-142 이메일

수신: 캐런 얀코프스키 〈kjankowski@metromail.net〉
발신: 셀마 아큐리 〈selma@boonerentals.com〉
날짜: 1월 4일
제목: 208호

얀코프스키 씨께,

1월 31일에 귀하의 임대차 계약을 **139종결하겠다는** 계획을 서면으로 알려주셔서 감사합니다. 절차 안내 정보를 첨부했습니다. 저희가 최종 점검을 위해 귀하의 아파트에 방문하기 **140전에** 건물에서 개인 소유물을 모두 치워 주셔야 합니다. 아파트를 깨끗이 청소할 수 있게 반드시 **141충분한** 시간을 두시기 바랍니다. **142아파트는 넘겨받으셨을 때와 동일하게 모든 표면의 먼지를 제거하고, 카펫을 진공 청소하고, 주방용 조리대는 문질러 청소한 상태여야 합니다. 이렇게 되어 있지 않으면 저희가 청소비를 청구합니다.**

질문이 있으면 언제라도 제게 이메일로 문의하시기 바랍니다.

셀마 아큐리
분 임대 건물 관리인

어휘 unit (아파트) 호실 written notice 서면 통지 lease agreement 임대차 계약 attach 첨부하다 process 과정, 절차 inspection 점검, 검사 personal belongings 개인 소유물 remove 제거[철거]하다, 없애다 property 재산, 부동산, 건물 be sure to+동사원형 반드시 ~하다 thoroughly 깨끗이, 철저하게 condition 상태 surface 표면 dust 먼지를 털다 vacuum 진공 청소하다 countertop 주방용 조리대 scrub 문질러서 닦다 property manager 건물 관리인 rental 임대

139 to부정사

해설 빈칸 뒤 명사(your lease agreement)를 목적어로 취하면서, 앞에 있는 명사(plans)를 수식하는 자리이다. plans는 to부정사의 수식을 받는 명사이므로, 정답은 (D) to terminate이다. 〈plan+to부정사〉의 형태로 묶어서 기억하자.

어휘 terminate 종결하다, 끝내다

140 부사절 접속사

해설 빈칸은 두 개의 완전한 절을 연결해 주는 부사절 접속사 자리이다. 문맥상 '최종 점검을 위해 귀하의 아파트에 방문하기 전에, 건물에서 개인 소유물을 모두 치워 주셔야 합니다'라는 의미가 자연스러우므로, 정답은 (C) Before(~ 전에)이다. 부사절 접속사 (A) Now that(~ 때문에, ~이므로), (B) As long as(~하는 한), (D) Even if(~에도 불구하고, 비록 ~일지라도)는 의미상 적합하지 않다.

141 형용사 어휘

해설 빈칸은 to부정사(to leave)의 목적어 역할을 하는 명사(time)를 수식하는 형용사 자리이다. 참고로, 명사(time)는 뒤에 나오는 to부정사 구문(to thoroughly clean the apartment)의 수식도 받는다. 문맥상 '아파트를 깨끗이 청소할 충분한 시간을 남기다'라는 의미가 자연스러우므로, 정답은 (D) adequate(충분한, 적절한)이다. (A) imperative(반드시 해야 하는, 긴요한), (B) complete(완성된, 완전한), (C) dependable(믿을 수 있는, 의지할 수 있는)은 의미상 적합하지 않다.

어휘 adequate 적절한, 충분한

142 문맥에 맞는 문장 고르기

번역 (A) 정돈된 생활 환경을 누리실 수 있습니다.
(B) 그러므로 마지막 임대료를 1월에 지불하게 됩니다.
(C) 가능하다면 저희 직원들이 수리해 드리겠습니다.
(D) 이렇게 되어 있지 않으면 저희가 청소비를 청구합니다.

해설 빈칸 앞 문장 '아파트는 넘겨받았을 때와 동일하게 모든 표면의 먼지를 제거하고, 카펫을 진공 청소하고, 주방용 조리대는 문질러 청소한 상태여야 한다(It should be in the same condition in which you received it, with all surfaces dusted, carpets vacuumed, and countertops scrubbed)'에서 아파트 임대 종료 후의 아파트 상태에 대한 요구사항을 밝히고 있다. 따라서 빈칸에는 이 요건을 충족하지 못했을 경우에 대해 언급하는 것이 문맥상 자연스러우므로, 정답은 (D)이다.

143-146 편지

월슨 스포츠용품
에코레인 1901번지
뉴욕 주 10601 화이트플레인스

담당자 귀하,

저는 최근에 잠수복과 그 밖의 몇 가지 서핑 장비를 구입하려고 귀사를 방문했습니다. 수상 스포츠 매장에서 켄에게 도움을 받았는데, 그의 인내심과 **143**정중한 태도에 감명을 받았습니다. 그는 시간을 내어 제게 선호하는 취향과 사용 목적을 물었습니다. 이런 **144**필요들을 고려하여 몇 가지 제품을 추천해 주더군요. 이런 개인적 관심에 제가 얼마나 **145**고마웠는지 말로 다 할 수 없습니다. **146**같은 규모의 대다수 점포에서는 질문에 답해 줄 사람을 찾기가 불가능합니다. 귀 점포는 그렇지 않아서 기쁩니다, 제 친구들과 가족에게 월슨 운동용품점을 확실히 추천하겠습니다.

홀리 매켄지

어휘 sporting goods 운동[스포츠]용품 to whom it may concern 담당자[관계자]에게 recently 최근에 purchase 구입하다, 사다 wetsuit 잠수복, 고무 옷 surfing gear 서핑[파도타기] 장비 assist 돕다, 지원하다 water sports department 수상 스포츠 매장 be impressed with ~에 감명을 받다, 좋은 인상을 받다 patience 인내심 behavior 행동, 태도 take the time to+동사원형 시간을 내어 ~하다 preference 선호(도) intended usage 사용 목적, 의도하는 용도 take ~ into consideration ~을 고려하다 recommend 추천하다 product 제품 personal attention 개인적 관심 impossible 불가능한 definitely 확실히, 분명히

143 형용사 자리 _ 명사 수식

해설 빈칸은 명사(behavior)를 수식하는 형용사 자리이므로, 정답은 (B) respectful이다. 명사/동사 (A) respects와 (D) respect, 부사 (C) respectfully는 품사상 적합하지 않다.

어휘 respectful 정중한

144 명사 어휘

해설 빈칸 앞에 있는 동명사(Taking)의 목적어 역할을 하는 명사 자리로, 앞의 지시형용사(these)의 한정 수식을 받는다. 앞의 지시형용사(these)는 앞 문장의 '선호하는 취향과 사용 목적(my preferences and intended usage)'을 가리키고 있으므로, 빈칸에는 이와 유사한 의미의 명사를 선택해야 한다. 따라서 정답은 (D) needs(필요, 요구)이다. (A) amounts(양, 총액), (B) complaints(불만, 불평), (C) assets(자산)는 의미상 적합하지 않다.

어휘 needs 필요

145 동사 어휘

해설 빈칸 앞에 있는 명사절 접속사(how much)가 이끄는 명사절의 동사 자리로, 빈칸 뒤에 나오는 명사구(this personal attention)를 목적어로 취한다. 문맥상 '이런 개인적 관심에 제가 얼마나 고마웠는지'라는 의미가 자연스러우므로, 정답은 (C) appreciated(고마워하다, 인정하다)이다.

(A) celebrated(경축하다, 기념하다), (B) satisfied(만족시키다, 충족시키다), (D) promoted(촉진하다, 홍보하다, 승진시키다)는 의미상 적합하지 않다.

어휘 appreciate 감사하다, 감상하다

146 문맥에 맞는 문장 고르기

번역 (A) 제가 구입한 물건은 품질이 좋아 보입니다.
(B) 그것들 중 일부가 이 편지로 해결되기를 바랍시다.
(C) 귀 점포는 그렇지 않아서 기쁩니다.
(D) 구비된 계절 상품들이 예상보다 좋았습니다.

해설 빈칸 앞 문장 '같은 규모의 대다수 점포에서는 질문에 답해 줄 사람을 찾기가 불가능하다(At most stores of your size, it is impossible to find someone to answer questions)'를 통해 빈칸에는 방문한 점포는 같은 규모의 대다수 점포와 달랐다는 내용이 이어지는 것이 문맥상 자연스러우므로, 정답은 (C)이다.

어휘 resolve 해결하다, 풀다 establishment 점포, 시설 better than expected 예상보다 나은

PART 7

147-148 양식

마리골라 인더스트리즈
정보통신기술 부서

148이름: 라비 세갈   사원 ID: 1394
부서: 마케팅   내선번호: 24

물품 #: 30429
147내역: 휴대용 프로젝터

내용: B 회의실에서 사용할 목적
147대출일자: 1월 18일

업무용으로만 사용
148주의: 24시간 이내에 사용자가 반납할 것. IT 팀에서 물품 수거하지 않음.
승인자: 크리스틴 네리   일자: 1월 18일

어휘 information technology 정보통신 기술 extension 내선(번호) portable 휴대용의 retrieve 되찾아오다

147 주제 / 목적

번역 세갈 씨는 왜 양식을 제출하는가?
(A) 회의 공간을 예약하기 위해
(B) 공급 주문을 하기 위해
(C) 장비를 대여하기 위해
(D) 수리 서비스를 요청하기 위해

해설 양식의 내역을 보면 1월 18일(Check-out Date: January 18)에 휴대용 프로젝터(Description: Portable projector)를 빌렸다는 것을 알 수 있으므로, 정답은 (C)이다.

▶▶ **Paraphrasing** 지문의 **Portable projector** → 정답의 **a device**

148 추론 / 암시

번역 세갈 씨는 무엇을 할 계획이겠는가?
(A) 회의실 조사
(B) 직접 물품 반납하기
(C) 부서 예산 수정하기
(D) 급행 배송 받기

해설 양식 하단의 주의 사항을 보면 24시간 이내에 사용자가 반납해야 한다(To be returned by user within 24 hours)고 했다. 따라서 사용자인 세갈 씨가 직접 물품을 반납할 것임을 알 수 있으므로, 정답은 (B)이다.

▶▶ **Paraphrasing** 지문의 **be returned by user**
→ 정답의 **Drop off an item in person**

149-150 광고

앤크워스 주식회사 – 최상의 보안서비스
www.ancworthincorporated.com

앤크워스 주식회사는 귀하가 귀하 및 임직원의 심적 평화뿐만 아니라 귀하의 부지를 지키고자 하시는 것을 잘 알고 있습니다. 저희는 유명 브랜드의 카메라와 경보장치부터 현장 직원에 이르기까지 다양한 보안 서비스를 제공합니다. **149 저희는 또한 실효성을 극대화하기 위해 지역 경찰서와 지속적인 관계도 유지하고 있습니다.** 24시간 보안이든 단순한 시스템 설치든 바로 앤크워스 주식회사를 찾으십시오. **150 쌍방향 온라인 양식에 기본적인 사항과 선호사항을 입력하셔서 무료 견적을 받아보세요.** 귀하를 모시기를 고대합니다!

어휘 incorporated 주식회사 premises (건물이 딸린) 부지 a wide range of 다양한 on-site 현장의 maintain 유지하다 constant 지속적인 maximize 최대화하다 effectiveness 효과, 유효성 round-the-clock 24시간 동안 계속되는 installation 설치 nothing less than 다름 아닌, 바로 그 quote 견적 preference 선호 interactive 상호의, 대화형의

---

149 사실 관계 확인

번역 앤크워스 주식회사에 대해 사실인 것은?
(A) 자사의 경보장치를 제조한다.
(B) 직원들이 경관 출신이다.
(C) 지역 관계 기관과 긴밀히 협력한다.
(D) 현재 보안 인력을 채용하고 있다.

해설 세 번째 문장에서 앤크워스 주식회사는 실효성을 극대화하기 위해 지역 경찰서와 지속적인 관계를 유지하고 있다(We also maintain a constant connection with the local police department to maximize our effectiveness)고 했다. 따라서 지역 관계 기관과 긴밀히 협력한다는 (C)가 글의 내용과 일치한다.

▶▶ **Paraphrasing** 지문의 **maintain a constant connection**
→ 정답의 **works closely**
지문의 **police department**
→ 정답의 **authorities**

---

150 세부 사항

번역 광고에 따르면, 독자들은 웹사이트에서 무엇을 할 수 있는가?
(A) 가격 견적 요청하기
(B) 장비 사진 보기
(C) 고객 추천글 읽기
(D) 시스템 테스트하기

해설 지문 후반부에서 온라인 양식에 기본적인 세부 사항과 선호 사항을 입력해서 무료 견적을 받아보라(Get a free quote by entering some basic details and preferences into our interactive online form)고 했다. 따라서 독자들은 웹사이트에서 가격 견적을 요청할 수 있음을 알 수 있으므로, 정답은 (A)이다.

▶▶ **Paraphrasing** 지문의 **Get a free quote**
→ 정답의 **Request a price estimate**

151-152 공지

알림: 콤덴 공공도서관에서 북클럽 신규회원을 모집 중입니다.

콤덴 공공도서관 북클럽의 모집 기간입니다. 흥미진진한 소설에서 흥미 넘치는 다양한 주제의 논픽션 작품까지 모두를 위한 책을 갖추고 있습니다. **151 개관하는 날 저녁마다 저희가 개최하는 북클럽 모임이 하나씩 있는데, 어떤 연령대이든 여섯 개 그룹 중 하나에 가입하실 수 있습니다.** 게다가 자신의 책을 가져오실 계획이라면 도서관 카드가 필요 없습니다. **152 그러나 프런트에서 등록서를 작성하시고 10달러를 납부해야 하는데, 이는 귀하의 평생 단체회원권 비용이 됩니다.** 이후 단체장이 연락을 드리고 다음 모임에 대해 알려드릴 것입니다.

오늘 가입하시고 책 읽는 사람들의 모임과 무한한 아이디어의 세계로 들어가 보세요!

어휘 recruitment 모집 stimulating (아주 흥미로워서) 자극이 되는 fill out 기입하다, 작성하다 be in touch 연락하다 upcoming 다가오는

---

151 추론 / 암시

번역 콤덴 공공도서관에 대해 암시된 것은?
(A) 독자들을 위해 온라인 포럼을 개최한다.
(B) 1주일에 하루 휴관한다.
(C) 중고 서적 일부를 판매한다.
(D) 현재 단체장을 찾고 있다.

해설 세 번째 문장에서 콤덴 공공도서관이 개관하는 날 저녁마다 북클럽 모임이 하나씩 있는데, 연령에 관계없이 여섯 개 그룹 중 하나에 가입할 수 있다(We have one book club meeting every evening that we're open, and readers of all ages are welcome in any of the six groups)고 했다. 따라서 콤덴 공공도서관은 일주일에 6일 개관하고 하루 휴관한다는 것을 추론할 수 있으므로, 정답은 (B)이다.

---

152 세부 사항

번역 북클럽 회원권의 자격 요건은 무엇인가?
(A) 특정 연령 이상일 것
(B) 유효한 도서관 카드를 소지할 것
(C) 일회성 비용을 납부할 것
(D) 면접을 볼 것

해설 첫 번째 단락의 후반부에서 프런트에서 등록서를 작성하고 10달러를 지불하면, 평생 회원이 된다(However, you must fill out a registration form at the front desk and pay a charge of ten dollars, which covers your group membership for life)고 했다. 따라서 회비 10달러를 한 번만 지불하면 된다는 것을 알 수 있으므로, 정답은 (C)이다.

153-154 문자 메시지

아르놀도 시아노 [오전 11:23]
¹⁵³리산드라, 다음달 데바노 오페라 컴퍼니의 리지웨이 방문에 갈 입장권을 사려고 보고 있는데요. 얼마나 빨리 판매되는지 정말 믿을 수가 없네요.

리산드라 콘도우 [오전 11:26]
놀랍지 않아요. ¹⁵³이 지역 사람들은 그들을 볼 기회가 없었으니까요.

아르놀도 시아노 [오전 11:27]
맞아요. ¹⁵⁴아무튼 입장권에 40달러 이상 지불하고 싶지 않으신 건 알지만, 그 가격대의 입장권으로는 금요일, 토요일, 일요일 밤은 모두 매진됐어요.

리산드라 콘도우 [오전 11:28]
다른 선택사항이 있나요?

아르놀도 시아노 [오전 11:31]
¹⁵⁴토요일 또는 일요일 주간 공연 중 하나에 갈 수 있어요. 아니면 60달러짜리 금요일 밤 입장권을 살 수 있고요.

리산드라 콘도우 [오전 11:33]
음, 저는 주말 내내 일해요.

아르놀도 시아노 [오전 11:36]
알겠어요. 금요일 입장권을 예매할게요. 외식 대신 집에서 저녁을 먹으면 돼요. 그러면 비용을 줄이는 데 도움이 될 거예요.

어휘 look into ~을 잘 살펴보다 price range 가격대 matinee (연극·영화 등의) 주간 공연, 상연

153 추론 / 암시

번역 데바노 오페라 컴퍼니에 대해 암시된 것은?
(A) 한 달 동안 전국 투어를 할 계획이다.
(B) 총 3회 공연을 할 것이다.
(C) 최근 입장권 가격을 올렸다.
(D) 리지웨이에서 최초로 공연할 예정이다.

해설 데바노 오페라 컴퍼니의 리지웨이 입장권을 사려고 보고 있는데 아주 빨리 판매되고 있다는 11시 23분 시아노 씨의 메시지에, 콘도우 씨는 이 지역 사람들이 그들을 볼 기회가 없었기(Locals have never had the opportunity to see the group before) 때문이라고 했다. 따라서 데바노 오페라 컴퍼니가 리지웨이에서 처음으로 공연할 것임을 추론할 수 있으므로, 정답은 (D)이다.

154 의도 파악

번역 오전 11시 33분에 콘도우 씨가 "저는 주말 내내 일해요"라고 쓸 때, 그 의도는 무엇인가?
(A) 시아노 씨가 초과 근무를 하지 않을 것이라서 놀랐다.
(B) 더 비싼 입장권을 구매할 의향이 있다.
(C) 시아노 씨가 다른 사람을 초대해야 한다고 생각한다.
(D) 자신의 동료 중 한 명과 근무시간을 바꾸었다.

해설 시아노 씨는 11시 27분 메시지에서 콘도우 씨가 입장권에 40달러 이상 지불하기를 원치 않는다는 것은 알지만, 그 가격대의 금요일, 토요일, 일요일 밤 입장권은 모두 매진되었다(Anyway, I know you didn't want to spend more than $40 for your ticket, but the tickets in that price range are sold out for Friday, Saturday, and Sunday nights)고 했으며, 11시 31분 메시지에서 토요일이나 일요일 주간 공연을 가거나 60달러짜리 금요일 밤 입장권을 살 수 있다(We could go to one of the matinees on Saturday or Sunday. Or we can get the $60 tickets for Friday night)고 했다. 그러자 콘도우 씨는 자신이 주말 내내 일해야 한다고 했으므로 60달러인 금요일 밤 공연 입장권을 구매하겠다는 의도이다. 따라서 정답은 (B)이다.

155-157 일정표

스펠서 무술센터

강사 일정: 5월 3일 월요일

	A 스튜디오	B 스튜디오	C 스튜디오
오전 7시	합기도 [초급반] 에릭 샤롱	합기도 [중급반] 알리시아 켄트	유도 [고급반] 제프리 미란다
오전 8시	쿵푸 [중급반] 제프리 미란다	태권도 [중급반] 에릭 샤롱	태권도 [초급반] 베로니카 로손
오전 9시	합기도 [중급반] 베로니카 로손	유도 [고급반] 이안 스칼리아	합기도 [초급반] 알리시아 켄트
오후 1시	태권도 [중급반] 에릭 샤롱	쿵푸 [초급반] 알리시아 켄트	유도 [중급반] 이안 스칼리아
¹⁵⁵오후 6시	태권도 [초급반] 베로니카 로손	¹⁵⁶크라브 마가 [초급반] 이안 스칼리아	¹⁵⁵태권도 [고급반] 레이먼드 알바레즈
¹⁵⁵오후 7시	쿵푸 [중급반] 제프리 미란다	¹⁵⁶유도 [초급반] 레이먼드 알바레즈	쿵푸 [고급반] 알리시아 켄트
¹⁵⁵오후 8시	¹⁵⁵유도 [초급반] 레이먼드 알바레즈	[없음]	태권도 [고급반] 베로니카 로손

주의: ¹⁵⁶크라브 마가를 수업 목록에 막 추가하여 몇 명이 수업에 참여할지 확실치 않습니다. 인기가 있으면 에릭 샤롱 씨가 이 수련법의 다른 저녁 수업 하나를 맡을 예정입니다. ¹⁵⁷각 수업 전에 매트, 머리보호대, 글러브(사용할 경우)가 수리되어 양호한 상태인지 확인해 주십시오.

어휘 martial art 무술 instructor 강사 intermediate 중급의 advanced 고급의 be in attendance 참석하다 take on 맡다 discipline 단련법, 수련법

155 추론 / 암시

번역 센터에 대해 암시된 것은?
(A) 고급반 수업은 C 스튜디오에서만 진행된다.
(B) 월요일은 한 주에서 가장 한가한 날이다.
(C) 합기도는 3개의 다른 레벨이 있다.
(D) 알바레즈 씨는 저녁에는 거기서만 수업을 한다.

해설 일정표를 보면, 알바레즈 씨는 Studio A에서는 오후 8시에 유도 초급반(Judo [Beginner])을, Studio B에서는 오후 7시에 유도 초급반(Judo [Beginner])을, Studio C에서는 오후 6시에 태권도 고급반(Taekwondo [Advanced]) 수업을 한다. 따라서 알바레즈 씨는 오후 6~8시에 수업을 하므로, 정답은 (D)이다.

156 세부 사항

번역 현재 신규 수업을 가르치고 있는 사람은?
(A) 샤롱 씨
(B) 로손 씨
(C) 미란다 씨
(D) 스칼리아 씨

해설 하단의 Notes 부분에서 크라브 마가를 수업 목록에 막 추가해서 몇 명이 수업에 참여할지 확실치 않다(Since we've just added Krav Maga to our class list, we're not sure how many people will be in attendance)고 했으며, 일정표를 보면 크라브 마가를 가르칠 사람은 이안 스칼리아(Krav Maga [Beginner] *Ian Scalia*)이므로, 정답은 (D)이다.

▶▶ **Paraphrasing** 지문의 **we've just added ~ to our class list**
→ 질문의 **the newest class**

157 세부 사항

번역 강사들은 무엇을 하라고 요청받았는가?
(A) 일정 오류를 관리자에게 보고하기
(B) 밤에 모든 스튜디오 문 잠그기
(C) 수강생 수 추적하기
(D) 일부 장비 손상 조사하기

해설 Notes의 마지막 문장에서, 강사들에게 각 수업 전에 매트, 머리보호대, 글러브 등의 수리 상태가 괜찮은지 확인하라(Before each session, make sure the mats, head guards, and gloves (if used) are in a good state of repair)고 요청하고 있다. 따라서 정답은 (D)이다.

▶▶ **Paraphrasing** 지문의 **the mats, head guards, and gloves**
→ 정답의 **some gear**

158-160 이메일

수신: 자스민 퀸
발신: 다니엘 쉬
날짜: 11월 9일
제목: 온라인 사전 프로젝트 투자

퀸 씨께,

다음 주가 저희 회사에서 제안한 온라인 사전 프로젝트 관련 투자자들과 갖는 첫 번째 회의입니다. **158**프로젝트에 쓰인 기술, 그리고 시스템과 상호작용하는 소비자 요구를 저희가 어떻게 예상하는지에 관해 강연하시는 데 동의해 주셔서 감사합니다. 회의 중 노트북 컴퓨터, 프로젝터, 프로젝션 스크린을 사용하실 수 있습니다. 따라서 강연에 수반될 글과 도표가 있는 슬라이드를 준비해 오셔야 합니다. 와이파이 연결에 접속하실 수 있으므로 본인에게 슬라이드를 이메일로 보내실 수 있습니다. 그러나 인터넷 문제가 있을 경우에도 강연이 진행될 수 있도록 USB 플래시 드라이브에 파일을 가져오실 것을 적극 권장합니다.

160또한 강연은 충분한 질의 시간을 포함하여 45분으로 제한해 주십시오. 그렇지 않으면 일정보다 늦어지기 쉬울 것입니다. 해당일에 네 분의 연사를 모실 예정이며 모두 저희 소중한 고객들과 공유할 생생한 정보를 갖고 계십니다. 회의

는 회사 밖인 윌링턴 플라자에서 열리므로 평소보다 더 광범위한 준비가 필요합니다. **159**해당 장소의 보안요원에게 제출하기 위해 귀하의 운전면허증 스캔이 필요합니다. 늦어도 금요일까지 제게 이메일로 보내 주세요.

본 행사에 관해 질문이 있으시면 이 주소로 언제든 편하게 연락 주십시오.

다니엘 쉬

어휘 investment 투자 investor 투자자 regarding ~에 관해 give a talk on ~에 대해 강연하다 anticipate 예상하다 interact with ~와 상호작용하다 accompany 동반되다, 딸리다 have access to ~에 접속할 수 있다 in the event of ~할 경우에는 complication 문제 be highly recommended 적극 권장되다 off-site 부지 밖에서 extensive 광범위한 venue 장소

158 주제 / 목적

번역 쉬 씨가 이메일을 쓴 이유는?
(A) 프로젝트 진행상황을 설명하려고
(B) 투자자에게 기회를 알리려고
(C) 발표자에게 지시사항을 알려주려고
(D) 일에 관해 도움을 구하려고

해설 이메일을 쓴 이유는 주로 지문 서두 부분에 제시되는 경우가 많다. 여기서도, 첫 번째 단락 초반부에서 강연에 동의해 주어서 감사하다(Thank you for agreeing to give a talk on the technology behind the project and the way that we have anticipated the needs of users interacting with the system)면서, 회의 중에 노트북 컴퓨터, 프로젝터, 프로젝션 스크린을 사용할 수 있으며, 슬라이드를 준비해 오라(A laptop computer, projector, and projection screen will be available at the meeting, so you should prepare slides with text and graphics to accompany the talk)고 했다. 따라서 정답은 (C)이다.

159 세부 사항

번역 퀸 씨는 주 말까지 쉬 씨에게 무엇을 보내야 하는가?
(A) 회의 장소로의 길 안내
(B) 슬라이드에 필요한 도표 목록
(C) 행사의 확정 참석자 수
(D) 신분증 이미지

해설 두 번째 단락 후반부에서 보안요원에게 제출할 운전면허증 스캔이 필요하다면서, 늦어도 금요일까지 이메일로 보내 달라(I will need a scan of your driver's license for the venue's security staff. Please e-mail it to me no later than Friday)고 했다. 따라서 (D)가 정답이다.

▶▶ **Paraphrasing** 지문의 **a scan of your driver's license**
→ 정답의 **An image of an identification card**
지문의 **no later than Friday**
→ 질문의 **by the end of the week**

160 문장 삽입

번역 [1], [2], [3], [4]로 표시된 곳 중에서 다음 문장이 들어가기에 가장 적합한 곳은?

"그렇지 않으면 일정보다 늦어지기 쉬울 것입니다."

(A) [1]
(B) [2]
(C) [3]
(D) [4]

해설 주어진 문장의 Otherwise와 fall behind schedule이 문제 해결의 단서이다. 주어진 문장은 '그렇지 않으면 일정보다 늦어지기 쉬울 것이다'라는 의미이므로, 주어진 문장 앞에는 강연 시간에 대한 내용이 와야 한다는 것을 알 수 있다. 따라서 주어진 문장은 충분한 질의 시간을 포함하여 강연 시간을 45분으로 제한하라(Also, please limit the talk to 45 minutes, including ample time for questions)는 내용 뒤인 [3]에 들어가야 글의 흐름이 자연스러워진다.

161-164 온라인 채팅

마뉴엘 로차 [오전 9:16]

모두 안녕하세요. HR 관리자가 저에게 선셋 롯지에서의 직원 피정 계획이 어떻게 되어가는지 확인해 달라고 요청했습니다.

라니 샤 [오전 9:18]

161최종 인원 확인이 있습니다. 직원 절반 가량이 개회 연회를 위해 그 전날 밤에 갈 계획입니다. 나머지는 아침에 이동해서 필참 워크숍에 늦지 않도록 오전 10시까지 도착할 겁니다.

리네트 크럼프턴 [오전 9:19]

영업부 누군가가 첫 번째 워크숍을 발표하나요?

라니 샤 [오전 9:20]

아니요, 그건 오후예요. **162**홍보 담당 직원이 첫 번째를 진행합니다.

리네트 크럼프턴 [오전 9:21]

알겠습니다. 그럼 그들을 위해 IT 부서 사람이 아침에 장비를 설치해야 할까요?

라니 샤 [오전 9:22]

162갈반 씨가 자신이 직접 설치할 수 있다고 했어요. 마이크만 필요할 거예요.

마뉴엘 로차 [오전 9:25]

지금까지는 좋군요. **163**출장요리 업체는요? 저희 규모의 단체를 위한 식사를 만들 업체를 찾았나요?

리네트 크럼프턴 [오전 9:26]

그건 포함되어 있지 않나요?

마뉴엘 로차 [오전 9:27]

163아침식사와 점심식사만요. 저녁식사는 출장요리가 필요합니다.

라니 샤 [오전 9:28]

볼크랜드 케이터링은 어떨까요? 다른 행사에서 저희를 도왔는데요. 타도시에서 일할 수 있는 것으로 알고 있어요. **164**여기 어딘가에 명함이 있습니다. 찾으면 연락처를 이메일로 보낼게요.

어휘 retreat 피정, 수행 head count 인원수 compulsory 의무의, 필수적인

161 추론 / 암시

번역 개회 연회에 대해 암시된 것은?

(A) 날짜가 변경되었다.
(B) 의무사항이 아니다.
(C) 오전 10시에 시작할 예정이다.
(D) 좌석이 제한되어 있다.

해설 9시 18분 샤 씨의 메시지에서 최종 인원을 확인했는데, 직원 중 반만 개회 연회를 위해 그 전날 밤에 갈 계획(About half of the employees plan to go there the night before for the opening reception)이라고 했다. 따라서 개회 연회가 꼭 참석해야 하는 필참 행사가 아님을 추론할 수 있으므로, 정답은 (B)이다.

162 추론 / 암시

번역 갈반 씨는 어느 부서에서 일하겠는가?

(A) 인사
(B) 해외 영업
(C) 홍보
(D) IT

해설 9시 20분 샤 씨의 메시지에서 홍보부 직원이 첫 번째 워크숍을 진행할(Public relations staff will hold the first one) 것임을 알 수 있으며, 9시 22분 메시지에서 갈반 씨가 직접 워크숍에 필요한 장비를 설치하겠다고 말했다는(Ms. Galvan said that she can set things up herself) 것을 알 수 있다. 따라서 갈반 씨가 첫 번째 워크숍을 진행할 홍보부 직원임을 추론할 수 있으므로, 정답은 (C)이다.

163 의도 파악

번역 오전 9시 26분에 크럼프턴 씨가 "그건 포함되어 있지 않나요?"라고 쓸 때, 그 의도는 무엇인가?

(A) 음식이 패키지의 일부라고 생각했다.
(B) 명단 내용에 대해 확신이 없다.
(C) 요청받은 서류를 이미 보냈다.
(D) 전 직원이 행사에 참여하기를 바란다.

해설 의도 파악 문제의 경우, 주로 인용문 앞뒤 문맥에서 문제 해결의 단서를 찾을 수 있다. 여기서도 로차 씨가 9시 25분 메시지에서 식사를 담당할 업체를 찾았는지(Have you found one that can make meals for a group of our size) 물었으며, 9시 27분 메시지에서는 아침식사와 점심식사만 포함되어 있으며, 저녁식사는 출장요리가 필요하다(Only breakfast and lunch. We need to have the dinner catered)고 했다. 따라서 크럼프턴 씨는 식사가 패키지에 포함되어 있는 것으로 생각했음을 알 수 있으므로, 정답은 (A)이다.

164 추론 / 암시

번역 샤 씨는 다음에 무엇을 하겠는가?

(A) 명함 찾기
(B) 일정을 이메일로 보내기
(C) 케이터링 업체에 연락하기
(D) 지역 지도 참고하기

해설 샤 씨는 9시 28분 마지막 메시지에서 볼크랜드 케이터링의 명함이 있다면서, 명함을 찾으면 연락처를 이메일로 보내주겠다(I have their business card around here somewhere. I'll e-mail you their contact details once I find it)고 했다. 따라서 샤 씨는 볼크랜드 케이터링의 명함을 찾을 것임을 알 수 있으므로, 정답은 (A)이다. 샤 씨가 이메일로 보내겠다고 한 것은 일정이 아니라 연락처이므로 (B)를 정답으로 혼동하지 않도록 유의한다.

165-167 웹페이지

http://www.teskdalefarms.com/ingredientsbox

테스크데일 팜즈 재료 상자

~ 신선한 식품이 댁까지 바로 배송됩니다. ~

테스크데일 팜즈는 전국적으로 잘 알려진 요리사 라몬 제이콥스 씨와 협력하여 저희 현지 및 지역 공급업체에서 받은 신선한 재료를 이용한 조리법을 만듭니다. **166B**재료 상자에는 2인 분량의 가정식 세 끼를 위한 재료가 들어 있으며 필수 양념과 단계별 설명이 적힌 조리법 카드도 포함되어 있습니다. **165**패키지는 월요일 또는 목요일마다 (선택 가능) 배송되며 배송비는 따로 없습니다.

1673개월의 입문 기간에 저희 서비스를 이용해 보세요. 이 기간 동안에는 계약 해지 비용이 없습니다. **166A, D**첫 번째 재료 상자에는 기준 물품 이외에도 조리법 카드를 담아 둘 수 있는 나무 상자, 대형 도자기 접시, 에반스 백화점에서 프라이팬 구매 시 50% 할인 쿠폰까지 들어 있습니다.

167고객에게 월별 청구합니다 (입문가 90달러, 표준가 120달러). 여기를 클릭하셔서 오늘 가입하시고 〈마이어스 푸드 먼슬리〉지가 "가정식의 미래"로 부르는 것들을 살펴보세요.

어휘 ingredient 재료 renowned 잘 알려진 supplier 공급업자 spice 양념, 향신료 step-by-step 단계적인 instruction 설명, 지시 introductory period 도입기, 입문 기간 terminate the contract 계약을 해지하다, 종료하다 in addition to ~에 덧붙여 platter 접시

165 세부 사항

번역 고객은 얼마나 자주 재료 상자를 받는가?
(A) 주 2회
(B) 주 1회
(C) 월 2회
(D) 월 1회

해설 첫 번째 단락 마지막 문장에서 고객은 선택해서 재료 상자를 월요일 또는 목요일마다 배송받을 수 있다(The package is delivered every Monday or Thursday (your choice), and there is no extra fee for delivery)고 했다. 따라서 주 1회 배송받을 수 있다는 의미이므로, 정답은 (B)이다.

▶▶ Paraphrasing 지문의 every Monday or Thursday → 정답의 Once a week

166 사실 관계 확인

번역 첫 번째 재료 상자에 포함되는 것으로 언급되지 않은 것은?
(A) 음식을 내는 접시
(B) 조리법 카드
(C) 목재 용기
(D) 프라이팬

해설 보기에 언급된 내용을 지문에서 찾아 하나씩 확인해 본다. 두 번째 단락의 마지막 문장에서 첫 번째 재료 상자에 조리법 카드를 담아 둘 수 있는 나무 상자(a wooden box)와 대형 도자기 접시(a large ceramic platter)가 포함되어 있다는 것을 확인할 수 있으며, 첫 번째 단락 두 번째 문장에서 단계별 설명이 적힌 조리법 카드(recipe cards with step-by-step instructions)가 포함되어 있다는 것을 알 수 있다. 두 번째 단락의 마지막 문장에서 프라이팬이 아니라 프라이팬의 50% 할인 쿠폰(a coupon for 50% off frying pans at Evans Department Store)이 포함되어 있다고 했으므로, 정답은 (D)이다.

167 추론 / 암시

번역 재료 상자 서비스에 대해 암시된 것은?
(A) 네 번째 달부터 요금이 오를 것이다.
(B) 시외 고객에게 요금이 부과된다.
(C) 업체는 단계별로 된 동영상을 제공한다.
(D) 고객은 음식 알레르기에 대해 질문을 받는다.

해설 두 번째 단락 첫 문장에서 3개월 동안 입문 기간에 이용해 보라(Try our service with our three-month introductory period)고 했으며, 세 번째 단락 첫 문장에서 고객에게 월별로 청구하는데 입문가는 90달러이고 표준가 120달러(Customers are billed monthly ($90 for the introductory rate, and $120 for the standard rate))라고 했다. 따라서 네 번째 달부터 120달러로 요금이 인상된다는 것을 알 수 있으므로, 정답은 (A)이다.

168-171 기사

지역 뉴스

(7월 11일) – **169**베밍턴 시는 지난주 이 지역을 강타한 심한 폭풍우의 영향을 여전히 받아 시간당 2~3인치의 비가 며칠째 쏟아지며 타이슨강의 강둑이 범람하고 있다. 홍수는 여러 행사의 취소 및 연기로 이어졌는데 이 중에서 가장 최근 행사는 연례 지역골프대회이다.

168, 169이 대회는 당초 7월 16일 토요일에 멘도자 파크에서 열릴 예정이었다. **169**유지보수 작업자들이 건조 과정을 앞당기기 위해 가장 피해가 심한 지역에서 강의 인근 구역들로 물을 다시 퍼냈다. 그러나 땅은 여전히 축축한 상태이다. 골프대회는 훨씬 지대가 높은 파인뷰 파크로 장소를 옮기지 못했는데, 해당 날짜에 야구대회가 이미 예정되었기 때문이다. **168**그 대신, 행사는 8월 6일 토요일로 연기됐다.

171작년 우승자 제임스 레만을 비롯한 대회 참가자들에게는 행사 기획자가 연락을 취할 예정이다. 참가자들은 참가와 환불 요청 중에서 선택할 수 있다. 지역업체 대표들은 대회가 관광객에게 큰 인기이기 때문에 이러한 변화가 행사 참가자 수에 영향을 미치지 않기를 바란다고 했다. **170**"언제든 베밍턴 시 방문객이 많으면 시에 좋은 거죠." 대회에 기금을 낸 강 샤오 씨의 말이다. "작년과 참가자 수가 비슷했으면 합니다."

어휘 bank 강둑 overflow 넘치다, 범람하다 result in ~을 야기하다, 그 결과 ~이 되다 postponement 연기 take place 개최되다, 열리다 affected 영향을 받은, 피해를 입은 adjacent 인근의, 인접한 damp 축축한 attendance 참가자 수 draw 인기를 끄는 것 contribute funding to ~에 기금을 내다 turnout 참가자 수

168 주제 / 목적

번역 기사는 주로 무엇에 관한 것인가?
(A) 스포츠 대회 변경
(B) 새로운 오락 시설
(C) 대회 등록절차
(D) 다가오는 모금 행사의 문제

해설 심한 폭풍의 영향으로 인한 행사 취소 및 변경을 알리는 기사문이다. 특히 두 번째 단락 첫 문장에서 대회가 애초 7월 16일 토요일에 멘도자 파크에서 열릴 예정(The tournament was originally scheduled to take place on Saturday, July 16, at Mendoza Park)이었다고 했으며, 마지막 문장에서 행사가 8월 6일 토요일로 연기됐다(Instead, the event has been moved to Saturday, August 6)고 했다. 따라서 정답은 (A)이다.

▶▶ **Paraphrasing** 지문의 **The tournament** → 정답의 **a sporting competition**

169 사실 관계 확인

번역 멘도자 파크에 대해 명시된 것은?
(A) 야구장이 있다.
(B) 시에서 가장 큰 공원이다.
(C) 강 근처에 위치해 있다.
(D) 8월까지 문을 닫을 것이다.

해설 첫 번째 단락에서 폭우가 쏟아져 타이슨강 강둑이 범람해 지역골프대회가 연기되었다(The city of Bemmington ~ Golf Tournament)고 했다. 두 번째 단락에서 대회가 7월 16일 멘도자 파크에서 열릴 계획이었으나 작업자들이 건조 과정을 앞당기기 위해 물을 퍼내고(The tournament was originally scheduled to take place ~ to speed up the drying process) 있지만 여전히 땅이 축축한 상태(However, the ground is still too damp)라고 했다. 따라서 멘도자 파크가 강 근처에 위치해 있다는 것을 알 수 있으므로, (C)가 정답이다.

170 추론 / 암시

번역 강 샤오 씨는 누구이겠는가?
(A) 시 공무원
(B) 유지 보수 작업자
(C) 프로 운동선수
(D) 행사 후원자

해설 지문 후반부에서 강 샤오 씨가 대회에 기금을 냈다(Kang Shao, who contributed funding to the tournament)고 했으므로, 강 샤오 씨가 행사 후원자임을 알 수 있다. 따라서 정답은 (D)이다.

▶▶ **Paraphrasing** 지문의 **who contributed funding to the tournament** → 정답의 **An event sponsor**

171 문장 삽입

번역 [1], [2], [3], [4]로 표시된 곳 중에서 다음 문장이 들어가기에 가장 적합한 곳은?

"참가자들은 참가와 환불 요청 중에서 선택할 수 있다."

(A) [1]
(B) [2]
(C) [3]
(D) [4]

해설 주어진 문장은 참가자들이 선택해서 참가를 하거나 환불 요청을 할 수 있다는 의미이므로, 주어진 문장 앞에는 참가자들이 행사 기획자에게 연락을 한다는 내용이 와야 문맥이 자연스러워진다. 따라서 주어진 문장은 작년 우승자 제임스 레만을 비롯한 대회 참가자들에게는 행사 기획자가 연락을 취할 예정(Participants in the tournament, including last year's champion James Lehman, will be contacted by the tournament's event planner)이라는 문장 바로 다음인 [4]에 들어가야 자연스럽다.

172-175 이메일

수신: 플로리안 크루거 〈f.krueger@kruegersconfections.com〉
발신: 한나 최 〈choihannah@almontebank.com〉
172날짜: 2월 10일
제목: 알몬테 은행으로부터

크루거 씨께,

172어제 귀하의 전화를 받지 못해 죄송합니다. 남기신 메시지의 질문에 대한 답을 드리자면, 귀하의 대출 신청이 잘 진행되고 있음을 확실히 말씀드립니다. 저희는 현재 귀하의 신용 점수 확정을 기다리고 있으며, 저는 본 대출 건에 대한 총부채상환비율도 적절하다고 결정하였습니다.

아직 요청드려야 할 몇 가지 서류가 있습니다. **173**귀하가 6년에 해당하는 영업세 기록을 가지고 있음을 알고 있습니다만, 저희 목적으로는 3년 것만 필요합니다. 재무부에서 발행한 단 하나의 연간 세금명세서 등본이 이에 해당됩니다. 아울러 자금이 어떻게 사용될지 세부적인 설명이 필요합니다. 귀하의 신청서에는 '건물 확장'이라고만 적혀 있지만 서비스와 자재를 항목별로 구별한 목록을 포함해 더 자세한 설명이 필요합니다. 필요하신 서류를 첨부했습니다. **174**www.almontebank.com/forms/b451.html을 방문하셔서 기입할 견본 서류를 확인하시면 어떻게 해야 하는지 아실 겁니다.

작성을 완료한 서류는 우편으로 제 사무실, 첨부한 서류 상단에 나와 있는 주소로 보내 주십시오. **175**서류는 상시 제출 가능하나 빨리 제출할수록 자금 대출이 더 빨라집니다. 질문이 있으시면 언제든 저에게 연락해 주십시오.

한나 최
알몬테 은행 대출 담당

어휘 in response to ~에 대한 응답으로 loan application 대출 신청 debt-to-income ratio 총부채상환비율 business tax 영업세 certified copy 등본 tax summary 세금명세서 National Treasury Department 재무부 account 설명 expansion 확장 thorough 철저한 itemized 항목별로 구분한 attach 첨부하다 completed 완료된 submit 제출하다

172 세부 사항

번역 크루거 씨가 2월 9일에 최 씨에게 전화한 이유는?

(A) 신청 건의 상태를 확인하려고
(B) 소기업을 소개하려고
(C) 기업 대출을 요청하려고
(D) 세금 서류에 대해 문의하려고

해설 첫 번째 단락 초반부에서 최 씨는 어제 크루거 씨의 전화를 받지 못해 미안하다(I'm sorry I missed your telephone call yesterday)고 했는데, 이메일 날짜(Date: February 10)를 보면 크루거 씨가 최 씨에게 2월 9일에 전화했다는 것을 알 수 있다. 또한 최 씨는 크루거 씨가 남긴 질문에 대한 답을 하자면, 대출 신청이 잘 진행되고 있다(In response to your question in the message that you left, I can confirm that your loan application is moving along nicely)고 했다. 따라서 크루거 씨는 대출 신청 건의 진행 상황을 확인하기 위해서 전화했음을 알 수 있으므로, 정답은 (A)이다.

173 추론 / 암시

번역 크루거 씨의 회사에 대해 암시된 것은?

(A) 사무실이 개조되었다.
(B) 6년간 영업 중이다.
(C) 알몬테 은행에 서비스를 제공한다.
(D) 최근 다른 장소로 이전했다.

해설 두 번째 단락 두 번째 문장에서 크루거 씨의 회사가 6년 간의 영업세 기록을 가지고 있다(I know that you have six years' worth of business tax records)고 했으므로, 크루거 씨의 회사가 6년째 영업 중임을 알 수 있다. 따라서 (B)가 정답이다.

어휘 in operation 영업 중인

▶▶ **Paraphrasing** 지문의 **six years' worth of business tax records** → 정답의 **has been in operation for six years**

174 세부 사항

번역 크루거 씨가 언급된 웹사이트를 방문해야 하는 이유는?

(A) 예시를 살펴보기 위해
(B) 계정을 만들기 위해
(C) 양식을 업로드하기 위해
(D) 개점시간을 보기 위해

해설 두 번째 단락 마지막 문장에서 웹사이트를 방문해서 기입할 견본 서류를 확인할 수 있다(You can visit www.almontebank.com/forms/b451.html to see a sample form that is filled out so you know what to do)고 했다. 따라서 정답은 (A)이다.

▶▶ **Paraphrasing** 지문의 **to see a sample** → 정답의 **To view an example**

175 사실 관계 확인

번역 관련 서류에 대해 명시된 것은?

(A) 스캔해서 이메일로 보내면 된다.
(B) 최 씨 앞에서 서명해야 한다.
(C) 장마다 여러 장의 사본이 있어야 한다.
(D) 제출 마감기한이 없다.

해설 마지막 단락 두 번째 문장에서 서류는 상시 제출 가능하나 빨리 제출할수록 자금 대출이 더 빨라진다(You may submit the documents anytime, but the sooner you do, the sooner we can issue the funds)고 했으므로, 서류 제출 마감 기한이 없다는 것을 알 수 있다. 따라서 정답은 (D)이다.

▶▶ **Paraphrasing** 지문의 **submit ~ anytime** → 정답의 **no deadline for its submission**

176-180 광고 + 청구서

메돌란트

청소 용품의 신뢰받는 상표인 메돌란트는 세제 용액을 업그레이드했음을 발표하게 되어 기쁩니다. **176**저희는 제조법에서 유해 물질을 빼고 대신 비독성 대체 물질로 대체했습니다. **177**하지만 저희 세제는 저렴한 가격을 유지하며 등록된 자선단체, 공립학교, 지원단체에는 여전히 15퍼센트의 추가 할인을 제공합니다.

178Bwww.medolant.com에서 온라인으로 주문을 받거나 전화 555-0178로 주문을 받습니다. **178A**고객은 선불로 지불하시거나 제품 도착 후 청구서를 요청하시면 됩니다. **180**배송 주소가 캘리포니아 주 내인 고객은 이틀 걸려 배송을 받게 됩니다. 기타 모든 주문은 주문이 접수된 후 약 5일 후에 배송을 받습니다. **178D**대량 주문 배송료는 면제됩니다.

제품:

카펫 세척제: 카펫 샴푸 (#093), 악취 흡수 파우더 (#097)

179욕실 세척제: 만능 표면 세척제 (#113), 비누 거품 제거제 (#114), 거울 및 창문 세척제 (#118), 변기 세척제 (#119), 개수대 및 배수관 젤 (#120)

주방 세척제: 만능 조리대 세척제 (#124), 스테인리스 스틸 연마제 (#125), 문지르지 않아도 되는 오븐 세척제 (#129)

—신제품!!!— 얼룩 제거제: 카펫 얼룩 처리제 (#136), 커버 얼룩 제거제 (#137)

어휘 commercial 상업적인 harmful substance 유해 물질 formula 제조법 replace ~ with ... ~을 …으로 교체하다 non-toxic 비독성의 charity 자선단체 settle 지불하다 up-front 선불의 approximately 약, 거의 shipping fee 배송료 bulk order 대량 발주, 일괄 주문 waive 면제하다 odor 악취 all-purpose 다목적의, 만능의 scum (액체 표면에 더러운 성분이 모인) 거품 drain 배수관

---

www.medolant.com/myorders/1021

고객: 살게로 호텔

전화번호: 555-0191

180배송 주소: 93705, 캘리포니아 프레스노 생 클레어 스트리트 501

청구 유형: 신용카드 XXXX-XXXX-XXXX-8859

180주문일자: 3월 18일

제품코드	수량	단가	총계
093	3	14.99달러	44.97달러
179113	2	3.99달러	7.98달러
179114	4	9.99달러	39.96달러
179120	1	12.99달러	12.99달러

| 125 | 2 | 29.99달러 | 59.98달러 |
| 136 | 4 | 8.99달러 | 35.96달러 |

[배송료 및 예상 시간을 보시려면 클릭하세요]

구매가 모두 만족스럽지 않으셨다면 30일 이내에 반품하고 전액 환불을 받으실 수 있습니다.

어휘 quantity 양 delivery fee 배송비 estimate 어림, 견적

176 세부 사항

번역 메돌란트는 최근 제품과 관련하여 무엇을 했는가?
(A) 재생 가능한 포장지를 도입했다.
(B) 새로운 주방 세척제를 추가했다.
(C) 다양한 병 크기를 제공하기 시작했다.
(D) 제품의 성분을 바꿨다.

해설 광고문 첫 번째 단락 두 번째 문장에서 제조법에서 유해 물질을 빼고 비독성 대체 물질로 대체했다(We've taken harmful substances out of our formulas and replaced them with non-toxic alternatives)고 했다. 따라서 메돌란트는 제품의 성분을 바꿨다는 것을 알 수 있으므로, 정답은 (D)이다.

177 추론 / 암시

번역 메돌란트에 대해 암시된 것은?
(A) 비영리단체에 할인을 제공한다.
(B) 시중 최다판매 제품을 가지고 있다.
(C) 주택용 세제 제품군을 따로 만든다.
(D) TV 광고를 통해서도 광고한다.

해설 광고문 첫 번째 단락 마지막 문장에서 등록된 자선단체, 공립학교, 지원단체에는 15퍼센트 추가 할인을 제공한다(we still offer 15% off to registered charities, public schools, and aid organizations)고 했다. 따라서 (A)가 정답이다.

▶▶ **Paraphrasing** 지문의 registered charities, public schools, and aid organizations → 정답의 nonprofit organizations

178 사실 관계 확인

번역 광고에서 명시되지 않은 것은?
(A) 고객은 주문품 수령 후에 지불할 수 있다.
(B) 주문에는 두 가지 방식이 있다.
(C) 주문품에는 설명용 소책자가 함께 들어 있다.
(D) 대량 주문은 배송이 무료이다.

해설 보기에 언급된 내용을 지문에서 찾아 확인해 본다. 광고문 두 번째 단락에서 확인할 수 있다. 고객은 선불로 지불하거나 제품 도착 후 청구서를 요청하면 된다(Customers may settle up-front or request to be billed once their goods have arrived)는 첫 번째 문장에서 (A)를, 온라인 www.medolant.com이나 전화 555-0178로 주문을 받는다(We welcome orders online at www.medolant.com or by phone at 555-0178)는 첫 번째 문장에서 (B)를, 대량 주문 배송료는 면제된다(The shipping fee for bulk orders will be waived)는 마지막 문장에서 (D)를 확인할 수 있다. 따라서 정답은 (C)이다.

▶▶ **Paraphrasing** 지문의 bulk orders → 보기의 large orders

179 연계

번역 살계로 호텔에서 가장 많이 구매한 것은 어떤 유형의 제품인가?
(A) 카펫 세척제
(B) 욕실 세척제
(C) 주방 세척제
(D) 얼룩 제거제

해설 청구서를 보면 살계로 호텔은 093 3개, 113 2개, 114 4개, 120 1개, 125 2개, 136 4개를 구입했다. 광고문의 제품(PRODUCTS) 항목을 보면, 113, 114, 120은 모두 욕실 세척제(Bathroom Cleaners: All-Purpose Surface Cleaner (#113), Soap Scum Remover (#114), Mirror and Window Cleaner (#118), Toilet Bowl Cleaner (#119), Sink and Drain Gel (#120)이므로, 정답은 (B)이다.

180 연계

번역 살계로 호텔은 언제 제품을 받겠는가?
(A) 3월 18일
(B) 3월 19일
(C) 3월 20일
(D) 3월 23일

해설 광고문 두 번째 단락 중반부에서 배송지 주소가 캘리포니아주 내인 고객은 이틀 걸려 배송을 받게 된다(Those whose delivery address is within the state of California will receive two-day delivery)고 했다. 청구서를 보면 배송 주소는 캘리포니아주(Shipping Address: 501 Saint Clair Street, Fresno, California, 93705)이고, 주문 날짜는 3월 18일(Order Date: March 18)이다. 따라서 살계로 호텔은 3월 18일에서 이틀 뒤인 3월 20일에 주문품을 받을 것이므로, 정답은 (C)이다.

181-185 정보문 + 양식

훌륭한 업적은 인정받아야 합니다!

오르몰라스 컨설팅 직원 시상이 다시 돌아왔습니다. [181]회사 웹사이트에 있는 양식을 작성하셔서 동료 직원 중 한 명을 추천해 주십시오. 후보 추천은 11월 20일까지 받습니다. [182]딘 록하트 CEO께서 연례 직원 연회에서 시상을 할 예정이지만, 귀하의 의견을 검토하고 시상자를 선정하는 것은 시상위원회입니다.

네 개 부문에서 상을 수여합니다.

상	설명	자격 기준
샤이닝 스타상	단기간 내에 긍정적인 평판을 얻은 신입사원에게 수여	지난 12개월 내에 채용
이노베이션상	창의적인 생각으로 회사에 이익을 가져다 준 직원에게 수여	없음
[183]파운데이션상	뛰어난 실적을 오래 보유한 직원에게 수여	[183]오르몰라스 직원으로 최소 5년 근무
비전상	지도력과 통솔력으로 팀을 더 우수하게 만드는 데 기여한 직원에게 수여	부서 관리자 또는 팀장만 해당

어휘 recognition 인정 nominate (후보로) 지명하다, 추천하다 coworker 동료 fill out a form 양식을 작성하다 present the award 시상하다 banquet 연회 eligibility criteria 자격 기준 reputation 명성, 평판 in a short time period 단기간에 innovation 혁신 track record 실적 direction 지휘, 통솔

Test 3

```
www.ormolasconsulting.net/forms/378
```

시상 후보 추천 양식

추천할 직원: 아만다 윌리스 **부서:** 마케팅
상 유형: ☐ 샤이닝 스타 ☐ 이노베이션 **183**☒ 파운데이션 ☐ 비전
183추천자가 자격 기준에 부합합니까? ☒ 예 ☐ 아니요

추천 이유: 저는 지난 3년간 윌리스 씨와 함께 근무했는데 윌리스 씨의 업무에 매우 만족했습니다. 그녀가 회사를 대표할 때면 언제나 좋은 인상을 줍니다. **184**윌리스 씨는 지난 달 신규 고객의 매장 개점 첫날을 기념하기 위해 부에노스아이레스를 방문했습니다. 여기에서 좋은 평을 받았고 다시 오라는 초대도 받았습니다. **185**또한 그녀의 업무 보고서는 항상 정확한데, 그것은 그녀가 실수가 없는지 꼼꼼히 검토하기 때문입니다. 윌리스 씨는 우리 모두에게 훌륭한 귀감이 된다고 확신합니다.

제출자: 라이언 드마르코

어휘 extremely 매우 make a good impression 좋은 인상을 주다 celebrate 기념하다, 축하하다 be favorably received 호평을 받다 accurate 정확한 meticulously 꼼꼼하게

---

181 추론 / 암시

번역 이 정보는 어디에 나와 있겠는가?
(A) 회사 소식지
(B) 홍보 안내책자
(C) 회의 프로그램
(D) 업계 잡지

해설 정보문 첫 단락에서 오르몰라스 컨설팅 직원 시상이 다시 돌아왔다면서 회사 웹사이트에 있는 양식을 작성해서 동료 직원을 추천해 달라(Nominate one of your fellow coworkers by filling out a form on the company Web site)고 했다. 따라서 회사 소식지에 실린 글임을 알 수 있으므로 정답은 (A)이다.

---

182 추론 / 암시

번역 록하트 씨에 대해 암시된 것은?
(A) 웹사이트에 기사를 썼다.
(B) 올해 새로운 상을 제정했다.
(C) 이전 연회에는 참석하지 않았다.
(D) 수상자 결정에는 관여하지 않을 것이다.

해설 정보문 첫 번째 단락 마지막 문장에서 CEO인 딘 록하트 씨가 연례 직원 연회에서 시상을 할 예정이지만, 시상자를 선정하는 것은 시상위원회(CEO Dean Lockhart will present the awards at the annual employee banquet, but it is the awards committee that will review your comments and choose the winners)라고 했다. 따라서 록하트 씨는 시상을 할 뿐 수상자 결정에는 관여하지 않을 것임을 알 수 있으므로, 정답은 (D)이다.

---

183 연계

번역 윌리스 씨에 대해 명시된 것은?
(A) 창의적인 아이디어를 내는 것으로 평판이 높다.
(B) 최소 5년간 회사를 위해 일했다.
(C) 마케팅 부서 팀장이다.
(D) 위원회에 들어가는 데 관심이 있다.

해설 추천서를 보면 윌리스 씨는 파운데이션상에 추천([X] Foundation)을 받았으며, 자격 기준에 부합한다(Does the nominee meet the eligibility criteria? [X] Yes)고 했다. 또한 정보문의 수상 부문을 보면, 파운데이션상의 기준은 오르몰라스 직원으로 5년 이상 근무(Minimum of five years of employment at Ormolas)한 것이다. 따라서 윌리스 씨는 회사에 5년 이상 근무했다는 것을 추론할 수 있으므로, 정답은 (B)이다.

▶▶ **Paraphrasing** 지문의 **Minimum of five years of employment** → 정답의 **has worked at the company for at least five years**

---

184 세부 사항

번역 윌리스 씨는 지난 달 부에노스아이레스에서 무엇을 했는가?
(A) 계약 체결
(B) 개업식 참석
(C) 수상
(D) 건물 부지 선정

해설 추천서 중반부에서 윌리스 씨는 신규 고객의 매장 개점 첫날을 기념하기 위해 부에노스아이레스를 방문했다(Just last month, she visited Buenos Aires to celebrate the first day of business for one of our new client's stores)고 했다. 따라서 윌리스 씨가 개업식에 참석했다는 것을 알 수 있으므로, 정답은 (B)이다.

▶▶ **Paraphrasing** 지문의 **the first day of business** → 정답의 **a grand opening**

---

185 사실 관계 확인

번역 윌리스 씨의 특징으로 언급된 것은?
(A) 다양한 언어에 관한 지식
(B) 팀워크에 대한 헌신
(C) 강력한 분석적 기술
(D) 세부적인 사항에 주의를 기울이는 것

해설 추천서 후반부에서 윌리스 씨는 실수가 없는지 꼼꼼히 검토하기 때문에 업무 보고서가 항상 정확하다(Also, her work reports are always accurate, as she reviews them meticulously to ensure they are error-free)고 했다. 따라서 (D)가 정답이다.

▶▶ **Paraphrasing** 지문의 **reviews them meticulously to ensure they are error-free** → 정답의 **Attention to detail**

186-190 기사 + 이메일 + 공지

노필드 (2월 15일) — **186**시 관계자들은 시 동쪽에 있는 어거스타 연못의 오염 수준이 이상적인 것으로 간주되는 수준의 거의 10배에 이른다는 사실을 확인했다. **189**농촌부(DRA)에서 2월 2일에 검사를 실시했다. 관계자들은 인근 농지에서의 농약, 비료 사용 증가가 이 문제의 원인이 된 듯하며 여가 목적으로 연못을 이용하는 사람들뿐 아니라 연못 안과 주변에 사는 야생동물에게 위협이 된다고 밝혔다.

시 의회는 새로운 규제를 통과시켜 농경지의 화학물질 사용을 제한하는 것뿐만 아니라 호수 정화 프로젝트의 기금 마련을 논의할 계획이다. 정화 프로젝트에는 무려 3백만 달러가 소요된다. 대부분의 의회 의원들은 보건 및 환경상의 이익을 들어 프로젝트를 찬성하지만 일부 의원들은 이 제안에 반대하고 있다. 제시 시에라는 재정적 부담이 마을을 파산 위험에 빠뜨릴 것을 우려한다. **187마저리 로우는 이 프로젝트로 인해 다른 중요한 프로젝트들이 지연될 것을 염려한다.** 의회는 곧 결정을 내리기를 바라고 있다.

어휘 contamination 오염 carry out 실행하다 determine 알아내다, 밝히다 pesticide 살충제, 농약 fertilizer 비료 pose a risk to ~에게 위험이 되다 wildlife 야생동물 recreational 여가의 debate 논의하다 regulation 규제 restrict 제한하다 as much as ~만큼이나 많이 be in favor of ~을 찬성하다 cite 인용하다 oppose 반대하다 financial burden 재정 부담 put ~ at risk ~을 위험에 처하게 하다 bankruptcy 파산

수신: 아냐 티그 〈a.teague@stel-mail.com〉
발신: 랜들 무어 〈moorer@lurmonincorporated.com〉
날짜: 2월 16일
제목: 어거스타 연못

티그 씨께,
지역 주민 여러 명이 어제 날짜 〈노필드 타임즈〉의 어거스타 연못 기사 관련해서 저에게 연락을 했습니다. **187저는 진술해 달라고 연락을 받지 못했습니다만 제안된 프로젝트에 관해 로우 씨의 의견과 뜻을 함께합니다.** 시 의회 의원으로서 우리가 지역사회 일원들이 의견을 나눌 수 있는 공개 포럼을 개최하는 것이 좋을 것 같습니다. 의회 전체가 이 문제가 심각한 사안임을 **188인식**하고 있어 가볍게 결정을 내리면 안 된다고 생각합니다.

랜들 무어

어휘 regarding ~과 관련하여 statement 진술, 성명 appreciate (제대로) 인식하다 complex 복잡한 take a decision 결정을 내리다

공지

노필드 시 의회는 3월 1일 화요일 오후 7시에 노필드 커뮤니티 센터에서 특별 회의를 개최하여 어거스타 연못 정화 프로젝트에 관해 논의할 예정입니다. **189셰릴 맥베이 씨와 그 팀이 지난달 실시한 시험에 따라 제안에 관해 의사결정이 이뤄져야 합니다.** 노필드 주민들과 다른 이해관계자들은 회의에 참석하여 피드백을 공유할 수 있습니다. **190뒤에 서 계시지 않으려면 일찍 도착하시는 것을 권장합니다.**

어휘 resident 주민 interested party 이해관계자 avoid 피하다

---

186 주제 / 목적

번역 기사의 목적은 무엇인가?
(A) 지역 수질오염 문제를 강조하는 것
(B) 사람들이 쓰레기를 줄이도록 독려하는 것
(C) 새 농업 규제를 도입하는 것
(D) 환경 단체 회원을 모집하는 것

해설 기사문 첫 번째 단락의 첫 문장에서 시 관계자들이 시 동쪽에 있는 어거스타 연못의 오염 수준이 이상적인 것으로 간주되는 수준의 거의 10배에 이른다는 사실을 확인했다(City officials have confirmed that the contamination levels at Augusta Pond, on the eastern side of town, are nearly ten times the level that is considered ideal)고 했으므로, 지역 수질오염 문제를 강조하기 위한 기사문임을 알 수 있다. 따라서 정답은 (A)이다.

187 연계

번역 무어 씨는 무엇을 염려하는가?
(A) 재정적 어려움
(B) 유권자 불만족
(C) 프로젝트 연기
(D) 서식지 유실

해설 기사문의 두 번째 단락 마지막 문장에서 마저리 로우는 이 프로젝트로 인해 다른 중요한 프로젝트들이 연기될 것을 염려한다(Marjorie Rowe is concerned that the work would cause other important projects to be postponed)고 했다. 무어 씨가 티그 씨에게 보낸 이메일 두 번째 문장에서 제안된 프로젝트에 관해 로우 씨의 의견과 뜻을 함께한다(I share Ms. Rowe's opinion about the proposed work)고 했다. 따라서 무어 씨는 로우 씨와 마찬가지로 프로젝트 지연에 대해 염려하고 있음을 알 수 있으므로, 정답은 (C)이다.

188 동의어 찾기

번역 이메일에서 첫 번째 단락 5행의 "appreciates"와 의미가 가장 가까운 단어는?
(A) 상승하다
(B) 감사하다
(C) 즐기다
(D) 이해하다

해설 해당 문장은 '의회 전체가 이 문제가 심각한 사안임을 인식하고 있다'는 의미로 해석되므로, 여기서 appreciates는 '인식하다, 이해하다'의 의미가 자연스럽다. 따라서 정답은 (D) understands이다.

189 연계

번역 맥베이 씨에 대해 암시된 것은?
(A) 노필드시 근처의 농부이다.
(B) 농촌부에서 일한다.
(C) 자원봉사 행사를 준비하도록 선정되었다.
(D) 최근 시 의회 의원이 됐다.

해설 기사문의 첫 단락 두 번째 문장에서 농촌부(DRA)에서 2월 2일에 검사를 실시했다(A test was carried out on February 2 by the Department of Rural Affairs (DRA))고 했다. 공지문에서 노필드 시 의회는 3월 1일에 특별 회의를 개최하여 연못 정화 프로젝트에 관해 논의할 예정인데, 셰릴 맥베이 씨와 그 팀이 지난달, 즉 2월에 검사를 실시했다(Following the test conducted by Cheryl McVey and her team last month)고 했다. 따라서, 맥베이 씨는 농촌부에서 근무한다는 것을 추론할 수 있으므로, 정답은 (B)이다.

190 추론 / 암시

번역 3월 1일 회의에 대해 암시된 것은?
(A) 좌석이 모두 찰 것으로 예상된다.
(B) 티그 씨가 검사 결과를 설명할 것이다.
(C) 노필드 주민들만을 위한 것이다.
(D) 언론이 시 의회 의원들을 인터뷰할 것이다.

해설 공지문 마지막 문장에서 뒤에 서 있지 않으려면 일찍 도착하는 것을 권장한다(To avoid standing in the back, early arrival is recommended)고 했으므로, 좌석이 모두 찰 것으로 예상하고 있다는 것을 알 수 있다. 따라서 정답은 (A)이다.

191-195 편지 + 이메일 + 웹페이지

앤드류 샐다나
시더 레인 814
콜럼버스, OH 43035

샐다나 씨께,

크렌턴 미술박물관을 대표하여, 저희 발표실 정비 기금 마련을 위해 다가오는 많은 행사들에 귀하께서 주목해 주시기 바랍니다. **191**특별 행사는 대개 박물관 회원에게만 제한되지만, 행사에 무료로 참가하셔서 발표를 위해 취재하실 수 있도록 귀하를 초청하는 바입니다.

9월 한 달간 매주 금요일마다 폐관시간 이후 투어를 제공할 예정입니다. 입장권 구매자들에게는 저희 정규 개관시간이 **192**적용되지 않습니다! **193**다스라스 페이텔이 매 투어 시작마다 발표를 하고, 이후 바바라 플레밍이 박물관의 여러 곳을 안내해 드릴 예정입니다. 입장권은 100달러이며 소규모를 유지하기 위해 행사당 25매로 제한됩니다. 각 투어 이후 다과가 제공됩니다.

제 사무실 555-0177로 전화 주셔서 참석 가능 여부를 알려주십시오.

캐리 브라이트

어휘 on behalf of ~을 대표하여 bring to one's attention ~가 주목하도록 만들다 upcoming 다가오는 raise money 모금하다 refurbishment 정비 at no charge 무료로 cover 취재하다, 보도하다 publication (신문 등을 통한) 발표, 공개 after-hours 근무 시간 후의 regular hours of operations 정규 영업시간 give a presentation 발표하다 refreshments 다과 be in attendance 참가하다, 참석하다

수신: 크렌턴 미술박물관 직원 〈stafflist@crentonart.net〉
발신: 캐리 브라이트 〈c.brighton@crentonart.net〉
날짜: 9월 3일
제목: 특별 행사

안녕하세요 여러분.

이번 금요일은 저희 박물관의 폐관시간 이후의 특별 기금 마련 행사가 시작되는 첫날입니다. 그래서 여러분께 몇 가지 새 소식을 알리고자 합니다. **193**플레밍 씨는 뜻밖의 상황 때문에 일하지 못할 예정입니다. 이에 따라 빈스 오스왈드 씨가 플레밍 씨의 일을 대신하겠다고 자원했습니다.

195좋은 소식을 전하자면 지역 기업가인 거액의 기부자가 저희 모금 노력에 부합하는 금액을 모두 제공해 주셨음을 알리게 되어 매우 기쁩니다. 정비 공사 목표에 훨씬 빨리 도달하는 데 도움이 될 것입니다. **194**또한 이번 달에 목표를 달성할 경우 디자이너 다이아나 커비 씨가 저희 10월 직원회의에 참석하여 발표실에 관한 자신의 시각을 보여줄 것입니다.

모두 수고해 주셔서 감사합니다!

캐리

어휘 fund-raising 모금 활동(의) due to ~ 때문에 unforeseen 뜻밖의, 예상치 못한 circumstance 상황 generous donor 거액의 기부자 entrepreneur 기업가 dollar for dollar 이 값으로 reach a goal 목표를 달성하다

---

http://www.crentonart.net

| 홈 | 전시품 | 후원 | **박물관 소식** | 연락처 |

10월 1일

<u>모금행사 목표 달성!</u>

1959월 모금행사와 함께 익명의 기부자에게서 아낌없는 기부를 받아 발표실 개조에 필요한 목표액 2만 달러에 도달했습니다. **194**직원들은 10월 10일 직원회의에서 새로운 디자인을 살짝 엿볼 수 있습니다. 진행 상황의 사진과 함께 향후 공지는 이곳 웹사이트에서 공개 게시될 예정입니다.

어휘 with a combination of ~의 조합으로 generous contribution 아낌없는 기부 anonymous 익명의 get a sneak peek 살짝 엿보다, 맛보다 along with ~와 함께

191 추론 / 암시

번역 샐다나 씨는 누구이겠는가?
(A) 전문 화가
(B) 박물관 후원자
(C) (신문·방송·잡지사의) 기자
(D) 관광 관계자

해설 캐리 브라이트 씨가 샐다나 씨에게 보낸 편지 첫 번째 단락 마지막 문장에서 특별 행사는 대개 박물관 회원에게만 제한되나 행사를 취재할 수 있도록 초청한다(Special events are usually limited to museum members only; however, we are inviting you to participate in them at no charge so you can cover them for your publication)고 했다. 따라서 샐다나 씨는 기자임을 알 수 있으므로, 정답은 (C)이다.

192 동의어 찾기

번역 편지에서 두 번째 단락 2행의 "apply"와 의미가 가장 가까운 단어는?
(A) 펴다
(B) 유효하다
(C) 열망하다
(D) 헌신하다

해설 해당 문장은 '입장권 구매자들에게는 정규 개관시간이 적용되지 않는다'는 의미로 해석되므로, 여기서 apply는 '적용하다, 유효하다'는 의미가 자연스럽다. 따라서 정답은 (B) be in effect이다.

193 연계

번역 오스왈드 씨는 특별 행사 중 어떤 책임을 맡을 것인가?
(A) 설문조사 실시
(B) 기부금 모금
(C) 투어 안내
(D) 발표

해설 편지의 두 번째 단락에서 바바라 플레밍이 박물관의 여러 곳을 안내할 예정(participants will be guided through the various sections of the museum by Barbara Fleming)이라고 했는데, 이메일에서 플레밍 씨가 뜻밖의 상황 때문에 일하지 못하게 되어, 오스왈드가 플레밍 씨의 일을 대신하기로 자원했다(Ms. Fleming will be unable to work due to unforeseen circumstances. Therefore, Vince Oswald has volunteered to take over her duties)고 했다. 따라서 오스왈드 씨가 플레밍 씨를 대신해 투어를 안내할 것임을 알 수 있으므로, 정답은 (C)이다.

194 연계

번역 커비 씨에 대해 암시된 것은?
(A) 10월 10일에 회의에 갈 예정이다.
(B) 자신의 웹사이트에 스케치를 게시할 것이다.
(C) 9월 모금행사 기획을 도왔다.
(D) 박물관의 다른 부분을 디자인했다.

해설 이메일의 두 번째 단락 마지막 문장에서 이번 달 목표를 달성할 경우 커비 씨가 10월 직원회의에 참석하여 발표실에 관한 자신의 시각을 보여줄 것(Also, if we meet the goal this month, designer Diana Kirby will attend our October staff meeting to show us her vision for the room)이라고 했다. 또한 웹페이지의 끝에서 두 번째 문장에서 직원들은 10월 10일 직원회의에서 새로운 디자인을 살짝 엿볼 수 있다(Staff members will get a sneak peek at sketches of the redesign at the October 10 staff meeting)고 했다. 따라서 커비 씨는 목표를 달성해 10월 10일 회의에 참석할 예정임을 추론할 수 있으므로, 정답은 (A)이다.

▶▶ **Paraphrasing** 지문의 **attend our October staff meeting** → 정답의 **go to a meeting on October 10**

195 연계

번역 익명의 기부자는 얼마를 기부했겠는가?
(A) 100달러
(B) 2,500달러
(C) 10,000달러
(D) 20,000달러

해설 이메일의 두 번째 단락 첫 문장에서 지역 기업가인 거액의 기부자가 모금한 금액과 같은 금액을 기부했다(On a happier note, I'm pleased to inform you that a generous donor, a local entrepreneur, has offered to match all funds raised dollar for dollar)고 했다. 웹페이지의 두 번째 문장에서 모금한 금액과 기부자가 기부한 금액을 합쳐 목표액 2만 달러에 도달했다(With a combination of September's fund-raisers and a generous contribution from an anonymous donor, we have reached our goal of $20,000 for the updating of our presentation hall)고 했다. 따라서 익명의 기부자는 전체 모금액인 2만 달러의 절반인 1만 달러를 기부했음을 알 수 있으므로, 정답은 (C)이다.

196-200 웹페이지 + 이메일 + 이메일

https://www.grandeylandscaping.com

| 홈 | 사진 갤러리 | 처리 정책 | 연락처 |

그랜데이 조경은 지난 20년 동안 주거용 건물과 사업장의 잔디 및 정원 유지보수에 필요한 최상의 서비스를 제공해 왔습니다. 저희는 아래를 포함하여 다양한 서비스를 제공해 드립니다.

- 잔디 씨 뿌리기, 잔디 깎기
- 정원 디자인 및 식물 관리
- 잡초 관리
- 나무 제거 및 관목 정리

저희는 린치버그, 블루밍턴, 핀우드 및 인근 지역에 조경 서비스를 제공합니다. **200주말 서비스는 핀우드 고객만 이용하실 수 있음을 알려 드립니다.**

그랜데이 조경이 여러분에게 적합한지 모르시겠다고요? **196저희 숙련된 직원이 귀하의 장소를 방문해 건물에 필요한 요구사항을 알려드립니다. 이 서비스는 무료로 해 드립니다.**

귀하의 연락을 기다립니다!

어휘 disposal 처리 maintenance 유지보수 residential 주거의 property 건물, 재산, 부동산 seeding 씨뿌리기 mowing 풀 베기 weed 잡초 experienced 숙련된, 노련한 at no cost 무료로

수신: 로버트 에르난데스
발신: 루이자 슈뢰더
날짜: 3월 25일
제목: 그랜데이 조경

에르난데스 씨께,

저는 블루밍턴 북서쪽에서 작은 상업용 건물을 관리하는데, 최근 소유주가 예산을 **198삭감하여** 조경 서비스 업체를 바꾸려고 생각하고 있습니다. **197현재 그랜데이 조경 서비스를 이용하는 사람의 추천 글을 요청했는데 직원이 귀하를 연결해 주었습니다. 199C꽃 정원을 디자인하는 업체의 절차에 대해 말씀해 주실 수 있는지 궁금합니다. 199B또한 청구서를 어떻게 받으며 청구서가 얼마나 정확한지도 알고 싶습니다. 199D아울러 장비가 저희 근로자들에게 너무 시끄러울지 우려됩니다.** 이것에 대한 의견을 알려 주십시오. 시간을 내어 질문에 답해 주시면 정말 감사하겠습니다.

감사합니다.

루이자 슈뢰더

어휘 cut the budget 예산을 삭감하다 testimonial 추천의 글 currently 현재 accurate 정확한

수신: 루이자 슈뢰더
발신: 로버트 에르난데스
날짜: 3월 26일
제목: RE: 그랜데이 조경

슈뢰더 씨께,

저는 주저 없이 그랜데이 조경을 추천합니다. **199C**그랜데이 조경은 저희 뒤뜰의 화단을 디자인했는데 그 부분이 받는 그늘의 양에 기반을 두고 추천해 주었습니다. 이 서비스에는 추가 요금이 있습니다만 충분한 가치가 있었습니다. 또한 제 집과 이웃 담장 사이에 죽은 나무가 있었는데 업체 직원이 주변 구조물의 손상 없이 제거해 줄 수 있었습니다.

200저는 현재 한 달에 두 번, 보통 토요일에 잔디 깎기와 정원 잡초 제거를 받습니다. **199D**장비는 그다지 시끄럽지 않고 작업자들이 가기 전에 항상 깎아 낸 잔디와 다른 쓰레기를 치웁니다. 이 서비스를 이용하신다면 실망하시지 않을 겁니다.

로버트 에르난데스

> **어휘** flowerbed 화단 make a recommendation 추천하다 extra charge 추가 요금 well worth 충분한 가치가 있는 surrounding 주변의 clipping 깎아낸 조각 debris 쓰레기, 잔해

196 추론 / 암시

번역 그랜데이 조경에 대해 암시된 것은?
(A) 최근 다른 도시에 지점을 열었다.
(B) 신규 고객에게 무료 상담을 제공한다.
(C) 주로 회사에 유지보수 서비스를 제공한다.
(D) 지난 30년간 영업해 왔다.

해설 웹페이지 세 번째 단락에서 그랜데이 조경의 숙련된 직원이 직접 방문해 건물에 필요한 요구사항을 무료로 알려준다(One of our experienced employees will visit your site and advise you about your property's needs. This is done at no cost to you)고 했으므로, 정답은 (B)이다.

> ▶▶ **Paraphrasing** 지문의 at no cost → 정답의 free

197 세부 사항

번역 슈뢰더 씨는 에르난데스 씨의 연락처 정보를 어떻게 얻었는가?
(A) 업체 단체를 통해
(B) 에르난데스 씨의 이웃을 통해
(C) 원예 취미 모임을 통해
(D) 그랜데이 조경을 통해

해설 슈뢰더 씨가 에르난데스 씨에게 보낸 이메일에서 슈뢰더 씨는 그랜데이 조경 서비스를 이용하는 사람의 추천 글을 요청했는데 직원이 에르난데스 씨를 연결해 주었다(I asked Grandey Landscaping for a testimonial from someone who is currently using its service, and an employee directed me to you)고 했으므로, 정답은 (D)이다.

198 동의어 찾기

번역 첫 번째 이메일에서 첫 번째 단락 3행의 "cut"과 의미가 가장 가까운 단어는?
(A) 중단시켰다
(B) 꿰뚫었다
(C) 삭감했다
(D) 단축했다

해설 해당 문장은 '최근 소유주가 예산을 삭감했다'라는 의미로 해석되므로, 여기서 cut은 '삭감했다, 줄였다'의 의미가 자연스럽다. 따라서 정답은 (C) decreased이다.

199 사실 관계 확인

번역 슈뢰더 씨가 언급한 화제 중 에르난데스 씨가 언급하지 않은 것은?
(A) 나무 제거
(B) 청구 방식
(C) 정원 디자인
(D) 소음 정도

해설 슈뢰더 씨가 에르난데스 씨에게 보낸 이메일을 보면, 슈뢰더 씨는 정원 디자인(I'm wondering if you could tell me about the company's process for designing a flower garden), 청구 방식과 청구서의 정확도(I'd also like to know how you receive your bills and how accurate these are), 장비의 소음 정도(I'm concerned that the equipment will be too noisy for my workers)에 대해 언급했다. 에르난데스 씨가 슈뢰더 씨에게 보낸 이메일을 보면, 정원 디자인(The company designed a flowerbed for my backyard)과 죽은 나무 처리(I also had a dead tree between my house and my neighbor's fence, and the company's employees were able to remove it), 장비의 소음 정도 및 쓰레기 처리(The equipment is not very noisy, and the workers always clean up the lawn clippings and other debris before leaving)에 대해서만 언급했다. 따라서 정답은 (B)이다.

> ▶▶ **Paraphrasing** 지문의 **how you receive your bills**
> → 보기의 **Billing methods**

200 연계

번역 두 번째 이메일이 에르난데스 씨에 대해 암시하는 것은?
(A) 현재 핀우드에 거주한다.
(B) 그의 부동산이 웹사이트용으로 촬영되었다.
(C) 슈뢰더 씨를 방문할 예정이다.
(D) 그랜데이 조경에서 잔디에 씨를 뿌렸다.

해설 세 번째 지문에서 에르난데스 씨는 현재 한 달에 두 번, 보통 토요일에 잔디 깎기와 정원 잡초 제거를 받는다(I currently have my lawn mowed and garden weeded twice a month, usually on Saturdays)고 했는데, 웹페이지의 두 번째 단락 마지막 문장에서 주말 서비스는 핀우드 고객만 이용할 수 있다(Please note that weekend services are available to customers in the town of Finwood only)고 했다. 따라서 에르난데스 씨는 핀우드에 거주한다는 것을 알 수 있으므로, 정답은 (A)이다.

> ▶▶ **Paraphrasing** 지문의 **customers in the town of Finwood**
> → 정답의 **is currently living in Finwood**

TEST 4

101 (D)	**102** (D)	**103** (C)	**104** (A)	**105** (C)
106 (C)	**107** (A)	**108** (B)	**109** (D)	**110** (D)
111 (D)	**112** (B)	**113** (B)	**114** (B)	**115** (D)
116 (B)	**117** (B)	**118** (A)	**119** (A)	**120** (B)
121 (B)	**122** (A)	**123** (C)	**124** (D)	**125** (B)
126 (A)	**127** (C)	**128** (C)	**129** (A)	**130** (B)
131 (A)	**132** (D)	**133** (D)	**134** (A)	**135** (B)
136 (D)	**137** (A)	**138** (B)	**139** (D)	**140** (B)
141 (C)	**142** (C)	**143** (D)	**144** (D)	**145** (B)
146 (A)	**147** (A)	**148** (D)	**149** (A)	**150** (C)
151 (D)	**152** (B)	**153** (A)	**154** (D)	**155** (D)
156 (D)	**157** (D)	**158** (C)	**159** (A)	**160** (B)
161 (C)	**162** (B)	**163** (D)	**164** (A)	**165** (D)
166 (C)	**167** (B)	**168** (A)	**169** (B)	**170** (B)
171 (A)	**172** (D)	**173** (D)	**174** (C)	**175** (B)
176 (B)	**177** (D)	**178** (C)	**179** (B)	**180** (A)
181 (C)	**182** (D)	**183** (D)	**184** (C)	**185** (C)
186 (A)	**187** (D)	**188** (A)	**189** (C)	**190** (C)
191 (A)	**192** (C)	**193** (D)	**194** (D)	**195** (B)
196 (A)	**197** (B)	**198** (B)	**199** (D)	**200** (C)

Test 4

Part 5

101 부사 자리 _ 동사 수식

해설 빈칸은 앞에 있는 동사(meets)를 수식하는 부사 자리로, 정답은 부사 (D) precisely이다. 명사 (A) preciseness와 (C) precision, 형용사 (B) precise는 품사상 적합하지 않다.

번역 귀하의 이력서를 저희에게 보내기 전에 반드시 저희 요건을 정확하게 충족하는지 점검하세요.

어휘 send 보내다 résumé 이력서 be sure to + 동사원형 반드시 ~하다 meet (요건 등을) 충족하다 requirement 요건, 요구조건 precisely 정확하게

102 상관 접속사

해설 빈칸은 앞에 있는 either와 짝을 이루어, 앞의 명사(the manufacturer)와 뒤의 명사(a freelance photographer)를 연결하는 접속사 자리이다. 따라서 정답은 (D) or이다.

번역 제품 사진 대부분은 제조업체 또는 프리랜서 사진가가 찍었습니다.

어휘 manufacturer 제조업체 either A or B A나 B 둘 중 하나 freelance 프리랜서

103 명사 자리 _ 주어

해설 빈칸은 뒤에 나오는 전치사구(about payments and account balances)의 수식을 받으면서, 동사(should be directed)의 주어 역할을 하는 명사 자리이다. 따라서 정답은 명사 (C) Inquiries이다. to부정사 (A) To inquire(문의하는 것)는 주어 자리에 올 수 있지만, 의미상 적

합하지 않고, 과거분사/과거시제 동사 (B) Inquired, 동사원형/현재동사 (D) Inquire는 품사상 적합하지 않다.

번역 지불금과 잔액에 대한 문의는 저희 청구서 담당 부서로 해주셔야 합니다.

어휘 inquiry about ~에 대한 문의[조회] payment 지불, 지불금 account balance 계좌[계정] 잔액 direct to ~로 향하다 billing department 청구서 담당 부서

104 전치사 / 부사절 접속사 구분

해설 빈칸 뒤의 명사(issues)를 목적어로 취하면서, 앞에 있는 동사 (suspended)를 수식하는 전치사 자리이다. 문맥상 '문제 때문에 중단했다'라는 의미가 자연스러우므로, 정답은 전치사 (A) due to이다. 전치사 (B) except for(~을 제외하고)는 의미상 적합하지 않고, 부사절 접속사 (C) whereas(~ 반면에)와 (D) although(~에도 불구하고) 뒤에는 주어와 동사로 이뤄진 완전한 절이 와야 한다.

번역 거머스 항공은 어제 항공기 문제 때문에 몇 차례 운항을 중단했다.

어휘 suspend 중단하다 flight 비행, 항공편 issue 문제(점) aircraft 항공기

105 동사 자리 _ 시제

해설 빈칸은 앞의 주어(Darablatt Ltd.)와 뒤의 목적어(its earnings figures) 사이의 동사 자리로, 뒤에 나오는 시간을 나타내는 부사(next Tuesday)의 수식을 받는다. 따라서 정답은 미래시제 동사 (C) will release이다. 현재분사/동명사 (A) being released는 동사 자리에 올 수 없다.

번역 대러블랏 사는 다음 주 화요일 이사회에서 수익 수치를 발표할 것이다.

어휘 earnings 수익, 소득 figure 수치 board meeting 이사회 release 발표하다, 공개하다

106 부사 어휘

해설 빈칸은 앞의 조동사(will)와 뒤의 동사(be reduced) 사이에서, 뒤의 동사를 수식하는 부사 자리이다. 문맥상 '머지 않아 줄어들 것이다'라는 의미가 자연스러우므로, 정답은 (C) soon이다. (A) recently(최근에)는 주로 현재완료 동사와 과거 동사를 수식하고, (B) more(더), (D) early(일찍)는 조동사와 be동사 사이에 올 수 없으므로 오답이다.

번역 새 도로 표지판 덕분에 길을 찾기 위해 운전자들이 도시 랜드마크 건물에 의존하는 것이 머지 않아 줄어들 것이다.

어휘 street sign 도로 표지판 dependence on ~에 대한 의존(도) landmark 랜드마크, (위치 파악의 기준이 되는) 주요 건물 navigation (운전하며) 길 찾기 reduce 줄이다, 줄다

107 전치사 어휘

해설 빈칸은 뒤에 나오는 목적어(audiences and critics alike)와 함께 앞의 명사(warm praise)를 수식하는 전치사 자리이다. 문맥상 '관객과 비평가 모두로부터 열렬한 찬사를 받았다'라는 의미가 자연스러우므로, 정답은 전치사 (A) from이다.

번역 영화 〈푸른 초원의 추억〉은 관객과 비평가 모두에게 열렬한 찬사를 받았다.

어휘 praise 칭찬, 찬사 audience 관객, 청중 critic 비평가
A and B alike A와 B 둘 다

108 명사 자리 _ 동사의 목적어

해설 빈칸은 앞의 형용사(sufficient)와 함께 동사(should provide)의 목적어 역할을 하는 명사 자리이므로, 정답은 명사 (B) reinforcement이다. 동사 (A) reinforce, 과거시제 동사/과거분사 (C) reinforced, 형용사 (D) reinforceable은 품사상 적합하지 않다.

번역 콘크리트 안에 박힌 철근들이 충분한 보강 작용을 해야 한다.

어휘 steel bar 철근 place 놓다, 두다 sufficient 충분한
reinforcement 강화, 보강

109 동사 자리

해설 빈칸은 앞의 주어(the new Hagoya Shopping Malll)와 뒤의 목적어(a variety of architectural styles and details) 사이의 동사 자리이므로, 정답은 현재동사 (D) incorporates이다. 명사 (A) incorporations, (C) incorporation과 동명사/현재분사 (B) incorporating은 동사 자리에 올 수 없다.

번역 금요일에 문을 여는 신축 하고야 쇼핑몰은 여러 가지 건축 양식과 세부 표현이 합쳐져 있다.

어휘 architectural style 건축 양식 detail 세부 사항 incorporate (부분으로) 포함하다, ～를 합해 전체를 이루다

110 인칭 대명사 _ 소유격

해설 빈칸 앞에 있는 전치사(of)의 목적어(authenticity and value)를 한정 수식하는 자리로, 앞의 명사(artwork)를 대신 가리킨다. 따라서 정답은 소유격 인칭대명사 (D) its이다. (A) what과 (B) whose 뒤에는 동사가 있는 절이 나와야 하고, 부사 (C) there는 품사상 적합하지 않다.

번역 미술품을 살펴본 뒤에는 작품의 진품 여부와 가치에 대한 귀하의 평가를 공유해 주세요.

어휘 assessment 판단, 평가 authenticity 진품임, 진짜임 inspect 조사하다 artwork 미술품 share 공유하다, 나누다

111 전치사 어휘

해설 빈칸은 뒤의 목적어(a large oak tree)와 함께 앞의 현재분사(leaning)를 수식하는 전치사 자리로, 전치사 (A) until(～까지), (B) between(～사이에), (D) against가 가능하다. 문맥상 '오크나무에 기대어'라는 의미가 자연스러우므로, 정답은 (D) against이다. 형용사 (C) contrary(반대의)는 전치사 to와 함께 쓰여 'contrary to(～에 반하여, ～에 상반되는)'로 쓰인다.

번역 현재 전시되고 있는 수상한 포스터 중 하나에서는 자전거 한 대가 큰 오크나무에 기대어 있는 것이 보인다.

어휘 prize-winning 수상한 currently 현재 exhibition 전시(회)
lean against ～에 기대다

112 부사 어휘

해설 빈칸은 뒤에 나오는 형용사구(likely to win the seat)를 수식하는 부사 자리이다. 문맥상 '당선 가능성이 동일한'이라는 의미가 자연스러우므로, 정답은 (B) equally이다. (A) normally(보통, 통상적으로), (C) formerly(이전에), (D) gradually(점차로)는 의미상 적합하지 않다.

번역 유권자 여론조사에 따르면 두 시장 후보자는 당선 가능성이 동일해 보인다.

어휘 voter 유권자 poll 여론조사 mayoral 시장의 candidate 후보자
be likely to + 동사원형 ～할 것 같다, ～할 가능성이 있다 win a seat 의석을 얻다, 당선되다 equally 똑같이

113 명사 어휘

해설 빈칸은 동사(enables)의 주어 역할을 하는 명사 자리로, 뒤의 절(Fiona Lim has acquired)의 수식을 받는다. 문맥상 '피오나 림이 얻은 경험'이라는 의미가 자연스러우므로, 정답은 (B) experience이다. (A) progress(발전, 진행), (C) graduation(졸업), (D) instance(예, 실례)는 의미상 적합하지 않다.

번역 피오나 림이 얻은 경험은 어떤 청중에게나 설득력 있는 강연을 할 수 있게 해준다.

어휘 acquire 얻다, 배우다 deliver a talk 강연[연설]을 하다
persuasive 설득력 있는

114 부사 자리 _ 동사 수식

해설 빈칸은 현재진행 시제를 나타내는 동사(is considering) 사이에서 동사를 수식하는 부사 자리이다. 따라서 정답은 부사 (B) strongly이다. 동사 (A) strengthen, 명사 (C) strength, 형용사 (D) strong은 품사상 적합하지 않다.

번역 포크 가수 캐런 왓슨은 다가오는 시즌의 인기 음악 프로그램에 출연을 열심히 고려하고 있다.

어휘 appear 출연하다, 나타나다 upcoming 다가오는 popular 인기 있는

115 동사 어휘

해설 빈칸 앞의 동사(have)와 함께 현재완료 시제를 나타내는 과거분사 자리이다. 뒤의 전치사구(at a superior level consistently)의 수식을 받아 앞에 있는 주어(they = employees)를 설명한다. 문맥상 '월등한 수준의 성취도를 보이면'이라는 의미가 자연스러우므로, 정답은 과거분사 (D) performed이다. (A) encountered(마주치다), (B) assured(보증하다), (C) understood(이해하다)는 의미상 적합하지 않다.

번역 세베티치 뮤추얼에서는 직원들이 지속적으로 월등한 수준의 성취도를 보일 경우 재택 근무가 허용되기도 한다.

어휘 permission 허락, 허용 telecommute 재택 근무하다 perform (일·과제 등을) 완수하다 consistently 지속적으로

116 형용사 자리 _ 명사 수식

해설 빈칸은 앞의 최상급(the most)과 함께 빈칸 뒤의 명사(novels)를 수식하는 형용사 자리이다. 따라서 정답은 형용사 역할을 하는 현재분사 (B) engaging이다. 명사 (A) engagement(개입, 종사, 약속), 부사 (C) engagingly(매력적으로), 동사 (D) engages(고용하다, 몰두하다)는 품사상 적합하지 않다.

번역 젊은 나이에도 불구하고 마크 브라운 씨는 최근의 가장 흥미로운 소설들 가운데 한 편을 저술했다.

어휘 novel 소설 engaging 매력적인, 흥미로운

117 명사 어휘

해설 빈칸은 부정관사(a) 뒤의 명사 자리이다. 앞의 부정관사(a)와 뒤의 전치사(of)와 함께, 뒤에 나오는 명사구(economic and political topics)를 가장 잘 수식하는 명사를 선택해야 한다. 문맥상 '다양한 경제 및 정치적 주제'라는 의미가 자연스러우므로, 정답은 (B) range이다. (A) material(물질, 재료), (C) type(유형), (D) distance(거리)는 의미상 적합하지 않다.

번역 베조트 사의 최근 조사는 다양한 경제 및 정치적 주제에 대한 응답자의 의견을 구했다.

어휘 latest 최신의 seek 구하다, 청하다 respondent 응답자 a range of 다양한 ~ economic 경제의 political 정치적인

118 부사 어휘

해설 빈칸은 주어(it = the final version of the product)를 보충 설명하는 형용사(different)를 수식하는 부사 자리이다. 문맥상 '완전히 다르지는 않다'라는 의미가 자연스러우므로, 정답은 부사 (A) fundamentally이다. 부사 (B) approximately(대략), (C) easily(손쉽게), (D) separately(별도로)는 의미상 적합하지 않다.

번역 디자인 팀에서 그 제품의 마지막 버전에 작은 변화를 주었지만, 전반적으로 시제품과 완전히 다르지는 않다.

어휘 minor 작은 overall 전반적으로, 대체로 prototype 원형, 시제품 fundamentally 근본적으로, 완전히

119 부사절 접속사

해설 빈칸은 뒤에 나오는 완전한 절을 이끌면서, 앞에 있는 to부정사 구문(to assist customers)을 수식하는 부사절 접속사 자리이다. 문맥상 '문의가 있을 때마다'라는 의미가 자연스러우므로, 정답은 부사절 접속사 (A) whenever이다. 접속사 (B) rather than(~보다는), (D) so that(~위해)은 의미상 적합하지 않고, (C) such as(~와 같은)는 주로 전치사로 쓰인다.

번역 제품지원 부서는 품질보증 조건과 관련해 문의가 있을 때마다 고객을 지원할 준비가 되어 있다.

어휘 on hand (필요할 때) 바로 이용할 수 있는 assist 돕다 arise 발생하다 concerning ~에 관해 warranty 품질보증

120 부사 자리 _ 형용사 수식

해설 빈칸 뒤에 나오는 형용사(risky)를 수식하는 부사 자리로, 정답은 부사 (B) intentionally이다. 형용사 (A) intentional, 명사 (C) intention, 동사 (D) intend는 품사상 적합하지 않다.

번역 베르소이 파이낸셜은 투자가 의도적으로 위험을 추구한다는 주장을 부인하고 있다.

어휘 claim 주장 investment 투자 intentionally 의도적으로 risky 위험한

121 명사 자리 _ 전치사의 목적어

해설 빈칸은 소유격 인칭대명사(his)와 함께 앞에 있는 전치사(for)의 목적어 역할을 하는 명사 자리이므로, 정답은 명사 (B) evaluation이다. 동사 (A) evaluate, (D) evaluates는 품사상 적합하지 않고, 과거시제 동사/과거분사인 (C) evaluated 역시 목적어 자리에 올 수 없다.

번역 이 서류는 자오 씨가 신입사원 평가를 위해 고려하는 요소들을 상세하게 나열하고 있다.

어휘 document 서류 detail 상세히 설명하다[나열하다] take into account 고려하다 evaluation 평가

122 형용사 자리 _ 명사 수식

해설 빈칸은 앞에 있는 동사(has)의 목적어 역할을 하는 명사(supply)를 수식하는 형용사 자리이므로, 정답은 형용사 (A) no이다. 부사 (B) not, 대명사 (C) nothing과 (D) none은 품사상 적합하지 않다. 참고로 (A) no는 형용사, 부사로 모두 쓰일 수 있다.

번역 한정판 지랍 차 선물 세트는 상점 재고에 남은 물건이 거의 없기 때문에 아마도 빨리 매진될 것이다.

어휘 limited-edition 한정판의 probably 아마도 sell out 매진되다 supply 비축량 inventory 재고

123 부사 어휘

해설 빈칸은 형용사(delicious)를 수식하는 부사 자리이다. 문맥상 '여전히 맛있다'라는 의미가 자연스러우므로, 정답은 (B) still이다. 부사 (C) far는 거리나 시간이 훨씬 멀다는 의미로 쓰이거나 형용사의 비교급을 주로 수식한다.

번역 그 식당의 요리가 매우 대담하고 모험적이 되었지만 손님들은 요리가 여전히 맛있다는 것에 동의한다.

어휘 cuisine 요리(법) bold 대담한 adventurous 모험적인 patron (식당·호텔 등의) 고객 still 여전히, 그럼에도 불구하고

124 동사 어형 _ 시제

해설 빈칸은 주어(The Sales Team) 뒤의 동사 자리로, 뒤에 나오는 과거시간을 나타내는 부사(last month)의 수식을 받는다. 따라서 정답은 과거사실에 대한 반대 의미를 나타내는 가정법 과거완료 동사 (B) would have participated이다. 현재완료진행 동사 (A) have been participating은 과거시간을 나타내는 부사(last month)의 수식을 받을 수 없다.

번역 영업팀은 지난달 전 직원회의에 참석했어야 하는데, 팀원 대부분이 출장으로 자리를 비웠다.

어휘 all-employee meeting 전 직원회의 away 자리에 없는 business trip 출장

125 형용사 어휘

해설 빈칸 앞에 있는 to부정사(to ensure)의 목적어 역할을 하는 명사(resolution)를 수식하는 형용사 자리이다. 문맥상 '문제의 신속한 해결을 위해'라는 의미가 자연스러우므로, 정답은 (B) prompt이다. 형용사 (A) steep(가파른), (C) identical(동일한), (D) vague(애매한, 모호한)는 의미상 적합하지 않다.

번역 우리는 문제의 신속한 해결을 보장하기 위해 정상 근무시간을 초과해 일하고 있다.

어휘 regular hours 정상 근무시간 resolution 해결 prompt 신속한, 즉각적인

126 형용사 어휘

해설 빈칸은 앞에 있는 동사(earned)의 목적어 역할을 하는 명사(Mauller Awards)를 수식하는 형용사 자리이다. 또한 뒤의 전치사구(for *Hand to Hand* and *The Renwicks*)는 동사(earned)를 수식한다. 따라서 전치사구의 수식을 받는 동사와 목적어의 의미가 가장 잘 통하는 형용사를 선택해야 한다. 문맥상 '연속 수상했다'라는 의미가 자연스러우므로, 정답은 (A) successive이다. (B) thorough(철저한), (C) mandatory(강제적인), (D) compatible(양립하는, 호환성의)은 의미상 적합하지 않다.

번역 감독 생활 중 한 인상적인 시기에 루 씨는 〈핸드 투 핸드〉와 〈더 렌윅스〉로 몰러 어워즈를 연속 수상했습니다.

어휘 direct 감독하다, 연출하다 earn (상·칭찬 등을) 받다 successive 연속적인

127 비교급

해설 빈칸은 to부정사(to gain)의 목적어(market share)를 수식하는 형용사 자리로, 뒤에 나오는 than과 어울리는 형용사의 형태를 선택해야 한다. 따라서 정답은 비교급 형용사 (C) higher이다. 부사 (A) highly는 품사상 적합하지 않고, 원급 형용사 (B) high, 최상급 형용사 (D) highest는 than과 함께 쓰이지 않는다.

번역 혁신적인 홍보 아이디어를 장려함으로써 그 회사는 이전에 가졌던 것보다 더 높은 시장 점유율을 얻기를 희망한다.

어휘 encourage 장려하다 innovative 혁신적인 promotional 홍보의 gain 얻다, 획득하다 market share 시장 점유율 previously 예전에

128 동사 어휘

해설 빈칸은 뒤에 나오는 목적어(their neighbors)와 함께, 앞에 있는 동사(will help)의 목적어(newly-arrived international residents)를 보충 설명하는 목적격 보어 자리이다. 문맥상 '갓 도착한 외국인 거주자들이 이웃과 교류하다'라는 의미가 자연스러우므로, 정답은 (C) interact with이다. (A) apply for(~을 신청하다, 지원하다), (B) reach out(연락하다, 손을 뻗다), (D) belong to(~에 속하다)는 의미상 적합하지 않다.

번역 그 도시는 언어 강좌가 갓 도착한 외국인 거주자들이 이웃과 교류하는 데 도움을 줄 것으로 기대한다.

어휘 resident 거주자 neighbor 이웃사람 interact with ~와 교류하다

129 명사 어휘

해설 빈칸은 앞의 to부정사(to provide)의 목적어 역할을 하는 명사 자리로, 뒤의 관계사절의 수식을 받는다. 문맥상 '참석자들이 환경 문제를 논의할 수 있는 포럼'이라는 의미가 자연스러우므로, 정답은 명사 (A) forum이다. 명사 (B) mission(사명), (C) safeguard(안전 장치), (D) prediction(예언)은 의미상 적합하지 않다.

번역 공원 생태 위원회의 주간 회의는 참석자들이 환경 문제를 논의할 수 있는 포럼을 제공하도록 기획되었다.

어휘 weekly 매주의 intended 의도된, 계획된 forum 포럼, 토론의 장 attendee 참가자, 참석자 environmental 환경의 issue 문제

130 동사 어휘

해설 빈칸은 앞의 동사(have)와 함께 현재완료 시제를 나타내는 과거분사 자리로, 뒤의 간접목적어(the crafts vendors)와 의미가 가장 잘 통하는 과거분사를 선택해야 한다. 문맥상 '판매상에게 통보하다'라는 의미가 자연스러우므로, 정답은 (B) notified이다. (A) announced(발표하다), (C) declared(선언하다, 신고하다), (D) expressed(표현하다)는 모두 직접목적어를 목적어로 취하므로 뒤에 바로 사람(the crafts vendors)이 올 수 없다.

번역 축제 주최측에서는 공예품 판매상들에게 행사 전에 설비 지원이 제공될 것이라고 통보했다.

어휘 organizer 주최자 craft 공예품 vendor 노점상 set-up (특정 목적을 위한) 설비 assistance 지원 notify 공지하다, 통보하다

Part 6

131-134 이메일

수신: 〈jordan.bartlett@sweettree.com〉
발신: 〈linhbui@critespackaging.com〉
날짜: 5월 4일
제목: 포장재 해법

발렛 씨께,

오늘 아침 저희 포장재 해법에 대한 논의 차 전화 주셔서 다시 한 번 감사드립니다. 스위트 트리 케이터링의 요구사항에 대해 알게 되어 매우 흥미로웠습니다. 약속 드린 대로 저희 디자인팀에 정보를 **131전달했습니다**. 디자인팀에서는 적합한 포장재를 만드는 일은 **132어렵지** 않을 것이라고 답변했습니다. **133사실 일주일도 채 걸리지 않아 샘플을 준비할 수 있을 것입니다.** 이 절차를 진행하고 싶으십니까? **133관심이 있으시면 다음 단계로 직접 만나는 회의를 마련해 134거기에서 디자인팀에게 더 자세한 요구사항을 직접 설명하실 수 있습니다.** 그렇게 하기를 원하시는지 전화 주시거나 이메일 답신으로 확정해 주십시오.

린 뷔
크라이티스 포장

어휘 as promised 약속한 대로 suitable 적당한 in-person 직접의 requirement 요구

131 동사 어형 _ 시제

해설 빈칸은 주어(I) 뒤에 나오는 동사 자리이다. 빈칸 뒤에 나오는 문장의 동사 (responded)를 통해 과거시제임을 알 수 있으므로, 정답은 과거시제 동사 (A) passed이다. 가정법 과거완료 동사 (D) would have passed는 과거에 하지 못한 일을 나타내므로, 의미상 적합하지 않다.

132 형용사 어휘

해설 빈칸은 부정어(not)와 함께 앞에 있는 that절의 주어(creating suitable packaging)를 보충 설명하는 형용사 자리이다. 빈칸 뒤에 나오는 문장 '사실 일주일도 채 걸리지 않아 샘플을 준비할 수 있을 것이다(In fact, they could probably have samples ready for you in as little as one week)'를 통해 어렵지 않은 일임을 알 수 있으므로, 정답은 (B) challenging(힘든, 어려운, 도전적인)이다. (A) responsible(맡고 있는, 책임지고 있는), (C) proportional(비례하는), (D) inaccurate(부정확한, 오류가 있는)는 의미상 적합하지 않다.

133 문맥에 맞는 문장 고르기

번역 (A) 샘플이 어디에 전시되는지 알고 계십니까?
(B) 일정이 정확한 것이 확실합니까?
(C) 문제점을 발견하셨습니까?
(D) 이 절차를 진행하고 싶으십니까?

해설 빈칸 앞 문장 '사실 일주일도 채 걸리지 않아 샘플을 준비할 수 있을 것이다(In fact, they could probably have samples ready for you in as little as one week)'에서 샘플 제작의 예상 소요시간을 언급하고 있고 뒤 문장에서는 '관심이 있으면 다음 단계로 직접 만나는 회의를 마련해 거기에서 디자인팀에게 더 자세한 요구사항을 직접 설명하실 수 있다 (If you are interested, the next step is to set up an in-person meeting at which you would describe your requirements in greater detail directly to the Design Team)'라고 했다 따라서 빈칸에는 샘플 제작 절차의 진행 여부를 확인하는 내용이 이어지는 것이 문맥상 자연스러우므로, 정답은 (D)이다.

134 전치사 어휘

해설 빈칸은 앞에 있는 명사(an in-person meeting)를 대신 가리키는 목적격 관계대명사(which=an in-person meeting) 앞에 오는 전치사 자리이다. 문맥상 '직접 만나는 회의에서'라는 의미가 자연스러우므로, 정답은 (A) at(~에)이다. (B) on(~ 위에, ~에 관해), (C) toward(~를 향해), (D) between(~ 사이에)은 의미상 적합하지 않다.

135-138 기사

시카고 (3월 19일) – **135**오늘 아침 인기 가수 커트 글레이즈가 현재 앨범의 두 번째 싱글은 스탠 웨버의 고전 "유리의 한숨"을 리메이크할 예정이라고 밝혔다. 이 발표는 WLV 라디오와의 인터뷰에서 이뤄졌다.

웨버 씨는 30년 전 이 노래의 **136**원곡을 발표하며 일약 스타덤에 올랐다. 이후 재즈, 록 등 다양한 음악 장르로 수 차례 리메이크된 바 있다. 그러나 어떤 **137**스타일도 글레이즈 씨에게 맞지 않았다. 젊은 가수(커트 글레이즈)는 자신의

싱글이 사실 웨버 씨의 노래와 꽤 비슷하다고 설명하며 전통 발라드에 대한 애정을 **138**드러냈다. "이미 정말 아름다운 노래입니다. 제가 한 일은 현대의 청중에 맞게 약간 업데이트한 것뿐입니다." 그의 설명이다.

어휘 reveal 드러내다, 밝히다 rise to fame 명성을 얻다, 일약 유명해지다 diverse 다양한 describe 설명하다 audience 청중

135 문맥에 맞는 문장 고르기

번역 (A) 4월 공연의 입장권은 아직 남아 있다.
(B) 이 발표는 WLV 라디오와의 인터뷰에서 이뤄졌다.
(C) 두 음악가는 각자 솔로 활동을 시작할 것으로 예상된다.
(D) 각 노래는 성인기의 다른 면모를 다룬다.

해설 빈칸 앞 문장 '오늘 아침 인기 가수 커트 글레이즈가 현재 앨범의 두 번째 싱글은 스탠 웨버의 고전 "유리의 한숨"을 리메이크할 예정이라고 밝혔다(Popular singer Kurt Glaize revealed this morning that the second single from his current album will be a remake of Stan Weber's classic "Sighs of Glass")'에서 발표 내용을 언급하고 있다. 따라서 빈칸에도 발표(The announcement)와 관련된 내용이 이어지는 것이 문맥상 자연스러우므로, 정답은 (B)이다.

어휘 deal with ~을 다루다 adulthood 성인기

136 형용사 어휘

해설 빈칸은 동명사(releasing)의 목적어 역할을 하는 명사(version)를 수식하는 형용사 자리이다. 빈칸 앞 문장 '오늘 아침 인기 가수 커트 글레이즈가 현재 앨범의 두 번째 싱글은 스탠 웨버의 고전 "유리의 한숨"을 리메이크할 예정이라고 밝혔다(Popular singer Kurt Glaize revealed this morning that the second single from his current album will be a remake of Stan Weber's classic "Sighs of Glass")'를 통해 웨버 씨의 원곡에 대한 설명임을 알 수 있으므로, 정답은 (D) original(원래의, 독창적인)이다. (A) newest(최신의), (B) adverse(부정적인, 불리한), (C) clarified(명확해진)는 의미상 적합하지 않다.

137 명사 어휘

해설 빈칸은 전치사(of)의 목적어 역할을 하는 명사 자리로, 앞에 있는 지시형용사(these)의 한정 수식을 받는다. 지시형용사(these)는 앞 문장 '이후 재즈, 록 등 다양한 음악 장르로 수 차례 리메이크된 바 있다(It has been remade several times since then, in musical genres as diverse as jazz and rock)'에서 다양한 장르로 수 차례 리메이크된 음악을 가리키고 있으므로, 빈칸에는 '장르(genres)'와 유사한 의미의 명사를 선택해야 한다. 따라서 정답은 (A) styles(스타일, 방식, 표현법)이다. (B) coupons(쿠폰), (C) instruments(기구, 도구, 악기), (D) designs (디자인, 도안)는 의미상 적합하지 않다.

138 분사구문

해설 빈칸은 명사(his love)를 목적어로 취하면서 앞에 있는 완전한 절을 접속사 없이 부가 설명하는 분사구문이므로, 정답은 현재분사 (B) reflecting이다. 접속사가 없으므로 동사 (A) has reflected, (C) reflects, (D) will reflect는 정답이 될 수 없다.

139-142 공지

> **고객 안내 말씀**
>
> 여러분 모두 아시겠지만 브라흐트 스토리지를 둘러싸고 있는 땅은 빈틈없이 울타리를 쳐 놓았고 모든 구역이 비디오 감시 시스템을 통해 계속 **139촬영됩니다.** 또한 꼼꼼하게 청소를 실시해 해충을 막고 있습니다. 그러나 **140안전**에 대한 저희의 노력은 거기서 멈추지 않습니다. **141추가 예방조치로 이제 브라흐트는 각 저장실의 내용물 보험도 들 것을 요청합니다.** 고객들은 저희를 통해 직접 기본 설계를 받으실 수 있습니다, 이 보험증서는 화재, 홍수, 기타 예기치 못한 사건들로 피해를 입은 모든 품목에 대해 부분적인 보상을 제공합니다. 더욱 포괄적인 보장을 원한다면 전문화된 보험회사에서 보험에 **142가입하는** 쪽을 선택해도 됩니다. 어떤 선택이 자신에게 적합한지 결정할 수 있도록 상담원이 도움을 줄 수 있습니다.

> **어휘** property 부동산, 땅 surrounding 둘러싸고 있는 fence 울타리를 치다 continuously 계속 surveillance 감시 meticulous 세심한, 꼼꼼한 practice 실행, 관행 deter 단념시키다, 막다 pest 해충 commitment 헌신, 노력 precaution 예방 조치 contents 내용물 insure 보험에 들다 policy 보험증서 compensation 보상 damage 손상을 입히다 flood 홍수 unexpected 예기치 못한, 뜻밖의 occurrence 발생, 사건 comprehensive 포괄적인 coverage (보험의) 보장 purchase a policy 보험증권을 구입하다, 보험에 들다 insurance carrier 보험회사

139 동사 어형 _ 태

해설 빈칸 앞 and는 접속사이므로 뒤에는 절이 와야 한다. and 뒤로 동사가 없으므로 빈칸은 동사 자리이고 주어는 all areas이다. 동사 자리에 올 수 있는 (B), (C), (D) 중에서 정답을 골라야 한다. 모든 구역은 촬영되는 것이므로 수동태인 (C), (D)가 정답 후보인데 and 앞 문장이 현재시제(the property surrounding Bracht Storage is fully fenced)이므로 현재시제인 (D) are filmed가 정답이다. 동사 자리에 단독으로 올 수 없는 to부정사구인 (A)는 정답이 될 수 없다.

140 명사 어휘

해설 지문 초반에서 울타리(fully fenced), 비디오 감시 시스템(video surveillance system), 해충 방지(deter harmful pests) 등 안전에 관한 장치들을 언급하고 있다. 따라서 '안전에 대한 노력'이 이어지는 것이 자연스러우므로 정답은 (B) security이다.

141 문맥에 맞는 문장 고르기

번역 (A) 그럼에도 불구하고, 많은 사람들이 실내 시설을 선호합니다.
(B) 추가 품목들에 대해서는 별도로 대여해야 합니다.
(C) 고객들은 저희를 통해 직접 기본 설계를 받으실 수 있습니다.
(D) 자격을 갖춘 수리 직원이 항상 대기하고 있습니다.

해설 빈칸 앞에서 추가 예방조치로 브라흐트는 각 저장실의 내용물 보험을 들 것을 요청한다(As an extra precaution, Bracht now requires storage unit contents to be insured)고 했다. 보험을 통한 예방조치를 언급하고 있으므로 빈칸에는 보험 가입 방법이 이어지는 것이 문맥상 자연스러우므로, 정답은 (C)이다.

142 to부정사

해설 빈칸 뒤의 명사(a policy)를 목적어로 취하면서 빈칸 앞에 있는 동사원형(opt)의 목적어 역할을 하는 자리이다. opt는 to부정사를 목적어로 취하는 동사이므로, 정답은 (C) to purchase이다. opt 뒤에 명사가 오려면 'opt for + 명사'의 형태가 되어야 한다.

143-146 회람

> **수신:** 도서관 전 직원
> **발신:** 책임자 카메론 미치
> **제목:** 예산 및 회의
> **날짜:** 12월 5일
> **첨부:** 제안서
>
> 올해 도서관의 "프로그램" 예산을 지출하는 여러 행사가 예상만큼 개최되지 않았습니다. **143그 예로** 2월로 예정됐던 작가 낭독회가 폭설로 취소됐습니다. 이로 인해 연말까지 프로그램에 사용해야 하는 상당한 금액의 돈이 남았습니다. 첨부에 이를 어떻게 할지 몇 가지 아이디어를 열거했습니다. 금요일 회의 전까지 **144검토** 바랍니다. 도서관이 공동체에 주는 도움을 **145강화하는** 목표를 어떤 아이디어가 가장 잘 뒷받침하는지 논의할 예정입니다. 그때 여러분도 제안해 주시기를 바랍니다. **146여러분의 소중한 의견 제시로 이 상황을 최대한 활용할 수 있을 것**이라고 확신합니다.

> **어휘** take place 개최되다, 일어나다 reading 낭독회, 낭송회 sizable 꽤 많은, 상당한 attachment 첨부 usefulness 유용함 take full advantage of ~를 십분 활용하다

143 부사 / 부사절 접속사 / 전치사 구분

해설 빈칸에는 앞뒤 문장을 자연스럽게 이어줄 접속부사가 필요하므로, 부사 (A) Otherwise(달리, 그렇지 않으면)와 (D) For instance(예를 들어, 그 예로)가 정답 후보이다. 앞 문장 '올해 도서관의 "프로그램" 예산을 지출하는 여러 행사가 예상만큼 개최되지 않았다(This year, several of the events on which we usually spend the library's "Programs" budget have not taken place as expected)'에서 행사가 예상대로 개최되지 않았다는 사실을 언급하고 있다. 빈칸 뒤에 나오는 문장 '2월로 예정됐던 작가 낭독회가 폭설로 취소됐다(our author readings scheduled for February were cancelled because of the heavy snowfall)'에서 예정대로 개최되지 않은 행사의 구체적인 예시를 제시하고 있으므로, 정답은 (D) For instance이다. 부사절 접속사 (B) As long as(~하는 한)와 전치사 (C) Owing to(~ 때문에)는 품사상 적합하지 않다.

144 동사 어휘

해설 빈칸은 앞 문장의 '몇 가지 아이디어(a few ideas)'를 대신 가리키는 목적격 인칭대명사(them=a few ideas)를 목적어로 취하는 명령문의 동사원형 자리로, 빈칸 뒤에 나오는 전치사구(before Friday's meeting)의 수식을 받는다. 문장상 '금요일 회의 전까지 검토 바랍니다'라는 의미가 자연스러우므로, 정답은 (D) examine(검토하다, 조사하다, 검사하다)이다. (A) transmit(전송하다, 전하다), (B) locate(위치시키다, 위치를 찾다), (C) reserve(예약하다, 보유하다)는 의미상 적합하지 않다.

145 동사 어형 _ 동명사

해설 빈칸 뒤 명사(the library's usefulness)를 목적어로 취하면서 앞에 있는 전치사(of)의 목적어 역할을 하는 동명사 자리이므로, 정답은 동명사 (B) enhancing이다. 명사 (C) enhancer는 명사를 목적어로 취할 수 없다.

146 문맥에 맞는 문장 고르기

번역 (A) 그때 여러분도 제안해 주시기를 바랍니다.
(B) 이 계획을 기획하는 데 든 여러분의 노고에 감사 드립니다.
(C) 더 최근에 있었던 고객 설문조사는 다른 영역에 대한 질문이었습니다.
(D) 예산 감축을 고려해야 한다는 점을 명심하십시오.

해설 빈칸 뒤에 나오는 문장 '여러분의 소중한 의견 제시로 이 상황을 최대한 활용할 수 있을 것이라고 확신한다(With your valuable input, I feel certain we will be able to take full advantage of this situation)'에서 제시된 의견의 활용을 언급하고 있다. 따라서 빈칸에서 의견의 제안을 요청하는 것이 문맥상 자연스러우므로, 정답은 (A)이다.

PART 7

147-148 이메일

발신: ⟨l.canfield@binniskphoto.com⟩
수신: ⟨j.pham@signeteffect.com⟩
주제: 직원 사진
날짜: 2월 19일

팜 씨께,

시그넷 이펙트 어소시에이츠 직원들의 공식 사진 촬영을 위해 비니스크 포토그래피를 선택해 주셔서 감사합니다. 저희가 귀사의 새로운 사업의 기업 이미지를 형성하는 데 도움이 되기를 기대합니다. 일정 약속을 잡을 때 말씀드린 것처럼, 사진 뒤 배경을 먼저 선택하시는 게 자연스러워 보이는 사진을 확실히 보장합니다. **148**저희의 사진 수정 서비스를 이용해 피사체의 얼굴이나 머리를 약간 바꿀 수는 있지만, 전체 배경을 대체하는 것은 안 됩니다. **147**여기에서 저희 배경 모음을 둘러보시고 약속한 날 전날 저녁까지 결정 사항을 알려 주십시오.

리어 캔필드
고객 서비스
비니스크 포토그래피

어휘 portrait 초상화, 인물 사진 public image 기업 이미지 book an appointment 약속을 잡다 backdrop (무대 등의) 배경 retouch (그림·사진을) 가필하다, 수정하다 subject 피사체 inform A of B A에게 B를 통지하다

147 주제 / 목적

번역 캔필드 씨가 팜 씨에게 편지를 쓰는 이유는?
(A) 선호하는 것을 알기 위해
(B) 그에게 사업을 추천하기 위해
(C) 약속 일정을 확정하기 위해
(D) 오해한 것을 사과하기 위해

해설 마지막 문장에서 여기에서 배경 모음을 둘러보고, 약속한 날 전날 저녁까지 결정 사항을 알려 달라(Please look over our background collection here, and inform us of your decision by the evening before the appointment)고 했다. 따라서 선호하는 것을 알기 위해 이 메일을 쓰고 있음을 알 수 있으므로, 정답은 (A)이다.

▶▶ Paraphrasing 지문의 your decision → 정답의 a preference

148 사실 관계 확인

번역 캔필드 씨는 무엇을 이용할 수 있다고 말하는가?
(A) 야간 촬영 작업
(B) 전문 메이크업 서비스
(C) 특별 조명 장비
(D) 디지털 사진 편집

해설 지문 중반부에서 사진 수정 서비스를 이용해 피사체의 얼굴이나 머리를 약간 바꿀 수는 있지만, 전체 배경을 대체하는 것은 안 된다(Our photo retouching service is useful for making small changes to a subject's face or hair, but not for replacing an entire background)고 했다. 따라서 사진 편집이 가능하다는 것을 알 수 있으므로, 정답은 (D)이다.

▶▶ Paraphrasing 지문의 photo retouching service
→ 정답의 Digital photograph editing

149-150 문자 메시지

발신: 알렉스 수
보낸 시각: 5월 31일 오전 10시 4분
수신: 로린 버튼

로린, 소소한 부탁이 하나 있어요. 여기 델프레이 아파트에서 지금 막 테클 씨를 만났는데, 그녀가 빈 작업실을 빌리는 데 관심이 있는 것 같아요. **149**테클 씨에게 건물을 안내하려던 참이에요. **150**그런데 방금 보니 임대차 계약서 견본을 하나도 안 갖고 있네요. 여기로 하나 가져다 주시겠어요? 우리는 한동안 여기 있을 거예요.

어휘 favor 부탁 lease 임차하다, 임대하다 be about to+동사원형 막 ~하려는 참이다 show around 둘러볼 수 있게 안내하다 rental contract 임대[임차] 계약서 a while 잠시, 얼마 동안

149 세부 사항

번역 수 씨는 곧 어떤 일이 있다고 밝히는가?
(A) 건물 둘러보기
(B) 기공식
(C) 안전 점검
(D) 교육

해설 지문 중반부의 테클 씨에게 건물을 안내하려던 참이다(I'm about to show her around the building)를 통해 곧 건물을 둘러본다는 것을 알 수 있으므로, 정답은 (A)이다.

150　세부 사항

번역　후 씨는 무엇을 하라고 요청을 받는가?
(A) 계약서 검토하기
(B) 방 청소하기
(C) **문서 갖다 주기**
(D) 초과근무하기

해설　지문 후반부에서 임대차 계약서 견본이 없으니 여기로 하나 갖다 달라 (But I just realized that I don't have any of the sample rental contracts with me. Would you mind bringing one over)고 했다. 따라서 계약서 견본을 요청했다는 것을 알 수 있으므로, 정답은 (C)이다.

▶▶ **Paraphrasing**　지문의 **the sample rental contracts**
→ 정답의 **a document**
지문의 **bringing one over**
→ 정답의 **Deliver a document**

151-152　정보문

더마크 DXR 디지털 카메라

151더마크 DXR 디지털 카메라 구입을 축하합니다. 디지털 카메라의 최신 기술을 통해 곧바로 고품질의 사진 촬영이 가능할 것입니다. 이를 실현하기 위해 첨부 설명서에 디지털 카메라 사용법과 제공되는 편집 소프트웨어 설치법이 나와 있습니다. 카메라 사용 전, 반드시 설명서 내용을 꼼꼼히 살펴보시기 바랍니다. **152**검색이 가능한 설명서도 여러 가지 전자 파일 포맷으로 이용 가능합니다. www.dermakk.com/support/manuals를 방문하셔서 페이지 상단의 박스에 "DXR 디지털 카메라"를 입력하십시오.

어휘　guarantee 보장하다　state-of-the-art 최신의
in no time 곧, 당장　facilitate 가능하게 하다　install 설치하다
thoroughly 철저하게　searchable 검색이 가능한

151　추론 / 암시

번역　정보는 누구를 위한 것이겠는가?
(A) 구입 결정을 내리려고 하는 소비자
(B) 디지털 편집 소프트웨어를 개발하는 기술자
(C) 제품 기능을 설명해야 하는 판매원
(D) **제품을 소유한 고객**

해설　첫 번째 문장의 더마크 DXR 디지털 카메라 구입을 축하한다 (Congratulations on your purchase of a Dermakk DXR Digital Camera)를 통해 제품을 소유한 고객을 위한 정보임을 유추할 수 있으므로, 정답은 (D)이다.

▶▶ **Paraphrasing**　지문의 **your purchase of a Dermakk DXR Digital Camera**
→ 정답의 **A customer who owns a product**

152　사실 관계 확인

번역　DXR 디지털 카메라에 대해 명시된 것은?
(A) 이전에 다른 제조업체가 판매했다.
(B) **인터넷에서 설명서를 찾을 수 있다.**
(C) 특정 기간 이내에는 수리 서비스가 무료이다.
(D) 사용자는 모든 표준 포맷으로 사진을 저장할 수 있다.

해설　지문 후반부에서 검색이 가능한 설명서도 여러 가지 전자 파일 포맷으로 이용 가능하다(A searchable version of the manual is also available in several electronic file formats)면서 설명서의 전자 파일 포맷을 언급하고 있으므로, 정답은 (B)이다.

▶▶ **Paraphrasing**　지문의 **A searchable version of the manual is also available**
→ 정답의 **be found on the Internet**

153-155　웹페이지

디나이푸르 식품 가공회사의 웹사이트

2월 2일자 최신 소식　　　　　　　게시자: 타일러 샤머, 업무팀장

153마지막 게시 이후 2주가 지나서 저는 우리 신규 공장 건설이 어떻게 진행되고 있는지 여러분께 알려 드리려고 합니다. 주 생산 구역에 바닥재를 설치하는 과정에서 몇 가지 차질이 있었지만, 지금은 그 작업이 마무리됐습니다. 배관과 전기 공사는 예정대로 진행되고 있고, 내부 칸막이 벽은 곧 설치될 예정입니다. 남은 작업이 계획대로 진행된다면 4월 말이면 공장이 가동될 것 같습니다.

저는 공장에서 일할 기술 지원 직원들을 모집하기 위해 인사팀과 긴밀하게 협조해 일하고 있습니다. **154**지난주에는 회사를 대표해 뭄바이 소재 나비-테크 대학에서 열린 직원 채용 박람회에 참석, 이 업종의 직업에 관심이 있는 유망한 젊은 지원자들을 면접했습니다. **155**또한 공장 작업장용 주문 제작 안전 표지판을 만드는 일을 처리하기 위해 제 예전 동료인 조지오 더트와 연락했습니다. 그가 소유한 인쇄 회사는 가시성 높은 작업 공간용 표지판을 전문으로 합니다.

더 소식이 들어오는 대로 모두에게 알려드리겠습니다.

어휘　inform 알리다　setback 걸림돌, 차질　installation 설치
flooring material 바닥재　plumbing 배관, 배관 작업　partition
wall 칸막이 벽　put in 설치하다, 들여놓다　proceed (계속) 진행되다
operational 가동 중인, 가동 준비가 된　recruit 모집하다　on behalf
of ~를 대표해　promising 장래가 촉망되는　candidate (일자리의)
후보자　custom 주문 제작한　floor 작업장, 층, 바닥　own 소유하다
specialize in ~을 전문으로 하다　high-visibility 가시성이 높은

153　추론 / 암시

번역　웹페이지를 쓴 이유는 무엇이겠는가?
(A) **건설 프로젝트에 대한 최신 소식을 전하려고**
(B) 새로운 제조 공정을 대략 설명하려고
(C) 기업의 구조조정 노력을 평가하려고
(D) 전 직원 회의를 더 자주 열자고 건의하려고

해설　첫 번째 단락 첫 번째 문장에서 마지막 게시 이후 2주가 지났으니 우리 신규 공장 건설이 어떻게 진행되고 있는지 알리려 한다(It's been two weeks since my last post, so I just want to inform everyone on what's going on with the construction of our new factory)고 했다. 따라서 건설 진행 상황을 알리기 위해 글을 썼음을 유추할 수 있으므로, 정답은 (A)이다.

> **▶▶ Paraphrasing** 지문의 **to inform everyone on what's going on with the construction of our new factory** → 정답의 **To provide updates on a building project**

154 세부 사항

번역 웹페이지에 따르면 사머 씨는 뭄바이에서 무엇을 했는가?
(A) 신제품을 시연했다
(B) 직원에게 상을 수여했다
(C) 지사를 둘러보았다
(D) 취업 박람회에 참가했다

해설 두 번째 단락에서 지난주에 회사를 대표해 뭄바이 소재 나비-테크 대학에서 열린 직원 채용 박람회에 참석해 이 업종의 직업에 관심 있는 유망한 젊은 지원자들을 면접했다(Last week, on behalf of the company, I attended the employment recruitment fair at Navi-Tech University in Mumbai to interview promising young candidates interested in careers in the industry)고 했다. 따라서 그가 뭄바이에서 열리는 채용 박람회에 참석했음을 알 수 있으므로, 정답은 (D)이다.

> **▶▶ Paraphrasing** 지문의 **attended the employment recruitment fair**
> → 정답의 **Participated in a job fair**

155 추론 / 암시

번역 더트 씨는 누구이겠는가?
(A) 비즈니스 출판물의 기자
(B) 본사 인턴 사원
(C) 식품 가공 공장 관리자
(D) 인쇄 회사 소유주

해설 두 번째 단락 마지막 문장들에서 공장 작업장용 주문 제작 안전 표지판을 만드는 일을 처리하기 위해 예전 동료인 조지오 더트와 연락했는데 그가 소유한 인쇄 회사는 가시성 높은 작업 공간용 표지판을 전문으로 한다(In addition, I have contacted a former colleague of mine, Giorgio Dutt, to handle the task of creating custom safety signs for the plant floor. The printing firm he owns specializes in high-visibility signs for work areas)고 했다. 따라서 더트 씨(he)는 인쇄 회사를 운영한다고 유추할 수 있으므로, 정답은 (D)이다.

> **▶▶ Paraphrasing** 지문의 **The printing firm**
> → 정답의 **a printing company**

156-158 양식

앨닥-D 주식회사

고객 피드백 양식

앨닥-D 주식회사는 저희의 청소 및 수리 서비스에 대한 고객 의견을 소중하게 생각합니다. 귀하의 의견을 아래에 공유해 주십시오.

고객명: 댄 마텔		서비스 품목: 검은색 가죽 구두	

	그렇다	모르겠다	그렇지 않다
직원들은 친절하고 도움이 되었다.		✓	
서비스 비용은 적당하다.		✓	
서비스가 제대로 완료되었다.	✓		
서비스가 신속하게 완료되었다.	✓		

의견:

서비스는 매우 신속했습니다. ¹⁵⁶제 신발은 서비스 센터에 맡긴 후 이틀 만에 찾을 수 있도록 준비됐습니다. 결과에도 만족합니다. ¹⁵⁷딱 한 가지 문제는 수선비가 제가 받은 원래 견적서보다 많이 나왔다는 겁니다. 이렇게 된 이유는 알고 있습니다. 예상보다 구두 상태가 나빴다고 기술자가 말해 주었으니까요. 하지만 저는 그것이 불만스러웠습니다.

의견 감사합니다. ¹⁵⁸귀하의 의견을 반영하여 신입 및 현직 직원과 기술자들을 위한 교육 방식을 개선하도록 하겠습니다.

어휘 reasonable (비용이) 적당한 swiftly 신속하게 exceed 초과하다 price quote 견적서 frustrating 불만스러운, 좌절감을 주는 current 현재의

156 사실 관계 확인

번역 마텔 씨에 대해 명시된 것은?
(A) 이메일로 양식을 받았다.
(B) 특급 배송에 대해 문의했다.
(C) 온라인 채팅으로 직원과 소통했다.
(D) 서비스 센터를 직접 방문했다.

해설 마텔 씨의 '의견:(Comments:)' 중 신발을 서비스 센터에 맡긴 후 이틀 만에 찾을 수 있도록 준비됐다(My shoes were ready for pick-up just two days after I dropped them off at the service center)를 통해 마텔 씨가 서비스 센터를 직접 방문했음을 알 수 있으므로, 정답은 (D)이다.

> **▶▶ Paraphrasing** 지문의 **dropped them off at the service center**
> → 정답의 **visited a service center in person**

157 세부 사항

번역 마텔 씨는 어떤 문제점을 이야기하는가?
(A) 헷갈리는 설명
(B) 조악한 품질의 수선
(C) 긴 대기 시간
(D) 맞지 않는 비용 견적서

해설 마텔 씨의 '의견:(Comments:)' 중 딱 한 가지 문제는 수선비가 제가 받은 원래 견적서보다 많이 나왔다는 것(The only problem is that the repair charges exceeded the original price quote I was given)에서 마텔 씨는 견적서보다 높았던 실제 수선비를 문제로 언급하고 있으므로, 정답은 (D)이다.

> **▶▶ Paraphrasing** 지문의 **exceeded the original price quote**
> → **An incorrect cost estimate**

158 세부 사항

번역 양식에 따르면, 앨닥–D 주식회사는 무엇을 할 것인가?
(A) 긍정적인 피드백을 받은 기술자에게 보상을 해 준다.
(B) 마텔 씨에게 전화해 양식 내용에 대해 이야기를 나눈다.
(C) 직원 교육 시스템을 개선한다.
(D) 마텔 씨에게 무료 액세서리를 보낸다.

해설 마지막 단락에서 귀하의 의견을 반영하여 신입 및 현직 직원과 기술자들을 위한 교육 방식을 개선하도록 하겠다(We will use them to further develop our training methods for new and current staff and technicians)고 했으므로 고객의 의견을 반영해 직원 교육 방식을 개선할 것을 알 수 있다. 따라서 정답은 (C)이다.

▶▶ **Paraphrasing** 지문의 **develop our training methods for new and current staff and technicians** → **Improve its employee education system**

159-160 문자 메시지

> **시몬 파월, 오전 10:34**
> 구스타보. 쉬는 날인데 귀찮게 해서 미안한데, 위블에서 방금 소식이 왔어요. **159**그들이 다른 시장을 겨냥하기로 했대요. 그래서 TV 캠페인에서 자사 상품을 고전적이고 전통적인 게 아니라 멋지고 젊어 보이게 하고 싶답니다. 그렇게 할 수 있을까요? 그들이 오늘 내로 대답을 원하는데요.
>
> **구스타보 리마스, 오전 10:35**
> 물론이죠. 기꺼이 수용하지만 쉽지는 않을 거예요. 티가든 게임즈 때 방송될 수 있게 광고를 만들려면 팀에서 도움이 좀 필요합니다. **160**다른 팀에서 사람을 지원해 달라고 부장님께 부탁해도 될지 모르겠네요.
>
> **시몬 파월, 오전 10:36**
> 안 될 것 없죠. 위블을 만족시키는 게 우리 대행사 전체에 이익이니까, 어떻게든 일이 되도록 해 볼 수 있을 것 같아요.
>
> **구스타보 리마스, 오전 10:37**
> 게다가, 제 시간에 마치기만 하면 이 광고가 틀림없이 훨씬 더 많은 시청자한테 노출될 거예요. 뭔가 인상적인 걸 만들어야겠네요. 내가 그에게 전화할게요.

어휘 bother 귀찮게 하다, 성가시게 하다 day off 쉬는 날, 비번 target 겨냥하다 present 보여주다, 묘사하다 accommodate (의견을) 수용하다 get + A(목적어) + 과거분사 A를 ~되게 하다 commercials 광고 (방송) in time to + 동사원형 ~할 시간에 맞게 air 방송하다

159 세부 사항

번역 위블은 무엇을 하고 싶어 하는가?
(A) 더 젊은 시장에 호소한다
(B) 대변인으로 유명인사를 고용한다
(C) 경쟁사 캠페인에 대응한다
(D) 시장 조사를 한다

해설 파월 씨의 오전 10시 34분 메시지에서 그들이 다른 시장을 겨냥하기로 했으며 TV 캠페인에서 자사 상품을 고전적이고 전통적인 게 아니라 멋지고 젊어 보였으면 한다(They've decided to target a different market, so they would like the TV campaign to present their products as cool and youthful, not classic and traditional)고 했다. 따라서 위블이 젊은 시장을 겨냥해 제품 홍보를 원한다는 것을 알 수 있으므로, 정답은 (A)이다.

▶▶ **Paraphrasing** 지문의 **target a different market** → 정답의 **Appeal to a younger market**

160 의도 파악

번역 오전 10시 36분에 파월 씨가 "안 될 것 없죠"라고 쓸 때, 그 의도는 무엇이겠는가?
(A) 광고가 성공적일 것이라고 생각한다.
(B) 추가 직원을 요청하고 싶다.
(C) 촬영 장비를 빌리고 싶다.
(D) 마감일이 연장되기를 기대한다.

해설 리마스 씨의 오전 10시 35분 메시지에서 다른 팀에서 사람을 지원해 달라고 부장한테 부탁해도 될지 모르겠다(I wonder if we could ask the director to lend us someone from another team)고 했다. 인용문은 이 말에 대한 반응이므로 파월 씨도 리마스 씨의 지원 요청의 필요성에 대해 동의한다고 볼 수 있다. 따라서 정답은 (B)이다.

161-163 기사

> *지역 비즈니스 뉴스*   3월 23일
>
> **161**작가로 유명한 카라반 카페가 곧 인근 건물을 인수해 매장 면적을 확장한다. 주인인 이브라힘 아카드는 인기 있는 자신의 레스토랑이 확장되어 매우 기쁘다고 말한다. 식당이 너무 작아 특히 주말이면 식사를 즐기러 오는 수많은 사람들을 다 수용할 수가 없기 때문이다.
>
> **162**아카드 씨는 클로버 가 72번지에 위치한 이 식당의 현재 식사 공간을 이미 개선하기 시작했다. 동시에 그는 이전에 카이너스 의류점이 차지하고 있던 바로 옆의 빈 구조물을 리모델링하느라 분주하다. 이웃한 더 넓은 상점 자리를 임차할 기회가 온 것은 한곳에서 23년간 영업해 온 주인 로즐린 카이너가 매럭스 쇼핑 플라자로 가게를 이전하기로 결정하면서였다. "제가 기회를 잡아 그곳을 임차했습니다."라고 아카드 씨는 말했다.
>
> **163**아카드 씨는 확장이 언제 완료될지 일정을 못박지는 않았지만 큰 행사로 완공을 축하하겠다고 말했다. 그는 그때까지는 식당이 평상시처럼 영업한다는 사실을 손님들이 알았으면 한다. 개점 시간, 메뉴, 기타 정보는 www.caravannecafe.com에서 찾을 수 있다.

어휘 floor space 바닥 면적, 매장 면적 take over ~을 인수하다 nearby 인근의 expansion 확장 eatery 식당 vacant 비어 있는 previously 이전에, 과거에 occupied 점유된 opportunity 기회 rent 빌리다, 임차하다 grab (기회를) 잡다 timeline 일정 completion 완성, 완료 celebrate 축하하다, 기념하다

161 주제 / 목적

번역 기사가 주로 논의하는 것은 무엇인가?
(A) 지역 비즈니스 행사
(B) 식당 메뉴 변경
(C) 업체 확장
(D) 주말 행사의 인기

해설 첫 번째 문장에서 작가로 유명한 카라반 카페가 곧 인근 건물을 인수해 매장 면적을 확장한다(The famously small Caravanne Café will soon increase its floor space by taking over a nearby building)고 했다. 따라서 업체 확장을 알리기 위한 기사임을 알 수 있으므로, 정답은 (C)이다.

▶▶ **Paraphrasing** 지문의 will soon increase its floor space → 정답의 The expansion of a business

162 추론 / 암시

번역 카이너스 의류점에 관해 암시된 것은 무엇인가?
(A) 아카드 씨가 운영한다.
(B) 과거 클로버 가에 위치했다.
(C) 과거 카라반 카페보다 더 작은 공간을 차지했다.
(D) 매럭스 쇼핑 플라자에 2호 지점을 열었다.

해설 두 번째 단락에서 아카드 씨는 클로버 가 72번지에 위치한 이 식당의 식사 공간을 이미 개선하기 시작했는데 동시에 이전에 카이너스 의류점이 차지하고 있던 바로 옆의 빈 구조물을 리모델링하느라 분주하다(Mr. Akkad has already begun updating the eatery's current dining area, located at 72 Clover Street. At the same time, he is busy remodeling the vacant structure next door, which was previously occupied by Kainer's Clothing Store)고 했다. 식당이 클로버 가에 있고 카이너스 의류점이 식당 바로 옆에 있었음을 알 수 있으므로, 정답은 (B)이다.

163 문장 삽입

번역 [1], [2], [3], [4]로 표시된 곳 중에서 다음 문장이 들어가기에 가장 적합한 곳은?

"그는 그때까지는 식당이 평상시처럼 영업한다는 사실을 손님들이 알았으면 한다."

(A) [1]
(B) [2]
(C) [3]
(D) [4]

해설 삽입 문장에서 '그때까지는(until then)'을 통해 앞에서 어떤 시점에 관해 언급하고 있음을 유추할 수 있다. [4]의 앞에서 아카드 씨는 확장이 언제 완료될지 일정을 못박지는 않았지만 큰 행사로 완공을 축하하겠다(Mr. Akkad has not set a timeline for the completion of the expansion, but said that it will be celebrated with a large event)고 했다. 따라서 완공 시점에 대한 언급 뒤에 식당이 평상시처럼 영업한다는 내용이 이어지는 것이 자연스러우므로, 정답은 (D)이다.

164-167 편지

바노트 안과
www.barnotte-ec.com

서먼 올소프
로열 로드1735
파르마, MI 48089

올소프 씨께,

164패트릭 마스든 박사가 40년의 진료 끝에 가족과 여행을 하며 시간을 보내기 위해 곧 진료를 그만둔다는 소식을 들으셨을 겁니다. 저를 비롯해 바노트 안과의 다른 의사들은 그가 파르마 지역에 있는 자신의 환자들을 계속 돌볼 수 있도록 저희를 선택해 발표한 것을 자랑스럽게 생각합니다. 동의하신다면 귀하의 눈을 돌볼 수 있게 되어 기쁩니다. 제 소개를 드리겠습니다.

저는 저의 가족 대다수가 아직 거주하고 있는 랜싱 인근에서 자랐으며 굿리치 대학교 의과대학을 졸업했습니다. **166**저는 의사 면허가 있으며 미시간 안과학회 계간지 〈최근 시각 연구〉에 정기 기고하고 있습니다. 바노트 안과에 들어온 직후부터 저는 지역사회를 위한 장기적 봉사에 힘써 왔습니다. 제 진료를 받기로 결정하시면 진료 이전에 귀하의 의료 기록을 검토하고, 진료 시 우려하시는 바에 대해 이야기하는 시간을 가질 것입니다. **165**그럼에도 불구하고 저희 병원의 "정시 의사상" 수상자로서 방문 시 귀하가 대기하지 않도록 약속드립니다.

167서로 더 잘 알아갈 수 있도록, 7월 15일 목요일 오후 5시 저희 병원에서 있을 마스든 박사의 환자들을 위한 연회에 귀하를 초대합니다. 즐거운 자리가 될 것이니 잠시 들러 주셨으면 합니다. 그렇지 않으면 저희 데스크 직원이 연락을 드려 곧 진료 예약을 잡을 수 있도록 하겠습니다.

만나 뵙기를 고대합니다.

힐러리 보스버그 박사

어휘 physician 의사 with one's consent ~의 동의하에 board-certified (의사 등 전문직 종사자가) 면허가 있는 regular contributor 정기 기고가 ophthalmology 안과학 quarterly 계간의 commit oneself to ~에 헌신하다 medical record 의료 기록 recipient 받는 사람 facilitate 가능하게 하다 affair 모임, 행사 set up an appointment 약속을 정하다

164 세부 사항

번역 편지에 따르면, 마스든 박사는 무엇을 할 것인가?
(A) 직업에서 은퇴
(B) 새 의료센터 시작
(C) 다른 도시로 이주
(D) 후배 의사 교육

해설 첫 번째 단락 첫 번째 문장에서 패트릭 마스든 박사가 40년의 진료 끝에 가족과 여행을 하며 시간을 보내기 위해 곧 진료를 그만둔다는 소식을 들었을 것(You may have heard that, after 40 years of service, Dr. Patrick Marsden will soon close his practice in order to travel and spend time with his family)이라고 했다. 따라서 마스든 박사가 곧 은퇴할 예정임을 알 수 있으므로, 정답은 (A)이다.

▶▶ **Paraphrasing** 지문의 close his practice → 정답의 Retire from the workforce

165 세부 사항

번역 보스버그 박사는 무엇에 대해 상을 받았는가?
(A) 연구
(B) 진료 역량
(C) 자원봉사 활동
(D) **시간 엄수**

해설 두 번째 단락 마지막 문장에서 저희 병원의 "정시 의사상" 수상자로서 방문 시 대기하지 않도록 약속한다(as a recipient of our clinic's "On-Time Doctor Award", I can assure you that you will not be kept waiting when you visit me)고 했다. 따라서 발신인(I)인 보스버그 박사가 시간 엄수에 대해 상을 받았다는 것을 알 수 있으므로, 정답은 (D)이다.

▶▶ **Paraphrasing** 지문의 **a recipient**
→ 질문의 **receive an award**
지문의 **On-Time** → 정답의 **punctuality**

166 추론 / 암시

번역 보스버그 박사에 대해 암시된 것은?
(A) 바노트 안과 설립자이다.
(B) 가족 몇 명이 의사이다.
(C) **전문지에 논문을 발표했다.**
(D) 과거에 굿리치 대학교에서 가르쳤다.

해설 두 번째 단락 두 번째 문장에서 의사 면허가 있으며 미시간 안과학회 계간지 〈최근 시각 연구〉에 정기 기고하고 있다(I am board-certified and a regular contributor to the Michigan Academy of Ophthalmology's quarterly *Current Vision Research*)고 했다. 따라서 발신인(I)인 보스버그 박사가 전문지에 논문을 기고하고 있음을 유추할 수 있으므로, 정답은 (C)이다.

▶▶ **Paraphrasing** 지문의 **a regular contributor to the Michigan Academy of Ophthalmology's quarterly *Current Vision Research***
→ 정답의 **published articles in a professional journal**

167 세부 사항

번역 올소프 씨는 무엇을 하라고 요청을 받았는가?
(A) 수신자 리스트에 들어가기
(B) **환영식에 참석하기**
(C) 전화해서 예약하기
(D) 의료 기록 사본 보관하기

해설 세 번째 단락 첫 번째 문장에서 서로 더 잘 알아갈 수 있도록, 7월 15일 목요일 오후 5시 저희 병원에서 있을 마스든 박사의 환자들을 위한 연회에 귀하를 초대한다(To further facilitate us getting to know each other, I invite you to come to a reception for Dr. Marsden's former patients at our office on Thursday, July 15 at 5 P.M.)고 했다. 따라서 수신인(you)인 올소프 씨를 환자들을 위한 연회에 초대하고 있으므로, 정답은 (B)이다.

▶▶ **Paraphrasing** 지문의 **come to a reception**
→ 정답의 **Attend a welcoming party**

168-171 기사

포탈라 경기장에서 USSL 올스타전 열려

US 축구 리그 (USSL) 위원 조셉 메이슨, FC 산타페 구단주 옥타비아 옐닉, 산타페 시장 이달리아 오티즈는 어제 공동 기자회견을 열고 산타페 시 포탈라 경기장이 리그의 다음 올스타전 개최지로 선정됐다고 발표했다.

168, 171올스타전은 선수와 코치 투표로 선정된 USSL 서부 지역과 동부 지역 최고 선수들 간 대회이다. 매년 6월에 개최된다. **168**작년에는 내슈빌에서 열린 접전에서 현재 FC 산타페 인기선수 에릭 기쿠누가 있는 서부팀이 동부팀을 근소한 차로 이겼다.

메이슨 씨는 리그의 이번 결정이 2년 전 FC 산타페 결성 후 지역 내 스포츠 인기가 급상승한 것을 반영했다고 설명했다. 그는 "산타페 시가 이번 행사에서 환영과 흥분의 분위기를 조성해 주리라 믿습니다."라고 말했다.

오티즈 시장은 자신의 발언 중 USSL에 영향을 미친 또 다른 요인으로 경기장 시설의 우수성을 꼽았다. **170**산타페 스트릭스 축구팀의 홈구장이기도 한 해당 경기장의 대규모 개조 프로젝트는 FC 산타페를 위한 공간을 마련하고자 시행됐으며, 오티즈 시장의 첫 임기 주요 계획이었다. 프로젝트는 높은 비용 때문에 지역 공무원들과 주민들의 우려를 **169**샀으나 완공 이후 성공적이라는 평을 받았다.

시에서는 경기뿐 아니라 경기가 열리는 한 주 내내 여러 가지 관련 특별 행사를 열 계획이다. 이에 관한 내용은 추후 발표될 예정이지만 콘서트와 선수 출연 등이 포함될 것으로 보인다.

어휘 commissioner 위원 joint press conference 공동 기자회견 poll 투표 narrowly beat 근소한 차로 이기다 thrilling 흥분되는, 아주 신나는 skyrocketing 치솟는 cite 인용하다 undertake 착수하다 accommodate 공간을 제공하다 initiative 계획 draw concern from ~의 우려를 사다 related 관련된 at a later date 후일에, 나중에

168 추론 / 암시

번역 기쿠누 씨에 대해 암시된 것은?
(A) **팀 선정 과정에 참여할 것이다.**
(B) FC 산타페의 새 선수이다.
(C) 기자회견에서 발언했다.
(D) 과거에 내슈빌 기반 팀에서 활동했다.

해설 두 번째 단락 첫 번째 문장에서 올스타전은 선수와 코치 투표로 선정된 USSL 서부 지역과 동부 지역 최고 선수들 간 대회(The all-star game is a competition between the best players of the USSL's western and eastern divisions as determined by a poll of players and coaches)라고 했다. 이를 통해 선수와 코치 투표로 올스타 선수를 뽑는다는 사실을 알 수 있다. 그리고 다음 문장에서 작년에는 내슈빌에서 열린 접전에서 현재 FC 산타페 인기선수 에릭 기쿠누가 있는 서부팀이 동부팀을 근소한 차로 이겼다(Last year, the Western Division Team, featuring current FC Santa Fe star Eric Gikunoo, narrowly beat the Eastern Division Team in a thrilling match in Nashville)고 했으므로 기쿠누 씨가 현역 선수임을 알 수 있다. 따라서 기쿠누 씨 또한 올스타 선정을 위한 투표에 참여할 것으로 유추할 수 있으므로, 정답은 (A)이다.

▶▶ **Paraphrasing** 지문의 **a poll of players and coaches**
→ 정답의 **a team selection process**

169 동의어 찾기

번역 네 번째 단락 9행의 "drew"와 의미가 가장 가까운 단어는?
(A) 끝맺었다
(B) 끌었다
(C) 계산했다
(D) 묘사했다

해설 해당 문장은 프로젝트는 높은 비용 때문에 지역 공무원들과 주민들의 우려를 샀으나 완공 이후 성공적이라는 평을 받았다(The project drew concern from local officials and residents because of the high costs involved, but has been considered a success since its completion)라는 의미로 해석되는데, 여기서 drew는 '끌었다'라는 의미가 자연스러우므로, 정답은 (B) attracted(끌었다, 끌어냈다, 매료했다)이다.

170 사실 관계 확인

번역 포탈라 경기장에 대해 언급된 것은?
(A) 콘서트장으로도 사용된다.
(B) 두 개의 스포츠 팀이 함께 쓴다.
(C) 현재 개조 공사가 진행 중이다.
(D) 오티즈 씨가 공사를 제안했다.

해설 네 번째 단락 두 번째 문장에서 산타페 스트릭스 축구팀의 홈구장이기도 한 해당 경기장의 대규모 개조 프로젝트는 FC 산타페를 위한 공간을 마련하고자 시행됐으며, 오티즈 시장의 첫 임기 주요 계획이었다(An extensive renovation project to the stadium, which is also the home of the Santa Fe Streaks football team, was undertaken to accommodate FC Santa Fe, and was a major initiative of Ms. Ortiz's first term in office)를 통해 산타페 스트릭스 축구팀과 FC 산타페가 함께 경기장을 사용한다는 것을 알 수 있으므로, 정답은 (B)이다.

171 문장 삽입

번역 [1], [2], [3], [4]로 표시된 곳 중에서 다음 문장이 들어가기에 가장 적합한 곳은?

"매년 6월에 개최된다."

(A) [1]
(B) [2]
(C) [3]
(D) [4]

해설 삽입 문장 '매년 6월에 개최된다'를 통해 앞에서 개최되는 행사(It)를 구체적으로 언급할 것임을 알 수 있다. [1]의 앞 문장, 올스타전은 선수와 코치 투표로 선정된 USSL 서부 지역과 동부 지역 최고 선수들 간 대회이다(The all-star game is a competition between the best players of the USSL's western and eastern divisions as determined by a poll of players and coaches)에서 올스타전이라는 행사를 구체적으로 제시하고 있으므로, 정답은 (A)이다.

172-175 온라인 채팅

라이언 에치슨, 오전 11:41 172여러분, 금요일에 있을 부서 영화 관람 입장권을 온라인으로 구매하려고 하는데요. 〈믿음의 문〉은 어때요? 비평가들에게 아주 좋은 평을 받았어요.
한나 키엘, 오전 11:42 그 영화는 오래 상영 중이라 대부분 이미 봤을 것 같아요. 저는 〈샘 드라이버의 모험〉이 더 좋은데요. 제 친구가 지난주말에 봤는데 적극 추천하더군요.
마크 개스킨스, 오전 11:43 173〈샘 드라이버의 모험〉이 괜찮은 것 같은데요. 후반부는 사실상 공포 영화라고 들었어요.
조이 래퍼티, 오전 11:44 좀 더 가벼운 내용의 영화는 어때요? 174〈금붕어 물통〉이 내일 개봉해요.
햄던 알 네야디, 오전 11:44 〈금붕어 물통〉이나 〈눈보라 속 연락〉을 보고 싶어요.
라이언 에치슨, 오전 11:46 175〈금붕어 물통〉이 4시 30분 상영편이 있는 것 같아요. 괜찮으세요?
한나 키엘, 오전 11:47 잠깐만요. 이후에 저녁을 먹을 예정인가요? 1757시 정각에 일어났으면 해서요.
라이언 에치슨, 오전 11시 48분 영화는 90분밖에 안 되니까 극장 옆 중식당에서 식사를 하죠. 괜찮으실 것 같은데요.

어휘 critic 비평가 highly recommend 적극 추천하다 second half 후반부 practically 사실상, 거의 lighthearted 편안한 마음으로 즐기는, 내용이 가벼운

172 세부 사항

번역 에치슨 씨가 영화를 추천해 달라고 한 이유는?
(A) 부서 관람을 위해
(B) 모금하기 위해
(C) 분석 기사를 쓰기 위해
(D) 장식 테마를 위해

해설 에치슨 씨의 오전 11시 41분 메시지에서 금요일에 있을 부서 영화 관람 입장권을 온라인으로 구매하려고 한다(I'm going online now to buy tickets for the department's trip to the movies on Friday)를 통해 부서 영화 관람을 위해 영화 추천을 요청하고 있음을 알 수 있으므로, 정답은 (A)이다.

▶▶ **Paraphrasing** 지문의 **the department's trip to the movies** → 정답의 **an office outing**

173 추론 / 암시

번역 개스킨스 씨가 〈샘 드라이버의 모험〉에 대해 암시한 것은?
(A) 지역 극장에서 상영하지 않는다.
(B) 비평가들에게 호평을 받지 못했다.
(C) 다른 영화의 속편이다.
(D) 무서운 장면이 있다.

해설 개스킨스 씨의 오전 11시 43분 메시지에서 〈샘 드라이버의 모험〉이 괜찮은 것 같은데 후반부는 사실상 공포 영화라고 들었다(*The Adventures of Sam Driver* does sound good, but I've heard that its second half is practically a horror movie)고 했다. 따라서 〈샘 드라이버의 모험〉에 무서운 장면이 있음을 유추할 수 있으므로, 정답은 (D)이다.

▶▶ **Paraphrasing** 지문의 **its second half is practically a horror movie**
→ 정답의 **It includes frightening scenes.**

174 세부 사항

번역 아직 개봉하지 않은 영화는 어떤 것인가?
(A) 〈믿음의 문〉
(B) 〈샘 드라이버의 모험〉
(C) 〈금붕어 물통〉
(D) 〈눈보라 속 연락〉

해설 래퍼티 씨의 오전 11시 44분 메시지, 〈금붕어 물통〉이 내일 개봉한다(*Goldfish Canteen* opens tomorrow)를 통해 〈금붕어 물통〉이 현재 개봉된 영화가 아님을 알 수 있으므로, 정답은 (C)이다.

▶▶ **Paraphrasing** 지문의 **opens tomorrow**
→ 질문의 **has not yet been released**

175 의도 파악

번역 오전 11시 47분에 키엘 씨가 "이후에 저녁을 먹을 예정인가요?"라고 쓸 때, 그 의도는 무엇인가?
(A) 배가 고프다.
(B) 일정에 대해 우려하고 있다.
(C) 자원해서 음식을 제공하고 싶다.
(D) 행사 예산이 너무 많다고 생각한다.

해설 에치슨 씨는 오전 11시 46분 메시지, 〈금붕어 물통〉이 4시 30분 상영편이 있는데 괜찮으냐(It looks like there's a 4:30 showing of *Goldfish Canteen*. Does that sound all right?)에서 영화 관람 시간에 대한 동의를 구하고 있다. 이에 대해 키엘 씨가 이후에 저녁을 먹을 예정인지(will there be dinner afterwards) 추후 일정에 대해 질문한 후, 자신은 7시 정각에 일어나야 한다면서 시간 제약에 대해 걱정하고 있으므로, 정답은 (B)이다.

176-180 웹페이지 + 이메일

http://www.ste-a.org/tcc

소도심 경연대회 정보

소도시 개발 협회에서는 미국의 소도시들을 지원하기 위해 연례 대회를 조직합니다. 쾌적한 도심을 만들기 위해 열심히 노력하는 지역사회를 알고 있다면 그것에 대해 듣고 싶습니다!

참가 신청은 <u>이곳</u>에서 해주세요. **176 A, C, D**제목을 붙여야 하며 도시의 과거와 현재에 대한 간단한 설명과 더불어 도시의 전체적인 특성을 보여주는 사진 두세 장을 포함시켜 주세요.

177주의사항: 소도시 개발 협회, 루드 웹 서비시즈, 사코스 하드웨어 직원들은 대회에 출전할 수 없습니다.

예전과 마찬가지로 접수는 3월 31일까지 받습니다. **178**4월에 www.ste-a.org/tcc/vote의 일반 투표를 거쳐 결선에 선정된 도시는 5월 중 하루 동안 심사위원들을 맞이하게 됩니다. 올해는 심사위원들이 다음과 같은 상을 수여할 예정입니다.

상 이름	내용
대상	수표 2만 달러
179금상	**루드 웹 서비시즈 1년 이용권**
은상	사코스 하드웨어 상품권 500달러
동상	품격 있는 감사패

어휘 welcoming 친절한, 쾌적한 entry 참가, 출품 submit 제출하다 enter 출전하다 finalist 결선 진출자[팀] popular vote 일반 투표(선거인단이 아닌 일반 유권자가 뽑는 투표) judge 심사위원 daylong 하루 종일 걸리는 yearlong 1년간의 subscription 정기 구독권[이용권] recognition (공로에 대한) 인정, 표창 plaque 명판, 패

발신: 〈r.ayers@ste-a.org〉
수신: 〈t.maddux@lio-mail.com〉
제목: 소도심 경연대회 결과
날짜: 6월 15일
첨부: 양식

매덕스 씨게,

축하합니다! **179**소도시 개발 협회 소도심 경연대회에서 금상에 입상하셨습니다. 심사위원들은 바르 힐스 지역 소유의 독특한 상점과 레스토랑에 깊은 인상을 받았습니다. 이 지역으로 더욱 많은 방문객을 유치하겠다는 여러분의 목표를 완수하는 데 이번 수상이 도움이 되기를 바랍니다. 제가 곧 연락해 상을 어떻게 받아 가실지 자세히 알려 드리겠습니다.

아울러, 귀하의 참가작 내용은 저희 웹사이트 "수상자 페이지"에 보존될 예정임을 양지해 주십시오. **180**내년 초에 저희에게 이메일로 한 단락의 글도 보내 주시기를 권합니다. 내용은 소도심 경연대회에 참가함으로써 바르 힐스에 어떤 도움이 되었는지에 관한 겁니다. 이 글은 귀하의 참가작에 첨부되어 귀하의 도시를 긍정적으로 알릴 것이며, 향후 많은 지원자를 대회로 끌어들이게 될 것입니다.

로즈 아이어스
소도시 개발 협회

어휘 locally-owned 지역 소유의 fulfill 완수하다 instruction 설명, 지침 claim 요구하다, 청구하다 contents 내용물, 콘텐츠 preserve 보존하다, 보호하다 paragraph 단락, 단문 benefit 이롭게 하다 publicity (언론 등의) 주목, 잘 알려짐

176 사실 관계 확인

번역 경연대회 제출물로 요구되지 않는 것은?
(A) 제목
(B) 도시 지도
(C) 지역 사진
(D) 역사 관련 정보

해설 웹페이지 두 번째 단락에서 제목을 붙여야 하며(They must be titled)에서 (A)를, 도시의 전체적인 특성을 보여주는 사진 두세 장(two to three photographs that show its overall character)에서 (C)를, 도시의 과거와 현재에 대한 간단한 설명(a brief explanation of the town's past and present)에서 (D)를 포함해야 한다는 것을 확인할 수 있으므로, 정답은 (B)이다.

▶▶ Paraphrasing   지문의 **be titled** → 보기의 **A heading**
지문의 **two to three photographs**
→ 보기의 **Some pictures**
지문의 **a brief explanation of the town's past and present**
→ 보기의 **Some historical information**

177 세부 사항

번역 웹페이지에 따르면 경연대회에 참가할 수 없는 사람은 누구인가?
(A) 최근 그곳에 이사 온 사람
(B) 과거에 대상을 받은 사람
(C) **특정 단체에 고용된 사람**
(D) 주민 2만 명 이상인 소도시에 사는 사람

해설 웹페이지 세 번째 단락의 주의사항에서 소도시 개발 협회, 루드 웹 서비시즈, 사코스 하드웨어 직원들은 대회에 출전할 수 없다(Note: Employees of the Small Town Enrichment Association, Rood Web Services, or Sakos Hardware may not enter the contest)고 했다. 따라서 특정 단체에 소속된 직원은 참가할 수 없음을 알 수 있으므로, 정답은 (C)이다.

▶▶ Paraphrasing   지문의 **Employees of the Small Town Enrichment Association, Rood Web Services, or Sakos Hardware**
→ 정답의 **People employed by certain organizations**

178 세부 사항

번역 웹페이지에 따르면 5월에 무슨 일이 있는가?
(A) 출품작을 모집한다.
(B) 규정이 결정된다.
(C) **심사위원들이 도시를 방문한다.**
(D) 일반인이 온라인 투표를 한다.

해설 웹페이지 네 번째 단락에서 4월에 www.ste-a.org/tcc/vote의 일반 투표를 거쳐 결선에 선정된 도시는 5월 중 하루 동안 심사위원들을 맞이하게 된다(Towns chosen as finalists in April by a popular vote at www.ste-a.org/tcc/vote then host our judges for daylong visits in May)고 했다. 따라서 5월에 심사위원들이 도시를 방문한다는 것을 알 수 있으므로, 정답은 (C)이다.

179 연계

번역 매덕스 씨는 무엇을 상으로 받았나?
(A) 장식용 명판
(B) **서비스 이용권**
(C) 상점 쿠폰
(D) 상품권

해설 아이어스 씨가 매덕스 씨에게 쓴 이메일 첫 번째 단락에서 소도시 개발 협회 소도심 경연대회에서 금상에 입상했다(You have won Gold Prize in the Small Town Enrichment Association's Town Center Contest)고 했다. 이를 통해 매덕스 씨가 금상을 받았다는 것을 알 수 있으므로, 웹페이지의 표를 참고하여 매덕스 씨가 받은 금상의 상품을 확인한다. 표에 따라 금상의 상품은 루드 웹 서비시즈 1년 이용권(A yearlong subscription to Rood Web Services)임을 알 수 있으므로, 정답은 (B)이다.

▶▶ Paraphrasing   지문의 **A yearlong subscription to Rood Web Services**
→ 정답의 **A service subscription**

180 세부 사항

번역 매덕스 씨는 다음 해에 무엇을 해달라고 요청을 받았나?
(A) **최신 정보에 대한 글 제공하기**
(B) 대회에 다시 지원하기
(C) 시상식에 오기
(D) 연구에 참여하기

해설 이메일 두 번째 단락에서 내년 초에 소도심 경연대회에 참가함으로써 바르 힐스에 어떤 도움이 되었는지에 관한 글을 보내 달라(We also encourage you to e-mail us a paragraph early next year about how participating in the Town Center Contest has benefitted Bahr Hills)고 했다. 따라서 대회 참가 후 도시의 근황에 대한 글을 요청받았음을 알 수 있으므로, 정답은 (A)이다.

▶▶ Paraphrasing   지문의 **e-mail us a paragraph**
→ 정답의 **Supply a written update**

181-185 웹페이지 + 전단지

http://www.valmirebooks.com

발마이어 서점
뉴스 및 업데이트

9월 23일 금요일

저희는 여러분의 매장 내 쇼핑 체험을 풍성하게 해 드릴 새로운 것으로 가을 시즌을 시작하려고 합니다. **182 C, D**다음 주 월요일부터 저희 서점 직원들이 강력하게 보증하는 서적들을 강조한 전단지를 매주 발행합니다. **182B**전단지에 소개되는 모든 책은 10% 할인이 됩니다. 하지만 할인 혜택을 누리려면 서점을 방문하셔야 합니다. 이 특가는 온라인 구매에는 적용되지 않습니다. **181**저희는 또한 여러분이 서점의 방대한 재고 품목을 훑어보시기를 권장합니다. 저희 웹사이트에는 판매되지 않는 책 수백 종이 있습니다.

첫 번째 전단지에서는 저희 서점의 비즈니스 부문에서 직원들이 가장 좋아하는 실용 입문서를 선별했습니다. **184**이 주의 선정작 중에는 그레첸 실바의 최신 인기 1위 서적과 잘 알려진 참고 서적 〈로고 디자인을 위한 영감〉이 있습니다. 선정된 서적은 모두 야심 있는 기업가들에게 틀림없이 도움이 되므로 방문하셔서 그것을 확인하세요.

발마이어 서점 – 9월 26일 주간 전단지

• 〈팀을 이끄는 방법〉, 데니스 냅
이해하기 쉬운 안내서로, 명확한 설명과 다채로운 흐름도의 도움으로 팀 관리가 쉬워 보이게 해 줍니다. 부록에 제공된 성격 검사를 통해 덤으로 통찰력을 얻으세요.

• **184**〈환경 친화적인 사업체 조성하기〉, 그레첸 실바
실제 사업 소유주들의 '친환경 실천' 경험에 관한 사례 연구로 가득한 이 책은 환경 친화적인 기업을 만들기 위한 6개 부문의 모델을 제시합니다.

• 〈로고 디자인을 위한 영감〉, 키스 제릴렉
권위 있는 이 책은 27개 국가의 로고가 담겨 있으며 새로운 아이디어를 **185**얻으려는 그래픽 디자이너들에게 귀중한 참고 도서 역할을 합니다.

• **183**〈소매점 진열 요령〉, 바트 던스탠
매우 유익한 이 책은 기억에 남는 진열장을 만들기 위한 단계별 지침을 담고 있으며, 상세한 스케치가 딸려 있습니다. **183**최신 판에는 온라인 상점을 위한 웹사이트 디자인을 다룬 장이 새로 추가되었습니다.

---

181 추론 / 암시

번역 발마이어 서점에 관해 암시된 것은?
(A) 여름철에는 연장 운영한다.
(B) 새로운 지점을 열 계획이다.
(C) 온라인과 오프라인 매장의 재고 상품이 다르다.
(D) 직원들이 근처 경영대학에 다닌다.

해설 웹페이지 첫 번째 단락 후반부에서 서점의 방대한 재고 품목을 훑어보시기를 권한다. 웹사이트에는 판매되지 않는 책 수백 종이 있다(We also encourage you to browse through our shop's vast inventory— including hundreds of titles that are not sold on our Web site)고 했다. 따라서 온라인 서점보다 오프라인 서점에 재고 상품이 더 방대하다는 것을 유추할 수 있으므로, 정답은 (C)이다.

▶▶ **Paraphrasing** 지문의 **our shop's** → 정답의 **offline store** 지문의 **on our Web site** → 정답의 **online**

182 사실 관계 확인

번역 웹페이지에서 전단지에 관해 언급되지 않은 것은?
(A) 매장 창문에 게시되어 있다.
(B) 할인되는 책이 적혀 있다.
(C) 직원들이 추천하는 책이 열거되어 있다.
(D) 매장에서 새로 하는 프로젝트이다.

해설 웹페이지 첫 번째 단락, 전단지에 소개되는 모든 책은 10% 할인되지만 할인 혜택을 누리려면 서점을 방문해야 한다(Every book featured in the flyers will be 10% off)에서 (B)를, 다음 주 월요일부터 저희 서점 직원들이 강력하게 보증하는 서적들을 강조한 전단지를 매주 발행한다(Starting next Monday, we will produce a weekly flyer high-lighting books that are strongly endorsed by our store's staff)에서 (C), (D)를 확인할 수 있으므로, 정답은 (A)이다.

▶▶ **Paraphrasing** 지문의 **10% off** → 정답의 **discounted** 지문의 **strongly endorsed by our store's staff** → 정답의 **recommended by staff** 지문의 **Starting next Monday** → 정답의 **a new project**

183 세부 사항

번역 개정판으로 재출간된 책은 무엇인가?
(A) 〈팀을 이끄는 방법〉
(B) 〈환경 친화적인 사업체 조성하기〉
(C) 〈로고 디자인을 위한 영감〉
(D) 〈소매점 진열 요령〉

해설 전단지 네 번째 단락에서 최신 판에는 온라인 상점을 위한 웹사이트 디자인을 다룬 장이 새로 추가되었다(Updated edition includes a new chapter covering Web site design for online shops)고 했다. 따라서 바트 던스탠이 저술한 〈소매점 진열 요령〉이 개정되었음을 알 수 있으므로, 정답은 (D)이다.

184 연계

번역 〈환경 친화적인 사업체 조성하기〉에 관해 암시된 것은 무엇인가?
(A) 재활용 종이에 인쇄되었다.
(B) 정확히 6개의 장으로 되어 있다.
(C) 최근 베스트셀러였다.
(D) 유익한 그림이 포함되어 있다.

해설 웹페이지 두 번째 단락에서 이 주의 선정작 중에는 그레첸 실바의 최신 인기 1위 서적과 잘 알려진 참고 서적 〈로고 디자인을 위한 영감〉이 있다(Among the selections for the week is the classic reference volume Inspirations for Logo Design, as well as Gretchen Silva's latest chart-topper)고 했다. 전단지에 보면 그레첸 실바의 저서는 〈환경 친화적인 사업체 조성하기〉(Make Your Business Eco-Friendly by Gretchen Silva)이므로 〈환경 친화적인 사업체 조성하기〉가 최신 베스트셀러였음을 알 수 있다. 따라서 정답은 (C)이다.

▶▶ **Paraphrasing** 지문의 **latest chart-topper** → 정답의 **a recent bestseller**

185 동의어 찾기

번역 전단지에서 세 번째 단락 2행의 "pick up"과 의미가 가장 가까운 단어는?
(A) 회복하다
(B) 가속화하다
(C) 얻다
(D) 제거하다

해설 해당 문장은 '권위 있는 이 책은 27개 국가의 로고가 담겨 있으며 새로운 아이디어를 얻으려는 그래픽 디자이너들에게 귀중한 참고 도서 역할을 한다'로 해석되는데 여기서 pick up은 문맥상 '얻다, 획득하다'라는 의미가 자연스러우므로, 정답은 (C) obtain(얻다, 획득하다)이다.

186-190 소책자 + 이메일 + 광고

올브라이트 포너 은행

소개

올브라이트 포너 은행은 불과 2년 전 오클랜드 피크 스트리트에 첫 지점을 개설한 이래, 황거레이, 타우랑가, 해밀턴 등지에 추가 지점을 설립했습니다. 이 과정 동안 훌륭한 서비스 성적을 유지했습니다. **186**글라스펠 얼라이언스가 주관한 뉴질랜드 국민 온라인 투표에서 올브라이트 포너는 최상의 고객 지원을 제공하는 은행으로 선정됐습니다.

신용카드 솔루션

믿을 수 있는 기관에서 발행하는 혜택 많은 신용카드를 찾으신다면 저희가 제공하는 하단의 카드를 확인해 보세요.

188AF 블루 카드	**187**AF 글린트 카드
모든 식료품점 구매 시 2% 캐시백을, 다른 모든 곳에서 1% 캐시백을 받으세요.	1달러를 사용할 때마다 항공, 호텔, 선박 등에서 사용할 수 있는 1.5포인트를 적립하세요.
AF 화이트 카드	AF 프리미엄 카드
카드 소지 후 최초 2년간 연간 0%의 금리를 누리세요.	소정의 연회비로 1달러 당 2포인트를 적립하고 어느 곳에서나 사용하실 수 있습니다.

어휘 maintain 유지하다 poll 여론 조사 institution 기관 grocery store 식료품점 interest rate 이자율, 금리 cardholder 카드 소지자

발신: 올브라이트 포너 은행
수신: 자이애나 해리스
날짜: 11월 22일
제목: 납부 확인

해리스 씨게,

189본 이메일은 귀하가 0821로 끝나는 귀하의 올브라이트 포너 보통예금 계좌로부터 7668로 끝나는 올브라이트 포너 신용카드 대금 결제를 승인하신 것을 확인하고자 발송된 것입니다. 보관용으로 본 정보를 저장하시기 바랍니다.

거래 요약:
참조번호: 41152
날짜: 11월 22일
결제금액: 436.09달러
188캐시백 적립액: 5.11달러

본 결제를 승인하지 않으셨거나 제공된 정보에 이의를 제기하시려면, 수신자 부담 전화 1-800-555-0176으로 전화 주십시오.

올브라이트 포너 은행

어휘 authorise 인가하다, 권한을 부여하다 savings account 보통예금 계좌 transaction 거래 dispute 이의를 제기하다 toll-free 수신자 부담

올브라이트 포너 은행
1월의 창립기념일

올브라이트 포너 은행은 이번 달에 3주년을 맞습니다. 이 중요한 시점을 기념하고자 신규 및 이전 고객 모두에게 혜택을 제공하는 특별 프로모션을 실시합니다. 1월 중 저희 지점 어느 곳에서나 당좌예금 계좌를 개설하고 최소 1,000달러를 예치하시면 예치금 200달러를 추가로 드립니다.

189아울러 모든 보통예금 계좌 보유자는 아큐리 N-680 신형 세단 당첨 기회에 응모되었습니다. **190**당첨자는 1월 25일 토요일 저희 오클랜드 지점 앞에서 열리는 고객 감사 파티에서 발표합니다. 오후 1시에 시작해 오후 5시에 있을 시상식까지 계속되며, 올브라이트 포너 고객 및 고객 가족 여러분께서는 게임과 다과를 이용하실 수 있습니다. 오셔서 성공적인 성장을 이룬 3주년을 축하해 주시고, 지역사회의 미래를 위한 관계를 구축하셨으면 합니다.

어휘 in honour of ~을 기념하여 milestone 중대한 시점 checking account 당좌예금 계좌 deposit 예치금 furthermore 게다가 brand-new 신형의 refreshments 다과 build relationship 관계를 구축하다

---

186 사실 관계 확인

번역 올브라이트 포너 은행에 대해 명시된 것은?
(A) 전국 설문조사에서 높은 순위를 기록했다.
(B) 지역 은행 인수를 통해 확장했다.
(C) 소기업 소유주에게 주로 서비스를 제공한다.
(D) 온라인 투자 툴을 출시할 예정이다.

해설 소책자의 첫 번째 단락에서 글라스펠 얼라이언스가 주관한 뉴질랜드 국민 온라인 투표에서 올브라이트 포너는 최상의 고객 지원을 제공하는 은행으로 선정됐다(In an online poll of New Zealanders by Glaspell Alliance, Albright Fonner was voted the bank with the best customer support)고 했으므로 뉴질랜드 국민 온라인 투표에서 최상의 고객 서비스를 제공하는 은행으로 선정되었음을 알 수 있다. 따라서 정답은 (A)이다.

▶▶ **Paraphrasing** 지문의 **In an online poll of New Zealanders** → 정답의 **in a nationwide survey** 지문의 **was voted the bank with the best customer support** → 정답의 **was highly ranked**

187 세부 사항

번역 소책자에 따르면, AF 글린트 카드 소지자들이 할 수 있는 것은?
(A) 잔액 자동이체 신청
(B) 1.5% 금리 지불
(C) 식료품 구매 시 추가 포인트 획득
(D) 여행 시 비용 절약

해설 소책자의 표 중 *AF 글린트 카드(AF Glint Card)*의 설명에서 1달러를 사용할 때마다 항공, 호텔, 선박 등에서 사용할 수 있는 1.5포인트를 적립하라(With every dollar you spend, earn 1.5 points that can be used on flights, hotels, cruises, etc.)고 했다. 따라서 카드를 사용할 때마다 여행 시 포인트를 이용할 수 있다고 했으므로, 정답은 (D)이다.

▶▶ Paraphrasing 지문의 **earn 1.5 points that can be used on flights, hotels, cruises, etc.**
→ 정답의 **Save money on travel**

188 연계

번역 해리스 씨는 어떤 신용카드를 가지고 있겠는가?
(A) AF 블루 카드
(B) AF 글린트 카드
(C) AF 화이트 카드
(D) AF 프리미엄 카드

해설 이메일의 두 번째 단락 '거래 요약:(Transaction summary:)' 중 '캐시백 적립액: $5.11(Cash back earned: $5.11)'을 통해 수신인(you)인 해리스 씨는 캐시백을 받을 수 있는 카드를 소지하고 있음을 알 수 있다. 소책자의 표 중 'AF 블루 카드(AF Blue Card)'의 설명 '모든 식료품점 구매 시 2% 캐시백을, 다른 모든 곳에서 1% 캐시백을 받으세요(Get 2% cash back on all grocery store purchases, and 1% cash back everywhere else)'를 통해 해리스 씨의 AF 블루 카드 소지를 유추할 수 있으므로, 정답은 (A)이다.

189 연계

번역 해리스 씨에 대해 암시된 것은?
(A) 오클랜드에 거주한다.
(B) 상담전화를 해야 할 것이다.
(C) 추첨에 응모됐다.
(D) 최근에 은행 계좌를 새로 개설했다.

해설 이메일의 첫 번째 단락, 0821로 끝나는 귀하의 올브라이트 포너 보통예금 계좌로부터 7668로 끝나는 올브라이트 포너 신용카드 대금 결제를 승인한 것을 확인하고자 이메일을 발송했다(This e-mail confirms that you authorised a payment to your Albright Fonner credit card account ending in 7668 from your Albright Fonner savings account ending in 0821)를 통해 해리스 씨가 보통예금 계좌를 보유하고 있음을 알 수 있다. 광고의 두 번째 단락, 아울러 모든 보통예금 계좌 보유자는 아큐리 N-680 신형 세단 당첨 기회에 응모되었다(Furthermore, all savings account holders have been entered into a lottery for a brand-new Arcuri N-680 sedan)를 통해 보통예금 계좌 보유자인 해리스 씨도 추첨에 응모되었다고 유추할 수 있으므로, 정답은 (C)이다.

▶▶ Paraphrasing 지문의 **a lottery** → **a drawing**

190 세부 사항

번역 창립일 기념식의 일환으로 알맞은 것은?
(A) 당좌계좌 보유자는 선물을 받는다.
(B) 일부 지점에 있는 직원들은 보너스를 지급 받는다.
(C) 은행 고객을 위한 모임이 열린다.
(D) 지역사회 단체를 위한 기부가 이뤄진다.

해설 광고의 두 번째 단락, 당첨자는 1월 25일 토요일 오클랜드 지점 앞에서 열리는 고객 감사 파티에서 발표한다(The winner will be announced at a customer appreciation party held in front of our Auckland branch on Saturday, 25 January)에서 고객 감사 파티를 언급하고 있으므로, 정답은 (C)이다.

▶▶ Paraphrasing 지문의 **a customer appreciation party**
→ 정답의 **A gathering will be held for the bank's customers**

191-195 이메일 + 문자 메시지 + 기사

발신: 서재용
수신: 데브라 크렉
날짜: 12월 4일
제목: Re: 요청

데브라 씨, 다시 소식을 듣게 되어 기쁩니다. 트랭퀼리티 트랜스포트 서비시즈가 잘 되고 있다니 기쁘네요. **191**요청하신 대로 저희가 현재 구비하고 있는 중고 미니밴을 살펴보니 귀하의 목적에 맞는 차가 몇 대 있습니다. 언제든 저희 부지에 나오셔서 옵션을 직접 확인해 보십시오.

1. 차량: 샤튼 무스그로브 SE 　　가격: **192A**41,500달러
설명: 휠체어 사용자를 위한 측면 문. 문과 램프 자동으로 작동. **192D**좌석 6개. 조수석 의자는 떼어내고 두 번째 휠체어를 실을 수 있음. 흰색에 실내는 검은색.

2. 차량: 올베라 트러스텔 　　가격: 38,850달러
설명: 초대형 휠체어 램프가 장착된 뒤쪽 문. 문과 램프는 리모콘이나 실내 스위치로 자동 작동. 휠체어 이용자 1인을 포함해 6인용 좌석. **193**검은색에 실내는 회색.

3. 차량: 네이첼 그랜드 옥스 　　가격: 37,720달러
설명: 휠체어 사용자를 위한 측면 문. 문과 램프는 수동으로 작동해야 함. 세 번째 줄의 편안한 "등받이 높은 의자" 때문에 차량 좌석은 휠체어 이용자용 1개를 포함해 총 5개. 흰색에 실내는 베이지색.

서재용
서 오토 세일즈

어휘 tranquility 고요, 평안 selection 선택(된 것), 구색 suit 맞다, 적합하다 purpose 목적 stop by 들르다 in person 직접 side entry (휠체어 등이 들어갈 수 있게 되어 있는) 측면 문 ramp 경사면, 램프 passenger seat 조수석 detach 떼어내다, 분리하다 accommodation 수용 manually 수동으로 comfortable 편안한, 안락한 captain's chair (밴) 등받이가 높은 의자

발신: 매트 폴크
수신: 데브라 클렉
12월 7일 오전 11시 10분에 수신됨

오늘 서 오토 세일즈로 차를 보러 같이 못 가서 미안하다는 말을 또 전하고 싶어요. 하지만 정말 도와 드리고 싶어서 밴에 관해 어떤 사항을 물어야 할지 조언을 좀 줄게요. **192A, D**비용처럼 명백한 질문과 더불어 휠체어 동반, 또는 휠체어 없이 각 밴에 몇 명이나 탈 수 있는지 알면 좋아요. **192C**이전에 밴이 어떤 수리나 서비스를 받았는지, 총 주행거리는 얼마인지도 알면 좋아요. 그럼, 내일 당신이 알아낸 정보에 대해 이야기해요. 행운을 빌어요!

어휘 vehicle 차량 help out 돕다 along with ~와 함께 obvious 명백한, 뻔한 cost 비용, 값 fit (들어가기에) 맞다 find out ~을 알아내다 repair 수리 in the past 이전에 mileage 주행거리

트랭퀼리티 트랜스포트 서비시즈 차량 이용하기

글: 스테파니 옥스너

룰리(12월 29일)—[193]룰리 주민들은 유쾌한 파란색 로고 스티커가 붙은 흰색 미니밴들을 좀 더 자주 보게 될 것이다. 트랭퀼리티 트랜스포트 서비시즈는 비상시를 제외한 의료 상황에서 장애인과 비장애인에게 교통 수단을 제공하는 지역 회사이다. 문을 연 지 6개월 만에 회사는 보유 차량을 1대에서 3대로 늘렸다.

나는 트랭퀼리티 트랜스포트 직원과 이 같은 인상적인 성장에 관해 이야기를 나누었다. [193]운전기사 매트 폴크는 회사에서 최근 구입한 올베라 트러스텔을 보여주면서 사업의 [194]토대는 신뢰였다고 설명했다. "우리가 시간을 잘 지키고 장비도 제대로 갖추고 있다는 점을 신뢰할 수 있음을 사람들이 알게 된 겁니다." 그는 이렇게 말했다.

[195]회사 소유주인 데브라 클렉은 회사의 미래가 매우 기대된다면서 이렇게 말했다. "우리는 이제 룰리 바깥, 예를 들어 에버린 병원까지 승객을 실어 나를 수 있습니다." 그녀는 관심이 있는 사람들은 555-0147로 전화해 트랭퀼리티 트랜스포트 서비시즈의 서비스를 확인해 달라고 권한다.

어휘 cheerful 유쾌한, 발랄한 non-emergency 비상시가 아닌, 일반의 medical 의료의 disability 장애 fleet (특정 조직에 속한) 한 무리의 차 growth 성장 recently 최근 foundation 기초 reliability 신뢰 properly 적당히, 제대로 equipped 장비를 갖춘 passenger 승객

---

191 주제 / 목적

번역 이메일의 목적은 무엇인가?
(A) 문의에 답하기 위하여
(B) 주문을 확인하기 위하여
(C) 앞으로 있을 할인을 광고하기 위하여
(D) 서비스 지연을 해명하기 위하여

해설 이메일의 첫 번째 단락에서 요청한 대로 현재 구비하고 있는 중고 미니밴을 살펴보니 귀하의 목적에 맞는 차가 몇 대 있다(As you asked, I looked into our current selection of used minivans and found some that might suit your purposes)고 했다. 따라서 문의에 대해 답하기 위해 쓴 것임을 알 수 있으므로, 정답은 (A)이다.

---

192 연계

번역 클렉 씨가 문의하라고 조언을 받은 정보 중 이메일에 제공되지 않은 것은?
(A) 차량의 가격
(B) 차량의 갤런 당 주행거리
(C) 차량의 정비 이력
(D) 차량의 좌석 수

해설 클렉 씨에게 문의하라고 조언했던 정보는 수신인이 클렉 씨인 두 번째 지문을 살펴야 한다. 비용처럼 명백한 질문(Along with obvious things like cost)에서 (A), 이전에 밴이 어떤 수리나 서비스를 받았는지(find out what kind of repairs and servicing the vans have had in the past)에서 (C), 휠체어 동반, 또는 휠체어 없이 각 밴에 몇 명이나

탈 수 있는지(know how many people can fit in each one, with or without wheelchairs)에서 (D)를 물어보라고 했다. 클렉 씨가 문의하라고 조언을 받은 정보는 갤런 당 주행거리가 아니라 총 주행거리(their total mileage)이므로 (B)는 문의 사항이 아니다. 이메일에 보면 41,500달러($41,500)에서 (A), 좌석 6개. 조수석 의자는 떼어내고 두 번째 휠체어를 실을 수 있음(Seats six. Front passenger seat can be detached to allow accommodation of second wheelchair)에서 (D)가 있으므로, 정답은 (C)이다.

---

193 연계

번역 트랭퀼리티 트랜스포트 서비시즈 차량에 대해 무엇이 사실이겠는가?
(A) 앞쪽 조수석을 없앴다.
(B) 비디오 오락기를 갖추고 있다.
(C) 도색을 다시 했다.
(D) 문은 손으로 열어야 한다.

해설 기사의 두 번째 단락 운전기사 매트 폴크는 회사에서 최근 구입한 올베라 트러스텔을 보여주면서(As driver Matt Paulk showed me an Olvera Trustel that the company had recently purchased)를 통해 트랭퀼리티 트랜스포트 서비시즈는 올베라 트러스텔을 구입했다는 것을 알 수 있다. 구입한 차량 올베라 트러스텔의 특징은 이메일을 통해 확인할 수 있다. 특징 중 검은색에 실내는 회색(Black with grey interior)과 기사의 첫 번째 단락 룰리 주민들은 유쾌한 파란색 로고 스티커가 붙은 흰색 미니밴들을 좀 더 자주 보게 될 것이다(Residents of Luley are about to see more white minivans with cheerful blue logo stickers)를 통해 검은색에서 흰색으로 색의 변화가 있었음을 유추할 수 있으므로, 정답은 (C)이다.

---

194 동의어 찾기

번역 기사에서 두 번째 단락 5행의 "foundation"과 의미가 가장 가까운 단어는?
(A) 부분
(B) 기관
(C) 설립
(D) 기반

해설 해당 문장은 '운전기사 매트 폴크는 회사에서 최근 구입한 올베라 트러스텔을 보여주면서 사업의 토대는 신뢰였다고 설명했다'라는 의미로 해석되는데, 여기서 foundation은 문맥상 '토대, 기반'이라는 의미가 자연스러우므로, 정답은 (D) basis(기반, 근거)이다.

---

195 세부 사항

번역 트랭퀼리티 트랜스포트 서비시즈는 어떻게 변화하고 있나?
(A) 가격 전략을 조정 중이다.
(B) 서비스 구역이 확대되고 있다.
(C) 이제 특별한 요구사항이 있는 승객들에게도 맞춰준다.
(D) 병원과 협력 관계를 형성하고 있다.

해설 기사의 세 번째 단락에서 회사 소유주가 한 말, 우리는 이제 룰리 바깥, 예를 들어 에버린 병원까지 승객들을 실어 나를 수 있다(We're now able to transport passengers to locations outside of Luley, such as Averin Hospital)를 통해 룰리 지역 밖으로 서비스를 확장하고 있음을 알 수 있으므로, 정답은 (B)이다. (C)는 처음부터 시행하고 있던 서비스이므로 정답이 될 수 없다.

Test 4

▶▶ Paraphrasing 지문의 to transport passengers to locations outside of Luley
→ 정답의 Its service territory is increasing.

어휘 oversee 감독하다 all aspects of ~의 모든 측면 occasional 가끔의 liaison 연락, 연락 담당자 student-run 학생이 운영하는 administer 집행하다

196-200 이메일 + 구인 광고 + 일정표

발신: 잔느 두보아
수신: 레이첼 프로인드
날짜: 5월 4일
제목: CLS 결과
첨부: CLS 요약

레이첼 씨께,

저는 이번 학기의 캠퍼스 라이프 설문조사를 마쳤습니다. 조사 결과에 대한 자세한 보고서가 본 이메일에 첨부되어 있으며 아래와 같이 중점 내용을 요약할 수 있습니다.

- 가장 낮은 지지율을 받은 서비스 또는 시설은 주차였습니다. 학생들은 특히 셰이드 강당 근처에 공간이 충분하지 않다고 말했습니다.

- **198**대다수 학생들은 가장 좋아하는 식당으로 모튼 카페테리아를 꼽았지만 너무 붐빈다는 점에 우려를 표했습니다. 학생들은 다른 식당들도 부리토와 같은 특별 음식을 제공했으면 합니다.

- **196**특히 과학 전공 학생들 사이에 특정 관심사를 공유하는 사람들을 위한 테마 기숙사에 대한 수요가 계속 있습니다.

첨부를 살펴보시고 언제쯤 만나 이 정보에 대해 논의할 수 있을지 알려 주십시오. 물론 제가 이 직책에 남아 있는 짧은 기간 동안 주요 프로젝트를 맡을 수는 없지만, 제 후임자가 제기된 모든 문제에 대해 잘 알 수 있도록 하겠습니다.

감사합니다.

잔느 두보아
주거 생활 담당관, 캐러웨이 대학교

어휘 finding (조사·연구 등의) 결과 approval rating 지지율, 지지도 auditorium 강당 express concerns about ~에 대해 우려를 표명하다 overcrowding 초만원, 과잉 수용 major in ~을 전공하다 themed 특별한 테마가 있는 take on (일 등을) 맡다 position 직책 successor 후임자

주거 생활 담당관

캐러웨이 대학교 - 피츠버그, 펜실베이니아

캐러웨이 대학교 학생 주거 생활부에서는 주거 생활 담당관(RLM)을 찾습니다. 주요 업무는 대학교 학생 생활관 내 모든 생활을 감독하는 일입니다. **197**RLM은 생활관 관련 문제가 발생하는 즉시 대응해야 하므로 때때로 야간 및 주말 업무가 요구됩니다. 아울러 해당 직책은 캠퍼스 생활 만족도 평가를 위한 피드백 조사 기획 및 실시뿐만 아니라 여러 학생 운영위원회와의 연락책 역할도 포함합니다. **199**지원자는 교육 관련 분야 석사 학위 이상을 보유해야 하며 최소 5년 간 대학교에서 일한 경력이 있어야 합니다. 해당 직책에 관한 더 자세한 내용은 www.carroway.edu/hr를 방문하십시오.

캐러웨이 대학교

신입생 오리엔테이션 일정표 – 제2일

시간	활동	장소
오전 7시 – 오전 8시 30분	조식	벨바 식당
오전 9시 – 오전 10시 30분	어색함 없애기 활동 – 기숙사 사감 주관	각 생활관
오전 11시 – 오후 12시	연설: "캐러웨이의 역사" (웬타오 리, 캐러웨이 대학교 총장)	셰이드 강당
오후 12시 – 오후 1시	**198**중식	**모튼 카페테리아**
오후 1시 15분 – 오후 2시 30분	**199**연설: "캠퍼스 생활의 기본" (피터 트라비스, 주거 생활 담당관)	셰이드 강당
200오후 2시 45분 – 오후 4시	연설: "강의실에서 해야 할 것과 하지 말아야 할 것" (크리스틴 렌 교수, 사회과학부)	셰이드 강당
오후 4시 – 오후 5시 15분	공개 토론회: "사회적 기회를 최대한 활용하기" (복학생들)	셰이드 강당
오후 6시 – 오후 7시 30분	석식	벨바 식당
오후 8시 – 오후 10시	환영 파티	슬로맨 광장

어휘 icebreaker 어색함을 누그러뜨리는 활동 lead 이끌다 social science 사회 과학 panel discussion 공개 토론회 make the most of ~을 최대한 활용하다 returning student 복학생

---

196 세부 사항

번역 이메일에 따르면, 캐러웨이 대학교 학생들은 무엇을 원하는가?
(A) 테마가 있는 주거 시설
(B) 주차요금 인하
(C) 캠퍼스 내 새 식당
(D) 과학 전공자를 위한 개인 지도

해설 이메일의 첫 번째 단락 중 세 번째 항목에서 특히 과학 전공 학생들 사이에 특정 관심사를 공유하는 사람들을 위한 테마 기숙사에 대한 수요가 계속 있다(Especially among students majoring in science, there continues to be demand for themed dormitories for those who share particular interests)고 했으므로 테마 기숙사에 대한 학생들의 수요가 있다는 것을 알 수 있다. 따라서 정답은 (A)이다.

▶▶ Paraphrasing 지문의 themed dormitories
→ 정답의 Themed housing

---

197 세부 사항

번역 광고에 설명된 해당 직책의 업무는 무엇인가?
(A) 문서를 다른 언어로 번역하기
(B) 정상 업무 시간 외 근무하기
(C) 직원 교육 프로그램 기획하기
(D) 가끔 장거리 운전하기

해설 구인 광고에서 생활관 관련 문제가 발생하는 즉시 대응해야 하므로 때때로 야간 및 주말 업무가 요구된다(Occasional night and weekend work will be required, as the RLM must respond to residence-hall related problems as soon as they arise)고 했으므로 야간 및 주말 업무가 요구될 수 있다는 것을 알 수 있다. 따라서 정답은 (B)이다.

▶▶ Paraphrasing 지문의 Occasional night and weekend work → 정답의 Working outside of normal business hours

198 연계

번역 신입생 오리엔테이션 중식에 대해 암시된 것은?
(A) 기숙사 사감들이 학생들을 식사 장소로 데려갈 것이다.
(B) 대학교에서 가장 인기 있는 식당에서 진행될 것이다.
(C) 대학교 총장이 주최할 것이다.
(D) 학생들은 미리 식사를 선택해야 한다.

해설 일정표를 통해 신입생 오리엔테이션 중식은 모든 카페테리아에서 진행된다는 것을 알 수 있다. 모든 카페테리아에 대한 정보는 이메일을 통해 확인할 수 있다. 이메일의 첫 번째 단락 두 번째 항목에서 대다수 학생들은 가장 좋아하는 식당으로 모든 카페테리아를 꼽았지만 너무 붐빈다는 점에 우려를 표했다(Most students rate Morton Cafeteria as their favorite dining hall, but express concerns about overcrowding there)를 통해 신입생 오리엔테이션 중식은 학생들이 가장 좋아하는 식당에서 진행될 예정임을 유추할 수 있으므로, 정답은 (B)이다.

▶▶ Paraphrasing 지문의 their favorite dining hall → 정답의 the university's most popular dining hall

199 연계

번역 트라비스 씨에 대해 암시된 것은?
(A) 대학교 캠퍼스 내에 거주한다.
(B) 재정위원회장이다.
(C) 사회과학 석사 학위가 있다.
(D) 최소 5년의 직장 경력이 있다.

해설 일정표의 '연설: "캠퍼스 생활의 기본"(피터 트라비스, 주거 생활 담당관)(Speech: "Basics of Campus Living" (Peter Travis, Residential Life Manager))'을 통해 트라비스 씨는 주거 생활 담당관임을 알 수 있다. 주거 생활 담당관에 대한 정보는 구인 광고를 통해 확인할 수 있다. 구인 광고의 지원자는 교육 관련 분야 석사 학위 이상을 보유해야 하며 최소 5년간 대학교에서 일한 경력이 있어야 한다(Candidates must possess a master's degree or higher in an education-related field, and have worked in a university setting for a minimum of five years)를 통해 주거 생활 담당관인 트라비스 씨는 적어도 5년의 직장 경력이 있음을 유추할 수 있으므로, 정답은 (D)이다.

▶▶ Paraphrasing 지문의 have worked in a university setting for a minimum of five years → 정답의 has at least five years of work experience

200 세부 사항

번역 오리엔테이션 참석자는 몇 시에 학업과 관련된 정책에 대해 듣기 시작하겠는가?
(A) 오전 11시
(B) 오후 1시 15분
(C) 오후 2시 45분
(D) 오후 4시

해설 일정표의 오후 2시 45분에 시작하는 연설: "강의실에서 해야 할 것과 하지 말아야 할 것"(Speech: "Classroom Do's and Don'ts")에서 렌 교수가 학교 정책을 다룰 것임을 알 수 있으므로, 정답은 (C)이다.

▶▶ Paraphrasing 지문의 Classroom Do's and Don'ts → 질문의 academic policies

TEST 5

101 (C)	**102** (C)	**103** (D)	**104** (B)	**105** (B)
106 (D)	**107** (C)	**108** (B)	**109** (D)	**110** (D)
111 (A)	**112** (C)	**113** (B)	**114** (B)	**115** (B)
116 (A)	**117** (A)	**118** (C)	**119** (D)	**120** (C)
121 (B)	**122** (B)	**123** (D)	**124** (B)	**125** (D)
126 (D)	**127** (A)	**128** (C)	**129** (D)	**130** (B)
131 (A)	**132** (C)	**133** (B)	**134** (A)	**135** (D)
136 (A)	**137** (D)	**138** (C)	**139** (B)	**140** (C)
141 (A)	**142** (D)	**143** (D)	**144** (D)	**145** (A)
146 (A)	**147** (D)	**148** (A)	**149** (C)	**150** (D)
151 (A)	**152** (A)	**153** (C)	**154** (A)	**155** (C)
156 (B)	**157** (A)	**158** (C)	**159** (D)	**160** (B)
161 (D)	**162** (B)	**163** (D)	**164** (B)	**165** (D)
166 (A)	**167** (B)	**168** (A)	**169** (C)	**170** (B)
171 (C)	**172** (D)	**173** (D)	**174** (C)	**175** (A)
176 (A)	**177** (C)	**178** (D)	**179** (D)	**180** (A)
181 (C)	**182** (A)	**183** (B)	**184** (B)	**185** (D)
186 (A)	**187** (D)	**188** (B)	**189** (B)	**190** (C)
191 (C)	**192** (B)	**193** (D)	**194** (A)	**195** (B)
196 (C)	**197** (D)	**198** (A)	**199** (B)	**200** (B)

PART 5

101 전치사 어휘

해설 빈칸은 명사구(a nutritional energy drink) 앞에 위치하는 전치사 자리이다. 문맥상 '에너지 영양 음료로 평가할 수 있다'라는 의미가 자연스러우므로, 정답은 (C) as(~로서)이다.

번역 엘름허스트 코퍼레이션에서 나온 새 음료는 에너지 영양 음료로 평가할 수 있다.

어휘 beverage 음료 describe 묘사하다, 평가하다 describe A as B A를 B로 묘사[평가]하다 nutritional 영양(상)의

102 부사 어휘

해설 빈칸 뒤 동사 구문(result in the creation of hundreds of jobs)을 수식하는 부사 자리이다. 문맥상 '궁극적으로 수백 개의 일자리 창출로 이어진다'는 의미가 자연스러우므로, 정답은 (C) ultimately(궁극적으로, 결국)이다. (A) commonly(흔히, 보통), (B) constantly(끊임없이, 언제나), (D) formerly(이전에)에는 의미상 적합하지 않다.

번역 제조 부문에 선행 투자하는 것은 궁극적으로 수백 개의 일자리 창출로 이어질 것이다.

어휘 upfront 선행의, 선불의 investment 투자 manufacturing sector 제조 부문 result in (결과로) ~이 되다, ~을 야기하다

103 to부정사 _ to + 동사원형

해설 빈칸은 뒤의 명사(the changes)를 목적어로 취하면서, 앞에 있는 타동사(hoped)의 목적어 역할을 하는 to부정사 자리이다. to부정사는 'to + 동사

원형'의 형태로 쓰이므로, 정답은 (D) clarify이다. 동명사 (C) clarifying은 전치사 to 뒤에 올 수 있으나 to부정사의 to 뒤에는 올 수 없다. to부정사의 to와 전치사 to를 혼동하지 않도록 주의하자.

번역 사무실 관리자는 회의에서 복장 규정 정책에 대한 변경사항을 명확히 하고 싶어했다.

어휘 dress code 복장 규정 policy 정책

104 동사 어휘

해설 빈칸은 앞에 있는 동사(made)의 진짜 목적어인 to부정사의 to 뒤에 나오는 동사원형 자리로, 목적격 보어(difficult)와 어울리는 어휘를 찾아야 한다. 문맥상 '소음은 집중하기 어렵게 만들었다'라는 의미가 자연스러우므로, 정답은 (B) concentrate(집중하다, 한곳에 모으다)이다. (A) lower(낮추다), (C) obtain(얻다, 구하다), (D) obstruct(방해하다, 막다)는 의미상 적합하지 않다.

번역 폴랑코 씨 사무실 밖에서 나는 공사 장비 소음 때문에 집중하기 어려웠다.

어휘 construction equipment 공사 장비

105 명사 자리 _ 동사의 목적어

해설 빈칸은 앞에 있는 동사(are seeking)의 목적어 역할을 하며, 형용사(new and unique)의 수식을 받는 명사 자리이다. 명사 (B) approaches와 (C) approach 중에서 골라야 하는데 approach는 '접근법'이라는 의미일 때 가산명사이다. 가산명사의 단수형 앞에는 한정사가 있어야 하는데 이 문장에는 빈칸을 수식하는 형용사(unique) 앞에 한정사가 없으므로 (C) approach는 정답이 될 수 없다. 따라서 정답은 복수형인 (B) approaches이다. 형용사 (A) approachable과 과거분사/과거시제 동사 (D) approached는 품사상 적합하지 않다.

번역 그 분야는 경쟁이 아주 치열한 유형이므로 관리자들은 소비자를 감동시킬 새롭고 독특한 접근법을 모색하고 있다.

어휘 due to ~ 때문에 competitive 경쟁적인 reach (~의 관심을) 끌다, 감동시키다

106 형용사 자리 _ 명사 수식

해설 빈칸은 명사(complaints)를 수식하는 형용사 자리이다. 과거분사 (A) numerated(계산된)와 형용사 (D) numerous(수많은) 중에 문맥상 '수많은 불만사항'이라는 의미가 자연스러우므로, 정답은 (D) numerous이다. 명사 (B) number와 동사 (C) numerate는 품사상 적합하지 않다.

번역 웨이본 일렉트로닉스는 기기 과열에 대한 수많은 불만사항을 접수한 후 신형 스마트폰을 회수했다.

어휘 complaint 불만 overheating 과열 recall (결함이 있는 제품을) 회수하다, 리콜하다

107 등위접속사

해설 빈칸 앞뒤에 완전한 절이 있으므로 빈칸은 절과 절을 연결하는 등위접속사 자리이다. 문맥상 '독창성은 부인할 수 없었지만, 결선까지 오르지는 못했다'라는 대조적인 의미가 자연스러우므로, 정답은 (C) yet이다. 참고로, yet 대신 but을 쓸 수도 있다.

번역 랭함 씨 출품작의 독창성은 부인할 수 없었지만 그녀는 미술 공모전 결선까지 오르지는 못했다.

어휘 originality 독창성 entry 출품작 deny 부인하다 make it to ~에 이르다 final round 결승 art competition 미술대회, 그림 공모전

108 인칭대명사의 격 _ 주격

해설 빈칸은 부사절 접속사(whenever)가 이끄는 부사절의 주어 자리이다. 주격 인칭대명사 (B) we와 소유대명사 (D) ours 중에 문맥상 '우리가 필요할 때마다'라는 의미가 자연스러우므로, 정답은 (B) we이다.

번역 이 회사의 모든 직원은 우리가 휴가로 일을 쉬어야 할 때마다 가능한 여유를 넉넉하게 두고 사전 통지를 해야 한다.

어휘 give much notice (촉박하지 않게) 여유를 두고 예고하다[사전 통지하다]

109 형용사 자리 _ 명사 수식

해설 빈칸은 비교급(more)과 함께 뒤의 명사(option)를 수식하는 형용사 자리이므로, 정답은 (D) costly이다. costly는 -ly로 끝나지만 부사가 아니라 형용사라는 점에 유의한다. 형용사의 비교급 (B) costlier 앞에는 비교급(more)이 또 올 수 없고 명사 (A) costing(원가 계산)과 동사/명사 (C) cost는 품사상 적합하지 않다.

번역 위원들은 제출된 두 건의 입찰을 검토한 후, 신뢰성에 대한 회사의 명성 때문에 비용이 더 많이 드는 쪽을 선택했다.

어휘 submit 제출하다 bid 입찰 council member (의회 등의) 위원 reputation for ~에 대한 명성 reliability 신뢰성

110 부사 어휘

해설 빈칸은 주어(a feeling of dizziness)와 동사(accompanies) 사이에서 동사를 수식하는 부사 자리이다. 문맥상 '종종 동반한다'라는 의미가 자연스러우므로, 정답은 (D) often(종종, 자주)이다. (B) either(또한)는 부사로 쓰일 수 있으나 주로 부정문에서 주로 사용되며, (C) much(많이)는 의미상 적합하지 않다.

번역 의사는 환자가 물을 충분히 마시지 않을 때 종종 갈증이 심해지고 현기증이 함께 올 수도 있다고 설명했다.

어휘 physician 내과의사 dizziness 현기증 accompany 함께 ~하다, 따르다 thirst 갈증

111 전치사 어휘

해설 빈칸은 주어(The emphasis)를 수식하는 과거분사 구문(placed _____ teamwork) 안의 전치사 자리로, teamwork에 중점을 둔다는 의미이므로, 정답은 (A) on이다. emphasis는 on과 함께 'place the emphasis on(~을 강조하다)'이라는 관용표현으로 많이 쓰인다. 전치사 (D) among 뒤에는 주로 복수명사가 나온다.

번역 팀워크가 강조되면 에스피노자 인터내셔널 직원들이 지지 받는다고 느끼는 데 도움이 된다.

어휘 emphasis 강조 support 지지하다, 뒷받침하다

112 동사 어휘

해설 빈칸은 조동사(must) 뒤의 동사원형 자리로, 목적어(the building)와 의미가 가장 잘 통하는 동사를 선택해야 한다. 문맥상 '화재 경보가 울리면 그 건물을 떠나야 한다'라는 의미가 자연스러우므로, 정답은 (C) vacate(비우다, 떠나다)이다. (B) dispose는 주로 전치사(of)와 함께 '처리하다, 처분하다'라는 의미로 쓰인다. (A) decline(거절하다)과 (D) suspend(매달다, 중단하다, 연기하다)는 의미상 적합하지 않다.

번역 안전상의 이유로, 화재 경보가 울리면 모든 직원과 고객은 그 건물을 떠나야 한다.

어휘 safety 안전 fire alarm 화재 경보

113 부사 자리 _ 형용사 수식

해설 빈칸은 형용사(similar)를 수식하는 부사 자리이므로, 정답은 (B) recognizably(곧 알아볼 수 있을 정도로)이다. 과거분사/과거시제 동사 (A) recognized, 형용사 (C) recognizable, 동사 (D) recognizes는 품사상 적합하지 않다.

번역 그 재즈 트리오의 첫 앨범을 잘 아는 사람들은 최신 발매 앨범이 곧 눈치챌 수 있을 정도로 비슷하다는 것을 알 것이다.

어휘 be familiar with ~을 익히 아는, ~에 친숙한 latest 최신의 release 발매

114 명사 자리 _ 동사의 목적어

해설 빈칸은 동사(will have)의 목적어 역할을 하는 명사 자리로, 앞의 부정관사(a)의 수식을 받는다. 따라서 정답은 단수명사 (D) demand이다. 복수명사 (A) demands는 앞의 부정관사(a)와 수일치하지 않고, 동명사 (C) demanding 앞에는 부정관사(a)가 나올 수 없다.

번역 분석가들은 볼만 오토모티브에 최소한 향후 몇 년간 하이브리드 차에 대한 수요가 있으리라고 예측한다.

어휘 analyst 분석가, 애널리스트 predict 예측하다 hybrid vehicle (휘발유, 전기 병용) 하이브리드 자동차 at least 최소한

115 부사 자리 _ 동명사 수식

해설 빈칸은 동명사구(handling the emergency procedures) 뒤에서 동명사구를 수식하는 부사 자리이므로, 정답은 (B) admirably(훌륭히)이다. 동명사/현재분사 (A) admiring, 명사 (C) admiration, 형용사 (D) admirable은 품사상 적합하지 않다.

번역 장 씨는 정전 중 비상조치를 훌륭하게 처리한 후 승진됐다.

어휘 promotion 승진 emergency procedure 비상조치 power outage 정전

116 형용사 자리

해설 빈칸은 명사(abilities)를 수식하는 형용사 자리이므로, 정답은 (A) athletic이다. 명사 (B) athlete, (D) athletes와 부사 (C) athletically는 품사상 적합하지 않다.

Test 5

번역 연례 지역사회 소프트볼 시합은 모든 연령대와 운동 능력의 팀들을 환영한다.

어휘 annual 연례의 of all ages 모든 연령대의 ability 능력 athletic 운동의

117 형용사 어휘

해설 빈칸은 전치사(Owing to) 뒤에서 명사(contents)를 수식하는 형용사 자리로, 문맥에 어울리는 어휘를 선택하도록 한다. 문맥상 '깨지기 쉬운 내용물 때문에, 쌓지 말아야 한다'는 의미가 자연스러우므로, 정답은 (A) fragile(깨지기 쉬운, 약한)이다. (B) sudden(갑작스런), (C) vivid(생생한, 선명한), (D) shallow(얕은)는 의미상 적합하지 않다.

번역 소포의 깨지기 쉬운 내용물 때문에 택배 직원은 그 위에 무거운 물건을 쌓지 말라고 지시 받았다.

어휘 owing to ~ 때문에 content 내용물 instruct 지시하다 stack 쌓다

118 부사 어휘

해설 빈칸은 수동의 과거완료시제 동사를 이루는 동사(had been)과 과거분사(worried) 사이에서, 동사구를 수식하는 부사 자리이다. 문맥상 '쓸데없이 걱정했다'라는 의미가 자연스러우므로, 정답은 (C) needlessly(쓸데없이, 불필요하게)이다. (A) obviously(명백히, 확실히), (B) lastingly(영구히), (D) strategically(전략적으로)는 의미상 적합하지 않다.

번역 영업사원들은 출시 제품이 예상을 뛰어넘었다는 사실을 통보 받자 쓸데없이 걱정했다는 사실을 깨달았다.

어휘 personnel 직원들 product launch 제품 출시 exceed 초과하다 projection 예상

119 명사 자리 _ 복합명사

해설 빈칸은 to부정사(to have) 뒤에서 명사 state와 함께 복합명사를 이루어 목적어 역할을 하는 명사 자리로, 정답은 (D) certification(증명, 자격증)이다. 동사 (A) certify(증명하다, 공인하다, 자격증을 교부하다), 과거시제 동사/과거분사 (B) certified, 형용사 (C) certifiable은 품사상 적합하지 않다.

번역 선셋 스파에서 일하는 모든 안마 치료사들은 3년의 경력뿐 아니라 유효한 주 정부 자격증을 갖춰야 한다.

어휘 therapist 치료사 be required to + 동사원형 ~하도록 요구되다 valid 유효한 state 주, 국가

120 부사 자리

해설 빈칸은 조동사(can)와 동사원형(arrive) 사이에서 동사(arrive)를 수식하는 부사 자리이므로, 정답은 (C) still(여전히, 그래도)이다. 접속사 (A) whether, 전치사 (D) despite는 품사상 적합하지 않다. (B) both(둘 다)는 둘을 지칭할 만한 것이 없으므로 적합하지 않다.

번역 놀랍게도 사라프 씨는 여전히 기차로 더 빨리 도착할 수 있는데, 비행기를 타면 긴 보안절차가 필요하기 때문이다.

어휘 surprisingly 놀랍게도 security procedure 보안절차

121 명사 어휘

해설 빈칸은 형용사(necessary)의 수식을 받는 명사 자리로, 문맥과 어울리는 어휘를 선택해야 한다. 문맥상 '필요한 예방조치를 취하다'라는 의미가 자연스러우므로, 정답은 (B) precautions(예방책, 예방조치)이다. (A) resources(자원, 재원, 수완), (C) announcements(발표), (D) descriptions(설명, 묘사)는 의미상 적합하지 않다.

번역 제트스키는 작동 중에 잘 뒤집히지 않지만 그럴더라도 이용자들은 필요한 예방조치를 취해야 한다.

어휘 flip over 뒤집히다 when in operation 작동 중에 nonetheless 그럴더라도

122 전치사 어휘

해설 빈칸은 명사(the addition) 앞 전치사 자리로, 문맥에 맞는 전치사 어휘를 선택해야 한다. 문맥상 '추가에 관한 결정'이라는 의미가 자연스러우므로, 정답은 (B) regarding이다. (A) since(~ 이래로), (C) into(~ 안으로), (D) underneath(~ 밑에)는 의미상 적합하지 않다.

번역 세입자 대다수는 측면 출입구 근처 동작 감지등 추가와 관련해 주인이 올바른 결정을 내렸다는 데 동의한다.

어휘 tenant 세입자 landlord (집, 사무실 등을 임대하는) 주인 make the right decision 올바른 결정을 내리다 addition 추가

123 동사 자리 _ 태

해설 빈칸은 명사절 접속사(that)가 이끄는 명사절 내 동사 자리이다. 동사 (C) will eliminate와 (D) will be eliminated 중에 문맥상 '악취가 제거되다'라는 수동의 의미가 자연스러우므로, 정답은 (D) will be eliminated이다. to부정사 (A) to eliminate와 (B) to be eliminated는 동사 자리에 단독으로 들어갈 수 없으므로 오답이다.

번역 제품을 만든 사람들은 카펫이나 커튼에 고르게 뿌리면 어떤 악취라도 몇 분 이내에 제거된다고 주장한다.

어휘 claim 주장하다 evenly 고르게 odor 악취

124 명사 어휘

해설 빈칸은 전치사(thanks to) 뒤에서 형용사의 수식을 받는 명사 자리로, 문맥에 어울리는 명사를 선택해야 한다. 문맥상 '수많은 중요한 기술의 진보 덕분에 확장할 수 있었다'는 의미가 자연스러우므로, 정답은 (B) advancements(발전, 진보, 승진)이다. (A) promotions(승진, 홍보, 판촉), (C) elevations(승진, 증가, 고도), (D) enlargements(확대, 확장)는 의미상 적합하지 않다.

번역 PG 인터넷은 수많은 중요한 기술의 진보 덕분에 네트워크를 기하급수적으로 확장할 수 있었다.

어휘 expand 확장하다 exponentially 기하급수적으로

125 분사 자리

해설 빈칸은 앞에 있는 목적어(a rare painting)를 뒤에서 수식하는 분사 자리이다. 현재분사 (A) estimating과 과거분사 (D) estimated중에 문맥상 '추정되는 진귀한 그림'이라는 수동의 의미가 자연스러우므로, 정답은 (D) estimated이다. 동사 (C) was estimated는 문법상 접속사가 한 개 더 있어야 하므로 오답이다.

번역 지역의 미술 애호가들은 박물관이 2백만 유로 이상의 가치가 있는 것으로 추정되는 진귀한 그림을 어렵게 구했다는 소식에 기뻐했다.

어휘 enthusiast 애호가   procure (특별히 어렵게) 구하다   rare 진귀한

126 형용사 어휘

해설 빈칸은 명사(currency)를 수식하는 형용사 자리로, 문맥에 어울리는 어휘를 선택해야 한다. 문맥상 '위조화폐를 유통시키는 것'이라는 의미가 자연스러우므로, 정답은 (D) counterfeit(위조의, 모조의)이다. (A) biased (편향된, 선입견이 있는), (B) negligent(태만한, 부주의한), (C) reckless (무모한, 신중하지 못한)는 의미상 적합하지 않다.

번역 관계자들은 몇몇 사람들이 위조화폐를 더 유통시키는 것을 막기 위해 특별 조치를 취하고 있다.

어휘 extraordinary measure 특별 조치   put ~ into circulation ~을 유통시키다

127 형용사 자리 _ 주격 보어

해설 빈칸은 복합관계부사(however)가 이끄는 부사절 내 주어(they=all battery packs)를 보충 설명하는 보어 자리이다. 복합관계부사 however 뒤에 올 수 있는 형용사와 부사 중 부사절이 be동사로 끝나고 있으므로 형용사 (A) operational이 정답이다.

번역 소비자들은 회수 기간 중, 아무리 배터리 팩이 작동하더라도 제조업체에 모두 반납하도록 장려되었다.

어휘 encourage 권하다, 장려하다   manufacturer 제조업체

128 부사 어휘

해설 빈칸은 등위접속사(but)가 연결하는 완전한 절 뒤에 나오는 부사 자리이다. 문맥상 '일반적인 여론이지만, 그렇지 않다는 것을 입증하려고 나섰다' 라는 대조의 의미가 자연스러우므로, 정답은 (C) otherwise(다르게, 달리, 그렇지 않으면)이다. (A) instead(대신에), (B) opposite(맞은편에), (D) else(그 밖에는)는 의미상 적합하지 않다. (B) opposite가 정답이 되려면 'prove the opposite'의 형태가 되어야 한다.

번역 수면시간에 임박하여 TV를 너무 많이 보는 것은 건강에 나쁘다는 것이 일반적인 의견이지만 아이버슨 박사는 그렇지 않다는 것을 입증하려고 나섰다.

어휘 general consensus 전반적인 합의, 일반적 여론   set out 착수하다, 나서다

129 부사절 접속사 / 등위접속사 구분

해설 빈칸 앞의 to부정사 구문(to take vacations overseas)과 뒤의 to가 생략된 동사원형 구문(stay closer to home)을 연결하는 등위접속사 자리로, 정답은 (D) rather than(~라기 보다는)이다. 부사절 접속사 (A) in order that(~하기 위해), (B) as if(마치 ~인 것처럼), (C) whereas(~인 데 반해) 뒤에는 완전한 절이 나와야 한다.

번역 페르난데스 씨는 다른 문화에 관해 배우기를 즐기기 때문에 고국에서 더 가까운 곳에 머물기보다는 해외 휴가를 선호한다.

어휘 enjoy 즐기다   culture 문화   prefer 선호하다   take a vacation 휴가를 보내다   overseas 해외에서, 해외로   rather than ~보다는 차라리   stay close to home 집[고국] 가까이에서 머물다

130 부사 어휘

해설 빈칸은 형용사(popular)를 수식하는 부사 자리이다. 문맥상 '지속적으로 인기가 있었다'라는 의미가 자연스러우므로, 정답은 (B) enduringly(지속적으로)이다. (A) willingly(기꺼이, 자진해서), (C) hastily(급히, 성급하게), (D) scarcely(드물게)는 의미상 적합하지 않다.

번역 앨리스 보이드의 아동도서는 아름다운 삽화와 매력적인 줄거리 덕분에 지속적으로 인기가 있었다.

어휘 illustration 삽화   storyline 줄거리

PART 6

131-134 공지

> 체스터스 스테이크하우스 고객 여러분께
>
> 체스터스 스테이크하우스는 여러분께 최고의 식사 경험을 드리기 위해 **131**전념하고 있습니다. 따라서 여름을 맞아 저희 테라스를 드디어 열게 됐다는 반가운 소식을 전합니다. 신선한 공기 속에서 식사하시는 동안 인근이 주거지역이라는 점을 명심해 주시기 바랍니다. 따라서 늦은 저녁, 특히 주 출입구 맞은편 아파트를 걸어 지날 때 목소리 성량을 살펴 **132**예의 있게 행동하셔야 합니다. 협조해 주셔서 미리 감사 드립니다. 이는 저희가 인근에 거주하는 분들과 긍정적인 **133**관계를 유지하는 데 도움이 됩니다. **134**실내로 들어오고 싶으시면 언제든 쉽게 공간을 내어드릴 수 있습니다. 종업원에게 실내로 들어가고 싶다고 알려주시기만 하면 됩니다.
>
> ---
>
> **어휘** patio (건물 뒤편의) 테라스   neighborhood 이웃, 인근   residential 주거의   therefore 그러므로   in advance 미리   maintain 유지하다   accommodate (살거나 지낼) 공간을 제공하다

131 동사 자리

해설 빈칸은 주어(Chester's Steakhouse) 뒤에 나오는 동사 자리이므로, 정답은 (A) is committed이다. 동명사/현재분사 (B) being committed 와 (D) committing, to부정사 (C) to commit는 동사 자리에 들어갈 수 없다.

132 형용사 자리 _ 주격 보어

해설 빈칸은 주어(you)를 보충 설명하는 형용사 자리이므로, 정답은 (C) courteous(공손한, 정중한)이다. 명사 (A) courteousness(예의 바름, 공손함)와 (D) courtesy(공손함, 정중함)는 사람 주어(you)와 동격 관계를 이룰 수 없고, 부사 (B) courteously는 품사상 적합하지 않다.

133 명사 어휘

해설 빈칸은 앞의 형용사(positive)의 수식을 받는 명사 자리로, 문맥에 어울리는 어휘를 찾아야 한다. 문맥상 '인근에 거주하는 분들과 긍정적인 관계를 유지하다'라는 의미가 자연스러우므로, 정답은 (B) relationship(관계)이다. (A) impact(영향, 충격), (C) proof(증거, 증명), (D) service(서비스, 봉사, 근무)는 의미상 적합하지 않다.

134 문맥에 맞는 문장 고르기

어휘 (A) 종업원에게 실내로 들어가고 싶다고 알려주시기만 하면 됩니다.
(B) 저희가 이 문제에 주목하게 해 주셔서 감사합니다.
(C) 결과적으로 테라스 개장은 지연될 예정입니다.
(D) 음식 준비하는 시간이 평소보다 더 걸릴 수도 있습니다.

해설 빈칸 앞 문장에서 실내로 들어오고 싶으면 언제든 쉽게 공간을 내어줄 수 있다(Should you prefer to move indoors at any time, we can easily accommodate you)고 했다. 따라서 빈칸에는 실내로 이동하려면(to do so) 어떻게 하면 되는지를 언급한 (A)가 정답이다.

어휘 appreciate 감사하다 bring to attention 주목하게 만들다 than usual 평소보다 더

135-138 이메일

수신: 아만도 미쇼 〈armando@michauddrycleaning.com〉
발신: 애슈빌 은행 〈loans@ashvillebank.com〉
날짜: 1월 18일
제목: 소기업 대출

미쇼 씨께,

저희 애슈빌 은행의 소기업 대출에 관심 가져주셔서 감사합니다. 첨부한 **135**양식에 기입해 주십시오. 이 양식은 저희에게 귀하의 개인 신용뿐 아니라 사업 모델에 대한 정보를 제공해 줍니다. 본 양식에 정확한 정보를 **136**제공하시는 것이 꼭 필요합니다. 그렇지 않은 경우 신청이 연기 또는 **137**거절까지 될 수 있습니다. **138**모든 요청사항에 부응하고자 최선을 다하겠지만 전액을 지급하지 못할 수도 있습니다. 그러한 경우, 귀하가 이용할 수 있는 다른 선택사항도 있을 것입니다.

애슈빌 은행 대출팀

어휘 small business 소기업 fill out 기입하다, 작성하다 afford 제공하다 essential 필수적인 accurate 정확한 rejection 거절 application 신청 accommodate (요구 등에) 부응하다 full amount 전액

135 명사 자리

해설 빈칸은 형용사(attached)의 수식을 받는 명사 자리이다. 이 명사는 뒤에 관계대명사절의 수식 또한 받고 있으므로 관계대명사절의 동사(afford)와 수를 일치시켜야 한다. 따라서 명사 (A) form과 (D) forms 중에 복수명사인 (D) forms가 정답이다. 명사 (C) forming(형성, 구성)은 의미상 적합하지 않으므로 오답이다.

136 동사 자리

해설 빈칸은 명사절 내 동사 자리로, 명사절 접속사 that 앞에 있는 형용사(essential)에 주목해야 한다. '필수적인', '중요한'의 의미를 가진 형용사 essential, necessary, important, imperative, vital 뒤에 that절이 오는 경우, 동사는 〈should + 동사원형〉의 형태로 나와야 하며, 이때 조동사(should)는 생략이 가능하다. 따라서 정답은 동사원형 (A) provide이다.

137 부사 어휘

해설 빈칸은 선택의 등위접속사(or)가 연결하는 목적어 중, 뒤에 나오는 목적어(the rejection)를 강조하는 부사 자리이다. 문맥상 '거절까지 야기할 수 있다'라는 의미가 자연스러우므로, 정답은 (D) even(~까지도, 조차, 심지어)이다. (A) more(더, 더 많이), (B) rather(다소, 약간, 차라리), (C) yet(아직)은 의미상 적합하지 않다.

138 문맥에 맞는 문장 고르기

번역 (A) 이러한 이유로 저희 은행은 높은 고객서비스 평점을 받았습니다.
(B) 그럼에도 불구하고 귀하의 신상을 고려했습니다.
(C) 그러한 경우, 귀하가 이용할 수 있는 다른 선택사항도 있을 것입니다.
(D) 그 대신에, 받았는지 확인하기 위해 귀하의 잔고를 확인하실 수 있습니다.

해설 빈칸 앞 문장에서 모든 요청사항에 부응하고자 최선을 다하겠지만 전액을 지급하지 못할 수도 있다(While we do our best to accommodate all requests, we may not be able to issue you the full amount)며 전액 지급이 되지 않을 가능성을 언급하고 있다. 따라서 빈칸에는 전액 지급이 되지 않는 경우(In that case)를 대비한 다른 선택사항도 있다는 내용이 이어지는 것이 문맥상 자연스러우므로, 정답은 (C)이다.

어휘 rating 평가, 평점 nevertheless 그럼에도 불구하고 take ~ into consideration ~을 고려하다 personal 개인적인 circumstance 사정, 환경 alternatively 대신에 balance 잔고

139-142 정보문

노크로스 수면센터

1200 하니판 레인 · 461-555-0138

최대 20퍼센트의 사람들이 수면 장애를 겪는 것으로 추산됩니다. 많은 수면 문제는 문제를 겪는 사람에게 **139**뚜렷하게 나타나지 않을 수도 있습니다. 따라서 심한 증세가 없더라도 스스로 검사해 보시기를 권합니다. 상태 평가를 받으시려면 저희 센터를 직접 방문하십시오. 전문가들이 다양한 수면장애를 **140**진단해 드릴 수 있습니다. 한편 모니터를 대여하여 집에서 **141**편안하게 수면 검사를 할 수 있습니다. 1주 후 저희가 데이터를 분석해 드립니다. **142**지속적 기도 양압기(CPAP) 같은 일부 기기들은 처방전이 필요합니다. 다른 기기들은 일반 소비자가 사용할 수 있습니다.

어휘 It is estimated that ~라고 추정되다 severe 심한 symptom 증상 assess 평가하다 in person 직접, 몸소 a wide variety of 다양한 sleep disorder 수면장애 analyze 분석하다 prescription 처방전 continuous positive airway pressure (CPAP) 지속적 기도 양압기

139 형용사 어휘

해설 빈칸은 주어(Many sleep issues)를 보충 설명하는 형용사 자리로, 뒤에 나오는 전치사구(to the affected person)의 수식을 받는다. 문맥상 '문제를 겪는 사람에게 뚜렷이 나타나지 않을 수도 있다'라는 의미가 자연스러우므로, 정답은 (B) apparent(뚜렷한, 명백한)이다. (A) susceptible(민감한, 영향 받기 쉬운), (C) tentative(잠정적인), (D) adequate(적절한, 충분한)는 의미상 적합하지 않다.

140 동사 어휘

해설 빈칸 뒤에 나오는 목적어(a wide variety of sleep disorders)와 의미가 가장 잘 통하는 동사를 선택해야 한다. 문맥상 '다양한 수면장애를 진단하다'라는 의미가 자연스러우므로, 정답은 (C) diagnose(진단하다)이다. (A) interpret(해석하다, 통역하다), (B) conduct(수행하다, 안내하다, 지휘하다), (D) inherit(물려받다, 상속받다)는 의미상 적합하지 않다.

141 부사 어휘

해설 빈칸은 조동사(may)와 동사원형(test) 사이에서 동사를 수식하는 부사 자리이다. 문맥상 '집에서 편안하게 수면 검사를 하다'라는 의미가 자연스러우므로, 정답은 (A) comfortably(편안하게, 수월하게)이다. (B) partially(부분적으로, 불완전하게), (C) evidently(분명히, 명백히), (D) abundantly(풍부하게, 매우)는 의미상 적합하지 않다.

142 문맥에 맞는 문장 고르기

번역 (A) 주마다 업데이트된 보고서를 받을 것입니다.
(B) 수 주 후 대다수가 성공을 알렸습니다.
(C) 가능한 한 빨리 이를 처리해주십시오.
(D) 다른 기기들은 일반 소비자가 사용할 수 있습니다.

해설 빈칸 앞 문장에서 지속적 기도 양압기 같은 일부 기기들은 처방전이 필요하다(A prescription is required for some of our devices, such as our continuous positive airway pressure (CPAP) machines)고 했다. 따라서 빈칸에는 다른 기기들(Others)은 처방전 없이 사용 가능하다는 내용이 이어지는 것이 문맥상 자연스러우므로, 정답은 (D)이다.

어휘 take care of ~을 처리하다 general 일반의 consumer 소비자

143-146 기사

10월 6일 – 니콜 월트가 국가 교통 자문 역할을 수락했다. 자신의 컨설팅 사업을 시작하기 위해 물러난 레온 힉스를 대체하는 자리다. 월트 씨는 인상적인 안전 전문 지식으로 143매우 존경 받고 있다. 나라의 남동부 지역에서 수 년간 교통을 144관리해 왔으며 지지자들은 규모가 더 큰 역할에 그녀가 쉽게 적응하리라 확신한다. 분석가들은 월트 씨가 곧 철도 부문을 기업체에 매각하도록 국회를 압박하리라 예측한다. 145이런 매각은 국가의 교통 시스템에 즉각 수익을 창출할 것이다. 또한 이동 시간에 대한 신뢰가 높아지리라 예상된다. 145그러나 월트 씨는 교통 시스템의 146민영화에 강력하게 반대하는 자들과 맞닥뜨릴 것이다. 공공이 이용하는 서비스는 공공의 손에 남아야 한다고 많은 사람들이 믿기 때문이다.

어휘 advisor 자문 replace 대체하다 step down 물러나다. 사임하다 highly respected 매우 존경 받는 expertise 전문 지식 adapt 적응하다, 맞추다 predict 예측하다 parliament 국회 generate 발생시키다 profit 이윤 opponent 반대자

143 부사 자리

해설 빈칸은 형용사(respected)를 수식하는 부사 자리이므로, 정답은 (C) highly이다. (A) high가 부사로 쓰일 경우 주로 동사 뒤에 쓰이며, (B) higher와 (D) height는 문법상, 품사상 적합하지 않아 오답이다.

144 동사 자리 _ 시제

해설 빈칸은 주어(She) 뒤에 나오는 동사 자리로, 뒤에 나오는 명사(transportation)를 목적어로 취한다. 또한 뒤에 나오는 전치사구(for several years)의 수식을 받는다. 문맥상 월트 씨의 과거부터 현재까지의 경력을 이야기하고 있으므로 정답은 능동의 현재완료진행시제 동사 (D) has been managing이다. 수동의 미래완료시제 동사 (A) will have been managed와 과거시제 동사 (B) was managed는 목적어를 취할 수 없고, 능동의 현재진행시제 동사 (C) is managing은 현재 또는 미래의 의미를 나타낸다.

145 문맥에 맞는 문장 고르기

번역 (A) 또한 이동 시간에 대한 신뢰가 높아지리라 예상된다.
(B) 다행히도 이는 개연성 없는 시나리오로 간주된다.
(C) 예를 들어 월트 씨는 승차권 발매를 현대화하는 데 집중할 계획이다.
(D) 각각 수천 명의 일일 승객에게 혜택이 돌아갈 것이다.

해설 빈칸의 앞 문장에서 이런 매각은 국가의 교통 시스템에 즉각 수익을 창출할 것(A sale such as this would generate immediate profit for the national transportation system)이라고 매각의 이점을 언급하고 있고, 뒤에 나오는 문장은 그러나 월트 씨는 강력한 반대자들과 맞닥뜨릴 것이다(However, Walt will face strong opponents)라고 매각에 반대하는 의견도 있다는 것을 언급하고 있다. 따라서 빈칸에는 앞 문장에 이어 매각의 이점을 하나 더(also) 제시하는 것이 문맥상 자연스러우므로, 정답은 (A)이다.

어휘 result in 결과가 ~이 되다 reliable 신뢰할 수 있는, 믿을 만한 unlikely 개연성이 없는 modernize 현대화하다 benefit 도움이 되다

146 명사 어휘

해설 빈칸은 관사(the)와 전치사구(of the system) 사이의 명사 자리이다. 앞에 있는 문장에서 월트 씨가 곧 철로 부분을 기업체에 매각하도록 국회를 압박할 것(she will soon push parliament to sell a section of the rail line to a corporation)이라고 했으므로, 빈칸에는 공공부분의 민간 매각과 유사한 의미의 단어를 선택해야 한다. 따라서 정답은 (A) privatization(민영화)이다. (B) renewal(갱신, 재개발, 회복), (C) evaluation(평가), (D) operation(운영, 작동, 실시)은 의미상 적합하지 않다.

PART 7

147-148 초대장

리전트 미술관이 개막 전 행사에 귀하를 진심으로 초대합니다.

밝음과 어둠
레슬리 디애즈 회화 전시회

1월 20일 금요일, 오후 7시

리전트 미술관은 이 놀라운 그림들을 전시하게 되어 기쁩니다. 147디애즈 씨의 최신 전시회는 그녀의 동남아시아 여행에서 영감을 받았습니다. 그곳에서 그녀는 그림의 핵심인 훌륭한 해변과 산악 풍경을 보았습니다. 148귀하는 회원이시기 때

문에 이 행사에 참석하시어 언론과 일반 대중보다 먼저 작품을 감상하실 수 있습니다.

> **어휘** museum 미술관, 박물관 cordially invite 진심으로[정중히] 초대하다 pre-opening 개막 전 행사, 사전 개막 행사 lightness 밝기, 명도 darkness 어둠, 암도 exhibit 전시회 painting 채색화 January 1월 be pleased to+동사원형 ~하게 되어 기쁘다 amazing 놀라운, 멋진, 훌륭한 on display 전시 중인 be inspired by ~에게 영감을 받다 travel 여행 observe 관찰하다, 보다 remarkable 주목할 만한, 눈에 띄는, 훌륭한 seaside 해변, 해안, 바닷가 landscape 경치, 풍경 be central to ~의 중심[핵심]이다, ~에 매우 중요하다 membership 회원권, 회원 신분 entitle 자격[권리]을 주다 attend 참석[참가]하다 event 행사 artwork 예술작품, 미술품 ahead of ~보다 먼저 press 언론 general public 일반 대중

147 사실 관계 확인

번역 디애즈 씨에 관해 명시된 것은?
(A) 리전트 미술관에서 데뷔전을 열고 있다.
(B) 그녀의 그림이 경매로 팔릴 것이다.
(C) 동남아시아에 살았었다.
(D) 작품이 자연의 경치를 묘사한다.

해설 디애즈 씨의 최신 전시회는 그녀의 동남아시아 여행에서 영감을 받았고, 그곳에서 그녀는 그림의 핵심인 훌륭한 해변과 산악 풍경을 보았다(Ms. Diaz's latest exhibition is inspired by her travels through Southeast Asia, where she observed the remarkable seaside and mountain landscapes that are central to her paintings)고 했으므로, 디애즈 씨의 작품은 자연 경관을 중점적으로 묘사한다는 것을 알 수 있다. 따라서 정답은 (D)이다.

▶▶ **Paraphrasing** 지문의 **the remarkable seaside and mountain landscapes that are central to her paintings** → 정답의 **Her artwork depicts scenes from nature.**

148 추론 / 암시

번역 초대장을 받는 사람은 누구이겠는가?
(A) 미술관 후원자
(B) 미술 평론가
(C) 미술학도
(D) 언론 종사자

해설 후반부에서 귀하는 회원이기 때문에 이 행사에 참석해 언론과 일반 대중보다 먼저 작품을 감상할 수 있다(Your membership entitles you to attend this event and see the artwork ahead of the press and the general public)고 했으므로, 초대장의 수령인이 미술관 회원이라고 유추할 수 있다. 따라서 정답은 (A)이다.

149-150 웹페이지

> **고객님의 계정이 갱신되었습니다.**
>
> **이름:** 다이애나 피터스
> **이메일 주소:** dpeters@kemberyco.com

[149]파이들랜트 의류 무료 월간 소식지를 성공적으로 **구독 해지하셨습니다.** 귀하의 주문 상태와 온라인 고객을 위한 저희의 이용 약관에 영향을 주는 정책 변동에 관해서는 파이들랜트 의류로부터 여전히 이메일을 받게 되실 것입니다. 이 해지 조치를 철회하기 원하신다면 **여기를** 클릭해 주십시오. 잠시 시간을 내어 귀하께서 왜 더 이상 소식지를 받아 보시고 싶지 않은지 알려주시기 바랍니다.

의견: [150]저는 수년 동안 파이들랜트 의류의 단골 고객이었지만, 최근의 가격 인상 탓에 제가 이 브랜드와 교류하는 방식을 바꾸었습니다. 특별한 경우에 입는 복장으로 여전히 파이들랜트 의류를 고려하겠지만, 제게는 다른 곳에서 캐주얼 의류를 구입하는 게 더 실용적입니다.

> **어휘** account 계정 update 업데이트하다, 갱신하다 successfully 성공적으로 unsubscribe 구독 해지하다 monthly 월간의 newsletter 소식지 clothing 의류 status 상태, 지위 place an order 주문하다 policy change 정책 변동 affect 영향을 미치다 terms of use 이용 약관 online customer 온라인 고객 undo 원상태로 돌리다, 무효화하다 action 조치, 행동 take a moment to+동사원형 시간을 내어 ~하다 no longer 더 이상 ~ 않다 regular customer 단골 고객 recent 최근의 increase in price 가격 인상 interact with ~와 교류하다, 상호작용하다 consider 간주하다, 고려하다 apparel 의류, 복장 special occasion 특별한 경우[때] practical 실용적인, 실제적인 purchase 구입[구매]하다, 사다 elsewhere 다른 곳에서

149 세부 사항

번역 피터스 씨가 웹페이지를 방문한 이유는?
(A) 주문품에 관한 후기를 남기려고
(B) 서비스에 대해 불만을 제기하려고
(C) 이메일 수신자 명단에서 자신을 빼려고
(D) 소식지 아이디어를 투고하려고

해설 첫 번째 단락에서 파이들랜트 의류 무료 월간 소식지를 성공적으로 구독 해지했다(You have successfully unsubscribed from the Piedlant Clothing free monthly newsletter)고 했으므로, 피터스 씨가 정기구독을 해지하기 위해 웹페이지를 방문했다는 것을 알 수 있다. 따라서 정답은 (C)이다.

▶▶ **Paraphrasing** 지문의 **unsubscribed from the Piedlant Clothing free monthly newsletter** → 정답의 **remove herself from a mailing list**

150 사실 관계 확인

번역 피터스 씨가 파이들랜트 의류에 관해 언급한 것은?
(A) 더 이상 캐주얼 의류를 팔지 않는다.
(B) 마케팅 전략이 구식이다.
(C) 고객들에게 이메일을 너무 자주 보낸다.
(D) 상품이 더 비싸졌다.

해설 두 번째 단락에서 피터스 씨는 수년 동안 파이들랜트 의류의 단골 고객이었지만, 최근의 가격 인상 탓에 이 브랜드와 교류하는 방식을 바꾸었다(I have been a regular customer of Piedlant Clothing for years, but the recent increase in prices has changed the way I plan to interact with the brand)고 했다. 의류 가격의 인상을 언급하고 있으므로, 정답은 (D)이다.

▶▶ **Paraphrasing** 지문의 **the recent increase in prices** → 정답의 **less affordable**

151-152 문자 메시지

찰스 로언솔 [오후 4:25] ¹⁵¹스테파니, 사무실에 몇 시쯤 돌아오나요?
스테파니 마틴 [오후 4:26] 실은, 사무실에 가지 않을 생각이었어요. 오후 6시경까지 코딜 엔터프라이즈와 회의를 할 거라서 바로 퇴근하려고요. 왜 그러시죠?
찰스 로언솔 [오후 4:28] ¹⁵²오늘 저녁에 카펫 청소를 하는데, 직원들이 자신의 사무 공간 바닥에 있는 개인 물건을 모두 치워 주기로 되어 있어요.
스테파니 마틴 [오후 4:29] 오, 이런! 까맣게 잊고 있었어요! ¹⁵²제 대신 치워 주시면 너무 번거로우실까요?
찰스 로언솔 [오후 4:30] 천만에요.
스테파니 마틴 [오후 4:31] 고마워요! 제가 신세를 지네요.

어휘 come back to the office 사무실에 복귀하다 actually 실은, 실제로 plan to+동사원형 ~할 계획[생각]이다 be in the meeting with ~와 회의를 하다 go straight home 곧장[바로] 퇴근하다 clean 청소하다 employee 직원, 사원 be supposed to+동사원형 ~하기로 되어 있다 remove 치우다, 제거하다 personal item 개인 물건 cubicle 칸막이 한 사무 공간 forget 잊다 inconvenient 불편한 Not at all. 천만에요. I owe you one. 신세를 졌네요.

151 세부 사항

번역 로언솔 씨가 마틴 씨에게 묻는 내용은?
(A) 그녀의 복귀 시간
(B) 그녀의 사무실 위치
(C) 회의 진행 상황
(D) 해야 할 업무

해설 오후 4시 25분 메시지에서 로언솔 씨가 스테파니 씨에게 사무실에 몇 시쯤 돌아오는지(Stephanie, do you know what time you're coming back to the office) 사무실 복귀 시간을 묻고 있으므로, 정답은 (A)이다.

▶▶ **Paraphrasing** 지문의 **what time you're coming back**
→ 정답의 **When she will return**

152 의도 파악

번역 오후 4시 30분에 로언솔 씨가 "천만에요"라고 쓸 때, 그 의도는 무엇인가?
(A) 그가 마틴 씨의 업무 공간을 치울 것이다.
(B) 그가 일부 물품을 다 써버렸다.
(C) 그가 몇몇 고객과 이야기를 나누지 못했다.
(D) 그가 청소 시간표를 수정할 것이다.

해설 로언솔 씨는 오후 4시 28분 메시지에서 오늘 저녁에 카펫 청소를 하는데, 직원들이 자신의 사무 공간 바닥에 있는 개인 물건을 모두 치워야 한다(The carpets will be cleaned this evening, so employees are supposed to remove all of their personal items from the floor of their cubicles)고 했다. 이에 대해 마틴 씨가 오후 4시 29분 메시

지에서 대신 치워 주면 안 되겠냐(Would it be too inconvenient for you to do it for me)며 부탁하는 말에, 로언솔 씨가 천만에요(Not at all)라고 응답했으므로, 정답은 (A)이다.

▶▶ **Paraphrasing** 지문의 **remove all of their personal items from the floor of their cubicles**
→ 정답의 **clear Ms. Martin's work space**

153-154 회람

수신: 론 주식회사 전 직원 발신: 라훌 셰베이드, 인사부장 날짜: 10월 6일 제목: 창업 25주년

직원 여러분께,

다음 달 말에 론 주식회사는 창립 25주년을 맞게 됩니다. 우리는 이러한 성취를 기념하기 위해 파티를 열고자 합니다. ¹⁵³우리가 이 행사를 준비할 수 있도록 저는 현재 준비위원회에 함께할 인원 6명을 찾고 있습니다. 이 기회는 모든 부서의 직원들에게 열려 있으니 알아 두시기 바랍니다. ¹⁵⁴관심이 있는 분이라면 언제 집단회의에 참석할 수 있는지 적어서 늦어도 10월 15일 수요일까지 제게 이메일을 보내주십시오. 마감 시한이 지난 후 제가 모든 사람의 참석 가능성을 확인하여 우리 모두에게 괜찮은 날과 시간을 정하겠습니다. 검토해 주셔서 감사합니다.

어휘 incorporated 유한책임[주식회사]의 employee 직원, 사원 Human Recourse Director 인사부장, 인력관리부장 in business 사업을 하는 celebrate (특별한 날을) 축하하다, 맞다 anniversary 기념일 hold a party 파티를 열다 commemorate 기념하다 achievement 성취, 업적 currently 현재, 지금 look for ~을 찾다 join 합류하다 planning board 준비위원회 make the preparations for ~에 대한 준비를 하다 event 행사 please note that ~을 유의하시기[알아 두시기] 바랍니다 opportunity 기회 be open to ~에게 열려 있다 staff member 직원 department 부서 interested 관심이 있는 no later than 늦어도 ~까지 notes 메모, 쪽지 take part in ~에 참석[참여]하다 deadline 마감시한 review 검토하다, 심사하다 availability 가용성, 참석 가능성 select 고르다, 택하다 work 유효하다, 괜찮다 consideration 검토, 고려, 배려

153 주제 / 목적

번역 이 회람의 목적은?
(A) 축하 행사에 직원들을 초대하려고
(B) 일자리를 공지하려고
(C) 위원회 구성원을 물색하려고
(D) 직원들의 성과를 축하하려고

해설 초반부에서 우리가 이 행사를 준비할 수 있도록 현재 준비위원회에 함께할 인원 6명을 찾고 있다(I am currently looking for six people to join our planning board so that we can make the preparations for the event)고 했으므로, 정답은 (C)이다.

▶▶ **Paraphrasing** 지문의 **looking for six people to join our planning board**
→ 정답의 **seek committee members**

Test 5

154 사실 관계 확인

번역 셰베이드 씨가 10월 15일이 지나 결정된다고 명시한 것은?

(A) 회의 시기
(B) 예산 규모
(C) 집단의 목표
(D) 연회장 위치

해설 관심 있으면 언제 집단회의에 참석할 수 있는지 적어서 늦어도 10월 15일 수요일까지 이메일로 보내달라(If you are interested, please e-mail me no later than Wednesday, October 15, with notes about when you would be able to take part in group meetings)고 했고, 마감 시한이 지난 후 모든 사람의 참석 가능성을 확인해 모두에게 괜찮은 날과 시간을 정하겠다(After the deadline, I will review everyone's availability and select a time and day that works for all of us)고 했다. 10월 15일이 지난 후 회의 날과 시간을 정하겠다고 언급했으므로, 정답은 (A)이다.

▶▶ **Paraphrasing** 지문의 **select** → 질문의 **be determined**
지문의 **a time and day that works for all of us** → 정답의 **The timing of a meeting**

155-157 송장

맥도웰 서플라이즈

www.mcdorwellsupplies.com s 1-800-555-0100

업체명: 애칠리스   담당자: 마이클 애칠리
전화번호: 901-555-0127   **156**주문일: 7월 9일
청구지 주소: 테네시 주 38018, 멤피스 시 머틀 애비뉴 875번지
배송지 주소: 테네시 주 38018, 멤피스 시 볼드윈 스트리트1299번지
156배송 종류: 익일 특급   반품 마감일: 7월 16일
157맥도웰 서플라이즈 고객 적립 제도 번호: 5498-7319

물품 내역	수량	단가	합계
15518인치 철사 옷걸이(500개 묶음)	5	21.99달러	109.95달러
155골판지 어깨 가드(500개 묶음)	3	28.49달러	85.47달러
155얼룩 제거액(5리터)	4	29.99달러	119.96달러
155다기능 세제(20리터)	3	189.99달러	569.97달러
구매해 주셔서 감사합니다. 저희가 고객님께 더 나은 서비스를 제공하는 데 도움이 되도록 잠시 시간을 내어 www.mcdorwellsupplies.com/ survey에서 간단한 고객 서비스 설문에 답해 주시기 바랍니다. 고객님의 의견은 저희에게 중요합니다.	소계		885.35달러
	세금 및 배송		83.75달러
	대금 총액		969.10달러

어휘 point of contact 연락처, (연락) 담당자 billing address 청구지 주소 shipping address 배송지 loyalty program 단골고객 보상 프로그램 overnight express 익일 특급 return cutoff date 반품 마감일 wire hanger 철사 옷걸이 cardboard 골판지, 두꺼운 종이 shoulder guard 어깨 가드(어깨 모양을 잡아주는 보형물) liquid 액체의 stain remover 얼룩 제거 all-in-one (두 가지 이상의 기능이) 하나로 된, 일체형의 detergent 세제 quantity 수량 price per unit 단가 tax 세금 delivery 배달, 배송 total due 대금 총액 purchase 구입, 구매 take a moment to+동사원형 잠시 시간을 내서 ~하다 complete 작성하다, 완성하다

brief 간단한   customer service questionnaire 고객 서비스 설문지   feedback 의견, 피드백

155 추론 / 암시

번역 애칠리스의 업종은 무엇이겠는가?

(A) 택배회사
(B) 옷 가게
(C) 드라이클리닝 업소
(D) 미용실

해설 물품 내역(Item Description) 항목에 있는 18인치 철사 옷걸이(18-inch wire hangers), 골판지 어깨 가드(Cardboard shoulder guards), 얼룩 제거액(Liquid stain remover), 다기능 세제(All-in-one detergent)로 보아 드라이클리닝 업소임을 유추할 수 있다. 따라서 정답은 (C)이다.

156 추론 / 암시

번역 애칠리 씨의 택배는 언제 도착하겠는가?

(A) 7월 9일
(B) 7월 10일
(C) 7월 11일
(D) 7월 16일

해설 주문일은 7월 9일(Date of Order: July 9)이고, 익일 특급 배송(Shipping Type: Overnight Express)을 신청했으므로, 애칠리 씨의 택배는 7월 10일에 도착할 것으로 유추할 수 있다. 따라서 정답은 (B)이다.

157 추론 / 암시

번역 송장에 암시되어 있는 것은?

(A) 애칠리스는 고객 적립 포인트를 모으고 있다.
(B) 애칠리 씨는 설문지를 작성했다.
(C) 배송비가 인하되었다.
(D) 주문품이 주소지 두 군데로 보내질 것이다.

해설 송장에 맥도웰 서플라이즈 고객 적립 제도 번호(McDorwell Supplies Loyalty Program Number: 5498-7319)가 나와 있으므로, 애칠리 씨가 맥도웰 서플라이즈의 고객 적립 제도에 참여하고 있음을 알 수 있다. 따라서 정답은 (A)이다.

158-160 공지

라이멜트 체육관 회원 안내문

158, 159구내 주차장을 이용하시는 라이멜트 체육관 회원께서는 9월 1일부터 7일까지 대체 공간을 알아 보셔야 합니다. 주차 구역을 재포장하고 경미한 균열을 메우게 될 작업반원들을 수용하기 위해 주차장 출입이 금지되기 때문입니다. **159**이 기간 동안 정문이 잠겨 있을 예정이니 모든 회원께서는 건물 서쪽 끝에 있는 직원 출입구를 이용하셔야 합니다. 주차장 작업 진척 상황에 관한 최신 정보가 저희 웹사이트에 게시될 예정입니다. 저희가 일주일 내내 제공하는 피트니스 수업들의 시간표는 영향을 받지 않을 것입니다.

사실 주차장 한 곳이 래드클리프 애비뉴에 체육관 근처에 있습니다. 안타깝게도, 비용이 발생해도 저희가 여러분께 변상해 드리지는 못합니다. 이번 작업으로 발생할 수 있는 모든 불편에 대해 사과드리며, 여러분의 인내에 감사합니다. 또한 이것은 저희가 향후 6개월 동안 실시하고자 하는 여러 공사 중 하나입니다.

¹⁶⁰저희는 여러분의 운동 경험을 더 즐겁게 해 줄 만한 추가적인 건물 개선 작업에 관해 항상 회원 여러분의 의견을 듣고자 합니다. 아이디어를 제안하시려면, 현장 관리인인 드웨인 베일리에게 직접 말씀하시거나 dbailey@reimeltgym.com으로 이메일을 보내주시기 바랍니다.

어휘 gym 체육관 on-site parking lot 구내 주차장 alternative 대안의, 대체의 make arrangements 수배하다, 준비하다 off limits 출입이 금지된 accommodate 수용하다 work crew 작업반 repave 재포장하다 section 구역 seal 메우다, 밀봉하다 minor 경미한, 사소한 crack 균열, 갈라진 틈 main entrance 정문 locked 잠긴 update 최신 소식 regarding ~에 관한 progress 진전, 진보, 향상 post 게시하다 offer 제공하다 throughout the week 일주일 내내 affect 영향을 주다 private 사설의, 민영의, 개인적인 be located near ~ 근처에 위치하다 unfortunately 안타깝게, 불행히 reimburse 변상[변제]하다 cost 비용 incur 초래하다, (빚을) 지다 apologize for ~에 대해 사과하다 inconvenience 불편 patience 인내, 참을성 project 사업, 과제 intend ~할 의향이 있다 be willing to+동사원형 기꺼이 ~하다 further 추가의 building upgrade 건물 개선 workout 운동 enjoyable 즐거운 put forward 제안[제시]하다 site manager 현장 관리자 directly 직접, 곧장

158 주제 / 목적

번역 무엇에 관한 안내인가?
(A) 주차장 확장
(B) 주차 정책 수정
(C) 주차 구역 보수
(D) 주차 요금 인상

해설 첫 번째 단락에서 구내 주차장을 이용하는 라이멜트 체육관 회원들은 9월 1일부터 7일까지 대체 공간을 알아 봐야 한다. 주차 구역을 재포장하고 경미한 균열을 메우게 될 작업반원들을 수용하기 위해 주차장 출입이 금지되기 때문(Reimelt Gym members who use our on-site parking lot should make alternative arrangements from September 1 to 7, as the lot will be off limits in order to accommodate work crews who will be repaving sections of the lot and sealing minor cracks)이라며 구내 주차장 보수를 알리고 있다. 따라서 정답은 (C)이다.

▶▶ **Paraphrasing** 지문의 repaving sections of the lot and sealing minor cracks
→ 정답의 Repairs to a parking area

159 추론 / 암시

번역 라이멜트 체육관 직원들에 관해 암시된 것은?
(A) 변화 관련 질문들에 답할 준비를 할 것이다.
(B) 한 주 동안 회원들과 출입구를 공유할 것이다.
(C) 9월에는 평소보다 수업을 더 적게 할 것이다.
(D) 체육관 부지에 있는 주차 공간을 배정받을 것이다.

해설 첫 번째 단락에서 구내 주차장을 이용하는 라이멜트 체육관 회원들은 9월 1일부터 7일까지 대체 공간을 알아 봐야 한다. 주차 구역을 재포장하고 경미한 균열을 메우게 될 작업반원들을 수용하기 위해 주차장 출입이 금지되기 때문이다. 이 기간 동안 정문이 잠겨 있을 예정이니 모든 회원들은 건물 서쪽 끝에 있는 직원 출입구를 이용해야 한다(Reimelt Gym members who use our on-site parking lot should make

alternative arrangements from September 1 to 7, as the lot will be off limits in order to accommodate work crews who will be repaving sections of the lot and sealing minor cracks. During this time, the main entrance will remain locked, and all members will need to use the employee entrance at the west end of the building)고 했다. 즉 일주일의 공사 기간 동안 직원들은 체육관 회원들과 함께 직원 출입구를 사용해야 한다는 것이므로, 정답은 (B)이다.

▶▶ **Paraphrasing** 지문의 all members will need to use the employee entrance → 정답의 They will share an entrance with members
지문의 from September 1 to 7 → 정답의 for one week

160 세부 사항

번역 안내에 따르면, 체육관 회원들이 베일리 씨에게 연락을 해야 하는 이유는?
(A) 회원 신분을 높이기 위해
(B) 시설물 개선을 제안하기 위해
(C) 변상을 받는 법을 공부하려고
(D) 공사의 진척 상황을 문의하려고

해설 두 번째 단락에서 여러분의 운동 경험을 더 즐겁게 해줄 만한 추가적인 건물 개선 작업에 관해 항상 회원들의 의견을 듣고자 한다. 아이디어를 제안하려면, 현장 관리인인 드웨인 베일리에게 직접 말하거나 이메일을 보내 달라(We are always willing to hear from our members about further building upgrades that would make your workout experience more enjoyable. To put forward your ideas, please talk to Site Manager Dwayne Bailey directly or e-mail him at dbailey@reimeltgym.com)고 했다. 즉 건물 개선 작업에 관한 아이디어를 제안하기 위해 베일리 씨에게 연락하라고 했으므로, 정답은 (B)이다.

▶▶ **Paraphrasing** 지문의 talk to Site Manager Dwayne Bailey directly or e-mail him → 질문의 contact Mr. Bailey
지문의 further building upgrades → 정답의 a facility improvement

161-163 이메일

수신: 테레사 버지스 〈burgess.t@monticello1.eu〉
발신: 버랜스턴 〈info@beranstoncamping.eu〉
^{162C}날짜: 2월 1일
제목: 마음에 들어 하실 제품들입니다!

버지스 씨께,

¹⁶¹저희는 캠핑 장비를 고를 때 선택할 물건이 엄청나게 많다는 점을 이해하고 있기에 고객님의 최근 주문에 기초해 몇 가지 제안할 제품을 모아 봤습니다. ^{162A}올드린은 버랜스턴 캠핑에 추가된 최신 브랜드이며 이미 베스트셀러가 되었습니다. ^{162C}이번 달에 올드린 제품을 구입하시면 배송료가 면제됩니다. 링크를 클릭하시고 저희 웹사이트에 오셔서 단 몇 분 만에 물품을 구매하세요!

- 올드린 배터리 랜턴 [45유로]: 이 랜턴은 텐트 안에서나 밖에서 안전하며, 한 번 충전하면 최저 전력 상태에서 최대 350시간까지 불을 밝힐 수 있습니다.

- 올드린 침낭 [150유로]: 편안함과 실용성이 완벽하게 조화된 이 침낭은 최저 기온이 영하 10℃까지 떨어질 때 안성맞춤이며 겨우 15 x 30센티미터 크기로 압축할 수 있어서 운반하기가 쉽습니다.
- **162D**올드린 스토브 [50유로]: 이 스토브는 가볍고 작지만 온갖 크기의 냄비에 꼭 맞아서 야외 취사가 쉽습니다.

163저희가 이제 반품을 구입일로부터 최장 45일 동안 받는다는 사실을 주목해 주십시오. 특히 선물로 받아서 즉시 개봉하지 않을지도 모르는 물품의 경우 30일로는 충분하지 않다고 저희 고객들이 의견을 주셨기 때문입니다.

즐거운 쇼핑 하시기를 바랍니다!

버랜스턴 팀 일동 드림

어휘 a vast array of 엄청나게 다양한[폭넓은] option 선택 사항 choose from ~에서 고르다 select 선택하다 camping gear 캠핑 장비 compile 모으다, 편집[편찬]하다 product 제품 suggestion 제안 based on ~에 근거[기초]해 addition 추가, 부가 purchase 구입[구매]하다 shipping fee 배송료 waive 탕감하다, 적용하지 않다 item 물품, 품목 in just minutes 겨우 몇 분 만에 battery-operated 배터리로 작동되는 charge 충전 provide 공급하다 up to 최대 ~까지 on the lowest setting 최저 전력 상태에서 sleeping bag 침낭 perfect 완벽한 blend 융합, 조화 comfort 편안함 practicality 실용성 be suitable for ~에 적합하다, 알맞다 temperature 기온 be compressed into ~으로 압축되다 easy transport 손쉬운 운반 lightweight 경량의, 가벼운 fit 꼭 맞다, 안성맞춤이다 size 크기 outdoor cooking 야외 취사 Please note that ~. ~을 유의[주목]하십시오. accept 받아들이다 purchase date 구입일 feedback 의견 customer 고객 indicate 표현하다, 지적하다 especially 특히 be opened 개봉되다 right away 당장, 즉시

161 세부 사항

번역 버지스 씨가 이메일을 받은 이유는?
(A) 그녀가 소셜미디어 페이지에 의견을 달아서.
(B) 그녀가 몇 가지 최신 제품 정보를 요청해서.
(C) 그녀가 고객 서비스 부서에 연락해서.
(D) 그녀가 예전에 웹사이트에서 구매한 적이 있어서.

해설 첫 번째 단락에서 캠핑 장비를 고를 때 선택할 물건이 엄청나게 많다는 점을 이해하고 있어서 고객님의 최근 주문을 바탕으로 제안할 제품들을 모아 봤다(We understand that there is a vast array of options to choose from when selecting camping gear, so we have compiled some product suggestions based on your recent orders)고 했다. 즉 버지스 씨의 최근 구매 이력을 바탕으로 제품을 추천하기 위해 이메일을 보냈음을 알 수 있으므로, 정답은 (D)이다.

▶▶ **Paraphrasing** 지문의 **your recent orders**
→ 정답의 **previously made purchases**

162 사실 관계 확인

번역 올드린 브랜드 제품에 관해 명시되지 않은 것은?
(A) 고객들에게 인기를 얻었다.
(B) 할인가에 판매된다.
(C) 2월에는 무료로 배송된다.
(D) 가열 장치를 포함하고 있다.

해설 첫 번째 단락에서 올드린은 버랜스턴 캠핑에 추가된 최신 브랜드이며 이미 베스트셀러가 되었다(Aldrin is our newest addition to Beranston Camping, and this brand has already become a best-seller)고 했으므로 (A)를, 날짜: 2월 1일(Date: February 1)과 이번 달에 올드린 제품을 구입하면 배송료가 면제된다(If you purchase any Aldrin products this month, their shipping fee will be waived)고 했으므로 (C)를, 올드린 스토브 제품 설명에서 가볍고 작지만 온갖 크기의 냄비에 꼭 맞아서 야외 취사가 쉽다(Aldrin Stove [€50]: This stove is lightweight and small, but it fits pots of all sizes to make outdoor cooking easy)고 했으므로 (D)를 확인할 수 있다. 따라서 정답은 (B)이다.

▶▶ **Paraphrasing** 지문의 **already become a best-seller**
→ 보기의 **become popular**
지문의 **their shipping fee will be waived**
→ 보기의 **free delivery**

163 세부 사항

번역 버랜스턴이 반품 정책에서 바꾼 것은?
(A) 얻을 수 있는 매장 포인트의 양
(B) 선물 반환에 필요한 서류
(C) 물품 반송 비용
(D) 반품 기간

해설 세 번째 단락에서 이제 우리는 반품을 구입일로부터 최장 45일 동안 받는다는 사실을 주목해 주기 바란다. 특히 선물로 받아서 즉시 개봉하지 않을지도 모르는 물품의 경우 30일로는 충분하지 않다는 고객들이 의견 때문(Please note that we now accept returned items for up to 45 days from the purchase date, as feedback from our customers indicated that 30 days was not enough, especially for items given as gifts that may not be opened right away)이라며 반품 기한이 늘어났음을 언급했다. 따라서 정답은 (D)이다.

▶▶ **Paraphrasing** 지문의 **we now accept returned items for up to 45 days from the purchase date**
→ 정답의 **The period for making returns**

164-167 안내문

가을 축제의 즐거움에 함께하세요!
프레리 공원, 10월 20일 토요일 오전 9시 - 오후7 시

가을 축제는 모든 연령에게 재미가 넘치는 연례 축제입니다. 올해는 10월 20일 토요일에 프레리 공원에서 열립니다. **164**모든 시민의 참석을 환영하며 축제의 여러 활동에도 참여하시기를 권합니다.

한 가지 참여 방법은 자신만의 허수아비를 만들고 장식해서 자신의 창의성을 보여주는 것입니다. 이 행사에는 업체, 학교, 자선단체 들도 출품할 수 있습니다. **165**등록비는 20달러이며, 이것에는 나무로 만든 틀(5인치×8인치)과 속을 채울 지푸라기가 작은 단으로 한 단 포함됩니다. 출전할 수 있는 자리의 수가 제한되어 있습니다. **167**되도록 많은 사람이 참여할 수 있도록 단체별로 한 점씩 출품해 주시기를 요청합니다. 등록을 하시고 정규 근무 시간 중 아무 때나 시청에서 재료를 받아 가실 수 있습니다. **165**자선단체는 10달러만 내면 됩니다.

빵 굽는 사람들은 모두 모이십시오! 축제에는 파이 굽기 대회가 포함될 예정입니다. 축제 당일 오전 10시에 공원 북단에 있는 축구장 인근 부스로 파이를 가져오십시오. 용기는 반환되지 않으니 파이를 위해 일회용 파이 틀을 사용하시기 바랍니다. 오후 2시에 심사가 진행되며 상위 3명이 100달러어치의 제빵 소품이 담긴 바구니를 받게 됩니다. 수상자들을 발표한 후 무료 파이와 아이스크림이 제공될 예정입니다. **166**제빵 행사는 사전 등록이 필요하지 않지만 출품작들을 비평하는 운 좋은 사람들 중 한 명이 되고 싶으시다면 555-0199번으로 캐시 쇼에게 전화해 주시기 바랍니다. 저희는 약 5명으로 된 패널을 찾고 있습니다.

축제 활동의 전체 목록은 시 웹사이트 www.westover.gov에서 찾아보실 수 있습니다.

어휘 join 함께하다, 합류하다 annual 연례의, 연간의 celebration 축하[기념] 행사 full of ~으로 가득한 take place 발생하다, 일어나다 be welcome to+동사원형 ~하는 것을 환영하다 attend 참석하다 encourage 장려[격려]하다, 권장하다 participate in ~에 참석[참여]하다(= take part in) creativity 창의성 decorate 장식하다 scarecrow 허수아비 charity 자선단체 enter 출품[출전]하다, 참가하다 registration fee 등록비 include 포함하다 wooden frame 나무 틀 a bale of straw 짚 한 단 stuffing 속[충전재] ask for ~을 요청하다 entry 출품작 register 등록하다 pick up 받아 가다, 찾아 가다 material 재료 anytime 언제라도 regular business hour 정규 근무시간 charge 요금을 물리다, 청구하다 baker 제빵사, 빵[케이크] 굽는 사람 contest 경연대회 booth 부스 soccer field 축구장 northern end 북쪽 끝, 북단 container 용기, 그릇 return 반환하다, 돌려주다 disposal 일회용의 pie tin 파이 틀 judge 심사하다, 판결하다 winner 수상자 worth of ~의 값어치가 있는 baking accessory 제빵 소품 serve 제공하다 announce 발표하다 advanced registration 사전 등록 necessary 필요한 critique 비평하다 look for ~을 찾다 a complete list of ~의 전체 목록

164 추론 / 암시

번역 이 공지는 어디에 게시되었겠는가?
(A) 참가 신청서
(B) 지역 신문
(C) 여행 웹사이트
(D) 취미 전문 잡지

해설 첫 번째 단락에서 모든 시민의 참석을 환영하며 축제의 여러 활동에도 참여하기를 권한다(Everyone in town is welcome to attend, and we encourage you to also participate in the festival's many activities)고 했으므로, 지역 신문에 게시된 공지임을 유추할 수 있다. 따라서 정답은 (B)이다.

165 사실 관계 확인

번역 비영리기관을 위한 혜택으로 언급된 것은?
(A) 자원봉사자 지원
(B) 팸플릿의 광고 지면
(C) 상을 받을 수 있는 기회
(D) 등록비 할인

해설 두 번째 단락에서 등록비는 20달러(The registration fee is $20)라고 언급했지만, 같은 단락의 마지막 문장에서 자선단체는 10달러만 내면 된다(Charities will only be charged $10)고 했으므로, 비영리기관은 등록비 할인의 혜택을 받는다는 것을 알 수 있다. 따라서 정답은 (D)이다.

▶▶ Paraphrasing   지문의 Charities
→ 질문의 nonprofit organizations

166 세부 사항

번역 사람들이 쇼 씨에게 연락해야 하는 이유는?
(A) 대회 심사위원으로 지원하려고
(B) 제빵대회에 출전하려고
(C) 재료를 찾아갈 약속을 잡으려고
(D) 전체 축제 시간표를 요청하려고

해설 세 번째 단락에서 제빵 행사는 사전 등록이 필요하지 않지만 출품작들을 비평하는 운 좋은 사람들 중 한 명이 되고 싶다면 캐시 쇼에게 전화해 달라(Advanced registration for the baking event is not necessary; however, if you would like to be one of the lucky people critiquing the entries, please call Cassie Shaw at 555-0199)고 했으므로, 정답은 (A)이다.

▶▶ Paraphrasing   지문의 one of the lucky people critiquing the entries → 정답의 a competition judge

167 문장 삽입

번역 [1], [2], [3], [4]로 표시된 곳 중 다음 문장이 들어가기에 가장 적합한 곳은?

"출전할 수 있는 자리의 수가 제한되어 있습니다."

(A) [1]
(B) [2]
(C) [3]
(D) [4]

해설 삽입 문장 '출전할 수 있는 자리의 수가 제한되어 있습니다(There are a limited number of spots available)'를 통해 뒤에서 공간상의 제약(a limited number of spots available)에 따른 해결방안을 제시할 것임을 알 수 있다. [2]의 뒤에 나오는 문장으로 되도록 많은 사람이 참여할 수 있도록 단체별로 한 점씩 출품해 주기를 요청한다(We ask for one entry per group so that as many people as possible can participate)며 공간 제약에 대한 해결방안을 언급하고 있으므로, 정답은 (B)이다.

168-171 온라인 채팅

| 버지니아 리츠 [오후 1:18] |
| **168**좋아요, 제가 아침 직원회의 후에 맥팔린 씨에게 전화해서 그가 계약 협상을 진행하기를 원하는지 알아봤어요. |

| 주드 도일 [오후 1:19] |
| 어땠어요? |

| 버지니아 리츠 [오후 1:19] |
| **169, 170C**음, 그는 루커 컴퓨팅이 업계에서 가격이 가장 낮아서 그곳을 쓰기로 결정했대요. |

| 메건 하월 [오후 1:20] |
| 우리가 며칠 동안 영업 활동을 했잖아요! |

버지니아 리츠 [오후 1:21] 알아요. 모두 아주 열심히 일했죠. 아주 허탈해요.
주드 도일 [오후 1:21] 170D솔직히, 맥팔린 씨가 신생기업보다 루커 같이 안정된 회사를 선호하는 것이 저는 놀랍지가 않아요. 170A그들은 우리보다 직원 수가 거의 다섯 배나 많아요. 하지만 그들은 고객들도 더 많죠. 우리가 제공하는 집중적이고 개인적인 서비스는 제공하지는 못할 거예요.
메건 하월 [오후 1:22] 맞아요. 대다수 고객들이 결국에는 비용을 약간 더 지불하고 우리 같이 믿을 수 있는 기술지원팀을 쓰는 게 좋다는 걸 알게 되죠.
버지니아 리츠 [오후 1:23] 맥팔린 씨가 1년짜리 계약을 했다고 제게 말했어요. 그러니까 내년에 갱신 기간 동안 우리가 계약을 따낼 기회가 또 있을 거예요.
메건 하월 [오후 1:26] 171제 생각엔 우리가 이번 패배를 뒤로 하고 스탠포드 인더스트리즈를 상대로 한 설명회에 집중해야 할 것 같아요.
주드 도일 [오후 1:27] 맞아요. 171설명 자료를 완전히 새로 만드는 대신 우리에게 있는 자료를 스탠포드의 특별한 요구조건에 맞게 손질하면 돼요.

어휘 ring 전화하다 staff meeting 직원회의 go forward with ~을 진행하다 contract negotiation 계약 협상[교섭], 거래 협상 decide to+동사원형 ~하기로 결심하다 hire 채용[고용]하다, 쓰다 the lowest price 최저가 in the industry 업계에서 sales pitch 구매 권유, 영업 활동 letdown 허탈, 실망 to be honest 솔직히 prefer A to B B보다 A를 선호하다 well-established 잘 자리잡은, 안정된 start-up 신생기업 employee 직원 provide 제공하다 personal service 개개인에 맞춘[개인적인] 서비스 You have a point. 일리가 있어요., 맞아요. customer 고객 eventually 결국 figure out 이해하다, 알아내다 worth ~의 가치가 있는 slightly 약간, 살짝 dependable 믿을 수 있는 tech support team 기술지원팀 inform 알려주다 sign 서명하다 opportunity 기회 secure a contract 계약을 확보하다[따내다] renewal period 갱신 기간 defeat 패배 put ~ behind ~을 뒤에 남기다, 뒤로 하다 focus on ~에 집중하다 prepare 준비하다 presentation 설명회, 프레젠테이션 Exactly. 맞아요. instead of ~ 대신에 completely 완전히, 아예 adapt 맞추다, 조정하다, 각색하다 address 다루다 specific need 특별한 요구조건

168 세부 사항

번역 리츠 씨가 오전에 한 일은?
(A) 전화 통화
(B) 맥팔린 씨의 회사 방문
(C) 이메일 수신함 확인
(D) 메모 작성

해설 리츠 씨는 오후 1시 18분 메시지에서 아침 직원회의 후에 맥팔린 씨에게 전화해서 그가 계약 협상을 진행하기를 원하는지 알아봤다(OK, I rang Mr. McFarlin right after our morning staff meeting to see whether he wanted to go forward with contract negotiations)고 했으므로, 정답은 (A)이다.

▶▶ **Paraphrasing** 지문의 **rang** → 정답의 **Made a phone call**

169 의도 파악

번역 오후 1시 20분에 하월 씨가 "우리가 며칠 동안 영업 활동을 했잖아요"라고 쓸 때, 그 의도는 무엇인가?
(A) 회의가 빨리 끝나서 놀랍다.
(B) 약속이 연기되어 답답하다.
(C) 고용 결정이 실망스럽다.
(D) 협상이 잘 진행되리라 확신한다.

해설 리츠 씨는 오후 1시 19분 메시지에서 그는 루커 컴퓨팅이 업계에서 가격이 가장 낮아서 그곳을 쓰기로 결정했다(Well, he decided to hire Rooker Computing instead since it has the lowest prices in the industry)고 계약이 성사되지 않았음을 언급하고 있다. 이에 하월 씨가 '우리가 며칠 동안 영업 활동을 했잖아요(We spent days on that sales pitch)'라며 노력에 따른 결과를 얻지 못한 것에 대한 실망감을 표현하고 있으므로, 정답은 (C)이다.

▶▶ **Paraphrasing** 지문의 **decided to hire**
→ 정답의 **an employment decision**

170 사실 관계 확인

번역 루커 컴퓨팅에 대해 명시되지 않은 것은?
(A) 대화 참여자들의 회사보다 직원이 더 많다.
(B) 훌륭한 고객 서비스를 제공하는 것으로 유명하다.
(C) 경쟁업체들보다 가격보다 더 낮다.
(D) 대화 참여자들의 회사보다 오래된 회사이다.

해설 도일 씨의 오후 1시 21분 메시지에서 루커 컴퓨팅은 우리보다 직원 수가 거의 다섯 배나 많다(They have nearly five times the number of employees we do)고 했으므로 (A)를, 리츠 씨의 오후 1시 19분 메시지에서 업계에서 가격이 가장 낮아서 그곳을 쓰기로 결정했다(Well, he decided to hire Rooker Computing instead since it has the lowest prices in the industry)고 했으므로 (C)를, 도일 씨의 오후 1시 21분 메시지에서 맥팔린 씨가 신생기업보다 루커 같이 안정된 회사를 선호하는 것이 놀랍지 않다(To be honest, I'm not surprised that Mr. McFarlin preferred a well-established business like Rooker over a start-up)고 했으므로 (D)를 확인할 수 있다. (B)에 대한 언급은 하지 않았으므로, 정답은 (B)이다.

▶▶ **Paraphrasing** 지문의 **nearly five times the number of employees** → 보기의 **more staff**
지문의 **the lowest prices in the industry**
→ 보기의 **Its prices are lower than those of its competitors.**
지문의 **a well-established business ~ over a start-up**
→ 보기의 **It has been in operation longer**

171 세부 사항

번역 도일 씨가 제안하는 것은 무엇인가?
(A) 서비스 계약 갱신
(B) 기술적인 문제 처리
(C) 설명회 자료 손질
(D) 스탠포드 인더스트리즈 고용

해설 하월 씨는 오후 1시 26분 메시지에서 이번 패배를 뒤로 하고 스탤포드 인더스트리즈를 상대로 한 설명회에 집중해야 할 것 같다(I guess we need to put this defeat behind us and focus on preparing the presentation for Stalford Industries)고 말했다. 이에 도일 씨가 설명 자료를 완전히 새로 만드는 대신 우리에게 있는 자료를 스탤포드의 특별한 요구조건에 맞게 손질하면 된다(And instead of making a completely new one, we can just adapt the one we have to address Stalford's specific needs)고 설명회 자료의 수정을 제안하고 있으므로, 정답은 (C)이다.

172-175 편지

칼스브룩 어린이병원
버지니아 주 20330 알링턴
그웬트 로드 1077번지

6월 15일

캐서린 제임스 박사
버지니아 주 22210 알링턴
카디프 스트리트 896번지

제임스 박사님께,

172특수질환 어린이를 위한 저희 신규 별관의 성공에 박사님의 자선단체가 기여한 것에 감사하는 이 감사편지를 받아 주십시오. 박사님의 지원이 없었으면 저희는 해내지 못했을 것입니다. 175또한 지난주 개원식에서 드디어 박사님을 친히 뵙게 되어서 참으로 좋았습니다. 박사님과 제가 같은 프로젝트를 다수 함께 했다는 점을 감안하면, 진작에 이렇게 만나지 않은 것이 놀라울 따름입니다.

173약속대로, 진행성 질환 어린이를 위한 양육 환경 조성에 관한 연구 결과를 박사님께 보내드립니다. 동봉한 첫 번째 연구는 위치타 대학교에서 스티브 채프먼 박사가 주도한 것으로서 색과 음악이 회복기에 미치는 효과를 설명합니다. 이 실험은 성인을 대상으로 진행되었지만, 저희는 그 효과가 더 어린 집단에도 비슷하리라고 생각합니다. 이는 병실에서 페인트 선택을 고려해야 한다는 뜻입니다. 동봉한 두 번째 연구는 저희 병원과 지역 기술대학의 공동연구입니다. 아델 디오프 교수가 주도한 이 연구는 전문 시설을 제공하는 것과 의료 성과 사이의 강한 연관성을 보여줍니다.

174이 연구들은 다음 달에 알링턴 병원이 어린이 시설 개선을 위한 지원금 신청서를 작성하는 일을 박사님께서 도와주실 때 박사님께 유용할 것입니다. 또한 박사님께서 첫 자문 작업을 하게 되신 것도 축하드립니다. 저희와 상대하는 전국의 여러 다른 병원 관계자들이 비슷한 프로젝트를 할 때 박사님의 도움으로 혜택을 받을 것이라고 저는 확신하고 있으니, 이 지원금 신청서 보조 작업을 더 하는 것에 관심이 있다면 제게 알려 주시기 바랍니다.

어슐라 어거스틴 박사 배상
소아과장, 칼스브룩 어린이병원
동봉물 있음

어휘 children's hospital 어린이병원 accept 받아주다, 수락하다 letter of appreciation 감사편지 charity 자선단체 contribute to ~에 이바지[기여]하다 annex 별관 special condition 특수질환 support 지원 wonderful 매우 멋진, 참으로 좋은 finally 마침내, 드디어 in person 직접, 몸소 opening ceremony 개원식, 개업식 as promised 약속된 대로 research 연구 nurturing environment 양육 환경 progressive condition 진행성 질환

enclosure 동봉물 describe 설명하다, 기술하다 effect 효과, 영향 recuperation period 회복기 trial 실험 adult 성인 similar 비슷한 as well 또한 mean 의미하다 choice 선택 patients' room 병실 take ~ into consideration ~을 고려[감안]하다 joint study 공동연구 technical college 기술대학 link between A and B A와 B 사이의 연관성 specialized facility 전문 시설 medical outcome 의료 성과 useful 유용한 grant application 지원금 신청서 upgrade 개선[업그레이드]하다, 등급을 높이다 congratulate+사람+on ~에게 …을 축하하다 consultancy 자문 counterpart 상대 benefit from ~에서 유익을 얻다, 혜택을 보다 assistance 보조, 지원 pediatrics 소아과

172 세부 사항

번역 제임스 박사가 근무하는 곳은?
(A) 어린이병원
(B) 실험실
(C) 기술대학
(D) 자선단체

해설 첫 번째 단락에서 특수질환 어린이를 위한 신규 별관의 성공에 박사님의 자선단체가 기여한 데 대해 감사드리는 이 편지를 받아 달라(Please accept this letter of appreciation for all the work your charity has done to contribute to the success of our new annex for children with special conditions)고 했으므로, 이 편지의 수신인인 (your)인 제임스 박사가 자선단체에 근무한다는 것을 알 수 있다. 따라서 정답은 (D)이다.

173 세부 사항

번역 어거스틴 박사가 하기로 한 일은?
(A) 단체에 돈을 기부한다.
(B) 몇몇 지역 대학에 연락한다.
(C) 의료 실험을 수행한다.
(D) 몇몇 연구 결과를 전달한다.

해설 두 번째 단락에서 약속대로, 진행성 질환 어린이를 위한 양육 환경 조성에 관한 연구 결과를 박사님께 보내드린다(As promised, I am sending you the research on creating a nurturing environment for children with progressive conditions)고 했다. 이 편지의 발신인 (I)인 어거스틴 박사가 연구 결과를 보내기로 약속한 것이므로, 정답은 (D)이다.

▶▶ Paraphrasing 지문의 As promised → 질문의 agree to do
지문의 sending you the research → 정답의 Forward the results of some studies

174 사실 관계 확인

번역 제임스 박사에 관해 명시된 것은?
(A) 경험 많은 고문 의사이다.
(B) 다음 달에 근무처를 바꿀 것이다.
(C) 일부 재원을 마련하는 일에 관여할 것이다.
(D) 의학 연구 수행을 책임지고 있다.

해설 세 번째 단락에서 이 연구들은 다음 달에 알링턴 병원이 어린이 시설 개선을 위한 지원금 신청서를 작성하는 일을 박사님께서 도와주실 때 유용할 것(These studies should be useful to you when you help Arlington Hospital write their grant application for upgrading their facilities for children next month)이라고 했다. 이 편지의 수신인(you)인 제임스 박사가 지원금 신청서 작성과 관련한 일을 돕고 있다는 것이므로, 정답은 (C)이다.

175 문장 삽입

번역 [1], [2], [3], [4]로 표시된 곳 중에서 다음 문장이 들어가기에 가장 적합한 곳은?

"박사님과 제가 같은 프로젝트를 다수 함께 했다는 점을 감안하면, 진작에 이렇게 만나지 않은 것이 놀라울 따름입니다."

(A) [1]
(B) [2]
(C) [3]
(D) [4]

해설 삽입 문장 '박사님과 제가 같은 프로젝트를 다수 함께 했다는 점을 감안하면, 진작에 이렇게 만나지 않은 것이 놀라울 따름입니다(It is amazing that this had not happened yet, considering that you and I have been working on many of the same projects)'를 통해 앞에서 만남과 관련한 이런 일(this)에 대해 구체적으로 언급할 것임을 알 수 있다. [1]의 앞 문장에서 지난주 개원식에서 드디어 박사님을 친히 뵙게 되어서 참으로 좋았다(It was also wonderful to finally meet you in person at the opening ceremony last week)고 두 사람의 만남에 대해 구체적으로 언급하고 있으므로, 정답은 (A)이다.

176-180 이메일 + 편지

수신: 레이먼드 모라 <rmora@berringley.gov>
발신: 킴 덴슨 <kdenson@berringley.gov>
날짜: 5월 8일
제목: 베링글리 주민 야유회

레이먼드에게,

176곧 있을 주민 야유회를 위해 밴드를 예약해 줘서 고마워요. 내 생각에는 그것이 현장 분위기를 확 바꿀 거예요. 가능하다면 우리는 새로 짓는 정자를 무대로 쓰려고 해요. 야유회 2주 전인 5월 15일까지는 완공이 되기로 되어 있어요. **179**하지만 작업을 맡은 콜브릿 건설이 예정보다 늦어지고 있어서 정자가 제때 준비되지 않을 수도 있어요. 만약 그런 일이 생기면, 로만토 서플라이즈에서 임시 무대를 빌릴 수 있는데, 그 업체 작업반이 무대를 설치하고 행사 후에 철거할 거예요. **177**또한, 우리가 행사에 많은 사람이 올 것으로 예상하고 있어서, 나는 주차 공간이 금세 없어질까 봐 염려하고 있어요. 그러니까 나는 당신이 사람들에게 대중교통 이용을 권장한다는 안내문을 시 웹사이트에 올려주었으면 해요.

고마워요!

킴

어휘 book 예약하다 upcoming 곧 있을, 다가오는 community picnic 주민 야유회 make a big difference 큰 차이가 나다 atmosphere 분위기 venue 장소 gazebo 정자 stage 무대 if possible 가능하면 be supposed to + 동사원형 ~하기로 되어 있다

complete 완성[완공]하다 construction 건설, 건축 hire 고용[채용]하다 behind schedule 예정보다 늦은 ready 준비된 in time 제때에 happen 생기다, 발생하다 rent 빌리다, 임대하다 temporary 임시의 crew 작업반 set up 설치하다 take down 해체하다, 철거하다 be worried that ~할까 걱정이다 run out of ~을 다 쓰다, 소진하다 space 공간 vehicle 자동차, 탈것 therefore 그러니까, 그러므로 post a message 메시지를 게시하다 remind 상기시키다, 일깨우다 public transportation 대중교통 recommend 권장하다, 추천하다

베라 플레밍
버몬트 주 베링글리
블랙웰 스트리트 214번지

플레밍 씨 귀하,

베링글리 행사 준비위원회를 대표해 저는 5월 30일에 열리는 제14회 연례 베링글리 주민 야유회에 귀하를 정중히 초대합니다. 음식은 손수 가지고 오시거나 지역 식당이 후원하는 부스 중 한 곳에서 구입하셔도 됩니다. **178, 180**시의원들을 위해 지정된 VIP 구역에 제가 기꺼이 귀하와 최대 3분을 위한 귀빈석을 따로 마련해 두겠습니다. **179**터너 공원 북단에 설치될 임시 무대를 완벽하게 관람하실 수 있을 것입니다. **180**참석을 원하신다면 동봉한 엽서를 5월 27일까지 반송해 주시기 바랍니다.

그 자리에서 뵙기를 희망합니다!

킴 덴슨 배상

어휘 on behalf of ~을 대표[대신]하여 event planning committee 행사 준비위원회, 행사 기획위원회 cordially 진심으로 invite 초대하다 annual 연례의 make a purchase 사다, 구입하다 sponsor 후원하다 local 지역의, 현지의 reserve 따로 잡아[남겨]두다, 예약하다 up to 최대 ~까지 VIP 귀빈 section 구역 designated 지정된 city council member 시의원 have a perfect view of ~이 완벽하게 보이다 temporary stage 임시 무대 set up 설치하다 attend 참석하다 send back 되돌려 보내다, 반송하다 enclosed 동봉된 postcard 엽서

176 세부 사항

번역 모라 씨가 한 일은?
(A) 라이브 공연 예약
(B) 야외 장소 예약
(C) 몇몇 음악 그룹 추천
(D) 광고 창작

해설 이메일에서 곧 있을 주민 야유회를 위해 밴드를 예약해 줘서 고맙다(Thanks for booking the bands for the upcoming community picnic)고 했다. 즉 이메일의 수신인인 모라 씨가 밴드를 예약했다는 것을 알 수 있으므로, 정답은 (A)이다.

▶▶ **Paraphrasing** 지문의 **booking the bands** → 정답의 **Arranged some live entertainment**

177 세부 사항

번역 덴슨 씨가 우려하는 것은?
(A) 불충분한 재원
(B) 낮은 참석률
(C) 주차 공간 부족
(D) 형편 없는 평가

해설 이메일에서 덴슨 씨는 행사에 많은 사람이 올 것으로 예상하고 있어서, 주차 공간이 금세 없어질까 봐 염려된다(Also, we're expecting a lot of people to turn up to the event, so I'm worried that we'll quickly run out of space for vehicles)고 했으므로, 정답은 (C)이다.

▶▶ Paraphrasing 지문의 **worried** → 질문의 **concerned**
지문의 **quickly run out of space for vehicles**
→ 정답의 **A lack of parking spaces**

178 추론 / 암시

번역 플레밍 씨는 누구이겠는가?
(A) 식당 주인
(B) 행사 기획자
(C) 시 정치인
(D) 유명 가수

해설 편지에서 시의원들을 위해 지정된 VIP 구역에 제가 기꺼이 귀하와 최대 3명을 위한 귀빈석을 따로 마련해 두겠다(I would be happy to reserve a seat for you and up to three guests in the VIP section designated for city council members)라고 했으므로, 편지의 수신인(you)인 플레밍 씨는 시의원임을 유추할 수 있다. 따라서 정답은 (C)이다.

▶▶ Paraphrasing 지문의 **city council members**
→ 정답의 **A city politician**

179 연계

번역 콜브릿 건설에 관해 암시된 것은?
(A) 정자에 안전 장치를 제안했다.
(B) 사무실이 터너 공원 근처에 있다.
(C) 정기적으로 시를 위해 작업한다.
(D) 공사를 제때 마치지 못했다.

해설 이메일에서 작업을 맡은 콜브릿 건설의 정자 건설 작업이 예정보다 늦어지고 있어서 제때 준비되지 않을 수도 있다. 만약 그런 일이 생기면, 로만토 서플라이즈에서 임시 무대를 빌릴 수 있다(However, Colbritt Construction, who was hired to do the work, is behind schedule, so it might not be ready in time. If that happens, we can rent a temporary stage from Romanto Supplies)고 했다. 편지에서 터너 공원 북단에 설치될 임시 무대를 완벽하게 관람할 수 있을 것(You would have a perfect view of the temporary stage, which will be set up at the northern end of Turner Park)이라고 했으므로, 콜브릿 건설이 작업을 제때 완수하지 못해 임시 무대를 설치했음을 알 수 있다. 따라서 정답은 (D)이다.

▶▶ Paraphrasing 지문의 **not be ready in time**
→ 정답의 **failed to finish a project on time**

180 세부 사항

번역 플레밍 씨가 엽서를 되돌려 보내야 하는 이유는?
(A) 특별석을 요청하려고
(B) 콘서트에 관해 의견을 보내려고
(C) 부스 임대에 관심을 보이려고
(D) 지역 문제에 관해 투표하려고

해설 편지에서 시의원들을 위해 지정된 VIP 구역에 제가 기꺼이 귀하와 최대 3명을 위한 귀빈석을 따로 마련해 두겠다(I would be happy to reserve a seat for you and up to three guests in the VIP section designated for city council members)며 참석을 원한다면 동봉한 엽서를 5월 27일까지 반송해 달라(If you would like to attend, please send back the enclosed postcard by May 27)고 했다. 즉 플레밍 씨는 시의원들을 위해 지정된 좌석을 요청하기 위해 엽서를 반송해야 한다는 것을 알 수 있으므로, 정답은 (A)이다.

▶▶ Paraphrasing 지문의 **the VIP section designated for city council members**
→ 정답의 **some special seats**

181-185 광고 + 양식

앤필드 퍼니싱즈에서 맞춤 커튼이 가능합니다!

182앤필드 퍼니싱즈는 새로운 맞춤 커튼 제품군인 브리커를 선보이게 되어 기쁩니다. 저희는 각 가정이 다르다는 사실과 저희의 표준 커튼과 가리개 제품들이 귀하의 가정에 딱히 어울리지 않을 수도 있다는 점을 이해하고 있습니다. 그래서 저희는 이 새로운 서비스를 제공하고 있습니다. **181**귀댁 창문의 정확한 사양에 맞춤 제작되는 것 외에 브리커 커튼은 실내에 온기를 잡아 두는 두꺼운 단열층까지 갖추고 있습니다. 이는 겨울철 가정 난방에 들어가는 에너지 비용이 줄어든다는 뜻입니다. 이 세련되고 품질 좋은 커튼은 색상이 여러 가지이며 무늬도 250가지입니다.

저희와 약속을 잡으시면 저희 직원이 귀하의 가정이나 사무실을 방문하여 정확한 치수를 측정할 것입니다. **184**측정에는 대략 30분이 걸리며, 저희가 며칠 내로 커튼 제작을 시작할 수 있으므로 신속 제작 서비스가 필요하지 않습니다! **183** 고객께서 약속을 잡을 때 25달러를 보증금으로 내셔야 하지만 이 돈은 구입비로 쓰실 수 있습니다.

더 자세히 알아 보시려면 1-800-555-0176번으로 전화하시거나 www.anfieldfurn.com을 방문해 주십시오. **182**저희가 대부분의 앤필드 퍼니싱즈 제품에 대해 구입일로부터 2개월 이내에 반품을 받지만, 브리커 제품군에는 이것이 해당되지 않는다는 사실을 유의하시기 바랍니다.

어휘 custom-made 맞춤 제작한 available 구할 수 있는, 이용할 수 있는 furnishing 가구, 비품 be pleased to+동사원형 ~해서 기쁘다 introduce 도입하다, 선보이다 line 제품군 curtain 커튼, 가리개 drapes 두꺼운 커튼 suit 어울리다, 알맞다 exactly 정확히, 딱히 offer 제공[제안]하다, 팔려고 내놓다 in addition to ~ 외에 customize 맞춤 제작하다 specification 사양 come with ~에 딸려 있다 insulated layer 단열층 keep heat in 열을 보존하다 stylish 세련된 high-quality 고급의 pattern 무늬 book an appointment with ~와 약속을 잡다 employee 직원 take a measurement 치수를 재다 precise 정확한 session 회기, 시간

last 지속되다 approximately 대략 produce 제작하다, 생산하다 within ~ 안에 express service 신속 서비스 put down a deposit 보증금[예치금]을 내다 fund 자금, 돈 accept returns 반품을 받다 purchase date 구입일 apply to ~에 적용되다

앤필드 퍼니싱즈
183치수 측정 예약 확인

183고객: 패멀라 알레시

전화번호: 555-0133

주소: 텍사스 주 78730 오스틴 시 타운즈 레인 6795번지

이메일 주소: allessip@balconeco.com

184약속 날짜/시간: 10월 8일 오후 1:30   부동산 유형: 주택

주의사항: 185자료 수집 과정에 속도를 내기 위해 창문과 소파, 탁자 등의 간격을 최소 2피트 정도 벌려 두어 기술자가 쉽게 접근할 수 있게 해 주시기 바랍니다.

어휘 confirmation 확인 appointment 약속 customer 고객 address 주소 property 부동산 residential 주택의, 주거의 expedite 더 신속히 처리하다 minimum 최소 space 공간 technician 기술자 have easy access to ~에 쉽게 접근하다

---

181 사실 관계 확인

번역 브리커 커튼에 관해 언급된 내용은?
(A) 회사에서 가장 잘 팔리는 품목이다.
(B) 가내 수공업으로 생산된다.
(C) 에너지 요금을 줄일 수 있다.
(D) 색상이 250가지이다.

해설 광고의 첫 번째 단락에서 브리커 커튼은 창문의 정확한 사양에 맞춤 제작되는 것 외에 실내에 온기를 잡아 두는 두꺼운 단열층까지 갖추고 있다. 이는 겨울철 가정 난방에 들어가는 에너지 비용이 줄어든다는 뜻이다(In addition to being customized to the exact specifications of your window, Bryker curtains also come with a thick insulated layer to keep heat in, meaning you'll pay less for energy to heat your home in the winter)라고 했으므로, 정답은 (C)이다.

▶▶ Paraphrasing 지문의 pay less for energy
→ 정답의 reduce energy bills

---

182 추론 / 암시

번역 앤필드 퍼니싱즈에 관해 암시된 것은?
(A) 맞춤 제작 제품은 반품을 받지 않는다.
(B) 웹사이트에 고객 토론장이 있다.
(C) 새로운 공급업체와 계약을 맺었다.
(D) 전시장에 두 달마다 새로운 물건이 들어온다.

해설 광고의 첫 번째 단락에서 앤필드 퍼니싱즈는 새로운 맞춤 커튼 제품군인 브리커를 선보이게 되어 기쁘다(Anfield Furnishings is pleased to introduce Bryker, our new line of custom-made curtains)고 했으므로, 브리커 제품이 맞춤 커튼임을 알 수 있다. 광고의 마지막 단락에서 대부분의 앤필드 퍼니싱즈 제품에 대해 구입일로부터 2개월 이내에 반품을 받지만, 브리커 제품군에는 이것이 해당되지 않는다(Please note

---

that for most Anfield Furnishing products, we accept returns within two months of the purchase date, but this does not apply to the Bryker line)고 언급해 맞춤 커튼 제품에 대해서는 반품을 받지 않는다는 것을 알 수 있다. 따라서 정답은 (A)이다.

▶▶ Paraphrasing 지문의 custom-made curtains
→ 정답의 customized products

---

183 연계

번역 알레시 씨에 관해 암시된 것은?
(A) 전화로 약속을 잡았다.
(B) 초기 비용을 지불했다.
(C) 그녀의 회사에서 상담하게 될 것이다.
(D) 신속 제작을 선택할 것이다.

해설 양식의 제목 '치수 측정 예약 확인(Confirmation of Appointment for Taking Measurements)'과 '고객: 패멀라 알레시(Customer: Pamela Alessi)'를 통해 알레시 씨가 치수 측정을 예약했음을 알 수 있다. 치수 측정에 대한 정책은 광고를 통해 확인할 수 있다. 광고의 두 번째 단락에서 약속을 잡을 때 25달러를 보증금으로 내야 하지만 이 돈은 구입비로 쓸 수 있다(Customers must put down a $25 deposit when booking the appointment, but these funds can be used toward your purchase)고 했으므로, 치수 측정을 예약한 알레시 씨는 보증금을 지불했음을 유추할 수 있다. 따라서 정답은 (B)이다.

▶▶ Paraphrasing 지문의 put down a $25 deposit
→ 정답의 made an initial payment

---

184 연계

번역 알레시 씨의 약속은 10월 8일 몇 시에 끝나겠는가?
(A) 오후 1시 30분.
(B) 오후 2시
(C) 오후 2시 30분
(D) 오후 3시

해설 양식에서 약속 날짜 및 시간은 10월 8일 오후 1:30(Appointment Date/Time: October 8, 1:30 P.M.)이라고 했고, 광고의 두 번째 단락에서 측정에는 대략 30분이 걸리며, 며칠 내로 커튼 제작을 시작할 수 있으므로 신속 제작 서비스가 필요하지 않다(The session will last for approximately half an hour, and we can begin producing your curtains within just a few days—no express service needed)고 했다. 따라서 알레시 씨의 약속은 오후 2시쯤 끝날 것으로 유추할 있으므로, 정답은 (B)이다.

---

185 세부 사항

번역 알레시 씨가 약속 전에 해야 할 일은?
(A) 방에서 가구 치우기
(B) 접속 비밀번호 제공하기
(C) 무늬와 천 선택하기
(D) 창문 근처 치우기

해설 양식의 주의사항에서 자료 수집 과정에 속도를 내기 위해 창문과 소파, 탁자 따위의 간격을 최소 2피트 정도 벌려 두어 기술자가 쉽게 접근할 수 있게 해달라(Notes: To expedite the data-collection process, please leave a minimum of two feet of space between the windows and any sofas, tables, etc. so that the technician has easy access to them)고 했다. 따라서 알레시 씨가 약속 시간 전에 창문 주변을 치워야 한다는 것을 알 수 있으므로, 정답은 (D)이다.

▶▶ Paraphrasing 지문의 leave a minimum of two feet of space between the windows and any sofas, tables, etc.
→ 정답의 Clear areas near the windows

186-190 공지 + 온라인 후기 + 기사

공지

콜바 풋웨어 고객들께 알림:

186콜바 풋웨어 나마라 빌딩 지점이 4월 30일 일요일을 끝으로 영업을 종료하게 됩니다. 186, 187저희는 기꺼이 이든데일 고객들께 캐주얼화와 정장화를 제공하고 있지만, 곧 있을 경기장 건설 공사를 위해 건물 소유주가 해당 건물을 매각할 계획이기 때문에 저희가 이렇게 점포를 폐쇄할 수밖에 없었습니다. (나마라 빌딩 지점만) 폐점을 앞둔 주에 상품을 할인해 판매할 예정입니다. 수년 동안 이 지점을 애용해 주셔서 감사드리며, 테니슨 몰 지점에서 계속 고객들께 서비스를 제공하기를 고대합니다. 해당 지점은 평소대로 영업을 지속할 것입니다.

—고라브 콜 배상
콜바 풋웨어 주인

어휘 attention 주목, 알림 footwear 신발 shopper 구매자, 쇼핑객 branch 지점 although 비록 ~일지라도 provide 제공하다 casual footwear 캐주얼화 formal footwear 정장화 customer 고객 cannot avoid ~할 수밖에 없다 closure 폐점, 폐쇄 owner 주인 plan 계획하다 structure 구조물 for the sake of ~을 위해 upcoming 다가오는, 곧 있을 stadium project 경기장 건설 공사 merchandise 상품 (= goods) discount 할인하다 lead up to ~에 차츰 가까워지다, 다가가다 patronage 애용, 후원 look forward to ~을 고대하다 serve 구매를 돕다, 시중을 들다 carry on 계속하다 as usual 평소대로

---

https://www.mylocalshopreviews.com/bellcity

벨 시티 》》 소매 》》 신발 》》 콜바 풋웨어

콜바 풋웨어는 188엄청나게 다양한 상품을 갖추고 있어서, 시에서 신발을 구입하기에 가장 좋은 곳이 아닌가 싶다. 친절한 점원들이 고객의 필요를 진심으로 들어주고 특정 상황에 맞게 신발을 추천해 준다. 187본점이 몇 주 전에 문을 닫는 바람에 사업이 현재 지점 하나로 줄었지만 두 번째 지점은 개장 시간이 훨씬 더 짧은데도 불구하고 동일한 수준의 서비스를 제공한다.

5월 18일 R.P.가 작성한 게시물

어휘 an impressive range of 엄청나게 다양한 attentive 친절한, 배려하는 salespeople 점원들, 판매원들 genuinely 진심으로 make recommendations 추천하다 tailored to ~에 맞춰진 specific 특정한 situation 상황 original store 본점 close 문을 닫다, 폐점하다 level 수준 despite ~에도 불구하고 amount 양

벨 시티 경기장 건설 진척되다

벨 시티, 5월 30일—모든 허가가 승인되고 부지 매입 거래도 마무리됨에 따라 이든데일 지역의 경기장 건설이 진척되고 있다. 186프로젝트를 주관하는 윌린스 개발은 해당 지역의 많은 건물을 매입했으며, 모든 건물을 헐어서 건축가 앤자 린델로프가 설계한 5만 석 규모의 경기장이 들어설 공간을 확보할 예정이다.

189경기장은 프로젝트에 들어갈 추가 수입을 마련하기 위해 일단 시 당국자들이 작명권을 매각하면 이름이 붙여질 예정인데, 경기장은 시 소유이며 스포츠뿐만 아니라 콘서트, 축제 등을 위해서도 사용될 터라 지역사회에 반가운 소식이 될 것이다. 경기장은 날씨 상태와 상관없이 일 년 내내 사용될 수 있게 개폐식 지붕을 갖출 예정이다. 190린델로프 씨는 "이 건물의 기능성은 물론 외관도 마음에 든다"면서 "이미 눈부시게 아름다운 벨 시티의 스카이라인을 해치지 않도록 주변 건물들 및 환경과 조화를 이룰 것"이라고 말했다.

어휘 stadium 경기장 move forward 진전[진척]되다 construction 건설, 건축 neighborhood 동네 permit 허가 approve 승인하다 land acquisition 토지 매입 deal 거래 finalize 마무리하다, 종결하다 development 개발 oversee 감독하다, 주관하다 purchase 매입[구입]하다 demolish 헐다, 파괴하다 make room for ~할 공간[여지]을 만들다 design 설계하다 architect 건축가 name 이름을 붙이다 city official 시 당국자 generate 생성하다, 만들어 내다 welcome addition 반가운[환영 받는] 것 community 지역사회 feature 특징으로 삼다 retractable roof 개폐식 지붕 year-round 일 년 내내 regardless of ~에 상관없이 weather condition 기상 조건, 날씨 상태 functionality 기능성 appearance 외관, 외모 blend in with ~와 조화를 이루다 so as not to + 동사원형 ~하지 않게 take away from ~을 깎아내리다, 훼손하다 stunning 눈부시게 아름다운

---

186 연계

번역 나마라 빌딩에 관해 사실인 것은?
(A) 헐릴 것이다.
(B) 테니슨 몰 근처에 있다.
(C) 콜 씨가 매각했다.
(D) 일요일마다 문을 닫는다.

해설 공지에서 콜바 풋웨어 나마라 빌딩 지점이 4월 30일 일요일을 끝으로 영업을 종료하게 된다(The Namara Building branch of Colba Footwear will hold its final day of business on Sunday, April 30)고 했고, 곧 있을 경기장 건설 공사를 위해 건물 주인이 해당 건물을 매각할 계획이기 때문에 이렇게 점포를 폐쇄할 수밖에 없다(we could not avoid this closure because the owner of our building plans to sell the structure for the sake of the upcoming stadium project)고 언급했다. 기사의 첫 번째 단락에서는 프로젝트를 주관하는 윌린스 개발이 해당 지역의 많은 건물을 매입했으며, 모든 건물을 헐어서 건축가 앤자 린델로프가 설계한 5만 석 규모의 경기장이 들어설 공간을 확보할 예정(Willins Development, the company overseeing the project, has purchased a number of buildings in the area, all of which will be demolished in order to make room for the 50,000-seat stadium designed by architect Anja Lindelauf)이라고 했으므로, 경기장 건설을 위해 나마라 빌딩을 헐 예정임을 알 수 있다. 따라서 정답은 (A)이다.

▶▶ Paraphrasing 지문의 be demolished
→ 정답의 be torn down

187 연계

번역 콜바 풋웨어에 관해 명시된 것은?
(A) 벨 시티에서 가장 오래된 신발 매장이다.
(B) 판매의 일부는 온라인에서 이루어진다.
(C) 직원 교육이 더 필요하다.
(D) 첫 번째 매장이 이든데일에 있었다.

해설 공지에서 이든데일 고객들께 캐주얼화와 정장화를 제공하고 있지만, 곧 있을 경기장 건설 공사를 위해 건물 소유주가 해당 건물을 매각할 계획이기 때문에 이렇게 점포를 폐쇄할 수밖에 없다(Although we enjoy providing casual and formal footwear for our Edendale customers, we could not avoid this closure because the owner of our building plans to sell the structure for the sake of the upcoming stadium project)며 이든데일 고객들께 서비스를 제공했던 콜바 풋웨어 지점의 폐쇄를 언급하고 있다. 콜바 풋웨어에 대한 온라인 평가에서는 본점이 몇 주 전에 문을 닫는 바람에 사업이 현재 지점 하나로 줄었다(The business is now down to just one branch, since its original store closed a few weeks ago)고 했으므로, 콜바 풋웨어의 본점이 이든데일에 있었음을 알 수 있다. 따라서 정답은 (D)이다.

> ▶▶ **Paraphrasing** 지문의 **its original store**
> → 정답의 **Its first store**

188 동의어 찾기

번역 온라인 후기에서 첫 번째 단락 1행의 "impressive"와 의미가 가장 가까운 단어는?
(A) 임박한
(B) 재능이 있는
(C) 의미 있는
(D) 광범위한

해설 해당 문장은 '콜바 풋웨어는 엄청나게 다양한 상품을 갖추고 있어서, 시에서 신발을 구입하기에 가장 좋은 곳이 아닌가 싶다(Colba Footwear has an impressive range of goods, and I believe it is the best place in the city to buy shoes)'라는 의미로 해석되므로, 여기서 impressive는 앞의 an, 뒤의 range of와 결합하여 '다양한, 광범위한'이라는 의미를 나타낸다. 따라서 정답은 (D) extensive(광범위한, 폭넓은)이다.

189 사실 관계 확인

번역 경기장에 관해 언급된 내용은?
(A) 회의용 복합건물을 대체할 것이다.
(B) 다양한 행사에 사용될 계획이다.
(C) 시 유권자들이 이름을 붙일 것이다.
(D) 기상 조건 때문에 공사가 연기되었다.

해설 기사의 두 번째 단락에서 경기장은 프로젝트에 들어갈 추가 수입을 마련하기 위해 일단 시 당국자들이 작명권을 매각하면 이름이 붙여질 예정인데, 경기장은 시 소유이며 스포츠뿐만 아니라 콘서트, 축제 등을 위해서도 사용될 터라 지역사회에 반가운 소식이 될 것(The stadium, which will be named once city officials sell its naming rights to generate further income for the project, will be owned by the city and will be used not just for sports, but also concerts, festivals, and more, making it a welcome addition to the community)이라고 경기장이 다양한 행사를 위해 사용될 예정임을 언급하고 있다. 따라서 정답은 (B)이다.

> ▶▶ **Paraphrasing** 지문의 **not just for sports, but also concerts, festivals, and more**
> → 정답의 **various events**

190 세부 사항

번역 린델로프 씨는 무엇을 마음에 들어 하는가?
(A) 견고한 지붕 설계
(B) 친환경 자재 사용
(C) 인근 구조물 보완
(D) 예산 목표 달성

해설 기사의 두 번째 단락에서 린델로프 씨는 이 건물의 기능성은 물론 외관도 마음에 든다(I'm pleased not only with the functionality of this building but also its appearance)면서 이미 눈부시게 아름다운 벨 시티의 스카이라인을 해치지 않도록 주변 건물들 및 환경과 조화를 이룰 것(It will blend in with the buildings and environment around it so as not to take away from the already stunning skyline of Bell City)이라고 말했다. 따라서 린델로프 씨가 경기장의 주변 건물들 및 환경과의 조화를 마음에 들어 한다는 것을 알 수 있으므로, 정답은 (C)이다.

> ▶▶ **Paraphrasing** 지문의 **blend in with the buildings and environment around it**
> → 정답의 **Complementing nearby structures**

191-195 광고 + 이메일 + 이메일

> ### 시간을 거슬러 에이버포스 성으로 여행을 떠나보세요!
>
> 에이버포스 성은 13세기 말 군사용 전초기지로 지어진 웅장한 석재 구조물입니다. **193**안내인과 함께 성 자체를 돌아보고 세심하게 손질된 부속 정원들을 둘러보는 여행이 날마다 있습니다. 20명이 넘는 단체에는 원활한 질의응답을 위해 안내인이 2명 배정됩니다.
>
> 매일 가능한 다른 활동들은 다음과 같습니다:
> – 프리츠 피너드의 사회로 진행되는 전통적인 점심식사에서 중세 요리 시식하기
> **195** – 소피 존스턴의 도자기 제작 시연 관람하기
> – 해당 유적지의 원예 전문가 매릴린 클레이튼의 강의 듣기
> – 에이자 데비와 함께 주변 나무숲에서 말 타기*
> **191** – 조지프 맨조의 검투 수업에 참여하기*
>
> **191**별표(*)가 된 활동은 사전 등록이 필요합니다.
>
> www.aberporthcastle.com에서 더 자세한 정보를 보실 수 있습니다.

어휘 take a journey 여행하다 back in time 시간을 거슬러 castle 성 majestic 웅장한, 으리으리한 structure 구조물 century 세기 military outpost 군사용 전초기지 guided tour 안내인이 딸린 여행 meticulously 세심하게, 꼼꼼하게 manicured 잘 손질된 daily 매일, 날마다 assigned to ~에 배정된 exceed 초과하다, 넘다 facilitate 촉진하다, 원활히 하다 activity 활동 available 이용 가능한 include 포함하다 the following 아래[다음] 사항 sample 시식하다 medieval 중세의

cuisine 요리, 음식   traditional 전통적인   host 사회를 보다, 주최하다
pottery-making 도자기 제작   demonstration 시범, 예시
lecture 강의, 강연   site 유적, 현장   master gardener 원예 전문가
horseback-riding 승마   surrounding 주변의
woodland 나무 숲   participate in ~에 참석[참여]하다
sword-fighting 칼 싸움, 검투   pre-registration 사전등록

수신: 모든 여행 안내인
발신: 토머스 휘트비 〈t.whitby@aberporthcastle.com〉
날짜: 4월 18일
제목: 갱신된 내일 일정

여러분, 안녕하세요.

매우 바쁜 한 주를 앞두고 평소보다 더 많은 업무를 감당하는 여러분의 협동정신에 감사를 드립니다. **192**사람들에게 성과 주변 부지를 둘러보게 할 때 선물 가게의 상품은 물론 현장 활동들을 상기시켜야 한다는 점을 기억하시기 바랍니다. 사무실에 갱신된 이번 주 일정을 붙여 놨습니다. **193**앨리사가 라일리와 함께 윌론 인스티튜트 팀을 맡게 될 것입니다. 그 외에, 알렉산드라가 오후 1시에 정문에서 몽고메리 대학교의 단체사진 촬영을 돕게 될 테니, 그 시간에 해당 지역은 피해 주시기 바랍니다.

고맙습니다!

토머스 휘트비 배상

어휘   tour guide 여행 안내인   updated 갱신된, 최신의   hectic 매우 바쁜   ahead of ~ 앞에   appreciate 감사하다   cooperative spirit 협동정신   take on ~을 맡다, 감당하다   than usual 평소보다   remember 기억하다   show around 보여주다   ground 부지, 정원   remind 상기시키다, 일깨우다   on-site 현장의   activity 활동   B as well as A A뿐만 아니라 B도   gift shop 선물가게   merchandise 상품   post 게시하다   join 합류하다   handle 다루다, 처리하다   institute 연구소   in addition 게다가, 덧붙여, 그 외에   group photo 단체 사진   main gate 정문   avoid 피하다

수신: 에이버포스 고객 서비스 〈service@aberporthcastle.com〉
발신: 베서니 헤이워드 〈b.hayward@willauninstitute.com〉
날짜: 4월 24일
제목: 저의 방문

담당자 귀하:

저는 4월 19일에 윌론 인스티튜트 학생들을 데리고 에이버포스 성을 방문했으며, 유적지에 대한 저의 인상을 **194**나누고자 합니다. 저는 이것이 모두에게 소중한 교육 경험이라고 생각했으며, 그 후로 많은 학생이 중세시대에 새로이 관심을 보였습니다. 우리는 시간 제약 때문에 한 가지 활동만 빼고 모든 현장 활동에 참여할 기회가 있었습니다. **195**저는 개인적으로 도기 그릇을 만드는 시연이 매우 흥미로웠으며, 가장 즐거웠던 활동이었습니다. 저는 에이버포스 성 여행을 우리 학교의 연례 행사로 삼고 싶으며, 제 친구들과 동료들에게도 여가 시간에 해당 유적지를 방문해 보도록 권하려고 합니다. 매우 근사하고 잊지 못할 시간을 보내게 해 주셔서 고맙습니다.

베서니 헤이워드 드림

어휘   To Whom It May Concern 담당자[관계자] 귀하   institute 학원, 연구소, 전문학교   share 나누다, 공유하다   impression 인상   valuable 소중한   educational experience 교육 경험   renewed 새로워진   medieval time period 중세시대   afterwards 그 후   have the opportunity to+동사 원형 ~할 기회를 가지다   with the exception of ~을 제외하고   due to ~ 때문에   time limitation 시간 제약[제한]   personally 개인적으로   demonstration 시연   clay bowl 도기 그릇   fascinating 매력적인, 매우 흥미로운   annual occurrence 연례 행사   encourage 권장하다, 장려하다   colleague 동료   spare time 여가 시간   unforgettable 잊지 못할

191 세부 사항

번역   광고에 따르면 방문객들이 검투 수업을 받기 위해 해야 하는 일은?
(A) 안전 장구를 착용한다.
(B) 추가 요금을 지불한다.
(C) 사전에 등록한다.
(D) 계약서에 서명한다.

해설   광고의 두 번째 단락의 마지막 부분에 조지프 맨조의 검투 수업에 참여하기(Participating in a sword-fighting lesson given by Joseph Manzo*)가 있고, 별표(*)가 된 활동은 사전 등록이 필요하다(Please note that starred activities (*) require pre-registration)고 명시되어 있으므로, 정답은 (C)이다.

▶▶ Paraphrasing   지문의 **pre-registration**
→ 정답의 **Register in advance**

192 추론 / 암시

번역   에이버포스 성에 관해 암시된 것은?
(A) 정문 보수 작업을 하고 있다.
(B) 소매점이 있다.
(C) 4월에는 항상 바쁘다.
(D) 여행 안내인이 전통의상을 입는다.

해설   첫 번째 이메일에서 사람들에게 성과 주변 부지를 둘러보게 할 때 선물 가게의 상품은 물론 현장 활동들을 상기시켜야 한다는 점을 기억하라(Remember that when you're showing people around the castle and grounds, they should be reminded about the on-site activities as well as the gift shop merchandise)고 언급했다. 즉 에이버포스 성에 선물 가게가 있음을 유추할 수 있으므로, 정답은 (B)이다.

▶▶ Paraphrasing   지문의 **the gift shop**
→ 정답의 **a retail establishment**

193 연계

번역   휘트비 씨가 윌론 인스티튜트의 단체 관광객에 관해 암시하는 것은?
(A) 구성원 일부가 13살 미만이다.
(B) 구성원들이 자세를 잡고 사진을 찍을 것이다.
(C) 특별한 식사 자리에 너무 늦게 도착할 것이다.
(D) 20명이 넘을 것이다.

Test 5

해설 휘트비 씨가 쓴 첫 번째 이메일에서 앨리사가 라일리와 함께 윌론 인스티튜트 팀을 맡게 될 것임(Alyssa will join Riley in handling the Willaun Institute group)이라며 두 명이 함께 윌론 인스티튜트 팀의 관광을 담당할 것임을 언급하고 있다. 관광에 대한 상세 정보는 광고를 통해 확인할 수 있다. 광고의 첫 번째 단락에서 안내인과 함께 성 자체를 돌아보고 세심하게 손질된 부속 정원들을 둘러보는 여행이 날마다 있는데, 20명이 넘는 단체에는 원활한 질의응답을 위해 안내인이 2명 배정된다(Guided tours of the castle itself and its meticulously manicured gardens are offered daily, with two guides assigned to groups exceeding 20 people to facilitate answering questions)고 했다. 따라서, 윌론 인스티튜트 팀은 20명이 넘는 단체임을 유추할 수 있으므로, 정답은 (D)이다.

▶▶ **Paraphrasing** 지문의 **exceeding 20 people**
→ 정답의 **more than 20 people**

194 동의어 찾기

번역 두 번째 이메일에서 첫 번째 단락 2행의 "share"와 의미가 가장 가까운 단어는?
(A) 표현하다
(B) 후원하다
(C) 배포하다
(D) 분할하다

해설 해당 문장은 '저는 4월 19일에 윌론 인스티튜트 학생들을 데리고 에이버포스 성을 방문했으며, 유적지에 대한 저의 인상을 나누고자 합니다(I visited Aberporth Castle on April 19 with a group of students from the Willaun Institute, and I wanted to share my impressions of your site)'라는 의미로 해석되므로, 여기서 share는 '함께 나누다, 말하다'라는 의미가 자연스럽다. 따라서 정답은 (A) express(표현하다, 나타내다)이다.

195 연계

번역 헤이워드 씨가 가장 즐거워한 활동을 이끈 사람은?
(A) 피너드 씨
(B) 존스턴 씨
(C) 클레이튼 씨
(D) 데비 씨

해설 헤이워드 씨가 쓴 두 번째 이메일에서 개인적으로 도기 그릇을 만드는 시연이 매우 흥미로웠으며, 가장 즐거웠던 활동이었다(I personally found the demonstration on creating clay bowls to be fascinating, making it the one I enjoyed most)고 언급했다. 활동에 대한 정보는 광고의 두 번째 단락에 있는 소피 존스턴의 도자기 제작 시연 관람하기(Watching a pottery-making demonstration by Sophie Johnston)에서 확인할 수 있으므로, 정답은 (B)이다.

196-200 안내문 + 이메일 + 토론방 게시글

펜슬러 하우스 런웨이 경연대회

축하합니다! 귀하의 디자인이 저희의 아마추어 패션쇼에 받아들여졌습니다. 이는 저희의 예선 심사위원단이 귀하가 제출한 스케치에 흥미를 보였으며 완성된 의상이 무대에 나오는 것을 보고 싶어 한다는 뜻입니다. **199**귀하에게는 이제 행사 당일 선발될 10명의 수상자 중 한 명이 될 기회가 있습니다.

완성된 출품작은 저희 본사(골트웨이 빌딩)에 3월 1일 오후 5시까지 도착해야 런웨이 쇼 전 주에 사진을 촬영할 수 있습니다. **196**의상을 분실하지 않도록 우편으로 보내지 말고 귀하가 가져와야 합니다.

귀하 자신과 출품작을 짧게 소개한 글을 mjensen@penslerhouse.com에 이메일로 보내 주시기 바랍니다. **197**모델을 직접 공급할 계획이라면 첨부된 연락 정보 카드에 해당 인물의 정보를 적어 저희에게 다시 보내 주십시오. 그렇지 않으면, 저희가 모델을 제공하겠습니다.

어휘 runway 런웨이, 패션쇼 무대 competition 경연대회 Congratulations! 축하합니다! accept 수락하다, 받아들이다 amateur 아마추어 preliminary 예선의, 예비의 judging panel 심사위원단 intrigue 흥미를 끌다 drawings 스케치, 소묘 submit 제출하다 finished outfit 완성된 의상[옷] have a chance to+동사원형 ~할 기회를 얻다 winner 수상자 select 선발하다, 고르다 event 행사 entry 출품작 headquarters 본부, 본사 photograph 사진(을 찍다) prior to ~에 앞서, ~ 전에 ensure 확실히 하다, 보장하다 clothing 옷, 의류 get lost 분실되다 through the mail 우편으로 description 설명 supply 공급하다 complete 작성하다, 완성하다 attached 첨부된 contact information 연락 정보 otherwise 그렇지 않으면

수신: 욜란다 산체스 〈yosanchez@ma103.com〉
발신: 맬컴 젠슨 (mjensen@penslerhouse.com)
날짜: 3월 3일
제목: 펜슬러 하우스 런웨이 경연대회

산체스 씨께,

197, 198다가오는 3월 7일에 있을 런웨이 쇼에 관해 저희가 연락 정보 카드는 받았지만, 여전히 귀하의 작품과 디자인 경력에 관한 짧은 소개를 기다리고 있습니다. 소개는 80~100단어 사이여야 합니다. 제게 가능한 한 빨리 이메일로 보내 주시기 바랍니다.

198모든 디자이너가 행사 전날 오후 5시에 펜슬러 하우스 본사로 방문해 모델에게 의상을 입혀 보고 필요하면 수정을 해야 합니다. 저희 회사 디자이너 중 한 명인 즈느비에브 매시가 가장 돋보이는 차림새를 연출하도록 추천해 줄 것입니다. 행사 당일 모든 사람이 모델들의 머리와 화장을 준비할 시간이 충분하도록 와일로나 센터에 오후 3시까지 도착해야 합니다.

추가 질문이 있으면 주저하지 말고 언제라도 제게 이메일을 보내시기 바랍니다.

맬컴 젠슨

어휘 regarding ~에 관해 upcoming 다가오는, 곧 있을 design history 디자인 경력 as soon as possible 가능한 한 빨리 try 시험 삼아 착용하다 make adjustments 조정하다, 수정하다 in-house 회사[조직] 내부의 make recommendations 추천하다 flattering 돋보이게 하는 fit 차림새, 매무새 report 도착을 알리다 plenty of 많은, 충분한 prepare 준비하다 makeup 화장

---
www.penslerhouse.com/events/runwaycompetition/forum

199게시일: 3월 8일 게시자: 젬마 바이럼

저는 어제 와일로나 센터에서 열린 펜슬러 하우스 런웨이 경연대회에서 아주 즐거운 시간을 보냈습니다. 런웨이에 독특한 디자인이 너무 많아서 아마추어들이

작업한 작품이라는 게 놀라웠어요. **199**쇼를 볼 기회가 없었더라도 앨미타 빌딩 로비에 오셔서 각 우승자가 만든 최고의 의상을 볼 수 있습니다. 런웨이 쇼 주최 측은 그 의상들이 이 달 남은 기간 동안 그곳에 전시될 것이라고 발표했습니다. 멋진 패션을 볼 수 있는 이런 기회를 **200**놓치지 마세요!

어휘 have a great time 즐거운 시간을 보내다 unique 독특한 remarkable 놀라운, 주목할 만한 catch the show 쇼를 보다 winner 수상자 outfit 의상 host 주최자 announce 발표[공표]하다 on display 전시 중인 pass up 놓치다, 포기하다 amazing 근사한, 멋진

---

196 사실 관계 확인

번역 안내문에 디자이너들이 해야 할 일로 명시된 것은?
(A) 가장 마음에 드는 의상을 선택한다.
(B) 옷감 목록을 작성한다.
(C) 물품을 직접 전달한다.
(D) 참가 자격을 증명한다.

해설 안내문의 두 번째 단락에서 의상을 분실하지 않도록 우편으로 보내지 말고 귀하가 가져와야 한다(To ensure that the clothing doesn't get lost, it must be brought by you; do not send it through the mail)고 언급했으므로, 정답은 (C)이다.

▶▶ **Paraphrasing** 지문의 must → 질문의 are required to 지문의 be brought by you → 정답의 Deliver items in person

---

197 연계

번역 산체스 씨에 관해 암시된 것은?
(A) 젠슨 씨에게 몇 가지 질문을 이메일로 보냈다.
(B) 그녀의 소개가 100단어를 넘었다.
(C) 그녀의 스케치를 매시 씨가 보았다.
(D) 런웨이 쇼에 설 모델을 구했다.

해설 이메일의 첫 번째 단락에서 다가오는 3월 7일에 있을 런웨이 쇼에 관해 저희가 연락 정보 카드는 받았다(Regarding the upcoming runway show on March 7, we have received your Contact Information Card)고 언급했다. 안내문의 세 번째 단락에서는 모델을 직접 공급할 계획이라면 첨부된 연락 정보 카드에 해당 인물의 정보를 적어 저희에게 돌려보내야 한다. 그렇지 않으면, 우리가 모델을 제공하겠다(If you plan to supply your own model, please complete the attached Contact Information Card for that person and send it back to us)고 언급했다. 따라서 산체스 씨는 모델을 직접 고용했음을 유추할 수 있으므로, 정답은 (D)이다.

▶▶ **Paraphrasing** 지문의 supply your own model → 정답의 recruited a model

---

198 세부 사항

번역 젠슨 씨에 따르면 3월 6일에 있을 일은?
(A) 의상 가봉
(B) 디자인실 구경
(C) 머리 및 화장 강의
(D) 런웨이 보행 연습

해설 젠슨 씨가 쓴 이메일의 첫 번째 단락에서 다가오는 3월 7일에 있을 런웨이 쇼에 관해 저희가 연락 정보 카드는 받았지만, 여전히 귀하의 작품과 디자인 경력에 관한 짧은 소개를 기다리고 있다(Regarding the upcoming runway show on March 7, we have received your Contact Information Card, but we are still waiting for the short description of your work and design history)고 했고, 두 번째 단락에서는 모든 디자이너가 행사 전날 오후 5시에 펜슬러 하우스 본사로 방문하여 모델에게 의상을 입혀 보고 필요하면 수정을 해야 한다(All designers should visit the Pensler House headquarters the day before the event at 5 P.M. in order to try the clothes on the models and make the necessary adjustments)고 언급했다. 따라서 행사 전날인 3월 6일에 디자이너들이 모델과 의상 가봉을 해야 함을 알 수 있으므로, 정답은 (A)이다.

▶▶ **Paraphrasing** 지문의 try the clothes on the models and make the necessary adjustments → 정답의 A clothing fitting session

---

199 연계

번역 앨미타 빌딩에 관해 암시된 것은?
(A) 펜슬러 하우스의 본사이다.
(B) 3월에 10점의 의상을 전시할 것이다.
(C) 바이럼 씨의 작업장이다.
(D) 런웨이 쇼가 열리는 장소였다.

해설 토론방 게시글에서 쇼를 볼 기회가 없었더라도 앨미타 빌딩 로비에 와서 각 우승자들이 만든 최고의 수상작들을 보라고 했고, 이 달 남은 기간 동안 그곳에 전시될 것(If you didn't get the chance to catch the show, stop by the lobby of the Almeta Building to see the best outfit made by each of the winners. The host of the runway show announced that they would be on display there for the rest of the month)이라고 했다. 게시일이 3월 8일이므로 앨미타 빌딩에서 3월의 남은 기간 동안 수상작들을 전시한다는 것을 알 수 있다. 또한 안내문의 첫 번째 단락에서 귀하에게는 이제 행사 당일 선발될 10명의 수상자 중 한 명이 될 기회가 있다(You now have a chance to become one of the ten winners that will be selected on the event day)고 했다. 따라서 수상작 10점이 앨미타 빌딩에 전시될 것으로 유추할 수 있으므로, 정답은 (B)이다.

---

200 동의어 찾기

번역 토론방 게시글에서 첫 번째 단락 6행의 "pass up"과 의미가 가장 가까운 단어는?
(A) 전달하다
(B) 놓치다
(C) 멈추다
(D) 앞지르다

해설 해당 문장은 '멋진 패션을 볼 수 있는 이런 기회를 놓치지 마세요(Don't pass up this opportunity to see some amazing fashions)'라는 의미로 해석되므로, 여기서 pass up은 '놓치다'라는 의미가 자연스럽다. 따라서 정답은 (B) miss(놓치다, 하지 못하다, 그리워하다)이다.

TEST 6

101 (B)	**102** (B)	**103** (C)	**104** (A)	**105** (D)
106 (D)	**107** (C)	**108** (C)	**109** (C)	**110** (C)
111 (C)	**112** (B)	**113** (D)	**114** (A)	**115** (C)
116 (D)	**117** (B)	**118** (B)	**119** (D)	**120** (D)
121 (D)	**122** (B)	**123** (B)	**124** (C)	**125** (D)
126 (D)	**127** (B)	**128** (D)	**129** (D)	**130** (C)
131 (C)	**132** (D)	**133** (D)	**134** (D)	**135** (D)
136 (A)	**137** (A)	**138** (C)	**139** (B)	**140** (C)
141 (C)	**142** (B)	**143** (C)	**144** (A)	**145** (B)
146 (B)	**147** (B)	**148** (C)	**149** (C)	**150** (A)
151 (A)	**152** (D)	**153** (C)	**154** (C)	**155** (D)
156 (B)	**157** (D)	**158** (B)	**159** (A)	**160** (A)
161 (B)	**162** (A)	**163** (C)	**164** (C)	**165** (B)
166 (D)	**167** (D)	**168** (B)	**169** (D)	**170** (A)
171 (B)	**172** (D)	**173** (D)	**174** (C)	**175** (A)
176 (D)	**177** (B)	**178** (C)	**179** (C)	**180** (C)
181 (B)	**182** (D)	**183** (A)	**184** (D)	**185** (C)
186 (A)	**187** (B)	**188** (C)	**189** (C)	**190** (A)
191 (A)	**192** (B)	**193** (C)	**194** (C)	**195** (B)
196 (D)	**197** (C)	**198** (B)	**199** (A)	**200** (D)

PART 5

101 접속사 자리 _ 접속사 / 전치사 구분

해설 빈칸은 절 두 개를 연결하는 접속사 자리이다. 따라서 전치사인 (A) along 과 (D) beyond는 정답에서 제외된다. 문맥상 '더 긴급한 일이 그의 주의를 필요로 하지 않는다면'이라는 의미가 되어야 하므로, 정답은 '만약 ~하지 않는다면'을 의미하는 (B) unless이다. (C) after(~ 후에)도 접속사이지만, 의미상 어색하므로 오답이다.

번역 원준 씨는 더 긴급한 일이 그의 관심을 필요로 하지 않는다면 접수 업무를 담당할 것이다.

어휘 handle 담당하다, 처리하다   receptionist 접수원, 안내원   urgent 긴급한, 급한   attention 관심, 주의

102 형용사 자리 _ 명사 수식

해설 빈칸은 뒤에 온 명사(clients)를 수식하는 형용사 자리이므로, '개별적인, 개인적인'이라는 의미의 형용사인 (B) individual이 정답이다. 명사 (A) individualization(개별화, 차별)와 (C) individuality(개성, 특성), 부사 (D) individually(개별적으로)는 품사상 맞지 않다.

번역 벡스캔 사의 컨설팅 프로그램은 개별 고객들의 필요에 맞게 만들어져 있다.

어휘 tailor to ~에 맞게 만들다   meet the needs of ~의 필요에 응하다, ~의 요구에 맞게 맞추다   client 고객

103 동사 어형 _ 태

해설 nonfiction manuscripts가 문장의 주어이고, are _____가 동사인 문장이다. be동사 뒤에는 현재분사(-ing)가 와서 진행형 시제가 되거나, 과거분사(p.p.)가 와서 수동태 문장이 되어야 한다. 주어가 주체적인 행위를

할 수 없는 nonfiction manuscripts이며, 빈칸 뒤에 목적어가 보이지 않으므로 수동태 문장이 되어야 한다. 따라서 정답은 (C) prepared이다.

번역 완료되는 대로 논픽션 원고는 전문 지식을 갖춘 편집자 팀에 의해 정성스럽게 출판 준비가 된다.

어휘 completion 완성, 완료   manuscript 원고   publication 출판(물)   expert 전문적인, 전문 지식을 가진; 전문가   editor 편집자

104 등위접속사

해설 빈칸은 형용사 regular와 special을 연결하는 접속사 자리이므로, '그리고'라는 의미의 등위접속사인 (A) and가 정답이다. (D) across(~을 건너서)는 전치사 또는 부사로, 두 형용사를 연결할 수 없으므로 정답이 될 수 없다.

번역 노스–메트로 교통공단의 승차권 발매기는 정기 및 특별 버스 승차권을 판매한다.

어휘 Transit Authority 교통공단, 교통국   ticket machine 승차권 발매기   regular 정기의   bus pass 버스 승차권

105 명사 자리 _ 주어

해설 The ------- to join the poetry workshop이 주어이며 will be handled가 동사인 문장이다. 빈칸 앞에 정관사 The가 있으므로 빈칸에는 명사가 들어갈 자리이다. 따라서 명사인 (C) application과 (D) applications가 가능하다. 뒤에 in the order that they arrive(도착하는 순서대로)에서 they가 복수 대명사이므로 복수 명사인 (D) applications가 정답이다.

번역 시 워크숍에 합류하기 위한 신청서는 도착하는 순서대로 처리될 것이다.

어휘 poetry 시   handle 처리하다

106 부사 자리 _ 분사 수식

해설 빈칸은 뒤에 나오는 과거분사 recorded를 수식하는 자리이다. 과거분사나 현재분사를 수식할 수 있는 품사는 부사이므로, 정답은 (D) systematically이다.

번역 이 소프트웨어 사용자들은 데이터베이스에 출장비를 체계적으로 기록하는 것에 대해 진가를 인정한다.

어휘 appreciate 진가를 알다, (가치를) 인정하다   travel expense 출장비

107 명사 어휘

해설 빈칸은 전치사 without의 목적어 자리로 앞에 나온 형용사 advance의 수식을 받는다. 따라서 빈칸 앞에 온 without advance와 잘 어울려 쓸 명사가 들어가야 한다. 문맥상 '사전 ~ 없이 과정이 취소될 경우'라는 의미가 되어야 하므로, '통지, 통고'라는 의미의 (C) notification이 정답이다. (A) contribution(기부, 기부금), (B) interruption(방해, 중단), (D) distribution(유통, 배포)는 의미상 적합하지 않다.

번역 과정이 사전 통지 없이 취소될 경우에는 참가자들에게 신속히 환불해 준다.

어휘 participant 참가자   swift 신속한, 재빠른   refund 환불, 반환   in the event that (만약에) ~할 경우에는   cancel 취소하다, 해지하다   advance 사전의, 미리 하는

108 동사 / 준동사 구분

해설 한 문장에 동사는 하나만 있어야 한다. 이 문장에는 이미 동사(is expected)가 있기 때문에, 빈칸에 더 이상 동사는 들어갈 수 없다. 따라서 준동사(to부정사)인 (C) to boost가 정답이다. be expected to부정사(~할 것으로 기대되다)는 토익에 자주 나오는 표현이니 알아두자.

번역 왈포 패션즈와의 합병으로 올해 천 만 달러까지 영업 순익이 늘 것으로 예상된다.

어휘 merger 합병　operating profit 영업 순익　boost 늘리다, 증대시키다

109 명사 자리 _ 관사 뒤

해설 Each potential client가 주어, is given이 동사이고 a ------- (of the gym's personal training programs)가 목적어인 문장이다. 또, 빈칸 앞에 관사 a가 있으므로 빈칸에는 명사가 들어가야 한다. 따라서 '설명, 설명서'라는 의미의 명사 (C) description이 정답이다. 형용사인 (A) descriptive(설명적인)와 (B) describable(기술할 수 있는)은 품사상 적합하지 않다.

번역 모든 잠재 고객은 체육관의 개인 지도 프로그램에 대한 설명을 받는다.

어휘 potential client 잠재 고객　gym 체육관

110 to부정사

해설 빈칸 뒤에 (more fully) understand라는 동사가 왔으므로, 빈칸에는 전치사구가 아닌 to부정사구가 들어가야 한다. 따라서 '~하기 위해'라는 의미의 to부정사구를 만들 수 있는 (C) In order to가 정답이다. (A) Based on(~에 근거하여), (D) Except for(~를 제외하고)에서 on과 for는 전치사이므로 이 뒤에는 명사가 와야 한다. (B) In case(만약 ~인 경우에)는 접속사로 쓰일 경우 뒤에 '주어＋동사'가 있는 절이 와야 한다.

번역 시장을 더 잘 이해하기 위해 파나스키 프로덕츠 사는 소비자 조사를 실시해 왔다.

어휘 undertake 착수하다　consumer survey 소비자 조사

111 접속사 자리 _ 접속사 / 부사 구분

해설 문장을 살펴보면 동사가 두 개(can result, are)이므로, 빈칸에는 두 절을 연결할 접속사가 필요하다. 따라서 접속사인 (C) Because(~ 때문에)가 정답이다. 부사 (A) Rather(오히려, 차라리), (B) Just(방금, 막), 형용사 (D) Any(어떤)는 품사상 적합하지 않다.

번역 어떤 실수도 심각한 결과로 이어질 수 있기 때문에 법률 문서는 번역하기가 아주 어렵다.

어휘 result in (결과로) ~이 되다　consequence 결과　legal 법적인, 법률의　document 문서, 서류　translate 번역하다

112 명사 어휘

해설 빈칸은 앞에 있는 is의 보어로 well-deserved의 수식을 받는다. 문맥상 '헌신을 마땅히 인정 받아 후보자로 선정되었다'는 의미가 되어야 한다. 따라서 정답은 (B) acknowledgment이다. acknowledgment of(~

을 인정하여, 감사의 뜻으로)는 토익에 자주 등장하는 표현이니 알아두자. (A) inspiration(영감), (C) allowance(수당), (D) depiction(묘사, 서술)은 의미상 정답이 될 수 없다.

번역 방 씨가 후보자로 지명된 것은 나이어 재단의 임무에 대한 유능한 헌신을 마땅히 인정받은 것이다.

어휘 nomination 후보로 지명됨, 추천　well-deserved 자격이 있는, 마땅한　commitment 헌신, 약속, 전념　foundation 재단, 협회　mission 임무

113 재귀대명사

해설 빈칸은 동사 will remove의 목적어 자리이다. 목적어 자리에 올 수 있는 목적격 대명사 (B) her, 소유대명사 (C) hers, 재귀대명사 (D) herself 중에 문맥상 '로리 레튼은 자기 자신을 위원회에서 배제할 것이다'라는 의미가 되어야 하므로 정답은 (D) herself이다. 주어와 동일한 사람이나 사물이 목적어가 되는 경우에는 재귀대명사를 써야 한다.

번역 로리 레튼은 바르가스 씨를 개인적으로 알고 있으므로 채용 위원회에서 자신을 배제할 것이다.

어휘 personally 개인적으로　remove 없애다, 제거하다　committee 위원, 위원회

114 부사 어휘

해설 빈칸은 be동사(is)와 보어(the top soft drink among teenagers) 사이 부사 자리이다. 문맥상 '현재 십대들 사이에서 최고의 청량음료'라는 의미로, 현재시제와 어울릴 수 있는 부사인 (A) now(현재, 지금)가 정답이다. (B) more(더 많은; 더 많이), (C) early(일찍), (D) long(긴; 길게)은 의미상 정답이 될 수 없다.

번역 데이터에 의하면 프로스타 라이트는 현재 십대들 사이에서 최고의 청량음료이다.

어휘 soft drink 청량음료　teenager 십대

115 부사 자리 _ 준동사(to부정사) 수식

해설 빈칸은 앞의 to부정사구(to spray the paint)를 수식하는 자리이다. to부정사구인 준동사를 수식하는 품사는 부사이므로, 정답은 부사인 (C) lightly(가볍게, 살며시)이다. 동사 (A) lightens, (B) lighten(~을 밝게 하다), 형용사의 최상급 (D) lightest는 품사상 정답이 될 수 없다.

번역 깡통 라벨에는 작은 페인트 기포가 생기는 것을 방지하기 위해 사용자들에게 페인트를 살짝 분무하라고 안내되어 있다.

어휘 direct 지시하다, 명하다, 유도하다　spray 뿌리다, 분무하다　prevent 방지하다, 막다　bubble 기포, 거품　form 생기다

116 소유격 대명사

해설 빈칸은 명사(multicultural themes)를 한정 수식하는 자리로, 명사 앞에서 명사를 수식할 수 있는 대명사는 소유격 대명사 밖에 없으므로 정답은 (D) its이다. (A) it은 주격[목적격] 대명사, (B) which는 관계대명사, (C) something은 (대)명사이다.

번역 과거 TV 스타였던 노아 씨는 다문화 주제 때문에 연극에 출연하기로 했다고 설명했다.

어휘 former 과거의, 이전의 choose to + 원형동사 ~하기로 선택하다 play 연극 multicultural 다문화의 theme 주제

117 부사 어휘

해설 빈칸은 뒤에 나오는 과거분사 opened를 수식하는 부사 자리이므로 opened와 문맥상 잘 어울리는 부사를 선택해야 한다. 문맥상 '새롭게 개장한 역사 공원'의 의미가 가장 자연스러우므로 정답은 (B) newly이다. (A) densely(빽빽하게, 밀집하여), (C) generally(일반적으로, 대부분은), (D) solely(오로지)는 의미상 정답이 될 수 없다.

번역 토요일에, 첫 방문객 단체들은 시내의 최근 개장한 역사 공원을 돌아보았다.

어휘 tour 여행하다, 돌아보다 historical 역사적인

118 전치사 어휘

해설 빈칸 뒤에 명사구(the date)가 왔으므로, 빈칸은 전치사 자리이다. 전치사 자리에 올 수 있는 (B) from과 (C) onto, (D) despite 중 문맥상 '발행일로부터 한 달'이라는 의미가 되어야 하므로, (B) from(~로부터)이 정답이다. (C) onto(~의 위에, ~쪽으로), (D) despite(~에도 불구하고)는 의미상 정답이 될 수 없으며, 접속사인 (A) when(~ 때) 뒤에는 주어와 동사를 갖춘 절이 와야 한다.

번역 크리츨리 유통의 가격 견적서는 발행일로부터 한 달 뒤 만료된다.

어휘 distributing 유통(업) price quote 가격 견적(서) expire (기한이) 만료되다 issue 발행하다

119 명사 어휘

해설 빈칸은 동사(bring)의 목적어 자리로 빈칸 뒤 전치사구(of their artistic skills)의 수식을 받는다. 전치사구의 their artistic skills(그들의 예술적 역량)가 빈칸에 들어갈 수 있는 단어를 파악할 수 있는 단서가 된다. 문맥상 '예술적 역량을 보여주는 증거'라는 의미가 자연스러우므로 '증거, 증명'이라는 뜻의 (D) evidence가 정답이다. (A) reduction(감소, 삭감), (B) cover(덮개, 표지), (C) reply(대답, 답변)는 의미상 정답이 될 수 없다.

번역 취업 면접에서 최상의 인상을 주려면 지원자들은 포트폴리오 형식으로 자신의 예술적 역량을 입증하는 증거를 가져와야 한다.

어휘 impression 인상 job interview 취업 면접 candidate 지원자, 응시자 artistic skill 예술적 역량 in the form of ~의 형태로 portfolio 포트폴리오

120 동사 어휘

해설 '____ A into B'의 형태로, 빈칸 뒤의 목적어(the list of reports)와 잘 어울릴 수 있는 동사를 골라야 한다. 문맥상 '보고서 목록을 연구 주제별로 나누다'라는 의미가 자연스러우므로 정답은 (D) divide(나누다)이다. 'divide A into B(A를 B로 나누다)'를 하나로 묶어서 외워두자.

번역 인턴사원들은 보고서 목록을 연구 주제별 부분으로 나누라고 요청 받았다.

어휘 be asked to + 동사원형 ~할 것을 요청 받다 section 섹션, 부분 research 연구, 조사

121 형용사 자리 _ be 동사의 보어

해설 빈칸은 be동사(are) 뒤의 보어 자리로 앞에 나오는 부사 readily의 수식을 받는다. be동사의 보어로는, 주어와 동격인 경우에는 명사가 오고 상태를 설명해 주는 경우에는 형용사가 온다. 명사인 (A) availability(유용성, 이용할 수 있는 것), (B) availabilities, 형용사인 (D) available(이용 가능한, 사용할 수 있는) 중 주어(all types of public transportation)가 '이용 가능한' 상태임을 설명해 주는 형용사 (D) available이 정답이다. 부사 (C) availably(유효하게, 쓸모 있게)는 품사상 적합하지 않다.

번역 시가 기반 시설에 넉넉하게 돈을 쓴 덕분에 멜우드 시티 중심에서는 모든 종류의 대중 교통을 쉽게 이용할 수 있다.

어휘 thanks to ~ 덕분에 generous 관대한, 후한 spend (돈·시간을) 쓰다 infrastructure 기반 시설 public transportation 대중 교통 readily 즉시, 쉽게

122 동사 어휘

해설 빈칸은 동사 decided의 목적어이면서 빈칸 뒤 our contract(우리 계약)를 목적어로 취하는 to부정사의 동사 자리이다. 따라서 our contract(우리 계약)와 잘 어울리는 동사를 골라야 한다. 문맥상 '계약을 종결하기로 결정했다'라는 의미가 가장 자연스러우므로 정답은 (C) terminate(끝내다, 종결시키다)이다. (A) insist(주장하다), (B) exceed(초과하다, 넘다)는 의미상 적합하지 않으며, (D) agree(동의하다)는 자동사로 목적어를 취하려면 전치사가 함께 와야 한다.

번역 어제 회의에서 이사회는 에그벨레 컨설팅 사와의 계약을 종결하기로 결정했다.

어휘 board of directors 이사회 contract 계약(서)

123 동사 어휘

해설 'be ____ with'의 형태로 쓸 수 있어야 하며, separate kitchens and work areas(별도의 주방 공간과 작업 공간)와 어울려 쓸 수 있는 동사를 골라야 한다. 문맥상 '별도의 주방 공간과 작업 공간을 갖추고 있다'라는 의미가 가장 자연스러우므로, 정답은 (B) equipped(갖추다)이다. be equipped with(~을 갖추다)는 토익에 자주 등장하는 표현이니 꼭 알아두자. (A) subscribed(구독하다, 구독 신청하다), (C) accelerated(촉진하다, 가속하다), (D) conducted(실행하다)는 의미상 적합하지 않다.

번역 호텔의 디럭스 스위트 전 객실은 별도의 주방 공간과 작업 공간을 갖추고 있습니다.

어휘 separate 별도의, 분리된, 떨어져 있는

124 동사 어형 _ 태

해설 빈칸은 접속사 so로 이어지는 절의 동사 자리이다. 빈칸 뒤에 목적어가 없고 '표준적인 서명 절차'는 '무시하는' 능동적 주체가 아니라 '무시되는' 대상이므로 수동태인 (C) was disregarded가 정답이다. (B) disregarding은 문장에서 동사 역할을 할 수 없으므로 정답이 될 수 없다.

번역 택배회사는 긴급 소포를 바로 음 씨에게 배송했으므로 표준적인 서명 절차는 무시되었다.

어휘 courier 택배회사 deliver 배송하다 urgent 긴급한 package 소포 directly 바로 sign-in 서명 protocol 관습, 절차

125 형용사 어휘

해설 문장 구조를 살펴보면, The need (to renovate some of the older store locations)가 문장의 주어이고, has been이 동사이며, 빈칸이 보어이다. 따라서 빈칸에는 has been의 보어 역할을 할 형용사가 들어가야 한다. 빈칸 뒤에 온 전치사 among이 단서로, 문맥상 '경영진의 우려 사항들 중 가장 중요하다'라는 의미가 자연스러우므로 정답은 (D) foremost (가장 중요한)이다. (A) attentive(배려하는), (B) maximum(최대의), (C) executive(관리직의)는 의미상 적합하지 않다.

번역 일부 오래된 매장을 수리해야 할 필요성은 우리 경영진이 가장 우려하는 사항이다.

어휘 renovate 수리하다, 새단장하다   management 경영진, 관리직   concerns 걱정, 염려, 관심사

126 명사 자리 _ 전치사의 목적어

해설 빈칸은 전치사 due to의 목적어 자리로, television과 함께 복합명사를 이루는 명사가 들어가야 한다. 따라서 '노출'이라는 의미의 명사인 (D) exposure가 정답이다. 현재시제 동사 (A) expose, (B) exposes, 과거시제 동사/과거분사 (C) exposed는 품사상 적합하지 않다.

번역 고수 잼의 브랜드 인지도 상승은 TV에 노출된 덕분인 듯하다.

어휘 increase 상승, 증가   brand recognition 브랜드 인지도   due to ~ 덕분에   receive 받다

127 명사 어휘

해설 빈칸은 to부정사(to stimulate)의 목적어 자리로 앞에 온 multimillion-dollar와 함께 어울려 쓸 수 있는 어휘를 골라야 한다. 문맥상 '수백만 달러의 투자를 촉진하다'라는 의미가 자연스러우므로, '투자(액), 출자'라는 의미의 (B) investment가 정답이다. (A) objective(목표), (C) affiliation(관계, 소속), (D) statement(진술, 설명)는 의미상 적합하지 않다.

번역 디라비는 시연을 통해 회사의 모바일 플랫폼에 수백만 달러의 투자를 촉진하길 바란다.

어휘 demonstration 시연, 설명   stimulate 촉진하다, 자극하다   multimillion 수백만의

128 접속사 자리 _ 접속사 / 부사 구분

해설 문장에 동사가 두 개(indicate, will personalize) 있으므로, 빈칸에는 두 문장을 연결할 접속사가 들어가야 한다. 따라서 접속사인 (A) Whether(~인지 아닌지), (D) Once(일단 ~하면) 중 문맥상 '일단 지역을 표시하면 ~ 개인의 필요에 맞추어 준다'라는 의미가 자연스러우므로 정답은 (D) Once이다. (B) Later, (C) Mostly는 둘 다 부사로 품사상 적합하지 않다.

번역 일단 지역을 표시하면, 웹사이트는 뉴스 공급 콘텐츠를 개인의 필요에 맞추어 드립니다.

어휘 indicate 표시하다, 나타내다   region 지역, 지방   personalize (개인의 필요에) 맞추다   contents 콘텐츠, 내용   feed 공급 (장치)

129 형용사 어휘

해설 빈칸 뒤의 products를 수식하는 형용사 자리이므로 products와 어울리는 어휘를 골라야 한다. CD players(CD 플레이어)와 before they disappear entirely(완전히 사라지기 전에)가 문제 해결의 단서이다. '사라지는' 것과 가장 어울리는 형용사를 생각해 보면, '시대에 뒤떨어진, 구식의, 더 이상 쓸모가 없는'이라는 의미의 (D) obsolete이 정답이다. (A) reversible(뒤집을 수 있는), (B) anonymous(익명의, 가명의), (C) tentative(시험적인, 일시적인)는 의미상 적합하지 않다.

번역 박물관에서는 휴대용 CD 플레이어와 다른 구식 제품들이 완전히 사라지기 전에 수집하려고 애쓰고 있다.

어휘 portable 휴대용의, 이동할 수 있는   entirely 완전히, 전적으로

130 동사 어휘

해설 빈칸은 조동사(will) 뒤의 동사원형 자리이다. that절의 주어인 the region's unusually plentiful orange harvest(지역의 이례적인 오렌지 풍작)와 빈칸 뒤의 목적어인 lower prices for the fruit(더 저렴한 과일 가격)의 관계를 생각해 보면, '~에 일치하다, ~와 들어맞다'라는 의미의 (C) correspond to가 정답이다. (A) inquire into(~을 조사하다), (B) complain about(~에 대해 불평하다), (D) participate in(~에 참석하다)은 의미상 적합하지 않다.

번역 경제학자들은 이번 시즌에 이 지역의 이례적인 오렌지 풍작으로 인해 슈퍼마켓의 과일 가격이 더 저렴할 것이라는 점을 지적해 왔다.

어휘 economist 경제학자   unusually 이례적으로, 유난히   plentiful 풍부한

PART 6

131-134 이메일

수신: 캐롤 냅튼 〈c-knapton@arf-mail.com〉
발신: 네드 베커 〈ned-becker@varpowbank.com〉
날짜: 7월 21일
제목: 귀하의 카드

냅튼 씨께,

바포우 은행은 귀하의 바포우 플래티넘 카드가 카드 기기에 더 이상 인식되지 않는다는 사실에 유감을 표합니다. 요청에 따라 카드를 **131취소했습니다.** 24시간 이내에 **132교체** 카드가 특급 우편으로 발송될 예정입니다. 영업일 기준 3일 이내에 받으실 수 있습니다. **134아울러 귀하가 지금까지 누린 혜택 및 보장은 새로운 바포우 플래티넘 카드로 133연장될 예정이니 안심하십시오.** 바뀌는 것은 신용카드 번호뿐입니다.

이 절차에 관한 질문이 있으시면 이 이메일에 답신으로 보내 주십시오.

네드 베커
고객 서비스

어휘 no longer 더 이상 ~ 않다   as per request 요청대로   rest assured that ~하니 안심하십시오

131 동사 어형_태

해설 빈칸은 주어(I) 뒤에 나오는 동사 자리로, 뒤의 목적격 인칭대명사(it)를 목적어로 취한다. 따라서 정답은 능동의 현재완료시제 동사 (C) have canceled이다. 동사원형 (A) be canceling은 동사 자리에 들어갈 수 없고, 수동의 동사 (B) was being canceled와 (D) would have been canceled는 목적어(it)를 취할 수 없다.

132 명사 자리_복합명사

해설 부정관사(A)와 명사(card) 사이에는 명사(card)를 수식하는 형용사 또는 명사(card)와 함께 복합명사를 이루는 명사가 나올 수 있으므로, (B) replaceability(대체 가능성)와 (D) replacement(교체)가 적합하다. 문맥상 '교체 카드'라는 의미가 자연스러우므로, 정답은 (D) replacement이다.

133 동사 어휘

해설 빈칸은 조동사(will) 뒤의 동사원형 자리로, 뒤에 나오는 전치사구(to your new Varpow Platinum card)의 수식을 받는다. 문맥상 '귀하가 지금까지 누린 혜택 및 보장은 새로운 바포우 플래티넘 카드로 연장될 예정이다'라는 의미가 자연스러우므로, 정답은 (B) extend(연장하다, 늘리다)이다. (A) share(공유하다, 나누다), (C) acquire(인수하다, 습득하다), (D) qualify(자격이 있다, 자격을 주다)는 의미상 적합하지 않다.

134 문맥에 맞는 문장 고르기

번역 (A) 월 이자율이 훨씬 낮습니다.
(B) 안전상의 이유로 카드를 폐기하실 것을 권장합니다.
(C) 보상 포인트는 연말까지 사용해야 합니다.
(D) 바뀌는 것은 신용카드 번호뿐입니다.

해설 빈칸 앞 문장 '아울러 귀하가 지금까지 누린 혜택 및 보장은 새로운 바포우 플래티넘 카드로 연장될 예정이니 안심하라(Also, please rest assured that the benefits and protections you have been enjoying up to this point will extend to your new Varpow Platinum card)'에서 혜택과 보장이 재발급 카드로 승계된다는 점을 언급하고 있다. 따라서 빈칸에는 재발급에 따른 불이익이 없음을 한 번 더 강조하는 것이 문맥상 자연스러우므로, 정답은 (D)이다.

135-138 사용설명서

브림 310 자동응답기로 보이스메일 인사말을 녹음하는 것은 간단합니다. 메시지를 준비한 후에, 기계의 붉은 색 '녹음' 버튼을 계속 누르고 있으면 됩니다. **136녹음 신호음이 135울리자마자, 말하기 시작하세요. 인사말은 최고 1분까지 가능합니다. 136편의를 위하여, 시간이 137단 10초 남아 있을 때 화면이 깜빡입니다.** 녹음을 끝내려면 버튼을 놓으면 됩니다. 새로운 인사말은 자동으로 **138작동할 것입니다.** 인사말이 마음에 들지 않으면, '녹음' 버튼을 다시 계속 누르기만 하면 됩니다. 인사말이 삭제된 것을 알려주는 신호음이 울릴 것입니다. 그러면 과정을 처음부터 다시 시작할 수 있습니다.

어휘 greeting 인사 answering machine 자동응답기 press 누르다 convenience 편의, 편리함 display 화면 flash 깜박이다 remain 남아 있다 release 놓아 주다, 풀어주다

automatically 자동으로 be unsatisfied with ~에 만족하지 못하다, 마음에 들지 않다 tone 신호음, 발신음 indicate 표시하다, 나타내다 delete 삭제하다, 지우다 process 과정, 절차 start over 다시 시작하다

135 접속사 자리

해설 문장을 살펴보면 동사가 두 개(sounds, begin)이므로, 빈칸에는 두 문장을 연결할 접속사가 필요하다. 따라서 '~하자마자, ~하자 곧'이라는 의미의 접속사인 (D) As soon as가 정답이다. (A) Even(평평한, 더욱)은 형용사 또는 부사, (B) Besides(~ 외에, ~에 더하여)와 (C) In spite of(~에도 불구하고)는 전치사(구)이다.

136 문맥에 맞는 문장 고르기

번역 **(A) 인사말은 최고 1분까지 가능합니다.**
(B) 그런 다음 화면 시간을 설정하시려면 "시간"을 누르세요.
(C) 음성 지시 메시지는 영어 또는 스페인어로 제공됩니다.
(D) 이렇게 하면 마이크가 손상될 수 있습니다.

해설 빈칸 바로 앞 문장에서 녹음 신호음이 울리자마자, 말하기 시작하라(As soon as the recording tone sounds, begin speaking)고 했고 빈칸 뒤 문장에서 편의를 위하여, 시간이 단 10초 남아 있을 때 화면이 깜빡인다(For your convenience, the display flashes when only ten seconds are remaining)고 했다. 따라서 빈칸에는 녹음할 수 있는 전체 시간과 관련된 내용이 들어가는 것이 자연스러우므로 정답은 (A)이다.

어휘 up to 최대 ~까지 prompt 지시 메시지, 프롬프트 microphone 마이크

137 형용사 어휘

해설 빈칸은 뒤에 온 ten seconds를 수식할 형용사 자리이다. 문맥상 '____ 10초가 남아 있을 때'라는 의미가 되어야 하므로, '오직, 다만'이라는 의미의 (A) only가 정답이다.

138 동사 어형_시제

해설 선택지를 보면 모두 시제가 다른 동사 형태이므로, 동사 시제 문제임을 알 수 있다. 지문 내용의 흐름상 앞으로 일어날 일에 대해 이야기하고 있으므로 '새로운 인사말은 자동으로 작동할 것이다'라는 미래 시제가 적절하다. 따라서 정답은 (C) will play이다.

139-142 통지

보식 치과 병원

저희는 치과 진료 서비스 개선을 위해 환자들로부터 방문에 관한 피드백을 **139수렴하고 있습니다. 141최근 저희 병원에서 정기 스케일링을 140받으셨으므로** 귀하의 경험에 대해 첨부한 설문지를 작성해 주시면 도움이 될 것입니다. 모두 작성하시는 데 10분 정도 걸립니다. 완료하시면 제공된 소인 찍힌 반신용 봉투에 설문지를 넣으시고 우편함에 넣어 주십시오. 참여는 철저히 자발적으로 이뤄지지만 시간을 내시어 충분하고 솔직한 답변을 해 주실 것을 권고합니다. 귀하의 노력이 결국 더 나은 서비스로 **142돌아옵니다.** 감사합니다.

---

139 동사 어휘

해설 빈칸은 동사(are)와 함께 현재진행시제를 이루면서 뒤의 명사구(feedback from patients about their visits)를 목적어로 취한다. 따라서 뒤의 목적어와 잘 어울리는 동사 어휘를 골라야 한다. 문맥상 '환자들로부터 방문에 관한 피드백을 수렴하고 있다'라는 의미가 자연스러우므로, 정답은 (B) gathering(모으다, 수집하다, 모이다)이다. (A) modifying(수정하다, 변경하다), (C) treating(다루다, 취급하다, 치료하다), (D) assisting(돕다, 도움이 되다)은 의미상 적합하지 않다.

140 부사절 접속사

해설 빈칸 뒤 절(you recently had a routine dental cleaning at our clinic)을 이끌면서 뒤에 나오는 주절을 수식하는 부사절 접속사 자리이므로, 부사절 접속사 (A) While(~ 동안, ~ 반면에), (B) Until(~까지), (C) As(~ 때, ~ 때문에, ~ 대로)가 가능하다. 문맥상 '최근 저희 병원에서 정기 스케일링을 받았기 때문에'라는 의미가 자연스러우므로, 정답은 (C) As이다. 접속부사 (D) Therefore(그러므로)는 절을 이끌 수 없다.

141 문맥에 맞는 문장 고르기

번역 (A) 귀하의 방문 시 종합적인 검사를 할 예정입니다.
(B) 이 단계는 모집 중인 직책에 지원할 때 필요합니다.
(C) 모두 작성하시는 데 10분 정도 걸립니다.
(D) 2주 전에 미리 진료 예약을 잡으십시오.

해설 빈칸 앞 문장 '최근 저희 병원에서 정기 스케일링을 받으셨으므로 귀하의 경험에 대해 첨부한 설문지를 작성해 주면 도움이 될 것입니다(As you recently had a routine dental cleaning at our clinic, it would be helpful if you would complete the attached questionnaire about your experience)'에서 설문지 작성을 요청하고 있다. 따라서 빈칸에도 설문지 작성과 관련한 내용을 언급하는 것이 문맥상 자연스러우므로, 정답은 (C)이다.

142 동사 어형 _ 시제

해설 빈칸은 주어(your efforts) 뒤에 나오는 동사 자리이므로, 미래시제 동사 (B) will be rewarded와 현재완료시제 동사 (C) have been rewarded가 가능하다. 설문지 작성을 요청하는 빈칸 앞의 내용을 통해 앞으로 일어날 일임을 알 수 있으므로, 정답은 미래시제 동사 (B) will be rewarded이다. to부정사 (A) to be rewarded와 동명사/현재분사 (D) having rewarded는 동사 자리에 들어갈 수 없다.

143-146 이메일

발신: 아시프 부이얀
수신: 인사부 전 직원
날짜: 3월 4일
제목: 워크숍

팀원 여러분, 안녕하세요

4월 17일에, 렙코 임플로이어스에서는 직원 평가의 혁신적 방법에 관한 워크숍을 개최할 예정입니다. 제가 받은 광고에서 보니 회사에서 **143**활용할 수 있을 것 같습니다. 이 **144**기법에 관해 심도 있게 배울 수 있도록 우리 팀원 두 명을 그곳에 보내고자 합니다. 참석자들은 나머지 부서원들을 위해 보고서를 작성해야 합니다.

145우리는 직원을 빨리 선정해야 합니다. 제 경험으로 보면 렙코 행사는 인기가 엄청납니다. 참석하고자 한다면 목요일 오전 11시까지 이 이메일로 회신해 주세요. 고참 사원들과 긴급한 프로젝트에 관여하지 않은 직원들에게 우선권이 부여됩니다. **146하지만 관심 있는 분들은 누구나 자원하시기 바랍니다.**

아시프

어휘 innovative 혁신적인 recognition 인정, 평가 attendee 출석자, 참석자 be responsible for ~의 업무를 맡다, ~에 대한 책임이 있다 rest 나머지 representative 직원 reply to ~에 대답하다 senior 선임의, 고참의 be involved in ~에 관여하다 urgent 긴급한 encourage 권장하다 volunteer 자원하다, 자원봉사하다

143 동사 자리

해설 문장 구조를 살펴보면, something 뒤에 목적격 관계대명사 that이 생략된 관계대명사절이다. that을 넣어서 생각해 보면 something that the company ------의 구조이다. 따라서 the company는 관계대명사절의 주어이고, 빈칸에는 동사가 필요하므로 (D) could utilize가 정답이다. (B) utilization(이용, 활용)은 명사이고, (C) utilizable(이용할 수 있는)은 형용사이므로 품사상 적합하지 않다.

어휘 utilize 이용하다, 활용하다

144 명사 어휘

해설 빈칸 바로 앞 문장을 살펴보면, 렙코 임플로이어스에서 직원을 평가하는 혁신적인 방법(an innovative method)에 관한 워크숍을 개최할 예정이라고 했다. 따라서 워크숍에 갈 팀원들이 배울 것은 '혁신적인 방법' 즉 '기법'임을 알 수 있으므로, 정답은 (A) technique이다. (B) recipient(수신자, 수령자), (C) behavior(행동), (D) profession(직업)은 의미상 적합하지 않다.

145 문맥에 맞는 문장 고르기

번역 (A) 회사에서 팀 전체의 교통비를 지불할 예정입니다.
(B) 제 경험으로 보면 렙코 행사는 인기가 엄청납니다.
(C) 마찬가지로 숙련된 강사들을 찾기가 어려울 수 있습니다.
(D) 그런 다음 최종 보고서를 공유 폴더에 올려야 합니다.

해설 빈칸 바로 앞 문장에 직원을 빨리 선정해야 한다(We will need to choose our representatives quickly)고 했다. 따라서 워크숍 참석 인원이 많다는 내용이 이어지는 것이 자연스러우므로 정답은 (B)이다.

어휘 transportation 교통 enormously 아주, 매우 likewise 마찬가지로 well-trained 숙련된 shared 공유된

146 부사 어휘

해설 빈칸 앞 문장에서는 고참 사원들과 긴급한 프로젝트에 관여하지 않은 직원들에게 우선권이 부여된다(Preference will be given to senior employees and those who are not involved in urgent projects)고 했으며, 빈칸 뒤에서는 관심 있는 사람들은 자원하라(I encourage anyone interested to volunteer)고 했다. 따라서 빈칸에는 서로 상반되는 내용을 연결하는 '대조'의 의미를 지닌 접속부사가 들어가야 하므로, 정답은 (B) However(그러나, 하지만)이다.

PART 7

147-148 송장

	쿠즈네초프 서비스			
청구지: 나이젤 윌콕스			송장: 85061	
린들러 파이낸셜			발행일: 7월 4일	
클라리 로드 42			지불 기한: 8월 4일	
런던 W11 2DY				

날짜	제공 서비스	수량	단가	소계
[147]6월 30일	다랴 쿠즈네초프가 러시아어로 된 회계 서류를 영어로 번역	1347단어	단어 당 0.08 파운드	1077.60 파운드
6월 30일	[148]작업 당일 완료 시 15% 할증			161.64 파운드
			총계	1239.24 파운드

어휘 invoice 송장, 청구서 payment due 지불 기한 translation 번역, 통역 surcharge 할증[추가] 요금 same-day 같은 날짜의

147 세부 사항

번역 쿠즈네초프 씨는 6월 30일에 무엇을 했는가?
(A) 투자 서비스 제공
(B) 문서 번역
(C) 윌콕스 씨를 위한 출장 준비
(D) 발표 문서 인쇄

해설 송장의 제공 서비스 중 다랴 쿠즈네초프가 러시아어로 된 회계 서류를 영어로 번역(Translation of financial document from Russian to English by Darya Kuznetzov)을 보면, 쿠즈네초프 씨는 6월 30일에 번역 작업을 했음을 알 수 있다. 따라서 정답은 (B)이다.

▶▶ Paraphrasing 지문의 Translation of financial document from Russian to English → 정답의 Converted the language of a text

148 세부 사항

번역 송장에 추가 요금이 부과된 이유는 무엇인가?
(A) 해외 배송 (B) 소량 주문
(C) 연체 (D) 빠른 서비스

해설 송장의 작업 당일 완료 시 15% 할증(15% surcharge for same-day completion of above)을 보면, 당일 서비스를 이용해 15%의 추가 요금이 발생했음을 알 수 있으므로, 정답은 (D)이다.

▶▶ Paraphrasing 지문의 same-day completion → 정답의 expedited service

149-150 웹페이지

http://eplincitymusicfestival.com

에플린 시 음악 축제

[150]에플린 시 음악 축제에서는 플래티넘 회원 이상 등급의 개인 및 사업체에게 무료 입장권을 드립니다. [149]이에 더해, 10인 이상 단체에는 구입 시 입장권 요금에서 15% 할인해 드립니다. 마지막으로, '축제 패스' 제도에 따라 3개 이상 행사에 참여하는 방문객들은 25% 할인해 드립니다. 예약 절차를 시작하기 전에 이 페이지를 방문하셔서 패스를 등록하십시오. 고객 1인당 또는 한 단체당 단한 번 할인됩니다. 중복 할인되지 않습니다.

어휘 complimentary 무료의 be eligible for ~에 해당되다, 자격이 있다 reduction 할인, 삭감 apply 적용하다 register for ~에 등록하다 book 예약 process 절차, 과정

149 주제 / 목적

번역 웹페이지의 목적은 무엇인가?
(A) 축제 후원자를 유치하기 위해
(B) 장소 시설을 비교하기 위해
(C) 입장권 판촉 행사를 설명하기 위해
(D) 예약 시스템을 설명하기 위해

해설 두 번째 문장에서 10인 이상 단체는 15%를 할인(audience groups of ten or larger are eligible for a 15% reduction in ticket price) 받을 수 있으며, 이어지는 문장에서는 3개 이상 행사에 참여하면 25%를 할인(visitors who plan to attend at least three events can receive a 25% discount) 받을 수 있다고 했다. 따라서 입장권 판촉 할인 행사를 설명하기 위한 것임을 알 수 있으므로, 정답은 (C)이다.

150 추론 / 암시

번역 회원 제도에 대해 암시된 것은?
(A) 등급별로 구별되어 있다.
(B) 온라인으로 구입할 수 있다.
(C) 기업 회원에게만 제공된다.
(D) 최소 출자금이 필요하다.

해설 첫 문장에서 플래티넘 회원 이상 등급의 개인 및 사업체에게 무료 입장권을 준다(supplies complimentary tickets to individuals and businesses with Platinum Sponsorship status or higher)고 한 것으로 미루어 보아, 회원 제도가 등급별로 나누어져 있음을 알 수 있다. 따라서 정답은 (A)이다.

151-152 공지

사물함 사용

151, 152최근 몇 차례 착오가 있은 후에, 아담스톤 피트니스에서는 회원 여러분들에게 사물함 사용 정책에 관해 다시 알려 드리고자 합니다.

사물함은 선착순으로 이용 가능합니다. **152**회원분들은 정기적으로 동일한 사물함을 사용하지 못할 수도 있으며, 1회 이용 기간이 지난 후에 사물함에 물품을 그대로 남겨 두셔도 안 됩니다. 사물함에 남겨 두신 소지품은 수시로 폐기 처리합니다. 모든 사물함에는 안전한 맹꽁이자물쇠가 달려 있으며, 열쇠는 안내원에게 받으시면 됩니다. 외부 자물쇠를 이용해 사물함을 잠그는 것은 금지되어 있습니다. 외부 자물쇠는 발견 시 잘라서 버릴 것입니다. 또 아담스톤 피트니스에서는 사물함을 남용하지 않도록 하기 위해 사물함 내용물을 검사할 권한도 갖고 있습니다.

규정을 준수해 주셔서 감사합니다.

– 아담스톤 피트니스

어휘 usage 사용, 사용법 in the wake of ~ 이후에, ~에 이어 refresh 새롭게 하다 policy 정책, 방침 available 이용 가능한 on a first-come, first-served basis 선착순으로, 순번대로 regularly 정기적으로 duration (지속) 기간 property 소유물, 부동산 dispose of ~을 폐기하다 at any time 수시로, 아무 때나 be outfitted with ~을 갖추고 있다 high-security 아주 안전한 padlock 맹꽁이자물쇠 attendant 안내원, 종업원 secure 안전하게 하다 prohibit 금지하다 reserve the right 권리를 갖다 inspect 검사하다 compliance 준수, 따름

151 주제 / 목적

번역 공고문을 게시한 이유는 무엇인가?
(A) 상기시키기 위해
(B) 제안을 요청하기 위해
(C) 상표를 추천하기 위해
(D) 서비스를 알리기 위해

해설 첫 번째 단락의 첫 문장을 보면, 피트니스 회원들에게 사물함 사용에 관한 정책을 알려 주기 위한(Adamston Fitness would like to refresh members' memory of our locker usage policies) 공고문임을 알 수 있다. 따라서 정답은 (A)이다.

▶▶ Paraphrasing   지문의 **refresh members' memory**
→ 정답의 **give a reminder**

152 추론 / 암시

번역 아담스톤 피트니스의 일부 회원에 대해 암시된 것은?
(A) 추가 안전 장치를 가져와야 한다.
(B) 사물함 사용에 추가 요금을 지불한다.
(C) 사물함 크기에 대해 불만을 제기해 왔다.
(D) 장기 보관용으로 사물함을 사용하려고 했다.

해설 첫 번째 단락에서 회원들의 사물함 사용에 착오가 있었다(some recent misunderstandings, ~ our locker usage policies)는 것을 알 수 있으며 이어지는 단락에서 사물함 사용 규정에 대해 설명하고 있다. 두 번째 단락에서 회원들은 정기적으로 동일한 사물함을 사용하지 못할 수도 있으며 1회 이용 기간이 지난 후에 사물함에 물품을 그대로 남겨 두면 안 된다(Members should not expect to be able to use the same locker regularly, or to leave items in a locker past the duration of a single visit)고 했다. 따라서 같은 사물함을 계속 사용하려고 시도한 회원이 있음을 알 수 있으므로, 정답은 (D)이다.

▶▶ Paraphrasing   지문의 **leave items in a locker past the duration of a single visit**
→ 정답의 **have attempted to use lockers for long-term storage**

153-154 문자 메시지

신시아 어윈, 오후 1:17
153프레드, 제가 루퍼트 씨의 집을 칠할 물품 비용 추산을 막 끝마쳐서, 우리는 입찰 준비가 됐어요. 이것을 이메일 첨부로 보내달라고 하셨죠, 그렇죠?

프레드 잘츠만, 오후 1:18
네, 우리가 루퍼트 씨에게 제시하기 전에 그것을 검토하고 싶습니다.

신시아 어윈, 오후 1:19
알겠습니다, 지금 보낼게요.

프레드 잘츠만, 오후 1:21
훌륭하군요. 하지만 작업자들이 작업을 시작할 시기를 루퍼트 씨에게도 알려야 한다고 생각해요. 루퍼트 씨에게 입찰가를 전달하기 전에 우리 프로젝트 일정 상에서 비어 있는 날을 찾아줄 수 있나요?

신시아 어윈, 오후 1:22
물론입니다. **154**사실 가능한 시작 날짜 몇 개를 그녀에게 보내서 다양한 선택의 여지를 주면 어떨까요?

프레드 잘츠만, 오후 1:23
좋은 생각이군요.

신시아 어윈, 오후 1:24
네. 이메일 내용에 해당 정보를 넣겠습니다.

어휘 estimate 추산하다 bid 입찰, 가격 제시 attachment 첨부 pass ~ on to ... ~을 …에게 전하다 a range of 다양한

153 세부 사항

번역 어윈 씨는 첫 번째 메시지를 보내기 전에 무엇을 했는가?
(A) 주택 소유주에게 답신하기
(B) 잠재 비용 계산하기
(C) 페인트 작업자 만나기
(D) 용품 찾아오기

해설 어윈 씨의 오후 1시 17분 메시지에서 루퍼트 씨의 집을 칠할 물품 비용 추산을 막 끝마쳐서 우리는 입찰 준비가 됐다(I just finished estimating the cost of the supplies for painting Ms. Rupert's house, so our bid is ready to go)라고 했으므로 칠 작업을 위한 물품 비용 추산을 마쳤음을 알 수 있다. 따라서 정답은 (B)이다.

154 의도 파악

번역 오후 1시 23분에 잘츠만 씨가 "좋은 생각이군요"라고 쓸 때, 그 의도는 무엇인가?

(A) 고객에게 몇 가지 선택사항을 주고 싶어 한다.
(B) 어윈 씨가 제안한 업체가 마음에 든다.
(C) 프로젝트 시작을 연기할 것이다.
(D) 어윈 씨를 위해 일정을 확인할 것이다.

해설 어윈 씨가 오후 1시 22분 메시지에서 가능한 시작 날짜 몇 개를 보내서 그녀에게 다양한 선택의 여지를 주면 어떨까(why don't I send her several possible start dates so that she can have a range of options)라고 하며 작업 시작 날짜에 대해 선택의 여지를 주자는 제안을 하고 있다. 이에 대해 잘츠만 씨가 좋은 생각(Good idea)이라며 동의를 표하고 있으므로, 정답은 (A)이다.

▶▶ Paraphrasing　지문의 **a range of options**
　　　　　　　　　→ 정답의 **some choices**

155-157 회람

즉각 실시되는 방침으로, 그 해 사용하지 않은 유급 휴가를 다음 해로 이월하는 것에 제한이 있을 것입니다. 직원들은 이전에 누적된 휴가 시간의 절반만 이월할 수 있습니다. **155**이 변경 사항은 병가나 흔치 않은 각종 휴가 등 무급 휴가에는 적용되지 않습니다.

156저희는 이 방침을 연초에 알림으로써 휴가 계획이 별 무리 없이 조정되기를 바랍니다. 만약 조정이 필요하면, 훨씬 전에 조정하시기 바랍니다.

방침에 관한 더 자세한 내용은 개정된 회사 편람을 참고하십시오. 오늘 아침 수신함에 들어갔을 겁니다. **157**받지 못하신 분은 내선 302로 제게 연락 주세요. 이 정책에 관해 문의하기 전에 규정을 먼저 읽어 보시기 바랍니다.

감사합니다.

조애나 도

어휘 immediately 즉시　limit 제한　paid vacation (time) 유급 휴가　roll over 이월하다, 연장하다　previously 이전에　accrued 누적된, 축적된　apply to ~에 적용되다　medical leave 병가　modify 수정하다, 변경하다　adjustment 조정, 조절　far in advance 훨씬 미리, 사전에　refer to ~을 참고하다　extension 내선 번호　submit 제출하다　inquiry 문의, 질문

155 사실 관계 확인

번역 병가에 대해 명시된 것은?

(A) 모든 유형의 직원들이 다 사용할 수는 없다.
(B) 의사의 통지가 필요하지 않다.
(C) 직원들이 자주 사용하지 않는다.
(D) 직원들이 보상을 받지 못한다.

해설 첫 번째 단락 마지막 문장에서 이 변경 사항은 병가나 흔치 않은 각종 휴가 등 무급 휴가에는 적용되지 않는다(This change does not apply to unpaid types of time off, such as medical leave and some less common varieties)고 했다. 이를 통해 병가는 무급 휴가임을 알 수 있으므로, 정답은 (D)이다.

▶▶ Paraphrasing　지문의 **unpaid**
　　　　　　　　　→ 정답의 **are not compensated**

156 세부 사항

번역 회람에 따르면, 직원들이 해야 할 일은 무엇인가?

(A) 도 씨에게 서류 제출하기
(B) 휴가 일정 조정하기
(C) 일부 경비 사전 승인받기
(D) 회사 규정에 대한 연례 교육 참석하기

해설 두 번째 단락에서 이 방침을 연초에 알림으로써 휴가 계획이 별 무리 없이 조정되기를 바라며, 조정이 필요하면 훨씬 전에 조정하라(We hope that by announcing this policy early in the year, vacation plans may be modified without much trouble. If an adjustment is necessary, please make it far in advance)고 했다. 따라서 직원들에게 휴가 일정 조정을 권하고 있으므로, 정답은 (B)이다.

▶▶ Paraphrasing　지문의 **vacation plans**
　　　　　　　　　→ 정답의 **vacation schedules**
　　　　　　　　　지문의 **an adjustment** → 정답의 **Rearrange**

157 문장 삽입

번역 [1], [2], [3], [4]로 표시된 곳 중에서 다음 문장이 들어가기에 가장 적합한 곳은?

"오늘 아침 수신함에 들어갔을 겁니다."

(A) [1]
(B) [2]
(C) [3]
(D) [4]

해설 삽입 문장이 오늘 아침에 편지를 보냈다는 내용이므로 수신에 관한 내용이 있는 곳을 찾아본다. 세 번째 단락 두 번째 문장에서 받지 못한 사람은 내선 302로 연락하라는 내용이 있으므로, 이 앞에 들어가는 것이 가장 자연스럽다. 따라서 정답은 (C)이다.

158-160 공지

공지

158, 160케트론 그린 콘도 주민들은 3월 26일 오후 7시에 본관 102호에 모여 곧 있을 공사 프로젝트에 대해 논의할 예정입니다.

최근 단지 이사회에서는 불필요한 물 사용을 줄이기 위해 서쪽 입구 근처에 있는 인공 폭포를 철거하기로 결정했습니다. **159**이사회에서는 몇 가지 선택 사항들을 검토한 후 중요한 인물의 조각상이 빈 공간을 이용하기에 보기 좋겠다고 결정했습니다. 이는 또한 장기간 유지비가 적게 든다는 이점도 있습니다.

따라서 직접 만나 논의하는 목적은 모든 단지 주민들이 나중에 선정할 수 있도록 조각상의 주제 목록을 작성하는 것입니다. ¹⁶⁰참석자 여러분은 미리 가능한 후보 목록을 조사해 보시고, 찬성하는 이유를 간단히 준비해 오시기 바랍니다.

감사합니다.

어휘 resident 주민 construction 건설, 공사 complex (아파트·공장 등의) 단지 board of directors 이사회 artificial waterfall 인공 폭포 reduce 줄이다 unnecessary 불필요한 usage 사용 sculpture 조각 figure 인물 attractive 매력 있는, 보기에 좋은 vacant 빈, 비어 있는 affordable (값이) 알맞은, 저렴한 long-term 장기(의) maintenance cost 유지비 come up with ~을 생각해 내다, 제시하다 shortlist 최종 (후보자) 명단 attendee 참석자 potential 잠재적인, ~의 가능성이 있는 in advance 미리, 사전에 in one's favor ~에게 유리하게

158 주제 / 목적

번역 공지의 목적은 무엇인가?
(A) 주민들에게 불편을 알리기 위해
(B) **주민들에게 곧 있을 모임을 알리기 위해**
(C) 이사회의 신임 이사를 환영하기 위해
(D) 환경 보존 캠페인을 지지하기 위해

해설 첫 번째 단락 첫 문장에서 케트론 그린 콘도 주민들은 3월 26일 오후 7시에 본관 102호에 모여 곧 있을 공사 프로젝트에 대해 논의할 예정 (gather in room 102 of the main building on March 26 at 7 P.M. for a special discussion on an upcoming construction project)이라고 했으므로, 정답은 (B)이다.

159 사실 관계 확인

번역 주거 단지에 관해 명시된 것은?
(A) **부지에 동상이 설치될 것이다.**
(B) 입구 중 하나가 임시 폐쇄될 것이다.
(C) 건물 관리 직원을 추가로 고용했다.
(D) 배수관이 파손되었다.

해설 두 번째 단락 중반부에서 이사회가 몇 가지 선택 사항들을 검토한 후 중요한 인물의 조각상이 빈 공간을 이용하기에 보기 좋겠다고 결정했다 (After considering several options, the board decided that a sculpture of an important figure would be an attractive use of the vacant space)고 했으므로, 정답은 (A)이다.

▶▶ **Paraphrasing** 지문의 **a sculpture** → 정답의 **A statue**

160 세부 사항

번역 주민들은 3월 26일 전에 무엇을 하라는 요청을 받는가?
(A) **제안 발전시키기**
(B) 동의서에 서명하기
(C) 단지 직원 방문하기
(D) 공동 구역에 있는 물건 치우기

해설 첫 번째 단락을 보면 주민들은 3월 26일에 공사 프로젝트를 논의한다는 것을 알 수 있다. 그리고 세 번째 단락 마지막 문장에서 참석자들은 미리 가능한 후보 목록을 조사해 보고, 찬성하는 이유를 간단히 준비해 오라(We urge attendees to research potential candidates in advance and prepare brief arguments in their favor)고 했으므로, 정답은 (A)이다.

161-163 기사

전국적인 숙박 일수 증가

더블린 (6월 23일)—아일랜드 통계청(SI)에서는 5월 내내 전국 숙박업체들의 투숙객이 약간 증가했다고 발표했다. ¹⁶¹SI 대변인에 따르면 투숙객의 증가는 주로 해외 여행객들 덕분이었다. 이 여행객들은 숙박 시설에서 470만 일을 보냈는데, 이는 작년 같은 달에 비해 1.8% 증가한 것이다. 이는 국내 여행객들의 투숙일이 2.3% 감소한 것을 상쇄했는데, 국내 여행객들의 투숙일은 260만 일로 하락했다.

SI는 또 가장 인기 있었던 숙박 시설의 유형도 발표했다. ¹⁶²호텔이 30%로, 가장 많은 일일 숙박을 차지했다. 하지만, 이 수치는 사실 작년 같은 달에 비해 다소 하락한 것이었다. 캠프장 같은 야외 숙박 시설(16%)뿐만 아니라 게스트하우스(23%), 유스 호스텔(11%)과 같은 좀 더 저렴한 시설에서의 일일 숙박 비율이 약간 증가했다.

¹⁶³여행객의 활동과 비용에 관한 세부 사항들을 포함하여 SI가 조사한 상세한 결과에 대해서는 IBN 방송 '아일랜드 이슈'의 오늘밤 에피소드에서 다룰 것이다.

어휘 nationwide 전국적인 guest night (호텔의 고객) 일일 숙박 accommodation 숙박 (시설) surge 급증, 폭증 spokesperson 대변인 due to ~ 때문에 overseas 해외 offset 상쇄하다 domestic 국내의 proportion 비율 alternative 선택, 대안 campground 캠프장, 야영지 detail 상세, 세부 사항 expenditure 지출, 경비, 비용

161 사실 관계 확인

번역 고객 숙박 일수 증가에 관해 명시된 것은?
(A) 음식점에서의 소비 감소를 상쇄했다.
(B) **해외 여행객들로 인해 증가했다.**
(C) 6월에 일어난 일이었다.
(D) 470만 유로의 추가 수익이 발생했다.

해설 첫 번째 단락 두 번째 문장에서 전국 숙박 시설에서 투숙객이 증가한 이유는 주로 해외 여행객 덕분(the increase was mainly due to visitors from overseas)이라고 했으므로, 정답은 (B)이다.

▶▶ **Paraphrasing** 지문의 **visitors from overseas** → 정답의 **international travelers**

162 세부 사항

번역 어떤 유형의 숙박 시설에서 숙박 비율이 증가하지 않았는가?
(A) **호텔**
(B) 게스트하우스
(C) 유스 호스텔
(D) 캠프장

해설 두 번째 단락의 두 번째 문장에서 호텔이 30%로, 가장 많은 숙박 비율을 차지했지만, 이는 작년 같은 달에 비해 다소 하락(a slight drop from the same month last year)한 것이었다고 했다. 따라서 정답은 (A)이다.

163 세부 사항

번역 기사문에 따르면, 독자들은 어디에서 이 주제에 관한 더 많은 정보를 얻을 수 있는가?
(A) 웹사이트를 방문해서
(B) 보고서 출력물을 주문해서
(C) TV 쇼를 시청해서
(D) 강의에 참석해서

해설 마지막 단락에서 SI가 조사한 상세한 결과에 대해서는 IBN 방송 '아일랜드 이슈'의 오늘밤 에피소드에서 다룰 것(on tonight's episode of *Ireland Issues*, broadcast by IBN)이라고 했으므로, 정답은 (C)이다.

▶▶ **Paraphrasing** 지문의 **tonight's episode of Ireland Issues, broadcast by IBN**
→ 정답의 **a television show**

164-167 온라인 채팅

> **다니엘라 레이 [오전 10:16]**
> 팀원 여러분, 문제가 생겼어요. ¹⁶⁵세미나실 조명 상태가 좋지 않아 결국 그곳에서는 일대일 팀원 인터뷰를 촬영하기 어려울 것 같아요.
>
> **질리안 허프 [오전 10:17]**
> 그것이 문제가 될 줄 알았어요. 블라인드를 내리고 천장 조명을 사용하면 어때요?
>
> **다니엘라 레이 [오전 10:19]**
> 흠… ¹⁶⁴아주 밝은 책상용 램프를 갖고 계신 분 있나요? 아직도 펠릭스의 얼굴에 달갑지 않은 그림자가 있네요.
>
> **수잔 민 [오전 10:20]**
> 아, 하나 있어요. 잠시만 기다리세요.
>
> **다니엘라 레이 [오전 10:21]**
> 고마워요, 수잔.
>
> **이오시프 사도비치 [오전 10:21]**
> 다니엘라, 미안하지만 이 모든 일들이 왜 아직 해결되지 않은 거죠? ¹⁶⁵제 일정표에 따르면 이미 펠릭스의 동영상을 찍기 시작했어야 해요.
>
> **다니엘라 레이 [오전 10:22]**
> ¹⁶⁶음, 세미나실 의자가 기획 회의에서 모두가 말한 것처럼 포개어 쌓아 올릴 수 있지 않다는 사실을 알게 됐습니다. 그래서 저희 두 명이 의자를 최대한 뒤쪽 창고로 끌고 가서 자리를 치워야 했어요.
>
> **이오시프 사도비치 [오전 10:22]**
> 알겠습니다. 이후에는 우리가 그것을 기억해야 할 겁니다.
>
> **다니엘라 레이 [오전 10:26]**
> 알겠습니다. 수잔의 램프가 꼭 맞네요. 이제 준비가 다 됐습니다. 배경은 좋고, 걸어 둔 담요 덕분에 방이 따뜻하고, 펠릭스는 준비가 됐어요.
>
> **이오시프 사도비치 [오전 10:27]**
> 안심이네요. 촬영이 잘 진행되길 바랍니다. ¹⁶⁷아, 일정이 끝나면 영상을 회사 서버에 올려서 제가 내일 아침에 검토할 수 있도록 해 주세요. 물론 모든 영상을 다 올릴 필요는 없고, 각 부분에서 제일 훌륭한 것들만 올려 주세요. 제 피드백은 이메일로 보내겠습니다.

어휘 one-on-one 일대일 unflattering 어울리지 않는, 호의적이지 않은 stackable 포개서 쌓아 올릴 수 있는 backdrop 배경 relief 안도, 안심 footage 화면, 영상

164 의도 파악

번역 오전 10시 20분에 민 씨가 "하나 있어요"라고 쓸 때, 그 의도는 무엇인가?
(A) 아직 고려하지 않은 아이디어가 있다.
(B) 물건 수리 방법을 알고 있다.
(C) 레이 씨에게 물건을 빌려줄 수 있다.
(D) 레이 씨와 같은 문제가 있다.

해설 레이 씨가 오전 10시 19분 메시지에서 아주 밝은 책상용 램프를 갖고 계신 분 있나요(does anyone have a really bright desk lamp, maybe)라고 하며 책상용 램프를 빌려줄 것을 요청하고 있다. 이에 대해 민 씨가 하나 있다(I've got one)며 긍정의 응답을 하고 있으므로, 정답은 (C)이다.

165 추론 / 암시

번역 펠릭스는 누구이겠는가?
(A) 화상회의 사회자
(B) 레이 씨의 팀원
(C) 객원 기술 컨설턴트
(D) 레이 씨 회사의 회장

해설 레이 씨의 오전 10시 16분 메시지, 세미나실 조명 상태가 좋지 않아 결국 그곳에서는 일대일 팀원 인터뷰를 촬영하기 어려울 것 같다(It looks like the lighting in the seminar room isn't going to be good enough to allow us to film the one-on-one team member interviews in there after all)와 사도비치 씨의 오전 10시 21분 메시지에서 제 일정표에 따르면 이미 펠릭스의 동영상을 찍기 시작했어야 한다(My schedule says you should have started filming Felix's video already)를 통해 펠릭스는 레이 씨의 팀원임을 유추할 수 있으므로, 정답은 (B)이다.

166 세부 사항

번역 준비 과정이 지연된 이유는 무엇인가?
(A) 보조자가 잘못된 장소로 갔다.
(B) 장비 일부가 창고에 있었다.
(C) 회의실이 세미나에 이용되고 있었다.
(D) 일부 가구를 옮겨야 했다.

해설 레이 씨의 오전 10시 22분 메시지, 세미나실 의자가 기획 회의에서 모두가 말한 것처럼 포개어 쌓아 올릴 수 있지 않다는 사실을 알게 됐다. 그래서 두 명이 의자를 최대한 뒤쪽 창고로 끌고 가서 자리를 치워야 했다(Well, it turned out that the seminar room chairs aren't stackable like everyone said at the planning meeting. The two of us had to drag most of them to the back storage room to clear out some space)를 통해 의자를 옮기는 작업 때문에 촬영이 지연되었음을 알 수 있으므로, 정답은 (D)이다.

▶▶ **Paraphrasing** 지문의 **the seminar room chairs**
→ 정답의 **Some furniture**
지문의 **had to drag**
→ 정답의 **had to be moved**

167 세부 사항

번역 사도비치 씨는 무엇을 하고 싶다고 말하는가?
(A) 회사 전체 이메일 전송하기
(B) 소셜미디어 페이지에 파일 업로드하기
(C) 피드백 읽기
(D) 동영상 일부 시청하기

해설 사도비치 씨의 오전 10시 27분 메시지, 일정이 끝나면 영상을 회사 서버에 올려서 제가 내일 아침에 검토할 수 있도록 해달라(remember to upload the footage to the company server at the end of the day so I can look over it tomorrow morning)를 통해 사도비치 씨가 영상 검토를 원한다는 것을 알 수 있으므로, 정답은 (D)이다.

▶▶ **Paraphrasing** 지문의 **the footage** → 정답의 **some videos**
지문의 **look over** → 정답의 **View**

168-171 이메일

수신: 트래비스 자레트
발신: 머나 애덤스
날짜: 10월 10일
제목: 신나는 소식

자레트 씨에게,

킹스턴 월콧 서비스를 이용해 주신 소중한 고객에 대한 감사의 표시로, 저희는 로빈슨 앤 자레트 어소시에이츠에 저희의 기쁜 소식을 가장 먼저 알려 드리고자 합니다. 저희는 서비스 패키지의 폭을 대폭 확장하고 있습니다. **168저희는 향후 경비 관리 서비스 외에 실외 관리 서비스도 곧 제공할 예정입니다.** 귀사는 저희가 건물 내부를 얼마나 성심성의껏 관리하는지 봐 오셨습니다. 이제 실외도 저희가 책임지겠습니다. **169저희의 확충된, 자격증을 완비한 인력은 지역 인가 요건에서 요구하는 이상의 교육을 이수했습니다.** 이것은 저희가 고객들에게 최상의 최첨단 서비스를 제공하는 것을 가능하게 합니다.

170저희의 새로운 서비스를 이용하기로 선택하신다면, 킹스턴 월콧에서는 현재 고객에게만 적용되는 할인 가격도 제공합니다. 실외 서비스와 실내 서비스를 결합한 비용은 월 17,000 자메이카 달러입니다. 각각 별도로 이용하실 경우 거의 총 22,000 자메이카 달러가 든다는 것을 고려하면, 매월 5,000 자메이카 달러를 절약할 수 있습니다. **171또한, 저희는 11월 5일부터 서비스를 제공해 드릴 수 있는데, 11월 5일은 귀사의 다음 달 청구 기간의 시작일입니다.**

저희는 귀사의 필요에 좀 더 부응하기를 바랍니다. 서비스를 이용할 의향이 있으시면 555-0194로 제게 연락 주시기 바랍니다.

머나 애덤스
킹스턴 월콧 서비스 판매 대리인

어휘 valued 귀중한, 존중되는 expand 확장하다, 확대하다 maintenance 관리, 유지 보수 on top of ~뿐만 아니라, ~ 외에 janitorial 관리인의, 수위의 conscientiously 양심적으로, 성심껏 responsibility 책임, 임무 enlarge 확충하다, 확대하다 certified 공인된, 자격증을 갖춘 workforce 노동력, 전체 종업원 수 licensing requirements 인가[허가] 요건 cutting-edge 최첨단의 make use of ~을 이용하다 reduced rate 할인 요금 exclusively ~만을 위한, 전용으로 combined 결합한 considering (that) ~을 고려하면 individually 개별적으로 savings 저축한 돈, 자금

168 주제 / 목적

번역 홍보하고 있는 서비스 중 한 가지는 무엇인가?
(A) 구내식당 운영
(B) 부지 관리
(C) 건물 보안
(D) 개별 교통 수단

해설 첫 번째 단락의 세 번째 문장에서 경비 관리 서비스 외에 실외 관리 서비스도 곧 제공할 예정(Starting immediately, we will offer outdoor maintenance services on top of our janitorial packages)이라고 했으므로, 정답은 (B)이다.

▶▶ **Paraphrasing** 지문의 **outdoor maintenance services** → 정답의 **Groundskeeping**

169 세부 사항

번역 킹스턴 월콧 서비스에 대해 강조된 것은?
(A) 넓은 지역까지 확장되었다.
(B) 본사가 이전 중이다.
(C) 실시간 업데이트를 제공한다.
(D) 직원들이 교육을 잘 받았다.

해설 첫 번째 단락의 끝에서 두 번째 문장에서 확충된, 자격증을 완비한 인력은 지역 인가 요건에서 요구하는 이상의 교육을 이수했다(Our enlarged, fully-certified workforce has been provided with training that goes far beyond local licensing requirements)고 했으므로, 정답은 (D)이다.

170 세부 사항

번역 이메일에 따르면 자레트 씨는 무엇을 할 자격이 있는가?
(A) 기존 회원들을 위한 할인 받기
(B) 전용 회계 담당자 요청하기
(C) 한 달 무료 서비스 받기
(D) 시설 견학 참여하기

해설 두 번째 단락 첫 번째 문장에서 새로운 서비스를 이용하기로 선택하면, 킹스턴 월콧에서는 현재 고객에게만 적용되는 할인 가격도 제공한다(Should you choose to make use of our new services, Kingston Walcott will even offer you a reduced rate available exclusively to current customers)고 했으므로, 정답은 (A)이다.

▶▶ **Paraphrasing** 지문의 **a reduced rate** → 정답의 **a discount**
지문의 **current customers** → 정답의 **existing customers**

171 세부 사항

번역 11월 5일에 무슨 일이 있을 것인가?
(A) 공식적으로 회사를 출범시킬 것이다.
(B) 재정 주기가 새로 시작될 것이다.
(C) 시연회가 있을 것이다.
(D) 체험 기간이 시작될 것이다.

해설 두 번째 단락의 마지막 문장에서 11월 5일부터 서비스를 제공할 수 있는데, 11월 5일은 로빈슨 앤 자레트 어소시에이츠의 다음 달 청구 기간의 시작일(November 5, the beginning of your next billing period)이라고 했다. 따라서 정답은 (B)이다.

familiarize 익숙하게 하다   shortcut 지름길, 손쉬운 방법
significantly 상당히   productivity 생산성   polished 세련된,
우수한   persuasive 설득력이 있는   function 기능   longtime
오랫동안의

172-175 웹페이지

http://www.beezleyeducation.com/mostpopular

비즐레이 에듀케이션

비즐레이 에듀케이션에서는 전문 단체들을 위해 현장 세미나를 실시합니다. **175**다양한 대인 관계 기술과 기술적인 능력을 다루는 저희 강좌는 전문 강사들이 교육합니다. 그 강사들은 해당 과목에 대해 수년간의 경력을 갖추고 있습니다.

아래 열거된 네 가지 세미나가 가장 인기 있습니다. 전체 강좌 목록은 여기에서 볼 수 있습니다. **172**특정 세미나에 대해 문의 사항이 있으시면, 관련 분야의 코디네이터에게 이메일을 보내세요. 세미나 일정을 정하실 준비가 되셨으면 이 양식을 작성하세요.

비즈니스 기술 172(코디네이터: 줄리엔 지토, j.zito@beezleyeducation.com)

173팀워크 기초 원리
이 세미나는 팀에게 효율적으로 함께 일하는 데 필요한 능력을 부여해 줍니다. 개성이 다른 사람들끼리 상호 작용하는 방법을 다루며, 의사소통 방식을 인지하는 법을 가르쳐 드립니다. **173**참석자들은 브레인스토밍과 갈등 해소에 관련된 시나리오를 실연합니다.

효과적인 관리
단체의 규모에 상관 없이 부서장이나 관리자들을 대상으로 하는 이 세미나는 아래 직원들과 좋은 관계를 유지하면서 권위를 지킬 수 있는 방법에 관해 알려 드립니다. 효과적으로 업무를 평가하는 것에 특히 중점을 둡니다.

컴퓨터 기술 (코디네이터: 그레이스 아데나이크, g.adenaike@beezleyeducation.com)
174귀사의 컴퓨터에 적당한 프로그램이 설치되어 있지 않다면, 추후 개별적으로 연습할 수 있도록 참석자들에게 인쇄된 설명서를 드릴 것입니다.

딜릴 데스크톱 출판 소프트웨어
이 세미나는 거의 상급 수준의 사용자들에게 유용할 것입니다. 참가자들이 딜릴에서 제공하는 다양한 툴에 정통하도록 해 줄 것이며, 또한 생산성을 상당히 증대시킬 수 있는 지름길도 알려 줄 것입니다.

페미아 프레젠테이션 소프트웨어
이 세미나에서는 매끄럽고 설득력 있는 프레젠테이션을 할 수 있도록 페미아 사용법을 설명해 드립니다. 오랫동안 페미아를 사용해 온 사용자들이 속도를 높일 수 있도록 소프트웨어의 더 새로워진 기능에 대한 섹션도 있습니다.

어휘 on-site 현지의, 현장의 a range of 다양한 interpersonal 대인 관계의, 사람과 사람 사이의 expert 전문가; 전문적인, 숙련된 relevant 관련된, 적절한 set up (시간을) 정하다, 준비하다 fill out 작성하다 efficiently 효율적으로 interact 상호 작용하다, 영향을 미치다 awareness 인식, 자각, 인지 dispute 갈등, 논쟁 supervisor 관리자, 상사 authority 권위자 cordial 다정한, 진심에서 우러나는 subordinate 하급자, 부하 effective 효과적인 performance evaluation 인사 고과 be equipped with ~을 갖추고 있다 instructions (사용) 설명서 advanced 고급의, 상급의

172 세부 사항

번역 웹페이지에 따르면, 독자들은 지토 씨에게 무엇을 요청할 수 있는가?
(A) 현장 세미나 준비하기
(B) 폭넓게 제공하는 회사 강좌 목록 등재하기
(C) 특정 세미나에 대한 세부 사항 제공하기
(D) 웹페이지의 기술적인 문제 해결하기

해설 두 번째 단락의 두 번째 문장에서 특정 세미나에 대해 문의 사항이 있으면, 관련 분야의 코디네이터에게 이메일을 보내라(For more information about a particular offering, send an e-mail to the relevant field coordinator)고 했으며, 세 번째 단락의 Coordinator: Julien Zito, j.zito@j.zito@beezleyeducation.com에서 지토 씨가 코디네이터임을 알 수 있다. 따라서 정답은 (C)이다.

173 사실 관계 확인

번역 팀워크 기초 원리 세미나의 일부로 언급된 것은?
(A) 성격 테스트 받기
(B) 동료 평가서 작성하기
(C) 그룹 목표 정하기
(D) 역할극에 참여하기

해설 세 번째 단락의 마지막 문장에서 팀워크 기초 원리 세미나의 참석자들은 브레인스토밍과 갈등 해소에 관련된 시나리오를 실연한다(Participants act out scenarios related to brainstorming and conflict resolution.)고 했으므로, 정답은 (D)이다.

▶▶ **Paraphrasing**   지문의 **act out scenarios** → 정답의 **role plays**

174 추론 / 암시

번역 컴퓨터 기술 세미나에 관해 암시된 것은?
(A) 소프트웨어 초보 사용자들에게는 적절하지 않다.
(B) 고객 선호도에 따라 세미나를 단축할 수도 있다.
(C) 비즐레이 에듀케이션은 세미나용 소프트웨어를 제공하지 않는다.
(D) 콘텐츠는 개인 지도를 통해서도 이용 가능하다.

해설 다섯 번째 단락에서 컴퓨터에 적당한 프로그램이 설치되어 있지 않으면 추후 개별적으로 연습할 수 있도록 참석자들에게 인쇄된 설명서를 준다(Please be advised that if your organization's computers are not equipped with the appropriate programs, participants will receive printed instructions)고 했다. 따라서 비즐레이 에듀케이션은 세미나를 위해 소프트웨어를 제공하지는 않는다는 것을 알 수 있으므로, 정답은 (C)이다.

175 문장 삽입

번역 [1], [2], [3], [4]로 표시된 곳 중에서 다음 문장이 들어가기에 가장 적합한 곳은?

"그 강사들은 해당 과목에 대해 수년간의 경력을 갖추고 있습니다."

(A) [1]
(B) [2]
(C) [3]
(D) [4]

해설 삽입 문장의 Each one이 무엇인지를 우선 파악해야 한다. Each one 이 해당 과목에 대해 수년간의 경력을 갖추고 있다고 했으므로, 강사들을 가리키는 말임을 짐작할 수 있다. [1] 바로 앞에 전문 강사들(expert lecturers)에 관해 언급했으므로 그 뒤에 삽입문의 내용이 이어지는 것이 자연스럽다. 따라서 정답은 (A)이다.

176-180 웹페이지 + 주문서

http://cierrasonthelake.com/catering

시에라스 온 더 레이크
출장 요리 패키지

177저희 출장 요리 패키지를 이용하시면 가렐 지역 내 어디에서든 시에라스 온 더 레이크의 군침 도는 요리를 맛보실 수 있습니다. 출장 요리 패키지는 세심하게 개발되었으며 아주 맛있으면서 균형 잡힌 식사로 구성되어 있습니다. **177**저희 식당 내에서 제공하는 식사와 마찬가지로, 가능한 한 신선함을 유지하기 위해 요리 재료는 가렐에 본사를 둔 업체에서 공급받습니다.

시에라스 온 더 레이크의 전문적인 물류 관리와 서비스로 고객들은 여유로운 **178**방식으로 먹는 즐거움을 누릴 수 있습니다. 뷔페를 선택하시든 자리에 앉아 먹는 식사를 선택하시든, 저희 직원들이 재빠르게 준비하고 치울 것이며, 도중에 생길 수 있는 문제를 가까이에서 처리할 것입니다. **176**하지만 저희는 음식 외에 접시, 유리컵, 포크와 수저, 그리고 냅킨만 제공해 드린다는 점에 유의하십시오.

웹페이지 하단에 제시되어 있는 연중 패키지 외에도, 여름철을 위해 특별히 고안된 두 가지 메뉴도 제공해 드립니다.

서머 프레시	서머 디럭스
콜드 치킨, 과일 샐러드, 그린 샐러드와 (통째) 구운 옥수수. 한여름 무더위를 식히기에 딱 좋은 요리.	구운 햄버거, 과일 샐러드, 그린 샐러드, 마카로니 샐러드와 (통째) 구운 옥수수. **179**전기를 이용할 수 있어야 함.

이 패키지에는 흔히 제공되는 음료 외에도 손으로 짠 레모네이드가 함께 나옵니다.

어휘 catering 출장 연회, 출장 요리 mouth-watering 군침이 도는 cuisine 요리(법) complimentary 칭찬하는, 찬사의 ingredient (요리의) 재료 supplier 공급업체 guarantee 보장[보증]하다, 확실히 하다 logistics 물류 관리, 상세한 계획 expertise 전문 지식[기술] edible 식용이 되는, 먹을 수 있는 leisurely 여유 있는, 한가로운 opt 선택하다 sit-down meal 의자에 앉아 먹는 식사 on hand 가까이에, 눈앞에 in between 중간에, 틈에 take care of ~을 처리하다 non-food 식료품 이외의 cutlery (나이프·포크·숟가락 등의) 날붙이류 year-round 연중 계속되는 devise 고안하다 cob 옥수수 속대 cool down 식히다 access 접속, 이용 권리 electricity 전기 hand-squeezed 손으로 짠

시에라스 온 더 레이크
출장 요리 주문서

고객명: 마자 카민스키	전화: (651) 555-0190
179패키지: 서머 디럭스	인원: 24
180서빙 방법: 뷔페 ✓	좌식 스타일 ___
날짜: 7월 29일	행사 시간*: 오후 1시 - 오후 3시
장소: 가렐 랭거 로드 1002, MN 55076	

특별 지시 사항: 정문 바로 앞에 주차하세요.

주문 접수자: 이안 오브라이언
담당자: 칼렙 아메스

* 행사 시간에 준비 및 청소 시간은 포함되지 않음

어휘 order form 주문 양식, 주문서 duration 지속 시간

176 추론 / 암시

번역 시에라스 온 더 레이크에 관해 암시된 것은?
(A) 가족이 운영하는 식당이다.
(B) 공식 행사에는 출장 요리를 제공하지 않는다.
(C) 최근에 출장 요리 사업에 진출했다.
(D) 손님용 좌석을 제공하지 않는다.

해설 첫 번째 지문의 두 번째 단락 마지막 문장에서 음식 외에는 접시, 유리컵, 포크와 수저, 그리고 냅킨만 제공한다(Please note, however, that the only non-food items we provide are plates, glasses, cutlery, and napkins)고 했으므로, 시에라스 온 더 레이크에서는 손님용 좌석을 마련해 주지 않는다는 것을 알 수 있다. 따라서 정답은 (D)이다.

▶▶ **Paraphrasing** 지문의 **provide** → 정답의 **furnish**

177 세부 사항

번역 시에라스 온 더 레이크는 음식 품질을 보장하기 위해 무엇을 하는가?
(A) 유기농 재료로 요리한다.
(B) 지역 판매상에서 구입한다.
(C) 자주 점검한다.
(D) 특별한 냉장 시스템을 이용한다.

해설 첫 번째 지문의 첫 번째 단락 첫 문장에서 출장 요리 패키지를 이용하면 가렐 지역 내 어디에서든 시에라스 온 더 레이크의 군침 도는 요리를 맛볼 수 있다(Our catering packages let you experience the mouth-watering cuisine of Cierra's on the Lake in any location within the Garrell area)고 했다. 따라서 이 식당은 가렐 지역에서 영업함을 알 수 있고, 같은 단락 마지막 문장에서 신선함을 유지하기 위해 요리 재료는 가렐에 본사를 둔 공급업체에서 받는다(the ingredients are obtained from Garrell-based suppliers to guarantee that they are as fresh as possible)고 했다. 따라서 같은 지역에서 재료를 공급받는다는 것을 알 수 있으므로, 정답은 (B)이다.

▶▶ **Paraphrasing** 지문의 **Garrell-based suppliers** → 정답의 **from local vendors**

Test 6

178 동의어 찾기

번역 웹페이지에서 두 번째 단락 2행의 "fashion"과 의미가 가장 가까운 단어는?
(A) 경향
(B) 틀
(C) 방식
(D) 범주

해설 in a leisurely fashion은 '여유롭게, 느긋하게'라는 의미이다. fashion은 '방식, 방법'이라는 의미로 쓰였으므로, 정답은 (C) manner이다.

179 연계

번역 카민스키 씨의 행사에서 출장 요리 업체는 무엇을 하겠는가?
(A) 닭 요리 차리기
(B) 두 시간만 머물기
(C) 전원 쓰기
(D) 실내에 주차하기

해설 두 번째 지문인 출장 요리 주문서를 보면 카민스키 씨는 서머 디럭스 패키지(Package: Summer Deluxe)를 선택했으며, 첫 번째 지문에서 서머 디럭스 패키지는 전기를 이용할 수 있어야 한다(Requires access to electricity)고 했다. 따라서 카민스키 씨 행사의 출장 요리 업체는 전원을 사용할 것임을 알 수 있으므로, 정답은 (C)이다.

▶▶ **Paraphrasing** 지문의 **Requires access to electricity.**
→ 정답의 **Use a power source**

180 사실 관계 확인

번역 주문서에 따르면, 카민스키 씨의 손님에 대해 사실인 것은?
(A) 결혼식에 초대되었다.
(B) 특별식을 요청했다.
(C) 음식을 스스로 가져다 먹기 위해 자리를 뜰 것이다.
(D) 오브라이언 씨에게 연락할 것이다.

해설 출장 요리 주문서를 보면 카민스키 씨는 서빙 방법으로 뷔페(Serving method: Buffet ✓)를 선택했으므로, 카민스키 씨의 손님들은 직접 음식을 가져다 먹을 것임을 알 수 있다. 따라서 정답은 (C)이다.

181-185 이메일 + 이메일

수신: 클린트 바이메르
발신: 매들린 스타인
날짜: 4월 10일
제목: 안내책자 출시

바이메르 씨에게,

181국제학생처에서 지난해에 '로이랜드 대학교 국제학생 가이드', 즉 'GRUIS'라고 부르는 종합 안내책자를 다시 제작했습니다. **182A, C**GRUIS에는 기숙사와 아파트, 보편적인 재정 및 언어 문제, 시내 버스 시스템 등의 광범위한 정보를 담고 있습니다. **182B**저희 학생처에서는 심지어 현지 모바일 네트워크 운영업체 직원들과 이야기를 나누어 계약 요건과 판매 상품에 대한 최신 정보까지 확인했습니다. 저희는 GRUIS로 인해 유학생들이 이곳에서 더 쉽고 완벽하게 적응할 수 있을 것이라고 확신합니다.

안내책자 출시를 축하하고 홍보하기 위해, 4월 23일 저녁 7시에 창간 파티를 열 예정입니다. **184**파르지알리 홀의 로비에 오셔서 GRUIS를 가져 가시고, 저희 국장님 또는 국장님께서 불가능하신 경우 제가 진행하는 간단한 프레젠테이션을 참관하세요. **183**로이랜드에서 최고 인기 있는 학생 단체의 회장으로 이 프로젝트에 대한 당신의 후원은 아주 소중합니다. 꼭 참석해 주시기를 바랍니다.

매들린 스타인
국제학생처

> **어휘** booklet 소책자 launch 출시, 개시 rework 재작업하다, 고치다 comprehensive 종합적인, 포괄적인 extensive 광범위한, 다방면에 걸친 dormitory 기숙사 municipal 시의 operator 운영업체 secure 확실하게 하다 up-to-date 최신의 contract requirements 계약 요건 offering 판매 상품 adjust 조정하다 celebrate 기념하다, 축하하다 publicize 공표하다, 발표하다 foyer 호텔, 로비 pick up 가져가다 director 임원, 책임자 unavailable (사람이) 만날 수 없는, 부재의 invaluable 매우 귀중한

수신: 매들린 스타인
발신: 클린트 바이메르
날짜: 4월 26일
제목: Re: 안내책자 출시

스타인 씨에게,

저는 지난밤 출간 파티에서 받은 GRUIS를 살펴볼 기회가 있었는데, 안내책자의 내용에 관한 제 생각을 말씀드리겠습니다. 안내책자에 로이랜드에서의 생활을 아주 잘 소개해 준 것 같아요. **184**스타인 씨가 프레젠테이션에서 말했던 것처럼, 우리 유학생들이 일반적으로 직면할 어려움을 최소화하는 데 도움이 될 겁니다. **185**저는 반드시 적극적으로 그것을 지인들에게 추천하겠습니다. 제가 향후에 국제학생처를 위해 할 수 있는 다른 일이 있으면 알려 주시기 바랍니다.

클린트 바이메르

> **어휘** look over ~을 살펴보다, 검토하다 minimize 최소화하다 challenge 난제, 도전 typically 대개, 일반적으로 face 직면하다 definitely 반드시 enthusiasm 열의, 열정 acquaintance 아는 사람, 친지

181 사실 관계 확인

번역 GRUIS에 대해 명시된 것은?
(A) 학생협회에서 작성했다.
(B) 초기 출판물을 개정한 것이다.
(C) 디지털 방식으로도 배포될 것이다.
(D) 다양한 언어로 발행되고 있다.

해설 첫 번째 지문의 첫 단락 첫 문장에서 국제학생처에서 지난해에 GRUIS를 다시 제작했다(reworking the *Information for International Students* to create a comprehensive booklet called *"Guide to Royland University for International Students"*, or "GRUIS")고 했으므로, 정답은 (B)이다.

▶▶ **Paraphrasing** 지문의 **reworking** → 정답의 **revision**

182 사실 관계 확인

번역 GRUIS에 포함되어 있는 목록이 아닌 것은 무엇인가?
(A) 주택
(B) 휴대전화 서비스
(C) 대중 교통
(D) 채용

해설 첫 번째 지문의 첫 단락, GRUIS에는 기숙사와 아파트(dormitories and apartments), 보편적인 재정 및 언어 문제(common financial and language issues), 시내 버스 시스템(the municipal bus system) 등의 광범위한 정보를 담고 있다고 했으므로 (A), (C)를, 심지어 모바일 네트워크 운영업체 직원들과 이야기를 나누어 계약 요건과 판매 상품에 대한 최신 정보(even spoke with local employees of mobile network operators to secure up-to-date details on their contract requirements and offerings)까지 수록했다고 했으므로 (B)가 있음을 알 수 있다. 채용에 대해서는 명시되어 있지 않으므로, 정답은 (D)이다.

▶▶ **Paraphrasing** 지문의 **dormitories and apartments**
→ 정답의 **Housing**
지문의 **contract requirements and offerings** → 정답의 **Mobile phone service**
지문의 **the municipal bus system**
→ 정답의 **Public transportation**

183 세부 사항

번역 바이메르 씨는 누구인가?
(A) 대학교 동아리 회장
(B) 대학교 관계자
(C) 유학생
(D) 관광학 교수

해설 첫 번째 지문의 두 번째 단락에서 스타인 씨는 로이랜드에서 최고 인기 있는 학생 단체의 회장(the president of one of Royland's most popular student organizations)인 바이메르 씨의 후원은 아주 소중하다고 했다. 따라서 바이메르 씨는 대학교 동아리 회장임을 알 수 있으므로, 정답은 (A)이다.

▶▶ **Paraphrasing** 지문의 **the president of one of Royland's most popular student organizations**
→ 정답의 **A university club leader**

184 연계

번역 창간 파티에 대해 암시된 것은?
(A) 모든 참석자들에게 주기에는 GRUIS가 충분하지 않았다.
(B) 프레젠테이션에 기술적인 문제가 있었다.
(C) 더 큰 건물로 변경되었다.
(D) 관리자가 참석하지 않았다.

해설 첫 번째 지문의 두 번째 단락에서 국장 또는 국장이 불가능할 경우 스타인 씨가 프레젠테이션을 진행할(a short presentation by our director, or by me if the director is unavailable) 것이라고 했다. 두 번째 지문 중반부에서 스타인 씨가 프레젠테이션을 했다(As you said during your presentation)는 것을 알 수 있다. 따라서 관리자가 참석하지 않았다는 것을 알 수 있으므로, 정답은 (D)이다.

▶▶ **Paraphrasing** 지문의 **the director**
→ 정답의 **An administrator**

185 세부 사항

번역 바이메르 씨는 무엇을 하겠다고 말하는가?
(A) 스타인 씨를 지인에게 소개하기
(B) 스타인 씨의 연구 작업 돕기
(C) 다른 사람에게 GRUIS를 읽으라고 조언하기
(D) 향후 GRUIS의 주제 제안하기

해설 두 번째 지문 후반부에서 바이메르 씨는 반드시 적극적으로 그것을 지인들에게 추천하겠다(I will definitely recommend it with enthusiasm to my acquaintances)고 했으므로, 정답은 (C)이다.

▶▶ **Paraphrasing** 지문의 **recommend** → 정답의 **Advise**

186-190 기사 + 보고서 + 이메일

신설 도서관 설문조사 열려

프랜턴 (9월 23일) - 촘슬리 주민들이 가장 가까운 도서관까지 무려 10마일이나 가야 했던 시절이 곧 막을 내릴 것으로 보인다. 어제 데이글렌 카운티 도서관 위원회는 이 지역에 신설 지점 부지로 선정됐다고 발표했다.

위원회는 첫 단계로 촘슬리 주민들이 신설 도서관에 포함되기를 바라는 특징들에 관해 여론조사를 실시할 예정이다. 이후 조사 결과를 프로젝트 제안서에 포함시켜 승인을 위해 카운티 감리위원회에 제출한다.

186, 188 "일곱 번째 지점의 공사와 유지보수로 카운티의 판매세 인상이 필요할지도 모릅니다." 9인 위원회 회장인 코린 스펙의 설명이다. "그래서 흥미로운 제안을 취합하는 것이 저희에게는 매우 중요한 일입니다."

어휘 as much as ~정도까지 많이   come to an end 끝나다
site 부지   commission 위원회   poll 여론조사를 하다
incorporate ~ into ... ~을 …의 일부로 포함시키다   submit
제출하다   board of supervisors 감리위원회   sales tax 판매세

보고서 요약

보스팅 어소시에이츠

보스팅 어소시에이츠는 데이글렌 카운티 도서관 위원회를 대표해 촘슬리 시 주민을 대상으로 신설 카운티 도서관의 잠재적 특징에 대한 설문조사를 실시했다. **187** 9월 28일부터 10월 27일까지 한 달 동안 전화 인터뷰를 통해 653명에게 데이터를 수집했다. 다음의 도표는 설문조사의 주요 결과를 요약한 것이다.

제안된 특징	흥미를 보인 주민 백분율
컴퓨터, 프린터, 스캐너	92%
개인 회의실	85%
189 시청각 자료와 미디어실	**74%**
카페	70%
어린이 놀이 공간	66%
자동 대출/반납 시스템	51%

어휘 on behalf of ~을 대표하여 potential 잠재적인 via ~를 통해, ~에 의해 finding (조사·연구 등의) 결과 respondent 응답자 audiovisual 시청각의 automated 자동화된

발신: 코린 스펙
수신: 도서관 위원회 위원
날짜: 11월 7일
제목: 설문조사 결과
첨부: 보고서

안녕하십니까 여러분,

보스팅 어소시에이츠에서 설문조사 보고서를 전송했습니다. 요약본의 도표에서 보시는 대로 응답자 과반수 이상이 선호하는 여섯 가지 특징이 제안되어 있습니다. **190**그럼에도 불구하고 저는 자동 대출 시스템은 고려하지 않아야 한다고 생각합니다. 선호도가 꽤 낮기 때문입니다. **188**아울러 마지막으로 신설된 러들리스 카운티 도서관에 포함된 사항에서 알 수 있듯이 이 시스템은 그다지 자주 사용되지 않을 것입니다. **189**다른 상위 결과는 대부분 예상했던 내용이나 DVD 및 CD 이용에 대한 요구는 예측했던 것보다 훨씬 많았습니다.

어쨌든 보고서를 검토하시고 다음 수요일에 있을 비공개회의에서 논의하도록 준비해 주시기 바랍니다.

코린

어휘 send over 전송하다 take ~ out of consideration ~을 고려 대상에서 제외하다 inclusion 포함시킨 것 mostly 대부분 predict 예측하다 closed meeting 비공개회의

186 세부 사항

번역 기사에 따르면, 스펙 씨는 무엇이 필요할 수도 있다고 말하는가?
(A) 납세 부담 증가
(B) 도서관 직원 급여 인상
(C) 카운티 부동산 매각
(D) 대책위원회 결성

해설 기사의 마지막 단락에서 일곱 번째 지점의 공사와 유지보수로 카운티의 판매세 인상이 필요할지도 모른다고 9인 위원회 회장인 코린 스펙이 설명했다(Construction and maintenance of a seventh branch would probably require raising the county sales tax," said Corinne Speck, president of the nine-member commission)를 통해 스펙 씨가 말한 판매세 인상의 필요성을 언급하고 있으므로, 정답은 (A)이다.

▶▶ Paraphrasing 지문의 would probably require
→ 질문의 may be necessary
지문의 raising the county sales tax
→ 정답의 An increase in a tax obligation

187 세부 사항

번역 보스팅 어소시에이츠 직원들이 설문조사를 실시한 방법은 무엇인가?
(A) 설문지를 우편으로 보냈다.
(B) 참여자들에게 전화했다.
(C) 촘슬리 주택지를 방문했다.
(D) 카운티 도서관에서 사람들을 면담했다.

해설 보고서의 첫 번째 단락 9월 28일부터 10월 27일까지 한 달 동안 전화 인터뷰를 통해 653명에게 데이터를 수집했다(Data was collected from 653 people via telephone interview during the one-month period from September 28 to October 27)에서 전화 인터뷰를 통한 자료 수집을 언급하고 있으므로, 정답은 (B)이다.

▶▶ Paraphrasing 지문의 Data was collected
→ 질문의 conduct the survey
지문의 via telephone interview
→ 정답의 called

188 연계

번역 러들리스 도서관에 대해 암시된 것은?
(A) 정기적인 이용자 수가 가장 적다.
(B) 촘슬리 시 경계에서 10마일 떨어져 있다.
(C) 건립된 여섯 번째 카운티 도서관이었다.
(D) 자동 대출 단말기를 정지했다.

해설 이메일의 첫 번째 단락에서 아울러 마지막으로 신설된 러들리스 카운티 도서관에 포함된 사항에서 알 수 있듯이 이 시스템은 그다지 자주 사용되지 않을 것이다(Also, as we know from its inclusion in the last new county library in Rudliss, it may not actually be used very often)를 통해 러들리스 카운티에 있는 도서관이 마지막으로 신설되었음을 언급하고 있다. 도서관 건립에 관한 정보는 기사를 통해 확인할 수 있다. 기사의 마지막 단락에서 일곱 번째 지점의 공사와 유지보수로 카운티 판매세 인상이 필요할지도 모른다고 9인 위원회 회장인 코린 스펙이 설명했다("Construction and maintenance of a seventh branch would probably require raising the county sales tax," said Corinne Speck, president of the nine-member commission)를 통해 러들리스 도서관은 여섯 번째로 건립된 도서관임을 유추할 수 있으므로, 정답은 (C)이다.

189 연계

번역 스펙 씨는 도표상의 어떤 수치가 예상 밖이라고 말하는가?
(A) 92% (B) 85%
(C) 74% (D) 70%

해설 스펙 씨가 쓴 이메일의 첫 번째 단락에서 다른 상위 결과는 대부분 예상했던 내용이나 DVD 및 CD 이용에 대한 요구는 예측했던 것보다 훨씬 많았다(The other top results are mostly what we expected, though the demand for access to DVDs and CDs is much greater than we had predicted)고 하며 DVD와 CD 이용에 대한 요구가 예상 밖이었음을 언급하고 있다. 보고서의 도표를 통해 시청각 자료와 미디어실(Audiovisual materials and media stations)에 대한 응답자의 선호도가 74%임을 확인할 수 있으므로, 정답은 (C)이다.

▶▶ Paraphrasing 지문의 much greater than we had
predicted → 질문의 unexpected

190 세부 사항

번역 스펙 씨는 이메일에서 위원회에게 무엇을 하라고 제안하는가?
(A) 상대적으로 인기가 없는 선택사항 배제하기
(B) 공공행사가 끝날 때까지 논의 연기하기
(C) 보스팅 어소시에이츠에 더 많은 정보 요청하기
(D) 간단한 시각 자료를 인쇄물로 준비하기

해설 이메일의 첫 번째 단락에서 그럼에도 불구하고 자동 대출 시스템은 고려하지 않아야 한다고 생각한다. 선호도가 꽤 낮기 때문이다(Despite this, I think we should take the automated borrowing system out of consideration, as its rating is still quite low)라고 했으므로 발신인 (I)인 스펙 씨는 선호도가 낮은 자동 대출 시스템을 고려대상에서 제외할 것을 제안하고 있다. 따라서 정답은 (A)이다.

▶▶ **Paraphrasing** 지문의 take ~ out of consideration
→ 정답의 Dismiss
지문의 its rating is still quite low
→ 정답의 a relatively unpopular option

191-195 이메일 + 일정표 + 평가

발신: 재스민 네스빗
수신: 드레이크 샌더스
날짜: 12월 8일
제목: 변경사항

샌더스 씨께,

제가 〈코미디 나이틀리 뉴스〉의 신임 제작 책임자가 되어 얼마나 기뻤는지 다시 한 번 말씀드리고 싶었습니다. **191**제가 전 출연진과 이야기를 나눠 본 바, 보다 젊은 시청자에게 어필하기 위해 프로그램을 현대적으로 만들려는 저의 계획이 성공을 거두겠다는 확신이 듭니다. 다른 프로그램에서의 제 경험을 살려 창의적인 스태프들과 저는 현 예산을 초과하지 않고 프로그램의 모습, 소리, 내용을 새롭게 만들기 시작할 것입니다. **192**저희가 논의한 대로 변경사항은 영향력을 높이기 위해 모두 한꺼번에 진행됩니다. 〈코미디 나이틀리 뉴스〉 새 버전의 첫 방송은 1월 4일을 목표로 잡았습니다.

기회를 주셔서 다시 한 번 감사드립니다.

재스민 네스빗

어휘 executive producer 제작 책임자 cast 출연진 modernize 현대화하다 exceed 초과하다 all at once 모두 함께, 동시에 premiere 첫 공연, 초연

오늘의 방영 프로그램
1922월 3일

오후 8시	(Ch. 5) *새로운 시선* "단 겟츠" 추상화가의 삶과 작품에 대한 소개.
오후 9시	(Ch. 40) *멜빈 스트리트에서* 고등학교에서의 마지막 해를 보내는 소녀의 이야기. 다수의 영화제 수상작.
오후 9:30	(Ch. 2) **194**프랭클린 패밀리 "바보 같은 짓" 롭과 할리가 동물원으로 가는 길에 곤경에 처한다.
오후 10시	(Ch. 8) *스페이스 넷* "허허벌판" S.S. '원더러' 선원들은 아무도 살지 않는 행성에 착륙한다.
오후 11시	(Ch. 24) **192**코미디 나이틀리 뉴스 뉴스 패러디 쇼가 몰라보게 바뀌어 첫선을 보인다. 게스트: 린 샘.

어휘 abstract painter 추상화가 monkey business 속임수, 장난, 바보 같은 짓 plain 평원, 평지 inhabitant 주민 debut 데뷔하다 transformation 변신, 변화

---

http://www.volpitvreviews.com/comedynightlynews

전문 비평가 　　　　　　　　　시청자 평가단

새로워진 〈코미디 나이틀리 뉴스〉
채드 프로쉬, 2월 3일

〈코미디 나이틀리 뉴스〉의 오랜 시청자로서 저는 프로그램의 변모에 대해 **193**복잡한 심정이었습니다. 오프닝 주제곡은 훨씬 더 힘찼고 지구의 디지털 사진이 나오는 모니터가 시대에 뒤떨어진 도시의 스카이라인 배경을 대체했습니다. **195**하지만 이렇게 긍정적인 변화가 정말 바보 같은 농담과 함께 나온다는 것이 문제입니다. **194**저는 제가 오늘 저녁에 먼저 본, 등장인물들이 동물들과 우스꽝스러운 행동을 했던 프로그램을 보는 것 같은 느낌이 들었습니다. 〈코미디 나이틀리 뉴스〉 제작자들은 대부분의 코미디 프로그램에 없는 수준 높은 유머 때문에 사람들이 수상에 빛나는 이 프로그램을 좋아한다는 사실을 모르나요? 그런 수준을 잃는다면 정말 유감일 것 같습니다.

어휘 mixed feeling 상반된 감정, 복잡한 감정 out-of-date 구식의, 시대에 뒤떨어진 backdrop 배경 accompany 수반하다, 동반하다 ridiculously 우스꽝스럽게 award-winning 상을 받은 sophisticated 세련된, 수준 높은 pity 유감

---

191 세부 사항

번역 네스빗 씨는 무엇을 하겠다고 썼는가?

(A) 새로운 시청자 층이 프로그램을 보게 하기
(B) 다른 프로그램에서 재능 있고 창의적인 스태프 영입하기
(C) 혼란을 막기 위해 점진적으로 변경하기
(D) 제작 비용 줄일 방법 모색하기

해설 네스빗 씨가 쓴 이메일의 첫 번째 단락에서 전 출연진과 이야기를 나눠 본 바, 보다 젊은 시청자에게 어필하기 위해 프로그램을 현대적으로 만들려는 저의 계획이 성공을 거두겠다는 확신이 든다(Now that I've spoken with the full cast, I feel I can guarantee that my plans to modernize the show to appeal to a younger audience will succeed)를 통해 젊은 시청자를 겨냥한 프로그램의 현대화 계획을 언급하고 있으므로, 정답은 (A)이다.

▶▶ **Paraphrasing** 지문의 appeal to a younger audience
→ 정답의 Attract a new group of viewers

---

192 연계

번역 프로그램의 변화에 대해 암시된 것은?

(A) 최근 주로 긍정적인 반응을 얻었다.
(B) 계획한 것보다 늦게 변경됐다.
(C) 에피소드가 더 길어졌다.
(D) 다른 프로그램들이 모방하고 있다.

해설 이메일에서 우리가 논의한 대로 변경사항은 영향력을 높이기 위해 모두 한꺼번에 진행된다. 〈코미디 나이틀리 뉴스〉 새 버전의 첫 방송은 1월 4일을 목표로 잡았다(As we discussed, the changes will be made all at once to increase their impact; I have set January 4 as the target date for the premiere of this new version of *Comedy Nightly News*)를 통해 〈코미디 나이틀리 뉴스〉의 새 버전의 첫 방영을 1월 4일 첫 방영을 목표로 한다고 언급하고 있다. 일정표의 날짜 2월 3일(February 3)과 코미디 나이틀리 뉴스(*Comedy Nightly News*)의 설명에서 뉴스 패러디 쇼가 몰라보게 바뀌어 첫선을 보인다(The news parody show

Test 6

debuts big transformations)를 통해 〈코미디 나이틀리 뉴스〉의 새 버전이 목표한 날짜보다 늦게 방영되었음을 확인할 수 있으므로, 정답은 (B)이다.

193 동의어 찾기

번역 평가에서 첫 번째 단락 1행의 "mixed"와 의미가 가장 가까운 단어는?
(A) 통일된
(B) 반복적인
(C) 상충되는
(D) 잘못된

해설 해당 문장은 '프로그램의 변모에 대해 복잡한 심정이었다(I have mixed feelings about the changes to the show)'라는 의미로 해석되는데, 지문을 읽어보면 긍정적인 변화와 부정적인 변화가 공존하는 데서 오는 복잡한 심정을 나타내고 있다. 따라서 정답은 (C) conflicting(모순되는, 상충된)이다.

194 연계

번역 프로쉬 씨는 〈코미디 나이틀리 뉴스〉를 어떤 프로그램에 비유하고 있는가?
(A) 〈새로운 시선〉
(B) 〈멜빈 스트리트에서〉
(C) 〈프랭클린 패밀리〉
(D) 〈스페이스 넷〉

해설 세 번째 지문인 평가에서 오늘 저녁에 먼저 본, 등장인물들이 동물들과 우스꽝스러운 행동을 했던 프로그램을 보는 것 같은 느낌이 들었다(I felt like I was watching that show I caught a moment of earlier tonight, where the characters were behaving ridiculously with some animals)를 통해 프로쉬 씨는 앞서 방영된 동물이 등장하는 프로그램과 〈코미디 나이틀리 뉴스〉를 비교하고 있다. 일정표의 프랭클린 패밀리(The Franklin Family)의 설명 '바보 같은 짓' 롭과 할리는 동물원으로 가는 길에 곤경에 처한다("Monkey Business" Rob and Harley get into trouble during a trip to the zoo)를 통해 프로쉬 씨가 언급한 동물이 등장하는 프로그램이 〈프랭클린 패밀리〉임을 확인할 수 있으므로, 정답은 (C)이다.

195 사실 관계 확인

번역 프로쉬 씨가 〈코미디 나이틀리 뉴스〉에 대해 언급한 것은?
(A) 출연진이 더 활발해 보인다.
(B) 유머의 수준이 낮아졌다.
(C) 새로운 배경은 매력적이지 않다.
(D) 진행자가 교체됐다.

해설 세 번째 지문인 평가에서 하지만 이렇게 긍정적인 변화가 정말 바보 같은 농담과 함께 나온다는 것이 문제이다(But the problem is that these positive changes seem to be accompanied by really silly jokes)를 통해 프로쉬 씨가 프로그램의 유머를 문제점으로 언급하고 있으므로, 정답은 (B)이다.

▶▶ **Paraphrasing** 지문의 **be accompanied by really silly jokes** → 정답의 **Its humor has become less sophisticated.**

196-200 공지 + 회람 + 이메일

고프니 커넥션즈

점검 실시

196해드릭 홈을 위해 가전 제품을 생산하기로 한 고프니의 가슴 벅찬 신규 계약의 일환으로, 정기적인 기계 점검이 필요합니다. 해드릭을 위한 생산에 참여할 두 공장은 공장의 기계를 테스트할 외부 감사관의 방문을 받을 것입니다. **197D**"불충분"을 의미하는 "U" 등급을 받은 장비는 교체하거나 수리해야 합니다.

197A첫 번째 방문은 이 공장들에서 다른 전자 제품 브랜드의 최근 주문을 마무리하는 동안 이루어질 예정입니다. **197B**달링턴 공장은 6월에 점검을 받을 것이며, 팬스빌 공장은 7월에 방문을 받을 예정인데, 정확한 날짜는 아직 확인되지 않았습니다. 이 기간 동안 생산은 속도를 늦추거나 일시 중단될 수도 있습니다. 관련 직원들은 이 공정 동안 조금 인내심을 가져 주시고, 이 중요한 고객을 기쁘게 할 수 있도록 좀 더 관심을 기울여 주시기 바랍니다.

어휘 inspection 점검, 검사 take place 발생하다, 열리다 manufacture 제조하다 appliances 가전 제품 call for ~을 필요로 하다 regular 정기적인 inspector 검사자, 감사관 unsatisfactory 불충분한, 불만족스러운 replace 교체하다 repair 수리하다 undergo 겪다 suspend 일시 중단하다 process 과정, 공정

발신: 샌드라 컬리, 부장
수신: 생산부
197B날짜: 6월 16일
제목: 점검 결과

197A, D, 199여러분이 들으신 대로, 최근의 공장 점검에 따르면 우리의 라인 중 한 곳에서 절단기와 거품 분사기의 부품을 교체해야 한다고 합니다. 필요한 부품을 주문했으며 내일 12시 전에 도착 예정입니다. 관련 라인의 관리자인 조시 페티가 직원들에게 통지할 것이며 우리의 표준 유지 보수 절차를 따를 것입니다.

197A이로 인해 칼루리 주문 배송 일정이 예정보다 조금 늦어질 수는 있겠지만, 저는 이미 스콧 폰세카와 이 문제를 해결하기 위해 이야기를 나눴습니다. 그의 라인에서 이를 보충하기 위해 야근을 할 것입니다. 이 상황에 대한 질문이나 문의 사항이 있으시면 제게 말씀해 주세요.

198마지막으로, 별 문제 없이 점검을 통과한 것에 대해 본사에서 축하 메시지를 보내 왔습니다. 고프니의 이름에 명예가 되도록 계속 노력합시다.

어휘 cutting machine 절단기 foam 거품 injector 인젝터, 분사 장치 component 구성 요소, 부품 replace 교체하다, 교환하다 parts 부품 maintenance procedures 유지 보수 절차 behind schedule 예정보다 늦게 work overtime 잔업하다, 야근하다 compensate 보상하다, 보충하다 address to ~에게 이야기하다 headquarters 본사, 본점 be a credit to ~의 명예가 되다

199발신: 조슈아 페티
199수신: 토마스 천
날짜: 6월 16일
제목: 부탁

안녕하세요 톰,

저녁에 방해해서 미안하지만, 보통 아침에 제일 먼저 공장에 도착하는 사람이 톰이잖아요. 다른 사람들이 도착하기 전에 입구 근처에 안내판을 게시해 줄래요? ¹⁹⁹내일 오후 12시부터 3시까지 라인이 가동 중지된다는 것을 운영자들에게 알려줘 해요. 안내판에는 라인 1의 직원은 점심 식사 후 직원 휴게실에서 기다렸다가 3시에 자리로 ²⁰⁰돌아와야 한다고 분명하게 써 주세요.

감사해요.

조쉬

어휘 operator 운영자 shut down (기계가) 멈추다, 문을 닫다 employee break room 직원 휴게실 station 담당 일터, 부서

196 세부 사항

번역 공지에 따르면 고프니가 최근에 한 일은?
(A) 새로운 장비 세트를 구입했다
(B) 기술자들에게 점검을 지시했다
(C) 두 번째 제조 공장을 열었다
(D) 새 고객과 거래했다

해설 첫 번째 지문의 첫 문장에서 해드릭 홈을 위해 가전 제품을 생산하기로 한 고프니의 가슴 벅찬 신규 계약의 일환으로, 정기적인 기계 점검이 필요하다(Part of Goffney's exciting new agreement to manufacture appliances for Hadrick Home calls for regular machinery inspections)고 했다. 따라서 새로운 계약을 체결했음을 알 수 있으므로, 정답은 (D)이다.

▶▶ **Paraphrasing** 지문의 **Goffney's exciting new agreement** → 정답의 **Made a deal with a new client**

197 연계

번역 절단기에 관해 암시된 것이 아닌 것은?
(A) 가전제품을 제조하는 데 사용된다.
(B) 달링턴 공장에 있다.
(C) 비싸다.
(D) "U" 등급을 받았다.

해설 첫 번째 지문 두 번째 단락의 다른 전자 제품 브랜드(another appliance brand), 두 번째 지문 첫 번째 문장, 우리의 라인 중 한 곳에서 절단기와 거품 분사기의 부품을 교체해야 한다(the cutting machine and foam injector on one of our lines need to have components replaced)에서 절단기가 가전제품 제조에 사용된다는 것을 알 수 있다. 따라서 (A)를 확인할 수 있다. 첫 번째 지문 두 번째 단락의 달링턴 공장은 6월에 점검을 받고, 팬스빌 공장은 7월에 방문을 받는다(The Darlington plant will undergo an inspection in June and the Fansville plant will be visited in July)고 했으며, 두 번째 지문의 날짜(Date: June 16)를 보면 6월이므로 절단기는 달링턴 공장에 있다는 것을 알 수 있다. 따라서 (B)를 확인할 수 있다. 첫 번째 지문에서 "U" 등급을 받으면 교체하거나 수리해야 한다(Any equipment that receives a "U" grade, for "unsatisfactory", will need to be replaced or repaired)고 했으며, 두 번째 지문에서 절단기와 거품 분사기의 부품을 교체해야 한다(the cutting machine and foam injector on one of our lines need to have components replaced)고 했으므로, 절단기는 "U" 등급을 받았음을 알 수 있다. 따라서 (D)를 확인할 수 있으므로 정답은 언급되지 않은 (C)이다.

198 추론 / 암시

번역 컬리 씨에 대해 암시된 것은?
(A) 폰세카 씨의 감독을 받는다.
(B) 메시지를 전달하라는 요청을 받았다.
(C) 야근 계획에 대해 우려하고 있다.
(D) 배송을 연기했다.

해설 두 번째 지문의 세 번째 단락에서 컬리 씨는 본사에서 점검을 통과한 것에 대한 축하 메시지를 보내 왔다(headquarters sends congratulations on passing the inspection with so few issues)는 소식을 전하고 있으므로, 정답은 (B)이다.

199 연계

번역 천 씨가 라인 1의 직원들을 휴게실로 보낼 이유는 무엇이겠는가?
(A) 수리할 시간을 벌기 위해
(B) 최신 일정을 보기 위해
(C) 안전 규칙에 대해 듣기 위해
(D) 원자재 배달을 기다리기 위해

해설 두 번째 지문의 첫 번째 단락에서 한 라인의 절단기와 거품 분사기의 부품을 교체해야 한다면서, 관련 라인 부장인 조시 페티가 직원들에게 통지할 것(As you may have heard, the recent inspection of our plant determined that the cutting machine and foam injector on one of our lines need to have components replaced ~ Josh Fetty, the line manager involved, will notify his employees and follow our standard maintenance procedures)이라고 했다. 세 번째 지문에서 조슈아 페티의 통지를 보면 오후 12시부터 3시까지 라인을 멈출 것이니 안내판에 라인 1의 직원은 점심 식사 후 직원 휴게실에서 기다렸다가 3시에 자리로 돌아와야 한다고 써 달라(the line will be shut down from 12 P.M. to 3 P.M. tomorrow. The sign should say clearly that Line 1 employees should wait in the employee break room after their lunch hour and then report to their stations at 3)고 했다. 따라서 부품 교체 때문에 라인 1의 직원을 휴게실에 대기시킬 것이므로, 정답은 (A)이다.

200 동의어 찾기

번역 이메일에서 5행의 "report to"와 의미가 가장 가까운 단어는?
(A) 모으다
(B) 알리다
(C) 반대하다
(D) ~에 나타나다

해설 지문에서 report to their stations at 3는 '3시에 자리로 돌아오다'라는 의미로, report to는 '~에 나타나다, ~로 출두하다'의 의미이다. 따라서 정답은 (D) appear at이다.

101 (A)	**102** (C)	**103** (B)	**104** (C)	**105** (A)
106 (B)	**107** (B)	**108** (A)	**109** (C)	**110** (C)
111 (B)	**112** (A)	**113** (D)	**114** (D)	**115** (B)
116 (B)	**117** (A)	**118** (C)	**119** (D)	**120** (A)
121 (C)	**122** (D)	**123** (B)	**124** (B)	**125** (C)
126 (A)	**127** (D)	**128** (D)	**129** (C)	**130** (C)
131 (C)	**132** (A)	**133** (A)	**134** (C)	**135** (C)
136 (B)	**137** (B)	**138** (D)	**139** (C)	**140** (B)
141 (A)	**142** (C)	**143** (C)	**144** (C)	**145** (C)
146 (C)	**147** (B)	**148** (C)	**149** (C)	**150** (C)
151 (A)	**152** (C)	**153** (A)	**154** (B)	**155** (B)
156 (D)	**157** (D)	**158** (A)	**159** (C)	**160** (C)
161 (A)	**162** (D)	**163** (C)	**164** (C)	**165** (C)
166 (D)	**167** (D)	**168** (C)	**169** (D)	**170** (D)
171 (B)	**172** (C)	**173** (A)	**174** (C)	**175** (A)
176 (A)	**177** (A)	**178** (B)	**179** (C)	**180** (C)
181 (C)	**182** (B)	**183** (D)	**184** (D)	**185** (A)
186 (B)	**187** (D)	**188** (C)	**189** (B)	**190** (D)
191 (C)	**192** (C)	**193** (B)	**194** (D)	**195** (A)
196 (C)	**197** (D)	**198** (D)	**199** (B)	**200** (C)

PART 5

101 인칭대명사의 격 _ 주격

해설 빈칸 바로 앞에는 목적격 관계대명사(that/which)가 생략되어 있다. 따라서 빈칸은 관계대명사절 내 동사(had opened)의 주어 자리이다. 주격 인칭대명사 (A) he와 소유대명사 (C) his 중에 앞에 있는 주절의 주어(Mr. Pritchard)를 대신 가리키고 있으므로, 정답은 (A) he이다.

번역 프리차드 씨는 자신이 지난달 개설한 예금 계좌에 대해 문의하고자 은행에 전화했다.

어휘 savings account 보통 예금 계좌

102 동사 어휘

해설 빈칸은 앞에 있는 동사(choose)의 목적어 역할을 하면서 빈칸 뒤 명사(the bus)를 목적어로 취한다. 따라서 '버스를 ~하는 것을 선택한다'는 문구이므로 문맥상 '버스를 타기를 선택한다'라는 의미가 자연스러우므로, 정답은 (C) ride(타다)이다. (A) travel(여행하다, 이동하다), (B) cross(건너다), (D) run(달리다, 운영하다)은 의미상 적합하지 않다.

번역 건물 근처에 주차 공간이 제한되어 있어서 사무실 사람 대다수가 버스로 출근하는 것을 선택한다.

어휘 choose to + 동사원형 ~하는 것을 선택하다   limited 제한된, 한정된

103 명사 어휘

해설 빈칸 앞 명사(kitchen)와 함께 복합명사를 이루어, 뒤에 나오는 동사(are not kept plugged in)의 주어 역할을 하는 명사 자리이다. 문맥상 '주방 기기는 전원을 연결해 두지 않는다'라는 의미가 자연스러우므로, 정답은

(B) appliances(가전제품, 기기)이다. (A) utensils(도구, 용품, 연장), (C) tiles(타일), (D) counters(판매대, 카운터)는 의미상 적합하지 않다.

번역 안전상의 이유로 전시실에 전시된 주방기기는 전원을 연결해 두지 않는다.

어휘 on display 전시된   plug in 전원을 연결하다, 플러그를 꽂다

104 비교급

해설 빈칸은 앞에 있는 주어(the cost of repairing the vehicle after the accident)를 보충 설명하는 형용사 자리이므로, 형용사의 원급 (B) great와 비교급 (C) greater가 가능하다. 뒤에 비교의 의미를 나타내는 접속사(than)가 있으므로, 정답은 (C) greater이다. 부사 (A) greatly와 명사 (D) greatness는 품사상 적합하지 않다.

번역 놀랍게도 사고 이후 차량 수리비용이 신차 구매 비용보다 높았다.

105 인칭대명사의 격 _ 소유격

해설 빈칸은 동사(helped)의 목적어(café)를 한정 수식하는 소유격 인칭대명사 자리이므로, 정답은 (A) our이다.

번역 레나타 은행의 소기업 대출은 우리 카페에 절실한 재단장을 하는 데 도움이 됐다.

어휘 much-needed 매우 필요한, 절실한   refurbishment 재정비, 개선

106 형용사 어휘

해설 빈칸 앞에 있는 동사(requires)의 목적어(understanding)를 수식하는 형용사 자리이다. 문맥상 '깊은 이해'라는 의미가 자연스러우므로, 정답은 (B) deep(깊은)이다. (A) sole(유일한, 단독의), (C) private(사유의, 사적인), (D) severe(극심한, 가혹한)는 의미상 적합하지 않다.

번역 협상가 직책은 조직의 내부 갈등에 대한 깊은 이해가 필요하다.

어휘 negotiator 협상가   internal 내부의   conflict 갈등, 분쟁   organization 조직

107 부사 자리 _ 형용사 수식

해설 빈칸은 형용사(identical)를 수식하는 부사 자리이다. 형용사/부사의 비교급 (A) nearer(더 가까이)와 최상급 (C) nearest(가장 가까이), 부사 (B) nearly(거의) 중에 문맥상 '거의 똑같은'이라는 의미가 자연스러우므로, 정답은 (B) nearly이다. 명사 (D) nearness는 품사상 적합하지 않다.

번역 두 개의 제품이 거의 동일했기 때문에 관리자는 가격이 더 싼 제품을 주문했다.

어휘 identical 똑같은, 동일한   order 주문하다

108 형용사 어휘

해설 빈칸 앞에 있는 전치사(for)의 목적어(time)를 수식하는 형용사 자리이다. 문맥상 '처음으로'라는 의미가 자연스러우므로, 정답은 (A) first(처음의)이다. 한정사 (B) each는 앞의 정관사(the)와 함께 쓰이지 않고, 부사/부사절 접속사 (D) once는 품사상 적합하지 않다. '처음으로(for the first time)'라는 관용적인 표현으로 묶어서 기억하자.

번역 세탁 시설을 처음 이용하는 고객은 기계를 작동하는 데 도움이 필요할 수도 있다.

어휘 laundry facility 세탁 시설 assistance 도움 operate 작동하다
machine 기계

109 동사 어형 _ 시제

해설 빈칸은 주어(Langley Software) 뒤의 동사 자리로, 뒤에 나오는 미래 시간을 나타내는 부사(later this year)의 수식을 받는다. 따라서 정답은 미래시제 동사 (C) will modify이다. 과거시제 동사 (A) modified는 시제가 일치하지 않고, 과거분사 (A) modified, 현재분사 (B) modifying과 (D) having modified는 동사 자리에 들어갈 수 없다.

번역 랭글리 소프트웨어는 고객들이 용어를 더욱 쉽게 이해하도록 올 하반기에 이용자 약관을 수정할 것이다.

어휘 user agreement 이용자 약관 term 용어

110 부사절 접속사

해설 빈칸 뒤 부사절 접속사(though)와 짝을 이루어 뒤에 나오는 완전한 절(he were unfamiliar with the company's history)을 이끌면서, 앞에 있는 완전한 절을 수식하는 부사절 접속사를 선택해야 한다. 따라서 정답은 (C) as이다. '마치 ~처럼(as though, as if)'이라는 관용적인 표현으로 묶어서 기억하자.

번역 대변인은 마치 회사의 내력을 잘 모르는 것처럼 기자의 질문에 응답하는 듯했다.

어휘 spokesperson 대변인 respond to ~에 응답하다 reporter 기자 inquiry 질문, 질의 be unfamiliar with ~을 잘 모르다, ~에 익숙하지 않다

111 명사 어휘

해설 빈칸 앞 명사(customer)와 함께 복합명사를 이루어 앞에 있는 동사(completes)의 목적어 역할을 하는 명사 자리이다. 문맥상 '고객 설문을 완성하다'라는 의미가 자연스러우므로, 정답은 (B) questionnaire(설문지)이다. (A) demand(요구, 수요), (C) loyalty(충실, 충성), (D) service(서비스, 근무, 봉사, 점검)는 문맥상 적합하지 않다.

번역 기간 내 고객 설문을 완료하는 모든 사람은 경품 추첨에 응모하게 된다.

어휘 time frame 기간 prize drawing 경품 추첨

112 전치사 어휘

해설 빈칸은 명사(the seat) 앞에 적합한 전치사를 묻는 문제이다. 선택의 등위접속사(or)가 연결하는 앞에 있는 전치사구(in the overhead compartments)와 함께 동사(can be placed)를 수식한다. 문맥상 '좌석 아래에 두다'라는 의미가 자연스러우므로, 정답은 (A) under이다. (B) between과 (D) among 뒤에는 주로 복수명사가 나온다.

번역 작은 가방은 머리 위 짐칸이나 앞 좌석 아래에 둘 수 있다.

어휘 overhead compartment (기내의) 짐칸

113 형용사 어휘

해설 빈칸은 명사(items)를 수식하는 형용사 자리이다. 문맥상 '귀중품을 두다'라는 의미가 자연스러우므로, 정답은 (D) valuable(귀중한, 값비싼)이다. (A) fluent(유창한), (B) attentive(주의를 기울이는), (C) prompt(즉각적인, 신속한)는 의미상 적합하지 않다.

번역 방에 귀중품을 두고 싶지 않은 투숙객은 외출 시 호텔 금고를 이용할 수 있다.

어휘 safe 금고

114 형용사 자리 _ 명사 수식

해설 빈칸 앞 전치사(of)의 목적어(information)를 수식하는 형용사 자리이므로, 정답은 (D) critical(중요한, 비판적인)이다. 명사 (A) critics(비평가), 부사 (B) critically(비판적으로, 결정적으로), 동사 (C) criticize(비판하다, 비평하다)는 품사상 적합하지 않다.

번역 예산에 관한 주요 정보가 누락됐기 때문에 보고서를 다시 써야 했다.

어휘 rewrite 다시 쓰다, 고치다 budget 예산 omit 누락시키다, 생략하다

115 동명사 / 명사 구분

해설 빈칸은 앞에 있는 전치사(in)의 목적어 자리이므로 동명사 (B) cultivating, 명사 (C) cultivation이 정답 후보이다. 그런데 빈칸 뒤 명사(produce)를 목적어로 취해야 하므로 정답은 목적어를 취할 수 있는 동명사인 (B) cultivating이다. 명사 (C) cultivation은 목적어(produce)를 취할 수 없고 뒤에 나오는 부사(organically)의 수식을 받을 수도 없다. 동명사는 부사(organically)의 수식을 받을 수 있다. 동사 (A) cultivates와 (D) cultivate(경작하다, 재배하다, 구축하다)는 전치사의 목적어가 될 수 없다.

번역 코티지 팜은 해로운 비료나 농약 없이 유기농으로 농작물을 재배하는 것이 전문이다.

어휘 specialize in ~에 전문이다 produce 농작물; 생산하다, 제작하다
organically 유기 재배로 harmful 해로운 fertilizer 비료
pesticide 농약, 살충제

116 전치사 어휘

해설 빈칸 뒤 목적어(a choice of side salad or the soup of the day)와 함께 앞의 동사(is served)를 수식하는 전치사 자리이다. 문맥상 '곁들임 샐러드나 오늘의 수프 중 하나와 함께 제공된다'라는 의미가 자연스러우므로, 정답은 (B) with이다.

번역 파라다이스 카페의 주중 점심 특선은 곁들임 샐러드 또는 오늘의 수프 중 선택하여 제공된다.

117 명사 자리 _ 복합명사

해설 빈칸 앞 명사(meal)와 함께 복합명사를 이루어 앞에 있는 동사원형(indicate)의 목적어 역할을 하는 명사 자리이므로, 정답은 (A) preference(선호, 애호)이다. 과거분사 (B) preferred(우선의, 발탁된), 형용사 (C) preferable(더 나은, 바람직한), 부사 (D) preferably(오히려, 가급적)는 품사상 적합하지 않다.

번역 초청에 답장하실 때, 참석할 예정이라면 선호하는 식단을 알려 주십시오.

어휘 indicate 나타내다, 내비치다 in attendance 참석한

118 부사 자리 _ 형용사 수식

해설 빈칸 뒤 비교급 형용사(safer)를 수식하는 부사 자리로, 정답은 (C) Demonstrably(명백히, 논증에 의해)이다. 명사 (A) Demonstration (실증, 설명), 동사 (B) Demonstrate(실증하다, 설명하다), 형용사 (D) Demonstrable(입증할 수 있는)은 품사상 적합하지 않다. 참고로 〈Demonstrably safer than ~〉은 부사절 〈Because it is demonstrably safer than ~〉이 축약된 형태로 볼 수 있다.

번역 Y-881은 확실히 시중에 나와 있는 다른 절단기보다 안전하므로 가장 잘 팔리는 사실이 놀랍지 않다.

어휘 on the market 시중에 나와 있는 top-selling product 가장 잘 팔리는 제품

119 부사절 접속사

해설 빈칸은 두 개의 완전한 절을 연결해 주는 부사절 접속사 자리이다. 문맥상 '로체스터 대로가 확장되었기 때문에'라는 의미가 자연스러우므로, 정답은 (D) Now that(~ 때문에)이다. (A) Whenever(~할 때마다), (B) Only if(~해야만), (C) Once(일단 ~하면)는 의미상 적합하지 않다.

번역 로체스터 대로가 확장되었기 때문에 그 지역에서 좀처럼 교통 체증을 볼 수 없다.

어휘 expand 확장하다 traffic jam 교통 체증 rarely 좀처럼 ~ 않는

120 형용사 어휘

해설 주어(raw meat and fresh vegetables)를 보충 설명하는 형용사 자리이다. 문맥상 '생고기와 신선한 채소는 따로 두어야 한다'라는 의미가 자연스러우므로, 정답은 (A) separate(따로 떨어진, 별개의)이다. (B) further(더 이상의, 추가의), (C) nearby(인근의), (D) opposite(맞은편의, 반대의)는 의미상 적합하지 않다.

번역 음식의 교차 오염을 막기 위해 날고기와 신선한 채소는 항상 따로 두어야 한다.

어휘 prevent 막다 cross-contamination 교차 오염 raw 날것인 at all times 항상

121 접속사 자리 _ 복합관계대명사

해설 빈칸 뒤 동사(wishes)의 주어가 없는 불완전한 절을 이끌면서 뒤에 나오는 동사(may do)의 주어 역할을 하는 명사절 접속사 자리이므로, 정답은 (C) Whoever이다. 대명사 (A) Anything과 (D) Those는 접속사의 역할을 하지 못하므로 적합하지 않고, 한정사 (B) Every는 품사상 적합하지 않다.

번역 일반석 표를 일등석으로 업그레이드하고자 하는 사람은 역에서 혹은 탑승해서 하면 된다.

어휘 standard class 일반석 on board 탑승한

122 명사 자리 _ 동사의 주어

해설 빈칸 뒤에 나오는 동사(are becoming)의 주어 역할을 하면서, 뒤의 과거분사 구문(made from plated copper)의 수식을 받는 명사 자리이다. 따라서 정답은 (D) Accessories이다. 과거분사/과거시제 동사 (A) Accessorized, 현재시제 동사 (B) Accessorizes와 (C) Accessorize는 품사상 적합하지 않다.

번역 요즘 패션계에서는 도금한 구리로 만든 액세서리가 더욱 인기를 끌고 있다.

어휘 plated 도금한 copper 구리 popular 인기 있는

123 부사절 접속사

해설 빈칸은 앞뒤에 나오는 완전한 절들을 연결해 주는 부사절 접속사 자리이다. (B) since(~ 이래로, ~ 때문에)와 (D) although(비록 ~하더라도) 중에 문맥상 '필요한 장비 일부가 제대로 작동하지 않았기 때문에'라는 의미가 자연스러우므로, 정답은 (B) since이다. 전치사 (A) through와 부사/형용사/대명사 (C) neither는 품사상 적합하지 않다.

번역 매디슨 박사는 필요한 장비 일부가 제대로 작동하지 않아 실험을 완료할 수 없었다.

어휘 be unable to + 동사원형 ~할 수 없다 complete 완료하다 malfunction 제대로 작동하지 않다, 고장 나다

124 동사 어형 _ 조동사 + 동사원형

해설 빈칸은 조동사(should) 뒤에 나오는 동사원형 자리로, 뒤의 명사(your luggage)를 목적어로 취한다. 따라서 정답은 능동의 동사원형 (B) have weighed이다. 수동의 동사원형 (C) be weighed와 (D) have been weighed는 목적어(your luggage)를 취할 수 없다.

번역 그 항공사의 발권 대행사는 체크인 시 저울로 당신의 수하물 무게를 재야 했다.

어휘 scale 저울 at the time of ~하는 시기에

125 부사 어휘

해설 빈칸은 등위접속사(so)가 이끄는 완전한 절(they should be packaged) 뒤에 나오는 부사 자리이다. 문맥상 '다른 제품들보다 깨지기 쉬워 그에 맞게 포장해야 한다'라는 의미로 앞의 원인에 따른 결과를 나타내는 것이 자연스러우므로, 정답은 (C) accordingly(그에 맞춰, 따라서)이다. (A) absolutely(전적으로, 완전히), (B) flexibly(유연하게, 융통성 있게), (D) mutually(서로, 상호간에)는 의미상 적합하지 않다.

번역 헨리에타 기프트가 판매하는 제품 일부는 다른 제품들보다 깨지기 쉬워 그에 맞게 포장해야 한다.

어휘 fragile 깨지기 쉬운 package 포장하다

126 동사 어휘

해설 빈칸은 주어(The team) 뒤의 동사 자리로, 뒤에 나오는 목적어(a memorable slogan)와 의미가 가장 잘 통하는 동사를 선택해야 한다. 문맥상 '인상적인 슬로건을 내놓았다'라는 의미가 자연스러우므로, 정답은 (A) came up with(찾아내다, 내놓다)이다. (B) took off(벗다, 뜯다), (C) ran out of(~을 다 쓰다), (D) relied on(~에 기대다, 의존하다)은 의미상 적합하지 않다.

번역 기번스 씨가 이끄는 팀은 웨스트베리 음료 광고에 사용할 인상적인 슬로건을 내놓았다.

어휘 memorable 기억할 만한, 인상적인 commercial 광고

127 명사 자리 _ 동사의 목적어

해설 빈칸 앞 동사(outlined)의 목적어 역할을 하는 명사 자리로, 뒤에 나오는 관계사절(that this songbird has made to adjust to living near highly populated areas)의 수식을 받는다. 따라서 정답은 (A) adaptations(조정, 수정, 적응)이다. 동명사/현재분사 (B) adapting, 동사 (C) adapt, 과거분사/과거시제 동사 (D) adapted는 품사상 적합하지 않다.

번역 강의에서 생물학자 조앤 마르케즈는 이 명금류 새가 인구 밀집도가 높은 지역 근처에서 서식하는 데 적응하기 위해 변한 것들을 설명했다.

어휘 biologist 생물학자 outline 개요를 서술하다 songbird 명금류(참새목의 새) make an adaptation 수정하다 adjust 적응하다 highly populated 인구가 밀집된

128 형용사 자리 _ 명사 수식

해설 빈칸은 명사(garage)를 수식하는 형용사 자리이다. 형용사와 같은 역할을 하는 현재분사 (B) converting과 과거분사 (D) converted 중에 문맥상 '개조된 창고'라는 수동의 의미가 자연스러우므로, 정답은 과거분사 (D) converted이다. 현재분사 (B) converting은 주로 능동의 의미를 나타내고, 동사 (A) convert(개조하다, 전환하다)와 (C) converts는 형용사 자리에 들어갈 수 없다.

번역 리차드 씨는 재택근무로 쓰는 개조된 창고에서 대부분의 집필을 한다.

어휘 majority 대다수 garage 차고

129 부사 자리 _ 동사 수식

해설 빈칸은 완전한 절(Most of the city council members nodded their heads) 뒤에서 동사(nodded)를 수식하는 부사 자리이므로, 정답은 (D) agreeably(기분 좋게, 흔쾌히)이다. 형용사 (A) agreeable(기분 좋은, 받아들일 수 있는, 알맞은), 명사 (B) agreement, 동사 (C) agree는 품사상 적합하지 않다.

번역 비달리아 씨가 세금 경감에 대한 필요성을 이야기하자, 시 의회 의원 대다수가 흔쾌히 동조했다.

어휘 city council 시 의회 nod one's head 고개를 끄덕이다, 동조하다 reduce 줄이다

130 동사 어휘

해설 빈칸은 주어(Mr. Conley) 뒤의 동사 자리로, 뒤에 나오는 부사(down)와 짝을 이루어 의미가 자연스러운 동사를 선택해야 한다. '네 개의 교육 시간으로 나눴다'는 의미가 가장 자연스러우므로 정답은 (C) broke이다. (A) withdrew(철수하다, 철회하다, 인출하다), (B) ensured(확실하게 하다, 보장하다)와 (D) shared(공유하다, 나눠 갖다)는 의미상 적합하지 않다.

번역 신입직원의 정보가 매우 복잡해서 콘리 씨는 교육 시간을 4개로 분리했다.

어휘 complicated 복잡한 break down into ~로 구분하다, 분리하다

PART 6

131-134 기사

국내 최대 음식 가공업체 중 하나인 엑터 푸드는 5년 이내에 재생 가능 자원을 통해 에너지 수요를 100% 충족하겠다는 ¹³¹야심 찬 계획을 밝혔다. 이러한 움직임은 회사의 3단계 환경 계획 중 첫 번째가 ¹³²된다. ¹³³해당 분야 전문가들은 엑터 푸드가 이러한 조치를 취한 업계 최초의 기업이라는 사실에 놀라지 않는다. 이 업체는 혁신에 있어 항상 업계를 선도해 왔다.

"저희는 책임감 있게 제품을 생산할 책임이 있습니다. ¹³⁴이것이 가볍게 취급되면 안 됩니다." 어제 기자회견에서 CEO인 모건 파커가 말했다. 엑터 푸드는 지역 내 풍력발전단지에서 전력을 구입하는 것과 더불어 현장 태양열 에너지를 사용할 예정이다.

어휘 food processing 음식 가공 meet the needs 수요를 충족시키다 renewable 재생 가능한 environmental 환경의 initiative 계획 expert 전문가 take a measure 조치를 취하다 responsibly 책임감 있게 press conference 기자회견 on-site 현장의 purchase 구매하다 electricity 전기 wind farm 풍력발전단지

131 형용사 어휘

해설 빈칸은 뒤에 나오는 명사(plans)를 수식하는 형용사 자리이며, 명사(plans)는 to부정사 구문(to meet 100% of its energy needs from renewable sources within five years)의 수식을 받고 있다. 문맥상 '5년 이내에 재생 가능 자원을 통해 에너지 수요 100%를 충족하겠다는 야심 찬 계획'이라는 의미가 자연스러우므로, 정답은 (C) ambitious(야심 있는, 야심 찬)이다. (A) altered(수선된, 바뀐), (B) similar(비슷한, 유사한), (D) motivated(의욕적인, 동기 부여된)는 의미상 적합하지 않다.

132 동사 자리 _ 시제

해설 빈칸은 주어(The move) 뒤의 동사 자리이다. 현재시제 동사 (A) marks와 미래완료시제 동사 (D) will have marked 중에 뒤에 나오는 문장의 현재시제 동사(are not surprised)를 통해 현재시제임을 알 수 있으므로, 정답은 (A) marks(표시하다, 나타내다, 기념하다)이다. 동명사/현재분사 (B) marking과 to부정사 (C) to mark는 동사 자리에 들어갈 수 없다.

133 문맥에 맞는 문장 고르기

번역 (A) 이 업체는 혁신에 있어 항상 업계를 선도해 왔다.
(B) 투자자들은 다른 업계로 확장하고자 한다.
(C) 변화를 위해 많은 지식이 필요하다.
(D) 개회식은 이번 달 말로 예정되어 있다.

해설 빈칸 앞 문장 '해당 분야 전문가들은 엑터 푸드가 이러한 조치를 취한 업계 최초의 기업이라는 사실에 놀라지 않는다(Experts working in the field are not surprised that Ector Foods is the first of its kind to take such measures)'에서 그 회사의 획기적인 조치가 놀랍지 않다는 의견을 제시하고 있다. 따라서 빈칸에는 그 의견을 제시한 이유를 밝히는 것이 문맥상 자연스러우므로, 정답은 (A)이다.

134 대명사

해설 빈칸은 동사(should not be taken) 앞의 주어 자리이다. 주어로 올 수 있는 (B) He와 (C) These, (D) It 중에 문맥상 빈칸은 앞에 있는 인용문장의 목적어(a responsibility to produce our goods responsibly)를 가리키고 있으므로, 정답은 (D) It이다. (B) He는 사람을 가리키므로 정답이 될 수 없고, 복수 지시대명사 (C) These는 대명사가 가리키는 'a responsibility to produce our goods responsibly'와 수일치하지 않는다. 명사절 접속사 (A) What 뒤에는 동사가 하나 더 나와야 한다.

135-138 이메일

수신: 애셔 라슨 <a.larson@ larsonflowers.com>
발신: 에밀리 아일러스 <emily@lilacvalleydeals.com>
날짜: 10월 10일
제목: 업체를 홍보하세요!

라슨 씨께,

이 지역 관광객의 수가 지난 몇 년 동안 **135꾸준히** 증가했습니다. 〈라일락 밸리 딜〉은 귀하의 업체가 돋보이도록 도와드릴 수 있습니다. 저희 잡지는 **136판매부수**가 2만 부이며 호텔, 관광객 정보 센터, 대중교통 시설 등에 들어갑니다. **137**1/4페이지, 1/2페이지, 또는 전면으로 귀하의 업체를 특가로 광고할 수 있습니다. 가장 큰 광고가 (가격 대비) 가치가 가장 좋습니다. 준비된 광고가 **138없더라도**, 저희 내부 그래픽팀이 만들 수 있으므로 광고가 가능함을 양지하시기 바랍니다. 관심이 있으시면 저에게 이메일로 회신해 주십시오.

에밀리 아일러스

어휘 over the past few years 지난 몇 년간 stand out 두드러지다, 빼어나다 public transportation 대중교통 facility 시설 advertise 광고하다 special offer 특가 판매 quarter 4분의 1 in-house (회사, 조직) 내부의

135 부사 자리

해설 빈칸은 현재완료시제 동사를 이루는 has와 increased 사이에서 동사를 수식하는 부사 자리이므로, 정답은 (C) steadily이다. 형용사 (A) steady, 과거분사/과거시제 동사 (B) steadied, 명사 (D) steadiness는 품사상 적합하지 않다.

136 명사 어휘

해설 빈칸 앞 동사(has)의 목적어 역할을 하는 명사 자리로, 뒤에 나오는 전치사구(of 20,000)의 수식을 받는다. 문맥상 '2만 부의 판매부수를 갖고 있다'라는 의미가 자연스러우므로, 정답은 (B) circulation(판매부수, 유통, 순환)이다. (A) deposit(보증금, 예금), (C) wage(임금, 급료), (D) turnout(참가자 수, 투표자 수)은 의미상 적합하지 않다.

어휘 circulation 판매부수

137 문맥에 맞는 문장 고르기

번역 (A) 귀사에 대해 알게 되어 즐거웠습니다.
(B) 가장 큰 광고가 (가격 대비) 가치가 가장 좋습니다.
(C) 이는 시즌 관광객 대다수입니다.
(D) 할인을 받으시려면 이 쿠폰을 제시하기만 하십시오.

해설 빈칸 앞 문장 '1/4페이지, 1/2페이지, 또는 전면으로 귀하의 업체를 특가로 광고할 수 있다(You can advertise a special offer for your business on a quarter, half, or full page)'에서 지면 크기에 따른 광고를 언급하고 있다. 따라서 빈칸에도 이 광고에 대한 추가 설명이 이어지는 것이 문맥상 자연스러우므로, 정답은 (B)이다.

138 부사절 접속사

해설 빈칸은 빈칸 바로 앞 명사절 접속사 that절 내에서 두 개의 완전한 절을 연결해 주는 부사절 접속사 자리로, 정답은 (D) even if(비록 ~하더라도)이다. 전치사 (A) owing to(~ 때문에)는 품사상 적합하지 않고, 부사절 접속사 (B) whether(~이든 아니든)는 or not과 같이 쓰이며, (C) before(~하기 전에)는 의미상 어색하다.

139-142 편지

니콜 허드슨
컵케이크 익스프레스
캐피탈 애비뉴 312
뉴캐슬, IN 47362

허드슨 씨께,

귀하를 뉴캐슬 베이킹 축제에 초대하고자 합니다. 저희는 이런 행사를 처음 준비합니다. **139하지만** 참가인원이 예상하는 수준에 도달할 경우 연례 행사로 만들 수 있습니다. 방문객들이 귀하의 **140조리법**을 체험해볼 것이므로 이는 귀사를 홍보하는 훌륭한 방법입니다. 행사에 대한 더 자세한 내용을 알아보시려면 www.newcastlebaking.org에서 온라인으로 **141** 짧은 동영상을 시청하십시오. 몇 분만 시간을 내시면 알아야 할 모든 것을 알려드립니다. 또한 축제에 **142참가할** 업체 명단도 게시할 계획입니다. 귀사를 목록에 더하게 되기를 바랍니다!

마야 피셔

어휘 reach 도달하다 participation 참가 annual 연례의 promote 홍보하다 post 게시하다 add 더하다, 추가하다

139 문맥에 맞는 문장 고르기

번역 (A) 작년 축제는 큰 성공을 거뒀습니다.
(B) 회신으로 참가 의사를 표시해 주십시오.
(C) 저희는 이런 행사를 처음 준비합니다.
(D) 각 부스마다 다양한 종류의 음식을 내놓습니다.

해설 빈칸 뒤에 나오는 문장 '하지만 참가인원이 예상하는 수준에 도달할 경우 연례 행사로 만들 수 있다(However, if we reach the level of participation that we are expecting, we can make it an annual tradition)'를 통해 빈칸에는 뒤에 나오는 긍정적인 기대와 달리 (However) 행사 진행과 관련하여 우려할 만한 사항을 먼저 언급하는 것이 문맥상 자연스러우므로, 정답은 (C)이다.

140 명사 어휘

해설 빈칸은 소유격(your) 뒤의 명사 자리이다. 첫 번째 문장(I'd like to invite you to the New Castle Baking Festival)을 통해 베이킹 축제에 초청받았다는 것을 알 수 있으므로, 빈칸에는 베이킹과 관련된 단어를 선택해야 한다. 문맥상 '귀하의 조리법을 체험하다'라는 의미가 자연스러우

므로, 정답은 (B) recipes(조리법)이다. (A) competitions(경쟁, 대회), (C) routines(일상, 관례), (D) methods(방법)는 의미상 적합하지 않다.

141 형용사 어휘

해설 빈칸은 명사(video)를 수식하는 형용사 자리이다. 뒤에 온 문장에 '몇 분만 시간을 내면 알아야 할 것을 다 알게 된다'고 했으므로 짧고 간단한 동영상임을 알 수 있다. 따라서 문맥상 '짧은 동영상을 시청하다'라는 의미가 자연스러우므로, 정답은 (A) brief(간단한, 짧은)이다. (B) live(생방송의, 살아 있는), (C) minor(사소한), (D) similar(유사한, 닮은)는 의미상 적합하지 않다.

142 동사 자리 _ 수 / 태

해설 빈칸은 주격 관계대명사(that)가 이끄는 관계사절 내의 동사 자리로 뒤에 나오는 명사(the festival)를 목적어로 취한다. 또한 빈칸은 주격 관계대명사(that)가 대신 가리키는 복수명사(businesses)와 수일치해야 하므로, 정답은 능동의 미래진행시제 동사 (C) will be attending이다. 수동의 미래시제 동사 (A) will be attended는 목적어를 취할 수 없고, 단수의 현재시제 동사 (B) attends와 현재진행시제 동사 (D) is attending은 주격 관계대명사(that)가 대신 가리키는 복수명사(businesses)와 수일치하지 않는다.

143-146 공지

글렌데일 서포트의 새 가족을 환영합니다

글렌데일 서포트는 현재 신규 회원을 모집 중입니다. 저희는 매월 첫째 주와 셋째 주 월요일에 모입니다. **143**하지만 모든 회의에 참석할 필요는 없습니다. 저희 단체는 지역사회 일원들에게 글렌데일 공공장소 개선을 위해 협력할 것을 **144**촉구합니다. 이 **145**협력적인 방법으로 학교, 도서관, 공원 등에 저희의 영향력을 최대화할 수 있습니다. 저희 단체의 일원이 되시려면 6월 18일 오후 7시 필버트 센터 104호에서 열리는 다음 회의에 참석하십시오. 또한 회원 관리자인 카일 톰슨 씨께 k.thompson@glendalesupport.org로 이메일을 보내셔도 됩니다. 저희 단체가 과거에 수행한 **146**프로젝트에 관해 더 알아보시려면 저희 웹사이트 www.glendalesupport.org를 방문하십시오.

어휘 currently 현재 seek 찾다, 구하다 attendance 참가, 출석 organization 단체, 조직 public site 공공장소 approach 접근법, 방법 maximize 최대화하다 carry out 수행하다

143 문맥에 맞는 문장 고르기

번역 (A) 각 프로젝트는 민간기금뿐 아니라 공공기금도 받습니다.
(B) 회비는 경우에 따라 면제될 수 있습니다.
(C) 저희는 매월 첫째 주와 셋째 주 월요일에 모입니다.
(D) 이 서비스는 인기가 높아지고 있습니다.

해설 빈칸 뒤에 나오는 문장 '하지만 모든 회의에 참석할 필요는 없습니다 (However, attendance at all meetings is not required)'를 통해 빈칸에는 회의 일정에 대해 먼저 언급하는 것이 문맥상 자연스러우므로, 정답은 (C)이다.

144 동사 어형 _ 수 / 태

해설 빈칸은 단수주어(Our organization) 뒤의 동사 자리로, 뒤에 나오는 명사(community members)를 목적어로 취한다. 동사 자리에는 (A) is urged, (C) urges, (D) urge가 올 수 있는데 단수주어이므로 복수동사 (D) urge는 올 수 없다. (A), (C) 중에 골라야 하는데 수동의 현재시제 동사 (A) is urged는 목적어를 취할 수 없으므로 정답은 (C) urges이다. to 부정사 (B) to urge는 동사 자리에 올 수 없다.

145 형용사 어휘

해설 빈칸 뒤 명사(approach)를 수식하는 형용사 자리이다. 문맥상 '협력적인 방법으로 영향력을 최대화할 수 있다'가 자연스러우므로, 정답은 (A) cooperative이다. (B) reversible(되돌릴 수 있는), (C) occasional (가끔의), (D) imaginary(상상의)는 의미상 적합하지 않다.

146 목적격 관계대명사

해설 빈칸은 동사(has carried out)의 목적어가 없는 불완전한 절을 이끌면서, 앞에 있는 사물명사(projects)를 수식하는 목적격 관계대명사 자리이므로, 정답은 (C) that이다. 명사절 접속사 (A) what이 이끄는 명사절은 앞에 있는 명사를 수식할 수 없고, 관계대명사 (B) who가 이끄는 관계사절은 앞에 있는 사람명사를 수식한다. 또한 관계부사 (D) where 뒤에는 완전한 절이 나와야 한다.

PART 7

147-148 영수증

- 고객 영수증 -
크로턴 홀
로제티 레인 1265 ▽ 555-0188

날짜: 8월 12일
구매 장소: Agent #081 매표소에서 직접 구매
고객명: 테사 포트니
지불 유형: 신용카드 XXXX-XXXX-XXXX-0734

내역
147부에노스아이레스 극장 오케스트라, 8월 31일 좌석 C51 £28,00
부에노스아이레스 극장 오케스트라, 8월 31일 좌석 C52 £28,00
취급 수수료 £1,50
148극장 복원 및 건설 비용* £5.00
합계 £62.50

148 *부가적인 기부금을 납부해 주셔서 감사합니다. 귀하의 기부금은 저희가 꼭 필요한 개조 공사를 시행하고 현 건축물을 증축하는 데 보탬이 될 것입니다.

어휘 box office 매표소 in person 직접, 몸소 handling charge 취급 수수료 restoration 복원 optional 선택적인 contribution 기부 carry out 수행하다 renovation 개조 build an extension 증축하다 existing 기존의, 존재하는

147 세부 사항

번역 포트니 씨는 어떤 행사의 입장권을 구매했는가?
(A) 학술 강연
(B) 음악 공연
(C) 영화 상영
(D) 코미디 쇼

해설 영수증의 내역(Description)을 보면, 포트니 씨는 부에노스아이레스 극장 오케스트라 공연 입장권(Buenos Aires Theatre Orchestra)을 구매했다는 것을 알 수 있으므로, 정답은 (B)이다.

▶▶ **Paraphrasing** 지문의 **Orchestra**
→ 정답의 **A musical performance**

148 사실 관계 확인

번역 영수증에서 포트니 씨에 대해 명시된 것은?
(A) 시 세금으로 1.50파운드가 부과됐다.
(B) 건축 프로젝트에 기부했다.
(C) 주문을 1개월 전에 했다.
(D) 전화로 입장권을 구매했다.

해설 영수증 내역을 보면 포트니 씨는 극장 복원 및 건설 비용(Theatre Restoration and Construction*)으로 5.00파운드를 지불했다. 또, 하단에서 기부금으로 꼭 필요한 개조 공사를 시행하고 건축물을 증축하는 데 보탬이 될 것이라면서 부가적인 기부금을 납부한 것에 감사한다(*Thank you for your optional contribution! Your support will help us to carry out essential renovations and build an extension to our existing structure)고 했다. 따라서 포트니 씨가 건축 프로젝트에 기부했다는 것을 알 수 있으므로, 정답은 (B)이다.

▶▶ **Paraphrasing** 지문의 **Theatre Restoration and Construction** → 정답의 **a building project**
지문의 **contribution** → 정답의 **donation**

149-150 문자 메시지

루치아노 가르시아 [오전 10:23]
¹⁴⁹안녕하세요. 사우스필드 인코퍼레이티드의 루치아노입니다. 오늘 댁으로 오후 12시 30분에서 1시 30분 사이에 배송할 예정입니다.

멜라니 월터스 [오전 10:26]
제가 집에서 배송을 받을 겁니다. ¹⁴⁹퀸 사이즈 매트리스죠, 그렇죠?

루치아노 가르시아 [오전 10:27]
맞습니다. 주문 번호는 95871입니다.

멜라니 월터스 [오전 10:28]
그런데 문제가 하나 있을 것 같아요. ¹⁵⁰저희 집은 4층인데 이 건물에 엘리베이터가 없어요.

루치아노 가르시아 [오전 10:29]
아, **두 사람이 갑니다.**

멜라니 월터스 [오전 10:30]
¹⁵⁰그럼 되겠네요. 이따가 뵙겠습니다. 감사합니다!

어휘 be scheduled to ~할 예정이다 make a delivery 배송하다

149 추론 / 암시

번역 사우스필드 인코퍼레이티드는 어디이겠는가?
(A) 차량 대여업체
(B) 전자제품 수리 서비스업체
(C) 부동산 중개업체
(D) 가구점

해설 10시 23분 메시지에서 사우스필드 인코퍼레이티드의 루치아노라면서 오후에 배송할 예정이라고 했으며, 10시 26분 메시지에서 월터스 씨는 집에서 배송을 받을 것이라면서 퀸 사이즈 매트리스가 맞는지(It's the queen-sized mattress, right) 확인하고 있다. 따라서 사우스필드 인코퍼레이티드는 가구점임을 추론할 수 있으므로, 정답은 (D)이다.

150 의도 파악

번역 오전 10시 29분에 가르시아 씨가 "두 사람이 갑니다"라고 쓸 때, 그 의도는 무엇인가?
(A) 서비스를 제공하는 데 경쟁이 있다.
(B) 어렵지 않게 제품을 옮길 수 있다.
(C) 행정상의 실수가 생겼다.
(D) 일부 제품은 따로 도착할 예정이다.

해설 인용문 앞뒤 문맥에서 문제 해결의 단서를 찾을 수 있다. 집이 4층인데 건물에 엘리베이터가 없다(My apartment is on the fourth floor, and there's no elevator in this building)는 월터스 씨의 10시 28분 메시지에 가르시아 씨는 두 사람이 간다고 했고, 10시 30분 메시지에서 그럼 괜찮겠다(That should be fine, then)고 했다. 따라서 가르시아가 두 사람이 간다고 말한 의도는 엘리베이터가 없어도 둘이 가니 침대 매트리스를 옮길 수 있다는 것이므로, 정답은 (B)이다.

151-152 편지

브라이언 실바
리버티 스트리트 403
포트워스, TX 76111

실바 씨께,

우편으로 귀하의 운전면허증 갱신 신청서를 받았습니다. 안타깝게도 저희의 갱신 기준에 부합하지 않아 귀하의 요청을 처리할 수 없습니다. ¹⁵¹운전자는 우편으로 연속 2회까지만 갱신을 할 수 있어, 이후에는 새로 촬영한 사진을 가지고 자동차 관리국 사무실을 방문해야 합니다. 이것은 반드시 면허증 만료 이전에 이뤄져야 합니다. ¹⁵²그렇지 않은 경우 귀하는 벌금 부과 대상이 될 수 있습니다. 주 운전면허증 발급 장소 목록이 이 문서의 뒷면에 나와 있습니다.

로버트 넬슨
갱신부

어휘 application 신청 process a request 요청을 처리하다 renewal 갱신 criteria 기준 consecutive 연이은 complete 완료하다 expire 만료되다 be subject to ~의 대상이다

151 세부 사항

번역 실바 씨의 요청이 거절된 이유는 무엇인가?
(A) 이미 우편으로 면허증을 2회 갱신했다.
(B) 크기가 틀린 사진을 보냈다.
(C) 필수 지불금을 넣지 않았다.
(D) 더 이상 같은 주소지에 살지 않는다.

해설 세 번째 문장에서 운전자는 우편으로 연속 2회까지만 갱신을 할 수 있으며, 이후에는 자동차 관리국 사무실을 직접 방문해야 한다(Drivers are only allowed two consecutive renewals by mail, after which they must visit a Motor Vehicles Authority office in person to have a new photograph taken)고 했다. 따라서 실바 씨가 이미 우편으로 연속 2회 면허증을 갱신했기 때문에, 실바 씨의 갱신 요청이 거절되었다는 것을 알 수 있으므로, 정답은 (A)이다.

▶▶ **Paraphrasing** 지문의 two consecutive renewals by mail
→ 정답의 renewed ~ by mail twice

152 세부 사항

번역 실바 씨가 현재 면허증이 만료되도록 둔다면 어떤 일이 발생할 것인가?
(A) 면허 시험을 봐야 할 것이다.
(B) 지원서가 거절될 것이다.
(C) 벌금이 부과될 것이다.
(D) 마감 기한이 연장될 것이다.

해설 지문 후반부에서 면허증 만료 이전에 갱신하지 않는 경우 벌금 부과 대상이 될 수 있다(Otherwise, you could be subject to a penalty charge)고 했다. 따라서 (C)가 정답이다.

▶▶ **Paraphrasing** 지문의 a penalty charge
→ 정답의 A fine may be imposed.

153-154 정보문

> **153**홈밀즈 팀과 함께해 주셔서 감사합니다. 저희는 연로하신 분들께 매일 따뜻한 식사를 배송하여 이들이 외롭지 않게 하고 자립성을 지킬 수 있도록 합니다. 근무를 배정받은 날은 오전 8시에 레스턴에 있는 업무용 주방으로 보고해야 합니다. **154**그곳에서 음식 준비를 거들거나 캘버턴 본사의 저장 시설로부터 물건을 옮겨 오도록 요청받을 것입니다. 음식이 준비되면 10~15 정거장 사이의 배송 노선에 배정을 받게 됩니다. 배송 노선에는 레스턴, 캘버턴, 페어팩스, 랜도버 인근 지역이 포함됩니다. **154**질문이 있으시면 근무 중인 관리자에게 이야기하거나 본사의 오드리 보겔에게 555-0176으로 연락하십시오.
>
> **어휘** the elderly 연장자들 isolation 고립, 외로운 상태 independence 독립, 자립 assign 할당하다 shift 교대 근무 neighborhood 인근 on duty 근무 중인, 당번인

153 추론 / 암시

번역 정보문은 누구를 위한 것이겠는가?
(A) 신입 직원
(B) 잠재적인 자원봉사자
(C) 자선 기부자
(D) 연장자

해설 첫 번째 문장에서 홈밀즈 팀과 함께해 주어 감사하다(Thank you for joining the Home-Meals team)고 한 후 업무에 대해 설명하고 있다. 따라서 신입 직원을 대상으로 한 정보문임을 알 수 있으므로, 정답은 (A)이다.

154 추론 / 암시

번역 보겔 씨는 어디에서 일하겠는가?
(A) 레스턴
(B) 캘버턴
(C) 페어팩스
(D) 랜도버

해설 마지막 문장에서 질문이 있으면 관리자에게 이야기하거나 본사의 오드리 보겔에게 연락하라(Should you have any questions, please speak to the manager on duty, or contact Audrey Vogel at the head office at 555-0176)고 했으므로, 보겔 씨는 본사에서 근무한다는 것을 알 수 있다. 또, 지문 중반부에서 본사는 캘버턴에 있다(at the head office in Calverton)고 했다. 따라서 보겔 씨는 본사가 있는 캘버턴에서 근무한다는 것을 추론할 수 있으므로, 정답은 (B)이다.

155-157 광고

> ### 자전거 투어 가이드 모집!
>
> 위들 파크 플러스의 자전거 투어 가이드가 되어 멋진 자연에서 여름을 보내세요. 가이드는 유티카 국립공원과 그 주변에서 투어를 안내하며 다양한 규모와 기량을 가진 단체를 담당합니다. **155**현대적인 기숙사 내 거주 시설이 하계 시즌 내내 제공되며 투어 및 위치에 따라 개인 비용 부담 없이 공원 근처의 호텔 또는 산장에서 머무를 수도 있습니다. 자전거 투어 가이드는 투어 진행일 하루당 95달러를 지급받으며 식사 일체를 제공받습니다. **156**보수에 관한 질문이 있으시면 1차 면접 시 답변해 드리겠습니다. 모든 가이드는 신체가 건강하고 자전거 유지 보수에 관해 잘 알아야 합니다. 지원하시려면 인사부장 필립 노리스 씨에게 pnorris@wiedl-pp.com으로 이메일을 보내 주시기 바랍니다. **157**해당 직책을 맡는 분들은 고용 첫날 이전에 여행 보험 증서를 발급받아야 함을 주지하시기 바랍니다.
>
> **어휘** conduct (특정한 활동을) 하다, 안내하다 a wide range of 광범위한 dormitory 기숙사 lodge 산장 at no cost 무료로 compensation 보상 initial 최초의 physically fit 신체적으로 건강한, 체력이 좋은 insurance policy 보험 증서, 보험 증권

155 사실 관계 확인

번역 자전거 투어 가이드에게 제공되는 숙박 시설에 대해 명시된 것은?
(A) 국립공원 내에 위치해 있다.
(B) 건물의 위치는 투어에 따라 달라진다.
(C) 투어 진행일에만 무료로 제공된다.
(D) 다른 가이드와 방을 같이 써야 한다.

해설 세 번째 문장에서 숙박시설은 하계 시즌 내내 제공되며 투어 및 위치에 따라 공원 근처의 호텔이나 산장에서 머무를 수도 있다(Housing in our modern dormitory is provided for the entire summer season; depending on the tour and location, you may also be housed at hotels or lodges near the park at no cost to you)고 했다. 따라서 정답은 (B)이다.

156 세부 사항

번역 급여에 관한 질문이 있는 지원자는 어떻게 해야 하는가?
(A) 노리스 씨에게 보내는 메일에 질문을 쓴다.
(B) 계약서 견본을 다운로드한다.
(C) 채용 동영상을 시청한다.
(D) 면접 시 질문한다.

해설 지문 중반부에서 보수에 관한 질문이 있으면 1차 면접 시에 답변해 주겠다(We are happy to answer any questions you may have about compensation at the initial interview)고 했으므로, 정답은 (D)이다.

▶▶ **Paraphrasing** 지문의 **compensation** → 질문의 **payment**

157 세부 사항

번역 광고에 따르면, 신입사원은 업무 시작 전 무엇을 해야 하는가?
(A) 신체검사 통과하기
(B) 회사의 안전 정책 검토하기
(C) 관련 경험 입증하기
(D) 여행 보험 가입하기

해설 마지막 문장에서 신입사원은 첫 업무를 시작하기 전에 여행 보험 증서를 발급받아야 한다(Please note that those who accept the position must purchase a travel insurance policy before the first day of employment)고 했다. 따라서 정답은 (D)이다.

▶▶ **Paraphrasing** 지문의 **before the first day of employment** → 질문의 **before starting work**

158-160 광고

BCP – 각자에 맞게 소포를 부치세요

소포가 제시간에 온전한 상태로 도착하도록 하시려면 BCP에 맡기세요. **158D**저희는 분실 또는 손상 물품 비율이 업계 최저이며 최근에는 상자 크기에 따른 정액 요금제로 변경하여 처음부터 정확한 가격이 나옵니다. **158C**저희 서비스 지점에서 봉투, 상자, 테이프를 무료로 이용할 수 있어 번거롭지 않게 소포를 준비할 수 있습니다. **158B**물품을 보낸 뒤 저희 웹사이트에서 실시간으로 배송을 추적할 수 있습니다. **159**특정 물건은 안전상의 문제 또는 국제법에 의한 제한 때문에 우편으로 운반할 수 없음을 알아두시기 바랍니다. 허가 물품과 금지 물품을 찾아보시려면 www.bcp-mail.com/before_sending을 방문하십시오.

저희는 항상 서비스 향상을 위한 방법을 모색하고 있습니다. **160**지난달 BCP에서 소포를 보낸 적이 있는 고객께서는 간단한 설문조사에 응답하시고 다음 거래 시 15% 할인을 받는 쿠폰을 받으세요. 응하시려면 1-800-555-0144로 전화하십시오.

어휘 parcel 소포 rely on ~을 믿다, ~에 의지하다 on time 정시에 flat fee 정액 요금, 고정 요금 hassle 귀찮은 상황, 일 shipment 배송 in real time 실시간으로 restriction 제한 complete a questionnaire 설문에 응답하다

158 사실 관계 확인

번역 BCP 고객이 이용할 수 있다고 언급되지 않은 것은?
(A) 분실 소포에 대한 보상
(B) 온라인 추적 시스템
(C) 무료 포장용품
(D) 단순화된 가격 체계

해설 보기에 언급된 내용을 지문에서 찾아 하나씩 확인해 본다. 두 번째 문장에서 최근에 상자 크기에 따른 정액 요금제로 변경하여 처음부터 정확한 가격이 나온다(we've recently changed to a flat fee based on box size so that the price is clear from the beginning)고 한 것을 통해 (D)를, 세 번째 문장의 서비스 지점에서 봉투, 상자, 테이프를 무료로 이용할 수 있어 번거롭지 않게 소포를 준비할 수 있다(At our service points, envelopes, boxes, and tape are freely available so that you can get your package ready without any hassle)고 한 것을 통해 (C)를, 네 번째 문장에서 물품을 보낸 뒤 웹사이트에서 실시간으로 배송을 추적할 수 있다(After your items are sent, you can track the shipment in real time on our Web site)고 한 것을 통해 (B)를 확인할 수 있다. 따라서 언급되지 않은 (A)가 정답이다.

▶▶ **Paraphrasing** 지문의 **envelopes, boxes, and tape are freely available**
→ 보기의 **Complimentary packing supplies**
지문의 **track the shipment in real time on our Web site**
→ 보기의 **An online tracking system**

159 세부 사항

번역 광고에 따르면, 언급된 웹페이지에서 찾을 수 있는 것은?
(A) 서비스 지점 약도
(B) 픽업 일정표
(C) 금지 물품 목록
(D) 예상 운송 시간

해설 첫 번째 단락 후반부에서 특정 물건은 안전상의 문제나 국제법에 의한 제한 때문에 우편으로 운반할 수 없다(Remember, certain things cannot be transported through the mail due to safety issues or restrictions set by international law)면서 허가 물품과 금지 물품을 찾아보려면 www.bcp-mail.com/before_sending을 방문하라(To find out what is and is not allowed, visit www.bcp-mail.com/before_sending)고 했다. 따라서 정답은 (C)이다.

160 세부 사항

번역 고객이 할인 쿠폰을 받을 수 있는 방법은 무엇인가?
(A) 친구 추천하기
(B) 서비스 자주 이용하기
(C) 우편물 수신자 명단에 들어가기
(D) 설문 작성하기

해설 두 번째 단락 중반부에서 간단한 설문조사에 응답하고 다음 거래 시에 15%를 할인받을 수 있는 쿠폰을 받으라(Customers who have sent a package through BCP anytime in the past month may complete a short questionnaire in May to receive a voucher for 15% off their next transaction)고 했다. 따라서 정답은 (D)이다.

161-163 이메일

수신: 캐리 키턴 (ckeaton@drilbyskiresort.com)
발신: 에반 바넷 (ebarnett@drilbyskiresort.com)
날짜: 9월 4일
제목: 잡지 광고
첨부: maxfuntravelsubmissions.doc

캐리 씨께,

〈맥스 펀 트래블〉 10월호에 게재될 저희 리조트 광고를 디자인하는 데 동의해 주셔서 감사합니다. **161**저희는 이번 시즌에 영향을 줄 변경 사항, 즉 저희 식당이 여름 동안 개조를 한 뒤 다시 개점하며 리프트 표마다 스키 강사와 함께하는 무료 강좌가 포함된다는 사실에 대해 신규 및 기존 고객 모두에게 알리는 광고를 하고 싶습니다.

저는 〈맥스 펀 트래블〉의 제출 부서에 연락을 취해 최근 지침을 요청했으며 귀하의 추천서 사본을 첨부했습니다. 저희 회사 데이터베이스에 있는 사진은 모두 자유롭게 사용하시기 바랍니다. **163**〈맥스 펀 트래블〉로 보내는 파일은 제출 시 출판할 준비가 완벽히 되어 있어야 하며 올바른 포맷이어야 합니다. 이 시점이 지나면 잡지사에서 변경에 관해 특별 요금을 청구합니다. 저희는 예산상 반 페이지짜리 광고를 집행할 여유밖에 없습니다. **162**컬러 광고여도 되지만 이 잡지는 반 페이지짜리 가로형 광고만 제공하므로 디자인은 위로 긴 것보다는 옆으로 넓어야 할 것입니다. 애로 사항이 생기면 주저 없이 저에게 이메일을 보내시기 바랍니다.

감사합니다.

에반

어휘　**advertisement** 광고　**namely** 즉, 다시 말해　**renovation** 개조, 보수　**complimentary** 무료의　**attach** 첨부하다　**reference** 추천서　**publication** 출판　**budget** 예산　**horizontal** 가로의　**run into** (곤경 등을) 만나다[겪다]　**obstacle** 장애물

161 세부 사항

번역　드릴비 스키 리조트는 무엇을 처음 제공하려고 하는가?
　　　(A) 무료 스키 강좌
　　　(B) 현장 식사
　　　(C) 하계 투어
　　　(D) 1박 숙소

해설　첫 번째 단락에서 이번 시즌의 변경 사항으로 식당이 여름 동안 개조를 한 뒤 다시 개점하며 스키 강사와 함께 하는 무료 강좌가 이제 제공될 것(namely, that our dining hall has reopened after renovations throughout the summer, and that a complimentary session with a ski instructor will now be included with every lift ticket)이라고 했다. 따라서 정답은 (A)이다.

▶▶ Paraphrasing　지문의 **a complimentary session with a ski instructor**
　　　　　　　　 → 정답의 **Free skiing lessons**

162 사실 관계 확인

번역　바넷 씨가 광고에 대해 언급한 것은?
　　　(A) 사진 여러 개가 들어가야 한다.
　　　(B) 월말까지 제출해야 한다.
　　　(C) 색상 수가 제한되어 있다.
　　　(D) 특정 형태를 갖고 있다.

해설　두 번째 단락 후반부에서 반 페이지짜리 가로형 광고만 제공하므로 디자인은 위로 긴 것보다는 옆으로 넓어야 한다(It can be in full color, but the magazine only offers horizontal half-page ads, so the design must be wider than it is tall)고 했다. 따라서 (D)가 정답이다.

▶▶ Paraphrasing　지문의 **horizontal half-page**
　　　　　　　　 → 정답의 **a specific shape**

163 문장 삽입

번역　[1], [2], [3], [4]로 표시된 곳 중에서 다음 문장이 들어가기에 가장 적합한 곳은?

　　　"이 시점이 지나면 잡지사에서 변경에 관해 특별 요금을 청구합니다."

　　　(A) [1]
　　　(B) [2]
　　　(C) [3]
　　　(D) [4]

해설　주어진 문장의 after that point가 문제 해결의 단서로, 주어진 문장은 특정 시점이 언급된 내용 뒤에 들어가야 한다. 따라서 주어진 문장은 파일 제출 시 완벽하게 준비가 되어야 하며 올바른 포맷이어야 한다(The file sent to *Max Fun Travel* must be completely ready for publication and in the correct format when it is submitted)는 문장 뒤인 [3]에 들어가야 문맥의 흐름이 자연스러우므로 (C)가 정답이다.

164-167 기사

히메네스-라이트 엔터프라이즈, 지평을 넓히다

7월 29일—운동용 의류 제조업체 히메네스-라이트 엔터프라이즈는 어제 열린 언론 발표에서 아동 의류 시장으로 분화하기 위해 신규 의류 제품군을 추가할 예정이라고 확정 발표했다. 이는 최근 CEO로 임명된 제시 스테그만이 추진한 계획이다. **166B, 167**히메네스-라이트 엔터프라이즈는 남성용 의류와 여성용 의류를 각각 국내 생산하는 인기 소매업체 채스켈과 크리스모어의 모회사다. **164**히메네스-라이트 엔터프라이즈는 작년 데이토나 비치에서 그들이 처음 개최한 비치발리볼 경기에 참가한 충성 고객들의 의견에 따라 아동에게 적합한 의류 개발을 시작했다.

165"지난 몇 년간 아동 비만율이 증가했습니다. 하루 종일 학교에 있으니 운동할 기회가 거의 없으니까요." 업체 컨설턴트인 소아과 의사 조던 다우니 씨의 설명이다. "다행히 부모들이 이 문제에 대해 각성하고 가족 전체에 건강한 생활 습관을 택하며 조치를 취하기 시작했습니다."

히메네스-라이트 엔터프라이즈는 5~13세 아동을 위한 운동용 의류 제품군인 메릴루를 도입함으로써 이러한 추세를 활용하고자 한다. **166B, C**해당 의류는 재생 가공한 플라스틱 병에서 얻은 천을 최대 40%까지 활용해 히메네스-라이트 엔터프라이즈의 기존 공장에서 생산된다. **166D**성인을 위한 매장의 제품 다수가 천의 기능을 유지하기 위해 손빨래를 해야 하는 제품이지만 메릴루의 모든 제품은 세탁기로 세탁할 수 있으며 얼룩에 강하다. **167**처음에는 고객의 관심을 알아보기 위해 업체의 여성용 의류 매장에서 출시할 예정이지만 메릴루만을 판매하는 소매점을 두는 것이 장기 계획이다.

> **어휘** press briefing 기자단 발표 activewear 야외용 의류, 운동용 의류 recently appointed 최근 임명된 parent company 모회사 domestically 국내에서 respectively 각각 suitable for ~에게 적합한 obesity 비만 pediatrician 소아과 의사 take action 조치를 취하다 capitalize on ~을 (기회로) 활용하다 apparel 의류, 의복 reprocessed 재생 가공된 resistant to ~에 저항하는 roll out 출시하다 long-term 장기간의 exclusively 독점적으로

164 사실 관계 확인

번역 히메네스-라이트 엔터프라이즈에 대해 사실인 것은?
(A) 최근에 경쟁 제조업체를 인수했다.
(B) 운동 장비를 개발 중이다.
(C) 작년에 스포츠 경기를 개최했다.
(D) 아동 스포츠 단체를 만들 예정이다.

해설 첫 번째 단락의 마지막 문장에서 히메네스-라이트 엔터프라이즈가 작년 데이토나 비치에서 처음 개최한 비치발리볼 경기에 참가한 고객들의 의견에 따라 아동에게 적합한 의류 개발을 시작했다(Based on feedback from loyal customers who attended Jimenez-Wright's first-ever beach volleyball competition at Daytona Beach last year, the company began developing clothing suitable for children)고 했다. 따라서 히메네스-라이트 엔터프라이즈는 작년에 스포츠 경기를 개최했다고는 것을 알 수 있으므로, 정답은 (C)이다.

> ▶▶ **Paraphrasing** 지문의 **Jimenez-Wright's first-ever beach volleyball competition**
> → 정답의 **a sports competition**

165 추론 / 암시

번역 다우니 씨는 누구이겠는가?
(A) 재무 컨설턴트
(B) 전문 의료인
(C) 학교 교장
(D) 회사 CEO

해설 두 번째 단락의 첫 문장에서 조던 다우니 씨는 소아과 의사(pediatrician Jordan Downey, a consultant for the company)임을 알 수 있다. 따라서 정답은 (B)이다.

> ▶▶ **Paraphrasing** 지문의 **pediatrician**
> → 정답의 **A medical professional**

166 사실 관계 확인

번역 메릴루 제품에 대해 암시되지 않은 것은?
(A) 세탁기를 이용하기에는 너무 약할 것이다.
(B) 국내 생산될 것이다.
(C) 일부 재활용 소재로 제작될 것이다.
(D) 얼룩에 강한 천으로 만들 것이다.

해설 보기에 언급된 내용을 지문에서 찾아 하나씩 확인해 본다. 첫 단락 두 번째 문장에서 히메네스-라이트 엔터프라이즈는 남성용 의류와 여성용 의류를 각각 국내 생산하는 인기 소매업체 채스켈과 크리스모어의 모회사(Jimenez-Wright Enterprises is the parent company of the popular retailers Chaskell and Krismore, whose clothing is produced domestically for men and women, respectively)라고 한 것을 통해 (B)를 확인할 수 있다. 마지막 단락 두 번째 문장에서 재생 가공한 플라스틱 병에서 얻은 천을 최대 40%까지 활용해 히메네스-라이트 엔터프라이즈의 기존 공장에서 생산된다(The apparel will be manufactured in Jimenez-Wright Enterprises' existing factories, with up to 40% of the fabrics made from reprocessed plastic bottles)고 한 것을 통해 (B)와 (C)를 확인할 수 있다. 또, 이어지는 문장에서 얼룩에 강하다(resistant to staining)고 한 것을 통해 (D)를 확인할 수 있다. 메릴루의 모든 제품은 세탁기로 세탁할 수 있다(all items in the Marilou line will be machine-washable)고 했으므로, 정답은 (A)이다.

> ▶▶ **Paraphrasing** 지문의 **up to 40% of the fabrics made from reprocessed plastic bottles**
> → 정답의 **will be partially made from recycled materials**
> 지문의 **resistant to staining**
> → 정답의 **stain resistant**

167 세부 사항

번역 메릴루 제품군은 어디서 처음 판매될 것인가?
(A) 특정 웹사이트
(B) 계절별 카탈로그
(C) 채스켈 매장
(D) 크리스모어 매장

해설 첫 단락의 두 번째 문장에서 남성용 의류를 판매하는 소매업체는 채스켈이고, 여성용 의류를 판매하는 소매업체는 크리스모어(Jimenez-Wright Enterprises is the parent company of the popular retailers Chaskell and Krismore, whose clothing is produced domestically for men and women, respectively)임을 알 수 있다. 세 번째 단락 마지막 문장에서 메릴루 제품은 여성용 의류(Initially, the line will be rolled out in stores with the company's women's clothing to test consumers' interest, but the long-term plan is to have retail stores that sell Marilou exclusively)임을 알 수 있으므로, 정답은 (D)이다.

168-171 공지

도로공사 공지

10월 7일 월요일에 세실 대로 약 2,000피트 지하 수로관에서 공사가 시작될 예정입니다. **168**수십 년 된 노후 콘크리트관이 아연 도금 강관으로 교체됩니다. 75만 달러가 소요되는 이번 프로젝트는 올해 초 시 의회에서 승인을 받아 기반 시설 개발을 위한 연방 정부 보조금에서 기금이 일부 지원됩니다.

프로젝트 진행 동안 특정 인근 지역의 물 공급을 중단해야 합니다. **171**이런 경우 고무 호스를 통해 임시로 물을 공급할 예정이며 각 가정은 최대 약 48시간 동안 영향을 받게 됩니다. 해당 주거 지역의 주민은 이미 시로부터 고지를 받았습니다.

세실 대로는 구획으로 나뉘어 도로가 일부 봉쇄되고 단일 차로만 사용 가능합니다. **169**작업자들이 오후 6시 30분부터 오전 6시 30분까지 작업하여 교통 흐름 방해를 최소화할 예정입니다. **170**그러나 대체 도로들이 평상시보다 혼잡하여 해당 지역 운전자들은 정체를 예상해야 하며, 우회를 지시하는 알림 및 표지판에 주목해야 합니다. 아울러 공사 구역에서는 과속 벌금이 두 배라는 점을 알립니다. 작업에 6주가 소요될 것으로 예상하나 악천후로 일부 작업이 지연될 수 있습니다. 봉쇄, 진행 상황, 대체 도로 추천 등에 관한 새로운 내용은 교통부 웹사이트에서 찾아볼 수 있습니다.

어휘 water pipe 수로관　boulevard 대로　aging 노후한 date back 거슬러 올라가다　galvanized steel 아연 도금 강판 city council 시 의회　federal grant 연방 정부 보조금 infrastructure 기반 시설　temporary 임시의　approximately 대략　at most 많아야　be torn up 갈기갈기 찢어지다, 나뉘다 interruption 방해, 중단　alternative 대체의, 대안이 되는　than usual 평소보다　signage 표지, 신호　adverse weather 악천후

168 주제 / 목적

번역 공지에서 알리는 사항은 무엇인가?
(A) 도로 철책 추가
(B) 세실 대로 폭 확장
(C) 노후한 수로관 교체
(D) 물 정화 필터 설치

해설 첫 번째 단락의 첫 번째 문장에서 지하 수로관에서 공사가 시작될 예정이라고 했으며, 이어지는 두 번째 문장에서 수십 년 된 노후 콘크리트관이 아연 도금 강관으로 교체된다(Aging concrete pipes that date back several decades will be swapped for those made of galvanized steel)고 했다. 따라서 노후한 수로관 교체를 알리는 공지문임을 알 수 있으므로, 정답은 (C)이다.

▶▶ **Paraphrasing**　지문의 **Aging concrete pipes that date back several decades** → 정답의 **outdated pipes**

169 사실 관계 확인

번역 작업자들에 대해 명시된 것은?
(A) 1개월 이내에 작업을 완료할 것이다.
(B) 진행 상황 사진을 온라인에 게시할 것이다.
(C) 혼잡한 시간에는 작업을 하지 않을 것이다.
(D) 혼잡한 도로를 완전히 봉쇄할 것이다.

해설 세 번째 단락의 두 번째 문장에서 작업자들이 오후 6시 30분부터 오전 6시 30분까지 작업하여 교통 흐름 방해를 최소화할 예정(Crews will work from 6:30 P.M. to 6:30 A.M. to minimize interruptions to the flow of traffic)이라고 했다. 따라서 혼잡한 시간에는 작업을 하지 않을 것임을 알 수 있으므로, 정답은 (C)이다.

170 세부 사항

번역 공지에 따르면, 운전자들은 공사 구역 내에서 무엇을 해야 하는가?
(A) 정보 제공 표지에 유의하기
(B) 창문을 닫아두기
(C) 속도 위반을 신고하기
(D) 우회도로 근처에 주차하지 않기

해설 세 번째 단락 중반부에서 대체 도로들이 평상시보다 혼잡하여 해당 지역 운전자들은 정체를 예상해야 하며, 우회를 지시하는 알림 및 표지판에 주목해야 한다(Still, motorists in the area should expect delays, as alternative routes will be busier than usual, and they should watch for notices and signage in the area indicating detours)고 했다. 따라서 정답은 (A)이다.

▶▶ **Paraphrasing**　지문의 **watch for notices and signage** → 정답의 **Look out for informational signs**

171 문장 삽입

번역 [1], [2], [3], [4]로 표시된 곳 중에서 다음 문장이 들어가기에 가장 적합한 곳은?

"해당 주거 지역의 주민은 이미 시로부터 고지를 받았습니다."

(A) [1]
(B) [2]
(C) [3]
(D) [4]

해설 주어진 문장은 '해당 주거 지역의 주민은 이미 시로부터 고지를 받았다'라는 의미이므로, 주어진 문장은 해당 지역이 어떤 영향을 받게 될지에 대해 언급한 문장(In those cases, a temporary water supply will be provided via a series of rubber hoses, and individual households will be affected for approximately 48 hours at most) 뒤인 [2]에 들어가야 문맥의 흐름이 자연스러워진다. 따라서 정답은 (B)이다.

172-175 온라인 채팅

시드니 리 [오전 11:25]
172우리 회사에서 새로 건설한 제조 시설 개소식이 8월 10일, 이번 금요일에 열립니다. 핀치 씨가 저희 팀에서 세 명이 참석하기를 바랍니다. 그래서 우리 네 명 중 누가 남을지 정해야 해요.

샬롯 맥켄지 [오전 11:27]
핀치 씨의 메모에는 다섯 명의 특별 손님이 올 예정이라고 되어 있어요. 다른 팀의 누군가를, 아마 마케팅 부장을 초대하는 것뿐만 아니라 우리 모두 갈 수 있어요.

나콜라 고얄 [오전 11:28]
173총 다섯 명이 올 거라는 건 맞지만, 메모에는 핀치 씨 자신도 참석할 계획이고 가이아 티벤 CEO도 간단한 연설을 하기 위해 동행할 것이라고 되어 있어요.

샬롯 맥켄지 [오전 11:29]
아, 제가 그 부분을 빠뜨렸나 봅니다.

민 쳉 [오전 11:31]
저는 공장에서 사용될 최신 기기를 보는 데 관심이 있지만, 가지 않는 한 명에 자원하겠습니다. **174**사실 저는 갈 수가 없어요. 직원 평가 보고서 기한이 곧 다가오거든요.

시드니 리 [오전 11:32]
알겠습니다. 그럼 됐어요. 핀치 씨와 티벤 씨는 알아서 공장으로 오실 겁니다. 거기서 바로 출장을 떠나시니까요. 샬롯, 나콜라, 어떤 교통 수단이 좋습니까?

나콜라 고얄 [오전 11:33]
175사무실에서 만나 차를 함께 타고 가죠.

샬롯 맥켄지 [오전 11:34]
좋은 생각입니다. 차로 두 시간 정도 걸리니 각자 가면 지루할 수도 있어요.

민 쳉 [오전 11:35]
즐거운 시간 보내세요! 어땠는지 제게 알려 주시고요.

어휘 grand opening 개업 manufacturing plant 제조 시설, 제조 공장 be in attendance 참석하다 figure out 알아내다 stay behind 뒤에 남다 give a speech 연설하다 brief 간단한 state-of-the-art 최신의

172 세부 사항

번역 8월 10일에 어떤 일이 있을 것인가?
(A) 공장 점검이 있을 것이다.
(B) 신제품이 출시될 것이다.
(C) 시설을 공식 개소할 것이다.
(D) 임원이 시상할 것이다.

해설 11시 25분 리 씨의 메시지에서 회사에서 새로 건설한 제조 시설 개소식이 8월 10일에 열릴 예정(The grand opening of our company's newly constructed manufacturing plant will take place this Friday, August 10)이라고 했다. 따라서 정답은 (C)이다.

▶▶ Paraphrasing   지문의 **The grand opening of our company's newly constructed manufacturing plant**
→ 정답의 **A facility will officially open.**

173 의도 파악

번역 오전 11시 29분에 맥켄지 씨가 "제가 그 부분을 빠뜨렸나 봅니다"라고 쓸 때, 그 의도는 무엇인가?
(A) 메모를 꼼꼼히 읽지 않았다.
(B) 핀치 씨가 보낸 문서를 잘못 두고 찾지 못했다.
(C) 행사에 참석했던 일을 기억하지 못한다.
(D) 기한이 지난 것을 깨달았다.

해설 인용문 앞뒤 문맥에서 문제 해결의 단서를 찾을 수 있다. 여기서도 11시 28분 고얄 씨의 메시지에서 총 다섯 명이 올 예정인 것은 맞지만 메모에는 핀치 씨 자신도 참석할 계획이고 가이아 티벤 CEO도 간단한 연설을 하기 위해 동행할 것이라고 되어 있다(You're right that there will be five people in total, but the memo said that Mr. Finch plans to be there himself and that CEO Gaia Tieben is going along as well in order to give a brief speech)고 했다. 따라서 '그 부분을 빠뜨린 것 같다'는 말의 의도는 메모를 꼼꼼히 읽지 않았다는 것이므로, 정답은 (A)이다.

174 세부 사항

번역 쳉 씨가 행사에 갈 수 없는 이유는 무엇인가?
(A) 평가에서 나쁜 점수를 받았다.
(B) 보고서 작성을 끝마쳐야 했다.
(C) 출장을 준비하고 있다.
(D) 도구 사용법을 모른다.

해설 11시 31분 쳉 씨의 메시지에서 쳉 씨는 직원 평가 보고서 기한이 곧 다가오고 있어서 행사에 갈 수 없다(I can't go, really—I've got an employee evaluation report due soon)고 했다. 따라서 정답은 (B)이다.

▶▶ Paraphrasing   지문의 **I've got an employee evaluation report due soon**
→ 정답의 **She has to finish writing a report.**

175 세부 사항

번역 고얄 씨는 무엇을 하자고 제안하는가?
(A) 대중교통 이용하기
(B) 장소로 함께 이동하기
(C) 두 시간 일찍 도착하기
(D) 회사 차량 대여하기

해설 11시 33분 메시지에서 고얄 씨는 사무실에서 만나 차를 함께 타고 가자(Let's meet at the office and then carpool there)고 제안했다. 따라서 정답은 (B)이다.

▶▶ Paraphrasing   지문의 **carpool there**
→ 정답의 **Traveling to a site together**

176-180 이메일 + 이메일

수신: 프레야 켄트 〈f.kent@abbotmail.com〉
발신: 해리슨 스타인 〈harrison_stein@colimabank.com〉
날짜: 2월 10일
제목: 콜리마 은행

켄트 씨께,

콜리마 은행을 대표하여 개인 은행 서비스 이용에 저희 은행을 고려해 주셔서 감사의 말씀을 드립니다. **176**오늘 오후 오로라 지점에서 귀하를 응대하여 반가 웠습니다. 약속 드린 대로, 저희가 제공하는 개인 보통 예금에 관한 세부 사항을 보냅니다. 계좌 개설을 진행하시려면 아래의 사항을 유의해 주십시오.

- 1인당 개인 계좌 수를 제한하고 있으나 계좌 유형은 언제든 변경 가능합니다.
- 귀하의 운전면허증으로 기본적인 개인 정보와 주소를 확인했습니다. **177**선택하시는 계좌 유형에 따라 추가 확인을 위해 여권의 정보가 있는 페이지 사본이 필요할 수도 있습니다.
- 지급 이자는 매월 말일에 귀하의 계좌에 자동으로 예치됩니다.

	최소 개설 예치금	이자율	연 최대 인출횟수
콜리마 베이직	50달러	.01%	5
콜리마 골드	250달러	.025%	8
179콜리마 프라이어리티	1,000달러	.03%	10
콜리마 플래티넘	$2,500달러	.05%	무제한

555-0175, 내선번호 33번으로 저에게 직접 연락하실 수 있습니다. 답신 기다리겠습니다.

해리슨 스타인

콜리마 은행 계좌 담당

어휘 on behalf of ~을 대표하여 savings account 보통 예금
move forward with ~을 진행하다 open an account 계좌를
개설하다 verify 확인하다 verification 확인 interest 이자
deposit 예치하다, 예금하다 interest rate 이자율 withdrawal
인출

수신: 해리스 스타인 ⟨harrion_stein@colimabank.com⟩
발신: 프레야 켄트 ⟨f.kent@abbotmail.com⟩
날짜: 2월 11일
제목: Re: 콜리마 은행

스타인 씨께,

179선택사항을 검토했으며 저에게 가장 잘 맞는 계좌는 콜리마 프라이어리티일 것 같습니다. **178**서비스 품질이 만족스럽다면 제 회사 계좌도 귀사로 전환하고자 합니다. 이자율도 중요하지만 저에게는 좋은 서비스가 정말 **180**중요합니다.

프레야 켄트

어휘 switch 전환하다, 바꾸다 corporate 회사의 count 중요하다

---

176 주제 / 목적

번역 스타인 씨가 첫 번째 이메일을 보낸 이유는?
(A) 약속을 이행하기 위해
(B) 실수를 바로잡기 위해
(C) 변경 사항을 설명하기 위해
(D) 약속을 확정하기 위해

해설 두 번째 문장에서 오늘 오후 오로라 지점에서 귀하를 응대하여 반가웠다면서 약속대로 개인 보통 예금에 관한 세부 사항을 보낸다(It was a pleasure speaking to you at the Aurora branch this afternoon, and, as promised, I am sending the details of the individual savings accounts we offer)고 했다. 따라서 스타인 씨가 첫 번째 이메일을 보낸 이유는 약속을 이행하기 위한 것임을 알 수 있으므로, 정답은 (A)이다.

▶▶ **Paraphrasing** 지문의 **as promised, I am sending the details of the individual savings accounts we offer**
→ 정답의 **To fulfill a promise**

---

177 사실 관계 확인

번역 스타인 씨가 자신이 보낸 이메일에 언급한 것은?
(A) 추가적인 신분 확인이 필요할 수도 있다.
(B) 서류 작업은 오로라 지점에서 완료해야 한다.
(C) 제공하는 내용은 한시적으로만 가능하다.
(D) 콜리마 베이직이 가장 인기 있는 계좌 유형이다.

해설 스타인 씨가 켄트 씨에게 보낸 이메일 중반부에서 선택하는 계좌 유형에 따라 추가 확인을 위해 여권의 정보가 있는 페이지 사본이 필요할 수도 있다(I may need a copy of your passport information page for additional verification, depending on the account type you choose)고 했다. 따라서 정답은 (A)이다.

▶▶ **Paraphrasing** 지문의 **need a copy of your passport information page for additional verification** → 정답의 **Further identification checks may be necessary.**

---

178 추론 / 암시

번역 켄트 씨에 대해 암시된 것은?
(A) 나중에 자신의 계좌를 업그레이드할 계획이다.
(B) 현재 자신의 사업을 운영하고 있다.
(C) 콜리마 은행 웹사이트에 평을 올렸다.
(D) 콜리마 은행 서비스에 실망했다.

해설 켄트 씨가 보낸 이메일 두 번째 문장에서 서비스 품질이 만족스럽다면 자신의 회사 계좌도 귀사로 전환하고자 한다(If I am pleased with the quality of service I receive, I may also switch over my corporate account to your bank)고 했다. 따라서 켄트 씨가 자신의 사업을 운영하고 있다는 것을 알 수 있으므로, 정답은 (B)이다.

▶▶ **Paraphrasing** 지문의 **my corporate account**
→ 정답의 **operates her own business**

---

179 연계

번역 켄트 씨가 선택한 계좌에 대해 사실인 것은?
(A) 특정 금액 이상은 예치할 수 없다.
(B) 선택사항 중 이자율이 가장 높다.
(C) 최초 잔고가 2,500달러여야 한다.
(D) 일 년에 10회 돈을 인출할 수 있다.

해설 켄트 씨가 보낸 이메일의 첫 번째 문장에서 켄트 씨는 선택사항을 검토했으며 자신에게 가장 잘 맞는 계좌는 콜리마 프라이어리티일 것 같다(I have reviewed the options, and I think the best account for me would be the Colima Priority account)고 했다. 스타인 씨가 보낸 이메일을 보면 콜리마 프라이어리티의 연 최대 인출 횟수(Maximum Annual Withdrawals)는 10회이므로, 정답은 (D)이다.

180 동의어 찾기

번역 두 번째 이메일에서 첫 번째 단락 4행의 "counts"와 의미가 가장 가까운 단어는?
(A) 계산하다
(B) 평가하다
(C) 중요하다
(D) 의지하다

해설 해당 문장은 '이자율도 중요하지만 저에게는 좋은 서비스가 정말 중요하다'라는 의미로 해석되므로, counts는 '중요하다'는 의미가 자연스럽다. 따라서 정답은 (C) matters(중요하다)이다.

181-185 웹페이지 + 온라인 양식

---

www.megaphotosearch.com

홈	검색	뉴스	가입	연락처

181메가 포토 서치(MPS)는 최초로 개인 및 소규모 업체들을 위한 사진 라이브러리를 오픈했습니다. 이전에는 대기업에게만 제공되던 사진 모음집이었으나, 더욱 대중적으로 사용될 수 있도록 저희 웹사이트를 바꿨습니다. MPS는 프리랜서 사진작가들을 대거 보유하고 있어 온라인상 가장 품질이 우수한 최대 규모의 사진 모음집으로 자리매김하고 있습니다. **182**아울러 온라인 채팅을 통해 24시간 내내 질문에 답할 수 있는 기술팀이 있어 고객 응대가 원활하다고 자부합니다.

저희는 사진을 낱장으로는 판매하지 않지만 가입하시면 예산에 맞는 적정 가격으로 이용하실 수 있습니다. 가입하여 다운로드하는 사진에 대해서는 라이선스(전용 아님)를 영구 보유할 수 있습니다. **183**가격은 하단에 명시되어 있으며 위약금 없이 언제든 계약을 해지할 수 있습니다. 첫 번째 청구서에는 등록비 25달러가 포함되며 이 시점부터 월 1회 청구서를 받게 됩니다.

가입 유형	월 다운로드 횟수	사용자 수	월 이용료	보너스
스탠다드	50	1	75달러	—
스탠다드 플러스	300	1	150달러	1년 후 사진 100장 증정
파트너	700	2	280달러	새로운 사진 입고 사전 통보
팀	700	3–5	**184**310달러	레인박스* 무료 접속

184*레인박스는 사진의 색상과 크기를 조정하고 여러 장의 사진을 하나로 통합할 수 있게 하는 MPS의 온라인 소프트웨어 프로그램입니다.

어휘 previously 이전에 adapt 맞추다, 조정하다 extensive 광범위한, 매우 넓은 around the clock 24시간 내내, 밤낮으로 subscription 가입 reasonably priced 가격이 적정한 budget 예산 retain 보유하다 permanent 영구한 exclusive 독점적인, 전용의 terminate an agreement 계약을 해지하다, 종료하다 sign-up fee 등록비 advance notice 사전 통보 multiple 다수의

---

www.megaphotosearch.com

홈	검색	뉴스	가입	연락처

메가 포토 서치 – 신규 가입자

이름: 데인 멀린스
회사 (해당되는 경우): 벨린 퍼블리싱
이메일 주소: dmullins@bellin-publ.com
주간 연락번호: 469-555-0172
청구지 주소: 마리온 애비뉴 975, 케임브리지, MA 02142

청구서 세부 내역: 등록비 25달러 + **184**월 이용료 310달러
5539로 끝나는 신용카드로 청구됨. 계속 발생하는 비용은 매월 해당 카드로 청구됨.

메가 포토 서치를 선택해 주셔서 감사합니다. **185**가입 축하 선물로 저희 사진 모음집을 효율적으로 검색하는 법에 관한 노하우를 드리는 무료 전자책을 드립니다. 다운로드하시려면 여기를 클릭하십시오.

어휘 if applicable 해당되는 경우 efficiently 효율적으로

181 주제 / 목적

번역 웹페이지에 있는 정보의 주요 목적은 무엇인가?
(A) 고객이 업그레이드를 하도록 장려하는 것
(B) 회사 합병에 관한 새 소식을 전하는 것
(C) 서비스 확대를 알리는 것
(D) 프리랜서 사진작가들에게 제출을 요청하는 것

해설 웹페이지 첫 두 문장에서 메가 포토 서치(MPS)는 최초로 개인 및 소규모 업체들을 위한 사진 라이브러리를 오픈했다(Mega Photo Search (MPS) is pleased to open our photo library to individuals and small businesses for the first time ever)면서 이전에는 대기업에게만 제공하던 사진 모음집이었으나 더욱 대중적으로 사용할 수 있도록 웹사이트를 바꿨다(This collection was previously only offered to large corporations, but we have adapted our Web site for more general use)고 했다. 따라서 서비스 확대를 알리기 위한 글임을 알 수 있으므로, 정답은 (C)이다.

182 사실 관계 확인

번역 MPS에 대해 명시된 것은?
(A) 다른 경쟁업체들보다 사진 모음집 규모가 크다.
(B) 24시간 고객 지원을 한다.
(C) 소규모 업체 소유주들을 위한 워크숍을 제공한다.
(D) 최근 케임브리지에 지점을 열었다.

해설 웹페이지 첫 단락 마지막 문장에서 온라인 채팅을 통해 24시간 내내 질문에 답할 수 있는 기술팀이 있어 고객 응대가 원활하다고 자부한다(Also, with our technical team available to answer questions around the clock via online chat, we are confident that we can serve our customers well)고 했다. 따라서 24시간 고객 지원을 한다는 것을 알 수 있으므로, 정답은 (B)이다.

▶▶ **Paraphrasing** 지문의 around the clock
→ 정답의 twenty-four hours a day

183 사실 관계 확인

번역 웹페이지상에서 가입에 대해 언급된 것은?
(A) 가입하면 사용자가 삽화를 다운로드할 수 있다.
(B) 개인만 가입할 수 있다.
(C) 매월 1일에 청구된다.
(D) 비용 발생 없이 취소할 수 있다.

해설 웹페이지 두 번째 단락의 세 번째 문장에서 가격은 하단에 명시되어 있으며 위약금 없이 언제든 계약을 해지할 수 있다(Prices are listed below, and you can terminate your service agreement at any time without penalty)고 했다. 따라서 정답은 (D)이다.

▶▶ **Paraphrasing** 지문의 **without penalty**
→ 정답의 **without incurring a fee**

184 연계

번역 멀린스 씨에 대해 암시된 것은?
(A) 일 년 후 무료 사진 100장을 받을 것이다.
(B) 계좌 이체로 정기 납부를 할 것이다.
(C) 사진이 추가될 경우 통지를 받을 것이다.
(D) 이미지 편집 소프트웨어에 접속할 수 있을 것이다.

해설 온라인 양식을 보면 멀린 씨의 월 이용료는 310달러($310 monthly fee)이다. 웹페이지를 보면 월 이용료가 310달러이면, 사진의 색상과 크기를 조정하고 여러 장의 사진을 하나로 통합할 수 있게 하는 MPS의 온라인 소프트웨어 프로그램(Rainbox is MPS's online software program that allows you to adjust the color and size of photos and combine multiple images into one)인 레인박스에 무료 접속(Free access to Rainbox)이 가능하다고 했다. 따라서 정답은 (D)이다.

185 세부 사항

번역 온라인 양식에 따르면, 다운로드 가능한 파일에 무엇이 들어 있는가?
(A) 검색 실행에 관한 조언
(B) 사진 촬영에 관한 책
(C) 저작권법에 관한 정보
(D) 가입 영수증

해설 온라인 양식의 마지막 문장에서 가입 축하 선물로 사진 모음집을 효율적으로 검색하는 법에 관한 노하우를 알려 주는 무료 전자책을 준다면서 다운로드하려면 여기를 클릭하라(As a welcome gift, we are offering a free e-book that gives you tips on how to search our collection efficiently. Click here to download it)고 했다. 따라서 정답은 (A)이다.

▶▶ **Paraphrasing** 지문의 **tips on how to search our collection efficiently**
→ 정답의 **Advice for conducting searches**

186-190 기사 + 일정표 + 전단지

다시 찾아온 러레이도 커뮤니티 페스티벌

러레이도 (5월 5일) – 점점 인기를 더하는 러레이도 커뮤니티 페스티벌(LCF)이 이번 여름에 6월 27일부터 6월 28일까지 롤랜드 파크에서 다시 개최될 예정이다. [186]올해는 항상 있었던 지역 식당 및 소매업체 부스에 더해, 기금 마련 및 홍보를 위한 자선단체 구역도 마련된다.

행사 기획자인 애니타 구티에레즈는 러레이도 주민의 의견에 따라 이러한 변경 사항이 [187]촉발됐다고 밝혔다. [188]"저희는 지역사회의 어려운 일원들을 지원할 기회입니다." 구티에레즈 씨의 설명이다. 그는 개회식에서 사진을 촬영하고 축제 중 촬영될 〈러레이도 라이브〉 에피소드의 시작 부분에서 연설할 예정이다.

부스 등록은 6월 1일까지 이뤄지며 많은 단체가 이미 등록을 마쳤다. 그중 하나는 커피-B로, 커피 재배 지역의 저소득층을 지원하는 데 헌신해 온 자선단체이다. [189]커피-B는 대표적인 커피 음료와 더불어 특별 음료, 즉 벌집을 얹은 에스프레소를 만들어 LCF 부스에서 독점 판매할 예정이다.

어휘 grow in popularity 인기가 높아지다 be scheduled to ~할 예정이다 charity 자선단체 registration 등록 sign up 등록하다 devoted to ~에 헌신하는 low-income 저소득의 topped with ~을 얹은 exclusively 독점적으로

러레이도 커뮤니티 페스티벌 특별 행사
6월 27일 토요일

러레이도 커뮤니티 페스티벌(LCF)은 지역 주민과 이들의 열정을 기념하는 자리입니다. 200개가 넘는 부스를 둘러보시고 주 무대에서 열리는 이 특별 행사도 놓치지 마세요.

오전 10시	개회식 시장 및 시 의회 의원들 참석
오후 1시	러레이도 말하기 대회 모든 연령대의 참가자들이 시, 단편소설, 연설 등을 공유
[188]오후 2시 30분	*러레이도 라이브* 촬영 트레이시 래트클리프가 진행하고 지역 특별 게스트들이 출연하는 1시간짜리 TV 프로그램
오후 7시	밴드 경합 지역 음악인들이 무료 야외 콘서트에서 재능 공개

어휘 passion 열정 browse 둘러보다 city council 시 의회 hour-long 한 시간의

커피-B와 함께 즐거운 시간을 보내세요!

커피-B는 커피 재배 지역 사람들에게 소득원으로 양봉법을 지도하는 자선단체입니다. 커피 꽃을 수분하는 벌은 커피에 완벽한 보완이 됩니다. [190]벌이 만드는 꿀과 밀랍은 양봉업자들이 토지를 소유하지 않아도 되는 방법으로 꾸준한 소득원을 만들어 줍니다.

롤랜드 파크에서 열리는 러레이도 커뮤니티 페스티벌에서 저희 부스를 둘러보세요. 저희는 꿀을 넣은 커피향 밀크쉐이크 허니 드림을 판매하여 기금을 마련할 예정입니다. **189**갓 내린 에스프레소에 진짜 벌집을 얹은 스위트 샷, 계피를 넣은 더블 에스프레소와 밀랍으로 된 젓는 막대가 제공되는 버지 밤, 다양한 향의 시럽과 함께 우러나는 아이스 커피 카페인 쿨러도 있습니다.

> **어휘** get a buzz 즐기다 source of income 수입원, 소득원 pollinate 수분하다 complement 보완물 raise money 기금을 조성하다 with a twist of ~을 넣은 honeycomb 벌집 beeswax 밀랍 stir 휘젓다 infuse 우리다, 우러나다

186 세부 사항

번역 기사에 따르면, 올해 LCF에서 달라진 점은 무엇인가?
(A) 초여름에 개최될 것이다.
(B) 새로운 유형의 단체가 포함될 것이다.
(C) 더욱 다양한 음식이 판매될 것이다.
(D) 기금 마련 대회가 포함될 것이다.

해설 기사문의 첫 단락 두 번째 문장에서 올해는 항상 있었던 지역 식당 및 소매업체 부스에 더해, 기금-마련 및 홍보를 위한 자선단체 구역도 마련된다(In addition to the usual booths from local restaurants and retail businesses, this year there will be a section for charities to raise money and promote their work)고 했다. 따라서 정답은 (B)이다.

187 동의어 찾기

번역 기사에서 두 번째 단락 2행의 "prompted"와 의미가 가장 가까운 단어는?
(A) 서둘렀다
(B) 확신시켰다
(C) 물었다
(D) 초래했다

해설 해당 문장은 '러레이도 주민의 의견에 따라 이러한 변경 사항이 촉발되었다'는 의미로 해석되므로, 여기서 prompted는 '(사람에게 어떤 결정을 내리도록) 유발했다, 촉발했다'라는 의미가 자연스럽다. 따라서 정답은 (D) caused(원인이 되었다)이다.

188 연계

번역 구티에레즈 씨는 6월 27일 몇 시에 연설할 것인가?
(A) 오전 10시
(B) 오후 1시
(C) 오후 2시 30분
(D) 오후 7시

해설 기사문 두 번째 단락에서 구티에레즈 씨는 개회식에서 사진을 촬영하고 축제 중 촬영될 러레이도 라이브 에피소드의 시작 부분에서 연설할 예정(who will take photos during the opening ceremony and speak at the start of the *Laredo Live* episode being filmed at the festival)이라고 했다. 일정표를 보면 러레이도 라이브 촬영(Filming of *Laredo Live*)은 오후 2시 30분에 있을 것임을 알 수 있으므로, 정답은 (C)이다.

189 연계

번역 LCF에서만 살 수 있는 음료는?
(A) 허니 드림
(B) 스위트 샷
(C) 버지 밤
(D) 카페인 쿨러

해설 기사문 마지막 단락 마지막 문장에서 커피-B는 대표적인 커피 음료와 더불어 특별 음료, 즉 벌집을 얹은 에스프레소를 만들어 LCF 부스에서 독점 판매할 예정(Along with its signature coffee drinks, Coffee-B has created a special drink—an espresso topped with honeycomb—that will be sold exclusively at its LCF booth)이라고 했다. 전단지 두 번째 단락에서 갓 내린 에스프레소에 진짜 벌집을 얹은 것은 스위트 샷(the Sweet Shot, a freshly-brewed espresso with real honeycomb on top)임을 알 수 있다. 따라서 LCF에서만 살 수 있는 음료는 스위트 샷이므로 정답은 (B)이다.

190 사실 관계 확인

번역 전단지에서 양봉업자에 대해 언급된 것은?
(A) 커피 재배업자들을 위한 밀랍을 생산한다.
(B) 커피-B에서 장비를 대여할 수 있다.
(C) 보통 커피 재배 지역에서 일한다.
(D) 토지를 소유할 필요가 없다.

해설 전단지 첫 번째 단락 마지막 문장에서 벌이 만드는 꿀과 밀랍은 양봉업자들이 토지를 소유하지 않아도 되는 방법으로 꾸준한 소득원을 만들어 준다(The honey and wax they produce create a steady source of income for beekeepers in a way that doesn't require land ownership)고 했다. 따라서 정답은 (D)이다.

> ▶▶ **Paraphrasing** 지문의 **that doesn't require land ownership** → 정답의 **do not need to own property**

191-195 웹페이지 + 웹페이지 + 고객 평가

> www.vivabotanicalgardens.com/customer_feedback
>
> ### 비바 식물원 고객 피드백
>
> ← 이전 게시물   금일 게시물
>
> 저는 열의 넘치는 정원사로서 비바 식물원의 매우 다양한 꽃과 식물을 무척 보고 싶었습니다. 하루 종일 전시물을 둘러볼 수 있어 입장료는 아주 적당합니다. **191**그러나 도심에서 식물원에 도착하기가 어렵습니다. 대중교통 버스나 기차가 없고 택시 요금은 매우 비쌉니다. **193**무척 친절한 관리자에게 말했고, 제가 여행 중 앞서 갔던 다른 관광지에 이용한 교통 서비스를 쓸 것을 제안했습니다. 그분이 제 조언을 고려하시길 바랍니다.
> – **193**크리스티나 선더스, 7월 18일
>
> 이 명소를 다른 사람들에게 추천할지는 잘 모르겠습니다. **191**입장료가 매우 비싸고 자가용이 있지 않은 한 가기가 어렵습니다. 굉장히 불편해요! 다음번에는 이 장소를 가지 않고 대신 애머스트 자연보호구역에 갈 겁니다.
> – 벤카타 타쿠르, 7월 18일

http://hi-pointshuttles.com

홈	추천글	견적 요청	소개	연락처

하이포인트 셔틀이 귀사 고객의 발이 됩니다!

귀사는 외진 곳에 위치해 있습니까? **192A**하이포인트 셔틀은 실속 있는 가격에 귀사까지 고객을 모셔 드릴 수 있습니다. **192B, D**저희는 지난 10년간 충돌 사고 없이 무사고로 운행해 왔으며, 저희 운전기사 전원은 최소 5년 이상 셔틀버스를 운행했습니다. 이는 업계 평균보다 두 배 이상 높은 경력입니다.

다음 패키지의 견적을 요청하시려면 여기를 클릭하십시오.

– 스탠다드: 직원 피정, 학교 야유회, 가족 모임 등의 행사를 위한 1회 셔틀.

– 비즈니스 라이트: 도심과 해당 지역을 일 2회 (오전, 이른 저녁) 운행하는 셔틀. 관광차 도심으로 가려고 하는 투숙객이 있는 소규모 숙박업소에 적합.

– **194**비즈니스 스탠다드: 주중 매시간 운행 또는 주말 주간에 운행하여 고객이 일정한 시차로 귀사까지 이동.

– 비즈니스 엘리트: 셔틀이 매 30분마다 출발함으로써 두 곳을 오가며 고객 이동 최대화.

하이포인트 셔틀
고객 평가 양식

이름: 데이브 베이츠 _____ 세부 사항: 비바 식물원 관리자 _____

총 평점: _5_ / 5

의견: **193**저희 고객 한 분이 직물 공장을 견학하며 하이포인트 셔틀을 이용한 후 추천했고, 기회를 드릴 수 있게 되어 매우 기쁩니다. **194**저희 고객들은 매 시간 있는 셔틀에 매우 만족하고 있으며 이로 인해 저희에게 많은 고객이 찾아왔습니다. 예상 이동 시간은 **195**정확도가 높고 셔틀버스는 편안합니다.

귀하의 평을 저희 웹사이트에 게시하는 데 동의하십니까? 예 _x_ , 아니요 ___

191 세부 사항

번역 첫 번째 웹페이지에서, 게시자 두 명 모두 비바 식물원의 어떤 문제를 언급했는가?
(A) 얼마 안 되는 전시물 숫자
(B) 비싼 입장권 가격
(C) 식물원으로 이동하기가 어려움
(D) 불편한 운영 시간

해설 첫 번째 웹페이지 첫 단락에서 도심에서 식물원에 도착하기가 어렵다(However, it is a challenge to reach the gardens from the city center)고 했으며, 두 번째 단락 두 번째 문장에서도 입장료가 매우 비싸고 자가용이 있지 않은 한 가기가 어렵다(it's hard to get there unless you have your own car)고 했다. 따라서 비바 식물원의 문제점은 그곳에 가기 어렵다는 것임을 알 수 있으므로, 정답은 (C)이다.

192 사실 관계 확인

번역 하이포인트 셔틀에 대해 명시되지 않은 것은?
(A) 적정한 가격이다.
(B) 직원들이 숙련되어 있다.
(C) 차량을 자주 청소한다.
(D) 안전 기록이 뛰어나다.

해설 보기에 언급된 내용을 지문에서 찾아 확인해 본다. 여기서는 두 번째 웹페이지 첫 단락에서 확인할 수 있다. 두 번째 문장에서 하이포인트 셔틀은 실속 있는 가격에 귀사까지 고객을 모셔다 준다(Hi-Point Shuttles can transport customers to and from your site at economical prices)고 한 것을 통해 (A)를, 이어지는 문장에서 지난 10년간 충돌 사고 없이 무사고로 운행해 왔으며 운전기사 전원은 최소 5년 이상 셔틀버스를 운행했는데, 이는 업계 평균보다 두 배 이상 높은 경력(We have had zero collisions and zero roadway incidents in the past ten years, and all of our drivers have been operating shuttle buses for at least five years, more than double the industry average)이라고 한 것을 통해 (B)와 (D)를 확인할 수 있다. 따라서 언급되지 않은 (C)가 정답이다.

▶▶ Paraphrasing 지문의 economical prices → 보기의 affordable rates
지문의 zero collisions and zero roadway incidents → 보기의 an excellent safety record
지문의 all of our drivers have been operating shuttle buses for at least five years → 보기의 Its staff members are experienced.

193 연계

번역 선더스 씨가 비바 식물원 이전에 방문한 곳은 어디인가?
(A) 꽃가게
(B) 직물 공장
(C) 자연보호구역
(D) 시립 박물관

해설 7월 18일 크리스티나 선더스(Christina Saunders, July 18)가 작성한 후기의 끝에서 두 번째 문장에서 무척 친절한 관리자에게 말했고, 제가 여행 중 앞서 갔던 다른 관광지에서 이용한 교통 서비스를 쓸 것을 제안했다(I spoke to the manager, who was very friendly, and suggested that he hire a transportation service that was used by another tourist site I had gone to earlier in my trip)고 했다. 세 번째 지문 첫 문장에서 고객 한 분이 직물 공장을 견학하며 하이포인트 셔틀을 이용한 후 추천했다(One of my customers recommended Hi-Point Shuttles after using it to visit a textile factory, and I'm so glad I gave the company a chance)고 했다. 따라서 정답은 (B)이다.

194 연계

번역 베이츠 씨는 어떤 서비스 패키지를 구매했는가?
(A) 스탠다드
(B) 비즈니스 라이트
(C) 비즈니스 스탠다드
(D) 비즈니스 엘리트

해설 세 번째 지문에서 고객들은 매시간 있는 셔틀에 매우 만족하고 있다(My customers love the hourly shuttle option)고 했다. 두 번째 지문에서 주중 매시간 운행하는 패키지를 찾아보면 비즈니스 스탠다드(Business Standard: Operating routes once per hour on weekdays or daily on weekends to keep customers moving to your business at regular intervals)이므로, 정답은 (C)이다.

195 동의어 찾기

번역 고객 평가에서 첫 번째 단락 4행의 "degree"와 의미가 가장 가까운 단어는?
(A) 정도
(B) 단계
(C) 학위
(D) 온도

해설 해당 문장은 '예상 이동 시간은 정확도가 높다'는 의미로 해석되므로, degree는 '정도'의 뜻으로 쓰였다. 따라서 정답은 (A) level(정도, 수준)이다.

196-200 정보문 + 편지 + 할인권

Q-리워드—쇼핑하시고 적립하세요!

퀸시 슈퍼마켓은 새로운 고객 보상 프로그램 Q-리워드를 도입했습니다. 프로그램에 가입하시고 퀸시 슈퍼마켓에서 지불한 금액 1달러당 1포인트, 저희 협력업체 어디에서나 지불한 금액 2달러당 1포인트를 받으세요. www.quincysupermarket.com/qrewards에서 프로그램에 등록하시면 이메일로 임시 카드가 즉시 발급되며 이후 우편으로 실제 카드를 받게 됩니다. **197신규 회원은 등록만으로도 300포인트를 지급받으며, 월간 소식지 및 다른 매장 특정 할인 소식의 수신을 등록하시면 이메일로 5달러 할인권도 보내 드립니다.** 프로그램에 등록하시면 귀하의 계좌에 1,000포인트가 쌓일 때마다 10달러 할인권이 자동 전송됩니다.

포인트를 받으시려면 계산 시 Q-리워드 카드를 제시하시면 됩니다. **196Q-리워드 스마트폰 어플리케이션도 다운하실 수 있습니다. 어플리케이션에서 발행 48시간 이내에 매장 영수증을 스캔하여 포인트를 신청할 수 있습니다.** 오늘 등록하시고 포인트가 쌓이는 것을 확인하세요!

어휘 loyalty program 고객 보상 프로그램 enroll in ~에 등록하다 instantly 즉시 temporary 임시의 sign up 등록하다 offer 할인 issuance 발행 pile up 쌓이다

캐럴 포크
웨스캠 애비뉴 1607
그로플랜, OH 45231

포크 씨께,

저희 Q-리워드 프로그램에 등록해 주셔서 감사합니다. **197받아야 하는 5달러 할인권과 함께 동봉한 Q-리워드 카드를 확인해 주십시오. 198본 할인권은 퀸시 슈퍼마켓 어느 곳에서나 사용 가능하며 온라인 www.quincysupermarket.com에서도 사용하실 수 있습니다. 199분실하실 경우 새 할인권을 발행해 드리지 않으므로 동일 금액에 상당하는 현금처럼 취급해 주시기 바랍니다.**

저희 제품 최신 브랜드도 꼭 확인해 주세요:
• 플린커스 청소용품: 조리대 세척제, 유리용 세척제, 목재용 광택제
• 비스팬트 고급 치즈: 프랑스에서 수입한 최상급 치즈
• **200랭크던 주스: 크랜베리, 사과, 포도 355밀리리터들이 병**
• 차킹 일일 비타민 보충제: 성인용과 아동용 별도 제조

퀸시 슈퍼마켓에서 곧 뵙게 되길 바랍니다!

토드 햄프턴
Q-리워드 팀 고객 서비스

어휘 enclosed 동봉된 be entitled to 자격이 부여되다 of equivalent value 동등한 가치가 있는 supplement 보충제 formula 제조법

$5	퀸시 슈퍼마켓	$5

본 할인권은 퀸시 슈퍼마켓에서 **5달러**의 금액만큼 유효합니다.

구매 금액이 5달러 이상이어야 하며 잔액은 환불되지 않습니다. **200가전제품 및 음료는 해당되지 않습니다.** 자세한 약관은 뒷면을 참조하십시오.

어휘 valid 유효한 exceed 초과하다 home appliance 가전제품 reverse 반대의, 뒷면 terms and conditions 계약조건, 약관

---

196 사실 관계 확인

번역 Q-리워드 프로그램에 대해 사실인 것은?
(A) 회원에게는 매월 할인권을 받을 자격이 부여된다.
(B) 회원은 지불하는 금액 1달러당 2포인트를 받는다.
(C) 포인트는 구매 이틀 후까지 적립할 수 있다.
(D) 포인트는 양식을 작성하여 신청할 수 있다.

해설 정보문 두 번째 단락에서 Q-리워드 스마트폰 어플리케이션도 다운할 수 있는데, 발행 48시간 이내에 매장 영수증을 스캔하여 포인트를 신청할 수 있다(You can also download the Q-Rewards smartphone application, which allows you to claim your points by scanning a store receipt within 48 hours of its issuance)고 했다. 따라서 정답은 (C)이다.

▶▶ **Paraphrasing** 지문의 **within 48 hours of its issuance**
→ 정답의 **up to two days after a purchase**

197 연계

번역 포크 씨는 무엇을 했겠는가?
(A) Q-리워드 등록에 관해 문의
(B) 보상 포인트 1,000점 적립
(C) Q-리워드 카드 손상
(D) 이메일 소식지 신청

해설 정보문의 첫 단락 후반부에서 신규 회원은 등록만으로도 300포인트를 지급받으며, 월간 소식지 및 다른 매장 특정 할인 소식의 수신을 등록하면 이메일로 5달러 할인권도 보내 준다(New members can get a bonus of 300 points just for signing up, and we'll also send you a voucher for $5 if you register to receive our monthly newsletter and other occasional store offers by e-mail)고 했다. 편지 첫 단락 두 번째 문장에서 받아야 하는 5달러짜리 할인권과 함께 동봉한 Q-리워드 카드를 확인하라(Please find enclosed your Q-Rewards card, as well as the $5 voucher that you are entitled to)고 했으므로 포크 씨는 이메일 소식지를 신청했다는 것을 추론할 수 있다. 따라서 정답은 (D)이다.

> ▶▶ Paraphrasing 지문의 **register to receive our monthly newsletter** → 정답의 **Signed up for an e-mail newsletter**

198 추론 / 암시

번역 퀸시 슈퍼마켓에 대해 암시된 것은?
(A) 그로플랜 최대 규모의 식료품점이다.
(B) 최근 온라인으로 물품 판매를 시작했다.
(C) 지역 식당과 제휴한다.
(D) 다수의 지점으로 구성되어 있다.

해설 두 번째 지문인 편지의 첫 단락 세 번째 문장에서 본 할인권은 퀸시 슈퍼마켓 어느 곳에서나 사용 가능하다(This voucher can be used at any Quincy Supermarket store)고 했다. 따라서 퀸시 슈퍼마켓은 여러 곳에 지점이 있다는 것을 추론할 수 있으므로, 정답은 (D)이다.

199 세부 사항

번역 햄프턴 씨가 포크 씨에게 주의를 준 것은 무엇인가?
(A) 할인권은 만료일이 지나면 유효하지 않다.
(B) 분실된 할인권은 매장에서 다시 발급해 주지 않는다.
(C) 할인권은 현금으로 교환할 수 없다.
(D) 할인권을 이용해 구매하면 보상 포인트를 받을 수 없다.

해설 편지의 첫 단락 마지막 문장에서 분실할 경우 새 할인권을 발행해 주지 않으므로 동일 금액에 상당하는 현금처럼 취급하라(Please treat it as you would treat cash of equivalent value, as we will not be able to issue you a new voucher if you misplace this one)고 했다. 따라서 정답은 (B)이다.

> ▶▶ Paraphrasing 지문의 **will not be able to issue you a new voucher if you misplace this one** → 정답의 **Lost vouchers will not be replaced by the store.**

200 연계

번역 할인권으로 구매할 수 없는 브랜드 제품은 어느 것인가?
(A) 플린커스
(B) 비스팬트
(C) 랭크던
(D) 차킹

해설 할인권을 보면 가전제품 및 음료는 해당되지 않는다(Not valid for home appliances or beverages)고 했는데, 두 번째 지문인 편지를 보면 랭크던은 주스, 즉 음료(Lankdon juices: cranberry, apple, and grape varieties in 355ml bottles)임을 알 수 있다. 따라서 할인권으로 구매할 수 없는 것은 랭크던 주스이므로, 정답은 (C)이다.

TEST 8

101 (D)	102 (D)	103 (B)	104 (C)	105 (B)
106 (C)	107 (B)	108 (C)	109 (C)	110 (C)
111 (A)	112 (B)	113 (A)	114 (D)	115 (B)
116 (B)	117 (C)	118 (D)	119 (A)	120 (A)
121 (D)	122 (D)	123 (A)	124 (D)	125 (A)
126 (D)	127 (D)	128 (B)	129 (B)	130 (A)
131 (A)	132 (A)	133 (B)	134 (C)	135 (D)
136 (B)	137 (C)	138 (B)	139 (D)	140 (C)
141 (B)	142 (A)	143 (D)	144 (A)	145 (C)
146 (D)	147 (C)	148 (C)	149 (C)	150 (C)
151 (A)	152 (C)	153 (D)	154 (D)	155 (A)
156 (A)	157 (B)	158 (D)	159 (D)	160 (C)
161 (B)	162 (D)	163 (A)	164 (C)	165 (D)
166 (C)	167 (A)	168 (A)	169 (D)	170 (D)
171 (B)	172 (D)	173 (C)	174 (C)	175 (B)
176 (D)	177 (A)	178 (C)	179 (D)	180 (A)
181 (D)	182 (C)	183 (D)	184 (C)	185 (A)
186 (A)	187 (B)	188 (D)	189 (A)	190 (D)
191 (C)	192 (A)	193 (B)	194 (D)	195 (B)
196 (B)	197 (C)	198 (B)	199 (D)	200 (A)

PART 5

101 인칭대명사의 격 _ 소유격

해설 빈칸은 형용사(own)와 명사(products) 앞에서 명사(products)를 한정 수식하는 소유격 인칭대명사 자리이므로, 정답은 (D) their이다.

번역 몇몇 지역 식품회사는 직원들에게 할인된 가격으로 자사 제품을 제공한다.

어휘 local 지역의, 현지의 food maker 식품회사 employee 직원, 사원 at a reduced price 할인된 가격에

102 명사 어휘

해설 빈칸은 동사(are explained)의 주어 역할을 하는 명사 자리로, 빈칸 뒤의 전치사 구문(on absences caused by medical issues)의 수식을 받는다. 문맥상 '의료 문제로 인한 결석에 관한 지침'이라는 의미가 자연스러우므로, 정답은 (D) guidelines(지침)이다. (A) solutions(해법, 해결책), (B) classrooms(교실), (C) instructors(강사)는 의미상 적합하지 않다.

번역 의료 문제로 인한 결석에 관한 폴리 아카데미의 지침이 학생 편람에 설명되어 있다.

어휘 absence 결석 medical issue 의료 문제 explain 설명하다 handbook 편람, 안내서 guideline 지침

103 부사 자리 _ 과거분사 수식

해설 빈칸 앞의 be동사(is)와 뒤의 과거분사(sealed) 사이에서 동사를 수식하는 부사 자리이므로, 정답은 (B) firmly이다. 명사/형용사/동사 (A) firm, 동명사/현재분사 (C) firming, 명사 (D) firmness는 품사상 적합하지 않다.

번역 내용물이 새는 것을 방지하기 위해 용기 뚜껑이 꽉 잠겼는지 확인하세요.

어휘 lid 뚜껑 container 용기 firmly 단단하게, 꽉 seal 밀봉[밀폐]하다 prevent 방지하다 contents 내용물 leak 새다

104 형용사 어휘

해설 빈칸 앞에 있는 It은 가짜 주어이고, 뒤에 나오는 that명사절(that the accuracy of measuring instruments be tested yearly)이 진짜 주어이다. 빈칸은 진짜 주어인 that명사절을 보충 설명하는 형용사 자리이다. 문맥상 '측정도구의 정확성을 해마다 점검하는 것은 필수적이다'라는 의미가 자연스러우므로, 정답은 (C) vital(필수적인, 중요한)이다. (A) active(능동적인, 활동적인), (B) initial(초기의, 처음의), (D) fluent(유창한)는 의미상 적합하지 않다. 참고로 필수/중요의 형용사가 that명사절을 보충 설명할 경우, 명사절의 동사원형(be tested) 앞에 있는 조동사(should)는 생략 가능하다.

번역 측정도구의 정확성을 해마다 점검하는 것은 필수적이다.

어휘 vital 필수적인 accuracy 정확성, 정밀성 measuring instrument 측정도구 test 점검[검사]하다 yearly 매년, 해마다

105 동사 어형 _ 수동태

해설 빈칸은 앞의 has been과 함께 whose절의 동사 자리를 이룬다. 주어 property(부동산)는 평가하는 능동적 주체가 아니라 평가되는 수동적 대상이므로, 정답은 수동태를 만드는 과거분사 (B) assessed이다. 동사원형 (A) assess는 동사(have been) 뒤에 나올 수 없고, 명사 (C) assessor(손해사정인)와 (D) assessment(평가)는 주어(property)와 동격 관계를 이루지 않으므로 정답이 될 수 없다.

번역 새로운 법률은 가치가 8만 달러 이하로 평가된 주택 소유자들에게는 영향을 미치지 않을 것이다.

어휘 law 법률 affect 영향을 미치다 homeowner 주택 소유자 property 부동산 less than ~ 이하 value 가치 assess 평가하다

106 부사 어휘

해설 빈칸은 조동사(should)와 동사원형(be used) 사이에서 동사를 수식하는 부사 자리이다. 동사원형(be used)은 뒤에 나오는 부사절(when there is cheaper alternative transportation available during your business travel)의 수식도 받는다. 문맥상 '더 저렴한 대체 교통편을 이용할 수 있을 때는 결코 이용하지 말아야 한다'라는 의미가 자연스러우므로, 정답은 (C) never(결코 ~아닌)이다. (A) overly(지나치게, 과도하게), (B) too(너무, 또한), (D) ever(줄곧, 항상)는 의미상 적합하지 않다.

번역 출장 기간 중 더 저렴한 대체 교통편을 이용할 수 있을 때는 택시 서비스를 결코 이용하지 말아야 한다.

어휘 cheaper 더 저렴한 alternative 대신하는, 대체의 transportation 교통 available 이용 가능한 business travel 출장

107 동사 어형 _ 태

해설 빈칸은 to be와 함께 동사 meant의 목적어를 이루는 자리이다. 앞에 있는 주어(This technique)와의 관계를 보면 기술은 '사용되는' 수동적 대상이므로, 정답은 과거분사 (B) employed이다. 주어와 능동 관계를 이루는 현재분사 (D) employing은 태가 적합하지 않다.

번역 이 기술은 근육 관련 통증을 치료할 때 사용하도록 되어 있다.

어휘 technique 기술 be meant to + 동사원형 ~하기로 되어 있다 treat 치료하다 muscle-related soreness 근육 관련 통증

108 전치사 어휘

해설 빈칸 뒤의 목적어(this summer's unusual weather)와 함께 뒤에 나오는 주절을 수식하는 전치사 자리이다. 문맥상 '올 여름의 기상이변을 감안하면'이라는 의미가 자연스러우므로, 정답은 (C) Given(~감안하면, 고려하면)이다. (A) Into(~ 안으로), (B) Until(~까지), (D) Amid(~ 가운데, ~ 중에서)는 의미상 적합하지 않다.

번역 올 여름의 기상이변을 감안하면 아이스크림 판매가 감소한 것은 놀랄 일이 아니다.

어휘 unusual weather 기상이변 it is no surprise that ~은 놀랄 일이 아니다 fall 하락하다, 감소하다

109 명사 자리 _ 동사의 주어

해설 빈칸은 동사(will require)의 주어 역할을 하는 명사 자리이므로, 정답은 (C) relocation(이전)이다. 동사 (A) relocate(이전하다)와 (B) relocates, 과거시제 동사/과거분사 (D) relocated는 품사상 적합하지 않다.

번역 관광업에 미치는 부정적 영향을 최소화하기 위해 그 유명한 동상을 이전하려면 세심하게 시기를 선정해야 할 것이다.

어휘 minimize 최소화하다 negative 부정적인 impact 영향, 충격 tourism 관광업 famous 유명한 statue 동상 require 필요하다 careful 세심한, 주의 깊은 timing 시기

110 부사 어휘

해설 빈칸 뒤의 전치사구(upon noticing errors)와 함께 앞에 있는 동사원형 (be made)을 수식하는 부사 자리이다. 문맥상 '실수를 알아채는 순간 신속히 이루어지다'라는 의미가 자연스러우므로, 정답은 (C) promptly(신속히, 즉시)이다. (A) accidentally(우연히), (B) chiefly(주로), (D) highly (매우, 몹시)는 의미상 적합하지 않다. 참고로 that명사절이 요구(asked) 동사의 목적어 역할을 하는 경우, 명사절의 동사원형(be made) 앞에 있는 조동사(should)는 생략 가능하다.

번역 미글리아치오 씨는 온라인 기사의 정정은 실수를 알아채는 순간 신속히 이루어져야 한다고 요청했다.

어휘 ask 요청하다 make a correction 정정하다 article 기사 upon -ing ~하자마자, ~하는 순간 notice 알아차리다, 인지하다 error 실수 promptly 신속히

111 형용사 어휘

해설 빈칸은 동사(undergo)의 목적어 역할을 하는 명사(inspections)를 수식하는 형용사 자리이다. 문맥상 '엄격한 검사를 거친다'라는 의미가 자연스러우므로, 정답은 (A) strict(엄격한)이다. (B) bent(휜, 굽은), (C) aware(인지하고 있는, 알고 있는), (D) vacant(빈, 공허한)는 의미상 적합하지 않다.

번역 우리 제품은 모두 높은 품질 기준을 반드시 만족시키기 위해 제조시설에서 엄격한 검사를 거친다.

어휘 undergo 거치다, 겪다 inspection 검사, 조사 manufacturing facility 제조시설 ensure 확실히 하다, 보장하다 strict 엄격한

112 형용사 자리 _ 명사 수식

해설 빈칸 앞의 정관사(the)와 뒤의 명사(effects) 사이에서 명사(effects)를 수식하는 형용사 자리이므로, 정답은 (B) advantageous이다.

번역 이타루 마츠다 박사의 연구는 환자에게 미치는 신약의 유익한 효과를 입증했다.

어휘 studies 연구 prove 입증하다 advantageous 유익한, 유리한 medication 약물 patient 환자

113 명사 어휘

해설 빈칸은 전치사(under)의 목적어 역할을 하는 명사 자리로, 뒤에 나오는 전치사구(of this agreement)의 수식을 받는다. 문맥상 '이 계약 조건으로'라는 의미가 자연스러우므로, 정답은 (A) conditions(조건, 상황)이다. (B) penalties(벌금, 처벌), (C) approaches(접근법), (D) phrases(구절)는 의미상 적합하지 않다.

번역 당신은 이 계약 조건으로 다음달 말까지 크롬비를 쓸 수 있는 사용권을 제공받는다.

어휘 provide 제공하다, 공급하다 license 사용권 until the end of ~말까지 agreement 계약, 협정

114 과거분사 / 현재분사 구분

해설 빈칸은 주격 관계대명사(that)가 이끄는 관계사절의 주어(that=A company)를 보충 설명하는 자리이다. 앞에 있는 주어(that=A company)가 '존경 받는 회사'라는 수동의 의미를 나타내므로, 정답은 과거분사 (D) respected이다. 주어(that=A company)와 능동 관계를 이루는 현재분사 (A) respecting은 의미상 적합하지 않다.

번역 기업 가치 때문에 존경 받는 회사는 자격 있는 구직자들을 모으는 데 더 크게 성공할 것이다.

어휘 corporate value 기업 가치 success 성공 attract 끌어모으다 qualified 자격 있는 job candidate 구직자 respected 존경받는

115 형용사 어휘

해설 빈칸은 주어(recreational bicycle use)를 보충 설명하는 형용사 자리이다. 문맥상 '여가를 위한 자전거 이용이 널리 퍼져 있다'라는 의미가 자연스러우므로, 정답은 (B) widespread(널리 퍼진, 광범위한)이다. (A) impatient(참을성 없는), (C) talented(재능 있는), (D) empty(빈, 공허한)는 의미상 적합하지 않다.

번역 설문에 응한 주민 중 자전거로 통근하는 사람은 비교적 적었지만 여가를 위한 자전거 이용은 널리 퍼져 있다.

어휘 although 비록 ~일지라도 relatively 비교적 few 적은, 거의 없는 survey 설문 조사하다 resident 주민 commute to work 통근하다 by bike 자전거로 recreational 여가 생활의 widespread 광범위한, 널리 퍼져 있는

116 부사절 접속사 / 전치사 구분

해설 빈칸 뒤의 절(their projects face delays)을 이끌면서 앞에 있는 절을 수식하는 부사절 접속사 자리로, 부사절 접속사 (B) when(~할 때)과 (D) whereas(~인 반면에)가 적합하다. 문맥상 '프로젝트를 연기해야 할 때'라는 의미가 자연스러우므로, 정답은 (B) when이다. 전치사 (A) behind(~ 뒤에)와 (C) over(~ 너머로) 뒤에는 절이 나올 수 없다.

번역 관리자들은 프로젝트를 연기해야 할 때 수정된 마감 일정표를 제출해야 한다.

어휘 submit 제출하다 revised 수정[개정]된 deadline schedule 마감 시간표 face 직면하다, 마주하다 delay 연기, 지연

117 부사 자리 _ 형용사 수식

해설 빈칸 뒤의 형용사(visible)를 수식하는 부사 자리이므로, 정답은 (C) clearly이다. 형용사의 최상급 (A) clearest와 비교급 (B) clearer는 품사상 적합하지 않다.

번역 그 교통 표지판은 도로에서 선명하게 보였으나 근처에 있는 나뭇가지 때문에 보이지 않게 되었다.

어휘 traffic sign 교통 표지판 visible 눈에 보이는 until ~하여 결국, ~할 때까지 branch 가지 nearby 근처의, 인근의 obscure 보이지 않게 하다, 흐릿하게 하다

118 동사 어휘

해설 빈칸 뒤의 목적어(27,000 square meters)와 함께 앞에 있는 명사(floor space)를 수식하는 현재분사 자리이다. 문맥상 '건평 2만 7000평방미터에 이르는'이라는 의미가 자연스러우므로, 정답은 (D) covering(~이르다, 덮다, 담당하다, 보도하다)이다. (A) finishing(끝내다, 완수하다), (B) obtaining(얻다, 획득하다), (C) developing(개발하다, 성장하다)은 의미상 적합하지 않다.

번역 디너드 수출입 주식회사는 건평 2만 7000제곱미터에 이르는 현대적인 창고를 운영한다.

어휘 import 수입 export 수출 operate 운영하다 warehouse 창고 floor space 건평, 매장 면적 square meter 제곱미터(㎡)

119 동사 어형 _ 과거분사 / 현재분사 구분

해설 빈칸은 동사(are) 뒤에서 주어(Clothing sales revenues)를 보충 설명하는 주격보어 자리이다. 앞에 있는 주어(Clothing sales revenues)와 '의류 판매 수입이 감소하고 있다'라는 계속/진행의 의미를 나타내므로, 정답은 현재분사 (A) declining이다. 주어(Clothing sales revenues)와 완료 관계를 이루는 과거분사 (C) declined는 의미상 적합하지 않다.

번역 매장의 가정용품이 여전히 인기를 끌고 있는데도 의류 판매 수입이 감소하고 있다.

어휘 clothing 의류, 의복 revenue 수입 decline 감소하다, 하락하다; 거절하다 even though 비록 ~이지만 home goods 가정용품 remain 여전히 ~이다, ~한 상태이다

120 인칭대명사의 격 _ 주격

해설 빈칸은 that명사절의 동사(will soon resume)의 주어 자리이므로, 정답은 주격 인칭대명사 (A) we이다.

번역 집행위원회는 곧 프루네다 홀딩스와 교섭을 재개할 것을 알리게 되어 자랑스럽습니다.

어휘 executive committee 집행위원회 be proud to + 동사원형 ~해서 자랑스럽다 announce 발표하다, 알리다 resume 재개하다, 다시 시작하다 negotiation 교섭, 협상 holdings 지주회사

121 부사 자리 _ 형용사 수식

해설 빈칸은 that절의 주어(staff in a majority of departments)를 보충 설명하는 형용사(absent)를 수식하는 부사 자리이므로, 정답은 (D) persistently이다.

번역 인사부는 대대수 부서의 직원들이 국경일을 포함하는 주 동안 지속해서 결근한다고 보고한다.

어휘 Human Resources 인사부, 인력관리부 report 보고하다 a majority of 대다수, 과반의 absent 결석한, 결근한 include 포함하다 national holiday 국경일 persist 지속하다, 고집하다 persistent 지속적인, 끈기 있는 persistently 지속해서, 꾸준히

122 동사 어형 _ 태

해설 빈칸은 주어(Tours of select apartments) 뒤에 나오는 동사 자리이다. 주어(Tours of select apartments)와 '최고급 아파트들을 둘러보는 것은 허용될 것이다'라는 수동의 의미를 나타내므로, 정답은 수동의 미래시제 동사 (D) will be allowed이다. 주어와 능동 관계를 이루는 동사 (A) are allowing과 (C) have allowed는 의미상 적합하지 않고, to부정사 (B) to allow는 동사 자리에 들어갈 수 없다.

번역 복합단지 공사가 완료되었으니 이제 최고급 아파트들을 둘러볼 수 있게 될 것이다.

어휘 select 선별된, 최고급의 now that ~이니까 construction 건설, 건축, 공사 complex 복합단지 complete 완료하다, 완성하다 allow 허락[허용]하다

123 부사절 접속사

해설 빈칸 뒤의 절(you find our mobile app satisfactory)을 이끌면서 뒤에 나오는 주절을 수식하는 부사절 접속사 자리이므로, 부사절 접속사 (A) If(~한다면)와 (D) So that(~하기 위해)이 가능하다. 문맥상 '저희의 모바일 앱이 만족스러우시다면'이라는 의미가 자연스러우므로, 정답은 (A) If이다. 대명사/한정사/부사 (B) Either와 부사 (C) Regardless(개의치 않고, 상관하지 않고)는 품사상 적합하지 않다.

번역 저희의 모바일 앱이 만족스러우시다면 아래 버튼을 살짝 눌러서 별 다섯 개짜리 후기를 남겨 주세요.

어휘 mobile app 모바일 앱 satisfactory 만족스러운 tap on ~을 가볍게 두드리다 leave 남기다 five-star review 별 다섯 개짜리 후기

124 형용사 어휘

해설 빈칸은 주어(The Karvex-K's advanced features)를 보충 설명하는 형용사 자리로, 뒤에 나오는 전치사구(with what professional photographers expect from a digital camera)의 수식을 받는다. 문맥상 '앞선 기능은 전문 사진가들이 바라는 바와 부합한다'라는 의미가 자연스러우므로, 정답은 (D) consistent(일치하는, 부합하는, 한결같은)이다. (A) incapable(할 수 없는, 무능한), (B) excited(흥분한), (C) thankful(감사하는)은 의미상 적합하지 않다.

번역 카벡스-케이의 앞선 기능은 전문 사진가들이 디지털 카메라에 바라는 바와 부합한다.

어휘 advanced 앞선, 진보한 feature 특징[특색], 기능 professional 전문의, 직업의 expect 기대하다, 바라다

125 부사절 접속사

해설 빈칸 뒤의 절(they decide not to purchase anything)을 이끌면서 앞에 있는 절을 수식하는 부사절 접속사 자리이다. 문맥상 '아무것도 사지 않기로 마음먹더라도'라는 양보의 의미가 자연스러우므로, 정답은 (A) even if(설령 ~일지라도)이다. (B) in case(~인 경우에), (C) now that(~이니까), (D) such as(~와 같은)는 의미상 적합하지 않다.

번역 쇼핑객들은 아무것도 사지 않기로 마음먹더라도 우리 매장의 전시장 전체를 둘러보도록 권장 받는다.

어휘 shopper 쇼핑객 be encouraged to + 동사원형 ~하도록 권장[장려] 받다 look around 둘러보다 entire 전체의 showroom floor 전시장 purchase 사다, 구입하다

126 동사 어휘

해설 빈칸 뒤의 목적어 역할을 하는 명사절(that all database systems be upgraded monthly)과 의미가 가장 잘 통하는 동사를 선택해야 한다. 문맥상 '모든 데이터베이스 시스템이 매월 업그레이드되어야 한다고 권고한다'라는 의미가 자연스러우므로, 정답은 (D) advises(권고하다, 조언하다, 알리다)이다. (A) expires(만료되다), (B) believes(믿다, 생각하다), (C) recalls(회상하다, 회수하다)는 의미상 적합하지 않다. 참고로 that명사절이 제안/요구/명령/주장 동사의 목적어 역할을 하는 경우, 명사절의 동사원형(be upgraded) 앞에 있는 조동사(should)는 생략 가능하다.

번역 IT 팀은 모든 데이터베이스 시스템이 매월 업그레이드되어야 한다고 권고한다.

어휘 database system 데이터베이스 upgrade 업그레이드하다, 개선하다 monthly 매월

127 부사 어휘

해설 빈칸은 앞에 있는 동사(found)를 수식하는 부사 자리로, 부사(just)의 수식을 받는다. 문맥상 '단 한 차례밖에 발견하지 못했다'라는 의미가 자연스러우므로, 정답은 (D) once(한 번)이다. 전치사 (B) for는 품사상 적합하지 않고, 부사/접속사 (A) yet(아직/그러나), 부사/전치사 (C) about(대략, 거의/~에 관해)은 의미상 적합하지 않다.

번역 품질관리 임원들은 방문 기간 일주일 동안 펑스 어패럴 물품에서 하자를 단 한 차례밖에 발견하지 못했다.

어휘 quality control 품질관리 official 담당자, 임원 find 찾다, 발견하다 defect 하자, 결함 apparel 의류 over the course of ~ 동안 weeklong 일주일간의 visit 방문

128 명사절 접속사

해설 빈칸 뒤의 to부정사 구문(to package a new food product)을 이끌면서 뒤에 나오는 동사(depends)의 주어 역할을 하는 자리이다. 문맥상 '새로 나온 식품을 포장하는 방법'이라는 의미가 자연스러우므로, 정답은 (B) How이다. 명사절 접속사 (A) Which(어떤 것)와 (D) Whatever(무엇이든), 대명사 (C) Nothing(없음)은 의미상 적합하지 않다.

번역 새로 나온 식품을 포장하는 방법은 상품의 브랜드 이미지와 목표 고객에 크게 좌우된다.

어휘 package 포장하다 depend heavily on ~에 크게 좌우되다[의존하다] item 물품, 상품 brand image 브랜드 이미지 target customer 목표 고객, 대상 고객

129 과거분사 / 현재분사 구분

해설 빈칸은 주어 역할을 하는 명사(Patient records)를 뒤에서 수식하는 형용사 자리이다. 앞의 수식을 받는 명사(Patient records)와 '글씨가 찍힌 진료기록'이라는 수동의 의미를 나타내므로, 정답은 과거분사 (B) stamped이다. 수식을 받는 명사와 능동 관계를 이루는 현재분사 (A) stamping과 관계사절 (C) that stamp는 의미상 적합하지 않고, 동사 (D) are stamped는 앞에 주격 관계대명사(that/which)가 나와야 한다.

번역 빨간 잉크로 "기밀"이라는 글씨가 찍힌 진료기록은 더 강력한 보호 조치의 대상이다.

어휘 patient record 진료기록 stamped with ~가 찍힌 confidential 기밀의 be subject to ~의 대상이다 protection measures 보호 조치 stamp (도장·스탬프를) 찍다

130 동사 어휘

해설 they 앞에는 목적격 관계대명사(that/which)가 생략되어 있고 빈칸은 관계대명사가 이끄는 관계사절의 조동사(may) 뒤 동사 원형 자리이다. 빈칸을 포함한 관계사절은 앞에 있는 명사(opportunities)를 수식한다. 문맥상 '직장에서 마주치는 기회들'이라는 의미가 자연스러우므로, 정답은 (A) come across(우연히 마주치다)이다. (B) take apart(분해[해체]하다), (C) go through(겪다, 경험하다), (D) back up(지지하다, 백업하다)는 의미상 적합하지 않다.

번역 스넬 헤럴드의 진로 상담란 덕에 독자들은 직장에서 마주치는 기회들을 잡을 수 있다.

Test 8

어휘 career advice column 진로 상담란 enable ~할 수 있게 하다 seize an opportunity 기회를 잡다 come across 우연히 마주치다[만나다, 찾다]

PART 6

131-134 이메일

발신: 해럴드 비오르네뷔 〈h.bjorneby@oue-mail.com〉
수신: 리바 셸튼 〈r.shelton@tpead.com〉
제목: 답신
날짜: 3월 18일

셸튼 씨께,

포리스트웨이 349번지에 있는 저의 방 2개짜리 부동산에 임대 신청을 해주셔서 감사합니다. 저는 귀하께서 해당 **131**가구에 잘 어울리는 분이라는 데 동의합니다. 허락을 하셨으니 귀하의 신용조회를 즉시 진행하겠습니다. **132**그렇지만, 이달 말 이전에 입주하기 원하시는 기대에 부응할 수 있다고 약속 드리지는 못합니다. 저의 최우선 과제는 세입자로서 귀하가 만족하도록 하는 것이니 양해해 주시기 바랍니다. **134**저는 필요한 만큼 시간을 들여서 그렇게 **133**해야 합니다. 그 과정이 마무리되면 다시 연락 드리겠습니다. 그 사이에 질문하실 일이 있으면 부담 갖지 마시고 제게 이메일을 보내시기 바랍니다.

해럴드 비오르네뷔

어휘 application 신청, 지원 property 부동산 located at/in/on ~에 위치한 a good match 잘 어울리는 것[사람] authorize 허가[허락]하다, 권한을 위임하다 proceed with ~을 진행하다 credit check 신용조회 move in 입주하다 accommodate (요구 등에) 부응하다 main priority 최우선 순위, 최우선 과제 confirm 확인[확정]하다 satisfactory 만족스러운, 훌륭한 tenant 세입자, 임차인 take time 시간이 걸리다 in the meantime 그 사이에, 그 동안에 feel free to+동사원형 부담 없이 ~하다

131 명사 어휘

해설 빈칸은 전치사(for)의 목적어 역할을 하는 명사 자리로, 빈칸을 포함한 전치사구는 앞의 명사(a good match)를 수식한다. 앞 문장 '포리스트웨이 349번지에 있는 저의 방 2개짜리 부동산에 임대 신청을 해주어서 감사한다(Thank you for your application to rent my two-bedroom property located at 349 Forest Way)'를 통해 방 2개짜리 부동산을 임대 신청했음을 알 수 있으므로, 빈칸에는 '방 2개짜리 부동산(my two-bedroom property)'과 유사한 의미의 단어가 들어가야 한다. 따라서 정답은 (A) unit(한 가구, 구성 단위)이다. (B) post(우편, 직책, 기둥), (C) major(전공), (D) vehicle(차량)은 의미상 적합하지 않다.

어휘 unit (공동주택 내의 한) 가구

132 부사 어휘

해설 빈칸에는 앞뒤 문장을 자연스럽게 이어줄 접속부사가 필요하다. 앞 문장 '허락을 했으니 귀하의 신용조회를 즉시 진행하겠다(As you authorized, I will proceed immediately with your credit check)'에서 신용조회의 즉시 진행을 언급하고 있다. 빈칸 뒤에 나오는 문장 '이달 말 이전에 입주하기 원하는 기대에 부응할 수 있다고 약속하지는 못한다(I cannot promise that your wish to move in before the end of the month can be accommodated)'에서 즉각적인 시행에도 불구하고 입주가 지연될 수 있다는 양보의 의미를 나타내고 있으므로, 정답은 (A) Still(그럼에도 불구하고, 그렇지만, 여전히)이다. (B) Therefore(그러므로, 그래서), (C) Furthermore(더욱이, 게다가), (D) Luckily(다행히도, 운 좋게)는 의미상 적합하지 않다.

133 동사 어형 _ 시제

해설 빈칸은 주어(I) 뒤에 나오는 동사 자리로, 뒤의 to부정사(to take)와 결합하여 '~해야 한다'라는 의미를 나타낸다. 문장 맨 뒤에 나오는 to부정사 구문(to do that)은 앞 문장의 to부정사 구문(to confirm that you will be a satisfactory tenant)를 대신한다. 따라서 시간을 들여 확인하는 일은 현재의 의무임을 알 수 있으므로, 정답은 현재시제 동사 (B) have이다.

134 문맥에 맞는 문장 고르기

번역 (A) 첨부된 보고서에 이번 거절 사유가 설명되어 있습니다.
(B) 귀하의 이메일에는 이 요금들을 어디에서 지불할 지가 분명하게 설명되지 않았습니다.
(C) 그 과정이 마무리되면 다시 연락 드리겠습니다.
(D) 저희는 계약서에 직접 서명하실 것을 요구합니다.

해설 빈칸 앞 문장 '저는 필요한 만큼 시간을 들여서 그렇게 해야 한다(I have to take as much time as necessary to do that)'와 앞에서 언급된 내용을 통해 신용조회 등 필요한 절차가 진행중임을 알 수 있다. 따라서 빈칸에는 절차가 종료될 때 취할 조치를 언급하는 것이 문맥상 자연스러우므로, 정답은 (C)이다.

어휘 refusal 거절, 거부 clarify 분명하게 설명하다 in person 직접, 몸소

135-138 회람

발신: 인사부
수신: 모든 직원
제목: Re: 설문조사

지난해, 여러분 중 일부가 **135**불만을 표출하면 경력에 부정적인 영향이 있을까 봐 우려하여 오칸 코퍼레이션의 연례 직원 만족도 조사를 작성하지 않았습니다. 하지만 솔직한 의견이 없으면 우리는 현 체계에 필요한 개선을 하지 못합니다. **136**따라서, 올해에는 설문 조사를 익명으로 하기로 했습니다. **138**여러분의 개인적인 응답은 라마고스 서베이즈만 **137**보게 될 것입니다. **138**이 회사는 작성된 양식을 취합해 종합 보고서를 만드는 것을 전문으로 하는 회사인데, 그 보고서가 오칸 경영진이 받게 될 유일한 문서입니다. 이로써 여러분의 우려가 사그라지기를 바랍니다.

참여하시려면 2월 19일에서 25일 사이에 www.ramagossurveys.com/2937을 방문하시기 바랍니다.

어휘 Human Resources 인사부, 인력관리부 survey 설문
refuse 거부[거절]하다 fill out 기재하다, 작성하다(= complete)
yearly 연례의(= annual) employee satisfaction survey 직원
만족도 조사 negative 부정적인 effect on ~에 미치는 영향[효과]
career 경력 candid 솔직한, 진솔한 feedback 의견 make an
improvement to ~을 개선[개량]하다 current 현재의 conduct
실행[수행]하다 anonymously 익명으로 individual 개별적인,
개인적인 specialize in ~을 전문으로 하다 compile 취합하다,
수집하다 completed form 작성된 양식 comprehensive
report 종합 보고서 management 경영진

135 명사 자리 _ 동명사의 목적어

해설 빈칸 앞 동명사(expressing)의 목적어 역할을 하는 명사 자리이므로,
정답은 (D) displeasure이다. 현재분사 (B) displeasing과 과거분사
(C) displeased는 형용사와 같은 역할을 하므로, 적합하지 않다.

어휘 displeasure 불만, 불쾌

136 부사 어휘

해설 빈칸에는 앞뒤 문장을 자연스럽게 이어줄 접속부사가 필요하다. 앞 문
장 '하지만 솔직한 의견이 없으면 우리는 현 체계에 필요한 개선을 하지
못한다(Without candid feedback, however, we cannot make
necessary improvements to our current systems)'에서 솔직
한 의견을 얻어야 할 필요성을 언급하고 있다. 빈칸 뒤에 나오는 문장
'올해에는 설문 조사를 익명으로 하기로 했다(we have decided to
conduct the survey anonymously this year)'에서 필요성에 따른 대
처 방법을 언급하고 있으므로, 정답은 (B) Accordingly(따라서, 그에 맞
춰)이다. (A) Namely(즉, 다시 말해), (C) Additionally(게다가, 또한),
(D) Formerly(이전에)는 의미상 적합하지 않다.

어휘 accordingly 따라서

137 동사 자리 _ 시제

해설 빈칸은 주어(Your individual answers) 뒤에 나오는 동사 자리로, 앞에
있는 주어(Your individual answers)와 '귀하의 대답은 보인다'라는 수
동의 의미를 나타내므로, 미래시제 수동태 (C) will be seen과 현재완료
시제 수동태 (D) have been seen이 가능하다. 앞 문장의 시간을 나타내
는 부사(this year)를 통해 앞으로 시행되는 일임을 알 수 있으므로, 정답
은 미래시제인 (C) will be seen이다.

138 문맥에 맞는 문장 고르기

번역 (A) 지난해에는 결과가 대체로 긍정적이었습니다.
(B) 이로써 여러분의 우려가 사그라지기를 바랍니다.
(C) 신중하게 응답하려면 시간이 걸릴지도 모릅니다.
(D) 마지막으로, 취합한 데이터를 그래프로 정리하십시오.

해설 빈칸 앞에 있는 두 문장 '여러분의 개인적인 응답은 라마고스 서베이즈만
보게 될 것이다. 이 회사는 작성된 양식을 취합해 종합 보고서를 만드는 것
을 전문으로 하는 회사인데, 그 보고서가 오칸 경영진이 받게 될 유일한 문
서이다(Your individual answers will be seen only by Ramagos

Surveys. It is a company that specializes in compiling sets of
completed forms to create a comprehensive report, which is
the only document that Oakhan management will receive)'에
서 직원들의 걱정을 덜어 줄 방법을 제시하고 있다. 따라서 빈칸에는 이 방
법에 따른 기대효과를 언급하는 것이 문맥상 자연스러우므로, 정답은 (B)
이다.

어휘 positive 긍정적인 put ~ to rest ~을 잠재우다 concerns
우려 take time 시간이 걸리다 thoughtful 사려 깊은, 신중한
organize 정리하다

139-142 이메일

애브란테스 씨께,

언더우드 홈 포럼즈에 오신 것을 환영합니다. 귀하께서는 이제 세계 전역에 있
는 사람들과 주택 개량 문제 및 공사에 관해 토론하실 수 있게 될 것입니다. 우
선 의견을 올리시려면, 관심 있는 토론방을 찾으시기만 하면 됩니다. 이용할 수
있는 139주제가 다양한 점을 감안하면 이는 어렵지 않을 것입니다.

140, 141하지만, 최적의 사용 경험을 위해 먼저 한 가지 조치를 취하실 수도 있습
니다. 본 사이트를 이용하시는 동안 익숙하지 않은 표현들을 마주칠 수 있습니
다. 오랫동안 게시자들이 외부인은 이해할 수 없는 수많은 줄임말을 만들어왔습
니다. 그 때문에 시작하시기 전에 저희 홈페이지의 "언더스피크" 아이콘을 통해
접근할 수 있는 맞춤 사전을 142살펴보시기를 권장합니다.

잘 되시기를 빕니다!

언더우드 홈 포럼즈 팀

어휘 home improvement 주택 개량 issue 문제 all around
the world 세계 도처에서, 전 세계에서 comment 논평하다,
견해를 밝히다 forum 토론장, 토론방 interest 흥미를 끌다, 관심을
불러일으키다 considering ~을 감안[고려]하면 take steps 조치를
취하다 poster 게시자 create 만들어내다 numerous 수많은
shorthand terms 줄임말, 약어 incomprehensible to ~가
이해할 수 없는 outsider 외부인, 제3자 recommend 권장하다,
추천하다 customized 맞춤형의 dictionary 사전 accessible
접근[이용]할 수 있는 via ~을 통해, ~에 의해 get started 시작하다

139 명사 어휘

해설 빈칸은 전치사(of)의 목적어 역할을 하는 명사 자리로, 빈칸을 포함한 전
치사구는 앞의 명사(the wide variety)를 수식한다. 앞에 있는 문장
'우선 의견을 올리려면, 관심 있는 토론방을 찾기만 하면 된다(To begin
commenting, simply find a forum that interests you)'를 통해 다
양한 토론방이 있음을 알 수 있으므로, 빈칸에는 '토론방(forum)'에서 다
루는 내용과 관련된 단어를 선택해야 한다. 따라서 정답은 (D) topics(주
제)이다. (A) estimates(추정, 견적서), (B) replacements(교체, 대체,
후임자), (C) venues(장소, 행사장)는 의미상 적합하지 않다.

140 부사 어휘

해설 빈칸에는 앞뒤 문장을 자연스럽게 이어줄 접속부사가 필요하다. 앞 문장 '이용할 수 있는 주제가 다양한 점을 감안하면 이는 어렵지 않을 것이다(This should not be difficult considering the wide variety of topics available)'에서 주제 선택이 어렵지 않음을 언급하고 있다. 빈칸 뒤에 나오는 문장 '먼저 한 가지 조치를 취할 수도 있다(there is one step you may want to take first)'에서 어렵지 않음에도 조치가 필요할 수 있다는 양보의 의미를 나타내고 있으므로, 정답은 (C) though(그렇지만, 하지만)이다. (A) for instance(예를 들어), (B) likewise(게다가, 마찬가지로), (D) in fact(사실은)는 의미상 적합하지 않다.

어휘 though 하지만(= however)

141 문맥에 맞는 문장 고르기

번역 (A) 이용 약관 동의에 따라 저희 콘텐츠의 복제는 금지되어 있습니다.
(B) 본 사이트를 이용하시는 동안 익숙하지 않은 표현들을 마주칠 수 있습니다.
(C) 토론이 장려될지라도 예의를 지켜 주실 것을 요청합니다.
(D) 저희는 회원 프로필이나 게시물에 제기된 주장들을 입증하지 않습니다.

해설 빈칸 앞 문장 '하지만, 최적의 사용 경험을 위해 먼저 한 가지 조치를 취할 수도 있다(For an optimal using experience, though, there is one step you may want to take first)'를 통해 빈칸에는 조치(step)가 필요한 상황을 구체적으로 언급하는 것이 문맥상 자연스러우므로, 정답은 (B)이다.

어휘 forbid 금지하다 encounter 마주치다 unfamiliar 익숙하지 않은 expression 표현 polite 공손한, 예의 바른 verify 입증하다

142 동명사

해설 빈칸 뒤의 명사(the customized dictionary)를 목적어로 취하면서, 빈칸 앞 동사(recommend)의 목적어 역할을 하는 자리이다. 제안의 타동사 recommend는 동명사를 목적어로 취하므로, 정답은 동명사 (A) reviewing이다. 명사 (B) a review와 (C) reviewers는 명사를 목적어로 취할 수 없다.

어휘 review 확인하다, 살펴보다, 공부하다

143-146 기사

사무실 커피 기계   리스넬 사보

우리 가운데 커피 애호가들이 현재 리스넬 사원의 새로운 혜택을 만끽하고 있다. **143**이달 초, 회사의 각 탕비실에 있던 커피 포트가 최신형 기계로 교체된 것이다. 이 조치는 일사분기 실적이 좋은 데 따른 보상 성격이다. 새 기계들은 헐포드 브루잉 시스템로서 다양한 풍미의 커피를 한 잔씩 제조한다. 커피 기계의 출현에 거의 모든 직원이 **144**기뻐했다. 몇몇 직원은 카페 모카가 그들이 맛본 커피 중 가장 맛있다고 한다. **145** 그 결과, 많은 부서에서 직원들이 탕비실을 찾는 발걸음이 더 잦아졌다. 그럼에도, 회사 총무부는 현재로선 커피 기계 **146**사용을 제한할 계획이 없다고 밝힌다. 오히려 모든 직원에게 한 잔씩 시음해 보라고 권고한다.

어휘 company newsletter 사보 benefit 혜택 earlier this month 이달 초 pantry 탕비실 be replaced with ~로 교체[대체]되다 state-of-the-art 최신식의, 최신형의

---

a variety of 다양한 flavor 풍미 appearance 출현, 등장 be greeted with ~한 반응을 얻다 nearly 거의 universal 보편적인, 전체적인 delight 기쁨, 즐거움 taste 맛보다 consequently 그 결과, 따라서 frequent 잦은, 빈번한 department 부서 regardless 그럼에도 불구하고 administration 행정, 총무 currently 현재 limit 제한하다 urge 촉구하다, 강하게 권고하다

143 문맥에 맞는 문장 고르기

번역 (A) 기계가 설치되는 동안 탕비실은 출입이 금지될 것이다.
(B) 재사용할 수 있는 컵은 정기적으로 세척해야 한다.
(C) 관심 있는 직원은 관리자에게 말해야 한다.
(D) 이 조치는 일사분기 실적이 좋은 데 따른 보상 성격이다.

해설 빈칸 앞 문장 '이달 초, 회사의 각 탕비실에 있던 커피 포트가 최신형 기계로 교체된 것이다(Earlier this month, the coffee pot in each pantry of the building was replaced with a state-of-the-art machine)'에서 회사의 개선된 점을 구체적으로 언급하고 있다. 따라서 빈칸에는 개선한 이유를 제시하는 것이 문맥상 자연스러우므로, 정답은 (D)이다.

어휘 off-limits 출입 금지의 reusable 재사용 가능한 move 조치, 행보 be meant as ~ 의도이다, ~ 성격이다 reward 보상 first quarter 일사분기

144 동사 어형_태

해설 빈칸은 주어(Their appearance) 뒤에 나오는 동사 자리이다. 앞에 있는 주어(This appearance)와 '커피 기계의 출현은 반응을 받았다'라는 수동의 의미를 나타내므로, 정답은 (A) was greeted이다. 동사 (B) will be greeting, (C) have greeted, (D) is greeting은 주어와 능동 관계를 이루므로, 의미상 적합하지 않다.

145 부사 어휘

해설 빈칸에는 앞뒤 문장을 자연스럽게 이어줄 접속부사가 필요하다. 앞 문장 '몇몇 직원은 카페 모카가 그들이 맛본 커피 중 가장 맛있다고 한다(Several employees say the café mocha is the best coffee they have tasted)'에서 직원들의 긍정적인 평가를 언급하고 있다. 빈칸 뒤에 나오는 문장 '많은 부서에서 직원들이 탕비실을 찾는 발걸음이 더 잦아졌다(trips to the pantry have become more frequent for members of many departments)'에서 긍정적인 평가로 인해 직원들의 방문이 늘었다는 결과의 의미를 나타내고 있으므로, 정답은 (B) Consequently(그 결과, 따라서)이다. (A) Nevertheless(그럼에도 불구하고), (C) Conversely(정반대로, 역으로), (D) Previously(이전에, 미리)는 의미상 적합하지 않다.

146 명사 어휘

해설 빈칸 앞 to부정사(to limit)의 목적어 역할을 하는 명사 자리로, 뒤에 나오는 전치사구(of the machine)의 수식을 받는다. 문맥상 '커피 기계 사용을 제한하다'라는 의미가 자연스러우므로, 정답은 (D) usage(사용량, 사용법)이다. (A) transportation(운송, 수송), (B) development(개발, 발달), (C) ranking(순위)은 의미상 적합하지 않다.

어휘 usage 사용, 이용

PART 7

출판사가 드리는 말씀

147이번 주, 〈드레이저스〉는 지난 수십 년 동안 새로운 경지를 개척한 과학자들 중 일부를 기리기 위해 시사를 잠시 쉽니다. 50쪽이 넘는 기사들은 다양한 분야에서 이 위대한 인물들의 업적을 설명하고, 그들이 오늘날 세계에 미친 영향을 고찰합니다. **148**저희는 또한 운 좋게도 그들 중 몇 명과 직접 그들의 경험에 관해 이야기를 나누었고, 그 전체 명단이 4쪽에 나옵니다. 그러므로 더 이상 길게 말하지 않고, 저희는 〈드레이저스 위클리〉의 이번 특집호를 즐기시도록 여러분을 초대합니다.

어휘 publisher 출판사 take a break from ~에서 잠시 손을 떼다, 일손을 쉬다 current affairs 최근 사건, 시사 honor 기리다, 영예롭게 하다 groundbreaking 획기적인, 새로운 경지를 개척한 decade 10년 article 기사 figure 인물 achievement 업적, 성취 a variety of 다양한 field 분야 effect 영향, 효과 fortunate 운이 좋은 directly 직접 available 입수할 수 있는, 이용할 수 있는 without further comment 더 이상 이렇다 저렇다 말하지 않고, 더 이상 길게 말하지 않고 unique 독특한 issue (신문·잡지 따위의) 호 weekly 주간지

147 추론 / 암시

번역 이 글은 어디에 실리겠는가?
(A) 과학 학회지
(B) 연구실 소식지
(C) 선집
(D) 뉴스 잡지

해설 지문의 첫 번째 문장에서 이번 주, 〈드레이저스〉는 지난 수십 년 동안 새로운 경지를 개척한 과학자들 중 일부를 기리기 위해 시사를 잠시 쉰다(This week, Drager's takes a break from current affairs to honor some of the groundbreaking scientists of the past decades)를 통해 〈드레이저스〉는 시사 내용을 다루는 잡지임을 유추할 수 있으므로, 정답은 (D)이다.

148 세부 사항

번역 언급된 페이지에서 찾을 수 있는 것은?
(A) 기념식 사진
(B) 재발행된 기사
(C) 일부 인터뷰 대상자의 이름
(D) 독자 투표 결과

해설 지문의 중반부에서 또한 운 좋게도 그들 중 몇 명과 직접 그들의 경험에 관해 이야기를 나누었고, 그 전체 명단이 4쪽에 나온다(We were also fortunate enough to speak directly with several of them about their experiences; a complete list is available on page four)를 통해 과학자들의 명단을 볼 수 있다고 언급하고 있으므로, 정답은 (C)이다.

▶▶ **Paraphrasing** 지문의 be available on page four → 질문의 be found on the page mentioned 지문의 a complete list → 정답의 The names of some interviewees

---

프라우스 K270 스피커

149음악이 빠진다면 어떤 뒤뜰 바비큐 파티나 수영장 파티가 완전할까요? 길이는 10인치밖에 안 되지만 K270 휴대용 스피커는 어디에 놓여 있든 수정처럼 맑은 소리를 냅니다. **150**튼튼한 알루미늄 외장은 햇빛과 여름 행사의 다른 위험들을 견디도록 해 주는 한편, 외장에 사용 가능한 눈부신 색조들이 재미를 더해 줍니다. 더욱이, K270은 다양한 기기와 호환되며 최대 30피트 범위까지 무선 연결이 가능합니다. 시험 삼아 사용해 보고 싶으신가요? 오늘 전국의 프라우스 전자 매장에 방문해 보세요.

어휘 backyard 뒤뜰, 뒷마당 complete 완전한, 완벽한 length 길이 portable 휴대할 수 있는 crystal-clear 수정처럼 맑은 place 놓다 tough 튼튼한 shell 껍데기, 외피, 외관 allow 가능하게 하다 withstand 견디다 sunlight 햇빛 hazard 위험 brilliant 눈부신, 환한 shade 색조 a touch of ~ 기운, 기미 what's more 더욱이, 게다가 compatible with ~와 호환되는 device 기기, 장치 wireless connectivity 무선 연결 range 범위 up to 최대 ~까지 try out 시험적으로 사용해 보다 electronics 전자 기기 nationwide 전국에, 전국적으로

149 추론 / 암시

번역 누구를 대상으로 한 광고이겠는가?
(A) 야외에서 즐겨 시간을 보내는 사람들
(B) 할인 전자제품을 찾고 있는 사람들
(C) 운전하며 음악을 듣는 사람들
(D) 직업으로 음악을 연주하는 사람들

해설 첫 번째 문장에서 음악이 빠진다면 어떤 뒤뜰 바비큐 파티나 수영장 파티가 완전할까(What backyard barbecue or pool party would be complete without music)를 통해 야외 활동을 즐기는 사람들을 위한 광고임을 유추할 수 있으므로, 정답은 (A)이다.

▶▶ **Paraphrasing** 지문의 backyard barbecue or pool party → 정답의 spending time outdoors

150 사실 관계 확인

번역 K270 스피커에 관해 언급된 것은?
(A) 크다.
(B) 온라인으로 판매한다.
(C) 색상이 밝다.
(D) 운반용 가방이 딸려 있다.

해설 지문 중반부의 튼튼한 알루미늄 외장은 햇빛과 여름 행사의 다른 위험들을 견디도록 해 주는 한편, 외장에 사용 가능한 눈부신 색조들이 재미를 더해 준다(A tough aluminum shell allows it to withstand sunlight and other hazards of summer events, while any of the shell's available brilliant shades add a touch of fun)에서 밝은 색상에 대해 언급하고 있으므로, 정답은 (C)이다.

▶▶ **Paraphrasing** 지문의 brilliant shades → 정답의 brightly colored

Test 8

151-152 문자 메시지

발레리아 권 [오전 10:24]
돈, 어디에 있어요?

돈 트루스데일 [오전 10:25]
개발 지역의 동쪽 끝에 있는 주택 중 한 곳에 있어요. ¹⁵¹세입자를 위해 헐거워진 문 손잡이를 수리해야 했어요. 왜 그러시는데요?

발레리아 권 [오전 10:25]
가능성 있는 주택 구매자인 폰티 씨가 방금 사무실에 도착하셨어요.

돈 트루스데일 [오전 10:26]
이런, 제가 복귀하려면 적어도 30분은 걸릴 거예요.

발레리아 권 [오전 10:27]
알았어요. ¹⁵²폰티 씨가 일정이 빡빡한 듯하니 우선 제가 직접 견본 주택을 보여 드리고 있을게요. 제게 열쇠가 있잖아요.

돈 트루스데일 [오전 10:28]
그러세요. 제가 뒤따라갈게요.

어휘 development 개발지 fix 고치다, 수리하다 loose 헐거운 tenant 세입자 potential 잠재적인 homebuyer 주택 구입자 at least 적어도 a half hour (미국식 어법) 30분(= half an hour) show+사람+around+장소 ~에게 …를 보여 주다[구경시키다] model home 견본 주택, 모델 하우스 Go right ahead. 진행하세요. 어서 하세요. catch up 따라잡다[따라가다]

151 추론 / 암시

번역 트루스데일 씨는 누구이겠는가?
(A) 부동산 관리인
(B) 전문 비서
(C) 잠재 고객
(D) 인테리어 디자이너

해설 트루스데일 씨의 오전 10시 25분 메시지에서 세입자를 위해 헐거워진 문 손잡이를 수리해야 했다(I had to fix a loose door handle for a tenant)를 통해 트루스데일 씨는 건물 관리인임을 유추할 수 있으므로, 정답은 (A)이다.

152 의도 파악

번역 오전 10시 28분에 트루스데일 씨가 "그러세요"라고 쓸 때, 그 의도는 무엇인가?
(A) 자동차를 대여하게 되어 기쁘다.
(B) 거리에 진입하지 못할 수도 있다.
(C) 권 씨가 집을 보여 줘야 한다.
(D) 나중에 권 씨에게 열쇠를 돌려줄 것이다.

해설 권 씨의 오전 10시 27분 메시지에서 폰티 씨가 일정이 빡빡한 듯하니 우선 내가 직접 견본 주택을 보여 주고 있겠다(It seems like Ms. Ponti is on a tight schedule, so maybe I could start showing her around the model home myself)를 통해 폰티 씨에게 견본 주택을 보여 주겠다고 제안하고 있다. 이에 대해 트루스데일 씨가 그러세요(Go right ahead)라며 동의를 표하고 있으므로, 정답은 (C)이다.

▶▶ **Paraphrasing** 지문의 showing her around the model home → 정답의 lead a house tour

153-154 설명서 발췌

창구 근무

¹⁵³고객에게 탁월한 서비스를 제공하기 위해 메어 론드리 전 지점의 창구 직원들은 아래 기본 절차를 준수해야 합니다.

- 고객을 친절하게 맞이한다.
- ¹⁵⁴고객의 물품을 받을 때 세탁할 품목과 드라이클리닝할 품목이 어떤 것인지, 얼룩 제거 같은 특별 서비스가 필요한지를 분명히 한다.
- 수집한 정보를 모두 전자 전표 시스템에 입력한다.
- ¹⁵⁴결과로 나온 가격을 고객에게 보여 주고 전액을 받는다.
- 전표를 출력한다. "이 부분은 고객 보관용"이라고 표시된 부분을 떼어 고객에게 준다. 물품을 찾을 때 그것을 보여 줘야 한다고 고객에게 설명한 후, "수령일"을 짚어서 알려 준다.
- 기분 좋게 대화를 마무리한다.
- 전표를 고객의 물품에 부착하고 물품을 적절한 통에 넣는다. (분류 방법은 다음 섹션 참조)

어휘 in order to+동사원형 ~하기 위하여 counter clerk 창구[계산대] 직원 laundry 세탁(소), 세탁물[빨래] location 지점, 지역 매장 adhere to ~을 준수하다, 지키다 following 아래의, 다음의 basic procedure 기본 절차 in a friendly manner 친절하게 clarify 분명히 하다 launder 세탁하다 stain removal 얼룩 제거 require 요구하다 gather 수집하다 electronic ticketing system 전자 전표[발권] 시스템 resulting 결과로 나온 obtain 얻다, 획득하다 full payment 전액 지불 detach 떼다, 분리하다 retain 보유하다, 보관하다 portion 부분 retrieve 회수하다, 찾다 point out 짚다, 지적하다 interaction 소통, 교류 attach 붙이다, 첨부하다 appropriate 적절한 bin 통, 함 sort 분류하다 instruction 지시, 방법

153 사실 관계 확인

번역 메어 론드리에 관해 명시된 것은?
(A) 영리기업들에게 서비스를 제공한다.
(B) 체인 사업체이다.
(C) 셀프서비스 기계들이 있다.
(D) 전자 통지서를 발송한다.

해설 첫 번째 단락에서 고객에게 탁월한 서비스를 제공하기 위해 메어 론드리 전 지점의 창구 직원들은 아래 기본 절차를 준수해야 한다(In order to provide excellent service to customers, counter clerks at all Maire Laundry locations should adhere to the following basic procedures)를 통해 메어 론드리는 여러 개의 지점을 가지고 있음을 알 수 있으므로, 정답은 (B)이다.

▶▶ **Paraphrasing** 지문의 all Maire Laundry locations → 정답의 a chain business

154 세부 사항

번역 직원들이 대금을 수령하기 전에 하도록 지시받은 일은?
(A) 보관증을 출력한다.
(B) 옷을 분류해 통 속에 넣는다.
(C) 완료일을 추산한다.
(D) 특별한 요청이 있는지 묻는다.

해설 대금 수령은 기본 절차의 네 번째 항목, 결과로 나온 가격을 고객에게 보여 주고 전액을 받는다(Show the resulting price to the customer and obtain full payment)에 있으므로 네 번째 항목 이전에 지시받은 일을 정답으로 골라야 한다. 두 번째 항목에서 고객의 물품을 받을 때 세탁할 품목과 드라이클리닝할 품목이 어떤 것인지, 얼룩 제거 같은 특별 서비스가 필요한지를 분명히 한다(Receive the customer's items, clarifying which are to be laundered and which are to be dry cleaned, and whether special services such as stain removal are required)를 통해 직원들은 전액을 받기 전에 특별한 서비스가 필요한지 확인해야 한다는 것을 알 수 있으므로, 정답은 (D)이다.

▶▶ **Paraphrasing** 지문의 **obtain full payment**
→ 질문의 **accepting payment**
지문의 **whether special services such as stain removal are required**
→ 정답의 **Ask about special requests**

155-157 광고

155버스비튼 몰이 넓어졌습니다! 새로 증축된 저희 매장들을 살펴보세요!

버스비튼 몰은 현재 55개가 넘는 점포와 넓은 주차장을 자랑합니다! 쇼핑객들께서 이곳에서 찾고 계신 것을 꼭 발견하실 수 있습니다. 또한 한가로이 둘러보시며 신상품을 발견하실 수도 있습니다. 156D쇼핑을 잠깐 쉴 때는 17곳의 구내 식당에 들르시거나, 1층 무대에서 자주 열리는 멋진 음악 공연을 보실 수도 있습니다.

그러나 그게 전부가 아닙니다. 버스비튼 몰은 역사적입니다: 156C100년 전에 지어진 저희의 아름다운 본관 건물은 수많은 디자인 출판물의 촬영 장소가 되어 왔으며, 나중에 지어진 구조물들은 본관을 보완하도록 세심하게 고안되었습니다.

어린이 친화적입니다: 156B저희의 실내 놀이터는 어린 방문객들에게 자유롭고 안전한 재미를 선사합니다. 또한 웬먼의 고전 만화들과 관련된 물건을 판매하는 웬먼 상점과 2층에 위치한 비디오 게임장도 이용하실 수 있습니다.

이미 팬이신가요? 157버스비튼 VIP 고객이 되십시오! 연회비를 조금만 내시면 전용 할인을 받게 되며, 저희의 VIP 라운지에서 편안히 모시겠습니다. 자세한 내용을 알아보시려면 안내 데스크를 방문하세요.

버스비튼 몰: 모두에게 즐거운 쇼핑!

어휘 addition 증축, 추가 boast 자랑하다, 뽐내다 ample 넓은, 풍부한 be sure to+동사원형 반드시[꼭] ~하다 browse 둘러보다 at a leisurely pace 천천히, 느긋하게 time-out 일시적 중단, 중간 휴식 on-site restaurant 구내 식당 take in 보다, 구경하다 sensational 환상적인, 멋진 performance 연주, 공연 frequently 자주 historic 역사적으로 중요한 numerous 수많은

publication 출판물 structure 구조물 conceive 구상하다, 고안하다 complement 보완하다 kid-friendly 어린이 친화적인 playground 놀이터, 운동장 available 이용할 수 있는 related to ~과 관련된 classic cartoon 고전 만화 video game arcade 비디오 게임장 located on[at, in] ~에 위치한 annual fee 연회비 gain access to ~을 이용하다, ~에 접근하다 exclusive 독점적인, 전용의 be invited to ~하도록 초청받다[모시다] unwind 느긋하게 쉬다, 긴장을 풀다

---

155 사실 관계 확인

번역 버스비튼 몰에 대해 명시된 것은?
(A) 최근에 확장했다.
(B) 월간지를 발행한다.
(C) 층수가 2층이 넘는다.
(D) 소유주가 바뀌었다.

해설 광고의 제목, 버스비튼 몰이 넓어졌습니다! 새로 증축된 저희 매장들을 살펴보세요(Busbyton Mall has grown! Check out our new additions)를 통해 버스비튼 몰이 확장했음을 알 수 있으므로, 정답은 (A)이다.

▶▶ **Paraphrasing** 지문의 **has grown** → 정답의 **expanded**

---

156 사실 관계 확인

번역 버스비튼 몰의 특징으로 언급되지 않은 것은?
(A) 대중교통 접근 용이성
(B) 어린이 놀이 시설
(C) 매력적인 건축 양식
(D) 콘서트 장소

해설 세 번째 단락의 실내 놀이터는 어린 방문객들에게 자유롭고 안전한 재미를 선사한다(Our indoor playground offers free, safe fun for younger visitors)를 통해 (B)를, 두 번째 단락의 100년 전에 지어진 저희의 아름다운 본관 건물은 수많은 디자인 출판물의 촬영 장소가 되어 왔으며, 나중에 지어진 구조물들은 본관을 보완하도록 세심하게 고안되었다(Built nearly 100 years ago, our beautiful main building has been photographed for numerous design publications, and later structures have been carefully conceived to complement it)를 통해 (C)를, 첫 번째 단락의 쇼핑을 잠깐 쉴 때 17곳의 구내 식당에 들르거나, 1층 무대에서 자주 열리는 멋진 음악 공연을 볼 수도 있다(For a time-out from shopping, stop by one of our 17 on-site restaurants, or take in the sensational music performances held frequently on our first-floor stage)를 통해 (D)를 특징으로 확인할 수 있으므로, 정답은 언급되지 않은 (A)이다.

▶▶ **Paraphrasing** 지문의 **Our indoor playground ~ for younger visitors**
→ 보기의 **A play facility for children**
지문의 **our beautiful main building**
→ 보기의 **Charming architecture**
지문의 **the sensational music performances held frequently on our first-floor stage** → 보기의 **A concert venue**

157 세부 사항

번역 특별 회원 자격이 있는 방문객에게 허용되는 것은?
(A) 경품 추첨 응모
(B) 휴게실 이용
(C) 보상 포인트 적립
(D) 근접 지역 주차

해설 마지막 단락의 버스비튼 VIP 고객이 되십시오! 연회비를 조금만 내면 전용 할인을 받게 되며, VIP 라운지에서 편안히 모시겠다(Become a Busbyton VIP! For a small annual fee, you will gain access to exclusive discounts and be invited to unwind in our VIP lounge)에서 VIP 고객이 되면 VIP 라운지를 이용할 수 있다고 언급하고 있으므로, 정답은 (B)이다.

▶▶ **Paraphrasing** 지문의 Become a Busbyton VIP
→ 질문의 hold special memberships
지문의 unwind in our VIP lounge
→ 정답의 Use a relaxation room

158-160 이메일

수신: 레이시 주 〈lacy.j@wic-mail.com〉
발신: 〈customerservice@fieldhughes.com〉
제목: 박스 구독 계획
날짜: 8월 1일

주 고객님께,

158필드 휴즈에서 3개월짜리 "매력 폭발" 박스 구독을 신청해 주셔서 감사합니다. 최신 유행 화장품, 패션 상품 등이 담긴 고객님의 첫 번째 상자가 곧 발송될 예정입니다. 요청하신 대로 고객님의 주소로 물품이 배송되는 당일에 문자 메시지를 받게 되실 것입니다.

159, 160또한 박스마다 내용물을 설명하는 카드가 들어 있으니 유의하시기 바랍니다. 알레르기 유발 제품으로 발생할 수 있는 문제들을 피하려면 사전에 카드를 자세히 살펴보십시오. 모든 화장품과 식품의 전체 성분이 기재되어 있습니다. 특정 품목을 특히 애호하시는 분들께는 어디에서 해당 품목을 더 구입하실 수 있는지 카드에 정보를 제공합니다.

마지막으로, 저희는 고객님께서 잠시 시간을 내어 다른 잠재 고객들을 필드 휴즈에 제안해 주시기를 소망합니다. 저희에게 세 명 이상의 친구들을 소개하시는 분들께는 최고급 월간 "매력 폭발" 박스 한 상자를 무료로 보내드립니다. 소개 양식은 저희 웹사이트 www.fieldhughes.com/referrals에서 찾으실 수 있습니다.

필드 휴즈 팀

어휘 sign up for ~을 신청하다, ~에 등록하다 burst 한바탕 터뜨림, 파열 trendy 유행하는 cosmetics 화장품 ship out 배송하다, 발송하다 request 요청하다 text message alert 문자 알림 deliver 배달[배송]하다 note that ~을 유의하다, 알아 두다 contain 포함하다 describe 설명하다 contents 내용물 closely 꼼꼼히, 자세히 beforehand 미리, 사전에 avoid 피하다

potential 잠재적인 allergy-inducing 알레르기를 일으키는 particular 특정한 supply 제공하다, 공급하다 purchase 구입[구매]하다, 사다 take a moment to+동사원형 잠시 시간을 내어 ~하다 suggest 제안하다 refer A to B A를 B에게 소개하다 premium 최고급의 referral form 소개 양식

158 주제 / 목적

번역 이메일의 목적 한 가지는 무엇인가?
(A) 문의에 답하려고
(B) 구독을 확인하려고
(C) 주 씨에게 배송 지연을 알리려고
(D) 신상품을 추천하려고

해설 첫 번째 단락의 필드 휴즈에서 3개월짜리 "매력 폭발" 박스 구독을 신청해 주셔서 감사하다(Thank you for signing up for a three-month "Burst of Glamour" box plan from Field Hughes)를 통해 정기구독 신청을 확인하기 위해 이메일을 쓰고 있음을 알 수 있으므로, 정답은 (B)이다.

▶▶ **Paraphrasing** 지문의 a three-month "Burst of Glamour" box plan → 정답의 a subscription

159 세부 사항

번역 주 씨가 자세히 읽도록 안내받은 것은?
(A) 웹페이지
(B) 제품 라벨
(C) 문자 메시지
(D) 상자 내용물

해설 두 번째 단락에서 박스마다 내용물을 설명하는 카드가 들어 있으니 유의하기 바란다. 알레르기 유발 제품으로 발생할 수 있는 문제들을 피하려면 사전에 카드를 자세히 살펴보라(Also, note that each box contains a card describing the contents inside. Please examine it closely beforehand to avoid any potential problems with allergy-inducing products)를 통해 이메일의 수신인(You)인 주 씨는 상자 안에 들어 있는 카드를 주의해서 읽어야 한다는 것을 알 수 있으므로, 정답은 (D)이다.

▶▶ **Paraphrasing** 지문의 examine it closely
→ 질문의 read carefully
지문의 each box contains a card describing the contents inside
→ 정답의 A package insert

160 문장 삽입

번역 [1], [2], [3], [4]로 표시된 곳 중에서 다음 문장이 들어가기에 가장 적합한 곳은?

"모든 화장품과 식품의 전체 성분이 기재되어 있습니다."

(A) [1]
(B) [2]
(C) [3]
(D) [4]

해설 삽입 문장 '모든 화장품과 식품의 전체 성분이 기재되어 있다(The ingredients of all cosmetics and edible goods are listed in full)'를 통해 앞에서 화장품과 식품의 전체 성분이 기재된 곳과 기재하는 이유를 구체적으로 언급할 것임을 알 수 있다. [3]의 앞 두 문장 또한 박스마다 내용물을 설명하는 카드가 들어 있으니 유의하기 바란다. 알레르기 유발 제품으로 발생할 수 있는 문제들을 피하려면 사전에 카드를 자세히 살펴보라(Also, note that each box contains a card describing the contents inside. Please examine it closely beforehand to avoid any potential problems with allergy-inducing products)에서 삽입 문장의 내용이 기재된 곳과 이유를 제시하고 있으므로, 정답은 (C)이다.

161-163 이메일

발신: 제인 라일리, 인사부
수신: 비데스 디자인 관리자들
날짜: 11월 3일
제목: 계획들

관리자들께,

비데스가 확장을 계속함에 따라 정기적으로 신입사원, 특히 그래픽 디자이너들이 더 필요해졌습니다. **161이를 염두에 두고 우리는 대학생을 대상으로 하게 인턴십 프로그램을 시작하기로 결정했습니다.** 이를 통해 우리는 재능 있는 직원들을 조기에 접촉해 우리의 체계를 교육시킬 수 있을 것입니다.

162이상적으로 말하자면, 우리는 내년 초에 보스트윅 대학교 취업 센터를 통해 지원자를 모집하기 시작할 것입니다. 처음에 이 대학교에 집중하기로 한 이유는 단지 우리 직원 다수가 이 대학 동문이기 때문입니다. 그렇다고 해서 우리가 장차 다른 기관들과 협력하지 않겠다는 뜻은 아닙니다.

우리는 부서마다 인턴 사원 한 명으로 시작할 예정입니다. **163여러분 각자가 가치 있게 여기는 인턴의 자질이 무엇이며, 여러분의 부서가 그 인턴에게 대가로 줄 수 있는 것이 무엇인지 우선 생각해 보기를 바랍니다.** 두 영역에 대한 여러분의 생각을 대략 정리해서 앞으로 몇 주 후에 제게 보내주시기 바랍니다. 참고로, 여러분이 기재한 내용이 인턴십 광고에 쓰이는 안내물의 기초가 될 것입니다.

– 제인 라일리

어휘 expand 확장하다, 팽창하다 supply 공급 with ~ in mind ~을 고려하여, 염두에 둔 decide 결정[결심]하다 make contact with ~와 연락하다, 접촉하다 talented 재능 있는 personnel 직원들 educate 교육하다 ideally 이상적으로 (말하면) recruit 모집하다 applicant 신청자, 지원자 career center 취업 센터 choose to+동사원형 ~하기로 하다 focus on ~에 집중하다, 초점을 맞추다 a number of 많은 alumnus 동문(pl. alumni) partner with ~와 협력하다 institution 기관 in the future 장차, 앞으로 per ~당, ~마다 quality 자질, 품질 valuable 소중한, 가치 있는 in return 대가로 rough 대략적인 for reference 참고로 advertise 광고하다

161 주제 / 목적

번역 이메일이 작성된 이유는?
(A) 연속 세미나의 연사를 모집하려고
(B) **인턴십 프로그램을 발표하려고**
(C) 신규 지점의 목적을 설명하려고
(D) 채용 과정에 대한 오해를 바로잡으려고

해설 첫 번째 단락 두 번째 문장, 이를 염두에 두고 대학생을 대상으로 하게 인턴십 프로그램을 시작하기로 결정했다(With this in mind, we've decided to begin a summer internship program for university students)를 통해 인턴십 프로그램의 시작을 알리기 위해 이메일을 쓰고 있음을 알 수 있으므로, 정답은 (B)이다.

162 사실 관계 확인

번역 보스트윅 대학교에 관해 명시된 것은?
(A) 뛰어난 그래픽 디자인과가 있다.
(B) 여름에 전문 개발 과정을 주도한다.
(C) 비데스 디자인이 이 학교와 공공미술 프로젝트를 협업하고 있다.
(D) **비데스 디자인 직원 몇 명이 이 학교 졸업생이다.**

해설 두 번째 단락에서 이상적으로 말하자면, 내년 초에 보스트윅 대학교 취업 센터를 통해 지원자를 모집하기 시작할 것이다. 처음에 이 대학교에 집중하기로 한 이유는 단지 우리 직원 다수가 이 대학 동문이기 때문이다(Ideally, we will begin recruiting applicants through the Bostwick University Career Center early next year. We chose to focus on this university first simply because a number of our staff are alumni of it)를 통해 직원 다수가 보스트윅 대학교 출신임을 언급하고 있으므로, 정답은 (D)이다.

▶▶ **Paraphrasing** 지문의 **a number of our staff are alumni of it** → 정답의 **Several Vides Design employees graduated from it.**

163 세부 사항

번역 이메일 독자들이 생각해 보도록 요청을 받은 것은?
(A) **가능성 있는 관계의 상호 유익**
(B) 성공적인 지도자의 자질
(C) 고객 불만의 근거
(D) 가장 좋은 일자리 광고 수단

해설 세 번째 단락의 여러분 각자가 가치 있게 여기는 인턴의 자질이 무엇이며, 여러분의 부서가 그 인턴에게 대가로 줄 수 있는 것이 무엇인지 우선 생각해 보기를 바란다(I'd like each of you to start thinking about what qualities you would find valuable in an intern and what your department can offer to him or her in return)에서 각 부서와 인턴 상호간에 도움이 되는 것을 생각해 보도록 요청하고 있으므로, 정답은 (A)이다.

▶▶ **Paraphrasing** 지문의 **thinking about** → 질문의 **consider** 지문의 **what qualities you would find valuable in an intern and what your department can offer to him or her in return** → 정답의 **The mutual benefits of a possible relationship**

소피아 홍과 함께하는 일일 워크숍에 오신 것을 환영합니다!

등록을 하셨으니 자리에 앉아 수강 준비를 해 주시기 바랍니다. **164, 166D**오전 10시부터 오후 12시 30분까지 홍 선생이 질문을 장려하는 대화 형식으로 성공적인 작가가 되는 길을 주제로 이야기를 들려줄 예정입니다. **165, 166B**오후 1시 30분부터 워크숍이 끝나는 오후 4시 30분까지 워크숍 참가자 다섯 분 모두에게 각자가 참가 전에 제출한 이야기 시안에 근거해 홍 선생이 개인별 조언을 해 줄 것입니다. **166A**점심 시간 1시간 외에 오전 11시 15분과 오후 3시에 10분간 휴식 시간이 있습니다. 저희 이용객들을 방해하지 않기 위해 대출 데스크 근처에 있는 로비에서 휴식을 취해 주실 것을 당부드립니다. 이 구역에는 여러분의 편안함과 편의를 위한 벤치와 안락의자가 있습니다.

167워크숍이 끝나고 아래 빈칸에 의견을 주시는 참가자들께는 기재된 선물들을 고를 수 있는 선택권을 드립니다.

―――――――――――― 절취선 ――――――――――――

의견:

선물: _____ 스프링 노트   **167**_____ 캔버스 책가방

어휘 now that ~이므로 check in 등록하다, 입실하다 prepare to+동사원형 ~할 준비를 하다 share 나누다, 공유하다 path to+동명사 ~하는 길 in a conversational format 대화 형식으로 encourage 장려하다, 권장하다 personalized 개인에 맞춘, 개인별 participant 참가자 based on ~에 근거하여 proposal 제안, 시안 submit 제출하다 prior to ~에 앞서, ~ 전에 in addition to ~에 덧붙여, ~외에 break 휴식 take place 발생하다, 일어나다 disturb 방해하다 patron (도서관 등의) 이용객, 고객 circulation desk 대출 데스크 lounge chair 안락의자 comfort 안락함, 편안함 convenience 편의, 편리 post-workshop 워크숍 이후의 list 기재하다, 열거하다 comment 논평, 견해[의견] spiral notebook 스프링 노트 bookbag 책가방

164 추론 / 암시

번역 워크숍의 주제는 무엇이겠는가?
(A) 효과적인 설명회를 하는 법
(B) 목공 사업 시작하기
(C) 작가로 성공하는 법
(D) 수공예품을 만드는 다양한 방법

해설 첫 번째 단락의 오전 10시부터 오후 12시 30분까지 홍 선생이 질문을 장려하는 대화 형식으로 성공적인 작가가 되는 길을 주제로 이야기를 들려줄 예정이다(From 10 A.M. to 12:30 P.M., Ms. Hong will share the story of her path to becoming a successful author, in a conversational format in which questions are encouraged)를 통해 작가가 되는 길에 관한 워크숍임을 유추할 수 있으므로, 정답은 (C)이다.

▶▶ **Paraphrasing** 지문의 **her path to becoming a successful author**
→ 정답의 **How to succeed as a writer**

165 세부 사항

번역 워크숍 전에 참가자들이 해야 했던 일은?
(A) 건물 로비에 집합한다
(B) 홍 선생에게 질문을 제출한다
(C) 필기도구 한 벌을 구입한다
(D) 앞으로 있을 프로젝트를 위한 아이디어를 준비한다

해설 첫 번째 단락의 오후 1시 30분부터 워크숍이 끝나는 오후 4시 30분까지 워크숍 참가자 다섯 명 모두에게 각자가 참가 전에 제출한 이야기 시안에 근거해 홍 선생이 개인별 조언을 해 줄 것이다(From 1:30 P.M. until the workshop ends at 4:30 P.M., she will supply personalized advice to all five of our workshop's participants, based on the story proposal that each of you submitted prior to attending)를 통해 워크숍 참가자 전원이 이야기 시안을 미리 작성해 제출했음을 알 수 있으므로, 정답은 (D)이다.

▶▶ **Paraphrasing** 지문의 **the story proposal**
→ 정답의 **ideas for a potential project**

166 사실 관계 확인

번역 양식에 포함되지 않은 정보는?
(A) 쉬는 시간 스케줄
(B) 참가자 수
(C) 워크숍 장소
(D) 오전 회의의 주제

해설 양식의 첫 번째 단락의 점심 시간 1시간 외에 오전 11시 15분과 오후 3시에 10분간 휴식 시간이 있다(In addition to the one-hour lunch period, ten-minute breaks will take place at 11:15 A.M. and 3 P.M.)를 통해 (A)를, 오후 1시 30분부터 워크숍이 끝나는 오후 4시 30분까지 워크숍 참가자 다섯 명 모두에게 각자가 참가 전에 제출한 이야기 시안에 근거해 홍 선생이 개인별 조언을 해 줄 것이다(From 1:30 P.M. until the workshop ends at 4:30 P.M., she will supply personalized advice to all five of our workshop's participants, based on the story proposal that each of you submitted prior to attending)를 통해 (B)를, 오전 10시부터 오후 12시 30분까지 홍 선생이 질문을 장려하는 대화 형식으로 성공적인 작가가 되는 길을 주제로 이야기를 들려줄 예정이다(From 10 A.M. to 12:30 P.M., Ms. Hong will share the story of her path to becoming a successful author, in a conversational format in which questions are encouraged)를 통해 (D)를 확인할 수 있으므로, 정답은 언급되지 않은 (C)이다.

▶▶ **Paraphrasing** 지문의 **ten-minute breaks**
→ 보기의 **rest times**
지문의 **all five of our workshop's participants**
→ 보기의 **The number of participants**
지문의 **the story of her path to becoming a successful author** → 보기의 **The topic**

167 사실 관계 확인

번역 의견을 주는 참가자들에 관해 명시된 것은?
(A) 천으로 만든 가방을 받을 수 있다.
(B) 아마도 워크숍을 싫어할 것이다.
(C) 양식을 우편으로 부쳐야 한다.
(D) 향후 행사에 등록할지도 모른다.

해설 두 번째 단락의 워크숍이 끝나고 아래 빈칸에 의견을 주는 참가자들에게 기재된 선물들을 고를 수 있는 선택권을 준다(Participants who provide post-workshop feedback in the box below will be given their choice of the gifts listed)와 선물:(Gift:)의 캔버스 책가방(canvas bookbag)을 통해 후기를 남기는 참가자들은 캔버스 책가방을 선택해 받을 수 있음을 알 수 있으므로, 정답은 (A)이다.

▶▶ **Paraphrasing** 지문의 **provide post-workshop feedback**
→ 질문의 **give feedback**
지문의 **be given** → 정답의 **receive**
지문의 **canvas bookbag**
→ 정답의 **a cloth sack**

168-171 온라인 채팅

안드레 존스, 오전 9:02
안녕하세요, 여러분. **168**볼릭 씨가 오늘 아침 우리 회의에 참석할 거라는 이야기를 방금 들었으니 준비하고 계세요.

바랏 라가리, 오전 9:02
네, 알려 줘서 고마워요. 제가 치사토에게 언제 간식을 가지고 올지 알려 줄게요.

캐럴 하우저, 오전 9:03
저는 회의실이 준비되었는지 살펴볼게요. **169**그리고 의사 일정을 수정해서 볼릭 씨에게 이야기할 시간을 줘야 할까요?

안드레 존스, 오전 9:04
아뇨, 그건 됐어요, 캐럴. 사실, 그는 자신이 자리에 없는 것처럼 우리가 행동하기를 원해요. **168**그렇지만 부사장급이 우리 주간 회의 자리에 앉는 게 오랜만이라서, 최소한 나쁜 인상은 주지 않았으면 좋겠어요.

이벳 컬리, 오전 9:05
170그렇다면 대상 소비층의 구매 습관에 관한 설명회를 혹시 다음 주로 옮길 수 있을까요? 제가 제품 출시 때문에 정말 바빠서요….

안드레 존스, 오전 9:05
제 생각에 그렇게 되면 회의가 너무 짧아질 것 같아요. **171**적어도 전자 슬라이드 쇼는 준비했죠?

이벳 컬리, 오전 9:06
171네. 하지만 좀 아쉬워요.

안드레 존스, 오전 9:07
음… 제게 그 파일을 이메일로 보낸 다음 제 사무실로 와서 상의하도록 해요. 캐럴, 결정 사항을 제가 알려 드릴게요.

어휘 get word (우연히) 알게 되다 **heads-up** 경고, 주의 **set up** 마련하다, 설치하다 **revise** 수정하다, 변경하다 **agenda** 의제, 의사일정 **actually** 실은 **as if** 마치 ~인 것처럼 **weekly meeting** 주간 회의 **ensure** 반드시 ~하게 하다, 보장하다 **at a minimum** 최소한 **make a bad impression** 나쁜 인상을 주다 **in that case** 그럴 경우, 그렇다면 **possibly** 혹시 **presentation** 설명회, 발표 **buying habit** 구매 습관 **target consumer** 대상 소비자 **be busy with** ~으로 바쁘다 **product launch** 제품 출시 **electronic slideshow** 전자 슬라이드쇼 **at least** 적어도

168 사실 관계 확인

번역 볼릭 씨에 대해 명시된 것은?
(A) 고위직 임원이다.
(B) 존스 씨에게 직접 전화했다.
(C) 발표할 내용이 있다.
(D) 장기 출장에서 돌아왔다.

해설 존스 씨의 오전 9시 2분 메시지, 볼릭 씨가 오늘 아침 우리 회의에 참석할 거라는 이야기를 방금 들었으니 준비하라(I just got word that Mr. Boliek will be attending our meeting this morning, so please be prepared)와 오전 9시 4분 메시지, 그렇지만 부사장급이 우리 주간 회의 자리에 앉는 게 오랜만이라서, 최소한 나쁜 인상은 주지 않았으면 좋겠다(But it's been a long time since someone at the vice-president level has sat in on our weekly meeting, so I'd like to ensure that, at a minimum, we don't make a bad impression)를 통해 볼릭 씨가 부사장급임을 알 수 있으므로, 정답은 (A)이다.

▶▶ **Paraphrasing** 지문의 **the vice-president level**
→ 정답의 **a high-ranking executive**

169 추론 / 암시

번역 하우저 씨가 맡은 일은 무엇이겠는가?
(A) 다과 준비
(B) 시간표 작성
(C) 전자 장비 준비
(D) 회의실 예약

해설 하우저 씨의 오전 9시 3분 메시지에서 의사 일정을 수정해서 볼릭 씨에게 말할 시간을 줘야 할까(And should I revise the agenda to allow time for Mr. Boliek to speak)를 통해 하우저 씨가 의사 일정과 관련된 일을 맡고 있음을 유추할 수 있으므로, 정답은 (B)이다.

▶▶ **Paraphrasing** 지문의 **revise the agenda**
→ 정답의 **Making a timetable**

170 추론 / 암시

번역 대화자들은 어떤 분야에서 일하겠는가?
(A) 법률
(B) 의료
(C) 회계
(D) 마케팅

해설 컬리 씨의 오전 9시 5분 메시지, 그렇다면 대상 소비층의 구매 습관에 관한 설명회를 혹시 다음 주로 옮길 수 있을까(In that case, could we possibly move my presentation on the buying habits of our target consumers to next week)를 통해 소비자를 연구하여 제품을 홍보하는 마케팅 분야에서 일한다고 유추할 수 있으므로, 정답은 (D)이다.

171 의도 파악

번역 오전 9시 6분에 컬리 씨가 "좀 아쉬워요"라고 쓸 때, 그 의도는 무엇인가?
(A) 존스 씨가 조사 결과에 실망할지도 모른다.
(B) 일부 작업의 현재 상태가 만족스럽지 않다.
(C) 시각 자료를 써서 일부 자료를 설명하기를 원한다.
(D) 존스 씨는 회의 취소를 고려해야 한다.

해설 존스 씨의 오전 9시 5분 메시지, 적어도 전자 슬라이드쇼는 준비했죠(Did you make an electronic slideshow, at least)라는 질문에 대해 컬리 씨가 네(Yes)라고 응답한 후 좀 아쉽다(it could be better)라고 했다. 따라서 준비한 전자 슬라이드쇼에 대한 실망감을 표현하고 있으므로, 정답은 (B)이다.

172-175 기사

아투소 푸드 트럭 축제 확대 예정

애비게일 데이비스

아투소 (8월 31일)—아투소 시는 5월에 처음 열린 아투소 푸드 트럭 축제의 놀라운 성공을 언급하며, 내년 행사를 하루 더 연장하는 한편 장소는 그대로 유지하겠다는 계획을 공개했다.

172첫 아투소 푸드 트럭 축제는 시가 1월에 건설 공사를 끝낸 몬타 공원에 방문객을 모으기 위해 조직되었다. 20대가 넘는 트럭이 약 천 명의 군중에게 다양한 음식을 내놓는 한편 음악가들과 미술 공예 천막들이 여흥거리를 제공했다.

변화는 축제 웹사이트 www.attuso-ftf.com에 어제 올라온 보도자료로 발표되었다. **175**시 당국자들은 하루가 추가되어 더 많은 방문객에게 참가 기회를 제공함으로써 두 번째 축제에 커다란 영향을 미칠 것이라고 적었다. <u>그들은 또 축제가 아투소 지역 외부에서 오는 트럭들에게도 더 매력적인 행사가 될 것이라고 내다보았다.</u>

올해 축제에 참가한 트럭 중 가장 많은 인기를 끈 김치 카레의 주인 드레이크 류는 이 소식에 흥분을 나타냈다. "우리는 내년 축제 자리에도 꼭 있을 거예요." 그는 말했다. "첫 축제가 우리 음식을 새로운 사람들에게 많이 **174**소개했는데, 상황이 더 좋아지기만 할 것 같네요."

시는 또한 제공되는 여흥의 선택 범위가 넓어지기를 희망한다. 추가적인 활동 천막들을 후원할 업체와 단체를 물색하고, 그룹과 개인의 음악 공연 기회가 많아질 것이다. **173**보도자료에는 지원 양식이 곧 나올 것이라고 약속하며 관심 있는 이들은 웹사이트를 정기적으로 확인해 볼 것을 권한다.

어휘 expand 확대[확장]하다 cite 언급하다, 인용하다 remarkable 놀랄 만한, 주목할 만한 inaugural 처음의, 최초의 reveal 공개하다, 밝히다 venue 장소 remain the same 똑같이[그대로] 유지하다 organize 조직하다, 구성하다 attract 끌어들이다, 유인하다 a variety of 다양한 estimated 추정된, 추산된

crowd 군중 arts-and-crafts 미술 공예의 entertainment 여흥, 오락거리 post 게시하다, 올리다 official 공무원, 관리 have a large impact on ~에 큰 영향을 미치다 participate in ~에 참가[참석]하다(= attend) voice 목소리를 내다, 표명하다 definitely 꼭, 분명히, 확실히 widen 넓히다, 확대[확장]하다 organization 단체, 조직 seek 모색하다, 찾다 sponsor 후원하다 additional 추가적인 opportunity 기회 individual 개인 application form 신청 양식 encourage 권장하다, 장려하다 regularly 규칙적으로, 정기적으로

172 추론 / 암시

번역 축제에 관해 암시된 것은?
(A) 데이비스 씨가 참가해 왔다.
(B) 류 씨가 주최자 중 한 명이다.
(C) 전에 두 차례 개최되었다.
(D) 공원에서 열린다.

해설 두 번째 단락에서 첫 아투소 푸드 트럭 축제는 시가 1월에 건설 공사를 끝낸 몬타 공원에 방문객을 모으기 위해 조직되었다(The first Attuso Food Truck Festival was organized to attract visitors to Montar Park, which the city had finished constructing in January)를 통해 축제가 공원에서 개최된다는 것을 유추할 수 있으므로, 정답은 (D)이다.

▶▶ Paraphrasing 지문의 **Montar Park, which the city had finished constructing** → 정답의 **a public park**

173 추론 / 암시

번역 웹사이트에 관해 암시된 것은?
(A) 아직 필요한 서류가 포함되지 않았다.
(B) 아투소 시가 관리하지 않는다.
(C) 도시 외부의 방문객을 위해 만들어졌다.
(D) 다음 축제 기간 동안 실시간으로 업데이트될 것이다.

해설 마지막 단락에서 보도자료에는 지원 양식이 곧 나올 것이라고 약속하며 관심 있는 이들은 웹사이트를 정기적으로 확인해 볼 것을 권한다(The press release promises that application forms are coming soon and encourages those interested to check the Web site regularly)를 통해 웹사이트에 현재 지원 양식이 없음을 유추할 수 있으므로, 정답은 (A)이다.

▶▶ Paraphrasing 지문의 **application forms are coming soon** → 정답의 **does not yet contain necessary documents**

174 동의어 찾기

번역 네 번째 단락 4행의 "introduced"와 의미가 가장 가까운 단어는?
(A) 시행했다
(B) 배정했다
(C) 제시했다
(D) 생성했다

해설 해당 문장은 첫 축제가 우리 음식을 새로운 사람들에게 많이 소개했는데, 상황이 더 좋아지기만 할 것 같다(The first one introduced our food to a lot of new people, and it sounds like it's only going to get better)라는 의미로 해석되는데, 여기서 introduced는 '소개했다, 내놓았다'라는 의미가 자연스러우므로, 정답은 (C) presented(제시했다, 소개했다, 보여 주었다)이다.

175 문장 삽입

번역 [1], [2], [3], [4]로 표시된 곳 중에서 다음 문장이 들어가기에 가장 적합한 곳은?

"그들은 또 축제가 아투소 지역 외부에서 오는 트럭들에게도 더 매력적인 행사가 될 것이라고 내다보았다."

(A) [1]
(B) [2]
(C) [3]
(D) [4]

해설 삽입 문장 '그들은 또 축제가 아투소 지역 외부에서 오는 트럭들에게도 더 매력적인 행사가 될 것이라고 내다보았다(They also predict that it will make the event more attractive to trucks from outside of the Attuso area)'를 통해 앞에서 그들(they)의 구체적인 대상과 그들이 예측하는 긍정적인 효과를 하나 더(also) 언급할 것임을 알 수 있다. [2]의 앞 문장, 시 당국자들은 하루 추가되어 더 많은 방문객에게 참가 기회를 제공함으로써 두 번째 축제에 커다란 영향을 미칠 것이라고 적었다(City officials wrote that the extra day will have a large impact on the second celebration of the festival by giving more visitors a chance to attend)에서 시 당국자들(they)에서 두 번째 축제에 대한 기대를 제시하고 있으므로, 정답은 (B)이다.

176-180 이메일 + 영수증

발신: ⟨promotions@aledonshoes.com⟩
수신: 그랜트 휴덕
날짜: 1월 29일
제목: 알레돈 슈즈 허클리

휴덕 씨께,

176, 178D저희는 알레돈 슈즈가 온라인에서 2년 동안 빠르게 성장한 끝에 첫 오프라인 매장 개점을 발표하게 되어 기쁩니다. 패션의 거리인 타피 스트리트에 위치한 알레돈 슈즈 허클리는 이번 주 토요일에 문을 열 예정입니다. 저희는 허클리 지역의 단골 고객이신 귀하께서 이 설레는 발전 소식을 가장 먼저 알게 되시기를 바랐습니다. **180**개점하는 주말에 들르셔서 모든 구매 고객께 드리는 무료 신발 세정제 세트를 받으세요!

178A하지만 그렇게 빨리 방문하실 수 없더라도 나중에 화요일부터 일요일까지 오전 10시에서 오후 7시 사이에 들러 주시기를 권합니다. **177**신발 디자인의 권위자가 상주하고 있어서 귀하께 직접 상담해 드릴 것입니다. 그리고 허클리 시 상공회의소의 자랑스러운 일원으로서 저희는 허클리 시 상공 우대 고객 카드 소지자들께 상시 10% 할인을 제공할 예정입니다.

곧 만나 뵙기를 바랍니다.

앨리사 쉽
알레돈 슈즈 CEO

어휘 be pleased to + 동사원형 ~하게 되어 기쁘다 rapid growth 빠른 성장 launch 시작하다, 출시하다 offline location 오프라인 매장[지점] located on ~에 자리 잡은[위치한] loyal customer 충성[단골] 고객 region 지역 development 발전 collect 받다, 수집하다 purchase 구입, 구매 even if 설령 ~일지라도 authority 권위자, 대가 footwear 신발류 on hand 출석해 있는 in-person consultation 직접 상담 Chamber of Commerce 상공회의소 standing 상시적인 holder 소지자 preferred customer 우대 고객

주문 영수증
알레돈 슈즈 허클리
타피 스트리트 907번지

고객명: 그랜트 휴덕 **179**날짜: 2월 3일
고객 번호: 000325 판매사원: 질리안 스태퍼드

알레돈 슈즈 허클리에서 구매해 주셔서 감사합니다. **178B**저희는 기재된 명세표와 저희가 측정한 치수를 사용해 아래 품목들을 제작하겠습니다. **179**주문하신 물품은 2월 12일 화요일이나 그 후에 찾으러 오시면 됩니다.

모델 번호	정보	수량	단가	합계
5439	최고급 가죽 정장화; 검은 실로 바느질한 검정색 구두	1	121달러	121달러
8167	캔버스 운동화; 밑창이 흰색인 남색 운동화	1	108달러	108달러
3402	**180**신발 세정제 세트	1	0.00	0달러
	할인			-0달러
	대금 총액			229달러
	받은 금액			-229달러
	미납 대금			0달러

지불 유형: __X__ 신용카드 ____ 현금 ____ 기타

어휘 receipt 영수증 construct 제작하다 specification 명세서, 명세표 list 기재하다, 열거하다 sizing measurements 크기 측정값, 치수 pick up 찾아가다 quantity 수량 price per unit 단가 leather 가죽 dress shoes 정장화 stitching 한 줄로 이어진 바늘땀 sole 밑창, 발바닥 shoe cleaner 신발 세정제 due 내야 할 돈, 대금 balance due 미납 대금[요금] payment 지불, 지급 cash 현금

176 주제 / 목적

번역 이메일에서 주로 광고하는 것은?
(A) 계절 할인 판매
(B) 제품군
(C) 고객 적립 카드
(D) 개점 행사

해설 이메일의 첫 번째 단락, 알레돈 슈즈가 온라인에서 2년 동안 빠르게 성장한 끝에 첫 오프라인 매장 개점을 발표하게 되어 기쁘다(We are pleased to announce that, after two years of rapid growth online, Aledon Shoes is launching its first offline location)를 통해 오프라인 매장의 개점을 알리기 위한 이메일임을 알 수 있으므로, 정답은 (D)이다.

▶▶ Paraphrasing   지문의 **launching its first offline location**
                     → 정답의 **A grand opening**

177 세부 사항

번역 이메일에 따르면 알레돈 슈즈 허클리 고객들이 이용할 수 있는 것은?
(A) 전문가의 조언
(B) 신발 수선
(C) 3D 족부 스캐닝 장치
(D) 어울리는 다양한 소품

해설 이메일의 두 번째 단락, 신발 디자인의 권위자가 상주하고 있어서 직접 상담해 줄 것이다(An authority on footwear design will always be on hand to give you an in-person consultation)에서 신발 디자인 권위자의 직접 상담을 언급하고 있으므로, 정답은 (A)이다.

▶▶ Paraphrasing   지문의 **An authority on footwear design**
                     → 정답의 **a specialist**
                    지문의 **an in-person consultation**
                     → 정답의 **Advice**

178 연계

번역 알레돈 슈즈 허클리에 관해 언급되지 않은 내용은?
(A) 주마다 하루는 문을 닫는다.
(B) 주문 제작 신발을 판매한다.
(C) 가정 배달 서비스를 운영한다.
(D) 인터넷업체에서 생겨났다.

해설 이메일의 두 번째 단락, 하지만 그렇게 빨리 방문할 수 없더라도 나중에 화요일부터 일요일까지 오전 10시에서 오후 7시 사이에 들러 주기를 권한다(But even if you can't visit us so soon, we encourage you to stop in later between 10 A.M. and 7 P.M., Tuesdays through Sundays)를 통해 (A)를, 영수증의 기재된 명세표와 측정한 치수를 사용해 아래 품목들을 제작하겠다(We will construct the items below using the specifications listed and the sizing measurements we have taken)를 통해 (B)를, 이메일의 첫 번째 단락 알레돈 슈즈가 온라인에서 2년 동안 빠르게 성장한 끝에 첫 오프라인 매장 개점을 발표하게 되어 기쁘다(We are pleased to announce that, after two years of rapid growth online, Aledon Shoes is launching its first offline location)를 통해 (D)를 확인할 수 있으므로, 정답은 언급되지 않은 (C)이다.

▶▶ Paraphrasing   지문의 **Tuesdays through Sundays**
                     → 보기의 **closed one day per week**
                    지문의 **using the specifications listed and the sizing measurements we have taken**
                     → 보기의 **custom-made**
                    지문의 **rapid growth online**
                     → 보기의 **grew out of an Internet business**

179 사실 관계 확인

번역 구입한 물품들에 대해 명시된 것은?
(A) 스태퍼드 씨가 선물 포장을 했다.
(B) 폭이 매우 좁다.
(C) 똑같은 재료로 만들어진다.
(D) 휴덕 씨가 2월 3일에 수령하지 않았다.

해설 영수증의 날짜: 2월 3일(Date: February 3)과 주문한 물품은 2월 12일 화요일이나 그 후에 찾으러 오면 된다(You may pick up your order on or after Tuesday, February 12)를 통해 2월 3일에 주문한 물건을 수령하지 않았다는 것을 알 수 있으므로, 정답은 (D)이다.

180 연계

번역 휴덕 씨에 관해 암시된 것은?
(A) 판촉 기간에 쇼핑했다.
(B) 지역 상공 카드를 소지하고 다닌다.
(C) 한때 타피 스트리트에 거주했다.
(D) 구매 대금을 현찰로 지불했다.

해설 영수증의 신발 세정제 세트(Shoe Cleaner Set)의 단가(Price unit: 0.00)를 통해 휴덕 씨가 신발 세정제 세트를 무료로 받았음을 알 수 있다. 신발 세정제 세트에 대한 정보는 이메일을 통해 확인할 수 있다. 이메일의 첫 번째 단락에서 개점하는 주말에 들러 모든 구매 고객에게 드리는 무료 신발 세정제 세트를 받으세요(Come by on opening weekend to collect a free Shoe Cleaner Set with any purchase)를 통해 휴덕 씨가 개점하는 주말에 신발을 구매했음을 유추할 수 있으므로, 정답은 (A)이다.

▶▶ Paraphrasing   지문의 **to collect a free Shoe Cleaner Set with any purchase**
                     → 정답의 **a sales promotion**

181-185 웹페이지 + 이메일

http://www.pursifull.com/businesses

홈	기업체용	구직자용	연락

퍼시풀
인력이 필요할 때

퍼시풀은 긍지를 가지고 캐나다 남동부 전역의 창고와 공장에 인력 알선 서비스를 제공합니다. 이런 체계 아래서 저희 직원들("내부 조달 직원들"로 호칭)이 귀사의 업장에서 귀사의 [182]감독 아래 필요한 기간만큼 근무합니다. [181B, C]이들 중 다수가 여러 해 동안 저희를 위해 일해 왔으며, 새로운 내부 조달 직원들도 반드시 귀사가 속한 업계에서 이미 경력을 갖추고 있는 사람들이라는 것을 저희의 철저한 평판 조회 시스템이 보장합니다. [181A]모든 직원이 산업 안전과 보건 법규에 관해 최신 정보를 받고 있습니다.

[184]귀사가 저희 서비스를 이용하고자 결정하신다면 컨설턴트가 귀사의 업장에 가서 내부 조달 직원들이 수행해야 하는 업무에 관해 상의할 것입니다. [183]이미 저희에게 고용된 직원들 가운데 적합한 인원을 선발하신 후에 남은 빈 자리가 있으면 저희가 "구직자용" 페이지에 구인 게시물을 올려 추가 인력을 모집하게 됩

니다. 그런 다음 자격을 갖춘 후보들이 저희의 효율적인 채용 및 교육 절차를 거칩니다. 필요한 근로자의 수에 따라 다르지만 전 과정이 일주일밖에 걸리지 않습니다.

퍼시풀에 만족하시는 많은 고객들 중 한 분이 되시겠습니까? 상단의 "연락"을 클릭하세요.

어휘 jobseeker 구직자 be proud to+동사원형 ~해서 자랑스럽다, 긍지를 느끼다 provide 공급하다, 제공하다 labour hire service 인력 알선 서비스 warehouse 창고, 창고형 매장, 도매점 throughout ~ 전역에 employee 직원, 사원 insourced 내부에서 조달한 as long as necessary 필요한 기간만큼 thorough 철저한 reference-checking system 평판 조회 시스템 have experience in ~에 경력[경험]이 있다 as well 또한 keep A up-to-date on B A를 B에 관해 최신 상태로 유지하다 occupational safety 산업 안전 health regulations 보건 법규 Should+주어+동사원형 혹시라도 ~한다면(= If+주어+should+동사원형) engage 고용하다 work site 업장 duty 업무, 임무 perform 수행하다 suitable 적합한 on one's payroll ~에게 고용된 recruit 모집하다 additional 추가적인 fill a gap 공백[빈 자리]을 메우다 via ~을 통해 job posting 구인 게시물 qualified 자격을 갖춘 candidate 후보 undergo 거치다, 겪다 efficient 효율적인 hiring 채용 procedure 절차 process 과정, 공정 as little as 겨우, 단지(= only, just) depending on ~에 따라 satisfied 만족한 client 고객

발신: 토냐 로스먼
수신: 키요시 블레인
날짜: 10월 25일
제목: 요청

키요시 귀하,

로나 웨어하우징에서 다시 인사드립니다! 약정한 대로 저희는 퍼시풀의 내부 조달 인력을 더 요청하려고 합니다. 회사 웹사이트를 거치지 않고 이렇게 귀하에게 연락해도 괜찮으면 좋겠습니다. ¹⁸⁴저는 저희와의 계약을 처음에 처리한 컨설턴트에게 직접 연락하는 게 더 빠를지도 모르겠다고 생각했거든요.

¹⁸⁵이번에 명절 쇼핑 기간에 오가게 될 많은 물량을 처리할 창고 직원들이 필요합니다. 11월 중순부터 12월 말까지 저희의 토론토 창고에서 근무할 수 있는 재고 관리 직원 다섯 명을 구해 주시기 바랍니다. 이 자리의 명세 사항은 전과 동일합니다. 추가로 필요한 세부 사항이나 조치가 있으면 알려 주시기 바랍니다.

감사합니다.

토냐 로스먼
로나 웨어하우징 인사부

어휘 warehousing 창고업 as promised 약속[약정]한 대로 contact 연락[접촉]하다 instead of ~ 대신에 go through ~을 거치다, 통하다 volume 양 stock 재고(품) holiday shopping season 휴일[명절] 쇼핑 기간 stock associate 재고 관리 직원 further 추가적인 details 세부 사항 action 조치, 행동

181 사실 관계 확인

번역 내부 조달 직원에 관해 명시되지 않은 것은?
(A) 안전 교육을 받는다.
(B) 관련 업무 경력이 있다.
(C) 취업 추천서를 제공했다.
(D) 전국 도처에 파견된다.

해설 웹페이지의 첫 번째 단락에서 모든 직원이 산업 안전과 보건 법규에 관해 최신 정보를 받는다(All are kept up-to-date on occupational safety and health regulations)를 통해 (A)를, 이들 중 다수가 여러 해 동안 저희를 위해 일해 왔으며, 새로운 내부 조달 직원들도 반드시 귀사가 속한 업계에서 이미 경력을 갖추고 있는 사람들이라는 것을 저희의 철저한 평판 조회 시스템이 보장한다(Many of them have worked for us for years, and our thorough reference-checking system ensures that new insourced employees already have experience in your industry as well)를 통해 (B)와 (C)를 확인할 수 있으므로, 정답은 언급되지 않은 (D)이다.

▶▶ Paraphrasing 지문의 kept up-to-date on occupational safety and health regulations
→ 보기의 given safety education
지문의 have experience in your industry
→ 보기의 have relevant work experience
지문의 our thorough reference-checking system ensures
→ 보기의 provided job references

182 동의어 찾기

번역 웹페이지에서 첫 번째 단락 3행의 "direction"과 의미가 가장 가까운 단어는?
(A) 경로
(B) 증거
(C) 감독
(D) 회복

해설 해당 문장은 '이런 체계 아래서 저희 직원들("내부 조달 직원들"로 호칭)이 귀사의 업장에서 귀사의 감독 아래 필요한 기간만큼 근무합니다(Under this system, our employees (called "insourced employees") work on your site and under your direction for as long as necessary)'라는 의미로 해석되는데, 여기서 direction은 '감독'이라는 의미가 자연스러우므로, 정답은 (C) oversight(감독, 관리)이다.

183 세부 사항

번역 웹페이지에 따르면, 퍼시풀 웹사이트에서 찾을 수 있는 것은?
(A) 구인 광고
(B) 학습 자료
(C) 구직자들이 올린 이력서
(D) 현재 고객 명단

해설 웹페이지의 두 번째 단락, 이미 저희에게 고용된 직원들 가운데 적합한 인원을 선발하신 후에 남은 빈 자리가 있으면 저희가 "구직자용" 페이지에 구인 게시물을 올려 추가 인력을 모집하게 됩니다(After selecting suitable employees who are already on our payroll, we will recruit additional workers to fill any remaining gaps via job postings on our "For jobseekers" page)에서 구직자를 위한 구인 게시물을 언급하고 있으므로, 정답은 (A)이다.

184 연계

번역 블레인 씨에 관해 암시된 것은?
(A) 재고 관리 직원 몇 명을 교육할 것이다.
(B) 퍼시풀의 토론토 지사로 전보되었다.
(C) 요청을 이행하려면 일주일 이상 필요할 것이다.
(D) 로나 웨어하우징 시설에 들어가 본 적이 있다.

해설 이메일의 첫 번째 단락, 저희와의 계약을 처음에 처리한 컨설턴트에게 직접 연락하는 게 더 빠를지도 모르겠다고 생각했다(I thought it might be quicker to go directly to the consultant who managed our first agreement)를 통해 수신인인 블레인 씨가 로나 웨어하우징과의 계약을 처리한 퍼시풀의 컨설턴트임을 알 수 있다. 컨설턴트에 대한 정보는 웹페이지를 통해 확인할 수 있다. 웹페이지의 두 번째 단락에서 귀사가 저희 서비스를 이용하고자 결정하신다면 컨설턴트가 귀사의 업장에 가서 내부 조달 직원들이 수행해야 하는 업무에 관해 귀사와 상의할 것이다(Should you decide to engage our services, a consultant will come to your work site and discuss with you the duties that insourced employees must perform)를 통해 컨설턴트인 블레인 씨가 로나 웨어하우징을 방문했음을 유추할 수 있으므로, 정답은 (D)이다.

185 세부 사항

번역 로스먼 씨의 요청 사유는 무엇인가?
(A) 연례 성수기에 대한 기대
(B) 신규 창고 직원 채용의 어려움
(C) 몇몇 기계의 오작동
(D) 일부 직원들의 이탈

해설 이메일의 두 번째 단락에서 이번에 저희는 명절 쇼핑 기간에 오가게 될 많은 물량을 처리할 창고 직원들이 필요하다(This time, we need extra warehouse staff to handle the large volume of stock that will be coming and going during the holiday shopping season)를 통해 발신인인 로스먼 씨가 명절 특수를 기대하고 있음을 알 수 있으므로, 정답은 (A)이다.

▶▶ Paraphrasing 지문의 **during the holiday shopping season** → 정답의 **an annual busy period**

186-190 웹페이지 + 이메일 + 기사

http://www.auengineeringconference.co.au/seminars/2204

오스트레일리아 토목공학 학술대회
6월 19일 금요일 세미나 일정표

더 자세한 정보를 원하시면 밑줄 그은 제목을 클릭하세요.

오전 9:00 – 오전 10:20　　**186"에너지 효율적인 철도"**
　　　　　　　　　　　　　정상우, 대한민국
　　　　　　　　　　　　　C동 102호

오전 10:40 – 오후 12　　**187"재료와 내구성"**
　　　　　　　　　　　　엘자 쾨니히, 독일
　　　　　　　　　　　　C동 105호

오후 1:30 – 오후 2:50　　**"토목공학의 윤리"** (추가 요금: 30호주달러)
　　　　　　　　　　　　지루 실즈, 오스트레일리아
　　　　　　　　　　　　C동 103호

오후 3:10 – 오후 4:30　　**186"물 공급 체계 개선하기"**
　　　　　　　　　　　　실비아 왓슨, 캐나다
　　　　　　　　　　　　C동 102호

어휘 civil engineering 토목공학 conference 학술대회, 학회 underlined 밑줄 그은 further 추가의 energy-efficient 에너지 효율적인 railway 철도 wing (건물의) 동 durability 내구성 ethics 윤리 improve 개선하다, 향상시키다 supply 공급

발신: 나이절 롤린스
수신: 웬디 빈센트
날짜: 6월 19일
제목: 질문

안녕하세요, 웬디

아시다시피 제가 오스트레일리아 토목공학 학술대회에 와 있는데, 한 가지 제안에 관해 당신의 의견을 구하려고 메일을 씁니다. **187**지금 제가 고성능 콘크리트와 여타 새로운 건설 자재에 관한 세미나 자리에 앉아 있어요. **189**우리가 그중 몇 가지를 스토빅 브리지 건설 사업에 포함시킬 수도 있겠다는 생각이 듭니다. 그 자재들이면 우리가 구들리 쪽 강변의 토지에서 겪고 있는 문제를 해결할 수도 있을 거예요. 세미나가 끝나면 발표자에게 교량 건설 위원회의 고문이 되어 달라고 요청하고 싶습니다. 어떻게 생각하세요?

조속히 답장해 주세요. 그런 인맥을 쌓기에는 남은 시간이 많지 않거든요. **188**제가 타는 열차가 오늘 저녁 일찍 출발합니다.

고마워요.

나이절

어휘 as you know 알다시피 get one's opinion ~의 의견을 구하다 proposal 제안(서) high-performance 고성능 construction material 건설[건축] 자재 incorporate A into B A를 B에 포함시키다[통합하다] solve (문제를) 해결하다, 풀다 act as ~로서 역할을 하다 consultant 컨설턴트, 상담역, 고문 committee 위원회 get back to ~에게 다시 연락하다, 회신하다 networking 인맥 쌓기, 네트워킹 depart 출발하다

스토빅 브리지, 일반에 공개되다

시드니 (4월 22일)—크리켓 애호가들이 다음 달에 열릴 웬델 컵 결승전에 가는 길이 이제 더 많아졌다. **189**어제 조촐한 기념식을 곁들여 보행자와 자전거들에 개방된 스토빅 브리지가 웨스트 크리켓 그라운드와 길모어 강 건너편에 있는 크레슬 인근 지역을 연결한다.

190 아름다운 무늬를 연출하는 다리 난간 덕에 방문객들이 바라보는 강의 경치가 돋보이는 한편, 중간 지점에 있는 25미터 구간이 90도로 회전할 수 있어서 대형 범선들이 지나갈 수 있도록 길을 낸다. 현지 주민과 기업들도 다리가 주요 자전거 길 두 개를 연결하는 점을 높이 평가한다.

스토빅 브리지는 해당 지역의 기반 시설을 크게 향상시키고, 웬델컵이 끝난 후에도 오랫동안 지역 경제에 도움이 될 것이다.

어휘 take place 발생하다, 일어나다　pedestrian 보행자　ceremony 기념식, 격식　connect A with B A를 B와 연결하다, 잇다　neighborhood 동네, 인근　railings 난간　enhance 향상시키다, 개선하다　segment 구간, 부분　midpoint 중간 지점　rotate 회전하다　pass through 통과하다, 지나가다　local resident 현지 주민, 지역 주민　enterprise 기업　appreciate 높이 평가하다, 진가를 인정하다　major 주요한　represent 나타내다, 상징하다　improvement 향상, 개선　infrastructure 기반 시설　benefit 유익[유용]하다　economy 경제, 경기　be over 끝나다

186　추론 / 암시

번역 웹페이지에서, "물 공급 체계 개선하기"에 관해 암시된 것은?
(A) 다른 세미나와 같은 방에서 열린다.
(B) 등록하려면 추가 요금을 내야 한다.
(C) 발표자가 오스트레일리아 출신이다.
(D) 원래 다른 날로 일정이 잡혀 있었다.

해설 웹페이지의 마지막 항목, 물 공급 체계 개선하기(Improving Water Supply Systems)의 세부 사항을 통해 첫 번째 세미나인 에너지 효율적인 철도(Energy-Efficient Railways)와 같은 장소인 C동 102호(Wing C, Room 102)에서 진행됨을 알 수 있으므로, 정답은 (A)이다.

187　연계

번역 롤린스 씨는 이메일을 작성할 때 누구의 세미나에 참석 중이었나?
(A) 정 씨의 세미나
(B) 쾨니히 씨의 세미나
(C) 실즈 씨의 세미나
(D) 왓슨 씨의 세미나

해설 이메일의 첫 번째 단락에서 지금 제가 고성능 콘크리트와 여타 새로운 건설 자재에 관한 세미나 자리에 앉아 있다(Right now, I'm sitting in a seminar about high-performance concrete and other new construction materials)를 통해 발신인(I)인 롤린스 씨는 건설 자재 관련 세미나에 참석 중이었음을 알 수 있다. 웹페이지를 통해 롤린스 씨는 엘자 쾨니히 씨가 진행하는 두 번째 세미나인 재료와 내구성(Materials and Durability)에 참석했음을 확인할 수 있으므로, 정답은 (B)이다.

▶▶ **Paraphrasing**　지문의 **sitting in** → 질문의 **attending**

188　세부 사항

번역 롤린스 씨가 저녁에 하겠다고 언급한 일은?
(A) 세미나를 진행한다.
(B) 학술대회장을 떠난다.
(C) 행사 진행 책임자와 이야기한다.
(D) 만찬에 가서 인맥을 쌓는다.

해설 이메일의 두 번째 단락에서 내가 타는 열차가 오늘 저녁 일찍 출발한다(My train departs early this evening)를 통해 발신인(My)인 롤린스 씨는 저녁에 학술대회장을 떠난다는 것을 알 수 있으므로, 정답은 (B)이다.

▶▶ **Paraphrasing**　지문의 **My train departs**
→ 정답의 **Leave a conference**

189　연계

번역 웨스트 크리켓 그라운드에 관해 무엇이 사실이겠는가?
(A) 구들리에 있다.
(B) 최근에 건설되었다.
(C) 항상 웬델컵을 주최한다.
(D) 회의장 복합 단지 근처에 있다.

해설 기사의 첫 번째 단락, 어제 조촐한 기념식을 곁들여 보행자와 자전거들에 개방된 스토빅 브리지가 웨스트 크리켓 그라운드와 길모어 강 건너편에 있는 크레슬 인근 지역을 연결한다(Storvick Bridge, which opened to pedestrian and bicycle traffic with a small ceremony yesterday, connects West Cricket Ground with the Cressell neighborhood across the Gilmour River)에서 스토빅 브리지의 웨스트 크리켓 그라운드와 크레슬 인근 지역의 연결을 언급하고 있다. 이메일의 첫 번째 단락에서 우리가 그중 몇 가지를 스토빅 브리지 건설 사업에 포함시킬 수도 있겠다는 생각이 든다. 그 자재들이면 우리가 구들리 쪽 강변의 토지에서 겪고 있는 문제를 해결할 수도 있을 것이다(I think we might want to incorporate some of them into the Storvick Bridge project. They could solve the problem we're having with the land on the Gouldley side of the river)를 통해 웨스트 크리켓 그라운드가 구들리 지역에 있음을 유추할 수 있으므로, 정답은 (A)이다.

190　사실 관계 확인

번역 스토빅 브리지에 관해 명시된 것은?
(A) 자동차 2차선 도로가 있다.
(B) 난간에 모형 배들이 장식되어 있다.
(C) 인기 있는 크리켓 선수의 이름을 따서 명명되었다.
(D) 중앙부를 움직일 수 있다.

해설 기사의 두 번째 단락, 아름다운 무늬를 연출하는 다리 난간 덕에 방문객들이 바라보는 강의 경치가 돋보이는 한편, 중간 지점에 있는 25미터 구간이 90도로 회전할 수 있어서 대형 범선들이 지나갈 수 있도록 길을 낸다(The bridge's beautifully-patterned railings enhance visitors' views of the river, while a 25-metre segment at its midpoint can rotate 90 degrees to give a clear way for tall ships to pass through)에서 스토빅 브리지의 중간 지점이 회전할 수 있음을 언급하고 있으므로, 정답은 (D)이다.

▶▶ **Paraphrasing**　지문의 **a 25-metre segment at its midpoint can rotate**
→ 정답의 **Its center section is movable.**

Test 8

수신: 린다 후퍼 〈lhooper@kelevac.com〉
발신: 아이번 멧캐프 〈imetcalf@kelevac-hr.com〉
날짜: 8월 23일
제목: Re: 인센티브 제도

후퍼 씨께,

귀하께서 자원봉사 프로젝트에 참여하는 직원들에게 유급 휴가를 주는 켈러백의 새로운 인센티브 제도에 관해 문의하신 내용을 접수했습니다. **191, 195**요청하신 정보는 옴스필드 지사에서 9월 3일에 열리는 전 직원 대상 설명회에서 얻으실 수 있을 것입니다. **195**행사 진행자인 에즈라 개프니가 그날 설명회를 인도하고 이후 귀하의 질문들을 다룰 예정입니다.

이 계획에 관심을 가져 주셔서 감사합니다.

아이번 멧캐프
인사 조정관

어휘 inquiry 문의 concerning ~에 관해 incentive program 인센티브 제도, 장려(금) 제도 paid time off 유급 휴가 participate in ~에 참가[참여]하다 volunteer project 자원봉사 프로젝트 request 요청하다 available 입수할 수 있는, 이용할 수 있는 information session 설명회 coordinator 행사 진행자 address 다루다 afterward 그 후에 initiative 실행 계획 human resources 인적 자원 coordinator 조정관

귀하의 휴가 요청이 승인되었습니다

이름: 린다 후퍼   부서: 경리부

시작일: 10월 13일   시간: 오후 1시
종료일: 10월 13일   시간: 오후 5시
전체 시간: 4
휴가 종류: 자원봉사 휴가

의견: **193**저는 그날 유나이티드 옴스필드가 **192**개최하는 행사를 돕는 데 시간을 쓸 예정입니다. 예전에는 자원봉사 휴가를 사용한 적이 없습니다.

심사: 올리비아 클라크
날짜: 10월 11일
승인 여부: 예 ☑   아니요 ☐
의견: 다음부터는 적어도 5일 전에는 통지해 주십시오. 또한 "자원봉사 확인서"를 출력해서, 귀하가 돕는 단체의 구성원에게 서명을 받고, 제게 제출해야 한다는 것을 기억하시기 바랍니다. 올해 남은 자원봉사 휴가: 36시간.

어휘 time-off request 휴가 요청 approve 승인하다 previously 전에 review 심사하다 give notice 통지하다, 알리다 at least 적어도 in advance 미리, 사전에 print out 출력하다 confirmation 확인 organization 단체 assist 돕다, 보조하다 submit 제출하다 remaining 남은

켈러백, 지역사회에 환원하다

옴스필드 (10월 30일)—**194**옴스필드가 이제 켈러백 사가 최근 채택한 신규 정책의 혜택을 받고 있다. 티엘버그에 본사를 두고 있는 이 대형 제약회사는 직원들이 자원봉사에 참여하도록 일주일간의 유급 휴가를 주기로 8월에 결정했다. 옴스필드 지사에서 근무하는 200명의 직원 중 다수가 이 기회를 활용하고 있다.

193지사 임원인 크리스 히메네스에 따르면, 켈러백 직원들은 옴스필드 해변 청소 작업에 자원봉사자로 참여해 왔으며, 유나이티드 옴스필드는 이달 초 경매를 열어 지역사회 푸드뱅크 모금 활동을 도왔다.

195품질 보증 보조원인 트리스탄 류는 옴스필드 지역 학교들에서 학업을 힘들어하는 학생들을 개인 지도하는 프로그램에 지원했다. "저는 막 오리엔테이션 과정을 마쳤는데, 어서 시작했으면 좋겠습니다." 그는 말했다.

히메네스 씨는 직원들이 동료들의 보람 있는 경험을 전해 들으면서 자원봉사자 수가 계속 증가할 것이라고 내다봤다.

어휘 reap 수확하다, 거둬들이다 benefit 혜택, 유익 policy 정책 adopt 채택하다 pharmaceuticals giant 대형 제약회사 be based in ~에 본사[근거지]를 두다 paid leave 유급 휴가 (= paid time off) engage in ~에 종사하다 take advantage of ~을 이용하다 opportunity 기회 volunteer 자원봉사하다; 자원봉사자 clean-up effort 청소 활동[작업] put on an auction 경매를 열다 raise money 모금하다 community 지역사회 food bank 푸드뱅크, 무료 급식소 quality assurance 품질 보증 tutoring 개인 지도 struggling student 학업을 힘들어 하는 학생 can't wait to + 동사원형 어서 ~하고 싶다 predict 내다보다, 예견하다 coworker 동료 직원 rewarding 보람 있는, 유익한

---

191 주제 / 목적

번역 이메일의 목적은 무엇인가?
(A) 어떤 계획의 성공을 보고하려고
(B) 프로그램에 등록한 데 대해 후퍼 씨에게 감사하려고
(C) 후퍼 씨에게 정보를 기다리도록 촉구하려고
(D) 자원해서 설명회를 하도록 제안하려고

해설 이메일의 첫 번째 단락, 요청한 정보는 옴스필드 지사에서 9월 3일에 열리는 전 직원 대상 설명회에서 얻을 수 있을 것이다(The information you requested will be made available to the Ormesfield branch at an all-staff information session on September 3)를 통해 수신인(your)인 후퍼 씨에게 추후 열릴 예정인 설명회에서 정보를 얻을 수 있음을 알리기 위한 이메일임을 알 수 있으므로, 정답은 (C)이다.

---

192 동의어 찾기

번역 통지문에서 첫 번째 단락 2행의 "holding"과 의미가 가장 가까운 단어는?
(A) 주관하는
(B) 진실로 남아 있는
(C) 파악하는
(D) 견디는

해설 해당 문장은 '저는 그날 유나이티드 옴스필드가 개최하는 행사를 돕는 데 시간을 쓸 예정입니다(I will use the time to help with an event that United Ormesfield is holding on that day)'라는 의미로 해석 되는데, 여기서 holding은 '개최하는, 주관하는'이라는 의미가 자연스럽 다. 따라서 정답은 (A) presiding over(주관하는, 주재하는, 사회를 보는) 이다.

193 연계

번역 후퍼 씨는 휴가 동안 무슨 일을 했겠는가?
(A) 지역 해변 청소
(B) 푸드뱅크 선반 정리
(C) 오리엔테이션 과정 참여
(D) 모금 행사 보조

해설 통지문의 그날 유나이티드 옴스필드가 개최하는 행사를 돕는 데 시간을 쓸 예정이다(I will use the time to help with an event that United Ormesfield is holding on that day)를 통해 후퍼 씨가 유나이티드 옴스필드가 개최하는 행사에서 자원봉사할 예정임을 알 수 있다. 유나이 티드 옴스필드가 개최할 행사에 대한 정보는 기사를 통해 확인할 수 있 다. 기사의 두 번째 단락 지사 임원인 크리스 히메네스에 따르면, 켈러백 직원들은 옴스필드 해변 청소 작업에 자원봉사자로 참여해 왔으며, 유나 이티드 옴스필드는 이달 초 경매를 열어 지역사회 푸드뱅크 모금 활동을 도왔다(According to Chris Jimenez, an official at the branch, Kelevac employees have volunteered for Ormesfield Beach clean-up efforts and helped United Ormesfield put on an auction earlier this month to raise money for its community food bank)를 통해 후퍼 씨는 유나이티드 옴스필드가 개최한 경매를 통 한 모금행사에서 자원봉사했음을 유추할 수 있으므로, 정답은 (D)이다.

▶▶ **Paraphrasing** 지문의 helped → 정답의 Assisted
지문의 to raise money → 정답의 a fundraiser

194 사실 관계 확인

번역 기사가 켈러백에 관해 명시한 것은?
(A) 본사가 옴스필드에 있다.
(B) 직원들이 일주일간 휴가를 갈 수 있다.
(C) 8월에 다른 회사를 인수했다.
(D) 의료 관련업계에 있다.

해설 기사의 첫 번째 단락 옴스필드가 이제 켈러백 사가 최근 채택한 신규 정책 의 혜택을 받고 있다. 티엘버그에 본사를 두고 있는 이 대형 제약회사는 직 원들이 자원봉사에 참여하도록 일주일간의 유급 휴가를 주기로 8월에 결 정했다(Ormesfield is now reaping the benefits of a new policy recently adopted by Kelevac. The pharmaceuticals giant, which is based in Thielberg, decided in August to allow its staff one week of paid leave to engage in volunteer work)를 통 해 켈러백이 제약회사임을 확인할 수 있으므로, 정답은 (D)이다.

▶▶ **Paraphrasing** 지문의 **The pharmaceuticals giant**
→ 정답의 **a healthcare-related industry**

195 연계

번역 류 씨에 관해 무엇이 사실이겠는가?
(A) 멧카프 씨의 이메일에 답장했다.
(B) 개프니 씨가 이끄는 회의에 참석했다.
(C) 히메네스 씨 담당 부서의 일원이다.
(D) 옴스필드에서 고등학교를 마쳤다.

해설 기사의 세 번째 단락, 품질 보증 보조원인 트리스탄 류는 옴스필드 지 역 학교들에서 학업을 힘들어하는 학생들을 개인 지도하는 프로그램 에 지원했다. "저는 막 오리엔테이션 과정을 마쳤는데, 어서 시작했으 면 좋겠습니다." 그는 말했다(Tristan Liu, a quality assurance assistant, has signed up for a program providing tutoring for struggling students at Ormesfield schools. "I just completed the orientation process, and I can't wait to get started," he said)에서 류 씨는 오리엔테이션 참석을 언급하고 있다. 오리엔테이션 에 대한 정보는 이메일을 통해 확인할 수 있다. 이메일의 첫 번째 단락, 요 청하신 정보는 옴스필드 지사에서 9월 3일에 열리는 전 직원 대상 설명 회에서 얻을 수 있다. 행사 진행자인 에즈라 개프니가 그날 설명회를 인 도하고 이후 귀하의 질문들을 다룰 예정이다(The information you requested will be made available to the Ormesfield branch at an all-staff information session on September 3. Coordinator Ezra Gaffney will lead the presentation and address your questions afterward on that day)를 통해 류 씨가 개프니 씨가 진행 한 설명회에 참석했음을 유추할 수 있으므로, 정답은 (B)이다.

▶▶ **Paraphrasing** 지문의 **Coordinator Ezra Gaffney will lead the presentation**
→ 정답의 **a meeting led by Mr. Gaffney**

196-200 웹페이지 + 양식 + 이메일

http://www.underbrinktours.com/tours-by-theme/city-tour-b

| 홈 | 명소 개관 | **주제별 관광** | 기간별 관광 | 자주 하는 질문 |

시티 투어 B

이틀짜리 일반 도시 관광 중 하나인 시티 투어 B는 비교적 짧은 시간에 종합적 으로 언더브링크를 경험하게 해줍니다. **196**이것은 시티 투어 A와 전부 동일한 활동을 제공하지만, 참가자들이 반드시 자신의 숙소를 마련해야 합니다. 참가자 들은 근처에 큰 호텔이 많은 로위스 역에서 차에 타고 내립니다.

시티 투어 B는 언더브링크의 역사적 명소인 브리스토 인근 지역을 걸어서 통 과하는 것으로 시작합니다. **197**오후에는 베스 이스텝의 고향인 시밍 힐을 방문 해 그녀의 소설을 좋아하는 팬들에게 즐거움을 선사하는 한편, 팬이 아닌 분들께 도 풍부한 볼거리를 제공합니다. 저녁에는 참가자들이 스테일린 강에서 유람선 을 타게 됩니다. 둘째 날에는 디네이토 미술관을 견학한 후 버스를 타고 인근에 있는 스테일린 계곡을 통과할 것입니다. 이 활동들은 각기 다른 전문 안내인이 인도하며 관광 인솔자는 필요에 따라 자유롭게 관광 참가자들을 돕습니다. 관광 기간 내내 다양한 점심식사와 저녁식사가 제공됩니다.

이 관광 여행의 가격은 계절에 따라 다릅니다. 가격 책정과 이용 가능 여부에 관 한 정보를 보시려면 여기를 클릭하십시오.

Test 8

attraction 명물, 명소 by theme 주제[테마]별 by length 길이[기간]별 FAQ 자주 묻는 질문(= frequently asked questions) relatively 비교적, 상대적으로 participant 참가자, 참여자 arrange 마련하다 accommodation 숙소 drop off 내려주다 delight 즐겁게 하다, 기쁨을 주다 novel 소설 plenty 풍부한 양, 풍성함 as well 또한 cruise 유람선을 타다 boast 내세우다, 뽐내다, 자랑하다 valley 계곡 tour director 관광 인솔자 as necessary 필요에 따라, 필요한 대로 throughout ~ 전반에 걸쳐 various 다양한 vary depending on ~에 따라 다르다 pricing 가격 책정 availability 이용 가능성

언더브링크 투어스 고객 만족도 조사

관광: 시티 투어 A   이름: 에이저 슬로먼

	나쁨	보통	좋음	매우 좋음
숙박 시설			X	
활동				X
안내인				X
식사		X		
교통			X	

의견:

음식이 소화가 잘 안 돼서 약간 곤란했다. **197**특히, 우리가 브리스토에서 먹은 점심 때문에 너무 불편해 시밍 힐에 가는 대신 호텔에서 쉬어야 했다. 그러나 내가 참여한 활동은 모두 매우 즐거웠다. 귀사에는 전문 안내인이 있어서 매우 좋다는 생각이 든다. **198**안내인 각자가 자신이 다루는 주제에 관해 아주 많은 것을 알고 있었다. 언더브링크 투어스를 친구들에게 꼭 추천할 계획이다.

customer satisfaction survey 고객 만족도 조사 meal 식사, 끼니 transportation 교통 have trouble with ~ 때문에 곤란을 겪다 heaviness 소화가 잘 안 됨 unwell 몸이 좋지 않은, 기분이 나쁜 rest 쉬다 instead of ~ 대신 participate in ~에 참여[참가]하다 enjoyable 즐거운 subject 주제 recommend 추천하다, 권하다

발신: 랜스 은초보 〈l.ntchobo@underbrinktours.com〉

수신: 모든 관광 안내인

날짜: 4월 27일

제목: 설문조사 결과

여러분 안녕하세요.

우리가 취합한 고객 설문지 덕분에 이제 우리가 제공하는 상품에 대한 고객들의 의견을 잘 **199**알게 됐습니다. **198**우선, 저는 여러분이 우리 관광 명소들에 대한 이해가 깊다는 칭찬을 꾸준히 받는다는 말을 전하게 되어 기쁩니다. 수고하셨습니다!

200그렇지만 여러분의 설명에 흥미와 유머가 부족하다는 의견도 일부 있었습니다. 저는 우리가 5월 9일 월요일 오후 4시에 사무실에서 모두 만나 이 문제를 해결할 방안을 논의했으면 합니다. 이 이메일에 회신하여 여러분의 출석을 확정해 주시기 바랍니다.

랜스 은초보

언더브링크 투어스 전무이사

---

survey form 설문지, 설문 양식 collect 취합하다, 모으다 give a good sense of ~을 잘 알게 해 주다 offering 제공하는 것 consistently 꾸준히, 일관되게 praise 칭찬하다 Well done! 잘했습니다!, 수고했습니다! That said 그렇지만, 그건 그렇다 치고 explanation 설명 lack 부족하다 resolve 해결하다 issue 문제 respond to ~에 답장하다, 회신하다 confirm 확인[확증]하다 attendance 참석, 출석 executive director 전무 이사

---

196 사실 관계 확인

번역 시티 투어 B에 관해 명시된 것은?
(A) 로위스 역 관광으로 시작된다.
(B) 숙박을 포함하지 않는다.
(C) 시티 투어 A보다 기간이 길다.
(D) 모든 계절에 운영되는 것은 아니다.

해설 웹페이지의 첫 번째 단락, 이것은 시티 투어 A와 전부 동일한 활동을 제공하지만, 참가자들이 반드시 자신의 숙소를 마련해야 한다(It offers all the same activities as City Tour A, but requires participants to arrange their own accommodations)를 통해 시티 투어 B는 숙소 미포함임을 알 수 있으므로, 정답은 (B)이다.

▶▶ **Paraphrasing** 지문의 **accommodations** → 정답의 **lodging**

---

197 연계

번역 슬로먼 씨가 참여할 수 없었던 활동은?
(A) 야외 도보 관광
(B) 저녁 강 유람선 여행
(C) 유명한 집 방문
(D) 미술관 견학

해설 양식의 의견(Comments) 중 브리스토에서 먹은 점심 때문에 너무 불편해 시밍 힐에 가는 대신 호텔에서 쉬어야 했다(the lunch we had in Bristaw made me feel so unwell that I had to rest in the hotel instead of going to Schimming Hill)에서 슬로먼 씨는 시밍 힐에 갈 수 없었음을 언급하고 있다. 일정에 대한 정보는 웹페이지를 통해 확인할 수 있다. 웹페이지의 두 번째 단락, 오후에는 베스 이스텝의 고향인 시밍 힐을 방문해 그녀의 소설을 좋아하는 팬들에게 즐거움을 선사하는 한편, 팬이 아닌 분들께도 풍부한 볼거리를 제공한다(An afternoon visit to Schimming Hill, the home of Beth Estepp, will delight fans of her novels, while giving plenty to see to non-fans as well)를 통해 슬로먼 씨는 시밍 힐에 있는 소설가의 집을 방문할 수 없었음을 알 수 있으므로, 정답은 (C)이다.

▶▶ **Paraphrasing** 지문의 **instead of going to**
→ 질문의 **unable to participate in**
지문의 **An afternoon visit to Schimming Hill, the home of Beth Estepp**
→ 정답의 **A visit to a famous house**

198 연계

번역 슬로먼 씨에 관해 암시된 것은?

(A) 언더브링크에서 친구를 만날 계획을 세웠다.
(B) **안내인에 대한 그의 의견을 다른 사람들도 대체로 공감한다.**
(C) 그의 설문지는 4월 26일에 제출되었다.
(D) 관광을 하는 동안 특별식을 선택했다.

해설 양식의 의견(Comments) 중 안내인 각자가 자신이 다루는 주제에 관해 아주 많은 것을 알고 있었다(Each one really knew a lot about their subject)에서 슬로먼 씨는 안내인들의 지식을 칭찬하고 있다. 안내인에 대한 의견은 은초보 씨가 안내인 전체에게 쓴 이메일을 통해 더 확인할 수 있다. 이메일의 첫 번째 단락, 여러분이 우리 관광 명소들에 대한 이해가 깊다는 칭찬을 꾸준히 받는다는 말을 전하게 되어 기쁘다(I'm happy to tell you all that you're consistently praised for your deep understanding of the attractions on our tours)를 통해 다른 관광객들도 슬로먼 씨의 의견에 공감한다는 것을 유추할 수 있으므로, 정답은 (B)이다.

199 동의어 찾기

번역 이메일에서 첫 번째 단락 1행의 "sense"와 의미가 가장 가까운 단어는?

(A) 능력
(B) 논리
(C) 의심
(D) **생각**

해설 해당 문장은 '우리가 취합한 고객 설문지 덕분에 이제 우리가 제공하는 상품에 대한 고객들의 의견을 잘 알게 됐다(The customer survey forms we've been collecting have now given us a good sense of customers' opinions about our offerings)'라는 의미로 해석되는데, 여기서 sense는 '의향, 생각'이라는 의미가 자연스러우므로, 정답은 (D) idea(생각, 견해, 발상)이다.

200 세부 사항

번역 은초보 씨가 회의에서 논의하고 싶어 하는 것은?

(A) **관광을 더 재미있게 하는 방법**
(B) 새로운 명소를 안내할 사람
(C) 여행 일정표 순서 변경 여부
(D) 고객 수 감소 이유

해설 이메일의 두 번째 단락, 그렇지만 여러분의 설명에 흥미와 유머가 부족하다는 의견도 일부 있었다. 5월 9일 월요일 오후 4시에 우리 사무실에서 만나 이 문제를 해결할 방안을 논의했으면 한다(That said, there have been some comments about your explanations lacking excitement and humor. I'm hoping we can all meet in our offices on Monday, May 9, at 4 P.M. to talk about ways to resolve this issue)에서 발신인(I)인 은초보 씨가 관광지 안내를 더 재미있게 할 방안을 다음 회의에서 논의하고 싶다고 언급하고 있으므로, 정답은 (A)이다.

▶▶ **Paraphrasing** 지문의 **talk about** → 질문의 **discuss**
지문의 **excitement and humor**
→ 정답의 **entertaining**
지문의 **ways to resolve this issue**
→ 정답의 **How to make tours more entertaining**

TEST 9

101 (B)	**102** (C)	**103** (C)	**104** (B)	**105** (A)
106 (C)	**107** (D)	**108** (C)	**109** (A)	**110** (C)
111 (D)	**112** (A)	**113** (A)	**114** (B)	**115** (D)
116 (A)	**117** (B)	**118** (D)	**119** (C)	**120** (B)
121 (C)	**122** (D)	**123** (A)	**124** (B)	**125** (D)
126 (B)	**127** (B)	**128** (C)	**129** (D)	**130** (A)
131 (A)	**132** (D)	**133** (D)	**134** (B)	**135** (C)
136 (C)	**137** (A)	**138** (D)	**139** (A)	**140** (C)
141 (C)	**142** (D)	**143** (C)	**144** (A)	**145** (D)
146 (B)	**147** (C)	**148** (A)	**149** (A)	**150** (D)
151 (D)	**152** (A)	**153** (C)	**154** (D)	**155** (B)
156 (D)	**157** (C)	**158** (C)	**159** (B)	**160** (D)
161 (D)	**162** (C)	**163** (B)	**164** (C)	**165** (B)
166 (D)	**167** (C)	**168** (C)	**169** (A)	**170** (C)
171 (B)	**172** (C)	**173** (A)	**174** (C)	**175** (C)
176 (C)	**177** (D)	**178** (A)	**179** (B)	**180** (D)
181 (D)	**182** (B)	**183** (D)	**184** (C)	**185** (A)
186 (C)	**187** (B)	**188** (D)	**189** (C)	**190** (D)
191 (B)	**192** (D)	**193** (C)	**194** (B)	**195** (D)
196 (D)	**197** (B)	**198** (D)	**199** (C)	**200** (D)

PART 5

101 전치사 어휘

해설 빈칸은 시점을 나타내는 목적어(the end of the week) 앞 전치사 자리로, 문맥에 맞는 전치사를 선택해야 한다. 문맥상 '이번 주말까지'라는 의미가 자연스러우므로, 정답은 (B) by(~까지)이다. (A) behind(~ 뒤에), (C) on(~(날)에), (D) across(~을 가로질러)는 의미상 적합하지 않다.

번역 초대 받은 내빈께서는 이번 주 말까지 연회 참석 의사를 알려 주셔야 합니다.

어휘 confirm 확인해 주다, 확정하다 intention 의도, 의사 banquet 연회

102 인칭대명사 _ 소유격

해설 빈칸은 뒤에 있는 전치사(of)의 목적어(accounting certification)를 한정 수식하는 자리이므로, 정답은 소유격 인칭대명사 (C) their이다.

번역 지원자는 첫 면접에서 회계업무 자격 증빙서류를 제시해야 합니다.

어휘 applicant 지원자 proof 증거(물), 증빙 accounting 회계 certification 증명, 인증

103 부사 자리

해설 빈칸 뒤에 있는 현재분사(resembling)를 수식하는 부사 자리이다. 문맥상 '매우 흡사한'이라는 의미가 자연스러우므로, 정답은 (C) Closely(면밀히, 밀접하게)이다. 형용사/부사의 비교급 (A) Closer, 원급 (B) Close (가까운, 가까이), 최상급 (D) Closest는 의미상 적합하지 않다.

번역 이전 시대들의 조각 작품들과 매우 흡사한 플로렌스 씨의 작품들은 일상의 장면들을 묘사한다.

어휘 resemble 닮다, 유사하다 era 시대 artwork 예술작품 depict 묘사하다, 그리다

104 명사 자리 _ 전치사의 목적어

해설 빈칸 앞의 명사(contract)와 복합명사를 이뤄 앞에 있는 전치사(in)의 목적어 역할을 하는 명사 자리이다. 명사 (B) negotiation(협상)과 (D) negotiator(교섭자, 협상자) 중에 문맥상 '계약 협상에 참여하다'라는 의미가 자연스러우므로, 정답은 (B) negotiation이다.

번역 파르자 씨는 인수의 세부 내역을 마무리하기 위해 싱가포르에서 열릴 계약 협상에 참여할 것이다.

어휘 take part in ~에 참여하다 contract 계약 finalize 마무리하다, 완결하다 acquisition (기업의) 인수 negotiation 협상

105 전치사 어휘

해설 빈칸은 명사(the stage) 앞에 위치하는 전치사 자리이다. 문맥상 '무대 위로'라는 의미가 자연스러우므로, 정답은 (A) onto이다. 전치사/접속사 (B) until(~까지), 전치사 (C) with(~와 함께), 전치사/접속사 (D) as(~로서, ~처럼)는 의미상 적합하지 않다.

번역 음악가들이 무대에 오르자 관객들은 열정에 찬 박수 갈채를 보냈다.

어휘 a round of applause 한 차례의 박수, 환호 enthusiastic 열정적인, 정열적인

106 명사 자리 _ 동사의 목적어

해설 빈칸 앞에 있는 동사(should bring)의 목적어 역할을 하는 명사 자리로, 빈칸 뒤에 나오는 절(they need with them)의 수식을 받는다. 참고로 빈칸 뒤에는 목적격 관계대명사(that)가 생략되어 있다. 문맥상 '필요로 하는 모든 것'이라는 의미가 자연스러우므로, 정답은 (C) everything이다. 부사절 접속사 (A) wherever 뒤에는 완전한 절이 나와야 하며, 부사 (D) then은 문장의 의미만 연결할 뿐 두 문장을 한 문장으로 연결할 수 없다.

번역 도보 코스에는 상점이 없기 때문에 도보여행자들은 필요한 물품을 모두 가지고 와야 합니다.

어휘 hiker 도보여행자, 하이커 trail (특정 목적으로 따라 가는) 코스, 경로

107 동사 어형 _ 시제

해설 빈칸 뒤에 나오는 과거를 나타내는 부사(last week)로 보아 정답은 (D) calculated이다. 참고로 빈칸 앞에 있는 명사(the figures) 뒤에는 목적격 관계대명사(which/that)가 생략되어 있으며, her department가 관계사절 내의 주어이고 빈칸은 동사 자리이다.

번역 검토를 하면서 서 씨는 지난주 자신의 부서에서 계산한 수치들이 틀렸다는 것을 발견했다.

어휘 examination 검사, 검토 figure 수치 incorrect 부정확한, 틀린 calculate 계산하다

108 명사 어휘

해설 빈칸은 앞에 있는 주어 역할을 하는 동명사 구문(Partnering with Apor Footwear)과 동격 관계를 나타내는 명사 자리로, 앞의 형용사(profitable)의 수식을 받는다. 문맥상 '아포어 풋웨어와의 제휴는 득이 되는 합의'라는 의미가 자연스러우므로, 정답은 (C) arrangement(합의, 배치, 준비)이다. (A) atmosphere(분위기, 대기), (B) content(내용), (D) source(원천, 근원)는 의미상 적합하지 않다.

번역 아포어 풋웨어와의 제휴는 이 소매업체의 훌륭한 평판 덕분에 파사디나 백화점에게는 득이 되는 합의가 될 수 있다.

어휘 partner with ~와 제휴하다, 협력하다 profitable 수익성이 있는, 이득이 되는 thanks to ~ 덕분에 retailer 소매업체 reputation 평판, 명성 arrangement 조정, 합의

109 부사절 접속사 자리

해설 빈칸은 콤마 앞뒤에 있는 두 개의 완전한 절을 연결하는 부사절 접속사 자리로, 정답은 (A) Before이다. 전치사 (B) Despite, 접속사/부사 (C) Nor, 명사절 접속사/관계 부사 (D) How는 품사상 적합하지 않다.

번역 합병이 이사회에 의해 승인되기 전에 해당 기업에 대한 공식 평가가 먼저 이루어져야 한다.

어휘 merger 합병 authorize 인가하다, 재가하다 board member 이사회 이사 valuation 가치 평가, 사정

110 동사 어휘

해설 빈칸 뒤의 목적어(standards)와 의미가 가장 잘 통하는 동사를 선택해야 한다. 문맥상 '전국보건안전협회가 세운 기준을 채택했다'라는 의미가 자연스러우므로, 정답은 (C) adopted(채택하다)이다. (A) insisted(주장하다), (B) conducted(수행하다, 안내하다, 지휘하다), (D) underwent(겪다)는 의미상 적합하지 않다. 참고로 conduct 뒤에는 'conduct research(연구를 수행하다)'처럼 주로 행위가 나온다.

번역 페어네이 매뉴팩처링은 화학물질의 노출에 관련해 전국보건안전협회가 세운 기준을 채택했다.

어휘 standard 기준 regarding ~에 대해 exposure (유해한 환경 등에) 노출 chemical 화학물질 adopt 채택하다

111 전치사 어휘

해설 빈칸은 명사(the need) 앞 전치사 자리로, 문맥상 앞의 동사(brought)와 짝을 이루어 '초래하다, 일으키다'라는 의미가 자연스러우므로 정답은 (D) about이다. (A) among(~ 사이에, ~ 중에) 뒤에는 주로 복수명사가 나오고, (C) down은 동사(brought)와 짝을 이루어 '낮추다, 떨어뜨리다'라는 의미를 나타낸다.

번역 휴대전화 사용의 증가로 운전 중 문자 주고받기를 금지하는 법을 더욱 강화할 필요성이 대두됐다.

어휘 usage 사용 bring about ~을 야기하다, 불러오다 strict 엄격한 text (휴대전화로) 문자를 주고받다

112 명사 자리 _ 주격 보어

해설 빈칸은 앞에 있는 사람 주어(Visitors to Bellucci Orchard)와 동격 관계를 나타내는 명사 자리로, 앞의 형용사(active)의 수식을 받는다. 따라서 정답은 사람명사 (A) participants(참가자)이다. 명사 (D) participation(참가)은 사람 주어(Visitors)와 동격 관계를 나타낼 수 없어 적합하지 않다.

번역 벨루치 과수원 방문객들은 VIP 투어를 신청하시면 수확 과정에 직접 참여할 수 있습니다.

어휘 orchard 과수원 active 능동적인, 적극적인 harvest 추수, 수확 register for ~에 등록하다, 신청하다

113 대명사

해설 빈칸은 'of+목적격 관계대명사(which)' 앞에서 선행사(a daily pass and a season ticket)를 대신 가리킬 수 있는 표현을 고르는 문제이다. 문맥상 '둘 중 어떤 것도 이용할 수 있다'라는 의미가 자연스러우므로, 정답은 (A) either이다. 지시대명사 (C) those(저것들)는 의미상 적합하지 않고, 명사절 접속사 (D) what은 품사상 적합하지 않다.

번역 리조트는 1일권과 정기권을 판매하는데 둘 다 스키 리프트를 이용할 수 있습니다.

어휘 pass 출입증, 탑승권 season ticket 정기권 access 접근하다, 이용하다

114 부사 자리

해설 빈칸은 자동사(reacted) 뒤에서 동사를 수식하는 부사 자리로, 정답은 (B) predictably이다. 형용사 (A) predictable, 동사 (C) predicts, 명사 (D) prediction은 품사상 적합하지 않다.

번역 그 회사 CEO는 주주들이 막판 회의를 요구했다는 소식에 예상대로 반응했다.

어휘 react 반응하다 stockholder 주주 call for ~을 요구하다 last-minute 막판의, 최종 순간의

115 동사 어형 _ 현재완료

해설 빈칸 뒤의 명사(the exit ramps)를 목적어로 취하면서, 앞의 조동사(has)와 함께 현재완료시제를 나타내는 자리이므로, 정답은 과거분사인 (D) broadened이다. 형용사 (A) broad, 동사원형 (B) broaden, 부사 (C) broadly는 품사상 적합하지 않다.

번역 17번 고속도로의 대규모 공사 프로젝트로 출구 램프가 확장되어 운전자 안전이 개선되었다.

어휘 extensive 광범위한, 대규모의 improve 개선하다, 높이다 motorist 운전자

116 부사 어휘

해설 빈칸은 동사(is)와 과거분사(supported) 사이에서 동사를 수식하는 부사 자리이다. 문맥상 '일부 지원을 받다'라는 의미가 자연스러우므로, 정답은 (A) partially(일부, 부분적으로)이다. (B) approximately(대략), (C) overly(너무, 지나치게), (D) briefly(잠시, 간단히)는 의미상 적합하지 않다.

번역 지역 농구 토너먼트 대회는 시 정부 자금으로 일부 지원을 받고 지역 기업들이 나머지를 부담합니다.

어휘 partially 부분적으로 support 지원하다 fund 기금, 자금 make up (요구되는 수, 양 등을) 채우다 remainder 나머지, 잔여분

117 형용사 자리

해설 빈칸 앞에 있는 전치사(with)의 목적어 역할을 하는 명사(sales)를 수식하는 형용사 자리이므로, 정답은 과거분사 (B) combined이다. to부정사 (C) to have combined와 (D) to combine은 전치사의 목적어 역할을 할 수 없고, 또한 명사를 앞에서 수식하지 않는다.

번역 국내 및 해외 물품의 합산 매출이 3만 달러 이상인 직원들만이 승진 자격이 있습니다.

어휘 employee 직원 sales 매출 domestic 국내의 be eligible for ~의 자격이 있다 promotion 승진

118 주격 관계대명사

해설 빈칸은 동사(wish)의 주어가 없는 불완전한 절을 이끌면서 앞의 사람명사(residents)를 수식하는 주격 관계대명사 자리이므로, 정답은 (D) who이다. (A) several과 (B) others는 문장들을 연결할 수 없다. 등위접속사 (C) but이 올 경우 뒤에 주어가 없으므로, 문장의 주어(The upcoming city council meeting)와 수가 일치해야 하는데, 복수형인 wish가 왔으므로 수가 일치하지 않는다.

번역 다가올 시의회 회의는 상업지구 확대안에 대해 우려를 표명하고자 하는 주민들을 위해 마련됩니다.

어휘 upcoming 다가올, 곧 있을 city council 시 의회 be intended for ~을 위해 의도되다 voice 목소리[의견]를 내다 concern 우려, 걱정 commercial district 상업지구 expansion 확장, 확대

119 부사 자리 _ 동사 수식

해설 빈칸은 부사절 접속사(Although)가 이끄는 부사절 내의 동사(differ)를 수식하는 부사 자리로, 정답은 (C) significantly(상당히)이다. 동사원형 (A) signify(의미하다, 나타내다), 형용사 (B) significant(상당한, 중요한), 동명사/현재분사 (D) signifying은 품사상 적합하지 않다.

번역 가장 잘 팔리는 하이브리드 차량들의 가격은 서로 큰 차이가 나지만 연비 결과는 거의 동일하다.

어휘 vehicle 차량 gas mileage 주행 마일 수, 연비 nearly 거의

120 접속사

해설 빈칸은 than과 짝을 이루어 앞에 있는 to부정사 구문(to travel solely with a carry-on bag)과 뒤에 나오는 구문(pay the required fee for checked luggage)을 연결하는 어휘를 찾아야 한다. 따라서 정답은 than과 함께 '~라기 보다는'이라는 의미를 나타내는 (B) rather이다. rather는 단독으로는 부사이지만 than과 함께 rather than의 형태로는 접속사 역할을 할 수 있다. 빈칸 뒤 than만 보고 (C) better를 고르지 않도록 주의한다.

번역 많은 승객들이 위탁 수화물에 요구되는 요금을 내기보다는 기내 휴대 가방만 가지고 여행하는 쪽을 택한다.

어휘 passenger 승객 choose to + 동사원형 ~하기를 선택하다 solely 오직, 단지 carry-on bag 기내 휴대용 가방 checked luggage 위탁 수화물

121 동사 어형 _ 시제

해설 빈칸은 주어(a number of new social media sites) 뒤의 동사 자리로, 뒤에 나오는 과거부터 현재까지의 의미를 나타내는 전치사구(in the past year alone)에 적합한 동사를 선택해야 한다. 따라서 정답은 현재 완료시제 동사 (C) have emerged이다. to부정사 (A) to emerge는 동사 자리에 올 수 없고, (D) will emerge는 시제가 맞지 않는다. 수동 현재시제 동사 (B) are emerged는 emerge가 수동으로 쓰이지 않으므로 적합하지 않다.

번역 신속한 정보 공유 방법에 대한 수요로 인해 지난 한 해만 해도 많은 소셜 미디어 사이트들이 새로 생겨났다.

어휘 demand 수요 share 공유하다 a number of 많은 emerge 생겨나다, 부상하다

122 명사 어휘

해설 빈칸은 정관사 the와 전치사(of) 사이에 올 수 있는 명사 어휘를 묻는 문제로, 문맥을 통해 적합한 어휘를 선택해야 한다. 문맥상 '집에서 편안하게'라는 의미가 자연스러우므로, 정답은 (D) comfort이다. (A) appreciation(감사, 감상), (B) decoration(장식), (C) layout(배치)은 의미상 적합하지 않다.

번역 온라인 교육 플랫폼 엘쉐이드는 사용자들이 집에서 편하게 기술 강좌를 수강할 수 있도록 해준다.

어휘 platform 플랫폼(컴퓨터 사용의 기반이 되는 하드웨어·소프트웨어 환경) allow 허락하다 comfort 안락, 편안

123 동사 어휘

해설 빈칸 뒤의 명사(the office picnic)를 목적어로 취하면서, 앞에 있는 동사(chose)의 목적어 역할을 하는 자리로, 문맥에 어울리는 어휘를 선택해야 한다. 문맥상 '악천후 예보 때문에 사무실 야유회를 취소하다'라는 의미가 자연스러우므로, 정답은 (A) call off(취소하다)이다. 참고로 동사 choose는 to부정사를 목적어로 취한다. (B) fill out(작성하다), (C) back up(지지하다, 뒷받침하다, 백업하다), (D) hand in(제출하다)은 의미상 적합하지 않다.

번역 경영진은 악천후 예보 때문에 사무실 야유회를 취소하기로 했다.

어휘 forecast 예보 adverse 불리한, 부정적인 adverse weather 악천후

124 부사 어휘

해설 빈칸은 등위 접속사(and)가 연결하는 완전한 절과 완전한 절 뒤에 나오는 부사 자리이다. 문맥상 앞뒤의 완전한 절이 순서대로 일어난다고 보는 것이 자연스러우므로, 정답은 (B) afterward(후에, 나중에)이다. (A) somewhat(어느 정도, 다소), (C) alike(비슷하게, 둘 다), (D) otherwise(달리, 그렇지 않으면)는 의미상 적합하지 않다.

번역 샌마리노 발레단은 웰번 극장에서 공연할 것이며 단원들은 공연 후 사인회를 가질 예정입니다.

어휘 perform 공연하다 troupe 공연단, 극단 autograph 사인

125 형용사 어휘

해설 빈칸은 전치사(from)의 목적어 역할을 하는 명사(cultural backgrounds)를 수식하는 형용사 자리이다. 문맥상 '다양한 문화 배경을 가지고'라는 의미가 자연스러우므로, 정답은 (D) diverse(다양한)이다. (A) ongoing(진행중인), (B) conscious(의식하는, 자각하는), (C) adjustable(조절 가능한, 조정 가능한)은 의미상 적합하지 않다.

번역 국제 통합 정상회담의 참석자들은 다양한 문화 배경을 가지고 있으며 다양한 언어를 사용합니다.

어휘 attendee 참석자 summit 정상회담 a variety of 다양한

126 형용사 자리 _ 주격 보어

해설 빈칸은 be동사(are) 뒤에서 앞의 주어(rush hour traffic downtown and the average congestion on Nicall Bridge)를 보충 설명하는 형용사 자리이므로 정답은 (B) comparable(비슷한, 비교할 만한)이다. 동사 (A) compares, 동명사 (C) comparing은 품사상 적합하지 않고 명사 (D) comparison은 주어와 동격 관계가 성립하지 않으므로 적합하지 않다. 참고로 demonstrated 뒤 that은 명사절 접속사이며 that 이하 절은 demonstrated의 목적절이다.

번역 보고서는 혼잡 시간대 시내 교통과 니콜 다리의 평균적인 교통혼잡이 거의 비슷한 수준임을 보여준다.

어휘 demonstrate 보여주다, 입증하다 congestion 혼잡 roughly 대략, 대충 comparable 비슷한, 비교할 만한

127 전치사구

해설 빈칸은 뒤에 나오는 명사구(the expiration date of his or her term of office) 앞에서 전치사(to)와 함께 전치사구를 이루는 어휘를 묻는 자리이다. 문맥상 '임기 만료일 이후에'라는 의미가 자연스러우므로, 정답은 (B) subsequent(다음의, 차후의)이다. 'subsequent to(~ 이후에)'를 묶어서 기억해 두자. (A) prospective(장래의, 유망한), (C) likely(~할 것 같은, 그럴듯한), (D) eager(열렬한, 열심인)는 의미상 적합하지 않다. 참고로 (C) likely(~할 것 같은, 그럴듯한)와 (D) eager(열렬한, 열심인)는 주로 to부정사와 함께 쓰인다. 빈칸 뒤에 to가 있을 경우, to가 전치사의 to인지, to부정사의 to인지를 구별하는 것이 중요하다.

번역 각 클럽 임원은 임기 만료일 이후에 후임자를 찾을 때까지 직을 유지해야 합니다.

어휘 remain in office 직을 유지하다, 유임하다 expiration date 만기일, 만료일 term of office 임기 successor 후임자, 승계자

128 동사 어형 _ 미래완료

해설 빈칸은 주절의 동사 자리이다. 문맥상 '6월 30일까지 백 곳이 넘는 생산 시설을 시찰하게 될 것이다'라는 의미가 자연스러우므로, 정답은 미래 이전부터 미래(June 30)까지의 의미를 나타내는 미래완료시제 동사 (D) will have inspected이다.

번역 애드리언 씨가 6월 30일 해외 근무를 마칠 때에는 백 곳이 넘는 생산 시설을 시찰하게 될 것입니다.

어휘 conclude 종결하다 assignment 과제, 임무 overseas 해외에서; 해외의

129 형용사 어휘

해설 빈칸 앞에 있는 전치사(of)의 목적어(value)를 수식하는 형용사 자리이다. 문맥상 '동일 가격의'라는 의미가 자연스러우므로, 정답은 (D) equivalent(등가의, 동등한)이다. (A) competent(유능한, 능숙한), (B) receptive(선뜻 받아들이는, 수용적인), (C) initial(처음의, 초기의)은 의미상 적합하지 않다.

번역 고객의 기대에 미치지 못하는 제품들은 반품해서 환불을 받거나 동일 가격의 제품으로 교환할 수 있습니다.

어휘 meet 충족하다 expectation 기대 refund 환불 merchandise 상품 equivalent 동등한

130 명사 어휘

해설 빈칸 앞에 있는 to부정사(to analyze)의 목적어 역할을 하는 명사 자리로, 뒤의 전치사구(of the change for faculty and students)의 수식을 받는다. 문맥상 '변화가 교수들과 학생들에게 미치게 될 영향을 분석하다'라는 의미가 자연스러우므로, 정답은 (A) implications(영향, 결과, 암시)이다. (B) alliances(동맹, 연합), (C) aptitudes(적성, 소질), (D) supplements(보충, 추가)는 의미상 적합하지 않다.

번역 대학 행정팀은 위원회에게 해당 변화가 교수들과 학생들에게 미치게 될 영향을 분석해 달라고 요청했다.

어휘 administration 행정[관리] 직원들 analyze 분석하다 implication 영향, 결과 faculty 교수단, 교수들

PART 6

131-134 공지

공사 공지

정기 선로 보수 작업이 10월 3일부터 7일까지 메트로폴리탄 지하철 3호선에서 실시될 **131**예정입니다. 일부 지연과 운행 차질이 예상되므로 공사기간 동안 지하철을 이용할 여행객 **132**누구나 온라인과 전 역에 걸쳐 게재된 업데이트된 운행시간표를 참고해 주십시오. 써니베일역과 캠벨 역 사이에는 열차 운행이 중단될 예정입니다. **133**정기적으로 운행되는 대체 버스 서비스가 제공될 것입니다. 승객들은 유효한 지하철 승차권을 제시하면 버스를 이용할 수 있습니다. 도움이 필요하거나 공사에 대해 우려 사항이 있는 분들은 저희 직원에게 말씀해 주십시오. **134**가능한 한 불편을 최소화하도록 노력하겠습니다.

어휘 routine 정기적인 post 게재하다, 올리다 delay 지연 interruption 방해, 차질 replacement 대체물 regularly 정기적으로, 주기적으로 minimize 최소화하다 inconvenience 불편, 폐

131 동사 어형 _ 태 / 시제

해설 빈칸은 주어(Routine maintenance work on the rail lines) 뒤 동사 자리이다. 문맥상 '정기 선로 보수 작업이 예정되어 있다'라는 수동의 의미가 자연스러우므로, 현재시제 수동태 (A) is planned와 과거진행시제 수동태 (B) was being planned 중에서 시제에 맞는 동사를 선택해야 한다. 뒤에 나오는 문장의 관계사절(who is traveling during the project)을 통해 앞으로 실시될 보수 작업이라는 것을 알 수 있으므로, 정답은 (A) is planned이다. to부정사 (C) to plan은 동사 자리에 들어갈 수 없고, 현재완료진행시제 동사 (D) has been planning은 능동의 의미를 나타내므로 적합하지 않다.

132 대명사

해설 빈칸은 뒤에 나오는 동사(should check)의 주어 역할을 하는 명사 자리로, 주격관계대명사(who)가 이끄는 관계사절(who is traveling during the project)의 수식을 받는다. 따라서 정답은 관계사절 내 단수동사(is traveling)와 수일치하는 (D) Anyone이다. '~하는 사람은 누구나'라는 의미로 'anyone who'를 묶어서 기억해 두자. 형용사 (A) Other(다른)는 품사상 부적합하고, (B) One another(서로서로)는 주어 자리에 들어갈 수 없고, 지시대명사 (C) Those는 동사(is traveling)와 수일치하지 않는다.

133 문맥에 맞는 문장 고르기

번역 (A) 공사 기간 동안 여러분이 보여주신 인내에 감사드립니다.
(B) 승객들은 유효한 지하철 승차권을 제시하면 버스를 이용할 수 있습니다.
(C) 지하철은 통근자들을 매일 실어 나릅니다.
(D) 경로는 운전 면허 종류에 따라 달라집니다.

해설 빈칸 앞 문장 '정기적으로 운행되는 대체 버스 서비스가 제공될 것이다(There will be a replacement bus service operating regularly)'를 통해 철도 공사 기간 중 대안으로 버스 이용이 가능하다는 것을 알 수 있다. 따라서 빈칸에는 버스 이용 방법과 관련된 내용이 이어지는 것이 문맥상 자연스러우므로, 정답은 (B)이다.

어휘 appreciate 감사하다 patience 인내 present 제시하다 valid 유효한 transport 운송하다, 실어 나르다 commuter 통근자

134 부사절 접속사

해설 빈칸은 뒤에 나오는 절(we can)을 이끌면서 앞에 있는 절을 수식하는 부사절 접속사 자리이다. (A) so that(~을 위해), (B) as much as(~ 만큼), (D) whether(~이든 아니든) 중에 문맥상 '우리가 할 수 있는 만큼 많이'라는 의미가 자연스러우므로, 정답은 (B) as much as(~ 만큼)이다. 'as much[many] as one can(누가 할 수 있는 만큼 많이)'을 묶어서 기억해 두자. 전치사 (C) aside from(~을 제외하고, ~이외에)은 품사상 적합하지 않다.

135-138 회람

수신: 뉴홀 사 전직원 발신: 지점 매니저 마빈 몬타노 날짜: 4월 14일 제목: 브라이언 휘터커

브라이언 휘터커 이사가 이번 달 말일 이사직에서 퇴임합니다. 그렇지만 여러분은 그를 사무실에서 정기적으로 보실 것입니다. 회사 135**자문역**으로 시간제 근무를 하시기 때문입니다. 자문역으로서 그는 기존 계약들의 136**수정** 제안뿐 아니라 재무 자문을 하게 됩니다. 퇴임 이후에도 137**그의** 전문지식을 활용함으로써 회사는 향후 수익성을 보장할 수 있습니다. 138**휘터커 씨가 계속 저희와 같이 근무하시지만 정식으로 그의 노고를 기리고자 합니다.** 축하 연회는 4월 30일 오후 4시에 열립니다. 연회에서 뵙겠습니다.

어휘 retire 은퇴하다, 퇴임하다 in spite of ~에도 불구하고 recommend 추천하다, 권고하다 existing 기존의, 현행의 expertise 전문지식 ensure 보장하다 profitability 수익성 going forward 장차, 앞으로 acknowledge 인정하다 contribution 기여, 공헌

135 형용사 어휘

해설 빈칸 앞에 있는 전치사(in)의 목적어(role)를 수식하는 형용사 자리이다. 문맥상 '자문 역할'이라는 의미가 자연스러우므로, 정답은 (C) advisory (자문의)이다. (A) adequate(적절한, 충분한), (B) estimated(추정된, 견적의), (D) equal(동등한, 같은)은 의미상 적합하지 않다.

어휘 advisory 자문의, 조언하는

136 명사 자리 _ 동명사의 목적어

해설 빈칸 앞에 있는 동명사(recommending)의 목적어 역할을 하는 명사 자리이므로, 정답은 (C) revisions이다. 과거시제 동사/과거분사 (A) revised, 형용사 (B) revisable, 동사 (D) revises는 품사상 적합하지 않다.

어휘 revision 수정, 변경

137 인칭대명사

해설 빈칸 뒤 명사(expertise)를 한정 수식하는 소유격 인칭대명사 자리이다. 첫 번째 문장 '브라이언 휘터커 이사가 이번 달 말일 이사직에서 퇴임한다(Brian Whitaker will be retiring from the position of director on the last day of this month)'를 통해 브라이언 휘터커 씨가 은퇴한다는 것을 알 수 있으므로, 정답은 브라이언 휘터커 씨를 대신 가리키는 (A) his이다.

138 문맥에 맞는 문장 고르기

번역 (A) 직원들 없이는 우리의 목표를 달성하지 못했을 것입니다.
(B) 축하 연회는 4월 30일 오후 4시에 열립니다.
(C) 몇몇 신규 고객들이 저희 회사에 등록했습니다.
(D) 그는 효율성 제고를 위한 정책들을 개발했습니다.

어휘 reception 축하 연회, 환영회

해설 빈칸 앞 문장 '휘터커 씨가 계속 저희와 같이 근무하지만 정식으로 그의 노고를 기리고자 한다(Although Mr. Whitaker will continue working for us, we want to acknowledge the contributions he has made in a formal celebration)'를 통해 휘터커 씨를 위한 행사를 준비한다는 것을 알 수 있다. 따라서 빈칸에는 그 행사와 관련된 내용이 이어지는 것이 자연스러우므로, 정답은 (B)이다.

어휘 reach 도달하다 reception 축하 연회, 환영회 enroll 등록하다 policy 정책, 규정 efficiency 효율(성)

139-142 광고

> **실바나 루쏘 관람 티켓을 구매하세요!**
>
> **139**6월 2일 오후 7시 램키 갤러리에서 화가 실바나 루쏘의 강연회를 열게 되어 매우 기쁩니다. 예술을 사랑하시는 분들에게는 흔하지 않은 기회입니다. **139**루쏘 씨는 대중에게 모습을 잘 드러내지 않는데 이번 행사에서는 호텔 메이드에서 세계적으로 저명한 미술가가 되기까지의 **140**여정, 수십 년간 성공적인 설치 미술 활동을 해온 그녀의 커리어 행로를 이야기할 예정입니다. 강연 후 관객들 질문에 답할 것입니다. 미리 질문을 전달하고자 하는 관객은 늦어도 5월 30일까지 이메일 info@ramkegallery.com으로 **141**제출해야 합니다. 이 **142**재능 있는 화가를 직접 만나기 위한 티켓을 구매하시려면 램키 갤러리 555-0144로 전화 주십시오.

> **어휘** host 개최하다, 열다 talk 강연, 연설 public appearance 공개석상에 출현함 housekeeper 호텔 객실 청소 매니저 renowned 저명한 art installation 설치 미술 hand in 제출하다, 내다 no later than 늦어도 ~까지 in person 직접

139 문맥에 맞는 문장 고르기

번역 (A) 예술을 사랑하시는 분들에게는 흔하지 않은 기회입니다.
(B) 각각은 미술가의 친필 사인이 되어 있습니다.
(C) 이 그림들은 수천 달러대로 평가됩니다.
(D) 정기 강연은 대중에게 정보를 알리는 데 도움이 됩니다.

해설 빈칸 앞 문장 '6월 2일 오후 7시 램키 갤러리에서 화가 실바나 루쏘의 강연회를 열게 되어 매우 기쁘다(The Ramke Gallery is pleased to host a talk by painter Silvana Russo on June 2 at 7 P.M.)'에서 화가의 강연회를 언급하고 있다. 또한 빈칸 뒤에 나오는 문장 '루쏘 씨는 대중에게 잘 모습을 드러내지 않는다(Ms. Russo does not often make public appearances)'를 통해 흔치 않은 기회임을 알 수 있다. 따라서 빈칸에는 화가의 강연회가 드문 기회임을 강조하는 내용이 이어지는 것이 자연스러우므로, 정답은 (A)이다.

어휘 rare 드문 opportunity 기회 lecture 강연

140 명사 어휘

해설 빈칸은 소유격(her) 뒤 명사 자리로, 문맥에 어울리는 어휘를 선택해야 한다. 문맥상 '호텔 메이드에서 세계적으로 저명한 미술가가 되기까지의 여정'이라는 의미가 자연스러우므로, 정답은 (C) journey(여정)이다. (A) involvement(관여, 개입), (B) absence(부재, 결핍), (D) release(출시, 공개)는 의미상 적합하지 않다.

어휘 journey 여행, 여정

141 동사 어형

해설 빈칸은 주어(Audience members) 뒤 동사 자리로 관계사절(who prefer handing in their questions in advance)이 주어를 수식하고 있다. 문맥상 '늦어도 5월 30일까지 이메일로 제출해야 한다'는 의미가 자연스러우므로, 정답은 (C) must submit이다. 미래시제 동사 (A) will submit(제출할 것이다), 과거완료시제 동사 (D) had submitted는 의미상 적합하지 않다. (B) be submitted는 동사 자리에 들어갈 수 없다.

어휘 submit 제출하다

142 형용사 어휘

해설 빈칸 앞에 있는 to부정사(to see)의 목적어(artist)를 수식하는 형용사 자리이다. 문맥상 '재능 있는 화가를 만나기 위한'이라는 의미가 자연스러우므로, 정답은 (D) talented(재능이 있는)이다. (A) rejected(거절 당한), (B) originated(비롯된, 유래된), (C) undiscovered(발견되지 않은)는 의미상 적합하지 않다.

143-146 이메일

> 수신: 베니타 양 〈vyang@crestonco.com〉
> 발신: 세바스천 나도 〈snadeau@crestonco.com〉
> 날짜: 2월 20일
> 제목: 직원 회의
>
> 베니타 씨께,
>
> **143**주간 직원회의에 참석하지 못하셨더군요. 그래서 제가 업데이트해 드리고자 합니다. **143**회의는 주로 새로운 로고 디자인 계획에 집중되었습니다. 저희 로고가 테릴린 엔터프라이즈의 로고와 **144**눈에 띄게 유사하기 때문입니다. 저희는 새 로고로 경쟁사들과 **145**차별화를 꾀하고자 합니다. 저희 사내 그래픽 팀이 BC 아트 디자이너들과 **146**협업해서 여러 샘플들을 제작할 예정입니다. 직원들은 추후 샘플들에 대한 의견을 나눌 기회를 갖게 됩니다.
>
> 세바스천 드림

> **어휘** notice 인지하다, 알아채다 staff meeting 직원 회의 be centered on ~에 집중되다, ~을 중심으로 하다 set A apart from B A를 B와 다르게 만들다 competitor 경쟁사

143 문맥에 맞는 문장 고르기

번역 (A) 그렇다고 하더라도 모두가 의무적으로 참석해야 합니다.
(B) 금요일 오후 4시로 일정이 재조정됐습니다.
(C) 그래서 제가 업데이트해드리고자 합니다.
(D) 귀하의 발표는 정말 유익했습니다.

해설 빈칸 앞 문장 '주간 직원회의에 참석하지 못하셨더군요(I noticed that you were not able to attend the weekly staff meeting)'를 통해 베니타 씨가 회의에 참석하지 못했다는 것을 알 수 있다. 빈칸 뒤에 나오는 문장 '회의는 주로 새로운 로고 디자인 계획에 집중되었다(The meeting was mainly centered on plans to have a new logo designed)'에서 회의 내용을 언급하고 있다. 따라서 빈칸에는 회의에 참석하지 못한 베니타 씨를 위해 회의의 세부 사항을 전해주고자 한다는 내용이 이어지는 것이 자연스러우므로, 정답은 (C)이다.

어휘 attendance 참석 mandatory 의무적인 extremely 정말, 매우 informative 유용한

144 부사 자리 _ 형용사 수식

해설 빈칸은 뒤에 있는 형용사(similar)를 수식하는 부사 자리이므로, 정답은 (A) strikingly이다. 동사/명사 (B) strike, 과거분사 (C) struck, 동명사/현재분사 (D) striking은 품사상 적합하지 않다.

어휘 strikingly 두드러지게, 눈에 띄게

Test 9

145 부사

해설 빈칸 앞에 있는 동사원형(set)과 짝을 이루어 '돋보이게 만들다, 다르게 만들다'라는 의미를 나타내는 부사를 선택해야 한다. 따라서 정답은 (D) apart이다. (B) against는 set과 짝을 이루어 '등돌리게 하다'라는 의미를 나타낸다.

146 동사 어휘

해설 빈칸 뒤의 전치사(with)와 결합하여 목적어(designers)를 취하는 자동사 자리이다. (B) collaborate(협력하다)와 (D) coincide(동시에 일어나다, 일치하다) 중에 문맥상 '디자이너들과 협업해서'라는 의미가 자연스러우므로, 정답은 (B) collaborate이다. 타동사 (A) identify(확인하다, 알아보다)와 (C) uphold(지지하다, 인정하다, 유지시키다)는 전치사 없이 바로 목적어를 취한다.

어휘 collaborate 협력하다, 협업하다

PART 7

147-148 광고

> 고등학교 졸업장을 가지고 계신가요? 본인이 팀워크가 뛰어난 사람이라고 생각하세요?
>
> 그렇다고 생각하신다면 Sandhill & Co.에서 일해 보시지 않겠습니까? 우리 회사는 50여 개의 대기업을 고객으로 보유하고 있는 위스콘신주 최고의 로펌입니다. 저희는 저희 전문 법률팀이 전국 최고라고 자부합니다.
>
> 회사가 지속적으로 성공을 거두고 있기 때문에 저희는 팀을 확장할 계획입니다. **147**그래서 새로이 문을 연 밀워키 사무실의 프런트 직원을 채용하고 있습니다. 담당 업무로는 방문 고객 응대, 전화 응대, 이메일 및 우편으로 고객과 소통, 그리고 저희 전문 법률 담당 직원 지원 등이 포함됩니다.
>
> **148**지원하시려면 최신 이력서 및 자기소개서를 인사 담당 앤디 스튜어트(asterwart@sandhill.com)에게 3월 31일까지 보내주십시오. 최종 심사 대상자들은 4월 10일까지 유선으로 통보될 것입니다.

> **어휘** diploma 졸업장 consider 여기다, 생각하다 represent 대변하다, 대표하다 client base 고객층 corporation 기업, 회사 expert 전문가 fine 우수한, 뛰어난 sustained 지속된 expand 확대하다, 확장하다 as such 이와 같이 responsibility 책임, 책무 greet 맞이하다, 인사하다 walk-in (손님 등이) 예약하지 않은 correspond 서신 교환하다 cover letter 첨부 편지, 자기 소개서 shortlist 최종 후보자 명단에 넣다 applicant 지원자

147 세부 사항

번역 어떤 자리의 채용 공고인가?
(A) 홍보 보조
(B) 변호사
(C) 접수 담당자
(D) 인사 부장

해설 구인 광고문으로, 세 번째 단락에서 새로 문을 연 밀워키 사무실의 프런트 직원을 채용하고 있다(As such, a position is available at the reception desk of our newly opened Milwaukee office)고 했으므로, 접수 담당자 채용 공고문임을 알 수 있다. 따라서 정답은 (C)이다.

148 세부 사항

번역 관심있는 사람들은 어떻게 하라고 하는가?
(A) 이메일을 보낸다
(B) 온라인 서식을 작성한다
(C) 회사를 방문한다
(D) 전화를 한다

해설 마지막 단락의 첫 번째 문장에서 지원하려면 이력서 및 자기소개서를 인사 담당 앤디 스튜어트에게 이메일로 보내라(To apply for this position, please send an up-to-date résumé and cover letter to our human resources manager, Andy Stewart, at astewart@sandhill.com by March 31)고 했다. 따라서 정답은 (A)이다.

▶▶ **Paraphrasing** 지문의 send ~ at astewart@sandhill.com → 정답의 **Send an e-mail**

149-150 회람

> **회람**
>
> 발신: 수 폴슨, 인사부장
> 수신: 렘리 은행 전직원
> 날짜: 3월 2일
> 주제: 스탠리 쿠퍼의 퇴직 연회
>
> 직원 여러분께,
>
> **149**아시다시피, 쿠퍼 씨의 퇴직 연회가 이번 주 금요일 저녁 시내의 다이아몬드 볼룸에서 열릴 예정이었습니다. 그렇지만 안타깝게도 내빈들이 너무 많아진 관계로 예약을 취소하고 다른 새로운 곳에 예약해야 했습니다. 그래서 행사는 메리골드 호텔의 연회장에서 열리게 됐습니다. 프랭크 그라이미가 직접 호텔 매니저와 이야기를 했는데, 그는 연회 음식들이 최상의 질이 될 것이라 약속했습니다. 음악은 지역 밴드인 〈더 펑키 플루츠〉가 맡게 될 것입니다. **150**프랭크가 수요일 여러분 각자의 자리를 찾아가 여러분이 원하는 메뉴를 조사할 것입니다. 많이들 아시겠지만 쿠퍼 씨는 30년이 넘게 영업팀 팀장으로 일하신 바 금요일 저녁을 그에게 잊지 못할 저녁이 되도록 만들어 봅시다!
>
> 감사합니다.
>
> 수 폴슨 드림

> **어휘** retirement 은퇴, 퇴직 take place 일어나다, 개최되다 reservation 예약 banquet 연회 obtain 얻다, 획득하다 preference 선호하는 것

149 주제 / 목적

번역 회람을 보낸 이유는 무엇인가?

(A) 직원들에게 준비 사항의 변경을 알리기 위해
(B) 직원들에게 행사에 직접 다과를 가지고 오도록 권장하기 위해
(C) 행사가 취소되었음을 알리기 위해
(D) 행사 오락 프로그램 추천을 요청하기 위해

해설 글의 목적은 주로 지문 서두 부분에 제시되는 경우가 많다. 여기서도 첫 세 문장에서 단서를 찾을 수 있다. 쿠퍼 씨의 퇴직 연회가 다이아몬드 볼룸에서 열릴 예정이었으나 내빈들의 인원 수가 많아져서 예약을 취소하고(Unfortunately, I have had to cancel this reservation and make a new one elsewhere, as the guest list has grown too large) 메리골드 호텔의 연회장에서 열리게 되었다고 했다. 따라서 직원들에게 퇴직 연회 장소의 변경을 알리기 위한 메모임을 알 수 있으므로, 정답은 (A)이다.

150 세부 사항

번역 프랭크 그라이미 씨는 수요일에 무엇을 할 계획인가?

(A) 음식 공급업체 매니저에게 연락하기
(B) 음악 공연 연습
(C) 영업 회의 참석
(D) 직원들에게 저녁식사 메뉴 설명

해설 on Wednesday가 문제 해결의 단서이다. 지문에서 on Wednesday가 언급되는 부분을 찾아보면, 프랭크가 수요일에 여러분 각자의 자리를 찾아가 원하는 메뉴를 조사할 것(Frank will visit each of you at your desks on Wednesday to obtain your menu preferences)이라고 했다. 따라서 정답은 (D)이다.

▶▶ **Paraphrasing** 지문의 **your menu preferences** → 정답의 **dinner options**

151-152 초대장

트위틀든 컨벤션 센터, C 회의실
11월 28일 (목) 오후 8시

트위틀든 시 의회는 주민 여러분 모두를 이번 주 목요일 트위틀든 컨벤션 센터에서 열릴 시상식에 초대합니다. 151이번 행사는 우리 청년 자원봉사자들의 공로를 기리는 자리가 될 것입니다. 이들 자원봉사자들은 거리에서 쓰레기를 치우고 어르신들을 위해 음식을 제공하는 활동에 열심히 임했습니다. 152B시상자로는 트위틀든 시의 토니 그리본스 시장님이 참석할 것입니다.

목요일 행사에 참석한 모든 분들에게는

– 152D무료 음료
– 시 의회 소식지 최신호 한 부
– 여러 지역의 업체에서 사용할 수 있는 할인 쿠폰북이 제공됩니다.

입장권은 빠르게 매진될 것으로 예상됩니다. 152C좌석 예약은 조 벅윗의 메일(j.buckwheat@twittledontc.net)로 이메일을 보내주세요.

어휘 resident 주민, 거주자 attend 참석하다 the elderly 노인들, 어르신들 complimentary 무료의 soft drink 탄산음료 booklet 소책자 voucher 할인권, 쿠폰

151 주제 / 목적

번역 행사의 주 목적은?

(A) 음식 공급업체의 개업 축하
(B) 신설된 쓰레기 수거 정책의 개요 설명
(C) 지역 기업들을 위한 건축 허가 논의
(D) 자원봉사자들의 공로 치하

해설 첫 번째 문단 두 번째 문장에 행사의 목적이 잘 나타나 있다. 청년 자원봉사자들의 공로를 기리는 자리가 될 것이라면서, 자원봉사자들은 거리에서 쓰레기를 치우고 어르신들을 위해 음식을 제공하는 활동을 열심히 했다(This event is to mark the achievements of our young volunteers, whose hard work has included clearing trash from our streets and providing a catering service to the elderly)고 공로를 치하하고 있다. 따라서 정답은 (D)이다.

▶▶ **Paraphrasing** 지문의 **to mark the achievements of our young volunteers** → 정답의 **To celebrate the achievements of volunteers**

152 사실 관계 확인

번역 행사에 대해 명시되지 않은 것은?

(A) 노령 거주민들은 무료로 입장할 수 있다.
(B) 시장이 참석할 것이다.
(C) 입장권은 이메일로 예매할 수 있다.
(D) 음료수가 제공될 것이다.

해설 보기에 언급된 내용을 지문에서 하나씩 찾아 확인해 본다. 첫 문단 마지막 문장에서 시상자로 토니 그리본스 시장이 참석할 것(Twittledon mayor Tony Gribbons will present the awards)이라고 한 것에서 (B)를, 세 번째 문단 마지막 문장에서 좌석 예약을 예약하려면 조 벅윗에게 이메일을 보내라(To reserve your place, please e-mail Jo Buckwheat at j.buckwheat@twittledontc.net)고 한 것에서 (C)를, 두 번째 문단 첫 항목에서 무료 청량음료(A complimentary soft drink)가 제공될 것이라고 한 것에서 (D)를 확인할 수 있다. 따라서 언급되지 않은 (A)가 정답이다.

▶▶ **Paraphrasing** 지문의 **Twittledon mayor Tony Gribbons will present** → 보기의 **It will be attended by the town mayor.**
지문의 **To reserve your place, please e-mail** → 보기의 **Tickets can be reserved by e-mail.**
지문의 **A complimentary soft drink** → 보기의 **Drinks**

153-154 문자 메시지

피터 레드먼드	오후 2:52

안녕, 수잔. 오늘 아침 교육 워크숍에서 안 보이시던데요. 전직원 필참이었는데. 깜빡했어요? 걱정하지 마세요, 다음 달에 보충하시면 됩니다.

수잔 바클리	오후 2:54

안녕 피터. 153오늘 아침에 회의에 가는 길이었는데 길이 꽉 막혔어요. 트럭 두 대가 사고가 나서 제시간에 가지를 못했어요.

피터 레드먼드	오후 3:02

아, 뉴스에서 그것에 대해 들었어요. 정당한 사유가 되겠네요. 9월 교육 워크숍으로 등록해 드릴까요?

수잔 바클리	오후 3:06

그 워크숍 날짜들을 봤는데 아마도 전 워크숍들이 있는 날 무역박람회에 참석해야 할 거예요. **154**제가 10월에 있는 워크숍에 참석하면 어떨까요?

피터 레드먼드	오후 3:21

물론 좋죠. **154**인사과의 로버트에게 연락해서 필요한 준비를 하도록 하겠습니다.

수잔 바클리	오후 3:33

고마워요, 피터. 오늘 오전 회의 회의록을 좀 팩스로 보내 줄래요?

피터 레드먼드	오후 3:38

회의록은 캐롤라인에게 요청하셔야 할 거예요. 제가 알기로는 오늘 아침 회의록 작성은 캐롤라인이 담당했습니다.

어휘 staff 직원 make up 보상하다, 보충하다 on one's way to ~로 가는 길에 traffic jam 교통 체증 involve 수반하다 on time 제시간에 valid 정당한, 타당한 book 예약하다 trade fair 무역박람회 arrangement 준비 minutes 회의록 in charge of ~을 맡아서, 담당해서

153 사실 관계 확인

번역 바클리 씨에 대해 알 수 있는 것은?
(A) 그녀는 현재 무역박람회에 참석하고 있다.
(B) 그녀는 오전에 워크숍을 이끌었다.
(C) 그녀는 지각 출근했다.
(D) 그녀는 차 사고가 났다.

해설 2시 54분 바클리 씨가 보낸 메시지에서 트럭 사고로 인해 길이 막혀 제시간에 출근할 수 없었다(I was on my way to the meeting this morning, but I got stuck in a traffic jam. There was an accident involving two trucks, so I couldn't make it in on time)고 했다. 따라서 정답은 (C)이다.

▶▶ **Paraphrasing** 지문의 **couldn't make it in on time**
→ 정답의 **was late**

154 의도 파악

번역 오후 3시 21분에 레드먼드 씨가 "물론 좋죠"라고 쓸 때, 그 의도는 무엇인가?
(A) 그는 인사부장이 자신의 사무실에 있을 것이라 생각한다.
(B) 그는 서류에 대한 바클리 씨의 요청을 받아들이고 있다.
(C) 그는 무역박람회가 많은 매출로 이어질 것이라 확신한다.
(D) 그는 바클리 씨가 10월 워크숍에 참석할 수 있다고 동의한다.

해설 3시 6분 메시지에서 바클리 씨가 워크숍이 있는 날짜에 무역박람회에 참석해야 한다면서 10월에 있을 워크숍에 참석할 수 있는지(How about I attend one in October)를 묻자, 가능하다면서 인사과의 로버트에게 연락해서 필요한 준비를 하겠다(I'll contact Robert in HR and get him to make the necessary arrangements)고 했다. 따라서 인용문 Sure thing이 의도하는 바는 바클리 씨가 10월에 워크숍에 참석할 수 있다는 것이므로, 정답은 (D)이다.

어휘 HR 인사부 (human resources)

155-157 기사

스탠버그 미술과 공예 박물관은 이번 주 모든 이용객을 위한 시설 개선 사업 계약을 체결했다고 발표했다. 박물관 대표 제시 캣젠 씨는 이를 가능하게 한 것은 지역 재계 거물인 찰리 해밀턴 씨의 후원금이라고 기자들에게 전했다. **155, 157**상당한 액수의 이 기부금은 박물관의 부속 건물 신축에 쓰일 예정인데, 이 건물에는 박물관이 보유한 르네상스 시대 미술품 및 공예품들을 전시할 계획이다. 이들 작품 중 일부는 공간 부족으로 인해 수개월 동안 창고에 보관되어 왔다.

캣젠 씨는 또 이번 투자가 스탠버그 박물관에는 그야말로 꼭 필요한 시기에 이루어졌다고 말했다. **156**그동안 박물관이 재정적 어려움을 겪고 있다는 추측이 무성했고 20명의 직원들은 상황이 개선되지 않으면 더 이상 운영이 불가능하다고 우려해 왔다. 이제 지역 주민들과 관광객 모두 앞으로 오래도록 눈부신 전시 작품들을 맘껏 누릴 수 있게 됐다.

어휘 announce 발표하다 patron 고객, 이용객 representative 대표자 grant 보조금 tycoon 거물 substantial (양이) 상당한, 많은 donate 기부하다 fund 자금을 제공하다 house 수용하다 era 시대 speculation 추측 viable 실행 가능한 rectify 수정하다, 교정하다 stunning 멋진, 훌륭한 for many years to come 앞으로 오랫동안

155 주제 / 목적

번역 기사의 주제는 무엇인가?
(A) 한 유명 예술가의 삶
(B) 박물관 확장
(C) 시청 회의
(D) 르네상스 시대의 미술

해설 첫 번째 단락 마지막 문장에서 기부금으로 박물관의 부속 건물을 신축할 것이며, 신축 건물에 박물관이 보유한 르네상스 시대 미술품 및 공예품들을 전시할 계획(The substantial sum of money donated will fund the building of a new museum wing, in which the museum plans to house its collection of arts and crafts from the Renaissance era)이라고 했다. 따라서 박물관 확장에 관한 기사임을 알 수 있으므로, 정답은 (B)이다.

▶▶ **Paraphrasing** 지문의 **the building of a new museum wing**
→ 정답의 **The expansion of a museum**

156 추론 / 암시

번역 스탠버그 박물관에 대해 암시된 것은?
(A) 현재 100명이 넘는 직원을 고용하고 있다.
(B) 이름을 찰리 해밀턴 박물관으로 변경할 것이다.
(C) 전시품들이 다른 건물로 옮겨졌다.
(D) 최근에 거의 파산 지경에 이르렀다고 여겨졌다.

해설 두 번째 단락 두 번째 문장에서 그동안 박물관이 재정적 어려움을 겪고 있다는 추측이 무성했으며 20명의 직원들은 상황이 개선되지 않으면 더 이상 운영이 불가능하다고 우려해 왔다(Speculation had been mounting that the museum was experiencing financial difficulties, with its twenty employees fearing it would not be viable for it to continue operating if the situation wasn't rectified)고 했다. 따라서 박물관이 재정적 어려움을 겪었다는 것을 알 수 있으므로, 정답은 (D)이다.

157 문장 삽입

번역 [1], [2], [3], [4]로 표시된 곳 중에서 다음 문장이 들어가기에 가장 적합한 곳은?

"이들 작품들 중 일부는 공간 부족으로 인해 수개월 동안 창고에 보관되어 왔다."

(A) [1]
(B) [2]
(C) [3]
(D) [4]

해설 삽입 문장 '이들 작품들 중 일부는 공간 부족으로 인해 수개월 동안 창고에 보관되어 왔다(Some of these pieces have been held in storage for several months due to a lack of space)'를 통해 삽입 문장 앞에는 작품 보관과 관련된 내용이 오는 것이 자연스럽다. 따라서 신축 건물에 박물관이 보유한 르네상스 시대 미술품 및 공예품들을 전시할 계획(the museum plans to house its collection of arts and crafts from the Renaissance era)이라는 문장 뒤인 [3]에 들어가야 흐름이 자연스러워지므로, 정답은 (C)이다.

158-160 회람

수신: 로버트 월시, 트레버 패트리지, 애니 테일러
발신: 케리 그래이엄, 교육 담당관
날짜: 8월 3일
주제: 필수 교육

레미컬 리미티드의 전직원들에게 분야 혁신의 최첨단을 점하기 위하여 우리의 시설들을 지속적으로 개선하고 새로이 업데이트하는 것은 아주 중요합니다. ¹⁵⁸어제 많은 실험실 장비들이 도착했습니다. 여기에는 새 계량컵, 실험관, 현미경 등이 포함되어 있습니다. 또한 고성능 가열기도 새로 들어왔습니다. ¹⁵⁸일단 설치가 끝나면 여러분들은 이 장비들을 실험에 사용할 수 있게 됩니다. 하지만 이 고가의 장비들을 사용하기 전에 모든 직원들은 필수 교육을 받아야 하며, 이 내용은 직원 핸드북에도 명시되어 있습니다. 교육은 금요일에 실시될 것입니다. ¹⁵⁹그때까지 제가 첨부해 드린 금요일 일정을 숙지해 주십시오. 거기에 나와 있듯이 오전 9시에 시작합니다. 꼭 이 시간에 맞추어 도착하실 것을 당부합니다.

또한 우리 회사 안전 감독관인 빌 켄라이트가 실험실에서 착용할 안전복을 새로 지급해 주었습니다. ¹⁶⁰ᴮ⁽ᶜ이 노란색 발광 작업복 착용은 중요한데, 시험을 통해 내열성이 입증되었기 때문입니다. ¹⁶⁰ᴬ안전복 사이즈는 소, 중, 대 중에서 고를 수 있습니다. 이메일로 원하는 사이즈를 저에게 알려주시면 금요일에 제가 직접 가지고 가겠습니다.

케리 그래이엄 올림

어휘 mandatory 강제의, 의무의 vital 극히 중대한, 불가결한 constantly 끊임없이, 항상 cutting edge 최첨단 innovation 혁신 lab 실험실 equipment 장비 microscope 현미경 high-powered 고성능의, 강력한 install 설치하다 conduct 실행하다 state 명시하다 familiarize 익숙하게 하다 agenda 의제, 일정 be due to ~하기로 되어 있다 promptly 정확히 제시간에 apparel 의상, 옷 luminous 빛이 나는, 야광의 outfit 옷, 복장 heatproof 내열성의 gear 장비, 복장

158 추론 / 암시

번역 메모는 누구를 대상으로 하겠는가?
(A) 과학자들
(B) 배송 운전기사들
(C) 안전 감독관들
(D) 교육 담당관들

해설 첫 번째 단락 초반부에서 계량컵, 실험관, 현미경, 고성능 가열기 등 주문한 실험실 장비를 어제 받았다(Yesterday, we received a delivery of a large volume of lab equipment)고 했으며, 이어지는 문장에서 장비 설치가 끝나면 실험을 하는 데 사용할 수 있을 것(Once this equipment is installed, you will be able to use it to conduct your experiments)이라고 했다. 따라서 실험을 하는 과학자들을 대상으로 한 메모임을 알 수 있으므로, 정답은 (A)이다.

159 세부 사항

번역 그래이엄 씨가 메모에 첨부한 것은?
(A) 명세서
(B) 교육 일정
(C) 새 장비
(D) 직원 핸드북

해설 첫 번째 단락 후반부에서 금요일에 교육이 있다며, 그때까지 자신이 첨부한 일정을 숙지하라(In the meantime, please familiarize yourselves with the agenda for Friday that I have attached)고 했다. 따라서 그래이엄 씨는 교육 일정을 첨부했음을 알 수 있으므로, 정답은 (B)이다.

▶▶ **Paraphrasing** 지문의 **the agenda**
→ 정답의 **A training schedule**

160 사실 관계 확인

번역 안전복에 대해 명시되지 않은 것은?
(A) 여러 사이즈로 제공된다.
(B) 밝은 색이다.
(C) 내열성이 있다.
(D) 직원들이 비용을 지불할 것이다.

해설 보기에 언급된 내용을 지문에서 하나씩 찾아 확인해 본다. 두 번째 단락에서 안전복(safety apparel)에 대해 언급하고 있는데, 노란색 발광 작업복(These luminous yellow outfits are important)이라고 한 것에서 (B)를, 시험을 통해 내열성이 입증되었다(they have been tested and found to be heatproof)고 한 것에서 (C)를, 소, 중, 대 사이즈 중에서 고를 수 있다(You can choose from small, medium, or large sizes of safety gear)고 한 것을 통해 (A)를 확인할 수 있다. 따라서 정답은 언급되지 않은 (D)이다.

▶▶ **Paraphrasing** 지문의 **luminous yellow**
→ 보기의 **brightly colored**
지문의 **heatproof** → 보기의 **heat resistant**
지문의 **choose from small, medium, or large sizes**
→ 보기의 **available in a range of sizes**

Test 9

161-163 기사

11월 1일 (존스빌) – 현 존스빌 자동차 공장 부지의 미래에 대한 추측이 무성한 가운데 오늘 부동산 개발업체 라이트홈 리미티드가 약 2천만 달러로 추산되는 금액으로 해당 부지를 매입했다. 부지 매입 후 **161**라이트홈은 해당 부지에 고급 아파트 100세대 건설 허가를 받기 위해 즉각적으로 시 도시계획과에 청사진을 제출했다. **163C**이 아파트들은 존스빌에 번창하고 있는 법조 분야에서 일하기 위해 이사 오는 많은 젊은 전문직 종사자들을 겨냥할 것이다.

162라이트홈 리미티드는 20년 전 미구엘 로페즈에 의해 설립됐다. 은퇴한 그는 아들인 파블로 로페즈를 후계자로 훈련시켰으며 현재 회사의 CEO를 맡고 있다. 어제 있은 기자회견에서 파블로 로페즈는 개발 프로젝트에 대해 더 상세하게 설명했다. 로페즈 씨에 따르면 멜우드 그로브라는 이름으로 5층짜리 콘도미니엄이 지어질 것이라 말했다. **163A**그뿐 아니라 모든 거주민들이 사용할 수 있는 공동 수영장, 체육관 시설들이 지어질 것이다. **163D**로페즈 씨는 또한 각 아파트 세대는 고속 인터넷을 무료로 제공받게 된다고 확인해 주었다. 그는 프로젝트의 일정을 설명하면서 기자회견을 마쳤는데, 그는 프로젝트가 18개월 내에 완료되기를 희망하고 있다. 이 최신의 부동산 개발은 최근 몇 년간 존스빌 도심에 눈에 띄게 활기를 불어 넣어 준 많은 프로젝트들 중 하나이다.

어휘 speculation 추측 plot 대지, 터 site 현장, 장소 property 부동산 purchase 구입하다 estimate 추산하다 submit 제출하다 blueprint 청사진 condo 콘도, 분양 아파트 be targeted at ~을 겨냥하다 thriving 번성하는 sector 분야, 부문 found 설립하다, 세우다 successor 계승자, 후계자 press conference 기자회견 complimentary 무료의, 공짜의 access 접속, 접근 outline 개요를 기술하다 yield 생산하다, 산출하다 rejuvenation 회복, 회춘

161 주제 / 목적

번역 기사는 주로 무엇에 관한 내용인가?
(A) 자동차 공장 건설
(B) 법률 회사 설립
(C) 체육관 개장
(D) 새로운 건축물의 건설

해설 첫 번째 단락 초반부에서 부동산 개발업체 라이트홈이 구입한 부지에 고급 아파트 건설을 허가받기 위해 시 도시계획과에 청사진을 제출했다(Righthome immediately submitted blueprints to the city's planning department in order to receive permission to build 100 luxury condos on the site)고 했으므로, 정답은 (D)이다.

▶▶ **Paraphrasing** 지문의 **build 100 luxury condos** → 정답의 **The building of some new structure**

162 추론 / 암시

번역 파블로 로페즈 씨는 누구이겠는가?
(A) 변호사
(B) 도시 계획가
(C) 부동산 개발업자
(D) 인터넷 영업직원

해설 두 번째 단락 초반부에서 20년 전에 라이트홈 리미티드를 설립한 미구엘 로페즈는 은퇴하고 현재는 아들인 파블로 로페즈가 라이트홈 리미티드의 CEO를 맡고 있다(Righthome Ltd. was founded by Miguel Lopez twenty years ago. After retiring, he trained as his successor his son, Pablo Lopez, who is now CEO of the company)고 했다. 첫 번째 단락 첫 문장의 property developer Righthome Ltd.를 통해 라이트홈 리미티드는 부동산 개발업체임을 알 수 있으므로, 정답은 (C)이다.

163 사실 관계 확인

번역 멜우드 그로브에 대해 명시되지 않은 것은?
(A) 레저 시설들이 포함된다.
(B) 키카로로 출입한다.
(C) 젊은 전문직 인구를 겨냥한다.
(D) 인터넷이 무료로 제공된다.

해설 두 번째 단락 중반부에서 주민들이 사용할 수 있는 공동 수영장, 체육관 시설들이 지어질 것(In addition, a communal swimming pool and gym facilities will be built on the site for all residents to use)이라고 한 것에서 (A)를, 이어지는 문장에서 각 아파트 세대에 고속 인터넷을 무료로 제공할 것(Mr. Lopez also confirmed that each apartment will be provided with complimentary high-speed Internet access)이라고 한 것에서 (D)를 확인할 수 있다. 또, 첫 번째 단락 마지막 문장에서 법조 분야에서 일하기 위해 이사 오는 많은 젊은 전문직 종사자들을 겨냥하고 있다(These properties will be targeted at the many young professionals moving to Jonesville to work in the thriving legal sector here)는 것에서 (C)를 확인할 수 있으므로, 정답은 (B)이다.

▶▶ **Paraphrasing** 지문의 **a communal swimming pool and gym facilities** → 보기의 **leisure facilities** 지문의 **complimentary** → 보기의 **free**

164-167 온라인 채팅

데일 윈저	오후 4:12
웨인, 안녕하세요. 저 지금 막 이사님들과 화상 회의를 했습니다. **164**이사님들이 우리 창고 신축에 진전이 없어 정말 심기가 불편해 보였습니다.	

웨인 헤네시	오후 4:14
165이사님들이 정확히 무엇이 불만인지 말씀을 하셨나요? 저는 완공 일정이 상당히 유동적이라 생각했었는데요.	

데일 윈저	오후 4:21
그랬었죠. 그런데 그분들이 이후 기한을 6월 1일로 정했습니다. **165**그렇게 하지 않으면 우리가 충분한 옷들을 보관하지 못하게 되고 고객에게 배송하는 데 시간이 더 걸릴 겁니다.	

웨인 헤네시	오후 4:29
잠시만요. 베스를 추가할게요…	

(베스 토디가 그룹 채팅창에 입장했습니다)	오후 4:30

웨인 헤네시	오후 4:34
안녕, 베스 **167**우리 창고 프로젝트를 위해 건축 회사를 새로 찾아야 할 것 같아요. 현 업체는 기한을 맞추는 데 애를 먹고 있습니다.	

| 베스 토디 | 오후 4:40 |

그거 골치 아프게 됐네요. **167**현 업체와 계약 조건에 합의하는 데 시간이 많이 걸렸어요. **166**이사님들이 건설업체 교체에 강경한 입장인가요?

| 데일 윈저 | 오후 4:46 |

그런 것 같아요. 제가 그분들에게 기한 변경이 불합리하다는 것을 설명하려 애썼지만 좀처럼 생각을 바꾸려 하지 않으시네요.

| 베스 토디 | 오후 4:50 |

알겠습니다. **166**그럼 다음 주 회의에서 이사님들에게 이 문제에 대한 제 의견을 말씀드려야겠네요.

| 데일 윈저 | 오후 4:57 |

잘 되길 빌어요. 그분들을 설득할 사람은 베스밖에 없어요!

어휘 conference call 화상회의 upset 마음이 상한, 속상한 progress 진전, 진척 warehouse 창고 completion 완수, 완공 flexible 유연한, 유동적인 deadline 마감 시한, 기한 source 공급자를 찾다 struggle 애를 먹다, 분투하다 a pain in the neck 골칫거리, 문제 인물 be set on -ing ~하기로 굳게 마음먹다 unreasonable 불합리한, 부당한 convince 설득하다

164 주제 / 목적

번역 이 논의의 주제는 무엇인가?
(A) 회의 준비
(B) 이사 선임
(C) 창고 건설
(D) 의류 생산

해설 주제를 묻는 문제로, 주제는 대개 지문 서두 부분에 제시되는 경우가 많다. 여기서도 4시 12분 윈저 씨의 메시지에서 이사들과 화상 회의를 했는데, 창고 신축에 진전이 없어 그들의 심기가 불편해 보였다(They are really upset about the lack of progress on building our warehouse)고 했다. 따라서 창고 신축 공사에 대해 논의할 것임을 알 수 있으므로, 정답은 (C)이다.

▶▶ **Paraphrasing** 지문의 building our warehouse
→ 정답의 The construction of a warehouse

165 세부 사항

번역 이사들이 우려하고 있는 한가지 문제는 무엇인가?
(A) 계약 조건들이 변경될 수 있다.
(B) 배송 시간이 증가할 수 있다.
(C) 건축 자재 가격이 더 비싸질 수 있다.
(D) 건축 허가가 승인되지 않을 수도 있다.

해설 이사들의 불만 사항이 정확히 무엇인지를 묻는 4시 14분 헤네시 씨의 질문에 윈저 씨는 충분한 옷을 보관할 수 없어 배송이 더 오래 걸릴 것(Otherwise, we won't be able to store enough clothes, and it will take longer to deliver our clothes to customers)이라고 했으므로, 정답은 (B)이다.

▶▶ **Paraphrasing** 지문의 it will take longer to deliver
→ 정답의 Delivery times may be increased.

166 추론 / 암시

번역 토디 씨에 대해 추론할 수 있는 것은?
(A) 의상 디자인에 관여한다.
(B) 오늘 화상 회의를 진행했다.
(C) 건설 회사의 매니저이다.
(D) 다음 주에 이사들과 만나 회의를 한다.

해설 건설업체 교체에 대한 이사들의 입장이 강경한지를 묻는 토디 씨의 질문에 윈저 씨는 기한 변경이 불합리하다고 이사들을 설득하려 했으나 이사들은 생각을 바꾸려고 하지 않았다고 했다. 그러자 4시 50분 메시지에서 토디 씨는 다음 주 회의에서 이 문제에 대해 이사들에게 자신의 의견을 말하겠다(Well, I'll have to tell them my opinion on the matter at the meeting next week)고 했으므로, 토디 씨는 다음 주에 이사들과 회의가 있다는 것을 추론할 수 있다. 따라서 정답은 (D)이다.

167 의도 파악

번역 오후 4시 40분에 토디 씨가 "그거 골치 아프게 됐네요"라고 쓸 때, 그 의도는 무엇인가?
(A) 그녀는 휴식 시간을 갖고 싶어 한다.
(B) 그녀는 건설 현장이 너무 멀다고 생각하다.
(C) 그녀는 변경이 불편을 초래할 것이라 생각한다.
(D) 그녀는 예산상의 제약에 대해 우려한다.

해설 의도 파악 문제는 인용문 앞뒤 문장에서 문제 해결의 단서를 찾을 수 있다. 여기서도 인용문 바로 앞인 4시 34분 메시지에서 헤네시 씨는 현 업체가 기한을 맞추는 데 애를 먹고 있다면서 창고 프로젝트를 위해 건축 회사를 새로 찾아야 할 것 같다(I think we're going to have to source a new construction company for the warehouse project)고 했으며, 인용문 바로 뒤에서 토디 씨는 현 업체와 계약 조건에 합의하는 데도 시간이 많이 걸렸다(It took a long time to agree on the contract with the current firm)고 했다. 따라서 토디 씨의 말이 의도하는 바는, 업체를 변경하는 것이 불편을 초래할 것이라는 (C)가 가장 적절하다.

168-171 웹페이지

| 패키지 상품 | CEO 프로필 | 고객 추천 | 여행지 |

170A저희 터치스타는 지난 25년간 모든 고객들이 꿈을 실현할 수 있도록 도와왔습니다. **168**저희는 지역 사회에서 최상의 패키지 투어 상품을 제공하는 것으로 잘 알려져 있고, 저희 고객님들은 친구들에게 저희 회사를 추천하는 일도 많습니다. **170D**CEO인 밥 앤더슨의 지휘하에 저희 직원들은 젊은 친구들의 단체여행이든 아니면 어르신 부부의 여행이든 고객에게 적합한 상품을 찾도록 도와드릴 수 있다고 자신합니다.

169고객이 상품을 선택하실 때, 저희는 이번 여름에 무엇을 가장 하고 싶은지에 대해 시간을 들여 잘 생각해 보시라 권해 드립니다. 아이가 아직 어린 가정의 고객이라면 체험이 많은 패키지 상품은 별로 적합하지 않다고 생각하실 겁니다. 마찬가지로 아드레날린이 샘솟는 여름을 원하는 고객이라면 저희의 가족 패키지 상품에는 실망하실 수 있습니다. **171**저희는 전담 전문가가 24시간 대기하며 예약 전 여러분이 갖게 되는 어떤 질문이라도 답해 드립니다. 그들은 당신의 전화를 받기 위해 대기하고 있습니다.

Test 9

저희는 이번 여름에 다양한 상품들을 안내하게 되어 기쁩니다. 저희의 캐리비언 드림라인 패키지는 일주일간 여러 섬을 방문하고 여러 가지 레저 활동을 할 수 있도록 해 드립니다. 이 패키지 상품은 대개 고래 구경 및 탐조 활동을 좋아하는 나이가 있는 여행객들에게 인기가 좋습니다. **170B**반대로, 저희의 트로피컬 러시 패키지는 스릴을 찾는 분들에게 스카이다이빙과 번지 점프와 같은 극한 스포츠 활동을 할 수 있도록 해 줍니다. 저희의 미니 어드벤처러 상품은 젊은 가족들에 가장 적합한데, 여기에는 전용 수영장이 딸린 5성급 리조트 숙박이 포함됩니다. 활동이 원활하게 진행되도록 모든 패키지 상품에는 전문 가이드들이 동행합니다.

> **어휘** testimonial 추천서, 추천의 글 destination 목적지, 행선지 fulfill 달성하다, 실현하다 well known 잘 알려진 supreme 최고의, 최상의 recommend 추천하다 권하다 confident 자신 있는 suit 적합하다, 어울리다 senior 노령의 reflect on ~에 대해 숙고하다 unsuitable 적합하지 않은 in search of ~을 찾아서 dedicated 전담의 book 예약하다 engage in ~에 관여하다 a number of 다수의 suited for ~에게 적합한 present (특정 장소에) 있는, 참석한

168 추론 / 암시

번역 터치스타는 어떤 회사이겠는가?
(A) 여행사
(B) 가족 법률 회사
(C) 회계 법인
(D) 신문사

해설 첫 번째 단락의 두 번째 문장에서 터치스타는 지역 사회에 최상의 패키지 투어 상품을 제공하는 것으로 잘 알려져 있다(We are well known throughout the local community for providing tour packages of supreme quality)고 했다. 따라서 터치스타는 여행사임을 알 수 있으므로, 정답은 (A)이다.

169 세부 사항

번역 웹페이지가 고객들에게 하라고 제안하는 것은?
(A) 자신들의 목적을 신중히 고려하기
(B) 고객 추천평 읽기.
(C) 경험 많은 직원 요청하기
(D) 전화로 납부 확인하기

해설 두 번째 단락 첫 문장에서 여행 상품을 선택할 때 이번 여름에 무엇을 가장 하고 싶은지에 대해 시간을 들여 잘 생각해 보라고 권한다(When making your choice, we recommend taking plenty of time to reflect on what you want from your summer)고 했다. 따라서 여행 목적을 신중히 고려하라고 제안하는 것이므로, 정답은 (A)이다.

> ▶▶ **Paraphrasing** 지문의 **taking plenty of time to reflect on what you want**
> → 정답의 **Consider their goals carefully**

170 사실 관계 확인

번역 터치스타에 대해 명시되지 않은 것은?
(A) 20년 이상 영업을 해 오고 있다.
(B) 신나는 활동들을 제공한다.
(C) 우호적인 언론의 평을 받았다.
(D) 다양한 연령대의 고객들을 대상으로 한다.

해설 보기에 언급된 내용을 지문에서 찾아 하나씩 확인해 본다. 첫 단락 첫 번째 문장에서 터치스타가 25년간 영업을 해 오고 있다(We at Touchstar have 25 years of experience helping all of our clients to fulfill their dreams)고 한 것에서 (A)를, 마지막 단락 중반부에서 스카이다이빙과 번지 점프와 같은 극한 스포츠 활동을 할 수 있도록 해 준다(Conversely, our Tropical Rush package allows thrill seekers to take part in a number of extreme hobbies, including skydiving and bungee jumping)고 한 것에서 (B)를 확인할 수 있다. 또한 첫 번째 단락 마지막 문장에서 젊은 친구들의 단체여행이든 어르신 부부의 여행이든 고객에게 적합한 상품을 찾도록 도와준다(our staff will be able to assist you in finding something to suit you, whether you are a group of young friends or a senior couple)고 한 것에서 (D)를 확인할 수 있다. 따라서 정답은 (C)이다.

> ▶▶ **Paraphrasing** 지문의 **25 years**
> → 보기의 **for over two decades**
> 지문의 **extreme hobbies, including skydiving and bungee jumping**
> → 보기의 **exciting activities**
> 지문의 **a group of young friends or a senior couple** → 보기의 **a range of age groups**

171 문장 삽입

번역 [1], [2], [3], [4]로 표시된 곳 중에서 다음 문장이 들어가기에 가장 적합한 곳은?
"그들은 당신의 전화를 받기 위해 대기하고 있습니다."

(A) [1]
(B) [2]
(C) [3]
(D) [4]

해설 주어진 문장의 They나 take your call이 문제 해결의 단서가 될 수 있는데, 주어진 문장 앞에는 누군가가 문의 전화를 받기 위해 항시 대기하고 있다(We have dedicated experts available 24 hours a day to answer any queries that you may have before booking)는 내용이 예상된다. 따라서 주어진 문장은 [2]에 들어가야 글의 흐름이 자연스러워진다. 주어진 문장의 They는 dedicated experts를 가리킨다.

172-175 일정표

> **볼티모어 헤럴드**
> *소개식 일정*
>
> **장소**: 헤럴드 오피스 트레이닝 스위트 – B 층
> **날짜**: 3월 19일 월요일
>
> **목적** **172**여러분이 자신의 업무를 곧 시작하기 전에 우리 신문사의 다양한 부서와 각 부서 업무를 파악하는 것이 중요합니다. 이번 소개 프로그램은 여러분에게 이러한 경험을 가장 효율적으로 선사하기 위해 마련되었습니다.
>
> **의제**: **175**이날 일정은 데니스 퍼맨 전무가 구성했으며 아래에 첨부되어 있습니다. 의제에 대한 질문은 퍼맨 씨에게 전화로 (내선 3299) 해 주십시오.

시간	활동	추가 상세 내역	장소
1759:00~10:00	인사 및 소개	**175**직원들은 전무와 직접 만나 소개를 한다.	브리즈데일 회의실
10:00~12:00	문제	우리 신문사가 공통으로 채용하는 서식 설정 방식 및 기술 소개	세미나실 C
1741:00~3:00	법률 문제	비밀 유지 등의 법적 의무에 대한 논의. **174**차 및 커피 제공됨.	야민 미디어 스위트
3:00~4:00	시스템 및 제어	**173**워드 프로세싱, 데이터베이스, 스프레드시트 프로그램 등을 포함한 다양한 소프트웨어 사용 소개.	레비 스위트
4:00~5:00	업계 윤리	취재 시 신문사의 평판과 업계 윤리를 지키는 방법에 대한 브라이언 크랜필드의 강연	세미나실 C

어휘 induction 소개식, 취임식 familiar 익숙한 various 다양한 commence 시작하다 efficient 효율적인 executive director 전무, 상무 agenda 의제 extension 내선(번호) in person 몸소, 직접 formatting style 서식 설정 방식 employ 채택하다, 채용하다 obligation 의무 confidentiality 기밀성, 비밀성 integrity 진실성, 정직 ensure 보장하다 reputation 평판 ethics 윤리 maintain 유지하다

172 주제 / 목적

번역 3월 19일 행사의 주 목적은 무엇인가?
(A) 공석 채용 공고
(B) 기사에 쓰일 정보 수집
(C) 신규 직원 교육
(D) 신문 판매 부수 통계 수집

해설 행사의 목적을 묻는 문제로, 행사의 목적은 Why 항목에 잘 나타나 있다. 자신의 업무를 시작하기 전에 우리 신문사의 다양한 부서와 각 부서 업무를 파악하는 것이 중요하다(It is vital that you quickly become familiar with the various departments of our newspaper company, and the work that they do, before commencing your role)고 했으므로, 신규 직원 교육을 위해 마련된 행사임을 알 수 있다. 따라서 (C)가 정답이다.

173 세부 사항

번역 직원들이 컴퓨터 사용 관련 활동에 참여하는 장소는?
(A) 레비 스위트
(B) 브리즈데일 회의실
(C) 세미나실 C
(D) 야민 미디어 스위트

해설 세부 일정표를 보면, 워드 프로세싱, 데이터베이스, 스프레드시트 프로그램 등을 포함한 컴퓨터 관련 활동(Instruction in using a variety of software, including our word-processing, database, and spreadsheet packages)은 3시에서 4시 사이에 레비 스위트(The Levy Suite)에서 열릴 것을 알 수 있으므로, 정답은 (A)이다.

▶▶ **Paraphrasing** 지문의 using a variety of software, including our word-processing, database, and spreadsheet packages → 질문의 activities related to computing

174 세부 사항

번역 음료는 언제 마실 수 있나?
(A) 9시에서 10시 사이
(B) 10시에서 12시 사이
(C) 1시에서 3시 사이
(D) 3시에서 4시 사이

해설 세부 일정표를 보면, 1시에서 3시 사이에 차와 커피가 제공될(Tea and coffee served) 것임을 알 수 있다. 따라서 (C)가 정답이다.

▶▶ **Paraphrasing** 지문의 Tea and coffee → 질문의 some beverages

175 추론 / 암시

번역 행사 참석자들은 오전 9시에 무엇을 하겠는가?
(A) 브라이언 크랜필드 강연 청취
(B) 법적 의무 사항 논의
(C) 데니스 퍼맨 만나기
(D) 기사 집필 연습

해설 9 A.M.이 문제 해결의 단서로, 일정표를 보면 행사 참석자들은 9시에 전무를 만나 소개를 할 것(Staff members will be introduced to the executive director in person)임을 알 수 있다. 또한 의제(Agenda) 항목을 보면 데니스 퍼맨 전무가 일정을 구성했다(The schedule for the day has been designed by executive director Dennis Furman)고 했다. 따라서 참석자들이 9시에 만나게 될 전무는 데니스 퍼맨임을 추론할 수 있으므로, 정답은 (C)이다.

176-180 기사 + 편지

허플튼 푸드 마켓 큰 인기

일리노이 주 허플튼 (7월 15일)—허플튼 시는 지난주 오랫동안 기다려 온 푸드 마켓을 개장했다. **176**주최측이 이제 매달 마지막 주말에 **177**운영하기를 희망하는 이 시장의 첫 개장 기간은 눈부시게 화창한 날씨에 만 명 이상이 시를 방문하면서 큰 성공을 거둔 것으로 간주되고 있다. 상인들이 판매한 음식에는 독일 소시지, 프랑스 치즈, 영국의 피시 앤 칩스, 터키의 케밥 등이 있었다. 푸드 마켓은 지역으로 더 많은 관광객을 유치하기 위해 허플튼시 시장이 펼치는 계획의 일환이었다. **178**행사를 홍보하기 위해, 지역 출신 영화 배우가 동원되어 손님들에게 무료 햄버거를 나눠 주었다.

푸드 마켓과 더불어 여러 음식 관련 행사들도 개최됐다. 그 중 가장 인기를 끈 행사는 일본인 셰프 아케미 수키의 요리 시연이었다. 수키 씨는 전문가의 손길로 썰기 기술을 선보인 후 생선을 기름에 조리하면서 넋을 빼놓는 밝은 색의 불꽃을 연출하면서 관중들을 매혹시켰다. **180**또 다른 인기 행사는 요리 대회였다. 경연 부문은 최고의 수프, 닭 요리, 샌드위치, 케이크였으며 각 부문 우승 요리사에게 상이 주어졌다.

어휘 long-awaited 오래도록 기다린 deem 여기다, 생각하다 attract 끌어들이다 gloriously 근사하게, 멋지게 vendor 행상인, 노점상 initiative 계획 promote 판촉하다, 홍보하다 recruit 모집하다 complimentary 무료의 patron 손님, 이용객 demonstration 시연 delight 기쁘게 하다 display 선보이다, 전시하다 slice 썰다, 저미다 mesmerizing 넋을 빼놓는, 마음을 사로잡는

아케미 수키
호스튼 가 86번지
일리노이 주 허플튼 60415

수키 씨께,

우선 지난주 제가 참석한 허플튼 푸드 마켓에서 저는 정말 즐거운 시간을 가졌다는 말씀을 드리고 싶습니다. **178**저와 제 가족은 많은 훌륭한 음식을 만끽했습니다. 저희는 그 유명한 데일 스프링필드에게 직접 햄버거를 대접받았다는 사실이 아직도 믿기지 않습니다!

179이 편지를 쓰는 이유는 제가 현재 허플튼 시내에 일본 식당 개점을 준비하고 있는데 수키 씨가 저희와 함께할 수 있을까 해서입니다.

저희 업체에 대해 조금 더 자세하게 말씀드리겠습니다. 저희는 작년에 문을 열었고, 아시아 대륙 전역의 맛에서 영감을 얻은 다양한 아시아 요리를 제공합니다. **180**저희는 디저트 메뉴를 위해 이미 요리사 샐리 버그스트롬 씨를 영입했습니다. 그녀가 푸드 마켓에서 열린 관련 요리 경연에서 우승을 한 것을 기억하실 텐데요. 수키 씨께서 저희와 함께한다면, 이 사업은 우리 모두에게 크나큰 성공이 될 것이라 자신합니다.

저희는 서로 나눌 이야기가 많을 것이라 생각됩니다. 되도록 빨리 560-2219-8282로 전화 주시면 감사하겠습니다.

파 이스턴 레스토랑
아델 월시 드림

어휘 attend 참석하다 in the process of ~의 과정 중에 cuisine 요리(법) flavor 맛, 풍미 inspire 영감을 주다 continent 대륙 come on board 승선하다 venture 사업, 사업상의 모험 appreciate 고맙게 생각하다

---

176 사실 관계 확인

번역 허플튼 푸드 마켓에 대해 명시된 것은?
(A) 시장이 참석했다.
(B) 시 거주민에게만 개방됐다.
(C) 이전에는 열린 적이 없다.
(D) 날씨가 안 좋아 연기되었다.

해설 기사문의 첫 번째 단락 두 번째 문장에서 허플튼 푸드 마켓의 첫 개장 기간 동안 만 명 이상이 시를 방문하면서 큰 성공을 거두었다(The first-ever session of the market, which organizers now hope to run on the last weekend of every month, was deemed a huge success, attracting over 10,000 visitors to the town on a gloriously sunny day)고 했다. 따라서 허플튼 푸드 마켓이 처음 열렸다는 것을 알 수 있으므로, 정답은 (C)이다.

▶▶ **Paraphrasing** 지문의 **The first-ever session**
→ 정답의 **had never been held before**

---

177 동의어 찾기

번역 기사에서 첫 번째 단락 2행의 "run"과 의미가 가장 가까운 단어는?
(A) 뛰다
(B) 흐르다
(C) 경쟁하다
(D) 운영하다

해설 해당 문장은 '주최측이 이제 매달 마지막 주말에 운영하기를 희망한다'라는 의미로 해석되므로, 여기서 run은 '운영하다'의 의미이다. 따라서 정답은 (D) operate이다.

---

178 연계

번역 스프링필드 씨에 대해 명시된 것은?
(A) 영화 배우이다.
(B) 시장이다.
(C) 유명한 요리사이다.
(D) 독일에서 태어났다.

해설 기사문의 첫 번째 단락 마지막 문장에서 행사를 홍보하기 위해, 지역 출신 영화 배우가 손님들에게 무료 햄버거를 나눠 주었다(To promote the event, a local film star was recruited to distribute complimentary hamburgers to patrons)고 했으며, 편지의 첫 번째 단락 마지막 문장에서 월시 씨는 유명한 데일 스프링필드에게 직접 햄버거를 대접받았다는 사실이 아직도 믿기지 않는다(we still can't believe we were served hamburgers by the famous Dale Springfield)고 했다. 따라서 스프링필드 씨는 영화 배우임을 알 수 있으므로, 정답은 (A)이다.

---

179 세부 사항

번역 월시 씨는 왜 수키 씨에게 연락을 했는가?
(A) 불만을 제기하기 위해
(B) 일자리를 제의하기 위해
(C) 메뉴에 대한 그의 조언을 얻기 위해
(D) 저녁 식사에 그를 초대하기 위해

해설 월시 씨가 수키 씨에게 보낸 편지의 두 번째 단락에서 월시 씨는 편지를 쓴 목적을 밝히고 있다. 월시 씨는 자신이 현재 허플튼 시내에 일본 식당 개점을 준비하고 있는데 수키 씨가 함께할 수 있는지(The reason I am writing is that I am currently in the process of opening a Japanese restaurant in the downtown area of Huffleton and would very much like it if you would join our team)를 묻고 있다. 따라서 월시 씨는 일자리를 제안하기 위해 수키 씨에게 연락한 것임을 알 수 있으므로, 정답은 (B)이다.

▶▶ **Paraphrasing** 지문의 **would very much like it if you would join our team**
→ 정답의 **offer him a job**

---

180 연계

번역 버그스트롬 씨는 어떤 경연에서 우승했겠는가?
(A) 최고의 아이스크림
(B) 최고의 수프
(C) 최고의 닭 요리
(D) 최고의 케이크

해설 편지의 세 번째 단락 후반부에서 디저트 메뉴를 위해 수상 경력이 있는 요리사 샐리 버그스트롬 씨를 영입했다(We already have recruited chef Sally Bergstrom to produce our desserts)고 했다. 기사문의 마지막 문장에서 요리 경연 부문에서는 최고의 수프, 닭 요리, 샌드위치, 케이크였으며 각 부문 우승 요리사에게 상이 주어졌다(Competition categories included making the best soup, chicken dish, sandwich, and cake, with prizes awarded to the winning chef in each category)고 했다. 요리 경연 부문에서 디저트 메뉴는 케이크이므로, 정답은 (D)이다.

181-185 이메일 + 영수증

담당자님께

지난주 저는 홈 컴포트의 가구 설비부에서 새 키친 유닛을 주문했습니다. **182**신속한 설치가 매우 만족스러웠습니다. 설비팀이 이번 주에 저희 집을 이틀 동안 방문해 주셔서 일정대로 설치를 마쳤습니다. **184**그런데 가구 한 부분(#9422)에서 표면 전체에 걸쳐 크게 긁힌 자국을 발견했습니다. 당연히 있어서는 안 될 흠이죠. **181**이 제품 스타일이 제 기대에 **183**맞기 때문에 가능한 한 조속히 동일한 제품으로 교체가 되었으면 합니다. 이메일에 첨부한 영수증을 참조하시기 바랍니다. 제 계정은 AG5929입니다.

미리 말씀드리자면, 저는 2주 후에 휴가를 가기 때문에 그 전까지 이 문제가 꼭 해결되기를 희망합니다. 이 기간 후에는 집에 아무도 없어서 설치팀에게 문을 열어 줄 수가 없으니 여행 전에 이것이 처리가 되었으면 합니다. 미리 감사드립니다.

찰리 맥리 드림

어휘 kitchen unit 키친 유닛, 주방 가구 일습 furnishing 가구, 비품 ecstatic 황홀한 prompt 신속한 installation 설치 notice 발견하다, 알아채다 scratch 할퀸 상처, 자국 surface 표면 unacceptable 받아들일 수 없는, 용납할 수 없는 meet one's expectations 기대에 부응하다 identical 동일한 replacement 대체물, 대체품 at one's earliest convenience 되도록 일찍 receipt 영수증 resolve 해결하다 take care of ~을 처리하다 prior to ~의 전에 in advance 미리, 사전에

영수증

고객 청구 및 배송 주소

이름: 찰리 맥리   계정 번호: AG5929
주소: 블랙 포레스트 가 302번지   전화: 501-533-6669
시: 포틀랜드
군/주: 오리건 97230
국가: 미국

구입 품목

#3218	대리석 주방 조리대	$800
#7032	화강암 바닥 타일 (24 팩)	$400
184#9422	금속 주방 싱크대	$350
#1305	퀵번 가스레인지	$900
	소계:	$2,450
	185설치비:	$300
	총계:	$2,750

홈 컴포트를 이용해 주셔서 감사합니다!

어휘 marble 대리석 granite 화강암 gas stove 가스레인지

181 주제 / 목적

번역 이메일의 목적은 무엇인가?
(A) 주소 변경 신고
(B) 환불 요청
(C) 지시 사항 전달
(D) 교환품 요청

해설 이메일 첫 번째 단락 후반부에서 주문품에 긁힌 자국이 있다면서 제품 스타일이 나의 기대에 맞으니 다른 동일한 제품으로 교체하고 싶다(The item's style meets my expectations, and I would therefore like an identical replacement installed at your earliest convenience)고 했다. 따라서 교환품을 요청하기 위해 쓴 이메일임을 알 수 있으므로, 정답은 (D)이다.

182 세부 사항

번역 맥리 씨는 무엇이 만족스럽다고 말하는가?
(A) 물품의 질
(B) 설치의 신속함
(C) 판매 직원의 친절함
(D) 웹사이트 사용의 용이성

해설 이메일 첫 번째 단락 두 번째 문장에서 맥리 씨는 신속한 설치가 매우 만족스러웠다(I was ecstatic with the prompt installation of the unit)고 했으므로, 정답은 (B)이다.

▶▶ **Paraphrasing**　지문의 **the prompt installation**
→ 정답의 **The speed of the installation**

183 동의어 찾기

번역 이메일에서 첫 번째 단락 5행의 "meets"와 의미가 가장 가까운 단어는?
(A) 수집하다
(B) 소개하다
(C) 동의하다
(D) 만족시키다

해설 해당 문장은 '제품 스타일이 나의 기대에 맞다'라는 의미로 해석되므로, 여기서 meets는 만족시키다'의 의미가 자연스럽다. 따라서 정답은 (D) satisfies이다.

184 연계

번역 맥리 씨의 구매품 중 이메일에서 구체적으로 언급되는 것은?
(A) 대리석 주방 조리대
(B) 화강암 바닥 타일
(C) 금속 주방 싱크대
(D) 퀵번 가스레인지

해설 이메일의 첫 번째 단락 중반부에서 제품 번호가 9422번인 제품(one piece (#9422))에 대해 언급하고 있다. 영수증의 구입 품목(Items Purchased)을 보면, 맥리 씨는 대리석 주방 조리대(3218번), 금속 주방 싱크대(9422번), 화강암 바닥 타일(7032번), 퀵번 레인지(1305번)를 구입했음을 알 수 있다. 제품 번호가 9422번인 것은 금속 주방 싱크대이므로, 정답은 (C)이다.

185 세부 사항

번역 품목들을 설치하면서 맥리 씨가 추가로 지급한 금액은?
(A) 300달러
(B) 350 달러
(C) 900 달러
(D) 2750 달러

해설 영수증을 보면 설치비는 300달러(Installation Fee: $300)이므로, 정답은 (A)이다.

186-190 이메일 + 웹페이지 + 기사

수신: 폴 람필드
발신: 트레이시 블랙하트
날짜: 4월 23일
제목: 출장

안녕하세요, 폴.

다음 주 화요일 인디애나폴리스에서 열리는 제품 출시 행사에 저와 같이 가신다고 들었습니다. 여기 덴버에서 출발하는 비행편들을 보고 있는데요. 지난달에 폴이 인디애나폴리스에 비행기로 가셨던 게 기억이 나서요. **186**항공사를 제안해주시면 제가 즉시 예약을 하겠습니다.

저희 발표 관련해서 말씀드리자면, 저희는 500명의 청중 앞에서 연설을 하게 됩니다. 그렇기 때문에 제시간에 그곳에 도착하는 게 중요합니다. **187**이름이 기억나지 않는데 그 프랑스 회사는 이용하면 안 될 것 같아요. 지난해 기계 결함 때문에 그 회사에 대한 좋지 않은 후기들을 읽었습니다. 또 터키 항공사 클라우드 서퍼가 사업을 접는다고 하는 기사도 읽었습니다. 저는 이 외에 다른 옵션은 다 괜찮아요.

190그리고 저희가 도착하면 기자들이 저희를 취재하도록 초대되었다는 사실도 알고 계셔야 합니다. 오페라 미디어 그룹은 저희 초대를 거절했지만 매가코아 인코퍼레이티드는 누군가를 보낼 거예요. CEO께서 레드펀 프레스와 비즈니스 인사이더의 인터뷰 요청은 거절하라고 지시를 내리셨습니다. 그 언론사들은 이미 저희 신제품에 대해 비판적이었기 때문이죠.

가급적 빨리 비행편에 대해 연락 주세요.

트레이시 드림

어휘 launch (제품 등의) 출시 booking 예약 with regard to ~에 관해서는 unfavorable 비판적인, 불리한 review 평, 후기 go out of business 폐업하다 decline 거절하다 instruct 지시하다 critical 비판적인

---

http://www.skysearcher.com/results/e0302555

래피드플라이 디럭스: 전체 점수 – 4.5/5. 최근 애비에이션 아너스 시상식에서 우수 고객 서비스로 수상을 한 독일의 래피드플라이는 여행업계에서 주요 기업으로 입지를 굳혔다. **188**그러나 그럼에도 올해 들어 지금까지 예약 건수가 줄었는데, 이는 기내 음식 서비스 중단에 기인한 것으로 보인다.

골든윙스: 전체 점수 – 2/5. **187, 188**프랑스 남부에 근거를 둔 이 항공사는 지난해 항공권 판매가 감소세로 돌아섰다. 로버트 피에르가 회사가 고비를 넘겼다라고 말했지만 많은 고객들의 신뢰를 회복하지 못했고 비행편들이 계속해서 승객들을 다 채우지 못하고 있다.

실버제트: 전체 점수 – 3/5. **188**감소하는 매출을 끌어올리기 위해 스웨덴 항공사 실버제트는 최근 여러 할인 항공편을 발표했다. **189**이 할인은 자사의 얼리버드 항공편에도 적용되는데 얼리버드 항공편은 매일 덴버를 출발해 점심시간 전에 인디애나폴리스에 도착하는 유일한 항공편이다.

어휘 recognize (공로를) 인정하다, 표창하다 outstanding 뛰어난, 훌륭한 sector 부문, 분야 decline 감소하다, 떨어지다 downturn 감소, 하락 unconvinced 확신하지 못하는, 납득하지 못하는 turn a corner 고비를 넘기다 undersubscribed 신청자[응모자]가 불충분한 dwindling 줄어드는 figure 수치 extend 관련시키다, 포함하다

테크노스파크 제품 출시를 위해 이사들 도착

190베벌리 시머

189오늘 오전 본 기자는 테크노스파크 이사인 폴 람필드와 트레이시 블랙하트를 오전 10시 30분 덴버에서 이들을 태운 비행기가 인디애나폴리스에 착륙한 후 만났다. 람필드 씨는 오후 제품 출시 행사에서 새 노트북 컴퓨터 모델을 선보이게 돼 "너무도 설레인다"라고 말하며 그것이 빠르게 시장 선두에 나서게 될 것이라 예측했다.

출시 제품의 독점 사진들을 포함한 람필드 씨와의 인터뷰 전체 기사를 보려면 5페이지로 가시오.

어휘 touch down 착륙하다 claim 주장하다 excited 신난, 흥분된 unveil 선보이다, 공개하다 predict 예상하다 exclusive 독점의, 특종의 forthcoming 다가오는, 곧 있을

186 주제 / 목적

번역 이메일의 목적은 무엇인가?
(A) 초대장 발신
(B) 일정 변경 논의
(C) 동료의 조언 요청
(D) 발표 원고 수정 제안

해설 이메일 첫 단락에서 다음 주 화요일 인디애나폴리스에서 열리는 제품 출시 행사에 같이 간다고 들었다면서 항공사를 제안해 주면 즉시 예약을 하겠다(If you could suggest an airline, I'll go ahead and make the booking right away)고 했다. 따라서 동료의 조언을 구하기 위해 쓴 이메일임을 알 수 있으므로, 정답은 (C)이다.

187 연계

번역 골든윙스에 대해 명시된 것은?
(A) 파산했다.
(B) 비행기들이 기계적으로 문제가 있었다.
(C) 최근에 상을 받았다.
(D) 다음 주 신제품을 출시한다.

해설 이메일 두 번째 단락에서 블랙하트 씨는 지난해 기계 결함 때문에 좋지 않은 후기들을 읽었다면서 프랑스 회사는 이용하면 안 될 것 같다(I don't think we should use the French firm. I can't remember the name, but I have read unfavorable reviews about them in the last year due to their mechanical problems)고 했다. 웹페이지의 골든윙스 부분을 보면, 프랑스 남부에 본사를 둔 골든윙스는 고객들의 신뢰를 회복하지 못해 지난해 항공권 판매가 감소세로 돌아섰다(The flight operator from the south of France has experienced a downturn in ticket sales in the last year)고 했다. 따라서 프랑스 항공사인 골든윙스 비행기들이 기계적으로 문제가 있었음을 추론할 수 있으므로, 정답은 (B)이다.

▶▶ Paraphrasing 지문의 **mechanical problems**
→ 정답의 **mechanical issues**

188 세부 사항

번역 웹페이지에 나온 회사들의 공통점은 무엇인가?
(A) 모두 항공편 판매가 감소했다.
(B) 같은 나라 회사들이다.
(C) 따뜻한 음식이 항공편마다 제공된다.
(D) 모두 같은 점수를 받았다.

해설 웹페이지를 보면 독일 항공사인 래피드플라이 디럭스는 여행업계에서 주요 기업으로 입지를 굳혔지만, 올해 들어 예약 건수가 줄었다(bookings have declined)고 했으며, 프랑스 항공사인 골든윙스 역시 지난해 항공권 판매가 감소세로 돌아섰다(has experienced a downturn in ticket sales)고 했다. 스웨덴 항공사 실버제트는 감소하는 매출(dwindling sales figures)을 끌어올리기 위해 할인 항공편을 발표했다고 했다. 따라서 웹페이지에 언급된 항공사의 공통점은 항공권 매출 감소이므로, 정답은 (A)이다.

189 연계

번역 람필드 씨는 블랙하트 씨에게 어떤 항공사를 추천했겠는가?
(A) 골든윙스
(B) 래피드플라이
(C) 실버제트
(D) 클라우드서퍼

해설 기사의 첫 번째 단락에서 시머 씨는 테크노스파크 이사인 폴 람필드와 트레이시 블랙하트를 오전 10시 30분 덴버를 떠난 비행기가 인디애나폴리스에 착륙한 후 만났다(This morning, I met with Technospark directors Paul Romfield and Tracy Blackheart shortly after their flight from Denver touched down in Indianapolis at 10:30 A.M.)고 했으며, 웹페이지를 보면 실버제트의 얼리버드 항공편이 매일 덴버를 출발해 점심시간 전에 인디애나폴리스에 도착하는 유일한 항공편(This offer extends to its Early Bird flight—the only flight to arrive into Indianapolis from Denver each day before lunchtime)이라고 했다. 따라서 람필드 씨는 블랙하트 씨에게 실버제트를 추천했음을 추론할 수 있으므로, 정답은 (C)이다.

190 연계

번역 시머 씨는 어느 언론사에서 일하겠는가?
(A) 레드펀 프레스
(B) 오페라 미디어 그룹
(C) 비즈니스 인사이더
(D) 매가코어 인코퍼레이티드

해설 이메일 세 번째 단락에서 기자들이 취재를 할 것이라면서 매가코아 인코퍼레이티드에서 누군가를 보낼 것(You should also know that reporters have been invited to interview us when we arrive. Opera Media Group has declined the offer, but I believe Magacore Incorporated will send somebody)이라고 했으며, 기사문을 보면 베벌리 시머(Beverly Shimmer)가 쓴 기사임을 알 수 있다. 따라서 시머 씨는 매가코어 인코퍼레이티드 기자임을 알 수 있으므로, 정답은 (D)이다.

191-195 공지 + 이메일 + 설문조사

럭셔홈 전직원 앞

191이 공지는 3월 19일 전 직원 필참 교육에 대해 다시 한 번 알려 드리기 위한 것입니다. 경영진은 전직원들이 임대를 할 때 우리의 새 판매 정책에 대해 숙지하고 있기를 바라고 있습니다. 안타깝게도 올해는 신시내티 컨벤션 센터를 예약하지 못했습니다. 또한 크리스탈 호텔의 회의실 대여를 문의해 봤지만 우리가 원하는 날짜에는 이미 전일 예약이 되었다고 합니다. 그래서 클라크 기술학교의 회의장을 임시로 예약해놓았습니다. **192**그러나 저희가 교육을 주말로 옮기게 되면 장소가 신시내티 대학의 회의장으로 변경될 것입니다.

195교육일에는 비즈니스 전문가 폴라 플로레스로부터 거래를 성사시키는 방법에 대한 조언을 듣게 됩니다. 라이언 버트랜드가 참석해 계약 협상 영역에 대해 그가 가진 전문 지식을 나누게 됩니다. 또한 테리 펠즈 씨는 신설된 시 부동산 규제에 대한 강연을 합니다. 마지막이긴 하지만 역시 중요한 순서로서, 아일린 래시모드가 성공적인 발표 방법에 대한 조언을 준비합니다.

교육일을 즐겨 주시기 바라며 교육에서 배운 정보들이 여러분들의 럭셔홈에서의 커리어에 도움이 되길 바랍니다.

어휘 reminder 상기시켜 주는 것 mandatory 의무의, 필수의 be aware of ~을 알고[의식하고] 있다 let 세를 주다 property 부동산 inquire 문의하다 provisionally 임시로, 일시적으로 alter 변경하다 expertise 전문 지식 lecture 강연, 강의 regulation 규정, 규제 last but not least 순서로는 마지막이지만 역시 중요한

Test 9

수신: 웨인 헨더시 〈w.hendersey@luxurhome.net〉
발신: 수잔 제펄린 〈s.zeperlin@luxurhome.net〉
주제: 교육일
날짜: 4월 5일
첨부: 설문지

웨인 씨께,

우선 최근 회사 교육일을 마련해 주신 데 대해 웨인 씨와 여타 경영진들에게 감사를 드립니다. **192연사들은 매우 해박했고 신시내티 대학의 마련된 시설들은 최고 수준이었다고 생각합니다.** 작성한 제 설문지를 아래에 첨부하오니 참고해 주십시오.

교육일을 제가 얼마나 즐겼는지에 대해서 다음 주 중에 찾아 뵙고 이야기 드리고 싶습니다. 신입직원으로서 저는 럭셔홈에서의 제 미래 커리어에 대해서 너무나 기대가 큽니다. 이번 기회에 웨인 씨와 제 커리어 개발 전략을 논의하고 싶습니다. 바쁘시겠지만 시간을 내어 저를 **193도와주실** 수 있다면 정말로 감사드리겠습니다.

수잔 제펄린 드림
영업사원

어휘 questionnaire 설문지, 질문서 knowledgeable 해박한, 많이 아는 meet with (논의를 위해) ~와 만나다 strategy 전략 accommodate (요구 등에) 부응하다, 협조하다

럭셔홈

	매우 동의함	다소 동의함	다소 동의 하지 않음	매우 동의 하지 않음
교육일은 내 미래 커리어를 위한 준비를 하게 해 주었다	✗			
교육일은 잘 구성되었다	✗			
교육 장소는 쉽게 찾을 갈 수 있었다				✗
연사들은 지식이 해박했다		✗		

추가 피드백: 아주 훌륭한 하루였습니다. 그러나 웹사이트상의 설명이 부정확해 장소를 찾다가 길을 잃었다는 점을 지적하고 싶습니다. **194그로 인해 두 번째 강연 시간이 되어서야 도착하게 되었습니다.** 폴라 플로레스 씨가 아주 유용한 정보를 제공했다고 생각합니다. **195테리 펠즈 씨가 아파서 참석을 하지 못했다는 사실을 알고 약간 실망했지만** 아멜리아 송 씨는 펠즈 씨의 원고를 이용해 매우 효과적인 강연을 했다고 봅니다.

수잔 제펄린

어휘 prepare 준비시키다 venue (회담·경기 등의) 장소 point out 지적하다 get lost 길을 잃다 invaluable 매우 귀중한 competent 유능한, 능숙한

---

191 주제 / 목적

번역 공지의 목적은?
(A) 교육 워크숍 연사 찾기
(B) **행사의 업데이트 사항 전달**
(C) 신규 회사 정책 기술
(D) 일정 변경 발표

해설 공지문의 첫 번째 단락의 첫 문장에서 3월 19일에 있을 전 직원 필참 교육에 대해 다시 한 번 알려 주기 위한 것(This is a reminder that all employees are to attend mandatory training on March 19)이라고 했으며, 마지막 문장에서는 교육 장소가 신시내티 대학의 회의장으로 변경되었다(However, this will be altered to the conference suite at Cincinnati University if we need to move the training to a weekend)고 했다. 따라서 정답은 (B)이다.

192 연계

번역 교육일은 어느 요일에 열렸겠는가?
(A) 월요일
(B) 수요일
(C) 목요일
(D) **토요일**

해설 공지에서 교육이 주말로 옮겨지면 교육 장소가 신시내티 대학의 회의장으로 변경될 것(However, this will be altered to the conference suite at Cincinnati University if we need to move the training to a weekend)이라고 했다. 이메일에서 교육에 대해 연사들은 매우 해박했고 신시내티 대학의 마련된 시설들은 최고 수준이었다(The speakers were all very knowledgeable, and I thought the facilities on hand at Cincinnati University were first class)고 언급해 교육이 신시내티 대학에서 열렸음을 알 수 있다. 따라서 교육이 주말에 열렸다는 것을 알 수 있으므로, 정답은 (D)이다.

193 동의어 찾기

번역 이메일에서 두 번째 단락 4행의 "accommodate"와 의미가 가장 가까운 단어는?
(A) 수용하다
(B) 포함하다
(C) **돕다**
(D) 맞추다

해설 해당 문장은 '바쁘시겠지만 시간을 내어 도와주면 감사하겠다'는 뜻으로 해석되므로, 여기서 accommodate은 '도와주다, 협조하다'의 의미가 자연스럽다. 따라서 정답은 (C) assist이다.

194 추론 / 암시

번역 제펄린 씨에 대해 암시된 것은?
(A) 그녀는 상무이사다.
(B) **그녀는 교육일 행사에 지각했다.**
(C) 그녀는 대학 강사가 되고 싶어 한다.
(D) 그녀는 교육일 구성이 엉망으로 짜여졌다고 생각했다.

해설 설문조사 하단에서 제펄린 씨는 웹사이트상의 설명이 부정확해 장소를 찾다가 길을 잃어 두 번째 강연 시간이 되어서야 도착했다(As such, I only arrived in time for the second lecture)고 했다. 따라서 제펄린 씨는 교육 시간에 늦었다는 것을 알 수 있으므로, 정답은 (B)이다. .

▶▶ **Paraphrasing** 지문의 **arrived in time for the second lecture**
→ 정답의 **was late to the training day**

195 연계

번역 아멜리아 송은 무엇을 주제로 강연을 했겠는가?
(A) 계약 협상
(B) 발표하기
(C) 거래 성사
(D) 부동산 규제

해설 설문조사 하단에서 테리 펠즈 씨가 아파서 참석을 하지 못해 아멜리아 송 씨가 펠즈 씨의 원고를 이용해 강연을 했다(I was a little disappointed to find out that Terry Felz was sick and couldn't make it, but thought Amelia Song delivered a very competent lecture using Mr. Felz's notes)고 했다. 공지문 두 번째 단락을 보면 테리 펠즈 씨는 신설된 시 부동산 규제에 대한 강연을 할 것(Terry Felz will give a lecture on the new city property regulations)이라고 했다. 따라서 아멜리아 송 씨는 테리 펠즈 씨 대신 부동산 규제에 대해 강연했다는 것을 추론할 수 있으므로, 정답은 (D)이다.

196-200 공지 + 웹페이지 + 영수증

기술 대회

보이즈 시는 3월에 시에서 열리는 연례 기술 대회에 참석하는 수천 명의 방문객을 맞게 됩니다. **196**지난해 7일간의 대회 기간에 열린 세미나와 강연에 3천 명이 넘게 참가하면서 행사는 대성공을 거두었습니다. 올해는 이미 사전 입장권을 1,500장이나 판매했기 때문에 지난해 참가인원 기록을 깰 수 있으리라 희망합니다. **196**올해 행사는 예년처럼 스티븐슨 홀에서 2주에 걸쳐 개최될 것입니다.

많은 참석자들이 우리 시와 사랑에 빠져서 기간을 연장해 머물면서 강변 풍광과 아름다운 주변 전원을 즐깁니다. 이를 고려할 때 지역 기업인 갤럭시 카스를 저희 행사의 공식 렌터카 기업으로 발표하게 되어 기쁩니다. 회의 참석자를 위한 특별 할인이 제공되며 이용객 편의를 위해 차량을 투숙 호텔로 직접 배차해 드립니다. 갤럭시 카스의 웹사이트는 www.galaxycars.com입니다.

올해 대회 참가 비용은 다음과 같습니다.

골드 패스 – 모든 강연, 세미나, 워크숍 참가 가능: 85달러
199실버 패스 – 저녁 행사만 참가 가능: 40달러
브론즈 패스 – 웹 방송 온라인 시청: 15달러

예약은 전용 직통 번호 208-555-0143을 이용해 주십시오. 여러분의 전화를 간절히 기다리며 대회에서 직접 만나 뵙기를 바랍니다.

어휘 convention (전문직 종사자, 혹은 정당 등의 큰) 대회 annual 연례의 spread over ~에 걸쳐 (퍼져) 있는 duration 지속 기간 attendance 참석, 출석 advance ticket 예매권, 사전 티켓 as usual 평상시처럼 extended (예상보다) 길어진, 늘어난 be delighted to ~하게 되어 기쁘다 eagerly 간절히

---

http://www.galaxycars.com

특가: 보이즈 기술 대회

197저희 갤럭시 카스는 항상 자동차 업계의 기술 진보를 수용하며 저희 렌터카에 최신의 기기를 제공하는 것뿐만 아니라 우리 고객들에게 최상의 고객 서비스를 제공하기 위해 노력합니다. 이것이 저희가 올해 기술 대회를 기쁘게 후원하는 이유입니다.

이 중요한 대회를 축하하기 위해 저희는 대회 참가자를 위해 보상 프로그램을 제공하기로 결정했습니다. **198**차량을 미리 예약하시면 렌트 가격의 특별 할인을 받으실 수 있습니다. 예약 시 코드 "SAVEDEAL"을 기입해 주시면 됩니다. 현재 다음과 같이 할인이 제공됩니다.

2009월 25일 이전 예약: 20% 할인

9월 25일과 9월 30일 사이 예약: 15% 할인
10월 1일과 10월 7일 사이 예약: 10% 할인
10월 8일 이후 예약: 5% 할인

어휘 embrace 수용하다, 받아들이다 advancement 진보, 발달 strive 노력하다, 힘쓰다 gadget 기계 장치, 도구 reward scheme 보상 제도, 보상 프로그램 entitle 자격[권리]을 주다 quote 인용하다

영수증 출력일: 9월 29일
고객: 테렌스 버네트
주소: 일리노이 주 시카고 시 비치 레인 49번지, 60605
199고객 패스 등급: 실버
차량 예약 여부 (예/아니요): 예
차량 제조사 및 모델: 어드밴스 스피드웨이 T400 디럭스
보상 프로그램 회원: 2388 MAH
총계: 169.95달러
차량 반납일: 10월 7일
200예약일: 9월 23일
은행 카드: XXXXXXXXXXXX5939
카드 유효기간 만료일: 10월 15일

패스는 행사 시작 전 공식 프런트 데스크에서 수령할 수 있습니다.

어휘 make 제조사 expiry 만료, 만기 prior to ~ 전에

196 추론 / 암시

번역 올해 기술 대회에 대해 암시된 것은?
(A) 보이즈 시의 새로운 장소에서 개최된다.
(B) 입장권이 이미 완전 매진됐다.
(C) 무료 공항 이동 차량이 포함된다.
(D) 지난해 행사보다 길게 열린다.

해설 공지문 첫 번째 단락에서 작년 행사는 1주일 동안 진행됐다(Last year's event was a huge success, with over 3,000 visitors attending seminars, and lectures spread over the duration of the seven day convention)고 했고, 뒤에 올해 행사는 예년처럼 스티븐슨 홀에서 열릴 것이지만, 행사 기간은 2주로 연장될 것(This year's event will be held in the Stephenson Hall as usual, and events will be spread over two weeks this time around)이라고 했다. 따라서 정답은 (D)이다.

197 추론 / 암시

번역 갤럭시 카스에 대해 암시된 것은?
(A) 대회에서 전시 부스를 운영할 것이다.
(B) 자사의 차량에 첨단 기기들을 장착한다.
(C) 개업 1주년을 기념하고 있다.
(D) 대회장에서 셔틀 버스를 제공할 것이다.

해설 웹페이지 첫 번째 단락에서 갤럭시 카스는 자동차 업계의 기술 진보를 수용하며, 렌터카에 최신 기기를 제공하는 것뿐만 아니라 고객들에게 최상의 고객 서비스를 제공하기 위해 노력한다(We at Galaxy Cars always seek to embrace technological advancements in the motor industry, and we strive to provide our customers with the best customer service as well as the latest gadgets in our rental cars)고 했다. 따라서 정답은 (B)이다.

▶▶ **Paraphrasing** 지문의 **the latest gadgets**
→ 정답의 **advanced devices**

198 세부 사항

번역 렌터카 할인을 받기 위해 고객들이 해야 하는 것은?
(A) 온라인 계정에 로그인
(B) 게스트 출입증 제시
(C) 특정 업체에서 호텔 객실 예약
(D) 참조 코드 기입

해설 웹페이지에서 차량을 미리 예약하면 렌트 가격의 특별 할인을 받을 수 있다면서, 예약 시 코드 "SAVEDEAL"을 기입하라(Please quote the code "SAVERDEAL" at the time of booking)고 했다. 따라서 정답은 (D)이다.

199 연계

번역 버네트 씨에 대해 사실인 것은?
(A) 올해 행사에 참석할 수 없다.
(B) 최근 갤럭시 카스로부터 채용 제의를 수락했다.
(C) 저녁 행사에만 참석할 수 있을 것이다.
(D) 기술 대회의 초빙 연사이다.

해설 영수증을 보면 버네트 씨의 고객 패스 등급은 실버(Guest Pass Level: Silver)이며, 공지문에서 실버 패스는 40달러로 저녁 행사만 참가 가능하다(Silver Pass–Attendance at evening events only: $40)고 했다. 따라서 버네트 씨는 저녁 행사에만 참석할 수 있다는 것을 알 수 있으므로, 정답은 (C)이다.

200 연계

번역 버네트 씨는 얼마만큼의 렌터카 할인을 받을 수 있을 것인가?
(A) 5%
(B) 10%
(C) 15%
(D) 20%

해설 영수증을 보면 버네트 씨의 예약일은 9월 23일(Date of Booking: September 23)이며, 웹페이지에서 날짜별 할인율을 보면, 9월 25일 이전 예약에 예약하면 20% 할인을 받을 수 있다(Bookings made before September 25: 20% discount)고 했다. 따라서 9월 23일에 예약한 버네트 씨는 20%를 할인받을 수 있다는 것을 알 수 있으므로, 정답은 (D)이다.

TEST 10

101 (A)	**102** (C)	**103** (B)	**104** (D)	**105** (D)
106 (A)	**107** (C)	**108** (D)	**109** (C)	**110** (A)
111 (B)	**112** (D)	**113** (B)	**114** (D)	**115** (A)
116 (D)	**117** (C)	**118** (A)	**119** (C)	**120** (D)
121 (C)	**122** (B)	**123** (D)	**124** (B)	**125** (A)
126 (B)	**127** (B)	**128** (B)	**129** (A)	**130** (C)
131 (B)	**132** (D)	**133** (D)	**134** (A)	**135** (C)
136 (D)	**137** (B)	**138** (C)	**139** (B)	**140** (D)
141 (B)	**142** (C)	**143** (A)	**144** (C)	**145** (C)
146 (C)	**147** (D)	**148** (D)	**149** (C)	**150** (D)
151 (C)	**152** (C)	**153** (C)	**154** (C)	**155** (D)
156 (D)	**157** (D)	**158** (B)	**159** (D)	**160** (D)
161 (A)	**162** (D)	**163** (D)	**164** (C)	**165** (B)
166 (D)	**167** (D)	**168** (B)	**169** (C)	**170** (D)
171 (D)	**172** (B)	**173** (D)	**174** (B)	**175** (D)
176 (C)	**177** (A)	**178** (D)	**179** (D)	**180** (B)
181 (C)	**182** (B)	**183** (C)	**184** (B)	**185** (C)
186 (C)	**187** (B)	**188** (A)	**189** (D)	**190** (D)
191 (B)	**192** (D)	**193** (C)	**194** (C)	**195** (B)
196 (B)	**197** (C)	**198** (A)	**199** (D)	**200** (A)

PART 5

101 인칭대명사 _ 소유격

해설 빈칸 앞 to부정사(to place)의 목적어(luggage)를 한정 수식하는 자리이므로, 정답은 소유격 인칭대명사인 (A) her이다.

번역 승객은 비행기 탑승 후 짐을 머리 위 짐칸에 넣도록 요청 받았다.

어휘 place 두다, 놓다 luggage 짐 overhead compartment 머리 위 짐칸 board (여객기 등에) 탑승하다

102 상관접속사

해설 빈칸 뒤에 나오는 등위접속사(and)와 짝을 이루어 and 앞의 명사(the initial prototype)와 뒤의 명사(the final model)를 연결하는 상관접속사를 선택해야 한다. 따라서 정답은 (C) Both이다. 상관접속사 (B) Either는 or와 짝을 이루어 쓰인다.

번역 키보드의 초기 시제품과 최종 모델 모두 맞춤형 미디어 키들을 갖추고 있었다.

어휘 initial 처음의 prototype 시제품, 원형 feature ~을 특별히 포함하다, 특징으로 삼다 customizable 맞춤형의

103 동사 어형 _ 시제

해설 빈칸은 주어(Executives at the Cedal Corporation) 뒤 동사 자리로, 뒤에 나오는 과거 시간을 나타내는 부사(two months ago)에 맞는 동사를 선택해야 한다. 따라서 정답은 과거시제 동사 (B) began이다. 동명사/현재분사 (C) beginning은 동사 자리에 올 수 없다.

번역 세달 코퍼레이션 임원들은 두 달 전 네빅스 인더스트리즈 인수를 위한 협상을 시작했다.

어휘 executive 임원, 중역 negotiation 협상 acquisition 획득, (기업) 인수

104 전치사 어휘

해설 빈칸은 명사구(some travel documents) 앞에 위치하는 전치사 자리로 문맥에 어울리는 전치사를 선택해야 한다. 문맥상 '여행 서류에서 분실한 영수증들을 찾아냈다'라는 의미가 자연스러우므로, 정답은 (D) among(~ 사이에, ~ 중에)이다.

번역 우리 동료들이 거의 한 시간 동안 파일 캐비닛을 뒤져 마침내 여행 서류에서 분실한 영수증들을 찾아냈다.

어휘 associate (사업, 직장) 동료 missing 분실한 receipt 영수증

105 부사 자리 _ 동사 수식

해설 빈칸 앞의 동사(will run out)를 수식하는 부사 자리로, 정답은 (D) entirely(완전히, 전부)이다. 형용사 (A) entire(전체의, 완전한)와 명사 (B) entirety(전체, 전부), (C) entireness(완전함)는 품사상 적합하지 않다.

번역 시 의회가 이를 최우선 과제로 다루지 않는다면 그 지역의 공원 유지 자금은 완전히 동이 날 것이다.

어휘 fund 자금, 기금 run out 다 떨어지다, 동이 나다 city council 시의회 top priority 최우선 과제[사항]

106 부정형용사

해설 빈칸 뒤에 나오는 주어인 복수명사(hotels)를 수식하는 자리이므로, 정답은 형용사 (A) Other이다. (B) Each와 (D) Another는 단수명사를 한정 수식한다.

번역 다른 호텔들은 체크인 24시간 내 예약 취소에 수수료를 부과하지만 레노라 인은 그렇지 않다.

어휘 charge 청구하다 fee 수수료 cancellation 취소

107 명사 자리 _ 동사의 주어

해설 빈칸은 뒤에 나오는 동사(can be proven)의 주어 자리로, 앞에 있는 부정관사(A)와 형용사(legitimate)의 수식을 받는다. 따라서 정답은 단수명사 (C) claim이다. 동사 (A) is claiming과 (B) claimed는 품사상 적합하지 않고, 복수명사 (D) claims는 앞의 부정관사(A)와 수일치하지 않는다.

번역 적법하게 시에 거주하고 있다는 주장은 유효한 아파트 임대 계약서를 통해 증명할 수 있다.

어휘 legitimate 정당한, 적법의 claim 주장 residency 거주 valid 유효한 rental lease 임대 계약서

108 동사 어휘

해설 빈칸은 명령문의 동사원형 자리로, 뒤에 나오는 목적어(the sources for all of the statistics)와 의미가 가장 잘 통하는 동사를 선택해야 한다. 문맥상 '모든 통계자료의 출처들을 인용하다'라는 의미가 자연스러우므로, 정답은 (D) cite(인용하다, 이유·예를 들다)이다. (A) base(근거를 두다), (B) direct(지시하다, 안내하다), (C) fulfill(충족시키다, 이행하다)은 의미상 적합하지 않다.

번역 보고서에 포함된 모든 통계자료의 출처들을 인용해 주십시오.

어휘 statistics 통계(자료) cite 인용하다

109 부사 어휘

해설 빈칸은 앞에 있는 대조의 의미를 나타내는 등위접속사(but)가 연결하는 완전한 절(The candidate had already won a majority by a large margin)과 완전한 절(election officials counted the rest of the votes) 뒤에 나오는 부사 자리이다. 문맥상 '그럼에도 불구하고 나머지 표를 개표했다'라는 양보의 의미가 자연스러우므로, 정답은 (C) nonetheless(그럼에도 불구하고)이다. (A) otherwise(달리, 그렇지 않으면), (B) ever(언젠가, 늘), (D) rather(다소, 약간, 차라리)는 의미상 적합하지 않다.

번역 그 후보는 이미 큰 표 차이로 과반을 차지했으나 선거관리위원들은 그럼에도 불구하고 나머지 표들을 개표했다.

어휘 candidate 후보 majority 과반수 by a large margin 큰 차이로 nonetheless 그럼에도 불구하고

110 명사 어휘

해설 빈칸 앞 전치사(in)의 목적어 역할을 하는 명사 자리로, 빈칸을 포함한 전치사구는 동사(remained)의 주어(its operator)를 보충 설명한다. 문맥상 '조종자는 제어 상태를 유지하다'라는 의미가 자연스러우므로, 정답은 (A) control이다. 참고로 in control은 '제어하는, 관리하는', in shape는 '건강한', in force는 '시행중인', in order는 '적법한, 적절한, 정돈된'이라는 의미를 나타낸다. 따라서 (B) shape, (C) force, (D) order는 의미상 적합하지 않다.

번역 드론이 예상치 못한 폭풍을 만났을 때에도 조종자는 제어 상태를 유지하고 드론이 경로를 벗어나지 않도록 했다.

어휘 unexpectedly 예상치 못하게 encounter 부닥치다, 만나다 operator 조작하는 사람

111 명사 자리 _ 전치사의 목적어

해설 빈칸 앞 전치사(to)의 목적어 자리로, 뒤에 나오는 사람명사를 수식하는 관계사절(who can complete the job more cost-effectively)의 수식을 받는다. 따라서 정답은 사람명사 (B) contractors이다. 사물명사 (D) contracts는 의미상 적합하지 않고, 부사 (A) contractually(계약상으로)와 형용사 (C) contractual(계약상의)은 품사상 적합하지 않다.

번역 많은 건설 회사들은 작업 일부를 더욱 비용효율적으로 업무를 완수할 수 있는 도급업체들에게 맡긴다.

어휘 delegate (권한 업무 등을) 위임하다 cost-effectively 비용효율적으로 contractor 하청업체, 도급업자

112 전치사 어휘

해설 빈칸은 명사구(the change in government policy) 앞 전치사 자리이다. 문맥상 '정부 정책 변화에 대해 알려 주기 위해'라는 의미가 자연스러우므로, 정답은 (D) about이다.

번역 지점 매니저는 직원들에게 정부 정책 변화에 대해 알려 주기 위해 긴급 회의를 소집했다.

어휘 call for ~을 요구하다 emergency 비상 사태, 비상시 policy 정책, 규정

113 형용사 어휘

해설 빈칸 앞 동사(had)의 목적어(levels of reserve supplies)를 수식하는 형용사 자리이다. 문맥상 '적정 수준의 예비 물품을 갖추고 있다'라는 의미가 자연스러우므로, 정답은 (B) acceptable(수용할 만한, 그런대로 괜찮은, 적정한)이다. (A) willing(기꺼이 하는, 자발적인), (C) skillful(솜씨 좋은, 교묘한), (D) rapid(빠른)는 의미상 적합하지 않다.

번역 다행히 원조기구가 실시한 재고 조사를 통해 보호소가 적정 수준의 예비 물품을 갖추고 있음이 드러났다.

어휘 fortunately 다행히 inventory 재고 조사 aid 원조, 구호 reserve 예비의 supplies 보급품, 물자 acceptable 수용할 만한, 그런대로 괜찮은

114 부사 어휘

해설 빈칸은 동사(must be marketed)를 수식하는 부사 자리이다. 문맥상 '공격적으로 마케팅해야 한다'라는 의미가 자연스러우므로, 정답은 (D) aggressively(공격적으로)이다. (A) consecutively(연속하여), (B) recently(최근에), (C) strictly(엄격히, 엄밀히)는 의미상 적합하지 않다. 참고로 부사 (B) recently는 주로 현재완료시제 또는 과거시제 동사와 함께 쓰인다.

번역 업계 내 심한 경쟁 때문에 바미언트 전자가 디자인한 새 스마트폰은 공격적으로 마케팅해야 한다.

어휘 owing to ~ 때문에 competition 경쟁 aggressively 공격적으로

115 동사 어형 _ 태

해설 빈칸 앞의 be동사(are)와 함께 동사구를 이루는 알맞은 어휘를 고르는 문제이다. 문맥상 '자연사 박물관의 VIP 회원은 입장이 허용된다'라는 수동의 의미가 자연스러우므로, 정답은 (A) permitted이다. (C) permits와 (D) permit가 동사로 쓰일 경우 be동사와 함께 쓸 수 없어 적합하지 않고, 명사로 쓰일 경우에는 주어와 동격이 될 수 없어 적합하지 않다.

번역 자연사 박물관의 VIP 회원은 워크숍에 입장하여 큐레이터의 작업을 직접 볼 수 있습니다.

어휘 curator 큐레이터(전시 책임자) permit 허락하다

116 부사절 접속사

해설 빈칸은 앞뒤에 위치한 두 개의 완전한 절들을 연결하는 부사절 접속사 자리로, 정답은 (D) so that(~하기 위해)이다. 'so that ~ can(~가 …할 수 있도록)'을 하나로 묶어서 기억해 두자. 전치사 (A) such as(예를 들어, ~와 같은), (B) regardless of(~에 관계없이)는 완전한 절을 이끌 수 없다. (C) no matter what(비록 무엇이 ~라고 하더라도) 뒤에도 완전한 절이 올 수 없으므로 적합하지 않다.

번역 룬랏 매뉴팩처링은 전력을 역내에서 자체 생산하기 위해 옥상에 태양 전지판을 설치했다.

어휘 install 설치하다 solar panel 태양 전지판 generate 발생시키다 on site 현장에서, 시설 내에서

117 형용사 자리 _ 명사 수식

해설 빈칸은 뒤에 나오는 명사(colleagues)를 앞의 최상급(Ms. Donnelly's most) 표현과 함께 수식하는 형용사 자리이므로, 정답은 (C) distant이다. 명사 (A) distances와 (B) distance, 부사 (D) distantly는 품사상 적합하지 않다.

번역 워낙 명망이 높은 상이기 때문에 도널리 씨와 아주 멀리 떨어져 사는 동료들까지 그녀의 수상을 보러 갔다.

어휘 prestigious 명망 있는, 일류의 colleague 동료

118 동사 어형 _ 조동사 + 동사원형

해설 빈칸은 조동사(may) 뒤의 동사원형 자리이므로, 정답은 (A) demolish 이다.

번역 헤들리 타워의 건물주는 곧 있을 안전 검사를 통과하지 못할 경우 건물을 허물지도 모른다.

어휘 inspection 검사, 점검 demolish (건물을) 헐다, 허물다

119 부사 자리 _ 동명사 수식

해설 빈칸은 동명사(warning)를 수식하는 부사 자리로, 정답은 (C) repeatedly 이다. 명사 (A) repetition, 형용사 (B) repetitive, 동명사/현재분사 (D) repeating은 품사상 적합하지 않다.

번역 IT 담당 이사가 회사 사장에게 이메일 시스템 관련 문제들에 대해 여러 차례 경고했지만 사장은 이를 바로잡기 위한 자금을 따로 할당하지 않았다.

어휘 warn A of B A에게 B에 대해 경고하다 allocate (특정 목적으로) 할당하다 fix 고치다, 바로잡다

120 동사 어휘

해설 빈칸 앞 to부정사의 to 뒤에 나오는 동사원형 자리로, 뒤에 나오는 목적어 (its status)와 의미가 가장 잘 통하는 동사를 선택해야 한다. 문맥상 '입지를 높일 수 있었다'라는 의미가 자연스러우므로, 정답은 (D) elevate(올리다, 높이다, 승진시키다)이다. (A) divide(나누다), (B) recruit(모집하다), (C) attach(첨부하다, 붙이다)는 의미상 적합하지 않다.

번역 크게 존경 받는 운동선수와 후원 계약을 맺으면서 퍼든 스포츠는 입지를 높일 수 있었다.

어휘 sponsorship 후원, 협찬 athlete 운동선수 elevate 올리다, 높이다 status 지위, 입지

121 형용사 자리 _ 명사 수식

해설 빈칸 앞 동사(offer)의 목적어(alternatives)를 수식하는 형용사 자리이다. 현재분사 (B) preferring과 형용사 (C) preferable(더 나은, 바람직한) 중에 문맥상 '더 나은 대안'이라는 의미가 자연스러우므로, 정답은 (C) preferable이다. 명사 (A) preferences와 동사 (D) prefer는 품사상 적합하지 않다. 참고로 동사 (D) prefer은 진행형으로 쓰이지 않는다.

번역 대다수 분석가들은 제안된 세 개의 세제안 모두 현재 시행중인 제도보다 더 좋은 대안이 될 수 있다는 데 동의한다.

어휘 analyst 분석가, 애널리스트 measure 조치, 방안 alternative 대안 currently 현재 in place 가동중인

122 형용사 어휘

해설 빈칸 앞 동사(left)의 목적어(scratches)를 수식하는 형용사 자리이다. 문맥상 '눈에 띄는 흠집을 남겼다'라는 의미가 자연스러우므로, 정답은 (B) visible(보이는, 눈에 띄는)이다. (A) vital(필수적인), (C) reduced (감소된, 할인된), (D) accessible(접근 가능한, 이용 가능한)은 의미상 적합하지 않다.

번역 그 고객은 우리 기사들이 그것을 운반하는 과정에서 유리에 눈에 띄는 흠집을 남겼다고 불평했다.

어휘 complain 불평하다 technician 기술자, 기사 scratch 긁힌 자국 in the process of ~하는 과정에 transport 운반하다

123 명사 자리 _ 동사의 주어

해설 빈칸 뒤에 나오는 동사(must have)의 주어 역할을 하는 명사 자리로, 뒤의 전치사구(for the economic summit)의 수식을 받는다. 명사 (B) Interpretation(해석, 설명)과 (D) Interpreters(통역사) 중에 문맥상 '경제 정상회담의 통역사들은 소지해야 한다'라는 의미가 자연스러우므로, 정답은 (D) Interpreters이다. 동명사/현재분사 (A) Interpreting과 동사 (C) Interprets는 품사상 적합하지 않다.

번역 경제 정상회담을 위한 통역사들은 전문 자격증을 소지하고 도착어 원어민이어야 한다.

어휘 summit 정상회담 certificate 자격증, 면허증 target language (통역, 번역에서의) 도착어

124 명사 자리 _ 복합명사

해설 빈칸 앞 명사(faculty)와 복합명사를 이루어 앞에 있는 전치사(of)의 목적어 역할을 하는 명사 자리이므로, 정답은 (B) dissatisfaction이다. 동명사/현재분사 (A) dissatisfying과 동사 (C) dissatisfies, (D) dissatisfy는 품사상 적합하지 않다.

번역 대학에서 승진 기회가 충분하지 못하면 교수들의 불만족도가 현저하게 상승한다.

어휘 promotion 승진 insufficient 불충분한 rate 비율 faculty 교수단, 교수진 significantly 현저하게, 크게

125 명사 어휘

해설 빈칸 앞에 있는 to부정사(to pass)의 목적어 역할을 하는 명사 자리로, 과거분사(proposed)의 수식을 받는다. 문맥상 '제안된 규제안을 통과시키다'라는 의미가 자연스러우므로, 정답은 (A) regulations(규정, 규제)이다. (B) transactions(거래), (C) affiliations(제휴, 가입), (D) admissions(입장, 인정)는 의미상 적합하지 않다.

번역 의회 의원들은 남서 지역 희귀종 새의 자연서식지를 보호하기 위해 제안된 규제안을 통과시킬 것으로 예상된다.

어휘 be expected to + 동사원형 ~하리라 예상되다 conserve 보호하다, 보존하다 habitat 서식지 rare 드문, 희귀한 species 종

126 부사 어휘

해설 빈칸 앞 to부정사(to stop)를 수식하는 부사 자리이다. 문맥상 '전면 중단하다'라는 의미가 자연스러우므로, 정답은 (B) altogether(전적으로, 완전히)이다. (A) lately(최근에), (C) almost(거의), (D) much(많이)는 의미상 적합하지 않다.

번역 코가라 과학재단이 프로젝트 보조금을 갱신해주지 않으면 연구실 연구는 전면 중단해야 할 것이다.

어휘 grant 보조금 renew 갱신하다 altogether 전적으로, 완전히

127 동사 어형 _ to부정사

해설 빈칸은 동사(were encouraged) 뒤의 준동사 자리로, 뒤의 명사 (their cubicles)를 목적어로 취한다. 따라서 준동사인 to부정사 (B) to personalize와 현재분사 (D) personalizing 중에 골라야 한다. 동사 encourage는 to부정사를 목적격 보어로 취하는 동사로, 〈encourage+목적어+to부정사〉의 형태로 쓰인다. 따라서 이를 수동의 형태로 나타낼 경우, 〈be encouraged+to부정사〉의 형태가 되므로, 정답은 (B) to personalize이다. 과거분사 (C) personalized는 목적어를 취할 수 없다. '~하도록 권장된다(be encouraged to+동사원형)'라는 관용적인 표현으로 묶어서 기억하자.

번역 소래큐 코퍼레이션에서는 즐거운 근무 환경을 조성하기 위해 직원들에게 칸막이 사무공간을 각자 기호에 맞추도록 권장했다.

어휘 encourage 권하다, 장려하다 cubicle 칸막이로 된 공간 personalize 개인의 기호에 맞추다

128 동사 어휘

해설 빈칸 앞 be동사(are)와 함께 수동태 동사를 나타내는 자리이다. 문맥상 '우승자가 선정될 때까지 참가자 신원을 비밀로 한다'라는 의미가 자연스러우므로, 정답은 (B) concealed(감추다, 숨기다)이다. (A) defined(정의하다, 분명히 밝히다), (C) verified(확인하다, 입증하다), (D) prohibited(금지하다)는 의미상 적합하지 않다.

번역 참가자들이 심사위원 패널에게 공정하게 대우 받도록 하기 위하여 우승자가 선정될 때까지 참가자 신원을 비밀로 한다.

어휘 participant 참가자 fairly 공정하게 identity 신원, 신분 conceal 숨기다, 비밀로 하다

129 부사절 접속사

해설 빈칸은 앞뒤에 있는 두 개의 완전한 절을 연결하는 부사절 접속사 자리이다. (A) whereas(~반면에)와 (C) before(~ 전에) 중에 문맥상 '젊은 소비자들은 무선 기술에만 의존하는 반면'이라는 대조의 의미가 자연스러우므로, 정답은 (A) whereas이다. 전치사 (B) instead of(~ 대신에) 뒤에는 완전한 절이 나올 수 없고, to부정사의 관용표현 (D) so as to 뒤에는 동사원형이 나온다.

번역 나이든 성인들의 반 이상이 여전히 가정에 유선 전화를 가지고 있는 반면 젊은 소비자들은 무선 기술에만 의존한다.

어휘 landline (지상 통신선을 이용한) 일반 전화, 유선 전화 whereas (접속사) ~인 반면

130 동사 어휘

해설 빈칸 앞 to부정사의 to 뒤에 나오는 동사원형 자리이다. 종속절에 양보의 부사절 접속사(Although)가 있으므로, 부사절과 대조되는 의미를 나타내는 동사를 선택해야 한다. 문맥상 '굉장한 성공을 거두었음에도 불구하고 가까운 미래에 수익이 감소할 것'이라는 의미가 자연스러우므로, 정답은 (C) shrink(감소하다)이다. (A) criticize(비판하다, 비평하다),

(B) revolve(돌다, 회전하다), (D) deduct(공제하다)는 의미상 적합하지 않다.

번역 개셋 제약은 지난 수년간 굉장한 성공을 거두었음에도 불구하고 가까운 미래에 수익이 감소할 것으로 예상된다.

어휘 predict 예측하다 foreseeable future 가까운 미래 shrink 줄어들다

PART 6

131-134 편지

1월 22일

카도소 씨,

귀하에게 스탠튼 어드바이저스의 선임재무분석가직을 제의하게 되어 기쁩니다. 채용 위원회는 적격자를 **131**찾고 있었습니다. 귀하는 저희의 기대를 가장 확실히 능가하는 후보였습니다. **132**귀하께서 보여주신 투자 포트폴리오는 균형이 잘 잡혀 있고 전문가적인 면모를 갖추었습니다. 더욱이 시장 상황에 대한 심도 깊은 이해를 보여 주었습니다. 또한 저희는 **133**귀하의 전 근무처에서 칭찬 일색의 추천서를 받았습니다. 표준고용계약서를 동봉합니다. 서명 **134**전 자세히 살펴보시고 질문 있으시면 저에게 연락 주십시오.

해롤드 카니

어휘 hiring committee 채용위원회 qualified 자격을 갖춘 surpass 능가하다, 초과하다 well-balanced 균형 잡힌 expertly 전문적으로 glowing 극찬하는 recommendation 추천(서) enclose 동봉하다 look over 살펴보다

131 동사 어형 _ 시제

해설 빈칸은 주어(The members of the hiring committee) 뒤에 나오는 동사 자리이다. 문맥상 '위원회가 적격자를 찾는다'라는 능동의 의미가 자연스러우므로, 미래완료시제 동사 (A) will have searched, 과거완료진행시제 동사 (B) had been searching, 현재진행시제 동사 (D) are searching 중에 시제에 맞는 동사를 선택해야 한다. 빈칸 뒤에 나오는 등위접속사(and)가 연결하는 절의 과거시제 동사(surpassed)를 통해 과거 이전에 일어난 일임을 알 수 있으므로, 정답은 (B) had been searching이다.

132 문맥에 맞는 문장 고르기

번역 (A) 그 직책의 잠재 소득은 구직자들에게 매우 매력적입니다.
(B) 마찬가지로 잠재적 문제를 방지하기 위해 우리는 엄격한 윤리 규정을 따르고 있습니다.
(C) 저희가 검토할 수 있도록 이력서 한 부를 제출해 주십시오.
(D) 더욱이 시장 상황에 대한 심도 깊은 이해를 보여 주었습니다.

해설 빈칸 앞 문장 '귀하께서 보여주신 투자 포트폴리오는 균형이 잘 잡혀 있고 전문가적인 면모를 갖추었다(The investment portfolios you showed us were well-balanced and expertly developed)'에서 카도소 씨(you)에게 일자리를 제안한 이유를 언급하고 있다. 따라서 빈칸에도 카도소 씨(you)의 장점과 관련된 내용이 이어지는 것이 문맥상 자연스러우므로, 정답은 (D)이다.

133 인칭대명사 _ 소유격

해설 빈칸 앞 전치사(from)의 목적어(former employer)를 한정 수식하는 소유격 인칭대명사 자리이다. 빈칸 앞에 나온 전반적인 내용을 통해 편지의 수신인(Mr. Cardoso=you)의 '전 고용주로부터 받은 추천서'라는 것을 알 수 있으므로, 정답은 (D) your이다.

134 전치사 어휘

해설 빈칸은 동명사 구문(signing it)을 목적어로 취하는 전치사 자리이다. 전치사 (A) Prior to(~ 전에), (B) Except for(~을 제외하고), (C) Because of(~ 때문에), (D) Such as(예를 들어) 중에 문맥상 '서명하기 전에 자세히 살펴보다'라는 의미가 자연스러우므로, 정답은 (A) Prior to이다.

135-138 편지

스콧 그레이엄
월윈 로드 859
핼리팩스
HX1 5TW

그레이엄 씨,

싱클레어 항공 마일리지 서비스 프로그램에 가입해 주셔서 감사드립니다. 탁월한 고객 서비스와 단골 고객들의 성원으로 우리 회사는 세계 15대 항공사의 하나로 **135**성장했습니다.

근래 대다수 항공사가 보상 프로그램을 제공하고 있지만 저희와 같은 혜택들을 제공하는 곳은 **136**드뭅니다. 저희는 호텔부터 렌터카 업체에 이르기까지 광범위한 협력업체 망을 보유하고 있습니다. 이들 **137**제휴 업체들마다 적립 포인트가 다릅니다. **138**이들 업체들을 지원하거나 비행 만을 이용하여 포인트를 적립할 수 있습니다. <u>어떤 방식이든 곧 무료 항공의 혜택을 누릴 수 있습니다.</u> 더 자세한 내용은 동봉된 소책자를 참고하십시오.

싱클레어 항공팀

어휘 frequent flyer program 마일리지 프로그램 loyal customer 단골 고객 rewards program 보상 프로그램 boost 올리다, 신장시키다 rely on ~에 의존하다 solely 오직 enclosed 동봉된

135 동사 자리

해설 빈칸은 주어(our business) 뒤의 동사 자리이므로, 정답은 (A) has grown이다. 과거분사 (B) grown, to부정사 (C) to grow, 동명사/현재분사 (D) growing은 동사 자리에 단독으로 들어갈 수 없다.

136 부정대명사

해설 빈칸은 복수동사(have) 앞 주어 자리이다. 복수 주어 (A) those와 (D) few 중에 문맥상 '거의 가지고 있지 않다'라는 부정의 의미가 자연스러우므로, 정답은 (D) few이다. (B) neither는 단수동사와 수일치하고, 명사절/형용사절 접속사 (C) which는 동사(have) 외에 동사가 하나 더 나와야 한다.

137 명사 어휘

해설 빈칸 뒤 동사(have set)의 주어 역할을 하는 명사 자리로, 앞에 지시형용사(These)의 한정 수식을 받는다. 지시형용사(These)는 앞 문장의 '광범위한 협력업체 망(a wide network of partners)'을 가리키고 있으므로, 이와 비슷한 의미의 명사를 선택해야 한다. 따라서 정답은 (B) affiliates (제휴업체, 계열사)이다. (A) subscribers(구독자), (C) passengers(승객), (D) attendants(안내원, 종업원)는 의미상 적합하지 않다.

어휘 affiliate 관계 단체, 제휴[자매] 회사

138 문맥에 맞는 문장 고르기

번역 (A) 사실 우리 회원 대다수는 그렇게 하는 편을 택합니다.
(B) 그러므로 편안함과 편의는 저희의 최우선 사항입니다.
(C) 어떤 방식이든 곧 무료 항공의 혜택을 누릴 수 있습니다.
(D) 그 결과 저희의 안전 비행 성적은 업계 최고입니다.

해설 빈칸 앞 문장 '이들 업체들을 지원하거나 비행 만을 이용하여 포인트를 적립할 수 있다(You can boost your points by supporting these businesses or rely solely on your points from flights)'에서 포인트를 적립할 수 있는 두 가지 방법을 언급하고 있다. 따라서 빈칸에는 포인트 적립을 통해 얻을 수 있는 혜택에 대한 내용이 이어지는 것이 문맥상 자연스러우므로, 정답은 (C)이다.

어휘 comfort 편안함 convenience 편의 top priority 최우선 사항 in no time 곧, 당장에

139-142 안내문

애너하임 연마봉 사용법

한 손으로 연마봉의 손잡이를 수직이 되게 **139**단단히 잡습니다. 다른 손으로는 칼끝이 위로 향하게 칼을 줍니다. 칼 가장 넓은 부분이 연마봉 아래 부분에 닿도록 위치시킵니다. **141**약간의 압력을 **140**가하면서 봉을 따라 20도의 각도를 유지하면서 칼날을 움직여 줍니다. <u>이렇게 해야 도구의 효과를 최대로 올릴 수 있습니다.</u> 균일한 연마를 위해 칼날 면을 한 번씩 교대로 갈아줍니다. 각 면을 15회 정도 간 **142**후 연마도를 시험해 보십시오. 칼 성능 향상을 위해 정기적으로 연마하실 것을 권장합니다.

어휘 sharpening steel 봉칼갈이, 연마봉 vertical 수직의 blade 칼몸 point 가리키다 pressure 압력 cutting edge 칼날 alternate 교대의, 번갈아 하는 even 평평한, 매끈한 approximately 대략 stroke 치기, 갈기, 타격 enhance 향상시키다 performance 성능

139 부사 자리 _ 동사 수식

해설 빈칸은 동사원형(hold)과 목적어(the handle of the steel)로 이뤄진 명령문 뒤에서 동사원형(hold)을 수식하는 부사 자리이므로, 정답은 (B) tightly이다. 동명사/현재분사 (A) tightening, 동사 (C) tighten, 명사 (D) tightness는 품사상 적합하지 않다.

140 동사 어휘

해설 빈칸은 명령문의 동사원형 자리로, 뒤의 목적어(light pressure)와 의미가 잘 통하는 동사를 선택해야 한다. 문맥상 '약간의 압력을 가하다'라는

의미가 자연스러우므로, 정답은 (D) Apply(힘을 가하다, 적용하다, 지원하다)이다. (A) Relieve(완화하다, 안도하게 하다), (B) Force(강요하다), (C) Withstand(견디다)는 의미상 적합하지 않다.

141 문맥에 맞는 문장 고르기

번역 (A) 예리한 칼은 빠른 음식 준비에 도움이 됩니다.
(B) 이렇게 해야 도구의 효과를 최대로 올릴 수 있습니다.
(C) 각 물품에 사용자 매뉴얼이 포함되어 있습니다.
(D) 충분히 뜨겁지 않으면 이 과정은 실행되지 않습니다.

해설 빈칸 앞 문장 '약간의 압력을 가하면서 봉을 따라 20도의 각도를 유지하면서 칼날을 움직여 준다(Apply light pressure as you move the blade up the steel along the cutting edge, maintaining an angle of twenty degrees)'에서 도구의 특이한 사용법을 언급하고 있다. 따라서 빈칸에는 도구를 이렇게(This) 사용하는 이유에 대한 내용이 이어지는 것이 문맥상 자연스러우므로, 정답은 (B)이다.

어휘 maximize 최대로 하다 effectiveness 효과, 효능

142 전치사 어휘

해설 빈칸은 명사구(approximately fifteen strokes) 앞 전치사 자리이다. 문맥상 '대략 15회 정도 간 후 연마도를 시험해 보다'라는 의미가 자연스러우므로, 정답은 (C) after이다. 전치사 (D) since(~ 이래로)는 주로 현재완료시제 동사와 함께 쓰인다.

143-146 이메일

수신: 미공개 수신자
발신: 골드스타인 치과 병원
날짜: 2월 1일
제목: 빅 뉴스!

골드스타인 치과병원 환자 여러분,

골드스타인 치과 병원의 새 웹사이트가 개설되었다는 사실을 알리게 되어 자랑스럽습니다. **144**이제 환자분들은 온라인으로 **143**예약을 할 수 있습니다. 계정을 만드는 데 특별한 컴퓨터 기술이 필요하지 않습니다. **144**여기를 클릭하여 텍스트 상자에 기입만 하면 됩니다. 잠깐이면 **145**손쉽게 환자 정보를 이용하는 편의를 누릴 수 있습니다. 예약 과정의 **146**자동화로 손이 빈 저희 프런트 데스크 직원들은 병원에서 더욱 양질의 서비스를 제공할 수 있게 됐습니다. 그러나 전화 예약을 선호하는 환자들께서는 앞으로도 계속 그렇게 하실 수 있습니다.

골드스타인 치과 병원

어휘 undisclosed 비밀에 붙여진, 미공개의 launch 개시하다, 시작하다 fill out 기입하다 convenience 편의, 편리 free up ~을 해방하다, 자유롭게 하다

143 동사 자리

해설 빈칸은 주어(patients) 뒤 동사 자리로, 앞에 있는 현재를 나타내는 시간부사(Now)의 수식을 받는다. 따라서 (A) can book과 (C) must book이 정답 후보이다. 앞 문장 '새 웹사이트가 개설되었다(our new Web site has been launched)'와 마지막 문장 '전화 예약을 선호하는 환자들은

앞으로도 계속 그렇게 할 수 있다(those of you who prefer to make appointments by phone will still be able to do so)'를 통해 온라인 예약은 선택 사항임을 알 수 있으므로, 정답은 (A) can book이다.

어휘 book 예약하다

144 문맥에 맞는 문장 고르기

번역 (A) 웹사이트 다운으로 혼선을 주었다면 사과 드립니다.
(B) 다음 달 새 치과의가 우리의 훌륭한 기존 팀에 합류하게 됩니다.
(C) 계정을 만드는 데 특별한 컴퓨터 기술이 필요하지 않습니다.
(D) 예약 확인서가 이 이메일에 첨부되어 있습니다.

해설 빈칸 앞 문장 '이제 환자분들은 온라인으로 예약을 할 수 있다(Now patients can book their appointments online)'에서 온라인 예약이 가능하다는 것을, 빈칸 뒤 '여기를 클릭하여 텍스트 상자에 기입만 하면 됩니다(Simply click here and fill out the text boxes)'에서 간편한 온라인 예약 방법을 언급하고 있다. 따라서 빈칸에는 온라인 예약 방법에 대한 의견을 밝히는 것이 문맥상 자연스러우므로, 정답은 (C)이다.

어휘 crash 사고, 고장 confusion 혼란 distinguished 유명한, 성공한 set up an account 계정을 만들다[열다] attach 첨부하다

145 부사 어휘

해설 빈칸은 앞에 있는 동명사(having)의 목적어(your patient information)를 보충 설명하는 형용사(available)를 수식하는 부사 자리이다. 문맥상 '환자 정보를 손쉽게 이용할 수 있도록 하다'라는 의미가 자연스러우므로, 정답은 (D) readily(손쉽게, 순조롭게)이다. (A) noticeably(두드러지게, 현저히), (B) widely(널리, 폭넓게), (C) primarily(주로)는 의미상 적합하지 않다.

어휘 readily 손쉽게 automation 자동화

146 명사 어휘

해설 빈칸은 정관사(The) 뒤 명사 자리로, 전치사구(of our booking process)의 수식을 받는다. 앞에 나온 '이제 환자분들은 온라인으로 예약을 할 수 있다(Now patients can book their appointments online)'를 통해 온라인으로 예약이 가능하다는 것을 알 수 있으므로, 온라인 예약과 관련 있는 단어를 선택해야 한다. 따라서 정답은 (C) automation(자동화)이다. (A) continuation(계속, 지속), (B) interval(간격, 중간 휴식), (D) stability(안정, 안정감)는 의미상 적합하지 않다.

PART 7

147-148 광고

힐락 쇼핑몰 – 소매 점포 임대

저희 쇼핑몰 1층과 2층에 여러 점포가 임대를 기다리고 있습니다. 2층에는 아르노트 강의 멋진 전망이 보이는 점포들이 있습니다. 모든 힐락 쇼핑몰 점포들에는 디스플레이 조명, 보안 시스템, 그리고 카운터를 포함한 최신 설비 및 비품들이 마련되어 있습니다. **147**저희 쇼핑 센터는 두 지하철 역 사이에, 그리고 센트로 파크 버스터미널 옆에 위치해 최상의 입지를 자랑합니다.

148저녁에 점포를 구경하실 분은 배리 갤러웨이 씨(bgalloway@starrealty. com)에게 연락해 시간 약속을 잡아 주세요.

점포 구경 가능 시간: 평일 오후 7시~10시, 주말, 오후 8시~11시

어휘 retail 소매의 boast 자랑하다 magnificent 최고의, 비길 데 없는 feature 특별히 포함하다, 특징으로 삼다 brand-new 아주 새로운, 신품의 fixture 붙박이 세간 fittings 반고정 세간 prime 최고의, 뛰어난 viewing (집을 사거나 얻을 때) 둘러보기

147 사실 관계 확인

번역 힐락 쇼핑몰의 장점으로 언급된 것은?
(A) 적정한 가격대의 매우 다양한 상점들이 있다.
(B) 다른 쇼핑몰들보다 영업 시간이 길다.
(C) 일부 상가 점포들은 복층으로 되어 있다.
(D) 대중교통을 이용하기 쉬운 위치에 있다.

해설 첫 번째 단락에서 쇼핑 센터는 두 지하철 역 사이에, 그리고 센트로 파크 버스터미널 옆에 위치해 최상의 입지를 자랑한다(Our shopping center is situated in a prime location, right in between two subway stations and next to Centro Park Bus Terminal)고 했으므로, 쇼핑 센터가 대중교통을 이용하기 편리한 곳에 위치하고 있음을 알 수 있다. 따라서 정답은 (D)이다.

▶▶ **Paraphrasing** 지문의 **situated in a prime location, right in between two subway stations and next to Centro Park Bus Terminal** → 정답의 **convenient access to public transportation**

148 세부 사항

번역 왜 사람들에게 이메일을 보내라고 하는가?
(A) 쇼핑몰 개점 시간을 문의하기 위해
(B) 쇼핑몰에서 행사 개최를 요청하기 위해
(C) 매장 할인에 대한 정보를 알아 보기 위해
(D) 비어 있는 점포를 볼 수 있도록 약속을 잡기 위해

해설 두 번째 단락에서 저녁에 점포를 구경하려면 배리 갤러웨이 씨에게 이메일을 보내 약속을 잡으라(Contact Barry Galloway at bgalloway@ starrealty.com to schedule an evening viewing)고 했으므로, 정답은 (D)이다.

▶▶ **Paraphrasing** 지문의 **to schedule an evening viewing** → 정답의 **To arrange to see vacant retail spaces**

149-150 안내문

149손상을 입기 쉬운 그림과 조각품들의 상태를 유지하고 다른 방문객들의 감상을 방해하지 않도록 갤러리 방문 시 배려와 예의를 지켜 행동해 주십시오.

✓ 모든 음식 및 음료 포장지와 용기들은 쓰레기통에 버립니다.
✓ 사진 촬영 시 플래시는 사용하지 않습니다.
✓ 전시관 투어 시에는 작은 소리로 이야기합니다.
✓ **150**전시물이나 조명 기구들을 만지거나 들어 올리지 않습니다.

협조해 주셔서 진심으로 감사드립니다. 고맙습니다.

어휘 delicate 연약한, 부서지기 쉬운 sculpture 조각, 조각상 spoil 망치다 respectfully 공손하게 courteously 예의 바르게 wrapper (식품 등의) 포장지 container 용기 exhibition 전시, 전시회 exhibit 전시품 apparatus 기구, 장치 appreciate 고맙게 여기다 cooperation 협력, 협조

149 주제 / 목적

번역 이 안내문의 목적은?
(A) 미술 갤러리로 가는 길을 알려주기 위해
(B) 방문객을 위한 지침을 안내하기 위해
(C) 새 전시물에 대해 방문객에게 알리기 위해
(D) 직원들에게 업무를 상기시키기 위해

해설 첫 번째 단락에서 손상 입기 쉬운 그림과 조각품들의 상태를 유지하고 다른 방문객들의 감상을 방해하지 않도록 갤러리 방문 시 배려와 예의를 지켜 행동해 달라(To preserve the delicate condition of all paintings and sculptures, and to avoid spoiling the enjoyment of other visitors, please behave respectfully and courteously while visiting the gallery)고 했으므로, 갤러리 방문객들이 지켜야 할 행동지침을 알리기 위한 안내문임을 알 수 있다. 따라서 정답은 (B)이다.

150 세부 사항

번역 어떤 행동이 금지되는가?
(A) 음식 먹기
(B) 투어 중 말하기
(C) 사진 촬영
(D) 전시품 만지기

해설 방문객들을 위한 행동지침 중 마지막 지침에서 전시물이나 조명 기구들을 만지거나 들어 올리지 말라(Do not touch or pick up any exhibits or lighting apparatus)고 했으므로, 정답은 (D)이다.

▶▶ **Paraphrasing** 지문의 **Do not** → 질문의 **is prohibited** 지문의 **touch or pick up any exhibits** → 정답의 **Handling exhibits**

151-152 이메일

발신: 린 코즐로우스키〈lkozlowski@filmfest.com〉
수신: 버넌 호건〈vhogan@widemail.net〉
제목: 영화제
날짜: 3월 9일

안녕하세요, 버넌.

지난주에 말씀 드렸듯이 저희는 5월 4일(토)과 5일(일) 양일간 개최되는 제4회 오리건 독립영화제의 준비 작업을 시작했습니다. 예년 영화제와 마찬가지로 여러 신문, 잡지, 웹사이트의 비평가와 평론가들이 초대될 것입니다.

151이전 내빈 목록을 확인해서 과거 영화제에 참석했던 모든 영화 평론가 명단을 저에게 보내 주세요. 그러면 제가 그분들에게 연락해서 올해 참석 여부를 확인하겠습니다. **152**올해 우리가 이용하는 영화관은 행사 개막일 밤 이름 별로 좌석을 지정한다고 하네요. 그래서 영화관 측에서 가능한 한 빨리 내빈 명단을 보내 달라고 했습니다. **151**이번 주 중에 제가 최종 내빈 명단을 보내 드릴테니 개막식 공

Test 10

식 초대장 준비를 시작하시면 됩니다. 초대장 배포를 위해 아니 루미스에게 3월 31일까지 제출하셔야 합니다.

고맙습니다.

린 드림

> **어휘** prepare for ~을 위해 준비하다 take place 일어나다, 개최되다 previous 이전의 critic 비평가, 평론가 attend 참석하다 confirm 확인하다 reserve 예약하다 proprietor 소유주, 경영주 distribution 배포, 분배

151 주제 / 목적

번역 코즐로우스키 씨가 이메일을 보낸 이유는?
(A) 축제 날짜를 변경하기 위해
(B) 호건 씨에게 축제에 참석하도록 권유하기 위해
(C) 극장이 왜 축제를 여는지를 설명하기 위해
(D) 축제 개최에 도움을 얻기 위해

해설 두 번째 단락에서 이전 내빈 목록을 확인해서 과거 영화제에 참석했던 모든 영화 평론가 명단을 보내 달라(Please take a look at our previous guest lists and e-mail me the names of all the film critics who attended past festivals)고 했고, 이번 주 중에 최종 내빈 명단을 보낼 테니 개막식 공식 초대장 준비를 시작하면 된다(Later this week, I'll send you the finalized guest list so that you can start preparing formal invitations for the opening night)고 했으므로, 영화제 준비를 위한 도움을 얻기 위해 이메일을 쓰고 있음을 알 수 있다. 따라서 정답은 (D)이다.

152 추론 / 암시

번역 이메일에 따르면 코즐로우스키 씨가 축제를 준비하기 위해 이미 한 일은 무엇인가?
(A) 개막일 밤에 상영할 영화 선정
(B) 특별 게스트에게 초대장 발송
(C) 극장주와 연락
(D) 참석하는 영화 평론가 명단 작성

해설 두 번째 단락에서 올해 우리가 이용하는 영화관은 행사 개막일 밤 이름별로 좌석을 지정한다고 해서 영화관 측에서 가능한 한 빨리 내빈 명단을 보내 달라고 했다(The movie theater we are using this year will reserve seats by name on the opening night of the event, so the proprietor asked me to send a guest list as soon as possible)고 했으므로, 코즐로우스키 씨가 영화관 측으로부터 이전에 연락을 받았음을 유추할 수 있다. 따라서 정답은 (C)이다.

▶▶ **Paraphrasing**   지문의 **the proprietor**
→ 정답의 **a theater owner**

153-154 문자 메시지

> **메건 데이비스**   오전 8:47
> 앤디. 오고 있어요? 직원들 대부분이 이미 도착했고, 교육 수업은 9시 정각에 시작하기로 돼 있어요.

> **앤디 폴러**   오전 8:53
> 알아요. 153출근길에 타이어 하나가 펑크가 나서 수리공을 불렀습니다. 1549시까지는 못 갈 것 같은데요. 메건이 워크숍을 진행하는 거 어때요?

> **메건 데이비스**   오전 8:56
> 제 전문 분야가 아닌데요. 게다가 앤디가 직원 매뉴얼과 유인물을 다 가지고 있지 않나요?

> **앤디 폴러**   오전 8:57
> 아, 맞아요. 알겠어요. 그럼 참석자들에게 짧게 개요를 소개해주세요. 최대한 빨리 갈게요.

> **어휘** on one's way 가는 길에, 가는 중에 be supposed to ~하기로 되어 있다 blow 펑크 나다 mechanic 수리공, 기계공 make it (어떤 장소에) 도착하다 specialty 전공, 장기 handout 유인물 attendee 참석자 introductory 도입의, 소개의

153 추론 / 암시

번역 폴러 씨에 대해 추론할 수 있는 것은?
(A) 워크숍 일정을 다시 잡고 싶어 한다.
(B) 데이비스 씨에게 차로 직장에 데려다 주겠다고 제의했다.
(C) 엉뚱한 장소로 갔다.
(D) 차에 문제가 발생했다.

해설 폴러 씨의 오전 8시 53분 메시지에서 출근길에 타이어 하나가 펑크가 나서 수리공을 불렀다(One of my tires blew on my way to the office, so I had to call out a mechanic)고 했으므로, 폴러 씨의 차에 문제가 생겼음을 알 수 있다. 따라서 정답은 (D)이다.

▶▶ **Paraphrasing**   지문의 **One of my tires blew**
→ 정답의 **trouble with his vehicle**

154 의도 파악

번역 오전 8시 56분에 데이비스 씨가 "제 전문 분야가 아닌데요"라고 쓸 때, 그 의도는 무엇인가?
(A) 그녀는 자신에게 교육이 더 필요하다고 생각한다.
(B) 그녀는 폴러 씨에게 어떠한 조언도 줄 수 없다.
(C) 그녀는 폴러 씨를 대신하기가 싫다.
(D) 그녀는 매뉴얼 작성하는 방법을 모른다.

해설 폴러 씨는 오전 8시 53분 메시지에서 9시까지는 못 갈 것 같은데 메건이 워크숍을 진행하는 게 어떠냐(I doubt I'll make it by 9. How do you feel about leading the workshop)며 데이비스 씨가 워크숍을 대신 진행할 것을 제안하고 있다. 이에 대해 데이비스 씨가 자신의 전문 분야가 아니라며(It's not exactly my specialty) 제안을 우회적으로 거절하고 있으므로, 정답은 (C)이다.

155-157 공지

> **인포텍 개발원**
> **탁월한 교육**
>
> 인포텍 개발원은 개원한 지 20년이 넘었습니다. 다양한 강좌와 세미나를 갖추고 저희는 법조인들에게 개발 기술을 익힐 수 있는 탁월한 기회를 제공합니다. 수천 명의 변호사와 검사들이 저희를 선택해 커리어의 다음 단계로 전진하는 데 도움을 받았습니다.

¹⁵⁵우리가 제공하는 10개의 강좌는 각각 한 달에 한 번 진행됩니다. 일부 강좌는 온라인으로 수강할 수 있지만 직접 참여해 토의와 실기 활동에 참여해야 하는 강좌들도 있습니다. ¹⁵⁷모든 유인물과 교육 자료들은 강의료에 포함될 것입니다. 이것들은 여러분이 개발원에 도착하면 제공될 것입니다.

^{156A, C}이달 말까지 인포텍 회원권을 구입하시면 여러분의 학습을 도와줄 인포텍 개인 튜터의 이메일 주소뿐만 아니라 고급 문구류 세트도 받게 됩니다. ^{156B}회원은 또한 수강하는 강좌에 대해 대폭 할인을 받을 수 있게 됩니다. 하지만 이제 공항과 개발원 간 교통편은 회원이 직접 마련해야 합니다. 그동안 제공되던 이 서비스가 이제는 중단되었기 때문입니다.

곧 여러분을 만나 뵙고 하루 빨리 여러분 커리어를 다음 단계로 상승시킬 수 있는 기술을 여러분에게 전수하게 되기를 고대합니다. 예약은 545-555-0125로 전화 주세요.

> **어휘** a range of 다양한 exceptional 비범한, 특출한 profession 직업 lawyer 변호사 attorney 변호사, 검사 access 접속하다, 접근하다 in person 몸소, 직접 take part in ~에 참가[참여]하다 complimentary 공짜의, 무료의 stationery 문구류 eligible 자격이 있는 generous 후한, 많은 transportation 수송, 운송 discontinue 중단하다 look forward to ~을 고대하다 book 예약하다

155 사실 관계 확인

번역 교육 강좌들에 대해 명시된 것은?
(A) 강좌 모두 웹사이트를 통해 원거리 접속이 가능하다.
(B) 의료인들을 대상으로 한다.
(C) 일 년에 여러 번 제공된다.
(D) 강좌 자료들은 추가로 구매해야 한다.

해설 두 번째 단락에서 우리가 제공하는 10개의 강좌는 각각 한 달에 한 번 진행된다(Each of our ten courses runs once a month)라고 했으므로, 강좌가 일 년에 여러 번 진행된다는 것을 알 수 있다. 따라서 정답은 (C)이다.

> **▶▶ Paraphrasing** 지문의 runs once a month → 정답의 are delivered several times a year

156 사실 관계 확인

번역 인포텍 회원의 혜택으로 언급되지 않은 것은?
(A) 직원의 연락처 정보
(B) 수강료 할인
(C) 무료 경품
(D) 무료 셔틀 서비스

해설 세 번째 단락에서 이달 말까지 인포텍 회원권을 구입하면 학습을 도와줄 인포텍 개인 튜터의 이메일 주소뿐만 아니라 고급 문구류 세트도 받게 된다(Until the end of the month, if you purchase an Infotec membership, you will receive a complimentary pack of luxury stationery, as well as be given the e-mail address of an Infotec personal tutor in order to help you with your learning)고 했으므로 (A)와 (C)가, 회원은 또한 수강하는 강좌에 대해 대폭 할인을 받을 수 있게 된다(Members are also eligible to receive generous savings on courses they participate in)고 했으므로 (B)가 회원 혜택임을 확인할 수 있다. 따라서 정답은 (D)이다.

> **▶▶ Paraphrasing** 지문의 the e-mail address of an Infotec personal tutor
> → 보기의 A staff member's contact details
> 지문의 generous savings on courses
> → 보기의 Discounted tuition fees
> 지문의 a complimentary pack of luxury stationery → 보기의 A free gift

157 문장 삽입

번역 [1], [2], [3], [4]로 표시된 곳 중에서 다음 문장이 들어가기에 가장 적합한 곳은?

"이것들은 여러분이 개발원에 도착하면 제공될 것입니다."

(A) [1]
(B) [2]
(C) [3]
(D) [4]

해설 삽입 문장 '이것들은 여러분이 개발원에 도착하면 제공될 것입니다 (These will be provided to you upon arrival at the institute)'를 통해 앞에서 제공되는 이것들(These)을 구체적으로 언급할 것임을 알 수 있다. [2]의 앞 문장에서 모든 유인물과 교육 자료들은 강의료에 포함될 것(All handouts and training packs will be included in the cost of the course)이라며 제공되는 것들을 구체적으로 나열하고 있으므로, 정답은 (B)이다.

158-160 광고

> ### 먹고-자고-놀고 — 곧 출간!
>
> ¹⁵⁸지역 식당, 호텔, 신나는 놀거리에 대한 추천을 받고 싶다면, '먹고-자고-놀고'를 찾아 주세요! ^{158, 159}창간호부터 '먹고-자고-놀고'의 지면은 하츠빌의 현지 주민과 급증하는 관광객들 모두에게 흥미 있는 심층 기사와 후기들이 가득합니다. 매달 저희는 생각을 요하는 진지한 소식을 전해 드릴 것이며 여러분은 어떤 호도 놓치고 싶지 않게 될 것입니다!
>
> '먹고-자고-놀고'는 가판대와 슈퍼마켓에서 구입할 수 있지만 못 읽고 건너 뛰는 일 없게 아예 구독을 할 수도 있습니다. 첫 월간호가 10월 1일에 출간됩니다. 여기에는 동종으로는 하츠빌의 유일한 업체인 잽 존 레이저 태그 소유주와의 인터뷰가 실립니다.
>
> 18개월 구독은 75달러이며 이는 일반 소매 가격과 비교해서 36달러가 절약되는 금액입니다. ¹⁶⁰이메일로 구독하시는 경우 제목에 행사 코드인 ESP111을 기입해 주세요. 창간호와 함께 무료 커피 머그잔을 드립니다. 지금 inquiries@eatsleepplay.com으로 연락 주세요. 채용 기회에 관심이 있다면 www.eatsleepplay.com/vacancies를 방문해 주세요.

> **어휘** recommendation 추천 issue (신문·잡지 등의) 호 feature 특징으로 삼다 in-depth 심층적인 local 지역의, 현지의 soaring 치솟는, 급증하는 thought-provoking 생각하게 만드는, 시사하는 바가 많은 miss out on ~을 놓치다 newsstand 가판대 subscribe 구독하다 laser tag 레이저 태그 (적외선 총으로 적을 쏘아 탈락시키는 서바이벌 게임) savings 절약 retail price 소매가 employment 고용

158 주제 / 목적

번역 광고의 주목적은?
(A) 회사 확장 발표
(B) 새 출판물 홍보
(C) 하츠빌의 업체들 추천
(D) 회사 신규 직원 구인

해설 첫 번째 단락에서 지역 식당, 호텔, 신나는 놀거리에 대한 추천을 받고 싶다면, '먹고-자고-놀고'를 찾아 달라(If you are looking for recommendations for restaurants, hotels, or fun activities around town, then *Eat-Sleep-Play* is for you)고 했다. 그리고 창간호부터 '먹고-자고-놀고'의 지면은 하츠빌의 현지 주민과 급증하는 관광객들 모두에게 흥미 있을 심층 기사와 후기들이 가득하다(Starting with our first issue, *Eat-Sleep-Play*s pages will feature in-depth articles and reviews that will be of interest to both local residents and the soaring number of tourists who come to Hartsville)고 했으므로, 새롭게 발간되는 출판물을 홍보하는 광고임을 알 수 있다. 따라서 정답은 (B)이다.

▶▶ **Paraphrasing** 지문의 **our first issue**
→ 정답의 **a new publication**

159 추론 / 암시

번역 하츠빌에 대해 암시된 것은?
(A) 레이저 태그 시설들이 여럿 있는 곳이다.
(B) 그곳의 요식업계가 점점 더 경쟁력을 갖추고 있다.
(C) 대중교통 체계가 편리하다.
(D) 관광업이 호황을 누리고 있다.

해설 첫 번째 단락에서 창간호부터 '먹고-자고-놀고'의 지면은 하츠빌의 현지 주민과 급증하는 관광객들 모두에게 흥미 있을 심층 기사와 후기들로 가득하다(Starting with our first issue, *Eat-Sleep-Play*'s pages will feature in-depth articles and reviews that will be of interest to both local residents and the soaring number of tourists who come to Hartsville)고 했으므로, 하츠빌로 오는 관광객의 증가로 관광업이 호황을 누리고 있음을 유추할 수 있다. 따라서 정답은 (D)이다.

▶▶ **Paraphrasing** 지문의 **the soaring number of tourists**
→ 정답의 **a rise in tourism**

160 세부 사항

번역 무료 경품은 어떻게 받을 수 있나?
(A) 웹사이트를 방문해서
(B) 특정 날짜에 구독신청을 해서
(C) 특별한 코드를 기입해서
(D) 1년 구독을 신청해서

해설 세 번째 단락에서 이메일로 구독하는 경우 제목에 행사 코드인 ESP111을 기입하면 창간호와 함께 무료 커피 머그잔을 제공(When subscribing by e-mail, provide the promo code ESP111 in the subject line to get a free coffee mug with your first issue)한다고 했으므로, 행사 코드를 기입하면 무료 경품을 받을 수 있음을 알 수 있다. 따라서 정답은 (C)이다.

▶▶ **Paraphrasing** 지문의 **get a free coffee mug**
→ 질문의 **receive a complimentary gift**
지문의 **provide the promo code ESP111**
→ 정답의 **entering a special code**

161-163 편지

> **코롤라스 비스트로**
> 캘리포니아주 샌프란시스코 글렌데일 파크 로드 3009번지
> 우편번호: 94118   Tel: 555-0133
>
> 9월 4일
>
> 애이다 유라왓
> 캘리포니아주 샌프란시스코 힐슨 애버뉴 237번지
> 우편번호: 94103
>
> 유라왓 씨,
>
> **161**귀하가 최근 저희 식당을 방문하고 종업원 중 한 명인 앨리스 리 씨에게 받은 훌륭한 서비스에 대해 주신 편지를 기쁘게 받아 보았습니다. **162**리 씨는 저희 식당에서 일한 지 오래되지 않았는데 그녀가 그러한 직업 정신과 고객에 대한 세심함을 보여줬다는 얘기를 듣게 되어 매우 기쁩니다. 저는 특히 그녀가 귀하가 주문한 음식이 일행의 음식과 바뀌었을 때 이를 어떻게 처리했는지 설명해 준 부분이 특히 좋았습니다.
>
> 식당의 주인으로 저는 고객들의 의견을 매우 소중히 생각합니다. 그런 의견들은 제가 식당을 개선하려 할 때 올바른 사업적 결정을 내리도록 도와주기 때문입니다. 리 씨에게는 이번 목요일 직원 회의에서 개인적으로 감사의 뜻을 전하겠습니다. **163**그리고 편지를 보내주신 것에 대한 감사의 뜻으로 편지에 쿠폰을 동봉했습니다. 다시 저희 식당을 방문하실 때 총액의 50%를 할인받을 수 있습니다.
>
> **161**저희 직원이 보여준 헌신과 전문적 태도를 저에게 상기시켜주셔서 다시 한 번 감사드립니다.
>
> 애드리언 코롤라 드림

어휘 bistro 작은 바, 식당 be delighted to ～하게 되어 기쁘다 regarding ～에 대해서, 관해서 wait staff (식당에서 시중드는) 종업원들, 웨이터들 pleasing 유쾌한, 즐거운 professionalism 전문성 attentiveness 정중함, 신경을 씀 handle 처리하다 mix-up 혼동, 뒤섞임 voucher 상품권, 쿠폰 envelope 봉투 bill 계산서 dedication 헌신, 전념

161 주제 / 목적

번역 편지의 목적은?
(A) 고객이 보내준 의견에 대해 고마움을 표시함
(B) 불만족스러운 서비스에 대한 고객 불만에 응대함
(C) 영업장에서 파티를 하겠다는 고객 요청을 승인함
(D) 메뉴 변경에 대한 고객 문의에 답변함

해설 첫 번째 단락에서 귀하가 최근 저희 식당을 방문하고 종업원 중 한 명인 앨리스 리 씨에게 받은 훌륭한 서비스에 대해 주신 편지를 기쁘게 받아 보았다(I was delighted to receive your letter regarding your recent visit to our restaurant and the excellent service provided to you by a member of our wait staff, Ms. Alice Lee)고 했고, 세 번째 단락에서는 저희 직원이 보여준 헌신과 전문적 태도를 저에게 상기

시켜주셔서 다시 한 번 감사드린다(Again, thanks for bringing my staff member's dedication and professional attitude to my attention)고 했으므로, 의견을 보내준 것에 감사를 표하기 위해 편지를 쓰고 있음을 알 수 있다. 따라서 정답은 (A)이다.

▶▶ **Paraphrasing**　지문의 **to receive your letter regarding your recent visit to our restaurant**　→ 정답의 **providing feedback**
지문의 **thanks** → 정답의 **express gratitude**

162　추론 / 암시

번역　리 씨에 대해 추론할 수 있는 것은?
(A) 그녀는 유라왓 씨를 위해 음식을 준비했다.
(B) 그녀는 상으로 보너스를 받을 것이다.
(C) 그녀는 식당 지배인이다.
(D) **그녀는 비교적 신입 직원이다.**

해설　첫 번째 단락에서 리 씨는 저희 식당에서 일한 지 오래되지 않았는데 그녀가 그러한 직업 정신과 고객에 대한 세심함을 보여줬다는 얘기를 듣게 되어 매우 기쁘다(Ms. Lee has not been with us long, so it is very pleasing for me to hear that she is displaying such professionalism and attentiveness to our customers)고 했으므로, 리 씨는 신입 직원임을 유추할 수 있다. 따라서 정답은 (D)이다.

▶▶ **Paraphrasing**　지문의 **Ms. Lee has not been with us long**
→ 정답의 **She is a relatively new employee.**

163　세부 사항

번역　코롤라 씨가 편지에 동봉한 것은?
(A) 수정된 계산서
(B) 일부 환불액
(C) 샘플 메뉴
(D) **할인 쿠폰**

해설　두 번째 단락에서 보내준 편지에 대한 감사의 뜻으로 편지에 쿠폰을 동봉했고, 식당을 재방문할 때 총액의 50%를 할인받을 수 있다(And, to thank you for your letter, I have included a voucher in the envelope. When you visit my restaurant again, you can use it to receive fifty percent off your total bill)고 했으므로, 정답은 (D)이다.

▶▶ **Paraphrasing**　지문의 **included a voucher in the envelope**
→ 질문의 **enclosed with the letter**
지문의 **receive fifty percent off your total bill** → 정답의 **discount**

164-167 온라인 채팅

레이철 베켓	오전 11:02
안녕하세요, 브래드. 저 지금 막 발표하려고 대회장에 도착했어요. 그런데 시작하려고 보니 뭔가 빠졌네요.	

브래드 네이벌	오전 11:07
뭐가 필요한가요? 발표 슬라이드는 다 가지고 있죠?	

레이철 베켓	오전 11:14
네, 가지고 있어요. ¹⁶⁴그런데 청중에게 나누어 줄 유인물이 없어요. ^{164, 165}그것들을 출력해서 오후 12시 30분에 가져다 줄 수 있나요?	

브래드 네이벌	오전 11:17
좀 너무 촉박한 것 같은데. 그곳에 출력할 수 있는 곳이 없어요?	

레이철 베켓	오전 11:21
벌써 체크해 봤죠. ¹⁶⁶여기 프린터가 이상이 있어서 할 수가 없어요. 기사가 와서 수리하기를 기다리고 있어요.	

브래드 네이벌	오전 11:28
아, 유감이네요. ¹⁶⁵저는 그 시간에 맞춰서는 못 갈 것 같은데. ¹⁶⁷그러지 말고 사람들에게 이메일로 유인물을 보내면 어떨까요?	

레이철 베켓	오전 11:31
네, 그게 최선이겠네요. 제가 가서 그렇게 할게요.	

어휘　last minute 마지막 순간의, 막바지의　fault 결함, 고장　service (기계 등을) 점검하다, 정비하다　make it (어떤 장소에) 도착하다, 가다　in time 시간 맞춰, 늦지 않게

164　세부 사항

번역　베켓 씨는 왜 네이벌 씨에게 연락했나?
(A) 그에게 자신이 길이 막혀 꼼짝 못하고 있다고 말하려고
(B) 장소의 주소를 확인하기 위해
(C) **그에게 문서를 가져다 달라고 요청하기 위해**
(D) 컴퓨터 로그인 암호를 요청하기 위해

해설　베켓 씨의 오전 11시 14분 메시지에서 청중에게 나누어 줄 유인물이 없다며 그것들을 출력해서 오후 12시 30분에 가져다 줄 수 있는지(But I don't have the handouts I was going to give to the audience. Could you print some and bring them over for 12:30 P.M.) 묻고 있으므로, 유인물을 가져다 달라고 요청하기 위해 연락했음을 알 수 있다. 따라서 정답은 (C)이다.

▶▶ **Paraphrasing**　지문의 **bring them over**
→ 정답의 **deliver some documents**

165　의도 파악

번역　오전 11시 17분에 네이벌 씨가 "좀 너무 촉박한 것 같은데"라고 쓸 때, 그 의도는 무엇인가?
(A) 그는 베켓 씨에게 잠시 기다리라고 말하고 있다.
(B) **베켓 씨가 부탁한 것을 하기에는 너무 늦었다.**
(C) 그것은 금방 할 수 있는 일이다.
(D) 그는 베켓 씨에게 몇 시인지를 묻고 있다.

해설　베켓 씨의 오전 11시 14분 메시지에서 그것들을 출력해서 오후 12시 30분에 가져다 줄 수 있냐(Could you print some and bring them over for 12:30 P.M.)는 요청에 네이벌 씨가 좀 너무 촉박한 것 같다(It's a bit last minute)며 우회적으로 부정적인 응답을 하고 있다. 또한 네이벌 씨는 오전 11시 28분 메시지에서 그 시간에 맞춰서는 못 갈 것 같다(I won't be able to make it in time)며 한 번 더 시간 부족을 언급하고 있으므로, 정답은 (B)이다.

Test 10

166 사실 관계 확인

번역 베켓 씨가 언급하는 문제는 무엇인가?
(A) 그녀는 자신의 이메일 비밀번호를 잊어버렸다.
(B) 일부 발표 자료에 오류가 있다.
(C) 어떤 기계가 고장이 나 있다.
(D) 청중이 아직 도착하지 않았다.

해설 베켓 씨가 오전 11시 21분 메시지에서 여기 프린터가 이상이 있어 할 수가 없다(I can't do it here because their printer is experiencing a fault)며 프린터 문제를 언급하고 있으므로, 정답은 (C)이다.

▶▶ Paraphrasing 지문의 their printer is experiencing a fault
→ 정답의 Some machinery is out of order.

167 세부 사항

번역 네이벌 씨가 제안한 것은?
(A) 행사 연기
(B) 다른 강연실로 가기
(C) 사무실에서 만나기
(D) 문서를 이메일로 보내기

해설 네이벌 씨가 오전 11시 28분 메시지에서 사람들에게 이메일로 유인물을 보내면 어떨지(How about we e-mail the handout to people instead) 제안하고 있으므로, 정답은 (D)이다.

▶▶ Paraphrasing 지문의 How about → 질문의 suggest
지문의 e-mail the handout
→ 정답의 Sending a document electronically

168-171 편지

브라이언 휴즈
영국 블랙풀
페어필드 애비뉴 14번지
우편번호: BL3 9FH

휴즈 씨

저는 이코노빌드의 오랜 고객이고 제 작업 용품들을 정기적으로 귀사에서 구입합니다. **168**저는 귀사에서 구매하는 부품들이 싱크나 변기 수리할 때 정말로 믿고 쓸 수 있는 제품이구나 하고 느끼는 경우가 많습니다. 하지만 애석하게도 이번 경우에는 몇 가지 불만사항을 제기하겠습니다.

169D첫째, 귀사에서 받은 택배는 예정보다 하루 늦게 도착했습니다. 기한을 엄격히 지켜야 하는 사람으로서 제 영업에 큰 지장이 발생했습니다. 일부 작업 예약들을 재조정해야 했기 때문입니다. 그러므로 귀사가 제게 급행 배송료 9.99파운드를 환불해주시면 감사하겠습니다. 귀사는 급행 서비스를 이행하지 못했기 때문이죠. 최소한 부품들이 평소처럼 고품질인 것에는 만족합니다.

둘째, 제가 전화로 귀사의 고객 서비스 직원 한 명과 연결이 되었는데 저를 고객 불만 접수 부서로 연결시켜 주었습니다. 저는 제 문제를 거기 직원에게 설명하려고 했습니다. **169A**그런데 그 직원 무척이나 무례하고 전혀 도움을 주지 않더군요. 더욱이 제 문제에 대해 별다른 해결책을 제시하지 않았습니다. 그래서 이 편지를 쓰게 됐습니다.

169B, 170마지막으로, 제가 제 잔액을 확인하려고 귀사의 웹사이트 회원 페이지에 로그인했더니 제 가장 최근 청구서에 제가 주문하지도 않은 물품에 대해 청구가 되어 있었습니다. **171**약 60파운드가 과잉 청구가 되어 있는 것 같습니다. 이 문제가 즉시 해결되도록 조처해 주시면 감사하겠습니다.

위에서 언급한 대로 저는 과거 귀사의 서비스에 늘 만족했던 사람으로서 이런 문제들이 발생한 것에 실망하지 않을 수 없습니다. 제가 지적한 것에 대해 저와 논의를 하시려면 558-555-0117로 연락 주십시오.

폴 그레이블 드림

그레이블 인더스트리즈

어휘 long-term 장기의 regularly 정기적인 supplies 물품, 물자 part 부품 reliable 신뢰할 수 있는 repair 수리하다 compliant 불만사항 deadline 기한, 마감 significant 커다란, 중요한 grateful 고마워하는 refund 환불 express delivery 급행 배송 fulfill (약속 등을) 이행하다 at least 최소한 rude 무례한 hence 그러므로 balance 잔액, 잔금 invoice 송장, 청구서 overcharge 과잉 청구하다

168 추론 / 암시

번역 그레이블 씨에 대해 암시된 것은?
(A) 그는 현재 실업자다.
(B) 그는 배관공이다.
(C) 청구서 대금 지불을 연체했다.
(D) 이코노빌드 일자리에 지원하고자 한다.

해설 첫 번째 단락에서 그레이블 씨가 귀사에서 구매하는 부품들이 싱크나 변기 수리할 때 정말로 믿고 쓸 수 있는 제품이구나 하고 느끼는 경우가 많다(I often find the parts I purchase to be extremely reliable to use when I am repairing sink and toilet units)고 했으므로, 그레이블 씨가 배관 수리와 관련된 일을 한다고 유추할 수 있다. 따라서 정답은 (B)이다.

▶▶ Paraphrasing 지문의 I am repairing sink and toilet units
→ 정답의 He works as a plumber.

169 사실 관계 확인

번역 그레이블 씨의 불만 사항이 아닌 것은?
(A) 직원의 행동
(B) 청구서 내역
(C) 일부 제품의 질
(D) 일부 물품의 배송 소요 기간

해설 세 번째 단락에서 그 직원이 무척이나 무례하고 전혀 도움을 주지 않았다(However, I found him to be extremely rude and unhelpful)고 했으므로 (A)를, 네 번째 단락에서 잔액을 확인하려고 귀사의 웹사이트 회원 페이지에 로그인했더니 가장 최근 청구서에 주문하지도 않은 물품이 청구가 되어 있었다(Lastly, when I logged in to check my balance on your Web site's member's section, I noticed I had been charged for some items that I did not order on my last invoice)고 했으므로 (B)를, 두 번째 단락에서 귀사에서 받은 택배는 예정보다 하루 늦게 도착했다(Firstly, the package I received from your company arrived a day later than scheduled)고 했으므로 (D)를 확인할 수 있다. 따라서 정답은 (C)이다.

▶▶ Paraphrasing 지문의 found him to be extremely rude and unhelpful → 보기의 The conduct of a staff member
지문의 arrived a day later than scheduled → 보기의 The time taken to deliver some items

170 사실 관계 확인

번역 이코노빌드에 대해 명시된 것은?
(A) 회원들에게 온라인 서비스를 제공한다.
(B) 여러 나라에 지점을 가지고 있다.
(C) 불만 접수 부서에는 직원이 없다.
(D) 배송 운전기사 채용 공고를 하고 있다

해설 네 번째 단락에서 잔액을 확인하려고 귀사의 웹사이트 회원 페이지에 로그인했더니 제 가장 최근 청구서에 주문하지도 않은 물품에 대해 청구가 되어 있었다(Lastly, when I logged in to check my balance on your Web site's member's section, I noticed I had been charged for some items that I did not order on my last invoice)고 했으므로, 웹사이트 회원 페이지를 운영한다는 것을 알 수 있다. 따라서 정답은 (A)이다.

▶▶ Paraphrasing 지문의 your Web site's member's section → 정답의 an online service to members

171 문장 삽입

번역 [1], [2], [3], [4]로 표시된 곳 중에서 다음 문장이 들어가기에 가장 적합한 곳은?

"이 문제가 즉시 해결되도록 조처해 주시면 감사하겠습니다."

(A) [1]
(B) [2]
(C) [3]
(D) [4]

해설 삽입 문장 '이 문제가 즉시 해결되도록 조처해 주시면 감사하겠습니다(I'd appreciate it if you would see to it that this is amended immediately)'를 통해 앞에서 이 문제(this)에 대해 구체적으로 언급할 것임을 알 수 있다. [4]의 앞 문장에서 약 60파운드가 과잉 청구가 되어 있는 것 같다(As such, I seem to have been overcharged by about £60)며 과잉 청구 문제를 명확히 제시하고 있으므로, 정답은 (D)이다.

172-175 안내문

제7회 먼로산 반딧불이 축제 – 6월 13일

공원 경비원들은 먼로산의 그 유명한 문화축제 〈반딧불이 축제〉 준비에 돌입했습니다! **173B**올해 행사는 6월 13일 오후 4시에서 10시까지 열리며 반딧불이를 보기에는 최상의 환경이 되리라 예상합니다. **172**행사 참석을 원하시는 분들은 다음을 숙지해 주십시오.

축제 기간 동안 일반에게 출입 금지되는 등산로:

스토니 브리지 코스: 방문객 센터 기점 전 코스

코니퍼 코스: 로완 대피소에서 더글라스 피크까지

맨포드 코스: 방문객 센터 기점 전 코스

에덴 코스: 셔우드 캠핑장에서 반스 리지까지

주차권 추첨:

인근 도로들의 혼잡을 예방하기 위해 방문객들은 반드시 저희 추첨 시스템을 통해 주차권을 받거나 대중교통을 이용하셔야 합니다. 주차권 신청은 5월 1일부터 6월 1일까지(조기 소진될 수 있음) 저희 웹사이트 www.munromountainpark.com/parking을 통해 받습니다. **173A**올해 추첨 응모는 무료입니다. **173C**추첨 결과는 6월 2일 이메일을 통해 발표됩니다. **173B**주차권은 환불, 양도가 불가하며 행사 당일에만 유효합니다.

주차장 및 방문객 센터

174허가를 받고 축제에 차량을 가지고 오시는 분들은 방문객 센터 앞 메인 주차장에 주차할 수 있습니다. 건물 자체는 행사 당일 저녁에 개방되지 않습니다만, 주차장 북쪽으로 임시 부스가 설치될 것입니다. 공원 직원이 배치되어 여러분의 질문에 답하고 팜플릿을 배포할 것입니다.

입장권:

입장권은 성인은 8.5달러, 어린이는 3.5달러입니다. **175**방문객 센터, 시청 공원 관리국 그리고 공공 도서관에서 구입할 수 있습니다. 모든 곳에서 현금과 신용카드를 사용할 수 있습니다. 입장권 구입은 일인당 4장으로 제한되어 있다는 것을 기억해주시기 바랍니다. 자세한 내용은 저희 웹사이트를 방문해 주세요.

어휘 firefly 반딧불이 park ranger 공원 경비원 peak 절정의, 최상의 aware 의식하고 있는, 알고 있는 trail (산책·등산 등의) 코스, 루트 congestion 혼잡 lottery 복권 (추첨) be subject to ~을 조건으로 하는 fee 요금 non-refundable 환불할 수 없는 non-transferable 양도할 수 없는 good 유효한 temporary 일시적인 on hand 출석한 form of payment 지불방법, 지불수단

172 세부 사항

번역 이 안내문은 주로 누구를 대상으로 하는가?
(A) 공원 직원들
(B) 행사 참가자들
(C) 주차장 요원들
(D) 축제 주최자들

해설 첫 번째 단락에서 행사 참석을 원하시는 분들은 다음을 숙지해 달라(Those interested in attending the event must be aware of the following)고 했으므로, 행사 참가자들을 위한 공지임을 알 수 있다. 따라서 정답은 (B)이다.

173 추론 / 암시

번역 주차권에 대해 암시되지 않은 것은?
(A) 추첨 응모는 무료로 할 수 있다.
(B) 주차권은 6월 13일에만 사용할 수 있다.
(C) 당첨자는 이메일로 통보될 것이다.
(D) 주차권은 특정 종류의 차량에만 적용된다.

해설 세 번째 단락에서 올해 추첨 응모는 무료(There is no fee for entering the lottery this year)라고 했으므로 (A)를, 첫 번째 단락에서 올해 행사는 6월 13일 오후 4시에서 10시까지 열리고(This year's event will be held on June 13, from 4 P.M. to 10 P.M.), 세 번째 단락에서 주차권은 환불, 양도가 불가하며 행사 당일에만 유효하다(Passes are non-refundable, non-transferable, and good only for the date of the event)고 했으므로 (B)를, 세 번째 단락에서 추첨 결과는 6월 2일 이메일을 통해 발표된다(The results of the lottery will be announced via e-mail on June 2)고 했으므로 (C)를 유추할 수 있다. 따라서 정답은 (D)이다.

▶▶ **Paraphrasing**
지문의 no fee for entering the lottery
→ 보기의 can be entered free of charge
지문의 good only for the date of the event
→ 보기의 only be used on June 13
지문의 be announced via e-mail
→ 보기의 be notified by e-mail

174 사실 관계 확인

번역 방문객 센터에 대해 명시된 것은?
(A) 주차장이 여러 곳이다.
(B) 행사 중에는 문을 닫는다.
(C) 공원 지도를 제공한다.
(D) 캠핑장 옆에 위치한다.

해설 네 번째 단락에서 허가를 받고 축제에 차량을 가지고 오시는 분들은 방문객 센터 앞 메인 주차장에 주차할 수 있다. 건물 자체는 행사 당일 저녁에 개방되지 않지만 주차장 북쪽으로 임시 부스가 설치될 것(Those permitted to bring a vehicle to the festival may park in the main parking lot in front of the Visitor Center. The building itself will not be open that evening, but a temporary booth will be set up on the north side of the parking lot)이라고 했으므로, 방문객 센터는 행사 당일 저녁에 문을 닫는 것을 알 수 있다. 따라서 정답은 (B)이다.

▶▶ **Paraphrasing**
지문의 not be open that evening
→ 정답의 be closed during the event

175 사실 관계 확인

번역 행사 입장권에 대해 사실인 것은?
(A) 수령자에게 우편으로 보내질 것이다.
(B) 웹사이트를 통해 예매할 수 있다.
(C) 반드시 신용카드로 지불해야 한다.
(D) 여러 곳에서 구입할 수 있다.

해설 마지막 단락에서 방문객 센터, 시청 공원관리국 그리고 공공 도서관에서 구입할 수 있고 모든 곳에서 현금과 신용카드를 사용할 수 있다(They may be obtained from the Visitor Center, the Parks and Recreation office at city hall, and the public library. In all cases, cash or credit cards are acceptable forms of payment)고 했다. 따라서 다양한 장소에서 행사 입장권을 구입할 수 있음을 알 수 있으므로, 정답은 (D)이다. 행사 입장권은 현금으로도 구매할 수 있으므로, (C)는 오답이다.

▶▶ **Paraphrasing**
지문의 may be obtained from the Visitor Center, the Parks and Recreation office at city hall, and the public library → 정답의 can be purchased at various locations

176-180 기사 + 이메일

삶을 위한 디자인
샘 맥스턴 기자

(10월 10일) 보스턴 — **176**캐롤라인 버지스는 거의 20년간 지역에서 인테리어 디자이너로 직장 생활을 했다. **176, 180**최근 그녀는 보스턴에서 자신의 회사를 설립하겠다는 결정을 내렸고, 이미 넓은 지역 고객층을 확보했다. "전 언제나 인테리어 디자인에 열정이 있었습니다"라고 버지스 씨는 말한다. "고객과 함께 무언가 특별한 것을 개발하고 그들이 진정으로 만족해 하는 생활 공간을 선사하는 데 큰 기쁨을 느낍니다." 버지스의 작업은 고객으로부터 극찬을 자아낸다. 최근 그녀는 매사추세츠 주지사의 사택을 개보수하는 프로젝트를 진행했다.

"제 회사가 잘 되고 있어서 매우 기쁩니다. 주지사의 저택 작업은 제 회사에 대한 관심을 불러일으키는 데 효과가 컸습니다. 그 이후 저는 많은 문의를 받았습니다." 버지스는 각 프로젝트마다 세부 사항까지 세심하게 신경 쓰는 것으로 알려졌다. 모든 면이 맞춤형으로 이루어지며 고객의 요구를 언제나 염두에 둔다. **177**그녀의 일에 단점이 있다면 그것은 그녀가 때때로 며칠이고 집에 들어가지 못하고 일해야 하는 것이라고 그녀는 말한다. "가끔 제 부모님과 형제들이 너무 보고 싶어요. 하지만 가족들이 많이 이해해 줍니다"라고 그녀는 말한다.

어휘 employ 고용하다 found 세우다, 설립하다 client base 고객층 attract 끌다, 유인하다 glowing 극찬의 governor 주지사 renovate 개조하다, 수리하다 inquiry 문의 well known 잘 알려진 take ~ into consideration ~을 고려에 넣다 downside 불리한 점, 부정적인 면 sibling 형제, 자매 understanding 이해심 있는

수신: 캐롤라인 버지스 〈burgessdesign@speedmail.com〉
발신: 토비 서미트 〈tsummit@globomail.com〉
날짜: 10월 20일
주제: 도면

안녕하세요, 캐롤라인

지난주 우편으로 캐롤라인 씨에게 디자인 도면을 받게 되어 너무 기뻤습니다. 예전에도 당신은 늘 우리 회사를 위해 훌륭히 작업을 해 주셨죠. 좋은 제안을 해 주신 것 같아요. 그런데 질문이 하나 있어요. **178, 179**우리가 회의실의 색깔 배치를 변경해도 괜찮을까요? 제안하신 색깔들이 상당히 밝은데 비즈니스 환경에는 어두운 색이 더 적합할 것 같아서요. 제 동료들과 저는 진청색 페인트가 벽 색깔로는 더 적당하지 않을까 생각합니다. 동의하시면 좋겠네요. **180**저는 다음 주 화요일 캐롤라인이 있는 시로 출장을 갑니다. 약속한 대로 제가 잠깐 당신의 사무실에 들러 프로젝트의 다른 세부 내용을 논의하도록 할게요.

토비 서미트 드림

어휘 plans 도면, 설계도 suggestion 제안 color scheme 색채 배합, 색 배치 suitable 적합한, 어울리는 appropriate 적절한 stop by 잠깐 들르다

176 주제 / 목적

번역 기사의 목적은?
(A) 채용 기회 발표
(B) 곧 있을 디자인 프로젝트 설명
(C) 기업가 소개
(D) 건물 개장 홍보

해설 기사의 첫 번째 단락에서 캐롤라인 버지스는 거의 20년간 지역에서 인테리어 디자이너로 직장 생활을 했고, 최근 그녀는 보스턴에서 자신의 회사를 설립하겠다는 결정을 내렸으며 이미 넓은 지역 고객층을 확보했다(Caroline Burgess has been employed locally as an interior designer for nearly two decades. Recently, she made the decision to found her own company in Boston, and already has a large client base in the local area)고 했다. 즉 최근에 회사를 차린 인테리어 디자이너 캐롤라인 버지스를 소개하는 기사임을 알 수 있으므로, 정답은 (C)이다.

▶▶ **Paraphrasing** 지문의 **to found her own company**
→ 정답의 **an entrepreneur**

177 세부 사항

번역 버지스 씨가 자신의 직업의 단점이라고 말하는 것은?
(A) 가족과 떨어져 시간을 보내야 한다.
(B) 일부 고객들은 같이 일하기 힘들다.
(C) 최근 임금 삭감을 당해야 했다.
(D) 종종 밤새 일해야 한다.

해설 기사의 두 번째 단락에서 그녀의 일에 단점이 있다면 그것은 그녀가 때때로 며칠이고 집에 들어가지 못하고 일해야 하는 것(The one downside of her role, she claims, is that she sometimes has to spend days away from home)이며, 가끔 부모님과 형제들이 보고 싶다(I miss my parents and siblings sometimes)고 했으므로, 가끔씩 집에 들어가지 못해 가족들이 보고 싶은 것을 자신의 일의 단점으로 언급하고 있다. 따라서 정답은 (A)이다.

▶▶ **Paraphrasing** 지문의 **The one downside of her role**
→ 질문의 **a disadvantage of her job**
지문의 **spend days away from home**
→ 정답의 **spend time away from her family**

178 세부 사항

번역 서미트 씨는 버지스 씨에게 무엇을 디자인하라고 요청했는가?
(A) 공연장
(B) 세미나 홀
(C) 개인 주택
(D) 사무실 공간

해설 이메일에서 서미트 씨가 회의실의 색깔 배치를 변경해도 괜찮을지(Is it okay if we change the color scheme in the boardroom)를 묻고 있으므로, 버지스 씨에게 회의실의 디자인을 요청했음을 알 수 있다. 따라서 정답은 (D)이다.

▶▶ **Paraphrasing** 지문의 **the boardroom**
→ 정답의 **An office space**

179 세부 사항

번역 서미트 씨가 버지스 씨에게 변경해 달라고 요청하는 것은?
(A) 일부 가구의 배치
(B) 커튼의 치수
(C) 방의 색 배치
(D) 이사회 시간

해설 이메일에서 서미트 씨는 회의실의 색깔 배치를 변경해도 괜찮을지를 물으며, 제안한 색깔들이 상당히 밝은데 비즈니스 환경에는 어두운 색이 더 적합할 것 같다(Is it okay if we change the color scheme in the boardroom? The colors you have suggested are quite light, and I think darker colors may be more suitable for a business environment)고 말했다. 즉 서미트 씨가 회의실 색 배치 변경을 제안하고 그에 따른 이유를 언급하고 있으므로, 정답은 (C)이다.

180 연계

번역 서미트 씨에 대해 알 수 있는 것은?
(A) 버지스 씨와 전에 같이 일해 본 적이 없다.
(B) 다음 주에 보스턴으로 여행을 간다.
(C) 그는 제품 샘플들을 버지스 씨에게 보냈다.
(D) 그는 버지스 씨가 자신의 직장을 방문하길 바란다.

해설 이메일에서 서미트 씨는 다음 주 화요일 버지스 씨가 있는 시로 출장을 가므로 약속한 대로 잠깐 그녀의 사무실에 들러 프로젝트의 다른 세부 내용을 논의하겠다(I'll be coming to your city on business next Tuesday, so I'll stop by your office, as we agreed, to discuss the other details of the project)고 했다. 버지스 씨가 있는 도시는 기사의 첫 번째 단락에서 최근 그녀가 보스턴에서 자신의 회사를 차리겠다는 결정을 내렸다(Recently, she made the decision to found her own company in Boston)는 내용으로 보아 보스턴이므로, 서미트 씨는 그녀가 있는 보스턴에 갈 것임을 알 수 있다. 따라서 정답은 (B)이다.

▶▶ **Paraphrasing** 지문의 **be coming to your city on business next Tuesday** → 정답의 **be traveling to Boston next week**

181-185 전단지 + 이메일

현대미술 애호가들이여
왓슨 전시회가 록포드에 옵니다!
시릴 왓슨은 새 시대를 연 그의 현대 회화 작품을 전시합니다

장소: 스티븐슨 컨벤션 센터
기간: **182, 184** 9월 16일 (월) ~ 9월 18일 (수)
시간: 오후 5:00~오후 8:00
관람료: 성인 25 달러 / 13세 미만 아동 무료

관람료 사전 예매를 원하시면 저희 티켓 관리부 번호 553-555-0195로 전화하셔서 ARS 안내 메시지를 듣고 3번을 선택해 주세요. **181A, B, 185** 지불 수단으로는 전화로 신용카드 결제, 혹은 본사에 우편환 보내기를 선택할 수 있습니다. 전시회 당일에는 남은 관람권을 판매하게 됩니다. **181D** 현장 판매 시에는 안타깝게도 현금 외에는 받을 수가 없습니다.

좀 더 자세한 내용은 저희의 정보 안내 번호 553-555-0132로 전화 주시거나 조니 콜맨(jcoleman@rockfordarts.org)에게 이메일 주십시오.

어휘 exhibit 전시(회) groundbreaking 신기원을 이룬, 획기적인
reserve 예약하다, 예매하다 automated 자동화된 opt 선택하다,
고르다 money order 우편환 head office 본점, 본사

181 사실 관계 확인

번역 지불 수단으로 언급되지 않은 것은?
(A) 신용카드 (B) 우편환
(C) 개인 수표 (D) 현금

해설 전단지의 첫 번째 단락에서 지불 수단으로는 전화로 신용카드 결제, 혹은 본사에 우편환 보내기를 선택할 수 있다(To pay, you can opt to use a credit card over the phone, or send a money order to our head office)고 했으므로 (A) 신용카드와 (B) 우편환이, 현장 판매 시에는 안타깝게도 현금 외에는 받을 수가 없다(Unfortunately, we are only able to accept cash as payment when tickets are purchased at the door)고 했으므로 (D) 현금이 지불수단으로 가능함을 확인할 수 있다. 따라서 정답은 언급되지 않은 (C)이다.

182 사실 관계 확인

번역 전단지에 명시된 것은?
(A) 관람권은 매진될 것으로 보인다.
(B) 전시회는 3일간 열린다.
(C) 화가가 질문에 답할 것이다.
(D) 주차장이 없다.

해설 전단지에서 9월 16일 월요일부터 9월 18일 수요일까지(Dates: Monday, September 16 to Wednesday, September 18) 전시회가 열린다고 나와 있으므로, 3일간 열린다는 것을 알 수 있다. 따라서 정답은 (B)이다.

183 동의어 찾기

번역 이메일에서 첫 번째 단락 2행의 "followed"와 의미가 가장 가까운 단어는?
(A) 찾았다 (B) 따랐다
(C) 관찰했다 (D) 전진했다

해설 해당 문장은 '저는 그의 첫 전시회부터 그의 이력에 관심을 가지고 지켜봐 왔고, 빨리 제 가족들에게 이번 기회를 알리고 싶습니다(I have

followed his career since his very first exhibition, and I cannot wait to share this opportunity with my family)'라고 해석되므로, 여기서 followed는 '지켜보다, 관찰하다'라는 의미이다. 따라서 정답은 (C) watched(지켜보다, 조심하다)이다.

184 연계

번역 링포드 씨는 무슨 요일에 전시회에 갈 계획인가?
(A) 월요일 (B) 화요일
(C) 수요일 (D) 목요일

해설 이메일의 두 번째 단락에서 링포드 씨는 전시 둘째 날의 관람권 4장을 구매하고 싶다(I would like to buy four tickets for the second evening of the exhibit)고 했고, 전시회 기간은 전단지를 통해 확인할 수 있다. 전단지의 기간에서 9월 16일 (월) ~ 9월 18일 (수)(Dates: Monday, September 16 to Wednesday, September 18)에 전시회가 열린다고 했으므로, 전시회 기간 중 둘째 날인 화요일에 전시회에 갈 것임을 확인할 수 있다. 따라서 정답은 (B)이다.

185 연계

번역 링포드 씨에 대해 알 수 있는 것은?
(A) 그녀는 이전에 다른 도시에서 전시회를 관람했다.
(B) 그녀는 영업 직원과 통화했다.
(C) 그녀는 관람권 비용을 우편으로 지불할 계획이다.
(D) 그녀는 전시회에서 작품 몇 점을 전시할 것이다.

해설 이메일의 두 번째 단락에서 링포드 씨는 티켓을 미리 수령하고 싶은데 신용카드를 쓸 수 없으니, 본사의 우편 주소를 자세히 알려달라(I'd like to receive my tickets well in advance, but I don't have access to a credit card right now. Can you please clarify the mailing address of your head office)고 요청하고 있다. 지불 수단은 전단지의 첫 번째 단락에서 전화로 신용카드 결제, 혹은 본사에 우편환 보내기를 선택할 수 있다(To pay, you can opt to use a credit card over the phone, or send a money order to our head office)고 했으므로, 우편환으로 관람권 비용을 지불할 계획임을 알 수 있다. 따라서 정답은 (C)이다.

▶▶ **Paraphrasing** 지문의 **send a money order**
→ 정답의 **pay for her tickets by mail**

186-190 편지 + 팸플릿 + 이메일

용하실 수 있습니다. **188**기업 고객들은 기업 고객 담당 직원인 헬렌 패터슨(번호 555-0179)과 상담하시기 바랍니다. **190**여기에 더하여 특별 홍보 행사로서 전화 예약 고객 전원에게 원하는 영화를 골라 볼 수 있는 무료 영화 관람권을 드립니다.

곧 고객으로 만나 뵙길 고대합니다.

로버트 하그로브
곰스 카 렌털스 영업 이사

곰스 카 렌털스
래피드라이브와 제휴

솔로 – 단 하루 차가 필요한 고객을 위한 상품
가격: 55달러
선택 가능 차량: 래피 마이크로, 래피 T100

189위크엔더 – 며칠 간(2~3일) 도시를 벗어나고자 하는 고객들에게 적합
가격: 하루 45달러
선택 가능 차량: 래피 T100, 래피 익스피리언스

로드 트립퍼 – 장기 여행(최소 10일)을 위한 차가 필요한 고객들에게 적합
가격: 하루 40달러
선택 가능 차량: 래피 익스피리언스, 래피 로드스터

익스플로러 – 더 장기의 렌털(최소 한 달)을 원하는 고객들에게 적합
가격: 하루 35달러
선택 가능 차량: 래피 로드스터, 래피 디럭스 플러스

수신: 로버트 하그로브 <rhargrove@gomescars.com>
발신: 로즈메리 리드 <r.reid@speedymail.net>
날짜: 8월 3일
제목: 최근 카 렌털 건

하그로브 씨께

저는 최근에 귀사의 신규 차량 중 한 대를 렌트했고, 제 렌트 경험에 대한 피드백을 드리면 좋아하지 않을까 생각했습니다. 제가 빌린 래피드라이브 차는 정말 운전하기 좋았고 실내가 깨끗하고 고급스러웠습니다. 이전 차량들과 비교하면 정말 업그레이드된 느낌이었습니다. 두 번째로, 귀사의 직원들이 정말 친절하더군요. **188**제가 7월 5일 상담사 중 한 명과 통화를 했는데, 그 분이 로드 트립퍼 상품을 예약해주시고 제 법인 계정으로 청구도 해 주셨어요. **189**그런데 제 출장 일정에 변경이 생겨 전화를 다시 했어야 했는데 출장이 3일로 줄어 버렸습니다. 상담사는 정말 친절하게도 즉시 저에게 더 적합한 상품을 선택해 주었습니다. **190**제가 대체로 좋은 경험을 했지만 광고하신 무료 영화 관람권을 아직 받지 못했습니다. 이것에 대해 좀 알아봐 주시겠습니까?

로즈메리 리드 드림

---

186 주제 / 목적

번역 편지를 보낸 이유는?
(A) 고객 피드백을 요청하기 위해
(B) 회사 이전을 공지하기 위해
(C) 서비스 개선을 설명하기 위해
(D) 신차 모델을 홍보하기 위해

해설 편지의 첫 번째 단락에서 곰스 카 렌털스의 단골 고객으로서 귀하는 저희 서비스의 최신 업그레이드 소식에 대해 관심이 있을 거라 생각된다(As a regular customer of Gomes Car Rentals, we thought you would be interested in hearing about the latest upgrades that we have made to our service)고 했으므로, 서비스 개선사항을 알리기 위한 편지임을 알 수 있다. 따라서 정답은 (C)이다.

▶▶ **Paraphrasing** 지문의 **the latest upgrades that we have made to our service**
→ 정답의 **service improvements**

187 사실 관계 확인

번역 곰스 카 렌털스에 대해 명시된 것은?
(A) 웹사이트에서 추가 할인을 해준다.
(B) 여러 지역에 매장이 있다.
(C) 래피드라이브에 매각됐다.
(D) 매장 내에 영화 스크린이 있다.

해설 편지의 첫 번째 단락에서 고객 서비스 직원인 빌리 캐롤에게 전화하거나 찰스톤, 앨버커키, 프린스빌 매장에 방문하시면 누구라도 이 상품들을 이용할 수 있다(Anybody can take advantage of one of our deals by calling our customer service representative Billy Carroll at 555-0178 or by stopping by one of our stores at Charleston, Albuquerque, or Princeville)고 했으므로, 곰스 카 렌털스는 여러 지역에 매장을 가지고 있음을 알 수 있다. 따라서 정답은 (B)이다.

▶▶ **Paraphrasing** 지문의 **our stores at Charleston, Albuquerque, or Princeville**
→ 정답의 **stores in multiple locations**

188 연계

번역 리드 씨는 7월 5일 누구와 통화했겠는가?
(A) 헬렌 패터슨
(B) 그렉 퍼킨스
(C) 빌리 캐롤
(D) 야스민 갈라스

해설 리드 씨의 이메일에서 리드 씨는 7월 5일 상담사 중 한 명과 통화를 했는데, 그 분이 로드 트립퍼 상품을 예약해주고 법인 계정으로 청구도 해 줬다(I spoke to one of your advisors on the phone on July 5, who was able to book the Road Tripper package for me and charge it to my business account)고 언급했으므로, 리드 씨는 기업 고객 상담사와 통화했음을 알 수 있다. 기업 고객 상담사에 대한 정보

는 하그로브 씨가 쓴 편지를 통해 확인할 수 있다. 편지의 첫 번째 단락에서 기업 고객들은 기업 고객 담당 직원인 헬렌 패터슨과 상담하길 바란다(Business clients are advised to speak to Helen Patterson, who manages the accounts of these customers, at 555-0179)고 했으므로, 리드 씨가 헬렌 패터슨과 통화했음을 알 수 있다. 따라서 정답은 (A)이다.

189 연계

번역 리드 씨는 어느 상품을 구매했겠는가?
(A) 로드 트립퍼 　　(B) 솔로
(C) 위크엔더 　　(D) 익스플로러

해설 리드 씨의 이메일에서 출장 일정에 변경이 생겨 전화를 다시 했어야 했는데 출장이 3일로 줄어 버렸다(However, I had to call back after some changes were made to my business trip, which meant it was shortened to last just three days)고 했으므로, 3일 일정으로 상품을 구매했음을 알 수 있다. 상품에 대한 설명은 곰스 카 렌털스의 팸플릿을 통해 확인할 수 있다. 팸플릿의 위크엔더(The Weekender) 항목에서 며칠 간(2-3일) 도시를 벗어나고자 하는 고객들에게 적합하다(Ideal for customers looking to escape the city for a few days(2-3 days))고 했으므로, 리드 씨는 위크엔더 상품을 구매했다고 유추할 수 있다. 따라서 정답은 (C)이다.

190 사실 관계 확인

번역 리드 씨가 그녀의 이메일에서 언급한 문제는?
(A) 직원 한 명이 그녀에게 무례했다.
(B) 차 실내가 깨끗하지 않았다.
(C) 차가 운전하기 힘들었다.
(D) 아직 무료 경품을 받지 못했다.

해설 리드 씨의 이메일에서 리드 씨는 대체로 좋은 경험을 했지만 광고한 무료 영화 관람권을 아직 받지 못했다(Although my experience was largely positive, I am yet to receive the complimentary cinema tickets that you advertised)고 했으므로, 정답은 (D)이다.

▶▶ **Paraphrasing** 지문의 I am yet to receive the complimentary cinema tickets
→ 정답의 She has not received a free gift.

191-195 회람 + 일정표 + 이메일

샤프라인 문구 회사 – 메모

수신: 전직원
발신: 에이미 와이트하우스, 인사과

팀원분들게,

여러분이 알고 계시는 대로, 연례 직원 MT가 다음 주말로 일정이 잡혔습니다. 이 행사는 여러 부서의 직원들이 아름다운 곳에서 즐거운 활동들을 하면서 서로를 개인적으로 알 수 있는 좋은 기회가 됩니다. MT는 이틀 동안 진행됩니다. 제가 선택할 수 있는 메뉴 문서를 보내드린 것을 **192기억하실** 텐데요. **191채식 주의자 메뉴**를 원하시는 분은 오늘 근무 시간 종료 때까지 저에게 알려주십시오.

195팀 빌딩 행사는 샤프라인 임원진들이 진행하게 됩니다. 로버트 폴슨은 장애물 코스 체력증진 행사를 진행하며 나탈리 포터는 지도 읽기 탐험 행사를 맡게 됩니다. **193에밀리 대가드와 콜린 히마는 퀴즈 행사 진행을 자원했습니다.** 이는 변경될 수도 있는데 대가드 씨가 급하게 처리해야 할 일이 생길 수도 있다고 저희에게 알려주셨습니다. 저희는 또한 수구 경기를 진행할 임원을 구하고 있습니다. 내일 있을 임원진 회의에서 이것이 확정되길 바라고 있습니다.

여러분에게 즐거운 MT가 되길 바랍니다!.

어휘 stationery 문구류　retreat 휴양, MT　personally 개인적으로　setting 배경, 환경　recall 회상하다, 기억하다　vegetarian 채식주의자(의)　obstacle 장애(물)　exploration 탐사, 탐험　volunteer 자원하다, 지원하다　host 주최하다　be subject to ~될[당할/걸릴] 수 있는　attend to ~을 처리하다[돌보다]　urgent 긴급한　water polo 수구　confirm 확정하다

샤프라인 문구 회사
직원 MT
4월 18일 (토)
웰링턴 리조트

이벤트	진행자	시작 시간	장소
오리엔티어링	나탈리 포터	오전 8:00	웰링턴 다운스
장애물 코스	로버트 폴슨	오전 10:30	블랙포레스트 우즈
수구 토너먼트	미정	오후 2:00	리조트 풀
193일반 상식 퀴즈	193콜린 히마 & 마이클 옥슬리	194오후 7:30	다이아몬드 대회의장

어휘 orienteering 오리엔티어링 (지도와 나침반으로 정해진 코스를 찾아가는 경기)

수신: 에이미 와이트하우스 〈amywhitehouse@sharpline.net〉
발신: 브래들리 웰시 〈bradleywelsh@sharpline.net〉
날짜: 4월 21일
제목: 회사 MT

안녕하세요 에이미,

회사 MT 준비하시느라 고생하신 데 대해 감사드립니다. 저는 주말이 정말 즐거웠고 다른 많은 직원들도 그랬다고 알고 있습니다. **195수구 경기 진행도 너무 즐거웠습니다.** 지금이야 말이지만, 처음에 회의에서 에이미가 그것을 제안했을 때 제가 수구를 해 본 적이 없어 약간 꺼려졌는데, 막상 너무 재미있어서 저도 놀랐습니다. **194또 제가 저녁 행사 전 급하게 자리를 뜬 것에 대해 사과를 드리고 싶습니다.** 제 딸이 몸이 안 좋아 병원에 데려가야 했습니다. MT 전체에 다 참석할 수 없어 아쉬웠지만, 위급한 가족 일을 우선적으로 처리해야 했어요. 이점 양해해 주시기 바랍니다.

다시 한 번 감사드립니다.

브래들리 웰시 드림

어휘 admit 시인하다, 인정하다　reluctant 꺼리는, 주저하는　apologize 사과하다　rush away 쏜살같이 달아나다　unwell 몸이 편치 않은, 아픈　emergency 위급한 상황, 비상 사태　take priority 우선하다, 우선권을 갖다

191 세부 사항

번역 샤프라인 문구 회사의 직원들에게 무엇을 하라고 권하고 있는가?
(A) 금액 납부
(B) 식사 요구사항 명시
(C) 가족 초대
(D) MT 이벤트 제안

해설 회람의 첫 번째 단락에서 채식주의자 메뉴를 원한다면 오늘 근무 시간 종료 때까지 저에게 알려달라(If anybody requires the vegetarian option, please let me know by the end of business today)고 요청하고 있으므로, 정답은 (B)이다.

▶▶ **Paraphrasing** 지문의 **the vegetarian option**
→ **dietary requirements**

192 동의어 찾기

번역 회람에서 첫 번째 단락 4행의 "recall"과 의미가 가장 가까운 단어는?
(A) 가지고 오다
(B) 찾다
(C) 주문하다
(D) 기억하다

해설 해당 문장은 '제가 선택할 수 있는 메뉴 문서를 보내드린 것을 기억하실 텐데요(You may recall I sent around a document with some menu choices)'라는 의미로 해석되므로, 여기서 recall은 '기억해 내다, 상기하다'라는 의미이다. 따라서 정답은 (D) remember(기억하다, 명심하다)이다.

193 연계

번역 MT에서 대가드 씨를 대신한 사람은 누구이겠는가?
(A) 로버트 폴스
(B) 브래들리 웰시
(C) 마이클 옥슬리
(D) 나탈리 포터

해설 회람의 첫 번째 단락에서 에밀리 대가드와 콜린 히마가 퀴즈 행사 진행을 자원했다(Emily Daggard and Colin Himaa have volunteered to host a quiz for us)고 했다. 하지만 MT 일정표에서 일반 상식 퀴즈(General Knowledge Quiz)를 진행한 사람은 콜린 히마와 마이클 옥슬리(Colin Himaa & Michael Oxley)라는 것을 확인할 수 있으므로, 정답은 (C)이다.

194 연계

번역 웰시 씨가 참석하지 못한 행사는 무엇이겠는가?
(A) 장애물 코스
(B) 수구 토너먼트
(C) 일반 상식 퀴즈
(D) 오리엔티어링

해설 웰시 씨의 이메일 첫 번째 단락에서 저녁 행사 전 급하게 자리를 뜬 것에 대해 사과를 드리고 싶다(I also just want to apologize for having to rush away before the evening event)고 했으므로, 웰시 씨는 저녁에 진행된 행사에 참석하지 못했음을 알 수 있다. MT 일정표에서 저녁 행사는 오후 7시 30분에 진행되는 일반 상식 퀴즈(General Knowledge Quiz)임을 확인할 수 있으므로, 정답은 (C)이다.

195 연계

번역 웰시 씨에 대해 추론할 수 있는 것은?
(A) 그는 프로 선수였다.
(B) 그는 샤프라인의 임원이다.
(C) 그는 자격증을 딴 의사이다.
(D) 그는 자녀가 여럿이다.

해설 이메일의 첫 번째 단락에서 웰시 씨는 수구 경기 진행이 너무 즐거웠다(I also really enjoyed hosting the water polo event)고 언급했고, 회람에서 팀 빌딩 행사는 샤프라인 임원진들이 진행하게 된다(Team-building events are to be led by Sharpline managers)고 했다. 따라서 수구 경기를 진행한 웰시 씨는 샤프라인의 임원진임을 유추할 수 있으므로, 정답은 (B)이다.

196-200 웹페이지 + 후기 + 응답

http://www.prestigehotel.com/roomrates

객실료	설명	고객 평	모임	연락처
1962층	– 일반 객실	–– $79	– 지금 예약 ▶	
1962층	– 욕실 딸린 일반 객실	–– $99	– 지금 예약 ▶	
1962층	– 프리미어 객실	–– $119	– 지금 예약 ▶	
1962층	– 디럭스 객실	–– $149	– 지금 예약 ▶	

현재 별관 건설 중 — 올해 개장!

각 객실에는 다음이 포함됩니다.
　조식
　호텔 수영장과 헬스장 이용
　컨시어지 서비스

199다음은 디럭스 객실에만 제공됩니다.
　옥상 테라스와 바 이용

어휘 standard 기준, 표준　en suite 욕실이 딸려 있는　on-site 현장의　concierge 호텔 안내원　rooftop 옥상

---

http://www.rateastay.net/4920/theprestigehotel

게재일: 5월 22일

저는 지난주 그곳에 출장 갔을 때 프레스티지 호텔에서 이틀 밤을 묵었습니다. 호텔은 정말 고급스러웠습니다. **197**제가 헬스장은 보지 못했지만 헬스장에 모든 최신 장비와 운동 기구들이 있다고 다른 투숙객들이 말하는 것을 들었습니다. **199**개인적으로 저는 지역 전원의 장관을 **198**볼 수 있었던 옥상 테라스가 정말 좋았고, 수영장은 수영하기에 딱 맞는 온도였습니다. 호텔 안내원도 정말 잘 도와줬습니다. 하지만 전 조식 뷔페의 질은 만족스럽지 못했어요. 음식은 이 정도 지명도가 있는 호텔에서 기대할 수 있는 수준이 아니었습니다. 불만을 제기할 직원을 찾을 수 없었고, 제 투숙 기간에 프런트 데스크는 종종 비어 있었습니다. **200**더욱이, 투숙한 기간 하루는 아침에 호텔에서 쓰는 기계 소리가 너무 커서 잠이 깼습니다. 다른 모든 좋은 점에도 불구하고 이러한 이유들 때문에 다시 이 호텔에 투숙하는 것을 망설일 것 같네요.

트레이시 앨드릿지

어휘 contain 포함하다, 함유하다 workout (건강·몸매 유지를 위한) 운동 spectacular 장관의 countryside 시골 지역, 전원 지대 temperature 온도 stature 지명도, 위상 pass on 전하다, 전달하다 unmanned 무인의, 사람이 배치 되지 않은 machinery 기계(류) feature 특색, 특징 hesitant 주저하는, 망설이는

---

http://www.rateastay.net/4920/theprestigehotel-aa01

게재일: 5월 26일

앨드릿지 씨께,

귀하의 프레스티지 투숙이 전적으로 만족스럽지 못하셨다니 죄송합니다. 저희는 모든 고객이 쾌적하고 즐겁게 투숙하고 만족스럽고 충분한 휴식을 취하고 돌아 가실 수 있도록 최선의 노력을 다합니다. 투숙하시는 동안 음식의 질이 좋지 않은 것에 대해 사과를 드립니다. 저희는 현재 채용 문제를 겪고 있고 고객님 투숙 날짜에는 주방장이 없었습니다. 이 문제는 현재 해결이 됐고 상근직 직원이 선발되었습니다. 불만을 전달할 사람을 찾을 수 없다고 하셨는데 사실 그런 일은 매우 이례적이라 하겠습니다. 이후에 저는 프런트 데스크 직원에게 지시를 했고, 이런 일이 다시는 일어나지 않을 테니 안심하십시오. **200**지적해 주신 다른 문제에 관해서 말씀 드리자면, 지금은 완료된 개보수 작업 때문이었습니다. 이후 그 기계는 프로젝트를 수행하던 회사로 반납됐습니다. 저희는 고객님께 프레스티지에서의 무료 투숙을 제공하고자 합니다. 부디 세계 최고로 알려진 저희의 서비스를 경험하시기 바랍니다. 무료 투숙 제의를 받으시려면 493-555-0122로 저에게 연락 주십시오.

그레타 산체즈 드림

프레스티지 호텔 고객 관리부

어휘 entirely 전적으로 strive 노력하다, 분투하다 ensure 반드시 ~하게 하다, 보장하다 well-rested 충분한 휴식을 취한 staffing 직원 채용 permanent 영구의, 상근의 appoint 임명하다 rest assured 안심하십시오 carry out 수행하다 take up an offer 제안을 받아들이다

---

196 사실 관계 확인

번역 웹페이지에 게시된 객실 목록에 대해 명시된 것은?
(A) 일부는 할인가에 제공된다.
(B) 모두 같은 층에 위치한다.
(C) 1층 객실은 더 비싸다.
(D) 일부 객실은 컨시어지 서비스를 받지 못한다.

해설 웹페이지의 객실 목록을 보면 모두 2층(2nd Floor)에 있다는 것을 알 수 있으므로, 정답은 (B)이다.

▶▶ **Paraphrasing** 지문의 **2nd Floor** → 정답의 **the same level**

---

197 사실 관계 확인

번역 앨드릿지 씨가 직접 이용하지 않은 것은?
(A) 호텔 안내원 서비스 (B) 수영장
(C) 헬스장 (D) 옥상 테라스

해설 앨드릿지 씨는 후기에 헬스장은 보지 못했지만 헬스장에 모든 최신 장비와 운동 기구들이 있다고 다른 투숙객들이 말하는 것을 들었다(Although I didn't see the gym, I heard other guests saying that it contained all the latest equipment and workout machines)고 언급했으므로, 정답은 (C)이다.

---

198 동의어 찾기

번역 후기에서 첫 번째 단락 4행의 "offered"와 의미가 가장 가까운 단어는?
(A) 제공했다 (B) 할인했다
(C) 자원했다 (D) 전달했다

해설 해당 문장은 '개인적으로 저는 지역 전원의 장관을 볼 수 있었던 옥상 테라스가 정말 좋았고, 수영장은 수영하기에 딱 맞는 온도였습니다(Personally, I really enjoyed using the rooftop terrace, which offered some spectacular views of the local countryside, and the pool was the perfect temperature to swim in)'라는 의미로 해석되므로, 여기서 offered는 '제공했다, 주었다'라는 의미가 자연스럽다. 따라서 정답은 (A) provided(제공했다, 주었다)이다.

---

199 연계

번역 앨드릿지 씨는 어떤 객실에 묵었겠는가?
(A) 일반 객실
(B) 욕실 딸린 일반 객실
(C) 프리미어 객실
(D) 디럭스 객실

해설 앨드릿지 씨의 후기에서 개인적으로 지역 전원의 장관을 볼 수 있었던 옥상 테라스가 정말 좋았고, 수영장은 수영하기에 딱 맞는 온도였다(Personally, I really enjoyed using the rooftop terrace, which offered some spectacular views of the local countryside, and the pool was the perfect temperature to swim in)고 언급해 옥상 테라스를 이용할 수 있는 방에 머물렀음을 알 수 있다. 웹페이지의 마지막 부분에서 옥상 테라스와 바 이용은 디럭스 객실에만 제공된다(For deluxe rooms only: Use of rooftop terrace and bar)고 했으므로, 앨드릿지 씨는 디럭스 객실에 머물렀다고 유추할 수 있다. 따라서 정답은 (D)이다.

---

200 연계

번역 산체즈 씨는 호텔 내의 기계에 대해 무엇이라고 말하는가?
(A) 기계가 이제는 철거됐다.
(B) 기계가 헬스장으로 옮겨졌다.
(C) 소음을 줄이기 위해 기계에 방음 처리를 했다.
(D) 기계를 수리하기 위해 직원이 고용됐다.

해설 앨드릿지 씨가 후기에 투숙한 기간 중 하루는 호텔에서 쓰는 기계 소리가 너무 커서 잠이 깼다(Furthermore, I was woken up by some loud machinery being used on site during one of the mornings)고 했다. 이에 대한 응답으로 산체즈 씨가 지금은 완료된 개보수 작업 때문이었고, 이후 그 기계는 프로젝트를 수행하던 회사로 반납됐다(Regarding the other issue you mentioned, this was due to renovation work that has now been completed, and it has since been returned to the company carrying out the project)고 응답했다. 따라서 현재 그 기계는 반납되고 호텔에 없다는 것을 알 수 있으므로, 정답은 (A)이다.